Architectural Conservation
in Europe and the Americas

NATIONAL EXPERIENCES AND PRACTICE

John H. Stubbs and Emily G. Makaš

Foreword by Mounir Bouchenaki

*With a contribution of images from the photo archive
of the World Monuments Fund*

WILEY

John Wiley & Sons, Inc.

Copyright © 2011 by John Wiley & Sons, Inc. All rights reserved.

Published by John Wiley & Sons, Inc., Hoboken, New Jersey.

Published simultaneously in Canada.

For general information on our other products and services, or technical support, please contact our Customer Care Department within the United States at 800-762-2974, outside the United States at 317-572-3993, or fax 317-572-4002.

Wiley also publishes its books in a variety of electronic formats. Some content that appears in print may not be available in electronic books.

For more information about Wiley products, visit our Web site at www.wiley.com.

Library of Congress Cataloging-in-Publication Data:

Stubbs, John H.
Architectural conservation in Europe and the Americas : national experiences
and practice / John H. Stubbs, Emily G. Makaš.
    p. cm.
  Includes index.
  ISBN 978-0-470-60385-7 (hardback); 978-0-470-90099-4 (ebk.); 978-0-470-90100-7 (ebk.); 978-0-470-90111-3
(ebk.); 978-0-470-95107-1 (ebk.); 978-0-470-95124-8 (ebk.)
  1. Architecture–Conservation and restoration–Europe. 2. Architecture–
Conservation and restoration—America. I. Makaš, Emily Gunzburger. II. Title.
  NA105.S793 2011
  363.6'909—dc22
                                                                            2010045252

Printed in the United States of America

10 9 8 7 6 5 4 3 2 1

Contents

Foreword

In every discipline, someone must step forward to document what has been accomplished thus far and take stock of contemporary practice. While architectural conservation is neither a particularly new discipline nor is this book the first attempt at such a survey, *Architectural Conservation in Europe and the Americas* is by far the most comprehensive and noteworthy effort to date. Its authors, John H. Stubbs and Emily G. Makaš have done an extraordinary job of assembling the stories of experiences in architectural conservation in the nearly ninety countries that comprise Europe and the Americas, presenting each in a remarkably clear, balanced, and intelligible manner.

Though much has been assembled here in an unprecedented manner, the authors are the first to admit that the scope and complexity of the topic in some places did not permit their describing every single relevant development. This would be impossible as in most countries of Western Europe alone there have been thousands of successful architectural conservation projects with scores that could be pointed out as exemplary. In an answer to this, the book's extensive endnotes and Further Reading Lists are present to support one of its main aims, which as John has described to me, is to be a convenient 'gateway' to more on most of the topics, examples and allied subjects addressed in this book.

So choices were made, and I think made wisely, in favor of a whole that provides a unique and evenly weighted overarching view while avoiding duplication and stressing the more influential accomplishments and solutions in architectural conservation practice in our time. As such, the book holds together as a remarkably readable and fascinating portrayal of the field at this juncture. It is sensibly organized, abundantly illustrated, and well-indexed. It should prove of interest to a wide audience, ranging from the curious lay person to the student, the professional, and the librarian.

I understand that the present book is the second in a series of probably three titles that will portray architectural conservation in all parts of the world. Along with its related predecessor volume, *Time Honored: A Global View of Architectural Conservation—Parameters, Theory and Evolution of an Ethos*, and an eventual additional title that documents the other parts of the world, the series holds great promise as a resource and reference for both teaching and reference.

The perspective of *Architectural Conservation in Europe and the Americas* is well suited for its task because its principal author John H. Stubbs is an active and accomplished practitioner in the field, trained with institutional perspectives of ICCROM's architectural conservation course and Columbia University's prestigious graduate program in historic prservation that he attended and where he has taught for many years. Dr. Emily G. Makaš, professor of architectural and urban history at University of North Carolina at Charlotte and an expert on cultural heritage conservation in southeastern Europe, serves as an excellent complement to Stubbs here as his coauthor. Adding to their erudition are the voices of several collaborators who have contributed signed specialty essays throughout the book. Many of these participants are distinguished figures in the field today.

As one who has mainly served the field in administrative capacities in several roles at UNESCO, including as Director of the World Heritage Center, and currently as Director General of ICCROM, I am particularly pleased to see that the authors have fairly represented the crucial roles of these institutions and others, such as ICOMOS, as among the key influences in architectural heritage conservation over the past half century. Indeed the educational aims of these institutions are well reflected in the present book. In their broad view of the subject where the authors discuss not just what has happened but also why Stubbs and Makaš have gone beyond describing what any of the above-mentioned institutions, and even his own—the World Monuments Fund—could, due to the limitations of their purviews.

I first met John Stubbs in relation to his extensive work at Angkor in Cambodia on behalf of the World Monuments Fund. His being at the center of most of WMF's many impressive initiatives for over two decades has given him a rare, if not unique, experience. WMF's leadership among international private not-for-profit organizations in advocating for architectural conservation and engaging the private sector in supporting architectural conservation is unparalleled. Bringing a production-oriented approach to WMF from work in the corporate world of architectural practice in New York City, it is his practical field experience that makes the observations of this book so special. Indeed, it is satisfying to see here how the system of the public and private, and the for-profit and not for profit sectors, have all found niches in architectural conservation practice that add to it being the robust and truly global concern that it is today. The solutions to conservation problems today that are cited in this book are both sensible and useful, and the prognosis for the future it suggests are particularly strong.

From reading this book I find it both amazing and reassuring to see how far the field has progressed, especially in the past few decades. As a result, it is a pleasure to introduce this new volume that I feel confident will be an especially useful new contribution to the field of cultural heritage management both now and for years to come.

MOUNIR BOUCHENAKI
Director General, International Centre for the Study of the
Preservation and Restoration of Cultural Property (ICCROM)

Preface

*A*rchitectural Conservation in Europe and the Americas; National Experiences and *Practice* explores the background and current status of the widespread efforts undertaken to ensure the survival of the rich architectural legacy of Europe, North and South America. This book addresses the sizable challenge of documenting these experiences by charting the history of the profession and its allied activities in these three continents from the early twentieth-century forward, with a special emphasis on key projects, participants, successes, and challenges of the past two decades. *Architectural Conservation in Europe and the Americas* offers a balanced view of architectural heritage conservation in the light of relevant cultural contexts and approaches to heritage protection involving all cultures on these three vast continents.

Organized architectural conservation—namely rationalized documentation, restoration, and preservation of historic architecture—has its origins in the Italian Renaissance, which by the mid-eighteenth century had radiated outward to France, England, Germany and Scandinavia and resonated elsewhere soon afterwards.[1] From the early nineteenth century, this thread of progressive extension gave way to an increasing number of simultaneous realizations and adoptions of cultural heritage conservation practice elsewhere in Europe, the Americas, and around the world. Since the last decades of the twentieth-century architectural conservation has been so pervasive that it is on the civic agenda of practically all countries of the world and global experiences have for several years now fed back and informed the Western European and American countries that so established the discipline. Today, the cross-fertilization of ideas in cultural resources management on a world-wide basis is commonplace.

Discussing developments in both Europe and the Americas together in this book is partly a practical matter: the authors and publisher want to produce this global series in as few volumes as possible, assuming that an additional book addressing Asia, Africa, Oceania, and the Polar Regions will follow. More importantly, the discussion of Europe and the Americas together respects certain historical and geopolitical realities. Of the various continents of the world, the histories and cultures of Europe and the Americas have been linked since the Age of Exploration in the early sixteenth century. With the spread of culture, including languages and religion, from one continent to the others, came the transmission of art, architectural and urban traditions between the Old and New Worlds. Heritage conservation practice has been a part of this intercontinental transfer and transmutation.

Today, professionals in both Europe and the Americas are faced by many of the same challenges and use many of the same tools and techniques on behalf of architectural heritage. On both sides of the Atlantic, the scope of cultural heritage protection has expanded to include intangible heritage as well as surviving artifacts, access to sites has been radically improved, developments in instant global communications have facilitated information sharing, including Web-based electronic aids to site interpretation, and documentation strategies and storage systems have improved tremendously. As a result, architectural conservation protection today in Europe and the Americas relies heavily on an electronic and institutional network and there has been significant movement towards institutionalized pan-European, and to a lesser extent, pan-American heritage protection programs and forums. The principal interests of the field in both Europe and the Americas have also evolved in recent years to noticeably include concerns for energy conservation—both in building anew and rehabilitating "green," as well as on sustainable heritage conservation in general. British architect and planner Dennis Rodwell has rightly called these two themes "the defining issues of our time."

Being Modern: The Currency of Conservation
Frank Matero

If there ever was a moment when heritage conservation had something to contribute to the current malaise of social and political strife, economic recession, and environmental destruction, it is now. On the surface conservation is concerned with the protection of historic and artistic works from loss and damage so they can continue to inspire, to admonish (from the Latin, *monere*, the root for monument) or simply to provide the same or different uses in the present. We advocate for conservation because objects and places hold important information, associations, and meaning; because they embody social and cultural memory which, if lost, would make the world less understandable.

Consider recent world events: the destruction of the Bamayan buddhas, the Mostar bridge, even the World Trade Towers-all potent cultural symbols whose targeted loss says more about the power and significance of these places than their existence ever did. Consider the current dilemma of if and how to rebuild the vernacular neighborhoods of New Orleans or the Haitian capital of Port au Prince in the aftermath of the 2010 earthquake, or the huge debate over the destruction of 2 Columbus Circle for the Museum of Design in New York City; a debate which has caused a serious reconsideration of how we view and define post war modernism and how we will pass on that legacy. All these examples engage in the phenomenon of loss or retention of cultural heritage and its implications.

For the general public, heritage conservation is fundamentally about the past. Long standing attitudes hold that true progress is about the new and the only real creativity is that which produces something novel. That which is existing or old is far from the new and therefore not part of real progress or progressive solutions. Of course this is untrue. Conservation is both creative and modern. In today's climate it is in fact subversive in its interest in mending the flawed rather than in discarding and starting anew. As Elizabeth Spelman has aptly observed, the capacity of professionals to repair things can scarcely be valued in any society whose economy is based on the production of and the desire for the new. Repair is at odds with the imperative of a capitalist society.[2]

To bring together the past and present by thinking and acting in ways different from the original processes that create new works, and to forge a new approach that is sensitive to all contexts are the very goals of conservation.

As an act of intervention conservation seeks to mediate and in that mediation it is creative. Conservation possesses a uniquely integrated set of knowledge and skills drawn from the sciences and the humanities and based on a values driven model.[3] Its concerns and methods of analysis, intervention, and especially prevention are part of the definition of *sustainability* and it has much to offer all professionals and the public in the ascendancy of that concept. While conservation has matured in response to larger social and environmental concerns, it has far to go in most countries to deeply influence local and global development.

Since the 1970s sustainability has evolved as a significant mode of thought in nearly every field of human intellectual activity. With its origins in the nature conservation movement in the early twentieth century, sustainability and sustainable development are about finding ways to design, plan, and manage that allow essential or desirable resources to be renewed faster than they are destroyed. In design and the building industry, sustainability has become synonymous with "green architecture" or new buildings designed with healthy work environments, energy conserving systems, and environmentally sensitive materials. Only recently, heritage conservation has been recognized as a concept compatible with the objectives of sustainability, emerging as a critical component of international development strategies now being advocated by some local and international government and non-government agencies.

Unlike the case for natural resources, sustainability for the built environment differs in that historic resources cannot be physically regenerated, only retained, modified, or lost.[4] Instead sustainability in this context means ensuring the continuing contribution heritage can make to the present through the thoughtful management of change responsive to the historic environment. Sustainability emphasizes the need for a long-term view. If conservation is to develop as a viable strategy for redevelopment, the larger economic and social dimensions need to be addressed, while at the local level, community involvement is central to sustaining conservation initiatives. In this case, sustainability means an investment in conserving human knowledge as much as historic buildings. Reconciling conservation and development is a prerequisite for achieving improvements in the quality of life in environmentally and culturally sensitive places. By shifting the focus on perception and valuation, conservation becomes a dynamic process involving public participation, dialogue, and consensus, and ultimately better stewardship. It calls for the retention and reinforcement (if necessary) of healthy existing social, cultural, and economic functions and the introduction of new uses as necessary in order to generate income for the local community. It requires the improvement of services and public open spaces, community–supported rehabilitation of historic housing and open spaces, employment opportunities, and promotion of local knowledge and craft.

If sustainability ultimately means learning to think and act in terms of interrelated systems, then heritage with its unique values and experiences must be contextualized and integrated with the new. In the transformation of our physical environment, what relationships should exist between change and continuity, between the old and the new? Are modernity and tradition truly oppositional? Only when history is rightly viewed as a part of that continuous change, can we speak of an integrated and sustainable built environment and conservation as an appropriate modern response to this current dilemma.

While Europe and the Americas share affluence, beliefs and social ambitions as well as legal bases for commonalities of approaches toward heritage protection, there are certainly significant differences in the histories, developments and current issues among the countries of these continents. Many of the developing countries of Eastern Europe, South America and the Caribbean have not had the same access to financial resources, training and information about conservation as those of North America and Western and Northern Europe. In some cases the varying foci of conservation practices among the Old and New World have also been theoretical. These differences stem back to the making of the Venice Charter of 1964, approved only tacitly by delegates from the United States and the United Kingdom because of a perceived continental European bias towards monuments that did not take fully into account some of the less monumental heritage found in all countries, or the vernacular and most indigenous heritage of the New World.[1] Since that time, the heritage protection efforts of the younger countries of the United States and Canada (and Australia) have led the quest for more representative strategies for their countries. The result is that the heritage protection management systems of North America and Europe, when viewed as a combined experience and capacity, cover most all the issues and are by any measure impressive in their robustness and influence.

Many European and American countries have shared ideas about architectural conservation through frequent assistance to the rest of the world. From exemplary projects at Abu Simbel and Nubia, Egypt in the 1960s to Borobudur, Indonesia in the 1970s to Angkor Wat in Cambodia since the 1990s—major sites of world architectural significance have been preserved with the assistance of European and American-based institutions. Through these projects training opportunities and information about best contemporary conservation practices have been disseminated globally. As such, the leading architectural conservation organizations, training institutions, several governments, and various practitioners in Europe and the Americas have played a central role in the internationalization of heritage conservation practice so successfully in the past half century that today the whole world is engaged in the activity. Though some imbalances in organized heritage protection exist between Europe and the Americas and the rest of the world—and some imbalances exist within the continents of Europe and the Americas themselves—these gaps have been closing with each passing year. Certain economic and technical advantages in some developing countries have even distinguished conservation efforts in those places. Especially in recent decades, Australia, New Zealand, India and Japan have emerged as leaders in Asia and the Pacific while impressive progress has also been witnessed in China, South Africa, Jordan and other countries in Western Asia.

There are certainly challenges to presenting Europe and the Americas together and separated from the rest of the world as is done here. This organization makes cross referencing more difficult, especially regarding the activities of European and American governmental and non-governmental organizations abroad as well as of those charters and ideas generated in the rest of the world that have since had an impact on European and American conservation practice and vice versa.

Architectural Conservation in Europe and the Americas is organized as a series of country profiles examining key issues, participants, sites and developments in the architectural conservation practices in the subject countries. The books two parts focus first on Europe and then on the Americas, and within these parts the discussion is divided into sections that group countries together by region based on geographical, historical, cultural, and linguistic ties. Part I includes five sections: Western Europe, Northern Europe, Central Europe, Eastern Europe and the Caucasus, and Southeastern Europe. Part II includes three sections that focus on North America, then on Mexico, the Caribbean and Central America, and finally on South America.

This current book is preceded by, but is not necessarily dependent on, a forerunner volume by John H. Stubbs, *Time Honored: A Global View of Architectural Conservation* (Wiley, 2009). That earlier book endeavored to more generally portray contemporary practice in architectural conservation, including its rationale, structure, early history, principles and practices, and likely future directions. *Time Honored* introduced many of the themes, terms, legal instruments, and the whats, whys, whos, and hows of architectural conservation that are explored in focused country-specific and specialty essays in *Architectural Conservation in Europe and the Americas*. Though both books are designed to be read independently of one another, readers seeking the broader picture and contextual framework for the portrayals of contemporary practice discussed herein will find *Time Honored* a useful companion. Two of four Appendices within *Time Honored*, a glossary of the field's nomenclature and lists of international resources, should prove especially helpful in relation to this book. The larger research initiative encompassing this book, its predecessor, and its probable successor is described on a companion website found at http://conservebuiltworld.com.

Architectural Conservation in Europe and the Americas provides the detailed country by country examination of the movement necessary to speak globally and generally about the field. It can be read in its entirety, offering a comprehensive scope to those seeking a comparative understanding of architectural conservation or a broad overview of global practices rich with specific examples. It can also be used as a reference, so that those seeking information about developments in a certain country or region may quickly access a thorough overview of that information with directions for further reading and online resources for additional research. Importantly, this book can also be studied as a source of solutions for effective architectural heritage management.

This book's content represents the views of its authors as researchers and practitioners in the field of heritage conservation, and does not necessarily reflect the positions and opinions of the organizations with which they are affiliated. As such the authors are responsible for its content.

This book is not the only recent publication to take an international view of architectural conservation, but the emphasis, scope, and contemporary nature of *Architectural Conservation in Europe and the Americas* varies from the other most significant of these studies and compendia. For example, in the 1980s James Marston Fitch's *Historic Preservation: Curatorial Management of the Built World* took a thematically broad and global view of the field's key facets, and under the auspices of US ICOMOS, Robert Stipe edited a series of bound reports on *Historic Preservation in Foreign Countries* that offered detailed profiles of developments in several European countries during the period before 1990.[6] Much has happened since these seminal studies were undertaken, however. More recently Giorgio Croci's *The Conservation and Structural Restoration of Architectural Heritage* and Bernard Feilden's *Conservation of Historic Buildings* primarily address technique and materials science. Jukka Jokilehto's *History of Architectural Conservation* provides a foundational portrayal of the history of the field and the contributions of key individuals primarily in Europe up until World War II.[7] *Architectural Conservation in Europe and the Americas* addresses these topics and others often in less detail, but contextualizes them within contemporary practice as well as broadens the geographic scope to include developments in every country in these three continents.

The impressive 11-volume thematically-organized compendium *Trattato di Restauro Architettonico* (Treatise on Architectural Restoration), coordinated and directed by Giovanni Carbonara over the course of the past decade and a half, is comprehensive in its scope and includes writings by different experts.[8] Particularly in volume nine, which discusses international practice in various countries and regions, its approach seems similar to *Architectural Conservation in Europe and the Americas*, though its compendium-like structure, its overall length and publication in Italian make it less accessible to many practitioners and students in the field today.

Country profiles focused on legislative and administrative frameworks, a component of *Architectural Conservation in Europe and the Americas*, have also previously been published by others as well as made available online. For the Council of Europe, Robert Pickard has brought together national experts to contribute to a number of edited books dedicated to this theme, beginning with *Policy and Law in Heritage Conservation* and the two-volume *European Cultural Heritage*, which examine representative countries from throughout Europe; these were followed in 2008 by three additional books focused specifically on Southeastern Europe.[9] The Council of Europe is also the sponsor of two online efforts to compile similar country profiles, including the European Heritage Network website, which focuses specifically on heritage management policies, and the Compendium of Cultural Policies in Europe, which discusses heritage protection in light of pan-European ambitions and broader cultural policies.[10] Both of these sites aim to comprehensively cover all of Europe (the former includes thirty country profiles and the latter forty-one to date) and are periodically updated.

Most of these publications and websites are focused on Europe, while similar comprehensive studies for the rest of the world, including the Americas are rare. UNESCO's World Heritage Center website compiles information about World Heritage Sites globally, and ICOMOS' series of *Heritage at Risk* publications highlights key threats in countries throughout the world on the basis of voluntary submissions.[11] Similarly, the website of the World Monuments Fund, particularly its component which profiles sites placed on its Watch® list of endangered sites since 1995, yields a wealth of information on threats to architectural heritage sites worldwide and solutions applied. However, none of these globally oriented sources managed by international organizations claims to be comprehensive in their presentation of the countries in which their projects are located.

Each of the aforementioned publications and institutional efforts has served as a valuable resource during the preparation of *Architectural Conservation in Europe and the Americas*. If the present book places these and other efforts to in a clearer context, it will have served its purpose.

ENDNOTES

1. For the history of architectural conservation in general and the origins of national practices in Italy, France, England and the German States through the early twentiety century, see: John H. Stubbs, *Time Honored: A Global View of Architectural Conservation* (Wiley & Sons: Hoboken, 2009), 183–226.

2. Spelman, Elizabeth V. *Repair: The Impulse to Restore in a Fragile World.* Boston, MA: Beacon Press, 2002.

3. Avrami, Erica, Randall Mason, and Marta de la Torre. *Values and Heritage Conservation.* Los Angeles: The Getty Conservation Institute, 2000.

4. Fairclough, Graham. *Cultural Landscape, Sustainability, and Living with Change? Managing Change: Sustainable Approaches to the Conservation of the Built Environment.* J. M. Teutonico and F. Matero, eds. Los Angeles: The Getty Conservation Institute, 2003, pp. 23–46.

5. According to the late British conservation architect Bernard M, Feilden, the delegates from Great Britain and the United States at the IInd International Congress of Architects and Technicians of Historic Monuments which met in Venice from May 25 to 31, 1964, dissented in their strong support for the Venice Charter on the basis of the limited types of architectural heritage that it addressed. Source: In review of the manuscript of the present book with Bernard Feilden at the Old Barn, Norwich, England, November 3, 2006.

6. James Marston Fitch, *Historic Preservation: Curatorial Management of the Built World* (New York: McGraw Hill, 1982); and Robert Stipe, *Historic Preservation in Other Countries,* vol. 1-5 (Washington, DC: US/ICOMOS, 1982-1990).

7. Giorgio Croci, *The Conservation and Structural Restoration of Architectural Heritage,* (Southampton: Computational Mechanics Publications, 1998); Bernard M. Feilden, *Conservation of Historic Buildings* (Oxford: Butterworth Heinemann, 2003); and Jukka Jokilehto, A *History of Architectural Conservation* (Oxford: Butterworth Heinemann, 1999).

8. Giovanni Carbonara (compiler), *Trattato di Restauro Architettonico,* vols. 1-11 (Torino: UTET, 1996-2008).

9. Robert Pickard, ed. *Policy and Law in Heritage Conservation* (London: Spon Press, 2000), *European Cultural Heritage Volume 1: Intergovernmental Cooperation: Collected Texts* (Strasbourg: Council of Europe Publishing, 2002), *European Cultural Heritage Volume 2: A Review of Policies and Practices* (Strasbourg: Council of Europe Publishing, 2002), *Analysis and Reform of Cultural Heritage Policies in Southeast Europe* (Strasbourg: Council of Europe, 2008), *Integrated Management Tools in the Heritage of South-East Europe* (Strasburg: Council of Europe, 2008), *Sustainable Development Strategies in South-East Europe* (Strasburg: Council of Europe, 2008).

10. "Home," The European Heritage Network, www.european-heritage.net/sdx/herein/index.xsp [accessed December 30 2009]; and "Compendium Country Directory," Compendium Cultural Polices and Trends in Europe, www.culturalpolicies.net/web/countries.php [accessed December 20 2009].

11. "World Heritage List," UNESCO World Heritage Center, http://whc.unesco.org/en/list [accessed December 30 2009]; and "Heritage at Risk," ICOMOS, www.international.icomos.org/risk/index.html [accessed December 30 2009].

Acknowledgments

THE ORIGINAL IDEA of a series that would document world efforts in global architectural conservation was conceived by John H. Stubbs in 1999: and, it has also principally been his efforts that have produced this book. Crucial among Stubbs' collaborators since 2006 has been architectural historian Emily G. Makaš, PhD. Makaš contributed so broadly toward research and writing during the book's early phases that she eventually was invited to join Stubbs as its co-author.

Much information was gained by John Stubbs via teaching courses in historic preservation within the Graduate School of Architecture Planning and Preservation at Columbia University in New York since 1984, a program he graduated from ten years earlier. Among other things, at Columbia Stubbs has researched the history of the field and "best practices" in foreign places. Also a graduate of Columbia's historic preservation program and later Cornell University's Ph.D. program in architectural and urban history, Makaš currently teaches in the School of Architecture at the University of North Carolina in Charlotte. She has also found that teaching, researching, and writing on architectural conservation is a matter of necessity, because in recent years the practice of physically conserving the built environment has far exceeded any efforts to actually document these activities. The authors are not alone in concluding that architectural heritage conservation practice is passing through a period of self-reflection, and sensed that they were in a good position to participate in assessing and documenting the field today.

The idea for this project was also inspired and informed by John Stubbs's work as Vice President for Field Projects at World Monuments Fund. From around 1990 Stubbs and his colleagues found themselves working in international architectural conservation practice at a time when the field rapidly expanded in major new ways.

So an important thanks for critical institutional support is extended to the World Monuments Fund, especially its president Bonnie Burnham and the organization's trustees, who supported John Stubbs's various levels of participation in scores of architectural conservation projects in dozens of countries throughout the world for a period of over two decades. In this connection it must be stated that this book was privately produced and the contents and opinions expressed herein are those of its authors.

In addition, World Monuments Fund colleagues Bonnie Burnham, Lisa Ackerman, Norma Barbacci, Jonathan Foyle, and Mark Weber helped more directly by reading and commenting on drafts, or parts thereof, of this book. The authors are especially grateful for the use of some 32 percent of the book's images that were sourced through the WMF Image Archives.

Another institution to which special gratitude is owed is the International Center for the Study of the Conservation of Cultural Property (ICCROM) especially Director General Mounir Bouchenaki for writing the Foreword for this book, and Paul Arenson and María Mata Caravaca who, respectively, direct ICCROM's Library and Image Archives and assisted the authors in their research.

In addition, special thanks are expressed to the contributors of specialty essays: Lisa Ackerman, Norma Barbacci, Eric Delony, Frank Matero, Theodore H.M. Prudon, Diana Ramiro, Dennis Rodwell, Carol D. Shull, Eduardo Rojas, Barbara Ross, and Donovan Rypkema. The additional voices and expertise provided by these colleagues has enriched the depth and detail of this book and the authors are grateful for their assistance.

Colleagues who assisted as readers, advisors, and providers of information in relation to Part I: Europe include Zeynep Ahunbay, Marek Baranski, Bonnie Burnham, Donough Cahill, Clementine Cecil, Cevat Erder, Tanja Damljanovic Conley, Lucy Der-Manuelian, Franca Di Valerio, Natalia Dushkina, Martin Dvorák, Tamás Fejerdy, Jacques Feiner, Donald Insall, Pamela Jerome, Maija Kairamo, Roman Koslowski, Pablo Longoria, Léon Lock, Bruno Maldoner, Arcady Nebolsine, Theodore H.M. Prudon, Didier Repellin, Gionata Rizzi, Dennis Rodwell, Werner Schmid, Chiara Siravo, Christopher Young, and Michael J. Walsh.

Colleagues who assisted as readers, advisors, and providers of information for Part II: The Americas include Bonnie Burnham, Anthony Butler, Elena Charola, Eric Delony, Frank Matero, Elias Mujica, Theodore H.M. Prudon, Diana Ramiro, Eduardo Rojas, Barbara Ross, Donovan Rypkema, Carol D. Shull, and Herb Stovel.

Various members of the production team served authors Stubbs and Makaš throughout the duration of this publishing project and provided invaluable help. Special thanks are expressed to patient and dedicated Sharon Delezenski Genin, general assistant to the project practically from the start, who served various roles ranging from maintainer and keeper of the manuscript to fact checker to indexer to organizer of the book's images and procurer of image use permissions.

Gratitude is also extended to Martha Wilkie for her help in procuring images for the book and consulting on matters related to a companion website, and to Guy Genin for his kind help in preparing a number of images for this publication. Elizabeth Puhl, cartographer, prepared the book's various maps, and graphic designer Ken Feisel procured two aerial images and is responsible for the cover design of the predecessor volume that this book emulates. The large number of colleagues, photographers, and others who helped by providing illustrations are gratefully acknowledged in the photo credits section of this book.

At different stages of the project writer-editors Ann ffolliott and Franca Di Valerio provided valuable help in improving the book's several drafts. Earlier researcher-writers who provided invaluable assistance included Brian Curran, Dorothy Dinsmoor, Catherine Gavin, Sharon Delezenski Genin, and Ian Morello.

The team at John Wiley & Sons, publishers including Amanda L. Miller, Paul Drougas, Sadie Abuhoff, Christine Gilmore, Amy Odum, Emily Cullings, and Walter Schwarz (book designer) are thanked for their expert oversight and support of—as well as their belief in—this multi-part publishing enterprise.

And finally, special thanks are extended to Linda K. Stubbs and Miran Makaš for their patience and countless other forms of support.

The accomplishment of this book was carried through by an extraordinary level of collegiality and cooperation among the above named colleagues and others too numerous to mention. Such generous collaboration may say the most about the enterprise of cultural heritage protection in our time: the field predominately consists of open, forward-looking, well-meaning, talented people who are eager to help.

JOHN H. STUBBS
EMILY G. MAKAŠ

PART I
Europe

To mark the fiftieth anniversary of the formation of the Council of Europe as well as the twenty-fifth anniversary of the Council of Europe's European Year for Cultural Heritage, a campaign to promote the natural and cultural heritage of Europe took place from late 1999 through the year 2000. The "Europe, A Common Heritage" campaign brought the twentieth century to a close: a century that is remembered in Europe for the destruction of the two world wars as well as for the historic buildings and environments preserved thanks to the maturation of the architectural conservation movement. The new millennium dawned in Europe with the recognition of escalating conservation challenges—such as pressures from economic development, tourism, and global warming—but also with unprecedented cooperation and coordination on behalf of cultural heritage across Europe.

Europe is a vast continent, a cultural sphere, and a political and economic union each with boundaries that differ and have shifted over time. In spite of diverse geographies, histories, cultures, and scales, today there is an ever-increasing unity of purpose and ideals within Europe and a shared concern for its architectural heritage. Europe stretches from the rolling Ural Mountains to the tip of Gibraltar on the Mediterranean Sea and from the expansive Caspian Sea to the fjords of Iceland. It includes countries that vary in area, population, climate, history, and culture ranging from the expansive Russian Federation to small Malta and Liechtenstein. Over the course of Europe's history, the ties and relationships among its disparate parts have evolved, and peripheral countries have participated to varying degrees. Countries or regions with geographical or cultural affinities toward Europe that might not always be considered part of the region proper, such as Caucasia, Greenland, Siberia, and Anatolia, will be considered along with Europe for the purposes of this book.

Europe's long and well-documented history led to an early appreciation of its cultural heritage, and as such, from a global perspective, it had an advanced start in architectural conservation practice. From the Renaissance's critical approach to the past and the birth of antiquarianism, to the eighteenth century's culture of rationalism, enlightenment, and international exploration, to the nineteenth century's interest in heritage values and protection for the social good, Europe has been the place where the ideas that underlie contemporary cultural heritage conservation practice emerged. In Europe, the development of administrative mechanisms and legal structures for the identification, protection, and preservation of cultural heritage has a unique and long history, clearly discernable patterns, and, as elsewhere, a constantly expanding scope.

Many of the global architectural conservation movement's principles and charters originated in Europe and it has always been a global leader in the field. Europe played an instrumental role in the establishment of two global cultural heritage protection institutions: the United Nations Educational, Scientific, and Cultural Organization (UNESCO) and the International Council on Monuments and Sites (ICOMOS). UNESCO was established in the wake of World War II as an intergovernmental organization aimed toward promotion of international dialogue, shared values, and respect for cultural diversity. In 1964 in Venice, at the Second Congress of Architects and Specialists of Historic Buildings, the International Restoration Charter, known as the Venice Charter, was signed, and ICOMOS was created as an international nongovernmental organization (NGO).[1] Half of the countries represented (and 90 percent of the delegates) at that foundational meeting were European.

Today forty-seven European countries are member states of UNESCO, and there are ICOMOS national chapters in almost all of them. Europe is still disproportionately represented on UNESCO's World Heritage List, with over half the inscribed cultural and mixed heritage sites found within its countries. Both UNESCO and ICOMOS are global in their scope, but the protective mechanisms and best practices they have developed—and the architectural conservation projects they have supported—have had a direct impact mainly on Europe.

Regional intergovernmental institutions such as the Council of Europe and the European Union (EU) have also played important roles in encouraging the sharing of experiences and expertise within Europe as well as the standardizing of policies and practices throughout the continent. The Council of Europe, founded in 1949 by ten countries, but today comprising forty-seven member states, has retained its original focus on promoting democracy, human rights, the rule of law, and European integration. The Council of Europe's active interest in heritage protection began with the European Cultural Convention, signed in Paris in 1954 by fourteen countries to promote mutual understanding and reciprocal appreciation for each other's cultures, as well as to protect their common heritage.[2]

To promote intergovernmental collaboration at the highest level, the Council of Europe has organized numerous Conferences of Ministers Responsible for the Cultural Heritage. At the first such conference, held in Brussels in 1969, discussions were initiated that eventually led to the European Charter of the Architectural Heritage that was signed as part of the activities of the Council of Europe's European Year for Cultural Heritage in 1975.[3] This charter's goal was "to make the public more aware of the irreplaceable cultural, social and economic values" embodied in the diversity of its built heritage.[4] The European Heritage Year program also encouraged local and national governments to actively inventory, protect, and rehabilitate their historic sites and to pay special attention to preventing insensitive changes to them.[5]

The 1975 charter led to the adoption in 1985 in Granada of the Convention for the Protection of the Architectural Heritage of Europe; however, this was not the first legally binding convention developed through the initiative of the Council of Europe. Indeed, a supplement to the 1954 European Cultural Convention had previously been enhanced with a specific convention to protect European archaeological heritage: it was signed in 1969 in London, and was revised in 1992 in Valletta, Malta.[6] In 2005 another convention (the Framework Convention on the Value of Cultural Heritage for Society) was drafted by the Council of Europe in Faro, Portugal, and it will soon have been ratified by enough countries to enter into force.[7] The various heritage charters and conventions and the European Year for Cultural Heritager laid the groundwork for coordinating conservation policies and fostering practical cooperation between government institutions and conservation professionals in Europe.

The European Union was formed in 1993; however, its executive body and predecessor, the European Commission, has been involved in cultural heritage programs almost since its inception in the 1950s. Today the EU includes twenty-seven member states, comprising most of Europe except for Norway, Switzerland, Iceland, Turkey, the Western Balkans, and some former states of the Union of Soviet Socialist Republics. In combination with other factors, the draw of membership to the EU has done much for the updating of heritage protection laws and the strengthening of relevant institutions throughout Central and Eastern Europe in the past decade. The EU's member states are less numerous and geographical extent is much smaller than that of the Council of Europe, but because its members have surrendered some sovereignty to this supranational body, it has greater authority to enforce regulations and coordinate activities. Viewing heritage "as a vehicle for cultural identity" and "as a factor in economic development," the EU has acted to promote awareness and access, the training of professionals, and the use of new technologies as well as to reduce the illicit trafficking in cultural objects.[8]

Through a collection of innovative interrelated programs the Council of Europe and the European Union have worked separately and collaboratively to promote cultural heritage concerns and a shared European identity. In 1985 the EU initiated its European Capital of Culture program, an idea that originated with the Greek Minister of Culture, Melina Mercouri, and led to the selection of Athens as the inaugural city for such international attention. Each year, one European city is honored and provided financial assistance to organize cultural heritage–related activities; however, in 2000, nine cites were designated in special recognition of the millennium, and since then pairs of cities have often shared the honor. Meant to highlight the diversity within Europe, promote tourism, and stimulate cultural initiatives in general, the program has encouraged the construction of elaborate new cultural facilities and significantly aided architectural and urban conservation efforts in many of the selected cities. According to the Palmer Report, issued by the European Commission in 2004 after a lengthy survey and evaluation of the program's first two decades by an independent consultant, the European Capital of Culture program proved "a powerful tool for cultural development that operates on a scale that offers unprecedented opportunities for acting as a catalyst for city change."[9] However, the report also noted that though good for individual cities and local political agendas, the program could be more coordinated and more focused on the "European dimension" of that heritage. Nevertheless, the program's success at spurring and popularizing conservation efforts in specific cities has led to its imitation beyond Europe: for example, since 1996, the Arab League has sponsored an Arab Capital of Culture program, and since 1997 the Organization of American States has designated an American Capital of Culture each year.

In 1991 the Council of Europe initiated its European Heritage Days program, which has been a joint venture with the EU's European Commission since 1999. Through this program, each September, important but usually inaccessible historic sites are opened to the public, and other museums and historic sites offer special activities in a pan-European celebration of heritage. Most countries develop specific themes to link the sites included in a given year, and preparations have prompted the completion of countless restoration and conservation projects throughout Europe. Various local and international NGOs have also coordinated activities to participate in this month highlighting heritage throughout Europe.

In the past twenty-five years, the European Heritage Days program's efforts have significantly raised public awareness for heritage and encouraged governments to prioritize this issue. In recent years, the focus of the European Heritage Days has shifted more and more to emphasize Europe's shared heritage and identity to further promote European integration. According to the 2009 *Handbook on European Heritage Days* (published by the EU and the Council of Europe), today's challenge is "to develop awareness of a common heritage, from Yerevan to Dublin and from Palermo to Helsinki, without negating the feeling of belonging to a specific region or country. In short, we must ensure that, in the words of Jean-Michel Leniaud, the European heritage is *the combined expression of a search for diversity and a quest for unity*."[10]

Launched in 1999, the Council of Europe's European Heritage Network (known as HEREIN) has served as a central reference point and resource for professionals, administrators, and researchers.[11] Designed to create a forum for the coordination of activities of government departments responsible for heritage in various European countries, it has mostly focused on maintaining a database on the cultural policies of those countries and promoting the digitization of cultural and natural heritage information and materials and the standardization of heritage language. Since 2001 it has focused on eastward expansion and integration of Europe as well as on expanding its thesaurus of heritage terms to include as many European languages as possible.

Informal intergovernmental cooperation has also been organized in recent years through the European Heritage Heads Forum (EHHF), which brings the leaders of state heritage protection agencies together to share ideas and strategies.[12] The first meeting was held in London in 2006 and proved so successful that it has been repeated annually. In 2007 a parallel European Heritage Legal Forum (EHLF) was formed by nineteen countries to research and monitor European Union legislation and its potential impact on cultural heritage.[13]

Under the auspices of the Council of Europe in 1963, various NGOs established Europa Nostra, the Pan-European Federation for Cultural Heritage.[14] Its prestigious awards were developed in the late 1970s; it undertook significant public surveying efforts in the 1980s, and it has since been recognized by the EU's European Commission as the premier cultural heritage protection umbrella organization in Europe. In 2002 Europa Nostra's European Heritage Awards for excellence in conservation, research, service, and education were combined with the EU Prize for Cultural Heritage. Recent laureates that reflect the range of honored projects and people have included the restoration of the Mátra Museum in Gyögyös, Hungary; a study on the effect of climate change on Europe's heritage; Glenn Murray, who has worked tirelessly for decades on behalf of Spain's Segovia Mint; and a Greek training program that involves the local population in sustainable urban conservation for economic development.

Europa Nostra's International Secretariat is based in The Hague, The Netherlands, and its efforts are financed by both the Council of Europe and the EU as well as by numerous corporate sponsors. Since 2010 Europa Nostra has been led by president Plácido Domingo, the renowned Spanish tenor and conductor, who has a deep interest and involvement in European culture. Today, Europa Nostra can proudly boast that it "represents some 250 non-governmental organizations, 150 associate organizations and 1500 individual members from more than fifty countries."[15] Europa Nostra campaigns vigorously on behalf of threatened structures, and both its reputation and the media attention it gathers have done much to save individual buildings and sites and to change local policies throughout Europe.

Other NGOs and networks of similar organizations have played a crucial role in promoting and protecting the architectural heritage of Europe. For example, an initiative that began in Flanders, Belgium, has sought to develop an inventory of key cultural heritage organizations throughout Europe to encourage collaboration and partnerships as well as to broaden the understanding of heritage. It has begun organizing meetings of heritage experts, and its bottom-up Inventory of Heritage Organizations of Europe has collected and categorized information about hundreds of NGOs concerned with heritage ranging from industrial to agricultural, from folk art to museology, and from the intangible to architectural.[16] A similar collection of information about European arts-and-heritage NGOs is housed by Culture Action Europe, another Belgium-based organization that was formerly known as the European Forum for the Arts and Heritage. Culture Action Europe is an advocacy group concerned more broadly with artistic production as well as conservation. It was founded in 1994 to provide networking opportunities for NGOs as well as a shared voice and resources when lobbying European policymakers on culture-related issues.[17]

This framework of international conventions, intergovernmental institutions, and NGOs has resulted in a great deal of coordination and shared resources among conservation professionals throughout Europe. In addition, every country in Europe today has long recognized the importance of architectural conservation and established state institutions to restore and oversee its historic sites. Across Europe, heritage legislation protects inventories of designated national monuments, though the terminology and definitions vary from country to country. In some countries, those laws are comprehensive; in others architectural, archaeological, and other components of heritage are protected separately.[18] While some countries have only one category of monument, others have multiple categories with varying levels of restrictions and available support; some also have protective buffer zones around these monuments; and many also have designated conservation areas, such as historic districts, city cores, building complexes, and archaeological sites.[19] In addition, most European countries support architectural conservation through direct grants, tax incentives, or a combination of these mechanisms; however, the particulars of how these funds are managed and distributed, as well as the amounts involved, varies from country to country.[20]

In addition, professionals in the field across Europe today face many of the same challenges. The current global economic crisis has reduced available funding for conservation projects from state and local budgets as well as tourism and the support it provides many sites. Tourism itself remains a double-edged sword, threatening many historic sites with overuse while providing much-needed revenue for research and conservation. The threat of global terrorism has created new security pressures on certain historic centers and sites and their visitors.

Though originally an "exclusivist, arrogant, and dominating" practice, as Costa Carras, vice president of Europa Nostra, characterized its origins, in recent years European conceptions of heritage have become increasingly accommodating of cultural diversity.[21] The early heritage conservationists perhaps never imagined all of the reasons for which historic sites are valued today, particularly how restoration of historic city centers and residential enclaves has contributed to urban regeneration, economic recovery, and the ever-growing cultural tourism industry. In addition, Europe's secularism, democratic traditions, and civil society have contributed to the formation of grassroots interest and involvement in heritage concerns from Great Britain to Greece—a phenomenon that has not always developed as fully elsewhere in the world.[22]

Despite these parallels, the coordination and collaboration facilitated by pan-European charters and institutions, and the globalization of heritage and the internationalization of debates on its issues, remarkably different emphases and characteristics of contemporary conservation practice are found in different countries, even within Europe. These variations are based on the particularities of national histories as well as the unique combinations of heritage found within them. For example, though culturally linked with Western and Northern Europe, the countries of central, eastern, and southeastern Europe have had very different histories, and thus have had differing conservation experiences. In these regions, the large, autocratic Habsburg, Russian, and Ottoman empires lingered into the early twentieth century, precluding the maturation of many of the populist forces that shaped the development of architectural conservation elsewhere in Europe, including aspects of the Renaissance and the Enlightenment in some areas. Yet the end of the Cold War in 1989 signaled a new era in European history, and ever since, similar patterns of interest have spread throughout eastern and southeastern Europe and the post-Soviet states, with the cultural reintegration of Europe as much a priority as its political reunion.

Indeed, Europe's greatest heritage challenge today is to strengthen national and cultural diversities within the framework of a reunited continent. Though initially seen as peripheral to the processes of integrating Europe, culture is playing an increasingly central and fundamental role in creating a true union by promoting European identity; because, to be sure, "Europe" is much more of a cultural entity than a political one.[23] Appreciating the protection of cultural heritage has gained a wider political audience as its benefits have become more and more obvious to European institutions and the international community at large. Today Europe shares and promotes cultural heritage conservation for the benefit of individual local cultures as well as for humanity in general, and European practice and principles have been imitated and adapted worldwide.

ENDNOTES

1. A nongovernmental organization (NGO), ICOMOS is not restricted by the official positions of its member states, and it has proven freer to campaign for broader heritage issues and develop doctrines. For fuller summaries of ICOMOS, UNESCO, and other NGOs and intergovernmental organizations (IGOs), see also John H. Stubbs, *Time Honored: A Global View of Architectural Conservation: Parameters, Theory, and Evolution of an Ethos* (Hoboken, NJ: John Wiley & Sons, 2009), 252–259.

2. Council of Europe, "European Cultural Convention" (Paris: Council of Europe, 1954), http://conventions.coe.int/Treaty/EN/Treaties/Html/018.htm (accessed June 28 2010).

3. Drafted occasionally by IGOs but more frequently by NGOs, the European Charter of the Architectural Heritage and other charters are recommendations of best practices that rely on the good will and cooperative spirit of participants to comply. Conventions, on the other hand, are drafted and ratified by the delegates of states' parties to IGOs—they are international agreements legally binding on the governments that sign them.

4. Council of Europe, "European Charter of the Architectural Heritage" (Amsterdam: Council of Europe, 1975), www.icomos.org/docs/euroch_e.html (accessed May 8, 2010). This in turn led to the "Convention for the Protection of the Architectural Heritage of Europe" (Granada, Spain: Council of Europe, 1985), http://conventions.coe.int/treaty/en/Treaties/Html/121.htm (accessed December 7, 2009).

5. Derek Linstrum, "The Conservation of Historic Towns and Buildings as a National Heritage," *Commonwealth Foundation Occasional Papers* 38 (1976): 15.

6. Council of Europe, "European Convention on the Protection of the Archaeological Heritage" (Valetta, Malta: Council of Europe, 1992), http://conventions.coe.int/Treaty/en/Treaties/Html/143.htm (accessed December 9, 2009).

7. The Council of Europe also signed a "Convention on Offences Relating to Cultural Property" in Delphi in 1985, but it has not been ratified because it duplicates a similar 1972 UNESCO Convention.

8. Through its Culture 2000 program, the European Union has supported specific restoration projects, such as post-earthquake conservation of frescoes at the St. Francis Basilica in Assisi, Italy. In addition, EU taxation, agricultural, and building construction laws also impact how heritage is protected in Europe.

9. Palmer/RAE Associates, *European Cities and Capitals of Culture: A Study Prepared for the European Commission*, part I (Brussels: Palmer/RAE: 2004), 23.

10. Michel Kneubühler, *Handbook on the European Heritage Days: A Practical Guide* (Strasburg and Brussels: Council of Europe and European Commission, 2009), 8.

11. "Home," European Heritage Network, www.european-heritage.net/sdx/herein (accessed December 9, 2009).

12. "European Heritage Heads Forum," English Heritage, www.english-heritage.org.uk/ehhf (accessed December 8, 2009).

13. European Heritage Legal Forum, "The EHLF," Riksantikvaren (Norwegian Directorate for Cultural Heritage), www.ra.no/ehlf (accessed December 8, 2009).

14. "About Europa Nostra, " Europa Nostra, www.europanostra.org/lang_en/index.html (accessed December 8, 2009).

15. "Mission," Europa Nostra, www.europanostra.org/mission (accessed December 8, 2009). Sneška Quaedvlieg-Mihailović and Rupert Graf Strachwitz, eds., "Editors' Foreword," *Heritage and the Building of Europe* (Berlin: Maecenata Verlag, 2004), 7.

16. "Heritage Organizations in Europe," Inventory of Heritage Organizations in Europe, www.heritage-organisations.eu/page?&orl=1&ssn=&lng=2&pge=2 (accessed December 10, 2009).

17. "About Us," Culture Action Europe, www.cultureactioneurope.org/network/about-us (accessed December 10, 2009).

18. Robert Pickard, "Review," in *Policy and Law in Heritage Conservation*, ed. Robert Pickard (London and New York: Spon Press, 2001), 318.

19. Ibid., 315–317.

20. Ibid., 333–334.

21. Costa Carras, "The Significance of the Cultural Heritage for Europe Today," in Quaedvlieg-Mihailović and Strachwitz, *Heritage and the Building of Europe*, 31.

22. Ibid., 54.

23. Ibid., 30.

Beginning in Italy with the Renaissance interest in the ruins of antiquity, the theory and practice of organized architectural conservation originated in Western Europe. These ideas spread outward during the eighteenth century as interest in deliberate architectural conservation was witnessed in France and England. Soon all of Western Europe was engaged in some variety of conservation activities, which began to mature in the late nineteenth and early twentieth century.

The separate but overlapping experiences of Italy, France, and Great Britain all provide substantial evidence that restoration practice in the nineteenth century was heavily imbued with scientific and nationalist implications, the hallmarks of the early industrial age. In Italy, as well as in Germany in central Europe, the restoration of key historic buildings instilled the populations with a collective cultural pride and reinforced enthusiasm for political unification, while French and British restoration practice was more reflective of a growing reaction against the societal changes wrought by the Industrial Revolution. In both France and Great Britain, this reaction was manifested in a glorification of everything medieval, because for many disturbed by the rising tide of unbridled capitalism and secular modernism the Middle Ages represented the core values of the state and church. In France and Great Britain medieval heritage was also looked to as a source in the search for national origins, while in Italy the great legacies of the Roman era and the Renaissance served a similar purpose in the late nineteenth and early twentieth century.

During this transition period for Western Europe, the "unity of style" movement was the paramount school of thought for architectural restoration. Through the efforts of its most fervent adherent, Eugène-Emmanuel Viollet-le-Duc, this approach elevated "restoration" from merely merging artistic additions with historic structures to a scientific and methodological practice. Viollet-le-Duc's prolific restoration work in France and voluminous scholarly endeavors quickly spread abroad, where architects, ecclesiastical societies, and government agencies adopted his ideas for restoring, correcting, and improving upon their historic monuments. His approach combined rationalism and creative license and was widely seen as the ideal solution for the treatment of damaged or unfinished historic structures in Western Europe, particularly in Belgium and Netherlands.

The contemporaneous Italian and British schools of conservation theory and practice, which advocated more conservative approaches to restoration, served as important counterpoints to "unity of style" ideas. This dialectic did much to define the philosophical parameters of the field in Europe and beyond.

The first half of the twentieth century introduced new challenges for Western European heritage, beginning with the destruction of sites during wartime on a scale unseen in modern history. The damage was compounded by subsequent post-war rebuilding projects, many of which seriously altered historic built environments by wholesale demolition and modernization. With the benefit of hindsight, we realize today that much of that new construction was inferior in workmanship, inadequate in function, and lacking in aesthetic quality.[1] By the mid-1960s there were increasing reactions across Western Europe to modern architecture's failure to provide compatibly designed new buildings in historic contexts.[2]

Local activists organized societies to save old buildings and prevent their replacement by mediocre modern architecture. Often, such activities engaged them in battles with a variety of interested parties, including planners, developers, architects, property owners, and the general public. Every country has had its struggles in this area, with the negotiated results—some more successful than others—constituting the architectural face of Europe that we see today.

As interest in conservation expanded, new conservation technologies, methodologies, and creative programs for action were developed. For example, many countries, such as Italy, France, Spain, and Portugal, which had been dependent on government funding for architectural conservation, eventually began to embrace schemes involving the private sector more significantly in the protection of architectural heritage. In fact, fund-raising for architectural conservation has become an increasing concern of individuals, historic sites, and NGOs in recent years.

Today, all Western European countries have well-developed legislation and listing procedures and a host of innovative heritage awareness and action schemes. Most also have well-established government offices to oversee, coordinate, and advise conservation efforts. Over the course of the twentieth century, they have amended and adapted their practices and laws to reflect broadening concepts of what is valuable and what deserves protection. In addition, most of these countries have also witnessed the emergence of networks of nonprofit and public advocacy groups that complement and act as monitors of government activities in the field of architectural conservation.

Despite these extensive parallels, each Western European country's particular conservation efforts developed from different combinations of factors in recent centuries and thus the contemporary practice of each has a slightly distinct character, with specific strengths and weaknesses. At the same time, in the second half of the twentieth century, increasing awareness of developments in neighboring countries as well as increasing collaboration both informally and through pan-European institutions has led to similarities in the architectural conservation experiences of Western European countries.

ENDNOTES

1. Certainly some post–World War II construction supplied urgently needed provisional architecture in circumstances where speed of erection and cost efficiency mattered more than aesthetics and longevity.

2. Probably the most thorough portrayal of reactions of heritage conservationists to new trends in twentieth century architecture is found in architectural historian Wim Denslagen's *Romantic Modernism; Nostalgia in the World of Conservation* (Amsterdam University Press, 2009)..

Figure 1.1 View of the Forum and Palatine from the Capitoline Hill, Rome, Italy, where 2,700 years of Roman architectural history are on view.

CHAPTER 1

Italy

Italy's extensive and significant surviving ancient and medieval-renaissance heritage, as well as its importance for Italian identity in the nineteenth and twentieth centuries, has meant that architectural conservation has been prevalent and a priority in this country for two hundred years. During this period, Italy has emerged as a leader in the global field, particularly in the specializations of conservation education and theory. Architectural conservation practitioners and theoreticians, from Camillo Boito in the nineteenth century to Cesare Brandi in the mid-twentieth century to Paolo Marconi in recent decades, have shaped the way contemporary architectural heritage protection is approached and understood in Italy today. The research institutes and graduate study programs with which they have been affiliated, including the Istituto Superiore per la Conservazione ed il Restauro (Higher Institute for Preservation and Restoration) and the Università degli Studi Roma Tre (University of Rome III)—and indeed many more could be named here—have trained specialists and advanced conservation theory and practice.

Italian conservators have also actively shared their experiences and expertise through work in projects around the world. Though caring for the extensive number of significant historic sites in Italy presents a challenge even for these global leaders and institutions, the importance of cultural heritage and the degree to which it is protected ensures that most of Italy's architectural patrimony should be secure in the years ahead.

EARLY ORGANIZED CONSERVATION EFFORTS

Following the social upheavals of the Napoleonic Wars at the beginning of the nineteenth century, especially after unification and industrialization at the end of that same century, Italian architectural conservationists joined their French and English counterparts in contributing to a growing body of theory and special methodologies. Among their principal concerns was the treatment of the vast number of ancient urban buildings, whose fabric was being negatively affected by various modernization schemes. The experience of adapting and restoring historic Roman buildings often served as the basis for developing this increasingly distinct aspect of the larger field of architecture.

Due to the widespread appeal of Rome's rich cultural patrimony, it is in the Eternal City where the most noticeable examples of a nascent professional architectural conservation specialization can be readily seen. Systematic restoration and heritage protection efforts in Rome began during the French occupation in 1798, and shortly thereafter excavation work at the Roman Forum initiated the close traditional linkage between Italian architectural conservation and the field of classical archaeology.[1]

As the nineteenth-century popes and the Roman Catholic Church hierarchy influenced both Rome's urban refurbishment and provided a legal framework for restoring and protecting key historic buildings, the treatment of individual buildings improved. The sensitive buttressing of the Colosseum by Raffaele Stern and Giuseppe Camporesi was the first great architectural conservation project of the nineteenth century in Italy.[2] Giuseppe Valadier's work at the Arch of Titus in 1821 skillfully blended old and new building fabric and successfully juxtaposed, where necessary, surviving original material with new marble elements that restored the structural and visual integrity of the damaged building. Valadier's sophisticated and carefully documented interventions focused on retaining as much original architectural fabric as possible. His work received much attention and set standards for the formalization of architectural restoration theory in Italy later in the nineteenth century.

By midcentury, the Italian architectural conservation movement had found itself in the center of the European philosophical debate on conservation approaches when Carlo Cattaneo's written opposition to the construction of Milan's cathedral square (Piazza del Duomo) imported John Ruskin's "less intervention is more" ideas into a locale that subscribed to Eugène-Emmanuel Viollet-le-Duc's approach of radical period restoration.[3] Energized by the enthusiasm of opposing positions, the Italian architectural conservation movement gained momentum. Conservation theories and methodologies were constantly publicly debated as legislation and architectural protection advocates created a vast body of literature, laws, and regulations for each small state and duchy.

The modernization of cities in the late nineteenth century, throughout Europe but especially in cherished historic centers such as Florence, helped give birth to today's public interest in architectural conservation. Proposals for street widening and cutting, as well as the insertion of modern infrastructure into near-perfectly preserved medieval and renaissance cities, inspired active campaigns to save these places. For example, in Florence, between 1885 and 1895, twenty-six streets, twenty squares, and twenty-one parks were destroyed, along with 341 dwellings, 451 shops, and 173 storehouses—in addition, 5,822 people were obliged to move elsewhere in order to open up broad avenues with calculated vistas.[4] When the threat of destruction turned to the Ponte Vecchio and other key sites within the city, concern was raised among city councillors, concerned Florentines, and others from throughout Europe (especially the United Kingdom) who had fallen in love with the city's charms. In 1898 the Society for the Defense of Old Florence was founded, and letter-writing campaigns and newspaper editorials questioned developments in both London and Florence. Finally, a petition was prepared with more than ten thousand signatures, including those of an astounding number of leading writers, artists, and governmental figures from across Europe and North America. Thus, one of the earliest international architectural conservation battles was witnessed in the campaign to prevent the modernization of Florence.

When the Kingdom of Italy was proclaimed in 1861, the groundwork for the organized protection of architectural heritage had already been laid. However, it took over forty years before the passage of Italy's first comprehensive law on architectural conservation: the Monument Act of 1902. Political unification both positively and negatively influenced Italian heritage conservation. It created the impetus for reorganizing the country's cultural property management system (which by definition included historically and artistically significant buildings, sites, and practically all surviving ancient monuments). At the same time, the new capital, Rome, once again saw its infrastructure and built heritage suffer. The Forum lost its romantic and picturesque mantle of earth and vegetation as archaeological excavations recommenced, and a controversial assault was launched on the Colosseum. Infrastructure demands seriously threatened the numerous historic buildings and districts that impeded modernization schemes such as the widening of boulevards, treatment of city walls, new embankments for the Tiber River,

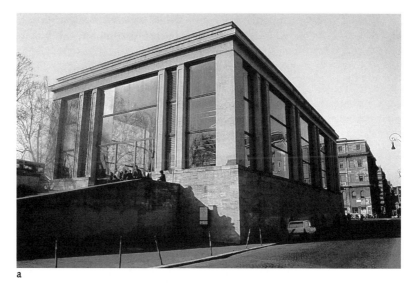

a

Figure 1-2 The enclosure built for the Ara Pacis (Altar of Peace) in Rome in 1938 (a) was replaced in 2005 (b). The vastly larger new structure, with the altar centered below a new high enclosure, is also meant to accommodate public exhibitions and cultural events: for example, a retrospective of couturier Valentino Garavani (c). This twenty-first century enclosure, designed by American architect Richard Meier, is one of the very few contemporary architectural interventions in the heart of Rome, and, as such, it has been the subject of a debate about whether conspicuous new construction is antithetical to preservation of the historic city.

b

c

and enlargement of public squares. It was within this atmosphere that today's contemporary architectural conservation practice in Italy developed its roots.

Benito Mussolini's rise to power in 1922 refocused national interest on the glory of the Roman Empire. The dictator, anxious to bathe his Partito Nazionale Fascista (National Fascist Party) in reflected imperial glory, ensured that the city's most valuable ancient structures remained unscathed by the extensive modernization programs being implemented by municipal authorities. He took an energetic and personal interest in using architecture as propaganda. Massive excavation and restorations projects were begun at many sites, including the Colosseum, the Capitol, the fora, the Tomb of Augustus, the Temple of Hercules, and the Pantheon.[5] A draconian approach was used on the chosen monuments: accretions were removed and neighboring buildings torn away to better present the structures to the public. A portion of the newly excavated Trajan market was reinstated as a marketplace. The discovery and the reassembly of the finely sculpted *Ara Pacis* (Altar of Peace), dating from the first century CE, and the raising of the galleys of Lake Nemi (used for mock sea battles in imperial Roman times) were among the most outstanding archaeological excavations and display efforts of the time.[6]

While Mussolini's heavy-handed approach was controversial, some architectural conservationists today view his actions in a positive light. Many of Rome's greatest antiquities today still stand in their glory, having been given comfortable viewing space for generations of onlookers. Only an autocrat could have done this.

KEY TWENTIETH-CENTURY THEORISTS AND METHODS

As Mussolini was attempting to redefine the Italian national psyche with the help of imperial Roman props, a generation of professional talent began to address international architectural heritage protection. The early twentieth-century approaches and conservation theory writings of Gustavo Giovannoni significantly affected the direction of conservation practice both domestically and beyond. His refinements of the principles of Camillo Boito, an Italian architect who tried to reconcile the ideas of Ruskin and Viollet-le-Duc, highlighted the need for a discernable difference between old and new work in style and materials used, the visible inscription and documentation of all new restoration work carried out on the historic building, and the display of removed surviving original elements near the restored building.[7] Giovannoni expanded the use of Boito's *restauro scientifico* (scientific restoration) approach (also called archaeological restoration) for all historic buildings, not just classical monuments, and encouraged the use of traditional techniques and "primitive materials" that were as close as possible to the original. He particularly emphasized the formerly discounted value of the "minor architecture" of historic urban centers and towns, which make an important contribution to the overall historic environment.

Giovannoni's revisions of Boito's principles helped create the 1931 Athens Charter and the Carta Italiana del Restauro (Italian Charter of Restoration) the following year. This Italian Charter initiated the practice of "philological restoration," a term derived from the Latin definition of monument as inscription or as document. A monument, in this sense, was built to carry a message, and it was itself seen as a document and therefore should not be falsified.[8] The views of art historian Tito Vespasiano Paravicini contributed significantly to the development of this approach.

By the 1930s, Italy's architectural conservation movement had gained sufficient momentum that the theories and methodologies of conservation were a constant subject of public debate and legislation. Instead of merely applying blanket concepts found in the 1931 Athens Charter, a more case-by-case, site-specific "critical restoration" approach began to develop. Giovannoni was among the first to stress the necessity of tailoring one's restoration approach to the needs of the building in question. As an example, ancient Greek monuments, which are constructed of cut stone, are appropriate candidates for

Figure 1-3 As a key center of professional architectural conservation, Italian examples of "best practices" over time can be readily observed, especially at sites such as the Roman Forum and ancient Pompeii and in the historic cities of Bologna, Venice, and Verona. The extensive ruins of Pompeii show a plethora of architectural, engineering, and scientific conservation approaches that have been used in the past century and half for conserving and featuring fragile ruins that are exposed to the elements. Three examples are shown here: a re-erected and structurally stabilized entablature fragment in Pompeii's forum where old and new are distinguished by use of different materials (a); extensive reconstruction based on archaeological evidence at the House of the Veti (both early twentieth century (b); and relatively conservative stone cleaning and consolidation at the Arch of Septimius Severus in Rome in 2002 (c).

a

b

c

anastylosis; that is, rebuilding using original materials. Most Roman monuments are not candidates for this method, because their assembly usually requires mortar or concrete.

In the mid-twentieth century, the theories of Boito and Giovannoni were joined by those of Cesare Brandi, the founder of Rome's highly regarded Istituto Centrale del Restauro (Central Institute for Restoration), now the Istituto Superiore per la Conservazione ed il Restauro (Higher Institute for Preservation and Restoration).

For Brandi, the restorer of any site must first relate to it as an artistic work (*opera d'arte*) and, second, recognize that it is an artistic creation (*istanza estetica*) created in a given space and time (*istanza storica*).[9] Once a restorer recognizes a site's artistic value, he or she is obliged to safeguard it for future generations. The type of intervention required is dictated by the site's aesthetic and historic uniqueness; one must never delete traces of its historic "evolution," including the patina acquired over years. The restorer must guard against artistic or historic forgery and keep the new intervention clearly distinct from the original fabric. Any work done, however, must permit and facilitate future interventions. For Brandi, how the site relates to its surrounding environment is also important: supports and structural frames may be added when necessary, but his approach forbade incorporating historic buildings within all new structures.

The degree of destruction caused by World War II in Italy significantly affected the country's post-war architectural conservation methodology. Triage decisions—based on a historic building's aesthetic value coupled with a cost-benefit assumption—prioritized work and determined what needed to be done. Most of the work done immediately after the war focused on saving significant historic buildings that could be restored or rehabilitated relatively easily; extensive rebuilding of collapsed buildings was rare, irrespective of their value.

Post-war recovery also required implementing a variety of architectural conservation approaches. Interventions covered the whole spectrum of possibilities, ranging from painstaking anastylosis and restoration to romantic imitation inspired by contemporary architectural fashion. Where documentation was missing, in-fill additions to the urban silhouette were often created according to the whim of the builder, often in the mode of Viollet-le-Duc. In other cases, new sympathetic designs in brick and travertine were used that respected the scale of surrounding buildings. Yet in other cases, such as the train station areas of Florence and Rome and the port areas of Naples and Genoa, all new designs replaced their extensively destroyed predecessor facilities.

Figure 1-4 The thirteenth-century Tempio Malatestiano (a), the cathedral church in Rimini, which had been transformed in the fifteenth-century by Leon Battista Alberti, suffered major damage (b and c) but remained standing despite the near-total destruction of the city around it as a result of heavy bombardment during World War II. The masonry walls of the Tempio Malatestiano shifted as a result of the attack on the city, causing major cracking, and after the war the stones were adjusted to restore Alberti's precise proportional arrangements. That early 1950s project was supported by the U.S.-based Samuel H. Kress Foundation, and the church has since been more thoroughly cleaned. The Tempio Malatestiano is one of many architecturally significant structures damaged or destroyed across Europe during the war that led to the reopening of the restoration versus conservation debate as architectural conservationists were faced with a desire to rebuild and recover the massive losses. Images courtesy Lisa Ackerman.

Pride in artistic traditions in both art and architecture in Italy, from the Renaissance forward, expressed itself in several ways. One of these forms of expression had profound and far-reaching significance: valued objects—both *naturalia* (objects from the natural world) and *artificialia* (objects made by humans, including artwork)—were collected and put on display in purpose-built spaces. This is the case with the gallery Florentine architect Bernardo Buontalenti built in the Uffizi Palace in 1581 to accommodate the Medici family's collections, which thereby became the original core of the renowned museum (Galleria degli Uffizi, or Uffizi Gallery).

At the same time, collections of antiquities and contemporary works of art were being amassed in Rome, a growing center of power, under the guidance of Vatican popes. The collections of antiquarians played a role as well in what evolved to be a new ethos and interest in featuring Italy's wealth of art, architecture, and history for didactic purposes. The motives fueling this new ethos ranged from the purely altruistic to the political, but the main development was that the collection, documentation, and presentation of art and architecture addressed a demand for such information from locals and foreigners alike.

Over the past five centuries, countless museums have been established in Italy and throughout Europe, so much so that museums have become essential to civic life. As such, the mission, collection policies, and methodology of museums are commonly encountered topics, especially among those working with or interested in cultural heritage. *Museology*, the discipline of museum organization and management, plays a central role in cultural heritage management today, and it is an essential element of many architectural conservation projects. The connections between museums and architectural conservation range from an architect and his or her advisors carefully accommodating a museum's collections in a restored historic building to museum and exhibition designers offering improved interpretations of historic sites. In this sense, the museums and most conserved architecture have similar aims—preserve and interpret cultural heritage for the public benefit.

Museums have also participated in architectural conservation through the preservation of elements and/or parts of buildings within their collections. Controversial cases include the Parthenon marbles in the British Museum in London and the Altar of Pergamum and Ishtar Gate on Berlin's Museum Island. Museums have been founded throughout Europe that are specifically dedicated to the decorative arts and focused on furnishings and interior architecture. In the United States, entire rooms have been transferred to and rebuilt in art museums when the buildings around them were destroyed.

In the past half century, architectural conservation has been enriched worldwide by international cooperation among museums and museum professionals. As a part of the wave of new international organizations formed following World War II, the NGO the International Council of Museums (ICOM) was established in 1946 to advise and work closely with UNESCO. With 115 national committees today, as well as individual participation in other countries and regional and thematic international cooperation among the national organizations, the Paris-based ICOM is active throughout the world. Its mission is to promote professional exchange, disseminate information, raise awareness, train personnel, improve professional standards and ethics, and preserve the heritage housed within museums as well as to fight the illicit traffic of cultural property.

Following years of careful research and as part of a global series documenting "One Hundred Missing Objects" from various parts of the world, ICOM published *Looting in Europe* in 2001.[10] As a result, numerous lost treasures have been found and returned to their established owners—for example, a late seventeenth-century sculpture of the Evangelist Mark was identified in a Viennese auction catalog and returned to its original place in St. Vitus Church in Jemnice, Czech Republic, and a wooden tabernacle stolen in 1996 was found in a private home in 2008 and returned to the Church of San Antonio Abate in Amatrice, Italy.

Today the conservation of architectural fragments in museums and of buildings and their artwork in situ is often separated by administrative organization. In many European countries, and indeed in much of the world, protection and conservation of immovable and movable cultural heritage is typically divided between separate branches within ministries of culture. For example, in France, responsibilities are separated between the Direction des Musées (Directorship for Museums) and the Direction de l'Architecture et du Patrimoine (Directorship for Architecture and Heritage). At the same level in Italy, these functions are combined under the Direzione Generale per la Valorizzazione del Patrimonio Culturale (Director General's Office for the Valorization of the Cultural Patrimony) that is responsible for both the country's museums and its architectural and urban heritage.

By the late 1950s, most of the crucial post-war rebuilding projects had been completed, and Italian architects and conservators regained the luxury of developing projects at a less urgent pace. During this period Carlo Scarpa emerged as one of the most creative and prominent modern Italian architects who specialized in adaptive reuse of buildings. He is well known for his sensitive and discrete incorporation of high-quality and detailed design elements into his restorations. One of his most notable projects is the 1958 to 1964 restoration and rearrangement of Castelvecchio in Verona, which amalgamated different phases of its construction, from the twelfth century through Napoleonic times. Carefully considered sight lines and the presentation of different periods of the castle's history in exposed architectural fabric are hallmarks of this project.

a

b

Figure 1-5 The Uffizi Gallery in Florence (a), which was built in the late sixteenth century in part to house the private collections of the Medici dynasty, became the first art museum in Europe once it opened to the public in 1765. In the twentieth century the Uffizi's extensive collection has been cramped for space in its controlled interior environment (b), leading to multiple extensions and the display of holdings in adjacent historic buildings, even on the walls of the adjacent enclosed Vasarian Corridor, the kilometer-long passageway that bridges the Arno River and leads to the Pitti Palace, which also houses part of the Uffizi's collection today.

▲ **Figure 1-6** Some of the more durable surviving architectural elements of the early fourth-century Baths of Diocletian are on display alfresco in a reinstated peristyle area. This largest bath complex in the ancient Roman world has since 1889 served as the National Roman Museum, housing collected ancient Roman artwork.

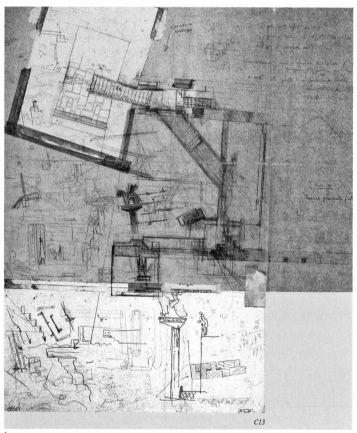

◄▲ **Figure 1-7** Architect Carlo Scarpa's widely hailed restoration of the Castelvecchio, adapting it into the City Museum of Verona between 1958 and 1964, demonstrates a remarkable ability to integrate new architectural elements and uses into historic buildings. His deep interest in history is evident in his skillful combining of old and new, with the hallmark of this project being the prominent positioning of the fourteenth-century equestrian sculpture of Cangrande I della Scala (a) in the museum's central space. Scarpa produced numerous design studies for the project (b).

a

b

Opportunities available to Italy's modern architects and architectural conservationists were expanded during the second half of the twentieth century as scientific advances created both new building materials and techniques for conserving historic architectural fabric. The prominent Florentine architectural conservationist Piero Sanpaolesi was particularly concerned with material durability. His research focused on the effect of chemical-hardening compounds on stone. For Sanpaolesi it was important to extend a historic building's "material existence" by protecting a site's original "autograph" material from further decay while still preserving the character it acquired over time.[11]

Sanpaolesi's research helped advance contemporary conservation architect and educator Giovanni Carbonara's restoration approach of minimal, potentially reversible, interventions. Carbonara mirrors Ruskin by equating conservation with preventive medicine and restoration with surgery.[12] For Carbonara restoration needed historical and critical judgment coupled with technical and scientific know-how.

Another important Italian player in the development of a theoretical architectural conservation approach was critic, historian, and conservator Roberto Pane, the country's representative on the ICOMOS working committee for the 1964 International Charter of Venice and a professor at the University of Naples. For Pane aesthetics were an important consideration in conservation decisions. An evaluation of the artistic merit of each historic building must be made in order to fashion an appropriate, site-specific conservation approach, observing that "any monument shall be seen as a unique case, because it is as such a work of art and such shall be also its restoration."[13] Pane was among the first to warn against overestimating the benefits of modern technologies, which he felt could obscure the authenticity of historic buildings. He recommended the removal of all accretions irrespective of their age or merit, although creative integrations that were made due to an aesthetic need could remain. Indeed, to Brandi's theory that any work of art or heritage object has two fundamental contexts in which it should be considered, the aesthetic and the historical (*istanza estetica* and *istanza storica*), Pane added a third—the psychological (*istanza psicologica*)—to stress the value of human integrity, aesthetic enjoyment, and memory. In addition, the prominent shapers of contemporary practice in Italian conservation through the 1960s and 1970s were a number of professional practitioners who made reliable contributions to the field through more specialized approaches and accomplishments. In contrast to Pane, an Italian conservation architect who looked to modern technology to solve one of the field's most pressing problems—how to protect excavated architectural sites from the detrimental effects of weather, sunlight, and vandalism—was architect Franco Minissi.

The Roman architect and professor Paolo Marconi has persuasively demonstrated that using traditional construction techniques in restorations and reconstructions, as at Pompeii, has both philosophical and practical merit. In 2003 Marconi also established an international graduate-level program at the University of Rome III (Università degli Studi Roma Tre) that primarily addresses the conservation of historic rural towns. Architect Andrea Bruno is among the many others who have produced award-winning designs for deftly blending finely detailed new design within, or adjacent to, historic building projects. Likewise, internationally renowned architects Renzo Piano and Gae Aulenti have made names for themselves in architectural circles with their bold rehabilitations, including the Morgan Library and Museum in New York City and the Musée d'Orsay in Paris. There are countless examples on a lesser scale, throughout Italy, of smartly detailed insertions of new design into historic contexts with some of the most successful found in relation to museums. The cleverly detailed insertions of circulation for visitors and displays in the subterranean Crypta Balbi, the new Palazzo Altemps Museum, and the Museum of the Aurelian Walls (Museo delle Mura), installed within a maze of ancient Roman walls by the Porta San Sebastiano, are but three examples in Rome alone.

Figure 1-8 Cement grout injection during a 1977 restoration as a structural stabilization measure at the Ospedale di San Michele complex in Trastevere, Rome, is illustrative of one of several conservation-engineering techniques developed in Italy.

a

b

Figure 1-9 The adaptive reuse of the former monastery cloister of the Palazzo delle Stelline in Corso Magenta in Milan (a) as offices for a cultural institution illustrates the discretion and talent of its designers in the mid-1970s. A view from the interior (b) through the enclosed arches of the cloister's former arcade shows sensitive detailing of glazing and air-conditioning systems and a bold new floor design in the foreground

The extraordinarily robust Italian architectural conservation system over the past two decades has produced a new breed of conservation architects. Notable are the Roman firm of Longobardi and Mandara, which has created computerized databases as conservation planning tools for ancient Pompeii, and Milanese conservation architect Gionata Rizzi, who is doing innovative conservation work and new design for amenities at archaeological sites in Italy and abroad.

Building large-scale shelters or enclosures over excavated archaeological sites to protect them from detrimental external effects has been a commonly employed solution since the 1950s. On Sicily, protecting its numerous ancient Greek and Roman sites, has largely been a successful endeavor thanks to innovative conservation interventions taken during the late twentieth century at key sites such as the earthen walls of the Greek colony at Gela and the Roman mosaics at Piazza Armerina. This work has influenced practices elsewhere and also led to thoughtful and continuous reevaluation of best practice methods used by the field.

In the mid-twentieth century, shelters were preferable to earlier treatments of archaeological sites: methods included *reburial*, which preserved the ruins but prevented continued research or viewing by tourists, to *reconstruction*, which usually destroyed part of the ruins and compromised their integrity. Shelters provided a much needed balance between prevention of deterioration of archaeological sites and accessibility for researchers and the visiting public.

In recent decades, a number of negative side effects generated by these shelters have raised questions about their effectiveness. Problems range from aesthetic intrusion to increased physical deterioration of the site or item(s) the shelters were meant to protect. While shelter design evolved, finding the perfect alternative solution remains a challenge today for archaeological site conservators and managers.

One of the earliest large-scale, permanent enclosures erected to protect an archaeological site was the steel and translucent plastic panel structure designed in 1957 by Franco Minissi and built over the Villa del Casale at Piazza Armerina in Sicily. The Villa del Casale was built in the early fourth century on the ruins of an earlier Roman country house, and it was destroyed by Norman invaders in the mid-twelfth century. Its ruins were rediscovered in 1881, largely excavated in the 1950s, and added to the World Heritage List in 1997. The Villa del Casale is renowned for its extensive floor mosaics, which have survived almost intact and in superb condition for centuries. Following their excavation, many were lifted and consolidated, using reinforced-concrete backing panels, to improve their display. This method of preserving mosaics is questioned by some today.

For all the good attention that Minissi's award-winning design has drawn to the topic of archaeological site protection, the greatest conservation problems facing Piazza Armerina's mosaics today, however, result from the protective enclosure he designed and built for them. Though built entirely out of modern materials, Minissi's enclosure is a conjectural recreation of the massing of the former palace, approximating its height and including typical Roman roof profiles. Metal walkways within the enclosure hover over the ancient walls and allow visitors to see the mosaics without intruding on the site itself.

While the enclosure's translucent roof panels offer protection from the elements and allow the mosaics to be viewed in natural light, they also create shadows that make viewing difficult. More importantly, they also create extreme fluctuations in temperature and humidity through their greenhouse-like effect. Although ventilation mechanisms were designed into the ceiling panels, air does not circulate well through the enclosure and contributes further to the negative environmental conditions at the site. The enclosure's microclimate is both uncomfortable for site visitors and detrimental to the mosaics themselves.[14] Today, conservation architect Gionata Rizzi's revisions to the original Piazza Armerina shelter are being implemented under the guidance of the director of the Centro Regionale del Restauro, architect Guido Meli. Both the Minissi and Rizzi designs for the sheltering and display of Piazza Armerina's mosaics illustrate the extreme difficulty of preserving and presenting fragile ancient building fragments in situ. In addition to the technical challenges, some heritage conservationists regard Minissi's original design to be historically significant in its own right and question today's interventions to the extent that Piazza Armerina was included in ICOMOS's *Heritage@Risk 2006/2007* list.[15]

Greater success is potentially being achieved through more recent shelter designs. For example, in 1998, a steel-and-glass enclosure was built over the ruins of the twelfth-century cathedral priory in Hamar, Norway. Designed by architect Kjell Lund, it has been praised as a work of art in its own right and as an important contribution to contemporary architecture. However, only time will tell if this and other more recent enclosures will eventually require additional maintenance attention or lead to the kind of environmental problems caused by the earlier generation of shelters.

The Getty Conservation Institute (GCI) has also contributed significantly to research efforts on protective shelters for archaeological sites. In 2001 GCI co-organized a conference on the topic, and the papers given there were published in a special issue of the journal *Conservation and Management of Archaeological Sites*. During the 1980s, GCI had also sponsored the development of an easily erectable, aesthetically appealing, and nonintrusive protective shelter for temporary use at archaeological sites. The modular design of the prototype "hexashelter" was based on tetrahedral geometry and included a fabric cover stretched over tension rods. After its use to protect the Orpheus mosaic in Paphos, Cyprus, and an adobe construction in Fort Selden, New Mexico, the "hexashelter" was praised for its neutral appearance and simple construction. Since the "hexashelter" does not fully enclose a site, it does not completely protect exposed archaeological material from the environment. Additionally, it has proven so lightweight that high winds and snowfall may threaten its stability and often prevent its use. Nonetheless, though intended to be a temporary structure, one of the original "hexashelters" still protects the archaeological site at Paphos almost twenty years after it was erected.

Though ideal solutions for protecting archaeological sites and making them publicly accessible remains an ongoing concern, GCI's efforts and those of contemporary designers have added to the important discussion of how to best protect this type of heritage and how shelters and enclosures can evolve to play a continuing role in this process.

FURTHER READING

Ashurst, John, "Protective Enclosures and Shelters." In *Conservation of Ruins* (Amsterdam: Elsevier, 2006), 177–191.

Aslan, Zaki. "Protective Structures for the Conservation and Presentation of Archaeological Sites." *Journal of Conservation and Museum Studies 3* (November 1997). http://cool.conservation-us.org/jcms/issue3/aslan.html (accessed May 19, 2010).

de la Torre, Marta. *The Conservation of Archaeological Sites in the Mediterranean Region: Proceedings of an International Conference organized by the Getty Conservation Institute and the J. Paul Getty Museum, 6–12 May 1995.* Los Angeles: Getty Conservation Institute, 1997.

Pesaresi, Paola, and Gionata Rizzi. "New and Existing Forms of Protective Shelter at Herculaneum: Towards Improving the Continuous Care of the Site." *Conservation and Management of Archaeological Sites 8*, no. 4 (2006):237–252.

Price, Nicholas Stanley, ed. "Special Issue on Protective Shelters." *Conservation and Management of Archaeological Sites 5* (2001): 1–2.

CONSERVATION LEGISLATION AND EDUCATION

Italy's comprehensive approach to architectural conservation began with the 1902 Monument Act, which established administrative branches, aided by a central commission of historians and archaeologists, to deal with key historic buildings, excavations, galleries, and objects of art. By 1905 the first superintendencies of national monuments were created to oversee, among other things, the exportation of antiquities and works of art, art galleries, and landscapes. This framework is operational even today, although chronic budgetary constraints and occasional moves to dilute its authority threaten its effectiveness.

In 1938 the Ministry of Education, influenced by the 1931 Athens Charter and the 1932 Italian Charter, published its first set of standards to regulate the restoration of ancient buildings. Recommendations included eliminating the subjective distinction between "dead" and "living" monuments, forbidding the conservation in situ of decorative elements (archaeological findings), and reconstructing structures in locations other than their original site.

By 1939 the Italian Parliament was debating wider issues: historic urban centers, gardens, and environments, which provided the basis for two important laws that remained in effect through the end of the twentieth century. Law N. 1089, Tutela delle Cose d'Interesse Artistico e Storico (Protection of Objects of Artistic and Historical Interest), focused on cultural heritage while Law N. 1497, Protezione delle Bellezze Naturali (Protection of Natural Beauties) protected the aesthetic value of the environment. These two laws further defined and reinforced the protection initially created by legislation passed earlier in the century. However, the unforeseen devastation Italy suffered during World War II created massive emergency rehabilitation and reconstruction needs that could not be met either by their conservative architectural conservation guidelines or by the Italian Charter's criteria.

a

b

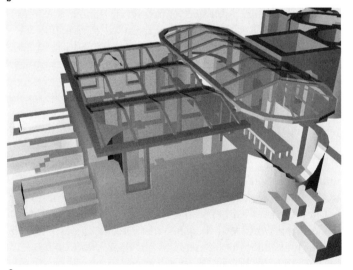

c

d

The post–World War II era saw for the first time a popular appreciation of the country's built heritage, as well as development of the concept that architectural heritage belongs to all. In 1958 and 1962, new key legislation facilitated the preservation of historic villas in the Veneto region by providing for their expropriation if an owner was unable or unwilling to maintain the property.[16] It started slowly, but in time it developed into a model program in Italy.

In 1955 Italy's premier nonprofit conservation organization Italia Nostra was formed to combat the planned destruction of Rome's historic core by municipal authorities. It gained media attention for a new concept—a "culture of conservation." Twenty years later, the idea of collective ownership of Italy's patrimony was accepted enough to facilitate the creation of the Fund for the Italian Environment (FAI)—Fondo per l'ambiente Italiano—to protect and manage Italy's natural and cultural heritage for the good of its general population. The Fund operates along the lines of Britain's National Trust; with the help of over 50,000 supporters and two hundred sponsors, this not-for-profit organization today maintains hundreds of historic buildings and sites acquired or donated by private owners.[17]

While Italians continued to refine and develop their conservation approaches during the last quarter of the twentieth century, the country's ongoing economic and political uncertainties have significantly affected the functionality of its extensive state-managed heritage conservation apparatus. Since 1978 the power of the superintendencies has weakened after a law was passed to decentralize their responsibilities.[18] In 2000 passage of a comprehensive new law, the *Testo Unico*, integrated and streamlined Italy's heritage policies. The new law encompasses the protection of listed ancient monuments, historic buildings, and archaeological sites as well as the contents of museums, libraries, and archives. Today, thin staffing means institutions have a difficult time adequately caring for all heritage sites, while the list of sites to be managed grows as various religious properties become secularized. A lack of funding impedes administrative action while external pressure from builders and real estate speculators intensifies, creating a growing risk for the country's built heritage.

In examining architectural conservation practice in Italy, as elsewhere in Europe, one must recognize the role of the closely allied field of art conservation. This venerable profession has been an integral part of the fine arts scene in Italy since the Renaissance, and it embraces a variety of media such as sculpture, paintings, mosaics, glass, wood, and metals. Architectural and art conservation are closely linked in many theoretical and technical areas, including how best to approach cleaning, integrate lacunae (missing portions), distinguish old and new elements, and intervene in ways that are reversible (re-treatable). Italians have been at the forefront of developments in methods of material conservation for art and architectural applications, notably relating to the conservation of applied finishes, such as sgraffiti—an artisan's decorative technique of cutting away parts of a surface layer to expose a different colored layer beneath—and *intonaco*—the final finish coat of fine plaster (made with white marble dust) to receive a fresco painting—have been promulgated by leading Italian architectural conservators Paolo Mora, Laura Mora, and Giorgio Torraca.[19] There are also many similarities in operational methods between architectural conservators and art conservators, including the areas of documentation, testing, preventative conservation, and maintenance. The two fields often work in tandem at the same site—for example, in the restoration of a church or other elaborate interior.[20]

Since Cesare Brandi established it in 1939, the Istituto Superiore per la Conservazione ed il Restauro (ISCR, previously the Instituto Centrale del Restauro) has researched conservation techniques, provided scientific advice to the ministry and superintendencies, taught conservation, and executed numerous complex conservation

◀**Figure 1-10** The remains of Roman Villa del Casale at Piazza Armerina (fourth century CE) in central Sicily (a) were protected in 1959 by a glass-and-metal-enclosure system (b) that approximated the geometry of the ancient villa's original roof-and-wall positions and allowed visitors to view the site's extensive floor mosaics from raised walkways. In 2009 construction began on a revised shelter system (c and d) that also approximates the form of the ancient villa but which additionally incorporates wood framing, translucent roofing, opaque walls, and improved natural ventilation. Images courtesy Gionata Rizzi, Architect

Following publication of the 1931 Athens Charter, the concept that important historic buildings and sites belonged to humanity in general became increasingly accepted in the international community, along with recognition of the importance of international cooperation in the field of heritage conservation. The acknowledgment that historic buildings embodied both human memory and identity helped define the philosophies of architectural conservation and made this activity more prominent in the agendas of both national governments and international concerns.

The first major trial for such international solidarity occurred in November 1966, when worldwide attention focused on the precarious position of much of Italy's historic treasures following the massive floods that inundated Florence and Venice. While at first glance the Arno River's Florentine destruction seemed more severe, it was Venice that proved the greater conservation challenge. British art historian John Pope-Hennessy noted that for the first time, the full extent of the city's problems was evidenced:

> It was not just a matter of the flood; rather, it was a matter of what the flood revealed, of the havoc wrought by generations of neglect. For centuries Venice lived off tourists, and almost none of the money they brought into the city was put back into the maintenance of its monuments. And that had been aggravated by problems of pollution, an issue of the utmost gravity.[21]

In response, several national and international organizations began working tirelessly in both Venice and Florence, making impressive progress in conserving various individual sites. Organizations at the forefront of activity included UNESCO, Venice in Peril, Save Venice, and the International Fund for Monuments (since renamed World Monuments Fund).[22]

Venice's precarious physical position was realized as early as the sixteenth century, when its doges attempted to protect the island city and its harbor by diverting rivers from the lagoon to prevent river silt from accumulating and blocking the lagoon. Over the centuries, as the mean sea level gradually rose and the foundations of many buildings settled further, the Venetians also gradually raised their islands, as evidenced by the deepest archaeological layer in St. Mark's Square, which is located approximately 10 feet below the present pavement.[23] Thus today's continuing flooding problem is exacerbated by a discontinued four-hundred-year old lagoon-dredging program and a sinking seabed.

Hopes for a permanent solution are now pinned on the Moses (*Mose*) project—a system of seventy-eight massive mobile floodgates that would close the inlet from the Adriatic Sea to the lagoon during storms, thereby shutting out the tidal changes that produce flooding.[24] The Moses project, introduced in 1989 by the Italian Ministry of Infrastructure and the Venice Water Authority, was only one piece of a general plan that also included raising quaysides and erosion-mediation activities around the lagoon. Despite these completed interventions, the Moses project was postponed for years in part due to fear that it might impede the natural tidal cleansing of the lagoon, causing related ecological problems. Construction of the mobile barriers finally commenced in 2003, and completion of this still controversial project is planned by 2012.

Venice's problem today is not only how to preserve its built patrimony from the forces of nature, air pollution, and multitudes of tourists, but also how to revitalize its core being. With the passing of each year, it remains home to fewer and fewer native Venetians, as its population abandons the islands to tourists and begins a more comfortable life on the mainland. Property improvements only increase taxes, and so they are rarely undertaken by home owners who are increasingly absentee landlords.[25]

The future of Venice, a jewel of human achievement, has been uncertain for many centuries. It remains so despite advances in modern technology and increased international support. Whether these efforts will be sufficient to maintain this disadvantageously sited city is anyone's guess.

works. Its activities are complemented by the Opificio delle Pietre Dure (OPD), whose antecedents are the sixteenth-century grand ducal workshops of the Medicis.[26] In 1975, all Florentine state conservation laboratories were consolidated into the OPD, which became prominent for rescue and conservation work done after the 1966 catastrophic floods. The OPD is one of the largest conservation institutions in Europe, and it has at its disposal an interdisciplinary team of conservators, art historians, archaeologists, architects, scientific experts, and documentary specialists.[27]

a

b

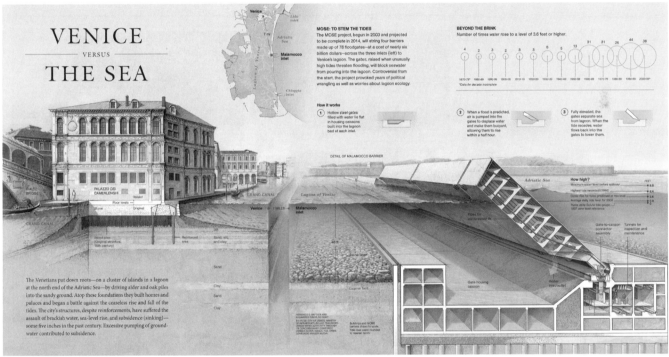

c

d

Figure 1-11 Venice's perilous relationship with the sea is clear in views of the record flood of 4 November 1966 (a) and of the Venetian lagoon from the Campanile of San Marco, showing Venetian islands. To protect the historic city from flooding as a result of its sinking seabed and future storms, construction is underway on the Moses project's submersible seawall system (c and d). Figures 1-11c by Virginia W. Mason/National Geographic stock and 1-11d by Engineria and Thetis.

RECENT ACCOMPLISHMENTS AND CHALLENGES

Land-development pressures on Sicily illustrate architectural heritage protection issues throughout Italy. While conservation of its diverse heritage has largely been handled admirably, a few challenges remain to be faced. Successful long-term maintenance led to the collective addition of eight late-baroque towns in southeastern Sicily to the World Heritage List in 2002. The city of Palermo has also continuously restored its many baroque palaces and churches, although some problems have been encountered, including extensive damage suffered during World War II. On the other hand, in 2002 UNESCO noted that Agrigento's well-preserved Greek temples were threatened by encroaching construction, much of which was illegal. Though previously surrounded by picturesque rolling hills, the temples are now obscured by concrete apartment buildings and hotels. Sprawl poses similar problems for many of Italy's other cities—both large and small.

Figure 1-12 The thirteenth-century cosmatesque-style cloister of the early Christian church of Santa Maria e Quattro Coronati in Rome was famously restored in 1913 by architect Antonio Muñoz and again nearly a century later by a team of conservators led by prominent conservation architect Giovanni Carbonara of the University of Rome, La Sapienza. Seen here is a composite representation of the chronology of finds and periods of construction at the cloister by the project's multidisciplinary research and conservation team. This didactic display reflects the approach used by an internationally funded conservation project that began in 1999, which addressed serious needs for improving the cloister's water-drainage system. Image courtesy of Giovanni Carbonara and World Monuments Fund.

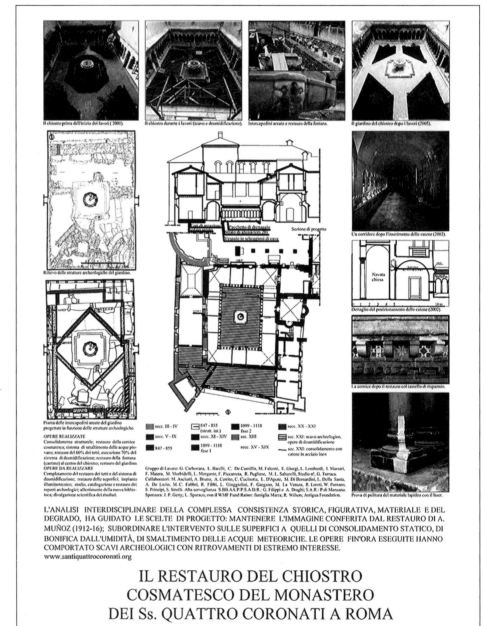

a

b

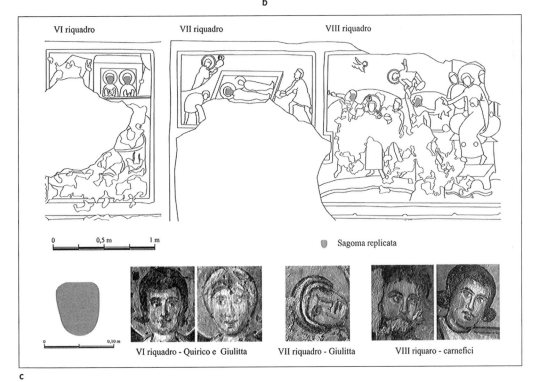
c

Figure 1-13 Conservation of eighth-century murals at the Theodotus Chapel at the Church of Santa Maria Antiqua at the west edge of the Roman Forum is part of program conducted by the conservation firm of Werner Schmid under the direction of the Soprintendenza Speciale ai Beni Archaeologici di Roma (Archaeological Superintendency of Rome) to preserve and present a rare surviving cycle of early medieval mural paintings that depict the Byzantine style of Christian art in Rome (a). The mural conservation team commenced work here with extensive documentation of every layer of visually accessible painted surface while simultaneously conducting various historical and nondestructive technical analyses in preparation for the conservation phase (b). One of several related art-historical examinations included research on the likely use of stencils depicting the heads and hands of many of the represented figures. In many cases, it was possible to prove that the same stencil was used for more than one figure by rotating or inverting the stencil. Among those depicted were the donor of the decorative scheme and his son (c). The conservation of the chapel paintings was completed in 2009 as part of a nine-year overall restoration and site-presentation project. Images courtesy Werner Schmid; stencil study image (Figure 1-13c) courtesy Valeria Valentini.

In 2000 Italy's capital celebrated the millennium and the jubilee of the Roman Catholic Church with a three-trillion-lire (approximately $900 million) urban restoration and improvement project. No grand monuments were erected to mark the jubilee; instead, Rome focused attention on the oeuvre of preceding generations. One hundred piazzas, including Giuseppe Valadier's early-nineteenth-century Piazza del Popolo, were reclaimed for pedestrians and horse-drawn carriages, as auto traffic was routed away. As well, the seventeenth-century facade of St. Peter's Basilica was cleaned and restored to its original appearance. The Colosseum was also substantially cleaned and readied to host a number of concerts; the Domus Aurea (Golden House) of Nero was opened after being closed for several decades.[28] Numerous other historic buildings were cleaned and restored, and they hosted exhibitions for jubilee attendees. The restored and improved post-jubilee Rome is expected to remain an enhanced treasure for locals and tourists for many years to come.

By the late twentieth century, the achievements of the Italian heritage conservation movement had become a topic of importance to most of the country's citizens. The development of numerous volunteer-based organizations in the last half of the century was

a

Figure 1-14 The tragic fire on April 11, 1997, (viewed here from the nearby Royal Palace) (a) that destroyed the dome (b) and adjacent areas of the Chapel of the Holy Shroud in Turin (c); the masterpiece of Piedmontese baroque architect Guarino Guarini has taken over a decade to restore. Post-disaster stabilization work (d) and subsequent restoration has entailed extensive analysis, planning, and the reconstruction of lost elements and conservation and every possible surviving architectural detail. Images courtesy Alessio Ré, SITI.

b

c

d

a

b

c

d

Figure 1-15 Restoration and rehabilitation, since the mid-1990s, of the extensive complex of the Royal Palace of Venaria on the outskirts of Turin, represents one of the most expensive single architectural conservation projects in Europe. In 2010 the complex holds an array of cultural facilities, including public meeting spaces, educational facilities, and the offices of the Environmental and Architectural Service of Piedmont (the region in which Turin is located). Numerous different teams of Italian architects, engineers, and conservation specialists have been involved in interventions ranging from the restoration of exteriors and interiors to inserting bold modern interior amenities. Images courtesy Alessio Ré, SITI.

timely, as Italy's continuing economic problems severely affected the government's ability to care for the country's wealth of extraordinary cultural patrimony. Fortunately, in some cases, other countries have contributed to architectural conservation efforts in Italy, most recently following the 2009 earthquake in the Abruzzo region that damaged the homes of tens of thousands as well as significant historic sites. The Italian Ministry for Cultural Heritage drew up a list of forty-five protected monuments requiring restoration after the earthquake and sought international donors to aid in their recovery. For example, the eighteenth-century Church of Santa Maria del Suffragio in L'Aquila, which had been built to replace one destroyed by an earthquake in 1703, is currently being restored with funds from the French government, and its collapsed early nineteenth-century dome, designed by Giuseppe Valadier, is also being reconstructed. Other large architectural and conservation projects in Italy are underway as well, with two in Turin in process since the 1990s: restoration of the famous Chapel of the Holy Shroud (Cappella della Sacra Sindone) and the huge complex of the Royal Palace of Venaria (Reggia di Venaria Reale).

Another recent architectural conservation success in Italy was the six-year reconstruction and restoration, and subsequent 2009 reopening, of the early twentieth-century, art nouveau–styled Teatro Petruzzelli in Bari, which was nearly destroyed by arson in 1991. Venice's La Fenice opera house was completely restored and reopened in 2004 after a fire similarly reduced it to its shell in the mid-1990s.

Italy leads other European countries in the quantity of historic rural towns that are nearly or completely abandoned. Hill towns, from the Alpine foothills to their counterparts throughout southern Italy, have nearly all faced questions of survival during the decades after the end of World War II, when traditional ways of life in walled towns, often dating to the Middle Ages, began to change as they became less dependent on adjacent agricultural activity. Industrialization, urbanization, and motorized transportation has had as much of an effect as anything else.

The geography of the Italian peninsula and the country's long history determined Italy's rural settlement patterns, and as such the architectural and cultural significance of these towns is often remarkable. Medium-sized towns dating to Etruscan and ancient Roman times, such as Orvieto in Umbria, Arezzo and Lucca in Tuscany, and Benevento and Salerno in Campania, are secure as regional seats of commerce and government. It is the multitude of smaller towns and villages that often struggle to survive, especially because younger members of the population have departed for university education, better work opportunities, and the lure of city life. Other issues affecting these towns and villages include economic stagnation, substandard infrastructure, and the expense of restoring aging structures of all types to modern safety and living standards.

The dying rural towns of Italy are not without their supporters or potential for future viability. Italia Nostra was the first to signal the issue on an international basis in an exhibition entitled: Italian Hill Towns, Too Late to be Saved? and has sustained focused on the issue since. Europa Nostra has also highlighted the importance of this heritage and since 1996 the World Monuments Fund has listed seven Italian towns on its biennial World Monuments Watch List of Endangered Sites: Pitigliano, Civita di Bagnoregio, Sorano, and Manciano in Central Italy and Matera, Craco, and the entire transhumance hill-town area in Southern Italy.

Solutions have been addressed recently via a growing number of specialty institutional research initiatives such as those conducted by the Istituto Superiore sui Sistemi Territoriali per l'Innovazione (SITI), based in Turin, which are focused on the cultural landscapes of Cinque Terre (Liguria) and Alberobello (Apulia). Restauro Architettonico e Recupero della Bellezza dei Centri Storici (Architectural Restoration and Rehabilitation of Historic Centers), situated within the faculty of architecture at the University of Rome III, is a university-level program that concentrates on training in conservation of Italian hill towns and rural architecture.

Perhaps the most noteworthy recent heritage conservation project in Italy, and one of the largest architectural restoration projects in European history, has been the series of interventions at the baroque complex of the Royal Palace of Venaria in Turin beginning in the 1990s.[29] Restoring this 80,000-square-meter complex cost over $365 million (€250 million) and involved a partnership of municipal, regional, and national political institutions as well as support from the European Union. In 2005 the former stables of the palace were converted into the Venaria Reale Center for Conservation and Restoration of Cultural Heritage, which works not only on the Venaria complex but also on projects in the region and includes conservation laboratories as well as a graduate training program in restoration. Though conservation is ongoing, the Venaria complex reopened to the public in 2007 and is slated to serve a central role in Turin's celebration of the 150th anniversary of Italian unification in 2011.

Despite the solid progress, Italian architectural heritage is still faced with an array of human and natural threats, notably including the same pressures for urban modernization that launched the earliest large-scale campaigns on behalf of conservation over a century ago in Florence. In that same city today, concerns are being raised about the construction of a new light rail network, the first line of which opened early in 2010. This first tram line has already undermined the design integrity and the fauna of Le Cascine Park, destroyed the remains of the city's first industrial district, The Pignone, and altered century-old views of the city and the river from the Arno River promenade.[30] As construction is planned for an additional two lines, whose paths threaten to involve trains passing within a few feet of the Duomo, Baptistery, and other iconic sites in Florence, a new petition is calling for "friends of Florence and the Florentines—in Florence and abroad" to join together "to help to preserve the city from wrong administrative choices such as the light rail project."[31] This international petition and battle seem an eerie repetition of the petition over a century ago that was motivated by similar threats to the same heritage, and it serves as a reminder that architectural conservationists must be ever vigilant in their efforts, even in countries such as Italy with longstanding traditions of respect and protection of heritage

ITALIAN CONSERVATION ABROAD

For centuries Italy has exported its talents in the arts, among them its extensive restoration and conservation skills.[32] Early examples include the Fossati brothers, Italian-educated Swiss nationals who restored the mosaics and other interior finishes at the Hagia Sophia complex in Istanbul in the 1840s, as well as the partial restorations of buildings at Italian-run archaeological excavations in Leptis Magna and Cyrene in Libya in the 1920s. More recent examples include Roman engineer Giorgio Croci's work at dozens of sites worldwide; the modifications for the contemporary use of the ancient Roman theater at Tarragona, Spain, in the 1990s by Torinese architect Andrea Bruno; and the documentation of Marmeshan Church in Gumri, Armenia, by the Milan-based Centro di Studi Armeni (Center for Armenian Studies), and its restoration in 2004 by architect Gaene Casnati.[33] In addition, Italian conservators are working on restoring mosaics at the ancient Roman site of Zeugma in Turkey under the direction of Italian conservation specialist Roberto Nardi and British archaeologist Richard Hodges.[34]

Italy's long-standing international perspective on architectural conservation is reflected in the participation of the country's leading figures at the seminal international conferences that resulted in the Athens Charter of 1931 and the Venice Charter of 1964. Since then, the Italian government has appreciated the importance and potential of its conservation talent. Both the Italian ministries of foreign affairs and for cultural heritage have been actively using this valuable national intellectual asset abroad and including cultural heritage efforts as a major component of Italian foreign policy.

◄Figure 1-16 The hill town of Civita di Bagnoregio, sited between Viterbo and Orvieto, is an especially picturesque example of Italy's rural historic townscapes. Located atop a pedestal of volcanic tuff that is prone to landslides, this town has faced centuries of deterioration. For the past few years, the Italian Ministry for Cultural Heritage and Activities has monitored subterranean conditions at Civita di Bagnoregio. Due to the efforts of an international partnership, the Northwest Institute for Architecture and Urban Studies in Italy has completed plans for conserving this hill town. Courtesy Norma Barbacci.

Figure 1-17 Mosaic retrieval at the ancient Roman site of Zeugma on the Euphrates in present-day Turkey by Italian conservators under the direction of Italian conservation specialist Roberto Nardi, vice president of the International Committee for the Conservation of Mosaics, and British archaeologist Richard Hodges.[34]

Such an approach fits well with UNESCO's aims in conserving heritage of universal value, which implicitly assumes international participation, often through both financial and technical assistance.

In the 1950s the Istituto Italiano per il Medio ed Estremo Oriente (ISMEO, Italian Institute for the Middle and Far East) was active in sponsoring foreign archaeological excavations and subsequent site-conservation efforts in Pakistan, Afghanistan, Iran, and numerous other countries. ISMEO, founded in 1933, merged in 1995 with the Istituto Italo-Africano (Italian-African Institute)—which had been conducting similar research in Africa since the 1980s—to form the new Istituto Italiano per l'Africa e l'Oriente (ISIAO, the Italian Institute for Africa and the Orient). ISIAO operates within the Italian Ministry of Foreign Affairs but in close association with the ministries for cultural heritage and of education as well as with Italian universities.

The Italian government has also worked for the protection of foreign cultural heritage through partnerships with international organizations. Within the Ministry of Foreign Affairs, the Directorate General for Development Cooperation funds Italy-UNESCO coordinated projects and the Directorate General for Cultural Promotion and Cooperation finances conservation-related research and field projects carried out by Italian universities and agencies. In addition, the World Bank's Italian Trust Fund for Culture and Sustainable Development was established in 2000 with a donation of $3.3 million from the Italian government. The Trust Fund, which stipulates that Italian conservation professionals should be involved in any projects it supports, has been involved in more than twenty projects in fourteen countries, including the reconstruction of the Old Bridge in Mostar, Bosnia and Herzegovina; the rehabilitation of the medina in Fez, Morocco; and the development of comprehensive heritage strategies for Chongqing and Sichuan in China. In 2004 the Italian Trust Fund received additional support targeted specifically for World Heritage sites in the Congo.

In 2005 the Italian Ministry for Cultural Heritage, the World Bank, and UNESCO coorganized a conference of cultural ministers from Southeastern European countries to discuss their region's shared heritage conservation concerns and efforts. Following this initial conference, the Italian Ministry of Foreign Affairs established a Southeastern Europe Trust Fund to be administered by UNESCO's Venice office. Additional funds were set aside for this trust by the Italian foreign minister in 2009.

The Italian Ministry for Cultural Heritage is also working closely today with UNESCO by coordinating its emergency heritage operations to improve efforts to respond quickly and effectively to natural disasters or conflicts that threaten cultural heritage worldwide. The agreement on what has been dubbed the "cultural blue berets" was reached in October 2004, but it was based on successful UNESCO and Italian cooperation on emergency projects the year before, including the transfer of expertise from professionals working on the Leaning Tower of Pisa in Italy to stabilization of Afghanistan's Minaret of Jam when it was in imminent danger of collapse.

An exhibition with catalogue entitled Excellence in Italian Restoration in the World held in Rome in November 2005 offered a summary of many of the important recent Italian achievements in architecture and art conservation abroad. The exhibition included descriptions of such diverse projects as the restoration of wall paintings at the Ellora and Ajanta caves in India; conservation of interiors in the Forbidden City in Beijing; restoration of national museum collections in Kabul, Afghanistan, and Baghdad, Iraq; the archaeological park for Carthage, Tunisia; church and mosque restorations in war ravaged Pec, Kosovo; and the return to Ethiopia of the restored 160-ton obelisk of Aksum, which stood near Porta Capena on the Caelian Hill in Rome since 1937 but was returned and reerected on its original site in 2008.

Such work does much toward extending international goodwill and improved trade and diplomatic relations. Today conservation assistance is also a notable part of the foreign relations of other Western European countries as well as Australia, Sweden, Finland, Canada, Japan, and Singapore. While others could be named, their participation in international conservation practice is better traced through the work of specialty heritage protection organizations such as the Geneva-based Aga Khan Trust for Culture and Paris-based Patrimoine Sans Frontières, as well as through the key professional membership organizations such as ICOMOS and the Association for Preservation Technology International.

ENDNOTES

1. Cevat Erder, *Our Architectural Heritage: From Consciousness to Conservation*, trans. Ayfer Bakalcioglu (Paris: UNESCO, 1986), 93.

2. Jukka Jokilehto, *A History of Architectural Conservation*, 2nd ed. (Oxford: Butterworth-Heinemann, 1999), 79.

3. In the nineteenth century, this debate was characterized as scrape versus antiscrape, pitting those in favor of restraint against the more heavy-handed who advocated "scraping" away later accretions to restore the alleged original, historic appearance of buildings. These diametrically

opposed positions were most notably associated with the approaches of Eugène-Emmanuel Viollet-le-Duc and John Ruskin. Ruskin advocated the laissez-faire approach of only simple maintenance while Viollet-le-Duc advocated "period" restoration that could entail restoring and rebuilding of a monument to an appearance it may have never had, consistent with his *stylistic unity* philosophy. See John H. Stubbs, *Time Honored: A Global View of Architectural Conservation,* 214–217 (Hoboken, NJ: John Wiley & Sons, 2009).

4. Walter Kaiser, "Saving the Magic City," *New York Review of Books,* December 3, 2009, 59–60; Bernd Roeck, *Florence 1900: The Quest for Arcadia* (New Haven, CT, and London: Yale University Press, 2009).

5. Mussolini himself inaugurated the work at the Tomb of Augustus, which he may have planned to use as his own monument.

6. The *Ara Pacis* dates from Augustan times and is perhaps the finest example of architectural sculpture surviving from ancient Rome. In an effort to feature it as part of Rome's 1930s urban renewal, it was excavated, restored, and enclosed in a bold modern glass building. This modern enclosure has itself become part of architectural history, especially in recent years, due to a resurgence of interest in architecture from that period. Its replacement in 2005 with a structure inspired by the International Style has disappointed many. Today, people are reevaluating the merits of the classically inspired Italian architecture from the 1920s and 1930s, which has proven remarkably congruent with other historic architectural styles in Rome.

7. John H. Stubbs, "The Forging of a Discipline: The Late Eighteenth to Early Twentieth Centuries," in *Time Honored,* 193–237. See also Erder, *Our Architectural Heritage,* 101.

8. Jokilehto, *History of Conservation,* 200.

9. Cesare Brandi, *Teoria del Restauro* (Rome: Edizioni di Storia e Letteratura, 1963), or the English edition: Cesare Brandi, *Theory of Restoration,* trans. Cynthia Rockwell (Rome: ICCROM, 2005), 6.

10. ICOMOS, *Pillage en Europe (Looting in Europe),* Cent objets disparus (One Hundred Missing Objects); 4 (Paris: ICOM, 2000).

11. Marco Dezzi Bardeschi, *Restauro: Punto e da Capo* (Milan: Franco Angeli, 1992), 245–246.

12. Giovanni Carbonara, *Avvicinamento al Restauro: Teoria, Storia, Monumenti* (Naples: Liguori, 1997), 384.

13. Ibid., 385.

14. Corrosion and expansion of the reinforcing rods in the new concrete backing panels that contain the floor mosaics has also distorted and damaged them. Likewise, the enclosure Franco Minissi designed to protect the ruins of the city walls, public baths, and other buildings of the Greek city of Gela, also on Sicily, has proven equally problematic decades later. In a recent restoration project, the glass panes of its roofs were removed, and the clay bricks of the ancient walls were themselves consolidated.

15. Marco Dezzi Bardeschi, "The Work of Franco Minissi at Piazza Armerina in Danger," *Heritage at Risk 2006/2007: ICOMOS World Report 2006/2007 on Monuments and Sites in Danger* (Paris: ICOMOS, 2008), 100.

16. The "Ente per la Villa Venete" legislation was administered by the Soprintendenza di Monumenti e Belle Arte.

17. Fondo per l'Ambiente Italiano, www.fondoambiente.it.

18. Dezzi Bardeschi, *Restauro,* 155.

19. Cyril M. Harris, *Dictionary of Architecture and Construction,* 4th ed. (New York: McGraw-Hill, 2005) and Paolo Mora, Laura Mora, and Paul Philippot, *Conservation of Wall Paintings* (Rome: ICCROM, 1984).

20. The main difference between art conservation and architectural conservation is that the former usually addresses objects in a controlled environment and the latter addresses buildings (their components, entire structures, or whole enclaves of structures) in uncontrolled environments.

21. John Pope-Hennessy, "Artistic Heritage Protection of Venice," conference proceedings, *Bulletin* (New York: Metropolitan Museum of Art, 1968), 165–75

22. The international post-disaster relief effort in Venice during the mid-1960s floods was only the first of many. During the 1970s, overseas aid helped Friuli recover from a devastating earthquake. Similar assistance was given to Assisi in the late 1990s and at L'Aquila in Abruzzo in 2009.

23. Robert Kunzig, "Turning the Tide," *U.S. News and World Report*, October 7, 2002, 38.

24. Ibid.

25. James A. Gray, Indro Montanelli, and Giuseppe Samonà, *Venice in Peril*, trans. Diana Sears (Florence: Sansoni Editore, 1970).

26. Today, the Opificio delle Pietre Dure (OPD) is an autonomous Institute of the Ministry for Cultural Heritage and a workshop for stonework, mosaics, tapestries, and various artistic objects.

27. Opificio delle Pietre Dure, www.opificiodellepietredure.it (accessed May 24, 2010).

28. However the Golden House of Nero was closed again in 2008 for further restoration.

29. For over a century, from the Napoleonic invasions in the early nineteenth century, the Reggia (Royal Palace) was used as a barracks, but it was sold to the Ministry of Culture by the Italian Army in the 1970s. It suffered from neglect and vandalism in the decades before the transfer of ownership; however, the first restoration projects were initiated in the 1960s.

30. Mario Bencivenni, "Environmental and Monumental SOS from Florence: Damages due to Wrong Ideas of Modernity and Embellishment," *Heritage @ Risk: 2006/2007* (Paris: ICOMOS, 2007), 98–99.

31. "About Us" (*Chi Siamo*), Salviamo Firenze, www.saveflorence.it/about_us.php (accessed May 23, 2010).

32. Mastrujeni, Grammenos, ed., *Preserving the World's Cultural Heritage* (Rome: Ministry of Foreign Affairs, 2004); also, Giuseppe Proietti, ed., *L'Eccellenza del Restauro Italiano nel Mondo*, exhibition catalogue for Vittoriano, 5 November–18 December 2005 (Rome: Gangemi Editore, 2005).

33. The Marmashan church stabilization project was funded by World Monuments Fund.

34. This project was conducted under the auspices of the Turkish Ministry of Culture by the University of Oxford Zeugma Conservation Project in an archaeological salvage operation necessitated by construction of the nearby Birecik Dam on the Euphrates River. Dr. Richard Hodges presently serves as director of the University of Pennsylvania Museum of Archaeology and Anthropology in Philadelphia.

Figure 2.1 Illustration of the threats to—and general state of—the Royal Abbey St. Denis near Paris in 1793 when the twelfth-century church suffered vandalism, and its tombs were looted during the French Revolution. In the early nineteenth century, it was restored and reopened by Napoleon. *Violation of the Royal Tombs at Saint-Denis in October 1793*, an oil painting by Hubert Robert at the Musée de la Ville de Paris, Musée Carnevalet, Paris, France. © Réunion des Musées Nationaux/ArtResource, NY.

CHAPTER 2

France

Over the past two centuries, France has steadily evolved as a global force in architectural conservation despite both internal and external political turmoil. Two of France's most important contributions to international architectural conservation practice were the establishment of administrative models for national administration of cultural heritage protection in the early nineteenth century and the work of Eugène-Emmanuele Viollet-le-Duc, whose nineteenth-century scholarship and restorations of many of France's key historic buildings produced novel technical methods of treating deteriorated medieval fabric. He pioneered a new, rational approach to architectural conservation that focused on idealized restorations to a particular period and broadly influenced official policy in France and throughout the European continent. He maximized the input of supportive nationalists and historians, who shared his enthusiasm for medieval architectural achievements. Viollet-le-Duc also played a central role in shaping the organization and procedures of France's developing administrative system for monuments restoration and protection.

In the twentieth century, France continued as a leader in legislation for cultural heritage protection, and has introduced the now global concepts of preserving a monument's context as well as conserving entire historic districts. France's remarkably strong commitment to the protection of its architectural heritage is demonstrated by the central government's support of a range of conservation projects and programs and its advanced system for the training of conservation architects. This plus a wide appreciation for cultural heritage protection held by most French citizens ensures that architectural conservation in France is secure for the foreseeable future.

CENTRALIZED LEGISLATION AND INCENTIVES

From the turn of the nineteenth century, as a result of destruction caused by the French Revolution and the ensuing Napoleonic Wars, individuals and eventually the government grew interested in inventorying France's architectural monuments and thinking about how they could be treated in an increasingly vital European country. Inventories, conditions surveys, and inclusion of France's omnipresent historic monuments in town-planning considerations grew in importance. Centralized rational planning and state support of France's arts and industries increasingly responded to growing questions of how France's distinguished architectural heritage should be accommodated in a modernizing society.

By 1837 the powerful Commission Nationale des Monuments Historiques (Historic Monuments Commission) was inaugurated. The Commission, the forerunner of today's Commission Supérieur des Monuments Historiques, gradually became a consultancy organization with real authority over France's built and cultural heritage was legislatively transferred to the Ministry of Culture.[1] The Ministry presently serves as the single most important government entity in charge of the country's architectural heritage. Its methods and clear system of administration is a concept of cultural heritage management that has since been freely adopted, and adapted, by many other countries.

Development of France's twentieth-century administrative structure is underpinned by various important legislations, beginning with the Act of 1913. The Act introduced two conservation categories: *monument classés* (classified monuments), which include buildings of great historic or artistic interest, and *monuments inscrits* (registered monuments), which is a supplementary inventory comprised of less important buildings whose conservation is desirable.[2] Today, there are over 14,300 historic buildings in France that are classified, and nearly 29,000 that are registered, with between 300 and 450 new monuments added to these lists annually.[3] Examples of classified monuments include everything from the prehistoric Dolmen tombs of Brittany to the castles of the Loire valley to the Eiffel Tower in Paris.

Classified monuments may never be demolished, moved, altered, restored, or repaired without approval from the Ministry of Culture, and official ministry architects (*architectes-en-chefs*) must supervise all authorized work on them. Costs incurred by private owners can be defrayed by preferential tax treatment. An annual inspection of each classed property by a specialized government architect (*architecte des bâtiments de France*) is required.

Under the Act of 1913, France became the first country to formalize the concept of "entourage," that is, protection of a monument's setting. Though the focus remained on the individual building itself, construction or demolition in the vicinity of a classified or registered site was also regulated. Height restrictions on new buildings were imposed, reflecting an awareness of the total impression created by the buildings of a city or town. In 1943, protection was also extended to a site's immediate surroundings, up to a perimeter of 500 meters or further, if decreed by the state council. Today, France has more than 30,000 such protected zones, within which work done in the visual distance of a classified historic building must be preapproved by the Ministry of Culture.

The Act of 1913 also rescinded the legal difference between secular and religious buildings and extended legal patrimonial protection to human-made archaeological remains and to *objets mobiliers*. These movable objects are protected whether or not they remain in their original location. To date, over 75,000 movable objects—including building components, furniture, and paintings—have been determined to be of national significance and are thus legally protected.[4] Like buildings, objets mobiliers can be either classified or, since 1970, registered.[5]

The scope of France's architectural conservation efforts was broadened again in 1930, when legal protection for natural sites and parks and landscapes of "artistic, historic, scientific, legendary or picturesque" interest was granted.[6] A new advisory body, the Commission Supérieur des Sites, Perspectives et Paysages (Commission of Sites, Views, and Landscapes), was created to assist the Ministry of Culture. The Commission's function and operations mirror that of the Commission Nationale des Monuments Historiques. Like monuments, these natural sites are protected under two categories depending on their value: today there are over 2,600 classified sites and 4,700 registered sites in France.[7]

The creation of a centralized, comprehensive financial incentive system was incorporated in French monument-protection legislation and its administrative apparatus throughout the twentieth-century. The Caisse Nationale des Monuments Historiques

(National Fund for Historic Monuments) was established in 1914 to supervise the allocation of funds for the purchase and repair of historic structures. By 1930 the majority of historic buildings were receiving some sort of government financial assistance due to a growing belief within the government that its regulatory position would be strengthened through outright ownership of historic buildings and sites or through financial control of them. The Ministry of Culture's Caisse Nationale has today become the Centre des Monuments Nationaux (Center for National Monuments) and currently maintains about 80 state-owned historic properties in France.[8]

In 1966 the law was altered to permit the minister of culture to compel private owners to carry out specified repairs on qualified historic buildings on the condition that the Ministry itself contribute grant aid to owners toward a portion of restoration expenses. In turn, the law encourages but does not require opening the building to the public. No third-party liens can attach to classified buildings, and the Ministry of Culture must be notified before their sale.

Due to these strict regulations, before a building can be designated as a classified monument, a detailed analytical study (*dossier de recensement*) must be compiled by the local *conservateur regional des monuments historiques* (regional conservator of historic monuments) either at owner's initiative or following a third-party request made jointly by an architect and an art historian. This dossier, along with a supporting opinion, is sent to the minister by the *inspecteur générale des monuments historiques*. There is also an exceptional fast-track procedure for urgent cases when a property is threatened by demolition, serious modification, or when it has reached a grave state of disrepair. Classification is announced in an ordinance after the proprietor's approval has been received. While it is possible for an owner to object to classification and petition against it at the state council, this rarely occurs. However, in these exceptional cases, the final decision is made by the prime minister.

Property can be registered on the supplementary inventory list without owner approval, because the obligations conferred by this designation are minimal in comparison to its tax benefits, which are the same as for classified buildings. The major responsibility for owners of registered historic properties is to notify the Ministry four months in advance of any planned alteration. Owners can request expert advice from the Ministry's specialist architects, but they are not legally obligated to follow their advice. The only option available to the Ministry to prevent harmful alterations to a registered site is to elevate it to the classified category of national monuments.

After World War I, international patrons began to pay for high-profile, costly restoration projects in France. Notable among these is the wealthy American philanthropist John D. Rockefeller Jr., whose investment of over 34 million francs (nearly $2 million) helped restore the palaces of Versailles and Fontainebleau and the Cathedral of Reims and encouraged further government investment in these key historic buildings. The concept continues today, with organizations such as the Friends of Versailles, French Heritage Society, and World Monuments Fund in France financially involved in conservation projects at many important sites.

AN INFLUENTIAL CONCEPT: *LES SECTEURS SAUVEGARDÉS*

Despite its well-established administrative network and long tradition of architectural appreciation and conservation, France was only partially shielded from many of the rebuilding excesses in post–World War II Europe. These traditions also laid the theoretical and technical foundation for several outstanding projects that have been completed over the past half century, particularly during the tenure of the dynamic writer, philosopher, and heritage advocate André Malraux as France's first minister of culture in the 1960s.

At this time, Malraux created France's first comprehensive listing of all objects of historic or artistic value, including many that were not legally protected by designation. He also activated a dormant legal provision that required the exteriors of Parisian buildings be periodically cleaned and initiated a massive program to liberate its most magnificent buildings—notably, the Louvre, Opéra Garnier, and Église Sainte-Marie-Madeleine—from centuries of dirt. The government at first encouraged, then later required, individual homeowners to undertake their own cleaning projects through a 1962 law—the Malraux Act—that helps maintain Paris as one of the world's most beautiful cities. Other French cities were similarly cleaned as a result of this legislation, and Malraux's most enduring legacy is this law that bears his name.

The Malraux Act was the first time that French conservation legislation focused on an *historic area* rather than on specific eminent historic buildings. Its radical conservation concept was that all components within a specific geographic area (*secteur sauvegardé*, or "safeguarded sector") be protected and restored irrespective of the importance of the individual buildings themselves. This longevity evidences the Act's conceptual validity, although administrative complexity and high costs have opened it to certain criticisms and reduced its overall effectiveness.

Initially, implementation of the Malraux Act was met with many complaints, particularly concerning its slow approval and implementation process, high costs, central government control at the cost of private and local initiative, lack of social objectives and public awareness, and often poor quality of the building work. But success has come at the expense of speed. The first secteur sauvegardé, Paris's Marais district, transformed a decaying neighborhood into one of the capital's most sought-after locations. During the Malraux Act's first decade, forty sectors were approved and eleven more were placed under consideration.[9] Today there are over 100 secteurs sauvegardés in France. Selection criteria include architectural and historical merit, receptiveness of local authorities, and economic feasibility, as well as town size, need, and style composition.[10]

Figure 2-2 View of Hotel de Sully in the Marais district in Paris, an early seventeenth-century private palace that was restored as an emblem of the Malraux Act. It was cited as a classified monument in 1862, bought by the state in 1944, and underwent an extensive restoration that was completed in the 1970s (it had become a subdivided property with a variety of later additions). Since 1967 it has housed what is now the Centre des Monuments Nationaux (Center for National Monuments). Image courtesy Europa Nostra.

In 1975— the European Architectural Heritage Year—one author stated that when making conservation plans, "the starting point in a historic city must be its historic quality and visual character, not secondary social, economic or even ecological arguments."[11] By contrast, in his seminal book *A History of Architectural Conservation,* first published in 1999, Jukka Jokilehto asked "whether modern conservation should not be redefined in reference to the environmental sustainability of social and economic development within the overall cultural and ecological situation on earth."[12] Or, as it was put even more succinctly a few years later, "conservation is not sustainable if it is only carried out for cultural reasons."[13]

Though the economic and energy efficiency of the "recycling" of buildings is not new—for example, the argument was made by American historic preservation educator and architect James Marston Fitch in the 1980s—sustainability has increasingly become an argument on behalf of architectural conservation in the twenty-first century, especially in urban areas. Sustainability has emerged as *the* issue of conservationists in general as it reveals an aligning of the interests of environmental ecologists, those of economic pragmatists, and the needs of communities. The challenge that this shifting focus poses is seen by some as a threat to established approaches to architectural and urban conservation but by others as an opportunity, especially in urban areas.

The world's demographic profile has now surpassed a defining threshold. For the first time, 50 percent of the world's population lives in cities. This proportion is forecast to increase steadily in the decades ahead. Moreover, in a world increasingly in search of ways to address the key agendas of our time—sustainability and climate change—this urban half of the human population accounts for three-quarters of the world's annual consumption of resources and discharge of wastes. In short, cities constitute an important starting point for a sustainable world. Their continuously accumulating heritage, ancient and modern, has a vital role to play in meeting this challenge.

Historic buildings and urban areas constitute not merely nonrenewable cultural resources, they also represent nonrenewable capital and material resources, embodied energies, and financial investments. Further, they comprise an essential functional resource, one that has been demonstrated time and time again to be highly adaptable to creative reuse.

By combining our concerns for the heritage value of historic buildings and urban areas (and their infrastructure) with the wider environmental imperatives of respecting the finite material resources of our planet and the threats posed by global warming and climate change, the rationale behind the protection and conservation of our heritage is reinforced and magnified many times over. Adopting a preservationist approach based on academically derived concepts such as "architectural or historic interest" offers only a very limited justification for conservation in a world in which so many other factors can also be brought into play, factors that demand a far more responsible approach than has hitherto been the norm in the developed world.[14]

Two further influences contribute to this reinforcement of the value of protection and conservation: firstly, increasing emphasis in our globalizing world on cultural diversity, and secondly, recognition not simply of tangible heritage values but also of the intangible values that attach to human traditions and practices. Thus, for urban conservationists, thinking about sustainability also means exploring the role of cultural heritage in sustaining distinctive cultures as well as how heritage conservation can meet the specific needs and interests of particular communities. The concrete expression of cultural diversity is supported through the use of locally and regionally distinctive building materials, architectural details and urban patterns, and—in parallel —they support an approach to cultural continuity that is focused at least as much on processes that must be sustained (or revived, where in jeopardy) as on museum-like artifacts from the past that are subject to curatorial care. This human approach, characterized as the anthropological vision of geocultural identity and cultural continuity, has much to commend it. At one and the same time it bolsters the safeguarding of historic objects by reinforcing the processes for conserving them and integrates this with the creative dynamics of evolving social and cultural processes. Thus, the concept of *heritage* is not seen as limited to a past that is fixed in time, but it is something to which each generation in turn is encouraged to contribute in a positive, additive sense. The anthropological vision focuses on people as both the custodians and creative vectors of cultural diversity and identity.

Today, cities pose one of the greatest challenges and opportunities for creating a more sustainable world. In the urban conservation field, Gustavo Giovannoni (see "Key Theorists and Methods in Italy," page 16) was one of the most important theoreticians and practitioners in the first half of the twentieth century. His response to the challenge of how to interrelate the historic areas of cities with their expanding modern counterparts was simple: mutually supportive, harmonious coexistence, that is, avoiding conflict and allowing the distinctive characteristics of both to be respected and given the freedom to evolve creatively.[15] His most successful legacies today, both directly and indirectly, include the strategic planning and detailed programs of conservation in cities across Italy and France.

Sustainable conservation requires closer alignment with other fields committed to the built and natural environments and the people who occupy them. Gone are the days when conservationists focused exclusively or primarily on the physical structures; today this must combined with attention to accommodating future use, various stakeholders, and social and cultural relevance. Urban planning needs to borrow principles of global and local ecological sustainability by, for example, regarding and managing cities as ecosystems including working with natural cycles of resource use and waste management. Other fundamental principles, such as minimum intervention, are already shared by conservation and sustainability practices. If properly managed and balanced, conflicts between development pressures and a city's most sensitive areas can be avoided, as exemplified by the careful juxtaposition of old and new and freedom of expression in Paris's Marais district.

FURTHER READING

Dennis Rodwell, *Conservation and Sustainability in Historic Cities.* Oxford: Blackwell, 2007.
——. "Conservation in a Changing Climate." In *Context*, Institute of Historic Building Conservation (May 2009).
——. "From Globalisation to Localisation." In *Context*, Institute of Historic Building Conservation (March 2008).

a

b

c

One of the reasons the Malraux Act has been successful is that is does not rely on negative sanctions to force compliance; rather, it emphasizes community benefits. When the Ministries of Culture and Communication and of Housing jointly decide to create a secteur sauvegardé, they first seek the approval of the local town council, since designation has far-reaching implications for the inhabitants. In many cases today, communes themselves request the designation of a secteur sauvegardé.[16] After obtaining local approval, the designation is formalized and nationally publicized by the Commission Nationale des Secteurs Sauvegardés (National Commission of Safeguarded Sectors), which the Malraux Act created to develop comprehensive urban conservation plans, called a Plan de sauvegarde et de mise en valeur (PSMV), to address the physical, economic, and social needs of the designated neighborhoods. Sweeping economic revitalization efforts are melded with financial incentives and a comprehensive evaluation of an area's historic assets in order to stimulate gentrification.[17] Once approved, a PSMV, which is linked to the local planning legislation, is a legal document and its land use and design provisions are binding and require that alterations to both interiors and exteriors within the designated district are regulated by a local commission and the architecte des bâtiments de France.[18]

RECENT CONSERVATION SUCCESSES

Contemporary France is rich with excellent examples of good architectural conservation. Its impressive public buildings, spaces, and monuments and its cathedrals and former royal properties are all maintained with assistance from accessible government staffing and financing. But even more modest buildings enjoy a formalized support system. There are approximately forty thousand privately held historic, unclassified structures in France, whose property value (notional capital value) for tax purposes is kept at a reasonable level to provide an economic offset against their heavy upkeep requirements. Since 1951 the government has also helped finance their maintenance through generous grants—up to 40 percent of the work undertaken.[19] Building owners can also receive advice about maintaining and rehabilitating their buildings from regional committees of conservation experts. This information is provided free by two important organizations—La Demeure Historique (1924) and Vieilles Maisons Françaises (1958).[20] Through several international amity groups, especially the American organization now known as the French Heritage Society (formerly Friends of Vieilles Maisons Françaises), founded in 1982, château owners have potential access to funding for conservation, primarily for exterior projects.

In the modern world, conserving historic town centers is challenging because of the difficulties involved with protecting enclaves of buildings and their original character while simultaneously introducing modern structures and infrastructure. The chateau towns of the Loire valley, one of France's premier tourist destinations, have become particularly adept at integrating old and new elements, to the benefit of both citizens and visitors. In Blois, imaginative and historically respectful planning has produced a harmonious result. Orléans, which suffered extensive damage in World War II, was reconstructed conservatively.

The importance of tourism revenues to the local economy has heightened the perception of conservation as economically attractive and socially desirable. Regionally, current planning practice encourages the protection and enhancement of tourist attractions, including such devices as the "son et lumière" (sound and light) productions at châteaus to dramatize the location's visual power.[21] Further to the north, the historic fabric encircling Amiens' important thirteenth-century cathedral was sensitively improved, with some work necessitated by war damage but most undertaken due to peacetime development needs. A refashioned urban plan both honors

◀**Figure 2-3** Contemporary insertions into the Marais quarter (a) in the center of Paris have respected the historic urban grain without slavishly imitating its architecture. Since the 1950s, the strategic plan for the Paris region has siphoned pressures for major development projects away from the historic core, thereby enabling formerly rundown quarters such as the Marais to evolve in ways that have not threatened their characteristic small-scale urban grain and typically Parisian way of life. This is exemplified in the Place des Voges (b) in the heart of the Marais District. The view of the Paris skyline, looking westward from the tower of Cathédrale Notre-Dame (c) illustrates how the general panorama of the city has been protected from modern intrusions— but not at the expense of modern development. The city's business and administrative center, La Défense (visible in this photograph on the horizon), was developed beginning in 1958, approximately 8 kilometers west of the Musée du Louvre (Louvre Museum) on the axis of the Champs Elysées. Images and captions courtesy of Dennis Rodwell.

Figure 2-4 At both the national and regional scales, planners of France's modern highways demonstrated restraint and foresight in carefully bypassing most historic towns along their routes instead of cutting through historic centers, as is commonplace elsewhere. This is evident in these aerial views of Nîmes (a) and Arles (b), where the historic centers of each town are easily spotted by the oval-shaped structures (in the upper center of each image)—each city's Roman amphitheater. Contemporaneous plans to conserve the centers of many of these smaller French towns resulted in most benefiting fully from national infrastructure improvement schemes.

a

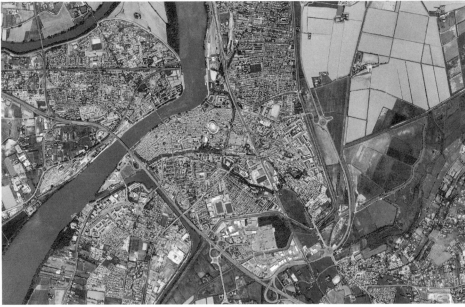

b

its historic buildings and sites and provides convenient new street arrangements and improved traffic circulation.[22]

Paris is home to one of the most controversial, yet successful restoration projects of recent decades: former President François Mitterrand's Grand Louvre Project (1981–1993). The project enhanced the Louvre Museum by adding vast underground spaces, with access provided by American architect I. M. Pei's striking glass pyramid entrance structure. This bold and highly contested design solution was initially derided but quickly became a beloved and proud symbol of the city. This modern entrance structure effectively improved visitor circulation, allowed for the addition of amenities, and gained new exhibition space for the Louvre.

a

b

c

Figure 2-5 The Napoléon Court at the Louvre (a), where the insertion of a bold new central entrance structure, the Pyramid, by American architect I. M. Pei, resolved a number of site-circulation issues while also giving one of France's most important and revered historic sites a new sense of excitement and purpose. The new entrance to the Louvre (b) and restoration of its original famous east facade (c) were parts of a larger vision: the Grand Louvre Project, which also entailed restoration of the Tuileries Garden complex (d) that extends from the Arc de Triomphe du Carrousel to the Arc de Triomphe de l'Étoile 2.3 kilometers away.

d

Figure 2-6 The twelfth-century Basilica of Saint Sernin in Toulouse was restored in the 1860s by Eugène Emmanuel Viollet-le-Duc utilizing his "unity of style" approach (according to these drawings, with the top being the east elevation), which included numerous conjectural additions and alterations attempting to make the structure more stylistically consistent with the time of its original construction. Amidst controversy, it was largely restored in the 1970s to its early nineteenth-century, pre-Viollet-le-Duc appearance.

Another conservation project of the past two decades that has encouraged debate on approaches to architectural heritage was the restoration of Basilica of Saint Sernin in Toulouse by Yves Boiret.[23] During an 1860s restoration of the eleventh- and twelfth-century Romanesque church, Viollet-le-Duc added an invented, medievalesque system of roofs as part of his "unity of style" approach. Boiret's proposal, which was approved by the Commission Supérieur Nationale des Monuments Historiques, returned the church to its early nineteenth-century appearance. Critics of this de-restoration have argued that it removed the work of a great French architect (Viollet-le-Duc), countered its own theoretical position of retaining later accretions and changes to the structure, and privileged authenticity over integrity.[24]

Conservation of twentieth-century architectural landmarks of modern design is also being addressed effectively and flexibly by authorities who understand that exceptional circumstances require special judgment calls. The most well-known solution to a sensitive contemporary heritage-protection issue occurred in 1959 in the Paris suburb of Poissy. Municipal authorities decided to replace the Villa Savoye, a highly regarded early work of the architect Le Corbusier, with a school. Under existing regulations, the house could not be preserved as a historic monument because the architect, one of the twentieth-century's most important, was still alive. Despite the lack of applicable legislation, Minister André Malraux prevented the Villa's destruction. The campaign to preserve the Villa Savoye began in 1960 at the urging of Le Corbusier himself, who hoped to remove later additions and turn it into a house museum, which was eventually done, largely without his involvement. The French state was at first reluctant to get involved, but an international campaign on behalf of this icon of International Style modernism—including an exhibition at the Museum of Modern Art in New York—contributed to its eventual restoration.[25] The Villa Savoye was declared a public building in 1963, and listed as a historic monument after Le Corbusier's death in 1965. Its restoration was finally completed in 1967; however, a re-restoration was carried out between 1985 and 1993 to counter this intervention, which was considered heavy-handed by the subsequent generation.[26]

Recent developments continue to refine France's architectural conservation practices and increase public appreciation of this work. The new focus on buildings of recent vintage presents distinct challenges. Architectural conservationists and builders face restoring and conserving unusual new materials and finishing details, such as synthetic sealants, plastics, composite building components, and a wide range of nontraditional, special finishes. For older buildings, technical advances in conservation methods, such as stone consolidants and a host of new diagnostic and documentation methods, provide new means of addressing traditionally problematic aspects of

a

b

c

Figure 2-8 The builders of Beauvais Cathedral (a) reached the limits of building in stone in the thirteenth century. A repaired structural failure at the time of the cathedral's construction showed signs of movement in 1988 when structural shoring (b and c) was added to enable modern structural repairs.

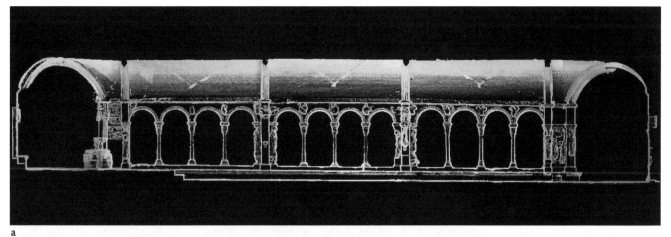

a

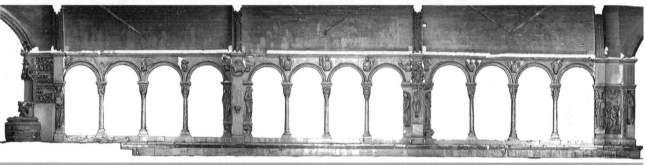

b

Figure 2-9 Conservation testing and planning at the twelfth-century Cloister of St. Trophime in Arles was aided by utilization of the CyArk laser-recording system. Shown here is the "cloud" of initial laser scan results on the east wing of the cloister (a) and the same image visually enhanced (b). The resulting three-dimensional laser scan of the cloister not only saved months of time, compared to other means of measurement, but its level of precision is 99.8 percent accurate or more. Images courtesy of WMF and CyArk.

conservation. Advanced technology is broadly applied in France: for example, it helped analyze the different types of pollutants affecting the Louvre's exterior statuary and the structural defects in Beauvais Cathedral, and it has provided extremely exacting measurements of the Cloister of St. Trophime in Arles.

From its first organized heritage-protection and restoration efforts at the turn of the twentieth century, France has been a leader in the development of international architectural conservation theories and techniques. Through constant analysis and revision of their approach to heritage protection, government committees and advisors have arrived at valuable insights that have proven applicable and useful in other countries.

Since inception, the complex government structure responsible for protecting built heritage in France has integrated the contributions of local experts with centralized direction from extensively trained architects and other professionals. In doing so, they have set the stage for a widespread appreciation of the benefits of conservation throughout French society. The architectural conservation profession is highly respected and rewarded, and it therefore attracts a talented pool of students and trainees eager to join their ranks. Since architectural education is centrally controlled, conservation training programs have little trouble receiving adequate funding and attention from government and educational authorities.

Many institutions and individuals comprise France's extensive heritage conservation network, including the managers and technicians who maintain and present the thousands of historic sites and museums throughout the country. Equally important are the specialist scientists working in stone, wood, metal, stained glass, and mural conservation in the Laboratoire de Recherche des Monuments Historiques (Laboratory for Research on Historic Monuments) as well as participants in France's famous master craftsman training program, the Compagnons du Devoir, which fosters centuries-old building craft traditions. In addition, an array of private practitioners specializes in conservation engineering, restoration and conservation of historic landscapes and interiors, and many other fields.

Figure 2-10 Members of France's master craftsman training program in the traditional building and restoration arts, the Compagnons du Devoir, at work using special tools to cut replacement stone (a) and restoring ironwork (b) at St. Antoine Abbey near Lyon.

a

b

In addition to the master craftsman training program, there are other significant vocational and graduate programs for conservation education in France. First among these is the École de Chaillot (Chaillot School), which offers a two-year program for architects specializing in conservation and restoration as well as shorter non-degree courses in architectural heritage. Founded in Paris in 1887, the École de Chaillot has existed under a number of different names in the past 130 years, and it is among most competitive conservation graduate programs in the world.[27] Its comprehensive program today covers the conservation of urban and rural structures in addition to constructed landscapes from all historical periods, as well as planning and legal aspects of heritage protection. Most graduates of this program join the French civil service, and indeed a graduate degree from the École de Chaillot is a prerequisite for two of the most important architectural conservation jobs in France: *architecte des bâtiments de France* and *architecte en chef des monuments historiques*. In addition to training French professionals, the École de Chaillot has partnered with other educational institutions worldwide to offer conservation training workshops in places such as Tongji, China; Damascus, Syria; Bucharest, Romania; and Angkor, Cambodia.

As in other western European countries and the United States, French architectural conservation professionals deal with historic buildings in a variety of ways. Their methods range from the conservative and practical approaches of the state-trained official *architectes-en-chef* for each of France's departments to the more radical approaches of private architects such as Jean Nouvel at the Lyon Opera House.[28] Nouvel renovated the nineteenth-century facades and lobby of the Opera House and added contemporary auditorium spaces and a dramatic steel-and-glass barrel-vaulted roof structure. No other country has bolder examples of consciously and carefully planned juxtapositions of old with the radically new in architecture in architectural and urban planning during the past two decades. Preceding Nouvel's Lyon Opera House rehabilitation were the insertions of I. M. Pei's aforementioned Pyramid at the Louvre in 1989 and the Centre Georges Pompidou (known as the Beaubourg due to its location) into the heart of Paris's Marais district by architects Renzo Piano and Richard Rogers in 1977. It is the high quality of these designs, their invigoration of urban environments, and their satisfaction of contemporary use needs that make them successful. In addition, and in hindsight, each can be said to have valorized the historic architectural ensembles in which they were placed.

Paris today proudly features its architectural heritage in an urban ambiance admired throughout the world. Under the national Journées du Patrimoine (Days of Heritage) program, France's most popular event, with over twelve million visitors, the government and other owners open select private historic spaces to the public each year, often accompanying this access with educational tours and presentations. Through a number of publicly funded programs, historic districts of the city are periodically enhanced by the integration of new construction, which is for the most part sensitively handled to introduce modern amenities without compromising an area's scale and special historic qualities.

France's impressive approach to managing its wealth of architectural heritage sites is a product of the priority the country places on culture in general and the importance of that culture to the French psyche. In addition, its centralized system of governance and long traditions in art and architecture, including its special experiences in restoration and conservation, further explain France's exemplary role in cultural heritage protection. Important as well is the remarkably high degree of financial support that the government provides, including the seventeen-year, $455 million (€675 million) restoration of the palace and gardens at Versailles now underway and slated for completion in 2020. This strong state support of architectural conservation is being increasingly joined by contributions from the private sector.

In Paris, "the past gnaws relentlessly into the future,"[29] philosopher Henry Bergson writes; without question, Parisian—and French—life is enhanced as a result. But the French system, which worked so well in the past, is now under pressure. New regulations imposed by the European Union in January 2009 require that all work must be opened to public tender, including structural work on classified buildings, which previously had been restricted to France's highly trained specialist *architectes-en-chef* and *architectes du patrimoine*. It is difficult to speculate on the future impact of this change, but it has the potential to be significant.

ENDNOTES

1. At various times in the past half century, this ministry has been the Ministry of Culture and, at other times, the Ministry of Culture and Communications, as it is currently called and organized. The most recent reorganization took place within this ministry in January 2010, when a Department of Heritage as part of a sweeping restructuring aimed at simplification and strengthening effectiveness. Within this umbrella department are four divisions focused on architecture, archives, museums and heritage. Further descriptions of France's prior system of cultural heritage management are found in: Anthony Dale and Robert E. Stipe, ed., *Historic Preservation in Foreign Countries*, vol. 1, *France, Great Britain, Ireland, the Netherlands and Denmark* (Washington, DC: US/ICOMOS, 1982), 10. See also Stubbs, "The Forging of a Discipline: The Late Eighteenth to Early Twentieth Centuries: France," *Time Honored*, 206–211.

2. Dale and Stipe, *Historic Preservation in Foreign Countries*, vol. 1, 11.

3. "Protection des monuments historiques," Institut national de la statistique et de études économiques, www.insee.fr/fr/themes/tableau.asp?reg_id=0&ref_id=NATnon05454 (accessed July 5, 2010). Nearly 9 percent of French listed monuments are located in Paris and its region, Ile-de-France. Other regions with high concentrations of French national monuments include Aquitaine, Bretagne, Centre and Midi-Pyrénées. "Regions," Architecture & Patrimonie, www.culture.gouv.fr/culture/inventai/patrimoine/index.htm (accessed July 15, 2010).

4. The largest number of items within this category is church fittings, including organs, which—due to their technical complexity—are specially treated under the Act of 1913. Stephen Jacobs, *Historic Preservation in Europe, the French and English; (in relation to) United States, the Government's Role* (Ithaca, NY: Cornell Center for Housing and Environmental Studies, 1966), 107.

5. Dale and Stipe, *Historic Preservation in Foreign Countries*, vol. 1, 20.

6. Ibid., 22.

7. "Les sites et monuments naturels classés et inscrits: des outils au service de la protection des paysages,"Ministère de l'écologie, de l'énergie, du développement durable et de la mer, www.developpement-durable.gouv.fr/Les-sites-et-monuments-naturels.html (accessed July 5, 2010).

8. "Monuments," Centre des Monuments Nationaux, www.monuments-nationaux.fr/en/monuments/monument-s-map/ (accessed July 5, 2010).

9. Adrian Stungo, "The Malraux Act, 1962–1972," *Journal of the Royal Town Planning Institute* 58, no. 8 (September–October 1972): 361.

10. Ibid.

11. Sherban Cantacuzino, ed., *Architectural Conservation in Europe* (London: Architectural Press, London, 1975).

12. Jukka Jokilehto, A History of Architectural Conservation. Oxford: Elsevier Butterworth-Heinemann, 2004; first published in 1999.

13. Silvio Mutal, "International Conservation Experience," paper presented at the conference Continuity of Urban Development in Historic Cities, Vilnius, Lithuania, June 2003.

14. "Architectural or historic interest" is the determining phrase in the United Kingdom for the national system of listing buildings and the local system of designation of conservation areas.

15. Gustavo Giovannoni, *L'urbanisme face aux Villes Anciennes* (Paris: Seuil, 1998).

16. Sebastian Loew, *Modern Architecture in historic Cities: Planning, Policy and Buidling in Contemporary France* (London: Routledge, 1998), 62. Property owners can personally undertake restoration and rehabilitation work with financial assistance from Credit Foncier, or they may have the work done by a special-purpose company. If the special-purpose company executes the work, the owner becomes eligible for a Ministry of Housing subsidy as well as for Credit Foncier financing. Refusal to allow the work to go forward incurs the risk of expropriation.

17. Ibid., 62–65.

18. See also Anthony M. Tung, *Preserving the World's Great Cities: The Destruction and Renewal of the Historic Metropolis* (New York: Clarkson Potter), 313.

19. Jacobs, *Historic Preservation in Europe, the French and English; (in relation to) United States, the Government's Role*, 202.

20. Ibid.

21. Ibid.

22. Ibid., 101.

23. Samia Rab, "The 'Monument' in Architecture and Conservation: Theories of Architectural Significance and their Influence on Restoration, Preservation and Conservation," doctoral dissertation, Georgia Institute of Technology (Spring 1997), 99–104.

24. Ibid., 103–4.

25. The 1966 Museum of Modern Art exhibition, "Destruction by Neglect," paired images of the Villa Savoye in the 1930s and the 1960s, contrasting its pristine original appearance with its disrepair. The exhibition was curated by Arthur Drexler, who had staged another exhibition on Le Corbusier's work just three years earlier at the same museum. Kevin D. Murphy, "The Villa Savoye and the Modernist Historic Monument," *Journal of the Society of Architectural Historians* 61, no. 1 (March 2002): 78–81.

26. Ibid., 82.

27. "The École de Chaillot," Cité de l'Architecture et du Patrimoine, www.citechaillot.fr/formation/the_ecole_de_chaillot.php (accessed December 14, 2009). The École de Chaillot is one of the three components of the Ministry of Culture supported City of Architecture and Heritage, which also includes the Museum of French Architecture and the French Institute of Architecture.

28. Training to become an architecte-en-chef within the Service des Monuments Historiques requires a degree from the École de Chaillot, plus approximately two-and-a-half years of specialized study. Successful candidates must pass a written examination in history, architecture, and restoration; prepare a thesis on a related topic; and then orally defend it to a jury of eighteen specialists before obtaining a diploma from the Chargé d'État, Haut Functionnaire. After entering the Bâtiments Monuments Historiques division, young architects advance—based on their performance—to the position of architect-en-chef. At that time, they are placed in charge of state-listed and state-controlled architectural heritage in one or more regions of France, or they are entrusted with restoration projects at French state–owned properties abroad. With one hundred departments in France and around fifty chief architects of historic buildings, on average each architect is responsible for two departments.

29. "Duration is the continuous progress of the past which gnaws into the future and which swells as it advances. And as the past grows without ceasing, so also there is no limit to its preservation." Source: Henri Bergson, *Creative Education*, ch. 1, 4. Translated by Arthur Mitchell. New York, Holt and Company, 1911.

a

b

CHAPTER 3

United Kingdom
England, Scotland, Wales, and Northern Ireland

The architectural conservation movement founded by the ideas of art critic and theorist John Ruskin and artist and social critic William Morris in the late nineteenth century spawned generations of architectural heritage protection activists. Their reactions to building restorations involving major interventions eventually spread from the United Kingdom to the continent of Europe. Since then the United Kingdom has remained a global leader in both architectural conservation theory and technology.

Within the United Kingdom, conservation became an established component of architectural and planning practices in the twentieth century. Steeped in a long history of conserving historic buildings in a country where tradition is an integral part of life, British conservationists found widespread popular support for their endeavors. Indeed, historian and social critic David Lowenthal described the British reverence for the past as "virtually a genetic trait."[1] The long-standing appreciation of authenticity, of easily discernable histories of objects, and of the special character of antiques has led to an almost religious respect for natural patinas on historic buildings in the United Kingdom. British sensitivity to these issues no doubt emerged from the romantic and picturesque traditions that developed in the eighteenth and nineteenth centuries.

Heritage conservation continues to transform the United Kingdom, as its dynamic and progressive society changes its view of architectural conservation from one that stresses conservation for cultural or aesthetic reasons to one that conserves heritage for the direct benefit of people and communities. The instrumental role of nongovernmental organizations of all sizes and types in architectural conservation distinguishes the field in the United Kingdom and has served as a model to which many countries without strong governmental support for heritage have aspired in the twentieth and twenty-first centuries.

LEGISLATION AND LISTING

Though a decentralized movement partly organized and carried out by private initiatives and citizens' groups, architectural conservation in the United Kingdom originated with and is still regulated by legislation and is guided by government-sponsored agencies. As American historian of the conservation field Stephen Jacobs noted, "In contrast to the organized and somewhat doctrinaire approach to architectural preservation used on the continent, English practices seem both complex and permissive."[2] Rather than a

◄ **Figure 3-1** A Scheduled Monument as well as a UNESCO World Heritage Site, world-renowned Stonehenge on the Wiltshire Plains (a) is a heritage site that requires utmost care and attention. A recently completed plan to improve visitor access and reroute traffic that passes nearby has taken over a decade to produce and gain approval. In contrast, in terms of age and recentness of listing, on February 23, 2010 the Abbey Road Studios (b) in St. John's Wood, London was listed as a Grade II site. It was home to several composers and musicians, most notably the Beatles during the 1960s.

single comprehensive law, multiple pieces of legislation, regulation, and oversight organizations govern and guide various aspects of heritage conservation in the United Kingdom. The way these frameworks are interpreted and implemented by national and local actors in the different parts of the country varies significantly. For example, Northern Ireland and Scotland are subject to laws separate from those applicable in England and Wales. Even within England, places of worship, archaeological sites, military remains, shipwrecks, and burial grounds are all protected separately.

Conservation legislation in the United Kingdom began in 1882 with the first Ancient Monuments Act. Initially restricted to prehistoric sites, successive amendments to the Act extended its coverage to significant ruins of later dates, provided that they were not in use. Following World War II, the Town and Country Act of 1947 allowed the Ministry of Housing and Local Government to identify and protect significant occupied historic buildings. The Historic Buildings and Ancient Monuments Act of 1953 ensured the maintenance and prevented demolition of historic sites, and it made Ministry funds available to assist building owners with conservation costs. The 1967 Civic Amenities Act expanded the protection beyond individual buildings to ensembles and complexes through the designation of Conservation Areas.

The contemporary framework for designating and maintaining the built environment in England and Wales is provided by the Ancient Monuments and Archaeological Areas Act of 1979 and the Listed Buildings and Conservation Areas Act of 1990. Through these two Acts, legal protection is extended for sites within three categories:

1. *Scheduled Monuments:* The central government maintains a list of archaeological sites, including ruins, that are no longer inhabited or economically useful and are deemed to be of national importance. These sites are placed on the Schedule of Monuments.[3] Recognized sites reflect the entirety of human history, from prehistoric through near contemporary times. Monuments are divided into two hundred separate classes; however, all receive the same high level of protection. The Schedule of Monuments currently includes about 18,300 entries, encompassing over 31,000 sites.

2. *Listed Buildings:* Sites of national architectural interest, historic interest, associative interest, or group value are placed on lists of buildings meriting statutory protection. Three grades of listed buildings—I, II*, and II—are awarded increasing levels of protection based on their comparative values and conditions. Grade I and II* sites are considered exceptionally important, and they may only be destroyed under exceptional circumstances. Consent for changes to listed buildings are granted by the relevant local authority. Buildings can be nominated for listing by the central government, local governments, amenity societies, or individuals. Decisions to list a building are taken by the relevant minister. Currently in England and Wales, there are nearly 500,000 listed buildings and sites, including over 9,000 Grade I sites in England alone.

3. *Conservation Areas:* Conservation areas are locally designated historic districts or ensembles of buildings, ranging from townscapes and villages to country houses and their estates to historic transportation links, such as canals. Within conservation areas, not just the buildings are protected but also all aspects that contribute to its particular character, including street patterns and paving materials, greenery, and street furniture as well as the historic mixtures of buildings types and balances of public and private spaces.

Oversight of Scheduled Monuments and Listed Buildings in England is carried out by the agency English Heritage, established in 1983 by the National Heritage Act.[4] Sponsored by the Department for Culture, Media, and Sport (DCMS), English Heritage recommends nominations to the lists and advises local authorities on applications for alterations to listed buildings and the minister on applications for works to scheduled monuments. English Heritage also maintains a register of Heritage at Risk to track conservation areas, scheduled monuments, and listed buildings threatened by neglect, decay, development, or redundancy.

English Heritage also manages more than four hundred historic properties and annually disburses over £29.3 million (about $47.5 million) on restoration projects and in conservation and archaeology grants.[5] Its priorities address a number of needs: conserving objects and buildings for the long term, involving local communities in heritage conservation, and extending protection to previously underserved categories of heritage sites, such as industrial cities and complexes, pubs, military sites, and post–World War II sites.

In Wales, the role of identifying, promoting, and conserving listed buildings is carried out by Cadw, founded in 1984 as a division of the Welsh Assembly Government. The word, Cadw, means "to keep" in Welsh.[6] Parallel government agencies also exist in the other major regions of the United Kingdom, including the Northern Ireland Environment Agency (formerly the Environment and Heritage Service), which maintains the Sites and Monuments Record that offers protection for over 15,000 sites.[7] Since the Town and Country Planning Act of 1969, Historic Scotland, a Scottish Government agency formerly called the Ancient Monuments and Historic Buildings Division of the Scottish Development Department, provides similar oversight for listed buildings, which are categorized as either Grade A or B.[8] As in England and Wales, Conservation Areas are also protected in Scotland, and they are similarly locally designated.

Figure 3-2 Historic Scotland, some powerful legislation, and the hard work and foresight of dedicated heritage conservationists have conserved the historic buildings and parks of Scotland's many historic cities and towns remarkably well. The juxtaposition of the Old and New Towns of Edinburgh, Scotland's capital city, provides a historical example of the principle of mutually supportive, harmonious coexistence that was articulated and promoted in Italy since the 1920s by the Roman architect and planner Gustavo Giovannoni. Image and text courtesy Dennis Rodwell.

Garden and Landscape Conservation in the United Kingdom

The United Kingdom was committed to protecting historic landscapes at least as early as any other country and has been more organized about their conservation than France, whose tradition of landscape design is longer. The United Kingdom has generated many good land conservation concepts, with purposes and methods similar to those of continental Europe and the United States. However, as is typically the case in the United Kingdom, strong public participation has always been crucial to the process. During the interwar period, innovative "green belts" were created to limit urban growth around many of the country's cities and, in effect, to preserve some of the rural landscapes around both new and historic towns. In some cases, local citizens identified sites of special scenographic or ecological interest and ensured their conservation. Since local economies and vitality are often connected to such sites, concerned citizens and government agencies alike regularly expend an untold number of hours to defend and maintain them. Consequently, numerous examples of legislation today exist to protect the country's land, seashore, and other natural features.

The rural conservation debate continues today as the United Kingdom's population increases and the need for more affordable housing grows. Calls for sustainable development have led to several experiments in new town development—for example, the town of Milton Keynes, which was created in 1967, and more recently Léon Krier's new urbanism development at Poundbury. Development has focused on the reduction of sprawl and the conservation of fields and open spaces. In the United Kingdom the need for such solutions is particularly urgent.

Despite its long tradition of rural landscape protection and sensitive new towns, the protection of parks and gardens was one of the last heritage issues to be addressed by the United Kingdom government. They were not covered by legislation until the passage of the National Heritage Act in 1983. Specialized groups such as the Garden History Society and the National Council for the Conservation of Plants and Gardens, among others, existed previously and were devoted and effective advocates for the inclusion of parks and gardens in the 1983 Act. With the Act, English Heritage and its parallel organizations throughout the United Kingdom were granted the authority to prepare registers of gardens, parks, and historic landscapes. Assistance in compiling the list was given by the Centre for the Conservation of Historic Parks and Gardens at the University of York. In addition, a more extensive inventory was prepared called the National Survey and Inventory of Gardens and Parks of Historic Interest. The net result of these initiatives has been to prevent the intrusion of new roads and housing developments on historic parks and gardens by raising awareness of their cultural value and requiring local authorities to take historic landscapes into account when planning.

Though the government was late in formally recognizing the significance of these initiatives, in its sensibility for landscapes, gardens, and the protection of land, the United Kingdom is well ahead of any other country in the world. It has numerous trusts devoted to specific land and nature conservation interests. Such trusts are based on private initiative, a very important ingredient in both architectural and nature conservation in England. Garden and land trusts that protect the scenographic qualities of special landscapes formed in local communities throughout the United Kingdom assist homeowners and community administrations with planning, lend practical assistance in garden creation and maintenance, and provide education and interpretation of the value of natural landscapes and gardens. These trusts illustrate the phenomenon of individuals taking matters into their own hands, for the public interest. They have influenced government decisions and are among the best guarantors of the conservation of sites, given their capacities to oversee the properties in question.

Though listed buildings and conservation areas are the most common designations of protected sites in the United Kingdom, most of these regional organizations also keep other specialized lists of additional sites within their geographic purview. For example, English Heritage maintains separate Registers for Historic Battlefields as well as of Parks and Gardens.[9] Cadw maintains separate lists for historic landscapes, maritime wrecks, and parks and gardens. The Northern Ireland Environment Agency maintains registers of historic parks and gardens as well as sites representing industrial, maritime, and defense heritage. In some cases, the owners of registered sites on these supplemental lists

a

b

Figure 3-3 The United Kingdom has been a leader in establishing legislation for protection of historic gardens and landscapes as complements to architectural and historic town conservation schemes. The far bank of Falmouth Harbor in Cornwall (a) is protected for its picturesque qualities and the great garden of Bodnant in Wales (b) for its well-maintained topiaries.

are under no obligation to maintain or make their sites publicly accessible; however, they may be eligible for special conservation grants.

Protection of the historic environment though the designation of areas, buildings, or monuments is only one part of the overall approach to heritage conservation in the United Kingdom. Equally important is the spatial planning system. The various national governments issue planning policy guidelines and planning policy statements that advise local authorities on how to prepare the spatial plans for the development of their area. For example, in England such guidelines concerning both historic buildings and archaeology have guided planning by local authorities for decades. In 2009 the government released the consultative draft of "Planning Policy Statement 15: Planning for the Historic Environment," which, for the first time, combined strategies for archaeological and architectural heritage and introduced a more rigorous preapplication stage for list-

Figure 3-4 The £7.18 million ($11.5 million) awarded in 2008 by the Heritage Lottery Fund to the People's History Museum in Manchester has been combined with additional funds from the Northeast Regional Development Agency to support the refurbishment of a nineteenth-century pump house and construction of a new addition to provide improved visitor facility and increased access to the museum's collections. The museum reopened in early 2010. Photo by permission of People's History Museum.

ing, with the aim of providing clarity on conservation principles and approaches.[10] This new Planning Policy Statement has been highly contested and is still being debated by conservation professionals in England.

The introduction of the Heritage Lottery Fund in 1993 as a key development by the government for the conservation of historic buildings and landscapes in the United Kingdom has already proven successful. Since 1994 a percentage of net proceeds from the National Lottery have been earmarked for qualified heritage conservation projects. To date, over £4.4 billion ($7.1 billion) in lottery funds has been distributed on a competitive basis in the form of matching grants intended to help conserve and maintain over 33,900 heritage sites of local, regional, and national significance.[11]

Notable recent projects supported by the Heritage Lottery Fund have ranged from the refurbishment of a nineteenth-century pump house in Manchester to serve as a labor history museum and the conservation of the SS *Great Britain* and its display in a dry dock, with an artificial water line below, that is an environmentally controlled area protecting the hull and showing the public the infrastructure required to conserve the ship. Heritage Lottery Fund monies are similarly being used to educate the public about the processes and techniques of architectural conservation as part of the restoration of the Gothic Revival Tyntesfield estate, near Bristol, including its original Victorian interiors and unrivaled collection of nineteenth-century decorative arts. Tyntesfield has been open to the public during the entire process, which began in 2006 and is scheduled for completion in 2011.

The complicated system of heritage protection in England and Wales, with its multiple agencies and separate legislation and lists for different types of protected sites may soon be changing. Because of the piecemeal and complicated nature of the system, and the resultant gaps and inefficiency, an extensive program of heritage protection review and reform was initiated in England and Wales by the Department for Culture, Media and Sport and the Welsh Assembly Government in 2003. A series of surveys, reports, and position papers was made, and some initial changes that did not require legislation have already been made, such as transferring review of listing applications to English Heritage and improving consultations with owners of listed properties. A new comprehensive heritage protection bill was drafted in 2008, setting "out the legislative framework for a unified and simpler heritage protection system that will be more open, accountable and transparent."[12] It remains to be seen whether this proposed bill will be presented to Parliament and enacted in the coming years.

PRIVATE, NOT-FOR-PROFIT ADVOCACY GROUPS

Since the late nineteenth century, private civic groups and amenity societies have played a major role in raising public awareness of architectural heritage in the United Kingdom as well as in carrying out actual conservation work.[13] The sheer number and variety of these groups and organizations in the United Kingdom is impressive. Though they all work to conserve the distinctive features of the built environment, they represent very diverse aspects of the field—from protest groups to the mainstream, and they include private homeowners, activist and advocacy groups, amenity and preservation societies, residents' associations in towns and villages, and funding bodies. In the words of conservation architect and educator Derek Linstrum: "In their activities, these enthusiastic groups embody a respect for the past and for their heritage that is far more complex and serious than mere nostalgia."[14] The most significant of these organizations continuously shape the architectural conservation landscape in Great Britain by influencing policy and the administration of heritage.

One of the earliest and most influential groups, one that helped shape the *scrape* and *antiscrape* debate of the nineteenth century, was the Society for the Protection of Ancient Buildings (SPAB), which firmly supported the antiscrape, laissez-faire approach to architectural conservation.[15] Founded by William Morris in 1877, the Society has broad interests and is perhaps the world's oldest, continuously operating nongovernmental architectural conservation organization. The number of other professional and private organizations modeled on the Society is testament to its sound approach to the protection and presentation of architectural heritage of a country.

An organization founded two decades later that remains a principal force in conservation in the United Kingdom is the National Trust for Places of Historic Interest or Natural Beauty, which was founded by three philanthropists in 1895 in response to the rapid disappearance of historic sites due to unbridled development and industrialization. Its mission remains the permanent conservation of areas of natural beauty and buildings of historical or architectural importance throughout England, Wales, and Northern Ireland. Since the period between the two world wars when social and economic changes seriously threatened countless important country houses, whose owners were forced to sell as a result of death duties and the relatively high cost of maintaining large estates, these national treasures have been a particular focus of the National Trust. Today, these houses are quite popular, and as a result of the National Trust's efforts to protect them, its membership had reached 3.5 million by 2007.[16]

The National Trust believes the best way to conserve a building or site is to control its ownership, so the organization primarily preserves heritage sites through bequest or, in exceptional cases, purchase—but it will generally not accept a property from a private donor without an endowment to cover its upkeep. The National Trust does, however, accept properties from the government, which received them often in lieu of taxes, and it depends largely on government grants for repair and maintenance of a few of its properties. Today this private charity is the second largest property owner in the United

Kingdom, after the Crown, owning 700 miles of coastline, more than 610,000 acres of land, over 5,000 prehistoric sites, and over 1,100 historic buildings.[17] Its holdings even encompass parts of six World Heritage Sites, ranging from Hadrian's Wall to Cornish mines. In recent years, the National Trust has developed a sophisticated management framework for its various properties, with unified systems of administration, ticket and product sales, advertising, and interpretation.

Another influential nongovernmental organization that worked in the heritage conservation field was the Civic Trust, founded in England in 1957. The Civic Trust was disbanded in early 2009, after a half century of campaigning to change policy and attitudes, administering an award program to raise standards of conservation work, and promoting a civic society movement that empowered communities to take responsibility for their local heritage. The Civic Trust served as an umbrella organization coordinating more than 850 voluntary local civic societies that focus on raising awareness of and solving local problems, restoring buildings, and acting as watchdogs for nearby scheduled and listed sites.

Though the Civic Trust itself is no longer extant, the civic societies it fostered and encouraged are still active. For example, activists in the English city of Norwich, which is known for its attractive Georgian main street, organized the Norwich Society in 1923. This membership organization, which does not accept funding from other sources to ensure its independence, aims "to encourage high standards of architecture and town planning in Norwich; to stimulate public interest in and care for the beauty, history and character of the city and its surroundings; to encourage the preservation, development and improvement of features of general public amenity or historic interest; [and] to pursue these ends by means of meetings, exhibitions, lectures, publications, other forms of instruction and publicity."[18]

The Scottish Civic Trust was formed a decade after the English Civic Trust, to take on parallel responsibilities promoting heritage and culture in Scotland, and it is still strong today. It also coordinates and encourages the activities of hundreds of local societies and organizes the Doors Open Days in association with the Council of Europe's European Heritage Days. At the request of Historic Scotland, the Scottish Civic Trust has maintained a register of Buildings at Risk, including listed as well as other sites. Today, that register includes nearly 2000 sites, over 100 of which are currently under restoration.[19]

The Association for Preservation Trusts is another umbrella organization that coordinates local conservation efforts throughout the United Kingdom. It was formed in 1989 to promote the sharing of information and strategies as the number of building preservation trusts grew.[20] The establishment of building preservation trusts dates back to 1934, when the first trust—the Bath Preservation Trust—was created. These registered charities are exclusively concerned with the preservation of buildings of historic or architectural merit in a specific county, district, or town. Buildings at risk are their first priority. Such trusts frequently operate as revolving funds: that is, they buy a property, repair it, sell it, and then buy another property. A series of conservation actions can take place under this arrangement; when two or more properties are under development at the same time, capital can be turned around efficiently.[21] A major source of funding for building preservation trusts are low-interest loans and grants from the Architectural Heritage Fund, a private philanthropic organization that has, since 1976, provided advice and financial assistance to these and other nonprofit organizations.[22]

Two other key organizations in the British architectural conservation field are the Ancient Monuments Society and SAVE Britain's Heritage. The Ancient Monuments Society, founded in 1924 to study the conservation of ancient structures in England and Wales, researches and publishes on historic architecture and works to prevent demolitions and damage to protected sites.[23] Founded in 1975, SAVE Britain's Heritage joined the Ancient Monuments Society in its mission. SAVE Britain's Heritage formulates arguments in support of conservation that, unlike those of most advocates, do not rest solely on aesthetic quality or historical value but rather focus on the practical use of society's heritage. The organization argues that all buildings "represent energy, labor, and materials, which either cannot be replaced or can only be replaced at high cost. The fight to save particular buildings is not the fancy of some impractical antiquarian. It is part of the battle for the sane use of all our resources."[24]

The work of SAVE Britain's Heritage is complemented in Northern Ireland by the Ulster Architectural Heritage Society (UAHS).[25] Founded in 1967, the organization's original aims were to secure government protection for historic buildings in Northern Ireland, a goal achieved in 1972. It also played a significant part in establishing a Historic Buildings Council, providing historic building grants, and creating a record of public buildings in Northern Ireland. Today the UAHS continues to promote public awareness for conservation issues through tours and publications, to lobby the government on behalf of particular sites and regarding planning legislation, and to provide a network for conservation resources and practitioners in Northern Ireland.

The work of these major organizations is complemented by several other smaller organizations established to promote more specific interests—the Council for British Archaeology, the Georgian Group (for buildings erected after 1714), the Victorian Society (for Victorian and Edwardian buildings), the Twentieth Century Society (for buildings from 1914 onward)—as well as several other societies focused specifically on conserving religious buildings.[26] In addition, the heritage conservation climate in Great Britain has produced many of the leading international NGOs in the field today, including the Landmark Trust, the Vivat Trust, the Headly Trust, Venice in Peril, and Jaisalmer in Jeopardy, all working in such diverse locations as Russia, Croatia, Italy, and India.

Figure 3-5 The Landmark Trust represents one of Britain's many specialty amenity groups and civic trusts devoted to heritage protection. It specializes in transforming unusual small-scale architectural wonders in England, Scotland, and Wales into holiday rental homes. The Pineapple House, the former conservatory on the estate of the John Murray, 4th Earl of Dunmore, in central Scotland, was converted in 1973 into self-catering holiday accommodations for weekly lease. It is one of the Trust's 186 restored heritage sites that can be leased for such use. Image courtesy Angus Bremner/The Landmark Trust.

CONTEMPORARY FOCI

The United Kingdom's most recent conservation efforts have focused on a number of specific types of sites, including historic townscapes, country houses, industrial sites, and gardens and parks. Despite variations in scale, aesthetics, and national importance, most British towns have managed to preserve their historical integrity despite modern commercial pressures, because sensitive infill and respectful new architectural design have long-standing traditions. The distinguished nineteenth-century Gothic Revival architect Sir Arthur Blomfield argued that "each genuine phase of architecture is indissolubly connected with the architecture before and after it; and it is only from this standpoint that it is possible to arrive at its true significance as a line in a long chain of developments."[27]

Bath, a city founded by the Romans and famously redeveloped in the eighteenth century, was declared a World Heritage List site in 1987. When one of the thermal baths for which the city is named was closed in 1978 because of hygienic concerns, Bath's historic center began to decline as its eponymous main attraction drew fewer tourists and got less attention.[28] In the following years, a number of proposals were suggested to encourage investment in the city center and to restore the city's function as a spa. In the late 1980s the City Council cleaned and repaired some of Bath's deteriorating and often abandoned historic structures. Donald Insall Associates' made emergency repairs and performed stone consolidation work at the Hot Baths; part of this work won a Diploma from Europa Nostra in 1993.

A decade later the city sponsored an international competition, won by Nicholas Grimshaw and Partners, to restore, update, and reopen the thermal baths themselves. The resultant intervention included careful conservation of the Georgian stone buildings as well as contemporary steel and glass additions that carefully and successfully negotiated the seemingly conflicting requirements of Bath's World Heritage status and the forward-looking Millennium Lottery grant that funded the development project. The dramatic project opened in August 2006, encouraged other investment in the city, brought tourists back to Bath by the tens of thousands, and rejuvenated the historic core of the city.[29]

At Oxford and Cambridge, a mixture of sympathetic classical architecture with older Gothic buildings testifies to the sensitive design approaches used even centuries earlier in Georgian England. The result creates picturesque ensembles that have won the lasting admiration of the British public and the many visitors to these university towns.[30] Today, even modern structures built at Oxford and Cambridge respect each university's architectural heritage; several successful additions have further enhanced these near pristine sites. Similarly, in the cathedral cities of Exeter, Durham, and York, the harmonious integration of buildings from a range of historic and contemporary periods is impressive.

In the twentieth century, Britain's medieval heritage has particularly attracted conservation attention, especially following the destruction of World War II. The cathedral city of Coventry is perhaps the most famous post-war redesign of a city complex around a historic structure. In a planning competition, the winning entry preserved the shell of the partially destroyed medieval cathedral and further arranged for the conservation of eighteen other historic structures as features of the new town design. Coventry today presents a harmonious assemblage of buildings old and new, with the ruins of the Gothic cathedral as its centerpiece.

In recent decades, one of the most visible proponents of the architectural conservation cause has been Prince Charles; he has tirelessly advocated sensible land use and architectural design that respects local traditions. Since the 1980s, Prince Charles has confronted members of the modern architectural and planning establishments who proposed designs for London buildings that he and others found objectionable.[31] The values expressed by the Prince and his attitudes toward heritage and historic cityscapes are derived from those articulated by the nineteenth-century founders of the architectural heritage protection movement. Despite criticism that his views are reactionary, a hindrance to progress, and an impediment to architectural creativity, he has had some influence on both Britain's con-

Figure 3-6 The sensitive stabilization and conservation of the ruined remains of Coventry Cathedral (its entrance area seen here) and retention of eighteen other historic structures that survived aerial bombardment during World War II are hallmarks of the city center's character since the 1960s. Coventry has been widely noted as an example of the successful integration of the old and new in modern urban planning.

Figure 3-7 In the spirit of William Morris's 1877 "Manifesto for Society for the Preservation of Ancient Buildings," Prince Charles argues in his 1989 book, *A Vision for Britain,* for changes to Britain's built environment that are rooted in historic building traditions. The controversy this book and Prince Charles' positions have stirred has polarized views and added visibility to heritage protection in Britain and abroad. Jacket cover from *A Vision of Britain* by HRH The Prince of Wales. Used by permission of Doubleday, a division of Random House, Inc.

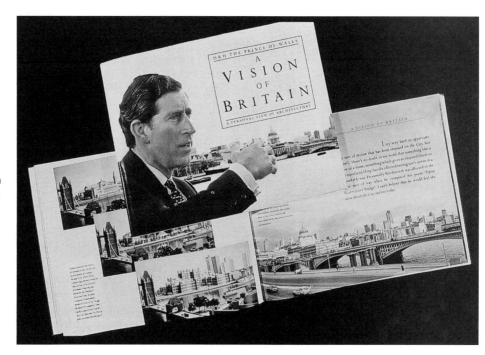

temporary architecture and architectural conservation movements and his positions reflect the opinions of much of the British public. Among the Prince of Wales's latest initiatives is the Prince's Regeneration Trust, established in 2006, which is dedicated to finding sustainable and commercially viable new uses for unused important historic buildings.

While late twentieth-century planning designs for London generally respected historic buildings, this usually only extended to buildings of exceptional significance and not necessarily to humbler historic structures or recent constructions. An awareness of the value of coordinating a variety of inherited architectural expressions with needed modern structures was also reflected in certain aspects of London's development during the 1960s and 1970s. Modern structures and developments such as Alison and Peter Smithson's complex for the *Economist* (1964) in the St. James area and Chamberlain, Powell, and Bonn's Barbican Estate (1969) either integrated themselves comfortably within a historic environment or incorporated historic structures into their plans.

English conservation architects, advocates, and developers followed the example of American large-scale conservation and adaptive-use projects that began in the early 1970s.[32] Some of London's examples of similar adaptive reuse projects include the mixed-use complex in the restored Covent Garden Marketplace, which opened in 1980, as well as the new Tate Modern art museum in the former Bankside Power Station, completed twenty years later. The adaptive use and judicious expansion of Covent Garden market has been the catalyst for a wider regeneration of the entire surrounding neighborhood. Its success has come at a price, however, as continuous throngs of tourists and revelers damage and vandalize such historic structures as Inigo Jones's classical church of St. Paul's Covent Garden. More recently the neo-Gothic St. Pancras Railway Station (now St. Pancras International), designated the terminus of Eurostar high-speed rail connection with Paris and Brussels through the "Chunnel" in 2007, was sensitively rehabilitated to accommodate the increased and international traffic. St. Pancras, which was nearly demolished in the 1960s, has once again become a vibrant transportation and urban hub. Even the adjacent hotel, designed by George Gilbert Scott, was refurbished and expanded and now includes both hotel rooms and loft apartments.

Figure 3-8 One of England's premier examples of adaptive reuse is the Tate Modern art museum in the former Bankside Power Station, designed by Giles Gilbert Scott and built between 1947 and 1963. In the year 2000, the architects Herzog & de Meuron converted the building to display the international art of the Tate collection, which had vastly outgrown the original gallery. The Tate specifically sought a suitable historic structure to reuse and then held an international competition for the project's design after selecting the Bankside Power Station. Herzog & de Meuron's design proposal was favored in part because of the degree of original building fabric they aimed to retain.

Figure 3-9 Exterior and interior views of the restored St. Pancras Railway Station and Midland Hotel, London. After standing empty for three-quarters of a century, the 1876 St. Pancras Midland Hotel, designed by George Gilbert Scott, has been restored and reopened as a combination of luxury flats and new hotel by the Manhattan Loft Corporation. The adjacent St. Pancras train shed, designed in 1868 by William Barlow, also witnessed a £800 million ($1.3 billion) restoration and extension to house the extra long Eurostar trains. Both buildings are Grade I listed sites.

St. Pancras train shed is not the only industrial building to receive conservation attention in recent decades. After much public and government debate, the 1960s loss of London's architecturally significant early nineteenth-century Euston Arch, the former entryway to the railway station of the same name, galvanized the architectural conservation field in England and raised awareness of its rich industrial-era heritage. Since that time, the United Kingdom has become a world leader in the conservation of industrial and infrastructural sites from the nineteenth and early twentieth century, including many early engineering marvels. The industrial archaeological site at Ironbridge Gorge, for example, is now a complex of museums and heritage sites, and attention has been lavished on other former industrial complexes such as the Albert Dock in Liverpool. Focusing on these sites was aided after 1987 when England adopted a controversial "thirty year rule" permitting the protection of more recent heritage under the Planning Acts.

There are, of course, other examples of conserved historic structures that today stand uncomfortably beside modern tourist accommodations. In William Shakespeare's birthplace of Stratford-upon-Avon, original seventeenth-century, half-timbered buildings coexist with imitations of inferior quality. Today, architects and planners have for the most part publicly accepted the purposes and principles of architectural conservation; however, the designs of new buildings in conservation areas are not always harmonious additions. In an unfortunate number of cases, they are isolated facades, poorly executed replicas, or grossly overscaled. The work of heightening awareness of the various kinds of values associated with architectural heritage protection clearly remains a priority for its advocates, if they are to maintain the atmosphere and special qualities of designated conservation areas.

Conserving Britain's Industrial Heritage
Dennis Rodwell

The United Kingdom's seminal role in the Industrial Revolution in the eighteenth and nineteenth centuries can be readily traced by both a local and an international audience through eight of the United Kingdom's total of twenty-four cultural sites featured on the UNESCO World Heritage List:

- *Ironbridge Gorge, England (inscribed in 1986):* notable for innovations in mining, ironworking, and structural and mechanical engineering; symbolized by the Iron Bridge.

- *Blaenavon Industrial Landscape, Wales (2000):* a landscape that has been powerfully shaped by humans and that bears witness to the preeminence of South Wales as the world's major producer of coal and iron in the nineteenth century.

- *Derwent Valley Mills, England (2001):* birthplace of the factory system of industrial-scale production and labor organization; inspired and developed by Sir Richard Arkwright.

- *New Lanark, Scotland (2001):* where David Dale and his partner Robert Owen pioneered the concept of a model industrial society; located in an idyllic setting on the banks of the river Clyde.

- *Saltaire, England (2001):* the planned model industrial village developed by Sir Titus Salt on the banks of the river Aire.

- *Liverpool Maritime Mercantile City, England (2004):* one of the world's foremost trading ports and a pioneer in the development of modern dock technology, warehouse design and construction, and port management.

- *Cornwall and West Devon Mining Landscape, England (2006):* prolific innovation in mining and related industries that enabled the region to produce two-thirds of the world's supply of copper.

- *Pontcysyllte Aqueduct and Canal, Wales (2009):* a masterpiece of civil engineering in a demanding geographical setting; designed by Thomas Telford.

Although under the United Kingdom protective systems there are no specific statutory controls for World Heritage Sites, each of these eight sites has a detailed management plan in place that is directed at safeguarding their outstanding universal value for future generations and managing change in a positive manner. Special care is taken in the application of controls over scheduled monuments, listed buildings, and conservation areas, as well as in the general consideration of proposals for new development both within the sites and in their settings.

World Heritage List status has increased the awareness of these sites for educational purposes and enhanced their profile as visitor attractions. In certain cases, most notably Blaenavon Industrial Landscape, the new international profile has had a catalytic effect in encouraging a significant level of investment from United Kingdom and European Union sources into the varied industrial components and, additionally, for upgrading the housing stock and in the provision of community facilities. The conversion of a former school into a World Heritage Centre, opened to acclaim in 2008, is an exemplar of its kind, presenting the history and importance of the site to audiences from near and far; it also supports understanding and continuity of the rich, intangible cultural heritage traditions of the area.

The United Kingdom experienced accelerating decline in its traditional industries in the decades following the First World War. The pace of decline varied, but across the country the legacy of this decline is enormous. Until the 1980s, it became fashionable to disparage the nation's industrial heritage as reminiscent of a dirty, noisy, unhealthy past that had no place in the contemporary world. Important regeneration initiatives at Ironbridge Gorge and New Lanark, however, predated their inscription on the UNESCO World Heritage List and showed a reevaluation of the country's industrial heritage.

This reevaluation was accompanied by countless other conservation initiatives across the United Kingdom. The country's railway heritage has seen significant revivals, including the regeneration of Swindon town railway station, founded in the 1840s by the great engineer Isambard Kingdom Brunel to serve his Great Western Railway; the restoration of George Gilbert Scott's St. Pancras Station; and countless smaller-scale projects of conversion and adaptive reuse, such as the restoration of Melrose Station in Scotland in the 1980s.

FURTHER READING

Dennis Rodwell, "Industrial World Heritage Sites in the United Kingdom." *World Heritage Review* 28 (2002): 4–23.

———. "The World Heritage Convention and the Exemplary Management of Complex Heritage Sites." *Journal of Architectural Conservation* 8, no. 3 (November 2002): 40–60.

———. "Urban Regeneration and the Management of Change: Liverpool and the Historic Urban Landscape." *Journal of Architectural Conservation* 14, no. 2 (July 2008): 83–106.

a

b

c

Figure 3-10 As the birthplace of the Industrial Revolution, the United Kingdom has numerous important nineteenth century manufacturing and infrastructure sites that have been preserved and protected. The Iron Bridge (a) crossing the Severn Gorge in Shropshire, constructed between 1777 and 1781 by Abraham Darby, pioneered the use of iron in bridge construction. The Albert Dock in Liverpool (b) represents the development of modern dock technology, warehouse design and construction, and port management. The Boar's Head Mills (c) at Darley Abbey, whose principal development took place from the early 1780s through the 1830s, comprise the most complete of the surviving cotton manufacturing complexes in the Derwent Valley Mills World Heritage Site. Saltaire (d), a planned model industrial village built between 1851 and 1876 by Sir Titus Salt, is dominated by Salts Mill and complemented by the tightly laid out workers' housing, allotments, public buildings, and open spaces. Images courtesy and copyright Dennis Rodwell.

d

Conserving Fine Architectural Interiors
Lisa Ackerman

Architectural conservation projects are complex activities requiring experts from many different fields, and the challenges grow as more elements of the building are taken into consideration. Often the most visible part of a project is the rehabilitation of the exterior, which alone can require art historians, architects, engineers, and specialists in scientific analysis of materials ranging from metal to stone, plaster, masonry, and mortar. While stabilization of the building envelope is essential, interior architectural restoration and conservation projects can prove to be even more thought provoking and require even more specialists. Conserving architectural interiors often necessitates deep discussions on the evolution of decorative campaigns, historic or cultural activities related to these interiors, and the need to reconcile interior and exterior as well as interior architecture with furnishings and fixtures, which may or may not be in evidence in the building at present.

Throughout Europe, and indeed the world, precious interiors are housed in great buildings: country houses, palaces, civic structures, and private homes may all be important structures with interiors that are distinctive and require attention. Startling examples can be found in any country, yet the British Isles are perhaps the obvious location for this discussion as issues of conservation of interiors began to be addressed there in the nineteenth century by figures such as William Morris.

A quintessential example of the complexities of conserving a site where grounds, interior, and exterior all vie for attention is Stowe House in Buckinghamshire, England, which was converted in the late seventeenth and eighteenth century into the impressive mansion that stands today. Its extensively painted and sculpted interiors include an elliptical marble salon designed by Vincenzo Valdrè (circa 1772) and a Gothic Revival library added by Sir John Soane. Stowe House and many other similar examples are only understood when one takes into consideration the grounds and its follies, the house, and the historic interiors together. Were one to restore only the building envelope, a great house would be saved, but the essence of what makes Stowe important would be lost.

Strawberry Hill is another such example. Horace Walpole's vision of a little Gothic castle for Strawberry Hill was so complete that the interaction of building, interiors, views from windows, and fine finishes created strong public interest, drawing people to the site during Walpole's lifetime and promoting the Gothic Revival aesthetic. The attention to detail and completeness of his vision still tantalizes visitors today. It would be unthinkable to restore the house's exterior without giving equal attention to the extraordinary interiors. The unusual use of materials as well as the blending of styles as the building evolved both during Walpole's life in the house and after his death fuel the desire to understand his artistic intent.

Similar discussions could easily focus on great interiors throughout Europe. Palaces, country houses, public architecture, and religious structures all were conceived to speak to visitors through the grandeur of the architecture and the impressive commissioned interiors. Yet it is in the United Kingdom where perhaps some of the earliest and most comprehensive conservation attention was paid to extraordinary interiors and their interpretation.

In recent years, the British government has realized the potential of architectural conservation to revive its most economically deprived urban and rural areas. The Heritage Economic Regeneration Scheme (HERS) and Conservation Area Partnership Scheme (CAPS), two matching grant programs run by English Heritage, help local authorities achieve economic development through conservation. Funded by the National Lottery, HERS focuses on a neighborhood's businesses and main streets, and CAPS focuses on groups of historic buildings within a conservation area. Under these programs, eligible property owners can receive a grant toward work for repairs that have been approved by the local authority and conservation officer. The appearance of a town, the ease of road and pedestrian traffic, and the town's appeal to residents, businesses, and visitors are all considered in evaluating the success of a town's regeneration. The concept seems highly appropriate for England, given the country's long-standing appreciation for the special characteristics of the townscape.

Figure 3-11 Stowe House is one of Britain's grandest country houses, and it displays the talents of several of the finest architects, landscape architects, and artisans of the Georgian period. Illustrated here is Stowe's premier interior space, the elliptical Marble Salon (a) that was restored in September 2005 as part of a phased conservation program for the house. Here conservation specialists and restorers are conserving the ornamented frieze using consolidation and a stucco infilling method (b and c) with finished results appearing in a lower portion of the coffered dome (d). Images courtesy of World Monuments Fund; Richard Houlttom, photographer.

Historic towns are only one of many focuses of conservation efforts in the United Kingdom in recent decades. Other typical and particular elements of Britain's heritage have also received attention, especially the country house, which is generally regarded as a national symbol today and "Britain's greatest single contribution to European civilization and the visual arts."[33] The traditional image of English country life usually features the English country house, with its architecturally imposing central structure, outbuildings, gardens, and vast surrounding acreage. Frequent representations of country houses in popular culture, especially films, have encouraged interest in their study and conservation and have in turn fueled tourism and new protection systems nationwide.

Though public and government awareness of the *museumization* and nationalization of country houses has increased in the past few decades, the effective management of country houses in the future is uncertain.[34] But their fate has improved significantly since activists, including Marcus Binney, John Cornforth, and others, presented a thorough discussion of related preservation issues in *Country Houses in Britain: Can They Survive?* (1974) and in the book (and the exhibition at the Victoria and Albert Museum) *Destruction of the Country House, 1875–1975*.[35]

a

b

Figure 3-12 Beginning in 2006 Horace Walpole's Strawberry Hill near London underwent extensive analysis and conservation planning aimed at making this Gothic Revival landmark more accessible to the visiting public. The conservation team led by the prominent conservation firm Inskip and Jenkins, under the guidance of the Strawberry Hill House Trust, discovered that several rooms were altered by Walpole in his efforts to apply the "Gothic taste." These changes posed a number of questions about which features from which period of Walpole's long residence in the house should be presented? The plan of Inskip and Jenkins ultimately resolved the question based on findings from rigorous historical and physical research and from surviving evidence viewed in light of new use requirements and a multifaceted interpretive program for the whole property. The unrestored "Long Gallery," which contains a number of sub-standard mid-twentieth century renovation interventions, is illustrated here (a) and the restoration in process in July 2009 is seen as well (b). Courtesy of World Monuments Fund; Richard Houlttom, photographer.

Today hundreds of country houses are under the management of the National Trust and English Heritage. The contents of houses such as Tyntesfield, an outstanding and nearly intact nineteenth-century Gothic Revival estate, would have been dispersed had it not been for a vigorous campaign by SAVE Britain's Heritage and the National Trust. In addition, the Historic Houses Association has proved an effective resource and lobbyist for many remaining privately owned houses. Other estates such as Chatsworth, home of the dukes of Devonshire, and Blenheim Palace, home of the dukes of Marlborough, have formed private trusts to allow access to public and private funds to help maintain these outstanding properties. Recipients of state aid are required to open their houses to the public, and new tax provisions provide relief for repair expenditures but encourage owners of historic houses to retain the inventoried contents of their houses. The objective of these new provisions is to stimulate preventative preservation through maintenance and repair, with the authorities committed to providing advice and financial help where needed.[36]

BRITISH CONSERVATION LEADERSHIP

Many prominent Britons are listed among the founders of the architectural conservation field, which has benefited from their distinctive and important contributions. The Ruskin-Morris schools of conservation philosophy in the late nineteenth century drew attention to the importance of discretion in restoring and maintaining historic buildings. Similarly bold personal initiatives of Sir Robert Hunter, Canon Hardwicke Rawnsley, and Octavia Hill—who were all, like Ruskin and Morris, motivated by concern for the loss of the country's historic built and natural assets—led to the establishment of England's National Trust in 1896. Their actions, focused on

Figure 3-13 Historic site interpretation specialists (a) are playing increasingly important roles at some restored national heritage sites in the United Kingdom in order to enliven their functions as places for learning. For example, actors playing Henry VIII and his last wife Catherine (a) greet guests at Hampton Court near London in 2009 (b). Prior to this moment, a few young girls in the audience were asked to serve as ladies in waiting to Queen Catherine to help her prepare for her public presentation, for which she gave each a coin (c). One mother in attendance, Mrs. Joanne O'Sullivan of Hertfordshire, said: "Prior to my daughter Gabrielle being asked to 'participate in history,' she was bored by it all. After this morning, no more." Images courtesy James Seger and Joanne O'Sullivan.

a

b

c

Figure 3-14 Due to their enormous size, complexity, and age, many of England's cathedrals require long conservation programs. Complex structural repair work and conservation begun in the 1970s at the Norwich Cathedral (illustrated here) and York Minster brought large-scale building conservation projects such as these to the fore as examples of "best practice" in architectural conservation at the time, not only because of their physical magnitude but due to the original solutions applied at each. Both projects were led by Bernard M. Feilden of Feilden + Mawson, Architects and Engineers. For instance, the failing stone tower and spire of Norwich Cathedral were consolidated using small-gauge wire rope (cable) set to give slightly and not to behave like a monolithic structure. Its carillon was reconfigured so that the cathedral's bells swung synchronously in opposite directions to minimize any swaying action. York Minster had equally serious problems, including foundation settlement and the failure of the stone tracery of its great rose window above the chancel, all of which had to be corrected while parts of the cathedral remained in operation.

solving problems, developed what proved to be a major contribution to global conservation. Not only did the new organization save historic sites, it also provided a workable framework for popular support of its cause. One innovation helped secure the Trust's future: public subscription, or dues-paying members.

Individual commitment to heritage conservation was an important theme again during the 1970s, when a new specialty of conservation architects began to distinguish itself. The firms of Donald Insall Associates and Feilden + Mawson, Architects and Engineers, headed a generation of professional pioneers in building conservation practice, whose high-quality work even today serve as exemplars both domestically and abroad. Sir Bernard M. Feilden drew on his skills both as an engineer and an architect when restoring some of the England's most significant religious buildings, notably Norwich Cathedral, York Minster, and St Paul's Cathedral in London.

Feilden and his team responded with insight, talent, and innovation to the complex engineering and material conservation challenges presented by other large projects. This accumulated knowledge is presented in Feilden's landmark publication, *Conservation of Historic Buildings*, originally published in 1982 and now in its third edition. A willingness to share his experiences led to Feilden accepting a position as the director general of the International Centre for the Study of the Preservation and Restoration of Cultural Property (better known as ICCROM) in 1977.[37] Since leaving that post in

1981, Feilden continued at the forefront of the field through his writing and international consulting work until his death in 2008.

Numerous other innovations and individuals could be named. That the British approach has been recognized so widely, and largely adopted in the United States, the Indian subcontinent, and Australia, is testament to the effectiveness of personal and institutional leadership in the field. In turn, British practice has been influenced by best practices and ideas, from other countries including Italy, Australia, India, and the United States.

A number of conservation technologies and methods used in the field were developed in Britain and exported throughout the world, particularly those involving masonry repair and cleaning, conservation of special architectural finishes, and conservation of ruins. In addition to Feilden's seminal work, texts by other British architects and scholars, such as John Harvey's *Conservation of Buildings*, have influenced the field far beyond the United Kingdom.[38] In addition, the National Trust, English Heritage, Historic Scotland, and the University of York all maintain conservation laboratories that regularly publish new findings and experiments. More recent scholarship, such as John Ashurst's *Conservation of Ruins*, John Warren's *Conservation of Earth Structures*, Dennis Rodwell's *Conservation and Sustainability in Historic Cities*, and the Michael Forsyth–edited *Building Conservation* series, reflect the very highly advanced state of the field of architectural heritage conservation in Britain as well as any other indicator.[39] In addition, English Heritage recently published their *Conservation Principles* that set out a logical approach to the identification and definition of significance in historic places and structures as well as the management of such places and structures.[40]

Of the dozens of distinguished architectural firms specializing in architectural conservation in Britain today one is particularly outstanding: Donald Insall Associates, whose fiftieth year of operation was commemorated in 2008 in an impressive monograph entitled *Living Buildings; Architectural Conservation Philosophy, Principles and Practice*. The portfolio of the Donald Insall Associates has included some of the most prestigious conservation projects in Britain on many of its most famous

Figure 3-15 Repairs and cleaning of the fire damaged Bartholomew Street facade of the Bank of England by Donald Insall Associates Ltd.

Figure 3-16 The interior of the Lords' Chamber (a) in the Palace of Westminster. Diagram (b) illustrates the elaborate ceiling structure and roof construction. The Chamber's gilded and coffered ceiling (c) was restored in 1984. Figure 3-16a image courtesy of the Historic Building and Monuments Commission for England (English Heritage)/National Monuments Record. Figures 3-16b and 3-16c are from Donald W. Insall, *Living Buildings; Architectural Conservation: Philosophy, Principles and Practice* (Mulgrave, Victoria: Images Publishing, 2008), copyright and courtesy of Donald Insall Associates Ltd.

a

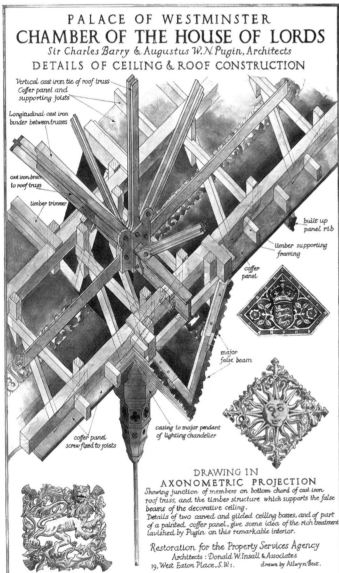

b

c

buildings, ranging from the restoration of Windsor Castle after its disastrous fire in 1992 and the ceiling of the Lords' Chamber in the Palace of Westminster to the afore-mentioned Georgian spas restoration in Bath and the Crown Estate's development plan for Regent Street in London. The robustness and seriousness of the field of architectural conservation in Britain can be seen in the range of projects taken on by Insall's London-based architectural firm. According to Donald Insall, through careful intervention, "every place may be truly more itself."[41] This serves as a guiding principle for the firm he founded, and reflects his attitude toward architectural conservation in the United Kingdom more generally.

ENDNOTES

1. David Lowenthal, "A Global Perspective on American Preservation," in *Past Meets Future: Saving America's Historic Environments*, ed. Antoinette J. Lee (Washington, DC: Preservation Press, 1992), 157.

2. Stephen Jacobs, *Historic Preservation in Europe, the French and English; (in relation to) the United States, the Government's Role* (Ithaca, NY: Cornell Center for Housing and Environmental Studies, 1966), 202.

3. There may be hybrid designations as well; some sites are both Listed and Scheduled, if they are currently not in use but could be potentially used—such as barns.

4. English Heritage was initially known as the Historic Buildings and Monuments Commission for England.

5. English Heritage, *English Heritage Annual Report and Accounts, 2008/2009* (London: English Heritage, 2009), 14–15.

6. "Welcome," Cadw, www.cadw.wales.gov.uk (accessed October 23, 2009).

7. "About Us," Department of the Environment, Northern Ireland Government, www.doeni.gov.uk/index/about_us.htm (accessed October 29, 2009).

8. "Home," Historic Scotland, www.historic-scotland.gov.uk (accessed October 29, 2009).

9. In addition, a separate Historic Royal Palaces agency oversees the crown's property, including both palaces inhabited by the Queen and those no longer in use.

10. "Planning Policy Statement for the Historic Environment," English Heritage, www.english-heritage.org.uk/server/show/nav.21135 (accessed December 8, 2009).

11. "About Us," Heritage Lottery Fund, www.hlf.org.uk/English/AboutUs (accessed October 23, 2009).

12. "Draft Heritage Protection Bill," Department for Culture, Media and Sport (DCMS), www.culture.gov.uk/reference_library/publications/5075.aspx (accessed October 23, 2009). As of November 2009, the proposed bill has not been enacted. It was omitted from the December 2008 Queen's Speech, which set out Parliament's legislative program for 2009, and it is uncertain when or if it will be presented to Parliament. There are, however, aspects in the bill that do not require legislation, which are being proceeded with. Updated information may be found at the DCMS, www.culture.gov.uk, or English Heritage, www.english-heritage.org.uk.

13. In the United Kingdom, voluntary societies "established with the express purpose of preserving the art and architecture of past centuries and promoting the appreciation of such buildings and the cultures that produced them" are known as amenity societies in government and other literature to distinguish them "from the many other local history and special interest societies which may become involved in the process of planning and listed building control." Joint Committee of the National Amenity Societies, www.jcnas.org.uk/ (accessed July 5, 2010). In keeping with the British tradition of private initiative leading the way to conservation, public appeals during the nineteenth century to restore London's Westminster Abbey, Somerset's Wells Cathedral, and Canterbury's Cathedral commenced the popular conservation process in those cities. Government support followed, but it was almost always in response to the initial impetus for the improvement of historic buildings cherished by the British people.

14. Derek Linstrum, "The Conservation of Historic Towns and Buildings," in *Architectural Conservation in Europe*, ed. Sherban Cantacuzino (London: Architectural Press, 1975), 26.

15. See also Stubbs, "The Forging of a Discipline: The Late Eighteenth to Early Twentieth Century," in *Time Honored*, pp. 218–226, on Great Britain for more on the landmark scrape versus antiscrape debates of William Morris, John Ruskin, and Sir George Gilbert Scott. The Society for the Protection of Ancient Buildings' *Manifesto*, one of the most influential documents of its type, can be viewed on its Web site: www.spab.org.uk/ (accessed October 30, 2009).

16. "Home," The National Trust, www.nationaltrust.org.uk/main/w-trust.htm (accessed October 23, 2009).

17. "Current Members," The National Trust, www.nationaltrust.org.uk/main/w-trust/w-support/w-currentmembers.htm (accessed October 23, 2009).

18. "The Society's Aims," The Norwich Society, www.thenorwichsociety.co.uk/html/aims.html (accessed October 30, 2009).

19. "Home," Buildings at Risk, www.buildingsatrisk.org.uk/BAR (accessed October 30, 2009).

20. "Welcome to APT—the UK Association of Preservation Trusts," Association of Preservation Trusts (APT), www.ukapt.org.uk (accessed October 30, 2009).

21. Anthony Haskell, *Caring for Our Built Heritage* (London: Taylor and Francis, 1993), 252.

22. "Home," The Architectural Heritage Fund, www.ahfund.org.uk (accessed October 26, 2009).

23. "About AMS," Ancient Monuments Society, www.ancientmonumentsociety.org/uk (accessed October 29, 2009).

24. Gavin Stamp, quoted by M. Hunter, in "The SAVE Report," *Architect's Journal* 17/24 (Dec. 1975): 96, and "Campaigning for Threatened Historic Buildings," Save Britain's Heritage, www.savebritainsheritage.org (accessed October 30, 2009).

25. "Home," Ulster Architectural Heritage Society, www.uahs.co.uk (accessed October 30, 2009).

26. The Twentieth Century Society was formerly known as the Thirties Society.

27. Jacobs, *Historic Preservation in Europe, the French and English; United States, the Government's Role*, 334.

28. Peter Carey, "Rebuilding the Spa in Bath," *Context* 99 (May 2007): 21–24. Under Sir Patrick Abercrombie's post–World War II restoration of the eighteenth-century town of Bath, Georgian terrace houses were tastefully converted into apartments. New architecture was placed discreetly at the base of the town, leaving the heart of Bath much as it had been for centuries.

29. Carey, "Rebuilding the Spa in Bath," 24.

30. York was the first city to institute control of building elevations under the guidelines of the Town Planning Act of 1925. Refer to Jacobs, *Historic Preservation in Europe*, 334.

31. The Prince of Wales's views on the proper handling of Britain's architectural heritage, including cultural landscapes, were initially presented in a widely publicized accusative speech to the Royal Institute of British Architects in 1984; in his remarks he criticized the effects of recent architecture on the historic built environment. He shared his views with the more general British public in 1988 on an episode of the BBC television documentary arts program *Omnibus*, entitled "A Vision of Britain," which he wrote and hosted. His book of the same name was published the following year.

32. Large-scale American rehabilitation and reuse projects in the early 1970s were inspired by similarly large schemes in Britain, for example, the transformation of Faneuil Hall Quincy Marketplace in Boston into a mixed-use complex and Union Station in Washington, D.C., into a visitor center for the U.S. bicentennial celebrations in 1976.

33. Linstrum, "The Conservation of Historic Towns and Buildings," 29.

34. P. Mandler, *The Rise and Fall of the Stately Home* (London and New Haven, CT: Yale University Press, 1997), 114.

35. John Cornforth, *Country Houses in Britain: Can They Survive?* (London: Country Life, 1974), and Roy C. Strong, *The Destruction of the Country House, 1875–1975* (London: Thames and Hudson, 1974).

36. Jacobs. *Historic Preservation in Europe, the French and English; (in relation to) the United States, the Government's Role*, 118.

37. Other influential Britons who served as director general of ICCROM were its first, Harold J. Plenderleith (1959–1971), and Nicholas Stanley-Price (2000–2005).

38. John Harvey, *Conservation of Buildings* (London: J. Baker, 1972).

39. John Ashurst, *Conservation of Ruins* (Boston: Elsevier, 2006); John Warren, *Conservation of Earth Structures* (Oxford and Boston: Butterworth-Heinemann, 1999); Dennis Rodwell, *Con-

servation and Sustainability in Historic Cities (Malden, MA: Blackwell Publishing, 2007); and Michael Forsyth, ed., *Materials & Skills for Historic Building Conservation* (Hoboken, NJ: Wiley-Blackwell, 2008), *Structures & Construction in Historic Building Conservation* (Hoboken, NJ: Wiley-Blackwell, 2007), and *Understanding Historic Building Conservation* (Hoboken, NJ: Wiley-Blackwell, 2007).

40. English Heritage, Paul Drury, and Anna McPherson, *Conservation Principles: Policies and Guidance for the Sustainable Management of the Historic Environment* (London: English Heritage, 2008), www.english-heritage.org.uk/publications/conservation-principles-policies-guidance-apr08/conservationprinciplespoliciesguidanceapr08web.pdf (accessed June 3, 2010).

41. "About Us," Donald Insall and Associates," www.donaldinsallassociates.co.uk (accessed October 23, 2009).

Figure 4-1 The megalithic passage tomb at Newgrange and other prehistoric sites were among the first protected heritage sites in Ireland. Newgrange was built over 5,000 years ago and excavated in the 1960s and 1970s. The tomb was extensively reconstructed through anastylosis and new infill in the 1980s. The site was added to the World Heritage List in 1993.

CHAPTER 4

Ireland

Ireland's late-twentieth-century economic revival facilitated increased appreciation for cultural heritage, as the country's new wealth allowed for the repatriation of Irish silver, paintings, and porcelain from overseas auction houses. Architectural conservation activities have also recently accelerated, and an improved political relationship with the United Kingdom in recent years has also expanded the types of sites the Irish value and their openness to foreign conservation models. Despite a lull in efforts in the mid-twentieth century, in the past few decades Ireland has joined the European trend toward architectural heritage conservation.

Ireland's 9,000-year history has generated a rich collection of heritage sites: Neolithic dolmens from about 4000 BCE that commemorate burials, Bronze Age earthen *henges* and stone circles from 2000 to 500 BCE that demarcate religious ceremonial sites, and Celtic hilltop or promontory fortresses and archaeological evidence of circular earthen and wood ritual buildings.[1] Thousands of small churches and hundreds of monasteries were established after Christianity was introduced in the fifth century. Medieval Ireland witnessed a great deal of architectural and urban development after colonization by twelfth-century Anglo-Norman lords and later by the English and Scottish planters in the sixteenth and seventeenth centuries. The Normans built lime-washed stone castles and monasteries with great axial cruciform churches as well as created walled market towns that emerged as centers of commerce. Ireland's British-inspired Georgian period was an artistic high point, as affluence and a rich craft tradition converged to create grand houses and furnishings in both Dublin and the countryside.

CONSERVATION LEGISLATION AND INSTITUTIONS

Throughout the nineteenth century, the scientific approach to the study of history that was popular in Europe was also evident in Ireland when it was still part of the United Kingdom. The first legislation in the United Kingdom protecting architectural heritage was the Irish Church Act of 1869, which required the Commissioners of Public Works to maintain medieval churches that had previously belonged to the Church of Ireland.[2] Five years later, the first site was purchased by the government to ensure its protection and preservation: the Rock of Cashel, a twelfth- and thirteenth-century hilltop castle complex that had been the traditional royal seat prior to the Norman invasion in the twelfth century.

The Ancient Monuments Protection Act of 1882, which focused primarily on archaeological sites, applied to Ireland as well as the rest of the United Kingdom. A series of local government and land-use laws in Ireland at the turn of the twentieth century also addressed archaeological site conservation, vesting protective authority in local authorities.[3] Broadening interest in Ireland's architectural inheritance continued after independence from the United Kingdom in 1922, as evidenced by George Petrie's pioneering work on early medieval Round Towers, the valuable information collected in an Ordnance Survey in the 1930s, and the foundation of local archaeological and historical societies.

An updated National Monuments Acts in 1930 charged the Office of Public Works with preserving Ireland's heritage, which included monuments predating the beginning of the eighteenth century. Initial Irish legislation mostly ignored the great streetscapes and monuments of the past two centuries, due in part to residual anti-British sentiment. British and Irish relations were historically difficult and led to civil war in the 1920s—they remained strained long after independence.

Although Ireland fortunately escaped destruction during the world wars that devastated much of Europe, mid-century modernization and road widening took a significant toll on the country's built patrimony, particularly in urban areas. When whole sections of historic urban building stock were cleared to accommodate new housing and government buildings during the mid-1960s, the country was ill prepared to deal with the new challenge. A coherent national conservation policy had still not been formulated, and not much thought had been given to the economics of conservation in Ireland.

In September 1964, when Dublin's Electricity Supply Board received authorization to demolish twenty-six Georgian terrace houses on Lower Fitzwilliam Street and erect an office block, local support for architectural conservation was galvanized, and urban conservation was dramatically brought into the public eye. At about the same time, a Local Government Planning and Development Act was passed; amended several times thereafter, it has used local spatial planning mechanisms to control development and offer further protection for Ireland's historic sites.[4]

In the 1980s Dublin witnessed several impressive large-scale conservation projects, including rerestorations of the prominent Custom House, the Bank of Ireland, the Four Courts, and the City Hall, all marvelous sites of monumental neoclassicism. The 1930 National Monument Act was amended and supplemented several times, including in

Figure 4-2 For much of the twentieth century, until the 1980s, the destruction of Ireland's eighteenth- and nineteenth-century heritage, built during the period of English rule, partly reflected a resentment of that colonization and hegemony. Scores of country houses were lost through this period, at first due to arson during the War of Independence and the Civil War of the early 1920s and later due to neglect and abandonment as properties ceased to be financially viable for their occupants. Castleboro House in Demsere, County Wexford was built in 1770, suffered an accidental fire in 1840, and was burnt in 1923.

1987 when the Register of Historic Monuments was established, in 1995 when the Heritage Council was formed as an advisory body to the Ministry, and in 1997 when Dúchas (the Irish Heritage Service) was created within the Ministry. Massive heritage inventorying efforts were also launched in the 1990s. Through the Archaeological Survey of Ireland, Dúchas created a documentary record of over 100,000 pre-1700 archaeological sites and monuments.[5] The Urban Archaeology survey included similar reports on all pre-1700 towns, with a special focus on identifying potential archaeological zones. The National Inventory of Architectural Heritage began similarly documenting the country's historic buildings in 1999. It was from the two archaeological surveys that sites were selected for the Record of Monuments and Places, and from the architectural inventory that buildings were selected for the Record of Protected Structures (RPS).

In the year 2000 the landmark Planning and Development Act was passed marking a new approach to heritage protection in Ireland.[6] In addition to encompassing new categories of sites, including architectural conservation areas, the Act compelled local authorities to compile lists of significant buildings and sites in the RPS and to note these in county development plans. The 2000 Planning and Development Act simultaneously empowered local authorities to require owners of properties in the RPS to maintain them, to offer grants to assist with this process, and to acquire endangered properties through compulsory purchase. Though not specified by the legislation, many local authorities have established conservation officers to implement its provisions. Though the 2000 Act "provides a robust means for protecting Ireland's architectural heritage through the stick and carrot approach..., in reality, a lack of available resources and the potential for legal challenges have resulted in insufficient protection for the most endangered sites."[7]

The updated Planning and Development Act of 2000 was soon followed by a new National Monuments Act in 2004. The National Monuments Service of the Department of the Environment, Heritage, and Local Government has replaced the former Ministry's Dúchas and is today responsible for identifying and designating archaeological sites as protected, licensing excavations and conservation interventions, and advising local planning authorities on their protection. The National Monuments Service also maintains the Archaeological Survey of Ireland, which today includes nearly 140,000 records.[8] The National Inventory of Architectural Heritage continues within the department, and its buildings list is regularly updated. It has also recently completed a Survey of Historic Gardens and Designed Landscapes in Ireland, for which it won a European Union/Europa Nostra award in 2009.

Today the Irish government directly owns almost one thousand of the recognized national monuments, representing a range of the country's houses, including everything from megalithic tombs to industrial mills.[9] These sites are maintained and presented by both the National Monuments Service and the Office of Public Works, which continues to play an active role in Irish architectural conservation. The Heritage Council also continues to advise the current Department for Environment, Heritage, and Local Government and other public authorities and educational institutions, as well as to propose policies and priorities and promote heritage appreciation through educational initiatives, grant programs, and cooperative projects with national and international partners.

ACTIVE NONGOVERNMENTAL HERITAGE ORGANIZATIONS IN IRELAND

Nongovernmental organizations have also played a role in the protection of Irish architectural heritage. In the early twentieth century, the Georgian Society completed the first systematic architectural survey of the country's architecture from that period and published this information between 1909 and 1913 as the *Georgian Society Records.*

In 1958 Desmond and Mariga Guinness founded the Irish Georgian Society as a membership organization interested in promoting awareness of and protecting the country's heritage. Despite its name and primary focus on this underappreciated component of Irish heritage, the Irish Georgian Society has always been concerned with conserving outstanding architecture from all periods of Irish history. In the past, it achieved its goals through property acquisition and restoration, but today the society focuses on research and publication, planning, advocacy, training, and grants for conservation.

The Irish Georgian Society also holds annual Training Building Skills exhibitions to promote best practices among owners of historic properties. Recently, in collaboration with the Irish Department of the Environment, Heritage, and Local Government, the Irish Georgian Society has organized seminars focused on improving energy efficiency in older buildings without compromising their historic integrity. The Society's annual journal, *Irish Architectural and Decorative Studies*, is the only publication focused on new research about the history of the country's built heritage.

Ireland's most important architectural archive is also run by a nongovernmental organization: the Irish Architectural Archive, established in Dublin in 1976, has collected and preserved documentation relating to Ireland's built environment and works to make this information accessible to the public.[10]

An Taisce, also known as the National Trust for Ireland, emerged as an important factor in the field of architectural conservation in the 1960s when it openly campaigned for the preservation of Lower Fitzwilliam Street in Dublin. Founded in 1948 and patterned after England's National Trust, An Taisce eventually took over a number of natural heritage sites. Despite its ambitious aims, it has only managed to acquire a few architectural heritage sites, including Kanturk Castle, a ruined sixteenth-century fortified house in County Cork.[11]

Figure 4-3 Castletown House in Celbridge, Ireland, a fine early eighteenth-century Palladian-style manor house, was taken on as a rescue and restoration project in 1967 by Desmond and Mariga Guinness, founders of the Irish Georgian Society, which celebrated its fiftieth anniversary in 2008.

Figure 4-4 The neoclassical Custom House (James Gandon, 1791) situated on the River Liffey in Dublin was extensively damaged by fire in 1921 but restored under the direction of the Office of Public Works in the 1980s. The restoration entailed complete reconstruction of the interiors, including its collapsed dome, and two campaigns of exterior stone restoration work. The building that currently houses the Department of the Environment, Heritage and Local Government, exemplifies Irish government support for architectural conservation from the 1980s forward.

The Dublin Civic Trust was established in 1992 and successfully restored a number of historic city buildings on a revolving fund basis.[12] In recent years it has focused less on conservation and restoration projects and more on indirect involvement in the field, such as consultancy services and publications. The Dublin Civic Trust has also completed important inventories of buildings in Dublin's historic core as well as of the city's churches.

Two other recently established nongovernmental organizations, Irish Landmark Trust and the Irish Heritage Trust have also been active participants in the field. Irish Landmark Trust was established in 1992 to purchase and rehabilitate smaller historic structures into self-catering holiday accommodations: it currently owns twenty-two properties, which range from lighthouses to farmhouses.[13] Using a similar model of acquisition and conservation, the Irish Heritage Trust was founded in 2006 and assumed responsibility for its first property—the Fota House and Gardens in County Cork—from the Fota Trust in late 2007.[14]

The Irish chapter of ICOMOS has proven yet another key nongovernmental organization actively promoting the country's architectural heritage. Established in 1984, it has focused on international coordination and the application of current theory and scientific techniques for heritage conservation.

In today's Republic of Ireland, this robust involvement of private organizations has contributed toward and reveals an increased interest and attention for architectural heritage. On the other hand, rapid modernization during recent decades has resulted in an unexpected and odd exploitation of the country's built heritage. Ironically, while the existing building stock is appreciated for its intrinsic worth, the unchecked popularity and quality of more ordinary home and commercial building renovations is worrisome. Architectural historian and architectural conservationist Ian Lumley of An Taisce is concerned about the recent plethora of ill-informed improvements, especially of lesser historic buildings, such as unlisted town architecture and commercial storefronts.[15] Lumley questions whether any authentic eighteenth-century storefronts and

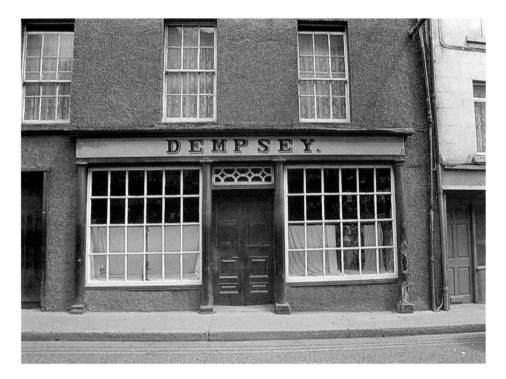

Figure 4-5 Subtle changes to the character of Ireland's historic towns and buildings through ad hoc modernization measures are of concern to the country's architectural conservationists. Illustrated is an example of a nineteenth-century storefront in Kilkenny County that was retained and sensitively restored.

exterior details will remain after the present mania to modernize. The preservation of authentic architectural details and finishes is a major issue in Ireland, as elsewhere in the world.

In recent decades, an improved political relationship with Great Britain has also expanded not only the types of sites valued by the Irish but also their openness to foreign conservation models. Architectural conservation activities have accelerated, and today's widespread ethos for things historic is a welcome replacement for years of neglect. Despite a late start, in the second half of the twentieth-century Ireland joined the European trend toward architectural heritage conservation and now the Republic is nearly on par with other western European countries in protecting its built patrimony.

ENDNOTES

1. The largest ritual building, the Navan Fort in County Armagh, Ireland, had a massive forty-three-meter diameter. Site adornments included sacred stones decorated with swirling and intertwining patterns, the earliest examples of Irish Celtic design.
2. Rachel MacRory and Sean Kirwan, "Ireland," in Robert Pickard, ed., *Policy and Law in Heritage Conservation*, 158–183. New York and London: Spon Press, 2001.
3. Ibid., 158–159.
4. Ibid., 162–163.
5. Ibid., 165.
6. Personal correspondence between J. H. Stubbs and Donough Cahill, December 2, 2009.
7. Ibid.
8. "The Archaeological Survey of Ireland," The National Monuments Service, www.archaeology.ie/en/ArchaeologicalSurveyofIreland/ (accessed December 9, 2009). According Donough Cahill (Irish Georgian Society), the information in the Archaeological Survey of Ireland archive was collected on a county by county basis between 1984 and 1992 as the Sites and Monuments Record, which was revised to become the Record of Monuments and Places in 1994.
9. "How Many Monuments Are in State Care?," National Monument Service, www.archaeology.ie/en/NationalMonuments/HowmanyNationalMonumentsareinStatecare/ (accessed December 30, 2009).

10. Originally called the National Trust Archive, this organization grew out of a successful photographic exhibition on Ireland's architecture in 1974 at Trinity College, but it soon expanded its collections to include drawings and documents as well as photographic records. "Origins and Development," The Irish Architectural Archive, www.iarc.ie/about/origins.html (accessed December 9, 2009).

11. "Home," An Taisce: The National Trust for Ireland, www.antaisce.org (accessed December 9, 2009).

12. "Welcome to the DCT Website!," The Dublin Civic Trust, www.dublincivictrust.ie/index.php (accessed December 9, 2009).

13. "About Us," The Irish Landmark Trust, www.irishlandmark.com/About.aspx (accessed December 9, 2009).

14. "Welcome to the Irish Heritage Trust," Irish Heritage Trust, www.irishheritagetrust.ie/display.php (accessed December 9, 2009).

15. Particular worries include the replacement of authentic and restorable doorways, shop fronts, upper-story windows, and cornices with modern approximations, all of which can result in a banal sameness. Despite attempts at historically appropriate signage as advocated in guidelines produced by the Civic Trust and others, modern signage in the old style is not the same, as anyone can see.

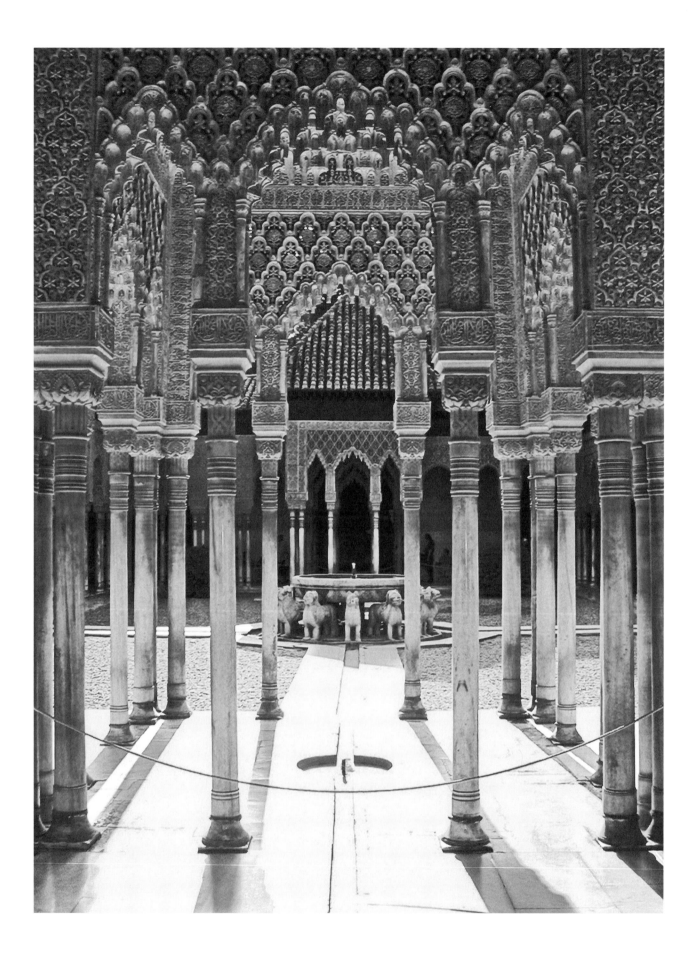

CHAPTER 5

Spain and Portugal

CHAPTER

In Spain and Portugal, legislation and involvement in architectural conservation developed in parallel for the past two centuries until the decentralization efforts in Spain of the past few decades. By the mid-nineteenth century, both countries began following organized European efforts and conserving their cultural heritage, which reflects the creative output of over 3,000 years of civilizations, including prehistoric cultures, the Celts, Phoenicians, Greeks, Carthaginians, Romans, Visigoths, Umayyads, and Abbasids as well as the medieval and modern Spanish and Portuguese kingdoms and republics. Sporadic interest in preserving the heritage of the Iberian Peninsula began early. In the fifteenth century, Spanish monarchs Ferdinand I and Isabella I acted to preserve certain historical monuments, and in Portugal during the eighteenth century the Royal Academy of History devoted its activities to the same purpose.

After an ill-fated alliance with France during the Napoleonic Wars, Spain suffered from a tumultuous century and half of wars of succession, revolutions, and short-lived republics culminating with the Spanish Civil War and the introduction of the fascist dictatorship of Generalissimo Francisco Franco in the 1939. Advances in conservation activities were impeded by this social and political unrest as well as by the subsequent insular fascist regimes in both countries. With Franco's death in 1975, the gradual transition to democracy began, and the constitutional monarchy established in the nineteenth century was restored. Portugal also became a democratic republic in the mid-1970s, and its twentieth-century political history has been no less chaotic than Spain's: it transformed from a constitutional monarchy to an ineffective and troubled republic, then to a conservative, authoritarian dictatorship, before its current government was established.

Despite this political turmoil in the nineteenth and twentieth century, both Spain and Portugal participated in pan-European architectural movements, including revival styles and modernism, and in recent decades both have quickly joined broader European trends in architectural conservation. Today the people of the Iberian Peninsula and the governments of Spain and Portugal are busy revitalizing the architectural heritage of their countries via both grand schemes and smaller projects designed to protect their historic cultural resources.

Figure 5-1 The restoration of the Alhambra in Granada, Spain, was among the first of its type in the country. The project was initiated in 1828, funded by the Crown, and was carried out by three successive generations of architects from the Contreras family.

SPANISH CONSERVATION POLICIES AND DECENTRALIZED STRUCTURE

The Spanish government was a pioneer in architectural conservation in Europe, sponsoring projects as early as the fifteenth century, including the restoration of the Roman aqueduct in Segovia, through which water ran normally until fifty years ago; however, more recent unsympathetic treatments have threatened this World Heritage Site.[1] By the early nineteenth century, ideas and actions related to heritage conservation developed amongst Spain's cultural establishment, as the romantic period of the 1830s inspired a general interest in Spain's history. The conservation-minded magazine *El Artista* was founded in 1835, and soon after the Academia de San Fernando began to protect convents and monasteries. This led to a series of government orders and lists for protection in 1836; in 1844 the first government commission was established to prepare inventories and evaluate the national cultural heritage. By midcentury, restoration activities, especially those addressing the country's numerous medieval monuments, began. Major restoration work was conducted at the Alhambra Palace in Granada, the Giralda bell tower in Seville, and the cathedrals at León and Burgos.[2]

During this early period of conservation in the nineteenth century, efforts focused on historiography and inventories, and approaches followed French models of conservation.[3] Eugène Emmanuel Viollet-le-Duc's theories advocating restoration to complete or extend the original style by removing or altering later additions were especially in vogue. Several cathedrals were restored according to such "unity of style" precepts, including San Vicente in Ávila and San Martín in Frómista. Spain's principal restoration architect at that time, Juan Batista Lázaro, was a proponent of such theories; his writings emphasized the historical importance of each building and criticized formalism in restoration.[4]

While Viollet-le-Duc's philosophies were avidly followed in conservation projects, ideas emerging from elsewhere in Europe began to be explored as well. By the 1920s there was strong debate in Spain between the schools of conservators and restorers. With the appointment of Leopoldo Torres Balbás as conservator of the Alhambra in 1923, the reliance on modern criteria favoring conservation rather than restoration developed.[5] Balbás claimed that modern conservation and repair efforts must always be distinguishable from the original work.

The republican government adopted this new direction as the national approach to heritage conservation, which led to a series of new laws to protect architectural patrimony. While there had been a number of previous laws devised to protect archaeological sites from pillage, Spain's key cultural heritage protection legislation was passed in 1933, and it embraced modern ideas of conservation.[6] This National Artistic Patrimony Law protected immovable and movable objects of artistic, archaeological, paleontological, or historical interest, and it served as the guiding principle for Spanish conservation projects for half a century. To be protected, objects had to be at least one hundred years old or display indisputable artistic or historic value. This law, in combination with subsequent decrees, binds the owner of historic properties to repair, maintain, and open the property to the public for visits on given days. Additionally, limits are placed on sales and exportation of the protected cultural property and its features.[7]

Under the auspices of the National Artistic Patrimony Law of 1933, many of the country's fortified castles, monasteries, and convents were converted into hotel facilities known as *paradores*. Such adaptive reuse resulted in the salvation of numerous properties and has served ever since as a hallmark of Spain's innovative approaches toward heritage conservation.[8]

Since Spain's transition to democracy in the late 1970s, radical changes have occurred in the policies and practices of cultural heritage conservation. Beginning with the new constitution of 1978, the Spanish government has increasingly decentralized

Paradores and Pousadas

Spain's innovative parador concept for adaptive use of monasteries, castles, and convents, in which these facilities are converted into guest lodging and hotels, emerged in the 1930s because of parallel needs to find viable new uses for these buildings, provide a network of hotel facilities throughout the country, and to promote tourism in Spain. Since then, this specialized type of state owned heritage hotel system has been operated through the Paradores de Turismo de España S.A. Most structures are located in small rural towns without adequate tourist facilities. In the 1930s and 1940s, their existence formed the basis of innovative and successful tourism development schemes. The first parador was not a rehabilitated structure, rather a new building that opened in 1928 in the Sierra de Gredos region. However, in 1930, a ruined palace in Oropresa gave rise to the idea of converting historical monuments into hotels to retain their value and provide necessary tourism amenities. The conversion of these properties incorporated appropriate interior decorating schemes and helped maintain regional traditions of art and folklore. This project inspired numerous others, and today Spain has a network of unique guest facilities to accommodate both national and international clientele.

Portugal's *pousada* program, run by Empresa Nacional de Turismo (ENATUR), similarly began as a way to boost tourism in areas that lacked proper facilities. It is an important factor in growth of the national tourism industry, which is now Portugal's second largest source of income. Unlike in Spain, the pousadas are not state owned; however, the state provides restoration grants to historic property owners if they agree to open rooms to guests once renovation is complete.

The accommodation of additions, parking facilities, and swimming pools has posed problems at some sites, especially tightly constricted ones with special design and amenity requirements. Nevertheless, the parador and pousada systems have accomplished many goals, and they have inspired similar schemes elsewhere, including the French-initiated international country estate hotel network, Relais et Chateaux. Spanish paradores and Portuguese pousadas remain popular tourist attractions today, and they provide visitors the opportunity to enjoy luxury hotel facilities in historic buildings that may date to the fifteenth century.

through the formation of seventeen autonomous communities, to which a variety of responsibilities have been transferred. Each autonomous community has a different internal structure and level of autonomy based on separately negotiated statutes with the central government. Cultural affairs, including heritage protection, is one aspect of governance over which these separate regions have in many cases assumed control and established their own laws, policies, and agencies.

Most of the autonomous communities have ministries or departments of culture, which have purview over cultural heritage concerns. For example, the Directorate General of Cultural Assets within the Ministry of Culture of the Andalusian Autonomous Government (Junta de Andalucía) is responsible for protection, conservation, research, and dissemination of information about the region's architectural and urban heritage. The Directorate General houses the Instituto Andaluz del Patrimonio Histórico (Andalusian Historical Heritage Institute, IAPH), which offers technical advice and training in conservation and restoration as well as prepares plans for and carries out projects.[9] The Institute's headquarters since 1992 have been in a fourteenth-century monastery complex on La Cartuja island on the Guadalquiver river at Seville. The monastic complex had been used as a ceramics factory from the mid-nineteenth-century until 1982, but it was thoroughly rehabilitated in the 1990s by the Andalusian government.

Other autonomous communities have taken a different approach. In Valencia, in addition to direct involvement in inventorying and conservation project implementation through its Dirección General de Patrimonio Cultural (General Directorate of Cultural Heritage) of its Department of Culture and Sport, the regional government established La Luz de las Imâgenes (Light of the Images) in 1999 as an independently run foundation responsible for the conservation of the region's artistic and architectural heritage.

The government of Valencia supports La Luz de las Imágenes financially and guides it in collaboration with other key regional institutions through a trust. In 2009 in recognition of a decade of successful conservation of thousands of objects at nearly fifty sites, ranging from elaborate cathedrals to rural structures, La Luz de las Imágenes received the European Union/Europa Nostra Dedicated Service award.

Despite this decentralization, the Spanish central government is still responsible for the countrywide catalog of protected buildings and sites and plays a significant role in architectural conservation throughout the country, especially because the majority of Spain's key historic places are state owned and state funded.[10] Two General Directorates of the Ministry of Culture administer these tasks, including the Subdirección General de Protección del Patrimonio Histórico (General Directorate of Protection of Historical Heritage), which oversees the legal framework, evaluates sites, and coordinates with the autonomous communities and international organizations. As necessary, architects, conservators, and other specialists of the Instituto del Patrimonio Cultural (Institute of Cultural Heritage) administer conservation projects at listed historic sites and have successfully conserved entire towns, industrial sites, and archaeological areas.

In 1985 a new law on Spanish Historical Heritage extended the protection and policies of the fifty-year-old legislation.[11] The new law protects and promotes properties of historical, artistic, scientific, or technical value reflecting Spain's contribution to world culture. It is around this concept that the basic measures of the law are structured and define intervention techniques. The law also defines illegal exportation of historic objects, provides financing to aid in protection and use regulation, and promotes public accessibility to sites to facilitate a greater understanding of heritage.[12]

The 1985 heritage law also more broadly defines cultural heritage to include not only movable and immovable historic property in general, but specifically museums and state-owned archives and libraries with document and bibliographic collections as well as archaeological and ethnographic objects. This enabled legal protection of numerous previously unprotected sites, including the archaeological complex of Guayadeque on the Canary Islands.[13] In 1986, after the government of Guayadeque developed and proposed a plan that included aspects of conservation, land use, and development, the sites comprising the complex were designated as a *zona arqueologica* (archaeological zone). The first stage of the Guayadeque site-protection program entailed fieldwork and analysis to understand the history and significance of the sites; a second stage encompassed conservation work and installation of a visitor center.[14]

Changes in legislation as well as in theory and practice have allowed Spain to widen its heritage conservation approach from focusing on specific buildings to focusing on districts and whole urban areas. The 1985 law allowed for protection of groups of buildings through designation, and 1992 land-use laws implemented planning mechanisms to protect these districts by requiring municipal councils to prepare special plans to maintain the character of each historic site or district. The law allows for programs to be developed between the national government, the autonomous regions, and the municipalities to provide funding, and it also gives municipal councils the responsibility of approving new developments.[15]

PORTUGUESE CONSERVATION POLICIES

Portugal's first move toward protecting its cultural heritage was taken in 1727, when the Royal Academy of History was assigned the task of protecting buildings of value from destruction. This mandate, unfortunately, was never put into practice, and many physical links to history were irretrievably lost. It was not until two centuries later, in 1932, that legislation in Portugal was passed allowing immovable property that represented "national values" or "public interest" to be designated a national monument and thereby

Figure 5-2 The Pousada Tavira Convento de Senora Graça in Portugal is representative of one of the Iberian Peninsula's major contributions to architectural conservation and the history of tourism: reuse of redundant castles, monasteries, and palaces through their conversion to hotels and guest facilities. The creation of paradores in Spain since the 1930s derived from the country's needs for a national quality hotel system.

to be protected and conserved.[16] In 1949, the scope of protection expanded to include properties of local value.

As in Spain in the 1930s and 1940s, a national hotel network was created by converting castles, monasteries, and convents into *pousadas*, which would be available as tourist accommodations. Restoration grants are offered by the government to property owners who want to restore their historic buildings, provided they open the property to overnight guests.[17] This program continues today as a key component of Portugal's hospitality industry, and it has become an important factor in making tourism a major income generator for the country.[18] Historically significant buildings such as this benefit from sensitive reuse, and the economic benefits of tourism are spread into the countryside.

In 1976 a broader definition of Portuguese cultural property was codified, and both natural and human-made sites of cultural, scientific, technical, ecological, or other values were protected. The phrase "other values" opened this new definition to wide interpretation, rendering the law applicable to many site types. As applied by the Ministry of Culture, Portuguese law enables anyone to propose an immovable object for designation, though the owner's opinion must be sought. If a property is considered ineligible for national level classification, it could still be registered as a site of "local value."[19]

In 1992 the government created the Instituto Português do Património Arquitectónico (Portuguese Institute of Architectural Patrimony and Archaeology, or IPPAR) within the Ministry of Culture to safeguard and promote designated properties. The Institute's duties included identifying properties through documentation and conservation activities and promoting the designation process by establishing conservation zones and the widening of criteria for site protection. Five years later, the Ministry of Culture launched a new Inventory of the Cultural Heritage, charging IPPAR and its parallel organizations—the Portuguese Institute of Archaeology (IPA), the National Library, the National Archive Institute, and the Portuguese Institute of Museums—to coordinate and integrate their efforts at documenting the country's vast heritage.

In 2007 the IPPAR and IPA merged to form the Instituto de Gestão do Património Arquitectónico e Arqueológico (IGESPAR; Management Institute of Architectural and Archaeological Heritage), which has also taken on some of the responsibilities of the former Directorate General for National Buildings and Monuments.[20] IGESPAR includes departments for safeguarding; for inventorying, studying, and disseminating information; and for projects and works. It also has management and research divisions dedicated to specific historic sites, including a convent, three monasteries, three churches, and the Côa Valley Archaeological Park.

IGESPAR nominates sites for designation as Portuguese national monuments, and if its advisory council agrees, the application is forwarded to the Minister of Culture for approval. The designation process also involves the preparation of supporting documentation, mandatory hearings with owners and local authorities, and the publication of information about the building or site. The separate IPPAR and IPA inventories are being merged, and today there are thousands of inventoried sites and buildings but only about 800 designated national monuments in Portugal.

The Ministry of Culture's protection mechanisms for designated properties include required maintenance, prior notice and approval for structural modifications, required notice of significant deterioration, and protection against full or partial demolition. If any modifications are made without prior authorization, the government may legally seize the property. Portuguese treatment of a designated national monument's surrounding area is similar to France's: restricted fifty-meter protective zones surround designated structures, and a permit is needed for any construction or modification within that area.[21] In certain cases, extended Special Protection Zones surround designated national monuments.

INTERNATIONAL AND PRIVATE PARTICIPATION AND RECENT REPRESENTATIVE PROJECTS

Spanish heritage sites became globally recognized for their important histories soon after the country joined UNESCO at the relatively late date of 1982. Today, forty-one sites have been designated, making Spain's inventory one of the largest in the world. Spain's sites on the World Heritage List include Paleolithic caves and paintings, Roman ruins, Gothic cathedrals, royal palaces, castles, Islamic sites, monasteries, natural sites, and modern architecture. In 1993 Spain's eleven UNESCO designated cities formed the Association of World Heritage Cities of Spain to defend their common interests, study solutions to shared problems, and carry out social and tourist promotion for their common benefit.[22]

Thirteen sites in Portugal have been added to the World Heritage List, including monasteries, historic cities, and archaeological areas. The richly layered World Heritage City of Porto has long been recognized for its careful integration of social and economic revitalization with high-quality urban conservation. Initiatives began in isolated neighborhoods in the 1970s but quickly spread throughout the city's historic center. In 2001 the wine-producing region of Alto Douro, famous for its port wine, was recognized as a cultural landscape, reflecting the heritage conservation field's continued maturation and embracing of new concepts. Over the course of centuries, landholders have modified the landscape, introducing terraces, villages, chapels, roads, highways, and railways.

Private initiatives for architectural heritage protection in Spain date to the founding in 1952 of the Spanish Association of Friends of Castles, which has worked to educate the public about the importance of preserving architectural patrimony. This association protects, preserves, restores, and refurbishes examples of Spanish military architecture and stimulates interest in the study and promotion of this heritage by organizing conferences, lectures, excursions, courses, and exhibitions and by publishing a scientific review containing news, articles, and reports on various castles.[23]

Other Spanish organizations and institutions active in architectural conservation include Hispania Nostra, ICOMOS Spain, and the Polytechnic University of Valencia. Hispania Nostra was founded in 1976 following the European Heritage Year, and since then it has been organizing conferences and courses and publishing, including the journal *Cultural Heritage and the Law*, first issued in 1997.[24] Hispania Nostra also

Figure 5-3 The Alto Douro region in northern Portugal has produced wine for over two thousand years, creating a specific topographical, social, and economic environment that demonstrates the evolution of wine-making over most of Europe's history. In 2001, the region was added to UNESCO's World Heritage List as a cultural landscape.

Figure 5-4 As with the nearby Tower of Belém, which served as a pilot project, the cloister of the sixteenth-century Jéronimos Monastery on the outskirts of Lisbon was restored in an international partnership led by the World Monuments Fund in Portugal in cooperation with the Portuguese Institute of Architectural Patrimony and Archaeology (IPPAR). Its uniquely Portuguese Manueline-style, named for King Manuel I, reflects its construction at the height of Portuguese maritime power. The project, including a ten-month study of the cloister and its conservation needs, mainly entailed stone cleaning and repointing (illustrated) and was completed in 2001.

maintains a Heritage Red List of Spanish sites in danger. Since 1985 the Department for Conservation and Restoration of Cultural Property at the Polytechnic University of Valencia has been a leader in research and the training professionals as well as in forming international partnerships.

Large conservation projects in Portugal have been made possible by linking government efforts with private donors, international organizations, and banks. Among the most active private organizations has been the World Monuments Fund in Portugal (WMF in Portugal), which has operated often in partnership with IPPAR, private investors, and other not-for-profit organizations. Their 1988 inaugural project, the cleaning and exterior conservation work on the Tower of Belém in Lisbon's outer harbor, received an European Union/*Europa Nostra* award in 1999.[25] The Tower, completed in 1520 to help protect the port of Lisbon, is one of the city's most recognizable landmarks and a symbol of the golden age of Portuguese culture and maritime exploration.[26]

The Spanish affiliate of WMF has also been active since its founding in 1992 after a decade of prior work in Toledo and other parts of Spain. One of WMF's most important completed projects in Spain was the conservation of the fourteenth-century cloister at the Royal Monastery at Guadalupe in the autonomous community of Extremadura. Built by Alfonso XI, the monastery was the location where Ferdinand and Isabella finalized the contract with Christopher Columbus to explore the New World.[27] The conservation of the *templete* (small temple), located within the complex's Mudejar cloister, was undertaken by WMF and its affiliate WMF Spain.[28] Three important aspects guided the completion of this project: enlargement of the scope of work from the original plan to restore the templete and its surrounding garden to including all the cloister's visible surfaces, accommodation of all interested parties to allow work to be divided into tasks and managed more easily, and institution of a one-year deadline to ensure restoration would be complete for the Columbus Quincentenary in 1992. The Spanish Ministry of Culture and WMF jointly completed the templete and garden restoration projects, while Extremadura's General Directorate for Cultural Heritage conserved the cloister walls.

Figure 5-5 The fifteenth-century Mudejar style *templete* (small temple) and its surrounding garden within the old cloister of the Royal Monastery of Guadalupe in Extremadura, Spain, were restored in a tripartite international technical and financial partnership. Due to the nature of the templete's design and the function of its various exterior surfaces, the top half of the structure was substantially restored to better protect the masonry and stucco structure from precipitation, while the better protected and carved stucco surfaces on the structure's lower half were simply stabilized and conserved.

The responsibility of looking after Europe's rich architectural heritage is immense and requires a broad range of professional talent. In the past century, numerous European countries have made outstanding achievements in the field of education in art and architectural conservation, and the activities of these programs are increasingly interactive.

The Polytechnic University of Valencia (UPV) in Spain hosts the Forum UNESCO–University and Heritage program, which was launched in 1995 and is jointly run by UPV and UNESCO's World Heritage Center. The program has created an informal network of university professors and students as well as other professionals concerned with architectural conservation. The network achieves its goals of disseminating information and encouraging links and exchanges between countries and between practitioners and academics in part by organizing annual international seminars on changing themes hosted by different universities around the world. Universities officially affiliated with the Forum UNESCO–University and Heritage program can be found in France, Italy, and the Netherlands as well as in Australia, Iran, the United States, and Senegal. In addition, the network has over 1,800 individual affiliated members from 114 countries, 75 percent of which are from Europe and the Americas.[29]

Advanced training for architectural conservation practice has a long history in Europe, and one of the earliest programs founded was the French École de Chaillot (Chaillot School), which was established in Paris in 1887 and has existed under a number of different names the past 130 years. Today it offers a two-year program for architects specializing in restoration and conservation as well as shorter nondegree courses in aspects of architectural heritage, and it remains among most competitive conservation graduate programs in the world.[30] Its comprehensive program covers the conservation of urban and rural structures and human-made landscapes from all historical periods as well as planning and legal aspects of heritage protection. In addition to training French professionals, the École de Chaillot has partnered with other educational institutions worldwide to offer conservation training in international locations including Tongji, China; Damascus, Syria; Bucharest, Romania; and Angkor, Cambodia.

In Italy the study of architectural restoration and conservation at the university level was introduced during the inter-war period by Gustavo Giovannoni and others, and today the country's heritage conservation education network includes state-supported training institutions located in Rome, Florence, Milan, Naples, and Venice, as well as a variety of postgraduate and doctoral conservation programs.

In Europe the extensive urban destruction of the Second World War contributed to a widespread interest in the postwar period in more training opportunities for architects and craftspeople in architectural conservation and restoration. Beginning in the 1960s, universities across Europe began establishing graduate-level courses in the field, and some of the earliest and continuing leaders in the field include Middle East Technical University in Turkey, University of York in England, and Catholic University of Leuven in Belgium. Today these countries, as well as others, notably including Netherlands, Germany, Slovakia, and the Czech Republic, continue to host a network of high-quality graduate programs for the study of architectural conservation. In the United Kingdom, for example, there are fourteen graduate programs in conservation today, which vary in their organization and emphasis, and half of which are located within schools of architecture.[31]

During the 1990s, many European training programs in architectural conservation also initiated specialist courses, and today's classroom lectures are often complemented by apprenticeships in traditional arts (stonemasonry, etc.) which have often been inspired by the French *compagnonnage* teaching method, wherein a master imparts traditional trade skills to apprentices during practical fieldwork. In addition to mastering time-proven methods, today's students also benefit from contemporary scientific advances. Increasingly, across Europe, introduction to architectural conservation practice is included in the regular education of all architecture students. This is in response to the fact that a large percentage of architectural work in Europe involves existing structures.

With the signing of the Bologna Accord in 1999, named for the University of Bologna where the idea originated, higher education across Europe is becoming increasingly coordinated to ensure similar standards and compatibility among degrees. The original accord had twenty-nine signatories, but has since expanded to include forty-seven participating countries. As education systems in these European countries adjust to what is known as the Bologna Process, architectural conservation centers that are not

(continued)

university-degree-granting institutions have come under pressure. Some degree programs have adjusted their structure to meet the new requirements. For example, in Portugal, where higher education training in architectural conservation was not introduced until the 1980s, some programs have closed and others, such as at the Polytechnic Institute of Tomar, have restructured, in part because of the Bologna Process. The harmonization and standardization in degrees and training will undoubtedly result in a loss of uniqueness among programs but will offer opportunities for improved coordination among architectural conservationists across Europe. This new chapter in university-based architectural conservation education in Europe reflects the continuing evolution of the field.

FURTHER READING

Cody, Jeffry W., and Kecia Fong, ed. "Built Heritage Conservation Education." Special issue, *Built Environment*, vol. 33, no. 3 (2007).

ICOMOS Guidelines on Education and Training in the Conservation of Monuments, Ensembles and Sites (Paris: ICOMOS, 1993), www.icomos.org/docs/guidelines_for_education.html (accessed December 30, 2009).

Oblasi, A. and Whitbourn, P. "Professional Training and Specialisation in Conservation." *Journal of Architectural Conservation*, vol. 8, no. 3, March 2002.

Preston, John. "The Context for Skills, Education and Training." *Journal of Architectural Conservation*, vol. 12, no. 3, November 2006, 35-48.

Stubbs, John H. "International Training in Architectural Conservation," in *Time Honored*, 272–274.

Among the most important Spanish conservation projects involving prehistoric sites is the work being done on Altamira's cave paintings. They were discovered accidentally in the mid-nineteenth century and were soon viewed by thousands of people. Visits to the Paleolithic gallery peaked in 1973, when 177,000 people passed through the cave. Due to rapid deterioration of the artwork, four years later, the Altamira cave was closed to the public temporarily to allow experts to decide on proper environmental conditions for the cave and to determine how many visitors it could safely sustain. In 1982 the cave was reopened to only 8,500 people per year—about thirty-five people per day. Many peak-season appointments were booked years in advance. To make the artwork of the caves more widely accessible, a full-scale replica was revealed in 2001. It utilizes cutting-edge modern technology, including the use of photogrammetry, to present three-dimensional paintings and recreate wall and ceiling contours.[32] Since the opening of the replica, the original Altamira cave paintings have been closed to public visitation for conservation purposes.

Figure 5-6 As a solution to overvisitation to Altamira Cave in northern Spain, a facsimile of the 18,500-to-14,000 year-old cave's interior surfaces, including its art representations of mammals and human hands, is offered to most visitors. The original caves are closed to ensure their protection. Getty Images/Luis Davila 26.4.06.

Figure 5-7 Rafael Moneo's award-winning National Museum of Roman Art in Mérida (a), completed in 1989, is a model of careful planning and discretion in a new design for Spain's most famous ancient Roman site. Moneo is a leader among several well-known European and American architects who have made a specialty of blending new with old architecture. His conference center for the City of Toledo solved an especially difficult problem of inserting a necessarily large building near the medieval town's center, which he adroitly and somewhat controversially accomplished by placing it alongside the town's citadel wall (b). Figure 5-7b courtesy of Pablo Longoria.

a

b

Mérida, the site of the imperial Roman capital of Iberia, is one of Spain's most important archaeological sites; it includes a theater, amphitheater, circus, triumphal arch, a temple, bridges, tombs, and multiple aqueducts. The site has been painstakingly conserved over the course of the twentieth century, and its theater was substantially reconstructed using the *anastylosis* method. Mérida's sixty-four arched Roman bridge over the Guadiana River still served as the principle entrance into the city until the city's Roman sites were inscribed on the World Heritage List in 1993 and a new bridge was constructed. Mérida's extensive and exceptional Roman remains were also carefully conserved and presented in the 1980s through the award-winning National Museum of Roman Art, designed by renowned Spanish architect Rafael Moneo. Through details, forms, and plans reminiscent of ancient Roman architecture, Moneo's museum partially incorporates Roman remains and is a sensitive and harmonious design for displaying artifacts and interpreting the site's history.

Spain's most impressive accomplishments in urban conservation have been the protection, preservation, and revitalization of whole historic towns such as Santiago de Compostela, Toledo, and Salamanca. For example, mechanisms for protecting and rehabilitating Santiago de Compostela, a UNESCO World Heritage Site, have included a general plan approved in 1988 and a supplemental plan in 1997. The key provisions of the plans called for the protection of valuable buildings while allowing for flexibility, rehabilitation of functions with the encouragement of economic and institutional uses, improvement of housing conditions through reuse of structures, and redevelopment of the environment for pedestrian use. Santiago de Compostela also developed a special heritage agency to coordinate efforts between its three levels of government, the University of Santiago de Compostela, and the Catholic Church. This organization has had significant success and has returned economic and social activity to the historic center, providing a positive example for other Spanish heritage cities.[33]

One of Portugal's most important recent urban conservation projects was the reconstruction of the Chiado district in Lisbon, the country's capital city, following a devastating fire in 1988. Lisbon had been devastated once before, in 1755, after a massive earthquake, which was followed by a tidal wave and fires. At that time, dozens of the city's churches, as well as its royal palace and recently constructed opera house were destroyed. Swift, massive, and highly effective reconstruction and recovery efforts were organized by the Marques de Pombral. Within a year the debris had been cleared and unplanned rebuilding had been prohibited; the Marques de Pombral's plan guided construction in the city until the nineteenth century.[34]

After the 1988 fire, local citizens requested that the district be restored to its historic eighteenth-century appearance, and the challenge was given to Portuguese architect Álvaro Siza, whose urban design scheme embraced the basic principles of the Marques de Pombral's earlier plan.[35] This precedent provided Siza with a strong justification to refuse the requests of modern building owners and their architects lobbying for significant changes. Siza called for the restoring of all facades according to their original design. Original building heights and floor levels were to be maintained, but owners could design their own interiors and create their own structural frames behind the facade.

To once again make the district suitable for living, a residential environment was fostered with the inclusion of cultural and leisure activities, a new metro station and pedestrian access to other parts of the city.[36] Siza both enhanced and revitalized the Chiado district through the addition of shops, restaurants, and cultural institutions. Two rundown department stores, the Grandella and Chiado buildings, were transformed: one became a hotel, and the other now holds a mixture of offices, shops, and a cultural center. The addition of a shopping street and creation of public courtyard has made Chiado a part of public city life. In 1989, Siza's flexible guidelines for the reconstruction were supported by the government, which saw them as a test for other future redevelopments.

The local government of the Portuguese city of Évora has taken a proactive stance in ensuring the city's position as culturally important. On the UNESCO World Heritage List, Évora has an unusually broad base of historic sites, in terms of quantity as well as age. In the plains surrounding the city are Paleolithic remains and megalithic monuments. Surviving Roman sites include the city walls and the ruins of a forum and baths. The largest concentration of historic architecture in Évora dates from the sixteenth century, when the Portuguese royalty moved the seat of power there. At this time, great buildings, universities, and convents were built, which fortunately were untouched by the industrial development of the city.[37]

Figure 5-8 Plans directed by the Marques de Pombral required rebuilding the Chiado district after Lisbon's major earthquake of 1755, including retention and reconstruction of collapsed facades to their prior appearance. A similar effort was required nearly two-and-half centuries later after a fire in the same neighborhood in 1988. Design guidelines developed at that time by architect Álvaro Siza for rebuilding the Chiado district required strict restoration of the damaged facades, but a flexible approach to modernizing the interiors of the historic buildings.

To preserve its built historic fabric, the city of Évora developed the first conservation-oriented municipal master plan in Portugal in 1978, which clearly outlined priorities for intervention.[38] The plan's proposals were discussed with the citizens to identify appropriate sites for improvement and restoration projects. Those projects most important to the public, such as housing and sanitation, were given priority status. Conservation interventions were delayed, which allowed studies to be done, best methods to be researched, and a detailed inventory of artwork, sites, and monuments to be undertaken prior to any action. Acknowledging that the 1986 designation as a World Heritage Site would lead to increased tourism, the city sought solutions for control of tourist activities. By maintaining a gradual pace of slowly completing large-scale projects, the city's population and resources have been able to adapt.[39]

Due to its positive approach to tourism and conservation of its heritage sites, Évora was selected to host the Fourth International Symposium of the Organization of World Heritage Cities in 1997. Mayors and representatives from seventy historic cities traveled to Évora to discuss solutions for improving the quality of life, access to social services, and maintenance of an adequate infrastructure in historic cities. Conference discussion centered on the need for tourism to be managed, controlled, and guided by the local city administrators.[40] Évora's leadership in sustained tourism, conservation, public awareness, and partnerships between the city government and the citizens provided an example of how historic cities can embrace their heritage and maintain their resources.

SPANISH AND PORTUGUESE CONSERVATION ASSISTANCE TO FORMER COLONIES

In the fifteenth century, as a result of their exploration of foreign lands, Spain and Portugal became two of the wealthiest kingdoms in the world. While Spanish-funded explorers introduced the Americas to European traders and colonists, Portuguese ships discovered Atlantic islands, explored the African coast, and opened a lucrative trade passage to Asia. Spain colonized the New World with numerous missions and fortified towns that are still extant throughout much of Latin America today. Portuguese colonial holdings extended from Brazil to Mozambique to India and Bahrain, and some of Portugal's settlements and fortifications date to the sixteenth century.

Both Spain and Portugal have participated in the conservation of colonial and indigenous heritage in the disparate parts of the world they once controlled. Some of Portugal's most impressive overseas cultural resources can be found in Macao, which was colonized in 1557 and served as an important Asian trade link. This island in the South China Sea was the first European settlement in the Far East; its colonists lived an Iberian lifestyle in grand houses, churches, and forts. Since China began governing Macao in 1999, Portugal has focused on conserving its historic resources to ensure they will not be diminished by modern development pressures.

The Calouste Gulbenkian Foundation is a particularly notable private organization that has generously supported the restoration and conservation of Portuguese heritage abroad, at sites ranging from castles on the east and west African coasts to Portuguese

Figure 5-9 The stabilized stone facade of the Mater Dei church in Macao, constructed at the turn of the seventeenth century as part of a now lost Jesuit college complex, is a component of the Portuguese legacy in the first European settlement in the Far East. After the expulsion of the Jesuits and a devastating fire in 1835, only the ruins of the steps and facade remained. A restoration project in the early 1990s stabilized the facade's structural condition and featured the church's foundations.

colonial buildings in India and Brazil. The Foundation's mission includes promoting Portuguese culture abroad through education, publications, and arts sponsorship, as well as heritage conservation.

In 1984 Spain established the Program of Heritage Conservation in Latin America to ensure the future of former Spanish colonial cultural sites and monuments in the Americas. Over 250 cities were established by the Spanish in their first century in the Americas, and many of these have expanded to become important modern urban centers over the centuries with deteriorated historic cores. The Spanish program gives financial and educational support to projects backed by local government heritage conservation institutions, which are expected to provide half of project financing. The Spanish program emphasizes revitalization of historic centers, restoration of cultural heritage, and training and education. Projects in historic urban centers require a master plan that defines the area's conservation actions and regulations and creates a local office to manage the project. Since 1999, more than twenty historic centers have instituted revitalization plans encompassing over thirty individual projects, and over forty projects have been completed outside of the historic cores. A total of eighteen Latin American countries have taken part in these conservation projects with the help of Spanish funding initiatives.[41]

In a similar initiative to the Program of Heritage Conservation in Latin America, the Spanish government made a sizeable donation to UNESCO's World Heritage Center in 2002 for architectural and urban conservation projects in Latin America and the Caribbean. Through the Spanish Funds-in-Trust, the World Heritage Center has spent €600,000 annually on projects that encourage community participation and on supporting the nominations of sites in the Americas to the World Heritage List.[42]

Another innovative Spanish initiative active throughout Latin America is the Escuela Taller (Workshop School) program, established in 1984 by Spain's National Institute of Employment and the European Social Fund to create job opportunities and provide training in traditional trades for Spanish youth.[43] The program was extended to Latin America in 1995. By 1999 it had twenty-seven workshop schools active in sixteen countries and had trained over three-thousand young people in the conservation of historic building fabric. Experience has proven that proper supervision of Escuelas Taller workforces is important, especially at the more technically challenging conservation projects where quality control is crucial.

Expanding upon this concept with a service that more specifically benefits Spain's architectural heritage is the Patrimonito youth program that began in Ávila in 2007. Young

Figure 5-10 The Patrimonitos en Ávila was organized by Spanish youth to help preserve and present the city of Ávila's architectural heritage; the program has been so successful since its founding in 2007 that it was replicated elsewhere in Spain, and it inspired an international initiative of the same name currently being developed by UNESCO World Heritage Center in several other countries. Courtesy of Rosa Ruiz, Patrimonitos en Ávila.

a

b

people in their teens and older are trained in proving services ranging from maintenance and repair to interpretation at architectural heritage sites. The program that is endorsed by Ávila's town council proved so successful, it was noticed by the UNESCO World Heritage Center, and the name and system is currently being applied to similar UNESCO-led initiatives in several other countries.

CURRENT ISSUES AND CHALLENGES

Despite these recent conservation successes, architectural conservationists in Spain and Portugal continue to be challenged by threats, especially development pressures in and around the peninsula's historic cities. For example, a 2006 Municipal Development Plan in Toledo calls for new construction in the protective zone surrounding the World Heritage City's historic center, and a proposed Cesar Pelli skyscraper threatens to irrevocably alter the skyline of Seville.[44] In Barcelona, planned construction of an underground tunnel for a high-speed train has professionals and citizens concerned for the future stability of Antonio Gaudí's masterpiece, the Sagrada Familia. Construction for the proposed tunnel will pass within a few meters of the church's foundations, and the planned mitigating concrete buffer wall has not satisfied those concerned as there has been inadequate research on the effects of the tunnel's construction or the vibrations of the passing trains on the massive church.[45] Despite these fears and proposed alternate routes for the train, the Spanish government approved the construction proposal in 2008.

In Spain, theoretical concepts for conservation have greatly evolved over the past twenty-five years. For example, today there is almost no blending of original fabric with new construction and no mimicry. A notable exception was the reconstruction of Ludwig Mies van der Rohe's Barcelona Pavilion, which had originally been built as part of a temporary international exhibition in 1929 and was disassembled the following year. In 1980 the urban planning department of the city of Barcelona initiated a project for the pavilion's reconstruction, which was carried out between 1983 and 1986 under the direction of Ignasi de Solà-Morales, Cristian Cirici, and Fernando Ramos.[46] This exception to the general

Figure 5-11 In 1980, the city of Barcelona reconstructed the Barcelona Pavilion, one of the most influential and iconic interwar buildings, which was designed by Ludwig Mies van der Rohe. The original Barcelona Pavilion was a temporary structure built as part of the German exhibits at the 1929 International Exposition.

disapproval of the reconstruction of lost heritage was justified by the city of Barcelona based on the building's potential for education and tourism.

Theoretically, it has been accepted that any intervention is a work of new architecture, and practitioners have recognized both the need for documentation and the cross-disciplinary nature of the work.[47] It seems that the polemics at the turn of the twenty-first century between restorers and conservators have found a way to coexist in modern Spanish architectural heritage conservation projects. Other major, recent changes in Spanish conservation practice include the involvement of many professionals in projects rather than just a few specialists, as well as the involvement of local and regional governments rather than just the central government. Both of these factors have allowed for a richer diversity of work.

Many architectural marvels built between the eighth and thirteenth centuries under the rule of the Islamic Caliphates have survived until today on the Iberian peninsula, particularly in the southern Spanish autonomous community of Andalusia. Few remnants of Islamic rule remain in Portugal, however, because subsequent Christian monarchs methodically eradicated traces of their presence. In Spain the most important sites have received significant attention. For example, extensive conservation efforts have been undertaken to retain much of the interior grandeur of La Mezquita, or the Great Mosque of Córdoba, whose construction begun in 784 CE, and which was spared destruction for centuries after conversion into a cathedral in the thirteenth century.[48]

Perhaps the best-known example of Islamic heritage in Spain is the Alhambra fortress and palace situated on a plateau overlooking Granada and built in phases between the ninth and sixteenth centuries. Its most elaborate architecture and interior decoration are superb examples of the late Andalusian art in the fourteenth century. After decades of conservation work in the nineteenth century, the Alhambra was first protected as a national, artistic monument in the 1870s by royal decree.

Today the Alhambra is maintained by an in-house conservation department, which coordinates programs focused on conservation, restoration, and archaeology as well as on ecology and biodiversity.[49] The restoration program includes the monument maintenance shop, where experts in masonry, wood, ceramics, paper, painting, and other materials care for the building complex, its collections, and its extensive gardens and grounds. Recent projects have included the conservation of the polychromatic domes of the Hall of Kings, including the removal of nineteenth-century alterations. This project, as well as others, including the conservation of the central basin and sculptures of the fountain as well as the water system in the Court of Lions, was completed in collaboration with the Andalusian Historical Heritage Institute.

Though the Mosque at Córdoba and the Alhambra have been protected and preserved for centuries, most Mudejar heritage in Spain has only come to be widely appreciated more recently. Although today Spain has embraced Islamic heritage sites and vigorously promotes them as tourist destinations, some official sources and tour guides remain hesitant to acknowledge the contributions of medieval Muslims to Spanish and European history, with the view that eight centuries of Islamic rule was an invasion and usurpation.[50]

Though in the early twentieth century Spain and Portugal fell behind in architectural conservation theory and practice, after political stability returned to these countries in the 1970s, they quickly established themselves as capable conservation forces by rapidly embracing new ideas in cultural heritage. Early laws for protection, charters, and the hosting of numerous conferences such as the First ICOMOS Conference on the Conservation, Restoration, and Renewal of Areas of Groups of Buildings of Historic Interest (held in Caceres in 1967) have helped Spain gain a position at the front of the field. Challenges, however, lie ahead. Critics argue that Spain needs to update its protection laws, promote heritage further through public outreach programs, and devise more financial incentives for building owners. While this may be true, recent innovative projects and solutions in both Spain and Portugal have provided some examples of best practices in architectural conservation that have been noticed across the world.

ENDNOTES

1. "Old Town of Segovia and Its Aqueduct," UNESCO World Heritage Center, whc.unesco.org/sites/311.htm (accessed December 9, 2009).

2. Jokilehto, *A History of Architectural Conservation*, 246–269.

3. Alfonso Muñoz Cosme, "Working with Old Buildings in Spain," *Architectural Review* 189, no.1138 (December 1991): 24.

4. Ibid., 24.

5. Ibid., 23.

6. Council of Europe, *Monument Protection in Europe* (Deventer, London, Boston, and Hingham, MA: Kluwer Law and Taxation, 1979), 83.

7. Ibid.

8. Gabriel Esteve Alomar, "The Spanish Paradores," *European Heritage* (RankXerox) no. 4 (1975): 13–14 and 18.

9. "Current Issues," Instituto Andaluz del Patrimonio Histórico, www.juntadeandalucia.es/cultura/iaph/nav/index.jsp (accessed December 30, 2009).

10. "Organización del Ministerio del Cultura," Ministerio del Cultura, www.mcu.es/organizacion/index.html (accessed December 10, 2009).

11. "Law 16/1985 dated 25 June, on the Spanish Historical Heritage (Official State Bulletin of 29 June 1985)," Heritage Laws, http://heritagelaw.org/Spain (accessed June 5, 2010).

12. Cosme, "Working With Old Buildings in Spain," 25.

13. Since the discovery of Guayadeque in the late nineteenth century, close to eight hundred skulls and mummies have been recovered from the site; however, since the site was not protected under any of the previous Spanish laws, it had been pillaged for artifacts for decades.

14. M. R. Eddy, "Heritage Conservation in the Canary Islands, Spain: The Guayadeque Archaeological Park and Other Proposed Parks," *Antiquity* 63, no. 238 (March 1989): 127–131.

15. Robert Pickard, "Area-Based Protection Mechanisms for Heritage Protection," *Journal of Architectural Conservation* 8, no. 2 (July 2002): 80–81.

16. Council of Europe, *Monument Protection in Europe*, 79.

17. "Three New Pousadas," *Daidalos* no. 62 (December 1996): 106–107.

18. Tom Fiorina, "Portugal's Pousadas: Housing Travelers, Preserving the Past," *Preservation News* 28, no. 3 (March 1988): 5–13.

19. Council of Europe, *Monument Protection in Europe*, 80–81.

20. "Legal Framework," Instituto de Gestão do Património Arquitectónico e Arqueológico (IGESPAR), www.igespar.pt/about/enquadramentolegal/ (accessed December 30, 2009).

21. Ibid.

22. "The Organization," Ciudades Patrimonio de la Humanidad de España, www.ciudadespatrimonio.org/DesktopDefault.aspx?tabID=8421 (accessed December 10, 2009).

23. "Home," The Spanish Association of Friends of Castles, www.castillosasociacion.es/ingles.htm (accessed December 9, 2009).

24. "Hispania Nostra: Información," Hispania Nostra, www.hispanianostra.es/hispania/quienes.htm (accessed December 9, 2009).

25. Frederick Winship, "Paulo Marques Leads Associaçao WMF Portugal," *Profile*, 8, Newletter of the World Monuments Fund, Spring, 1998–9.

26. "Home," World Monuments Fund Portugal, www.wmfportugal.pt/en_index.html (accessed December 9, 2009).

27. "Royal Monastery at Santa María de Guadalupe," UNESCO World Heritage Center, http://whc.unesco.org/sites/665.htm (accessed December 9, 2009).

28. The Royal Monastery of Guadalupe cloister restoration project and the aforementioned Tower of Belém and Jéronimos Monastery restorations in Lisbon were substantially funded by the World Monuments Fund.

29. "Members," Forum UNESCO—University and Heritage, http://universityandheritage.net/eng/Miembros/Individuales.html (accessed December 30, 2009).

30. "The École de Chaillot," Cité de l'Architecture et du Patrimoine, www.citechaillot.fr/formation/the_ecole_de_chaillot.php (accessed December 14, 2009). The École de Chaillot is one

of the three components of the Ministry of Culture–supported City of Architecture and Heritage, which also includes the Museum of French Architecture and the French Institute of Architecture.

31. ICOMOS-UK Education and Training Committee, "Conservation in Architectural Education: Making a Case," Workshop Report, University of Bath, September 2005, 3.

32. Paul G. Bahn, "At the Museums: Cloning Altamira," *Archaeology* 52, no. 2 (March/April 2001): 72–73.

33. It appears that the efforts to revitalize Santiago de Compostela have been too successful in some respects. Some of the legendary pilgrimage routes and road systems that led to Santiago de Compostela are threatened by uncontrolled development in the region. These systems were listed on WMF's World Monuments Watch list in September 2009.

34. B. W. Colenbrander, *Chiado Lisbon: Alvaro Siza and the Strategy of Memory* (Rotterdam: Dutch Architectural Institute, 1991), 12–13.

35. Manuel A. C. Teixeira, "Lisbon After the Fire: The Reconstruction of the Chiado District," *A/R/C, Architecture, Research, Criticism* 1, no. 2 (Fall 1990), 13–14; and Bernard Colenbrander, *Chiado, Lisbon : Álvaro Siza and the Strategy of Memory* (Rotterdam : Dutch Architectural Institute, 1991.), 17–19.

36. Ibid.

37. Mario Bravo, "The Culture of Civic Participation: A Conversation with Abilio Dias Fernandes," *Conservation: The GCI Newsletter* 12, no. 2 (Fall 1997) www.getty.edu/conservation/publications/newsletters/12_2/profile1.html (accessed June 7, 2010).

38. The Town Council of Évora, *The Town of Évora from Its Foundation (2059 B.C.) to the Present* (Paris: UNESCO, 1985), http://unesdoc.unesco.org/images/0006/000649/064982EB.pdf (accessed June 7, 2010).

39. Bravo, "The Culture of Civic Participation."

40. "Tourism and World Heritage Cities," *Conservation: The GCI Newsletter* 12, no. 3 (Fall 1997), www.getty.us/conservation/publications/newsletters/12_3/gcinews1.html (accessed June 7, 2010).

41. Maria Rosa Suárez-Inclán Ducassi, "Spain's Ongoing Foreign Technical Assistance for the Conservation of Historic Heritage Worldwide," www.icomos.org/usicomos/sym99/suarez-inclan.htm (accessed June 7, 2010).

42. "Spanish Funds-in-Trust," UNESCO, http://whc.unesco.org/en/sfit (accessed December 16, 2010).

43. Maria Rosa Suárez-Inclán Ducassi, "Spain's Ongoing Foreign Technical Assistance."

44. Michael Petzet, "Toledo and Its Setting: World Heritage in Danger," and María Rosa Suárez-Inclán Ducassi, "Seville: Comments on the Planned Construction of a Skyscraper by Cesar Pelli," *Heritage@Risk 2006–2007* (Paris: ICOMOS, 2007), 141 and 149.

45. ICOMOS Spain, "Possible Impact of the Spanish High-Speed Train (AVE) on the Church of the Sagrada Familia in Barcelona," *Heritage@Risk 2006–2007* (Paris: ICOMOS, 2007), 143–144; and "The High-Speed Train that Can Collapse the Sagrada Familia (and the Milà House)," SOS Sagrada Familia, http://www.sossagradafamilia.org (accessed December 15, 2009).

46. Theodore H. M. Prudon, *Preservation of Modern Architecture* (Hoboken, NJ: John Wiley & Sons, 2008), 185–193.

47. Cosme, "Working With Old Buildings in Spain," 25.

48. "Historic Centre of Córdoba Page," UNESCO World Heritage Center, http://whc.unesco.org/sites/313.htm (accessed December 9, 2009).

49. "Conservation Department," La Alhambra y el Generalife, http://www.alhambra-patronato.es/index.php/Conservation-Department/7+M5d637b1e38d/0/ (accessed December 30, 2009).

50. S. M. Ghazanfar, "Spain's Islamic Heritage: A Muslim's Travelogue" (Manchester: Foundation for Science, Technology and Civilization, March 2004), 11. Available as a pdf at www.muslim-heritage.com/uploads/Main_Spain1.pdf.

a

b

Figure 6-1 The Town Hall in Brussels, built in successive phases over the course of the fifteenth century, has been subjected to numerous restorations during its six-hundred-year history, including after extensive destruction by the French in 1695 and a century of neglect and deterioration in 1840 (a). The nineteenth-century restoration of the Town Hall's facades involved repairs of existing fabric as well as some inventive embellishment, including the addition of some three-hundred statues of local notables in formerly empty niches and the adjustment of those niches to fit the new sculptures. In the late twentieth century, the nineteenth-century facade was itself restored (b). Images courtesy of and copyright Musée de la Ville de Bruxelles-Hôtel de Ville. Figure 6-1b by Mirjam Devriendt, photographer.

CHAPTER 6

Belgium, Luxembourg, and the Netherlands

The geographically linked countries of Belgium, Luxembourg, and the Netherlands share historic, economic, and linguistic ties—yet they have maintained strong, individual cultural identities. Each country achieved its highest point of financial and cultural success through foreign trade and advantageous, central geographical locations in Western Europe. That historic prosperity is visible in the abundance of well-preserved historic buildings throughout the region.

The architectural conservation tradition in these three countries is analogous to experiences elsewhere in Western Europe, where a heritage consciousness heavily imbued with nationalist overtones emerged in the nineteenth century and gradually became more scientific over the course of the twentieth century. While debates about the relative merits of restoration and conservation have continued in Belgium and the Netherlands for over 150 years, the very small, highly centralized country of Luxembourg did not even begin to focus on conserving its built heritage until the mid-twentieth century. Following the disproportionate devastation in these countries during the world wars, when their central location between France and Germany proved unfortunate, focus on rebuilding and heritage protection received renewed interest.

The consistent and systematic government concern for architectural conservation that occurred in Belgium, the Netherlands, and Luxembourg in the twentieth century was firmly rooted in the earlier initiatives that had laid the groundwork for the later formal protection. In recent decades, each country's experiences have reflected their individual nature: in Belgium, government architectural heritage conservation efforts have typically been multicentered and community focused; in the Netherlands they have been efficient and involved high-quality design; and in Luxembourg they have been centralized and oriented towards a broad, European image. Today all three countries struggle with development pressures and continuing tendencies toward stylistic restoration, but they have growing conservation communities and ample legislation in place to protect their heritage.

EARLY CONSERVATION DEBATES IN BELGIUM AND THE NETHERLANDS

While throughout Europe in the mid-nineteenth century, Eugène Emmanuel Viollet-le-Duc's "unity of style" restoration approach had many adherents, nowhere outside of France were his ideas adopted so readily, nor held so strongly, as in Belgium and the Netherlands. These countries joined Viollet-le-Duc's movement to restore national monuments in the late 1850s, as news of his works and ideas filtered into their architectural circles.

The spread of stylistic restoration was facilitated in the Netherlands by the Roman Catholic Church's many projects and its interest in the neo-Gothic style, following its official resurgence in the mid-nineteenth century after centuries of suppression since the Reformation. The neo-Gothic style was also actively promoted by Victor De Stuers, a member of Parliament who wrote and campaigned for the protection of Dutch heritage. However, it was one particular architect, Pierre Cuypers, a fervent admirer of Viollet-le-Duc's, who ensured the primacy of this approach throughout his home country of the Netherlands on his return from France. Cuypers was equivalent to Great Britain's Sir George Gilbert Scott in terms of both his influence in the profession and the sheer number of buildings he designed and restored. His radical approach often involved the demolition of all or part of historic churches, and the addition of neo-Gothic replacements.[1] For example, his work in the 1850s and 1860s on St. Petrus Stoel van Antiochie in Sittard, St. Servaas in Maastricht, and Munsterkerk in Roermond destroyed their nonmedieval elements and added new interior decorations and towers. Because church congregations generally approved of his grandiose embellishments, there was little protest about the destruction involved.

At the same time in Belgium, several prominent restoration projects created fervent proponents of the stylistic unity approach, such as Jean-Baptiste Bethune, fueled by Englishman A.W.N. Pugin's writings, which promoted both neo-Gothic new architecture as well as detailing in restoration projects. Pugin was particularly popular among Flemish Catholic architects, who transformed the old city centers of Brussels, Bruges, and Ghent in imitation of his theories and practices. One of the earliest buildings restored in the "unity of style" approach in Belgium was the fifteenth-century Town Hall on Brussels' Grand-Place, whose restored medieval facade was embellished with scores of neo-Gothic statues in the mid-nineteenth century.

As exposure to the works of Viollet-le-Duc increased, Belgian architects grew even bolder. Belgium's most extreme case of a nineteenth-century stylistic restoration was the Maison du Roi (King's House) in Brussels. The original thirteenth-century building, a marketplace bakery, had been wholly subsumed by centuries of rebuilding and additions. In 1873 the city fathers ordered another restoration, and architect Victor Jamaer extensively studied the building before beginning his work. His use of all available reference materials, including city archives and other similar edifices, made this project one of the first attempts to create a scientific restoration methodology in Belgium. Though his plans called for the demolition of most of the building and the addition of new turrets and galleries for visual drama, many of the sixteenth-century elements were reused, and the building's proportions were unchanged. The new and improved Maison du Roi, completed in 1878, became the Museum of the City of Brussels.

When attention turned to similar civic structures in the Netherlands, the first serious debates about such restoration practice began, even though the "unity of style" approach had been unquestionably applied to churches through most of the nineteenth century. For the thirteenth-century Ridderzaal (Hall of Knights) in the center of the Binnenhof, a former seat of government in The Hague and still one of the country's most important ceremonial buildings, state architect W. N. Rose designed an iron neo-Gothic ceiling in the spirit of the original. Reaction was immediate against the proposed destruction of the "authentic" ceiling to make way for this "whimsical renovation."[2] However, despite a protracted debate among art historians and other scholars, the government supported Rose's stylistic restoration.[3]

Twenty years later, more criticism of restoration practices in the Netherlands emerged, when a small-town judge, J. ver Loren, publicly questioned the addition of a staircase turret to a sixteenth-century gate in Hoorn. For the first time, a written case was made that additions altered a historic structure's appearance, which compromised

a   b

Figure 6-2 After careful study, the accumulated changes to the Maison du Roi (King's House) market building in Brussels (a) were mostly removed during the building's restoration and neo-gothic enhancement (b) in the late 1870s by architect Victor Jamaer using Viollet-le-Duc's "unity of style" approach. Image copyright Musée de la Ville de Bruxelles-Maison du Roi.

its historic integrity.[4] The debate about the Hoorn gate was published in open letters in the magazine *Kunstbode* (Art Messenger).[5] At about the same time, the British art historian James Weale openly criticized the attitude of Flemish architects who, he felt, destroyed or disfigured their heritage rather than preserved as much of the authentic fabric as possible.

Like Weale, Charles Buls, mayor of Brussels and Belgium's first theoretician on restoration practice, was influenced by art and social critic John Ruskin's passion for preservation and careful maintenance of historic buildings. While he criticized restorations that demolished historic accretions and recreated historic details using Viollet-le-Duc's approach, he was not inflexible. He justified the Maison du Roi project by claiming the removal of the building would alter the scale of the Grand-Place and harm the overall historic environment. In 1903 Buls published *La restauration des monuments anciens* (Restoration of Ancient Monuments), in which he tried to formulate a harmonious position between Viollet-le-Duc's and Ruskin's opposing viewpoints.[6] While he promoted Viollet-le-Duc's scholastic examination of historic structures, he also advanced Ruskin's concept of minimal physical interventions.

Buls made another important contribution to the debate with his classification of historic structures as either "living" or "dead" monuments based on the ideas of the Belgian Louis Cloquet. For Cloquet, "dead" monuments were important because of their documentary value and thus should be preserved, while "living" monuments possessed contemporary uses and therefore should be restored, including the removal of historic accretions and a return to their original state.[7] Buls, on the other hand, argued more along the lines of Viollet-le-Duc: "when treating 'dead' monuments: consolidate rather than restore; and when it comes to 'living' monuments, restore rather than rebuild, rebuild rather than embellish."[8] However, it was Cloquet's views supporting stylistic restoration of all but "dead" monuments that were published at the 1904 International Congress of European and American Architects and that, once again, tipped the scales Buls had attempted to balance.[9]

a

b

Figure 6-3 Belgium was caught in the middle of German and French fighting during World War I, and historic cities such as Ypres were extensively damaged. In November 1914 Ypres' thirteenth-century Lakenhal, or Cloth Hall, a remarkable surviving example of medieval civic architecture (a), was set on fire and completely destroyed (b). Reconstruction of the city began immediately after the war in 1919. The Lakenhal was reconstructed from the 1930s through the 1960s by architects J. Coomans and P. A. Pauwels.

Another classification system was proposed in 1938 by a professor at the University of Leuven, Canon Raymond Lemaire, who in his *La restauration des monuments anciens* (Restoration of Ancient Monuments) characterized the two sides of the debate as maximalists and minimalists.[10] Recalling Austrian art historian Alois Riegl, Lemaire identified four classes of monuments based on their values, including *use, artistic, historical-archaeological*, and *picturesque value*, and he argued that any restoration project should preserve and amplify the specific value attributed to a site.[11]

The debate about conservation approaches in Belgium and the Netherlands in the early twentieth century was also profoundly affected by the destruction of the two world wars and the postwar rebuilding climates. During the German invasion of Belgium in 1914, historic Leuven was sacked and looted, and its world-renowned library of ancient manuscripts was burned. Belgium rebuilt Leuven and its other destroyed cities, but in the heightened emotional postwar context, the government gave little thought to the theoretical debate over whether to restore or conserve: ruined churches and public buildings were reconstructed in imitation of their prewar appearances. In 1927 Leuven's town center, the university library and the Tafelrond (guild hall) were meticulously restored, and, where necessary, completely reconstructed.

In response to the predominant "period restoration" approach of the time, in the Netherlands a new generation of architectural conservationists presented revolutionary antirestoration concepts, most notably in the 1917 publication *Grondbeginselen en voorschriften voor het behoud, de herstelling en de uitbreiding van oude bouwwerken* (Principles and Regulations for the Preservation, Restoration, and Extension of Old Buildings). This publication was sponsored by a private advocacy organization, the Nederlandse Oudheidkundige Bond (Dutch Archaeological League), which was founded in 1899 and still exists today. Inspired by the works of Ruskin, Morris, and Riegl, the *Grondbeginselen* espoused the sanctity of any original structure, which should be preserved rather than "creatively" restored. Acceptance of its principles led to the promotion of its principal author, Jan Kalf, to the head of the new Rijksbureau voor de Monumentenzorg (Department for Monument Conservation).

Kalf and the Rijksbureau, however, were soon severely criticized for their work at the Janskerk in Gouda, one of the first monuments treated according to the new principles. Kalf and the department supported preserving the historic edifice and its accretions but also believed that, because earlier architects and craftsman could not be adequately imitated, all new interventions "should not exhibit the forms of an earlier age, and should be the work of an artist of today."[12] These clearly contemporary additions, revealed a paradox in the new Rijksbureau methodologies. Cuypers and De Stuers had been demonized for creating neo-Gothic additions to Gothic buildings, but there seemed little difference between their approach and additions of a contemporary design. Both were "creative" solutions that evolved from an architect's imagination.

Kalf and his colleagues had imbued the *Grondbeginselen* with their fervent distaste for the neo-Gothic and historicism in general and used it to promote International Style modernism.[13] The ideological debate they ignited immediately undermined the Rijksbureau's authority and plans for contemporary additions or replacements of unsalvageable elements at the Grote Kerk in Breda, the Wijnhuisstoren in Zutphen, and the Leiden Town Hall were intensely resisted and ultimately abandoned. Traditionalist restoration techniques in the manner of Cuypers and De Stuers again led to historicized recreations and the "scraping" off of historic additions. It is unfortunate that the first serious Dutch effort to codify respect for the preservation of existing forms and protect them from damaging and misleading stylistic additions was lost because of Kalf's parallel attempt to promote modern artistic principles.

In May 1940 Belgium was again occupied, and its built heritage again suffered, this time during the war liberation phase, when damage inflicted by the Germans was compounded by Allied forces air bombardment. Tournai, Mechelen, and Nivelles lost much of their historic fabric. As for the furnishings and fittings that adorned such places, the label *movable* culture lived up to its name when the German army retreated laden with art treasures looted from historic sites, private homes, and public museums. Throughout the war, the efforts of the Royal Commission on Monuments protected Belgium's built heritage as best they could, even carrying out some restoration projects. When the British and American armies arrived in Belgium, as well as in France, Italy, and the Netherlands, they included so-called monuments officers whose task it was to locate, secure, and protect works of art and other historic heritage and sometimes to guide repairs to historic structures. Recent publications on the British and American historians, art historians, and others that comprised the units of heritage protection officers underscore their often heroic efforts and their fortunate accomplishments.[14]

Belgium again rebuilt, and this time advocates of conservation seemed to overcome proponents of stylistic restoration. While postwar planners demolished many damaged historic urban centers, ensembles, and individual monuments, many other important historic structures were preserved. Although returning the country's most significant monuments to their prewar appearance, as had been done after the previous war, was still important, architects and conservation specialists tried to introduce more conservative approaches, encouraging consolidation and conservation of as much original fabric as possible. Paul Coremans, the foremost among this group, also promoted the use of new technological advances to aid conservation efforts, believing that restoration methods could be improved by technicians, engineers, and scientists. Both Coremans and his colleague Paul Philippot ardently defended the principles of multidisciplinary work and proper training and were devoted to restoration and conservation ethics.

Philippot was a proponent of Cesare Brandi's approach in Italy, which urged respect for original structures both as historical documents and as aesthetic creations. Brandi had noted that lacunae (missing elements) disrupted the unity of an image and stood out aggressively, calling attention to themselves. Thus, filling in these small gaps during the conservation process should, he felt, be done in such a way as to invert this relationship and cause the lacuna to recede into the background.[15] Paul Philippot and his father, Albert, the chief restorer at Belgium's Royal Museums of Fine-Arts, effectively transformed these theories into conservation practice, first using these techniques on paintings and later when reintegrating losses in three-dimensional objects. In all his specific suggestions Philippot tried to reduce the visual annoyance caused by lacunae and "give back to the aesthetic structure the clarity of perception it had lost."[16] The art conservation problems of lacunae, "retouching," and conserving patina were all hotly debated issues in the analogous field of architectural reconstruction in post–World War II Europe.

One notable postwar reconstruction project that represents these ideas of sensitive and conservative intervention is the 1964 preservation plan for the thirteenth-century Great Beguinage of Leuven prepared by Baron Raymond Lemaire, nephew of the Raymond Lemaire who wrote *La restauration des monuments anciens*. The younger Lemaire saved as much of the original structures as possible at the Great Beguinage while also creating modern housing flats for university staff and students. His work resulted in one of Belgium's finest examples of postwar adaptive reuse.

Immediately following World War II, the Dutch also began a comprehensive reexamination of their vast collection of historic architectural resources, which revealed the devastation of entire cities and towns as well as of the country's ports, its vital means of trade. The debate over stylistic restoration was again reopened in the Netherlands in the postwar decades. In some cities, such as the extensively destroyed Rotterdam, Dutch architects seized the moment as an opportunity to rebuild on what had become a tabula rasa with modern and functionalist designs.[17] In other cities, such as Amsterdam, Utrecht, and Rhenen, postwar reconstruction paid more attention to surviving monuments and historic urban ensembles, which were mercifully spared from extensive bombing—more conservative reconstruction approaches were taken in these cities. City ordinances ensured the retention of the historic scale and traditional forms in Amsterdam, and a master plan in Utrecht prevented new construction from proceeding at the expense of the remaining historic fabric.

a

b

c

Figure 6-4 The 2004 adaptive reuse of the Van Nelle factory complex, originally designed by architects Brinkman and Van der Vlugt in the 1920s (d), to become a "Design Factory," consisting of multipurpose conference and trade-fair facilities provided Rotterdam with a distinctive amenity of its type (a, b, and c). The restoration and reuse project, accomplished by a consortium of conservation architects led by Hubert-Jan Henket and Wessel de Jonge, won a European Union/ Europa Nostra award for conservation in 2008. Figures 6-4a, b, c, courtesy and copyright T.K. mcClintock, TKKM Studios. Figure 6-4d courtesy Van Nelle Factory.

d

LEGISLATION AND ADMINISTRATION IN BELGIUM

Following the chaos of the Napoleonic period and a fifteen-year unhappy union with the Netherlands, Belgium gained its independence in 1830. Eager to emphasize its cultural as well as political distinctiveness, King Leopold I established the Royal Commission on Monuments in 1835 to examine the state's historic resources. Its provincial offices were entrusted with the task of documenting significant art and antiquities in their areas. Work on the inventories progressed at different rates in different parts of the kingdom and started and stopped periodically throughout the nineteenth century.[18] The Royal Commission's concerns were refocused in 1918 to include historic sites and landscapes, and in 1931 it was given the power to enforce the protection of monuments when Belgium's first heritage legislation was passed. This law still governs heritage protection in most of Belgium, though it has been supplemented more recently in the Flanders region. In the 1950s, the inventories of historic sites and objects started more than a century earlier by the Royal Commission and its provincial offices were finally complete and publishable; however, by 1972, only 2,500 sites in Belgium were actually legally protected.[19]

In the late 1960s and in the revised Belgian constitution of 1970, a complicated political system was developed that simultaneously granted autonomy to Belgium's three cultural communities: the Dutch-speaking Flemish, the French-speaking Walloons, and the minority German speakers, as well as created three separate governing regions: Flanders, Wallonia, and the Brussels-Capital Region. Political necessity required dividing up various departments and governmental bodies and devolving formerly centralized responsibilities to the communities and regions. Power over cultural issues, including heritage conservation, was transferred to the communities, while power over property issues were transferred to the regions. Unfortunately, this has proven to be sometimes problematic and complicated for architectural heritage protection in Wallonia and Flanders and detrimental for heritage concerns in Brussels, where community and regional policies are often in conflict.

The government of the Brussels-Capital Region only recently enacted architectural heritage protection legislation. The Town Planning Act of 1991 created architectural heritage zones and permitted local authorities to refuse demolition requests based on cultural, historic, or aesthetic reasons.[20] The Heritage Conservation Act of 1993 enabled the government of the Brussels-Capital Region to create a list of protected historic buildings. As a result of limited funding and personnel, the Brussels-Capital Region's Monuments and Sites service has still only completely surveyed three of its nineteen municipalities, while surveys are currently in progress in three others, including Brussels City. This means the inventory contains only around seven-hundred sites to date.

While the government of the Brussels-Capital Region has authority and expertise over listing and protecting historic buildings, the nineteen municipalities within it hold the power to grant permission for demolition, and these two levels of government were often at odds until the "permis unique" was introduced. Political disputes between the Flemish and Brussels-Capital Region governments have also exacerbated the area's problems. In addition, because it is politically isolated from the rest of Belgium, the Brussels-Capital Region has little tax base and therefore little money for conservation efforts.

As a result of this confusion and lack of allocated funds for architectural heritage protection, in the second half of the twentieth century, the Brussels-Capital Region has undergone extensive redevelopment far exceeding the post-war reconstruction of typical European cities. Urban renewal began due to the need for highway access to the 1958 World's Fair, and the establishment of the European Commission headquarters in 1959. New construction demolished hundreds of nineteenth-century buildings, including architectural masterpieces, such as Victor Horta's art nouveau Maison du Peuple.

a

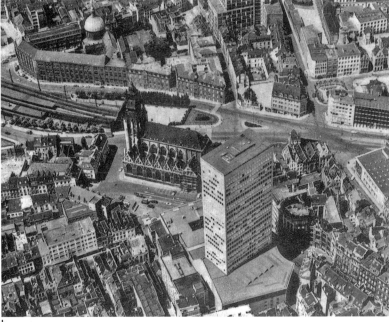

b

Figure 6-5 During the second half of the twentieth-century, planners and architects in Brussels replaced extensive areas of the capital's historic architectural fabric with new construction. Victor Horta's Maison du Peuple (a), which could have been restored after a disasterous fire, was a casualty of this philosophy of modernization in 1965. In its place the Blaton Tower (b) was constructed the following year.

Indeed, the term "Brusselization" (French: bruxellisation, Dutch: verbrusseling) has become internationally synonymous with the "senseless destruction of urban and cultural values in an historical town center."[21] Developers purchased listed or historic buildings, neglected them for a decade, and then applied for demolition permits because of the extensive disrepair of their sites. Another problem highlighted by André Loits, principal engineer of Brussels' Monuments and Sites Service, is that a decision about whether or not to protect a valuable building in Brussels usually occurs after a developer has already made plans for its demolition. Loits laments that these decisions, therefore, include either impossible attempts to restore already destroyed structures or last-minute, reactionary legal proceedings to block demolitions. According to Loits, "In the best cases, when popular protest against demolition becomes too high, a compromise is found in the way the developer can go on," and all too often this compromise includes retaining only the most valuable facade and razing the rest of the historic structure.[22]

Within Belgium's other two semiautonomous regions, Flanders and Wallonia, government conservation efforts have developed along different courses. Belgium's northern provinces, collectively known as Flanders, are home to some of its most historic and well-preserved cities: Ghent, Leuven, Tongeren, Mechelen, and the World Heritage city of Bruges. When given responsibility for cultural matters in 1968, Flanders enthusiastically took up the challenge of managing its own architectural heritage. In 1972 the first Flemish Public Service for the Conservation of Monuments and Sites was established and given the authority to enforce protection laws, including the 1976 Decree on Monuments and Landscapes passed by the Flemish Parliament.[23]

In the 1980s as the regional government grappled with its increased responsibilities following its merger with the Flemish community, support for heritage policy and monuments protection in Flanders declined. Funding for conservation projects was gradually cut, the number of designations fell, and the Division for the Conservation of Monuments and Sites could no longer fully execute its duties. In 1984 Flanders passed ineffective tax incentive schemes for conservation in response to a critical report published by the Foundation Roi Baudouin / Koning Boudewijnstichting (King Baudouin Foundation), a nonprofit organization established during the Belgian monarch's twenty-fifth year on the throne in 1976. The report had criticized the weak heritage legislation and enforcement throughout Belgium as well as the country's dearth of financial incentives and funding for conservation projects.[24]

The popular attitude toward cultural heritage protection gradually began to improve in Flanders, and in 1991 government interest in the subject revived and conservation funding was increased.[25] Scores of historic structures and townscapes were listed and restored, as government funding was made available for up to 25 percent of total conservation costs. Flemish heritage policy today is the responsibility of the Afdeling Monumenten en Landschappen (Division for Monuments and Landscapes), which oversees matters of legislation, regulation, policy, documentation, and public education.[26] It also supervises and coordinates the activities and inspections carried out by its five province-level cells and ten special issue offices.[27] The Royal Commission on Monuments continues to advise the Division on its work.

Belgium's French-speaking southern provinces comprise the region of Wallonia, whose built heritage is protected and conserved by the Division du Patrimoine (Heritage Division) of the regional government's Direction Générale de l'Aménagement du Territoire, du Logement, du Patrimoine, et de l'Energie (General Directorate for Land Settlement, Housing, Patrimony, and Energy). Like its parallel Division in Flanders, Wallonia's Heritage Division is also advised by the Royal Commission. Within the Division, the Direction de la Protection (Directorate for Protection) is responsible for listing immovable sites of historic, archaeological, scientific, social, artistic, or technical interest. It is the contact point for management of Wallonia's four World Heritage Sites and participates in the Council of Europe's Heritage Network program. The Division's Direction de l'Archaeologie (Directorate for Archaeology) oversees work and research at archaeological sites, and the Direction de la Restauration (Directorate for Restoration) administers technical and financial aid for listed buildings as well as coordinates the conservation efforts of the separate communes.

The Institut du Patrimoine Wallon (Institute for Walloon Patrimony) was created in 1999 to provide physical and consultation assistance to owners of listed buildings. By 2004, the organization had identified almost one hundred buildings suffering from serious decay and neglect, and it had begun work on their conservation. One of the Institut's first major pilot projects was the rehabilitation of the thirteenth-century Cistercian Paix-Dieu Abbey near Huy, which now serves as a training institute for heritage professionals.[28] Since inception, the Institut has also successfully collaborated with a number of public agencies and nongovernmental organizations to conserve the region's agricultural and mining culture.

A federal government agency that continues to provide much valuable support for heritage management and restoration is the Royal Institute for Historic Heritage, Brussels, that not only contains the national online photographic survey of about one million images (including most of the country's historic buildings) but also large-scale restoration workshops and laboratories.[29]

LEGISLATION AND ADMINISTRATION IN THE NETHERLANDS

In the Netherlands the Koninklijke Akademie van Wetenschappen (Royal Academy of Sciences) formed a heritage commission in 1860 to take up the cause of conservation, marking the first organized attempt to document and publish information about the country's architectural heritage. An advisory council was founded within the Ministerie van Binnenlandse (Ministry of the Interior) in 1874 in response to an inflammatory essay on the state of Dutch heritage published the previous year by Victor de Stuers: the advisory council—largely comprised of "unity of style" proponents, including Cuypers and De Stuers—advised the government on the treatment of historic sites.[30] In 1903, the Rijkscommissie voor de Monumentenzorg (State Commission for Monument Conservation) was formed to create a more formal inventory of all significant structures built before 1850 and to advise the government on their treatment.[31] Though extending no formal protection, the Dutch government began offering restoration grants to owners of historic buildings in exchange for unenforceable promises to maintain them.

Immediately following World War I, the Dutch government established the Rijksbureau voor de Monumentenzorg (Department for Monument Conservation), within the Rijkscommissie, to focus specifically on overseeing restoration projects. In the 1920s the cause of Dutch architectural conservation was advanced by the publication of the first national inventory of historic architecture, which had been started two decades earlier under the direction of De Stuers and Cuypers. As planned, it caught the public's attention and encouraged regulation of the country's architectural heritage, including the passage of local ordinances prohibiting the demolition or alteration of inventoried structures.[32]

After World War II the Dutch government took even greater steps to protect surviving historic buildings. By the order of the Army's chief of staff, no historic structure included on the interwar inventory of historic architecture could be demolished or altered without permission.[33] In 1947 authority for the protection of historic structures was transferred from the military to the Ministry of Arts and Sciences, and the venerable Rijksbureau was reconstituted and renamed the Rijksdienst voor de Monumentenzorg (State Service for Monument Conservation, or RDMZ).[34]

In 1961 the Netherlands passed its first comprehensive legislation for the protection of significant buildings, the Monumentenwet (Historic Buildings and Monuments Act). This law called for each municipality to create an updated list of buildings over the next two decades. Though restricted to buildings built before 1850, this new list for the first time included vernacular buildings, and the list totaled over 39,000 sites.[35] Later the inventory was further expanded to include sites built after 1850 but that were at least fifty years old, and it also added two new listing categories: townscapes, which are historic districts within larger cities, and historic town centers, which have retained their physical appearance for over a century.[36]

In 1988 a new Monumentenwet replaced the 1961 law. Though the state ministry was still charged with maintaining the list of historic sites, with this new law most decisions about alterations to listed sites were transferred to the municipal level, which already had authority over other land-use issues.[37] In 2005, in the Netherlands, the Rijksdienst (State Service) for listed monuments merged with similar inspectorates for archaeology, public records, and cultural heritage to form a new umbrella Erfgoedinspectie (Cultural Heritage Inspectorate) within the reconstituted Ministry of Education, Culture, and Science. In 2009 the system was revised again, and a Rijksdienst voor het Cultureel Erfgoed (State Service for Cultural Heritage) was formed with responsibility for archaeology, cultural landscapes, and monuments.[38]

Rijksdienst officials are constantly reexamining and expanding heritage definitions to incorporate a broader scope of Dutch history. Currently, the more than 165,000 inventoried Dutch sites include more than 62,500 protected monuments (rijksmonumenten), including private homes, farms, churches, windmills, and numerous other types.[39] This list is augmented by protection of 30,000 additional sites at the local authority level (gemeentemonumenten) as well as the designation of 350 towns and historic town centers and seven World Heritage sites.

In the Netherlands today, the Rijksdienst identifies and lists sites that warrant state protection; educates the public about the cultural value of built heritage; consults with municipalities, private owners, and organizations about conservation; and awards financial aid to restoration projects. In 1985 the National Restoration Fund was established to promote private and institutional investment in heritage conservation and cooperation with the Dutch government in this area. The Fund offers grants and low-interest loans and mortgages to owners of historic properties.

The Rijksdienst has become increasingly involved with urban planning and land-use issues, as these decisions are integral to the protection of not only monuments but their historic contexts as well. It has also taken advantage of new technologies to continuously update its listing process, such as the digitalization of approximately 400,000 photographs and the use of Geographic Information Survey (GIS) data management systems.[40]

ARCHITECTURAL CONSERVATION IN LUXEMBOURG

Although a Commission Nationale pour les Sites et Monuments (National Sites and Monuments Commission) was established in 1927, the Grand Duchy of Luxembourg's formal architectural conservation movement began only in the last quarter of the twentieth century.[41] In 1977 the Service des Sites et Monuments Nationaux (National Sites and Monuments Service) was created within Luxembourg's Ministry of Culture, Higher Education, and Research to oversee cultural heritage protection. It maintains an inventory of archeological, artistic, aesthetic, and scientifically important individual sites and conservation areas that are to be protected, as well as a supplemental list of other important sites. The Monuments Service organizes Luxembourg's heritage into four categories: châteaus and rural, religious, and industrial sites. Soon after its establishment, the Monuments Service launched a campaign specifically aimed at restoring Luxembourg's rural heritage with traditional building methods and materials.

The earlier Commission Nationale still exists and collaborates with the Monuments Service on proposing new legislation and protective measures. Since 1980 the Ministry and its Monuments Service have also been advised on cultural heritage issues by the Conseil Supérieur des Sites (High Council for Sites), which is comprised of professionals representing relevant private institutions and nongovernmental organizations. The National Cultural Fund, established in 1982 within the Ministry, oversees Luxembourg's grant program for heritage conservation. The funding for these grants comes from private donations and from a national lottery, as in the United Kingdom. Luxembourg's governmental structures and procedures were strengthened significantly in 1983, when a comprehensive new law enhanced the scope of the earlier legislation and provided the framework for today's heritage protection system. In 1988 Luxembourg's cultural institutes were reorganized so that the Monuments Service has since shared responsibility for archaeological sites with the National Museum of History and Art, which overseas excavations and studies at those sites.

Within Luxembourg City, restrictive urban plans provide an additional layer of protection for its historic sites. The history of the Grand Duchy of Luxembourg is inextricably linked to its capital's architectural heritage as its history traditionally begins with the construction of Luxembourg Castle by Count Sigefroid of Ardennes in the tenth century. This mighty castle, and the fortified town that gradually grew up around it, were built upon the ruins of a Roman fort at a strategic point in the heart of Europe. The fortified center of Luxembourg City was designated a UNESCO World Heritage Site in 1994.

In 1993 the Projet Général d'Aménagement (General Management Plan) established protected zones within Luxembourg City, each with strict use, building, and design controls. The Plan also restricted development within a wide buffer area around these zones, which effectively includes most of the city. Extensive research and archeological excavations began earlier, when Luxembourg City's entire historic center came under control of the Monuments Service in 1989. This was followed by a five-year major restoration program to prepare for its role as European Capital of Culture in 1995. In addition to the work of city authorities and the Monuments Service, conservation in

Figure 6-6 The fortified center of Luxembourg City , dramatically situated on multiple hilltops separated by deep river gorges and built on a site dating to Roman times, was placed on the World Heritage List in 1994, one year after a comprehensive new General Management Plan established protected zones within the city.

Luxembourg City has also been undertaken by the Administration of Bridges and Roadways, which maintains and restores many of the city's precipitously sited 110 bridges.

In 2002 ICOMOS Luxembourg argued that a lack of clarity within Luxembourg's legislative framework had permitted the demolition of a significant medieval building in the market town of Larochette and threatened the integrity of its historically charming assemblage of buildings.[42] In 2004 a new law was passed coordinating the work of the National Library and the National Museums of History and Art and of Natural History. Each maintained their separate purviews, but they were united in their mission and the new priorities of finalizing inventories and digitizing heritage. A new unified "cultural portal" was proposed to bring Luxembourg's heritage into the twenty-first century by providing a single point for information. It remains to be seen whether this new government structure will protect other cities and sites in Luxembourg from the real estate development pressures to which Larochette was subjected.

CONTEMPORARY CONSERVATION AND THE ROLE OF NONGOVERNMENTAL ORGANIZATIONS

Protecting built heritage in the late twentieth and early twenty-first century has been a continuing challenge for conservation communities in the Netherlands, Belgium, and Luxembourg. In the Netherlands, a number of publicly owned monuments and sites are suffering from deferred maintenance and poor management, as cities and municipalities struggle with growing populations and other urban issues. Many expansive sites—such as Amsterdam's Defense Line (the city's water-control fortifications) and the network of windmills at Kinderdijk-Elshort, both on the World Heritage List—need comprehensive attention ranging from maintenance to sympathetic development. The situation is somewhat better for the country's 31,000 privately held monuments, whose upkeep is often expensive. Although state funds are provided for private restoration, there are few incentives in place for owners to maintain their properties. This is especially the case for historic interiors, though they are well protected under Dutch law.[43]

In addition to the government's traditional role protecting architectural heritage, Dutch NGOs also actively bridge the gap between the public and private sectors. Through advocacy and public awareness campaigns and direct restoration and conser-

a

b

c

Figure 6-7 The restoration of individual houses in Amsterdam (a) is a tradition that gained significant momentum through organized conservation efforts beginning in the 1960s. A variety of technical, administrative, and funding solutions for protecting the city's domestic structures are being addressed by public and private sectors working in harmony. The result is retention of Amsterdam's special architectural character, including its numerous canal houses (b) with their distinctive gables (c), as one of Europe's most notable achievements in architectural heritage protection.

vation efforts, these groups are a testament to the high value placed by the Dutch public on their historic and cultural resources. Over one thousand private organizations deal with cultural heritage sites, varying from vast cultural landscapes to windmills. The oldest of these NGOs is the Hendrick de Keyser Society, founded in 1918, which operates similarly to the British National Trust by acquiring and restoring significant buildings. Today the society owns over two hundred buildings, including seventy in Amsterdam.[44]

In 2007, on the suggestion of the Ministry of Culture, the Stichting Erfgoed Nederland (Netherlands Foundation for Heritage) was formed when four nonprofit organizations with parallel agendas joined together.[45] The new organization promotes other organizations, provides training, conducts research, and advises on heritage policies. It is broadly concerned with all types of heritage: from archaeological to documentary, from intangible traditions to historic buildings. Erfgoed Nederland set an ambitious program for the years 2008 to 2012 with a focus on reinforcing and promoting heritage as cultural capital, developing creative and innovative methods to showcase heritage, and providing a platform for linking the work of others concerned with heritage protection.[46]

Architectural and Social Preservation in Amsterdam

Tenacious Dutch ingenuity and engineering carved Amsterdam's complex, organic structure from the Zuider Zee, an inlet of the North Sea. The city exists thanks to a sophisticated network of seawalls and dikes, some of which were begun in the twelfth century. As a result, a major conservation issue for Amsterdam property owners has been the rotting of wooden pilings supporting its historic buildings.[47] Such restoration work is expensive and delicate because of fragile facades, the proximity of each building to adjacent ones, and the potential for destabilizing entire parts of the city.

Amsterdam's complex seawall networks have successfully separated the city from the sea over the centuries because of the unflagging maintenance given by cooperative public effort. According to Anthony Tung, this common interest and cooperative spirit constantly underscores the importance of a centralized government and has even formed a Dutch national persona, which is known for tolerance, public equality, and a wide social conscience.[48] In particular, a social consciousness has pervaded both Amsterdam's urban development and conservation efforts.

Over the years, Amsterdam has become what some have termed a laboratory for town planning experiments. When its seventeenth-century glory faded into a gentrification process in which the wealthy gradually relocated their economic interests to the city's outskirts, Amsterdam's built infrastructure deteriorated. At the turn of the twentieth century, the city's economic outlook was improving, but inner city living conditions remained dire. In response, private developers encircled the city with poorly designed, substandard housing tracts and speculative housing projects, which initiated a popular outcry for development that was more aesthetically pleasing and better managed. Both the private and government sectors responded. Architect H. P. Berlage attempted to reconcile the historic city's plan with modern urban development by introducing urban planning concepts that incorporated efficient circulation patterns with aesthetically pleasing new housing and communal open spaces. Berlage's ideas became the catalyst for the dramatic, high-quality buildings created by architects of what became known as the Amsterdam School.

In 1901 a Housing Act mandated a joint approach between civic authorities and nonprofit groups to create low-cost housing compliant with modern standards of health, safety, aesthetics, and planning. Amsterdam's attempts to alleviate human suffering as a result of crowded housing conditions were unusual for that time. By 1925 fifty-eight officially recognized mutual benefit housing corporations were actively addressing social improvements and welfare, reflecting the Calvinist concepts of thrift, hard work, and individual responsibility.[49]

In 1957 Amsterdam passed a series of ordinances to ensure retention of the character and silhouette of its historic center by regulating the size, height, and design of all new construction in the old town. This marked a continuation of its City Council's interest in design and beauty: for decades Amsterdam's public works department included an aesthetic advisor, and long before national heritage protection legislation, the city had formed a Committee on Urban Beauty, which reviewed proposals for alterations to historic structures and made detailed suggestions for design revisions.

From the 1970s through the 1990s, urban rehabilitation in Amsterdam replaced demolition as the preferred method of treating deteriorated neighborhoods and reinforcing central residential areas. An important player in this process was the organization Vereniging Vrienden van de Amsterdamse Binnenstad (Friends of Downtown Amsterdam, or VVAB), which was formed in 1975 to encourage quality work and living conditions in the inner city. The organization is still an active advocacy and watchdog group in Amsterdam today and continues to purchase and restore properties. Other urban renewal efforts saw underutilized parcels of land enhanced by sensitive new designs, including some that displayed remarkable sensitivity to urban context. Public efforts to improve the quality of life of Amsterdam's citizens with new housing developments in former industrial areas have been augmented by the initiatives of about sixty business–minded neighborhood revitalization groups. In turn private investors are engaged.[50]

Today's Amsterdam also has several corporations that address a range of housing needs though architectural conservation. The Jan Pieters Haus Foundation restores buildings for musicians and the Aristiles Foundation converts buildings into condominiums for artists. Nonlisted historic buildings are restored and converted into subsidized housing by Stadsherstel (the Company for City Restoration), which remains involved as landlord. Stadsherstel's goal to sensitively revitalize neighborhoods has been so successful, for nearly fifty years, that property prices rise when one of their bronze medallions is placed on a building—proof that quality architectural heritage protection can be profitable as well as socially responsible.[51]

Figure 6-8 The Dutch organization Monumentenwacht (Monument Watch) was founded in 1973 to assist property owners with the upkeep of their historic sites. Its aims and methods have been adapted in neighboring countries. The emblem of Monumentenwacht is shown here.

One of the most active Dutch NGOs concerned with architectural conservation for the past few decades is Monumentenwacht (Monument Watch), which was founded in 1973 to assist property owners with the upkeep of their historic sites. Based on a philosophy that preventative maintenance and continuous care saves buildings and reduces expenses, the Monumentenwacht system involves inspecting buildings, completing small-scale repairs immediately, and preparing prioritized maintenance plans for historic sites. Monumentenwacht is funded through donations, payment from building owners, and subsidies from provincial level governments. Its more than fifty teams of inspectors visit more than 15,000 buildings each year—over 25 percent of listed buildings in the Netherlands—whose owners subscribe to Monumentenwacht's services.

The Monumentenwacht strategy has influenced the Dutch government's policies and moved it "away from expensive disruptive repair and restoration campaigns and toward encouraging and subsidizing regular systematic maintenance."[52] In addition, over the course of nearly forty years of service, similar Monumentenwacht inspection organizations have been established in many other parts of Europe, including Denmark, Germany, and Flanders. Groups in additional countries are considering adopting variations of the Monumentenwacht model. Even conservators in the United Kingdom, with its plethora of NGOs seemingly addressing all possible conservation concerns, have studied the Dutch Monumentenwacht system and begun implementing it.

Monumentenwacht Vlaanderen (Monument Watch Flanders) was founded in 1991 by a group of Belgian private and public institutions. With funds from the National Lottery and the King Baudouin Foundation, it operates similarly to its sister organization in the Netherlands with its teams of conservators who inspect and advise the owners of historic buildings. Another NGO concerned with the protection of Flemish cultural heritage is Erfgoed Vlaanderen (Flanders' Heritage), founded in 1994. Like the British National Trust or the Dutch Hendrick de Keyser Society, it administers and restores threatened historic properties and makes them publicly accessible, complete with site interpretation. As of 2010 it holds twelve properties within its trust and aims to add to them. In 2011, Erfgoed Vlaanderen will merge with its sister organizations Open Monumentendag Vlaaderen and the Forum voor Erfgoedverenigingen, and has plans to also eventually merge with the Monumentenwacht Vlaanderen.[53]

Nongovernmental organizations have also played a role elsewhere in Belgium. During the 1990s grass roots organizations such as Pétitions-Patrimoine (Heritage Petitions) protested the demolition of specific historic structures in Brussels, such as the interwar modern Radio and Television Building. Though successful at blocking the destruction of 80 percent of the projects they oppose, the limited resources of Pétitions-Patrimoine permits it to focus its efforts and energies only on the most significant sites. Another Belgian NGO, La Fonderie, promotes the social and economic history of the Brussels region, with a focus on industrial development, was active in the battle to save the early twentieth-century Tour and Taxis transportation terminal. The careful redevelopment of this structure won an European Union EU/Europa Nostra award for conservation in 2008.

The following year, the Maison du Patrimoine Médiéval Mosan in Bouvignes, Belgium won an EU/Europa Nostra Award for education, training, and awareness. This new local museum, focused on medieval civilization in the Meuse River valley, opened in 2008 in a sixteenth-century Spanish-style house. It combines the latest research and excavations from the region with interactive displays "to create dynamic links between the past and the present involving local life, tourism, and culture...for tourists and school visitors alike."[54]

Another long-standing NGO that advocates the conservation and restoration of Belgian heritage held in private hands is the Association royale des Demeures historiques et des Jardins de Belgique (Royal Association of Historic Residences and Gardens of Belgium), operating within a federation of European associations of its kind (Union of European Historic Houses Associations). Its latest initiative concerns a public-private partnership for saving the castle of the 900-year-old family estate of the princes de Chimay at Chimay, following the approach of the British practice of keeping the original family deeply involved in the day-to-day running of the operation, both on an estate management and a tourist level.

Since 1988 the Cultural Heritage Items Fund of the King Baudouin Foundation has been more broadly concerned with conservation of heritage throughout Belgium. With funds from the National Lottery, it purchases movable objects and loans them permanently to museums, with the aim of preserving this heritage and keeping it in Belgium. In addition, the King Baudouin Foundation has financed architectural conservation projects abroad, most notably in Southeastern Europe, including conservation initiatives in Romania, Bulgaria, and Macedonia.

For larger projects, the King Baudouin Foundation organizes tax deductibility for heritage conservation projects, while smaller projects are usually handled by a society that was founded in 1977 on the initiative of the then Minister of Finance, Jean-Charles Snoy: Patrimoine Culturel Immobilier/Onroerend Cultureel Erfgoed (Immovable Cultural Heritage), an effective solution to avoid complicated state bureaucracy had this tax deductibility been organized directed by the central government.[55]

In Holland the Prince Claus Foundation for Culture and Development has played a similar role to the King Baudouin Foundation in Belgium. It has been active in emergency conservation projects around the world, most recently in Gaza and Indonesia (the former Dutch East Indies), where it was among the first to support inventorying damage and rebuilding of heritage following human-made and natural disasters in 2008

Figure 6-9 Aerial view of the Tour and Taxis transportation hub in Brussels that was saved by the efforts of the La Fonderie cultural center that first nominated it to WMF's World Monuments Watch list in 1996 and then again in 1998 and 2000. The local and international pressure to save the terminal resulted in new plans in late 2007 to convert most of the complex for mixed-use cultural and commercial activities.

and 2009.[56] In fact, both the government and NGOs in the Netherlands have been involved in a variety of foreign conservation efforts, particularly though not exclusively in former colonies. The Netherlands vast overseas colonial architectural heritage includes seventeenth-century Caribbean fortresses, urban ensembles, plantation complexes, and ruins. Like Spain and Portugal, the Netherlands and Dutch NGOs have concerned themselves with the conservation of this colonial heritage, including the historic city center and harbor of Willemstad, Curaçao, a World Heritage Site (Figure 31-3). Balancing the needs of profitable tourist development with the simultaneous protection of heritage sites in the fragile economies of the Netherlands Antilles has proven to be no simple task. While certain islands, such as Saint Eustatius, are implementing conservation plans, other islands—such as Curaçao—have significantly reduced conservation efforts because of their faltering economies. The Netherlands aids heritage conservation in some of its former colonial possessions in Southeast Asia as well, particularly through the Foundation for Exploration and Conservation of Monuments of the Dutch West India Company (MOWIC), which is active worldwide. The Nieuw Nederland Erfgoed Stichting (New Netherlands Heritage Foundation) is focused on the Dutch architectural legacy in North America, and it has been active in surveying Dutch barns and houses in New York State as well as in creating a three-dimensional digital model of New Amsterdam (New York City) as it appeared in 1660.[57]

One of the most important global NGOs concerned with architectural conservation, the International Committee for the Documentation and Conservation of the buildings, sites and neighborhoods of the Modern Movement (DOCOMOMO), was founded in the Netherlands. Originally the 1988 idea of Hubert-Jan Henket and Wessel de Jonge of the School of Architecture of the Technical University in Eindhoven, the Netherlands, DOCOMOMO's mission and goals were articulated two years later in the Eindhoven Statement, drafted at the organization's foundational conference.[58] These goals included raising public awareness and funds for the conservation of modern architecture, developing appropriate conservation techniques and advocating for these sites, and documenting and researching this period. In 2002 the DOCOMOMO International Secretariat moved to Paris, and this global organization today includes over fifty chapters from every continent and has proven to be a key specialized NGO in the field in the past few decades.

Exciting recent architectural conservation projects in the Netherlands include not only the rehabilitation of the Van Nelle factory in Rotterdam (Figure 6-4) but also the restoration of the neoclassical Town Hall in Utrecht and the reuse of building elements from a demolished adjacent structure in the new addition in 2000.[59] Maastricht is home to a series of exciting recent reuse projects, including a hotel in the fifteenth-century Kruisheren cloister and adjacent church. In addition, the thirteenth-century Gothic Dominican church in Maastricht was carefully transformed into a bookstore by the Dutch architects Merkx + Girod in 2007. The change of use was not controversial as the Dominicanen (or Dominican church) had not been used as a church in over two centuries (it has been used for bicycle storage, as stables, a boxing arena, and a car showroom, among other things). The insertion of contemporary steel shelves and staircases was paired with the cleaning of the paintings in the medieval ceiling vaults.

In part, because of its small size, conservation in Luxembourg has primarily been the purview of the Grand Duchy's government, and few significant private initiatives or nongovernmental organizations have emerged in the field of cultural heritage conservation. Luxembourg is home, however, to the European Institute of Cultural Routes, a nonprofit organization founded jointly by the Council of Europe and the Grand Duchy in 1997. At the completion of Luxembourg City's tenure as a European Capital of Culture in 1995, it wanted to stay involved in European cultural policy integration, and thus took the lead in forming this Institute, which promotes heritage tourism and cultural partnerships throughout Europe, as well as organizes conferences and exhibitions, conducts studies, and publishes information on issues of heritage, society, and identity in Europe.

Figure 6-10 The medieval Dominican church in Maastricht was rehabilitated in 2007 by the Dutch architects Merkx + Girod to become the Selexyz Dominicanen Bookstore. The project won the Lensvelt Prize for Interior Architecture in 2008 for the dramatic juxtapositions created by the church's restored features and the strikingly contemporary bookstore furnishings and fittings. The British newspaper *The Guardian* also named it the best bookstore in the world that same year. Images courtesy and copyright of Roos Aldershott, photographer and Merkx + Girod.

Luxembourg's post–World War II record of caring for its most significant monuments and sites has been good. Other than its capital, few other cities developed in the Grand Duchy until the eighteenth century. Indeed, until the Industrial Revolution and the establishment of an investment friendly climate, most of the country was rural, agricultural, and isolated. Luxembourg's villages and historic châteaus have largely preserved their traditional appearance successfully, and proper architectural heritage planning and conservation is highly valued. For example, the Château Bettembourg was transformed into a congressional center, both preserving it for public use and ensuring its future maintenance.

Overall management of the Grand Duchy's architectural patrimony today faces new challenges posed by the economic success of its steel industry. Recent national prosperity has placed the country's heritage inventory under pressure. The growing financial sector workforce, coupled with the office space requirements of many European Union institutions, has created a high demand for quality new housing and office space, some of which must be met by Luxembourg City's historic building stock. Insensitive adaptive reuse of historic structures is common because of conversion deadlines and budgetary constraints. Renovation work often demolishes original interiors and structural elements, leaving only the historic facades intact. Rising land prices have also led to the purchase and demolition of smaller old buildings, which are then razed and replaced by larger structures that are less sympathetic to the local character. Alternatively, according to ICOMOS *Heritage@Risk 2000* report, buildings are being overrestored by enthusiastic new owners, whose zeal has turned humble farm houses into mini manor houses.[60]

On the other hand, the Adolphe Bridge in Luxembourg City has been the focus of conservation attention in recent years and is slated to undergo an exciting and complicated restoration and reconstruction in the coming years. The sandstone bridge was built in 1903 across the deep gorge of the Petrusse River, and an investigation in the early 1990s revealed extensive damage to the stone and steel from a century of weathering as well as problems arising from concrete interventions intended to raise and widen the deck in the 1960s.[61] Emergency stabilization through the insertion of additional steel bars was carried out in 2003 and 2004. After additional study and public hearings revealing widespread support for conservation of the bridge, a popular tourist destination and symbol of Luxembourg, a complete reconstruction is planned. A temporary bridge will be built to reroute traffic and a scaffold will be erected to support the main stone arch while the stone balustrades, piers, and relieving arches above are completely disassembled. Then the main arch will be reinforced with concrete and the balustrades, piers and roadway above will be rebuilt.[62]

In all, the countries of Belgium, Luxembourg, and the Netherlands represent a very important facet of contemporary European architectural conservation practice. Each country has a wealth of historic architectural resources that each has managed to preserve, often in difficult circumstances, including war. Over the past century and a half, conservation practice in Belgium, Luxembourg, and the Netherlands has evolved from methods of restoration and conservation borrowed from France and England to each country developing and refining its own system of heritage protection today. Commitment to architectural conservation in the region is evidenced in a number of ways, but mainly by the appearance and appeal of historic centers and through some of their remarkably innovative architectural heritage protection schemes.

ENDNOTES

1. "Architects: P. J. H. Cuypers (1827–1921), part 1/2," Archimon: The Virtual Museum of Religious Architecture in The Netherlands, www.archimon.nl/architects/pjhcuypers.html (accessed December 9, 2009); Hetty Berens (ed.) P.J.H. Cuypers (1827-1921), *The Complete Works* (Rotterdam: NAi Publishers, 2007); AJC van Leeuwen, Pierre Cuypers architect (1827-1921) (Zwolle: Waanders, 2007)

2. Wim Denslagen, *Architectural Restoration in Western Europe: Controversy and Continuity*, trans. Jane Zuyl-Moores (Amsterdam: Architectura & Natura Press, 1994), 189.

3. The Ridderzaal building underwent yet another restoration in 1895–1905 which replaced the iron Gothic ceiling with a wooden one of a different design. It also received a new neo-Gothic exterior, complete with turrets.

4. Denslagen, *Architectural Restoration in Western Europe*, 210.

5. Ibid., 205.

6 Charles Buls, *La restauration des monuments anciens* (Brussels: P. Weissenbruch, 1903) , www.kikirpa.be (accessed July 21, 2010).

7. Jokilehto, *A History of Architectural Conservation*, 250.

8. Buls, vol. XLIV, 498–503 and vol. XLV, 41–45.

9. Jokilehto, *A History of Architectural Conservation*, 250.

10. Ibid., 250.

11. Alois Riegl, "The Modern Cult of Monuments: Its Character and Its Origins," trans. Kurt W. Forster and Diane Ghirardo, *Oppositions* 25 (1982): 24. See also Stubbs, "Riegl and the Meaning of Monuments," in *Time Honored*, 38.

12. Theodore H. M. Prudon, "Architectural Preservation in the Netherlands," *Curator* 16, no. 2 (1973): 107–137.

13. Beginning in the 1920s, Dutch architecture became influenced by French (Le Corbusier), American (Frank Lloyd Wright), and German (Bauhaus) styles. Functionalism became an obsession for some architects, and it would become especially popular after World War II. However, the debate between Dutch traditionalists and modernists was abruptly halted by the outbreak of war in May 1940 and the Netherlands' subsequent German occupation.

14. Lynn H. Nicholas, *The Rape of Europa: The Fate of Europe's Treasures in the Third Reich and World War II* (New York: Vintage, 1995), 295. Firsthand accounts of the search for pillaged art and the outcome are offered in Robert Edsel and Brett Witter's *The Monuments Men: Allied Heroes, Nazi Thieves, and the Greatest Treasure Hunt in History*, Center Street Books (Hachette), New York, 2009.

15. Alessandra Melucco Vaccaro, "Introduction to Part VI: Reintegration of losses," in *Historical and Philosophical Issues in the Conservation of Cultural Heritage*, eds. Nicholas Stanley Price, M. Kirby Talley Jr., Alessandro Melucco Vaccaro (Los Angeles: Getty Conservation Institute, 1996), 325–421.

16. Albert Philippot, "Le problème de l'intégration des lacunes dans la restauration des peintures," *Bulletin de l'Institut royal du patrimoine artistique* 2 (1959): 73.

17. Today Rotterdam is one of Europe's most thoroughly contemporary cities, a stark visual contrast to Amsterdam, Maastricht, or Utrecht. Postwar architects designed a new city center from the ground up, incorporating sensible design elements. Tower blocks and wide thoroughfares improved civic life, and broad sidewalk overhangs offer weather protection to pedestrians during the country's long rainy winters. It is a haven for those interested in modern architecture and transport: Europoort makes it the busiest port city in the world.

18. Luc Devliegher, "The Inventories of the Belgian Artistic Heritage," *Monumentum* 20–21–22 (1980): 69; www.international.icomos.org/monumentum/vol20-21-22/vol20-21-22_6.pdf (accessed June 11, 2010). After World War I, Professor Maere suggested abandoning "the system of separate initiatives for the individual provinces in favor of a central publication on the same lines as in Germany, Austria and Holland"[(Devliegher, 69.) Though a Joint Inventorying Committee was established, it was underfunded and understaffed, and the provincial commissions continued their work, with interruptions from both the world wars.

19. André de Naeyer, "Preservation of Monuments in Belgium since 1945," *Monumentum* 20–21–22 (1980): 158; www.international.icomos.org/monumentum/vol20-21-22/vol20-21-22_13.pdf (accessed June 11, 2010).

20. André Loits, "Brussels Social and Economic Integration of Heritage," in *European Research on Cultural Heritage: State-of-the-Art Studies*, vol. 1, ed. Miloš Drdácký (Prague: Advanced Research Centre for Cultural Heritage Interdisciplinary Projects [ARCCHIP], 2004), 31. Originally presented as: "*Social and Economic Integration of Cultural Heritage in Europe*" (paper, 1st Ariadne Workshop, Prague, Czech Republic, April 23–29, 2001).

21. Ibid.

22. Ibid.

23. One of the first Ministers of Flemish Culture, Rika de Backer-Van Ocken, and her chief private secretary Johan Fleerackers, created the new Flemish policy toward heritage protection. Their efforts were bolstered by the launch of the European Architectural Heritage Campaign in 1975, which successfully promoted the appreciation of architectural heritage throughout the European Community. A year later Backen-Van Ocken's policies were incorporated into the Decree on Monuments and Townscapes. Her efforts toward this legislation were aided by Raymond Lemaire and the representatives in Parliament from Antwerp, Bob Cools and André De Buel.

24. Loits, "Brussels Social and Economic Integration of Heritage," 34–6.

25. Ibid., 36. Popular interest was invigorated by Flanders' first annual Monuments Day and the official promotion of monuments and heritage sites. In 1991 Louis Waltniel, Minister for Environmental Planning, Housing, and the Conservation of Monuments, was responsible for renewed government interest.

26. What is today the Afdeling was established in 1972 as the Rijksdienst voor Monumenten en Landschappen (State Service for Monuments and Landscapes), which during a reorganization of the Flemish Government in 1980 became the Bestuur (Directorate) within the Administratie voor Ruimtelijke Ordening en Leefmilieur (Administration for Physical Planning and Environment). In 1991 the Bestuur was moved into the Departement Leefmilieu en Infrastructuur (Environment and Infrastructure Department), and finally, in 1995, the Bestuur was renamed the Afdeling (Division).

27. "Home," Onroerend Erfgoed, www.onroerenderfgoed.be (accessed December 9, 2009).

28. "Home," Institut du Patrimoine Wallon (IPW), www.institutdupatrimoine.be (accessed December 9, 2009); "Home," Direction générale opérationnelle—Aménagement du territoire, Logement, Patrimoine et Energie, Ministère de la Région wallonne, http://mrw.wallonie.be/dgatlp/dgatlp/default.asp (accessed July 15 2010).

29. "Home," Royal Institute for Cultural Heritage, www.kikirpa.be (accessed December 18, 2010).

30. Jokilehto, *A History of Architectural Conservation*, 251.

31. Rob Berends, *Monumenten Wijzer: Rijksdienst voor de Monumentenzorg* (The Hague: Sdu Uitgeverij Koninginnegracht, 1995), 10, 12.

32. Dale, A. "France, Great Britain, Ireland, the Netherlands" in vol. 1, 106 of Stipe, R. (Ed.) *Historic Preservation in other countries*. Washington, DC: ICOMOS.

33. Prudon, *Preservation of Modern Architecture*, 117.

34. Dale and Stipe, *Historic Preservation in Other Countries*, vol. 1, 17.]

35. Marieke Kuipers, "Dutch Developments in Documenting Built Heritage," in *European Research on Cultural Heritage: State-of-the-Art Studies*, vol. 2, ed. Miloš Drdácký (Prague: ARCCHIP, 2004), 93. Originally presented as: "Documentation, Interpretation, Presentation and Publication of Cultural Heritage" (paper, 5th Ariadne Workshop, Prague, Czech Republic, September 17–23, 2001.

36. Dale and Stipe, *Historic Preservation in Other Countries*, vol. I, 112; Denslagen, *Architectural Restoration in Western Europe*, 233.

37. Kuipers, "Dutch Developments in Documenting Built Heritage," 95; also, Ministry of Education, Culture and Science in the Netherlands, *Cultural Policy in the Netherlands* (The Hague: 2003), 96.

38. "Home," Rijksdienst voor het Cultureel Erfgoed, www.cultureelerfgoed.nl (accessed December 9, 2009).

39. Ministry of Education, Culture and Science in the Netherlands, *Cultural Policy in the Netherlands*, 97.

40. Kuipers, "Dutch Developments in Documenting Built Heritage," 94.

41. The legislation that created this commission and that concerned Luxembourg's heritage was amended in 1930, 1945, and 1968.

42. ICOMOS Luxemburg, "Luxemburg: Larochette, A Disappearing Historic Town," *Heritage@Risk 2002–2003* (Paris: ICOMOS, 2003), www.international.icomos.org/risk/2002/luxemburg2002.htm (accessed December 9, 2009).

43. The listing of a building Dutch law implies obtaining permission, even for interior works that do not affect the exterior; this is unlike Flanders and Wallonia, where listing of only the facades and roofs means no protection at all for the interiors.

44. Dale and Stipe, *Historic Preservation in Other Countries*, 120.

45. "About the Netherlands Institute for Heritage," Erfgoed Nederland, www.erfgoednederland.nl/english (accessed December 14, 2009). The four NGOs that merged to form the Netherlands Institute for Heritage were the National Contact Monuments, Foundation for Netherlands' Archaeology, Association for Documentary Information Supply and Archiving, and the Foundation for Cultural Heritage.

46. "Missions and Objectives," Erfgoed Nederland, www.erfgoednederland.nl/english/organisation/mission-and-objectives (December 14, 2009).

47. Tung, *Preserving the World's Great Cities*, 222–3.

48. Ibid., 212.

49. Ibid., 228. Although the government eventually retracted from its partnership position in developing social housing, Amsterdam remains committed to providing aesthetically pleasing, modern housing for everyone.

50. Ibid.

51. Ibid., 237. Tung further describes the social good resident in sound urban preservation and design: "When contrasted with the armadas of repetitive, mass-produced urban housing built in the decades to come, in communist, capitalist and democratic societies—the social housing experiment in Amsterdam in the early twentieth-century conveyed an enduring message; that people of all classes deserved good design."

52. Nigel Dunn, "Maintaining Europe's Built Cultural Heritage" (paper, From Cataloguing to Planned Preservation, Politecnico di Milano, Milan, Italy, November 23, 2000).

53 Contract signed by Flemish Minister Geert Bourgeois at Sissinghurst, Kent, 22 June 2010.

54. Maison du Patrimoine Médiéval Mosan, Bouvignes-sur-Meuse, Belgium, *2009 Laureates: The European Union Prize for Cultural Heritage/Europa Nostra Awards* (The Hague: Europa Nostra, 2009), 54.

55. "Presentation," Patrimoine Culturel Immobilier / Onroerend Cultureel Erfgoed, www.cultural-heritage.be (accessed December 18, 2010).

56. "Cultural Emergency Response," The Prince Claus Foundation for Culture and Development, www.princeclausfund.org/en/what_we_do/cer/index.shtml (accessed December 9, 2009).

57. "New Netherland Heritage," New Netherlands Heritage Society, www.newnetherland.net/Home.html (accessed December 14, 2009).

58. "Home," Royal Institute for Cultural Heritage.

59. Prudon, *Preservation of Modern Architecture*, 462–72.

60. ICOMOS Luxemburg, "Luxemburg," *Heritage@Risk 2000* (Paris: ICOMOS, 2000), www.international.icomos.org/risk/world_report/2000/luxem_2000.htm (accessed December 9, 2009).

61. ICOMOS Luxemburg, "Luxemburg: Le Ponte Adolphe," *Heritage@Risk: 2006–2007* (Paris: ICOMOS, 2007), 111.

62. Ministry of Public Works, Administration of Bridges and Roads, "Réhabilitation du Ponte Adolphe à Luxembourg," Press Conference, June 28, 2006 (Luxembourg City: Ministry of Public Works, 2006), 7–13.

a

b

c

Figure 7-1 Conservation of the deteriorated sandstone facades of the Basel Munster (a and b) has been a multiyear project conducted by the Institut für Denkmalpflege (Institute of Monument Conservation) of the Swiss Federal Institute for Technology in Zurich. Conservation work has entailed a range of interventions from cleaning and in situ consolidation, as required, to replicating (c) severely deteriorated or missing elements with physically and visually compatible new composite stone. Figure 7-1a courtesy of Basler Denkmalpflege, © 2006 Erik Schmidt. Figures 7-1b and 7-1c courtesy and copyright of Basel Munster construction hut 2009.

CHAPTER 7

Switzerland and Liechtenstein

Over the course of the twentieth century, architectural conservation practices and policies have matured in Switzerland and Liechtenstein, two countries that share many historical and cultural traditions as well as borders in the Alps. In Switzerland, a balance between the central government and the cantons ensures the protection and conservation of historic sites, while in the small principality of Liechtenstein the responsibility for cultural heritage protection has resided with the state.

SWITZERLAND

According to the 1998 Swiss Constitution, the protection of cultural and natural heritage is relegated to the cantonal level; however, the Swiss Federation is also given the authority to support conservation efforts and to acquire properties of national significance, even through appropriation.[1] The Sektion Heimatschutz und Denkmalpflege (Section for Heritage and Preservation of Historic Monuments) of the Swiss Federation's Bundesamt für Kultur (Federal Office for Culture) oversees these activities.[2] In collaboration with the twenty-six cantons, it provides financial assistance for restoration projects and also organizes exhibitions and conferences to raise public awareness of cultural heritage.

Since 1973 the Sektion Heimatschutz und Denkmalpflege has been completing an inventory of important historic sites in Switzerland, known as the Inventar der Schützenswerten Ortsbilder der Schweiz (ISOS). The multidecade inventory—the first effort by the Swiss to make a comprehensive list—is ongoing and today includes approximately 5,800 sites, categorized as of local, regional, or national importance.[3] The list of nationally significant sites was approved by the Federal Council, the chief executive of the Swiss confederation. Inclusion on the ISOS is merely honorary and has no legal implications on property owners, except in cantons that have passed separate legislation outlining specific restrictions, such as Uri and Grisons. Most cantons do, however, use the federally organized ISOS as a regional and urban planning tool.

At the Eidgenössische Technische Hochschule (ETH), the renowned Swiss Federal Institute for Technology in Zurich, the Institut für Denkmalpflege (Institute for Monument Conservation) was established in 1972.[4] The institute maintains a scientific laboratory for testing and researching historic materials and conservation techniques and an extensive research library on science and technology in architectural conservation. Its conservators also provide consulting services for on-site projects. In recent years, they have organized major, multiyear studies and conservation efforts on the Carolingian frescos at the Monastery of St. John in Müstair and the sandstone at the Cathedral of Basel. The fragile facades and Martin tower of this fourteenth-century cathedral are being consolidated and conserved, stone by stone. In addition, the ETH Institute of Monument Conservation has worked extensively on projects outside of Switzerland, including in Egypt, Georgia, Norway, and China.

Pro Helvetia, the Arts Council of Switzerland, was founded by the government in 1939 to promote Swiss cultural identity and to advocate a cultural policy independent from, and opposed to, that of Nazi Germany. Pro Helvetia continued as an important

Figure 7-2 The restoration of the Haus Hauptgasse at Nr. 2, 16 in the 1960s (seen here before and after restoration) is exemplary of long-standing interest in Switzerland in improving historic town architecture in Werdenberg (St. Gallen), one of the country's most famous historic towns. Courtesy Kantonale Denkmalpflege St Gallen/Walter Fietz, photographer.

organization in Swiss cultural life after World War II, and in 1965 its organization and mission were expanded to reflect changing political times and cultural needs. Still funded by the Swiss Parliament, though acting relatively autonomously, Pro Helvetia began offering extensive grants for cultural projects, including heritage conservation, with total awards in recent years exceeding 23 million Swiss Francs ($23 million) annually. In addition to promoting Swiss culture, Pro Helvetia has also played a significant role in advocating cultural exchange among Switzerland's different linguistic communities as well as with foreign countries as many of the projects Pro Helvetia supports are abroad.

A number of NGOs have also been active in Swiss heritage conservation, including the National Organization for the Preservation of Monuments (or NIKE), Patrimoine, Pro Patria, and the Swiss Association for Industrial and Technological History (SGTI). This last organization has launched ISIS, an online "information portal of significant industrial sites in Switzerland," which includes over three hundred sites and is focused on promoting and studying this component of Swiss architectural heritage.

One of the oldest and most important of the NGOs for heritage protection in Switzerland is the Schweizer Heimatschutz (Swiss Heritage Society), which was founded in 1905 to promote architectural conservation and new high-quality design.[5] It provides consulting and advisory services as well as property appraisals, pursues legal action to protect heritage sites, provides financial support for a small number of projects, publishes a quarterly magazine, and administers a prestigious awards program. In celebration of its centennial, in 2005 the Swiss Heritage Society proposed creating a new foundation to purchase and restore historic buildings for use as small hotels.

The first four Swiss cultural sites on UNESCO's World Heritage List, reflecting the country's rich medieval heritage, are the Carolingian convents in Müstair and St. Gall, castles in Bellinzona, and the historic town of Berne. More recent successful nominations promoted by the Swiss government demonstrate a broader spectrum of Swiss history. In the past few years, UNESCO recognized as cultural landscapes vineyard terraces on Lake Geneva, a nineteenth-century railway, and the watchmaking city of Le Locle.[6]

One of the most impressive early architectural conservation projects in Switzerland was the restoration of the Benedictine Convent of St. John in Müstair. Perhaps founded by Charlemagne himself, this complex contains elements from the early ninth century, though most of the construction dates from the eleventh and sixteenth centuries. The complex's remarkable Romanesque wall paintings were discovered in the late nineteenth century after centuries of obstruction by later paintings, and were completely uncovered between 1947 and 1951. In 1969 the Pro Koster St. Johann Foundation was established to coordinate and raise funds for the convent's conservation, and the work has been ongoing ever since.

Conservation interventions in Switzerland since the 1970s reflect the evolution of best practices and theoretical approaches in late twentieth and early twenty-first century. In the early 1990s, the well-known Swiss architect and landscape architect Eduard Neuenschwander completed the successful rescue and renovation of the Rindermarket 7 building in Zurich's Old Town.[7] Other more recent noteworthy architectural conservation projects in Switzerland include the restorations of the baroque Convent of Einsiedeln and the small pilgrimage chapel of Hergiswald. At the latter, the chapel and its unusual, colorful painted ceiling with 324 mid-seventeenth century pictographs of the Virgin Mary, was completely restored between 2003 and 2006 through the support of the Pro Hergiswald and the Albert Koechlin Foundations. Public entities in Switzerland have also been active in architectural conservation abroad, including a partnership between Zurich and Kunming, China, in the 1990s that led to restoration of Shaxi Village in Yunnan Province; the Swiss Department of Culture's work at the Adadi Mariam Church near Addis Ababa, Ethiopia, and the Bantea Srei temple in Angkor, Cambodia; and the Swiss government and experts involvement in decades of urban conservation in Sanaa, Yemen.

LIECHTENSTEIN

Architectural conservation in the principality of Liechtenstein, the small Alpine country nestled between Switzerland and Austria, is overseen by the Denkmalpflege (Cultural Heritage Division) of the Abteilung des Hochbauamts (State Building and Fire Authority).[8] Based in Vaduz, the division is responsible for protecting and maintaining historic artifacts, buildings, and groups of buildings as well as for archaeology throughout the principality. It maintains an inventory of Liechtenstein's most significant cultural assets, which numbers about 175 items, including both cultural heritage sites and archaeological objects.

The Cultural Heritage Division also conducts research and serves as a resource for property owners seeking information about building histories and technical advice on the maintenance and repair of historic buildings. It has been particularly active in promoting the economic benefits of cultural heritage conservation and works with other cultural institutions within the principality. Liechtenstein's Kommission bei Restaurierungsmassnahmen (Historical Preservation Commission) assists the Cultural Heritage Division with the allocation of state funds for conservation projects.

The Cultural Heritage Division and the contemporary cultural heritage conservation framework were established by the Historical Preservation Act of 1977, a law developed in response to the 1975 European Year of Architectural Heritage. However, the tradition of heritage protection in Liechtenstein originated at the beginning of the twentieth century with the founding of the private Historical Society of the Principality in 1901. Established to compile Liechtenstein's history as well as to collect and preserve its cultural heritage, this society was instrumental in instigating the country's first conservation efforts and its earliest archaeological research as well as the establishment of the National Museum.

The Historical Society of the Principality also sponsored the passage of Liechtenstein's first heritage protection legislation in 1944 and successfully encouraged the government to play a more active part in architectural conservation, and heritage protection in general, in the 1960s.[9] The Kulturbeirat (Cultural Advisory Council) a government commission to promote, coordinate, and document cultural activities in Liechtenstein—was established in 1964. The Kulturbeirat also administers grants for cultural projects and oversees Pro Liechtenstein, a public foundation that acquires and maintains properties.

Liechtenstein's largely agricultural past has resulted in a rich heritage of farm houses, dating from the sixteenth century onward, and parish churches and town halls scattered throughout its eleven municipalities. A number of more substantial medieval fortress complexes can also be found in the principality's mountains, including the castle of Vaduz, one of its most important historic structures. Between 1905 and 1912, Prince Johann II undertook an extensive restoration of this castle complex, which dates originally from the twelfth century but is mostly comprised of sixteenth- and seventeenth-century buildings. Since 1938 the castle of Vaduz has served as the permanent residence of the princes.

Another of Liechtenstein's key heritage sites, the ruins of the Schellenberg fortress, was restored in the 1950s by the Historical Society. Examples of more recent successful conservation projects in Liechtenstein include the eleventh-century Gutenberg Castle in Balzers, which was acquired by the state in the 1990s and restored for use for cultural and social events. The Romanesque chapel of St. Mary (Marienkapelle) in Triesen was also meticulously restored in time to serve as the centerpiece of the 2003 European Architectural Days in Liechtenstein.

Because of the country's cultural connections with its neighbors and its small size, consisting of only 160 square kilometers, Liechtenstein has been particularly active among regional and pan-European conservation organizations. Liechtenstein is also proudly aware of the fact that it has few extraordinary sites but, rather, an architectural heritage that reflects the developments of farm communities in Europe over the past few hundred years. The principality recognizes that the economic, technological, and historic value of this heritage is as important to preserve as sites of perhaps greater artistic or architectural value found elsewhere.

Figure 7-3 The Romanesque Marienkapelle in Triesen was carefully restored to serve as the centerpiece of Liechtenstein's celebration of European Architectural Days in 2003. Courtesy Patrik Birrer, Curator of Monuments, Principality of Liechtenstein.

ENDNOTES

1. "Switzerland Constitution," International Constitutional Law, www.oefre.unibe.ch/law/icl/sz00000_.html (accessed December 9, 2009).

2. "Patrimoine culturel et monuments historiques," Office Fédéral de la Culture, www.bak.admin.ch/themen/kulturpflege/00513/index.html?lang=fr (accessed December 9, 2009).

3. "Welcome!" Inventory of Swiss Heritage Sites, www.isos.ch/en/index.asp (accessed December 9, 2009).

4. "Institute," Institute of Historic Building Research and Conservation, Department of Architecture, www.idb.arch.ethz.ch/4-1-institute.html (accessed December 9, 2009).

5. "Swiss Heritage Society," Swiss Heritage Society, www.heimatschutz.ch/index.php?id=904&L= (accessed December 9, 2009).

6. "Five Sites Vie for Heritage Status," SwissInfo, December 10, 2004, www.swissinfo.ch/eng/index/Five_sites_vie_for_heritage_status.html?cid=1288590 (accessed December 9, 2009).

7. Eduard Neuenschwander, *Abbruchprojekt Rindermarkt 7* (Zurich: Baukultur and Benteli-Werdverlag, 2009).

8. "Preservation of Historic Sites," Principality of Liechtenstein, www.liechtenstein.li/en/eliechtenstein_main_sites/ portal_fuerstentum_liechtenstein/fl-kuk-kultur_kunst/fl-kuk-staat/fl-kuk-staat-denkmalpflege.htm (accessed November 30 2009).

9. European Forum for Arts and Heritage and InterArts, "Liechtenstein," in *Report on the State of Cultural Cooperation in Europe* (Brussels: European Union, 2003), 256; http://ec.europa.eu/culture/pdf/doc940_en.pdf (accessed May 31, 2010).

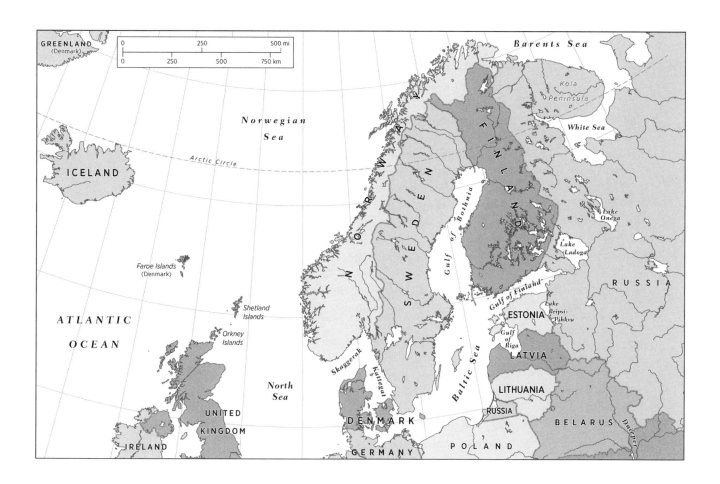

The Nordic and Baltic countries of Northern Europe share many aspects of their geography, climate, heritage, and history. In recent centuries, they were all part of two major multinational powers, the kingdom of Sweden and the Russian empire, only emerging as distinct independent states in the twentieth century.[1]

The countries of Scandinavia, including Sweden, Norway, and Denmark, as well as Finland and the islands of Iceland and Greenland, have closely interrelated histories, beginning with the shared legacy of the Vikings, the Old Norse warriors whose lands in the tenth through thirteenth centuries stretched from Scandinavia to the British Isles and as far west as the arctic shores of North America. In the later Middle Ages, the growth of maritime trade, Lutheranism, and political alliances further linked the peoples of Northern Europe.

These relationships continue into the present, and the overlapping cultural heritage of the Nordic countries means that they are faced with many of the same heritage-protection issues today. Viking long houses, shipwrecks, and historic wooden towns are among the many shared aspects of the region's heritage. Despite the commonalities in history and culture, these countries each have unique traditions and each has taken distinct approaches to caring for their historic sites.

The same can be said for the Baltic states, which like the Nordic countries, have intertwined political and cultural histories, and thus have similar architectural heritage and conservation challenges today. As in Scandinavia, despite these links, Latvia, Lithuania, and Estonia also have unique aspects to their history and have been eager to forge individual identities and have focused on different priorities since independence from the Soviet Union two decades ago.

Former political unions resulted in shared cultural and architectural traditions and have encouraged remarkable regional cooperation on heritage policies and practices in the late twentieth and early twenty-first centuries. Regional integration is evidenced in the Nordic Council and Council of Ministers, which were founded in 1952 and 1971 to coordinate the parliamentary and governmental activities of Denmark, Finland, Iceland, Norway, and Sweden. Since 1999 officials from the three Baltic states have participated in the meetings and working groups of the Nordic Council.

It is through these institutions that these countries have also coordinated their cultural policies. Though the primary goals of the Nordic Council and Council of Ministers have always been to promote regional cooperation and collaboration, in recent years they have also focused significant attention on promoting Nordic culture and establishing partnerships outside Scandinavia and the Baltic states.

A declaration of the Nordic Council Ministers of Culture established the Baltic Sea Heritage Co-operation in 1997 to coordinate regional cultural heritage ideas, research, and efforts.[2] It maintains four working groups that focus on architectural conservation and maintenance, sustainable historic towns, coastal and maritime heritage, and underwater heritage.[3] In addition to harmonizing state policies and practices, it raises awareness of heritage threats and issues and organizes training seminars for craftspeople and workshops on conservation theory and regional identity. A series of workshops held by the Sustainable Historic Towns working group led to an important report in 2003 on regional urban identities, sensitive development in historic centers, and national conservation practices in Northern Europe.[4] In recent years this working group has focused its efforts on investigating and promoting the role of urban heritage in economic development and in establishing guidelines and planning tools to further this goal.

A successful recent project of the Coastal and Maritime Heritage working group was the Baltic Lights poster and internet exhibition focused on regional lighthouses.[5] Today many of these structures, most dating from the seventeenth and eighteenth centuries, are designated landmarks within their countries. However, since their functions have been superseded by fully automated lights and satellite navigation systems, many are threatened by neglect. The Baltic Lights exhibition attempted to promote public awareness of the importance of lighthouses to Northern European regional history and identity and to highlight the importance of actively protecting and using these sites.

In 2003 the Baltic Sea Heritage Co-operation began hosting biannual Cultural Heritage Forums, gathering together distinguished speakers and concerned architectural conservation professionals from the region to give presentations focused on a particular broad theme. The most recent meeting, the Fourth Baltic Sea Region Cultural Heritage Forum, took place in Riga, Latvia, in September 2010, and addressed contemporary conservation challenges in the region under the theme "Cultural Heritage—Contemporary Challenge".

The Nordic Council of Ministers was the primary financier of the Nordic-Baltic Industrial Heritage Platform (IHP), a three-year program through which the countries of the region cooperated in the field of conservation between 2000 and 2003. The IHP was administered by the Finnish National Board of Antiquities, with representatives from each participating country as members of a coordinating group.[6] Aiming to "increase and strengthen knowledge, appreciation and appropriate use of industrial heritage in the Baltic Sea region," the IHP focused on training and networking.[7]

Groundbreaking contributions to the global development of architectural conservation have come from the Nordic countries. The region is the birthplace of the world's first modern law to protect cultural sites and of a now ubiquitous heritage presentation concept: the open-air museum. Respect for built and natural heritage has always been part of the Northern European tradition. Locale-based commitments to architectural conservation and comprehensive national heritage-protection legislation help ensure effective conservation of significant structures and sites in the Nordic countries.

Despite the important and well-coordinated architectural conservation efforts of Northern Europe, the region still faces many heritage threats today. Northern Europe's rapidly modernizing towns and infrastructure have had a repercussive effect on its natural and built heritage; several underground sites in Norway have already been damaged or destroyed due to these changes. Migration from the countryside to urban centers also poses threats to the region's heritage, as many cultural resources located in rural areas are abandoned, potentially allowing many cherished structures and landscapes to succumb to a lack of upkeep and other protections. However, Northern Europe's long-standing and pioneering efforts in architectural conservation ensure that current challenges are being addressed by the region's conservation professionals.

ENDNOTES

1. Norway and Denmark separated from the kingdom of Sweden in 1905, and Finland separated from the Russian empire in 1917. Iceland remained part of Denmark until 1944, and Greenland is still today, though it has had autonomous home rule since 1979. Lithuania, Latvia. and Estonia gained independence from Russia with the dissolution of the Soviet Union in 1991.

2. Countries participating in the Baltic Sea Heritage Co-operation include: Denmark, Estonia, Finland, Germany, Latvia, Lithuania, Norway, Poland, Russia, and Sweden.

3. "Baltic Heritage Co-operation," Baltic Sea States Heritage Co-operation, www.baltic-heritage. net (accessed October 31, 2009).

4. *Baltic Sea Region Co-operation on Sustainable Urban Heritage Management: Activities of the Working Group Sustainable Historic Towns: 2000–2001* (Copenhagen: The Nordic Council of Ministers, 2003); www.nba.fi/tiedostot/c7e2a3b6.pdf (accessed June 12, 2010).

5. "Lighthouses," Baltic Lights—A Guarantee of Safe Passage, www.cmm.pl/balticlights/index. html (accessed October 31, 2009).

6. Countries participating in the Industrial Heritage Platform (IHP) include: Denmark, Estonia, Finland, Latvia, Lithuania, Norway, and Sweden.

7. The IHP also supports conservation of industrial heritage, including a 2002 project involving strength analysis and consolidation of badly corroded reinforced concrete vaults at a 1916–1917 hydroplane hanger in Tallinn, Estonia: "General Information on the Nordic-Baltic Industrial Heritage Platform (IHP) Program 2000–2002," Nordic-Baltic Industrial Heritage Platform, http://msi.lms.lt/ihp/platform/htmlib.html (accessed October 31, 2009)..

Figure 8-1 Monumental remains, such as the burial markers at the cultural landscape of Hornborga in the Swedish province of Västergötland, were among the priorities for protection of King Gustav II Adolph's 1630 proclamation to create a Director General for Antiquities and King Charles XI's 1666 proclamation protecting historic monuments. Today several additional laws and protection agencies have purview over the site, including the Act Concerning Ancient Monuments and Finds, the Historic Building Act, and the Building Statute and Nature Conservancy Act. Photo courtesy of Antikvarisk-topografiska arkivet, Swedish National Heritage Board; photo by Iwar Anderson.

CHAPTER 8

Sweden

Sweden has one of the longest continuous traditions of state protection for cultural heritage, beginning with legislation, a responsible government official, and research institutions in the seventeenth century. These legal and administrative mechanisms have been continuously revisited and strengthened in the centuries since, including repeatedly in the second half of the twentieth century. As a result, Sweden today has one of the most comprehensive cultural heritage protection systems in Europe. In addition to this well-supported state apparatus, in recent decades architectural conservation in Sweden has been promoted and carried out by an increasingly engaged population as well as through the activities of a variety of nongovernmental organizations. Sweden has always been a leader in the field in Northern Europe and has recently become active in important heritage projects abroad.

LEGISLATION AND STATE-ORGANIZED HERITAGE PROTECTION

Sweden's tradition of legal protection for cultural resources is among the oldest in Europe. In 1630 King Gustav II Adolph appointed the first Director General of Antiquities and allocated to the position responsibility for recording and collecting runic inscriptions and ancient stones from the kingdom's numerous prehistoric sites.[1] Information determined from this inventory was later used to compile the first early histories of Sweden.

In 1666, King Charles XI issued another royal decree calling for the protection of ruins and prehistoric sites, including stone circles, monumental tombs, and burial mounds. Further support for heritage protection developed when the College of Antiquities was founded in Uppsala in 1667. For the next twenty-five years its members researched Sweden's ancient cultural heritage and managed and cared for its historic sites.

In these early years, however, it was impossible to halt the destruction of sites: the legislation in place provided little authority for effective site protection, and the small number of historians and researchers at the College meant it was limited in its ability to implement actual conservation measures. Compounding the problem was the lack of a comprehensive list of protected sites. Lists of significant sites were being compiled with the help of local parish ministers; this exercise, however, was not very thorough or systematic.[2] In 1786 responsibility for cultural heritage protection passed to the newly formed Kunglig Vitterhets, Historie och Antikvitets Akademien (Royal Academy of Letters, History, and Antiquities). An academic approach to cultural heritage documentation and protection dominated in Sweden from this point through the first decades of the nineteenth century, when support for strengthening heritage protection measures began to grow. In 1828 the Ordinance of 1666 was revised and the first National Antiquary, J. G. Liljengren, was appointed.[3]

Liljengren was heavily influenced by the German romantic movement's glorification of the Gothic and its promotion of the revival of medieval architectural styles. Such influence translated architecturally into French architect Eugène Emmanuel Viollet-le-Duc's newly developed restoration method of "stylistic unity," as evidenced by the mid-1830s postfire restoration of Stockholm's Riddarholm church spire in Gothic form.[4] Swedish architects—such as Carl Georg Brunius and Helgo Nikolaus Zettervall, who jointly restored Lund's twelfth-century Romanesque Cathedral—also reflect the gathering momentum of Viollet-le-Duc's influence.[5] Zettervall's appointment as director of the kingdom's Office of Antiquities allowed him to extend his preference for stylistic unity throughout the country.[6] He went on to extensively restore the cathedrals in Linköping, Skara, and Uppsala as well as the castle in Kalmar.

Though numerous radical restorations were officially approved and carried out by leading restoration architects throughout the nineteenth century, voices of dissent were also heard. One opponent was poet and nationalist Verner von Heidenstam, whose 1894 treatise criticized modern restoration methods and declared (in the spirit of Ruskin and Morris): "what was not done by barbarians was done by architects!"[7] Heidenstam's work ignited a resistance movement against stylistic unity. Ultimately, the stylistic zeal that had dominated the field for decades across northern Europe was tempered, and more conservative treatments for historic buildings were introduced.

Sweden's law for the protection of antiquities was revised several times in the late nineteenth and early twentieth centuries to expand the responsibilities and regulatory powers of cultural heritage authorities and to establish the Central Office of National Antiquities, which has been the country's primary cultural heritage governing body

Figure 8-2 Architect Helgo Zettervall's restoration of Lund's twelfth-century Romanesque Cathedral in the 1860s and 1870s, including the significant enlargement of its towers and embellishment of its facade, reflects the early influence in Scandinavia of Viollet-le-Duc's "unity of style" approach.

Skansen and the Open-Air Museum Tradition

Skansen Village, perhaps the world's best known open-air museum, was designed, promoted, and opened in 1891 by the eminent Swedish folklorist, ethnographer, and patriotic school teacher Artur Hazelius. It was a radical departure from the typical nineteenth-century European anthropological and ethnographical museums, and it revolutionized the display of historic artifacts, including rural architecture.

As Sweden urbanized and industrialized in the late nineteenth century, Hazelius began collecting artifacts that reflected Sweden's disappearing agrarian way of life, including traditional craft items, costumes, and farm implements.[8] In 1873 he opened a private museum in Stockholm to display these items, which later became the Nordic Museum.

By the 1880s Hazelius had made plans to replace the museum's dioramas, models, and re-creations of farmsteads with a collection of real farm buildings organized as a typical agricultural community. He acquired buildings from throughout Sweden's provinces, moving and rebuilding them on Skansen hill in suburban Stockholm. In this architectural setting, costumed docents demonstrated traditional cultural activities and handicrafts to visitors. Thus, Skansen offered museum officials a unique alternative way to preserve and interpret vernacular architecture in a rapidly modernizing society.

Hazelius was influenced by parallel developments in Norway, where King Oscar II had opened a small collection of wooden buildings near Oslo as a museum in 1881. In the early twentieth century these structures were incorporated into the Norsk Folkemuseum (Norweigian Musuem of Cultural History), which had been opened by Hans Aall in the 1890s. The model developed at the Norsk Folkemuseum and Skansen spread quickly, particularly to elsewhere in Scandinavia and in Eastern Europe, where forty-four similar open-air museums were opened before World War I. By 1980 over five hundred similar museums could be found throughout Europe.[9] Within a century, this early Scandinavian heritage protection and education tool was applied in diverse locations and for different populations around the world—from Colonial Williamsburg in the United States to South Africa's Tsongakraal Museum near Letsitele. These museums have not only allowed the public to see and experience past ways of life in historic settings, but also served as important locations for innovative research on the documentation, maintenance, and restoration of wooden architecture.

since 1886. Under the 1917 reorganization, the National Board of Building and Planning became involved in heritage conservation efforts through the acquisition of the Department of Cultural History. This department partnered with the Central Office to manage historically significant state-owned buildings, to restore churches, and to develop old towns.[10] Under the 1920 Proclamation Concerning Public Buildings, it received the regulatory power necessary to designate state-owned properties and list them in an inventory of significant structures.[11]

Five years later, Sweden's system of heritage protection was streamlined when the Central Office became the sole government authority responsible for the protection of historic sites. It divided oversight between two complementary departments: one for prehistoric sites and the other for historic buildings, churches, castles, and ruins that dated from the medieval period onward.[12] Under its contemporary name, the Riksantikvarieämbetet (National Heritage Board), it continues with the same mission today.

In the early twentieth century, the staff at the Central Office's Stockholm headquarters was assisted in their work by an extensive network of volunteers. County-level operations were run by individual representatives, or regional inspectors, who were experts in related fields (such as archaeology or history) and also directors of county museums. They were responsible for carrying out Central Office mandates in their locality, including the initiation and supervision of investigations and restorations. They also offered expert advice on planning issues that directly affected historic environments or monuments.[13] Interoffice cooperation was an important factor in the conclusion of an updated National Inventory, which was launched at Parliament's request in 1937.

Figure 8-3 Restoration of Gamla Stan (Old Town) in Stockholm in the 1930s represented an early example of conserving an entire district of historic buildings in Northern Europe.

The 1930s also saw the first concerted efforts to preserve Stockholm's medieval center, the Gamla Stan (Old Town). A special-purpose, not-for-profit company organized the restoration and reconstruction of the district's historic buildings, and low-interest loans from the city and national government funded the project.[14] The work entailed the coordinated restoration of the district's primary street facades as well as the secondary facades forming Gamla Stan's deep and narrow side streets.

In 1942 Swedish heritage laws were again strengthened with yet another revision of the Act Concerning Monuments and Finds, which boldly stated that all fixed monuments could not be "altered, displaced, damaged or removed."[15] The Act extended legal protection automatically to all prehistoric sites, ruins of churches, castles, fortifications, old bridges, and sign posts, as well as to all of the ecclesiastical buildings of the Church of Sweden "irrespective of age."[16] This greatly expanded the number of state-owned sites protected and whose conservation was overseen by the Central Office.

The next major revision of the Act occurred in 1960, when amendments allowed, for the first time, the designation of private property as legally protected sites. The Historic Building Act of 1960 also broadened the definition of significant structures to include buildings that exemplify a particular method of construction or an important historical event. Thus sites could be protected and preserved based on historical factors as well as architectural significance or age. Once a privately owned structure was designated as a national monument, the Central Office issued a conservation order describing the requirements for care and maintenance of the building and often its adjacent land, which—since the 1942 Act—could also be protected.[17] Only the director general of the Central Office could order the demolition or alteration of these sites; all approved work would be borne by the owner of the protected site.[18] Owners who felt unduly burdened by these responsibilities, or who believed that the designation overly restricted the use of their property, could request financial compensation for their perceived economic loss.[19]

Although the Act of 1960 allowed for greater protection of individual buildings, it still lacked the power to protect larger historic environments. The conservation of cultural landscapes, streetscapes, and significant urban ensembles continued to challenge

Swedish conservation authorities. This challenge became a crisis in the 1970s, as two decades of urban renewal took an inevitable toll on city centers undamaged by the two world wars, in which Sweden did not participate. Thousands of old buildings were demolished across Sweden as historic urban centers fell under modernization schemes. At the same time, a decline in traditional craft and building trades became apparent as utilization of traditional materials and techniques was increasingly considered dated and anachronistic. This attitude tended to undermine historic building conservation. At the same time, the attempts by restoration architects to use modern techniques and materials to preserve historic structures often led to the destruction of original fabric and chronic building maintenance problems.[20]

Slowly but surely, a counterreaction critical of urban renewal projects and the loss of valuable historic buildings across Sweden gained momentum. An early sign of this response was evident during the restoration of Skokloster Castle in the early 1970s when the chief architect, Ove Hidemark, took the radical position that only traditional materials, tools, and techniques would be used. This directive required a serious analysis of the castle's structure and fabric before work began to identify appropriate materials to be used and to ensure that traditional building practices were successfully replicated. The principles used during the project were published in 1974 and have been an important guide for Sweden's conservation practice ever since.[21]

Increased public interest in architectural heritage in the 1970s encouraged the Swedish government to reform and decentralize its cultural heritage management systems. Beginning in 1976 the Central Office established County Administration regional inspection offices staffed by conservators trained at the University of Gothenburg.[22] The Swedish government also began to actively encourage local governments to consider historic buildings and ensembles in their planning processes, to set aside areas of architectural significance, and to establish principles for conservation.[23] Flexible financing terms were instituted on government loans covering conservation costs of privately owned historic buildings restored under its housing program.[24]

The Planning and Building Act of 1987 and the National Heritage Act of 1988 further increased national and local governmental responsibility for historic buildings and

Figure 8-4 Restoration of Skokloster Castle in the region north of Stockholm using traditional materials in the 1970s marked a turning point in the country's approach to the restoration of significant historic buildings. The techniques used by the chief architect, Ove Hidemark, including employing traditional materials and restoration methods, are considered a best practice in Sweden today.

cultural sites and clarified the powers of these various cultural heritage authorities. Sweden's cultural heritage management system was further decentralized during the 1990s, as the twenty-one county administrations became responsible for the direct funding, designation, and supervision of their local historic sites. In 1993 a National Property Board was established to conserve state-owned heritage properties, which allowed the Central Office, now known as the Riksantikvarieämbetet, to concentrate on coordinating cultural heritage regulation and education. The following year a Commission on Cultural Heritage was established to review the country's architectural heritage protection and to recommend ways to further strengthen it.

The long tradition and growing focus and commitment to heritage conservation in the past two decades has resulted in Sweden's system of cultural heritage protection ranking among the best in Europe today. Though strong, it continues to evolve in important ways—for example, with the Environmental Code of 1999, Areas of National Importance, including cultural landscapes, were extended protection. Sweden now has seventeen hundred protected natural and historic environments.[25] Still, legislation only automatically protects state- or church-owned landscapes and leaves the fate of other designated sites to their owners or to local planning authorities.

NGOs, INTERNATIONAL INVOLVEMENT, AND CURRENT CHALLENGES

Fortunately, heritage values have become deeply ingrained in Sweden due to the government's long-standing concern for the protection of its patrimony, and the public has been increasingly involved in the architectural conservation movement in the past half century. Sweden's institutionalized honor system for private historic properties is successful, in contrast to elsewhere in Europe, where legislation is the primary means for enforcing protection of privately held historic properties. Nevertheless, problems have arisen in some areas, such as in the protection of historic country house estates, farmsteads, parks, and industrial heritage. Development pressures also cause ongoing threats to Sweden's cultural heritage.[26]

When the Council of Europe launched the European Architectural Heritage Year in 1975 to raise awareness and appreciation of Europe's historic and traditional architecture, this campaign had the desired effect in Sweden. It led to greater public interest in the country's architectural heritage and gave further momentum to a nascent private conservation movement. A reflection of this advocacy effort was the creation of the Byggnads vårds Föreningen (Swedish Association for Building Conservation), which garnered the support of architects, cultural heritage officials, and, more importantly, enthusiasts interested in preserving their locality's historic resources.[27]

Sweden is also home to the internationally focused nongovernmental organization, Cultural Heritage without Borders, which was founded in 1995 in response to the destruction of historic sites during the political breakup of Yugoslavia.[28] It remains active in Bosnia and Herzegovina and in Kosovo today by financing specific reconstruction and training projects. In 2002 it also began working in Tibet, and in 2005 it won a EU/Europa Nostra Medal for its dedicated service to the cause of cultural heritage conservation and protection. The Swedish International Development Cooperation Agency is the organization's main donor.

Sweden is also taking the lead in new and expanded areas of heritage conservation, notably the study of underwater cultural heritage and the protection and development of the shared cultural heritage of the Baltic Sea region.[29] Both issues represent opportunities for international cooperation and exchange that will benefit Sweden, Scandinavia, and the broader region as well as provide impetus for further improvement in one of Europe's oldest and most treasured cultural heritage conservation systems.

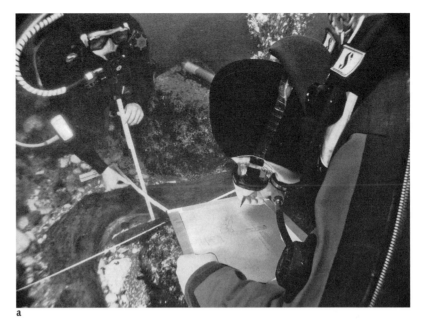

a

Figure 8-5 Sweden currently plays a leadership role in promoting the protection of underwater cultural heritage in the Baltic Sea region, a measure that fosters international cooperation. The interest in conserving maritime heritage is long-standing, going back at least to the study and raising in the 1970s of the *Vasa* warship (a and b), which sank in Stockholm harbor on its maiden voyage in 1628. Its timbers and other woodwork were conserved using the polyethylene glycol method (see also page 173), and the hull of the vessel was put on display in a specially built museum enclosure (c) that facilitates viewing and interpretation.

b

c

Figure 8-6 The restoration of Hans Asplund's Eslöv Civic Hall by Barup Edström Architects won a European Union/Europa Nostra Award in 2006.

A firm whose work epitomizes the increasing private involvement in architectural conservation in Sweden is Barup Edström Architects, based in Lund. Both Mats Edström and Kerstin Barup teach and research at Lund University's Department of Architectural Conservation and Research. In addition, they both consult with foreign universities and the Norwegian government and participate in international conferences. Some of their recent conservation projects demonstrate the range of sites being preserved in Sweden today as well as the high-quality of work being done. For example, in the past few years, Barup Edström Architects has restored the interior of the thirteenth-century Linköping Cathedral and Hans Asplund's 1950s Eslöv Civic Hall. For the Eslöv project they were awarded a EU/Europa Nostra Award in 2006.

Today the work of the Swedish Ministry of Culture's Riksantikvarieämbetet has expanded well beyond the conservation and oversight of protected historic properties. An established Council for Research and Development focuses not only on interdisciplinary investigation to improve conservation techniques but also on disseminating and making this information accessible. The Riksantikvarieämbetet conducts research itself as well as sponsors research at Swedish universities.

a

Figure 8-7 Under the direction of the Statens Fastighetsverk (National Property Board), structural stabilization work at the ruin of the baroque Borgholm Castle (a, b, and c) in 1996 included re-creation of a lime production process similar to the originally used process. The hydraulic lime that was produced enabled modern restorers to correct damage done by earlier restoration work, which used cement mortar. A traditional lime kiln (d and e) was specially constructed and limestone pieces were transformed into powder form. High-quality hydraulic lime was a key constituent in formation of structurally and visually compatible repair mortars used in masonry conservation at the site. Images courtesy of Mark Weber.

b

c

e

d

In the period 2006 to 2010, the Riksantikvarieämbetet focused on three broad research themes: place and tradition, landscapes with history, and modern cultural heritage.[30] The first investigates regional traditions, heritage, place-making, promotion, and tourism; the second researches connections between historic environments and biodiversity, climate change, and mediating conflicts between culture, nature, and business; and the third analyzes modern urban environments, urban changes over time, and twentieth-century building materials.

In addition, the Riksantikvarieämbetet has become increasingly active in the realm of public policy as it relates to its mission and research agenda, acting to encourage programs and government activities that responsibly involve cultural heritage in sustainable development, regional economic growth, and tourism. In combination with the increasing activity of NGOs and activists in Sweden, these broad new research and policy directions of key state institutions suggest the country's heritage will remain carefully protected and conserved in the years ahead.

Endnotes

1. Gösta Selling, "Legal and Administrative Organisation in Sweden for the Protection of Archaeological Sites and Historic Buildings" (The Monument for the Man: Records of the II International Congress of Restoration, Venice, Italy May 25–31, 1964).
2. Ibid.
3. Jokilehto, *A History of Architectural Conservation*. Oxford: Elsevier Butterworth-Heinemann, 2004, p. 252; first published in 1999.
4. Ibid.
5. Brunius' incremental improvements eventually yielded to Zettervall's full-scale restoration and reconstruction of the Cathedral, which proceeded according to the theory of stylistic unity.
6. Ibid. Mälmo's Town Hall and the cathedrals of Kalmar, Uppsala, and Skara were all restored during Zettervall's tenure.
7. Ibid.
8. Eva Nordenson, "In the Beginning…Skansen," *Museum* 175 [XLIV, no. 3] (1992): 149–150.
9. Paul Oliver, "Re-Presenting the Vernacular: The Open-Air Museum," in *Consuming Tradition, Manufacturing Heritage*, ed. Nezar Alsayyad (Milton Park, UK: Routledge, 2001).
10. Selling, "Legal and Administrative Organization in Sweden…"
11. *Protection of the Architectural Heritage of Sweden* (Stockholm: Riksantikvarieämbetet, Central Office of National Antiquities, 1975), 15.
12. Selling, "Legal and Administrative Organization in Sweden."
13. Ibid.
14. Ibid.
15. Ibid.
16. *Protection of the Architectural Heritage of Sweden*, 14.
17. Selling, "Legal and Administrative Organization in Sweden."
18. *Protection of the Architectural Heritage of Sweden*, 14.
19. Ibid., 16.
20. Henrik Larsson, "From Training to Employment: Wooden Skills in Sweden," in *Living Wooden Culture Throughout Europe*, ed. Nuriz Sanz (Strasburg: Council of Europe, 2002), 181.
21. Ibid.
22. Ibid.
23. *Protection of the Architectural Heritage of Sweden*, 17.
24. Ibid., 21.
25. Brigitta Hoberg, "Sweden," *Heritage @ Risk 2001–2002* (Paris: ICOMOS, 2002), www.international.icomos.org/risk/2001/swed2001.htm (accessed December 9, 2009).

26. Ibid.

27. Ibid.

28. "Home," Cultural Heritage Without Borders, www.chwb.org (accessed December 9, 2009).

29. Monitoring Group on Cultural Heritage in the Baltic Sea States, *Cultural Heritage Co-operation in the Baltic Sea States, Report* 3 (Stockholm: Riksantikvarieämbetet, 2003), 12, www.baltic-heritage.net/reports/report3.pdf (accessed July, 6, 2010).

30. "Research and Development," Riksantikvarieämbetet / Swedish National Heritage Board, www.raa.se/cms/en/our_mission/research_and_development.html (accessed November 1, 2009).

CHAPTER 9

Finland

Finland's longstanding tradition of heritage conservation began in 1666, when—as part of the Swedish empire—its ancient monuments and prehistoric sites were placed under government protection by a royal directive. The country's centuries of experience and history of architectural conservation education and training are combined with the ability of Finnish heritage protection officials to think critically about their policies and to mold them into appropriate solutions for specific issues and cases. Due to the nature of its historic built environment, special foci on wooden and modern heritage have emerged in Finland.

EARLY LEGISLATION AND CONSERVATION EFFORTS

Twenty Finnish sites were included in the first inventory of the kingdom of Sweden in the seventeenth century. In the mid-eighteenth century, Swedish legislation reinforced the importance of Finnish antiquities in the kingdom's cultural heritage, but it would take 150 years before a national oversight organization was created.

Swedish legal traditions continued throughout Finland's period of Russian rule, which began in 1809. In the autonomous Grand Duchy capital of Helsinki, romanticism developed in tandem with an enormous campaign of building in the neoclassical style, and several medieval churches were renovated to meet new liturgical requirements. By the mid-nineteenth century, Finnish nationalism, inspired by Germany's national movement, encouraged the identification and protection of sites and monuments of national importance. In particular, Finns became increasingly concerned about deteriorated medieval castles and stone churches. National pride also helped establish the Finnish Antiquarian Society in 1870, which in turn greatly influenced the future development of Finnish heritage legislation and administration.

Government action to identify, protect, and conserve cultural heritage began in the Grand Duchy of Finland with the Decree on the Protection of Ancient Monuments in 1883. This law, which is the basis for today's conservation policies and practices, protected the remains of ancient forts, churches, public buildings, inscriptions, wall paintings, and decorations and also emphasized the use of original technology and materials in conservation practice. The Archaeological Bureau, the antecedent of the institutions still responsible for Finnish heritage today was founded a year later to administer conservation policies.

CONTEMPORARY HERITAGE FRAMEWORK AND STATE ACTIVITIES

Passage of the comprehensive Antiquities Act of 1963 did much to shape contemporary conservation efforts in Finland, though it only extended to archaeological sites. The Act created an effective means for identifying and protecting these sites, all with a minimum of administrative activity. As a result, ancient sites are protected immediately upon discovery, as in Sweden, without cumbersome and time-consuming paperwork. There is also no age restriction for protected antiquities—the Finnish definition of such antiquities is far from typical, as it includes even "sacrificial springs, trees or stones and other worship sites and ancient places."[1] The Act also covers the conservation and protection of ancient monuments, ships and other vessels, and movable objects.

To supplement the 1963 Act which protected government-owned archaeological sites, the long-awaited Historic Buildings Act was passed by the Finnish Parliament the following year. This 1964 Act extended protection to privately held properties throughout the country; however, even with the grants to property owners made available two years later, the Historic Building Act has proven less effective than mechanisms for protecting historic sites owned by the government or by dedicated conservation organizations in Finland. At the time in the 1960s, only seven sites were protected as a result of this legislation.[2]

A dynamic legislative approach keeps Finland very current on heritage protection: a new land-use law was passed in 2000 to ensure that the conservation of nature, biodiversity, and the environment is compatible with international agreements concerning cultural and natural heritage. While thousands of wooden structures have been protected and restored through town planning, the law calls for more direct efforts at combining conservation and planning initiatives. In the last quarter of the twentieth century, the Finnish government also mandated creation of a state inventory, protection of historic buildings beyond planned development zones, protection of movable prehistoric artifacts, and protection of all ecclesiastical buildings built prior to 1917. The evolving needs for protection of cultural heritage resources remains a national priority in Finland.

Figure 9-1 The small island and municipality of Hailuoto in west-central Finland is an example of a protected and conserved rural townscape in Finland. Vernacular buildings with modest but distinctive detailing, such as this two-storey residence, define the area's architectural character. High standards of maintenance are essential for the wooden buildings comprising sites such as Hailuoto.

Figure 9-2 The late-eighteenth-century Petäjävesi wooden church in the Finnish lake district, a World Heritage Site since 1994, is a well-preserved example of Lutheran log architecture in Scandinavia. Restoration and conservation of the church has been ongoing since the 1920s and has influenced conservation practice in Finland.

In 1972, the nineteenth-century Archaeological Bureau was reorganized into the Museovirasto (National Board of Antiquities), overseen by a Director-General and an Advisory Council, and it remains today the primary agency responsible for the conservation of material culture and environment within three categories: archaeological sites, built heritage, and museums.[3] The Museovirasto identifies and develops conservation plans, guides projects, and disseminates knowledge to the general public. It receives specific financial allocations from the Finnish government for museums, restoration projects, and conservation efforts.

The Museovirasto's centralized oversight of Finland's 150 museums ensures a coordinated flow of information among institutions, which operate under the concept that an educated populace best facilitates the advance of conservation goals. The Museovirasto also protects the country's rapidly growing roster of ancient sites, which are still being discovered at modern construction sites in industrialized regions. Local teams under the direction of a Museovirasto curator excavate, monitor, and manage archaeological areas.

In part because of construction predominately in wood, a fragile material, few Finnish medieval structures survived to the twentieth century, and in fact, less than 150,000 structures built prior to 1921 still stand in Finland.[4] Therefore significant attention is paid to the rare surviving older sites, such as the fifteenth-century Olavinlinna Castle, which was restored in the 1960s and 1970s, and the fourteenth-century Häme Castle, on which decades of work was completed in the late 1980s. The Old Town of Rauma, added to the World Heritage List in 1991, is one of the best preserved wooden towns in Northern Europe, though most of its medieval heritage was rebuilt in the eighteenth century after a series of fires.

Another significant wooden site in Finland is the eighteenth-century Old Church in Petäjävesi, which combined Romanesque and Gothic styles to exemplify how Finnish builders skillfully adapted European ecclesiastical architecture to the vernacular log jointing technique. In the 1920s, the church's interior and furnishings were restored, and in the 1950s its roof was replaced. Despite years of neglect in the late nineteenth century, good maintenance throughout the twentieth century has spared Petäjävesi

Church the need for a major exterior restoration. Today it stands as a remarkably intact and authentic example of late log-church architecture in Finland, and it has also been designated a World Heritage Site.

Fire remains one of the most significant threats to Finland's wooden heritage, as was evidenced in 1997 when the medieval St. Olof Church of Tyrvää in Vammala was burnt by arsonists. The original trusses and wood-shingle roof and the eighteenth-century interior tempera paintings were all lost, leaving only the stone walls remaining. The parish decided to reconstruct the lost elements, and volunteer carpenters and painters used traditional methods to recreate the vaulted wooden ceiling and interior paintings. Funds for the project were raised from throughout Finland, and the reconstruction was completed in September 2009.

Earlier that same year, the restoration of the wooden bell tower of Kesälahti Church in eastern Finland was completed. The early nineteenth-century tower was all that remained of the church after bombing during World War II, and it is the oldest surviving example in Finland of such wooden construction in its original state. The tower's restoration won a EU/Europa Nostra Grand Prize for conservation for the "strict methodology" and "skillful craftsmanship" employed in the installation of handmade replacement shingles in the historic patterns that had been carefully documented before damaged pieces were removed.[5]

CONSERVING MODERN HERITAGE IN FINLAND

The vast majority of Finnish built heritage is young in comparison with the rest of Europe, with much of its urban construction occurring after World War II. As a result, Finland's government is well underway in addressing the conservation needs of its aging interwar and postwar heritage, in addition to its surviving pre-twentieth century sites. Pioneers of modernism in the early twentieth century, the Finns have also been leaders in the conservation of this heritage in the late twentieth century.

Finland's heritage regulations have no age requirement, so modern-era sites, including power plants, churches, museums, conservatories, and housing projects, are all eligible for protection. In particular, many works by the avant-garde architect Alvar Aalto have been recognized for their importance to architectural history. Particularly admired are Aalto's clean-lined, organic designs that helped develop the International Style in the 1920s and 1930s. Because his work illustrates Finland's historical, technical, and economic development and because it represents a peak in international recognition of Finnish design, retention of Aalto's structures has been a priority for Finnish conservators in the past half century.[6] The Alvar Aalto Foundation, established in 1968, ensures that his structures are properly maintained and preserved, and it is involved in conservation efforts when additions and alterations threaten their technological integrity. The Foundation also cares for Aalto's architectural drawings and writings and has instituted an academy to promote education and serve as an international discussion forum in environmental culture and contemporary architecture.[7]

A major battle ensued around the conservation of the 1960s marble facade of Aalto's Finlandia Hall. The Carrara marble, which was the building's primary original facade material, had deteriorated in Helsinki's harsh environment, and after only thirty years

▶**Figure 9-3** The restoration of Alvar Aalto's Viipuri Library in the Russian city of Vyborg on the Karelian Isthmus is being accomplished via an international partnership that began in the early 1990s and is slated for completion in 2012. Prior to the start of conservation work in the 1990s, this treasure of modern architecture was significantly deteriorated (a). Projects completed between 2002 and 2010 at the Viipuri Library included restoration of the roof and skylights (b), the reading room (c), and the lecture hall's undulating ceiling (d). Courtesy of The Finnish Committee for the Restoration of Viipuri Library.

a

b

c

d

the structure required recladding. Aalto devotees lobbied for new Carrara marble to maintain the concept and original look of the buildings, while others claimed that more durable replacement granite of a similar color was preferable. After considerable debate, a public vote chose the more expensive, but more authentic, option: Carrara marble. The recladding was completed in 1999. The populace's overwhelming desire to retain the physical ideas behind the structure pays homage to Aalto's architectural designs and is tangible evidence of the national importance of that heritage in Finland.

Finnish heritage conservationists have also focused on the conservation of Aalto's works abroad, including the 1930s Viipuri Library in Vyborg, Russia, which exemplifies his concepts: the free plan, undulating surfaces, sectional space, and innovative use of light, wood, and plantings in design. The building's Karelian Isthmus location was lost to the Soviet Union during World War II, and consequently the structure suffered from war damage and neglect. The Soviet authorities renovated the building as a library; however, the attempt to correct water drainage problems and deteriorating concrete and to install different air-conditioning technologies resulted in new problems for the Viipuri Library

Beginning in 1992, a concerted international effort between the Finnish Committee for the Restoration of Viipuri Library and the St. Petersburg Committee for the Preservation of Historical and Cultural Monuments (KGIOP) has restored the library building on a phased basis, with financial help from overseas donors.[8] As funds are raised the Viipuri Library is restored room by room: in 2003 the skylights and roof of the reading hall were repaired, in 2006 the periodicals room and entrance to the children's hall were completed, and in 2009 the undulating wood paneled ceiling of the lecture hall was restored.[9] In 2010 the Finnish Committee for the Restoration of Viipuri Library published a well-illustrated study of this ongoing project titled *Alvar Aalto Library in Vyborg—Saving a Modern Masterpiece.*[10]

Not all Finnish modern architectural heritage has enjoyed the same level of protection and success, however. The Helsinki-Malmi Airport, which was developed in the early days of commercial aviation and served an important role in the Helsinki 1952 Olympics, was placed on the World Monuments Fund's 2004 and 2006 Watch list of endangered sites. Threatened by proposed demolition to provide space for housing and urban development, a campaign was launched by the Friends of Malmi Airport Society to preserve the site due to its cultural significance. A compromise solution was reached; the airport would be converted into an office building and the former airfield and runways transformed into a residential and commercial development. An environmental impact study of the proposed airport facility retention plan commenced in 2009 and its outcome may spell more uncertainty for the future of the Helsinki-Malmi Airport.

From modern architecture to stone castles, historic wooden churches, and Bronze Age burial cairns, Finland's broad and extensive cultural heritage has been protected and conserved for centuries by a flexible and dynamic system. Finland's traditional openness to outside influences and ideas for heritage protection has allowed its conservation approaches to benefit from lessons learned from the experiences of other countries, and these countries have also benefited from Finnish experience and input.

ENDNOTES

1. "The Antiquities Act." National Board of Antiquities, www.nba.fi/en/antiquitiesact (accessed December 9, 2009).
2. Maija Kairamo, "Developments in Restoration and Building Conservation in Finland since the Second World War," *Monuments and Sites: Finland* (Paris: ICOMOS, 1996).
3. "The Organization of the National Board of Antiquitie." National Board of Antiquities, www.nba.fi/en/organization (accessed December 9, 2009).

4. K. Niskala, "The Built Cultural Milieu in Finland," in Drdácký, *European Research on Cultural Heritage: State-of-the-Art Studies*, 57. Originally: "Social and Economic Integration of Cultural Heritage in Europe" (paper, 1st Ariadne Workshop, Prague, Czech Republic, April 23–29, 2001); and "Finnish Built Heritage," National Board of Antiquities, www.nba.fi/en/finnishbuiltheritage (accessed July 7, 2010).

5. "The Kesälahti Church Bell Tower, Kesälahti (Finland." *2009 Laureates: The European Union Prize for Cultural Heritage / Europa Nostra Awards* (The Hague: Europa Nostra, 2009), 8.

6. Maija Kairamo and Hanni Sippo, "Repairing Alvar Aalto's Buildings." *Arkkitehti* 5 (2001), 24–25.

7. "Alvar Aalto Foundation." Alvar Aalto, www.alvaraalto.fi/foundation/ (accessed December 9, 2009).

8. The Getty Grant Program, Finnish Restoration Committee, Finnish Ministry of Environments, Leningrad Region (Oblast), Vyborg City Administration, Russian Federation, and World Monuments Fund have all contributed funds to various restoration efforts.

9. "Works Completed." Viipuri Library, www.alvaraalto.fi/viipuri/completed.htm (accessed November 1, 2009).

10. Markku Karjalainen, *Alvar Aalto Library in Vyborg: Saving a Modern Masterpiece* (Helsinki: Rakennustieto Publishing, 2010).

CHAPTER 10

Norway

Architectural heritage conservation efforts in Norway began in an influential way in the mid-nineteenth-century, while it was still part of the kingdom of Sweden. Among the first names in Norwegian conservation is that of Johan Christian Dahl, an internationally trained artist from Bergen whose rural painting expeditions introduced him to the country's numerous deteriorating wooden stave churches. Dahl became so enthralled by their beauty that he produced the first publication on this uniquely Norwegian building type.[1] Fearing this would not be enough to ensure their future, he established Norway's first conservation organization in 1841, the Society for the Preservation of Norwegian Ancient Monuments. Dahl's efforts in raising architectural awareness led to the reconstruction of a traditional Norwegian farm building on a royal estate near Oslo in 1882 that was opened to the public as a museum.[2]

The nineteenth century also witnessed the stylistic restoration of Trondheim's Nidaros Cathedral, which was begun in 1869 by architect Heinrich Ernst Schirmer. The Chapter House of the cathedral was fully restored, but the cathedral remained incomplete until the twentieth century, by which time Schirmer's design had been altered by other architects. Over the course of the twentieth century, Norway has established government institutions and passed a series of legislative measures to protect its architectural heritage. Norway has been very active in international partnerships and funding for conservation abroad, and alongside Finland, has emerged as a global leader in the conservation of wooden architecture.

LEGISLATION AND STATE CONSERVATION INSTITUTIONS

Norway's independence from Sweden in 1905 sparked a revival of appreciation for, and interest in, specifically Norwegian history and culture. While initially only scholars and enthusiasts had studied historic sites, eventually ancient monuments became popularly valued for their ties to Norway's cultural roots and burgeoning national identity. Norway's new government acted quickly to protect its cultural heritage by passing its first legislation concerning archaeological sites of national significance, such as its Viking settlements.[3] In 1912 a state Riksantikvaren (Directorate for Cultural Heritage) was established and made responsible for the protection of historic buildings, though legislation directly pertaining to these sites was not passed until 1920. The 1920 law was reinforced by a series of later laws, including the 1951 Act, which protected ancient and medieval archaeological sites; the 1965 Town Planning Act, which provided limited protection for historic urban areas; and the 1970 Nature Conservation Act, which protected landscapes of cultural as well as natural value.[4]

In 1972 the Riksantikvaren became a division of the new Ministry of the Environment, and throughout the 1970s the management and protection of cultural heritage became a priority in Norway. This position was tangibly proven by Norway's 1977 ratification of the World Heritage Convention and successful nomination of four World Heritage Sites: Bergen's medieval Bryggen wharf, the mining town of Røros, Alta's prehistoric rock carvings, and Urnes' Stave Church. In addition, a new Cultural Heritage Act was passed in 1978, extending automatic protection to any wooden structure built prior to 1650 and all sites and structures predating 1537 (the end of Norway's medieval period, when Protestantism and Danish control came to the country); however, more recent sites require a protection order from the Riksantikvaren. To date, 5,700 of the over 300,000 registered buildings built before 1900 have been afforded legal protection in Norway, and the Riksantikvaren estimates that 1 percent of the unprotected buildings are lost each year.[5]

Amendments to the Cultural Heritage Act made in 1992 and in 2000 protect sites relating to Norway's indigenous minority, the Sami people, and also structures built before 1946 on Svalbard archipelago, surrounded by the Arctic Ocean and the Barents, Greenland, and Norwegian seas. The 1992 amendment also added protection for "cultural environments," that is, for cases where an additional layer of cultural significance has been created by grouping several buildings together.[6] Such sites were only nominally protected before, but Norway now has four official cultural environments: Havrå Farm (Hordaland); Utstein Monastery (Rogaland); Neiden, an East-Sami Settlement in Finnmark; and the Kongsberg Silver Mines.

Today, the Riksantikvaren is mainly responsible for policy and administration; everyday operations are carried out through a closely coordinated system of decentralized agencies. These several ancillary agencies include a network of eighteen county service offices that advise upon, and implement, heritage policy at the regional level. These service offices ensure that heritage sites are considered in county planning and issue protection orders for sites threatened with demolition.

The cultural heritage of the indigenous and autonomous Sami peoples is looked after by the Council for Sami Cultural Heritage, which operates much like a county service office on Sami lands. The conservation of historic buildings and sites in arctic Svalbard is administered directly by the governor's office. Five archaeological museums oversee the excavation and investigation of archaeological sites throughout Norway, and regional maritime museums monitor and investigate heritage in the North Atlantic Ocean, including shipwrecks and underwater archaeological sites.

In 1994 the Norsk Institutt for Kulturminneforskning (NIKU, Norwegian Institute for Cultural Heritage Research), which is partially funded by the Riksantikvaren, was created to assist these agencies in proper documentation and the study of specific sites.[7] NIKU is well regarded for its technical laboratories, photographic and documentation services, as well as geographic information system (GIS) and archaeological excavation expertise. NIKU also maintains up to date registers of its historic buildings and archaeological sites, all of which are protected under the Cultural Heritage Act.[8]

CURRENT CHALLENGES AND SUCCESSES

There are a number of urban conservation successes in Norway, including the restoration and protection of medieval Stavanger, nineteenth-century Haugesund, the seaport district of Bergen, and various historic areas. A common problem with successful conservation areas such as these is their interface with adjacent modern commercial districts and new developments. For instance, there is current concern among architectural conservationists in Bergen about the compatibility of the design and density changes posed by new housing in the immediate proximity of Bergen's historic harbor area, a World Heritage Site.

▲ **Figure 10-1** Conservation in the 1970s and 1980s of Stavanger, Norway, Scandinavia's largest historic wooden town, entailed restoration of building facades lining the town's irregularly shaped streets. At the edges of the historic district, which dates from the eighth and ninth centuries, are modern commercial facilities.

▶ **Figure 10-2** According to local architectural conservationists, increasing numbers of floods each winter in Bergen, Norway, can be attributed to rising sea levels due to global warming. The floods and resultant dampness create significant challenges for the wooden architecture of this and other historic coastal cities.

Local architectural conservationists have also noted an apparent effect of global climate change on the heritage of these coastal cities. For example, in recent years at Bryggen (wharf) in Bergen, rising sea levels have caused increasingly frequent floods during winter storms—especially when combined with high tides.[9] Bergen floods fifteen to twenty times each winter. Not only do the storms cause damage in the historic city, but the constant wetness of the timber structures makes them more susceptible to rot and fungal growth.[10]

Other urban centers in Norway have participated in pilot projects for investigating new methods of analysis and documentation and planning for simultaneous conservation and change due to development pressures. In the town of Røros and Mosjøen, a team comprised of local architects and researchers from the Riksantikvaren, NIKU, the State Housing Bank, and other institutes developed an analytical approach known as DIVE, for Describe, Interpret, Valuate, and Enable.[11] The project led to a two-phased master plan for the Øra district of Røros in 2004 and 2005, and in subsequent years the DIVE approach was expanded to projects in other cities under the supervision of the Riksantikvaren.

In 2006 the Riksantikvaren also launched its Creating New Assets in the Cultural Heritage Sphere program to promote the use of historic sites and landscapes in the social, cultural, and economic development of local communities.[12] The first phase of the program, scheduled for completion in 2010, has focused efforts on ten pilot projects selected from over seventy applications from local agencies and villages throughout Norway. For example, in one of those pilot projects, the Riksantikvaren and Nordland County have started a campaign for community building through the cooperative conservation of coastal heritage.

Several NGOs and quasi-governmental organizations also play active roles in Norwegian architectural conservation. For example, the Society for the Preservation of Norwegian Ancient Monuments participates in conservation advocacy and serves as custodian of several important sites. Among its collection are eight stave churches and the eclectic home of Ole (Bornemann) Bull, Norway's most famous violin virtuoso.

The stave church at Urnes is an example of the unique building typology that peaked Dahl's interest in the nineteenth century and has continued to impress visitors ever since. These stave churches are among Norway's most important contributions to the history of architecture and a fundamental component of its cultural heritage. They are named for their construction technique. Stave walls consist of a series of vertical planks with their bases set into a groove in the floor sill beam and their tops fitted into a wall plate. Solid posts at each corner hold the sill and plate together to create the church's basic structure. This method of construction evolved from Viking longhouse and longship construction. The lavish carved decorations of the stave churches fuse Christian and Viking traditions, with Nordic symbols and motifs mixed with dragons and gargoyles. Many different types of stave churches were built between 1100 and 1300, but the most common had simple plans consisting of only a nave and a narrow chancel. The more complex examples mimic Viking longhouses, with long rectangular forms, soaring spires, and tiered roofs.

Though as many as two thousand stave churches may have originally been built, only twenty-eight have survived to the present due to the harsh Northern climate and to Reformation iconoclasm. In the twentieth century, some were moved from remote locations to open air museums to ensure their protection; however, many of these now receive tens of thousands of visitors annually, resulting in significant deterioration from overuse. Others suffer from a lack of routine maintenance, and all of the remaining stave churches are also continuously threatened by natural decay from the severe northern climate.[13] Norway has taken significant steps to protect and conserve these stave churches over the past two centuries, and their uniqueness was internationally recognized in 1979 when the stave church in Urnes was inscribed on UNESCO's World Heritage List.

Even today, fire remains the greatest danger for Norway's predominately wooden medieval heritage, although Norway's fire abatement technology is second to none. Protecting historic farm buildings and ensembles is challenging, as traditional rural environments and cultures have been transformed by modernity and rural depopulation. Mechanized forestry industries and services threaten unrecorded archaeological sites as formerly virgin territories are now more easily exploitable.

Figure 10-3 The stave churches of Norway are among the country's most distinctive cultural features. The rate of deterioration of these structures versus masonry structures makes them special conservation challenges, especially with regard to fire and biodeterioration. Attention has been focused on these two challenges in recent years. As a result, the installation of preventive methods such as improved fire detection and suppression systems has helped to increase the survival rates of these distinctive structures. Shown here is the early twelfth-century stave church in Urnes, whose restoration was completed in 2009.

In March 2002 the Norwegian government, in cooperation with UNESCO, established the Nordic World Heritage Foundation to serve as a focal point for Scandinavian efforts to implement the World Heritage Convention.[14] The Foundation supports regional activities toward this end and ensures the distribution of information from the World Heritage Center. It has also been active in mobilizing funds for assisting conservation efforts in developing countries, such as working on a multiyear project to promote cultural tourism and retain local Buddhist traditions in ten countries of Southeast and South Asia in collaboration with UNESCO's Bangkok, Thailand office. In 2003 the Foundation began to work with Kyrgyz authorities on UNESCO's behalf to nominate Kyrgyzstan's first World Heritage Site, the Sulaiman–Too Sacred Mountain, a project partially underwritten by the Norwegian government and successfully achieved in 2009. Nearly one-quarter of the projects supported through the EEA (European Economic Area) Norway Grants program, a joint project of the governments of Norway, Liechtenstein, and Iceland, have gone to support conservation projects, education, and capacity building through Europe.[15] Nearly 75 percent of the 250 million Euros spent has been directly to architectural and urban conservation and restoration.[16] Poland and the Baltic states have been major recipients of this funding, which has been used to restore manor houses in Estonia and Lithuania, cellars in Warsaw's Old Town, and wood heritage in Latvia.

Scandinavian history and culture have always been strongly linked with the region's natural environment and resources. Wood as a building material has largely defined the region's built fabric; it was not until the mid-twentieth century that other materials surpassed it in use. Considering that nearly 60 percent of Scandinavia is still covered in forests, the predominance of wood construction is understandable. However, wood deteriorates rapidly, is easily altered, and is highly susceptible to insect and fire damage. On the other hand, the possibility of dismantling, moving, and re-erecting wooden structures in part explains why it was this region that saw the invention and rapid spread of open air museums as a revolutionary way to conserve exemplary pieces of vernacular architecture.[17] (See "Skansen and the Open-Air Museum Tradition," page 149.)

Although reliance on the fragile material has affected the ability of many of Scandinavia's significant structures to withstand the test of time, many other wooden buildings still exist today thanks to innovative efforts by the region's conservators to maintain this essential component of their heritage. In particular, Norway and Finland have pioneered wood conservation and preventive maintenance techniques, both for individual historic structures and for historic wooden towns.

State-of-the-art fire protection systems that can withstand the difficult climate conditions were developed and installed in each Norwegian stave church. In 2001 the Norwegian government started a program to restore all twenty-eight remaining churches, regardless of ownership, to ensure their continued protection and that trained craftspeople familiar with the techniques and materials of these medieval wooden buildings completed the work.[18] It is expected that all of Norway's stave churches will have been rehabilitated by 2015.

Taking care of Norway's vast wooden architectural heritage has made Norway a leader in wood conservation. Throughout many of the country's historic towns, fire protection systems have been installed based on developments at stave churches as well as on new innovations, including early detection devices, sprinklers, frost-proof fire hoses, and fire engines designed to navi-

gate medieval streets.[19] Since the 1960s, four towns have been fitted with these systems, including the Bryggen district in Bergen as well as Røros, Risør, and Tvedestrand, and plans are underway to install similar systems in additional historic wooden towns.

Historic wooden towns are also one of the most distinctive architectural features of Finland; however, these Finnish towns have been threatened by dwindling rural populations and a lack of economic viability. Nevertheless, more than ten small wooden towns and numerous wooden historic districts in bigger cities have been preserved in Finland, including the country's oldest city and major thirteenth-century regional trade center, Turku. Although extensively rebuilt on its original foundations, Turku is today one of only a handful of locations that exemplifies pre-nineteenth-century Finnish building techniques and that underwent major rehabilitation in the 1970s and 1980s.[20]

Old Rauma in western Finland, the largest, best-preserved wooden town in Scandinavia, has over six hundred unique shops and houses scattered throughout a medieval street pattern. Though most of these structures date from the nineteenth century, their facades, plans, and building technology reflect centuries-old vernacular tradition. Modern urban development has ringed the town's medieval core and adaptive reuse schemes have developed buildings within the historic center, but concerned building owners and local preservation laws have minimized the potential negative impact on Rauma's historic center.[21] Since 1981 the town plan has included provisions to protect these wooden houses, and since 1991 Old Rauma has been included on UNESCO's World Heritage List.

Conservation of the late-seventeenth-century wooden log church of Sodankylä in the Finnish Lapland contributed significantly to the international debate about authenticity and reconstruction of impermanent materials. In the course of the church's history, numerous alterations had been made, including the addition of an external paneling and wood shingle roof system in the eighteenth century. Various restoration projects undertaken during the twentieth century left the structure's interior detailing intact, but the exterior was rebuilt using long-abandoned traditional medieval techniques, which had been revived for the project. The Sodankylä Church restoration is an important contemporary interpretation of the Venice Charter's principles, which address revived building traditions within the scope of modern conservation efforts.

Sweden has led efforts in the conservation of underwater wooden heritage. The *Vasa*, discovered in Stockholm harbor in 1956, is the most intact seventeenth-century warship in the world today and the largest historic object ever conserved (see Figure 8-5). It was saved in the decade following its discovery thanks to cutting-edge analysis, reclamation, and conservation technology, and it is now the central exhibit in Sweden's most visited museum: the Vasa Museum opened in 1990 to house the battle galleon and over four thousand artifacts retrieved from it.[22] Evidence of new chemical deposits on the *Vasa's* surface due to centuries of submergence as well as iron used during its restoration were recently discovered and have led to the use of even more advanced, twenty-first century conservation techniques. Beginning in 2005, Swedish conservationists have worked to remove sulfur and iron deposits and to neutralize the breakdown of the wood itself. The search for an effective and permanent solution continues today.

The important wood conservation efforts taking place in Scandinavia have been recognized and appreciated outside of the region. For example, in 2004 the European Union and Europa Nostra awarded Dedicated Service medals to two Norwegian conservators, Arne Berg and Håkon Christie, for their research and work on medieval wooden architecture. As curator of the Norsk Folkemuseum, Berg had relocated and conserved hundreds of rural wood buildings, and Christie had worked for more than sixty years on stave churches.

In addition, the countries of Scandinavia have actively sought to share their extensive knowledge and experience in wood conservation with the world. Since 1984, the Norwegian Riksantikvaren and numerous Norwegian universities and research institutes have hosted a biannual six-week ICCROM course on wood conservation in which experts teach state-of-the-art wood diagnostic and treatment techniques to conservators from around the world. Finland and Sweden have taken the lead in the wooden culture theme as part of the Council of Europe's "Europe—A Common Heritage" program. Both countries hosted international training workshops on premodern wooden construction in 2002. In addition, Norwegian institutions have proposed the conservation of wooden structures and fire protection for historic buildings as two areas in which they could collaborate with organizations and agencies in other European countries in the field of cultural heritage protection.

The government of Norway demonstrated its prioritization of and commitment to architectural and related conservation by designating 2009 as the official Year of Cultural Heritage. This was done "hoping to encourage close, quality cooperation between voluntary, public and private organizations to highlight the diversity of Norway's cultural heritage and to place focus on the fact that working with cultural conservation and promotion is an asset in itself."[23] Focused around the theme of cultural heritage in everyday life, the year of activities included an online encyclopedia, tours, and school projects as well as sought to involve local, regional, and international partners.

Over the past century, cultural heritage management in Norway has become a dynamic local and regional force. Norwegian experts have explored new boundaries of conservation, such as underwater heritage, rock art, and industrial heritage, and they work closely with other countries that share not only a common heritage but also common problems and concerns. Norway's cultural heritage authorities can be proud of the progress and achievements made during the past century and a half, and they continue to seek improved means of cultural heritage protection today.

ENDNOTES

1. Jokilehto, *A History of Architectural Conservation.* Oxford: Elsevier Butterworth-Heinemann, 2004, p. 252; first published in 1999.

2. Ibid.

3. ICOMOS Norway, "Norway," *Heritage@Risk 2002–2003* (Paris: International Council on Monuments and Sites [ICOMOS], 2004), www.international.icomos.org/risk/2002/norway2002.htm (accessed December 9, 2009).

4. Dennis Rodwell, "Conservation Legislation," in *Architectural Conservation*, ed. Sherban Cantacuzino (New York: Billboard Publications, 1975), 137.

5. "Architectural Heritage," State of Environment Norway, www.environment.no/Topics/Cultural-heritage/Architectural-heritage1/ (accessed December 18, 2009).

6. "Cultural Environments," State of Environment in Norway, www.environment.no/Topics/Cultural-heritage/Cultural-environments/ (accessed December 19, 2009). The individual structures that form significant architectural ensembles are often not in isolated buildings that would justify individual designation.

7. "Championing Cultural Heritage," Norsk Institutt for Kulturminneforskning (NIKU), www.niku.no (accessed December 19, 2009).

8. Thomas Hanell, Christer Bengs, Hólmfríður Bjarnadóttir, Holger Platz, and Klaus Spiekermann, "Appendix 1: Administration of Cultural Heritage in the Baltic Sea Region," *The Baltic Sea Region Yesterday, Today and Tomorrow* (Stockholm: Nordreigo, 2000).

9. ICOMOS Norway, "Norway: Climate Change and the Effect on Norwegian World Heritage Sites," *Heritage @ Risk 2006–2007* (Paris: ICOMOS, 2007), 117.

10. Ibid.

11. Gisle Erlien, "Sustainable Historic Towns: Problems and Possibilities," in *Urban Heritage—Collective Privilege*, ed. Marianne Lehtimäki (Helsinki: National Board of Antiquities of Finland, 2005), 62–63; *Urban Heritage* is a report on the 2nd Baltic Sea Region Cultural Heritage Forum, held in Helsinki, Finland, June 7–11, 2005. Also, see "DIVE-Analyses of Urban Heritage," National Board of Antiquities, www.nba.fi/en/suhito_diveanalyses (accessed December 20, 2009).

12. "Creating New Assets in the Cultural Sphere," Riksantikvaren, www.riksantikvaren.no/English/New_assets (accessed November 1, 2009)

13. ICOMOS Norway, "Norway."

14. "About Us," The Nordic World Heritage Foundation, www.nwhf.no, (accessed December 27, 2010).

15. "Cultural Heritage Fact Sheet," European Economic Area (EEA) Grants / Norway Grants (October 2009), www.eeagrants.org/asset/1483/1/1483_1.pdf (accessed December 19, 2009).

16. Ibid.

17. Rural architecture in southern Europe is usually constructed of more durable materials, such as stone and clay brick, which makes these structures more long lived and useful for longer periods of time.

18. "Stave Churches," State of the Environment in Norway, www.environment.no/Topics/Cultural-heritage/Architectural-heritage1/Stave-churches (accessed December 19, 2009).

19. ICOMOS Norway, "Norway."

20. The town's numerous conservation projects have included the major restoration effort in 1979 on its stone cathedral, which serves as the seat of the Lutheran Church of Finland and is the country's most important medieval religious building. The recent restoration not only returned Turku Cathedral to its original splendor but also exemplified best restoration practices and served as a guide for other cathedral works in region. Today its museum exhibits a collection of articles that survived a nineteenth-century fire and subsequent looting. Jokilehto, *A History of Architectural Conservation*, 254–255, and "Turku Cathedral," Turku and Karrina Parishe Union, www.turunsrk.fi/portal/en/turku_cathedral (accessed December 19, 2009).

21. "Old Rauma," UNESCO World Heritage List, http://whc.unesco.org/sites/582.htm (accessed December 19 2009).

22. The *Vasa* sank in a storm on its maiden voyage in 1628 when water poured into its gun ports, which had been left open after firing a salute. In the seventeenth century, waste dumping into Stockholm harbor had created a highly polluted environment whose high bacteria content, fortunately for the *Vasa*, created a largely anaerobic environment that prevented the growth of the microorganisms that break down wood. Before the *Vasa* emerged from the harbor in April 1961, it took five years of undersea preparation and consolidation efforts that included Swedish Navy divers flushing with water under pressure six tunnels below the vessel, through which were drawn steel cables attached to surface lifting pontoons. Restoration of the *Vasa* began while it was still fifty feet underwater to prevent its wood from decomposing upon exposure to the air. During the *Vasa's* 333 years of submergence, a layer of hydrogen sulfide had been deposited on its wood. Eventually the hydrogen sulfide turned into elemental sulfur, and it is today oxidizing into sulfuric acid, probably because of a chemical reaction with iron deposits left in the wood from its original meter-long bolts. These bolts rusted away and were replaced during the 1950s salvage effort by approximately 5,500 new iron bolts. "Preservation," The Vasa Museum, www.vasamuseet.se/sitecore/content/ Vasamuseet/InEnglish/Research/Preservation.aspx (accessed December 1, 2009).

23. "The Norwegian Year of Cultural Heritage 2009," Kulturminneäret 2009, www.kulturminneaaret2009.no/english (accessed December 20, 2009).

a

b

Figure 11-1 Frederiksborg Castle (a,b) in Zealand, Denmark, required major restoration after a disastrous fire in 1859. From 1863 to 1876, under direction of Danish authorities, a team led by architect Niels Lauritz Hoyen restored the complex to an extraordinarily high level of accuracy. Restoration of the castle's baroque gardens (c) occurred in 1998.

c

CHAPTER 11

Denmark, Iceland, and Greenland

From the thirteenth through the seventeenth centuries, Denmark's seafaring prowess made it the locus of Scandinavian power: it ruled Sweden, Norway, Iceland and far off Greenland, and spread its culture and influence throughout the region. Denmark began losing ground to the growing Swedish empire in the seventeenth century, witnessed continued losses in the aftermath of the Napoleonic wars, and in the mid-nineteenth century lost much territory and population to Prussia. In the aftermath of such political change, a national reexamination of the country's cultural and architectural heritage instigated a call for protection. Since the nineteenth century, Denmark's cultural heritage conservation system has evolved into one of the most comprehensive in Europe. Beginning in the early twentieth century, architectural conservation efforts in Denmark have been connected to the administration of the country's museums. This relationship influenced developments in Iceland and Greenland, where the respective national museums remain key administrative entities for architectural conservation.

EARLY DANISH CONSERVATION EFFORTS

Organized efforts to conserve Denmark's architectural heritage began in 1807, when King Frederik VI set up a royal commission to preserve antiquities. After the Napoleonic Wars, artistic and architectural influences from other countries, especially from Italy and France, entered Denmark, including ideas for restoring and conserving historic buildings. This was contemporaneous with Danish sculptors, painters, and architects traveling to Rome and Greece to study the artistic works and great monuments of the classical era.[1] Especially well-known was the sculptor Albert Thorvaldsen, who became prominent as an early archaeologist and restorer; he directed the restoration of the Colosseum as head of the Roman Academy of Archaeology in 1827.[2]

Another early pioneer in Denmark was Niels Lauritz Hoyen, who translated Victor Hugo's 1820s polemic, *Guerre aux Démolisseurs* (War on the Demolishers), which castigated the French church, state, and other powers for neglecting to protect the country's architectural heritage.[3] Inspired by Hugo's call to action (but evidently ignoring Hugo's warnings about the destructiveness of some early nineteenth-century French restorations), Hoyen planned to restore Viborg Cathedral by removing all accretions prior to 1726 in order to return it to its original Nordic Romanesque form.[4]

Hoyen and others worked to ensure the preservation of Denmark's great medieval cathedrals, not only at Viborg but also at Aarhus, Ribe, and Roskilde. In 1861 a law was passed calling for their protection, care, and maintenance and specifying the need for annual inspections and the establishment of a special advisory board to make recommendations regarding the conservation of these sites.[5] The advisory board was to include an historian and two architects. The law supported Hoyen's recommendation and strong conviction that any restoration should return a church to its "original" style to the detriment of later additions.

Hoyen participated in nineteenth-century Denmark's highest profile restoration: that of Frederiksborg Castle, which was originally built in 1602. This lavish royal compound, spanning three islands, was nearly destroyed by fire in 1859. Following the tragedy, the Danish government ordered that the castle be restored and preserved as a national museum, with private funding from the brewer J. C. Jacobsen and the Carlsberg Foundation. From 1863 until 1876, Hoyen and two other restoration architects, N. S. Nebelong and H. B. Storck,[6] reconstructed Frederiksborg Castle to an extraordinary degree of accuracy, based on information gleaned from historical records and archaeological evidence. Today, this early example of a scientific restoration is the National History Museum at Frederiksborg Castle, and it has become Denmark's most popular historic building outside of Copenhagen.

Following completion of the Frederiksborg restoration, Storck continued Hoyen's preferred "unity of style" approach during his restoration of two churches, Copenhagen's Helligandskirken and Bjernede's round church. Bjernede's church was radically altered when its attractive, original saddleback roof was replaced by a more historically accurate conical one.[7]

English ideas about architectural conservation arrived with the establishment of the Danish Society for the Preservation of Old Buildings in 1907, which was based on William Morris's London prototype, the Society for the Protection of Ancient Buildings.[8] This initiated an activist phase in the Danish heritage conservation movement, when an increased public consciousness demanded greater protection of historic monuments.

In 1908 the Danish activist, teacher, and translator Peter Holm dismantled a large merchant's house, which had been threatened with demolition and reerected it a year later at a special exhibition in Aarhus.[9] Inspired by the popular enthusiasm that greeted his effort, Holm dedicated himself to preserving ancient market-town houses, which were rapidly disappearing as Denmark industrialized. In 1914 he founded an open-air museum, Den Gamle By (the Old Town) in Aarhus, which specialized in the preservation of traditional Danish urban domestic architecture. By the time Holm retired from being its curator in 1945, he had saved over fifty houses and re-erected them in his museum town.[10] Today, Den Gamle By maintains a collection of seventy-five buildings complete with their restored historic interiors, furniture, and objects.

HERITAGE LEGISLATION AND ADMINISTRATION IN THE TWENTIETH CENTURY

The destruction of a Renaissance townhouse in Copenhagen in 1913 was seen as scandalous, leading to an increased public concern for architectural heritage and helping to lay the groundwork for relevant legislation and government action.[11] Denmark's first protective measure, the Preservation of Buildings Act of 1918, recognized historic sites as significant national resources worthy of government attention and established a consulting body, the Historic Buildings Council, to advise the minister of education on compiling a list of secular buildings more than one hundred years old that were of outstanding artistic and historic quality.[12] The 1918 Act remained Denmark's central piece of heritage legislation until the 1960s.

A successive piece of legislation affecting Denmark's historic sites was the reformed Protection of Churches Act of 1922. The original statute had encouraged restoring historic churches to their "original" state, but Danish architectural conservationists, led by architect Mogens Clemmesen, argued that architectural restoration and preservation should be based on detailed "building-archaeological" studies rather than on speculative concepts of "period restoration."[13] The 1922 law adopted Clemmesen's position, representing the continuation of John Ruskin's and William Morris's influence in Denmark, and it also required the advice of the National Museum on all proposed demolitions, alterations, or improvements of select churches.

Half a century later, in 1966, new protective laws were required to stem the loss of the country's historic architecture as a result of urban renewal and regeneration. The 1966 Act organized listed buildings into a two-tier grading system: Grade "A" buildings were considered to be of the highest significance; Grade "B" buildings were considered to be of slightly lesser value.[14] Sites for potential listing could be nominated by individuals and voluntary societies, and their status is to be updated in the public Tinglysningsretten (Land Registry), a legal system that has tracked ownership and other property

Figure 11-2 Village houses and their maintenance in Hillerød, Denmark, represent the typically high degree of maintenance and care with which most Danish town architecture is treated.

concerns in Denmark since 1845. Work on, or additions to, Grade "A" buildings were highly regulated while only facade works were regulated for Grade "B" listed structures.[15] The 1966 law also required that if the state refused an owner's request to demolish a listed building, the state was compelled to purchase it.[16] Loans to homeowners of listed buildings were made available from the government's Preservation of Buildings Fund, which also provided financial support for restoration.

During the late 1960s and 1970s, additional legislation further enhanced the protection of Danish historic buildings and sites. The 1969 Slum Clearance Act provided for adaptive reuse of old buildings and encouraged cooperation between municipalities and the Historic Buildings Council.[17] The Conservation of Nature Act of 1975 followed the 1913 French concept of *entourage* (protecting a site and its immediate environment) by authorizing the protection of the surroundings of a designated site within a radius of 100 meters.[18] The 1977 Municipal Planning Act authorized localities to inventory buildings they wished to protect. When these lists are included in local planning codes, the inventoried buildings cannot be demolished without permission from the local authority.

The Preservation of Buildings Act was amended in 1980 to expand the government's powers. The state gained the authority to compel the sale of surrounding land when purchasing a Listed Building threatened with demolition and to restore a neglected listed building at the owner's expense—at the same time, the state also began to offer grants for property owners to cover up to 20 percent of costs.[19] The 1980 law combined the two former grade ranks, which extended the protection formerly afforded only to Grade "A" sites to all Listed Buildings. Today, the Det Kulturhistoriske Centralregister (Central Register of Cultural History) includes over nine thousand Listed Buildings and about thirty thousand additional Protected Sites and Monuments (prehistoric, ancient and other archaeological heritage as well as shipwrecks).[20] Over half of the Listed Buildings in Denmark are urban houses; public and vernacular buildings together comprise another 25 percent.

Denmark's Listed Buildings and its Protected Sites and Monuments of national significance have been supplemented with another list of regionally and locally valued heritage as identified either by the state heritage agency or by individual Danish municipalities. This secondary list grew out of the Survey of Architectural Values in the Environment (SAVE) National Inventory, set up in 1987, following the recommendations of the 1985 Convention for the Protection of Cultural Heritage in Europe.[21] SAVE called for the evaluation of sites and buildings based on five parameters: architectural value, historic value, environmental value, originality, and condition. This secondary list was created to guide municipal surveys of architectural heritage for the purpose of preparing local planning regulations and for developing criteria for new buildings in historic areas. Three-hundred thousand sites and cultural environments (districts) on the SAVE inventory are deemed "worthy of preservation," meaning that they are subject to certain regulations. This designation affects only the exterior of buildings, unlike listing which extends also to interiors, and requires local authorities' permission for demolition. Though being designated "worthy of preservation" does not necessarily ensure protection, municipal authorities must consider the impact of any new plans on these sites.

For most of the twentieth century, the Historic Buildings Council was the main government agency responsible for Denmark's immovable heritage. However, through the 1980 amendments, jurisdiction for inventorying and monitoring sites and for buildings transferred to the National Agency for the Protection of Nature, Monuments and Sites, part of the Ministry of Environment (which, with a new Preservation of Buildings Act in 1997, became the National Forest and Nature Agency of the Ministry of the Environment and Energy). The Historic Buildings Council became an advisory body whose approval is necessary to add new buildings and sites to the protected list.

CONTEMPORARY CONSERVATION PARTICIPANTS AND SUCCESSES IN DENMARK

In 2002 heritage protection in Denmark was completely reorganized once again to a system more similar to that seen elsewhere in Europe: While the Ministry of the Environment and Energy retained jurisdiction over conservation of natural sites, a *Kulturarvsstyrelsen* (Heritage Agency) was formed within the Ministry of Culture to take over matters concerning built heritage. A series of executive orders in the following years outlined the responsibilities of the Kulturarvsstyrelsen regarding overseeing state-owned and subsidized museums as well as the administration and registers of Listed Buildings and Protected Monuments and Sites.

The Kulturarvsstyrelsen is also charged with advising the Church of Denmark on the conservation of many historic properties. Ecclesiastical buildings owned by the Danish National Evangelical Lutheran Church are not protected by the Preservation of Historic Buildings Act unless they have been secularized.[22] An inventory of historic churches indicates there are over 1,800 surviving churches built between 1100 and 1850, the oldest of which are subject to a special Church Commission, while the rest are still covered under the Maintenance of Churches Act of 1861.[23]

Municipal reform in 2007 further decentralized the protection of architectural conservation in Denmark. Since the Museum Act of 1977 (updated in 2001), municipalities had been required to consult with the experts at local cultural heritage museums on the potential impact of any new town plans on Listed Buildings or Protected Monuments and Sites. With the new reform in 2007, municipalities became primary stewards of Danish cultural heritage, required to protect individual sites on the national lists as well as the sites and cultural environments worthy of preservation from the SAVE inventory. Thus, while the Kulturarvsstyrelsen is the responsible party for Listed Buildings and Sites and Monuments, the sites worthy of preservation officially fall under the purview of the municipalities.

In addition to the role played by the municipalities, a number of other government bodies assist the Kulturarvsstyrelsen with implementing Danish heritage protection policy today. The Ministry of Finance's Palaces and Properties Agency cares for the conservation and operation of state-owned buildings used as royal residences, government departments, and museums. This agency has directed several large restoration campaigns: restoring King Christian VII's Palace at Amalienborg; rebuilding Christiansborg Palace Church; restoring the Christiansborg Riding Ground Complex, including the Marble Bridge and the pavilions; and renovating the baroque gardens at Frederiksborg Castle.[24]

Recent architectural conservation successes in Denmark have also resulted from the contributions of nongovernmental actors. Local conservation activists successfully lobbied to save a historic area of Copenhagen known as Christiania when it was threatened by development pressures in 2005. The city council considered approving the construction of six high-rise towers despite municipal height restriction regulations; however, the activists persuaded the authorities that the new building disfigured the city and would set a dangerous precedent.[25] Their cause was supported by local residents, international media coverage, and Europa Nostra, whose president wrote to Danish public officials on Christiania's behalf. He argued that "it is the human scale of Copenhagen's inner city and its unspoilt character that draw vast numbers of tourists to your city annually. Therefore, we believe that a disfigured Christiania will not only lose its intrinsic value, but also negatively affect Copenhagen's tourist, and hence economic, potential."[26]

Elsewhere in Denmark's capital, the Copenhagen City Museum has been active in archaeological site conservation in recent decades. Before the construction of the Copenhagen Metro, which began in 1996 and was completed in 2007, the City Museum oversaw excavations at impacted sites throughout the city, including Kongens Nytorv,

Figure 11-3 Restored waterfront buildings (a) and the locally led initiative to protect the eighteenth-century Christiana district (b) represent both public and private interests in architectural conservation in Copenhagen.

one of the city's largest public squares, where the remains of fifteenth- and sixteenth-century quays and ships were found.[27]

For more than a century, the Danish system of heritage protection has evolved and expanded its purview over as many monuments and sites as possible. This progress continues, as over one hundred sites are added annually to the national inventories.[28] At the same time, with the development of Denmark, threats to its built heritage persist: towns and small communities depopulate leaving historic buildings abandoned while urban centers grow; modern agriculture and industrial techniques threaten archaeological heritage; and high building taxes add to restoration costs, especially for owners of large country houses and castles.[29] The traditional responsiveness of the Danish government and public to the protection of their heritage will likely lead to these challenges being addressed.

ICELAND AND GREENLAND

Though Iceland is considered part of Europe and Greenland part of North America, these two island countries share an arctic climate, cultural histories, and historical political ties to Denmark. The shared legacy of Viking conquests from around the year 1000 CE also links Iceland and Greenland to Scandinavia. From their settlements in Iceland, Old Norse explorers had gone on to conquer Greenland and establish communities in North America, as is recounted in the great Icelandic sagas. Both Iceland and Greenland were colonies of the Danish-Norwegian combined kingdoms and of Denmark after it separated from Norway in 1814. Iceland became an independent country in 1944; Greenland obtained autonomous home rule in 1979.[30]

Both Iceland and Greenland have very low population densities, with nearly all settlements concentrated on their coastlines. Eighty percent of Greenland's territory is covered in ice, but its indigenous Inuit population and colonial settlers built on the fjords at the southern end of the island. Iceland's natural riches—vast glaciers, majestic geysers, and impressive fjords—are also complemented by its traditional turf buildings; Viking settlements; nineteenth-century, Danish-influenced churches and houses; and twentieth-century, Swiss-inspired chalets. Harsh climates on both islands regularly threaten historic sites; additionally, Iceland's heritage is endangered by earthquakes and other effects that often accompany the activity of its many volcanoes, and climate change may increasingly affect coastal settlements.

Since obtaining its independence, Iceland has passed no specific or comprehensive law to protect or list the country's architectural heritage, but many sites have been conserved and are managed through a combination of regulations and state institutions. The Danish Royal Commission for the Preservation of Antiquities began surveying Iceland's cultural heritage sites as early as 1817. Nearly a century later, in 1907, a National Antiquarian was appointed and a Preservation of Antiquities Act was passed for Iceland. During the 1920s and 1930s, the Danish government placed protection orders on the majority of sites associated with the ancient Norse settlements, which to this day make up the majority of listed sites. In 1994 a systematic survey of archaeological sites was initiated by the Institute of Archaeology, which aims to identify every archaeological site on the island.[31]

Today, the National Museum of Iceland, operating with the Division of Cultural Affairs of the Ministry of Education, Science, and Culture, is the main authority respon-

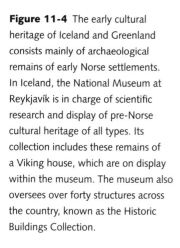

Figure 11-4 The early cultural heritage of Iceland and Greenland consists mainly of archaeological remains of early Norse settlements. In Iceland, the National Museum at Reykjavík is in charge of scientific research and display of pre-Norse cultural heritage of all types. Its collection includes these remains of a Viking house, which are on display within the museum. The museum also oversees over forty structures across the country, known as the Historic Buildings Collection.

▲ **Figure 11-5** Due to a scarcity of trees on the island, houses made of cut pieces of soil attached to birch-wood frames and built on stone foundations were once a common sight in Iceland. Today, the few remaining Icelandic turf houses, such as these eighteenth- and nineteenth-century examples at the Glaumbaer Skagafjörður Folk Museum, an open air museum in the Skagafjörður area, are registered and are under protection of Iceland's National Museum.

▶ **Figure 11-6** The Árbaejarsafn open air museum was founded in a suburb of Reykjavík in 1957 using historic buildings, mostly from the nineteenth century, which were brought to the central location from various sites around the country. It is now part of the Árbaer Museum.

sible for cultural heritage protection in the country.[32] A Building Preservation Committee also advises the Ministry on architectural conservation issues, and a Building Preservation Fund awards grants for the conservation of buildings of cultural value.[33]

Prior to 2001, the National Museum of Iceland's holdings also included all of the major archaeological finds of the past several centuries, as well as numerous Viking relics; however, those now fall under the purview of the newly formed Archaeological Heritage Agency of Iceland. The National Museum, however, still oversees the Historic Building Collection, which includes over forty buildings located throughout the country. The collection includes a few unusual early stone and wooden structures, but it mostly comprises turf houses and churches. This building tradition once encompassed most of Iceland's structures but was gradually abandoned in the twentieth century, as building materials were imported, and more earthquake-resistant technologies were adopted.[34]

Between 2006 and 2008, through the collaboration of a number of folk museums and universities, an archaeological survey of the Skagafjörður fjord area in the north was completed to uncover the ruins of turf houses. In addition, a late nineteenth-century turf farmhouse, known as Tyrfingsstaðir, was rebuilt according to traditional techniques and using traditional materials.

In addition to the buildings owned by the National Museum, Iceland's traditional rural buildings are also preserved in another open air architectural and cultural museum.

This museum opened as Árbaejarsafn in a Reykjavík suburb in 1957 through the purchase of a deteriorating farm and was consolidated with the Reykjavík Historic Museum in 1968 to form the Árbaer Museum. Additional old buildings of historical value, mostly from the nineteenth century, were moved to the Árbaer Museum from central Reykjavík and various sites around the country.[35]

Though Norse settlements and traditional rural buildings comprise a significant portion of the prserved architecture of Iceland, other types and periods of heritage sites have also received attention from conservationists in the early twenty-first century. For example, restoration of the impressive tower of the Hallgrímskirkja, or Church of Hallgrímur, in Reykjavík began in 2008. The church was designed in 1937 by Guðjón Samúelsson and built over nearly four decades, beginning in 1945. The tower was completed in 1974, and it is one of tallest buildings in Iceland. An outstanding example of concrete expressionist architecture, the stepped tower is considered by some to be suggestive of the jagged volcanic landscape of the country.

In a system similar to that of Iceland's before its restructuring, the National Museum of Greenland has purview over archaeology as well as building and site preservation. The museum is the central institution for research and documentation of cultural history, and it is the central archival institution for public archives and offices. Its collections cover the island's 4,500-year history and include fine ethnographical material as well as more recent colonial period artifacts.[36] The National Museum also advises the autonomous government on archaeological excavations; maintains national files about conserved ruins, graveyards, and buildings; and participates in nature conservation and town planning decisions.

The National Museum is part of Greenland's Home Rule Ministry of Culture and Education, which since the 1983 Act of Landsting Concerning the Preservation of Ancient Monuments and Buildings, protects buildings and sites that existed prior to 1900.[37] A three-member Building Preservation Council advises on the protection of buildings and sites for the national register, which is maintained by the National Museum of Greenland.

Treatment of the island's early Norse and colonial heritage in the late twentieth and early twenty-first centuries ranges from consolidation to total reconstruction. In the south, the ruins of the fourteenth-century stone Hvalsey Church are the country's largest and best-preserved Viking site. The twelfth-century bishop's residence and the cathedral near Narsarsuaq have been renovated. In Brattahlid, Erik the Red's longhouse and his wife Tjodhilde's church were reconstructed. The late-tenth-century wooden structures had turf roofs and comprised the first Norse settlement and Christian buildings not only in Greenland, but anywhere in North America. Adaptive reuse has also been a common preservation strategy in Greenland, including the location of tourist offices in a former missionary residence in Sisimiut and the National Museum's use of a number of historic structures in the capital city of Nuuk to house its collections and offices.[38]

Figure 11-7 The expressionist Lutheran church of Hallgrímskirkja in Reykajavík, designed in 1937 by Guðjón Samúelsson and completed in 1986, is an example of modern Icelandic architectural heritage that is protected by national legislation administered by the Division of Cultural Affairs of the Ministry of Education, Science, and Culture.

In 2009, a survey and salvage archaeology report was prepared by the National Museum of Greenland to assess the impact of a planned aluminum smelter and hydroelectric power stations, which will involve building dams and creating new reservoirs in a cultural landscape important to the country's Inuit history around Lake Tasersiaq, Greenland's longest lake, located inland from the western coast.[39] The area includes base camps with stone foundation walls on which tent super-structures were built as well as stone cairns (used for herding caribou), hunter's blinds, and traps, used from prehistoric times through the nineteenth century. The report concluded that the large concentration of remains was significant to Greenland's history and identity and should be preserved. The Lake Tasersiaq sites are just north of the Aussivissuit–Arnangarnup Qoorua Inuit hunting area, which Denmark proposed for nomination to the World Heritage List as a cultural landscape in 2003. The report also included recommendations for mapping, excavating, and documenting the sites should the reservoirs be built.

The people of Greenland have been debating whether to move forward with the project, including a study carried out by the government at the Parliament's request, which in a November 2010 White Paper supported the Lake Tasersiaq project so long as the National Museums documentation recommendations were followed.[40] Well-attended public meetings have been held since 2007 to discuss the project, and debate continues on the subject in Greenland: in late 2010 an aluminum-project opposition group was founded in Maniitsoq to lobby for further research. The engaged public and thoughtful studies by various government agencies regarding the fate of the Inuit hunting landscape around Lake Tasersiaq suggest that whatever the final outcome of this particular case, architectural and cultural heritage is a priority concern in Greenland, and will continue to be documented, protected, and conserved in the decades ahead.

ENDNOTES

1. Jokilehto, *A History of Architectural Conservation*, Oxford: Elsevier Butterworth-Heinemann, 2004, p. 252; first published in 1999.
2. Ibid., 87.
3. Ibid., 252.
4. Ibid.
5. Ibid, 253.
6. Ibid., 252.
7. Ibid., 253.
8. Anthony Dale, "Denmark," in Stipe, *Historic Preservation in Foreign Countries* vol. 1, 125.
9. "History," Den Gamle By, www.dengamleby.dk/history.htm (accessed December 19, 2009).
10. Ibid.
11. Peter Pearson, "We Must Pay to Protect Our Heritage," *The Sunday Business Post Online*, November 19, 2001, http://archives.tcm.ie/businesspost/2001/11/18/story641828.asp (accessed December 19, 2009).
12. Ibid.
13. Jokilehto, *A History of Architectural Conservation*, 253.
14. Dale, "Denmark," 125.
15. Ibid.
16. Ibid., 126.
17. Ibid., 133.
18. Ibid., 129.
19. Ibid., 126, 129.
20. "Listed Buildings" and "Protected Sites and Monuments," Heritage Agency of Denmark, www.kulturarv.dk/english/listed-buildings/ and www.kulturarv.dk/english/sites-and-monuments/protected-sites-and-monuments/ (accessed July 13, 2010).

21. Robert Pickard, "Area-Based Protection Mechanisms for Heritage Conservation: A European Comparison," *Journal of Architectural Conservation* 5, no. 8 (2002): 73; and "Buildings Worthy of Preservation," Heritage Agency of Denmark, http://www.kulturarv.dk/english/listed-buildings/buildings-worthy-of-preservation/ (accessed July 13, 2010).

22. Dale, "Denmark," 129–130.

23. Ibid.

24. "Castles and Gardens," Palaces and Properties Agency, www.ses.dk/en/SlotteOgHaver/OmSlotteneOgHaverne.aspx (accessed December 19, 2009).

25. The area is composed of an eighteenth-century naval fort that has been occupied by a dissenting bohemian community since 1971; the area was recognized by the Danish government as a "social experiment." The luxury high-rise apartment buildings were to replace this alternative commune, where the government and police are not welcome.

26. Letter from Andrea H. Schuler, executive president of Europa Nostra to Anders Fogh Rasmussen, prime minister of Denmark, "Re: Serious threats to the historic integrity of the inner City of Copenhagen," www.talkingpoints.dk/Files/DK%20Prime%20Minister,%2001.07.08%20_1_.pdf (accessed December 18, 2009).

27. Morten Gøthche, "Copenhagen: From Harbour to Housing," in *Urban Heritage—Collective Privilege (Report on the 2nd Baltic Sea Region Cultural Heritage Forum Helsinki, June 9–12, 2005)*, ed. Marianne Lehtimäki (Helsinki: National Board of Antiquities of Finland, 2005), 86.

28. Stig Enemark, *The Danish Way: Land and Environmental Management in Denmark* (Frederiksborg, Denmark: The Danish Association of Chartered Surveyors, 2002), 12.

29. ICOMOS Denmark, "Denmark," *Heritage@Risk!* (Paris: ICOMOS, 2000), www.international.icomos.org/risk/world_report/2000/denma_2000.htm (accessed December 19, 2009). The experience of England's Historic Houses Association, which is actively lobbying its government to authorize preferential value-added tax (VAT) treatment for renovation works on listed buildings may help Danish owners, since in the years following the establishment of the European Union, close relationships have developed among various national organizations through the Council of Europe's Union of European Historic Houses Association.

30. In 1998 Greenland received the right to independence, if its population should ever choose to request it.

31. "Welcome to the Institute for Archaeology," Institute for Archaeology, www.instarch.is/instarch/english/ (accessed December 19, 2009).

32. "About the Museum," National Museum of Iceland, www.natmus.is/english/about-the-museum/ (accessed December 19, 2009).

33. Ministry of Education, Science and Culture of Iceland, *Culture*, Reports and Opinions 26, trans. Jeffrey Cosser (Reykjavík: The Ministry of Education, Science and Culture of Iceland, 2002); http://bella.stjr.is/utgafur/enskan.pdf (accessed November 2, 2009).

34. ICOMOS Iceland, "Iceland," *Heritage@Risk!* www.international.icomos.org/risk/world_report/2000/icela_2000.htm (accessed December 19, 2009).

35. "Reykjavík Museum—Árbaejarsafn," Randburg, http://randburg.com/is/arbaejarsafn/ (accessed December 19, 2009).

36. "Welcome: The Museum," The National Museum of Greenland, www.natmus.gl/Default.aspx (accessed December 19, 2009).

37. Landsting is the Danish word for Greenland's parliament. "Pertinent Legislation," Danish Polar Center, www.dpc.dk/sw1099.asp (accessed December 19, 2009).

38. Joanne Lewis, "Monuments and Buildings in Greenland," *USA Today*, http://traveltips.usatoday.com/monuments-buildings-greenland-11733.html (accessed December 26, 2010).

39. Pauline K. Knudsen and Claus Andreasen, "Culture Historical Significance on Areas Tasersiaq and Tarsartuup Tasersua in West Greenland and Suggestions for Salvage Archaeology and Documentation in Case of Damming Lakes: Report Prepared for ALCOA" (Greenland National Museum, May 2009). Cultural Heritage Greenland, www.kulturi.org/Rapporter/NKA%20report%20EN%20full%20version.pdf (accessed December 26, 2010).

40. Department of Business and Employment, "White Paper on the Aluminium Project Based on Recent Completed Studies, Including the Strategic Environmental Assessment (SEA)" (Government of Greenland, September 2010). Greenland Development, www.aluminium.gl/media(770,1033)/White_Paper_2010.pdf (accessed December 26, 2010).

CHAPTER 12

The Baltic States

Due to their contiguous coastal geography on the Baltic Sea and a history of domination by Poland and Russia, the countries of Estonia, Latvia, and Lithuania share certain heritage qualities and traditions. However, now that each country has its independence, each is eager to express its unique cultural identity, which it is striving to maintain in the face of modern pressures.

Government interest in architectural conservation was relatively restrained when Estonia, Latvia, and Lithuania were part of the Soviet Union, but today all are actively working to protect their historic resources. With the dissolution of the Soviet Union in 1991, the Baltic states gained control of their own heritage policies, and the recent architectural conservation efforts of each of these new countries have epitomized the reclamation of culture and traditions from foreign domination.

SHARED CONTEMPORARY CHALLENGES

Though Estonia, Latvia, and Lithuania have begun to identify their important cultural and historic sites, each country must now begin to incorporate their conservation into comprehensive development plans. Political and economic instability and urban growth and development have posed the largest threats to the historic resources of the Baltic states since the early 1990s. In addition, in both town and countryside, the privatization of properties that has accompanied the political and economic transition from socialism has affected conservation efforts as some owners modernize historic buildings in insensitive ways, as new construction is introduced into historic architectural settings, or as buildings remain neglected during the slow process of property restitution when ownership has been unclear.

Integrative legislation is an important component for the future of Baltic conservation policies, as can be seen in the attempt of Latvian authorities to relate cultural heritage and environmental protection laws. Another positive mutual concern of Estonia, Latvia, and Lithuania is cultural tourism, as successful rehabilitation and restoration of historic areas redefines their tourism economies. While these countries realize tourism can bring significant revenue, they are also beginning to address its negative impact on heritage sites.

Initial post-independence conservation projects in the Baltic states focused on the capital cities and major urban centers, and efforts have since expanded to include the region's many historic rural settings, with their rich collection of wooden buildings, as well as some twentieth-century industrial complexes. While the majority of conservation efforts in the Baltic States remain centered on structures more than a century old, today officials are beginning to confront more recent built environments, with protect-

189

Figure 12-1 The Dominican monastery in Palevene, Lithuania, is an example of numerous religious heritage sites in the Baltic states whose functions were disrupted by political change in the twentieth century.

ing the remnants of the Soviet era being one of the most sensitive recent developments in the region's practice of cultural heritage conservation.

Other conservation issues of critical concern to Estonia, Latvia, and Lithuania are shared with their northern European neighbors across the Baltic Sea. Wooden vernacular architecture, both rural and urban, is as major a component of the built heritage of these countries as it is in Scandinavia. It provides modern Baltic society with a sense of history and belonging, and its protection is a priority. In Lithuania, in particular, where nearly 30 percent of all buildings are constructed of wood, the government has launched an active campaign to list and protect these structures. Latvia hosted Europa Nostra's September 2001 forum, "Wooden Architecture in Cities," and the resulting Riga Declaration highlighted the problems of conserving and protecting wooden architectural elements as well as the need for policy solutions and properly trained craftspeople.[1]

Since regaining independence, the Baltic states have collaborated to establish educational programs in conservation that address the practical and theoretical aspects of the field.[2] These training programs allow them to avoid the problems experienced elsewhere, where inadequate conservation techniques have contributed to the decay of historic sites. UNESCO's World Heritage Fund has provided financial support for this conservation training and helped create the Academy of Cultural Heritage in Vilnius. Although located in Lithuania, the Academy is supported by the Ministries of Culture of Lithuania, Latvia, Estonia, Belarus, and Ukraine. Seminars and training courses at the Academy have also been supported by ICCROM.[3]

In addition, UNESCO, ICOMOS and the World Bank have provided financial and technical support for specific conservation projects in the region as have private organizations such as World Monuments Fund, the Ronald S. Lauder Foundation, and the Canadian Urban Institute (CUI). The CUI's Canada-Baltic Municipal Assistance Program, for example, helps develop urban planning and management systems that function in accordance with principles of democracy, market economy, and sustainable development.[4] The Lauder Foundation focuses its efforts on restoring Jewish heritage in eastern and central Europe, including in the Baltic States. The World Monuments Fund conservation projects in the region include the Church of St. John's in Tartu, Estonia; a street in the historic town of Jūrmala and the cathedral in Riga, Latvia; as well as a monastery and synagogue in Kalvarija, Lithuania. Numerous other successful architectural conservation projects, which often incorporate economic development benefits, have resulted from collaborative efforts of local not-for-profit groups and international organizations. One early example in 1994 involved the U.S.-based St. John's University and the World Monuments Fund assisting the Archbishop of Vilnius by conducting a charrette to assess and plan for the conservation of the Bernadine church and monastery complex in Lithuania's capital.[5]

The importance of the Baltic States' contribution to global architectural patrimony is evidenced by the fact that their three capitals have all become UNESCO World Heritage Sites since independence. The historic center of Vilnius, Lithuania, was listed in 1994 because it retains its medieval plan, including its city walls and many historic buildings. Riga, Latvia, was also included in 1997 for its intact medieval core and also for its nineteenth-century suburbs with their unusual neoclassical wooden buildings and for its art nouveau–style inner ring. Tallinn, Estonia, was added in 1997 due to its especially well-preserved churches and merchant houses.

LITHUANIA

Lithuania has a long history of concern for its cultural and architectural heritage. In 1855, while part of the Russian empire, the Temporal Archaeological Commission was created to oversee its archaeological resources. Other developments occurred while Lithuania was briefly independent, between the two World Wars: in 1919 the State Archaeological Commission was founded, and in 1936 the Department of Cultural Heritage Conservation was established to administrate the Great Culture Museum in Vytautas. In 1940 the Lithuanian Parliament adopted its first conservation legislation: the Law on Cultural Monument Protection.

Even during the Soviet era, when cultural heritage conservation efforts slowed in other Baltic states, Lithuania managed to keep the issue at the forefront of the political agenda, and restoration projects were initiated in its historic capital, Vilnius, in the mid-1950s. In response to threats of loss or compromised integrity of historic structures due

Figure 12-2 In the 1970s the walls and gateways of Vilnius were stabilized and restored. They stand today as one of the most intact medieval city defense systems in Europe.

a

b

c

Figure 12-3 Four years after Lithuania's independence from the Soviet Union, the Roman Catholic archbishop of Vilnius sought help in assessing and planning for the conservation of church properties, especially the Bernardine church and monastery (a). The challenges faced included the expected: an undermaintained church and its support facilities (b). To plan for the revitalization and conservation of the site, the archbishop agreed to have an international planning charrette (an intensive on-site workshop) (c) that succeeded in articulating a number of viable new uses and a strategic action plan.

to neglect, insensitive renovations, and general development, Lithuania established an official list of significant buildings and sites in 1961.[6]

Article 42 of the Lithuanian Constitution makes the protection of the country's history, art, architecture, and other cultural heritage a national priority. Since independence, Lithuania has passed a continuous succession of legislation to protect its historic resources. Specific laws protecting cultural heritage include: the Law on the Protection of Immovable Cultural Properties (1994), the Laws on Archives and the Law on Museums (both 1995), and the Law on the Protection of Movable Cultural Properties (1996). In 2005 an updated Law on the Protection of Immovable Cultural Heritage strengthened mechanisms for financial support of protected properties.

Since 2006, owners of protected properties open to the public are eligible for financial support for conservation and maintenance. These policies are all overseen and enforced by the Ministry of Culture, through the Kultūros Paveldo Departamentas (Department of Cultural Heritage) and its ten territorial divisions.[7] The Departamentas maintains a register of sites of national and local significance; in 2010 the register included more than 15,600 sites and buildings.

The Kultūros Paveldo Departamentas has also been involved in major conservation projects at protected sites in recent years. For example, in 2003 it initiated a multiyear project to excavate, research, and conserve the Dubingiai Castle area, including the ruins of an evangelical reformed church. Excavations have explored the church's cellars, helped establish the building complex's chronology, and led to the discovery of the burial place of the Radvila family and the remains of their sixteenth-century palace. As excavations near an end, plans are underway to conserve the church and palace foundations and build elevated pathways above them to open the important historical site for cultural tourism.

The restoration of historic Vilnius has been one of the most successful recent projects in Lithuania. Renewed architectural heritage protection efforts in the city began with support from UNESCO and the United Nations Development Programme (UNDP) in the early 1990s to sustain tourism and economic development and to promote civil society participation in heritage conservation. In 1998 the Vilnius Old Town Renewal Agency (OTRA) was created by the municipality to oversee the rehabilitation of its architectural heritage in the light of the capital city's general plan. With a rich architectural history of churches and monasteries from the fifteenth century, Gothic- and Renaissance-style buildings from the sixteenth century, and neoclassical buildings and cathedrals from the eighteenth century, Vilnius's historic center represents the broad spectrum of styles and types found throughout the country. Through a major initiative in its first few years, OTRA made improvements to over thirty streets between 1998 and 2005 and as well oversaw the exterior restorations of over three hundred buildings by private property owners, developers, and the government.[8]

Today, OTRA continues to develop and implement conservation and renewal programs in Vilnius, coordinate various involved parties and groups, and promote investment and cooperation locally as well as with international partners such as UNESCO.[9] Nevertheless, Vilnius still faces threats that concern its architectural conservationists, including new construction in the early twentieth-century suburbs just beyond the boundaries of the World Heritage district.[10] In 2004 the thirty-three-story Europa Tower in the Šnipiškės area of Vilnius became the tallest building in the Baltic states and dramatically altered the historic city's skyline. The project was approved by the city despite protests from heritage protection groups.

Another threatened component of Lithuanian heritage is the hundreds of surviving manor estates found throughout its countryside. These manorial estates are the legacy of an institutional system integral to Lithuania's economic and political history, especially its period of medieval statehood. Only 125 of the over 4,000 recorded manors were protected during the Soviet period, when many were nationalized and either adapted to other uses or neglected.[11] When independent Lithuania's State Register was completed in 1995, 823 manor houses were listed, although over two hundred have since been removed from that list.[12] The Kultūros Paveldo Departamentas drafted principles for conserving the country's historic manor houses in 2002; however, today many remain in a precarious state due to continuing ownership questions and a lack of funding and maintenance.[13]

More successful conservation projects in Lithuania have focused on its strong industrial heritage, including historic wind and water mills, breweries and distilleries, worker housing blocks, agricultural infrastructure, and canals. Much of the country's industrial heritage has severely deteriorated as a result of the neglect that followed political, economic, and lifestyle changes during and after the two world wars. Adaptive reuse has been especially helpful in conserving a number of these sites, with several structures being converted into restaurants, museums, or other public uses.[14]

The strong Lithuanian commitment toward architectural conservation is epitomized by the 1996 Law on the Basic Elements of National Security, which defines cultural heritage—combined with civil rights, fundamental freedoms, and state independence—as an issue of national security.[15] The high value placed on cultural heritage protection and conservation by the Lithuanian government indicates it is not only a priority but a vital necessity to the country's identity.

LATVIA

Concern for conservation of cultural heritage in Latvia began in the seventeenth century, when Sweden's King Gustav II Adolph commanded Martinš Ašaneus, a Swedish antiquarian, to record all epitaphs and church inventories in the Vidzeme region.[16] During the early nineteenth century, another registration of cultural heritage was made by several Latvian antiquity and art societies. Organized oversight of historic sites was introduced in 1923, when the Board of Monuments was formed by the new Latvian republic; however, heritage protection waned during the Soviet era.

In the post-Soviet period, protection of Latvia's cultural heritage and administrative systems for its regulation were established in December 1992 when the Latvian parliament adopted the law On the Protection of Cultural Monuments. This law, the first of its kind in any former Soviet republic, delineates the responsibilities of the Valsts Kultūras Pieminkļu Aizsardzĭbas Inspekcija (State Inspection for Heritage Protection), which had been established in 1989. As in Lithuania, these duties are also outlined in a number of other legal instruments, including the 1995 regulations On Enumeration, Protection, Use, and Restoration of Cultural Monuments and the 1996 Statute of State Inspection for Heritage Protection Regulation.[17] The Inspekcija maintains a cabinet-approved list of buildings considered cultural heritage of national value, provides tax incentives and support to the owners of these properties, and imposes penalties on persons who damage them. The Inspekcija appoints inspectors for every major region and city in Latvia to administer its policies on a local level and encourages municipalities to establish their own conservation agencies to aid in this process.

Latvian cultural heritage is broadly defined as "material or non-material evidence of a person's intellectual activity," including "works of artists, architects, musicians, writers and scientists as well as expressions of the spirit of humanity and system of values that imports meaning of life."[18] Latvia's protected immovable heritage is classed as being either of national or local importance and is divided into four categories: archaeological, urban, artistic, and historic value. Thus, protected sites in Latvia range widely, from entire cultural landscapes, cemeteries, archaeological sites, and urban ensembles to individual structures.[19] In 2009 the over 8,500 significant sites and objects under state protection in Latvia included 2,494 archaeological, 3,395 architectural, and 45 urban sites.[20] In addition, the Inspekcija often designates protection zones around historic buildings and sites to ensure the preservation of their context. Economic activity and interventions in these zones are controlled.

Conservation of listed sites is the responsibility of property owners, and despite effective procedures for requesting state financial aid, available funds from either state or local governments are limited. Municipalities, therefore, stress the importance of maintenance as a preventive measure. Unfortunately, this does little to help the many castles, manors, farms, and mills that lie in ruins from years of neglect.[21] A 1998 technical survey showed Latvia's heritage inventory to be in need of attention: 55 percent was classified as in satisfactory or good condition; 37 percent were in poor condition, 7 percent in catastrophic condition, and 1 percent (totaling 520 objects) partially or entirely destroyed.[22] In the five years following that survey, conservation problems at more than a quarter of Latvia's designated sites were addressed by the Inspekcija.

Due to the rapid privatization of property since independence, 85 percent of Latvian heritage sites are privately owned, as opposed to 15 percent in 1990. This has placed historic sites at risk because the limited economic resources of many owners leave little funds available for upkeep or improvements. Land privatization has posed a dilemma for the Abava Valley cultural landscape and region, which was first developed during the Middle Ages along a major route to Germany. The broad range of historical and

Figure 12-4 The protection of the Abava Valley cultural landscape after Latvia's return to a free market economy in the early 1990s thus far represents a successful example of rural landscape conservation attributable to planning, advocacy, and effective legislation. Threats to such pristine rural areas from subdivision and development are always a possibility, making vigilance and enforcement of planning regulations a crucial matter.

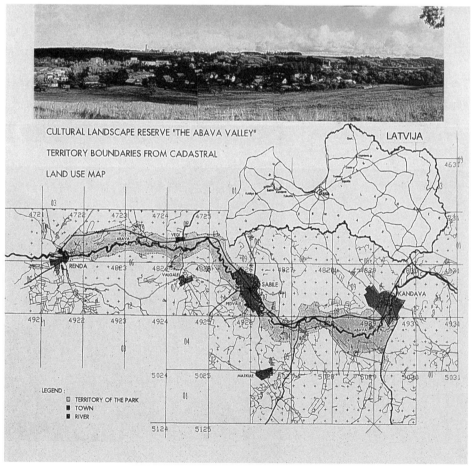

natural features surrounding the town of Kandava typifies the countryside that supported medieval centers. The Sabile vineyards played a central role in regional economic development and enabled the construction of many country estates and churches. In 1996 the Abava Valley was designated a protected cultural territory, but unfortunately the area remains threatened by the division of land into small parcels for unregulated private development.

A noteworthy recent conservation project in Latvia was the early twenty-first-century stabilization of the fifteenth- and sixteenth-century fortress in Bauska. The structure has

a

Figure 12-5 An emergency conservation effort between 2000 and 2003 at the fifteenth- and sixteenth-century fortress (a) in Bauska, Latvia, stabilized the ruined structure and enabled its reopening as a local and international visitor destination (b).

b

Figure 12-6 The conserved town architecture of Riga as exemplified here characterizes the ambience of Latvia's internationally recognized historic capital city.

been a ruin since a Russian invasion of the region in the early eighteenth-century Great Northern War. Three centuries of exposure to the elements caused significant masonry deterioration, threatening the stability of the structure and resulting in its closure to the public.[23] Emergency work was completed with support from the European Commission in 2000, and an international symposium gathered experts to plan for the fortress-ruin's complete conservation. A team of Czech architects and craftspeople carried out additional conservation projects in 2002 and 2003 and provided technical training for Latvian workers. The project won an Annual Award from the Latvian Inspekcija as well as a 2004 EU/Europa Nostra Award.

Riga, the capital of Latvia and one of the great cultural centers of the Baltic states, holds an eclectic mix of architectural resources, including its World Heritage–recognized medieval center and a significant number of nineteenth-century neoclassical wooden buildings.[24] Riga's post-independence conservation efforts have concerned these sites as well as incorporated the city's many modern architectural marvels. Pre–World War I art nouveau buildings with ribbon windows, horizontal balconies, and technically innovative reinforced concrete as well as interwar International Style structures are appreciated and conserved in Riga today. In addition, DOCOMOMO has listed many of the city's modern structures on its international register.

The legislative prominence and protection that Latvia has given to its intangible cultural heritage—such as language, folklore, song, and dance—has not yet been mirrored in Estonia or Lithuania. These traditions, however, became especially significant in all three Baltic states during the twentieth century, when the Soviet regime sought to separate Latvians from their heritage traditions. Today, all Baltic peoples are proudly reviving folk traditions to maintain and recreate a sense of place and national identity. By focusing attention on all aspects of heritage, from modern architecture to folk traditions, Latvia aims to retain a complete record of its cultural history as a statement of its contemporary identity.

Figure 12-7 Building heights and roof construction in the World Heritage city of Tallinn (a) are controlled by Estonia's national heritage protection laws as well as by a local Preservation Board, which has in the past been called to give opinions about controversial proposals for high-rise buildings near historic sites. The city has a long history of architectural and urban conservation, including the restoration of key sites in the nineteenth century, becoming the first protected urban district in the Soviet Union in the 1960s and expanding to an ever-increasing protected historic center (b) in the late twentieth century.

ESTONIA

The history of architectural conservation in Estonia began over a century ago, with the late-nineteenth-century restoration of the ruins of Tartu Cathedral in the south central part of the country. Destroyed by warfare and fire in the seventeenth century, a library for the University of Tartu had been built within the cathedral's ruins in 1807 and expanded in the 1960s. The nineteenth-century library was restored in the 1980s and converted into a historical museum.

Conservation in Tallinn, the capital of Estonia, has also occurred continuously for over a century, beginning with the city council's formation of a Built Monuments Preservation Commission in 1891 and Georg Dehio's and Walther Neumann's restoration at the same time of numerous key structures in the city, including the House of the Black Hands, a medieval guild house. In the interwar period, additional structures were restored. Tallinn became the first recognized and protected conservation area in the Soviet Union in 1966, and the first regulation plan was drafted in 1971.

In Estonia, cultural heritage played a direct and significant role in the national identity and independence movement in the late Soviet period, particularly through the advocacy of the Eesti Muinsuskaitse Seltsi (EMS, Estonian Heritage Society), founded in 1987 by Trivimi Velliste.[25] Establishing an independent Estonia was one of EMS's goals, and in addition to supporting architectural conservation, it drafted the Estonian language act, lobbied for the release of political prisoners, and in 1988 flew the historic Estonian flag for the first time in defiance of the Soviet Union as part of the Taertu Heritage Days.[26] Numerous Estonian intellectuals joined the EMS, and many of the members of the new government after independence were members, including one of the first prime ministers, the historian Mart Laar.[27]

Today, Estonian cultural resources—whether archaeological, architectural, historic, technological, or artistic—are protected by the Ministry of Culture and managed by the Muinsuskaitseamet (National Heritage Board).[28] County inspectors from the Muinsuskaitseamet issue permits, supervise conservation projects, and develop public awareness programs to inform local authorities and residents about issues and concerns in architectural conservation. In accordance with the Estonian Heritage Conservation Act of 1994, the Muinsuskaitseamet maintains a national register of cultural monuments. Thus far, over 27,600 historic objects, buildings, and sites have been added to the register, including over 5,200 buildings, with the majority located in major urban centers.[29] The government has also established twelve heritage conservation areas, primarily in the historic cores of each of Estonia's main cities, but it also uses village planning and land cultivation as conservation tools.[30] In the past few years, the Muinsuskaitseamet has shifted its focus to positively reinforcing the appreciation of heritage by supporting exemplary projects, in addition to ensuring conservation guideline compliance.[31]

The Survey of Architectural Values in the Environment (SAVE), a joint initiative of the Danish and Estonian Ministries of the Environment based on the Danish precedent, also documents important sites in Estonia's historic towns and specifically addresses localities whose identities are threatened or being transformed by modern additions or changes to historic structures. SAVE's main goal is to create plans that will appropriately integrate new buildings into the historic fabric of Estonian cities, towns, and villages.[32]

Architectural conservationists in Estonia are trained in the Department of Cultural Heritage and Conservation at the Estonian Academy of Arts, which offers bachelor's, master's and doctoral degree programs in both building and artifact conservation.[33] The institution has changed names and configurations numerous times, but it was originally established in 1914. It has been the only school in Estonia to offer courses in all art and architectural fields since 1966, but it only began offering conservation courses in 1997.

New regulations were enacted for the already well-preserved capital city in 1993 and a master plan by the Tallinn Heritage Preservation Department followed in 1995. Two years later, the Old Town of Tallinn was inscribed on UNESCO's World Heritage List. One of the most important and noteworthy conservation projects in Tallinn has been the decades-long restoration of the Raekoda, or Town Hall, which in 2005 won an EU/Europa Nostra medal. The current configuration of this limestone building, with its arcaded ground floor, crenellated parapet, and skyline-dominating tower, was completed in 1404, and the current restoration was completed in time for the building's six hundredth birthday. The project began in 1958 and was overseen by the late architect and historian Teddy Böckler, one of Estonia's key architectural conservationists.[35] The Gothic structure is the oldest surviving town hall in northern Europe, and it is still a city administrative building, though primarily used for official events and ceremonies now.

Despite the layers of protection for Tallinn's Old Town, in recent years heritage conservation professionals in Tallinn and elsewhere in Estonia must contend with the market-dominated building boom that began in the mid-1990s as well as the accompanying attitude—that preservation sometimes hinders the newly independent country's progress. In Tallinn, new construction is only permitted on empty lots or the sites of buildings

Figure 12-8 The Museum of Estonian Architecture in a rehabilitated early twentieth-century Salt Storehouse near Tallinn's harbor is an excellent example of the reuse of industrial heritage for museum and educational purposes. Courtesy and copyright of Museum of Estonian Architecture.

damaged during World War II, and conservationists have struggled to shape these twenty-first century interventions. They had little impact on the WW Passaaž, a shopping center built in 1997 in the center of Tallinn, but they were able to issue design guidelines for the 2001 De La Gardie department store, though these guidelines were only marginally successful at increasing the design compatibility of the new building to the historic city.[36] Though the design for the department store incorporated the limestone commonly used in Tallinn, its expanses of glass and merging of three building lots into one large structure reflected a contrasting material and scale. However, other urban approaches can also be witnessed in Tallinn; after decades of debate over what to build on the empty lot in Harju Street, in 2006 the city purchased the property and converted it into an urban park.[37]

Tallinn's suburban industrial heritage has also been threatened by development pressures in the past two decades. St. John's quarter, outside the city walls, served as a manufacturing center since the Middle Ages, and it still contains mills from this early period as well as notable late nineteenth-century factory buildings. In 2000, Tallinn was threatened by insensitive new construction, road development projects passing through a historic cemetery, and plans to demolish nineteenth and early twentieth-century additions to the district's thirteenth-century hospital for infectious diseases.[38] The major new road was built, despite the concerns of archaeologists, and a small underground museum was built in 2004 to showcase walls revealed during its construction.[39] The district's eighteenth-century St. John's Almshouse Church was overshadowed by the construction of Tallinn's first skyscraper—the Ühispank headquarters—in 1999, and additional tall buildings have been constructed since in this vulnerable wooden neighborhood.[40]

Industrial suburbs of Tallinn, such as Kalamaja, which is known for its late nineteenth-century wooden apartment and manufacturing buildings, have been the object of a number of international partnerships, not all of which have been entirely successful. The NGO called PRO Kapital reconstructed a listed wooden factory with Italian funds, but it demolished other, less old, nearby historic masonry buildings and built dense apartment blocks in their place.[41] A Swedish team acquired a nearby 1860s wooden house that had deteriorated due to neglect, fires, and occupation by homeless squatters,

Figure 12-9 The manor house of Riisipere is one of a number of similar manors located near the Bay of Matsula that represent a special heritage type in Estonia. The functions of nearly all of these houses changed during the country's communist years, and while several have been restored since independence, many still require viable new uses. New development on former estate lands has affected conservation potential—both negatively and positively—of several of these sites.

and its restoration in 2000 has served as an example for other projects in Kalamaja.[42] The late nineteenth- and early twentieth-century wooden districts of Tallinn and other Estonian cities have in fact become increasingly valued in the past decades, despite the fact that arson was a common aid to redevelopment as recently as the 1990s.[43] Entire neighborhoods, such as the Süda district, once at risk, are now well preserved thanks to the efforts of local architectural conservation advocates.

Concern for the conservation and rehabilitation of industrial heritage in Estonia has not been limited to Tallinn, although many of the most noticeable projects have been in the capital city. Significant research has been done on the country's engineering and technology history, and a number of important industrial sites have been conserved. For example, the Estonian Museum of Architecture has converted Rotterman's Salt Storehouse—near Tallinn's harbor and built in 1908 by a German engineer—into exhibition space for its collections. The museum, established in 1991, was first housed in the medieval Loewenschede tower in Old Tallinn. In 1996 the museum acquired the Salt Storehouse from the Estonian government, and the building was rehabilitated by the architects Ülo Peil and Taso Mähar.[44]

The Estonian government has recognized the need for adaptive reuse solutions for other structures whose original purposes are no longer viable or appropriate. This is particularly true for the numerous eighteenth- and nineteenth-century manor houses that were nationalized and fell into disrepair during the Soviet era. The restoration of seventy manor houses and their surrounding landscapes illustrates the Estonian commitment to reinforcing positive conservation attitudes, especially among its youth, while simultaneously repairing damaged built heritage. It is hoped that this government conservation program will be successful in teaching students about their artistic and cultural traditions.[45]

The Estonian Heritage Society (EMS) continues to play an active role in cultural heritage protection and preservation. Today it organizes tours and workshops, issues publications, houses a library, and promotes civic awareness and volunteer work for architectural conservation.[46] The EMS also coordinates its work closely with the Muinsuskaitseamet, ICOMOS Estonia, and various international partners as well as serves as an umbrella organization for over fifty other NGOs active in heritage-related issues throughout the country.

In 2001 EMS opened a Sustainable Renovation Center that offers training courses and expert advice to homeowners, and it has been active in promoting the use of natural materials and effective practice in architectural conservation.[47] The EMS center is located in the Kalamaja district of Tallinn and inspired the formation of the independent *Säästva Renoveerimise Infokeskus* (Sustainable Renovation Information Center, or SRIK), a network of similar centers in six other Estonian cities.[48]

Estonia's post-independence progress in architectural conservation continues to emphasize the country's desire to define and promote a national identity, though today the "romantic national slogans" of the late Soviet period have given way to "practical work."[49] The important role of architectural heritage in Estonian cultural identity is the focus of a number of state-sponsored programs, such as its annual "Heritage Protection Month," which since 1984 has promoted conservation awareness from April 18 to May 18 through seminars, conferences, and public events.

Connections between heritage, architectural conservation, and cultural identity are prevalent not only in Estonia but throughout northern Europe, where increasing regional cooperation bodes well for the future of the region's cultural heritage. Economic development combined with new legislation, administrative structures, and active civil society participation in the Baltic states have all enabled a rapid alignment of architectural conservation practice in these countries with long-standing successful cultural traditions in Scandinavia.

ENDNOTES

1. "The Riga Declaration," Europa Nostra, www.europanostra.org/UPLOADS/FILS/THE%20 RIGA%20DECLARATION.pdf (accessed November 3, 2009).

2. J. Leinjeks, "Latvia Training System in Field of Cultural Heritage," in Drdácký, *European Research on Cultural Heritage: State-of-the-Art Studies*, 100. Originally: "Cultural Heritage in Urban Areas" (paper, 3rd Ariadne Workshop, Prague, Czech Republic, June 11–17, 2001).

3. Audrone Kasperavičienė, "Revitalization of Vilnius Old Town: Social and Economic Integration," in Drdácký, *European Research on Cultural Heritage*, 97. Originally: "Social and Economic Integration of Cultural Heritage in Europe" (paper, 1st Ariadne Workshop, Prague, Czech Republic, April 23–29, 2001).

4. "Canada-Baltic Municipal Cooperation Program: Strategic Urban Management, Phase I and II," Canada Urban Institute (2006), www.canurb.com/programs/int_programs_ceurope_baltic.php (accessed June 16, 2010).

5. The charrette was sponsored by the New York–based St. John's University with technical assistance from the World Monuments Fund.

6. Kasperavičienė, "Revitalization of Vilnius Old Town," 97.

7. The Cultural Heritage Inspection and the Monument Management Department were created immediately after independence, and in 1994 they were combined into the Department for the Protection of Cultural Properties, which was renamed the Department of Cultural Heritage in 2005. "Department of Cultural Heritage Protection under the Ministry of Culture," Department of Cultural Heritage Protection, www.kpd.lt/en/node/49 (accessed November 3, 2009).

8. "Vilnius Old Town Revitalization Programme," European Urban Knowledge Network, www.eukn.org/eukn/themes/Urban_Policy/Urban_environment/Cultural_heritage/Preservation_of_historic_city_quarters/Vilnius-old-town_1036.html (accessed November 3, 2009).

9. Kasperavičienė, "Revitalization of Vilnius Old Town," 97.

10. Jurate Jureviciene, "Threats to Cultural Values, Historic Suburbs of Vilnius," in Lehtimäki, *Urban Heritage—Collective Privilege*, 52.

11. Algimantas Gražulis, "Lithuania: Lithuanian Manor Heritage and Problems of Its Protection," *Heritage@Risk 2006–2007* (Paris: ICOMOS, 2007), 108.

12. Ibid.

13. Ibid., 109.

14. Jurate Markeviciene, "Industrial Heritage in Lithuania," Gateway to Industrial Heritage, http://msi.lms.lt/ihp/gateway/lt/index.html (accessed November 3, 2009).

15. Ibid.

16. Juris Dambis, "Latvia," in *Policy and Law in Heritage Conservation*, ed. Robert Pickard (London: Spon Press, 2001), 208.

17. Ibid., 216.

18. Ibid., 208.

19. Ibid., 209.

20. "Heritage Statistics," Valsts Kultūras Pieminkļu Aizsardzības Inspekcija, http://mantojums.lv/?cat=592&lang=lv (accessed November 3, 2009).

21. Liga Kravale, "Latvia's Culture Programme's Subprogram 'Cultural Heritage," in Drdácký, *European Research on Cultural Heritage: State-of-the-Art Studies*, 89. Originally: "Social and Economic Integration of Cultural Heritage in Europe" (paper, 1st Ariadne Workshop, Prague, Czech Republic, April 23–29, 2001).

22. Dambis, "Latvia," 216.

23. "Bauska Castle Museum: Conservation of Bauska Fortress-Ruin: Renaissance of the Historical Handicrafts in Conservation of the 15th-century Bauska Fortress-Ruin." The Best in Heritage, www.thebestinheritage.com/presentations/2006/conservation-of-bauska-fortress-ruin-renaissance-of-the-historical-handicrafts-in-conservation-of-the-15-th-century-bauska-fortress-ruin,70.html (accessed December 19, 2009).

24. ICOMOS, "World Heritage List: Riga (Latvia), No. 852: The Historic Centre of Riga," *World Heritage List Advisory Body Evaluation* (Paris: UNESCO, 1996), http://whc.unesco.org/archive/advisory_body_evaluation/852.pdf (accessed December 15, 2009).

25. Karin Hallas-Murula, "A Changing Society, A Changing City: The Building Boom and Heritage Protection in Tallinn, Estonia," in *Cultural Heritage in the 21st Century: Opportunities and Challenges*, eds. Monika Murzyn and Jacek Purchla (Krakow, Poland: International Cultural Centre, 2007), 117.

26. Ibid., 118.

27. Ibid.

28. "Welcome!" Muinsuskaitseamet, www.muinas.ee (accessed November 3, 2009).

29. "Monuments by Type and Number in Counties (21.09.2009)," Muinsuskaitseamet, www.muinas.ee/413 (accessed November 3, 2009).

30. Urwe Russow, "Cultural Heritage in Local and Regional Social and Economic Stability," in Drdácký, *European Research on Cultural Heritage: State-of-the-Art Studies*, 31. Originally: "Cultural Heritage in Local and Regional Social and Economic Stability" (2nd Ariadne Workshop, Prague, Czech Republic, May 9–15, 2001).

31. Hallas-Murula, "A Changing Society, A Changing City," 125.

32. Anton Pärn, "Social and Economic Integration of Cultural Heritage within Cities," in Drdácký, *European Research on Cultural Heritage: State-of-the-Art Studies*, 53. Originally: "*Social and Economic Integration of Cultural Heritage in Europe*" (1st Ariadne Workshop, Prague, Czech Republic, April 23–29, 2001).

33. "Department of Cultural Heritage Conservation," Estonian Academy of Arts, www.artun.ee/index.php?lang=eng&main_id=365 (accessed December 19, 2009).

34. ICOMOS, "Tallinn (Estonia)," *World Heritage List Advisory Body Evaluation* (Paris: UNESCO, 1996), http://whc.unesco.org/archive/advisory_body_evaluation/822bis.pdf (accessed December 19, 2009); and *Helmi Üprus*, "The 'Old Town' of Tallinn and its Future," *Monumentum* 8, no. 4 (1972), www.international.icomos.org/monumentum/vol8/vol8_4.pdf (accessed June 17, 2010).

35. Teddy Böckler, "The Building," Tallinn Town Hall, http://veeb.tallinn.ee/raekoda/uus/index.php?id=36 (accessed December 19, 2009).

36. Hallas-Murula, "A Changing Society, A Changing City," 120.

37. Ibid., 121.

38. Andri Ksenofontov, "The Industrial Heritage in Estonia 1999," Henrik Wagner, ed. *Industrial Heritage in the Nordic and Baltic Countries*, proceedings of the Seminar on Cooperation in Strategies, Research and Training, Helsinki, October 1–3, 1999 (Copenhagen: Nordic Council of Ministers, 2000), 59.

39. Hallas-Murula, "A Changing Society, A Changing City," 122.

40. Ibid., 122.

41. Ksenofontov, "The Industrial Heritage in Estonia 1999," 57.

42. Ibid., 58.

43. Hallas-Murula, "A Changing Society, A Changing City," 124.

44. "History," The Estonian Museum of Architecture, www.arhitektuurimuuseum.ee/eam/english/index.htm (accessed December 19, 2009).

45. Russow, "Cultural Heritage in Local and Regional Social and Economic Stability," 31.

46. "Estonian Heritage Society: Cultural Heritage—the Past and Future of Civil Society" (description of project), KÜSK (National Foundation of Civil Society), www.kysk.ee/?s=152 (accessed December 15, 2009).

47. "Sustainable Renovation Center," Säästva Renoveerimise Infokeskus (SRIK), www.renoveeri.net (accessed December 19, 2009).

48. "Sustainable Renovation Information Center," Säästva Renoveerimise Infokeskus, www.srik.ee (accessed December 19, 2009).

49. Hallas-Murula, "A Changing Society, A Changing City," 118.

CENTRAL EUROPE

Between the Baltic Sea and the Alps, central Europe is a region whose eastern and western borders have shifted constantly in recent centuries and whose parameters have been defined in many different ways by scholars and politicians. In the late nineteenth-century, the German concept of *Mitteleuropa* referred to the recently united German states as well as the Austro-Hungarian Empire, which shared Germanic traditions, and had expanded eastward to include Hungarians and Western Slavs. During the Cold War, central Europe conceptually ceased to exist as Europe was polarized between the North Atlantic Treaty Organization (NATO) and Warsaw Pact countries. However, since the early 1990s and the loosening of Soviet control over what was the Eastern Bloc, central Europe has reemerged as an important cultural region united once again by its shared past and shared current political, economic, and cultural interests.

The architectural heritage of central Europe, particularly of its urban centers, is remarkably similar as a result of the region's shared traditions and interrelated histories. The establishment and growth of cities in the region, beginning in the ninth century and expanding notably between the thirteenth and fifteenth centuries, was characterized by the founding of new economic centers in relation to traditional seats of regional power. This process established the two essential and characteristic components of central European cities: a stronghold of a local ruler, typically on high ground, adjacent to a separate market center with a surrounding street network, usually enclosed in its own walls across a river from the castle.

As it steadily expanded, the Austrian Habsburg dynasty brought relative stability and clearly recognizable cultural and architectural traditions to central Europe during the seventeenth and eighteenth centuries. In the eighteenth century, Empress Maria Theresa passed an edict protecting movable heritage—it was one of the earliest such laws.[1] In the nineteenth century, the Habsburg rulers also introduced an interest in historic architecture and the idea of cultural heritage protection to the region. The Zentral Kommission zur Erforschung und Erhaltung der Baudenkmale (Central Commission for Research and Conservation of Historical Monuments) was established in 1850 to inventory, document, and protect sites within the empire. Though the Commission's effectiveness varied from place to place, by the late nineteenth century, documentation and registration of significant historic architectural sites had begun, conservation institutions had been formalized, and expertise in the subject had emerged throughout the empire.

Parallel developments were also witnessed in the separate German states at the same time. Legislation protecting historic buildings was passed in the eighteenth century in numerous German states, and in the nineteenth century one of the many facets of the German national movement, spurred on by the Napoleonic invasions, was the formation of voluntary groups and state commissions to study and protect historic German architecture. For example, architect Karl Friedrich Schinkel led the Ober-Bau-Deputation (General Directorate) in Prussia, and his projects resembled those in other German states, where the "unity of style" approach—called *purifizierung*—was popular. This attitude is epitomized by the decades-long project to complete the facade and towers of the Cologne Cathedral, a restoration and new construction project that was of key importance for growing German national sentiments.

Bavarian Leo von Klenze experimented with new approaches while in Greece and championed anastylosis and conspicuous differentiation between new and old materials. Though his more sensitive ideas were introduced in Prussia in the 1840s, it was not until the early twentieth century that the balance shifted away from purifizierung. The tide turned from restoration to conservation during debate over the restoration of the Heidelberg Castle and due to the promotion of architects and German supporters of John Ruskin, such as Hermann Muthesius and Georg Dehio.

While the twenty-five separate German states were uniting to form one Germany centered in Prussia in 1871, the Austrian Empire was beginning to fragment. In 1867, it became Austro-Hungary, divided into two halves and each with its own parliament. Then in 1918—in part as a result of the rise of nationalism among its diverse peoples and its transition from a feudal autocratic system to a capitalist economy with modern administrative structures—Austria, Hungary, Czechoslovakia, and Poland emerged as independent countries.[2] Each of these new countries began forming its own cultural heritage protection policies, based on the frameworks established within the Habsburg Empire and rational approaches and categorizations developed by Viennese art historian Alois Riegl.[3]

After World War II, in all of these countries except Austria and the western half of Germany, heritage legislation and administrative institutions developed under the influence of communist ideology and Soviet models. Following the collapse of the Soviet Union, the region began the difficult process of transition to democratic governments and market economies, and Czechoslovakia split into two separate countries: the Czech Republic and Slovakia. For architectural conservation the changes of the past two decades has meant a loss of significant state subsidies but a new openness to outside donors. It has also meant a renewed interest in certain time periods and types of architecture—such as religious buildings—that were typically neglected during the forty years of communist rule. Today, the German states have been united for a second time, with the merger between the Federal Republic of Germany and the German Democratic Republic in 1990; the countries of Hungary, Poland, the Czech Republic, and Slovakia have joined Austria and Germany in the European Union; and contemporary architectural conservation throughout central Europe reflects pan-European ideals and practices.

ENDNOTES

1. Jokilehto, A *History of Architectural Conservation*, 163. See also Stubbs, *Time Honored*, 226–233, for early history of architectural conservation in the German and Austrian states.
2. Poland was reformed by combining the part of it in Austro-Hungary with Polish territories from within Russia and Germany. Other parts of the Habsburg Empire, including modern-day Slovenia, Croatia, and Bosnia and Herzegovina, joined fellow south Slavs to become part of the newly formed Kingdom of Serbs, Croats, and Slovenes. Parts of modern-day Ukraine, Moldavia, and Romania were also in the Austro-Hungarian Empire.
3. See also "Riegl and the Meaning of Monuments," in Stubbs, *Time Honored*, 38.

Figure 13-1 Aerial view of Hamburg, Germany, in 1945 after air raids conducted by the Allied forces laid waste not only to the port and industrial district but also to the city's historic medieval center. Image: akg-images Ltd., London/Ullstein Bild; photo by Hugo Schmidt-Luchs.

CHAPTER 13

Germany

I n its historic July 4, 2002, decision, Germany's Bundestag (national parliament) voted 384 to 133 in favor of reconstructing the Berliner Stadtschloss, the capital's lost royal palace. This vote was the crescendo of a decade of debate over the controversial project and its implications, and it initially appeared to end a half century of polemics over the need for postwar reconstruction in Germany. With this decision, the unified Federal Republic of Germany formally reclaimed its history and architectural heritage, even if that meant choosing reconstruction over physical authenticity. Now, nearly a decade later, the fate of the palace site in central Berlin is still in question: it has been cleared, a design has been selected, but construction has been continuously delayed. The philosophical struggle over "authentic" restorations and "reconstructed" facsimiles was born out of the debates of the late nineteenth and early twentieth centuries. It was revived as a result of the devastation wrought by World War II, which called all previous theories into question and demanded new solutions appropriate for a Germany in ruins, and this conservation debate has reemerged in a united Germany due to the new and reopened discussions of German identity and history.[1]

POST–WORLD WAR II DEBATES

When the Nazi high command capitulated in May 1945, occupied and devastated Germany stood at zero hour. With cities laid waste, towns decimated, and monuments in ruins, Germans inherited a bleak landscape with few familiar features. In a typical example, nearly 90 percent of the 2,580 historic structures in Nuremberg were destroyed.[2] Dresden and Hamburg were equally shattered—their historic centers dating to medieval times had been made into fields of charred ruins.

Almost immediately, conservation professionals were called upon to join in the reconstruction process and aid in the recovery and emergency conservation of the few monuments and significant structures that remained standing. Immense resources were necessary for the reconstruction efforts in both East and West Germany. In each country, economic survival required that it rebuild and recover necessary housing and commercial buildings as soon as possible. According to architectural historian Wim Denslagen, during this postwar period, professional architectural historians, conservation architects, and engineers had a "collective nervous breakdown" while facing the problem."[3] The reality that thousands of monuments were either completely destroyed or extensively damaged polarized the professional community. While some clung to the nineteenth-century "conservation not restoration" principles of Max Dvořák and Georg Dehio, others believed that such wholesale destruction demanded a less conservative response, one that permitted the re-creation of significant monuments and architectural ensembles.[4]

Hence, the nineteenth-century debates, thought to have been resolved at the 1906 symposium on approaches to restoration of Heidelberg castle, began anew. As the debate grew in both East and West Germany in the late 1940s, conservation purists arguing for "authenticity" sought to protect remaining monuments and urban spaces and attempted to prevent the reconstruction of others sites that had been completely destroyed, arguing that these replicas or fakes would have little historic or artistic value. Their views were bolstered by art historians schooled in the doctrine of the Deutsche Werkbund, which believed that art and imitation were inherently antithetical.[5]

While these arguments led to the implementation of modern planning and reconstruction in several German cities, they did not succeed universally. The post-war reconstruction of the sixteenth-century Knochenhaueramtshaus (Butcher's Guild House) in Hildesheim was postponed, but the structure was eventually rebuilt between 1986 and 1989. In many instances, popular opinion supported the re-creation of destroyed monuments and the rebuilding of towns and cities. Faced with psychologically fragile populations, stunned by a disconnection to their physical past, many civic authorities opted to re-create lost historic structures and reconstruct urban environments along traditional street patterns. New construction was often required to make reference to the historical past through the use of materials and traditional building forms.[6] These officials rejected the arguments of modernists who sought the wholesale replacement of the old, although late-twentieth-century architecture—mostly in the International Style—would be built in abundance in nonhistorically designated areas in the immediate postwar period.

THE EAST GERMAN CONSERVATION APPROACH

As the Cold War political reality settled in, differences appeared between the postwar reconstruction approaches of the two Germanys. In still Soviet-occupied East Germany (the German Democratic Republic, or GDR), officials passed the Reconstruction Act of 1950. Its Sixteen Principles of City Planning were heavily infused with Soviet ideology, which argued against urban decentralization and heavily emphasized the importance of the city's visual aspects.[7] The new communist government politicized reconstruction and conservation for its ideological purposes. Even before the formalization of the division of Germany, restoration began on the early-eighteenth-century Prussian *Zeughaus* (Armory), a baroque masterpiece on Berlin's Unter den Linden, which opened as the Museum für Deutsche Geschichte (Museum of German History) in 1952.[8]

Soviet influence is also apparent in the GDR's choice of restoration projects, which deliberately left many sites in ruins, most notably Dresden's Frauenkirche (Church of Our Lady). This symbol of the city was destroyed along with most of the heart of Dresden in February 1945. Designed and built by George Bähr in the 1720s through the 1740s, it was patterned after Santa Maria del Fiore in Florence. Considered a masterpiece of baroque architecture, the Frauenkirche was shown prominently in Bernardo Bellotto's series of Dresden city view paintings in 1750. The Fraunkirche's destroyed shell remained as an unofficial war memorial throughout the Cold War. On the other hand, Dresden's heavily damaged Zwinger, a former royal festivity court built in the early eighteenth century, was rapidly returned to use as a concert venue. Its conservation and restoration was a state imperative; substantial funds were slated for the project, begun in 1945. It was given priority even over housing reconstruction.[9] Karl Friedrich Schinkel's early nineteenth century Neue Wache, a Prussian guardhouse in Berlin that had been converted to a war memorial after World War I, was also restored during the 1950s, and rededicated as the Memorial to the Victims of Fascism and Militarism.

When GDR officials did approve restoration, the final products were not always faithful to the structure's original appearance. The 1960s reconstructions of the late-eighteenth-century St. Hedwig's Cathedral and turn of the twentieth-century Berlin

a

Figure 13-2 Restoration of the Zwinger royal festival court (a) in Dresden, destroyed by bombing by Allied forces in February 1945, began immediately after Soviet occupation of Germany—later in 1945—and was completed in 1963. Its armory collection is featured in one of the restored interior rooms (b).

b

Figure 13-3 Dresden's Frauenkirche as it appeared in 1994, left as a ruin since 1945 as a reminder of World War II. Its reconstruction was completed in 2005. (See also Figures 13-9 and 13-10.)

Cathedral included austere domes remade in accordance with the GDR's Institute for the Preservation of Monuments, which stressed the "modification or removal of details with strong ideological content."[10]

Ideological content was also used to justify the destruction of historic buildings to consciously eradicate all signs of German militarism or imperialism.[11] Aside from the deliberate demolition of the ruined remains of Hitler's Third Reich Chancellery in 1949, the destruction of the Berlin Stadtschloss is perhaps the most tragic case of this period. The palace was begun in 1443, transformed in the late eighteenth century, and badly damaged by the conflagration that engulfed its interior as a result of Allied forces bombing in February 1945. The majority of its shell remained intact at the end of the war and cultural events continued to be held in its White Ballroom. Several members of the art and conservation fields argued for its preservation, but GDR officials ordered its demolition in 1950. Walter Olbricht, the German Communist Party's General Secretary, argued the symbol of Germany's imperial past would be removed to make room for an open space for public demonstrations.[12]

Despite the debate and controversy, and a concerted effort to save the palace, arguments fell on deaf ears. Architectural historian Richard Hamann pleaded to save the palace, exclaiming that both the Louvre and the Kremlin survived their royal occupants to serve and become "possessions of the people."[13] By December 1950 the palace was reduced to rubble, with only a few sculptural elements and one gateway preserved for use elsewhere. The vast Marx-Engels Platz occupied this central Berlin site throughout the Cold War, and key government buildings were erected around its perimeter.

It was not until 1975 that the GDR passed it first General Monuments Preservation Law. It prescribed the protection of key historic buildings because as witnesses to the country's historical and political development, "their protection is of great interest for the socialist society."[14] Communist elites realized that continued destruction of monuments, whether by active demolition or neglect, could actually backfire against them and that by encouraging a milder form of patriotism through cultural appreciation they could further bolster the regime.[15] Under the watchful eye of the Ministry of Culture, the new Institut für Denkmalpflege (Institute for Monuments) oversaw the protection and conservation of historic buildings and sites of international importance. Monuments of national and regional importance were the responsibility of local and civic authorities. From the 1970s until the collapse of the communist regime in 1989, economic conditions improved, and the GDR government and local authorities actively pursued a policy of architectural restoration and completed projects at numerous key sites.

THE WEST GERMAN CONSERVATION APPROACH

Many post-war city planners and architects saw the reconstruction of Germany's western regions, the new Federal Republic of Germany (FRG), as a golden opportunity to create new cities based on modernist principals. Some devastated cities such as West Berlin, Cologne, Frankfurt, and the industrial cities of the Ruhr valley chose to rebuild much of their urban fabric in the modern style and retain only small historic quarters or individual monuments. But many other major cities, such as Munich, Münster, and Hamburg, were rebuilt along their historic street patterns with building designs based on those cities lost and historic architecture. This decision was widely derided by British and American planners, who believed that such "sentimental romanticism" for a restoration of the past constituted a missed opportunity and a waste of money.[16]

Immediately after the war, the FRG, like the GDR, also displayed distaste for monuments associated with Germany's Nazi and military-imperial past. A rapid decision was made to demolish objects of high Nazi symbolism that had been built in Munich in the 1930s, including Paul Ludwig Troost's Ehrentempel and the Feldherrnhalle memorial to those killed in the Munich Putsch of 1923. Action taken toward certain monuments such as Berlin's 1873 Victory Column, which celebrated Germany's defeat of the French in the Franco-Prussian War, was especially controversial. Great Britain, France, and the United States, the FRG's Allied occupiers, were offended by this massive reminder of German militarism. This was particularly the case for the French, who went so far as to remove the relief sculpture of the Battle of Sedan from its base and demanded the Victory Column's demolition.[17] Cooler heads prevailed and the column was saved. It is today a popular landmark and tourist attraction in Berlin's Tiergarten.

An historic building with both monarchist and militarist connotations was Berlin's Kaiser-Wilhelm-Gedächtniskirche (Kaiser Wilhelm Memorial Church), a neo-Romanesque church built in the 1890s that symbolized the empire and a unified Germany. A 1943 air raid reduced it to a shell with a truncated tower rising above the ruins. The ruined site became a post-war symbol of resistance and of freedom in central West Berlin. Popular outcry met every suggestion of demolition made by the Berlin au-

Figure 13-4 Since stabilization and partial reconstruction in 1963, the Kaiser Wilhelm Memorial Church in west Berlin, has served as a popular reminder of war and symbol of Germany's hope for peace.

thorities, who searched for another option. Finally, the decision was made to restore the church, which ignited one of the most heated design and conservation debates of the post-war era. Architect Egon Eiermann's winning design was completed in 1963. The new church, foyer, belfry and chapel, with walls of honeycomb blue glass block, were grouped around the conserved ruined tower. The complex became one of West Berlin's great monuments, a symbol that remembered the destructive past while looking towards a new future.

During the period of Germany's division, the GDR's individual states (*länder*) had no autonomous conservation authority with the country's centralized administrative system that mirrored that of the Soviet Union. In contrast, the FRG, wary of its authoritarian past, chose a decentralized system that devolved much administrative power, including the protection of monuments, to individual länder.[18] Each state had its own monument conservation laws and shared responsibility for building conservation oversight with local cities and towns. The operations of each State Conservation Office were assisted by local branch networks that carried out a wide array of conservation activities, including historic building and site listing and documentation, advising on conservation and restoration projects, and distributing public subsidies for architectural heritage protection.[19]

UNIFIED CONSERVATION EFFORTS AND CURRENT CHALLENGES

Following the opening of borders and democratic elections in the GDR, Germany's two halves reunited in 1990. The new unified Bundesrepublik Deutschland (Federal Republic of Germany) adopted a system based on that of the FRG, and the former centralized GDR system with its Institut für Denkmalpflege was abolished. From unification onwards, each of the 16 German länder became primary controller of its own heritage. Similar yet distinct administrations exist in each state, including for example the Bayerisches Ländesamt für Denkmalpflege (Bavarian State Heritage Office), the Ländesdenkmalamt Berlin (Berlin Monument Authority), the Ländesamt für Kultur und Denkmalpflege (State Office for Culture and Heritage) in Mecklenburg-Vorpommern, and the Ländesamt für Denkmalpflege und Archäologie Sachsen-Anhalt (Sachsen-Anhalt State Office for Heritage and Archaeology).

In 1951, in the FRG, the Vereinigung der Ländesdenkmalpfleger (Association of Conservation Authorities) was formed to coordinate activities of the various state agencies.[20] This association continues to function today in reunified Germany. It organizes thematic working groups to share information and expertise from specialists from different states and it publishes the journal *Die Denkmalpflege* (The Heritage). Since 2001 the Vereinigung has partnered with the private Deutsche Stiftung Denkmalschutz (The German Foundation for Monument Protection) to co-edit the *Dehio Handbuch der deutschen Kunstdenkmäler* (Dehio Handbook of German Historic Monuments), a series of books inventorying and documenting key historic sites in Germany, organized into volumes by city or region.[21]

While today Germany's federal government has less control over individual historic buildings and sites when compared to the individual länder, it contributes to architectural conservation on a broader scale through its participation in international cultural heritage treaties. The federal government also exerts influence on architectural conservation through countrywide legislation. Reunified Germany has retained the FRG Federal Building Law of 1960, which requires local authorities to consider cultural assets when proceeding with building projects and permits federal intervention in development and building disputes.[22] Also, the FRG 1971 Law on Renovation and Development in Town and Country is still in force and requires that the opinions of federal and state authorities on any disputed local building project be heard and that the effect on historic buildings, sites, and districts be publicly presented.[23]

Funding programs through its Commissioner of Cultural Affairs and Media and Ministry of Buildings as well as tax incentives are other ways the German federal government encourages architectural conservation projects throughout the country. Federal funding programs have been particularly successful in assisting conservation efforts in the former GDR states and the former East Berlin. Within a decade, over 120 "large-size monument areas," including historic districts, towns, ensembles, and complexes, received funding through the urban conservation grant program administered by the Federal Ministry of Buildings.[24] Today, many of Germany's million-plus listed historic buildings are owned by local, state, or the federal government; however, a substantial number are not—ownership of some remains unclear, while others are dependent on private owners for care and maintenance. State and federal tax legislation provides tax incentives to assist owners in conserving and properly maintaining their historic properties. Further incentives encourage investment in historic properties for residential and commercial adaptive reuse projects.

Thirty-three World Heritage Sites are located throughout Germany and represent the country's broad range of built heritage from prehistoric times through the twentieth century. Its medieval castles, cathedrals, and town centers are particularly rich and have been protected. In his book *Architectural Conservation in Western Europe: Controversy and Continuity*, architectural historian Wim Denslagen refers to both the theoretical and technical complexities that have been faced in Germany, when he argues that: "In Germany, restoration on the whole is carried out with great scientific accuracy, but the tendency to revive archetypes at the expense of the later, chiefly nineteenth-century alterations is no less widespread than in other countries."[25] He notes that Germany's medieval heritage, particularly half-timbered buildings, has frequently been restored to reflect earlier appearances.

During the last two decades, private participation in the support and funding of historic sites in Germany has increased, and the German public strongly supports conservation of their cultural heritage. Since its inception, the Deutsche Stiftung Denkmalschutz, founded in 1985 under the patronage of the federal president, has channeled over €390 million ($570 million) from state, private, and lottery sources to over three thousand conservation projects throughout Germany.[26] For example, at the fifteenth-through eighteenth-century village church of Schöngleina, which was badly neglected and unused for decades while within the GDR, walls and interior fittings were restored and the roof replaced in the early 2000s.

Another private German conservation financier has been the Messerschmitt Stiftung (Messerschmitt Foundation), a foundation established in 1978 by the Messerschmitt family, whose wealth derived from the manufacture of German aircraft. While originally the Messerschmitt Stiftung limited its activities to restoring and preserving Bavarian monuments, its trustees expanded their project range after the collapse of the Soviet Union and its sphere of influence in Eastern Europe. Since 1990, the Messerschmitt Stiftung also supports preservation of German art and cultural monuments in Hungary, Poland, and Romania.

Since its establishment in 1995, the Ostdeutsche Sparkassenstiftung (East German Savings Bank Foundation) has supported over thirteen hundred cultural heritage projects promoting regional identity in four eastern länder. Recent grant recipients have included conservation work at the New Palace in the Sanssouci Park in Potsdam and the restoration of the early renaissance bay window at Hartenfels Castle in Torgau.

Another trend in private participation in German conservation has been the establishment of several voluntary private heritage trusts. Some like the Stiftung Dessau-Wörlitz and the Stiftung Preußische Schlösser und Gärten Berlin (Trust for Prussian Chateaux and Gardens in Berlin) concentrate on an individual site or group of sites, raising their popular awareness and funding specific conservation projects. Others focus on particular historic building types. For example, the group Dorfkirchen in Not (Village Churches in Need) is concerned with wooden religious structures in Mecklenburg-

Figure 13-5 The scrupulous restoration of Erich Mendelsohn's 1921 expressionist Einstein Tower in Potsdam by Pitz & Hoh Werkstatt für Architecktur und Denkmalpflege GmbH, Berlin was completed between 1997 and 1999. The project is representative of an unusual subspecialty of German architectural conservators lead in—the ability to restore modernist architecture to highly exacting standards.

Vorpommern. Some of these churches date to medieval times, and are often the only remaining historical focus in a rural area that has been otherwise totally changed.[27]

Germany's position as a leader in both the Industrial Revolution and International Style modernism is represented by sites such as the Völklingen Ironworks and the Bauhaus school and faculty housing in Dessau. These and other projects have acted as models of best practices for the conservation of modern architecture elsewhere in Europe. The Wüstenrot Stiftung (Wüstenrot Foundation), a foundation interested in research related to the built environment, has been particularly active in the conservation of modern architecture, including the €3 million ($4.4 million) restoration of Erich Mendelsohn's Einstein Tower in Potsdam between 1997 and 1999.

Sustainability and "green" practices have also become increasingly a part of the conservation trends—and general culture—in Germany in recent years. In historic Marburg in 2008, the City Council mandated the installation of solar panels not only on new construction but also on existing properties being renovated. While most are in favor of the energy- and cost-saving sentiments of the new ordinance, many of Marburg's citizens are concerned with its compulsory character, especially because the city is only offering minimal financial subsidies. Some fear that it will lead owners of historic properties to neglect major maintenance projects so as not to incur the initial cost of installing the solar panels, though some historic structures have been granted exceptions.

a

Figure 13-6 The reuse of obsolete industrial sites has been done creatively and dramatically in Germany in recent years. In Jena, Thuringia, the enormous complex of the now protected nineteenth- and early twentieth-century Carl Zeiss optics factory was transformed in the early 1990s into the Goethe Gallery shopping and commercial center. The project involved rehabilitating the early industrial buildings and the enclosure of Goethe Street with a glass and steel roof (a). An even greater juxtaposition is evident in the use of the Zeche Zollverein Coal Mining Complex in Essen in the Ruhr valley, a World Heritage Site, as an ice skating complex (b) in the winter. Other athletic- and design-related activities take place at the complex as well.

b

Because the main objective of architectural conservation practice is to slow or arrest the decay process of buildings, that is, to extend their physical existence, the task often entails sophisticated technical material interventions developed from the work of art restorers, scientists, restoration architects, and engineers. Conservation science has played a major role in shaping today's architectural conservation practice as an interdisciplinary field involving the close cooperation of a wide variety of specialists. It has helped to replace the traditional, mainly empiric approach to conservation with a more scientific one. A tangible result is the current practice of preceding any conservation treatment with a preliminary scientific survey. The specialized methodologies of architectural conservation science have grown to meet the needs of architectural heritage protection and have occurred simultaneously in several different places.

Some early names in the formative years of modern European art and architectural conservation included the Swiss Italian brothers Gaspare and Giuseppe Fossati, who restored the mosaics and painted finishes of Hagia Sophia in Istanbul in the 1840s. A succeeding generation of pioneers in architectural conservation science and technology included Belgians Albert Philippot and the director of the Institut Royal du Patrimoine Artistique in Brussels, Paul Coremans; Italians Roberto Longhi, Piero Sanpaolesi, Cesare Brandi, Giorgio Torraca, and Paolo and Laura Mora; and Harold James Plenderleith of the British Museum, later the first director of ICCROM, from 1959 to 1971. These conservators had their counterparts elsewhere, especially in North America. As the larger field of architectural conservation developed from the mid-twentieth century forward, the work of these pioneers grew in importance, and their students and others who followed went on to define and populate today's robust field of architectural conservation science and technology.

The emergence of architectural conservation as a profession in Europe in the 1960s is directly related to extensive contemporaneous developments in science and technology and its applications. Modern conservation practice in Europe and elsewhere derives not only from firsthand experiences in technical problem solving by conservation architects, chemists, engineers, archaeologists and restorers-conservators, but also from artistic and crafts traditions of collecting and museum management and developments in the building industry over the past century.[28] However, the scientific research of practitioners in the field has played a particularly key role in preserving authentic historic building materials and systems.[29]

Hand in hand with the scientific- and laboratory-based aspects of conservation science are the concomitant issues of research and methodology. Examples of diagnostic and survey techniques include photogrammetric and geodetic, endoscopic, ultrasound and thermographic analysis, and laser scanning. Usage of such nondestructive methods of scientific investigation have rapidly expanded in the past two decades, and this change has been the result of numerous international meetings as well as development and refinement of portable instruments. Other examples include multispectral analysis, special photographic techniques (infrared and ultraviolet), and X-ray fluorescence (XRF) spectrometry for elemental analysis.

The transfer of knowledge in architectural conservation science is one of the field's most impressive characteristics. For instance, American fact-finding missions to Europe in the early 1960s to observe architectural restoration practices brought back news of model government commitment to—and school training in—architectural conservation practices. Today, scientists and restorers continue to share new ideas with their colleagues via work-related travel. But by far the most effective means of transmitting information on conservation science and practice has been through formal educational training at research institutes and universities as well as through published research, often from experts at these same institions.[30]

From the 1980s on, specializations in conservation science were seated at national or regional institutes such as the Laboratoire de Recherche des Monuments Historiques in Champs-sur-Marne, France; the Geological Institute of the Rheinish-Westfälische Technische Hochschule (RWTH) in Aachen, Germany; the Center for Architectural Conservation of the Bundesdenkmalamt in Mauerbach, Austria; English Heritage in the United Kingdom and the distinguished Opificio delle Pietre Dure (OPD) in Florence. Other key Italian institutions are the Istituto Centrale per il Restauro in Rome and the Istituto Superiore per la Conservazione ed il Restauro (ISCR), which recently began training students at the university level. The work of these institutions today is represented by experts with extraordinary expertise in a single genre of materials. The leading work in stone conservation by German stone scientist Erhard M. Winkler, affiliated with the University of Notre Dame in the United States, is a prime example.

Other initiatives included a nationwide stone conservation survey begun in the 1970s that extended across West and East Germany, the work of the Swedish Riksantikvarieämbetet, the conservation facilities of the Middle Eastern Technical University in Ankara, Turkey, and the Academy of Fine Arts of the University of Ljubljana, Slovenia. In some cases, particularly large conservation projects such as the recent Acropolis conservation program conducted by the Acropolis Restoration Service have elevated technical capacities to a higher level in one country and had wider influence. Most of these institutions were and remain state-supported organizations of scientists and scholars responsible for the scientific aspects of the protection of state monuments.

Beyond the nationally oriented work of these institutions, and others like them, is a supranational capacity that exists in multiple forms. Significant scientific and technical expertise is present in the worldwide network of ICOMOS national and scientific committees. In addition, today's practice of architectural conservation science is served by several other professional interest groups, including the Association for Preservation Technology International (APTI). Three major institutions on both the American and international scenes are the Getty Conservation Institute (GCI) in Los Angeles, the American Institute of Conservation (AIC), and the Canadian Conservation Institute (CCI).

One of the most important international initiatives for the advancement of conservation science is ICCROM, which was initially established by specialists primarily from Europe and is based in Rome, Italy. During its first decades of existence, one of the principal aims of ICCROM was to compensate for the lack of basic conservation science training worldwide. Over the last quarter century, though more national and academic institutions have incorporated conservation science in their service and training offerings, ICCROM remains a global leader in conservation science research and information exchange. Over its nearly fifty years of existence, ICCROM has excelled in offering supplementary training, or refresher courses, for midcareer professionals with requisite basic training.

The building industry also played a key role in the development of conservation sciences, as specialists within research and development branches of product manufacturers responded to market needs. The industry has made considerable contributions in masonry, wood, glass, and paint conservation. Various independent chemists, scientists, and technicians have become associated with the field through their interests in the building trades.

The proliferation of the architectural conservation industry throughout Europe and beyond is reflected in the increasing number of specialty publications and discussion of conservation projects in the mainstream architectural press. Examples of specialized regular publications that have extensively covered the full range of scientific and technical solutions for architectural conservation include the *Association for Preservation Technology International Bulletin,* the *Architectural Conservation Journal,* and publications of the International Institute for Conservation of History and Artistic Works. Dozens of other relevant journals and sources include: *Studies in Conservation,* published by the International Institute of Conservation (IIC); the *International Journal of Architectural Heritage;* and proceedings of international conferences, bulletins, and special issues of national institutes such as OPD, Instituto Centrale per il Restauro, Bayerisches Ländesamt für Denkmalpflege, English Heritage, and so forth.

In addition, monographs have documented advances the field of conservation science, with notable examples including Bernard M. Feilden's *Conservation of Historic Buildings;* Martin E. Weaver's *Conserving Buildings;* the Butterworth-Heinemann series on architectural conservation edited by John Ashurst; Giorgio Croci's *The Conservation and Structural Restoration of Architectural Heritage;* and Harold James Plenderleith's *The Conservation of Antiquities and Works of Art.*[32] It is among these and others sources, including well-indexed bibliographies on the World Wide Web, that the constantly evolving developments in architectural conservation science and methodology are best researched.

Conservation science, its related technologies, and its application serve as the basis of cultural heritage protection in Europe today, in large part because conservation scientists have cooperated with one another, sharing information with the building trades and at professional conferences and journals. In light of the numerous and often sizable and successful architectural conservation projects undertaken annually in Europe and other countries, it is clear that establishing a scientific basis within the profession has reinforced and distinguished it.

In the densely populated state of Nordrhein-Westfalen, which has been a leader in German economic development and creativity since World War II, a collection of very varied projects have reflected this new sensibility.[31] The reuse of industrial structures is widely practiced; for example, the Thyssen steelworks, closed in 1999, has been transformed into new cultural and outdoor recreation facilities that include theatres, a convention center, and bike trails as well as a diving center in a former gas tank and a climbing wall on a chimneylike former storage structure. The project, called the Duisburg-Nord Landschaftspark, is repeated elsewhere in the region, including at the Küppersmühle Museum, also in Duisburg, where Swiss architecture firm Herzog & de Meuron transformed a former corn mill into a contemporary art museum. Abandoned coal mines, such as the Zeche Zollverein near Essen and the Zeche Zollern near Dortmund, have also become cultural facilities, schools, and recreation centers.

SYMBOLIC HERITAGE IN A NEW GERMANY

After the reunification of Germany in 1990, cultural heritage has continued the highly politicized and symbolic role it played immediately after World War II and throughout the Cold War. Given Germany's complicated contemporary sociopolitical context and its controversial nineteenth- and twentieth-century history, today's architectural conservationists have been faced with an unusual set of challenges. Some of the most sensitive sites have dealt with the preservation and reuse of Nazi-era buildings, the restoration of the Reichstag, the reconstruction of the Berlin Stadtschloss, and the reconstruction of the Frauenkirche in Dresden. Each reflects the continuing struggle of both the German public and the international conservation community to come to terms with the past, define a new identity for Germany today, and retain conservation values that can be carried into the future.

Following the 1991 decision to move the federal capital from Bonn in western Germany back to the former capital of Berlin, the rush to restore the city began. Still divided and scarred, Berlin was not ready to take up its new role. Billions of Deutsche marks were required to build, restore, and refurbish enough buildings to house all of the functions of the German government, and this initiative transformed Berlin into a forest of cranes. Even as relocated ministries searched for office space and land in the city, most monumental Nazi-era buildings were slated for demolition as distasteful surviving relics of the Third Reich, unsuitable for reoccupation.[33] Such action was met with unexpected protests from conservationists who opposed the further destruction of Berlin's already diminished historic resources, arguing that "there were alternatives more appropriate to the culture of Berlin and Germany than disposing of history by tearing down buildings."[34] To assist its decision making, Berlin's city government sponsored a report about the 1930s buildings constructed to house the Reichsbank, Aviation Ministry, and Popular Enlightenment and Propaganda Ministry. Despite their ignoble pasts, each was declared a significant architectural monument of the first rank.[35]

Not surprisingly, German authorities were wary of reusing these buildings in an official capacity for fear of projecting the triumphant stance of Fascist-period architecture. In the end, historians pointed out that the Nuremberg parade grounds, the former Central Nazi Party Headquarters, and the House of German Art in Munich had all been reused for cultural or popular activities. The soaring costs of other new buildings forced the government to refurbish these structures, and though initially a few ministries vociferously objected at being housed in former Nazi buildings, the debates eventually receded. The original style of the refurbished buildings has been toned down through contemporary interior decoration, and the buildings have become comfortable work spaces.

The rehabilitation of Paul Wallot's late-nineteenth-century Reichstag to house the Bundestag of the reunited Germany was similarly controversial. Burned by arsonists in 1933, it provided the catalyst for the Nazi consolidation of dictatorial powers, and its ruined shell stood for decades until it was partially restored in the 1960s and occasionally used for meetings or exhibitions. The renewed interest in the Reichstag in 1995 inspired the artists Christo and Jeanne-Claude to completely wrap the building in fabric as the latest in their oeuvre of abstract, site-specific art involving applying layers of fabric to highlight buildings and landscapes.

a

b

Figure 13-7 After a troubled twentieth century, the Reichstag (a) has housed the united German Bundestag (Parliament) since 1999. British architect Norman Foster's abstract reconstruction of the Reichstag's former central dome (b) references its war damaged predecessor in spirit. The original was a steel-and-glass engineering wonder of the 1890s, as is Foster's new dome, which takes a different form and incorporates new energy-efficient technologies of the twenty-first century. Envisioned as a symbol of the transparency of the new government, the dome is open to the public, who can see panoramic views of Berlin as well as watch democracy in progress below them in the Bundestag debating chamber. Figure 13-7b Courtesy of Michael W. Ellis.

The Berlin Stadtschloss: Emblem of Germany's Reconstruction Debates

The most contentious restoration project yet for the reunified Germany has been the proposed reconstruction of the former imperial residence, the Stadtschloss, in central Berlin. The palace was damaged during World War II, then completely demolished in 1950, and its site remained empty for over two decades until 1973, when the East German government used the site to build the Palast der Republik, a "people's parliament." During the final decades of the Communist regime, the new palace's many restaurants and public spaces became festive popular venues for general socializing and celebrating important events.

Soon after the collapse of the GDR and reunification, the Palast was closed due to the presence of hazardous asbestos. Demolition plans were approved, but questions were raised as to whether or not the important role it played for the communist regime as well as its popularity among the East German people warranted its preservation. The fate of significant GDR-era buildings in Berlin has proven uneven: while buildings such as the 1964 East German Council of State and the landmark television tower were deemed worthy of continued protection, the 1967 GDR Foreign Ministry and other Communist-era structures have been demolished.

At the same time the fate of the Communist-era Palast was being debated, a campaign spearheaded by Hamburg businessman Wilhelm von Boddien was launched to rebuild the former royal palace on the same site. In 1993 those proceeding down the Unter den Linden were greeted by a life-sized reproduction of the former palace's baroque facade, which was painted on a canvas sheet hung on scaffolding on the parts of its original site not occupied by the Palast. For passersby, this recreated a view of Berlin's prewar center, which had been lost for fifty years. Both supporters of the Palast and those who wished to see it replaced by a new structure argued against the idea of a historicist re-creation of the baroque imperial palace, claiming that it sent a confusing message about the intentions of the new Germany.[36]

Financial pragmatism prevented the Palast's immediate demolition. However, the site's future remained uncertain, and the campaign for the Stadtschloss continued. In July 2002, after twelve years of debate, the Bundestag decided to rebuild portions of the Stadtschloss, and that sealed the fate of the Palast der Republik. Many former East Berliners received the news of the demolition with great resentment, because it intensified their sense of dislocation in a post-Communist world. For them, the demolition of a building that held such fond memories was yet another sign of imposed Western hegemony. By 2008, the Palast had been completely removed from the site. Today the empty lot includes the exposed remains of the Stadtschloss' basement walls as well as an open air exhibit on the complicated past and possible future of the site.

Along with a collection of modern interiors, the new Stadtschloss, to be known as the Humboltforum, will contain exhibition space displaying artifacts from the collections of major state and regional libraries and art and scientific museums. The competition for its design was won by Italian architect Franco Stella. As per the competition brief, Stella's design for the Humboltforum replicates three of the exterior facades of the baroque palace, as well as three of the facades that enclosed the famous Schlüterhof (Schlüter's Court). In 2007 the Bundestag determined that the cost of the Stadtschloss' estimated $600 million (€450 million) reconstruction would have to be largely met by private and corporate sponsors and public donations. Construction was slated to begin in 2010, but has been delayed due to ongoing financing concerns as well as continued debate on the concept itself, on grounds both of authenticity in architectural conservation and what it says about contemporary German identity.

a

Figure 13-8 The Berlin Stadtschloss (a), severely damaged in World War II, was demolished in 1950 by the GDR government to make way for a large public space and later the Palast der Republik (1973). In 2008, demolition of that Palast was completed by the unified German government, and the site today (b) awaits an uncertain future that will likely include partial reconstruction of the imperial Stadtschloss.

b

The wrapped Reichstag underscored the increasing public attention the historic building was drawing and contributed to the debate about its plight and potential meaning in the new Germany. German authorities were eventually forced to deal with the question of the Reichstag's future, and an international architectural competition was organized in 1992 to solicit proposals for its restoration. The competition was won by the British architect Norman Foster, who based his design solution on an updated reconstruction of the former glass dome in a twenty-first century style. Spiral stairs gave access to its upper reaches, and views down into the central debating chamber, literally and symbolically suggesting the transparency of the German government. Foster's design team honored the building's turbulent history by presenting wherever possible its war-damaged fabric, including graffiti added in 1945 by its Russian occupiers. The project was conducted between 1995 and 1999.

Figure 13-9 Salvaged, catalogued, and temporarily stored original stone (a) from the destroyed Frauenkirche in Dresden in November 1996 awaiting reinstatement in their original positions in the reconstructed building. A new cross and orb (b) designed by English sculptor Alan Smith, son of one of the British aerial bombers of Dresden, symbolizes reconciliation and was displayed on site before its erection as the pinnacle of the reconstructed dome of the Frauenkirche.

Probably the most heroic late postwar effort in architectural conservation in reunified Germany was the extraordinary recent effort to rebuild Dresden's Frauenkirche, which began in 1994. The destroyed shell and rubble pile that had served as a memorial for decades also allowed for the preservation of many of its stone fragments in situ. Thus the possibility of a faithful re-creation through anastylosis remained. After excavating and carefully cataloging every salvageable fragment, reconstruction was begun with scrupulous accuracy under the direction of architect Eberhard Burger. Every stone that could be rescued was measured and documented using a computer graphics system. The challenge of meeting the project's projected $175 million (€133 million) cost was met by a number of local and international fundraising initiatives, including the English charity, the Dresden Trust. The clean, new infill pieces of stone were differentiated from the dark patination on the 3,800 reused originals—over time the stark patchwork contrast between old and new will soften.

The Frauenkirche's reconstruction is a remarkable example of a postwar initiative not only because of the project's scale and technical complexity, but also because it occurred some fifty years after the church's destruction. In mobilizing the project, its advocates answered others, including several experts positioned in the highest levels of German heritage protection, who questioned the wisdom of the project and the theoretical basis for it. It was finally decided that while total reconstruction is normally a dubious action, the mitigating circumstances here were that the remains of the structure had remained in situ, and extensive prewar documentation, including the original plans for the building, were available. But most importantly, Dresden's citizens no longer wanted a pile of rubble in their midst to remind them of their once beautiful city and the atrocities of war. The rebuilding of the Frauenkirche is not only a symbol of the rebuilding of Dresden but the rebuilding of a reunified Germany as well.

▶**Figure 13-10** The reconstructed Frauenkirche in Dresden in 2005, the year of its rededication. The replaced original stone elements are noticeable, because the darker colored stones were purposefully not cleaned to conserve their authenticity and to demonstrate the degree to which the original and new building fabric are combined.

ENDNOTES

1. A summary history of architectural conservation in Germany from the eighteenth- through the early twentieth- centuries is found in John H. Stubbs, *Time Honored, A Global View of Architectural Conservation*, Hoboken: John Wiley & Sons, 2009 226–253. For details on the past century see: Rudy J. Koshar. "On Cults and Cultists; German Historic Preservation in the Twentieth Century," in *Giving Preservation a History*, edited by Max Page and Randall Mason (New York: Routledge, 2004), 45–81.

2. Regine Dölling, *The Conservation of Historical Monuments in the Federal Republic of Germany: History, Organisation, Tasks, Case-Histories: A Contribution to European Architectural Heritage Year 1975* , trans. Timothy Nevill (Bonn-Bad Godesberg: Inter Nationes, 1974), 35.

3. Wim Denslagen, *Architectural Restoration in Western Europe: Controversy and Continuity* (Amsterdam: Architectura & Natura Press, 1994), 146.

4. Ibid., 143. See also Stubbs, *Time Honored*, 232–233.

5. Denslagen, *Architectural Restoration in Western Europe*, 147–148.

6. Dölling, *The Conservation of Historical Monuments in the Federal Republic of Germany*, 27.

7. Brian Ladd, *The Ghosts of Berlin: Confronting German History in the Urban Landscape* (Chicago: University of Chicago Press, 1997), 183.

8. Robert R. Taylor, *Hohenzollern Berlin: Construction and Reconstruction* (Port Credit, Ontario: P. D. Meany Publishers, 1985), 47.

9. Rene Elvin, "The Reconstruction of East German Cities," *Architect and Building News*, February 14, 1968, 233.

10. Mark McGee, *Berlin: A Visual and Historical Documentation form 1925 to the Present* (New York: The Overlook Press, 2002), 80.

11. Taylor, *Hohenzollern Berlin*, 33.

12. McGee, *Berlin*, 19–20.

13. Taylor, *Hohenzollern Berlin*, 36.

14. Ludwig Deiters, "Historic Monuments and the Preservation of Monuments in the German Democratic Republic," *Architectural History* 38 (1979): 142.

15. Olivier Bernier, "The Ideal City," *Preservation* (May/June 1998): 38–40.

16. E. A. Gutkind, "Report on a Void: Notes on the Reconstruction of Germany," *Town Planning Institute Journal* 35 (January/February 1949): 53–59.

17. Taylor, *Hohenzollern Berlin*, 126.

18. ICOMOS Germany, "Germany," *Heritage@Risk: 2001–2002* (Paris: ICOMOS, 2003), www.international.icomos.org/risk/2001/germ2001.htm (accessed November 6, 2009).

19. Ibid.

20. "Vereinigung der Landesdenkmalpfleger," Vereinigung der Landesdenkmalpfleger in der Bundesrepublik Deutschland, www.denkmalpflege-forum.de/Vereinigung/vereinigung.html (accessed July 14, 2010).

21. This most recent editon of the volumes of the Dehio Handbuch is based on the series of volumes published by Georg Dehio between 1905 and 1912 that documented key German historic sites by region. In the 1930s, after Dehio's death, Ernest Gall revised, reorganized and expanded the original volumes and republished them. In the 1950s, the GDR government initiated a new updated edition, which was published in successive volumes in the 1960s through 1990s.

22. Dölling, *The Conservation of Historical Monuments in the Federal Republic of Germany*, 11.

23. Ibid.

24. ICOMOS Germany, "Germany."

25. Denslagen, *Architectural Conservation in Western Europe*, 15.

26. "So the Past has a Future," Deutsche Stiftung Denkmalschutz, www.denkmalschutz.de/home.html?&L=2 (accessed November 6, 2009).

27. ICOMOS Germany, "Germany."

28. The professional title conservator-restorer was determined by the European Confederation of Conservators-Restorers' Organization (ECCO) in the 1990s. With the aid of national associations and national legislators, ECCO has succeeded since its founding to upgrade the profes-

sion to an academic one. All study programs for conservator-restorers offered in Europe are at the university level and entail five years of training toward a university degree. A fewer number of institutions offer doctoral degrees.

29. See Stubbs, *Time Honored,* see esp. chap. 8, "Scale of Possible Physical Intervention," 125–130.

30. See Stubbs, *Time Honored,* chap. 15 and 16.

31. Im Hye-ji, "Nordrhein-Westfalen's Culture of Sustainability," *Asiana* (February 2009): 14–25.

32. Giorgio Croci, *The Conservation and Structural Restoration of Architectural Heritage* (Southampton, UK, and Boston: Computational Mechanics Publications, 1998), and Harold James Plenderleith, *The Conservation of Antiquities and Works of Art* (London, New York, Oxford University Press, 1956).

33. Michael Z. Wise, *Capital Dilemma: Germany's Search for a New Architecture of Democracy* (New York: Princeton Architectural Press, 1998), 89.

34. Ibid., 90.

35. Ibid.

36. Ibid., 115.

CHAPTER 14

Austria

As the center of the expansive former Habsburg Empire, Austria witnessed active and successful architectural conservation efforts and has been a regional leader in restoration theory since the mid-nineteenth century. Its long tradition was reinforced when its current legislation and administrative structure were established following World War I and the founding of the Republic of Austria. The country's stable tradition of heritage protection has meant that these same laws and administrative bodies have been responsible for documenting and preserving Austria's architectural sites with only slight modifications and updates in the past century.

LONG-STANDING LEGAL AND ADMINISTRATIVE STRUCTURES

In 1923 the Law on the Protection of Monuments replaced the former empire's Zentral Kommission zur Erforschung und Erhaltung der Baudenkmale (Central Commission for Research and Conservation of Historical Monuments) with the Bundesdenkmalamt (Federal Office for the Protection of Monuments), which continues today as a department within the Federal Ministry for Education, Arts, and Culture. The Bundesdenkmalamt has responsibility for researching, documenting, and preserving Austria's rich cultural heritage through a central office in Vienna as well as through branches in each of the country's nine provinces.[1] This second tier of Landeskonservatoren (Provincial Conservators) monitors ownership changes and alterations and provides expert consultants for the conservation of historic sites in their region. Ten departments within the central office of the Bundesdenkmalamt focus on specific types of heritage, including gardens, libraries, museums, archaeological sites, auditory (church organs and bells), and industrial sites. They also handle specific tasks, including making inventories, monitoring exports, consulting as experts with property owners and local governments, and conducting laboratory research. The Restaurierwerkstätten (Restoration Workshops) were established in 1938 to coordinate the conservation of painting, sculpture, wood, and stone.

In 1975 a scientific laboratory was added to test materials, develop new conservation techniques and technology, and advocate and support traditional crafts and trades. Nine years later a workshop focused specifically on architectural conservation was established, the Restaurierwerkstätten Baudenkmalpflege (Architectural Conservation Workshops). The architectural workshops are housed in the fourteenth- through eighteenth-century Kartause Mauerbach (Mauerbach Charterhouse), whose extensive complex is used as a training ground for conservation professionals.[2]

The protective mechanisms established by the 1923 law still govern architectural conservation in Austria today. According to this law, all property owned by the state,

◀ **Figure 14-1** The restoration of the mostly fourteenth- and fifteenth-century St. Stephen's Cathedral in Vienna, Austria, including typical nineteenth-century additions and alterations, was completed in 1872 by Friedrich von Schmidt, who had earlier worked on the completion of the Cologne Cathedral. The project is an example of one of the first major historic building restorations by the Habsburg empire's Zentral Kommission. Severely damaged portions of St. Stephen's were reconstructed after World War II, and the multiyear restoration of the church's south tower was completed in 2008.

Figure 14-2 The protected Hallstatt-Dachstein/Salzkammergut cultural landscape in western-central Austria represents a special combination of a pristinely conserved natural site and well-preserved evidence of deep human history.

provinces, or religious communities was protected *"ex lege,"* meaning these sites were automatically listed.[3] As the concept of monument has widened over the twentieth century, Austria's protective legislation has been amended numerous times. Changes in the late 1960s facilitated the creation of protection zones within cities, with the first designated zone in the center of Salzburg. Amendments in 1999 extended federal protection to ensembles of buildings and to historic gardens and parks, including Vienna's famous tree-lined boulevard, the Ringstrasse, as well as enabled direct designation of state-owned property as protected.[4]

The inventory of historic sites in Austria worthy of preservation is based on the initiative begun by Georg Dehio in 1905 in Germany. Beginning in the 1930s, successive updated editions of the *Dehio-Handbuch der Kunstdenkmäler Österreichs* (The Dehio handbook for Historical Monuments of Austria) have been published in volumes based on cities or geographical regions of the country.[5] This list is supplemented by the *Österreichische Kunsttopographie* (Austrian Art Topography), which since 1907 has been a more detailed compilation of sites organized by town or district that includes visual documentation, scientific evaluation, and research bibliographies.[6] Today roughly 41,000 sites are registered in Austria. Of these, 50 percent are owned by federal, provincial, or local governments, 25 percent by churches, and 25 percent are private property.[7]

Austria only ratified the World Heritage Convention in 1993, however, it quickly added eight sites to the World Heritage List, including the historic cities of Salzburg, Graz, and Vienna, the palace and gardens of Schönbrunn, and the Semmering railway—a nineteenth-century engineering marvel. Three Austrian cultural landscapes have been recognized by UNESCO for demonstrating the intertwining of cultural and natural heritage, including the evidence of prehistoric culture in Hallstatt-Dachstein/Salzkammergut, of medieval monastic and urban life in Wachau, and of continuous rural existence in the Neusiedler See area.

One of these World Heritage Sites, Schönbrunn Palace and its extensive gardens, is also one of Vienna's most well-known building complexes. It has also been conserved since 1992 through an experimental and innovative financing scheme in which an independent but state-owned company, the Schloss Schönbrunn Kultur- und Betriebsges.m.b.H (Schönbrunn Palace Culture and Operating Company), manages the site as an economically self-sustainable tourist attraction. Funds for conserving and presenting Schönbrunn Palace to the public are raised by the company and through proceeds from the site, without any subsidies from the state. The late eighteenth-century Roman Ruin's folly in the palace gardens recently underwent a major restoration, but it is the constant conservation research and maintenance at Schönbrunn that has kept the palace and its extensive grounds in excellent condition.

URBAN CONSERVATION IN AUSTRIA

Austria's monumental capital city has benefited from additional layers of legal protection for its historic sites. The Vienna Building Code of 1930 requires owners of historic properties to seek permission from the city before making any alterations. In 1972 the Old Town Conservation Act created protection zones and enabled the city to take over responsibility for decision making about historic sites from the federal government.[8] Structures within protection zones may not be demolished and facades may not be altered without the city's consent. Today, 8 percent of buildings in Vienna are included within 118 separate zones. In 2001 the protective zones of the Inner City and the Ringstrasse were collectively inscribed on the World Heritage List, along with a buffer area, adding yet another layer of protection and recognition.

Vienna's 1972 Conservation Act also created the exemplary Old Town Conservation Fund with revenues from television and radio licensing fees. The Fund is used to supplement maintenance and restoration costs of historic sites; its monies are distributed equally between city owned property, privately owned property, and religious properties, one third for each. In its first thirty years, the Fund dispensed almost 170 million euros for architectural conservation in Vienna, and it continues to be a key source of funding for protected sites in Vienna today.

Vienna's conservation structures are paralleled in other Austrian cities: for example, both Graz and Salzburg have also passed Old Town Conservation Acts to protect their historic cores and create buffer areas around them. These and other Austrian cities have also established commissions to coordinate and regulate conservation in these protected zones as well as funds to support these efforts. Salzburg, the birthplace of Mozart and an important surviving example of the architecture of an ecclesiastical city-state, became Austria's first protected city center in 1967. In the 1980s protection was extended to interiors and public spaces, and in 1995 the boundaries of the conservation zone were extended to included adjacent late-nineteenth-century neighborhoods around the medieval center. Major restoration projects were completed in the 1990s, including the seventeenth-century Salzburg cathedral, the first major baroque church north of the Alps, and the Hohensalzburg Palace, the largest intact medieval fortress in central Europe.

During the September 2002 flood that inundated many historic central European cities, Salzburg and its environs were among the most severely affected in Austria, with more than 10,000 houses seriously damaged or destroyed. Emergency support came quickly from the Austrian government, the recently established EU Solidarity Fund, and numerous international charities and humanitarian organizations. Austrian cultural heritage was most severely harmed in the small historic town of Steyr, between Salzburg and Linz, where 150 listed buildings were damaged and the ground floor of the Arbeitswelt Museum was flooded.

In Graz, the Old Town Conservation Fund was established in 1974 and is supported by the city (55 percent) and by the Province of Styria (45 percent). In its first thirty-five years, it provided 1,450 grants toward the restoration of exterior facades of privately owned buildings in the cities five protective zones.[9] The Fund's €4.9 million ($7.1 million) expenditure thus far has encouraged an additional €150 million ($217 million) in private spending on conservation in Graz. In 2007 a Management Plan for the World Heritage Site of Graz was integrated into the city's planning procedures. The plan involves proactive monitoring and controls development in the core and a buffer zone.

Figure 14-3 The installation of starkly new additions to the roofs of several historic architectural landmarks in Vienna stirred debate in the early twenty-first century among traditionalists and those preferring instances of contemporariness in Vienna's historic center. A similar debate had raged over a decade earlier when Hans Hollein's postmodernist glass-and-concrete Haas-Haus (shown here) was completed in 1990 on Vienna's central square, directly across from St. Stephen's Cathedral in the heart of the historic city center.

Developmental pressures and economic growth have posed the greatest threat to Austrian urban heritage in recent years. In 2004 ICOMOS Austria noted that the historic roofscapes of Vienna were threatened by recent trends toward making attic spaces usable as well as building upward from existing buildings.[10] A loophole had been found within legislation, which, while protecting historic facades, allowed for rooftop additions, even to buildings within protective zones. Nineteenth-century buildings, which form a large percentage of Vienna's building stock, have been particularly at risk. Though measures were taken to arrest this skyline-changing trend in Vienna's historic Inner City, by 2009 ICOMOS Austria was concerned that the same trend had become prevalent in Graz as a result of planned alterations to a nineteenth-century department store in the city's historic core.[11] Despite several revisions to the design as a result of the concerns of architectural conservationists, critics still argue the project will ruin the integrity of the World Heritage district in Graz.

Graz has also made headlines in recent years for a controversial new building in the historic center of the city: the 2003 Kunsthaus addition to a listed nineteenth-century cast-iron building by architects Colin Fournier and Peter Cook. The Kunsthaus' amorphous black glass structure with raised porthole-like nozzles contrasts markedly with the city's traditional red-tiled and gabled roofs. Known affectionately as "the alien" and criticized as "the blob," Graz's new contemporary art museum had been noted as part of a "damaging trend" by UNESCO, causing them to question the city's World Heritage status.[12] On the other hand, this same Kunsthaus has led others to praise the local authorities' nontraditional vision, which has encouraged risk taking and has prevented the "mummification" of the historic city.[13]

Evaluating Graz's Kunsthaus perhaps requires time, considering how the Loos House across from Vienna's Hofburg shocked architectural critics, traditionalists, and the public in 1909, but has since become an icon of modern architecture and a revered component of Vienna's historic cityscape. Hans Hollein's New Haas House across from St. Stephen's Cathedral was similarly skeptically received while being built in the late 1980s, but it, too, has become a key site on architectural tours of Vienna today. Indeed, UNESCO originally designated the center of Graz as a World Heritage Site because within it "each epoch is represented by typical architectural styles which form a harmonious whole."[14]

Local and international heritage conservation lobbyists have been unsuccessful in their challenge of intrusive new construction in the outskirts of Salzburg, where after ten years of planning and controversy, a large sports stadium and parking facility were constructed immediately across from the gates of the Klessheim Palace. Since Klessheim is one of the best known works of the baroque master Johann Fischer von Erlach and one of Austria's most important historic palaces, conservation activists argued that the stadium, completed in 2003, fundamentally altered its historic context and obstructed views between it and Salzburg's other monuments, including the city's fortifications and the steeple of the Müllner Church.[15] Through efforts by UNESCO and ICOMOS, the stadium's total height was reduced to mitigate its impact; however, modifications to accommodate Austria's hosting of the UEFA EURO 2008 soccer championships extended Salzburg stadium's capacity from 18,300 to 30,400 seats and its height to a total of 10.5 meters (35 feet), basically negating the contextual preservation victory negotiated only a few years earlier.

OTHER RECENT CHALLENGES AND DEVELOPMENTS

Partnerships among various government entities have resulted in successful conservation projects in Austria. For example, the City of Krems, Province of Lower Austria, and Federal Office of the Preservation of Historic Monuments worked together to restore the Gozzoburg, one of the country's most important medieval residential structures. A 2006 competition solicited ideas for the restoration of this fourteenth-century urban mansion and its conversion into a museum. The recently completed project uncovered a number of interior murals and won a EU/Europa Nostra award for conservation in 2009.[16]

Figure 14-4 Adaptive use of four obsolete nineteenth-century gasometers (a) as housing, with commercial amenities, by architects Jean Nouvel, Coop Himmelblau, Manfred Weldorn, and Wilhelm Holzbauer helped redefine the Simmering district of Vienna as mainly residential. Flexibility and cooperation on the part of the architects, owners, and heritage administrators who produced this project is reflected in the successful resolution of differing conservation philosophies used in the same project, namely, careful restoration of the distinctive facades of these unusual structures and a much freer and more imaginative treatment of the formerly void spaces within. The interior of Gasometer B (b) was designed by the architects Coop Himmelblau.

a

b

Figure 14-5 Various historic interiors in the former Niederösterreichisches Landhaus (State House of the Federal Province of Lower Austria), with elements dating to 1513, were sensitively restored by architect Gerhard Lindner for use by the Governor of Vienna and the Federal Minister of European and International Affairs. Other parts of the complex became conference facilities. Completed in 2005, the work was supervised by the Bundesdenkmalamt assisted by specialty conservation consultants.

In recent years, architectural conservation has also been overseen and undertaken by the private sector in Austria. Most notably, in 2000, the Baukulturstiftung Osterreichische (Austrian Building Trust) was founded as a nonprofit organization interested in purchasing and restoring historic sites and making them publicly accessible.[17] Demonstrating its interest in a broad range of periods and building types, its initial projects included the ruins of a Romanesque church in Graz, a Renaissance country house in Styria, and Gustav Klimt's last atelier in Vienna.

Other voluntary organizations working for Austria's heritage include the Österreichische Gesellschaft für Denkmal-und Ortsbildpflege (Austrian Association for the Preservation of Monuments and Views), which has branches throughout the country and is focused on publications and public education; the Initiative Denkmalschutz (Monument Protection Initiative), which maintains a list of sites in danger and seeks to increase community participation in architectural conservation; the Gemeinnützige Österreichische Baukultur Privatstiftung (Private Trust for Austrian Building Culture), which is based on the British National Trust model and protects endangered properties through purchase and restoration; and the Österreichische Gesellschaft für Historische Garten (Austrian Association for Historic Gardens), which focuses on this single aspect of Austria's built heritage.

As a result of the significant interest and extensive protective measures in Austria's historic cities, today it is the country's rural architecture that is most at risk.[18] Austria's traditional farm houses and their landscapes are threatened by changing socioeconomic patterns and development. Decline in church attendance has led to the abandonment of rural ecclesiastical buildings whose disuse means a lack of regular maintenance and upkeep.

Despite these new challenges for Austria's conservation professionals, having marked a century and a half of successful, organized heritage protection in 2000 in celebration of the 150th anniversary of the Emperor Franz Josef's establishment of the Zentral Kommission, Austria can assuredly look forward to new successes in the field in the twenty-first century.

ENDNOTES

1. "Organization," Bundesdenkmalamt, www.bda.at/organisation (accessed November 6, 2009). The influential earlier history of architectural conservation in Austria is described in Stubbs, *Time Honored*, "The Forging of a Discipline: The German States and Austria," 226–238.

2. "Abteilung Restaurierwerkstätten Baudenkmalpflege," Bundesdenkmalamt, http://bda.at/organisation/885 (accessed December 30, 2009).

3. City of Vienna (on Behalf of the Republic of Austria), Report on the Requests and Recommendations Made by the World Heritage Committee Regarding the World Heritage Site "Historic Centre of Vienna (Austria)" September 2002 (Wien, Austria: 2002), 18; www.wien.gv.at/english/urbandevelopment/pdf/report05.pdf (accessed June 17, 2010).

4. Manfred Wehdorn, "Social and Economic Integration of Cultural Heritage in Austria," in Drdácký, *European Research on Cultural Heritage: State-of-the-Art Studies*, 23–30. Originally: "Social and Economic Integration of Cultural Heritage in Europe" (paper, 1st Ariadne Workshop, Prague, Czech Republic, April 23–29, 2001).

5. The multiple volumes of the *Dehio-Handbuch der Kunstdenkmäler Österreichs* are edited and prepared by the Bundesdenkmalamt and published by Verlag Berger, based in Horn, Austria. Currently there are 17 available volumes, with publication dates ranging from 1983 (Graz) through 2009 (Linz). The original Dehio guide, which focused on historic sites Germany, is totally separate. It has also been periodically updated and republished in multiple volumes covering cities or regions of Germany. Since 2001 new editions have been prepared and published as the *Dehio Handbuch der deutschen Kunstdenkmäler* (Dehio Handbook of German Historic Monuments) by the Vereinigung der Landesdenkmalpfleger (Association of Conservation Authorities) in association with the private Deutsche Stiftung Denkmalschutz (The German Foundation for Monument Protection).

6. The multiple volumes of the *Österreichische Kunsttopographie* are also edited and prepared by the Bundesdenkmalamt and published by Verlag Berger, based in Horn, Austria. Currently there are 20 available volumes, with publication dates ranging from 1973 (Oberwölz) through 2009 (Wels).

7. "Austria," European Heritage Network, www.european-heritage.coe.int/sdx/herein/national_heritage/voir.xsp?id=intro_AT_en (accessed November 6, 2009).

8. City of Vienna, "Report on the Requests and Recommendations Made by the World Heritage Committee," 20.

9. URBACT II Thematic Network HerO, "City of Graz, Austria: Graz: Fund for the Preservation of the Old Town," *HerO—Heritage as Opportunity: Sustainable Management Strategies for Vital Historic Urban Landscapes: Good-Practice Compilation* (2009), 10–11, http://urbact.eu/fileadmin/Projects/HERO/outputs_media/HerO_-_Good_Practice_Compilation.pdf (accessed June 17, 2010).

10. ICOMOS Austria, "Austria: Vienna Roofscape and Roofspace," *Heritage at Risk 2004–2005* (Paris: ICOMOS, 2004), 41–45

11. ICOMOS Austria, "Austria: Roof Alteration to the Department Store Kastner & Öhler—An Attack on the Roofscape of Graz," *Heritage@Risk 2006–2007* (Paris: ICOMOS, 2006), 35.

12. ICOMOS Austria, "Austria," *Heritage@Risk 2000* (Paris: ICOMOS, 2000), www.international.icomos.org/risk/world_report/2000/austria_2000.htm (accessed December 30, 2009).

13. UNESCO-ICOMOS Mission to Graz, *Report on the Mission to Graz (World Heritage Site in Austria)* (Paris: UNESCO, 2005), http://whc.unesco.org/archive/2005/mis931-2005.pdf (accessed December 30, 2009).

14. Blaise Gauquelin, "Graz: The World Heritage of Tomorrow," *URBACT Newsletter* no. 21 (March 2006); www.mie.ro/urbactII/urbact/projects/chorus/chorus-report1.html (accessed December 30, 2009).

15. ICOMOS, "Graz (Austria)," Advisory Body Evaluation No. 931 (Paris: ICOMOS, 1998), http://whc.unesco.org/archive/advisory_body_evaluation/931.pdf (accessed December 30, 2009).

16. "Gozzoburg, Krems (Austria)," *European Union Prize for Cultural Heritage/Europa Nostra Awards 2009* (Paris: Europa Nostra, 2009), 16–17.

17. "Geschichte des National Trust in Großbritannien," Die Gemeinnützige Österreichische Baukultur-Privatstiftung, http://baukulturstiftung.at/ (accessed December 30, 2009).

18. ICOMOS Austria, "Austria," *Heritage@Risk 2000*.

Figure 15-1 Hollókö castle and its surrounding lands represent a seventeenth- and eighteenth-century rural agricultural settlement of the Palóc ethnic minority in northeast Hungary. Due to its high degree of intactness as a cultural resource of its type it was protected by Hungary's Országos Műemléki Felügyelősé (National Inspectorate for Historic Monuments) in the 1970s. Hollókö is not an open air museum so much as a living community; it was the first historic village to be added to the UNESCO World Heritage List in 1987.

15

Hungary

From prehistory onward, a landlocked position at the confluence of several important trading routes placed Hungary at the forefront of central European history. Unfortunately, its location also resulted in numerous conflicts on Hungarian soil to the detriment of its built heritage. Thirteenth-century Mongol invasions destroyed Romanesque churches during medieval Hungary's architectural zenith, and sixteenth-century Ottoman invasions destroyed numerous Gothic towns and Renaissance palaces. In turn, at the end of the seventeenth century, the Ottomans were ousted in a series of wars that destroyed the mosques, tombs, and baths they had built.[1] During World War I, demands for metal resulted in the loss of numerous church bells, brass roofs, and historic drainage systems.[2] Though most of Hungary was spared by the destruction of World War II, its capital, Budapest, suffered.

The historic sites and artifacts in Hungary that have survived this difficult history are thus highly revered, as evidenced by the meticulous care given to the country's built patrimony. Hungary has a long history of legal protection of its cultural heritage and an ever-improving organizational system for overseeing it—a promising new, comprehensive law was unveiled in 2001.

LEGISLATION AND GOVERNMENT FRAMEWORK

When the Habsburg empire absorbed Hungary in the early eighteenth century, art and culture flourished, and internationally educated nobility for the first time had the luxury of turning their attention to Hungary's cultural heritage. Several edicts were passed to protect movable heritage in the ensuing century, including an 1802 export ban on objects from castles and ruins.

The respect shown to heritage throughout the empire by the Habsburg authorities during the eighteenth century became an issue of popular concern in mid-nineteenth-century Hungary, especially as the Hungarian national movement gained ground. Even before the empire-wide Zentral Kommission was established, Imre Henszlmann, an art historian and architectural conservation advocate, appealed to the Hungarian Academy of Sciences in 1846 for the protection of built heritage in Hungary.[3] The Academy's Archaeological Committee began identifying historically significant sites and acquainting the general public with them. In the 1850s and 1860s, this work was taken over by the Vienna-based Zentral Kommission.

A return to local oversight and formal institutional protection of buildings in Hungary began after the 1867 Compromise, which created a separate Hungarian Parliament. In 1872 the Provisional Committee for Historical Monuments of Hungary was established within the Ministry of Religion and Education and was headed by Henszlmann. Medieval architecture, particularly churches, was its first priority. One of its first projects was the restoration of the thirteenth- through fifteenth-century Virgin Mary Church in Buda Castle, today's Matthias Church, which was intensively rebuilt over the next twenty years. The Provisional Committee became the Műemlékek Országos Bizottsága (MOB, National Committee for Historic Monuments) with the passage of the Historic Monuments Protection Act in 1881. This legislation provided for site care, expropriations for maintenance, and punitive sanctions to those who defaced historic sites. The MOB worked to implement these policies and the first official registration of sites; however, it was unfortunately lacking in the ability to enforce its mandates.[4]

During World War I, Hungary became an independent country, and after the war in the 1920s, the MOB's scope gradually expanded from a focus only on medieval buildings to include vernacular and folk architecture, building groupings, industrial sites, and districts of national interest such as Hollókö, the world's first World Heritage-listed village. Under the direction of the dynamic MOB Chairman Tibor Gerevich in 1949, authorities passed the country's first integrated legislation, which covered both movable and immovable heritage, and expanded the protection given to ancient sites and artifacts to artistic and historic ones. The value of the natural environment was also recognized and the concept of "aesthetic and safety zones" introduced.

Between 1945 and 1989, Hungary's Communist government frequently altered the country's complex organizational structures. Architectural heritage conservation suffered as a result of confusing and overlapping responsibilities. In 1957 Országos Műemléki Felügyelősé (National Inspectorate of Historic Monuments), operating within the Ministry of Housing and Public Construction and City Planning but acting with input from the Minister of Culture, was established. Responsibility for the capital city resided with the autonomous Budapest Inspectorate for Historic Monuments, which existed until 1992 when it was absorbed into the National Inspectorate, which was renamed the Országos Műemlékvédelmi Hivatal (OMvH, Bizottsága National Office for the Protection of Historic Monuments).

Soon after Hungary's democratic transition, a new law in 1997 significantly altered the relationship of the state toward its built heritage inventory. At that time, about 60 percent of the 10,500 listed buildings were state owned, and conservation work was directly undertaken by the government. The new legislation encouraged privatization and looked to alleviate chronic funding shortfalls by substituting private individuals as "good proprietor" owners and conservators for almost all of its holdings.[5] However, this also made built heritage susceptible to mistreatment from negligent and market-driven investors. Today, the risk of preserving only historic facades has become more widespread as entrepreneurs seek to maximize the value of their holdings by modernizing interiors while retaining charming external architectural features to suit the tastes of both locals and tourists.[6]

In 2001, a comprehensive new Law on Protection of Cultural Heritage simplified official processes and embraced a broader definition of cultural heritage, from human-made landscapes to art objects. With the passage of this new law, responsibility for the protection of historic sites and artifacts moved to the Kulturális Örökségvédelmi Hivatal (KÖH, National Office for Cultural Heritage) within the Ministry of Education and Culture.[7] The KÖH was established by merging the OMvH with the Kulturális Örökség Igazgatósága (Directorate of Cultural Heritage), thereby consolidating all heritage agencies within a single institution as the former had been responsible for most immovable heritage and the latter for archaeological and movable heritage. The KÖH operates through seven regional offices and an additional thirteen subcounty offices, and it has a division focused on the conservation of Hungarian cultural heritage outside the country's current geographic boundaries. With its clear, legally defined scope, national authority, and local presence, the KÖH today provides Hungary with a heritage protection system sufficient to cope with the demands on historic sites in the country today.

SENSITIVE CONSERVATION APPROACHES

Respect for authenticity has been a key interest to Hungarian heritage conservation since the late nineteenth century, when architect Istvan Möller opted for preserving authentic remains rather than reconstructing what had been destroyed at the thirteenth-century Premontrian cathedral in Zsámbék.[8] Hungary's "conserve rather than restore" approach was further refined over the course of the twentieth century and continues in the twenty-first century as a result of philosophical preferences and funding realities.[9]

In the 1930s MOB Chairman Tibor Gerevich introduced modern, scientifically based restoration to Hungary through the conservation of wall paintings. Originally, many of Hungary's Byzantine and Renaissance buildings were beautifully adorned with murals and frescos executed by some of the best artisans of their time. Unfortunately, early restorations of them were poorly executed: damaged sections were removed, faded sections repainted, and destroyed sections re-created.[10] An appropriate and sensitive approach toward wall paintings was first taken in 1935, when the MOB commissioned the talented Italian Mauro Pellicoli to restore the murals at Esztergom palace and the medieval Benedictine Abbey church at Ják. Today, only the highest restoration standards prevail in Hungary: even faintly surviving fresco portions are respected, retouchings minimal, abrasions no longer covered or colored over, and new work made discernible.[11]

Because the inventory of Hungary's architectural heritage was so affected by successive waves of destruction and very few artistic and historic treasures remain intact, conservators have emphasized the retrieval and conservation of original fabric. The careful treatment of even fragments of historic and artistic materials is today one of the most widely known Hungarian conservation policies. "Indirect anastylosis," in which obviously modern support frameworks display fragments in their original positions, was pioneered by architects Emmerich Kálmán and Géza Lux in the 1930s.[12] Though used globally today, this approach, which permits the conservation, exhibition, and interpretation of highly fragmentary ruins, is still closely associated with Hungary.

In 1961 "indirect anastylosis" was used at the site of the second-century Roman Temple of Isis in Szombathely. The important discovery of sculpted cornice fragments made a conjectural reconstruction of the temple's facade possible.[13] A reinforced concrete structure approximating the portico's silhouette was built over the excavated foundations and fitted with marble fragments placed in their original positions. The unobtrusive support structure serves as an interpretive guide to the temple without deflecting attention away from the original fabric.[14] Indirect anastylosis has been used at other Roman archaeological sites in Hungary such as at Aquincum's Amphitheater and at medieval sites such as the Árpád dynasty's castle in Esztergom.

Because of Hungary's long interest in effective architectural conservation, the 1964 publication of the Venice Charter struck a resonant chord for its heritage protection professionals. As soon as the charter was translated into Hungarian, the Hungarian Academy of Science Commission on the History and Theory of Architecture held a conference to ensure that their methodologies were fully consistent with the new recommendations. Hungary became one of the first countries to actively adopt the Venice Charter precepts and has risen to the challenges it posed. In 2004 Hungary celebrated the charter's fortieth anniversary by hosting an ICOMOS conference in the historic city of Pécs. The Charter's call to conserve sites by making them socially useful without modifying a building's layout or decoration required inventive solutions from conservation architects.[15] Wherever possible, a site's former function was retained—as was done at Budapest's sixteenth-century Turkish Kiraly baths, where today centuries-old bathing rituals continue to live on. The site, enlarged in the nineteenth century, was restored in the 1950s.

Hungary's tradition of sensitive conservation interventions continues today at sites like the Mátra Museum, Gyöngyös, which won an EU/Europa Nostra cultural heri-

a

b

c

Figure 15-2 The practice of "indirect anastylosis," or the repositioning of displaced fragments of seriously damaged buildings to their original position and selectively using distinctly contemporary materials to support these elements was developed in Hungary in the 1930s. In the latest of four restorations at Visegrád castle in over a century, as part of post-fire repairs to the Solomon tower, architect János Sedlmayr aimed to make a clear distinction between the original structure and later additions on both the exterior (a) and interior (b). Necessary replacement elements, such as the tower's winding stair were built in carefully detailed reinforced concrete-and-steel construction, and the former vaulting of the tower's fourth level was abstractly depicted in stretched fabric mesh (c). Images courtesy National Office of Cultural Heritage, Budapest; Tamás Fejérdy.

tage Grand Prize in 2009. The jury argued the project was "an outstanding example of harmonious coexistence of a careful historical restoration and the incorporation of contemporary architecture. The ensemble has regained the authentic complexity and completeness of the property while employing high levels of standard and quality."[16] The restoration of the baroque and neoclassical eighteenth- and nineteenth-century mansion and its gardens, which involved the construction of a new glass roof over the former courtyard, was partially financed by the European Union.

ADDITIONAL PROJECTS AND SUCCESSES

Until the 1940s, few medieval buildings were thought to still exist in Hungary, but war damage unearthed this "lost" inventory in several instances; the newly discovered medieval remains had been embedded in later structures, especially around the historic center of Buda. Budapest's Castle District suffered significant damage during World War II, and its repair was Hungary's first major postwar restoration project and, at the time, Europe's largest archaeological excavation.[17] As soon as the war ended, medieval and Renaissance ruins, including thousands of stone carvings and ceramics, were unearthed under the castle's nineteenth-century remains. Today, the fortress' defensive system and Knight's Hall have been restored.[18]

To maximize the impact of the miscellaneous architectural features that had been discovered—a Gothic door, an arcade cornice, window decorations—medieval elements were left evident wherever possible. Though undoubtedly additional fragments exist, they have not been sought, for the Hungarian approach respects the value of a building's subsequent alterations. More recent architectural features would rarely be destroyed to feature older details.

The post–World War II rescue of baroque mansions and palaces in Hungary proved extremely difficult, as war damage often compounded long-term problems caused by inadequate maintenance and new uses were difficult to find. Insensitive adaptive reuse created more problems than it solved at several sites; however, some renovations were successful, including the conversion of Prince Eugene of Savoy's palace in Ráckeve, built in 1702 by the Austrian architect Johann Lukas von Hildebrandt, into an architects' retreat.

The restoration of the baroque Eszterháza mansion, Hungary's largest residence, is the country's most high-profile architectural conservation project to date after the Buda Castle restoration.[19] Following years of meticulous research, Esterháza, near Fertőd, Hungary, was restored in 1958. Its wings house an agricultural vocational school and scientific research institute, while the main building holds a museum dedicated to longtime resident composer Franz Joseph Haydn and includes furnished eighteenth-century rooms. The palace where Haydn created many of his masterpieces is once again the scene of classical concerts, both on its grounds and in its large public rooms.

Figure 15-3 For over a decade the Hungarian government has been restoring the late eighteenth-century Baroque Eszterháza Palace in Fertőd, and it is once again a classical concert venue in honor of a former resident of its grounds, Franz Joseph Haydn.

Figure 15-4 The oldest extant iron-smelting foundry in Hungary at Újmassa, dating from 1811, was restored in 1952, joining the country's several other conserved industrial heritage sites. Image courtesy National Office of Cultural Heritage, Budapest; Tamás Fejérdy.

Because Hungary does not link historic status to a structure's age, significant buildings from the modern era were granted protection long before such measures were implemented in other countries. By 1952, early modern buildings were officially protected, including several buildings erected just prior to World War II. Adorned with some of the decade's finest progressive artwork, a notable example is Budapest's Heart of Jesus Church, which was begun by Aladár Arkady in 1931 and completed by his son Bertalan in 1935.

The conservation of the country's industrial heritage is also important in Hungary since late twentieth-century modernization demolished or made many such sites obsolete. Only twenty-four out of an estimated ten thousand mills that were extant in 1900 survived through the twentieth century. Today, many of those preserved display their machinery and other installations. Other historically significant industrial sites under government protection include the country's first foundry in Újmassa: a blue-dye factory in Pápa, an early eighteenth-century bakery in Sopron, and machine works from the mid-nineteenth century.

The imposition of modern safety specifications at nineteenth-century railroad stations has significantly affected their conservation and reuse. Budapest's Nyugati Pályaudvar (West Railway Station), with its 42 meters (138 feet) long train shed, was among the world's largest buildings when erected by Gustav Eiffel's engineering firm in the 1870s. Its averted demolition and subsequent renovation was a major achievement for Hungarian conservationists, who overcame many structural difficulties to ensure the station's continued use.

While heritage conservation is important to the government and the public, and even if Hungary has one of the strongest economies among the former Eastern Bloc countries, competition for funding with numerous domestic needs is great. Nonetheless, to reinforce popular appreciation of Hungary's historic patrimony, the cultural ministry initiated various programs for its cities and significantly increased its church building conservation budget to Ft 4 billion (approximately $18.5 million).[20] Such tangible support for heritage protection, coupled with the earlier encompassing heritage protection legislation passed in 2001, points to a bright future for architectural conservation in Hungary.

ENDNOTES

1. Notable exceptions include the Turkish Király and Császár Baths, which were built over Buda's thermal springs. They have survived almost intact and continue their original medieval function today. The few mosques that still exist do not retain their religious usage; for example, the important sixteenth-century Yakovali Hassan Mosque in Pécs is a museum.

2. In 1915 the Hungarian Royal Defense Ministry issued a requisition order for these metal objects. Much destruction of Hungary's artistic patrimony had already occurred by 1917, when the government's heritage oversight group, the National Committee for Historic Monuments (MOB), succeeded in having an exemption passed for bells cast prior to 1700 or that had a cultural or historic significance. However, there was no sparing the metal building components. According to military commanders, "many such buildings are of value because of their interior decoration, while in the case of others, namely those which are simply and plainly covered, their artistic and other values are not always going to manifest themselves in material." Corvina Kiadó, *Historical Monuments and Their Protection in Hungary* (Budapest: Egyetemi Nyomda, 1984), 64.

3. Ibid., 261.

4. The 1881 Act also did not extend protection to movable cultural artifacts, for which comprehensive legal protection was not passed until 1929. Judit Tamási, ed., *Heritage Protection within the Compass of Legal Regulation* (Budapest: Ministry of National Cultural Heritage, National Board for the Protection of Historic Monuments, 2001), 7 and 13.

5. Jokilehto, *A History of Architectural Conservation*. Oxford: Elsevier Butterworth-Heinemann, 2004, p. 262; first published in 1999.

6. ICOMOS Hungary, "Hungary," *Heritage@Risk 2000* (Paris: ICOMOS, 2000), www.international.icomos.org/risk/world_report/2000/hunga_2000.htm, (accessed December 30, 2009).

7. "National Office of Cultural Heritage," Kulturális Örökségvédelmi Hivatal, www.koh.hu/english.html (accessed December 30, 2009).

8. Miklós Horler, "The Charter of Venice and the Restoration of Historical Monuments in Hungary," *ICOMOS Bulletin* no. 1 (1971): 79.

9. Ibid, 69.

10. Tamási, *Heritage Protection within the Compass of Legal Regulation*, 92.

11. Kiadó, *Historical Monuments and Their Protection in Hungary*, 10.

12. Horler, "The Charter of Venice and the Restoration of Historical Monuments in Hungary," 81.

13. The remains of Aquincum, Emperor Hadrian's first-century provincial seat, are found in Budapest, while digs at Sopron unearthed Roman Scarbantia and at Pécs, Roman Sopianae. These archaeological sites include remnants of murals, mosaics, amphitheaters, baths, temples, shops, and houses, and they are among the oldest and most valued heritage sites found in Hungary today.

14. Horler, "The Charter of Venice and the Restoration of Historical Monuments in Hungary," 95.

15. Article 5, "The Venice Charter," ICOMOS, www.icomos.org/venice_charter.html (accessed December 30, 2009).

16. "Mátra Museum, Gyöngyös (Hungary)," *European Union Prize for Cultural Heritage/Europa Nostra Awards 2009* (Paris: Europa Nostra, 2009), 10–11.

17. Kiadó, *Historical Monuments and Their Protection in Hungary*, 18.

18. Due to damage sustained during the Turkish wars, only a medieval keep and chapel survived. The chapel now houses a unique collection of Gothic statues, which were discovered in 1974.

19. In 1760–67 Miklós Esterházy, called "the Magnificent" for the splendor of his court, converted a small hunting lodge into the huge Esterházy castle, a 126-room mansion in Fertöd, with the probable help of architects Girolamo Bonn, Miklós Jakoby, and Menyhért Hefele. The mansion, surrounded by a 250-acre, French-style park, became the era's most famous center of aristocratic society. Court composer Franz Joseph Haydn and others performed in its 200-seat theatre. Grand living at the mansion survived until Duke Nikolas Esterhazy's death in 1790, when the family moved to Austria and allowed the building to decay. One-hundred-fifty years later, it sustained major damage as the Germans' last World War II headquarters. Among the special features found during its restoration in the 1950s and 1960s were its original chinoiserie wall paintings, which were restored.

20. Tamási, *Heritage Protection within the Compass of Legal Regulation*, 188.

a

Figure 16-1 The sixteenth-century Church of the Assumption of the Virgin Mary in the north Bohemian town of Most was moved to a new location some 840 meters away (a). The decision was made to relocate the entire town in order to excavate coal deposits beneath it in the 1960s. The church was one of the few historic buildings that survived, and moving it after seven years of preparation was an example of the high technological capacity in architectural conservation in 1975. The church, with its supporting steel girdle, was moved along four sets of rails, at a rate of approximately one inch per minute. The interior was extensively braced to withstand the moving process (b). One of fifty transporting rail trolleys and servos supported and carried the church as it traveled to its new location (c). Courtesy Susan Schur, *Technology & Conservation Magazine of Art, Architecture and Antiquities*, Boston, Massachusetts.

b

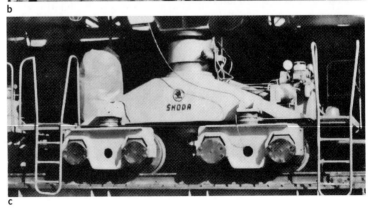

c

CHAPTER 16

Czech Republic and Slovakia

Until 1993 the Czech Republic and Slovakia shared both a government and an architectural conservation tradition. Both were part of the Habsburg empire until 1918 when the country of Czechoslovakia was established and, following a brief separation during World War II, was reformed as a centralized communist country under the influence of the Soviet Union in 1948. The democratic Czechoslovakia established by 1989's Velvet Revolution lasted only a few years, until the country voluntarily and peacefully separated into the Czech Republic and Slovakia in December 1992.

Prior to the formation of Czechoslovakia, architectural heritage was subject to the regulations of the Austro-Hungarian Empire. The Czech population in particular was well aware of the value of its heritage and proud of its richness and variety. The cultural importance of architectural conservation can be seen in the Czech building restoration tradition and by the establishment in 1854 of a still-extant journal dedicated to archaeological and historic sites. Shortly thereafter, the region of Bohemia began a voluminous listing of its architectural, artistic, and historic buildings. This list was actively maintained until the outbreak of World War II in 1937.[1]

The scope of contemporary architectural conservation challenges in these countries is extensive as a result of neglect and inadequate resources during the Communist period, and large percentages of their historic sites require attention. While the situation today is improved due to progress over the past two decades and to growing interests in sustainable conservation, the volume of cultural heritage sites in the Czech Republic and Slovakia still requiring attention remains high.

ARCHITECTURAL CONSERVATION IN CZECHOSLOVAKIA

After the formation of Czechoslovakia, State Monument Offices were established for Bohemia as well as for Moravia and Silesia in 1918. Czechoslovakia's first law protecting historic monuments was enacted in 1948, along with the establishment of regional centers for the preservation and protection of the natural environment.[2] The 1960 constitution linked built and natural sites together as among the country's heritage to be protected, giving the country's conservation professionals a sweeping range of sites to consider. In 1987 two new laws simultaneously established three types of protection areas at three different government levels, including a central government–defined "complex of monuments," a more flexible regional government–defined "monument zone," and a less significant district government–defined "buffer zone."[3] These laws required that listed buildings be maintained by their owners, which at that time was mostly the state government.

In communist-era Czechoslovakia, two institutions within the Ministry of Culture and Education were responsible for the country's architectural heritage. The Státni ústav památkové péce (State Institute for the Care of Historic Monuments) surveyed, evaluated, and inventoried sites and prioritized projects at those deemed worthy of listing and protection. The State Office for the Restoration of Historic Towns and Buildings, with offices in Prague and Bratislava, actually carried out the conservation projects.

In the mid-twentieth century in Czechoslovakia, conservation efforts were primarily channeled toward projects that met various socialist agendas rather than toward the most historically signficant or needy sites. During the forty years of communist rule, state policies also harmed certain categories of Czech and Slovak heritage. For example, the communist-era abolition of religious orders and secularization of society broadened the threat of dilapidation to churches, temples, monasteries, convents, and other religious sites. In addition, the nationalization of nearly three-thousand properties formerly owned by the nobility turned countless formerly elegant baroque manor houses into insensitively adapted public buildings.[4] While their agricultural land holdings were absorbed into communes or cooperative farming schemes, the buildings themselves became available to various government and social organizations for use as country retreats for high-ranking officials or as hospitals and asylums. Though many country houses were kept in service in this way, many others were severely neglected and left to deteriorate.

Initial architectural restoration efforts were significant in Czechoslovakia, with thousands of conservation projects carried out in the 1950s and early 1960s at sites such as the nineteenth-century National Theater in Prague and the Gothic-hall church in Kurtna Hora. Some of the best examples from the period are the remarkably well restored Moravian town and hinterland of Telč and the Bohemian town Jičín. Telč was later designated as a World Heritage Site and inspired the creation of protective legislation in the Czech Republic.[5] The buildings surrounding the central square of the walled medieval town of Jičín were carefully restored in a phased conservation plan that also called for new construction to be sensitive to the historic context. Czechoslovak conservation approaches in the early communist period were noted for their lack of reconstruction of missing or damaged elements, clear demarcation between old and new elements, and even for rejecting historicist new building designs.[6] An exemplary project, for instance, for care and technical achievement was the relocation of an architecturally significant stone church in Most, which originally stood above a particularly valuable coal mine. At great cost, the building was held together with a concrete band, hydraulically lifted onto cribbing and gently moved via railway to the relocated town in 1975. Restoration of the church continued for over a decade after the move was completed.

On the other hand, much damage was done through neglect or poorly conceived property adaptations during the Communist period. According to Josef Stulc, former director of the State Institute for the Care of Historic Monuments, between 1958 and 1988, ten percent of Czechoslovakia's built heritage—3,500 sites—was lost due to decay and neglect.[7] Innumerable significant buildings were never listed by authorities, because there were no funds available to maintain them, as would be required for designated sites. The economic costs of maintaining cultural heritage was never incorporated into government agencies or a tax system, which remains today a major impediment toward large-scale architectural conservation in both the Czech Republic and Slovakia.

CZECH REPUBLIC

Heritage conservation responsibilities in today's Czech Republic are still defined by the 1987 Czechoslovak State Preservation Act, which has been amended numerous times, most recently in 2004. The law provides for the designation and protection of monuments and monument zones to which interventions require approval. Since Czechoslovakia split in the early 1990s, responsibility for overseeing built cultural heritage in the Czech Republic has resided with the Ministry of Culture's Monument Institute, which in 2001 was renamed the Národní památkový ústav (National Heritage Institute). The Národní památkový ústav has a main office in Prague, centers in two castles, and thirteen regional training centers, and it is also assisted by district and municipal authorities located in the country's major cities. The ústav maintains the Central List of Cultural Monuments of the Czech Republic, which includes over 38,700 historic sites and 800,000 movable objects.

Training of conservation professionals in the Czech Republic is carried out at specialized educational institutions such as the State Conservation Institute and the Prague Conservation Institute.[8] Programs at various secondary and higher education institutions ensure a continued supply of local conservation professionals. The most internationally well known is the restoration program of the Akademie výtvarných umění (Academy of Fine Arts), which was established in 1947, as well as that of the Faculty of Restoration at the University of Pardubice in Litomyšl, which was established in 2005. These are complemented by local training opportunities offered by the Společnost pro technologie ochrany památek (Society for Monument Preservation Technologies), the Asociace restaurátorů (Restorers Association), and by the Czech committees of ICOMOS, ICCROM, and ICOM.

The lack of financial assistance for conservation efforts has become especially important in the past two decades. Complicated restitution laws, enacted during the 1990s, returned many privatized estates to their pre-1948 owners in a dilapidated or altered state. Legally, their appearance cannot be changed without government approval, and repairs must be made in line with advice obtained from the Národní památkový ústav.[9] However, while the government can settle ecological claims related to privatized properties by drawing on its National Property Fund, these funds are not allocated to finance private rehabilitation projects. There are currently no tax deductions allowable for restoration expenses, irrespective of whether a building will eventually be opened to the public. Additionally, there are no institutions such as the British National Trust to centralize efforts for sourcing and disseminating funds for approved private projects.

Estates not returned to private ownership remain the responsibility of the state, which now technically has no legal requirement to protect them.[10] Thus, with no private, centralized capacity to purchase and maintain important state-owned buildings and a weak legal framework and lack of institutional capacity to manage these properties, the situation for government-owned historic sites in the Czech Republic is not significantly better than for privately owned properties.[11]

The little attention given to Czech historic town centers for half a century meant there was no investment in repairs and that many sites were lost due to neglect. But it also meant that there was usually no detrimental new development, so that historic urban forms were spared the redevelopment suffered by many western European cities in the 1950s and 1960s. Since 1989 this situation has dramatically reversed: Czech cities are building and developing at unprecedented speed.

This is true nowhere more so than in the capital city of Prague, which faces significant architectural conservation challenges today despite its championing as a cultural tourism destination. Unlike many other major European cities, Prague's historic center survived World War II almost completely intact, and it is today renowned for a dense cultural environment that is unique in both quality and quantity of extant medieval buildings. The historic Staré Město (Old Town), including the Church of Our Lady before Týn and old Town Hall, rests on the eastern bank of the Vltava River and has been recognized as a World Heritage Site. Across the famous Charles Bridge with its statuary and towers, lies the Malá Strana (Lesser Town), dominated by Pražský hrad (Prague Castle) and St. Vitus Cathedral. Following extensive restorations, some funded by international organizations, Prague Castle now houses the administrative and social offices of the president and serves as a popular venue for cultural programs and exhibitions and as a major tourist destination.

a

Figure 16-2 Properties offered to their former owners after the Czech Republic's economic transition in 1989 were in many cases claimed, and the descendants of their former owners often found themselves faced with extensive conservation projects as the aristocratic homes had often been severely damaged by neglect or misuse during the Communist period. Members of the Lobkowicz family from the United States claimed their ancestral home, Nelahozeves Zamek (a), along with several other properties, and through great effort have restored this sixteenth-century fortified manor in Bohemia as a self-sustaining estate museum and cultural heritage attraction. Of the manor's interiors, the most noteworthy are the south-facing Arcade Hall on the first floor and a grand room with a very well-preserved Renaissance interior dating to 1564 (b). Known as the Knight's Hall, it is decorated with frescoes of larger-than-life military figures. The ceiling's theme is Titus Livius' description of the five examples of Roman virtues. Courtesy The Lobkowicz Collections.

b

Figure 16-3 Restoration of the elaborate mosaic ornamentation (a) above exterior portals of St. Vitus Cathedral (b) at Prague Castle was made possible by technical analysis and funding provided by the Getty Conservation Institute in 1999. The project included a training component for local conservators and extensive monitoring has been ongoing since its completion.

a

b

The economic boom of the late twentieth century has done more to negatively affect Prague's historic integrity and structural authenticity than any overtly hostile act. Though miraculously spared by war and neglected by an insensitive government rule for nearly a half century, the nearly completely intact historic center of the city has been rapidly eroded by new investment projects since the Velvet Revolution. Inappropriately scaled buildings built from discordant modern materials occupy infill sites. Some old structures are modified beyond recognition in new commercial zones, as modernized glass-fronted ground-floor spaces are created to attract shoppers. The conservation of Prague's Staré Město and its promotion as a tourist center has also driven out permanent residents and non-tourist-related businesses, socially altering the character of the city and reducing the historic identity for which it is praised and visited.

Perhaps most disfiguring of all is the much wider array of colors applied to Prague's buildings. Historically, the buildings of Prague, many of which date to the medieval period, were adorned with limited range of exterior colors, but, in their zeal to clean up the town, modern renovators have chosen a variety of historically inaccurate colors for building exteriors. These not only impact the city's ambiance, but the paint's chemistry is also potentially destructive. Modern nonporous paints trap moisture, which may cause historic building surfaces to deteriorate. Fortunately, since the late 1990s more physically compatible exterior applied finishes consisting of silicates and lime-based paints are being used.

During the early 1990s, the stress of modernization quickly outpaced the ability of local administrators to handle the deluge of applications for new construction projects, and an overwhelmed network approved several projects that should have been more carefully considered. The placement of Prague on World Monument Fund's 1998 Watch List focused attention on the problem, as did the devastating

a

b

Figure 16-4 The rapid opening of Prague to a free market economy after the country's economic and political transition in 1989 brought with it rapid change to the city's almost completely intact historic center (a). A plethora of relatively minor changes in the form of upgraded storefronts, new paint colors, and discordant signage (b) adds to the historic areas on both sides of the Vltava River having a newer, less authentic character.

Figure 16-5 The distinctive glass conservatory built by Johannes Lichtenstein in 1850 as an adjoining structure to Lednice Zamek in southern Moravia was restored in 2002 under the direction of Pamatkovýústav of Brno through a funding partnership between the World Monuments Fund and one of the biggest Czech banks—Československá Obchodni Banka (ČSOB). This was one of several priority conservation projects since the early 1990s at the Lednice-Valtice cultural landscape that derived from two international charrettes (planning sessions) that addressed conservation issues and opportunities ranging in scale from conserving paintings in the baroque chapel at Valtice Zamek to development of the Czech Greenways system that connects this World Heritage List site to several neighboring countries through reactivation of historic road and trail systems.

floods of August 2002, which inundated basements of historic structures through much of Prague, as well as other historic Czech towns such as České Budějovice and Plzeň. International assistance was offered and accepted to aid in repairing damage to the heritage of these fragile cities.

Today, ongoing educational and media campaigns actively reinforce the value of historic Prague to both its citizens and to the world, as public awareness is seen as the most effective force against the threat of inappropriate development. Hopes that recent trends in Prague have been abated were raised by the Czech Ministry of Culture's December 2005 overruling of a building permit issued by the city's Department for the Preservation of Monuments for a new luxury apartment building in the Hradčany (Castle District) conservation area. However, development economics being as attractive as they are, preservation of Prague's historic integrity will likely remain a constant battle.

In the Czech Republic, years of aggressive strip mining has eradicated or irreparably defaced some of Bohemia's built and natural heritage and left behind a scarred landscape and memories of over 150 villages and settlements.[12] Unfortunately, most ecological problems remain to be rectified and most mining-related sites worthy of preseration have not been protected. Current land-use-planning concepts for this region include the creation of extensive green zones—or reclaimed land—that may be connected by revived picturesque heritage routes (greenways) and that will tie into a national ecologically sensitive network. Though some Czech industrial sites are considered significant patrimony in their own right, conservation of such sites is not easy to arrange and alternative uses seem limited. A need for funding for industrial heritage sites such as Vitkovice's 1828 Ironworks complex is critical—without significant financial support little can be done to conserve it or similar sites.

Though no sites in Czechoslovakia were included on UNESCO's World Heritage List, the Czech Republic has been very active and successful in nominating sites in the past two decades. Between 1992 and 2003, twelve Czech cultural sites were added to UNESCO's list, covering a broad range of types, ages, and scales. These sites include parts of the historic centers of Český Krumlov, and Prague, Sedlec, Telč, Třebíč and the village of Holašovice; the castles of Kroměříž and Litomyšl; as well as the eighteenth-century Holy Trinity Column in Olomouc and Pilgrimage Church of St. John of Nepomuk at Zelená Hora, Mies van der Rohe's 1930 Tugendhat Villa in Brno, and the Lednice-Valtice Cultural Landscape.[13]

SLOVAKIA

Of the two states formed by Czechoslovakia's political dissolution in 1992, Slovakia's transition from a socialist, Soviet satellite to a modern market economy reliant on private investment has been slower and much more difficult than that of the Czech Republic. A weaker economic base, coupled with divisive ethnic, religious, and social pressures, has also affected its ability to erase the loss of its built patrimony by years of war, neglect, and insensitive care.

Today, cultural heritage protection in Slovakia is centrally organized within three state administrative organizations whose responsibilities are delineated by Law 49/2002: the Ministry of Culture and the Pamiatkový úrad (Monuments Board) through its offices in eight of the country's regions. Assistance in protecting monuments and historic sites—defined to include both movable and immovable property—is also provided by two relatively new professional advisory bodies, the Pamiatková rada (Monuments Council) and the Archeologickej rady (Archaeological Council), whose members are appointed by the Ministry to three-year terms.

While the 2002 law retains the concept of three protection categories established in Czechoslovakia in 1987, their titles have changed to *historic reserve*; *historic zone*; and *buffer zone*. The 2002 law also centralizes the authority of designating sites to the Central Register with the Ministry of Culture, following its receipt of a proposal from the Pamiatkový úrad. Theoretically, the broadly defined protection zones should facilitate the inclusion of minority ethnic and religious sites into the Central Register, but to date they have had limited effect. The country's current listing remains largely reflective of only the ethnic Slovak majority, although there have been discussions about listing sites relating to other important twentieth-century personages.

Listing does not, however, ensure certain conservation of historic buildings and other heritage in Slovakia. The combination of an extensive number of deteriorated historic buildings and sites and limited economic resources means that little can be done except on the most important sites, or those that have generated external interest and funding. In 2000 the ICOMOS Heritage@Risk program estimated that seven hundred of Slovakia's twelve thousand listed sites were at risk, as was a "remarkable amount" of the country's movable heritage.[14] That same year, Slovakia indicated that a third of its cultural monuments were in desolate or damaged condition, a figure that included the few sites under restoration.

The Pro Slovakia Fund, created in 1991 by Czechoslovakia's post-Communist Ministry of Culture, was the country's first governmental source of funding for architectural conservation, as well as a variety of educational and cultural programs. Shortly after creation, it received a minimal 0.5 percent ($4 million) allocation of the state budget to be used for matching funds for restoration projects. Within a few years and the independence of Slovakia, funding dropped considerably, to less than $750,000 per year.[15] The Fund has not yet been replaced by a workable financing mechanism.

For many years, this lack of funds has also impeded private investment in architectural conservation in Slovakia, resulting in a loss of several historic sites. In 1991 alone, the number of listed buildings decreased by ten percent, as inspection demonstrated many had already been destroyed or irreparably damaged.[16] During the 1990s, budget cuts reduced the number of heritage conservation professionals in the field, and made it extremely difficult to monitor adherence to heritage protection laws. The problem was confounded by absurdly low financial penalties for infractions that were, consequently, no deterrent to developers: The maximum fine imposed due to any legal infraction is capped at the equivalent of about $3,000.[17]

Financial constraints are not limited to private owners of historic buildings. Municipalities have limited access to tax revenues, and must depend on state favor, or administrative creativity, to find funding resources.[18] Since the 1990s, the conservation-supportive mayors of Bratislava and Košice have implemented a variety of actions to achieve this goal. Two notable approaches have included marketing the town's opportunities to private national and international investors, and funding restoration projects with municipal rent monies. Work on a state-level tax incentive system for architectural conservation also began in the 1990s but has not yet been employed.

Slovakia's past heritage management approach is a major contributing factor to the poor state of its built patrimony today. A focus on reconstruction rather than maintenance has distorted public understanding of the methods and aims of appropriate architectural conservation, and even today this view continues to impede the growth of a collaborative approach between central authorities and local officials on conservation projects. Though the nongovernmental sector in general has been slow to develop in Slovakia in recent years, there are a few private organizations assisting the Pamiatkový úrad. Among these is the National Trust for Historic Places and Landscapes of Slovakia, established in 1996 and renamed the Narodný Trust (National Trust) in 2002.[19] The Narodný Trust's focus on public education is exemplified by the summer youth training at a nineteenth-century blast furnace it owns in Podbiel. Public and private partnerships have also been pursued by the Trust, and the results can be seen in the work at the eighteenth-century vernacular structures in Bartošova Lehôtka, which were given to the Trust by the Slovak government.

Figure 16-6 Despite being on UNESCO's World Heritage List and being protected by Slovak law, the local population of the historic silver-mining town of Banská Štiavnica still struggles to balance heritage stewardship, local pride and enthusiasm about the place, and the desire for new forms of development. A more robust national cultural heritage management system for Slovakia in general would likely help to solve these problems.

The historic structures are being restored in collaboration with other NGOs and with state support.[20] In addition to managing these and other historic properties, the Narodný Trust is helping to prepare formalized strategies for sustainable development and for the use and protection of historic buildings.

Conservation education is also a significant component of the mission of the Academia Istropolitana Nova (AINova), which was established in 1996 as an independent institution after the disbanding of the Ministry of Education's short-lived Academia Istropolitana, founded in 1990. In addition to seminars, short courses, and consultancies, AINova organizes and operates year-long graduate programs in a number of fields, including architectural conservation. With support from a number of international organizations, foreign governments, and the Slovak Ministry of Culture, AINova has completed research studies and monitoring projects as well as offered training seminars for public officials. In recognition of its important role and significant contribution to conservation education in Slovakia, AINova won an EU/Europa Nostra prize in 2009.[21]

After neglect and widespread destructive renewal in the late Communist period, Bratislava's heritage appeared protected by the introduction of historic districts shortly after Slovakia's independence. However, the boundaries of the protective zone created in 1992 in the city's Staré Mesto (Old Town), with its significant medieval, renaissance, baroque, and more recent structures, were reduced by half in 2005 because of the poor conditions of many of its building and the unwieldiness of the large protected area. No master plan has been prepared for the protective zone, and its individual buildings and overall integrity has been repeatedly threatened by demolition, unregulated alterations and construction, addition of extra floors on historic buildings, and inappropriately scaled or designed infill in and adjacent to the district.[22] These same threats are experienced in other protected zones throughout Slovakia as a result of frequent disregard for heritage legislation by developers and property owners and the failure of government agencies to enforce these policies.[23]

Banská Štiavnica, a rare and remarkably intact enclave of historic buildings and industrial sites in an impressive natural setting, is a Slovak heritage site that epitomizes the weakness of legal instruments and other threats to Slovakia's heritage. For centuries Banská Štiavnica was one of central Europe's most important gold and silver mining towns due to its extensive ores and its highly developed mining technology and natural science education centers. However, years of economic decline haven taken a toll on this historic industrial townscape. While its 1993 World Heritage listing has brought international conservation interest and funding, working tensions between local authorities and central conservation officials continue to negatively affect conservation efforts. In addition, the minimal financial penalties for breaking heritage conservation regulations have led to Banská Štiavnica's gradual decline.

Banská Štiavnica is only one of the five cultural sites in Slovakia that have been inscribed on UNESCO's World Heritage List in the past two decades. Other recognized Slovak urban sites include the fortified medieval city of Bardejov and the well-preserved centers of Levoča and Spišský Hrad. In addition, the traditional log houses of the typical central European village of Vlkolínec and the sixteenth- through eighteenth-century Catholic, Protestant, and Greek Orthodox churches of the Carpathian Mountain area represent two significant components of Slovak wooden architecture that has also been recognized by UNESCO.

Slovakia's historic built environment has long been threatened by the tension between the Ministry of Culture's professional field teams and powerful, locally elected district officials with the authority to approve development permits and make planning decisions. However, the clearer language in the 2002 Law bodes well for the future of Slovak cultural heritage protection. The state's authority over architechtural heritage and the oversight it exercises through the decentralized Pamiatkový úrad appears stronger, and for the first time the possibility of financial assistance from the Ministry or local municipalities to property owners has been introduced. In addition, membership in the EU since 2004 ensures that Slovakia's heritage protection policies and mechanisms will continue to strengthen and benefit the country's historic resources.

Figure 16-7 An example of purely local efforts to conserve cultural heritage in Slovakia is seen in the current program to stabilize and better present Lietava Castle and its rural setting in Slovakia's Žilina district. The site dates to prehistoric times and includes the ruins of the present thirteenth- through sixteenth-century castle, which reflects the region's strategic position. The Foundation for Cultural Heritage Preservation Slovak Republic started working to conserve the site on a largely voluntary basis in 2008.

Conserving Jewish Heritage in Central Europe

Since the early 1990s, the countries of central and eastern Europe have reopened their borders for tourists and international investment. With critical distance and new transparent, democratic governments, central Europe has begun the difficult process of preserving the traumatic sites of the Holocaust. At the same time, local authorities and Jewish communities are focusing on the few surviving synagogues and other historic sites as important evidence of the region's once-flourishing Jewish culture.

In addition to local and federal governments, international Jewish and cultural heritage organizations have taken an active interest in the restoration of Jewish sites in central Europe. The World Monuments Fund established its Jewish Heritage Program in 1988 and was among the first to raise awareness for conservation of Jewish heritage sites in the region, to survey and prioritize the most significant sites in the most urgent need of attention, and to award grants for exemplary restoration projects. Other active organizations have included the Ronald S. Lauder Foundation, the International Survey of Jewish Monuments, and the Getty Grant Program. Symposia, such as the one sponsored by Paris's Museum of Art and History of Judaism in 1989, and programs, such as the European Association for the Preservation and Promotion of Jewish Culture and Heritage's European Day of Jewish Culture each September since 2001, have also helped promote conservation of this heritage throughout the continent.

From Sachsenhausen in the former East Germany to Jasenovac in Croatia to Riga-Kaiserwald in Latvia, the physical remains of the horrific Nazi concentration and death camps have posed an emotionally charged challenge for heritage protection professionals. During the communist era, certain Holocaust sites whose interpretation coincided with state-sponsored ideologies were preserved and numerous monuments were erected; however, their "antifascist" aspects were often privileged at the expense of their Jewish components. In more recent years, these sites have been reexamined, and throughout central Europe new interpretive and conservation projects have begun.

The most notorious of all the Holocaust sites, the death camp at Auschwitz-Birkenau near Kraków, Poland, has been preserved as a museum since 1947 and has been a World Heritage Site since 1979; however, the Polish communist authorities did not actively plan for or sufficiently fund its maintenance. In the 1990s, thanks to the initiative of private foundations and a significant investment from the German government, a massive preservation program was initiated. A conservation committee of survivors, reli-

gious leaders, museum professionals, and architectural conservators created a preservation plan that took a moderate approach, calling for the maintenance of the camp's slightly deteriorated state as a potent reminder of unspeakable horror. Today, a master plan guides and prioritizes site stabilization and conservation measures; however, as the December 2009 theft of the notorious *Arbeit macht frei* ("Work makes you free") sign over Auschwitz's gateway revealed, heritage conservationists must still be ever vigilant against all sorts of potential threats.

Though other camps have not received as much international attention from funders and international visitors as Auschwitz-Birkenau, many have been protected by local legislation and received renewed conservation attention in recent years. For example, at Terezín, in the Czech Republic, new exhibitions were installed in the Ghetto Museum, which reopened in 1991, and a secret, wartime synagogue discovered in 1997 has since been restored and opened to the public.

Many of the historic synagogues, ghettos, and other Jewish heritage sites in Central Europe were destroyed during World War II by the Nazis or their supporting regimes. During the Communist era, other sites were razed for ideological reasons or as part of massive redevelopment schemes, or they were converted to new uses—from museums to theaters to churches. In post-Communist privatization efforts, most surviving synagogues have been returned to local Jewish communities, ensuring they will be respected and preserved. However, conserving and interpreting these sites is complicated by the fact that much of the region's Jewish population was decimated or emigrated away half a century ago. These small surviving and returning communities have begun surveying, documenting, restoring, and publicizing their heritage. For example, the two-towered, late nineteenth-century synagogue in Trnava, Slovakia, was restored and converted into a concert hall in a project notable for its preservation of all traces of the building's history, including the extensive damage it incurred during World War II.

In recognition of the region's extensive losses, a few of the better-preserved Jewish districts have been identified by local governments and included within the boundaries of the UNESCO World Heritage Cities of Třebíč in the Czech Republic, Kraków in Poland, and Bardejov in Slovakia. The Jewish community in Prague has painstakingly restored the Josefov quarter of the city, with its sixteenth-century Jewish town hall, early twentieth-century Jewish museum, and Jewish cemetery. The district also includes

(continued)

six synagogues, including the oldest synagogue in Europe still in use for prayer, which though repeatedly rebuilt over the centuries, still retains some element of its original thirteenth-century construction. Today, Jewish heritage, from museum artifacts to historic districts, is finally receiving long overdue attention as well as a prominent place in the history of central and eastern Europe.

FURTHER READING

European Association for the Preservation and Protection of Jewish Heritage, www.jewishheritage.org (accessed December 31, 2010).

"The Future of Jewish Heritage in Europe: An International Conference," Prague. Czech Republic, April 24–27, 2004. www.jewish-heritage-europe.eu/confer/prague04/Programm.pdf (accessed December 31, 2010).

Gruber, Ruth Ellen. *National Geographic Jewish Heritage Travel: A Guide to Eastern Europe.* (Washington, DC: National Geographic, 2007).

The International Survey of Jewish Monuments, www.isjm.org (accessed December 31, 2010).

Jacques and Jacqueline Levy-Willard Foundation. *The Cultural Guide to Jewish Europe.* (Paris: Editions du Seuil, 2004).

Memorial Museum Auschwitz-Birkenau. "Preservation." http://en.auschwitz.org.pl/m/index.php?option=com_content&task=view&id=583&Itemid=37 (accessed December 31, 2010).

a

Figure 16-8 A wide range of Jewish heritage sites in central Europe have been addressed though conservation and interpretation programs since the early 1990s. Some, such as Auschwitz-Birkenau (a) in southern Poland, reflect the horrors of the Holocaust. Others, such as the late nineteenth-century synagogue in Trnava, Slovakia, (b) are testament to the region's long and rich Jewish history.

b

ENDNOTES

1. Eliška Fučiková, "The Need for Institutions for Historic Preservation in the ČSFR," *Architectural Conservation in the Czech and Slovak Republics* (New York: World Monuments Fund, 1993), 79.

2. Ibid.

3. Law 27/1987 and Czech National Council Law No. 20/1987. Marek Šarišský, "Preservation of Cultural Heritage in Urban Areas: Slovak Republic," in Drdácký, *European Research on Cultural Heritage: State-of-the-Art Studies*, 397–400. Originally: "Cultural Heritage in Urban Areas" (paper, 3rd Ariadne Workshop, Prague, Czech Republic, April 23–29, 2001).

4. Miroslav Burian, "Bohemia's Raddled Face," *The Economist,* June 18, 1992, 89.

5. James Marston Fitch, "The Preservation of Historic Architecture in Czechoslovakia." *Journal of the Society of Architectural Historians,* vol. 25, no. 2 (May 1966), pp. 119–135. One of Fitch's most favorable impressions of Czechoslovakia's architectural conservation capacity at the time was of SURPMO (Státní ústav rekonstrukce měst a památkových objektů) that comprised several large ateliers of highly skilled architects and restoration craftspeople.

6. Josef Štulc, "Czech Republic," in Robert Pickard, ed., *Policy and Law in Heritage Conservation* (London: Spon Press, 2001), 62.

7. The Prague Conservation Institute's roots began in 1707 with the establishment of central Europe's first public engineering school. Karel Kibic, Alena Horynová, and Jaroslav Petru, "Les Intervenants: La Formation, la Restauration, les Publications," *Monuments Historiques* no. 188 (January-February 1993): 21.

8. Burian, "Bohemia's Raddled Face," 89.

9. ICOMOS Czech Republic, "Czech Republic," *Heritage@Risk 2000* (Paris: ICOMOS, 2000), www.international.icomos.org/risk/world_report/2000/czech_2000.htm (accessed December 2, 2009).

10. Fučiková, "The Need for Institutions for Historic Preservation in the ČSFR," 79.

11. Stubbs, *Time Honored,* 20 and 255.

12. ICOMOS Czech Republic, "Czech Republic," *Heritage@Risk 2000.*

13. Stubbs, *Time Honored,* 299, and the Friends of Czech Greenways Web site: www.pragueviennagreenways.org (accessed December 31, 2010).

14. ICOMOS Czech Republic, "Czech Republic," *Heritage@Risk 2000.*

15. Ibid.

16. Phyllis Myers, *Democracy in Development: A Reconnaissance of Monuments Protection Law and Cultural Diversity in Poland, the Czech Republic, and Slovakia* (Washington, DC: State Resource Strategies, 1996), 15.

17. The National Council of the Slovak Republic, "Act 49: On the Protection of Monuments and Historic Sites," *Slovak Law* 49/2002 (December 19, 2001), www.unesco.org/culture/natlaws/media/pdf/slovakia/sk_actprotecthistoricmontsites2001_engtof.pdf (accessed December 30, 2009).

18. Myers, *Democracy and Development,* 25.

19. "Our Objectives," National Trust Slovakia, www.nt.sk/en/ont.html (accessed November 11, 2009).

20. Michaela Chalupova, "The Civil Society and Heritage Conservation in Slovakia," in Monika A. Murzyn and Jacek Purchla, eds., *Cultural Heritage in the 21st Century: Opportunities and Challenges* (Kraków, Poland: International Cultural Centre, 2007), 273–274.

21. "Academia Istropolitana Nova, Sväty Jur (Slovakia)," *European Union Prize for Cultural Heritage/Europa Nostra Awards 2009* (Paris: Europa Nostra, 2009), 58–59.

22. Jana Gregorová and Pavel Gregor, "Slovakia: Bratislava—Protected Area of Central Urban District at Risk," in *Heritage@Risk 2006/2007: ICOMOS World Report 2006/2007 On Monuments and Sites in Danger,* eds. Michael Petzet and John Ziesemer (Paris: ICOMOS, 2008), 138–139.

23. Lubica Pičíková, "Slovakia: Risk from Development: Threats to Monuments Caused by Ignoring Valid Legislation," in *Heritage@Risk 2006–2007,* 139–140.

Figure 17-1 The Church of Our Lady and the medieval Cloth Hall in Kraków's main market square, both restored in the 1890s, were among Poland's earliest restoration projects.

CHAPTER 17

Poland

Poland's tumultuous past has typified the political changes and divisions of central and eastern Europe in recent centuries. For over a century Poland did not exist—it was partitioned in 1795 as a spoil of war by neighboring Prussia, Russia, and Austria. Poland was reconstituted as a separate country after World War I; however, independence was brief, lasting only until the German invasion of September 1939. Statehood returned after World War II; but as a closely watched satellite of the Soviet Union, Poland remained under heavy foreign political domination. True sovereignty and autonomy in the modern era has only been experienced in Poland since 1989.

Because Poland as a political entity has existed only sporadically over the past millennium, the importance of preserving its national built heritage has been dependent on the political agendas of its various foreign rulers. Since World War II, and in part because of the overwhelming destruction in Poland during that conflict, the country has focused a significant amount of effort and resources on cultural heritage protection. In the past two decades as Poland has quickly redefined itself as a democratic republic, it has emerged as one of the most successful countries in eastern Europe and has only strengthened its commitment to architectural conservation.

HERITAGE PROTECTION IN PARTITIONED AND SECOND REPUBLIC POLAND

In the nineteenth century, three very different approaches to architectural heritage protection developed in Poland in its three separately controlled parts. By 1843 Prussia had established a conservator for Poland's northern and western regions, but one who only concentrated inventory and restoration efforts on sites of Germanic interest.[1] Polish cultural sites, including those in the important medieval trading centers of Warsaw and Gdańsk, were ignored. Little architectural conservation was carried out during the nineteenth century in the Russian-held parts of Poland either. Only the Austrians focused attention on preserving a broad range of significant built heritage, irrespective of its provenance, in Galicia, the part of Poland they controlled.

Fortuitously, Austria's Galicia was the historic seat of Polish sovereignty during its medieval golden age. Consequently, this region was exceptionally rich in a broad range of architectural heritage, including important market towns and the fortified Wawel royal castle and cathedral complex in Kraków. By 1856 the Austrian authorities had established the position of Conservator of Kraków to oversee an architectural restoration program for the city's most prominent sites.[2] These were systematically inventoried by the Academy of Sciences beginning in 1887, and the first restorations of the medieval

Church of Our Lady and the Cloth Hall began before the turn of the twentieth century. Wawel Castle's restoration was begun in 1905 as Habsburg troops gave up residence there, but the project was not completed until after the World War II.

In the first quarter of the twentieth century, the Polish architects, historians, and restorers began to operate cohesively on conservation projects despite the territory's political division. After the reunited and independent Poland was established in 1918, informal dialogues and information exchanges among conservation experts in the three formerly separate areas spurred the further development of a national heritage protection strategy and the push to codify the protection of historic assets. The devastation of World War I contributed to the imperative for such interaction. District conservators were nominated in 1918 by the newly established Ministry of Culture and Arts, and the provisional government began drafting comprehensive heritage protection legislation.

By 1928 Poland's first architectural conservation law called for the protection not only of individual buildings and sites but also quarters and towns of historic importance. Thus, according to Anthony M. Tung, it was "the earliest modern preservation statute to recognize the significance of protecting entire historic neighborhoods."[3] Compliance was overseen by a nationally responsible Conservator General. Although this law was technically in effect until 1962, differing government priorities and the German invasion in 1939 precluded its enforcement in its initial decades.

The strength of the Polish national spirit, honed over centuries of conflict, was put to its greatest test during the German occupation in World War II. Under Adolf Hitler's specific instruction, German invaders were ordered not only to eradicate "inconvenient" Polish citizens and all of the country's Jewish population but also to break Poland's spirit by methodically razing two centers of resistance: the beautiful early modern capital of Warsaw and the historic Hanseatic port of Gdańsk. Under the Pabst Plan, Gdańsk's Gothic, brick-faced city center was 75 percent destroyed by air raids, and Warsaw was even more extensively damaged.[4]

However, the genius loci in the hearts of the citizens of these two picturesque cities survived and even strengthened. Today, both have been largely reconstructed and restored to exacting standards as tangible expressions of Polish defiance, love for their past, and need for a cogent sense of place. In both cities, reconstruction efforts focused on replicating the original exterior appearance of lost buildings, while building interiors were renovated to permit modern conveniences and better light, heat, and space.

COMPREHENSIVE COMMUNIST-ERA CONSERVATION ACTIVITIES

Post-war liberation did not mean a complete return to political independence. Instead Poland was heavily influenced by the Soviet Union for more than forty years, and the country began reconstituting its heritage conservation programs within newly instituted socialist economic privations. The centralized planning system was a mixed blessing for architectural conservation because it facilitated the wholesale channeling of resources into certain approved architectural restoration projects, irrespective of economic cost or impact. Between 1974 and 1979, these resources amounted to $150 million; by the 1980s, Poland was spending almost 7 percent of its national budget on restoration, nearly ten times more than what was spent in France.[5] When considering Poland's heritage protection efforts during its Communist era, it is worth noting that its government exerted far more leverage for restoration and preservation than would have been the case in a democratic country.[6]

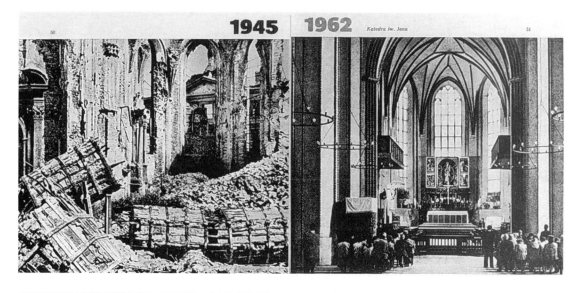

Figure 17-2 Three views of historic buildings in Stare Miasto, Warsaw, in 1945 and after reconstruction in 1962, proudly demonstrating the remarkable recreation of the city in the book *Varsovie Reconstruite*. Ciborowski, Warsaw, Polonia, 1962.

Warsaw's national importance, and its role as a center of underground resistance activity during Hitler's campaign in Poland, unfortunately made it a first target for German reprisals. With a prewar population of over one million people, Adolf Hitler envisioned that Warsaw be leveled and rebuilt as a minor German garrison town of less than 150,000 inhabitants. From late 1939, preparations were made to demolish the most significant buildings in the city center. Following the failed Warsaw Ghetto Uprising in 1943 and the expulsion of the remaining population, special German demolition squads used flamethrowers and explosives to methodically destroy building after building. Special attention was paid to eliminate historical monuments, national archives, religious buildings, and other places of cultural significance. Their orders were concise: nothing was to be left. Estimates of the destruction of Warsaw's built heritage range from 70 percent to as high as 96 percent. Of approximately 1,000 significant historic buildings in existence before the war, 780 were totally destroyed. After 1945, only 40 of the 750 legally protected monuments in prewar Warsaw were still standing.[7]

In anticipation of the capital's possible complete destruction and the damage it would cause to the Polish psyche, courageous members of Warsaw's architectural community undertook a heroic and highly dangerous task. While the war continued, clandestinely produced measured drawings and analytic studies were made by architects and students of the Warsaw Technical University to supplement the existing photographic and textural documentation of the city. The defunct Department of Town Planning, in direct violation of German orders, continued to train about 150 students in planning and architecture under the guise of mechanical drafting exercises, predating the work so as to avoid reprisals should the plans for rebuilding the city be discovered. In an action of extraordinary patriotism, several Technical University faculty members obtained special passes from the German occupiers to enable them to reenter their school and secretly remove several truckloads of historical and architectural documentation, which was safely hidden elsewhere until 1945, when the Allied forces liberated Poland.

Almost immediately after the war, and after much consideration, the Polish leadership focused on the importance of rebuilding the capital guided by the idea of carefully and rapidly reconstructing the city's lost architectural heritage. The acute sense of loss, national pride, and a sense of defiance focused Warsaw's population on reconstructing the city's heritage rather than building anew. By 1946 a general policy for Warsaw's recovery and that of other historic landmarks had been adopted and made operational. At its height, Poland's postwar Biuro Odbudowy Stolicy (Capital Reconstruction Bureau) had engaged nearly 16 percent of Warsaw's populace in the task. While the country bore the costs of the Bureau's administration, site work was supported by thousands of unpaid volunteers, whose national fervor enabled the completion of rubble clearance and reconstruction projects in record time.

By 1953 reconstruction work in the Stare Miasto (Old Town) square and adjacent streets was finished. Facades of traditional burgher residences dating from the Renaissance through the baroque periods had been painstakingly reconstructed, although with modified floor plans to accommodate modern amenities, improved sanitation systems, and better light and air circulation. In the seventeenth-century New Town, a more economical reconstruction approach was followed. Only buildings on the primary road regained their original appearance; the rest were constructed in a modern style. Work there was completed in 1965, and between 1971 and 1988 the Royal Castle—which was dynamited in 1944—was reconstructed to its pre-1939 state. Today it houses one of Poland's leading museums, and its Royal Apartments were painstakingly restored, using as many original decorative elements as possible.

Though the loss of the original historic city and so many of its citizens was a trauma of unimaginable proportion, there were a few unintended positive consequences. The city's extensive destruction exposed historic underground caverns and other features that permitted construction of a new, subterranean access roadway through the Old Town. It also partially exposed the medieval town walls, moat, and original barbican foundations, permitting their restoration, which was a long-standing goal of the city. In retrospect, the need for a wide variety of skilled craftsmen to rebuild historic Warsaw proved fortuitous: It required the transfer of restoration and architectural craft skills to young apprentices from an older generation whose talents were being threatened with obsolescence due to advances in modern building methods.

In 1980 Warsaw's Stare Miastro received UNESCO World Heritage listing, a tribute to the talents of innumerable Polish architects, artisans, and others who worked on the decade-long reconstruction project. This honor emphasized the cultural importance of the location and validated the methods by which a city of high historic and artistic value was re-created. It is especially significant because initially, the decision of Warsaw's planners to reconstruct the town to its earlier appearance met with a mixed response. There was debate in the beginning as to whether or not such action was justified and whether it would reflect sound planning and architectural practice. Today, however, few would disagree that re-creating Warsaw's Stare Miastro was appropriate given the circumstances and the care with which the task was undertaken. In any case, the action was insisted upon by Polish citizens who yearned for their lost city, with the result being the greatest effort to date in re-constructing a destroyed historic urban center.

FURTHER READING

Baranski, Marek. "The Monuments of Warsaw 50 Years After." *Transactions: Association for Studies in the Conservation of Historic Buildings* 19 (1994): 39–49.

Borowiec, Andrew. *Destroy Warsaw! Hitler's Punishment, Stalin's Revenge.* (Westport, CT, and London: Praeger, 2001).

Jankowski, Stanislaw. "Warsaw: Destruction, Secret Town Planning 1939–44, and Postwar Reconstruction." In *Rebuilding Europe's Bombed Cities,* edited by J. M. Diefendorf. (New York: St. Martin's Press, 1990).

Konopka, Marek, ed. *Destroyed but Not Lost: Materials of Conference on the 25th Anniversary of the Old Town's Entry onto the UNESCO Heritage List.* (Warsaw: Capital City of Warsaw, Heritage Protection Department, 2006). See esp. Marek Baranski, "Foreign Views on the Reconstruction," 129–135.

Tung, Anthony M. "The Heritage of War: Warsaw." In *Preserving the World's Great Cities,* 77-99. (New York: Three Rivers Press, 2001).

Poland's initial architectural conservation legislation of 1928 was not altered until 1962, when following a new examination of heritage preservation policies, the comprehensive Law on the Protection of Cultural Property and on Museums was passed. This law affirmed the value of historic buildings, sites, and objects and delegated a system of regional and national administrative responsibilities over the country's cultural inventory and museum network. The definition of Poland's "cultural assets" was broadened to encompass buildings and works of architecture and town planning; sites of ethnological interest; and places of historic interest, such as battlefields. For the first time, prohibitions were established and imposed via administrative penalties and fines. To ensure that national treasures would be preserved in good condition, the law was structured to integrate sites "into contemporary life so that this legacy will constitute a durable feature of our national culture."[8]

Under the 1962 law, each *voivodship* (district) conservator was required to maintain a register of buildings and sites ranked in order of importance from a high of "0" to a low of "5". After the Council of Ministers approved a site for listing, a comprehensive dossier was created for it, including full archaeological and architectural details, drawings and photographs, written studies of its social history, and proposals for its conservation and use.[9] Of the 45,000 buildings and sites that were so documented and deemed worthy of protective listing, the fifty-two "0"-level-ranked sites became Poland's top conservation priorities. An additional two hundred thousand historically significant buildings and sites were noted but were not listed. Unfortunately, over the past forty years, many of the category "4" and "5" sites were either demolished or altered.[10]

Poland's efforts to create an inventory of its cultural property was mirrored in a project focused on historic ensembles launched a decade later by the Polish Academy of Sciences. In 1973 the Academy analyzed nearly two thousand towns and villages and identified approximately ten percent as being especially worthy of conservation for their historic architectural or landscape architectural significance.[11] The Academy's recommendations were taken into account by Poland's central planning authority.

Figure 17-3 Polskie Pracownie Konserwacji Zabytków (PP PKZ, Polish Monuments Restoration Laboratories) has been successfully conserving the country's architectural heritage since it was established in 1945. The organization operated as a government entity within the Ministry of Culture until it became an independent state enterprise in 1951. Zamek Królewski (Warsaw Castle) was extensively restored by PP PKZ as part of the general Stare Miasto reconstruction effort, with roof repairs and rebuilt interiors. Extreme attention was paid to above-grade archaeological evidence and historical accuracy. The rebuilding of different elements of Zamek Królewski, from exterior envelopes to painted finishes, is illustrated here (a–d). PP PKZ has worked internationally since the 1960s, and was privatized and renamed PKZ Zamek in 1989. Images courtesy Archive PP PKZ/Marek Baranski

a

The world-renowned Polskie Pracownie Konserwacji Zabytków (PP PKZ, Polish Monuments Restoration Laboratories) has been successfully conserving Polish architectural heritage since it was established in 1945 as part of the Communist-era Ministry of Culture. It became an independent state enterprise in 1951 and was semiprivatized in 1989.[12] Despite these structural reorganizations and several name changes, its services have always included research, technical and feasibility studies and the conservation of architectural stone, wood, metals, and paintings.[13]

In 2002 PP PKZ was reacquired by the Polish state, but it continues to function as a sophisticated, professional international enterprise whose sizable staff of eight thousand includes art historians, conservators, archaeologists, architects, and engineers operating via a network centered in Warsaw. They are organized into five national branches and an international division. PP PKZ's ateliers specialize in everything from materials conservation (wood, masonry, ceramics, and glass) to historic district planning and technical conservation services. Recently, its focus has expanded to include new building projects. The PP PKZ's apprenticeship system ensures the continuation of valuable conservation skills, and its talent pool is also regularly refreshed by graduates of several universities, including the respected Institute of Preservation and Conservation of Works of Art in Toruń and the Academies of Fine Arts in Warsaw and Kraków.

PP PKZ's primary client remains the Polish Ministry of Culture and Arts, but ever since it began using its conservation expertise abroad in 1967, it has orchestrated numerous projects for prominent private and governmental clients in such diverse locales as Egypt, Cuba, Cambodia, Vietnam, Ukraine, and Russia. PP PKZ's interest in expanding this global role is evidenced by the establishment of its foreign division in Saint Petersburg, Russia.

b

c

d

CONTEMPORARY ISSUES AND CHALLENGES

It is no surprise that during the first half of the twentieth century, Polish restoration and preservation choices consistently reflected a strong national bias and emphasized an independent Polish identity, therefore focusing on the country's medieval "golden age." Throughout Poland, most eighteenth- through twentieth-century buildings remind the populace of its successive foreign authorities, and none were given much attention when the country's conservation inventory was reorganized in the 1960s. However, almost simultaneous with—or because of—the overthrow of Soviet domination in the 1990s, there arose a new appreciation for nineteenth-century architecture. Polish conservators are now also even considering the quality of the Socialist Realist architecture of the 1950s, reflecting the maturing of a confident and proud country.

The economic realities of today's open market-driven society have altered Poland's architectural conservation efforts, as they have done throughout central and Eastern Europe. The subsidies and economic insulation of the former Eastern Bloc system have disappeared. Today's privatization schemes have taken many aging buildings and sites—such as factories, mines, foundries, and state-owned agricultural cooperatives—away from government control and maintenance. Widespread staff "rationalizations," modernizing technologies, and a new focus on corporate financial goals have often meant fewer inhabitants for these complexes, some of which have been abandoned. Likewise, military-related structures, fortifications, and buildings erected for defense, are now deteriorating because of the retracted military presence. In a 1997 interview, then PP PKZ director Przemysław Woźniakowski noted that "the biggest threat to these old buildings is the lack of an owner. A bad user is better than no owner."[14]

Figure 17-4 High-conservation science was used to support and monitor conservation at the fifteenth-century wooden Church of the Archangel Michael in Dębno, a World Heritage Site in southern Poland. The renewal of the wooden roof shingles and the external weatherboarding (siding) (a), as well as the conservation of the church's elaborate painted finishes (b–d), was completed in 2006 under the direction of Jaroslaw Adamowicz, painting conservator and lecturer at the renowned Faculty of Conservation of the Academy of Fine Arts in Kraków.

a

But this is presumably a temporary phenomenon resulting from the complexities of economic and political transition. As was poignantly demonstrated in Warsaw's Old Town, the Polish people's psyche is closely tied to its physical heritage, and they will not tolerate its loss. Through hard work and resilience, in the past decade Poland has become one of the most successful of the former Eastern Bloc countries, making numerous adjustments in preparation for joining the EU, including strengthening its commitment to cultural heritage protection.

b

c

d

Endnotes

1. Robert Stipe, Paul H. Gleye, and Waldemar Szczerba, eds., *Historic Preservation in Other Countries*, vol. 3, *Poland* (Washington, DC: US/ICOMOS, 1989), 3.

2. Ibid., 1.

3. Anthony Tung, *Preserving the World's Great Cities: The Destruction and Renewal of the Historic Metropolis.* (New York: Three Rivers Press, 2001), 75. Poland's legislation predated even the historic district declarations of the U.S. Cities of Charleston and New Orleans in the early 1930s.

4. The plan was named for Friedrich Pabst, the German army architect who promoted the concept of destroying an enemy's national identity by destroying all of its physical manifestations—art, architecture, archives. The destruction of this strategic port city, Gdańsk, was also the result of aerial and naval bombings by the British and the Soviets. While its rebuilding was probably less an act of defiance than in Warsaw, the care that was taken to reconstruct the historic center as it appeared before the war was just as considered and deliberate. See also: James Marston Fitch, *Historic Preservation: Curatorial Management of the Built World* (Charlottesville: University of Virginia Press, 1990), 53, 57, and 77.

5. Krystyna Puc, *Poland's Commitment to Its Past: A Report on Two Study Tours* (Washington, DC: Partners for Livable Places, 1985), 11.

6. Ibid, 39.

7. Ibid, 12.

8. Ibid.

9. Stipe, Gleye, and Szczerba, *Historic Preservation in Other Countries*, 36.

10. Ibid, 35.

11. Ibid, 39.

12. Its pride in the extensive and professionally acclaimed restoration work done on Kraców's Zamek Królewski is reflected in its new name, PKZ Zamek.

13. "Historia i Działalność," PPKZ, www.ppkz.pl/historia.html (accessed December 30, 2009).

14. Puc, *Poland's Commitment to Its Past*, 36.

EASTERN EUROPE AND THE CAUCASUS

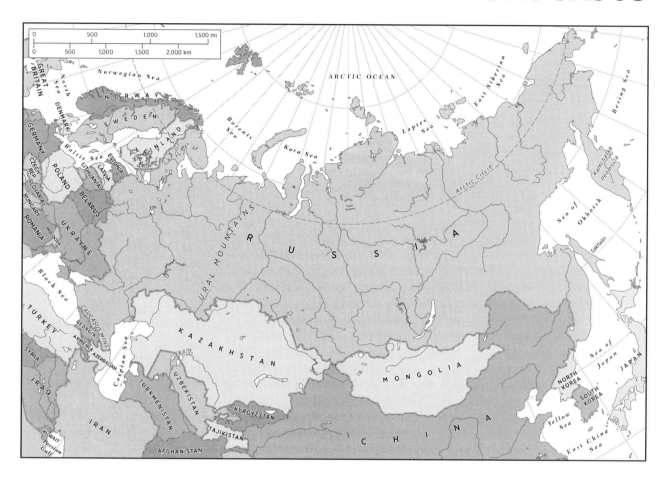

In 1991 the Union of Soviet Socialist Republics (USSR) collapsed in the midst of internal political turmoil and following successful independence movements in the Baltic region. In its place the Commonwealth of Independent States (CIS) was formed by leaders of eleven of the fifteen former Soviet republics, each now an independent country. These included all of the central Asian republics as well as Russia, Ukraine, Belarus, Moldova, Armenia, and Azerbaijan. Georgia joined the CIS in 1993. Through the CIS, these countries retained a loose alliance that eased the process of separation and allowed for continued coordination of foreign and economic policies.

Though having embarked on independent paths of architectural conservation since their independence in the early 1990s, several of the countries comprising the former Soviet Union have done so within the legacy of the Soviet system as well as of traditions inherited from the Russian empire.[1] This prolonged foreign hegemony both contributed to their architectural heritage and imbued a strong desire to assert and promote their cultural uniqueness once independent.

Despite short histories of political independence, each of these countries has a long cultural history, and much of the heritage of the region's prehistoric peoples, Byzantine Greek settlers, and medieval kingdoms has survived. As with the central European countries that were members of the former Eastern bloc, most of the countries of eastern Europe have remarkably long records of achievement in cultural heritage protection. It is not surprising, therefore, that architectural conservation and heritage promotion are relatively high priorities in this region today. Nonetheless, in the Russian Federation, as well as in the European countries of the CIS, architectural heritage is threatened by continued political instability and crime; corruption, economic hardship, and limited state funding; highly centralized systems with unclear priorities; and failure to adhere to international guidelines and recommended techniques at many sites.

Endnotes

1. Ukraine and Belarus were integral parts of the early medieval Kievan Rus'—however, both were controlled by Poland-Lithuania between the mid-fourteenth and mid-seventeenth centuries, at which time they returned to Russian control. Empress Catherine the Great's armies penetrated Caucasia as early as 1770, at the cost of both the decaying Ottoman Empire and the Persians. After a century of gradual conquest, the whole region was part of the Russian empire by 1878. Russia took Moldova from the Ottomans in 1812; however, between 1918 and 1945, it was part of Romania until reannexed by the Soviet Union.

CHAPTER 18

Russia

Architectural conservation of selected sites emerged as a government concern in imperial Russia, which controlled a vast territory stretching from eastern Europe to the Pacific Ocean. In the Union of Soviet Socialist Republics (USSR), which was established in 1917 and dissolved in 1991, resources for architectural conservation increased, documentation and protection efforts were extended and made more comprehensive, and conservation projects became more scientific. However, the Soviet era also witnessed periods of significant destruction, especially during the rule of Joseph Stalin in the 1930s and during World War II.

In the Russian Federation, which was established in 1991 as all other republics became independent from the Soviet Union, architectural conservation has remained a priority, though resources dedicated to the cause have in general lessened and the focus has been sporadic. While some historic sites deteriorate, other examples of lost heritage have been reconstructed at enormous expense. Though architectural conservation can be argued to have declined in Russia since the Soviet era of broad concern and centralized control, the past two decades have witnessed the rise in active local nongovernmental organizations concerned with heritage protection as well as increased international funding and support for architectural conservation in Russia.

IMPERIAL AND REVOLUTIONARY CONSERVATION EFFORTS

Sporadic interest in Russia's architectural heritage and concern for its conservation began early, including the reconstruction of the Cathedral of St. George in Yuriev-Polskoi in 1471 by Vasily Ermolin and in the early eighteenth century the personal concern of Tsar Peter I (Peter the Great), for the preservation of his wooden cabin, one of the first structures built in St. Petersburg, the city he founded. Initial attempts to preserve this modest house, fusing traditional Russian and Dutch styles, included a shelter to shield the structure from the weather, which was later replaced by a brick enclosure building.[1] In addition, interest in church and cathedral repairs and preservation occurred regularly throughout the eighteenth and nineteenth centuries.[2]

It was also during the reign of Peter the Great that the first Russian law on antiquities preservation was issued in 1704.[3] A century later, in 1805 under Alexander I, a register of protected ancient Greek and other archaeological sites on the Black Sea was prepared, and under Nicholas I in 1829 a register for all of Russia was initiated.[4] In the 1850s, building codes required special treatment of historic structures and an Imperial Russian Archaeological Society was established in 1846, followed by an Imperial Archaeological Commission in 1859, to maintain the registry of significant sites . This responsibility was soon taken over by the private Moscow Archaeological Society in 1864.[5]

◀ **Figure 18-1** One of the earliest acts of deliberate architectural preservation in eastern Europe resulted from Tsar Peter the Great's order in 1711 to move his original wooden cabin in the city that bears his name to a new site and to preserve it. He also ordered a roofed gallery constructed around the house to protect it from the elements in 1723. In the 1780s, Catherine II (Catherine the Great), Empress of Russia, replaced this with a brick enclosure, which was reconstructed in the 1840s. The wooden cabin itself was most recently restored in the 1970s.

During the late nineteenth and early twentieth century, other private organizations and efforts were initiated in the declining Russian empire. In its Asian east, a church archaeological society was established in Irkutsk in 1912 to focus on the conditions of religious heritage in the harsh Siberian climate.[6] In the empire's European west, architects, historians, and artists lobbied for more rigorous legal protection of historic sites and began more systematic documentation of Russia's extensive heritage.[7] In 1910 the Society for Defense and Preservation of Russian Monuments of Art and Ancient Times was established and started investigating and conserving medieval sites. Between 1909 and 1916, the painter and academic Igor Grabar published the comprehensive, multi-volume *History of Russian Art* (five volumes were published, though twelve volumes were originally planned) in which he surveyed Russian architecture as well as other forms of art. Equally accomplished Russian architectural historians and architectural conservationists include Vladimir Suslov, Petr Pokryshkin, Alexei Schusev, and Nikolai Rerikh (or Nicholas Roerich), among others.

Though certain key sites associated with the monarchy, or with religious significance for the Russian Orthodox Church had been protected by the tsar beginning in the mid-nineteenth century, it was not until the monarchy was overthrown in 1917 that widespread, systematic government action was taken.[8] Tsar Nicholas II's abdication resulted in the establishment of a provisional government, which was in turn overthrown by Vladimir Ilyich Lenin and the Bolsheviks only eight months later. Civil war and instability followed, culminating in eventual communist victory and the formation of the Union of Soviet Socialist Republics in 1922. Over its seventy-year history, the official Soviet response to conservation erratically ranged from destruction of important sites having inconvenient histories to carefully reasoned and highly sophisticated conservation solutions, and often these policies operated contemporaneously.[9]

During the revolution and the early Soviet period, systematic, rapid, and unprecedented destruction and changes in the use of historic structures were experienced throughout the former Russian empire. As relics of the past and symbols of tyranny, many imperial palaces were looted and burned, along with aristocratic towns and country estates. Great numbers of these residences, as well as churches, monasteries, and civic buildings were commandeered, collections gathered over centuries were dispersed, and venerated sites were desecrated and demolished.[10] However, it was also in this chaotic atmosphere that the country's modern architectural conservation practice was born. In the mid-1920s, despite revolution, restoration practice in Russia operated on the same level as in Western Europe.

The short-lived provisional government established a Fine Arts Committee of professionals and connoisseurs to inventory the imperial residences and their contents.[11] The committee did not, however, have long to complete its task before it and the entire government was replaced by the Communist authorities. The country's architects and historians, led by writer and philosopher Anatoly Lunacharsky, began to speak vociferously against the damage to cultural property done in the name of the revolution, and they quickly sent a delegation to ask Lenin to intervene. In November 1917, immediately after his acquisition of power, Lenin issued a directive urging a halt to the destruction by arguing:

> Citizens, the former overlords have gone and left us a great heritage which
> now belongs to the people…. Preserve this heritage, preserve the pictures, the
> statues, the buildings: they are the incarnation of your might and of the spiritual
> might of your ancestors…Do not touch a single stone, preserve the monuments,
> the buildings, the antiquities, the writings; they are the soil of which your new
> people's art will grow.[12]

Figure 18-2 Former imperial Russian palaces and their contents, such as the eighteenth-century baroque Winter Palace—now the Hermitage Museum—in St. Petersburg, were threatened by revolutionary fervor and backlash, but they were protected in 1917 by the first of several timely decrees from Vladimir Lenin at the urging of concerned architects, writers, and historians.

Lunacharsky was appointed the first Soviet Commissar of Education, and his many responsibilities included overseeing the Department of Museums and Preservation, within which the Commission on the Restoration of Art Treasures was created by the 1918 decree On Inventorying and Protection of Works of Art and Historical Monuments. Thus the first heritage management structure on the territory of the former Russian empire was established. The commission, headed by Igor Grabar, had three departments focusing on architecture, painting, and textile conservation.

During the early 1920s, the commission systematically documented and registered six thousand buildings and restored and rehabilitated a significant number of those.[13] Between 1918 and 1923, Moscow's Kremlin underwent an extensive restoration to repair damage from the recent civil war as well as damage sustained during the prior century in relation to Napoleon's invasion.[14] Other commission projects not only led to the unfortunate removal of significant nineteenth-century additions from many medieval structures but also to the fortunate exploration and documentation of the architectural resources of remote areas of the Soviet Union. In 1924 the commission was renamed the Central State Restoration Studios (Central Studios).

The early Soviet attitude toward heritage protection, however, was far from consistent. While the Central Studios conserved some sites and objects, the Antikvariat, established by Lenin in 1921, sold other Russian imperial treasures to the West in exchange for desperately needed hard currency.[15] The riches of the Russian Orthodox Church were also a focus of the new government's nationalization of private property. In 1922 Lenin ordered the removal of all objects of value from churches.[16] Although there was widespread resistance to this policy in rural areas, opposition was silenced and hundreds of icons were torn apart for firewood, their silver and gold melted down, and their precious stones sold to fund new industrial enterprises and machinery imports.[17] Church buildings themselves fared slightly better: while some were demolished, many remained open, and others were converted to new uses and occasionally even restored under the auspices of the Central Studios.[18]

THE FATE OF HERITAGE UNDER STALIN AND DURING WORLD WAR II

The conclusion of the civil war in 1923 and the death of Lenin in 1924 marked the end of the revolution and the beginning of a new era. The city of St. Petersburg was renamed Leningrad, and Joseph Stalin became general secretary of the Communist Party. His harsh reign had profound consequences on the Soviet Union's historic monuments and heritage sites. Stalin disbanded the Central Studios, and many heritage conservationists were among those banished to Siberian work camps.[19]

Much of the progress witnessed in preceding years was undone in the late 1920s and 1930s through insensitive adaptations and deliberate destruction of buildings representing politically incorrect values or historic periods. Between 1925 and 1935, the registry of significant sites worthy of protection decreased from two thousand to twelve hundred sites.[20] In addition, after 1929 religion was severely repressed, hundreds of additional churches were closed, and even more were demolished or plundered for reusable building materials.[21] The Russian Academy of Architecture estimates that between 1924 and 1940, Moscow alone lost nearly half of its historic buildings, including over two hundred churches, and several principal streetscapes were destroyed.[22] The nineteenth-century Cathedral of Christ the Savior, designed by Konstantin Thon as the prototypical example of the imperial Russian national architectural style, was one of Moscow's most conspicuous losses. Stalin insisted on its removal to clear the site for his never completed Palace of the Soviets. Despite these depredations, Stalin recognized that certain monuments of outstanding significance could be useful in promoting national identity, and among the buildings he reprieved were St. Basil's Cathedral on Red Square and the adjacent Kremlin itself, with its rich array of religious structures.[23]

The German invasion in 1941 spurred a new wave of destruction and systematic looting in the Soviet Union, especially in its westernmost regions. Within three years, nearly 1.5 million freight loads of treasure had been sent by train and 500,000 tons of objects sent by sea to Germany.[24] In addition to this organized pillage, German occupation forces stole what could be carried and attempted to destroy the rest. The cities of Minsk and Kiev—including their museums, universities, and libraries—were completely destroyed. Historic Novgorod, with its Kremlin and Cathedral of St. Sophia, was heavily bombed: Only forty out of nearly twenty-five hundred residential buildings were left standing. The homes of Pushkin, Tolstoy, Tchaikovsky, and Chekhov were ransacked and burned. The oldest monastery in the Soviet Union, the Kiev-Pechersk Lavra Monastery and the magnificent New Jerusalem Monastery near Moscow were both bombed.[25] By the time the Nazis withdrew, over four hundred museums and historic sites as well as almost three thousand churches, synagogues, chapels, and other religious structures were gone.

The herculean effort to reclaim Russia's built heritage from utter destruction started gradually but picked up momentum after the war. In 1944 the Central State Restoration Studios were resurrected and, due to an acute shortage of trained professionals, a conservation school was established in Leningrad to train teenagers in the various traditional buildings crafts.[26] The restoration workshops in Moscow and Leningrad were soon known as centers of eighteenth- and nineteenth-century craftsmanship in a twentieth-century world. Minsk, Novgorod, Stalingrad, and Kiev were all substantially rebuilt using state funds. Even before the war ended, Leningrad's residents began preparing reconstruction and restoration efforts; by 1945, 10 percent of the city budget was earmarked for restoration and reconstruction projects.[27] Moscow's oldest religious structure, the Redeemer Cathedral in the Andronikov Monastery, was painstakingly restored in the early 1950s.[28]

In 1948 the Soviet Council of Ministers passed a new law "On the Improvement of the Protection of Cultural Monuments," reinforcing earlier legislation on identification, cataloging, maintenance, conservation, and the use of historic buildings and sites.[29] Protection was extended to freestanding structures as well as ensembles of buildings and architectural artwork (frescoes, tapestries, sculptures, iconostases, furniture, etc.). Interventions at sites of significance to the Soviet Union as a whole required approval from the Central Administration for the Protection of Architectural Monuments of the Soviet Council of Ministers, while decisions about repair and restoration of republic-level monuments could be made by local architectural administrators. The 1948 law called for the repair or restoration of these sites and defined restoration as either the re-creation of lost elements and/or removal of later accretions.

In the immediate aftermath of the German occupation, many doubted that the imperial palaces could ever be restored, and some questioned if they should be, since the

a

b

Figure 18-3 Pavlovsk Palace (a) and the Catherine Palace at Tsarskoe Selo, near St Petersburg, required complete reconstruction and extensive restoration after World War II. Anatoly Kuchumov (b), the former Alexander Palace curator and postwar director of museum monuments at Tsarskoe Selo, is shown here with author John Stubbs. Kuchumov led dozens of other experts and hundreds of workers and artisans in the task.

Soviet Union was still at war and tens of thousands of people were without housing. Yet Anatoly Kuchumov, the former Alexander Palace curator and postwar Director of Museum Monuments, persevered. Along with a few of his colleagues, he managed to appeal directly to Stalin on behalf of the palaces. When presented with photographs of the ruins of the Catherine Palace at Pavlovsk, near St. Petersburg, Stalin surprised even his closest advisors by agreeing to fund the restoration efforts.[30]

LATE-SOVIET POLICIES AND INSTITUTIONS

In the Soviet Union's final decades, interest in conservation again peaked, and a strong, centralized system was gradually established for protecting and restoring built heritage. Beginning with Stalin's death in 1953, many of his policies, including his destruction of architectural heritage, were denounced by his successors, setting the stage for a new period of heritage protection in the Soviet Union. This period was characterized by strong centralization, including Moscow's selection of sites for restoration or conservation and close supervision of activities, as the authorities looked to promote and control a common Soviet heritage. For example, extensive conservation work on the churches of Kiev and its noted medieval Kiev-Pechersk Lavra monastery was supported by this centrally regulated plan and completed by a joint effort of Russian and Ukrainian architectural conservationists.[31]

Though, in the late 1950s, renewed religious persecution, postwar urban development, and the low prioritization of heritage issues again threatened architectural conservation efforts throughout the Soviet Union, during the 1960s and 1970s, public interest in restoration grew. Centralized control and ownership of property greatly facilitated Soviet conservation efforts during this period. In 1961 a universal Soviet restoration methodology was developed, and in 1967 the Ministry of Culture began inventorying sites requiring attention. In the early 1960s this list included thirty thousand sites, and by 1991 the Register of Historical and Cultural Monuments of the Peoples of the USSR included eighty thousand sites. Because of the existence of all the earlier Russian monument registries, this late Soviet list—and the 1974 version—never really offered a guarantee of protection. In addition, the register was riddled with errors, listed sites were frequently delisted, and the state itself was often the worst offender, altering and demolishing listed buildings.[32]

In 1965 the Council of Ministers of the USSR and a number of cultural activists, who were concerned about the state of cultural heritage, founded the All-Russian Society for the Preservation of Historical and Cultural Monuments (VOOPLiK). Under the watchful eye of the Ministry of Culture, the independent Society raised funds from membership dues and donations and provided volunteers to document historic structures and their contents.[33] During the Soviet period, its membership grew to nearly fifteen million, and branches representing special or regional interests were established throughout Russia. The Society's greatest contributions to architectural conservation have been to elevate public concern and to advocate in favor of the issue. In 1971, the group successfully forced authorities to scale back proposed urban redevelopment plans in Moscow to lessen the impact on historic structures and neighborhoods.[34] Similarly, public outcry against the demolition of the Angleterre Hotel in Leningrad in 1987 galvanized opposition to the demolition of the nearby Astoria Hotel, which was instead restored.[35] With its fifty branch offices and expert restoration center, VOOPLiK remains an active nongovernmental participant in architectural conservation in Russia today.

Figure 18-4 Founded in 1965, the All-Russian Society for the Preservation of Historical and Cultural Monuments (VOOPLiK) grew to nearly fifteen million members during the Soviet era and continues, with reduced numbers, as an active membership organization working for the conservation of Russia's architectural heritage today. The restoration of the late nineteenth-century Church of the Spilled Blood in St. Petersburg was among the first projects of the organization.

Growing concern for the fate of historic structures resulted in the inclusion in the 1977 Soviet constitution of an article declaring it each citizen's patriotic duty and obligation to protect and preserve cultural heritage.[36] Revised comprehensive architectural conservation legislation followed in 1978 in the Soviet Union. The law On Protection and Application of Historic and Cultural Monuments regulated the use and conservation of historic sites, which were categorized as being of global, Union, republic, or local importance and were also ranked as to the level of intervention permissible.[37]

In an extension of the ensemble provisions of the 1948 law, the new legislation provided for the designation of "historic and cultural reserves," which included ensembles of buildings in museumlike settings, as well as "reserved territories," which included historic districts and streets in active urban areas. Each "reserved territory" had individually designed controls to allow for continued use but limited new construction and change. An inventory system was also created by the 1978 law, giving each protected building, reserve, or territory an "identity card" containing pertinent information about its history, status, and treatment.[38]

The collapse of the Soviet Union in 1991 ended the centralized, Communist government that had both supported and threatened its historic resources for three-quarters of a century. Leningrad suddenly found itself called St. Petersburg again, as former street and place names returned to use in the fifteen separate countries that emerged from the USSR. Moscow's responsibility for heritage protection and conservation was partitioned among these newly independent countries, many of which initially retained the cultural and historic resource laws and frameworks inherited from the Soviet system, only gradually supplementing and updating them.

CURRENT CONSERVATION CHALLENGES IN THE RUSSIAN FEDERATION

The post-Soviet government of the Russian Federation has indicated a strong belief in the cultural as well as economic benefits of heritage conservation, and it is slowly revaluating and updating the conservation laws and frameworks established under the former regime.[39] On the eve of the Soviet Union's collapse, the architectural conservation climate in Russia was as contradictory as ever. Neglect of cultural heritage in the 1980s resulted in a reduction in hours of operation at (or the closure of) some of the country's most important historic sites due to poor physical conditions and lack of financial support. Yet at the same time, restoration projects of unimaginable cost and sophistication were being carried out at other sites, such as the re-creation of the expensive amber wall panels and decorations in the Amber Room at the Catherine Palace in Tsarskoe Selo, which had mysteriously disappeared during World War II.[40] This same inconsistency exists in Russia today—there are neglected and undersupported sites as well as sites undergoing exemplary, state-of-the-art conservation interventions.

Despite interest and appreciation for architectural conservation, the realities of post-Soviet Russia present its heritage management system with an almost overwhelming set of challenges. Enormous threats to Russia's historic cultural resources have been created by the privatization of historic properties, a lack of funding, inefficient bureaucracy and project mismanagement, uncontrolled development, and the propensity to reconstruct lost heritage, as well as by armed conflict and corruption.[41] The administrative structure for protection and conservation of architectural and historic sites in Russia is itself also a threat to the country's heritage. The 1978 Soviet law was replaced in 2002 by the Federal Law On Objects of Cultural Heritage, which designated the Ministry of Culture's Federal Service for Monitoring Compliance with Cultural Heritage Protection Law, known as the Rosokhrankultura, as having primary responsibility for heritage concerns in Russia.

Figure 18-5 The mid-eighteenth-century baroque Catherine Palace in Tsarskoe Selo outside St. Petersburg, designed and built by Italian architect Francesco Bartolomeo Rastrelli in the 1750s, was destroyed by retreating German forces during World War II. The vestibule and ballroom (a and b) were among the damaged spaces. The Catherine Palace's interior, including the ballroom (c), was restored in the 1960s and required the dramatic airlift of roof trusses (d). Conservation work was also done in the early 2000s. Figure 18-5b from *Saving the Tsars' Palaces* (2005) by Christopher Morgan and Irina Orlova, courtesy and copyright of Polperro Heritage Press, London.

Figure 18-6 The Amber Room is lined with decorative amber and gold leaf wall panels, a gift from the Prussian government in the early eighteenth century; but the extraordinary wall panels mysteriously disappeared from the Catherine Palace during World War II. The expensive and detailed reconstruction process began in 1979 and was completed in 2003. Shown here is the restored west interior elevation, a view looking upwards

The Rosokhrankultura is charged with maintaining the Register of Russian Heritage, a list that since 2002 includes buildings, ensembles of buildings, archaeological sites, and cultural landscapes more than forty years old. The list itself was inherited from the Soviet-era Register of Historical and Cultural Monuments, including all its inconsistencies and errors, and was first reevaluated in 1995, seven years before the new legislation. More than 100,000 sites are included on the Register, 42,000 of which are designated as being of federal importance.[42] The remainder are classified as having regional or local significance. All archaeological sites are automatically categorized as being of federal significance.

Ownership issues related to listed sites have proven obstacles to their restoration and maintenance. Some opportunities are lost because regional governments are legally forbidden to finance projects at federally significant sites, and municipal governments are prevented from financing projects at either regionally or federally significant sites.[43] In addition, the ongoing process of denationalization of property in the Russian Federation has meant ownership of many sites is still unresolved. In St. Petersburg, ownership—by federal, regional, or local government—of over 1,200 listed sites is still in dispute; consequently, no funding is provided for their upkeep, and disuse contributes to their deterioration.[44] Also common is the practice of nominating a building to be considered for listed status (as so-called "newly revealed monuments"). As soon as these sites are put forward, they theoretically enjoy the same protection as listed monuments; but often retain this in-between status for years, during which they lack proper conservation attention.[45]

Celebrating the anniversary of St. Petersburg's founding by Peter the Great provided a perfect opportunity for the country's new regime to present its modern face to the world. The federal government, headed by Vladimir Putin, a former ranking official of St. Petersburg's city government, allocated millions of rubles to fund a variety of restoration and conservation projects throughout the city and its environs on a scale reminiscent of the Soviet era. However, gross underestimation of necessary funds and time frames meant that none of the most significant projects were completed in time for the 2003 celebrations, and a great deal of the work accomplished in the city was only superficial.

The inefficiencies and poorly managed post-Soviet system has been nowhere more clearly demonstrated than in Moscow, where local authorities have defied federal regulations and policies in pursuit of business development and misunderstood notions of conservation. The municipal authorities, through the Moscow Commission for Cultural Heritage, have issued approvals for conservation-oriented projects to numerous developers who destroyed the historic buildings instead. In other cases, facades have been retained and the interiors gutted. The city of Moscow also funded the $50 million restoration of the early-nineteenth-century Manezh Exhibition Center after a fire gutted the building in 2000; however, expert advice was ignored in the interest of completing the project in just thirteen months. Thus, the rehabilitated exhibition center bears little resemblance to the original. It has an underground exhibition hall with services, and its magnificent original 60-meter-long roof beams have been replaced with glue-laminated wood beams. Another controversial project in Moscow was the completion of the neo-Gothic Tsaritsyno Palace, commissioned but abandoned before its completion by Catherine the Great. Though it stood as a picturesque ruin for two centuries, its construction was completed in 2007, its appearance largely based on conjecture and invention.[46]

Modernist Soviet-era architecture has long been under threat in Russia: a lack of temporal distance and the disinclination toward defining recent structures as historic has obliterated their value for many.[47] Though most of the interwar structures are certainly eligible for registered protection under Russia's forty-year rule, few have been listed. An initial group of thirty avant-garde buildings were added to the Register of Historical and Cultural Monuments by the Soviet authorities in 1987 and seven others two year after that. But this component of the architectural heritage has not continued to receive state support or attention in the Russian Federation.

Plans to demolish and replace the 1930s Moskva Hotel on Red Square were protested to no avail, and local architectural conservationists learned the hard way that the quest for five-star profit is an extremely potent adversary. The new Moskva Hotel has an updated interior, but the exterior only approximates the former building. Icons of Soviet Modernism have survived, but they have been altered beyond recognition. Examples include Barshch and Sinyavsky's 1929 Planetarium, whose dome was raised 20 feet (6.3 meters) in 2004 and Konstantin Melnikov's 1927 Bakhmetrvsky Garage, which was overwhelmed by an addition and lost its steel-and-glass roof while being converted to serve as a Museum of Jewish History in 2001. Since then a more sensitive treatment of the building is evidenced by installation of the Garage Gallery of contemporary art, which entailed less-than-perfect restoration, but does celebrate Melnikov's original design.

The plight of Russia's modernist heritage has received increased attention in the early twenty-first century on a global scale. The ICOMOS Heritage at Risk conference held in Moscow in 2006 was organized under the theme "Preservation of 20th-Century Architecture and World Heritage" and focused significantly on Russia's modern architecture. DOCOMOMO, WMF, International Union of Architects (UIA), and other organizations as well as over two hundred experts worldwide participated in this international dialogue, which was continued in Berlin the following year. The Museum of Modern Art in New York also hosted a conference and photography exhibition in 2007 dedicated to lost and deteriorating Soviet constructivist architecture.

Russian architectural conservationists have also been actively involved in lobbying on behalf of interwar architecture. In 2006, *Twentieth Century: Preservation of Cultural Heritage* was published in Moscow, and it was soon followed by the report *Moscow Heritage at Crisis Point,* coauthored by SAVE Europe's Heritage and the Moscow Architecture Preservation Society (MAPS). In addition, two nongovernmental organizations concerned with modern architectural heritage were established in 2007, including the Russian Avant-Garde Foundation and the Narkomfin Foundation. The Russian Avant-Garde Foundation has been actively pursuing the inclusion of architecture of the 1920s and 1930s on the state Register, and the Narkomfin Foundation has focused its attention on achieving a positive outcome for a single iconic modernist site, Moisei Ginsburg and Ignati Milinis's 1928–1930 Narkomfin Building.

There are some signs that the heightened international and local awareness and appreciation of Russia's avant-garde architecture will translate into increased attention to the conservation needs of threatened sites. The Russian Avant-Garde Foundation has had success registering the Red Professor's Institute hostels and a number of housing blocks and recent conservation plans for the Narkomfin Building and other sites are more sensitive to the original materials and designs than earlier projects in the Russian Federation. While progress has been made on some fronts, setbacks have occurred on others, including newly raised ownership and legal issues as well as financial uncertainties.

FURTHER READING

Cecil, Clementine. "Narkomfin" and "Monuments of Constructivism Today," Narkomfin Foundation. http://narkomfin.ru/Eng/Narkomfin.aspx and http://narkomfin.ru/Eng/Architecture/Today.aspx (accessed June 25, 2010).

Haspel, Jörg, Michael Petzet, Anke Zalivako, and John Ziesemer, eds. *The Soviet Heritage and European Modernism: Heritage at Risk Special Edition* (Berlin and Paris: Hendrik Bäßler Verlag/ICOMOS, 2007), www.international.icomos.org/risk/2007/pdf/Soviet_Heritage_FULL_100dpi.pdf (accessed June 24, 2010).

Kudryavtsev, Alexander, and Natalia Dushkina, eds. *Preservation of 20th Century Architecture and World Heritage,* Moscow, April 17-20, 2006, Proceedings of Scientific Conference, Abstract Collection. Moscow, 2006.

Kudryavtsev, Alexander, and Natalia Dushkina, eds. *20th Century: Preservation of Cultural Heritage.* Moscow: n.p., 2006.

Moscow Architecture Preservation Society (MAPS) and SAVE Europe's Heritage. *Moscow Heritage at Crisis Point, updated expanded edition.* Edited by Edmund Harris, Clementine Cecil, and Mariana Khrustaleva. (Moscow: SAVE Europe's Heritage, MAPS, and DOCOMOMO, 2009), www.maps-moscow.com/index.php?chapter_id=173&data_id=237&do=view_single (accessed June 25, 2010).

Museum of Modern Art. Lost Vanguard: Soviet Modernist Architecture, 1922–1932; photographs by Richard Pare. Exhibition, Museum of Modern Art, New York, July 18–October 29, 2007, www.moma.org/visit/calendar/exhibitions/47 (accessed December 31, 2010).

Figure 18-7 The condition of architects Moisei Ginsburg and Ignati Milinis's Narkomfin Building (a), an apartment block constructed in Moscow between 1928 and 1930, declined slowly from the time of its construction due to changed attitudes about the avant-garde during the Stalin era. Increased rates of vacancy and dereliction after privatization in the early 1990s presented such a problem that demolition was considered. Now, after nearly two decades of indecision about how to proceed, a sensitive restoration project has been proposed based on the designs of Alexei Ginsburg, the master's grandson, and some dedicated colleagues. One scenario is to restore the building as apartments, a hotel, and a few offices, including those of the Narkomfin Foundation; another scenario is to restore it and offer it as apartments only. In any case, the building's distinctive and influential single-loaded corridor and apartment mezzanine entrance system (b) should be carefully preserved. Figure 18-7b courtesy and copyright Richard Pare.

a

b

a

Figure 18-8 The 1929 Chekist Housing Scheme (a) by architects Ivan Antonov, Veniamin Sokolov, and Arseni Tumbasov in Yekaterinburg, central Russia is an example of a well-preserved building from the Soviet constructivist era located outside of the capital. The building's location, beyond the pressures of land development, is likely the main reason it survived. Its spiraling, so-called KGB stairway (b) and the building's other character-defining details (including the balconies) have been carefully restored, using materials and detailing identical to that which was originally used. Courtesy and copyright Richard Pare.

b

These and many other recent projects in the Russian capital led Boris Pasternak, chief architect of the Urban History Studies Center, to conclude in 2005 that "There is not a single major preservation project in Moscow's recent history where the historical integrity of the site had been maintained."[48] A recent project that has given others reason to hope, however, is the restoration of Dom Pashkova, one of Moscow's most magnificent palaces, which was built in the early nineteenth century in a neo-Palladian style after its predecessor had been destroyed by fire during the French invasion. Because the mansion houses part of the complex of the Russian National Library and is located immediately adjacent to the Kremlin, for twenty years it stood in derelict condition and served for many as symbol of the attitude toward cultural heritage of the new Russian government. The careful restoration was completed in 2008 with state funds and was overseen by the Ministry of Culture's Federal Agency for Culture and Cinematography.

The 2009 report *Moscow Heritage at Crisis Point*, coauthored by SAVE Europe's Heritage and the Moscow Architecture Preservation Society (MAPS), argues that conservationists in Russia must battle the prevailing attitude that new replicas are more desirable than old buildings. This disregard for integrity and historic fabric in approaches toward architectural heritage is also evident in the propensity to reconstruct lost heritage, an old tradition in Russia, which continues to threaten heritage today, both through the channeling of scarce resources toward these massive projects as well as through the misrepresentations of the past by these inauthentic re-creations.

The most extraordinary and well-known of Russia's recent reconstructions is Moscow's massive Cathedral of Christ the Savior. The original early nineteenth-century building was demolished in 1931 by Stalin but recreated in the 1990s on the initiative of Mayor Yuri Luzhkov, who raised $300 million from state, municipal, and corporate funds.[49] Unlike in St. Petersburg, this project was completed in time to serve as the centerpiece of the 1997 celebrations of the 850th anniversary of Moscow's founding. Though hailed as an architectural preservation project, material integrity and historic authenticity were not issues of high importance in the building of new Cathedral of Christ the Saviour. In fact, the first project architect was fired in part because his interest in documentation was slowing the project down and his insistence on using historic materials was too expensive.[50]

A similar church reconstruction in Yaroslavl caused UNESCO to question the local government's commitment to protect the city, just one month after it was added to the World Heritage List.[51] Despite a new master plan in 2006 and new local regulatory legislation in 2008, these concerns were reiterated by the World Heritage Committee in 2009 as Yaroslavl's skyline was threatened by new high rise construction and the rebuilding of the seventeenth-century Cathedral of the Dormition and its distinctive five-story bell tower destroyed by Stalin in 1937.[52] Yaroslavl's radial plan is an outstanding surviving example of the design principles dictated by Catherine the Great's mid-eighteenth-century urban planning reforms. Its historic form, as well as its numerous sixteenth- and seventeenth-century churches, survived the destruction of the two world wars and Stalin's antireligious campaigns.

Many of the high-rise projects in Yaroslavl have been halted, and the careful restoration of the Peter and Paul Park is underway by a team from Netherlands and Russia: the park was originally laid for Peter the Great by his Dutch gardener Jan Roosen. At the same time, the reconstruction of the Cathedral of the Dormition is complete and there are still active discussions of plans to rebuild a few other of Yaroslavl's lost elements, including a wing of the department store trading rows and a bell tower at the Kazan monastery. International and Russian experts question the cathedral's reconstruction, as the winning entry in the controversial design competition proposed neither a historically accurate replica, nor a modern interpretation; rather, the new Cathedral is an oversized, historicist mélange of elements.

Figure 18-9 The Church of the Icon of the Sign at Dubrovitsy near Moscow suffered a slow decline from the 1930s. It still awaits restoration today despite its considerable historical significance—it was erected by Tsar Peter I's tutor, Boris Golitsyn. The church is architecturally significant as a transition piece from medieval- to western-European influenced Russian styles. It was listed on the World Monuments Fund's 2010 Watch list of endangered sites.

In addition to concerns over authenticity, the tendency to rebuild churches destroyed by the Soviets has been controversial among historians and architectural conservationists who lament that, while lavish funds are spent to create historically inaccurate facsimiles, extant and authentic churches crumble. The post-Communist restoration of religious freedom has led to the return of thousands of religious buildings to their original uses and to the ownership of the Russian Orthodox Church. In many cases, this has benefited historic churches through increased attention and regular maintenance. However, some religious buildings have presented challenges to their new congregations, as they struggle to meet the needs of their upkeep and conservation. Thus, while millions are spent on reconstructing lost churches, those that have survived are often left to deteriorate. Another problem has been the clergy's inattention to proper conservation methods when attending to historic religious buildings and objects.[53] For instance, in March 2010 the Russian Orthodox Church announced a project that stunned both Russian and international heritage conservationists: Plans to build a large Russian Orthodox cemetery and cathedral at the site of the burials of Tsar Nicholas II and his family after their murder in Yekaterinburg would effectively obliterate its historic and archaeological value.[54] Of this astonishing idea Russian-American architectural scholar and historian Arcady A. R. Nebolsine said: "We thought in recent years that Russia's rapidly disappearing cultural heritage had suffered every conceivable indignity, and now there is this…and it is the Church that is behind it."[55]

Though a few major restoration projects received significant federal support during the 1990s, government funding for conservation has been severely cut since the Soviet era, prohibiting cities from budgeting for care and maintenance of their historic sites. The shortcomings led St. Petersburg's authorities to court foreign investment and to begin leasing select historic buildings. Although the need for private participation to financially support conservation projects is widely recognized, the issue has also led to popular protests from citizens concerned that their city is being sold to outside interests. From another side, national and international investors and donors are frustrated with the system and continue to be wary of funneling restoration monies into a place where both property laws and political jurisdictions over state and private property remain unclear.[56]

Increased growth and demands for luxury housing and commercial real estate in Moscow, St. Petersburg, and other Russian cities has led to several clashes between developers and architectural conservationists over size and scale of buildings neighboring on historic districts, as well as to debates over new historicist buildings that are replacing authentic historic structures.[57]

Architectural sites in the Russian Federation have also been damaged as a result of armed conflict in the post-Soviet period. This has been particularly the case in Chechnya, whose heritage is still at risk from continuing civil unrest and instability, even though the region seems to have settled down from the wars of the mid-1990s, and rebuilding has begun.[58] In 2003 a ten-year urban plan for the Chechen capital of Grozny was introduced that simultaneously outlined the postwar reconstruction and future growth of the city as well as the accommodation of returning refugees. An inventory of sites and their conditions has begun, with sixty-nine federally and twelve hundred locally important sites on the preliminary list. The current Chechen constitution calls for joint jurisdiction over cultural heritage concerns between the local government and the Russian Federation.

The Cultural Heritage Minister of Chechnya has called for international assistance both to rebuild war-damaged sites and to care for long-neglected sites, such as the hundreds of medieval fortress towers and 150 historic settlements in the Archun State Conservation Area along the Georgian border. Despite their recognition by the Soviet Union in 1988 and their continued importance in post-Soviet Russia, these towers and settlements have not received conservation attention in decades. The structural integrity of these unique tenth- to fifteenth-century stone towers was also seriously compromised by Russian aerial and artillery bombardment during the 1990s conflict. UNESCO responded to Chechnya's request for international aid with a grant for its museums, including the National History Museum in Grozny, which was allegedly ransacked and looted by Russian soldiers in 1995.[59] However, most of Chechnya's heritage is still in dire need of financing for conservation and maintenance, and organizations and investors will likely be reluctant to provide the necessary funds until there is less civil unrest and more political stability.

Government attitudes and policies have shifted away from valuing preservation, especially in Moscow, whose budget for conservation has dwindled from nearly $240 million between 1989 and 2004 to less than $13 million.[60] In addition, Russia's framework of legislation, oversight bodies, and policies are still poorly implemented. While the Soviet-era government applied its policies selectively and often exempted itself, these same polices have not been adequately funded or enforced in the post-Soviet period.[61]

Figure 18-10 War-ravaged Grozny, Chechnya, produced a ten-year reconstruction and restoration plan in 2003; however, implementation of the plan is behind schedule due to continued political instability. Chechnya's most distinctive architectural features are its tenth- to fifteenth- century stone watch towers within the Archun State Conservation Area, along the Georgian border. The towers suffered in the recent conflict and are in need of stabilization and repair.

Located on the remote Lake Onega in the northern part of Russia, Kizhi Island is home to two magnificent wooden, early eighteenth-century churches and a mid-nineteenth-century octagonal bell tower in a wooden enclosure called a *pogost*. This site was first measured and surveyed in 1876 and came under state protection in 1920. Restorations to combat rot and insect damage were carried out in the 1920s and the late 1950s.

Other historic wooden buildings were moved to Kizhi beginning in 1951, including the Church of the Resurrection of Lazarus, the oldest wooden ecclesiastical building in Russia, which was brought from the Muromsk Monastery and reassembled and restored. Other chapels as well as houses, farms, and smith buildings were also relocated to form part of the Kizhi State Open-Air Museum of History, Architecture, and Ethnography, which opened in 1966.

Today, Kizhi Pogost is the site of an extensive, multidecade restoration project at the Church of the Transfiguration, one of the site's two main and original churches. Fear of collapse in the 1980s led to the removal of its interior furnishings and fittings, the placement of its iconostasis in storage, and the insertion of a metal support frame in its interior. This unsightly steel scaffold was a temporary solution to stabilize the church, which was originally built during the reign of Tsar Peter the Great with twenty-two onion domes and not a single nail.

Between 1992 and 1995, ICOMOS hosted a series of workshops focused on finding acceptable solutions for stabilizing the Church of the Transfiguration, in which experts studied and discussed possibilities and made recommendations. International financial support and technical assistance has also been provided at various times since 1995 by the Finnish Committee of ICOMOS, World Monuments Fund, and the Samuel H. Kress Foundation. Important contributions have also been made by the Russian Ministry of Culture and the Norwegian and German governments.

But it was the St. Petersburg based Spetsproektrestavratsia (Scientific Research Institute) that ultimately designed the unique and technologically advanced solution to be used to stabilize the church. This strategy involves dividing the church into seven horizontal bands to be lifted one by one, starting from the top, and hung from the metal scaffolding. Once the entire church is suspended in the air, it will be disassembled, consolidated, and reassembled from the bottom up.

In October 2004 the uppermost part of the church—weighing 30 tons and equivalent in height to a four-story building—was lifted 20 centimeters (about 8 inches) in a successful test of this remarkable conservation plan, which is being carried out by the Russian Ministry of Culture and its regional office in Karelia. By 2014, in time for the Church's three-hundredth anniversary, Kizhi's Church of the Transfiguration will have been restored from its foundation to its roof shingles—and, amazingly, it will have remained open to tourists throughout the entire stabilization project.[62]

RECENT RUSSIAN CONSERVATION SUCCESSES

Despite the many daunting challenges and threats facing architectural conservationists in the Russian Federation today, a few notable successes have occurred in the post-Soviet period. In 2006 the Presidential Culture and Art Council launched a pilot project in the Tver' region based on Britain's National Trust in which state-owned listed properties will be restored and converted into hotels and other self-sustaining uses to ensure their continued maintenance in the future.[63] Since 1990, UNESCO has added fifteen cultural sites in Russia to the World Heritage List, including districts in St. Petersburg, Novgorod, and Yaroslavl as well as Moscow's Kremlin and Kizhi Pogost.

The emergence of a diverse collection of concerned nongovernment participants is an important post-Soviet development that has furthered architectural conservation efforts in the Russian Federation. The All-Russian Society for Protection of Monuments launched new initiatives in the 1990s focused on wooden, monastic, and literary heritage sites in the Russian countryside. This older society has also been joined by a significant number of active foundations, nongovernmental organizations, and private companies.

a

b

c

d

Figure 18-11 After much research and expert consultation, the ingenious solution devised for the restoration of the wooden Church of the Transfiguration at Kizhi Pogost (a) involves the suspension of the church from a metal scaffolding and consolidation of its wooden members from the bottom up. The process requires the installation of temporary structural shoring and new wooden members (b, c, d).

Figure 18-12 The issue of building height control in and around Russia's historic cities was exemplified by the 2006 proposal to construct the 403-meter-tall Gazprom office building in the Smolny Cathedral area, within the historical perimeter of St. Petersburg. Architectural conservation professionals and institutions in St. Petersburg, concerned about its impact on the city's skyline, fought vigorously, with the support of UNESCO and others, to prevent its construction or find acceptable alterations to the proposed design. In December 2010, the state gas company and the city of St. Petersburg decided to find an alternate site for the tower. Image courtesy RMJM Architects, London, © 2008.

Some of these private organizations promote certain building types, such as the Village Church of Russia Society, while others have focused their attention on certain cities or regions, such as the Moscow Architecture Preservation Society (MAPS). Since its establishment in 2004, MAPS has battled against great odds for all Moscow's heritage, but it has been a particularly strong advocate of Russia's unique avant-garde architecture dating from the interwar years. The Russian Cultural Heritage Network, founded in 1995, organizes conferences, standardizes information, and facilitates domestic and international cooperation of heritage museums and professionals. Since 1988 the Scientific and Design Institute for Reconstruction of Historic Towns has created numerous, comprehensive urban rehabilitation plans for Russian cities. One of these plans has been implemented and has developed the tourist potential of Suzdal. A very active new preservation organization in Moscow, Arkhnadzor, has brought together many small organizations and individuals. Also, Zhivoi Gorod (Living City), another preservation-minded NGO in St Petersburg, spearheaded the successful campaign against building the Gazprom skyscraper within the city's historic center.

In addition, many internationally based NGOs have assisted Russian heritage conservation in recent years. The American Friends of the Russian Country Estate promotes and assists former Russian country houses, many of which are in a desperate state. The American and British Friends of the Hermitage raise funds internationally for that deteriorating and impoverished museum, which houses some of the world's finest artworks. The World Monuments Fund has initiated conservation projects at the Alexander Palace, Yelagin Palace, and at Catherine the Great's Chinese Palace at Oranienbaum.[64] Efforts such as the Getty Conservation Institute–funded St. Petersburg International Center for Preservation and the International Foundation for the

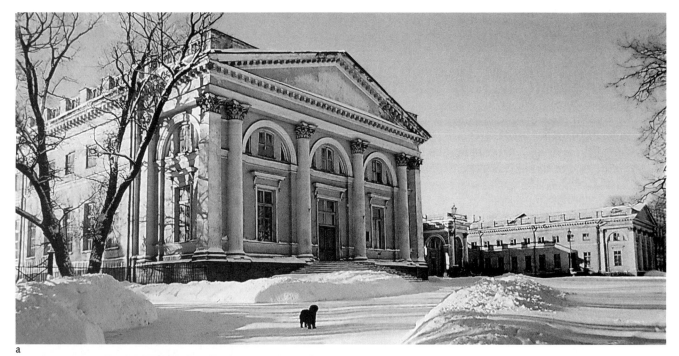

a

b

c

Figure 18-13 The neoclassical Alexander Palace in Tsarskoe Selo (a) near St. Petersburg was built by Empress Catherine II in the late eighteenth century; it became the favored home of the last Russian tsar, Nicholas II and his family. Work on the palace with the assistance of the World Monuments Fund began in 1995 and included restoration of the palace's western wing roof (b and c). Soon after, the restored wing opened as a museum dedicated to the last tsar and his family.

Salvation of St. Petersburg also work with local groups and donors to carry out conservation projects.[65]

In Moscow a positive trend is noticeable in the process of reclamation and reuse of industrial sites. The careful attention paid to these sites evidences a small and potentially growing art and architectural community interested in architectural conservation. In one of the most acclaimed and successful of Moscow's industrial conversion projects, the Russian Ministry of Culture created the State Centre for Contemporary Art from an interwar lamp factory. This bold intervention uses color, material, and textures to provocatively juxtapose new and old in a project inspired by 1930s constructivists and contemporary western European projects like London's Tate Modern.[66] Such projects are making the industrial aesthetic more popular; however, because most of these recent adaptive reuse projects have been motivated by tight budgets rather than concern for the specific sites in question, the history and integrity of these nineteenth- and early twentieth-century industrial buildings has not been a major priority.

Figure 18-14 Despite numerous losses to the architecture of Moscow in the last decade, there are examples of imaginative adaptive reuse, usually by members of the arts community. An example of such an adaptation is Winzavod, a former wine factory in east Moscow that was converted in 2008 into an art gallery, shop, and office space. Since the conversion, Winzavod has become a trendy and popular place.

Russia's contemporary cultural heritage conservation scene has many positive characteristics—including decentralization, the introduction of NGOs, and private architectural conservation firms (still a weak point, as restoration skills are scarce at the moment), increasing popular interest in heritage protection, nonideological approaches to sites and their interpretation, and well-trained, creative professionals who devise thoughtful solutions. However, the diverse built heritage found throughout the vast Russian Federation remains vulnerable today as the period of transition and national reorganization continues. Furthermore, training in the restoration skills that were in prior times state-supported are now in decline. Although increased funding in certain sectors and broadened international cooperation has aided Russia's conservation community, a comprehensive and sustainable heritage system is only in its initial stages of development.

ARCHITECTURAL CONSERVATION IN SIBERIA

The seemingly boundless frontier of Siberia—with its frozen tundra, bountiful conifer forests, icy river network, and highest concentration of active volcanoes in the world—stretches for 13.1 million square kilometers (5.1 million square miles), from the peaks of the Ural Mountains to the north Pacific Ocean. Russian hunters and trappers began making small inroads into Siberia in the sixteenth century; however, it was not until the nineteenth century that large-scale colonization of the region took place. Due to its size, Siberia's vernacular and ecclesiastical architecture is mostly concentrated in the few cities established by these Russian settlers, as well as along the Trans-Siberian Railroad, built in imperial Russia's final years. These tiny accessible outposts of economic development offer Siberia's only chance of leveraging its heritage for tourism purposes.

One of Siberia's primary resources, wood, is the principle building material of most of its historic buildings. In the nineteenth century, Cossack settlers built wooden forts and towns for protection from Tatar raiders and to secure the lucrative fur trade. These towns included many splendid churches with steeply slanted roofs to deflect snow. This architectural heritage is today plagued by a host of problems typical to wood architecture in colder climes, including attacks from microorganisms and deterioration from continuous freeze-thaw cycles. At the same time, the constant cold in Siberia's northern reaches has also helped preserve other buildings in their original form, much like the wooden explorer huts in the Antarctic and Arctic regions.[67] Unfortunately, though the early cities of East Russia and Siberia were spared the devastation of World War II, they were allowed to deteriorate during the Soviet era.

Siberia's later industrial and mining towns as well as their infrastructure, quickly built to extract the region's resources and quickly abandoned when exhausted, are a ghostly legacy of Soviet economic plans. Those industrial towns that are still producing do not fare much better, because the companies that grow rich from extracting Siberia's oil and other resources pay taxes directly to the federal government in Moscow, which returns little of these funds to support, let alone conserve, Siberia's urban centers. In addition, the constant pollution of still-functioning Siberian industries threatens the historic architecture and environment of the entire region.[68]

Many Trans-Siberian Railroad towns have nevertheless managed to protect their own unique architectural heritage. While other cities in Russia lost much of their historic architecture to wide-scale redevelopment, insensitive planning, and the ubiquitous concrete residential building blocks, Irkutsk's poor infrastructure staved off Soviet redevelopment, inadvertently protecting its neoclassical vernacular wooden buildings. Yekaterinburg and Novosibirsk boast an impressive array of preserved Soviet constructivist buildings, and Verkhoturye in the north has managed to preserve its Trinity Church, with its Ukrainian baroque, Italian Renaissance, and medieval Muscovite elements.

While action might be taken to save historic architecture along the Trans-Siberian Railway and in large cities like Vladivostok and Krasnoyarsk, sites outside these major urban centers are difficult to access and unlikely to receive any of the limited conservation funding. However, many of these remote regions are home to unique and important heritage sites of some of Siberia's over thirty indigenous groups. In some places, especially along Siberia's southern edge, a distinctive Chinese and Mongol culture still permeates, even though the people have converted to the Russian Orthodox Church. Sadly, very little of the physical remains of this Buddhist legacy still exist, though a few monasteries styled after those in Tibet and Mongolia have survived in various states of disrepair, including the late eighteenth-century temples of the Goose Lake Monastery, which survived Stalin's attacks and multiple reuse attempts.[69] Another one of these historic monasteries, the seat of Russian Buddhism in Ulan-Ude, was reconstructed in the 1940s. In addition, if protected, the cultural landscapes of native Siberian groups such as the Tuvans and the Khanty could serve as a model for both those west and east of the Urals.

For many foreigners, Siberia is synonymous with the system of Gulag prison camps established in its isolated wilderness in the mid-twentieth century. The bleak, improvised architecture of its hundreds of work camps was abandoned or dismantled following the Soviet Union's collapse. While many Russians would like to forget this odious part of their history, there is a movement to conserve what is left of the Gulag legacy.

Perm 36, which operated from 1947 to 1987 as a prison for human rights activists and political dissidents, is one of the most complete and significant of the remaining

Figure 18-15 Perm 36 is the best surviving example from among hundreds of former Soviet work camps in Siberia. Preserving the poignant character of the tangible and intangible conditions of such places poses special conservation and curatorial challenges. With international support, including from the U.S. Ambassador's Fund for Preservation and the U.S. National Park Service, the Memorial Center of the History of Political Repression Perm 36 has begun to conserve the remains as a "site of conscience" for future generations.

Gulag camps. In 1994 site protection began and the Memorial Center of the History of Political Repression at Perm 36 was established, and the Gulag Museum opened two years later. In 1999 the U.S. National Park Service began cooperating with the Memorial Center to conserve the eighteen surviving wooden buildings and to create a long-term site plan to counteract threats from piling snow, timber decay, and fire. The maintenance of Perm 36 as an open air museum will hopefully serve as an enduring reminder of the Gulag system and educate a new generation of Russians who did not grow up under the threat of its brutal camps. While Perm 36 is located on the western border of Siberia, its conservation offers a model for the more distant camps that held the political prisoners of a generation.

Despite the attention and progress at Perm 36, it was placed on the 2004 Watch List of the World Monuments Fund. Similarly, though the Center for the Preservation of Historical and Cultural Landscapes in Irkutsk actively works toward long-term management plans for the city's urban vernacular fabric, the Historic Center of Irkutsk was also placed on the World Monuments Fund's Watch List in both 1998 and 2000. Thus, while locals in Perm, Irkutsk, and other Siberian cities have raised what scant money they can for their endangered heritage, more needs to be done on both federal and international levels to support Siberia's unique heritage. International recognition has drawn attention to Siberia's woes and opportunities, but additional intervention is needed to explore and preserve this hidden part of Russia. Only then can Siberia acknowledge its own special place in history.

ENDNOTES

1. Boris Ometev and John Stuart, *St. Petersburg: Portrait of an Imperial City* (New York: Vendome Press, 1990), 54.

2. For details on the earliest efforts in Russian architectural restoration and preservation see: Alexei Schenkov, ed., *Monuments of Architecture in Prerevolutionary Russia: Essays in the History of Architectural Restoration* (Moscow: Terra Book Club, 2002) (*Pamyatniki arkhitektury v dorevolutsionnoi Rossii. Ocherki istorii arkhitekturnoi restavratsii. Pod obschei redaktsiei doktora arkhitekturi*). Published in Russian with a short resume in English, it is richly illustrated and represents much new original research.

3. This law was restated in 1718–1722. The most tangible results of these laws was establishment of the Kunstcamera collection in St. Petersburg; though this was not a full-scale architectural conservation per se, the inclination to collect, document, preserve, and present Russian objects (including models of buildings) represents an important beginning and groundwork for monument protection laws that followed.

4. "Russian Cultural Heritage Register," *Wikipedia*, http://en.wikipedia.org/wiki/Russian_cultural_heritage_register (accessed November 20, 2009).

5. The Russian Imperial Archaeological Commission was in charge of the protection of architectural monuments until 1889.

6. "Architectural and Cultural Monuments," Irkutsk Ancient and Modern, www.manus.bailal.ru/eng/es18.htm.

7. Anthony Tung, *Preserving the World's Great Cities: The Destruction and Renewal of the Historic Metropolis.* (New York: Clarkson Potter), 151.

8. The Church of St. Nicholas in Demre on the south-central coast of Turkey, was restored by Alexander II in the 1860s in honor of his father, and it is one of the first examples of international architectural conservation.

9. For the history of architectural restoration and conservation during the Soviet period, see: Elena Kulchinskaya, Kjnstantin Rytzarev, and Alexei Schenkov, *Monuments of Architecture in the Soviet Union: Essays in the History of Restoration* (Moscow: Terra Book Club, 2004) that is richly illustrated in the Russian language with a brief English summary.

10. Under Lunacharsky's January 1918 ordinance: "All buildings and structures, as well as art and historical monuments, are considered property of the republic, valid immediately, regardless of what institution or organization, including churches, cathedrals and monasteries, owns or uses them at present. Notable collections that were protected intact include the Hermitage in St. Petersburg and the Alexander Palace in nearby Tsarskoe Selo, both of which experienced hard times later. Irina Rodimzeva, et al., *The Kremlin and Its Treasures* (New York: Rizzoli, 1986), 60.

11. Suzanne Massie, *Pavlovsk: The Life of a Russian Palace* (Boston: Little, Brown and Company, 1990), 132–33.

12. Vladimir Ivanov, *Monuments and Society* (St. Petersburg: Leningrad Colloquium of ICOMOS, 1969). Additional decrees on culture and heritage protection were issued by Lenin in 1918–1922.

13. Tung, *Preserving the World's Great Cities*, 152.

14. Rodimzeva, et al., *The Kremlin and Its Treasures*, 57. During the 1812 French occupation the Kremlin's Water, Middle Arsenal, Peter, and Nikolskaia towers were all destroyed on Napoleon's orders.

15. During the 1920s and 1930s, thousands of pieces of furniture, jewelry, paintings, and objects from private and imperial collections found their way into the hands of American millionaires Armand Hammer, J. Paul Getty, Mathilde Geddings Gray, and Marjorie Merriweather Post, as well as foreign monarchs such as King Farouk of Egypt and Queen Mary of Great Britain. Even the famous jeweled eggs created by the Fabergé studios for Tsar Nicholas were sold off—although many have since been repurchased by some of Russia's new elite and returned to the country.

16. Orlando Figes, *A People's Tragedy: The Russian Revolution 1917–1924* (London: Jonathan Cape, 1996), 748–49.

17. Brian Moynahan, *The Russian Century* (New York: Random House, 1994), 134.

18. William Brumfield, *Lost Russia* (Durham, NC: Duke University Press, 1995), 8.

19. Ibid., 10.

20. "Russian Cultural Heritage Register."

21. Blair Ruble, "Russian Reform and Historic Preservation in a Provincial City," in Jodi Koehn, ed., *Issues of Historical Preservation in Central Europe and Russia: Conference Proceedings*, Kennan Institute for Advanced Russian Studies, Occasional Paper #259, 3-14 (Washington, DC: The Woodrow Wilson International Center for Scholars, 1993).

22. Tung, *Preserving the World's Great Cities*, 155. In the decade between 1926 and 1936, urban renewal projects destroyed whole medieval quarters in Moscow. About 260 of the city's churches were razed for modernization projects, including nine in and around the Kremlin. Brumfield, *Lost Russia*, 9; and Ruth Daniloff, "Restoring a Russian Heritage Turns Out to Be a Byzantine Task," *Smithsonian Magazine* 13, no. 12 (March 1983): 66.

23. Brumfield, *Lost Russia*, 10.

24. Massie, *Pavlovsk*, 223. In the German-occupied territories of Russia, Ukraine, and Belarus, the Einsatzstab Reichleiter Rosenberg für die Besetzten Gebiete (ERR) was created to identify and collect important cultural treasures for the Reich.

25. Ibid., 221.

26. Ibid., 323–324.

27. Ibid., 281; and Harrison E. Salisbury, *The 900 Days: The Siege of Leningrad* (New York: Da Capo Press, 1969), 556.

28. Daniloff, "Restoring a Russian Heritage," 67.

29. "The USSR's 1948 Instructions for the Identification, Registration, Maintenance, and Restoration of Architectural Monuments under State Protection," *Future Anterior* 5, no. 1 (Summer 2008): 64–72.

30. Massie, *Pavlovsk*, 281. After the war, recovery efforts began almost immediately at the palace complexes on the outskirts of St. Petersburg to protect what remained of the structures and gather whatever objects or fragments had been hidden by the staff or left behind by the retreating Germans. Anatoly Kuchumov followed the path of the retreating army and retrieved portraits, furniture, architectural fragments, even sections of parquet floors that had been abandoned en route.

31. Katrina Durbak "Architectural Conservation in Ukraine" (master thesis, Columbia University, 2006), 7.

32. "Russian Cultural Heritage Register."

33. Daniloff, "Restoring Russian Heritage," 67.

34. Ibid., 69.

35. Steve Raymer, *St. Petersburg* (Atlanta, GA: Turner Publishing, Inc., 1994), 100.

36. Daniloff, "Restoring Russian Heritage," 69.

37. "1973 Law of the Union of Soviet Socialist Republics: On the Protection and Use of Historic and Cultural Monuments," *Future Anterior* 5, no. 1 (Summer 2008): 74–80.

38. Information on the card included title, location, type, date, character of use, category. Manana Simonishvili, "Georgia," in Pickard, *Policy and Law in Heritage Conservation*, 118; and Pickard, *Management of Historic Centres*, 93.

39. Many Russian architectural conservationists today feel the government, during post-Soviet times, has operated without adequate long-term planning, and as well it has been slow to respond with the actual investment and action necessary to ensure effective architectural heritage protection.

40. Restoration of Amber Room was largely underwritten by the German government.

41. According to Russian conservation experts, the government's effective addressing of these issues only began recently, and it remains to be seen if it will be successful.

42. "Russian Cultural Heritage Register."

43. Ibid. There are exceptions; For instance, in the financing of the post-fire restoration of the Manezh, Mayor Luzhkov declared that if the state were in charge of the restoration, it would take years—so the City of Moscow undertook the effort, creating some controversy in the process.

44. Ibid.

45. Another issue has been the need for transparency about what is listed on Russian historic building registers. In Moscow the historic buildings register was only made public after the publication of a report in 2007 by the private Moscow Architecture Preservation Society (MAPS)—and

that was after three years of debate on the matter. The report states that the Ministry of Culture and the Rosokhrankultura's decision-making abilities are also still burdened by Soviet-era bureaucracy, and consequently its operations are far from efficient, as was painfully obvious from its handling of St. Petersburg's high-profile tercentenary restoration program.

46. "Tsaritsino' Readies Itself for Guests—*Izvestia*," Moscow Architecture Preservation Society, May 25, 2006, www.maps-moscow.com/index.php?chapter_id=149&data_id=253&do=view_single (accessed December 30, 2009).

47. Natalia Dushkina, "Russia: 20th-Century Heritage," *Heritage@Risk: 2002/2003* (Paris: ICO-MOS, 2002), www.international.icomos.org/risk/2002/russia2002.htm (accessed December 30, 2009).

48. Conor Humphries, "Activists Rally in Historic Buildings' Defense," *The Moscow Times*, November 1, 2005, www.maps-moscow.com/index.php?chapter_id=149&data_id=140&do=view_single (accessed December 30, 2009).

49. David Hoffman, "The Man Who Rebuilt Moscow," *Washington Post Foreign Service*, February 24, 1997, A1; and Thanos Pagonis and Andy Thornely, "Urban Development in Moscow: Market/State Relations in the New Russia," *European Planning Studies* 8, No. 6 (December 2000), 751–66.

50. Other important examples of rebuilding heritage sites in Moscow include the reconstructed Kazan Cathedral and the Resurrection Gates on Red Square. Natalia Dushkina, "Reconstruction: Recent Russian Experience," *Quaderni ARCO. Restauro, Storia e Tecnica* (Roma: Gangemi, 1998), 47–58, and "Historic Reconstruction: Prospects for Heritage Preservation or Metamorphoses of Theory?" in Price and King, *Conserving the Authentic*, 83-94.

51. "Heritage Revival in Yaroslavl," Moscow Architecture Preservation Society (MAPS), August 28, 2005, www.maps-moscow.com/index.php?chapter_id=151&data_id=25&do=view_single (accessed December 30, 2009).

52. UNESCO, *Report of the World Heritage Committee, 33rd Session, Seville, Spain 22–30 June 2009* (Paris: UNESCO, 2009), 129–133.

53. According to Clementine Cecil of MAPS, in correspondence with John H. Stubbs, December 3, 2009: "The Soviets actually conserved a lot of religious objects well, by putting them in museums. At the other extreme, a lot of clergy today actually use sacred objects with no concern for the preserving them." "Ditto with their churches—they treat them roughly and have no training in conservation—they do not know the problems that using concrete instead of lime bring, or inserting plastic windows. They are concerned with patching up their ragged churches as quickly and as cheaply as possible. This leads to a huge number of problems."

54. Clifford J. Levy, "Where Some Envision Czar's End, Church Sees Building Site." *New York Times*, March 13, 2010, A4.

55. Private conversation, John H. Stubbs, March 19, 2010. Arcady A.R. Nebolsine represents an influential circle of seminal philosophers and activists in twentieth century Russian architectural heritage protection. The late D. S Likhachev, famed for his belief in 'cultural ecology' (the belief that Nature is not in conflict but in friendly collaboration with Mankind), was viewed as leader of this circle.

56. Raymer, *St. Petersburg*, 98.

57. Sophia Kishkovsky, "Should Stalinist Hotel Be Saved?" *The Art News Paper*, August 16, 2002.

58. As of 2009 instability in Chechnya appears to be shifting to the regions of Ingushetia and Kabardino-Balkaria to the west.

59. Carlotta Gall and Thomas de Waal, *Chechnya: Calamity in the Caucasus* (New York: New York University Press, 1998), 235.

60. "Russian Cultural Heritage Register."

61. Vladimir Krogius, "The Historic Towns of Russia and Problems of Their Conservation," *Context* no. 43 (September 1994), 15; www.ihbc.org.uk/context_archive/43/Vladimir.htm (accessed June 26, 2010).

62. "In Front of the World: The Restoration of the Church of the Transfiguration at Kizhi Island (1990–2014)," The Kizhi Museum, http://kizhi.karelia.ru/carpenter_world/index_e.htm.

63. John Varoli, "Putin Looks to UK to Save Listed Buildings—The Art Newspaper," March 23, 2006, www.maps-moscow.com/index.php?chapter_id=149&data_id=177&do=view_single (accessed December 30, 2009.

64. WMF's World Monuments Watch program has also stimulated restoration at modernist landmarks such as the Rusakov Club in Moscow (K. Melnikov, 1927–29) and the Viipuri Library (Alvar Aalto, 1927–35) in Karelia, Vyborg, Russia.

65. The St. Petersburg Institute for Conservation was established through a partnership of Russian Academy of Sciences, the city of St. Petersburg, and the Getty Conservation Institute in 1996 and offered training and other courses for about seven years .

66. Ibid., and "New Life: The State Center for Contemporary Art," Moscow Architecture Preservation Society, December 15, 2004, www.maps-moscow.com/index.php?chapter_id=164&data_id=17&do=view_single (accessed December 30, 2009).

67. See Stubbs, "The Polar Regions," *Time Honored*, 358–365.

68. Fiona Hill and Clifford Gaddy, *The Siberian Curse* (Washington, DC: Brookings Institution Press, 2003), 132.

69. Anna Reid, *The Shaman's Coat: A Native History of Siberia* (New York: Walker Publishing, 2002), 88.

CHAPTER 19

Ukraine, Moldova, and Belarus

Ukraine, Moldova, and Belarus are all independent countries in eastern Europe that were formerly part of the Soviet Union and are currently active members of the Commonwealth of Independent States. Centuries of Russian czarist and Soviet control shaped early architectural conservation efforts throughout the region as well as witnessed periods of extensive destruction. With independence in the early 1990s came strong nationalism that focused much needed attention on the heritage of these countries. At that time, all three passed cultural heritage legislation, established responsible government agencies, and created registries of sites worthy of protection. Though the end of Soviet state subsidies, weak economies, and negligent owners threaten architectural heritage in each of these three eastern European countries, prospects vary among them. Cause for hope for the future of heritage conservation can be found in Belarus due to a relatively stable economy and in the Ukraine due international assistance and reforms aimed at European Union integration; however, insufficient international or local interest in Moldova is cause of concern for that country's heritage.

UKRAINE

Some of the most extensive archaeological remains in the world are located on the Crimean peninsula in Ukraine, including the 500 hectare fifth-century BCE Greek city of Tauric Chersonesos. However, the most important historic period for many of today's Ukrainians is their early medieval golden age, when the prosperous Slavic princedom, Kievan Rus', was one of the most powerful states in Europe. Many architectural masterpieces were created during this period, including the Kiev-Pechersk Lavra monastery, a World Heritage Site. This independent and thriving medieval kingdom ended with the Mongol invasion in 1240. From that time until the collapse of the Soviet Union, Ukraine was ruled by foreigners, including the Polish-Lithuanian kings, the Russian czars, and the Soviets. As a result, since independence in 1991, Ukraine has been marked by the promotion of national identity, including a deep concern for its heritage.

The earliest organized architectural conservation efforts in Ukraine took place in the seventeenth century, when Cossacks stationed in the region to enforce Russian rule brought prosperity and financed large-scale restorations of long-neglected architectural sites. Kiev benefited the most from this interest. Many of its eleventh-century wooden churches were rehabilitated or rebuilt in stone to counter the decay of their original material. These first attempts at restoring Ukraine's grand past created a new architectural style known as Cossack baroque; but, unfortunately, they also facilitated twentieth-century Soviet arguments that certain historic buildings were inauthentic and should be removed.

During the Stalinist attacks on religious and imperial heritage, countless significant historic buildings and churches were demolished in Ukraine to promote Soviet unity. For example, Kiev's twelfth-century Monastery of Saint Michael of the Golden Domes, which was rehabilitated and enlarged during the seventeenth and eighteenth centuries, was demolished

◀**Figure 19-1** Architectural heritage protection in Ukraine has endured numerous inconsistencies over the past four centuries, from careful restorations to fanciful reconstructions to politically motivated demolitions of cherished sites. An example of successful architectural restoration during the post-Stalin Soviet era is the Cathedral of the Assumption in Kiev, whose exterior (a) and interior (b) were extensively restored using original documentation.

297

in 1935. Also lost was the Church of St. Basil, built in 1183 at the apex of Kievan Rus' culture and reconstructed in the late seventeenth century. Fortunately, St. Basil's clergy had received advance notice of its impending destruction and were able to dismantle much of it and transport the pieces to other churches for safekeeping.

In the post-Stalin Soviet era, centrally regulated architectural conservation projects carried out in Ukraine included extensive work at the St. Sophia Cathedral and Cathedral of the Assumption in Kiev, which were completely restored using original documentation to ensure authenticity. Not every late Soviet conservation project, however, adhered to international standards. For example, documentation suggests that Kiev's reconstructed Golden Gate—completed to commemorate the city's 1500th anniversary in 1982—shares little more than its name and location with the historic gate. While Soviet-era policies lavished attention on projects such as these, others received no attention at all, including the Church of Our Savior of Berestove, which continues today to suffer from cracking stone walls and rotting wood foundation pilings. As in the Russian Federation, conservators in independent Ukraine still struggle with their preference for funding the reconstruction of lost monuments while existing historic structures deteriorate.

Upon independence in 1991, centralized Soviet work in Ukraine ended, and local heritage protection advocates were left to their own devices. In a zealous effort to protect what remains, Ukrainian authorities have spent many years digging into Soviet archives to discern what methods were used in past projects and which sites had been destroyed or historically discredited. Unfortunately, such meddling has often erased valuable information from archival records and instilled a sense of hopelessness in many professional researchers who are today tackling the issue of what to preserve.

Architectural conservation policies in the independent Ukraine were not clearly outlined until the 1999 Law on Cultural Heritage, which charged the Ministry of Culture and Arts (now the Ministry of Culture and Tourism) with the task. The Ministry was given focused responsibilities, including fulfilling the country's contractual responsibilities under international agreements, administering state-owned property, and registering and protecting archaeological sites and art artifacts. A separate State Department for Construction and Architecture was responsible for architectural and urban heritage inventorying and protection. Enforcing the protection of these sites and objects has been severely limited by insufficient funding and the lack of fines, punishments, or incentives to encourage compliance.

In 2002 the heritage protection system was consolidated under the purview of the Ministry of Culture and Arts, which assumed responsibility for listing and protecting architectural and urban heritage sites as well as archaeological reserves and art objects. The State Service for the Protection of Cultural Heritage was established within the Ministry, with branches in major Ukrainian cities. Today, a wide variety of sites are included among the 130,000 listings on the State Register of Immovable Memorial Objects, including over 57,000 archaeological sites, 51,000 objects, nearly 6,000 artworks, and 16,800 buildings. Only 3 percent of all these listings are ranked of national importance; however, 85 percent of those that are valued as such are buildings.[1] In addition, over four hundred towns are separately recognized on the List of Historic Settlements.

In 2004 this system was again updated and legislation amended, and cultural heritage protection was identified as a priority of the Ukrainian government. That same year another initiative was proposed: the All-Ukrainian Programme of the Preservation and Use of Cultural Heritage Objects for the Period of 2004–2010. This program called for tax exemptions for heritage sites, investment incentives, increased conservation research and training institutions and centers, improved legislation, and increased international cooperation. Despite the admirable intentions and suggestions of this initiative, it was not implemented as a result of insufficient financial support.

Indeed, the weak economic situation in Ukraine since independence has left limited funds available for restoring and conserving historic sites, despite their importance to the country and their prioritization by the Ministry of Culture. Much that has been accomplished in architectural heritage conservation in Ukraine since 1991 has, therefore, been the result of international assistance, which has focused on the most important and most needful sites. Both the Getty Conservation Institute and the World Monuments Fund have provided grants for specific sites, and the Institute of Classical Archaeology at the University of Texas at Austin's work at Tauric Chersonesos has provided not only funding but also training and research.

Europa Nostra is one of the most vocal of the international agencies that today offers Ukraine logistic and financial help. In 1997 Europa Nostra voiced its dissatisfaction with the Ukrainian government and garnered important publicity when a plan to construct a skyscraper hotel in the vicinity of Kiev-Pechersk Lavra monastery threatened the site's foundation and the stability of several historic structures. Due to Europa Nostra's intervention, this project was revised, as were plans in 2000 to reconstruct the Desjatinna Church, which had been destroyed in 1240 by Mongol invaders.

Emergency measures have recently been taken at the mid-thirteenth-century World Heritage List site of L'viv, whose collection of built heritage from a variety of cultures is at serious risk. Lenient immigration policies in early medieval L'viv helped create a multicultural city, and today one can see evidence of this in the presence of its Armenian and Latin cathedrals, several Jewish synagogues, Orthodox Church, and its many Polish sites. Some of these important historic structures are suffering from unstable foundations due to hydrogeological instability. Many lesser-known sites have deteriorated to an extreme degree. Though only one in ten is said to be currently unsalvageable, immediate assistance is required to prevent further losses.[2]

In the past decade, looting and vandalism of Ukrainian archaeological ruins have increased because site security has weakened. Damage from the natural elements, unregulated tourism, and local development also threaten heritage sites today, even at important archaeological complexes like the 6th century BCE Greek colony of Chersonesos. The site, which is more widely known as Tauric Chersonesos after the Greek and Roman name for the entire Crimeria region in which it is located, includes the only known Greek theater on the Black Sea and the tenth-century basilica where Christianity was allegedly introduced to the eastern Slavic world. Tauric Chersonesos had been shielded from the many potential destructive elements due to its publicly inaccessible location within the military zone of Sevastopol. But now that the region has become more and more unrestricted, tourism, property development, and looters are arriving and threatening Tauric Chersonesos and its hinterland as well.

Figure 19-2 The town of L'viv, in western Ukraine, has a remarkably intact range of eighteenth- and nineteenth-century buildings that reflect its multicultural past. As conservation efforts and modernization efforts increase, L'viv would benefit from studying the architectural conservation experiences of Prague, Czech Republic, and Kraków, Poland, over the past two decades.

This ancient Greek city has a long conservation history, beginning with its initial excavations in 1827.[3] Between 1969 and 1980, protective efforts focused on how to keep its fortresses standing: The weak tower was reinforced by the insertion of a steel pipe, and other walls were shored up using large stones mined from the surrounding rubble. These interventions were invasive and aesthetically insensitive, and today it is nearly impossible to distinguish which sites have survived the centuries intact and which were improved recently with recycled rubble.[4]

In 1993 a presidential decree established the National Preserve of Tauric Chersonesos as a state-level center of archaeological scholarship and methodology.[5] Joint projects have been formed with experts in Poland, Austria, Canada, the United States, and other countries to transfer conservation expertise to Ukrainian officials. While Tauric Chersonesos has begun to attract donations from the international conservation community, it is uncertain whether it will be able to mount a successful campaign against a new powerful enemy: the Russian Orthodox Church. The Church claims ownership of parts of the Tauric Chersonese region because of its religious importance and hopes to create a pilgrimage center there, potentially at the expense of its nonreligious and pagan elements.[6]

Under the auspices of the Council of Europe, an extensive cultural policy review of Ukraine was conducted and published in 2007.[7] The report, which was prepared locally but accompanied by an expert report prepared by delegates of the Council of Europe, concluded that Ukraine should focus on: rethinking its administrative structures and polices to broaden the activities and understandings of its culture; integrating heritage into sustainable economic development policies; and strengthening its civil society to create more effective partners in cultural endeavors. It also noted that due to insufficient funding, 50 percent of the listed sites in the Ukraine were inadequately maintained and 10 percent in emergency condition.[8] Ukraine responded by launching a National Cultural Development Program for the years 2008 through 2012 aimed at promoting cultural tourism, stricter standards, and increased funding for general and heritage culture.

If this recent initiative is indeed funded more successfully than previous proposals, it bodes well for the future of Ukraine's architectural heritage. On the other hand, it is likely that heritage conservation and protection efforts in the Ukraine will continue to be impeded by domestic economic weakness and the high cost of addressing chronic problems. Yet, with reforms aimed at European integration, continued promotion of cultural tourism, growing public interest in heritage conservation, and sustained financial support from international organizations and wealthy Ukrainians living abroad, the prospects for protecting Ukraine's built patrimony are brighter today than ever before.

MOLDOVA

Moldova, a small independent country nestled between Ukraine and Romania, was part of the Russian empire in the mid-nineteenth century, then part of Romania, and annexed after World War II to the Soviet Union, under whose control it remained until 1991. Ties between Moldova and Russia remained strong after independence, especially between 2001 and 2009 when Moldovans returned the communist party to power. Though the communist party continues to receive the most votes in public elections, a coalition of smaller parties has governed Moldova since 2009, resulting in civil unrest and constitutional reforms.

Shortly after independence, the Law of Monument Protection was enacted in Moldova in 1993 indicating the importance of both movable and immovable heritage to the country's identity and setting up a register of state-protected sites and objects. With the Law on Culture of 1999, the Directorate of Cultural Heritage and the Arts of the Moldovan Ministry of Culture was made responsible for registering monuments and protective zones to be brought under the state's protection, as well as for conserving

a

b

c

Figure 19-3 As elsewhere, architectural conservation in Moldova is directly related to the country's economic situation. Following the former Soviet model for heritage protection, Moldovans have addressed conservation at their country's earlier Christian monasteries, such as Humor Monastery, where the International Centre for the Study of the Preservation and Restoration of Cultural Property (ICCROM) conducted an on-site workshop in murals conservation in the mid-1980s (a–c). The monastery's painted exterior murals were documented, stabilized, and conserved. Other sites require urgent attention, and Moldova is especially open at the present time to international aid in addressing challenges to its cultural heritage. Courtesy ICCROM Image Archives.

and maintaining these sites.[9] Between 2005 and 2009, when the Moldovan government reorganized to form a Ministry of Culture and Tourism, and cultural heritage was overseen by its Heritage and Tourism Resources Division. Today, responsibilities lie with the Ministry of Culture's Direcţia Patrimoniu Cultural şi Arte Vizuale (Directorate for Cultural Heritage and Visual Arts) and its Agenţia de Inspectare şi Restaurare a Monumentelor (Agency for Inspection and Restoration of Mouments). The Direcţia has also been charged with supervising archaeological excavations and researching Moldovan heritage sites.

Perhaps the greatest threat to architectural heritage in Moldova is the lack of financial resources for the restoration and maintenance of sites. Less than one percent of the state budget is allocated for the entire cultural sector in Moldova, and this amount is mostly spent paying the salaries of state employees.[10] However, the Ministry of Culture has continuously prioritized cultural heritage protection, and spends a large percentage of what little it has on securing and maintaining sites on the protected registry.

Threatened historic sites have had little chance for conservation in this context. For example, the seventeenth-century Barbary-Bosia Monastery Complex in Buteceni, which is in part carved into a limestone cliff and includes early Christian and pre-Christian sanctuaries as well as the fourth-century BCE Geto-Dacian fortifications, is threatened by industrial development and groundwater erosion. The complex's icons are also under biological attack from mosses and lichens that cling to the consistently wet surface of the cave walls.

Even the Moldovan capital of Chisinău, developed primarily between the seventeenth and nineteenth centuries, has been left to deteriorate.[11] Though it was a recognized historic city within the Soviet Union and in 1993 became a protected site within independent Moldova, a lack of documentation, public interest, and resources have caused the rapid loss of the city's historic architecture. Buildings are demolished for new construction, others are renovated beyond recognition or added on to unsympathetically, and still others sit as slowly deteriorating ruins without funds for basic maintenance. In addition, city street-widening plans threaten individual buildings and the overall scale and character of Chisinău.

Like its much larger neighbor Ukraine, Moldova has recognized the potential role of cultural heritage in economic development and has even suggested that cultural tourism is one of its development priorities; however, the country simply does not have the resources to conserve its heritage and develop its tourism potential.[12] With a per capita income of only $450, agrarian Moldova is one of the poorest countries in Europe, although its population is highly literate. The minimal funds available for conservation projects have usually been generated from limited international support and the Ministry of Culture's attempt to supplement its state allocations by establishing a fund supported by renting out historic properties and charging fees for technical assistance and copyright usage.

Given its financial situation, the future prospects for competent heritage conservation in Moldova seem unpromising. International partners have been scarce and an interested nongovernmental sector or concerned public is currently lacking in Moldova. These factors, combined with the absence of state resources, have brought architectural conservation in Moldova to an urgent situation.

Admirably, the government continues to optimistically establish a regulatory and protective structure in line with European standards, and is currently drafting four separate pieces of new legislation addressing built, archeological, intangible, and movable heritage. In addition, a new Ministry initiative for 2005 through 2015, called "Moldovan Village," focuses on decentralization and supporting locally important architectural heritage as well as regional museums, libraries, and other cultural institutions.[13] Despite these efforts, due to the country's relative insularity, the deterioration of heritage in Moldova will probably continue unabated unless important changes are made to find more international partners, regulate land ownership, and most importantly, establish concrete, sustainable financing mechanisms.

BELARUS

The architectural heritage of Belarus includes early medieval planned cities and red brick houses, churches, and defensive towers predating the twelfth-century Mongol invasion. Economic development in the later Middle Ages led to more complex town squares and the replacement of the ancient Rus' style with Gothic, Renaissance, and baroque architecture. The wide range of extant buildings includes classically styled estates built for Russian nobility in the seventeenth and eighteenth centuries, large-scale baroque cathedrals, Jewish synagogues and community centers, and hundreds of factories built in the industrialized era.

Belarusian cultural heritage policies have varied in the twentieth century. Organized conservation began in the early Soviet era when the most important sites were researched and officially recorded during the 1920s, and a first state list of historic, artistic, and natural sites—including ninety-four buildings—was approved in 1926.[14] This listing offered no legal protection, and the potential importance of this inventory was overshadowed by indiscriminate demolition by the Soviet authorities for urban renewal projects in the following decades.

By the 1930s, suppression of Belarusian pride by the central Soviet government atrophied cultural heritage protection and fostered an environment of destruction. However, the large-scale losses suffered during World War II caused the government to reexamine the protection of cultural heritage throughout the Soviet Union, including in Belarus. A new survey was financed, a number of specialist scientific missions were sponsored, and in 1947 a new state registry of the most significant sites in the Belarusian Soviet Republic was approved.[15]

As the war seemed more distant, interest in heritage again waned. In the 1960s, many historic structures, such as the Vitebsk Church and the Gothic Cathedral in Grodno, were inexplicably destroyed. But at that time, the public response to this most recent set of losses led to the establishment of the Belarusian Voluntary Society for the Protection of Monuments of History and Culture. Through its branches in six regions and in the city of Minsk, the Voluntary Society is still active today raising money for sites in need and serving as a watchdog organization to keep the Ministry of Culture vigilant against infringements on Belorussian cultural heritage law.

Figure 19-4 Restoration of the Radziwill family estate in Nesvizh, southwest of Minsk, is the most prominent restoration in Belarusian history. It was placed on the World Heritage List in 2005.

In 1967 the Special Scientific-Restoration Workshops were founded, and the first Belarusian law addressing the protection of cultural and historical sites was passed. These restoration schools were unfortunately closed in the 1980s, and Belarus today still suffers from poorly executed conservations projects as a result of the lack of trained professionals. However, the 1980s witnessed the publication of another official registry that included more than 16,000 sites of archaeological, historical, urban, and architectural significance.[16]

Soon after separation from the Soviet Union, a detailed and comprehensive Law of the Republic of Belarus on the Protection of Historical and Cultural Heritage was enacted in November 1992. The law outlined procedures and authorities for overseeing the newly independent country's tangible and intangible heritage.[17] This law entrusted the State Scientific and Methodological Council of the Ministry of Culture with designating objects and sites for inclusion on the State Register, preserving these sites and their surroundings, monitoring changes to them, and controlling their use. Coordinating the repatriation of Belarusian heritage that has been taken abroad is also within the purview of the Council, and these objects are eligible for inclusion on the State Register even when located outside of Belarus. The responsibilities of owners of historic properties and artifacts included on the State Register are also clearly articulated in the law.

Belarus's 1992 heritage protection law also established a data bank to maintain and systemize the documentation and research on heritage sites, and in addition it established the Foundation for the Preservation, Protection, and Restoring of the Heritage and Culture of the Republic of Belarus to act as a repository for funds to be used exclusively for heritage concerns. These funds are collected from the Belarusian state budget; from institutions, individuals, and international organizations in the form of grants; from heritage site proceeds, when used for commercial purposes; and from fines for infringements on the treatment or use of protected historic sites and objects. With the return of authoritarian rule in 1994 under President Alexander Lukashenko, heritage conservation became less of a priority. Though the 1992 heritage protection law remained in force, it proved ineffective in practice, since connections between the administrative framework it established and other heritage institutions were severed.[18]

Beginning as early as 1988, a joint effort of the Voluntary Society, the Belarusian Cultural Fund, and the Ministry of Culture prepared a list of valuable cultural heritage sites for potential nomination to the UNESCO World Heritage List. So far three culturally significant sites have been inscribed, including the late-fifteenth-century Gothic Mir Castle, which was added in 2000. This medieval complex was reconstructed and expanded in Renaissance and baroque styles, then abandoned for almost a century following the Napoleonic wars. It was restored in the late nineteenth century, when a number of elements were added or altered.

In 2005 a second site, which similarly reflected the succession of cultural influences in Belarus, was added to UNESCO's World Heritage List: the Radziwill Complex at Nesvizh. This family castle, which remained in the Radziwill dynasty's hands from 1523 to 1939, was gradually expanded over that time. The complex consists of ten interconnected buildings, including fortifications, palaces, and the Mausoleum Church of Corpus Christi. It was protected under Belarusian law in the mid-1990s. The complex has witnessed numerous conservation projects in the past century and a half, including a nineteenth-century renovation by the Radziwill family, the repair of war damage to the church in the 1950s, the extensive restoration of the park and gardens in the late 1980s and the castle complex in the late 1990s, and the reconstruction of palace galleries after a fire in 2002. Recent efforts have been financed by the Belarusian government and the local Roman Catholic parish.[19]

Belarus is also included within the ten-country Struve Geodetic Arc, added to the World Heritage List in 2005. This is a collection of sites triangulated by the German astronomer Friedrich Struve in the mid-nineteenth century along the first long segment of a meridian, every segment accurately measured. Thirty-four of the original 265 station points marked in various ways by Struve have survived, including four in Belarus at Lopati, Ossowinitza, Tshekutsk, and Leskowitschi.

In 2003 through the U.S. Ambassador's fund, the U.S. Embassy in Minsk restored the boyhood home of Thaddeus Kosciuszko, a Belarusian native who was a friend of Thomas Jefferson and a heroic participant in the American Revolution. Kosciuszko's home near Kossova (also Kosava), Belarus, was rehabilitated and converted into a museum in a project cofinanced by the regional government in Brest, Belarus.

Located just north of Minsk, the "Zaslavl" Reservation Museum of Culture and History is another example of conservation success in Belarus. Established in 1986 and affiliated with the state museum, its collection includes the centers of two tenth- and eleventh-century villages, a variety of archeological sites, and medieval castles, fortifications, and churches. As at other open-air museums, Zaslavl's approaches have included moving sites from other locations and total reconstructions of no longer extant sites, and have also involved the successful restoration and reuse of historic structures as exhibition space and museums. Notable projects include the conservation of the Catholic Church of the Nativity in Val and the reuse of an early twentieth century mill building to house an ethnographic center.[20]

For many buildings, restitution to private owners in the post-independence period has led to worse fates than Communist-era neglect. This has especially been the case with churches that have been returned to the Orthodox Church. A rush to repair buildings with minimal investment has placed sites in jeopardy. For example, while the twelfth-century Kalozha church was saved only by local activists, the Zaslaue Savior Transfiguration Cathedral remains at risk by its proposed reconstruction.[21]

Figure 19-5 The boyhood home of Thaddeus Kosciuszko, a Belarusian native who fought in the American Revolution, was restored with aid from the U.S. Ambassador's Fund, showing the reach of innovative funding in international architectural conservation.

Like the other members of the Commonwealth of Independent States (CIS), Belarus is today challenged by the financial and technological realities of managing its patrimony in an uncertain and expensive world. On the other hand, because Belarus started out as one of the wealthiest, most developed Soviet republics at the time of independence, it has fared comparatively well economically, and this has been aided by its ongoing stable trade and close relationship with Russia since Lukashenko assumed power in 1994. Though still poorly funded by European standards, the continued centralization and state control of the Belarusian economy has enabled far more support and organization of architectural heritage conservation than has occurred in its neighboring CIS countries.

ENDNOTES

1. Ukrainian Center for Cultural Studies, *European Programme of Cultural Policy Reviews: Cultural Policy in Ukraine: National Report* (Strasbourg: Council of Europe, 2007), 47.

2. "Ukraine," *Heritage@Risk 2001–2002* (Paris: ICOMOS, 2001), http://international.icomos.org/risk/2001/ukra2001.htm (accessed December 30, 2009).

3. It also contains valuable information about the central Asian building techniques used by fourteenth-century Crimean Tatars, who remained behind when the Mongol hoards departed the region. *World Monuments Watch 2004* (New York: World Monuments Fund, 2004), 83.

4. Katrina Durbak, "Architectural Conservation in Ukraine." Thesis, Master's Degree in Historic Preservation, School of Architecture, Planning and Preservation, Columbia University, Spring 2006, 9.

5. "Home," National Preserve of Tauric Chersonesos, Sevastopol," http://chersonesos.org/?p=index&l=eng&res=nf (accessed December 30, 2009).

6. Durbak, "Architectural Conservation in the Ukraine," 9.

7. Ukrainian Center for Cultural Studies, "European Programme," 50.

8. Ibid., 50.

9. "Moldova: 4.2.9 / Heritage Issues and Policies," *Compendium of Cultural Practices and Trends in Europe*, 10th ed. (Strasbourg: Council of Europe, 2009), www.culturalpolicies.net/web/moldova.php?aid=429 (accessed November 19, 2009).

10. Yael Ohana, "Culture and Change in Moldova," East European Reflection Group, 2007, www.eurocult.org/uploads/docs/753.pdf (accessed November 19, 2009).

11. Sergius Ciocanu, "Chisinau: A Historic City in the Process of Disappearing," *Heritage at@ Risk 2006/2007* (Paris: ICOMOS, 2007), www.international.icomos.org/risk/world_report/2006-2007/pdf/H@R_2006-2007_32_National_Report_Moldova.pdf (accessed November 19, 2009).

12. Ohana, "Culture and Change in Moldova."

13. "Moldova: 4.4.1 / Main Cultural Policy Issues and Priorities," Compendium of Cultural Practices and Trends in Europe, 10th ed. (Strasbourg: Council of Europe, 2009), http://www.culturalpolicies.net/web/moldova.php?aid=41 (accessed December 31, 2010).

14. Vladimir Denisov, "Belarus," *Heritage@Risk 2001–2002* (Paris: ICOMOS, 2001), www.international.icomos.org/risk/2001/bela2001.htm (accessed November 19, 2009).

15. Ibid. Many claim that this work was undertaken to gain compensation from the German government for war damage inflicted on select sites, including Minsk's Dominican Monastery. This opinion is supported by the Belarusian authorities' frequent destruction of both records and buildings after documentation and compensation.

16. Ibid.

17. "Law of the Republic of Belarus on the Protection of Historical and Cultural Heritage," UNESCO Cultural Heritage Laws Database, http://portal.unesco.org/culture/fr/files/25262/11061239243Belarusian_CH_law_EN.pdf/Belarusian_CH_law_EN.pdf (accessed December 30, 2009).

18. Denisov, "Belarus."

19. ICOMOS, "Radziwill complex (Belarus)," UNESCO World Heritage Center, http://whc.unesco.org/archive/advisory_body_evaluation/1196.pdf (accessed December 30, 2009).

20. "History of Zaslavl," "Zaslavl" Reservation Museum of Culture and History, http://www.zaslaue.by/page.php?issue_id=6&parent_id=0&lang=en (accessed December 31, 2010).

21. "Belarusian Architecture," Virtual Guide to Belarus, www.belarusguide.com/culture1/visual_arts/Architecture.html_(accessed December 30, 2009).

Figure 20-1 The Caucasus Mountain Region.

The Caucasus

The imposing Caucasus Mountains, which stretch between the shores of the Caspian and Black Seas, are home to ancient trade routes linking Asia and Europe. The region's built heritage reflects the many successive peoples who came and went over the centuries. Many of the empires that established control in the area left substantial, tangible remnants of their power, while others left only minor imprints on regional building traditions.

Regardless of their provenance, the inherent value of all historic sites is recognized by the three modern Transcaucasian republics—Armenia, Azerbaijan, and Georgia, although each approaches the question of architectural heritage conservation in a somewhat different manner. In Georgia and Armenia, these efforts have a long history, but sites of national importance increased in value in response to repressive Soviet-era policies. Heritage conservation became an even more important issue in all three countries in 1991, when each gained its independence following the dissolution of the Soviet Union.

Instability—both seismic and political—has been the region's primary obstacle to architectural conservation. Earthquakes are a constant threat, for the region lies at the juncture of four tectonic plates. Much of the structural instability and failing walls of historic churches in the Caucasus is the result of past earthquake activity. Armenia suffered a disastrous earthquake in 1988. Another earthquake in 2002 damaged the historic center of Tbilisi, Georgia's capital, deferring its World Heritage listing. While Azerbaijan does not suffer the same extreme depredations as its neighbors, its built heritage is vulnerable to the often severe aftershocks of these earthquakes. Other natural disasters, such as floods and avalanches from the high peaks of the Caucasus Mountains, have also affected historic sites in the region. After a recent severe storm, the dome of Georgia's ninth-century Kanchaeti Kabeni Church collapsed.[1]

Political factors also impede the restoration of deteriorating sites in the region, even as the relative importance of built heritage has increased with each successive government. In Georgia, insurrection from the autonomous republic of Abkhazia, spillover from neighboring Chechnya, and a history of voting irregularities have resulted in continued instability. Armenia and Azerbaijan's protracted conflict over Nagorno-Karabakh has stunted economic growth in both countries, and mass migrations of Armenian and Azeri refugees fuel bitter cross-border resentment. Russia's 2008 invasion of South Ossetia, another autonomous region in Georgia, also took a toll on its cities and heritage sites.

As also happened during the breakup of Yugoslavia in Southeastern Europe, raw emotion has beentranslated into attacks on and desecration of ethnic symbols, such as Armenian churches and Azeri mosques located in the disputed enclave and Azerbaijan itself. While international examiners have not been allowed to assess damage in the region, a known casualty of this inter-Caucasian conflict is the Ağdam Mosque, which was vandalized and is currently used as a cattle stable by Armenian villagers.[2] Entire towns in the Nagorno-Karabakh region, such as Ağdam, which had 150,000 residents who fled the city in 1993, have been destroyed by the conflict. Efforts to stem such senseless acts have been largely unsuccessful, and they continue today.

An additional challenge that the region's architectural conservationists share with other former Soviet republics include economic stagnation, which substantially limits funding for conservation, as well as inappropriate interventions, which often cause irreparable harm. Armenia's sixth-century Church of Saint Astvatsatsin of Artik, which has been deformed and is decaying following problematic reconstruction efforts and insensitive additions, is an example of a mistaken intervention.[3]

Much-needed financial capital has begun to enter the cash-strapped region thanks to the Baku-Tbilisi-Ceyhan (BTC) oil pipeline through Azerbaijan, Georgia, and Turkey, which was completed in 2006. Even before it opened, work on the BTC pipeline directly benefited the region's cultural heritage by providing for archaeological excavations along its path.[4] The pipeline's original route was modified to avoid nationally and internationally recognized heritage sites and important archaeological areas based on investigations carried out in all three countries.[5]

Lesser sites that could not be avoided, such as the Tsalka district of Georgia, were thoroughly excavated and studied before the BTC pipeline's construction began. In addition, cultural management experts served as monitors to each construction unit in the event that any unanticipated archaeological sites were found. These cultural monitors had the authority to halt construction or make minor reroutes in the pipeline's course to investigate any discovered sites.[6] In a very real sense, the BTC pipeline project has thus presented a positive opportunity for studying heritage in the region, not only through the millions of dollars it has channeled into archaeology but also through the impetus it has provided for investigating remote regions. In Azerbaijan alone, three previously unexplored Bronze Age settlements and one medieval village were discovered and researched.

ARMENIA

Armenia's intermittent periods of prosperity facilitated the increasing size and scope of building projects, which incorporated Persian, Greek, Byzantine, and Armenian designs. Many of the ecclesiastical structures, built after Armenia's official adoption of Christianity in the fourth century, endure to this day, including three World Heritage Sites: the monasteries of Haghpat and Sanahin, with their blend of Byzantine and vernacular styles; the churches and cathedral of Echmiatsin and archaeological site of Zvarnots; and the medieval monastery of Geghard in the Upper Azat valley.

Armenia's tradition of cultural heritage protection is among the oldest in the region, and numerous restoration projects were completed while it was an independent medieval kingdom. Because of the frequent earthquakes, stone churches were often repaired, using approaches that were remarkably modern. For example, during the thirteenth-century restoration of the Marmashen monastery, careful attention was paid to the reintegration of old and new building fabric, and much effort was expended in restoring its original appearance. The descriptions of the components of the restoration inscribed on the church's rebuilt west transept prove as interesting and preservation-worthy as the restored buildings themselves.[7] At the southern end of the church, Prince Vahram Pahlavuni's construction of the main Katoghike Church of Marmashen Monastery beginning in 988 is detailed, while a similar inscription on the northern end intricately describes its restoration by his descendants in 1225, indicating who oversaw the project and who paid for which components.

The historic fluidity of regional political borders and conflicts with neighbors have complicated Armenia's conservation efforts in the past century. Long before its recent

Figure 20-2 The World Heritage listed cathedral in Echmiatsin, a key symbolic structure for the Armenian Church, was built in the early fourth century and altered periodically in the succeeding 1,600 years. The general Echmiatsin site contains three churches. Armenia has had an exraordinarily long-standing interest in protecting both its artistic and religious heritage.

Figure 20-3 The Temple of Helios at the Roman site of Garni in southern Armenia was built near the end of the first-century CE. Its ruins were investigated in 1910, and the temple was extensively reconstructed using the anastylosis method between 1969 and 1975. It stands today as one of a very few whole religious buildings from antiquity.

invasion of Nagorno-Karabakh in Azerbaijan to its east, Armenia has had problems with Turkey to its west. As many as a million Armenians living in Anatolia died in the final years of the Ottoman Empire, and it was not until 2009 that relations between the two countries reached a point where Armenian heritage sites in easternmost Turkey might be accessible for Armenian nationals and possible joint conservation efforts.

One such site is Ani, which was founded as a frontier outpost by Armenian settlers in the fifth century but became the flourishing capital of the kingdom by the tenth century. It has been abandoned and untouched since Mongol invasions and a severe earthquake in the early fourteenth century, but the twentieth century witnessed the gradual deterioration of its citadel, churches, cathedral, palaces, and immense fortifications. While briefly part of the Russian empire in the early twentieth century, the documentation of Ani's built heritage began. But since 1917, Ani has been located within Turkey and deserted, except for the occasional border guard or ambitious tourist.

While Armenia was part of the Soviet Union, two notable conservation and heritage management initiatives were accomplished successfully. One was the complete in situ anastylosis (reconstruction using original components) of the first-century CE ancient Roman temple at Garni in the south, and the other was the establishment of a heritage tour route around Armenia that featured the country's wealth of well-preserved medieval buildings.

Today in Armenia, the Historical and Cultural Monuments Conservation Agency, under the purview of the Ministry of Culture, is responsible for architectural conservation and implementing cultural heritage legislation. With support from the UNESCO, the Agency has enhanced its operations and used international best practices, including stabilizing structures at a number of important sites against seismic tremors. The board has been proactive in its search for outside aid, especially in the aftermath of the 1988 earthquake.

Following this devastating disaster, the Armenian Soviet Socialist Republic found its international plea for assistance answered by the World Monuments Fund (WMF), the U.S. National Park Service, and the U.S. Information Agency. A general needs assessment survey of over thirty sites in 1991 recommended three as suitable priority conservation projects and subsequent work focused on emergency work at one of them: the fifth-century Basilica of Ererouk, an excellent example of a typical early medieval, Armenian, three-naved basilica with transversal arches over the central bay. The remains of this stone church were in danger of collapsing from heavily weakened walls, but they were stabilized in 1995 by a joint effort coordinated by WMF with support from the Getty Grant Program and the Samuel H. Kress Foundation.[8]

Lacking suitable funds from the Ministry of Culture, the Historical and Cultural Monuments Protection Agency has received aid from the World Bank and UNESCO for the development of Armenia's cultural tourism resources and has attracted more attention and money for conservation projects from the international Armenian diaspora. A three-year plan for cultural tourism prepared in 2003 included documenting and categorizing historic sites and better preparing them for visitors by developing maps, guides, and a Web site to familiarize potential tourists with Armenia's cultural history.[9] However, given the myriad obstacles faced—ranging from earthquake tremors to economic stagnation to isolation due to its occupation of Nagorno-Karabakh—attracting tourists to Armenia will be a difficult task in the near future.

Figure 20-4 The fifth-century church of Ererouk in western Armenia is the country's earliest freestanding basilican form. A corner of the building that was in danger of collapsing in 1992 was temporarily shored in 1993, in an American-funded effort, until economic conditions in the country improved to permit more extensive measures. Preparation for this interevention included development of a site management plan.

Traditions of extensively repairing and reconstructing historic monuments in the Caucasus Mountain region could be considered a specialty subtopic within today's increasing dialogue on the validity of historic building reconstructions. Such practices in Armenia and Georgia and their former lands represent unbroken building traditions since medieval times. Frequent earthquakes and conflicts throughout the region's history often necessitated building restoration—and, in many instances, the complete reconstruction of extensively damaged structures. In some cases, the new structures reflected the changing styles of the later periods, but in other cases the reconstructed churches and other buildings were faithfully restored or built to approximate their predecessors. Caucasia's distance from Western Europe, where most of today's conservation doctrine discouraging reconstruction was developed, is likely why conservation experiences and traditions in the Caucasus Mountain region are not widely appreciated.[10]

The Christian religious architecture and the civic buildings in the Caucasus have historically consisted of remarkably well-integrated spatial forms that were typically solidly built, sparely ornamented, and majestic in appearance. Wall construction consisted of finely fitted, rectilinear stonework applied to cemented rubble wall cores, and space was created by a variety of stone vault types. Roof surfaces were usually also finished stonework laid over fill. Mathematically reasoned designs and construction details as well as accommodation for earth tremors were no doubt incorporated in building plans from the fifth century through the nineteenth century. As elsewhere, religious buildings were constructed with the utmost care, and many were extraordinary for their time, such as the Armenian Holy Virgin Cathedral and Church of the Holy Redeemer at Ani, now in easternmost Turkey; St. Thaddeus in the Iran's northwestern province of West Azerbaijan; and the numerous churches in Echmiatsin and nearby Zvardnots and Ererouk, all in modern-day Armenia. A comparable genre of architectural styles survives in Georgia, a region that held similar views of restoration and preservation of its churches since medieval times. Georgian examples include Ikort'a of the Archangel church in the Mtskheta-Mtianeti region, Timotesubani Virgin church in the Borjomi region, and Kanchaeti Kabeni church in the Alkhagori region.

Throughout the Caucasus, when disaster struck—whether earthquake, accident, or social calamity—and large parts of buildings collapsed, there seemed little choice but to rebuild to make structures whole and functional again. For over a millennium, the only questions likely centered on whether to rebuild what had existed or attempt to improve upon the earlier design. The notion of conserving ruins for aesthetic reasons, an interest deriving from the eighteenth-century picturesque tradition in western and central Europe, was and still is an unappealing concept in the Caucasus. Though well-informed about tenets of conservation versus reconstruction as practiced in the West today, most conservation architects, ministries of culture, and Eastern Orthodox Church officials in the region consider reconstruction as the preferred choice within the range of possible architectural conservation interventions.[11] In spite of modern, international conservation charters, this long-established practice is a distinctive and instructive technique of architectural conservation practice in this region. As with traditions of anastylosis and partial reconstruction of classical ruins in the Mediterranean region, extensive restoration and reconstruction is a Caucasian tradition worth respecting.

On the other hand, the reconstruction trend throughout eastern and southeastern Europe in the past twenty years, since the renewal of religion in the post-Communist period, has raised concerns about authenticity, the use of limited resources for heritage, and the fate of archaeological sites. Moscow's Church of Christ our Savior, Dresden's Frauenkirche, Kiev's Monastery of Saint Michael of the Golden Domes and the Orthodox Church of the Holy Trinity in Banja Luka, Bosnia and Herzegovina, are only a few of the hundreds of similar projects throughout the region of rebuilt churches destroyed decades or centuries prior. These types of projects have given rise to various levels of debate among historians, archaeologists, and conservation professionals.

A number of key publications in recent years have thoughtfully explored the large and complex issues surrounding contemporary discussions of conservation versus restoration versus reconstruction of damaged or destroyed historic buildings. These include *Conservation of Ruins* (2007), edited by John Ashurst; *Architectural Imitations: Reproductions and Reproductions in East and West* (2005), edited by Wim Denslagen and Neils

(continued)

Gutchow; and "The Reconstruction of Ruins: Principles and Practice" by Nicholas Stanley Price in *Conservation Principles, Dilemmas and Uncomfortable Truths* (2009), edited by Alison Richmond and Alison Bracker. All of these publications correctly view the topic in historical terms, although the aims and approaches of each of these studies represents three different perspectives on the matter: empirical reporting and synthesis with recommendations for applied practice; discussions of the theoretical implications of reconstructions in the context of both past and present artistic and socio-cultural contexts; and reconstruction of monumental archaeological remains in the light of established conservation doctrine.

AZERBAIJAN

While Azerbaijan's history bears much in common with its neighbors in the Caucasus, its Islamic heritage makes Azeri culture and architecture distinctive in the region. Islam came to Azerbaijan with the Seljuk and Oguz Turks in the eleventh century, and as it flourished, it produced beautiful mosques, hammams (Turkish baths), and caravanseries. Minorities such as Jews, Russians, Circassians, and Turks added their own distinct cultural flavor to Azeri cities. Though most of Azerbaijan's earliest cultural heritage sites have been destroyed, a rich array of vernacular, military, and religious buildings still remain today, including many intricately designed mosques and numerous elaborate mansions built by early-twentieth-century oil barons. Major threats to this heritage include general decay, insensitive restoration, and modernization, as well as pollution from the industrial zone of the Azeri capital city of Baku.

The protection of cultural heritage is a relatively new endeavor in Azerbaijan. During the Soviet period, Azeri Ministry of Culture's Department for Protection of Monuments oversaw architectural conservation. In 1992, it was replaced with the State Commission for Protection of Historical and Cultural Monuments within the New Republic of Azerbaijan's Ministry of Culture. Legislation was passed in 1998 to address growing concern over the current conditions of Azeri historic sites. This law included specific regulations against damaging or altering important buildings on a proposed new register.[12] Sites of both local and national significance have been inventoried and registered. In 2000, another government reorganization followed, and the Tarix və mədəniyyət abidələrinin mühafizəsi, bərpası və istifadəsi üzrə Baş İdarə (Central Department for Protection, Restoration and Use of Historical and Cultural Monuments) was established within the new Ministry of Culture and Tourism. The Baş İdarə's mandate is to identify, restore, and protect Azerbaijan's heritage. It is advised by the Institute of Architecture and Art of the Azerbaijan Academy of Sciences and the Azerbaijan University of Architecture and Construction.

Though interest in conserving historic architecture is new, sporadic efforts occurred throughout the twentieth century in Baku's historic Ichari Shahar (Inner City), which is best known for its twelfth-century defensive walls and Maiden Tower as well as for its fifteenth-century Shirvanshah palace complex. The Russian tsarist authorities identified a buffer area in Ichari Shahar, and the Soviet Union recognized it as a national monument and successfully prevented alterations in this historic district. However, property sales and construction in the post-independence period have posed a significant threat as insensitively designed and out-of-scale new buildings have been built in Ichari Shahar.

In 2000 the center of Baku was recognized as a World Heritage Site by UNESCO, but continued uncontrolled new construction coupled with slow recovery from an earthquake that same year resulted in its placement on the List of World Heritage Sites in Danger by 2003. Soon thereafter, a presidential decree established strict guidelines for construction in Ichari Shahar; however, these have gone unheeded, and Baku's historic center remains threatened today.

Figure 20-5 Architectural heritage conservationists trying to preserve the scale and character of historic Baku's Ichari Shahar (Inner City) are fighting an uphill battle against uncontrolled development and other pressures to modernize.

In 2001 the World Bank gave a cultural heritage support grant to Azerbaijan to promote its conservation efforts. In addition to strengthening local institutional capacities to protect cultural heritage, the World Bank grant funded the conservation of four priority projects in the cities of Baku, Sheki, and Nakhichevan. Azerbaijan's conservation abilities have been further strengthened by its participation since 2002 as a member state of ICCROM, which subsequently co-organized a training course for Azeri heritage site managers.

Its large undeveloped petroleum resources and its location on the oil-rich Caspian Sea combine to create a positive future economic outlook for Azerbaijan. The new regional BTC pipeline is already bringing investors to this impoverished country, and it has already begun to benefit architectural conservation.[13] The philanthropic fund of the Russian oil company LUKOIL, which is actively working in Azerbaijan, rehabilitated Baku's Russian Orthodox Cathedral in 2001, and this church's rededication was attended by the Patriarch of the Russian Orthodox Church. A few years earlier, LUKOIL contributed to the reconstruction of the Bibi-Heybat Mosque in a suburb of Baku, which Stalin had destroyed in 1934. This mosque had originally been built in the 1260s to mark the seventh-century grave of one of Mohammad's descendants and reflected the typical Azeri mosque type: a stone cubic form covered with a low, central dome.

As revenues from the new pipeline begin to arrive in Azerbaijan and improve all aspects of its economy, there is hope that the government will allocate increased funding for the conservation of its historic sites. In addition, by promoting its diverse cultural heritage to both its own citizens and foreign visitors, the Azeri government can ensure the future of these sites while creating a self-sustaining national asset.

GEORGIA

In the late eleventh century, under King David the Builder, a great patron of the arts and learning, Georgia successfully resisted a Turkish invasion, expanded its borders, captured Tbilisi, and ushered in a golden age. During the century and a half of peace that followed, large construction works, such as the monastery of Vardzia, were carried out in beautiful Byzantine, Armenian, and Syrian styles. Many splendid churches

a

Figure 20-6 Restoration of the twelfth-century Ikorta of the Archangel church (a, b) in the Mtskheta-Mitianeti region of eastern Georgia was accomplished by the staff of the Georgian Ministry of Culture in work that began in 1998—seven years after an earthquake damaged its dome, roof, facade masonry, and murals—and was completed in 2004.

b

and monasteries still remain to this day, although many more were destroyed when the Mongols invaded in 1231. Other religious buildings in multiethnic Georgia include synagogues, mosques, and the remains of Zoroastrian fire temples. Tbilisi, the capital, contains many splendid examples of vernacular architecture, bathhouses, and inner-city fortifications. In the countryside, Persian influences from the fifteenth to the seventeenth centuries are found in the brick citadels and towers.

Georgia has been one of the most active proponents of cultural heritage conservation in the Caucasus. During the Soviet era, while conservation efforts in other republics stagnated, Georgian experts delved into new projects and developed the republic's professional resources, advanced its conservation techniques, and raised popular support for their efforts. During the 1970s and 1980s, the Central Department for Monuments Protection, the Georgian Soviet Republic's primary conservation institution, prioritized conservation, and set and implemented state conservation policies. The Central Department's operations were governed by strong Soviet legislation, including an inventory system that facilitated recording information about whole areas and enclaves, easing the way for contemporary heritage conservation planning for defined areas, as in Old Tbilisi.

After independence, new legislation streamlined cultural heritage protection, organized a network to safeguard both movable and immovable heritage, and conformed local restoration and conservation mechanisms to international standards, such as those outlined in the Venice Charter. In 1991, the Department of Cultural Heritage of the Georgian Ministry of Culture and Monuments Protection and Sport became responsible for documenting significant sites, collaborating with other institutions to address threats, and financing conservation programs. Since the Georgian government was restructured in 2008, it has been the National Agency for Cultural Heritage Preservation of the Georgian Ministry of Culture and Monument Protection that has administered and conserved state-owned architectural heritage sites as well as inventoried, researched, and promoted the country's cultural heritage. A cultural heritage council recommends sites for inclusion on the Ministry's state register of significant heritage. In 1999 the Georgian Parliament adopted the comprehensive Law on Cultural Heritage Protection, which safeguards all types of heritage—movable, immovable, fragmentary, archaeological, and natural—as well as building complexes and buffer zones. This protection, which was made effective by relatively strict penalties, is provided irrespective of ownership.

In 2002 a concordat was signed between the Georgian government and the Georgian Apostolic Autocephalous Orthodox Church, acknowledging that the latter was the owner of all church and monastery buildings within the country as well as of all ecclesiastic objects in state museums.[14] The same concordat recognized these buildings and artifacts as part of the national cultural heritage that the Georgian government has the responsibility to protect and conserve. Under this joint trusteeship arrangement, the state retains the right to set legal parameters and terms of restoration and maintenance of these properties owned by the Georgian Orthodox Church.

International aid has been sought where local initiatives have been unsuccessful or funding has been insufficient. International organizations have supported a substantial array of projects and have also helped encourage and coordinate the use of best practices among the Georgian authorities. The restoration of the Ikorta Church of the Archangel in Zeno Artsevi, South Ossetia, is one project that has received a significant amount of international aid and attention. An earthquake in 1999 damaged this twelfth-century stone church, which is one of the earliest examples of the traditional Georgian domed style and is noted for its well-preserved medieval interior murals and exterior ornamentation. Funding for various phases of the church's stabilization and conservation have come from the Open Society Georgia Foundation, the Kress Foundation European Preservation Program, administered by the World Monuments Fund, and the Fund for Preservation of Cultural Heritage in Georgia, which was established by presidential decree in 1998 with a start-up grant of $4.5 million from the World Bank.[15]

The Fund for Preservation has restored numerous projects throughout the country, and its initial resources were used for emergency stabilization projects and for priority sites.[16] As a result of its successes, in recent years the Fund for Preservation has been supplemented by the Georgian government. The current economic and political situation in the country has prevented the revival of tourism that these conservation projects

a

b

Figure 20-7 Urban conservation in Old Tbilisi has been an ongoing effort since the 1980s. A plethora of competent Georgian architectural conservation professionals and national and international heritage-protection organizations have participated in projects ranging from the maintenance of well preserved historic districts (a) to emergency stabilization and extensive restoration (b).

were meant to stimulate; however, the Fund for Preservation's activities did encourage the development of NGOs and private sector conservation companies in Georgia.

Its active private sector working to study, protect, and promote heritage issues distinguishes Georgia from its neighbors in the Caucasus and from other members of the CIS in Europe. Since independence, numerous nongovernmental cultural heritage organizations have been established, including Save Old Tbilisi, the Restoration Centre of Architectural Heritage, Heritage and Modernity, the Georgian Arts and Culture Centre (GACC), and the Georgian Cultural Heritage Information Centre (GCHIC). The GACC won an EU/Europa Nostra medal in 2006 for diagnostic studies, conservation planning, and emergency repairs at the Church of the Virgin in Timotesubani, which was carried out in collaboration with the Conservazione Beni Culturali from Rome.[17] The GCHIC, funded by the Council of Europe and the Fund for Preservation, has documented hundreds of sites and sponsored research expeditions and international exhibitions of a few exceptional sites.[18]

Local and international efforts have focused on the deteriorating historic district of the Georgian capital, Tbilisi. Immediately after independence in the early 1990s, facades along Freedom Square and Rustaveli Avenue were restored, as were major public buildings in the area, including the parliament, town hall, and other structures damaged during the civil violence that occurred as the first post-Soviet government was formed.[19] In 1997 the Tbilisi Pilot Project was launched as part of a World Bank and Georgian government cooperation, and the following year the WMF placed Old Tbilisi on its Watch List of Endangered Sites.[20] Its nomination for World Heritage listing in 1999 was deferred because of the lack of plans for the district's management or conservation. However, in more recent years, prospects for Tbilisi's future and its potential international recognition have improved. Following earthquake damage in 2002, ICCROM, UNESCO, and the Council of Europe offered conservation assistance to the city, and in 2004 a moratorium on new construction in historic districts was declared until a regulation plan could be devised.

A new Law on Cultural Heritage was introduced in 2007 to better address the concerns of historic towns, to reorganize and refocus Georgia's heritage priorities, and to alleviate confusion about overlapping responsibilities. The new law is more comprehensive than the 1999 legislation and is more specific regarding the obligations of property owners and the principles for determining eligibility for protective listing.[21] The Ministry of Culture, Monument Protection and Sport's most important focal areas now include historic towns, establishing protective zones in specific cities and around key archaeological sites and monuments, developing a register of protected movable objects, and initiating programs for funding restoration projects and the monitoring of heritage sites.[22] Inventories and rehabilitation plans have already been made for Tbilisi and Batumi, seven protective zones have been established, and the current conditions of over fifty monuments have been documented. New research initiatives and museum reforms were also recently launched, as well as an increased promotion of Georgian heritage and the creation of heritage database.

Despite Georgia's conservation advances, the continuing conflict in neighboring Chechnya has spilled over into its territory, and some Chechen sites in the Pankisi Gorge area of Georgia have been damaged. (See Chechnya, page 284.) In addition, important medieval sites have been destroyed in the still unresolved conflict in the Abkhazia region. On the other hand, new technologies developed to stabilize fragile structures from further earthquake damage or to prevent such damage from occurring will help Georgia address another of its major heritage threats. In the long run, Georgia's strong cultural heritage institutions, plethora of new heritage conservation initiatives, involved civil society, increased income from the BTC pipeline, and assistance from international organizations combine to indicate that the future of the country's cultural heritage is in good hands.

ENDNOTES

1. Nato Tsintsabadze, Marine Kenia, and Maya Foty, "Georgia," *Heritage@Risk: 2002–2003* (Paris: ICOMOS, 2002), www.international.icomos.org/risk/2002/georgia2002.htm (accessed December 30, 2009).

2. Mark Elliott, *Azerbaijan with Excursions to Georgia* (Hindhead, Surrey, UK: Trailblazer Publications, 2001), 253.

3. ICOMOS Armenia, "Armenia," *Heritage@Risk: 2002-2003* (Paris: ICOMOS, 2002), www.international.icomos.org/risk/2002/armenia2002.htm (accessed December 30, 2009).

4. The pipeline was built by the Azerbaijan International Operating Company (AIOC) in association with the State Oil Company of Azerbaijan (SOCAR). AIOC is a consortium of eleven oil companies from seven countries, including Great Britain, United States, Russia, Norway, Turkey, Japan, and Saudi Arabia.

5. "BTC Section—Construction Begins: The Pipeline is On Its Way Now!" *Azerbaijan International* 11.2 (Summer 2003): 72–81; http://azer.com/aiweb/categories/magazine/ai112_folder/112_articles/112_btc.html (accessed December 30, 2009).

6. "BTC Section—Construction Begins."

7. Gaiané Casnati, "Report on the Restoration of Marmashen Church, Gumri, Republic of Armenia," submitted to World Monuments Fund, April 10, 2002, 12. See also Stubbs, *Time Honored*, 176–177.

8. *World Monuments Fund: The First Thirty Years* (New York: Christie's Publication, 1996), 75. Since 2005 the Getty Grant Program is referred to as the Getty Foundation.

9. Lisa Scorsolini, Gordon Adams, Aideen Mannion, and Gayane Dallakyan, eds., *Armenia's Tourism Development Initiative, 2001–2003* (Yerevan: IESC/Armenia, 2003).

10. The Caucasus region's relative political isolation from the West through most of the twentieth century is another reason why architectural conservation practice in the region was so underappreciated by a wider world until recently. This is changing, though, due to increasing numbers of international scholarly research projects and conservation assistance programs.

11. Stubbs, "Scales of Intervention," *Time Honored*, 125–127.

12. "New Legislation to Protect Azerbaijani Architecture," *Azerbajian International* 6.4 (Winter 1988): 49; www.azer.com/aiweb/categories/magazine/64_folder/64_articles/64_legislation.html (accessed December 30, 2009).

13. Douglas Frantz, "Shirvan Steppe Journal; Gift from Oil to Archaeology: Pipeline to the Past," *The New York Times*, September 19, 2001.

14. "Georgia: 5.3.10 / Other Areas of Relevant Legislation," *Compendium of Cultural Practices and Trends in Europe*, 10th ed. (Strasbourg: Council of Europe, 2009), www.culturalpolicies.net/web/georgia.php?aid=5310&cid=1180&lid=en&curl=533 (accessed November 19, 2009); Manana Simonishvili, "Georgia," in Pickard, *Policy and Law in Heritage Conservation*, 126.

15. "About Us," Cultural Heritage Preservation Fund," www.culturalheritage.ge/english/eng-about.html (accessed November 19, 2009).

16. "Georgia: Cultural Heritage Project," *Summaries of Investment Projects under Implementation or in Preparation* (Washington, DC: The World Bank, 2003), 26.

17. "Church of the Virgin, Timotesubani (Georgia)," *European Union Prize for Cultural Heritage/ Europa Nostra Awards 2006* (Paris: Europa Nostra, 2007, 9.

18. "About Us," Georgian Cultural Heritage Information Center, www.heritage.ge/aboutus_e.html (accessed November 19, 2009).

19. *Urban Rehabilitation Policy in Tbilisi (Georgia)* (Strasbourg: Council of Europe, 2002), 44.

20. After the Tbilisi Pilot Project, the World Bank supported other conservation projects throughout the country through its Fund for the Preservation of the Cultural Heritage of Georgia.

21. "Georgia: 5.3.3 / Cultural Heritage," *Compendium of Cultural Practices and Trends in Europe*, www.culturalpolicies.net/web/georgia.php?aid=533&cid=1180&lid=en&curl=429 (accessed November 19, 2009).

22. Council of Europe, "Georgia: 4.2.9 / Heritage Issues and Policies," *Compendium of Cultural Practices and Trends in Europe*, www.culturalpolicies.net/web/georgia.php?aid=429 (accessed November 19, 2009).

SOUTHEASTERN EUROPE

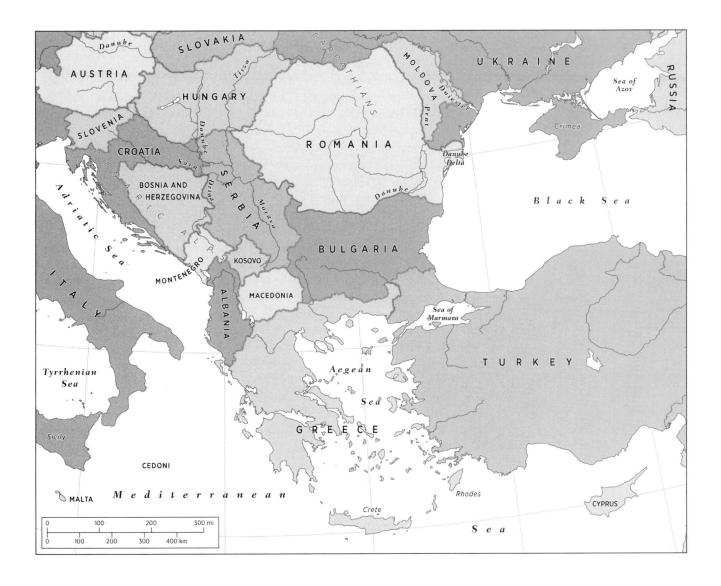

Southeastern Europe, a strategic region that was one of Europe's first inhabited areas, has long been contested by many of the most powerful empires in European history. Architectural relics found in the rugged mountains and along the extensive coastlines of the Balkan and Anatolian peninsulas attest to a colorful existence during Illyrian, Thracian, Greek, Roman, Byzantine, Venetian, Genovese, Ottoman, and Austro-Hungarian rule as well as to the independent kingdoms that existed throughout the region in the Middle Ages.

Greece was the first southeastern European country to gain its independence, followed by Romania and Bulgaria later in the nineteenth century. After the Balkan Wars and World War I, Albania, Turkey, and Yugoslavia emerged as independent countries. The islands of Malta and Cyprus were British protectorates until the 1960s, and Yugoslavia separated into several distinct countries (Bosnia and Herzegovina, Croatia, Serbia, Slovenia, Macedonia, Montenegro, and the still-disputed Kosovo) in the 1990s and early twenty-first century. That time also marked the transition of Bulgaria, Romania, Albania, and the Yugoslav successor states from Communist rule to participation in wider European political and cultural endeavors.

Despite their overlapping histories and heritages, there is great variation in the current economic and political conditions of the countries of southeastern Europe. Countries with relatively strong economies that are members of the European Union—such as Greece, Slovenia, and Malta—neighbor others that are heavily dependent on foreign aid, such as the Republic of Macedonia (accepted to the United Nations as the Former Yugoslav Republic of Macedonia, or FYR Macedonia) and Albania. At the same time, countries with unstable political situations and continued ethnic divisions—such Cyprus, Bosnia and Herzegovina, Montenegro, and Serbia—exist alongside strong, stable governments, such as Turkey, Romania, Bulgaria, and Croatia.

These differences within the region have resulted in disparate contemporary architectural conservation scenes, as well as different expectations from the world about how this heritage will be handled. For those diverse southeastern European countries not yet members of the EU, its magnetic pull is helping them catch up with their neighbors. Though broad-based support and secure financing for architectural conservation is still absent in most of these countries, slow economic growth, increased tourism, and growing public awareness of the economic and intrinsic values of maintaining cultural heritage bodes well for future conservation efforts.

The changes of the past two decades have freed the region from the centralized and ideologically based conservation policies and approaches of the Communist era, yet the same changes have introduced altogether new threats, such as the sudden loss of both financing for restoration and protection for privatized sites as well as dramatically increased pressures from tourism and often uncontrollable, illegal new construction. On the other hand, nationalism in Eastern Europe has been a powerful force in recent decades and has both fueled heritage conservation efforts and caused the neglect and destruction of sites not fitting new national narratives.

Cooperation in the region has also been widely promoted by international, European, and regional initiatives. The Council of Europe's Regional Programme for Cultural and Natural Heritage in South East Europe, initiated in 2003, has been working to share technical expertise with the region as well as to integrate the heritage policies of southeastern European countries with each other and with European standards. Its program for 2004 through 2008 focused on institutional capacity building, surveying and planning for architectural and archaeological sites, and pilot projects using heritage as a tool in local development strategies.[1]

UNESCO's program called South Eastern Europe Heritage Conservation and Management, launched in 2003, aims to build partnerships and promote reconciliation and development in the region through collaboration in the restoration of cultural heritage. As part of UNESCO's program, the ministers of culture from nine southeastern European countries and from Italy met in Mostar, Bosnia, in July 2004 to witness the opening of its newly reconstructed Stari Most (Old Bridge) and to sign a joint declaration on cultural heritage cooperation. Known as the Mostar Declaration, it reveals a commitment of the region's governments to work independently and together on "the enhancement of cultural heritage for the stabilization and sustainable development of the region."[2]

In the fall of 2009, Slovenia's capital, Ljubljana, hosted a conference of 170 participants from eastern and southeastern Europe and the Caucasus region coorganized by the Slovene Ministries of Culture and Foreign Affairs, the Council of Europe, and the European Union. The conference focused on regional cooperation and also included an exhibition titled "Ljubljana Process: Rehabilitating our Common Heritage" that highlighted sites destroyed during the breakup of Yugoslavia that have been successfully restored with European support. The exhibition was a product of the Integrated Rehabilitation Project Plan/Survey of the Architecture and Archaeological Heritage project of the Council of Europe and the European Union. Conference discussion focused on funding strategies for 186 key sites still needing restoration in the region proposed by participating countries.[3] Regional integration programs such as this, as well as UNESCO's and Council of Europe's initiatives, have helped keep a sustained focus on architectural conservation in southeastern Europe, and have done much to ensure progress is made despite the limited resources and other factors that have troubled most of the region in the past few decades.

Endnotes

1. Council of Europe, "Regional Programme for Cultural and Natural Heritage in Southeastern Europe," www.coe.int/t/dg4/cultureheritage/cooperation/SEE/default_en.asp (accessed November 25, 2009).

2. "Joint Declaration of the Ministers Responsible for Culture in South-East Europe and Italy Concerning the Enhancement of Cultural Heritage for the Stabilisation and the Sustainable Development of the Region" (declaration, Mostar, Bosnia and Herzegovina, July 19, 2004).

3. "The Ljubljana Process," Ministry of Culture, Government of the Republic of Slovenia, www.mk.gov.si/en/ljubljana_process/ (accessed December 1, 2009); and *The Ljubljana Process: Funding Heritage Rehabilitation in South-East Europe* (Belgium: European Commission, 2009), http://ec.europa.eu/culture/archive/culture_program/pdf/CE_precatalogue_Ljubljana_E.pdf (accessed December 1, 2009).

Figure 21-1 View of the Tower of the Winds monument in Athens as it appeared in 1758 in French architect Julien-David Le Roy's publication *Les Ruines des Plus Beaux Monuments de la Grece.* The "rediscovery" and wider appreciation of ancient Greek architecture from the mid-eighteenth century did much to shape the course of architectural history as well as the country's future, contributing to its becoming the first of the southeastern European countries to gain independence in 1821.

CHAPTER 21

Greece

The ruins of classical Greek monuments and sites have inspired awe, reverence, and poetry, prose, and emulation for more than two thousand years.[1] With help from the European powers, the autonomous Greek state emerged from its War of Independence against the Ottoman Turks in 1821. The new government, headed by Otto von Wittelsbach, son of King Ludwig of Bavaria, wasted no time in establishing an official position on the importance of Greece's classical heritage to its new national identity. Just one year after independence, the state established legislation to protect the country's treasured antiquities, which was one of the most comprehensive heritage laws in Europe at the time. It declared that "all objects of antiquity in Greece, being the productions of the ancestors of the Hellenic people, are regarded as the common national possession of all Hellenes."[2]

The conservation of the country's ancient classical monuments was an overwhelming priority of the new Greek state in the nineteenth century. In 1834 Leo von Klenze, architect to the Bavarian court, was invited by the Greek government to travel through the country and determine the condition of its ancient ruins. In addition to the Acropolis, von Klenze identified twelve sites outside of Athens that he believed should be supervised (to prevent looting) and that should be ultimately restored. The European archaeologists and restoration architects who came to work on these sites in the nineteenth century actively adhered to a doctrine of stylistic "purism" in which buildings or architectural elements from later periods that intruded into a classical monument were to be summarily removed.

In addition to its revered and influential sites from ancient Greece, modern Greece's architectural heritage also includes the contributions of a host of foreign invaders, including the Romans, Byzantines, French crusaders, Venetians, Florentines, and Ottoman Turks. Though each left their imprint on the built environment of Greece, until recently conservation interest focused solely on the country's classical and Byzantine heritage, especially key sites such as the Acropolis in Athens and the palace at Knossos. In recent decades, contemporary archaeologists and conservation professionals in Greece have gradually become concerned with protecting the historical evidence of these foreign, later presences as well.

THE ATHENIAN ACROPOLIS

In 1834 Leo von Klenze prepared detailed guidelines for restoring the buildings on the Acropolis in Athens, and work began immediately. Over the next five decades, the remains of Roman, Byzantine, medieval, and Ottoman construction projects were methodically cleared. Sixth-century alterations made to the Parthenon and the Erechtheion to facilitate their conversion to churches were undone. Fortifications around the Propylaea, a garrison village of utilitarian houses, and a late seventeenth-century mosque and minaret within the Parthenon itself—all built by the Ottomans—were removed. The so-called Frankish tower above a corner of the Propylaea, actually a Florentine work from the thirteenth-century, was also removed.

In 1837 the Archaeological Society of Athens was established, and one of its primary tasks was financing and supervising the restoration of the Acropolis. Athenian archaeologist, Kyriokos Pittakis, assumed responsibility for directing the restoration of the Acropolis monuments and the extensive excavations then under way at the site. The excavators were rewarded with the discovery of a sizable collection of sixth-century BCE sculptures, including freestanding Archaic maidens and pedimental figures from earlier temples. A critical period in the treatment of the Acropolis began when the role of chief conservator was assigned to civil engineer Nikolaos Balanos, who led its restoration from 1895 to 1940, amidst ceaseless debate over his working methods. He practiced a technique that came to be known as *anastylosis*, the "reassembling of existing but dismembered" architectural elements.[3]

The restoration principles advocated—if not always followed—by Balanos anticipated the recommendations of the First International Congress of Architects and Technicians of Historic Monuments, which was held at Athens in 1931. This conference produced the Athens Charter, the first document to provide specific guidelines for the restoration and conservation of historic sites, and recommended anastylosis, which stressed, among other things, that new materials and methods used should be recognized for their potential benefits in restoration.

In his eagerness to transform the Acropolis ruins, Balanos often disregarded the respectful spirit of his own anastylotic method. Unconcerned with determining the original positions of the fragments he selected for use in his restorations of portions of the Parthenon, Erechtheion, and Temple of Athena Nike, he freely cut and adjusted the ancient members that lay scattered about the hill to produce a better fit. In addition to the questionable approach taken, which involved extensive reconstruction, problems were caused by the iron cramps and rods he used to link the ancient fragments to each other and to new material. Unshielded or carelessly shielded with lead, the cramps and rods oxidized, expanded, and eventually split much of the ancient marble. Similar problems occurred when iron beams inserted in the undersides of soffits and beams began to corrode. As decades passed, problems with the stones of the Acropolis buildings were exacerbated by the steadily rising levels of air pollution in Athens. The extent of the problems of this well-intended but unfortunate major restoration campaign was not fully recognized until 1970, when international alarm prompted the UNESCO intervention and the production of a detailed report. In 1975 the Greek government convened an interdisciplinary team of experts, the Committee for the Preservation of the Acropolis Monuments (ESMA), to oversee a meticulous conservation and restoration operation unmatched in archaeological history. It called for highly detailed documentation of every unidentified ancient fragment, and the dismantling and reassembly, to varying degrees, of every structure on the site. This time, all connecting elements were joined by noncorroding titanium, which replaced Balanos's iron cramps.[4] No other modern consolidation materials were used for lack of long-term proof of their safety and effectiveness, though the project still involved extensive reconstruction. In developing specific points to be followed during the work, the team of international experts was consulted about exactly how many columns to reerect, and to what height.

Figure 21-2 The recent restoration of the Parthenon, the Erechtheion, the Temple of Nike, and the Propylaea on the Athenian Acropolis represents the highest possible quality of restoration of marble buildings of their kind. The work is in effect a "re-restoration" that incorporates both lessons learned during the earlier efforts and today's state-of-the-art conservation science and methods. Parthenon re-restoration (a); Parthenon stone conservation detail (b); Erechtheion re-restoration (c); Erechtheion stone conservation detail (d); and column restororation at the Temple of Nike and Propylaea (e).

a

b

c

d

e

Restitution of artifacts of cultural heritage taken from one country to another as a result of trade long ago or more recent theft or wartime pillage is a hotly contested issue that raises questions about who owns heritage and often pits developing countries against the world's leading museums and most powerful governments. Restitution has been the subject of numerous international conferences and bilateral, regional, and international treaties. The Vatican, the J. Paul Getty Museum, and other high-profile institutions have returned contested objects to their countries of origin in recent years.

For passionate rhetoric and longevity, few restitution debates can compete with the one regarding the Parthenon marbles, also known as the Elgin Marbles, which primarily reside in London's British Museum. Pieces of the Parthenon can be found in ten museums in eight countries; however, the British collection comprises approximately half of the Parthenon's surviving sculpture, including portions of the frieze, more than a dozen metopes, and seventeen pedimental figures. These and more were removed by agents of Thomas Bruce, seventh Earl of Elgin, between 1801 and 1810 and were dispatched by ship to England. The British Parliament purchased the marbles and presented them to the British Museum in 1816.

The struggle between Greece and the United Kingdom for possession of the marbles has continued for over a century. Learned experts on both sides claim to demonstrate beyond all doubt that the marbles belong in the location they advocate. Knowing that the marbles were stripped from the Parthenon with crude tools and no concern for the structure's integrity is often enough to generate support for their return to Greece. Greece also hopes to reunite the fragmented Parthenon marbles from Britain with those already in their possession to create a cohesive, historically accurate, and complete presentation of these valued sculptures near their original context. Advocates of retaining these marbles in the British Museum argue they are part of a collection of world heritage brought together and made accessible to a greater audience. Advocates also argue that returning these items would set a precedent that would result in the emptying of many of the world's greatest museums as the majority of their contents are from somewhere else. In addition, as British art historian Mary Beard points out, "it is quite wrong to imagine Elgin removing works of art from the equivalent of a modern archaeological site—it was more of a seedy shanty town," and that "whatever Elgin's motives, there is no doubt at all that he saved his sculpture from worse damage," because the Acropolis was being used as a stone quarry at the time.[5]

Greece's perceived inability to appropriately care for the Elgin Marbles was an important element in the British refusal to return them throughout the twentieth century. However, a new internationally acclaimed museum was designed specifically to house these marbles in state-of-the-art conditions. It opened without them at the base of the Acropolis in 2009. Though the new museum eliminates the most potent argument against bringing the Parthenon marbles home to Athens, the British Museum, with the support of the British Parliament, remains steadfast in its decision to keep this international heritage.

In 1999 ESMA became more of an advisory body and the Acropolis Restoration Service (YMSA) formed, and both institutions are located within the Greek Ministry of Culture today.[6] Funding for YMSA's extensive work has come in part from the European Union but mostly from the Greek government.

By the end of 2003, most of the ancient sculptures that remained at the Parthenon and Erechtheion had been transferred to the Acropolis Museum for conservation and display in a climate-controlled interior environment. Fiberglass and cast-stone replicas replaced the originals on the Acropolis itself. Interventions have been carried out at every ancient structure on and around the base of the Acropolis—from soil and rubble clearing at the House of the Arrhephoroi to consolidation of stone at the major monuments to the cataloging of scattered building fragments all over the site. Demonstrating the vast

Figure 21-3 Resulting from an international design competition won by Bernard Tschumi Architects, the new Acropolis Museum (a) opened in June 2009. An area (b) is reserved within the museum to accommodate the hoped-for return of the so-called Elgin Marbles, which have resided in the British Museum since the early nineteenth century.

distance between today's approach and the theories that shaped the first Acropolis restorations, YMSA decided to retain and conserve a staircase in the Parthenon's southwest corner built centuries after its original construction. Even the marks of Venetian cannonballs that devastated the temple during the siege four centuries ago were kept.

Today, most of the major restoration projects at the Athenian Acropolis have been completed after more than thirty years of complications, financial difficulties, and debates about conservation methodology. Some projects are still underway or planned, such as reroofing the Erechtheion and conserving parts of the Temple of Athena Nike. Over 250 architects, engineers, archaeologists, architectural conservationists, and other specialists of YMSA continue to carry out monitoring, maintenance, ongoing conservation, research, and educational outreach on the monuments of the Acropolis.

EXPANDING CONSERVATION PRIORITIES

Though early restoration programs specifically for the heritage of ancient Greece were prominent, the Greek government, as well as its scholars and public, eventually came to appreciate the components of their heritage reflecting several historic cultures. Classical and preclassical heritage from Roman, Minoan, and Mycenaean sources were the first to receive conservation attention after ancient Greek sites, and collectively this ancient heritage still dominates attention in modern Greece.

Investigation and conservation of the ancient heritage of the Greek island of Crete began at the turn of the twentieth century. Since Sir Arthur Evans began excavating Knossos in 1900, the site has continuously delivered finds from its seven thousand years of history. Evans valued the didactic possibilities the Bronze Age Minoan palace at Knossos provided, and he preserved and presented certain ancient architectural features in a way that would make the site intelligible to visitors. Until his efforts, it was unheard of for an archaeologist to undertake such extensive site interpretation and presentation. Today, Knossos is second only to the Athenian Acropolis in the number of visitors it attracts each year in Greece.

The work done by Evans represented advanced and widespread approaches to restoration theory and technology for the early twentieth century. He replicated charred remains of tapered cypress columns in concrete, reerected fallen walls, and stabilized or reattached their painted plaster finishes. Certain spaces, including the remarkable Throne Room, were extensively reconstructed. Some original fabric was used, but the upper walls and a full second and third story were built entirely of concrete and new stonework to reflect Evans's vision of what the structure might have looked like.

Over time, the largely irreversible interventions at Knossos, with their liberal use of reinforced concrete, have proved less durable than many had expected. Modern conservationists have also criticized the relatively heavy-handed and subjective quality of the reconstruction, which was clearly influenced by the art deco style of the day and compromised the site's historic authenticity. At the time, however, there were few precedents for conserving and presenting in situ archaeological sites—today, conservators are restoring Evans's reconstructions, which are now deteriorating and largely regarded as part of architectural history in their own right.

Byzantine-era Greek sites, reflecting a period of regional power before the Ottoman conquest, have also been of interest to Greek architectural conservationists for over a century. Today, one-third of the protected monuments in Greece and four of its seventeen World Heritage Sites are of Byzantine origin. Medieval Byzantine churches, with their cross in square plans, golden mosaic interiors, and polychromatic stone exteriors, were sources of design inspiration for national style architecture and commanded limited restoration efforts in the late nineteenth and early twentieth centuries.

In 1919, the Society for Byzantine Studies was founded and headquartered in Athens. From the Peloponnese to the Cyclades, the remains of Byzantine art and architecture were excavated and conserved including the eleventh-century monasteries of Hosios Loukas and Nea Moni of Chios. In Athens twelve small Byzantine parish churches were restored by 1938 and put to immediate use by the surrounding communities. In the 1950s, the monastery at Daphni outside Athens was restored: Its twelfth-century church had been built on the ruins of a sixth-century predecessor and previously restored in the 1880s. All three monasteries were added to the World Heritage List in 1990. Especially since the 1960s, archaeological exploration of sites yielding Byzantine treasures has made significant advances.

More recently, conservation efforts in Greece have extended to the country's Ottoman Islamic heritage as well. Fortunately, the Greek authorities' different priorities over

a

b

c

Figure 21-4 The Throne Room at the Palace of Minos at Knossos, Crete, reconstructed by Sir Arthur Evans in the first decade of the twentieth century, represents one of the first extensive archaeological reconstructions in Europe. Its frescoes were largely creations based on fragmentary evidence of Evans's assistants, the father and son team Émile Gilliéron et fils. The reconstructions by Evans were probably informed by contemporary, though less conjectural, examples at Pompeii and Herculaneum. Evans's projects included restoration of the interior of the Throne Room (a) as well as its exterior (b), and the replication of a former inverted tapered wooden column in concrete (c).

the past century and half resulted in neglect of these sites. However, except for the initial wave of mosque destruction in Greek cities shortly after independence in the early nineteenth century, Greece launched no other sustained efforts to eliminate this history. This has meant that some of these sites have survived but are in poor condition, and they have sometimes been converted to new, often insensitive, uses.[7] Of Greece's over eight hundred protected monuments, only a small percentage are of Ottoman construction, including two mosques and a few bridges and fortifications.

To date, relatively few Ottoman-era sites have been protected or restored, including the Imaret Castle in Kavala, whose complex of buildings was constructed in 1817 by an Egyptian viceroy as a seminary and inn with a mosque and baths, was restored in 2004. Plans for its conservation were begun in 1954, when it was listed as a protected building; however, the plans were never carried out until Anna Missirian completed the largest private restoration project in Greek history and converted the complex into one of Greece's few hotels operating in a historic building.

The oldest mosque in Europe outside Spain, the Great Temenos (or Çelebi Sultan Mehmed Mosque) in Didymoteichon on the Turkish border near Edirne, which was built by Ottoman Sultan Mehmed I in the early fifteenth century, is currently being restored by the Greek Ministry of Culture. Its partially wooden roof structure and interior mural paintings have decayed significantly because of water penetration and neglect, but it is being reinforced with a metal tower and its lead roof is being replaced. The Ministry as well as the EU and the Turkish government are also completing numerous other projects at Ottoman-era sites in Greece, including various mosques, hammams, markets, and aqueducts.

Since the end of World War II, much impressive work has been done to preserve historic towns and their environments on the Greek mainland, on the Peloponnese, and on several islands, notably Mykonos, Hydra, Santorini, and Crete. Island architecture often includes simple eighteenth- and nineteenth-century vernacular buildings in local stone. On the Cyclades, the traditional architecture's distinctive whitewashed organic

Figure 21-5 The Turkish hammam in Mytilene, Lesvos, was restored in 2004–5 by the 14th Ephorate of Byzantine and Post Byzantine Antiquities (a Greek government official) and was converted into a gallery for art exhibits. The mottled look of the facade comes from the use in the restoration of a lime wash instead of paint. In the past two decades, there has been an increase in the number restorations of such buildings representing the heritage of former foreign rulers and current minority ethnic groups in modern Greece. Courtesy Pamela Jerome.

forms are protected through regulations that require new construction to be of the same style, but they also must be reinforced for seismic protection.

Currently across Greece, some four hundred of the estimated two thousand historic towns thought to merit protective measures are actually protected. An obstacle to completing the listing is the lack of a comprehensive national inventory of towns, villages, and surrounding historic areas. The limited resources available to the Ministry of Planning, which has responsibility for compiling the needed data, coupled with the size of the task restrict the rate of progress. Nonetheless, it is encouraging to note that for many historic towns, firm building regulations governing new construction are already in place. In addition, in some towns small conservation projects are beginning to serve as catalysts for urban regeneration. For example, in Veria, a medium-sized town in north-eastern Greece, a new modern art and civic history museum in a restored manor house, a new Byzantine museum in a historic mill, and a restored Jewish quarter have combined to revive culture and tourism.[8]

CURRENT CONSERVATION FRAMEWORK AND CHALLENGES

In 2002 Greece passed a comprehensive law for the Protection of Antiquities and Cultural Heritage in General. The law broadened the scope of heritage such that sites—whether ancient or modern, movable or immovable, intangible or tangible—can be listed and legally protected. The law also introduced fiscal incentives for private property owners and stricter penalties for offences. It remains to be seen if the Greek authorities will follow through with enforcement of its regulations, providing private owners of listed buildings the necessary incentives to maintain them and carrying out additional conservation and restoration projects.

The Ministry of Culture is the only major actor for cultural heritage in Greece. Local governments, interested voluntary organizations, and private financing have contributed to architectural conservation only minimally. Since 1971 the Ministry's General Directorate of Antiquities and Cultural Heritage has been directly responsible for heritage protection. The Directorate includes numerous divisions, called Ephorates, with varying foci, including prehistoric and classical antiquities, Byzantine and post-Byzantine antiquities, and modern cultural heritage and conservation. In the 1980s, campaigns were launched to link cultural heritage to regional development that involved opening new museums, initiating new archaeological excavations, and a wave of nominating new World Heritage Sites. By the 1990s, this program had lost its momentum, as infrastructure and other costs made it increasingly difficult. Today the Ministry of Culture protects and conserves sites throughout Greece, but many of its major projects have focused on the capital city of Athens, where 50 percent of Greeks live.

After World War I and the collapse of the Ottoman Empire, an influx of Greeks from its former territories doubled the size of Athens overnight, creating housing and development pressures that have not yet ceased. Sadly, innumerable vernacular buildings were lost to unchecked illegal housing developments, especially after World War II. Today, with national and local preservation laws irregularly enforced at best, and conservation policies and initiatives changing dramatically with each new government, there is little realistic hope of saving more than a few of the delightful neoclassical houses that once graced the winding streets of nineteenth-century Athens. While the smaller vernacular buildings are few and far between in Athens today, there are a number of art nouveau, art deco, and Bauhaus-style apartment buildings. While such buildings are presently unprotected, they are relatively secure as they are multifamily residences.

Figure 21-6 The Unification of Archaeological Sites project completed in time for the 2004 Olympics created the country's largest archaeological park. This 4-kilometer path weaves through the city of Athens, linking archaeological sites and encouraging greater interaction with cultural heritage among both Athenians and tourists.

In 2004 Athens hosted the Summer Olympic Games, and though every four years the choice of a location for this international event can be counted on to provoke controversy, few sites in recent memory have generated as much opposition as the selection of the Marathon battlefield area, northeast of Athens, as the site for a water sports complex. Construction of this permanent facility with several buildings and two artificial lakes was protested by archaeologists and environmentalists from several countries. They claimed it represented a major threat to the highly symbolic historic site where an outnumbered Greek contingent successfully defended themselves against the Persian invasion in 490 BCE. Many people also raised ecological concerns, citing possible damage to nearby coastal wetlands and their bird populations.

In the end, Olympic organizers were backed by the European environmental commissioner, which subdued the storm of protest and allowed the project to move steadily ahead. Today the site is a national park. In any event, later studies showed that the site was not, in fact, the location of the historic battle that it was thought to be.[9]

The Olympics also forced Greece to commence a long overdue urban improvement program for both modern and classical Athens. Related funding was channeled into various works, from the ongoing Acropolis restoration to altogether new projects, such as the restoration of Hadrian's arch in Athens and the Philippeion in Olympia. Tourists and locals alike will long benefit from the Unification of Archaeological Sites project, which created Greece's largest archaeological park with a network of safe paved walkways linking key sites within the city.[10] A cooperative program between the Ministry of Culture and the Ministry of the Environment, Physical Planning, and Public Works, the unification project was first proposed in 1985 but was energized and accelerated with the coming of the Olympic Games to Athens.

With the ongoing restoration of the Acropolis, the broadening of heritage concerns, and the first signs of conservation as a stimulus for the regeneration of historic districts, prospects for Greek heritage have never seemed more positive. While the country's ancient sites and artifacts have been protected and preserved for nearly two centuries, and its Byzantine heritage has long since caught up in importance and protection, the rest of its extensive architectural heritage is beginning to make the same claims.

ENDNOTES

1. The neoclassical movement, which began in the mid-1700s, gathered momentum after architects James Stuart and Nicholas Revett published their four-volume work, the *Antiquities of Athens* (between 1762 and 1816), and Revett published his two-volume study of the *Antiquities of Ionia* (in 1769 and 1797). These books included precisely measured drawings of the ancient ruins of the Acropolis, images of certain buildings "restored," and picturesque views that depicted their physical contexts at the time. These works were influential in shifting contemporary European scholarly and popular views towards a aesthetic and theoretical preference for the simpler, more "original" architecture of ancient Greece, as opposed to the derivative architecture of Rome that had been popular since the Renaissance. Equally significant was the fact that these and other similar publications stimulated a new interest in first-hand examination of archaeological evidence by architects, a practice that significantly influenced styles and theories of architecture.

2. Jokilehto, A *History of Architectural Conservation*. Oxford: Elsevier Butterworth-Heinemann, 2004, p. 89; first published in 1999.

3. Fifty years before Balanos began his highly public restorations, anastylosis was used on the Acropolis by the archaeologist Ludwig Ross, who worked with architects Edouard Schaubert and Christian Hansen. But the method has long been associated with Balanos, whose forceful implementation of the technique produced the most striking changes in the Parthenon, the Erechtheion, and the Propylaea in Athens. Using this method, a conservator would reconfigure blocks from a temple column or other cut pieces of stone, using little or no mortar. New material could replace missing stones when needed but was to be kept to a minimum, and such interventions should be obvious.

4. Tung, *Preserving the World's Great Cities*. "The City of the Gods Besieged: Athens." In *Preserving the World's Great Cities*, p. 268 (New York: Three Rivers Press, 2001).

5. Mary Beard, "Lord Elgin—Savior or Vandal?" BBC, www.bbc.co.uk/history/ancient/greeks/parthenon_debate_01.shtml (accessed December 2, 2009).

6. "Welcome," Acropolis Restoration Service, www.ysma.gr/ysma/Default.aspx?id=1 (accessed November 25, 2009).

7. Christine Pirovolakis, "Greece Rediscovers Islamic Treasures," *InFocus News* (January 8, 2006), www.infocusnews.net/content/view/9792/82/ (accessed December 2, 2009).

8. Nikos Vatopoulos, "Restoration Project in Veria a Focus for Urban Regeneration and Culture," *Kathimerini English Edition*, April 27, 2002, www.ekathimerini.com/4dcgi/news/content.asp?aid=15916 (accessed December 2, 2009).

9. "Ambassador George Savvaides on 2004 Olympics at National Press Club" (press release, Hellenic Republic, Embassy of Greece, December 17, 2002), www.greekembassy.org/embassy/content/en/Article.aspx?office=2&folder=168&article=12369 (accessed December 2, 2009).

10. "The Unification of the Archaeological Sites of Athens," Hellenic Ministry of Culture, www.yppo.gr/4/e40.jsp?obj_id=90 (accessed December 2, 2009).

CHAPTER 22

Turkey

Turkey has witnessed the ebb and flow of numerous civilizations in its long history mainly as a result of its geographic location, straddling Europe and Asia and bordering the Aegean, Black, and Mediterranean seas. Migration and trade routes have traversed the Anatolian Peninsula for 80,000 years, and in eastern Turkey the headwaters of the Tigris and Euphrates rivers form the northernmost reaches of the Fertile Crescent, the "cradle of civilization," one of the global locations where farming and urban life originated. The numerous coastal and inland areas of modern Turkey long ago attracted Greek and Roman colonies, which were often established on the foundations of earlier settlements. Many of Turkey's historic towns and cities, whether abandoned or still inhabited, contain evidence of these successive layers of occupation, and their physical legacies comprise Turkey's extensive cultural heritage today.

Three of the Seven Wonders of the Ancient World—the Temple of Diana at Ephesus, the Colossus of Rhodes, and the Tomb of Mausolus at Halicarnassus—were located in Anatolia or its nearby islands. One was destroyed by fire, the second collapsed in an earthquake, and the third was dismantled so its stones could be reused. That these Hellenistic marvels no longer exist is an indication of the natural and human hazards threatening even the most renowned sites, and their slim chances of survival if left unprotected. The Ottoman authorities were the first to pass legislation concerning historic sites and archaeological artifacts in what is now Turkey—first in 1869 and the again in 1912. In 1891 the Ottomans also made an initial attempt to gather and preserve the region's antiquities by establishing an Archaeological Museum in Istanbul's Topkapı Palace.

Today, the Republic of Turkey is charged with protecting and conserving its important and far-reaching heritage so that it can continue to be appreciated by future generations. These goals have been significantly achieved as a result of the country's comprehensive heritage network and broad legislation; however, this rapidly modernizing country has also lost many historic sites and artifacts to large-scale development, industrialization, and infrastructure projects.

HAGIA SOPHIA

◀Figure 22-1 Water-damaged ceiling and pendentives at Hagia Sophia, Istanbul, Turkey in 1999, before restoration.

The city of Istanbul, located on both sides of the Bosporus strait that separates Europe and Asia, epitomizes the country's layered history and its position as a crossroad between continents. The broad accumulation of architectural heritage in this city, originally founded by the Greeks, reflects the successive empires of which it was the center—including the Eastern Roman, Byzantine, and Ottoman. Centuries of reuse, conservation, and restoration have occurred in this city, especially at its most well-known site—the Hagia Sophia.

Built as a cathedral in the early sixth century, Istanbul's Hagia Sophia (Holy Wisdom) has been extensively altered in its fifteen-hundred-year history, yet it remains one of the city's most magnificent sites. It was by far the grandest structure of its day: To adorn it, colorful columns and marble veneers were brought from ancient sites in Egypt, Greece, and Anatolia. Soon after its completion in 537 CE, a series of earthquakes weakened the Hagia Sophia's structure, and in 558 CE its eastern arch and most of its dome collapsed. Repairs were completed with only minor modifications, but a later earthquake again caused severe damage. In 1334 the architect Trdat, from Armenia, restored the dome again, adding buttresses to the exterior of the building and enhancing the legendary golden mosaics covering the Hagia Sophia's four acres of interior walls and ceilings.

After the 1453 Ottoman conquest of Istanbul, Hagia Sophia was converted into a mosque. In the sixteenth century, its interior mosaics were covered with plaster, Koranic inscriptions were added by a noted Ottoman calligrapher, and its altar was moved to the eastern end. Thereafter it was called Ayasofya Çamii (Mosque of the Holy Wisdom). The architect Sinan added more structural buttressing and two new minarets later in the sixteenth century. Relatively few changes were made to the Hagia Sophia in the following centuries, until the Swiss architects Gaspare and Giuseppe Fossati undertook extensive repairs and redecoration in the nineteenth century. Their work included consolidating the dome, straightening some columns, and cleaning, recording, and replastering over the mosaics.

In 1932, after the collapse of the Ottoman Empire and the establishment of the Turkish Republic, President Mustafa Kemal Atatürk closed the mosque, uncovered many of the mosaics and reopened it as a secular, historical museum two years later. Since then, restoration and conservation interventions on the Hagia Sophia have been almost continuous, beginning with the efforts in the 1940s of the Byzantine Institute of America at Dumbarton Oaks in Washington, DC.

In the late 1990s, the Turkish government began discussing needs and methods of protecting the structure from earthquakes. At about the same time, a UNESCO mission made recommendations for improving the environmental conditions of the interior, tourist use, and interpretation of the site's history. The partial restoration of the Hagia Sophia's roof and exterior wall repairs by a team led by conservation architect Zeynep Ahunbay soon followed. Stabilizing and restoring the mosaics and painted finishes beneath the structure's 183-foot (55-meter) high dome began at the same time through the collaboration of UNESCO-provided experts and conservators from the Central Laboratory for Restoration and Conservation.[1] This project also involved a training program in mosaic conservation for young Turkish craftsmen.

Nonetheless, due to the enormity of the building, today the Hagia Sophia's interior still suffers from water seepage, additional windows require repair, marble needs to be cleaned, and stucco needs partial replacing.[2] In addition, its location on a seismic fault line puts it at constant risk of major damage from an earthquake, and there have also been calls recently for returning the structure to functioning as a mosque, which could potentially threaten some interior decorations. However, the greatest threat to the Hagia Sophia today is that there remains no viable overall conservation and restoration plan, no comprehensive survey of conditions and threats, and no prioritization of projects to be completed. As Ahunbay has noted, there is also no permanent restoration staff working regularly on the Hagia Sophia, and budgets for its conservation fluctuate widely from year to year.[3]

Though not as consistently maintained as would be desirable, the power of Hagia Sophia's grand design endures despite the range of major changes imposed over time. Today it is appreciated simultaneously for being the distinctive embodiment of a seminal moment in architectural history and for being a collection of styles tracing architectural history, as well as for reflecting fifteen centuries of conservation consciousness and restoration techniques.

Figure 22-2 Scaffolding was installed in 1999 to facilitate restoration of Hagia Sophia's high dome and pendentives (a). The painted Koranic inscriptions on the ceiling of the high dome of Hagia Sophia were restored in 2002 by the Istanbul Conservation and Restoration Laboratory (b). In addition, the structure's extensive mosaics were conserved between 2002 and 2010 (c). Photos courtesy Cemal Hoyuk and the World Monuments Fund

CONSERVATION FRAMEWORKS AND PROJECTS IN MODERN TURKEY

With the establishment of the republic in 1923, concerns for cultural heritage on Turkish soil were given renewed focus, and many sites were officially recognized as part of the common national heritage.[4] The post–World War I modernization campaign initiated more changes to Turkey's built environment within eighty years than it had experienced in its entire previous history. Though the twentieth century in Turkey has largely been characterized by rapid development and extensive new construction, it has also included concern for its historic sites.

Atatürk—who said that had he not been head of state he would have chosen to be cultural minister—fostered the development of Turkish culture and the preservation of its heritage. He created a Department of Antiquities just two weeks after calling the first National Assembly in 1920. Among the department's earliest efforts were the identification and preservation of Turkey's most significant historic buildings and sites. A Supreme Council on Monuments was formed in 1951, followed twenty years later by the establishment of the Ministry of Culture, now the Ministry of Culture and Tourism, within which today the *Kültür Varliklari ve Müzeler Genel Müdürlüğü* (General Directorate of Cultural Heritage and Museums) is responsible for conserving the country's architectural heritage.

Through its thirty-one regional directorates (including six in Istanbul and two in Izmir), the Genel Müdürlüğü registers buildings and sites and supervises any interventions at them. However, because Turkey's protected built heritage includes 7,800 archaeological sites, nearly 85,000 buildings, 80 ancient cities, and over 750 other urban sites,[5] most regional councils have staffs of only a few persons with hundreds of sites to administer. Municipal governments are tasked with implementing and monitoring the decisions of the regional councils, but they typically cannot afford to hire the necessary technical personnel and often do not enforce decisions they disagree with.[6]

Comprehensive new legislation to protect natural, historic, and archaeological artifacts and sites was passed in 1983 and amended four years later. The law strengthened state support and tax benefits for conservation and increased financial and other penalties for noncompliance. The 1983 law also introduced Conservation Areas around key historic buildings to preserve their historical context and to ensure that the ambience of historic city centers is maintained.[7] Several historic districts have been designated (including those in Istanbul, Izmir, and Bodrum), and entire historic towns, such as Trabzon and Safranbolu, have been conserved.

Unfortunately, a comprehensive survey to better understand and document Istanbul's physical history is difficult because of the prohibitive cost of such a study, logistical difficulties posed by later constructions, and competing claims for funding. However, in 1985, "Historic Areas of Istanbul," including the Hagia Sophia, Theodosian Walls, and the Süleymaniye and Zeyrek mosques, were added to the World Heritage List. The recognized area contained surviving sites and buildings from all layers of the city's long history. The fourth-century Hippodrome of Constantine, the Aqueduct of Valens, the archaeological park, and the early ramparts of the city all represent its ancient roots; the Hagia Sophia, the Hagia Eirene (Holy Peace church), and the Zeyrek Camii (the former Pantocrator Monastery) represent its Byzantine era; and hundreds of wooden vernacular buildings as well as the Topkapı Palace and the Blue (Sultan Ahmed), Şehzade, and Süleymaniye mosques represent its Ottoman heritage.

The abundance of cultural property meriting protection, and the related need to prioritize, has been a concern of the Ministry of Culture since its inception. However, insufficient funding and staffing has impeded action even at the most important sites. Because the countrywide survey of cultural property is still incomplete, many buildings that require attention remain unlisted and vulnerable to unsympathetic change or loss. Much historic architecture has been lost to development because of the high value of inner-city land and a public that tends to look unfavorably on older, often wooden, structures. Historic site razing is often the most viable economic alternative for owners and investors.

Despite these pressures, individual historic structures have been successfully conserved, including the Topkapı Palace, Kalenderhane Mosque, and Lengerhane industrial plant, where chains and anchors were produced for the Ottoman navy. Another extensively restored Istanbul site is its massive sixth-century underground water reservoir, known as the Yerebatan Saray (Basilica Cistern).[8] When originally constructed, 336 ancient columns were reused to support its vast vaults, and the cistern served as a water source for the city until the fifteenth century. In the 1980s, the Yerebatan Saray was restored and today has footbridges above its 9,800 square meters of water surface, providing visitors with a fascinating subterranean experience of what is perhaps the most complete and unchanged of Istanbul's early buildings.

Turkey made conservation history in 1964 by establishing the world's first university-based graduate-level architectural conservation training program at Middle East Technical University (METU) in Ankara. It was the creation of archaeologist Cevat Erder, who later served as director general of ICCROM in Rome. Today the faculties of architecture at Istanbul Technical, Mimar Sinan, and Yildiz universities in Istanbul also offer excellent heritage conservation training opportunities at the graduate level. Thus Turkey today is home to a vast number of well-trained professionals who are often called upon by international organizations to share their expertise abroad.

Individual Turkish citizens and private organizations have also been actively involved in the conservation of Turkey's heritage. The Touring and Automobile Club of Turkey, established in 1923, has one of the longest traditions in this regard, and it was joined in the 1960s by the Chamber of Architects of Turkey, which has focused more on sharing expertise than sponsoring field projects.[9] One of the most active advocacy groups in the country is the Türkiye Anıt Çevre Turizm Değerlerini Koruma Vakfı (TAÇ Foundation, (TAÇ Foundation, Foundation for the Preservation of Turkish Monuments and Environment), which was established in 1976 as an NGO, though it receives regular financial support from the Ministry of Culture. Like the British National Trust, the TAÇ Foundation acquires and restores properties and provides expert consultancy services to property owners.[10]

For his efforts and advocacy on behalf of cultural heritage, Metin Sözen has won numerous Turkish and international awards, including the prestigious Aga Khan Trust for Culture award in 1984 for the restoration of Ottoman palaces in Istanbul when he served as director of the regional offices of the National Palaces Trust. More recently, he has served as an advisor to the Turkish government and founded a number of important and active NGOs in the country. As part of the "Europe, A Common Heritage" campaign in 2000, he was involved in the establishment of the *Tarihi Kentler Birligi* (Union of Historical Towns), which began with an agreement between fifty-four Turkish cities and has since grown to two hundred members.[11] In 1990 Sözen was one of the founding members of the Çevre ve Kültür Değerlerini Koruma ve Tanıtma Vakfı (ÇEKÜL, Foundation for the Promotion and Protection of the Environment and Cultural Heritage), where he continues to serve as director. ÇEKÜL is one of the largest NGOs in Turkey today, and it works to promote awareness, educate, and organize communities to the benefit of their architectural and other heritage.[12]

One of the most important and high-profile recent conservation initiatives in Istanbul was the idea of another dedicated individual, Çelik Gülersoy, a lawyer with imagination, determination, and a passion for the history of his city. In the early 1970s, Gülersoy devised a number of innovative means of financing architectural restoration projects, including the introduction of a registration fee on vehicles entering or leaving the country. The proceeds were divided between the government and the Turkish Touring and Automobile Association, of which Gülersoy was managing director. Sufficient funds were raised to complete a variety of restoration projects in Istanbul proper as well as on the Bosporus before this special excise tax was suspended in 1990.

a

b

c

Figure 22-3 Through an innovative funding scheme devised by heritage protection advocate Çelik Gülersoy, as well as through his own initiative, dozens of architectural conservation projects were completed in Turkey in the 1970s and 1980s. Among these were the restorations of a traditional Bosporus yali, shown here with work in progress (a), and two pensions: the Green Hotel (b) and the Hagia Sophia (c).

In recent years, Turkish specialists, universities, firms, and organizations have especially been involved in the restoration of heritage built during the Ottoman period throughout southeastern Europe. In 1989, the Turkish Ministry of Foreign Affairs published the book *Ottoman Architectural Works Outside of Turkey*, which included thorough descriptions of the history and current condition of structures in the Middle East and Central Asia as well as southeastern Europe. The Turkish Cooperation and Development Agency (TIKA), affiliated with the Prime Minister's Office, as well as the Directorate of Religious Affairs, have supported numerous conservation projects in every formerly Ottoman country in Europe.

The Turkish Ministry of Culture and Tourism announced plans in 2005 to restore numerous buildings in Bulgaria and Kosovo, including some large mosque projects in Kostendil and Razgrad, Bulgaria, and hundreds of sites in the historic center of Prizren, Kosovo. A number of years earlier, a similar agreement had been reached between the Turkish and Macedonian Ministers of Culture on restoration of sites in that country. Initial projects have included mosques, a caravansary, a clock tower, and an Ottoman-era administration building, which was converted into a contemporary Turkish Cultural Center. In addition, through the Turkish Embassy in the Republic of Macedonia, the Stone Bridge, which has spanned the Vardar River in Skopje since 1451, is being restored. Lost elements such as its tower, cobblestone pavers, and Ottoman insignia were reconstructed.

In 2001 Greece and Turkey signed a cultural exchange agreement that included the formation of a joint working group to collaborate on the study and conservation of Turkish sites in Greece and Greek sites in Turkey. Almost four hundred Ottoman structures or ruins were identified in Greece that could potentially be restored as part of this program. In 2005 plans were announced to restore the childhood home of Mustafa Kemal Atatürk, in Thessaloníki.

In addition to the support for the Ottoman heritage of southeastern Europe, which has come from various branches of the Turkish government, religious organizations based in Turkey, such as the Vakfı, and private Turkish companies have also invested in restoration projects throughout southeastern Europe. The Turkish History Institute conducted a survey of Ottoman heritage in Romania in 2002, with the support of the Romanian State Planning Organization. Ankara University is in the process of restoring Ottoman manuscripts at the Fethi Pasha Library in Rhodes, Greece. The Research Center for Islamic History, Art, and Culture (IRCICA), an Istanbul-based international organization, has also been active in supporting research as well as specific projects on Ottoman heritage sites in southeastern Europe.

Perhaps the best known of Gülersoy's work today is his mid-1980s restoration of a row of nineteenth-century wooden houses along the south wall of the Topkapı Palace, facing Hagia Sophia. In implementing these impressive projects, he overcame a variety of obstacles and demonstrated the reuse for commercial purposes potential of Istanbul's historic wooden architecture. His work has increased tourism to the area and has done much to preserve the character of Istanbul's historic center.

Gülersoy's efforts have also contributed to an impressive private initiative to save the few remaining *yali*, the old wooden houses that have lined the European and Asian shores of the Bosporus since the seventeenth century. These spacious summer home-and-garden complexes were built by senior Ottoman officials to accommodate extravagant entertainment programs designed to impress the Sultan and his international guests. Over the centuries, countless yali have been lost to the hazards of their waterside environment or to fire, pollution, or development. Due to their graceful proportions and striking locations, those that have survived have become popular residences for Istanbul's elite. While yali have been considered central to the scenographic quality of this famous waterway since the nineteenth century, it was not until the 1970s that individual property owners organized to promote their protection. The TAÇ Foundation has been one of the most active advocacy groups working to save the yali.

ARCHAEOLOGICAL SITE CONSERVATION AND MUSEUMS IN TURKEY

Ani is only one of hundreds of archaeological sites in Turkey that is currently the focus of conservation interest from Turkey and abroad. The legacy of foreign participation in Turkish archaeological heritage concerns began in the nineteenth century. Heinrich Schliemann's discovery of Troy in the 1880s is perhaps the most famous example of a foreign archaeological intervention, although there were many earlier foreign exploration and conservation teams, including the Swiss Fossati brothers and numerous French examples.

Today, foreign research centers support almost a hundred different archaeological excavations in Turkey each year and, further, some of the country's most impressive conservation efforts. Ongoing work at Ephesus, which was begun in the nineteenth century by Britons John T. Wood and David G. Hogart, is now led by an Austrian team. American-sponsored projects include Harvard University's reconstruction of Sardis and New York University's site conservation and museum creation at the ancient city of Aphrodisias. The Byzantine Institute of America at Dumbarton Oaks continues scholarly architectural conservation studies at various sites and organized several conservation interventions in Istanbul from the 1950s through the 1980s. From 2001 until 2004, Dutch archaeologists from the University of Amsterdam conducted site

Figure 22-4 The Church of Agthamar situated on an island in Lake Van in eastern Turkey is one of several Armenian heritage sites in eastern Turkey that has been or is in the process of being restored. Other regional heritage sites deserving special attention in Eastern Turkey include the Syriac Orthodox churches in Turabdin in southeastern Turkey and the Greek Orthodox religious buildings located in and near ÇEKÜL.

conservation work at Nemrut Dağ, and an effective multidisciplinary approach to conserving and presenting the Neolithic site of Çatalhöyük is led by British archaeologist Ian Hodder with technical conservation assistance provided by the University of Pennsylvania.

While the various international archaeological and architectural conservation concessions have been hosted by the Ministry of Culture, their financial support has been provided almost exclusively by guest institutions and private philanthropic foundations, which are often specifically created to aid a particular site. The work at Çatalhöyük and Aphrodisias, for example, is backed in part by an international friends group. With funds from the Munich-based Studiosus Foundation, the German Archaeological Institute has been working for four years on conservation and cultural tourism promotion projects at the ancient Hellenistic and Roman city of Pergamum, whose famous Great Altar of Zeus was moved in the early twentieth century to a museum built to showcase it in Berlin: the Pergamon Museum. Recent successful projects at Pergamum have included the consolidation of the stone dome of the round tower of the Red Hall and topping it with protective lead sheeting.

The archaeological museum in Istanbul's Topkapı Palace has one of the finest collections of Archaic, Hellenis-

Figure 22-5 Partial reconstruction using the *anastylosis* method was conducted in 1996 at the Temple of Trajan at Pergamum by the German Archaeological Institute. In 2009 similar stabilization and partial reconstruction of the southern round tower of the Red Hall at Pergamum was completed.

Figure 22-6 The Yesemek Open Air Museum in southeast Turkey displays a Hittite stone quarry and workshop dating from approximately 1400 BCE. Its upkeep and presentation has been supported by a consortium of local tour companies.

tic, and Roman sculpture in the world. Its highlights include prehistoric objects from Anatolia and finds from different levels of the excavations at Troy. Ankara's Museum of Anatolian Civilizations offers a compelling presentation of the range of cultures that settled in the area during its long history. Its exhibitions include an eight-thousand-year-old goddess figurine from the ruins of Çatalhöyük, the world's first settlement of sufficient size to be considered a city. Turkey's southeastern hills are the expansive setting for the Yesemek Open Air Museum, site of a Hittite stone quarry and workshop dating from approximately 1400 BCE, which has been excavated since the 1950s. The museum presents an intriguing collection of more than three hundred stones carved in the shapes of sphinxes, lions, mountain gods, war chariots, and figurative relief sculpture groups.

Hundreds of other archaeological sites and historic settlements in southeast Turkey, however, have less positive fates awaiting them. Many are destined for extinction under a master plan begun in the late 1980s, and still being implemented, that calls for the construction of twenty-two dams and associated hydroelectric plants and irrigations systems to help develop this impoverished region. Thanks to the work of several Turkish journalists, the plight of cultural heritage jeopardized by this plan made world news in 2000, when construction of the Birecik power plant and dam threatened to flood the remains of the Roman garrison city of Zeugma, which is comprised of scores of town buildings and buried villas with walls and floors decorated with exquisite mosaics and frescoes.[13] Though extensive publicity stimulated widespread public concern, ultimately the decision to build the new energy source proved irreversible.

The resulting reservoir inundated almost twenty-six square miles, including about 8 percent of Zeugma. In the months before the site was submerged, salvage archaeology was done by a consortium of archaeologists led by the University of Oxford, with funding from the Packard Humanities Institute in Los Angeles. The international rescue effort also served as an impetus for the nearby community of Gaziantep to display the discoveries in their regional museum. In addition to bringing global attention to this formerly little-known part of Turkey, the improvement of this museum is viewed by local officials as an opportunity to stimulate tourism and bring its economic benefits to the entire region (Figure 1-18).

In a similar case, archaeologists, art historians, and researchers today are working at the medieval city of Hasankeyf to do what they can before this listed site is flooded by the Ilisu Dam, whose construction will be complete around 2013, also in spite of international outcry. The possibility of moving select buildings to higher ground is being studied; however, the project's budget was conceived and approved without funds for relocating Hasankeyf's irreplaceable architectural riches.[14]

CHALLENGES AHEAD

UNESCO has advocated for heritage conservation in Turkey since 1985 by sponsoring reports, including an inventory of Istanbul's threatened heritage, and providing minor support for individual projects. In 1974 the Turkish Committee of ICOMOS was established, and has since become one of that organization's strongest country affiliates. However, the costs of maintaining Turkey's massive inventory of historic sites and buildings are immense and a heavy financial burden for its still developing economy. The government has failed to prioritize architectural conservation, allocating only a small percentage of its budget to the Ministry of Culture and Tourism, of which only a small amount is used for heritage. Despite the many impressive accomplishments to date by Turkish conservation professionals, they would certainly benefit from more prominent political and public support.

Thousands of archaeological sites remain unexcavated, and overworked archaeologists tend to mostly perform crisis-mode salvage operations at urban construction sites or rural locations threatened by land-development schemes or infrastructure projects. In addition, natural disasters—from oil spills in the Bosporus to massive earthquakes—regularly take their toll on Turkey's heritage and deflect funding from planned conservation projects to emergency interventions.

Many losses could have been avoided, however, and Turkey will continue to lose its irreplaceable culture unless the government requires development projects to incorporate appropriate treatment for the country's patrimony. Especially in the past thirty years, Turkish authorities have underserved the needs of heritage protection in their planning decisions. In addition to risks from major infrastructure projects, the new road systems, airports, hotels, and housing developments along the country's largely pristine southern coast threaten not only the cultural landscape but specific historic sites as well. Accommodating and attracting mass leisure and cultural tourism is important for the Turkish economy; however, it has led to questionable practices, such as adapting ancient Hellenistic and Roman amphitheaters for modern cultural gatherings.

Inadequate controls over rampant illegal construction have also long represented a crisis for the country's archaeological and historic architectural patrimony. Half the new housing in Istanbul, for example, is estimated either to lack a building permit or be in violation of zoning requirements. These squatter housing settlements, known as *gecekondus*, can be found in all of Turkey's major urban areas.

Contemporary conservation efforts in Turkey are also challenged by the potential shift in heritage priorities that may result from the increasing centrality of religion to Turkish culture and politics. Stephen Kinzer, an ardent observer of Turkey, noticed in 2001 a possibly lamentable trend among "some conservative politicians who believe that the government should not worry too much about preserving pre-Islamic heritage because that heritage contradicts Muslim beliefs."[15] On the other hand, other recent activities seem to contradict this potential direction. For example, conservation has begun in recent years on Turkey's wider "shared heritage," including the ancient Armenian capital city of Ani. In addition, the Ministry of Culture recently restored portions of Istanbul's Byzantine defences and a few of the city's grander churches. And while it may seem that the Turkey's many historic mosques receive significantly more attention than its churches, responsibility for preserving Turkey's Islamic religious buildings rests with their owner, the Islamic community, as it does in most predominately Muslim countries. Most buildings have Vakfı foundations, the traditional Islamic charitable institution, associated with them that carry out routine maintenance as well as major restoration projects.[16]

A public climate that places more value on historic sites and appreciates the aesthetic, economic, and social benefits of heritage conservation is not as strong in Turkey as in other European countries today. The development of such a public consciousness and interest would do much to keep Turkish developers in check. As Atatürk remarked in 1935, "it is necessary that the people themselves—who are the real owners of our historical and national monuments—become the protectors of antiquities."[17]

ENDNOTES

1. This work was begun through a UNESCO initiative and has been supported in successive partnership funding phases by the World Monuments Fund and the Turkish Ministry of Culture.

2. Fergus M. Bordewich, "A Monumental Struggle to Preserve the Hagia Sophia," *Smithsonian* (December 2008), www.smithsonianmag.com/travel/Fading-Glory.html (accessed November 30, 2009).

3. Ibid.

4. Jokilehto, *A History of Architectural Conservation*. Oxford: Elsevier Butterworth-Heinemann, 2004, p. 245; first published in 1999.

5. "Immovable Cultural and Natural Heritage," *Kültür Varliklari ve Müzeler Genel Müdürlü ü*, www.kulturvarliklari.gov.tr/Genel/BelgeGoster.aspx?F6E10F8892433CFF20F60137B44E34F 5A9D8DAD33E7182F1 (accessed December 10, 2009).

6. Ö. Başağaç, E. Köşgeoğlu, and Ş. Güçhan, "Problems in Management of Urban Site Conservation in Turkey: A Case Study in Antakya" (paper, The International Scientific Committee for Documentation of Cultural Heritage [CIPA]) 19th International Symposium, September 30–October 4, 2003, Antalya, Turkey).

7. Jo Ramsay Leimenstoll, *Historic Preservation in Other Countries*, vol. 4, *Turkey* (Washington, DC: US/ICOMOS, 1989), 17.

8. Evidence of how Constantinople's ancient heritage was pillaged and reused can also be seen far from today's Istanbul. In 1204 the city's riches proved irresistible to the leaders of the Fourth Crusade, who stripped it of its wealth and artistic treasures. The famous bronze horses atop the Cathedral of St. Mark in Venice were taken from the *spina* of Constantinople's Hippodrome, which had survived since antiquity. Other war trophies and relics from Constantinople that adorn the Cathedral of St. Mark include a porphyry sculpture of Constantine's sons and the remains of St. Mark himself, which were secretly spirited out of Alexandria, Egypt, and brought to Venice in the ninth century.

9. Nezvat Ilhan, "Legal Forms: National Approaches in Turkey," in *Legal Structures of Private Sponsorship: International Seminar on Legal Structures of Private Sponsorship and Participation in the Protection and Maintenance of Monuments, Weimar, April 17-19, 1997*, eds. Floriane Fiedler and Werner von Trützschler (Munich: ICOMOS Germany, 2008), 82.

10. Leimenstoll, *Historic Preservation in Other Countries*, 45.

11. "Union of Historical Towns," Tarihi Kentler Birligi, www.tarihikentlerbirligi.org/icerik/icerik. asp?ID=50 (accessed December 30, 2009).

12. "We Exist through Nature and Culture," Çekül Vakfı, www.cekulvakfi.org.tr/icerik/content.asp?sayfaID=55 (accessed December 30, 2009).

13. Office of the Prime Minister, Directorate General of Press and Information, "The Zeugma Mosaics Will Not be Surrendered to the Euphrates," *Newspot* (July-August 2000), www.byegm.gov.tr/YAYINLARIMIZ/ta%C5%9Finan-newspot/2000/Jul-Aug/N25.htm (accessed December 2, 2009).

14. ICOMOS Turkey, "Turkey," *Heritage@Risk 2000* (Paris: ICOMOS, 2000), www.international.icomos.org/risk/world_report/2000/turkey_2000.htm (accessed December 2, 2009).

15. Stephen Kinzer, "Border to Border, Turkey's a Kaleidoscope of Art and Culture," *The New York Times*, May 2, 2001, H30.

16. The Turkish work *vakfı* is derived from the Arabic word *waqf*, which means hold, confinement, or prohibition. Under Islamic law, it refers to a perpetual religious, philanthropic, or family endowment of nonperishable property (e.g., real estate, jewelry, or other goods of value) made within a strictly regulated trust structure. Waqf trusts exist throughout the Islamic world.

17. As quoted by Hillary R. Clinton in "Remarks on Cultural Preservation by First Lady Hillary Rodham Clinton" (speech, Aspendos, Turkey, November 18, 1999), http://clinton4.nara.gov/WH/EOP/First_Lady/html/generalspeeches/1999/19991118a.html (accessed December 4, 2009).

CHAPTER 23

Cyprus and Malta

Cyprus and Malta, two island countries in the Mediterranean Sea, have served as stopover points and backdrops for numerous historic empires on the move, including Phoenician, Grecian, Roman, Venetian, Frankish, Genoese, and Ottoman, and as well as British trading and military expeditions. Over the centuries, these islands became melting pots for the many cultures who sought out their ports of call. While most Mediterranean islands are today integrated into continental countries such as Greece, Italy, or Turkey, both Cyprus and the Maltese archipelago became sovereign states when their British protectors granted them independence in the third quarter of the twentieth century—Cyprus in 1960 and Malta in 1964. On both island countries, layers of cultural heritage provide today's citizens and tourists much to appreciate and their conservationists much to protect. Despite their overlapping histories, heritage protection in Cyprus and Malta varies significantly due to their very different contemporary political contexts.

ARCHITECTURAL CONSERVATION IN A DIVIDED CYPRUS

The prime location of Cyprus in the eastern Mediterranean Sea—between the coasts of Turkey and the Levant—has throughout history been sought after by numerous empires attempting to dominate the sea around it. Many civilizations have influenced Cypriot cultural heritage in its nearly 40,000 years of inhabitation. Two of Cyprus's ancient sites have been included on the World Heritage List, including the Neolithic settlement at Choirokoitia (also known as Khirokitia) that reveals evidence of how civilization spread from Asia and the Near East to Europe. The second ancient site is Paphos, the alleged birthplace of Aphrodite and thus an important religious center in ancient Greece. The site includes many exceptional palace, villa, fortress, and tomb ruins and extraordinary mosaics that are among the best-surviving in the world.

In the Middle Ages, Cyprus was controlled by the Byzantines, and Cyprus's third World Heritage Site—the ten painted churches of the Troödos region—comprise one of the largest extant groups of Byzantine churches and monasteries. The Byzantines were followed by the Ottomans, whose waves of Muslim Turkish settlers joined the island's Latin, Greek, and Armenian populations. While the Orthodox Church was allowed to retain much of its possessions, most Catholic churches were converted into mosques.[1]

In the first century of Ottoman control, many bastions and defensive towers throughout the island were restored, and a series of laws to protect cultural heritage in Cyprus were passed in 1843, 1865, and 1874. However for most of the period of

◀Figure 23-1 The restoration of the monastery of Machairas, an example of nineteenth-century vernacular architecture outside of Lefkosia, is one of several Greek heritage sites supported by the Anastasios G. Leventis Foundation.

Turkish rule, which lasted until 1878, the administrators spent very little money on maintaining most historic Cypriot sites. In the 1860s and 1870s, the American consul to Cyprus, Luigi Palma di Cesnola, explored Cyprus's archaeological sites and returned to the United States with thousands of objects that were sold to the newly formed Metropolitan Museum of Art in New York. As a result of this plunder, and the increased awareness of Cypriot heritage it created, stricter legislation was passed under British rule. During this period, scientific archaeological excavations were also initiated, Cyprus's first museum was founded, and a Department of Antiquities was established in the 1930s.

In 1974 an attempted Greek military coup d'etat was countered by a Turkish military intervention, and the island was partitioned into two sides, mediated by a United Nations (UN) peacekeeping force. The separation of Cyprus into Greek and Turkish sides, divided by the Green Line, has created a significant obstacle to effective conservation planning.

Today, the architectural and urban heritage of Cyprus's two halves is threatened by very different sources.[2] In the Greek-Cypriot south, which is part of the EU, excessive tourism and development have already transformed most of the coastline and most of the historic cities into monotonous landscapes of modern hotels and high-rise buildings. In addition, wealthy monasteries have tended toward overrestoration of their buildings and extensive collections of icons. Northern Cyprus has not witnessed this same development, and in addition to a lack of resources and technical expertise, political isolation of the unrecognized territory threatens its architectural heritage.

Battling against the theft of art and historical objects, an industry that has deep roots in Cyprus, has significantly occupied Cypriot conservation professionals on both the Greek and Turkish sides. Both sides have denied the specific allegations that they allow the destruction and desolation of each other's treasured historic sites. However, Greek Cypriots have clearly allowed mosques in the south to deteriorate and their artifacts to be illicitly sold, and Turkish Cypriots have done the same to Orthodox Churches in the north. Major examples include the looting of mosaics from the Byzantine church of Kanakaria in North Cyprus, which later turned up in the United States, and icons stolen from the Byzantine-era Monastery of Christ Antiphonitis.[3] According to the Cypriot government, 133 churches have been damaged, 77 converted into mosques, and 33 to other uses, including the Church of Agia Anastasia in Lapithos, which allegedly has become a luxury hotel.[4] Sadly, looting continues throughout the island, despite the best efforts to prevent it by both sides. Most of the items on today's black market are from the Turkish-controlled part of Cyprus; but because there is little transfer of information across the Green Line, it is difficult to ascertain the extent of the problem.

Conservation efforts in the Republic of Cyprus, the southern Greek-controlled two-thirds of the island, have since 1990 been guided by the Town and Country Planning Law, which was passed in 1972, shortly before the island's division. This law authorizes the minister of the interior to issue Preservation Orders requiring the protection of Cyprus's most significant heritage sites and authorizes the Ministry's Department of Town Planning and Housing to create an Architectural Heritage Inventory of additional important historic sites, which today includes over 10,000 entries. In 1985 and again in 1992, generous incentives were introduced, offering a combination of grants, low-interest loans, and tax credits to assist owners of historic properties with their maintenance and restoration.

In Greek Cyprus, the primary government institution concerned with the protection and conservation of cultural heritage is the Department of Antiquities. This agency is responsible for both the documentation and restoration of historic sites and artifacts, including archaeological excavations and their display. It also maintains the Cyprus

Museum, where innumerable objects discovered at Cyprus's many archaeological sites are kept.

Nicosia's architectural and archaeological heritage in Greek Cyprus has been threatened in recent years by governmental construction projects. Construction of a new town hall on a former parking lot within the old town walls of Nicosia began in 2002, but it was stalled for four years for excavations of the archaeological remains of structures from the Byzantine medieval period. Local experts argue work at the site, known as Palaion Demarcheion, was rushed and proceeded without a management plan, and the site is now exposed to the elements, subject to floods, and not opened to the public.[5] In addition, the municipality still has not officially given up plans to build on part of the site. Similarly, the proposed new Cypriot House of Representatives is still planned for St. George Hill, despite the discovery and excavation of remains from the prehistoric through Hellenistic periods as well as the much later Venetian period on that site.[6]

Private assistance for conservation in Greek Cyprus is provided by organizations such as the Anastasios G. Leventis Foundation, which was established in Nicosia in 1980. The foundation, a branch of the Greek Leventis Foundation, supports Cypriot cultural heritage by financing projects at archaeological and historic sites. Its particular concern is rescuing artifacts from looting and trading, and it actively purchases ancient Cypriot objects from overseas markets and donates them to the Cyprus Museum. The Foundation's many other current projects include collaboration with the Department of Antiquities for the preservation of vernacular architecture.[7]

The independence of the Turkish Republic of Northern Cyprus, which comprises the northeast third of the island, has only been recognized by Turkey; however, it functions as a de facto separate entity. Though amendments were made to the Antiquities Law in 1975 and 1994 in Turkish Cyprus, conservation efforts have been less extensive and less organized than in the south, because it has significantly fewer resources. The UN embargo against Turkish Cyprus has further augmented this problem.[8] For many years, its conservationists only interacted with colleagues in Turkey, not with the international programs of the ICOMOS and ICCROM. The region's cultural heritage has suffered as a result of this isolation. In 2002 the Council of Europe issued a report calling for the allowance of internationally supported surveys and emergency protection measures for heritage sites in northern Cyprus and suggested that the destruction of cultural heritage through neglect is collateral damage in the political standoff in Cyprus.[9]

Nonetheless, conservation projects have been completed in recent decades in the Turkish-controlled part of Cyprus with funds both from its own government and from private initiatives. In the early 1990s, an extensive rehabilitation of the deteriorated Arabahmet quarter of Nicosia—with its late-Ottoman-era residential buildings and tight network of streets—was carried out. The project included the restoration of numerous houses, the construction of community facilities, and the reorganization of traffic connections with the rest of the city.

In addition, the Evkaf, the charitable foundation of the Islamic community, has contributed to the restoration of several sites, including the Gothic Lala Mustafa Pasha Mosque in Famagusta, which was built as the St. Nicholas Cathedral by crusaders in the fourteenth century. Famagusta's impressive cathedral, palace, tower, and other fortifications were neglected for centuries after the sixteenth-century Ottoman conquest of the then Venetian city. These sites in Northern Cyprus continue to suffer from neglect, due to a lack of funding for their conservation. Support has begun to arrive for Famagusta, including from the EU for rehabilitating the covered market place and for work on the Venetian Palace; from SAFE (Saving Antiquities for Everyone) for a structural survey of the church of Saints Peter and Paul; from Global Heritage Fund for the Sea Gate and Othello's Tower; and from the University of Minho in Portugal to conduct scientific tests

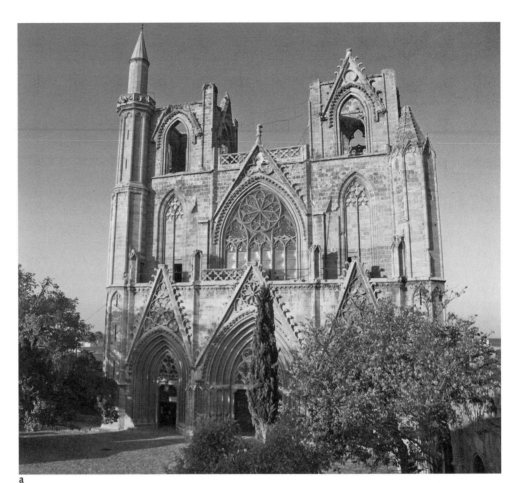

a

Figure 23-2 Restoration of the
Lala Mustafa Pasha Mosque (a)
in Famagusta, which was built as
the St. Nicholas Cathedral in the
fourteenth century, was sponsored
by Evkaf, the local charitable
foundation of the Islamic
community. The building reflects
the mélange of styles (b) and uses
typical of Cypriot heritage.

b

on the churches to judge resistance to seismic activity. As British art historian Michael J. K. Walsh, who teaches at Eastern Mediterranean University in Famagusta, has argued: International organizations must play an even greater role in architectural conservation at other sites in Northern Cyprus if this heritage is to survive.[10]

COOPERATIVE CYPRIOT CONSERVATION PROJECTS

Despite the current political situation and Walsh's dire predictions, both the Greek- and Turkish-controlled parts of Cyprus have made efforts to conserve the island's extensive heritage and have even begun slowly working together on restoration projects, often with international aid. Though little has been accomplished to reunite the island politically or socially, cultural heritage cooperation seems to have outpaced political settlements.

The first joint conservation efforts occurred in 1981, when teams of planners and specialists from both the north and south prepared a master plan for Nicosia under the mediation of the United Nations Development Program (UNDP). In this breakthrough plan, conservation and development on both sides of the divided capital were coordinated in such a way that they would complement one another and facilitate the eventual reuniting of the city. Because the Green Line bisected historic Old Town Nicosia, this former city center had become the deserted periphery of both sides and had significantly deteriorated. As part of the Master Plan, pedestrianization and rehabilitation projects on both sides of the city have been carried out in the past few decades.

In 1998 the Bi-Communal Development Programme was established by the UNDP and United States Agency for International Development (USAID) to promote cooperative efforts between the two Cypriot entities. Over the course of seven years, $67 million was spent on joint educational, cultural, and environmental projects. One of the projects completed as part of the Programme was the simultaneous restoration of two neglected monuments: the Hala Sultan Tekke on the Greek side, and the Apostolas Andreas Monastery on the Turkish side. Both were important religious structures before they were isolated by the 1974 partition, and the project was implemented by religious authorities on both sides of the island. In 2004 conservation architects, also from both sides, coordinated plans for the restoration of these sites in an attempt to demonstrate how heritage conservation can overcome political differences.[11] Unfortunately, little work was ever carried out at the Apostolas Andreas Monastery and the project proved less an opportunity for reconciliation than had been hoped.

Nonetheless, cooperative efforts for architectural conservation on Cyprus have been increasingly common. In 2003 a UN intervention helped the Greek Cypriot Department of Antiquities initiate the first restoration of a monument in the buffer zone, and Turkish Cypriots and Greek Cypriots worked together to shore up the Roccas Bastion, part of the Venetian city walls of Nicosia.[12] That same year, the EU donated considerable funds for projects in Famagusta and Kyrenia, two walled cities in Northern Cyprus in serious need of conservation attention. And, because of the Bi-Communal Development Programme's successes, upon its completion in 2005 a similar initiative was begun under UNDP management with funds from USAID, this time called the Action for Cooperation and Trust.

The UNDP-sponsored study of the history and proposed restoration of the Bedesten, also embedded in the walls of Nicosia, was awarded the EU/Europa Nostra Prize for Cultural Heritage for Research in 2009 for its focus on the site's past, present, and future and strategies for reintegrating it into the life and fabric of the city.[13] Built in the twelfth century as a church dedicated to St. Nicholas, the building was later used as a marketplace and has been rehabilitated today to serve as a multicultural meeting and

Figure 23-3 The wealth of religious architecture in Nicosia makes it an especially attractive potential tourist destination. Illustrated here is the portal of St. Nicholas, Nicosia, built originally as the Chapter-House of the Knights of St. John, and rehabilitated today to be a multicultural meeting center and exhibition space.

exhibition space as part of the EU's Rehabilitation of Old Nicosia project with additional support from the Evkaf.

Though a political solution to the current stalemate in Cyprus seems distant after the failure of the Annan Plan of 2004 and the evident disinterest in follow-up reunification negotiations, in the interim there are reasons for optimism for the future of Cyprus's architectural heritage. Both sides have recognized the economic and social benefits of heritage conservation and the importance of sensitive cultural tourism to their futures. They have also recognized that the extensive development and modernization, which has occurred primarily in the wealthier south, needs to be managed to minimize its negative effects on historic sites.[14] More importantly, the recent cooperative projects between conservation professionals from both sides of the island and the increasing international scholarly and professional interest in Cypriot heritage indicate positive trends for heritage on Cyprus.

MALTA

Malta's culture and history have been shaped by the many visitors who have left their mark on its small islands, including the Phoenicians, Romans, Arabs, Normans, and Anjevins and the apostle Paul (who converted the inhabitants to Christianity). The monastic Knights of St. John arrived following the first Crusade, fleeing from Rhodes after being expelled by an Ottoman fleet.[15] They brought with them their substantial treasury and a collection of artifacts from Jerusalem, as well as the will to protect Malta and develop it into a Mediterranean bastion of Christendom.

The knights' capital city, Valletta, was largely planned and constructed in a blend of Renaissance concepts and local styles by Michelangelo's pupil, Francesco Laparelli, and his Maltese assistant, Gerolamo Cassar.[16] Its substantial early seventeenth-century fortifications and sea walls, as well as financial support from the European mainland, protected Valletta and its impressive Cathedral of St. John (now a World Heritage Site) from the constant Ottoman threat, and the knights' Order retained control of Malta until they were expelled by Napoleon in 1798.

From the beginning of the nineteenth century until independence in 1964 Malta was a British protectorate, and it was during this period that its architectural conservation efforts began. In 1903 the British Governor established a central Museum Department to collect and protect antiquities as well as to protect Malta's ancient sites.[17] Heritage protection legislation followed seven years later, when an initial and simply framed Preservation of Antiquities Ordinance was drafted along the lines of the recently enacted Italian law.

In 1925 this initial law was replaced by a new Antiquities Protection Act, which (until 2002) regulated Malta's vast movable and immovable heritage of over fifty years old.[18] The Act strengthened the Museum Department's responsibility for these sites and objects and established an Antiquities Committee as an advisory body. The 1925 Antiquities Protection Act also defined regulations on the sale or export of art and archaeological artifacts, the demolition or alteration of historic buildings, the control of excavations and the creation of a list of protected heritage.[19] It codified penalties for persons found destroying or damaging historic sites or artifacts and gives the government preferential buying power for those deemed to be in danger.[20]

In the 1990s, two important acts of legislation broadened Malta's heritage conservation approach: the 1991 Environment Protection Act and the 1992 Development Planning Act. The first closely parallels the principles of the EU's Grenada Convention, by placing cultural heritage issues within an environmental context. It initiated the designation of conservation areas and the preservation of historic centers and assemblages in Malta. The Development Planning Act, based on current British planning legislation, similarly treated heritage issues within the broader context of developmental control.[21] It initiated the concepts of listing and grading of historic buildings, urban conservation areas, and protective zoning.[22]

In 2002 the Maltese Parliament passed a comprehensive new Cultural Heritage Act that transformed the country's entire system for architectural protection and conservation. Within the Ministry of Education, Culture, Youth, and Sport, the new Act created the Cultural Heritage Fund, Malta Centre for Restoration, Superintendence of Cultural Heritage, National Heritage Forum, Heritage Malta, and a Committee of Guarantee to oversee the interactions of these new entities.[23] The Committee of Guarantee is also responsible for distributing monies for conservation and research projects from the Cultural Heritage Fund, which receives monies from fines and other specifics of the new Act.

The superintendence is responsible for managing the excavating, documenting, and evaluating cultural assets and of international commitments and heritage relationships, including with UNESCO; monitoring the import and export of cultural goods; coordinating with other government agencies on land-use planning; initiating public awareness and education campaigns; and developing national heritage policy, standards, and guidelines.[24] The superintendence also prepares for the annual National Forum at which all the agencies created by the 2002 act meet with one another and with local government officials, NGOs, educational institutions, representatives of heritage commissions of religious communities, and other architectural conservationists to discuss the state of heritage in Malta.

The agency with day to day responsibility for the country's architectural conservation and protection is Heritage Malta, which manages Malta's most important sites and its museum network. Taking over from the former Museum Department, which had overseen Malta's heritage for one hundred years, Heritage Malta's main responsibilities include the management, conservation, interpretation, and promotion of cultural heritage.[25] Education, combined with recognition of the revenue potential of Malta's unique patrimony, is a keystone to its approach. Since 2005 Heritage Malta has also managed the Malta Centre for Restoration, a training and research institution that provides conservation, maintenance, and site-management consulting services for public and private sites as required.

One of Heritage Malta's most important initial challenges is improving the protection of the country's seven World Heritage Sites, including the oldest freestanding megaliths in the world. Malta's twenty-three known prehistoric sites are sacred temples dating from around 3700 BCE, which considerably predate other better-known prehistoric structures, such as England's Stonehenge.[26] Today, these megaliths are threatened by vibrations from neighboring quarries, and the structural integrity of their porous limestone has been weakened by Malta's constant, salty marine winds. They have also been defaced several times, including in 2003 when vandals armed with crowbars cut through the flimsy wire netting around the Mnajdra Temple and toppled sixty megaliths. Within two months, damage at Mnajdra had been repaired and broken stones were consolidated using a new reversible hydraulic lime restoration technique, which is almost invisible and does not deteriorate with exposure, unlike the hard cement used in the repairs at the site in the 1920s. The perimeter fence has been replaced with one twice as large and made of thicker steel wire, and security cameras and surveillance points have been added at Mnajdra and other sites.[27]

After completion of a site management and conservation plan, a Heritage Park has been built at Mnajdra as well as at Hagar Qim, comprising visitors' centers and archaeological site shelters over the temples. The designs of the completely reversible, long-term temporary shelters were the result of an international competition in 2004, and construction was completed in the summer of 2009. Though widely questioned by the Maltese public, it is expected that these protective measures will deter future vandals and protect Malta's impressive architectural and archaeological heritage from the salty rain, enabling further study and exploration of these sites.

In addition to the various entities within the Ministry of Culture and Tourism with direct jurisdiction over museums and historic sites, other government entities in Malta are also concerned with heritage issues and actively pursue architectural and urban conservation projects. These include the Restoration Unit of the Ministry of Resources and Infrastructure, which frequently completes rehabilitation projects in historic town centers; the Government Property Division within the Ministry for Justice and Home Affairs, which is responsible for state-owned properties irrespective of age; and the Malta Environment and Planning Authority within the Ministry for Rural Affairs and the Environment, which promotes sustainable development throughout the Maltese islands.

There are many challenges ahead for Maltese architectural heritage protection. Local training opportunities in both architectural conservation and planning are limited,

Figure 23-4 Though only about 300 square kilometers (115 square miles), the Maltese archipelago is home to seven World Heritage Sites, including the oldest freestanding megaliths in the world. Mnajdra is one of twenty-three known prehistoric sites and sacred temples that date from around 3700 BCE. In 2009 new protective shelters were built over this archaeological site and the nearby Hagar Qim.

although improvements have been made in the past fifteen years by Malta's sole university.[28] The government, while designating heritage conservation a high priority for the future of its largely tourist-based economy, has traditionally focused more on urban centers such as Valletta and on its prehistoric sites. At the same time, most of Malta's vernacular architecture has not yet been catalogued or protected. Nevertheless, the well-organized government structure, especially including the newly established Heritage Malta, as well as the integration of heritage concerns into the government's diverse activities, indicates that this small Mediterranean country successfully maintains and conserves its cultural heritage.

ENDNOTES

1. Ian Robertson, *Blue Guide: Cyprus* (London: Ernest Bend Ltd., 1981), 21.

2. Josef Štulc, "Report on a Mission to Cyprus," *Report to the Council of Europe*, November 15, 2000, http://assembly.coe.int/Mainf.asp?link=/Documents/WorkingDocs/Doc02/EDOC9460.htm (accessed December 2, 2009).

3. "Destruction of Cultural Heritage," *Embassy of the Republic of Cyprus in Washington, DC*, www.cyprusembassy.net/home/index.php?module=page&pid=? (accessed December 1, 2009).

4. Ibid.

5. ICOMOS Cyprus, "Cyprus," *Heritage@Risk 2006–2007* (Paris: ICOMOS, 2006), 48.

6. Ibid., 47.

7. "Major Projects," The A. G. Leventis Foundation, www.leventisfoundation.org (accessed December 2, 2009).

8. Michael J. K. Walsh, "Cultural Welfare and Political Stalemate: The Case of Northern Cyprus" (paper, College Art Association, 92nd Annual Conference, Seattle, Washington, February18–21, 2004).

9. Michael J. K. Walsh, "Famagusta 2007: An Appeal for International Cooperation," *Heritage@Risk 2006–2007*, 51.

10. Ibid., 52.

11. Jon Calame, "Architects Bridge Diplomatic Gap in Cyprus," *Christian Science Monitor Online*, April 30, 2003, www.csmonitor.com/2003/0430/p09s02-coop.htm (accessed December 1, 2009); Jon Calame and Esther Charlesworth, "Nicosia," in *Divided Cities: Belfast, Beirut, Jerusalem, Mostar and Nicosia* (Philadelphia: University of Pennsylvania Press, 2009).

12. Sophocles Hadjisavvas, "Cyprus: Preserving the Medieval Walls of Nicosia," *Heritage@Risk 2002–2003* (Paris: ICOMOS, 2002), www.international.icomos.org/risk/2002/cyprus2002.htm (accessed December 1, 2009).

13. "Study, Assessment and Design for the Structural and Architectural Restoration of the Bedestan, Nicosia (Cyprus)," *European Union Prize for Cultural Heritage/Europa Nostra Awards 2006* (Paris: Europa Nostra, 2007), 40–41.

14. An example of a successfully averted development project that infringed on protected heritage in Cyprus was a planned underground car park near the moat of the Venetian wall in the capital city Nicosia. The project was approved by the Town Planning Bureau and the Municipality of Nicosia, but it was then opposed by the Department of Antiquities.

15. In the sixteenth century the Holy Roman Emperor Charles V settled the Order permanently on the Maltese islands. Joseph S. Abela, *Malta: A Panoramic History: A Narrative History of the Maltese Islands* (San Gwann, Malta: Publishers Enterprises Group [PEG], 1999), 127.

16. Simon Gaul, *Malta: Gozo & Comino* (London and Old Saybrook, CT: Cadogan Guides and Globe Pequot Press, 1998), 107–108.

17. Anthony Pace, "Malta," in Robert Pickard, *Policy and Law in Heritage Conservation*, 228 (New York and London: SPON Press, 2001).

18. Ibid., 235.

19. Ibid., 229.

20. Ibid., 243. Unfortunately, the extensive damage to Valletta caused by German shelling and bombing during World War II occurred outside the purview of such penalty and reparation provisions.

21. Ibid., 230.

22. Ibid., 229.

23. "Other Entities Established by the Cultural Heritage Act," Superintendence of Cultural Heritage, www.culturalheritage.gov.mt/page.asp?p=3071&l=1 (accessed December 30, 2009).

24. Functions," Superintendence of Cultural Heritage, www.culturalheritage.gov.mt/page.asp?p=3072&l=1 (accessed December 30, 2009).

25. "Who We Are," Heritage Malta, www.heritagemalta.org/aboutus/aboutus.html (accessed December 2, 2009).

26. Linda Eneix, *Tell Me About The Maltese Temples* (Sarasota, FL: OTS Foundation, 2000), 4–7.

27. Two years prior to Mnajdra being vandalized the site was listed on the World Monuments Watch list.

28. Pace, "Malta," 247.

Figure 24-1 The complete restoration and adaptive reuse of Ljubljana Castle in Slovenia's capital between 2000 and 2003 involved an update of the complex's infrastructure, archaeological excavations, the reconstruction of some battlements and parapets, and the restoration of the roof, chapel, and bridge.

CHAPTER 24

The Former Yugoslavia

The fratricidal conflicts of the 1990s destroyed communities and cultural heritage throughout the former Yugoslavia. Especially in Croatia, Bosnia and Herzegovina, and Kosovo, cultural and religious buildings were wantonly destroyed as were those reflecting the region's shared history and traditional role as a crucible of cultures. The overall future of the region's built heritage today depends largely on the fragile and disparate economies of each of the countries created from Yugoslavia's political breakup (Bosnia and Herzegovina, Croatia, Kosovo, Macedonia, Montenegro, Serbia, and Slovenia). While slowly returning to normalcy, the process of rebuilding has been slow, expensive, and painful for most of these countries except Slovenia, which escaped most of the conflict, and Croatia, which recovered quickly. Both Slovenia and Croatia have fared much better than their southern neighbors who have fewer resources available for architectural conservation. In addition, residual ethnic posturing has made outside assistance almost a prerequisite for heritage conservation and restoration in most of the former Yugoslavia. Fortunately, the conflicts have garnered substantial publicity in the international media, which has channeled an enormous amount of overseas funds and expertise to selected projects in the region.

CONSERVATION POLICIES IN THE FORMER YUGOSLAVIA

These newly independent countries actually have long and strong architectural conservation histories and have all adapted the comprehensive infrastructure and policies of the former Yugoslavia to meet their current needs. The Socialist Federal Republic of Yugoslavia was established after World War II by Marshal Josip Broz Tito, who had led the multicultural group of Communist partisans that liberated the country from the Italians and Germans and their puppet governments. Even before hostilities ended, Tito took a proactive approach toward the region's cultural heritage by passing an order through his temporary government concerning its protection and directing military units to avoid destroying important buildings.[1]

Keen to unite Yugoslavia's disparate peoples, after the war Tito actively encouraged the restoration of sites from various eras of southeastern European history. To accomplish this tremendous feat, regional institutes were created in each of Yugoslavia's six republics, as soon as the war ended, and loosely controlled by a central Zavod za zaštitu spomenika kulture (Institute for Protection of Cultural Monuments) in Belgrade. The first heritage law was passed in 1949, and in 1965 its regulations and Yugoslavia's conservation institutions were further strengthened by the new Fundamental Law for the Protection of Monuments. At that time, the Central Registry of Protected Cultural Monuments was established as an inventory of the country's most important historic sites. As Yugoslavia moved toward a looser federal system in the 1970s, the central institute was dissolved and the regional institutes each independently oversaw efforts in their respective republics.

Architectural conservation was taken seriously in Yugoslavia by all layers of society, from the federal, republican, and local authorities to individual citizens. Its practitioners were well-trained leaders in the field who often worked abroad, sharing their expertise and hosting international conferences.[2] By the late 1980s, much of Yugoslavia's historic architecture had been well conserved, comprehensive legal protection had long been in place, and was strictly enforced. Inventories of historic resources had been completed, and a variety of traditional craft and professional conservation training programs had been established. Unfortunately, this illusion of a secure future for Yugoslavia's built heritage was short lived.

The rise of nationalism and separatist movements in the former Yugoslavia resulted in part from the increasing transfer of competencies from the federal Yugoslav government in Belgrade to its constituent republics in combination with the introduction of multiparty elections following the death of the charismatic and popular Tito in 1980. Slovenia and Croatia were the first to declare independence in late 1990, followed quickly by the Republic of Macedonia (accepted into the United Nations as the Former Yugoslav Republic of Macedonia) and Bosnia and Herzegovina. Serbia and Montenegro contested most of these separations in an attempt at first to keep Yugoslavia together, and later to keep together all parts of Yugoslavia where Serbs lived.

As former republics broke away, a reduced Yugoslavia—comprising only Serbia and Montenegro—continued on, and was restructured in 2003 into a loose federation between these two remaining republics, which finally separated into two independent countries in 2006. However, for most of the past two decades, Serbia and Montenegro addressed cultural heritage separately. Kosovo (a former autonomous province in Serbia) also declared independence in 2008, and though Serbia has not recognized this change in status yet, most of the rest of the world has accepted this as the probable final step in the breakup of Yugoslavia.

Yugoslavia's violent collapse in the early 1990s took an overwhelming toll on cultural heritage. Many historic buildings and sites in the region, which had survived for centuries, were ruined or eradicated by the conflict and by destructive political policies. The hard work of Yugoslav conservation professionals unraveled as the remnants of the Yugoslav Army and Serb paramilitaries targeted Catholic and Islamic sites and Croats and Muslims attacked Orthodox sites. In addition, entire villages and historic cities were destroyed by shelling and fighting within them. The 1954 Hague Convention for the Protection of Cultural Property in the Event of Armed Conflict, which ironically Yugoslavia was one of the first countries to sign, was ineffective against this wholesale destruction of cultural heritage in the heart of Europe in the late twentieth century.

SLOVENIA

After achieving independence in 1991, Slovenia established its own Ministry of Culture, within which a Direktorat za kulturno dediščino (Directorate for Cultural Heritage) was added in 1994 to provide guidelines for the care of historic sites, prepare financing plans for conservation, and cooperate with international organizations. Heritage conservation is a clear priority for Slovenia, and its prospects are particularly bright as a result of its robust economy, stable democracy, and accession to the EU in 2004.

Architectural conservation in Slovenia actually began during the nineteenth century, when the Zentrale Kommission (Central Commission) in Vienna instituted restoration guidelines and projects for the entire Austro-Hungarian Empire. A separate regional office for Slovenia was established in 1913. Few new developments occurred during the interwar period in royal Yugoslavia, but after World War II and the formation of Tito's Yugoslavia, a Regionalni zavod za zaštitu spomenika kulture (Regional Institute for Protection of Cultural Monuments) was created in Ljubljana, Slovenia's capital city. Among its many early projects was one of the final works of Jože Plečnik, one of the most important central European architects of the twentieth century and one of Slovenia's most famous native sons. His restoration of the Krizanke Monastery in Ljubljana during the 1950s returned its thirteenth-century church to its former splendor but also converted the complex into a cultural center whose design bears clear marks of his unique architectural style.

When the Yugoslav republic level branches were reorganized in the 1960s, Ljubljana's regional institute was supplemented with additional offices in other Slovene cities. Multidisciplinary groups of professionals at the seven regional offices documented, researched, evaluated, and planned for the protection of historic sites as well as actively promoted public interest in architectural heritage. In the 1970s and 1980s, the historic centers of numerous medieval Slovenian towns were studied and restored, and in 1982 a restoration center was founded to carry out conservation projects on sites and objects throughout Slovenia. The thoughtful urban conservation programs of the 1970s and 1980s were interrupted by the changes of the early 1990s in Slovenia, and many additional towns could benefit from that attention today.[3]

In 1999 independent Slovenia passed new legislation to again reorganize the government institutions responsible for heritage and to strengthen the country's protective guidelines. Today, the Direktorat za kulturno dediščino oversees the overall governance structure of heritage protection in Slovenia; makes legal recommendations and strategical plans; coordinates financing; and interacts with international organizations such as UNESCO and ICOMOS. Within the Direktorat, the interdisciplinary experts and specialists at what is now called the Zavod za Varstvo Kulturne Dediščine Slovenije (ZVKDS, Institute for the Protection of Cultural Heritage of Slovenia) are responsible for conservation and other interventions at sites, and the laboratories at the restoration center carry out research on architectural and object conservation. The restoration center also organizes workshops for professionals and secondary students. Slovenia's strong conservation science field also has a private sector counterpart in the Društvo restavratorjev Slovenije (Association of Slovene Restorers, which was founded in 1993 as a professional voluntary organization for knowledge sharing.

A Central Registry of Cultural Heritage was also established by the new 1999 legislation, which revised the inherited Yugoslav-era listing structure and today includes over 25,300 sites and objects, representing the most important archaeological, historical, art-historical, settlement, ethnological, technological, and natural (parks and gardens) components of Slovene heritage.[4] The Central Registry—and related documentation on its sites—is maintained by the INDOK Cultural Heritage Center and Library, which is a division of the Ministry of Culture that also houses a publically accessible specialized professional library.

The Direktorat's permission is required for any alterations to these registered sites, and impact studies are required when any new development or planning takes place in their vicinity. A Culture and Media Inspectorate ensures legal compliance and has the authority to issue serious fines and to order owners to complete conservation projects.[5] On the other hand, owners of historic sites included on the Central Registry are eligible for government grants of up to 50 percent of restoration costs.

Slovenia has actively participated in the European Heritage Days, a program of the "Europe, A Common Heritage" program, since its inception in 1991, with annual themes reflecting its broad range of historic sites and revealing its commitment to all types of heritage. These themes have included Roman army sites, vernacular architecture, medieval towns, monasteries, parks and gardens, Viennese Secession sites, and twentieth-century architecture.

Slovenia is home to hundreds of fortifications and castles that were built during the early Austrian era, at the time of frequent Ottoman encroachments. Many of these have been extensively restored in recent years, including the Kenda Manor in the village of Spodnja Idrija, which has been converted into a luxury hotel by the Austrian-based Schlosshotel chain. At Ljubljana Castle, the symbol and center of Slovenia's capital, between 2000 and 2003, major conservation work was completed that included extensive archaeological excavations; restoration of the roof, chapel, and bridge; and reconstruction of some battlements and parapets. The project also updated the castle's facilities by making it accessible for the disabled and discretely adding major power, water supply, and climate-control infrastructure beneath its courtyard. Though certainly one of Ljubljana's main tourist attractions, especially considering the unequalled views it offers of the city, the castle's dramatic setting and architecture are increasingly used to host weddings, concerts, performances, exhibitions, and other cultural activities.

The state-of-the-art project at Ljubljana Castle is only one of many similar recent restorations in Slovenia, and in fact the country has become a regional leader in the use of

▲ **Figure 24-2** The well-preserved Adriatic town of Piran, Slovenia, boasts numerous examples of medieval architecture, including the recently restored Church of St. George, situated on a cliff overlooking the town and the sea.

▶ **Figure 24-3** The roofscape of Koper, a coastal Slovenian town with significant surviving medieval-renaissance urban architecture, has been successfully conserved. Image courtesy of Roy Graham.

recent technological developments in architectural conservation.[6] At the Rotunda Carmine in Koper, a Romanesque baptistery in Slovenia's main port city, photogrammetric and geodetic methods were used to document the site, and endoscopic, ultrasound, and thermographic analytical methods were used at the baroque ecclesiastical complex of St. George in Piran, another picturesque historic town on the Adriatic coast.

Despite Slovenia's strong position vis-à-vis other former Yugoslav republics, preserving its architectural heritage has not always been easy. Modernization and economic vibrancy endanger town centers: "Façadism" has often accompanied building renovations, and privatization has returned real estate to former owners who often do not have the financial means to provide adequate upkeep.[7] Nevertheless, Slovenia has accomplished much in the way of architectural conservation and restoration in its short period of independence. With a booming economy geared toward tourism and sufficient financial resources and mechanisms, it appears likely that local conservators will be able to address these deficiencies in an appropriate manner in the near term.

CROATIA

Perhaps nowhere in the former Yugoslavia does the cultural environment and built heritage figure as prominently as in Croatia, in large part because cultural tourism has been one of its largest and most important industries throughout the twentieth century. Today Croatia's heritage conservation network is highly professional and competent, and the outlook for conserving Croatia's splendor, which encompasses six World Heritage Sites and a large stretch of the lush Adriatic coastline, is promising.

Like Slovenia, Croatia's history of conservation began when it was part of the Austro-Hungarian empire, under the Vienna-based Zentrale Kommission, and today's institutions responsible for conservation are outgrowths of ones founded within the former Yugoslavia. New heritage legislation was passed in 1999 and amended in 2003, and the former Yugoslav-era Regionalni zavod za zaštitu spomenika kulture (Regional Institute for Protection of Cultural Monuments) has been renamed the Uprava za zaštitu kulturne baštine (Directorate for the Protection of Cultural Heritage) and reports to the Croatian Ministry of Culture.[8]

The Uprava today has twenty regional conservation centers throughout the country and five specialized departments in Zagreb for archives, inspections, archaeological sites, built heritage, and movable and intangible heritage. In recent years, the Uprava's focus has included inventorying assets, preparing a new Registry of Cultural Property, unifying documentation on historic sites, publishing, sponsoring exhibitions, and pursuing international partnerships and cooperation opportunities.

In 1997 the Hrvatski restauratorski zavod (Croatian Conservation Institute) was founded by merging a number of organizations with similar and overlapping specializations throughout the country.[9] Its materials conservation specialists are well-trained experts who restore everything from mosaics, murals, stucco, paper, and textiles to wood and stone. The Restauratorski zavod includes departments for conserving museum objects, archaeological sites, and historic structures. Recent architectural restoration projects of the Restauratorski zavod have included the Croatian National Theater in Varaždin, the Chapel of Saints John and Paul in Gora, and the Monastery of Our Lady of the Snows in Kamensko. Also overseen by the Ministry of Culture, the Restauratorski zavod collaborates closely with the Uprava za zaštitu kulturne baštine.

The Ministry of Culture has also embarked on creating a comprehensive Web portal on Croatian cultural heritage that involves the digitization of archival, photographic, and other museum materials related to all aspects and forms of the country's cultural legacy.[10] To complete the project, the National and University Library, the Croatian State Archives, and the Museum Documentation Center partnered up in 2007.

Figure 24-4 Vukovar incurred severe damage in the 1991 battle in this Danube River city during Croatia's war for independence from Yugoslavia. Though many structures in Vukovar have been repaired, the restoration of socioeconomic conditions may take even longer, and the region may never return to prewar economic and multicultural social conditions.

Figure 24-5 Damage to buildings and streets during the 1991 shelling of Dubrovnik, including shell marks on its renowned stone-paved Stradun, was repaired with remarkable speed after the conflict.

The Croatian Ministry of Culture is still in the process of cataloging the damage from the 1991 war, when the country's built heritage and its museums were shelled, looted, and otherwise attacked.[11] In 2002 ICOMOS Croatia established a system of six categories of damage, from superficial facade and shrapnel-broken windows to total destruction, and estimated that a total of over 2,400 cultural monuments protected through the Yugoslav-era designation system were damaged, including 136 in the most severe category.[12] The city of Vukovar, on the Danube River directly across from Serbia, was particularly harshly assaulted and extensively destroyed during the war, and much of the city still lies in ruins almost twenty years later, with the cost of rebuilding estimated at over $2.5 billion.[13] The city has gradually moved along the path to recovery and many buildings have been repaired, one by one. However, numerous other buildings remain in ruins, and the cultural divisions within the city are still a source of friction.

Museums have been opened in the few partially restored large-scale buildings in Vukovar, including a museum dedicated to atrocities of the recent war in a former hospital and the Vukovar City Museum in the Eltz Manor. The roof of this mid-eighteenth-century agricultural manor was repaired in 2005 when the ground floor was converted into the museum, and today the facades and upper stories are undergoing complete restoration with support from the Council of Europe and the Croatian Ministry of Culture. Despite this major project, Vukovar remains largely forgotten by the international media and aid organizations, which have focused on Croatia's picturesque Dalmatian cities, though their destruction was small in comparison to the damage in Vukovar.

After its rapid repair, the World Heritage city of Dubrovnik has once again become one of Croatia's top tourist destinations. When the Yugoslav Army and Navy bombed Dubrovnik with more than 2,000 artillery shells in 1991, almost 70 percent of buildings in the historic core of this walled medieval city were hit, including the early-fifteenth-century Old Synagogue, Europe's second oldest synagogue, and the sixteenth-century Sponza Palace, home to Dubrovnik's historical archives.[14] The placement of blue shield markers on sites protected by the 1954 Hague Convention was not only ineffective but seemed to draw fire from the attackers. Such deliberate targeting in Dubrovnik, repeated throughout the former Yugoslavia, was the subject of a war crimes trials that resulted in convictions.[15]

Fortunately, Croatia's extensive international ties and Dubrovnik's worldwide renown enabled the swift garnering of support for the city's reconstruction. The city was added to World Monument Fund's Watch list of endangered sites in 1996. UNESCO estimated the cost of rebuilding the Old City at $10 million and established a Commission for the Rehabilitation of Dubrovnik composed of international experts and local officials. International aid flowed in and new relief organizations were formed, including the Rebuild Dubrovnik Fund, established in 1991 by the American Society of Travel Agents and one of Croatia's largest tour operators, Atlas Ambassador. The Fund raised money through innovative schemes with catchy names like "Buy a Tile" and "Adopt a Monument."[16] The Croatian government and international partners restored the city's distinctive red tile roofs and significant architectural heritage. Efforts have paid off, and Dubrovnik has regained its previous splendor and is once again the "Jewel of the Adriatic," complete with a robust return of tourism.

Split, another World Heritage City on Croatia's Dalmatian coast, has perhaps the longest and strongest conservation history in the country.[17] The city was founded in the seventh century, when local Slavs took refuge inside the ruins of Emperor Diocletian's retirement palace, which had been built three hundred years earlier. The fortified palace on a beautiful natural harbor was constructed of Egyptian white stones, marble, and columns, materials imported by Diocletian at great expense. It remains today a uniquely well preserved and continuously used example of Roman architecture. During the nineteenth century, this palace was one of the first sites in Croatia to benefit from Austrian conservation policies: In 1853 restoration projects were completed by the Honorary Conservator for the city, Vicko Andrić.[18]

Andrić and Frane Bulić, who founded an Archaeological Museum in Split later in the nineteenth century, were Croatia's first modern conservators, initiating a tradition of leadership in the field that continues today. The Universities of Zagreb and Split cofounded a graduate program in architectural conservation there in 1975. The program's research arm was headed by Tomislav Marasović, a prolific author on the city's heritage and an active council member of ICCROM in the 1980s and early 1990s. In 1991 the research center was renamed the Mediterranean Center for Architectural Heritage.

In Split reconstruction projects have been carried out consistently since World War II, including the removal of medieval additions to the Roman-era walls in the 1950s, excavation of Diocletian's palace's basement halls and construction of passageways between key public spaces during the 1960s, and the restoration of the late nineteenth-century Croatian National Theater in the 1970s. A new phase of rehabilitation and management began in 1994 after Croatian independence with the formation of a special Agency for the Historic Core of Split. Medieval houses and monastery complexes have since been restored, the basement halls of Diocletian's palace have been further cleared of centuries of rubble and opened to the public, and the south front of the palace has been consolidated from the inside to prevent further degradation. In the hope that these ambitious efforts will increase cultural tourism and reenergize Split's economy, these projects were in part financed through a $9 million loan from the World Bank.[19]

Though the century of conservation efforts in Split have often included the removal of later additions and the reconstruction of missing elements, the city today is still an extraordinary resource for tourists and scholars. The residents of Split are willing to

Figure 24-6 The famous fourth century Roman peristyle (a) at Diocletian's Palace in Split was restored recently via a financial partnership between the Croatian Ministry of Culture and the World Monuments Fund, among other sources. Because of the extreme historic significance of this part of the complex, conservation work included centimeter-by-centimeter laser cleaning (b) of "black crust" (solidified airborne particulates) from every surface of the peristyle's Egyptian limestone columns and entablatures.

continue paying for improvements to their historic city, as is true in many localities in Croatia, thus it is likely that even without future international aid, community involvement and interest will continue to prioritize restoration efforts in Croatia.[20] Combined with Croatia's strong administrative structure, numerous well-trained professionals, and strengthening economy, it will surely lead to the completion of the significant amount of work left to be done in Croatia.

BOSNIA AND HERZEGOVINA

Bosnia and Herzegovina's declaration of independence in 1992 was followed by a four-year war that was by far the longest and most destructive of Yugoslavia's violent breakup. The three-way conflict between Bosnia's Muslims, Croats, and Serbs, with significant involvement from neighboring Serbia and Croatia, included the deliberate destruction of a large percentage of the country's religious and cultural heritage as well as of many of its historic cities. This extensive damage has created an enormous challenge for the impoverished, multilayered postwar Bosnian government created by the Dayton Peace Agreement in 1995.

In its eighth annex, the Dayton Agreement established the Komisija/Povjerenstvo za očuvanje nacionalnih spomenika (Commission to Preserve National Monuments) with responsibility for designating sites based on their artistic, symbolic, townscape, uniqueness, authenticity, or integrity values.[21] The Komisija drafted a List of Provisional Monuments, including almost eight hundred movable objects and immovable sites, more than half of which are religious in nature, and has also accepted nomination petitions for additional potential sites. Anyone may submit a petition, and the Komisija must make a decision on the proposed site within one year. To date, the Komisija has issued official decisions designating more than 550 sites as National Monuments of Bosnia and Herzegovina. The Komisija monitors the treatment and threats to these sites and maintains a list of Heritage at Risk that currently includes almost forty sites, such as the medieval fortresses in Jajce and Banja Luka, the Mehmed-Paša Sokolovic Bridge in Višegrad, and the St. Nicholas Orthodox Church in Stolac.

Specific regulations for protecting historic sites, as well as for protecting the environment, are also governed by separate legislation in the Federation of Bosnia and Herzegovina and Republika Srpska, the two autonomous entities in Bosnia and Herzegovina established as part of the Dayton Agreement. In the Federation, a Yugoslav-era law from 1985 is still in effect (with amendments from 1987, 1993, and 1994) and in the Republika Srpska the Law on Cultural Property was passed in 1995.[22] In 2002 both entities passed coordinated spatial planning legislation requiring municipal development plans to consider architectural heritage.[23] A preliminary draft of a new state-level law to better coordinate policies and administration throughout all of Bosnia and Herzegovina was prepared in 2004; however, it has not moved forward.[24]

Today, responsibility for actually protecting and conserving designated sites and enforcing the decisions of the Komisija resides with the two autonomous entities. The Republički zavod za zaštitu kulturno- istorijskog i prirodnog nasljeđa (Republican Institute for Protection of Cultural, Historical, and Natural Heritage) of the Republika Srpska Ministry of Education and Culture is responsible for research, prioritizing projects, authorizing conservation and alteration work, and approving archaeological investigations, as is the Zavod za zaštitu spomenika (Institute for the Protection of Monuments) of the Federation Ministry of Culture and Sport. While in recent years the Federation of Bosnia and Herzegovina has managed to fund a number of restoration projects, the Republika Srpska has only very minimally budgeted for heritage concerns.[25]

In addition, three of the ten cantons within the Federation have adopted additional heritage protection laws and established their own local institutes to document, research and conserve historic sites. The Zavod za zaštitu kulturno, historijskog i prirodnog nasljeđa Kanton Sarajevo (Sarajevo Institute for the Protection of Cultural, Historic and Natural Heritage) has been particularly well organized and productive in recent years. The city's first heritage institution, established in 1963, had successfully documented and conserved many historic structures, but it was reorganized in 1997 to reflect the changing times and current concerns and now serves all of the Sarajevo Canton, not just the city. Sarajevo was extensively damaged during its four-year siege in the early 1990s. No building type or area of the city was spared from the indiscriminate shelling,

Figure 24-7 Restoration of the multi-domed and enclosed Bruza Bezistan market building and conversion into the Museum of Sarajevo is one of the city's most successful post-war reconstruction and adaptive reuse projects.

and a few key sites were even targeted for destruction. In its reconstruction efforts, Sarajevo's Zavod has been particularly attentive to the city's multicultural heritage, focusing on churches and mosques, as well as historic bridges and streetscapes.

One of Sarajevo's successful projects includes the restoration of the Bruza Bezistan, a late-sixteenth-century, six-domed, enclosed marketplace built during the Ottoman era, and its conversion into an exhibition space for the Museum of Sarajevo. Since the war ended, this museum, whose mission is to preserve and present the city's multicultural history, has also restored a number of other sites throughout Sarajevo and opened them to the public. Some of these projects include Svirzina Kuća, a typical Muslim family house, and Despića Kuća, a typical nineteenth-century Orthodox family house, as well as the old Jewish Synagogue.[26]

Continued ethnic divisions in Bosnia and Hercegovina pose a major problem for protecting and restoring the country's architectural heritage. Gaining permission to restore historic sites from local governments often controlled by exclusive nationalists has sometimes proved impossible for expelled minorities. For surviving sites, instead of proactive destruction, today's demolition is quiet and subversive: Restoration experts have been denied access, especially to Islamic sites in the Republika Srpska, and such lack of attention will eventually cause fragile mosques and other buildings to deteriorate beyond practical retrieval.

Though Banja Luka, one of Bosnia's largest cities and the current capital of Republika Srpska, witnessed little fighting during the war, important sites like the sixteenth-century Ferhadija Mosque were deliberately destroyed nonetheless. Initial attempts to rebuild mosques in Banja Luka and other cities were met by obstruction from local authorities and rioting from the local Serb population.[27] In 2007 after years of negotiations, court battles and fundraising, work finally began. Stone fragments were carefully analyzed and documented through photogrammetry for potential reuse in the mosque's reconstruction.

Many other historic religious sites throughout Bosnia and Herzegovina have been restored and maintained by their owners: the Catholic, Orthodox, Jewish, and Islamic communities. Most of the major Orthodox churches in the Republika Srpska have been rebuilt in this way, as have most Catholic churches and a few mosques in the Federation. However, many of these restoration or reconstruction projects, including the Church of Jesus the Savior in Banja Luka and the Franciscan Church in Mostar, have resulted in new buildings that only slightly resemble their predecessors, and they certainly have not followed internationally accepted architectural conservation principles and approaches.

In addition to these locally initiated projects, significant progress has been made toward the reconstruction and restoration of Bosnia's heritage with the aid of the international community. Numerous foreign governments and cultural heritage NGOs have invested in projects throughout the country. The World Monuments Fund supported conservation planning for Počitelj, a village dramatically sited on a steep cliffside and used as an artist community until its devastation during the war. The Swedish NGO Cultural Heritage without Borders has participated in the restoration of a tower at Banja Luka's fortress, the Franciscan Monastery of Kraljeva Sutjeska, the National Musuem in Sarajevo and other projects. In 2004 the Council of Europe sponsored preliminary technical assessments for the reconstruction of the Aladža Mosque in Foča and the Serb Orthodox Monastery Complex in Vozuca, as well as the actual conservation of Sarajevo's Jewish cemetery, the ruins of the Catholic Monastery in Plehan, and the medieval tombstones at Radmilja.

No city or site in Bosnia and Hercegovina has received as much international attention in recent years as Mostar and its Stari Most (Old Bridge), built by the Ottomans in the sixteenth century and destroyed by Bosnian Croats in 1993. The damage in Mostar was the most extensive anywhere in Bosnia and Herzegovina and perhaps in all of the former Yugoslavia. The Stari Grad (Old Town), which had undergone a major, Aga Khan Trust for Culture award-winning restoration during the 1980s, was devastated—but soon thereafter, Amir Pašic, a dedicated local architect, began a crusade to gather international support for its rebuilding. He organized a successful series of summer workshops for international architectural conservation students, called Mostar 2004, as an innovative way to bring attention to the city and plan for its rebuilding within a decade.

The workshops were in part sponsored by the Aga Khan Trust for Culture and the World Monuments Fund. The Stari Most and the Stari Grad of Mostar's prewar reputation inspired the collaborative efforts of these two NGOs, UNESCO, NATO peacekeepers, and numerous foreign governments to aid the city in the bridge's reconstruction, which was organized and significantly financed by the World Bank.[28] Though Mostar was listed in 2000 and 2002 on the World Monument Fund's Watch list of endangered sites, in 2004 its reconstructed Stari Most was inaugurated amid great fanfare, and in 2005 the bridge and Stari Grad were inscribed on the UNESCO World Heritage List. The $15.4 million restoration project was hailed as a symbol of reconciliation and focused the world's attention on Bosnia and Hercegovina for a positive reason for the first time in decades. However, in the context of such widespread and traumatic social change associated with the war in Mostar and other locales in the region, some scholars have argued that the reconstruction process is not playing the reconciliatory and inspirational role as effectively as the international supporters of some of these projects have suggested.[29]

Figure 24-8 The fifteenth-century Old Bridge in Mostar was destroyed in 1993 but reconstructed by 2004 thanks to a partnership that involved numerous international organizations and foreign governments. The carefully executed project involved using traditional building techniques as well as stone from the same quarry that was used during the construction of the original bridge.

Success stories such as the efforts of the Museum of the City of Sarajevo and the rebuilding of Mostar and its bridge are models not just for Bosnia and Herzegovina, but for conservationists in post-conflict societies worldwide. However, these achievements must also be seen alongside the obstructionism (and other complications) that still exists in Bosnia and Hercegovina today. In addition to continued ethnic division, Bosnia's heritage is also threatened by the loss of documentation on many sites during the war, dire economic conditions, poorly executed and historically irresponsible reconstructions, and hastily conceived and illegal new construction that is dramatically changing Bosnia's townscapes.[30] While some of the country's highest profile sites have received lavish international attention since the war's end, others—such as Sarajevo's Vijećnica and Višegrad's Mehmed Paša Bridge—have only recently begun to receive the support they need. Dozens of less well-known sites throughout Bosnia and Herzegovina still languish in various states of ruin. It will be a difficult road forward, but many Bosnians, whether Serb, Croat, or Muslim, consider conservation part of their time-honored tradition, and partnerships with international organizations will help them overcome the perils that now face the splintered country's historic sites.

MACEDONIA

Like the other former Yugoslav republics, Macedonia (also known as the Former Yugoslav Republic of Macedonia, or FYR Macedonia) has had a strong tradition of architectural conservation throughout the twentieth century. Its Yugoslav-era Republički zavod za zaštitu similarly fulfilled a variety of conservation objectives, including identification of sites, raising public awareness of heritage issues, and the completion of conservation studies and projects.

Macedonia's capital, Skopje, was the epicenter of massive earthquake in 1963 that destroyed two-thirds of the city's buildings, including much of its architectural heritage. Fortunately the city's famous fifteenth-century Stone Bridge, its expansive

Figure 24-9 The reconstruction of the Old Railway Station in Skopje after a particularly destructive earthquake on July 26, 1963 entailed preserving a ruined portion of the building in its appearance moments after the event. The building now houses the Museum of the City of Skoplje, and the clock on its facade has for half a century displayed the time of the earthquake, when it stopped.

Ottoman-era marketplace, and a few historic churches and mosques survived, and an international aid effort organized by the UN helped with reconstruction efforts. In 1970, when the modernist Old Railway Station was converted into the Museum of the City of Skopje, it was left partially in its half-destroyed state as a reminder of this tragic event in the building and city's history.

In the earthquake's aftermath, the Institute of Earthquake Engineering and Engineering Seismology (IZIIS) was established in 1965 at Skopje's University of Cyril and Methodius with the support of UNESCO. In the decades since, it has been a global leader in researching earthquake resistance, and its consultants have worked in advisory capacities throughout the region as well as in Canada, Azerbaijan, and elsewhere.[31] In 1990 the Getty Conservation Institute partnered with IZIIS and Macedonia's Republički zavod za zaštitu to launch a research project focused on emergency preparedness measures for protecting architectural heritage from seismic disasters. The phased project involved structural analyses and thorough documentation of over fifty Byzantine churches in the area, followed by in-depth material capacity studies including testing a scale model of the early-fourteenth-century Church of St. Nikita "on a seismic simulation shake table."[32] Testing revealed the vulnerability of St. Nikita and similarly constructed churches to earthquakes, and recommendations for preventative retrofitting measures were made. IZIIS continues to carry out similar research today.

After its uncontested declaration of independence from Yugoslavia in 1991, FYR Macedonia's Ministry of Culture assumed responsibility for cultural policy in the new country. In 2004 a Law on Protection of Cultural Heritage was passed establishing a National Council for Cultural Heritage to advise the Ministry in matters of policy, as well as a Cultural Heritage Preservation Department to manage state-owned property, develop heritage inventories, and classify, monitor, and plan for protected sites. The Department also oversees the National Conservation Center in Skopje and its six local branches throughout Macedonia. The Soros Foundation has contributed significant funds toward capacity building within the Department to improve its effectiveness in the upkeep of Macedonia's treasured past, which includes sites of Roman, Greek, Slavic, Byzantine, and Ottoman provenance.

The 2004 law and its 2007 amendments offers protection for Macedonia's movable, immovable, and intangible heritage in two categories: special and significant, with the former referring to sites and objects of universal or national value and the latter sites and objects of a secondary level of importance.[33] Designated types of immovable heritage were divided into monuments, monumental entireties (ensembles and urban centers), and cultural landscapes. In addition, archaeological zones (reserves) can be protected in Macedonia, including areas around known heritage sites that might also contain other as yet undiscovered archaeological sites. Macedonian law also calls for a list of cultural heritage in danger, forbids the sale of state-owned listed properties, obligates private owners to maintain and conserve properties with the Department's authorization for any interventions, and requires municipalities to make heritage protection a goal of both urban and rural land planning.[34]

Numerous international organizations and foreign governments have also assisted Macedonia with specific restoration projects. Through the Ambassador's Fund for Cultural Preservation program, the U.S. Embassy supported the restoration of the stone walls of Skopje's Church of the Holy Savior in 2004 to their original unstuccoed appearance. At the Treskavec Monastery near Prilep, restoration of paintings and a faulty roof began in 2005 through funding provided by the World Monuments Fund. Through special agreements, the Turkish Ministry of Culture and the Turkish Embassy have completed several projects throughout Macedonia, including the current restoration of Skopje's fifteenth-century Stone Bridge. In addition, the World Bank's Community Development and Culture Project has renovated and prepared diverse sites throughout Macedonia for reuse.

a

b

c

Figure 24-10 After being devastated by an earthquake in 1963, Skopje has become a global leader in research on the vulnerability of architecture to this type of natural disaster through the Institute of Earthquake Engineering and Engineering Seismology (IZIIS) at the University of Cyril and Methodius. In the early 1990s, IZIIS partnered with the Getty Conservation Institute to develop strategies for retrofitting Byzantine churches to withstand seismic activity. This project involved shake testing a scale model of the early-fourteenth-century Church of St. Nikita (a, b, and c). Image a. courtesy Stephen Kelley, and images b. and c. courtesy Predrag Gavrilovic, IZIIS, at the University of Cyril and Methodius.

A variety of Macedonian sites have recently been proposed for potential inclusion on the World Heritage List. These range from Byzantine monasteries to the Old Turkish Post Office in Strumica to the Roman Thermal Spas in the Bansko area. However, the mixed natural and cultural Lake Ohrid region, which was added in 1980, remains the Republic of Macedonia's only World Heritage List site today. Some of the historic structures encompassed within the Lake Ohrid site are the thirteenth-century Church of St. Clement, with its extraordinary frescoes and extensive icon collection, and the numerous vernacular medieval buildings in the city of Ohrid, which maintains its historic street pattern. According to a UNESCO report from 1998, the historic buildings included in the Ohrid designation were extremely well maintained; however, general development and new construction threatened the region. It was recommended that the city of Ohrid integrate natural and cultural heritage concerns into its development plans and consider forming buffer zones around specific sites.[35]

One of the many difficulties with which heritage conservationists in Macedonia must contend is interethnic violence, which began after an influx of Albanian refugees from the conflict in nearby Kosovo inspired an Albanian separatist movement in Macedonia. The conflict turned violent in 2001, and as in other parts of the former Yugoslavia, unfortunately involved frequent attacks on cultural heritage. Arson by militant groups has claimed a number of historically significant sites, including the Church of St. Gjogjija, a fourteenth-century Byzantine structure with several important frescoes. Islamic sites, such as the fifteenth-century Charsi Mosque in Prilep, have often been targeted in retaliation. ICOMOS sponsored a fact-finding mission in 2001 to evaluate the extent of the damage in Macedonia, and their report brought international attention to the issue.[36]

A lack of public awareness and interest also poses a threat to cultural heritage in the republic. To combat this problem, the Skopje-based NGO Seizmo (the Association for Highlighting and Popularization of Heritage and Heritage Education) initiated an innovative program in 1999 called "One School—One Monument" in cooperation with the Council of Europe. The concept, based on a similar program begun in Naples in 1992, simultaneously educated the local community about Macedonia's historic sites and introduced the younger generation to its heritage in a dynamic and proactive way. Nine Skopje schools were paired with nine historic sites, including the Skopje Fortress and the Mustafa-Paša Mosque.[37] The "One School—One Monument" project was so successful that it was continued the following year and repeated in a number of other Macedonian cities. It also stimulated the restoration of the tower and west gate of the Skopje Fortress in 2005.

Another innovative recent project in Macedonia is the Living Heritage Network that aims to promote sustainable community regeneration through the development of cultural resources.[38] The project was initiated in 2000 by the Belgian King Baudouin Foundation with additional funds from the Open Society Institute. Through the Living Heritage Network, numerous conservation related projects have been completed, including the publication of books, the organization of craft workshops, the development of Web sites for historic buildings, sites, and towns, and the restoration of a neo-baroque mansion in Bitola and a monastery in Lesnovo.

Figure 24-11 The Lake Ohrid region in the Republic of Macedonia was listed in 1980 as one of UNESCO's first World Heritage Sites under the newly termed mixed (cultural and natural) heritage category. The town of Ohrid is home to well-preserved late-Ottoman urban residential architecture as well as medieval churches and a monastery with an important collection of Byzantine icons.

Figure 24-12 The Living Heritage Network in the Republic of Macedonia initiated in 2000 by the King Baudouin Foundation with additional support from the Open Society Institute promotes sustainable community regeneration through the development of cultural resources. Publications, workshops, Web sites, and two building restorations, including of the Lesnovo monastery (illustrated) have resulted from the initiative.

As a result of its successes, it too was later extended to include projects in Bulgaria, Romania, and Bosnia and Herzegovina.

These projects reflect the interesting ways Macedonia is dealing with the overlapping difficulties of lacking public interest and economic destitution. The successful development and implementation of programs such as these as well as strict legislation and oversight agencies, has meant that despite Macedonia's weak economy, it has demonstrated resourcefulness in its efforts to protect its architectural heritage and offer hope for the future of its built environment. Rarely are students anywhere given an opportunity to combine educationally focused, hands-on work with the remains of their history. Such experiences can instill pride in a shared national history as well as an appreciation of cultural heritage in general and will, in turn, help to mold a future generation sensitive to the needs of those historic sites in the years to come.

SERBIA

Serbia also has a long history of commitment to architectural conservation, beginning after independence from the Ottomans in 1840 when a list of Serbia's important historic sites was made and initial efforts to conserve medieval churches took place. In 1844 King Alexander Karađorđević passed a law protecting ruins and other sites, which was one of the earliest examples of this type of legislation in Europe. However it was during the 1870s and 1880s that Mihailo Valtrović and Dragutin Milutinović introduced institutionalized methodologies establishing the disciplines of architectural conservation, archaeology, and museum studies in Serbia based on the central European models they had become familiar with when studying in Germany.

The earliest experiences in cultural heritage protection in the mid-nineteenth century in Serbia tended to focus on ancient and medieval sites, especially the buildings of the Serbian Orthodox Church. However, throughout the Federal Yugoslav and post-Yugoslav periods, vernacular sites, Ottoman heritage and other urban architecture from the eighteenth through the twentieth century has received significant attention from conservation professionals. For example, mosques in Novi Pazar, including the Altum Alem, were conserved in the 1950s and 1960s, the city's historic center was one of the first urban areas protected in Yugoslav in 1979, and more recently a management plan has been prepared for this intact Ottoman town in the Sandjak region of Serbia. Unfortunately, despite this careful state concern, the heritage of Novi Pazar has begun disappearing in the past few years as a result of protectionism and skepticism by locals of the mostly Belgrade-based specialists and their plans.

As a result of the changing political context, in 1994 the new Cultural Properties Law outlined revised responsibilities of various government institutions as well as new inventory procedures, categories, and heritage valuations. Today the Sektor za Zaštitu Kulturne Baštine (Sector for the Preservation of Cultural Heritage) of the Ministry of Culture and Media oversees designation and protection of architectural and archaeological sites in Serbia. The Sector has maintained the inherited system of designating sites to be protected as Cultural Property of Great Importance, which is now divided into four categories. In Serbia today this list includes over 150 Monuments (individual buildings), eleven Cultural-Historic Spatial Units (districts, cities, and building complexes), sixteen Historic Landmarks (mostly battlefields), and eighteen Archaeological Sites.[39] Unfortunately, the Serbian Ministry of Culture has spent less than 8 percent of its budget on heritage protection in recent years, making it the lowest priority of the Ministry's major responsibilities.[40]

Within the Sektor za Zaštitu, the agency responsible for actual conservation and restoration work at the country's historic sites is the Belgrade-based central Republički zavod za zaštitu spomenika kulture originally established in 1947. The well-staffed but underfunded institute manages to complete nearly one hundred projects at monasteries, castles, and archaeological sites each year.[41] For example, it undertook extensive documentation of the historic town of Sremski Karlovci on the Danube River in the 1990s, prepared a phased conservation plan in 2003, and is currently seeking support for implementation of the town's restoration.

The Republički zavod za zaštitu's work is complemented by that of a network of eleven other heritage-protection institutes located throughout the country, including two focused on the cities of Belgrade and Novi Sad, eight on various regions in Serbia, and one in Kosovo.[42] Each of these regional institutes was founded separately over the past few decades and operates independently. For example, with financial support from the Serbian government in the past few years, the regional institute in Valjevo has explored a Bronze Age archaeological site in Jaričište, restored a rural church in Ljubovija, and carried out conservation work at the nineteenth-century Nenadović Tower.

In Subotica, the regional institute documented and developed a plan for the total conservation and reuse of the city's magnificent five-domed, Hungarian art nouveau synagogue, built in 1902. Conservation professionals in Subotica and elsewhere in Vojvodina, the autonomous province in northern Serbia, have numerous sites representing the region's former Jewish population as well as of its still significant Hungarian minority. Despite stabilization efforts in the 1980s, the Subotica synagogue was in dire condition in the 1990s. As soon as sanctions against Serbia were lifted and prior to the regional institute's proposals, the World Monuments Fund supported priority roof and exterior repairs at the synagogue in 2000 by a team from ICOMOS Hungary.

Another of the independent regional and urban heritage protection institutions in Serbia is the Zavod za zaštitu spomenika kulture grada Beograda (Institute for the Protection of Cultural Monuments of Belgrade), which was established in 1960. Its first projects included restoring the house of Jevrem Grujič, a participant in the nineteenth-century Serbian independence movement; stabilizing the fifteenth-century

Figure 24-13 As in other former Yugoslav republics, Serbia has a long tradition of architectural conservation with numerous important projects completed during the federal Yugoslav period—an example is the stabilization of the fifteenth-century Nebojša Tower at Belgrade's Kalemegdan Fortress in the 1960s by the Institute for the Protection of Cultural Monuments of Belgrade.

Nebojša Tower at Kalemegdan Fortress; and rebuilding the minaret of the Bajrakli Mosque. Belgrade's cultural heritage institute was extremely productive in the 1970s and 1980s, and it became a leader for documentation and conservation methodologies in Yugoslavia.[43] However, with the political changes in the 1990s, illegal construction as well as the institute's marginalization within the country and isolation from international contacts reduced its effectiveness. Without funding for projects, it focused on publishing research studies and staging exhibitions; however, since 2000 its work has returned to normalcy, and it aspires be a regional leader in the conservation field again.

Though its decentralized heritage protection system would seemingly place Serbia right in step with contemporary European trends, it is actually creating problems for the country. The need for a clearly outlined and consistent heritage policy as well as for better legal protection and enforcement, standardized systems of documentation and categorization, and coordinated presentation and interpretation of historic sites has been recognized by the country.[44]

Yugoslavia's legacy of conservation professionalism left Serbia well situated to preserve its heritage. However, its position as an instigator of violent regional conflicts left it isolated, and it is only slowly beginning to recover. Economic sanctions against Serbia in the 1990s prevented the international aid that enabled the restoration of cultural heritage in other former Yugoslav republics in the first postwar decade. Funding for conservation has also been lacking from the Serbian government, whose other priorities and poor administration complicate the tasks of conservation professionals. Today Serbian heritage conservationists are reestablishing relationships with international organizations and professional networks and beginning to gain international aid for restoration projects. Though Serbia has made tremendous strides in trying to improve its international standing, foreign investment and assistance have been slow in coming. For those committed to protecting architectural and archaeological sites in Serbia, the wait is difficult.

MONTENEGRO

Montenegro held a referendum on independence in 2006, and by the narrowest of margins (half a percentage point over the required 55 percent) chose to separate from Serbia. It had already established many independent institutions, including a Ministry of Culture in 1993, which had absorbed the two existing heritage protection institutes in Montenegro. These include the larger Republički zavod za zaštitu spomenika kulture based in Cetinje, which is responsible for most heritage sites in the country, and the Regionalni zavod za zaštitu spomenika kulture (Regional Institute for Protection of Cultural Monuments) based in Kotor, which is responsible for sites in the municipalities of Kotor, Herceg Novi, and Tivat. As in the other former Yugoslav republics, these institutes had existed in various forms and under various names since the end of World War II.

Montenegro passed its own Law on Protection of Cultural Monuments in 1991 that classified heritage sites in four categories: World Heritage sites, sites of special importance (I), of high importance (II), and of importance (III). This law also assigned the responsibility for designating protected sites to the Montenegrin parliament, which has proven a highly ineffective arrangement, though the Republican Institute has submitted numerous proposals, the Parliament did not designate a single site for a decade and a half.[45] Today there are over 350 protected immovable cultural monuments on the Central Registry, which is managed by the Republican Institute.[46]

Architectural conservation efforts in Montenegro have also been hampered in recent years by frequent administrative changes and a lack of professional training opportunities. In addition, the blatant disregard for regulations by property owners, including the Serbian Orthodox Church, complicates heritage protection in Montenegro as it does in Serbia. Looting of Montenegro's archaeological sites is a persistent problem despite stricter policing and consequences for those caught stealing antiquities.

Damage to many important sites in Kotor, which was added to the World Heritage List in 1979 and damaged by an earthquake that same year, was not addressed for decades and was aggravated by long-term exposure to the elements. The rehabilitation of the northern sector of the ramparts did begin in 1983 and was followed in 1990 with plans to develop the complex into a tourist-centered ensemble.[47] In 2001, after sanctions against Serbia and Montenegro were lifted, UNESCO began preliminary cleaning and maintenance efforts at the Kotor Fortress; the U.S. Ambassador's Fund, Japanese government, and Cultural Heritage without Borders also financed additional projects in Kotor. In 2005, under the auspices of the Council of Europe, a preliminary technical assessment of the fortress was carried out to create a comprehensive plan for its conservation and management.[48]

Though Montenegro, like Serbia, has well-established professional heritage conservation organizations, the lack of higher education training in architectural conservation perhaps means fewer heritage professionals in the future. Montenegro also faces an uphill battle to regain lost financial support for their work, because the local economy is weak and the government overstretched in coping with pressing social concerns. Montenegro has realized the need to develop its cultural tourism resources, especially along its Adriatic coast, and to increase international exchanges now that its relations with the world have normalized.[49] Hopefully, its heritage will receive increased attention in the years to come.

a

Figure 24-14 After an earthquake in 1979, the same year that Kotor Fortress in Montenegro was placed on the World Heritage List, various components of the fortress received extraordinary attention and support for conservation from international funders. Figure 24-14a courtesy of ICCROM, Alessandro Balderama, photographer; 24-14b courtesy of Turist Komerc Zagreb; 24-14c courtesty of ICCROM, Jukka Jolikehto, photographer.

b

c

KOSOVO

Prior to 2008, Kosovo was an autonomous entity within first the Yugoslav Republic of Serbia, then Serbia-Montenegro, and then Serbia. Before the breakup of Yugoslavia, architectural heritage protection in Kosovo was limited due to a lack of funding, expertise, and adequate inventories and policies.[50] In the past decade, conflict, political stalemate, and economic stagnation have meant little progress has been made on behalf of Kosovo's cultural heritage, and legal mechanisms and effective management systems are still lacking.

Since the NATO intervention in 1999, Kosovo has been governed by the United Nations Interim Administration Mission in Kosovo (UNMIK). In 2008, after two years of negotiations and proposals, Kosovo declared independence. While over sixty countries have recognized this status, Serbia still has not—so the territory remains contested. Under the auspices of the UNMIK, UNESCO took on the safeguarding of Kosovo's heritage, organizing a series of conferences for donors at which over $3 million was pledged for the reconstruction of Kosovo's important Ottoman Islamic, Serbian Orthodox, and secular sites.[51]

In 2003 UNESCO recommended the formation of a Kosovo Ministry of Culture to assume responsibility for its multicultural heritage, but only recently have administrative powers begun to be slowly transferred to what is now called the Kosovo Ministry of Culture, Youth, and Sport and its Divizioni i Trashëgimisë Kulturore (Division of Cultural Heritage). Four regional conservation institutes also currently exist, and two additional ones will soon be established. However, these institutes are understaffed and underfunded, and their management and training deficiencies are an unfortunate by-product of the region's animosities. According to one expert on heritage policies in the region: "[T]he Kosovo Albanians were excluded from management responsibilities before 1999, which prevented them from being able to acquire experience and training in this field. The Serbians in their turn have been excluded since 1999, taking with them a great body of knowledge and expertise."[52]

The Law on Cultural Property was passed in Kosovo in 1994 but nullified by UNMIK, along with all other legislation in the province passed between 1989 and 1999.[53] Therefore, the Yugoslav-era law from 1977 remained technically in effect in Kosovo, though not followed closely. Based on that law, over four hundred buildings in Kosovo were awarded state recognition and protection, with the most recent addition made in the early twenty-first century. The types of sites on this list was not balanced or reflective of the complexity of Kosovo's heritage; it included 132 churches and monasteries but only 23 mosques, and 96 archaeological sites but no structures from the past century, and only one architectural ensemble.[54]

In 2002 a team representing Kosovo's different communities and including foreign consultants began working on a new law that encompasses architectural, archaeological, movable, and intangible heritage. The Council of Europe organized workshops to help draft the law and made recommendations on the need for financial incentives to encourage private sector involvement in architectural conservation, something that is currently completely absent.[55] After thorough vetting, including a public hearing, the Kosovo Assembly passed the Cultural Heritage Act in 2006.[56]

The 2006 Cultural Heritage Act established the Kosovo Council for Cultural Heritage to make recommendations about sites and to determine which restoration and conservation projects should be funded by the government. The act also called for the creation of a new, more comprehensive inventory of sites to be protected, known as the List of the Cultural Heritage, as well as standardized documentation procedures and a centralized, public collection of this information. Architectural heritage protected by the 2006 act includes monuments, ensembles, and conservation areas, for which state permission is required for any alterations and fines are imposed for infractions (by owners or vandals). Owners of protected properties are required to maintain and conserve their properties, and the state reserves the right to appropriate neglected monuments in exceptional circumstances. Additionally, alterations and new construction within a 50-meter protective zone around architectural monuments also requires state permission.

The administrative complications in Kosovo are compounded by the dire conditions of its architectural heritage; both the multicultural population and cultural heritage of Kosovo were decimated by conflict in the late 1990s. Serbian forces burned homes, mosques, and public buildings in attacks on the region's ethnic Albanians. The ethnic-Albanian Kosovo Liberation Army destroyed many Orthodox churches, monasteries, and homes and expelled many Serbs.[57] The Serbian Orthodox Church estimates that seventy-four churches and monasteries were attacked in the four months between June 13, 1999—the day NATO forces arrived in Kosovo—and October 20, 1999. Another figure estimated that one-third of Kosovo's six hundred Ottoman Islamic mosques were damaged during the 1998–1999 conflict.[58]

A variety of international organizations visited Kosovo and prepared reports in the immediate aftermath of the conflict, including the European Commission in 2000 and the Council of Europe in 2001.[59] In addition to European and global government organizations, the Turkish and Italian governments, Ankara and Harvard universities, as well as NGOs supported by the Swedish, Danish, Norwegian, and Dutch governments have all been involved in documentation and research projects on damaged historic sites in Kosovo. Only a very few conservation projects have actually been carried out, including many mosques that have been restored with support from Islamic charities, in some cases not in adherence with international standards and not to their former appearances.[60]

One ongoing conservation success in Kosovo has been the restoration of the Hadum Mosque complex in Gjakovo, which is being managed by Cultural Heritage without Borders, which established an office in Pristina in 2001.[61] During the conflict in 1999, the wooden portico of the sixteenth-century Hadum Mosque was burnt, the top of its minaret shot off, and its adjacent library with hundreds of books and manuscripts from the seventeenth century onward completely destroyed. The conservation of the mosque has responded to this recent damage as well as ongoing rising damp, exposure issues, and problems caused by earlier conservation attempts. To date, the minaret has been reconstructed with a combination of new and reused stones, holes in the stone columns of the portico were patched and replastered, moss was removed from window and door frames, and incompatible cement from an earlier restoration was removed.[62] In addition, in 2005, the lead covering of the dome was replaced by master craftsmen from Turkey, who trained local workers in traditional construction techniques. In 2008 and 2009,

Figure 24-15 The early seventeenth-century Sinan Pasha Mosque dominates Shadervan Square in the center of Prizren and is noted for its interior paintings of landscapes, floral motifs and Koranic inscriptions, as well as for its well-preserved stone floor and wooden furniture. However, years of water infiltration have resulted in severe deterioration of its interior walls. In 2009, restoration work began at the Sinan Pasha Mosque.

Figure 24-16 Political instability in the Kosovo region has left Dečani Monastery, part of Kosovo's only World Heritage Site, inaccessible and under special protection measures provided by UNESCO.

in partnership with UNESCO, Cultural Heritage without Borders completed the restoration of the mosque's interior paintings and wooden decoration.

Churches, monasteries, and other Orthodox Christian sites are not under the jurisdiction of the Ministry of Culture or the regional institutes—rather, they are directly protected by the Serb Orthodox Church. The religious community has been unable to conserve its properties on its own, and many are in urgent need of attention, but unfortunately the Serbian authorities and other interested parties have for the most part had little access or opportunity to initiate projects at these damaged and endangered sites. The Zavod za zaštitu spomenika kulture in Serbia and an NGO called Mnemosyne, with offices in both Belgrade and Pristina, have tried to start work at sites, including the fourteenth-century Dečani Monastery, which—along with three other groups of churches—is Kosovo's only World Heritage Site. In association with the Central Institute for Conservation in Rome, Mnemosyne published a report on the Metohija region of Kosovo to help publicize the plight of Orthodox churches and monasteries.[63]

In 2006 three other Serbian Orthodox building complexes in Kosovo, including Gračanica and Peć monasteries and the Church of the Virgin of Ljeviša in Prizren, were added to the Dečani World Heritage Site by UNESCO and immediately placed on the List of World Heritage in Danger, due to the management difficulties resulting from political instability. Today these thirteenth- and fourteenth-century churches are Europe's only World Heritage Site on that threatened list. At the Church of the Virgin of Ljeviša, a combined Greek and Czech team completed a preliminary survey of the conditions of the medieval frescoes.

Unfortunately, since Kosovo's de facto independence in 2008, the context for architectural heritage conservation has not improved. Kosovo's political status is still uncertain for some sites, and vandalism against cultural heritage sites still occurs. With few trained conservationists and a weak economy that generates little financial support, prospects are currently bleak. However, on the positive side, there is widespread public interest in architectural heritage in Kosovo as well as continued international assistance.

ENDNOTES

1. Tomislav Marasovic, *Zaštita Graditeljskog Nasljeđa* (Zagreb/Split, Croatia: Drustvo Konservatora Hrvatske, 1983), 181.

2. During the 1960s, Yugoslavia sent a national delegation to Egypt to assist with the relocation of ancient Nubian monuments located upstream from the Aswan Dam. V. Madarić, "La Yougoslavie dans la Campagne Internationale pour la Sauvegarde des Monuments de Nubie," *Commission Nationale Yougoslave Pour L'UNESCO. Tire du Recueil des Traveaux sur Protection des Monuments Historique*, vol. 16 (Paris: UNESCO, 1965).

3. "Heritage Preservation and Restoration," *Slovenia Cultural Profile*, www.culturalprofiles.net/slovenia/Directories/Slovenia_Cultural_Profile/-6825.html (accessed December 1, 2009).

4. "Register of Slovene Cultural Heritage," Kultura—Republika Slovenija, Ministrstvo za Kulturo, http://rkd.situla.org (accessed December 1, 2009); Jovo Grobovšek, "Slovenia: Social and Economic Integration of Cultural Heritage," in *European Research on Cultural Heritage: State-of-the-Art Studies*, 121–6. Originally: Jovo Grobovšek, "Social and Economic Integration of Cultural Heritage in Europe" (paper, 1st Ariadne Workshop, Prague, Czech Republic, April 23–29, 2001).

5. The 1999 laws also gave the Slovenian government the right to appropriate any registered sites it felt could not otherwise be protected, as well as the right to purchase any newly discovered archaeological sites.

6. Mojca Guček, "Modern Conservation Research as Guidelines for Conservation Projects in Slovenia," in Drdácký, *European Research on Cultural Heritage*, 551–558; originally: "Vulnerability of Cultural Heritage to Hazards and Prevention Measures" (paper, 4th Ariadne Workshop, Prague, Czech Republic, August 18–24, 2001).

7. ICOMOS Slovenia, "Slovenia," *Heritage@Risk 2001–2002* (Paris: ICOMOS, 2002), www.international.icomos.org/risk/2001/sloven2001.htm (accessed December 1, 2009).

8. "Cultural Heritage," Ministry of Culture of the Republic of Croatia, www.min-kulture.hr/default.aspx?id=6 (accessed December 2, 2009).

9. "Activity," The Croatian Conservation Institute, www.h-r-z.hr/index_en.asp (accessed December 1, 2009).

10. "Croatian Cultural Heritage," Ministry of Culture of the Republic of Croatia, www.kultura.hr/eng (accessed December 1, 2009).

11. During the conflict, relevant institutions and professionals took extensive steps to protect both Croatia's movable and immovable heritage, including building wooden and sandbag protective structures around important buildings, closing all museums and archives in the country and moving much of their collections to safe locations. In addition, the Yugoslav Army and Serb paramilitaries looted numerous sites and transferred a significant amount of movable heritage to Serbia. Much of this is still unaccounted for and the return of other objects is still being negotiated. Another important question yet to be resolved concerns the future of objects removed from churches that were subsequently completely demolished. Vlado Ukrainčik,"Croatia: War Damage to Cultural Monuments in Croatia," *Heritage@Risk 2001–2002*, www.international.icomos.org/risk/2001/croa2001.htm (accessed December 1, 2009).

12. Vlado Ukrainčik, ICOMOS Croatia, "Croatia: War Damage to Cultural Monuments in Croatia," *Heritage@Risk 2001–2002*, www.international.icomos.org/risk/2001/croa2001.htm (accessed July 15, 2010).

13. Jeanne Oliver, *Lonely Planet: Croatia* (Melbourne: Lonely Planet Publications, 1999), 108.

14. Ibid., 250.

15. Sylvia Gottwald-Thapar and Katherine Rosich, *The Destruction of Art and Architecture in Croatia* (Washington, DC: Croatian Democracy Project, 1992), 2–5.

16. Council of Europe, "War Damage to the Cultural Heritage in Croatia and Bosnia-Herzegovina presented by the Committee on Culture and Education," *2nd Information Report*, doc. 6869 rev. (Strasbourg: Council of Europe, 17 July 1993).

17. Duško Marasović, ed., *Rehabilitation of the Historic Core of Split 2* (Split, Croatia: The City of Split, 1998).

18. John H. Stubbs, "Picking up the Pieces: Heritage Site Conservation in the Former Yugoslavia" (paper, Archaeological Institute of America, Philadelphia, PA, January 4, 2002). Between 1882

and 1908, the bell tower of St. Doimus Cathedral, which was originally built as Diocletian's mausoleum, was reconstructed in a project that was extremely advanced for the time. However, in addition to stabilizing the tower, the intervention resulted in extensive replacement of historic material and the conversion of its uppermost story from its original Gothic-Renaissance appearance to being more in the Romanesque style.

19. Maha Armaly, Stefano Pagiola, and Alain Bertaud, "Economics of Investing in Heritage: Historic Center of Split," in *Historic Cities and Sacred Sites: Cultural Roots for Urban Futures*, eds. Ismail Serageldin, Ephim Shluger, and Joan Martin-Brown (Washington, DC: World Bank, 2001), 166.

20. Ibid, 171.

21. According to the Dayton Agreement, the Commission's five members were originally appointed as follows: two by the Federation, one by Republika Srpska, and two by UNESCO. In 2001 this procedure was revised, and now all five members are appointed by the Bosnian Presidency, but the Commission still includes one member representing each of Bosnian's three ethnic groups and two international members. *The General Framework Agreement: Annex 8 Agreement on Commission to Preserve National Monuments*, Dayton, Ohio, December 1995.

22. Robert Pickard, ed., Report: "Bosnia and Herzegovina," *Analysis and Reform of Cultural Heritage Policies in Southeast Europe* (Strasbourg: Council of Europe, 2008), 31.

23. The High Representative, the international administrator overseeing implementation of the Dayton agreement, forced Republika Srpska to pass this new heritage law in coordination with the Federation, after repeated stalling on the issue. Within Bosnia and Hercegovina, the Brčko District is an independently governed city that has its own Commission for Heritage within its Department of Town Planning.

24. Pickard, "Bosnia and Herzegovina," 32.

25. Ibid., 35.

26. "Muzej Sarajeva/Museum of the City of Sarajevo," Muzej Sarajeva, www.muzejsarajeva.ba (accessed December 1, 2009).

27. The foundation-stone-laying ceremony for the Ferhadija in 2001, as well as a similar ceremony in Trebinje that same year, were interrupted by attacks from angry protesters. The Osman Paša Mosque in Trebinje and a number of other mosques in Banja Luka have since been reconstructed.

28. Emily Gunzburger Makaš, "Interpreting Multivalent Sites: New Meanings of Mostar's Old Bridge," *Centropa* 5, no.1 (January 2005): 62, and *Reclaiming Historic Mostar: Opportunities for Revitalization* (New York: World Monuments Fund/Aga Khan Trust for Culture, 1999), 3–4.

29. For more information, see: Emily Gunzburger Makaš, "Representing Competing Identities: Building and Rebuilding in Mostar" (doctoral dissertation, Cornell University, 2007); Makaš, "Interpreting Multivalent Sites: New Meanings of Mostar's Old Bridge," 59-69; Jon Calame and Kirsten Sechler, "Is Preservation Missing the Point?" *Future Anterior* 1, no. 1 (Spring 2004): 58-64; and Jon Calame and Amir Pašić, "Post-Conflict Reconstruction in Mostar: Cart Before the Horse?" *Divided Cities/Contested States Working Paper No. 7, 2009* (Cambridge, UK: Conflict in Cities, 2009), www.conflictincities.org/workingpaper07.html (accessed December 3, 2009).

30. "Bosnia and Herzegovina," *Heritage@Risk 2000* (Paris: ICOMOS, 2000), http://www.international.icomos.org/risk/world_report/2000/bosni_2000.htm (accessed July 15, 2010).

31. "Building Structures and Material: Design, Analysis and Testing," Institute of Earthquake Engineering and Engineering Seismology (IZIIS), www.iziis.edu.mk/departments/dep222.htm (accessed December 30, 2009).

32. William S. Ginnell, "Coping with the Seismic Threat: Byzantine Churches in the Balkans," *Getty Conservation Institute Newsletter* 9, no. 3 (Fall 1994), www.gettymuseum.us/conservation/publications/newsletters/9_3/balkans.html (accessed July 15, 2010).

33. "Law on Protection of Cultural Heritage," Ministry of Culture of the Republic of Macedonia, http://uzkn.gov.mk/dokumenti/Law on Cultural Heritage.pdf (accessed December 20, 2009).

34. Ibid.

35. Because of its importance to the history of the Macedonian Orthodox Church and to the country, the ninth-century Monastery of St. Panteleimon, the oldest known Slav monastery, was completely reconstructed on its ruined foundations beginning in 2000. Though the project seems to have disregarded accepted treatment of archaeological sites, it has had one unquestionably

positive outcome: Floor mosaics from a fourth-century church were discovered in the monastery's courtyard during the course of the reconstruction. UNESCO World Heritage Committee, "Ohrid Region with its Cultural and Historical Aspect and Its Natural Environment (Macedonia, Former Yugoslav Republic of)," *State of Conservation Report—1998* (Paris: UNESCO, 1998).

36. ICOMOS's investigation focused on the fourteenth-century Orthodox Monastery at Matejce, which had been taken over and used as a headquarters for a separatist militant group and whose murals had been defaced and roof seriously damaged. Lazar Sumanov, "Macedonia: Matejce Mission Provisional Report," *Heritage@Risk 2001–2002*, www.international.icomos.org/risk/2001/mace2001.htm (accessed December 3, 2009).

37. "One School—One Monument," Edno Učilište—Eden Spomenik, www.unet.com.mk/school-monument/sdefault-e.htm (accessed December 2, 2009).

38. "Living Heritage —Network: Community Development through Cultural Resources," Living Heritage Network—Macedonia, www.zivonasledstvo.org.mk/default_en.asp (accessed December 2, 2009).

39. "Kulturna Dobra od Izuzetnog Značaja," Ministarstvo Kulture, www.kultura.sr.gov.yu/?jez=&p=561 (accessed December 30, 2009).

40. In recent years, the Serbian Ministry of Culture has spent significantly more on the performing arts, radio and television, museums, and libraries than it has on the conservation and protection of cultural heritage. In addition to underfunding, built heritage in Serbia today faces numerous additional risks, both natural and human-made. Frequent earthquakes continue to compromise the structural integrity of historic buildings, including to the fifteenth-century Church of St. Elijah, which was damaged by tremors in 1998. "Serbia/6. Financing of Culture: 6.4 Sector Breakdown," *Compendium: Cultural Policies and Trends in Europe* (Strasbourg: Council of Europe, c2005), www.culturalpolicies.net/web/serbia.php?aid=64 (accessed December 2 2009); ICOMOS Yugoslavia, "Yugoslavia," *Heritage@Risk 2001–2002*, www.international.icomos.org/risk/2001/yugo2001.htm (accessed December 2, 2009).

41. "Serbia/4.2. Recent Policy Issues and Debates: 4.2.9 Heritage Issues and Policies," *Compendium: Cultural Policies and Trends in Europe*, www.culturalpolicies.net/web/serbia.php?aid=429 (accessed December 2, 2009)

42. Serbia does not recognize the independence of Kosovo (a former autonomous region in Serbia that declared independence and was internationally recognized in 2008), and maintains a Kancelarija za obnovu i očuvanje kulturne baštine na Kosovu i Metohiji (Office for the restoration and protection of cultural heritage in Kosovo and Metohija), based in the north-Kosovo town of Leposavić.

43. "Brief History," Institute for the Protection of Cultural Monuments of Belgrade, www.belgrade-heritage.com/eng/onama/?conid=2 (accessed December 2, 2009).

44. "Serbia/4.2. Recent Policy Issues and Debates," *Compendium: Cultural Policies and Trends in Europe*, www.culturalpolicies.net/web/serbia.php?aid=421 (accessed July 2, 2010).

45. Steering Committee for Culture, "Cultural Policy in Serbia and Montenegro: Part II: Republic of Montenegro, National Report," European Programme of National Cultural Policy Reviews: MOSAIC Project, (Strasbourg: Council of Europe, 2004), 13.

46. Lidija Ljesar and Vasilije Busković, "Montenegro," in Pickard, *Integrated Management Tools in the Heritage of South-East Europe*, 87–88.

47. Ilija Lalošević, *Kotor Fortress: Studies, Conservation and Revitalization* (Kotor: Regional Institute for the Protection of Cultural Heritage, 2003), 22.

48. Lidija Ljesar, *Preliminary Technical Assessment (PTA): Fortifications of Kotor, Kotor, Montenegro, Serbia and Montenegro* (Strasbourg: European Commission and the Council of Europe: 2005).

49. "Protection of Cultural Monuments."

50. Robert Pickard, "Kosovo/UNMIK," in Pickard, *Analysis and Reform of Cultural Heritage Policies in Southeast Europe*, 65.

51. "Protection and Preservation of Cultural Heritage in Kosovo," UNESCO Cultural Sector (2005), http://portal.unesco.org/culture/en/ev.php-URL_ID=36086&URL_DO=DO_PRINTPAGE&URL_SECTION=201.html (accessed December 2, 2009).

52. Pickard, "Kosovo/UNMIK," 66.

53. Ibid., 64.

54. *A Future for Pristina's Past* (Pristina: IKS/European Stability Initiative, 2006), 9.

55. Ibid., 67.

56. "Cultural Heritage Law (2006/02-L88)," Kosovo Assembly, www.assembly-kosova.org/?cid=2,191,205 (accessed December 30, 2009).

57. Robert Fisk, "NATO Turns a Blind Eye as Scores of Ancient Christian Churches Are Reduced to Rubble," *The Independent*, Nov. 20, 1999, www.yuheritage.com/indy.htm (accessed December 2, 2009).

58. Andras Riedelmeyer and Andrew Hersher, "Architectural Heritage in Kosovo: A Post-War Report," September 2000, http://cool.conservation-us.org/byform/mailing-lists/cdl/2000/1124.html (accessed December 10, 2009).

59. Council of Europe, *Study on the State of Cultural Heritage in Kosovo* (Strasbourg: Council of Europe, 2001); European Commission, *Kosovo Damage Assessment CD-ROM* (Brussels: European Commission, April 2000).

60. Rita Gaber, "Preserving Sacred Sites in Kosovo After The War," *Site Saver: The Newsletter of Sacred Sites International* 11, no. 2 (Winter 2001): 6.

61. The conservation of the Hadum Mosque was initiated by the American organization Kosovo Cultural Heritage Project, with funding from the Packard Foundation; since 2003, though, it has been coordinated by Cultural Heritage without Borders.

62. Andrew Hersher, ed., *Heritage After War: The Hadum Mosque Restoration* (Prishtina: CHwB Kosovo Office, 2007), 57–71.

63. Pickard, "Kosovo/UNMIK," 68.

a

b

Figure 25-1 Since the 1990s, the international response to the need for assistance at Butrint, Albania's most famous archaeological complex and only World Heritage Site, has come mainly from the UK-based Butrint Foundation. Conservation planning has addressed issues of general site interpretation. In addition, various components have been conserved, such as the theater (a) and the exposed Roman mosaics in the Baptistery (b). Courtesy of and copyright the Butrint Foundation.

CHAPTER 25

Albania

Many important historical buildings and archaeological sites can be found in Albania's mountains and along the eastern shores of the Adriatic and Ionian seas, reflecting the succession of conquering empires and rulers who arrived to profit from the region's strategic trade location and mineral wealth. The ancient Illyrians, who originally inhabited what is today Albania, left little material evidence—however, remains of the Greek settlers, who began establishing colonies in the area in the fourth century BCE, can be found at the ancient cities of Epidamnus (now Durres) and Apollonia. The Romans also founded cities whose ruins still mark the Albanian countryside. In addition, Byzantine-era churches and Ottoman-era mosques enrich many Albanian cities.

Today this diverse legacy is threatened by economic stagnation in Albania. However, certain developments suggest cause for new hope for the future of architectural heritage in Albania. International assistance has increased in recent years and Albania has begun participating in international organizations that share information and expertise related to cultural heritage and architectural conservation since the democratic transition in the early 1990s. Also in the past two decades, Albania has frequently reorganized its new administrative structures for cultural heritage protection as it moves to learn from and catch up with European best practices.

EARLY EFFORTS AND COMMUNIST ERA ACCOMPLISHMENTS AND SETBACKS

Albania's rich heritage of archaeological sites has been explored since the early nineteenth century, when the Ottoman viceroy, Ali Pasha, began excavating them to acquire treasures for his personal collection. François Poqueville, Napoleon's consul-general to the pasha's court, and Martin Leake, a local British agent, systematically investigated and recorded the region's archaeological monuments, publishing their findings in 1821 and 1835, respectively.[1] By the turn of the century, French archaeological missions were exploring Epidamnus and Apollonia, and Austrian archaeologists arrived just prior to World War I.

Following a long struggle, Albanian independence was finally achieved in the early twentieth century. Ahmet Zog, a former army officer elected president in 1925, proclaimed himself king three years later and soon instituted legislation to protect cultural heritage. Albanian archaeology received a boost when Mussolini, one of Zog's supporters who was suspicious of the French missions, sent Luigi Maria Ugolini to excavate several sites.[2] King Zog closed the important archaeological site of Butrint to the public in order to protect it, yet allowed Italian archaeologists to continue excavations and conduct special tours there.

After World War II, Albania's Marxist dictator Enver Hoxha sealed the country's borders and isolated its population. Today Albania's built patrimony includes over 750,000 concrete pillbox bunkers built to protect its shores from foreign invasions that never came. This seclusion separated the country from the postwar industrialization experienced by most of Eastern Europe, an economic disadvantage from which Albania is still trying to recover. Though the Hoxha era may have been detrimental to Albania's social development, it provides today's heritage conservationists with a host of potential projects on which to work and learn, because the retention of a static agricultural society kept much of Albania's historic sites intact and largely unspoiled.

In 1948 the Instituti Shqiptar i Arkeologjisë (AIA, Albanian Institute of Archaeology) was opened on the initiative of Ugolini and with Hoxha's support. Hoxha hoped its work would glorify the country's past and link the population to its illustrious Illyrian roots. The AIA was charged with archaeological research, study, and excavation, and it also administered the country's five archaeological museums in Tirana, Durres, Apollonia, Butrint, and Korce as well as their archives.

Hoxha's approach to Albania's valuable patrimony was sadly inconsistent. Though he supported the AIA and refused Nikita Khrushchev's request to build a submarine base in Lake Butrint because it would destroy Greek, Roman, and Byzantine sites, after his return from Asia he emulated China and its Cultural Revolution by confiscating mosques, churches, monasteries, and shrines.[3] Even worse, his ban on religion was accompanied by a call to desecrate and damage the country's religious institutions. Many historic mosques, Orthodox and Catholic churches, and unique Bektashi dervish monasteries called *tekkes*, were destroyed or damaged.[4] Tragically, these sites—which had survived centuries—were lost in the 1960s. A full assessment of the damage cannot be made until sealed records in Tirana and Moscow are searched—consequently, the extent of this destruction of Albanian heritage remains unknown.[5]

ARCHITECTURAL CONSERVATION IN ALBANIA TODAY

In the early 1990s, the new democratic rulers were keen to invest in the country's cultural inheritance, which today includes 1,500 "First Class" cultural heritage sites. These include archaeological remains, fortresses, town centers, and religious and other buildings.[6] Though Hoxha had formally ratified the Convention that established the World Heritage Committee in 1979, Albania only began to adhere to its principles in 1989. Two years later, within the new democratic government, the Ministry of Culture, Youth, and Sports was formed by presidential decree, and in 1998 a Drejtoria e Trashëgimisë Kulturore (Directorate of Cultural Heritage) was formed within the Ministry to oversee most of Albanian cultural heritage.[7] The first post-Hoxha law concerning heritage was passed in 1994, but it was soon supplanted by the Cultural Heritage Act of 2003, which was amended in 2006 to include a National Committee on National Heritage as an advisory body. In privatization cases concerning registered buildings, the Albanian state has typically either purchased the properties outright or returned them to their former owners and then rented them.

Since 2007, the administrative structure in Albania has been reorganized within the Ministry of Tourism, Culture, Youth, and Sport, in a way that clearly recognizes the economic development potential of protection, conservation, and presentation of historic sites through its combined Directorate of Tourism and National Heritage. Within the Directorate, the Institute of Monuments and its eight regional departments manage the protected sites and buildings, while Albania's nine national museums are concerned with movable cultural heritage.

The Albanian government has also taken important steps to secure sites that were in danger from overdevelopment, decay, and, most seriously of all, theft. In response to the widespread looting of archaeological sites that accompanied the 1997 economic collapse, the government passed a Law for the Protection of Cultural Property in 1999, which brought attention to the issue of preserving Albania's heritage and designated Butrint and its surrounding area as a national park.

With the transition to democracy in 1990, financial assistance weakened as resources were redeployed into the impoverished economy, and the state stopped funding the AIA and its museums and publications.[8] Many young scholars emigrated and architectural conservation began to depend on the few foreign missions still working in the country. International aid has continued to be the primary source of support for architectural heritage in Albania until the present.

As early as 1993, the United Kingdom–based organization the Butrint Foundation was formed by Lord Jacob Rothschild and Lord John Sainsbury to answer the growing threat of unrestricted development of the coast and deterioration of the many structures located within the newly listed World Heritage Site of Butrint.[9] The city of Butrint, the ancient Greek settlement, is one of the Mediterranean's most important classical archaeological sites: Homer places its origins at about the twelfth century BCE, although recent archaeological evidence suggests that the settlement was not constructed until about four centuries later. This important cultural center became an integral part of the Roman empire when Julius Caesar colonized it in 44 BCE and settled his veteran soldiers there. Today evidence of several Roman villas, theaters, bathhouses fed by aqueducts, and the grid street pattern have all survived, as have Byzantine-era churches and fortifications, which were later complemented by houses and a triangular fortress constructed by the Ottomans.[10]

Over 10,000 visitors come each year to see this layered city, and it is hoped that with careful management a tenfold rise in visitors over the next few years can be sustained without damaging the site and its surroundings.[11] The Butrint Foundation's work at Butrint both promotes archaeological research and creates a tourist destination attractive to visitors from Corfu and from Mediterranean cruise ships. In 1999 the California-based Packard Humanities Institute also started supporting work at Butrint, and within five years had contributed about $5 million for research there as well as in support of the Albanian Rescue Archaeology Unit.[12]

Butrint is not the only site to benefit from international aid. The Hebrew University Institute of Archaeology has partnered with a delegation of American Institute of Architects to work at the fifth- and sixth-century synagogue uncovered at Saranda, the oldest discovered in the region. The U.S. National Endowment for the Humanities, the National Geographic Society, and the Institute of Aegean Prehistory are among the other institutions that hae been active in supporting research and protection of Albanian architectural heritage.

The seventeenth-century Voskopoja churches of Korca, built when the town was a prosperous *entrepôt* of Venetian-Constantinople trade, have also received increased attention as a result of efforts by Patrimoine sans Frontières, a French organization. The churches' precious frescoes are threatened by dampness, as imperfect roofs and structural decay have contributed to their deterioration. Funds from Patrimoine sans Frontières, as well as from the World Bank, the World Monuments Fund, and the Institute of Cultural Monuments, have allowed the structural repair of the foundations and roof, conservation of its frescoes, and measures for improved protection against earthquakes.

Several Islamic organizations and the governments of some Islamic countries have restored and rebuilt some of Albania's mosques, many of which are in disrepair after a half century of disuse. The Orthodox Church is also reasserting itself by restoring surviving historic churches, though to date many churches either remain in a state of disrepair or have been converted to other uses. Both Orthodox and Muslim leaders in Albania have condemned the flagrant destruction of religious sites by extremists.[13] The most notorious case of vandalism occurred in 1995 when the eighteenth-century frescoes in the St. Michael Church in Voskopoja were allegedly destroyed by students at a nearby Iranian

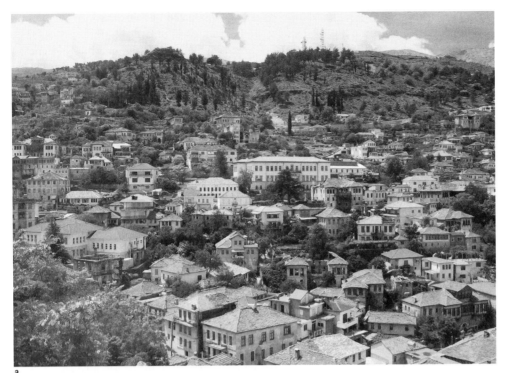

Figure 25-2 The Ottoman residential and commercial architecture in Gjirokastër (a) has been recognized and conserved by UNESCO in recent years. The city is significant for many eras of Albanian history, as it is home not only to significant early modern heritage but also to a medieval citadel (b) and other elements of such towns, including a house museum at the birthplace of Enver Hoxha.

a

b

school. The Albanian Ministry of Culture reacted quickly, ordering the Islamic schools in the country to close and establishing a commission to restore the remaining frescoes at the church.

St. Michael's and four other seventeenth- and eighteenth-century churches in Voskopoja are all that remain of this vibrant Christian center from the Ottoman period. Centuries of conflict, earthquakes, and inclement weather in the region have caused the loss of twenty churches from the period as well as the severe deterioration of those that have survived into the early twenty-first century.

Other sites and historic cities remain in immediate danger from very different threats. Hoxha's birthplace, the historic city of Gjirokastër, was an important Ottoman-era administrative center, and its heritage includes splendid examples of Bektashi and Ottoman structures overlooked by a thirteenth-century citadel. Today the citadel houses the National Museum of Arms. Despite Gjirokastër's significance, it was threatened by a lack of financial support and attention and was slowly deteriorating and losing its architectural integrity.[14] In 2005 Gjirokastër was added to the World Heritage List, and UNESCO intervened to assist the conservation of the town's historic core, including its characteristic *kule*, or tower houses, as well as its mosques and bazaar.

Throughout the 1990s negligible state funds were allocated for the restoration of the late-nineteenth-century Korca Bazaar, the most intact market of its kind in southeastern Europe. Today the complex is in a state of disrepair, though it has been placed under state protection.[15] Another endangered site is the twelfth- or thirteenth-century Byzantine church and monastery of Shen Nout, which is located in the traditionally Catholic Mirdita region in the north. Restoration of the church was completed in 1999, with support from the Austrian Ministry of Culture; however, no funds were earmarked for its monastery, which is deteriorating and vulnerable to the elements.[16]

Prospects for heritage conservation in Albania are positive, yet the threats are real and immediate. The government, seeking to attract tourist money, has begun to prioritize the restoration of its built environment. However, the looting of heritage sites needs to be curbed by proper security measures at important archaeological sites. Although Albania has escaped the mass destruction that occurred in the former Yugoslavia, it still must cope with a multireligious population with extreme elements that occasionally attack sites important to others. Finally, the government's approach to funding by Islamic and Christian charities is unbalanced, and it should more actively consult with professionals regarding which approaches and practices best meet their heritage conservation needs.

As in other newly independent European nations, a number of government officials and ministers have worked in fields closely related to cultural heritage conservation.[17] The first prime minister after Hoxha's death in 1985 was an archaeologist. The son of Hasan Ceka, a pioneer of Albanian archaeology, is today the director of Albania's Institute of Archaeology and a founding member of the Democratic Alliance, a political party that is part of the post-1997 government. This mélange of professionalism and politics will hopefully ensure that the efforts of ICOMOS Albania and other organizations are ultimately successful in preserving its cultural landscape and historic built environment. This Adriatic Sea country is a nexus of civilizations that deserves to have the world see its innumerable and intriguing heritage sites. Though small and not widely known because of its twentieth-century isolation, Albania "is not a backwater but an archaeological hotspot."[18]

ENDNOTES

1. Diana Michelle Fox, "Under Albanian Soil," *Archaeology*, August 12, 2004, www.archaeology. org/online/features/albania/index.html (accessed December 2, 2009).

2. Ibid.

3. Richard Hodges, "Archaeology in Albania after Kosovo," *History Today* 50, no. 3 (March 2000): 3–4.

4. These *tekkes* were constructed by members of the Islamic Bektashi sect and incorporated elements from Zoroastrianism, Buddhism, Christian, and some pagan religions in their designs.

5. James Pettifer, *Blue Guide: Albania & Kosovo* (London: A & C Black, 2001), 94.

6. ICOMOS Albania, "Albania," *Heritage@Risk 2000* (Paris: ICOMOS, 2000), www.international.icomos.org/risk/world_report/2000/alban_2000.htm (accessed December 3, 2009).

7. "Albania/1. Historical Perspectives: Cultural Policies and Instruments," *Compendium: Cultural Policies and Trends in Europe* (Strasbourg: Council of Europe, 2005), www.culturalpolicies.net/web/albania.php (accessed December 1, 2009).

8. Fox, "Under Albanian Soil."

9. Listing of Butrint on the World Monuments Fund's Watch list in 1996, 1998, and 2000 helped raise concern and stimulate the formation of the Butrint Foundation. Both Jacob Rothschild and David Sainsbury were WMF Hadrian awardees in 1995 and 1999, respectively.

10. "Butrint: A Brief Introduction," The Butrint Foundation, www.butrintfoundation.co.uk/history.htm (accessed December 2, 2009).

11. Richard Cavendish, "Butrint's Byzantine Heritage: Archaeological Wonders in the Mediterranean," *History Today* 45, no. 3 (March 1995): 3–4.

12. Fox, "Under Albanian Soil."

13. The Society Farsarotul, "Attack on Our Cultural and Spiritual Monuments in Albania," *Newsletter* (1995), www.farsarotul.org/nl19_5.htm (accessed December 2, 2009).

14. ICOMOS Albania, "Albania," *Heritage@Risk 2000*.

15. ICOMOS Albania, "Albania," *Heritage@Risk 2002–2003* (Paris: ICOMOS, 2002), www.internationa.icomos.org/risk/2002/albania2002.htm (accessed December 2, 2009).

16. Pettifer, *Blue Guide*, 178–179.

17. Scholars, artists, and others working in the humanities tended to be the people most trusted as new leaders in a number of Europe's fledgling democracies in the 1990s, a prime example being playwright-politician Václav Havel in the Czech Republic.

18. Fox, "Under Albanian Soil."

Figure 26-1 The restoration in 1983 of the Basilica of Hagia Sophia in Bulgaria's capital city of Sofia was carried out with assistance from the Soviet Union in connection with the celebration of Bulgaria's 1300th anniversary.

CHAPTER 26

Bulgaria

As is true for most southeastern European countries, Bulgaria's cultural heritage is a mixture of styles and types reflecting the series of successive cultures that have dominated the region. Treasured architectural sites today include: Thracian royal tombs with Hellenistic decorative influences, early medieval stone and wood monasteries from the "golden age," smaller and later medieval churches with beautiful murals, grand mosques of the Ottoman era, and late nineteenth- and early twentieth-century expressions of national independence. Following the meeting of the great powers of Europe at the Congress of Berlin in 1878, Bulgaria gained autonomy within the Ottoman Empire, with full independence coming in the early twentieth century. After World War II, Bulgaria fell under the heavy influence of the Soviet Union.

Conservation has had a long and treasured history in Bulgaria, especially for sites associated with the Orthodox Church. During the Ottoman era, prominent Bulgarian merchants donated funds to revitalize damaged monasteries. The first statutes regarding heritage were passed in 1888 and 1890—just after autonomy—and legislation followed in 1911 and 1936, protecting sites and calling for state ownership of the most important among them.[1] During the Communist era, architectural heritage protection was characterized by strong centralization, an ideological approach to culture, and the nationalization of sites. Few individuals or private organizations participated in architectural conservation and restoration projects, and the state had a monopoly in the field except for a few church projects sponsored by religious organizations.[2]

Today architectural conservation is achieved in Bulgaria through the cooperation of state and local governments with international organizations, foreign governments, and local nongovernmental organizations. Comprehensive new legislation in 2009 has streamlined the oversight and protection of Bulgaria's heritage, and the country is poised to take greater leadership role in the field now that Bulgarian diplomat Irina Bokova is director general of UNESCO.

LATE TWENTIETH-CENTURY FRAMEWORKS AND CHALLENGES

Though the Bulgarian National Committee of ICOMOS was founded in 1960, modern heritage protection in Bulgaria had little momentum until 1969, when the Institute for Cultural Monuments was created within the Ministry of Culture and comprehensive legislation to protect cultural heritage was passed. The Monuments of Culture and Museums Act provided for government financial responsibility for private properties, though owners were required to maintain their properties, and there were restrictions on sales. In celebration of Bulgaria's 1300th anniversary in 1983, the Soviet Union channeled resources to restore cultural heritage that reflected the Bulgarian spirit—conspicuously absent from these efforts were Ottoman-era mosques.

Bulgaria's economy was hit hard when the Soviet Union dissolved in 1991 and its subsidies ended. The severe drop in funding had a harsh effect on the country's historic sites: The staff of the National Institute for Monuments of Culture dropped from three thousand to sixty within a year. Though in 1981 the Bulgarian government spent the equivalent of $29 million on cultural heritage, that amount plummeted to the equivalent of $200,000 annually by the mid-1990s.[3] According to Dimitar Kostov, this is "barely enough to meet the emergency conservation needs of a negligible number of monuments."[4] Since Bulgaria's socialist government was overthrown in 1996, the economy has markedly improved, although high unemployment, poverty, and inflation are still serious problems. This stagnation has significantly reduced the already minimal funds allocated to restoration projects at several key sites.[5]

Physical factors compound the negative effects of insufficient resources for architectural conservation in Bulgaria today. The Communist-era drive to industrialize created numerous factories that are polluting air and water in some areas of the country. Such health hazards also accelerate rates of deterioration of rock structures, including two of Bulgaria's nine World Heritage Sites: Ivanovo, a thirteenth-century Eastern Orthodox rock-hewn monastery, and the Madara Horseman relief, carved on a cliff face in the Madera plateau in northeastern Bulgaria. Both were originally placed on the World Monuments Watch list of endangered sites in 1996 and appeared again on subsequent lists. Unfortunately, Bulgaria's rich archaeological treasures are also of major interest to looters. The government's normal response to archaeological thefts is damage control and emergency security, and its efforts at significant preventative action have been uneven. Seismic activity coupled with inadequate site maintenance has also endangered sites such as the historic churches of St. Nickola in the Seslavtzi Monastery, St. Georgi in Arbanasi, and Bachkovo Monastery. The murals at these sites are in danger of disappearing from the damage caused by water infiltration and inappropriate whitewash.[6]

Until 2009 the separate National Institute for Monuments of Culture, the Archaeological Institute, and the National Museum were the three primary organizations concerned with managing and conserving Bulgarian immovable, archaeological, and movable heritage, respectively. These institutions categorized and protected the country's over 40,000 buildings, sites, and objects of historical and cultural significance as well as maintained archives with over 800,000 documents related to that heritage.[7] Monuments in Bulgaria are classified as of world, national, or local importance and include about 15,500 buildings and 15,550 archaeological sites; however, many of these sites have not been assessed or maintained for decades.[8] Due to what ICOMOS Bulgaria describes as "an extremely insufficient budget," the inventory of sites has never been exhaustive, and the documentation on sites is not kept up to date.[9]

Critics long argued that the 1969 legislation was outdated and that reevaluating it should be more of a priority for lawmakers of the new Bulgaria.[10] An amendment in 1995 introduced tax deductions for research, conservation, and protection to promote private participation. Though over twenty-five heritage-focused NGOs have been founded, with limited resources, only those focused on specific, individual sites have been even moderately successful.[11] In 1998 the possibility of buffer zones around sites on certain conditions was introduced through a new regulation, and in 2004 another amendment expanded the definition and scope of cultural monuments of Bulgaria.[12]

As a result of these and other piecemeal updates to the 1969 legislation, the overall system remained unclear and convoluted, and numerous issues were still unresolved. For example, the activities of the National Institute for Monuments of Culture were not legally regulated but rather based on orders from the Bulgarian Council of Ministers. Thus the Institute's organization and responsibilities were not clearly defined and were subject to change, leaving the country's cultural heritage at potential risk.[13] Overlapping responsibilities of local governments and agencies were also unclear—for example, all were authorized to impose sanctions for misuse of protected sites, but due to the confusion few seldom did.[14]

In 2009 the Bulgarian parliament finally passed a comprehensive new cultural heritage law that, while still controversial and much debated, takes important steps toward reorganization of the country's heritage management system to bring it in line with recent European trends. The law broadened the scope of what is protected to include intangible, industrial, and underwater heritage as well as cultural landscapes. Archaeological excavation is now controlled more tightly, and looting and other unauthorized activities at sites are more strictly punished. In addition, a decentralized, transparent management system was introduced through the dissolution of the National Institute for Monuments of Culture and the transfer of all responsibility for inventorying, listing, managing, and conserving Bulgaria's architectural heritage to the Ministry of Culture's new Inspectorate for the Protection of Cultural Heritage, with a main office in Sofia and branches in each of the country's six planning regions responsible for research, promotion, and conservation of immovable heritage. Municipalities are also charged with creating strategies and allotting funds for cultural heritage protection.

RECENT SUCCESSES AND TRENDS

Despite financial shortages and an ambiguous legal situation until very recently, numerous governmental, private, and international initiatives have significantly aided Bulgaria's architectural heritage in the past two decades. The "Beautiful Bulgaria" project, begun in earnest in 1998 with the support of the European Union, is a good example of how the Bulgarian state has partnered with foreign institutions and local governments to promote tourism while addressing unemployment issues. Five municipalities have taken part in this scheme, which both employs the jobless and improves the appearance of cities to attract tourists. For example, in Veliko Turnovo the Swiss government and the United Nations Development Program (UNDP), one of the initiative's main sponsors, employed townspeople to upgrade their urban fabric and public facilities and renovate their decaying buildings. This program was overseen by the Ministry of Labor and Social Policy, rather than the Ministry of Culture, so its focus was on job creation and training rather than best conservation practices.[15] Nevertheless, following an economically successful initial phase, a "Beautiful Bulgaria II" program was launched in 1999 in nine additional cities and thirteen new sites. Though conservation purists may question some of the interventions, especially their durability, overall the program has been a noteworthy example of sustainable development and the benefits that can be gained from restoration activities, both through increased employment and tourism opportunities.[16]

Other positive steps have been taken piece by piece. Since 1999, Bulgaria has been participating in the annual European Heritage Day initiative, sponsored by the Council of Europe and the European Union. The program, which includes free public access to many museums and monuments of culture, has become a popular and successful way to increase public awareness of national cultural riches and the need to conserve them. The Phare program was launched in Assenovgrad between 2003 and 2005 to study possibilities for natural and cultural tourism.[17] In 2005 a conservation research laboratory opened at the University of Architecture, Civil Engineering, and Geodesy in Sofia with support from the British Council in Bulgaria and the British Council Fund for South-East Europe.[18]

Though more could be done to court international aid for architectural conservation and to promote cultural tourism, in recent years international organizations have contributed to the conservation of Bulgarian architectural heritage at many important

a

b

Figure 26-2 Financial support to Bulgaria provided by the British-based Headley Trust enabled the restoration and improved presentation of the Thracian sepulcher, Kazanlak, in the village of Sveshtari. Conservation challenges addressed in such projects include humidity control (as seen in air circulation piping installed along the floor of the tomb's entrance passage in image a), structural stabilization, and conservation of painted wall and ceiling surfaces (b).

sites. The World Monuments Fund funded stabilization and restoration of the rock-hewn churches near Ivanovo and conserved the St. Dimitar church in Boboshevo. The American-Bulgarian Foundation for Cultural and Economic Development was created in 1997 and has since done extensive work in Blagoevgrad, while the British Headley Trust financed the restoration of the Thracian sepulcher in the village of Sveshtari by ICOMOS Bulgaria.[19] A private Russian society has restored the Russian Church in Shipka, which was built in 1877 to commemorate the Russian and Bulgarian soldiers lost in a nearby battle against the Ottomans.

In Plovdiv, whose old town includes a second-century Roman theater as well as a remarkable ensemble of early nineteenth-century Ottoman-style houses, UNESCO's Venice office is carrying out emergency stabilization at a number of sites and exemplary and thorough pilot conservation projects at three others supported by the Japanese Trust Fund and ICOMOS Japan. The city of Plovdiv has witnessed numerous interventions in the past thirty years that have threatened its architectural heritage, including a highway built in 1985 that passes under the Roman Forum. However, recent developments in the city are more promising: in addition to the UNESCO-sponsored projects, in 2003 a Conservation Steering Plan and Comprehensive Management Plan were drafted and the following year, Plovdiv was added to Bulgaria's tentative list of World Heritage Sites.[20]

Restoration projects at the few surviving mosques in Bulgaria were only periodically carried out before 1990, such as during the 1970s at the early seventeenth-century Ibrahim Pasha Mosque in Razgrad; however, numerous mosque conservation projects have been completed in the past two decades with support from Turkey, Arab countries, and the United States.[21] In 1999 Turkey and Bulgaria signed an agreement to cooperate on the financing and works for the restoration of Ottoman mosques in Bulgaria and Bulgarian Orthodox churches in Turkey.

It is not just international organizations and foreign governments who have been active in architectural conservation in Bulgaria but local NGOs and religious communities as well. An organization that has worked on behalf of archaeological heritage in Bulgaria is the Stara Zagora–based Balkan Heritage Foundation. Since 2003 it has operated a Balkan Heritage Field School that achieves its goals of preserving and promoting the region's heritage by offering study tours, workshops, and lecture courses and providing practical training in archaeological excavations, conservation lab work, and similar field projects, typically in partnership with local history museums or other organizations.[22] Thus far most completed projects have been in Bulgaria, but the Balkan Heritage Field School has also included sponsorship of a youth work camp at the ancient archaeological site of Heraclea Lyncestis near Bitola in the Republic of Macedonia. Projects in Bulgaria have included excavation of the Roman forum and an aqueduct at Stara Zagora, work at a sixth-century early Christian monastery at Varna, and documentation of medieval frescoes in the western part of the country.

In Bulgaria, responsibility for restoration and conservation of churches that are in use is the responsibility of the Synod of the Orthodox Church of Bulgaria, which must consult the Ministry of Culture when intervening on historic structures. However, in some cases, prior to the new legislation, restoration projects have been carried out by the Church without expert advice, and in others, funds given by the state at the time the structures were restituted to the Church were not used for their physical upkeep.[23] Thus, despite their preferred status, many of Bulgaria's medieval churches—such as at Tunovo, Nesseber and Cheven—today suffer from neglect and insensitive restorations as well as from problematic reconstructions carried out in the nineteenth and early twentieth century.[24]

In addition, development pressures in the Bulgarian capital of Sofia have threatened protected sites, and in most cases little has been done to safeguard them by the authorities. For example, after a 2007 fire, the protected Serdika Hotel (now the

Arena di Serdica Residence Hotel) was dramatically altered during restoration, and the early-twentieth-century house of Nicola Moushanov, a prominent interwar politician, was destroyed after the National Institute reduced its listing category. A six-story hotel was built in its place: a replica of one of the original house's facades was incorporated into the new hotel.[25] This trend has alarmed the architectural community in Sofia, and in November 2007 the Union of Architects of Bulgaria hosted a debate and exhibition on the threat titled "Heritage at Risk." There is evidence the tide may be slowly turning, as the 1906 house of architect Georgi Fingov was threatened in late 2008 by redevelopment, which would incorporate it into a larger structure, damaging significant historic fabric and destroying its integrity. However, partly in response to public outcry, in early 2009, the Sofia Municipality ordered the property owner to restore the protected building instead.[26]

The government of Bulgaria may not have been as proactive in architectural conservation as many of its neighbors, but there is a genuine desire within the Ministry of Culture to reclaim and conserve the country's cultural heritage from the years of neglect and disintegration. With new legislation and a reorganized administrative framework, Bulgaria is poised to enter a new, more positive chapter in its history of architectural conservation. One of the most important and commendable characteristics of contemporary practice in Bulgaria is the effort to rehabilitate sites of many origins: Roman, Thracian, Byzantine, and Orthodox buildings but also Islamic and Jewish heritage sites.[27] By raising public awareness, prioritizing international partnerships in heritage protection and tourism development, and committing additional resources to the effort, Bulgarians will likely continue to make positive headway in their efforts to conserve the country's rich cultural heritage in a sustainable way.

ENDNOTES

1. Dimitar Kostov, "Heritage Conservation in Bulgaria: Issues Relating to Private Sponsorship," in *Legal Structures of Private Sponsorship (International Seminar on Legal Structures of Private Sponsorship and Participation in the Protection and Maintenance of Monuments)*, eds. Floriane Fiedler and Werner von Trützschler, 29–31 (Munich: ICOMOS Germany, 2008), 29.

2. Kostov, "Heritage Conservation in Bulgaria," 29.

3. Pickard, "Bulgaria," in Pickard, *Analysis and Reform of Cultural Heritage Policies in South-East Europe*, 41; and Kostov, "Heritage Conservation in Bulgaria," 30.

4. Kostov, "Heritage Conservation in Bulgaria," 30.

5. Todor Krestev, "Cultural Heritage and Cultural Policy," Kultura (2002), www.online.bg/kultura/my_html/2222/cp-nasled.htm (accessed December 2, 2009).

6. ICOMOS Bulgaria, "Bulgaria," *Heritage@Risk 2002–2003* (Paris: ICOMOS, 2002), www.international.icomos.org/risk/2002/bulgaria2002.htm (accessed December 3, 2009).

7. Dimitar Tepavitcharov, "Problems of the Bulgarian Cultural and Historical Heritage (CHH) in the Context of the Regional Development," in Drdácký, *European Research on Cultural Heritage*, 173–8. Originally: "Cultural Heritage in Local and regional Social and Economic Stability" (paper, 2nd Ariadne Workshop, Prague, Czech Republic, May 9–15, 2001).

8. Pickard, "Bulgaria," 40.

9. ICOMOS Bulgaria, "Bulgaria: Heritage in Danger," *Heritage at Risk: ICOMOS World Report 2006/2007 on Monuments and Sites in Danger* (Paris: ICOMOS, 2008), 42.

10. ICOMOS Bulgaria, "Bulgaria: Heritage in Danger," 42.

11. Ibid.

12. Ibid. 43.

13. Svetozara Petkova, "Cultural Heritage Legislation in the Transition Countries of Southeastern Europe" (International Policy Fellowship Research Paper, July 2005), Open Society Institute—Budapest, www.policy.hu/petkova/Research 20Paper.htm (accessed July 2, 2010).

14. Ibid.; Pickard, "Bulgaria," 42; and Todor Krestev, "Integrated Conservation in Bulgaria," in Pickard, *Integrated Management Tools in the Heritage of South-East Europe*, 222.

15. Pickard, "Bulgaria," 50.

16. "News and Events," Beautiful Bulgaria, December 31, 1999, www.beautifulbulgaria.com/en/ (accessed December 2, 2009).

17. Phare started as the program for "Poland and Hungary: Assistance for Restructuring their Economies (PHARE)," specifically to support central and eastern Europe; however, since its overhaul, the European Union program is now understood as the "Programme of Community aid to the countries of Central and Eastern Europe" and to countries that have made application for membership in the European Union. For more information, see: http://europa.eu/legislation_summaries/enlargement/2004_and_2007_enlargement/e50004_en.htm (accessed July 2, 2010).

18. Krestev, "Integrated Conservation in Bulgaria," 220.

19. Tepavitchaov, "Problems of the Bulgarian Cultural and Historical Heritage," 174.

20. Krestev, "Integrated Conservation in Bulgaria," 221.

21. Pickard, "Bulgaria," 42.

22. "Balkan Heritage (BH) Field School," Balkan Heritage Field School, www.bhfieldschool.org/index.html (accessed December 30, 2009).

23. Pickard, "Bulgaria," 41.

24. Alexander Fol, ed., *Bulgaria: History Retold in Brief* (Sofia: Riva Publishing, 1999), 97.

25. ICOMOS Bulgaria, "Bulgaria: Heritage in Danger," 45.

26. Nick Iliev, "Georgi Fingov's Architectural Gem in Sofia to Be Renovated," Bulgaria Propertywise, March 18, 2009, www.propertywisebulgaria.com/article/georgi-fingovs-architectural-gem-in-sofia-to-be-renovated/id_3182/catid_24 (accessed December 1, 2009).

27. These sites are of particular importance to the Jewish community, as Bulgaria was one of the only members of the German alliance that refused to forcibly deport Bulgarian Jews during World War II.

CHAPTER 27

Romania

One of the Thracian tribes, the Dacians, flourished on the shores of the Black Sea in what is today Romania and built numerous military forts in an unsuccessful attempt to stave off the Romans. Some of these fortresses are evidenced today either in situ, including the ruins of the six Dacian fortresses in the Orăştie Mountains that became World Heritage Sites in 1999, or depicted in art as found on Trajan's Column in Rome, whose relief sculptures detail the Roman empire's eventual victory in Dacia. The Romans built roads, fortresses, and other public projects throughout what is now Romania.[1] By the time of the first Ottoman incursions in the fifteenth century, Dacia had split into the three separate feudal principalities: Wallachia, Moldavia, and Transylvania, which mostly remained autonomous for centuries by paying tribute to Istanbul.

The principalities of Wallachia and Moldavia merged in 1859 and took their first steps toward preserving their cultural heritage. The first architectural restoration and protection law—based on French models—was passed in 1892, shortly after full autonomy from the Ottomans was granted and after the principalities assumed the collective name Romania. The Comisia Naţională a Monumentelor Istorice (National Commission of Historic Monuments) was established within the then Ministry of Public Instruction, which—despite a few interruptions—still advises the government on heritage conservation today.[2]

The protection of historic sites had begun nearly a half-century earlier in Transylvania, when as part of the Austro-Hungarian Empire, it had created its own commission to protect cultural heritage and to compile an inventory of sites in 1850. During World War I, Romania acquired Transylvania and Bucovina from Austria-Hungary and Bessarabia from Russia. Thereafter, conservation efforts broadened to include the Saxon, Dacian, and Hungarian architecture found in these regions, including fortifications such as the fourteenth-century Bran Castle.

COMMUNIST-ERA INSTITUTIONS, KEY PROJECTS, AND CHALLENGES

As in most of Europe, World War II was a time of destruction in Romania. Numerous historic Jewish sites—including Bucharest's Choral Temple Synagogue—were destroyed by the Iron Guard, a Romanian fascist group. Serious damage was also incurred in Romania as the retreating German invaders fled the Russian army, including the burning of the sixteenth-century Bánffy Castle, Transylvania's largest castle. Such degradations continued until Soviet troops invaded Romania, exiled the king, and installed a Communist government. Initially, Romania's new postwar government treated its cultural heritage with respect and actively sought to preserve its historic sites, particularly those

◀**Figure 27-1** Benefiting from international membership cooperation and training via ICOMOS and ICCROM, programs were initiated to restore the intricately painted churches of Moldavia, the northeastern region of Romania. The Church of St Nicholas of the Probota Monastery in South Bucovina is one of seven fifteenth- and sixteenth-century painted churches on the World Heritage List.

403

that promoted links with its Slavic neighbors. With the withdrawal of Russian troops in 1958, sites integral to the Romanian spirit became increasingly important.

The state institution responsible for architectural conservation changed names and was reorganized repeatedly during the communist period, with changes taking place in 1952, 1959, 1974, and 1978. For much of this period, it was the Directia Monumentelor Istorice (Directorate of Historic Monuments) that monitored and intervened for the protection of Romania's heritage. In 1969, Romania joined ICCROM, and two years later formed an ICOMOS national committee. Programs were undertaken to catalog and preserve the intricately painted fifteenth- and sixteenth-century Moldavian churches, Transylvania's fortified monasteries, and numerous examples of wooden vernacular architecture. In the two decades following the war, over one hundred sites were restored by the Romanian government, and the listing of historic sites deserving state protection was carried out.[3]

In 1974 a new law protecting Romania's cultural heritage was passed decentralizing the Directia Monumentelor Istorice with main offices in Bucharest and regional offices in each county. This new system was never able to accomplish much, and it was rendered impotent by an earthquake that devastated the country in March 1977. The destruction of much of Bucharest's urban fabric gave President Nicolae Ceauşescu an opportunity to modernize the capital, and at the same time terminate any dialogue with conservationists, whom he felt were opposing progress. Ceauşescu disbanded the Directia Monumentelor Istorice; but fortunately, while state efforts to conserve cultural heritage had ceased, civil and church authorities continued to work undeterred on many sites.

Ceauşescu's new construction projects in Bucharest's center, especially the People's Palace, which was to be one of the largest structures in the world, caused further damage to the country's heritage. In preparation for its construction, twelve churches, two monasteries, two synagogues, and thousands of homes were bulldozed in the 1980s. Most of these buildings were listed protected sites, and former members of the Directia Monumentelor Istorice, as well as foreign institutions and organizations, protested their losses to no avail.[4] This urban destruction was joined by a program that threatened the country's rural built heritage by proposing half of Romania's rural population should be relocated into Bucharest's newly constructed apartment blocks. The resultant population drain jeopardized the future upkeep of the countryside's distinctive vernacular architecture.[5] Before either plan was completed, a general uprising in 1989 deposed Ceauşescu, who was later executed, and the People's Palace, a symbol of his excesses, was left half finished. Debate about the site's future ranged from completing the project to tearing it down, with the former solution eventually winning out. The building now houses the Romanian Parliament.

THE CONTEMPORARY CONSERVATION SCENE

Post-communist Romania has made a tremendous effort—albeit with a slow start—to recoup the losses suffered under Ceauşescu. In 1990, the 1974 protective legislation was abolished, initiating a decade-long period of confusion and unclear responsibilities. New legislation was constantly being discussed, and the text of the Law Regarding the Protection of Historic Monuments, which was eventually passed in 2001, was revised at least fifteen times during this period. One of the main issues holding up its passage was the decision that the new legislation and new list of protected sites should go into effect at the same time; thus, a time-consuming update of the inventory was a prerequisite to the law.[6]

This situation basically left cultural heritage without legal protection for eleven years. Most important historic sites managed to survive, because they remained under government control. Their privatization was another point of contention during the drafting of the new legislation. In the end, it was decided that protected properties would be divided into two classes, with most of the sites of *national* or *universal value* kept in the government's ownership; while others, mostly of *local* or *regional value*, would be sold to private owners entrusted with their maintenance.[7] Protected properties are also divided into three types by the 2001 law: constructions or part of constructions, groups, and sites. Under the Romanian system, sites are roughly synonymous with cultural landscapes, as they include the land as shaped by human-use patterns.

The current heritage protection legislation in Romania conforms to many of the international standards as stipulated in the Venice Charter and other international conservation doctrine. It mandates private owners conserve their protected properties, criminalizes unauthorized interventions, and offers in exchange free technical consultations from the government as well as financial support if necessary. Since 1995, with updates in the 2001 law, three institutions within the Ministry of Culture and National Heritage have shared responsibility for architectural heritage in Romainia: the Directia Monumentelor Istorice (Directorate of Historic Monuments), which inspects sites, mandates repairs, and authorizes funding; the Institutul National al Monumentelor Istorice (National Institute of Historic Monuments), which conducts research and proposed strategies for interventions; and the Oficiul National al Monumentelor Istorice (National Office of Historic Monuments), which carries out actual conservation and restoration projects at historic sites. In 2009, to simplify the system, these later two institutions were combined into the Institutul National al Patrimoniului (INP, National Heritage Institute). Their recommendations are made to the Commission of Historic Monuments for its decision, which is then passed to the Minister of Culture for final approval.[8] In 2005 the Ministry established the National Cultural Fund as an autonomous granting institution that has proven a valuable source of funds for restoration projects in Romania.

The Institutul de Memorie Culturală (cIMeC, Institute for Cultural Memory) was established in 1978, within the then Ministry of Culture, and it is still responsible for collecting and disseminating information about Romanian cultural heritage as well as new cultural output. Since 1996 this has included maintaining comprehensive online databases as well as publishing books and guides. Online records are kept for over 32,500 historic sites and 1,000 archaeological site excavations, as well as for its museum objects, rare books, museums, theatres, and other cultural venues and products.[9]

Despite its rapid progress in recent years, many obstacles still complicate architectural conservation practice in Romania today. Pollution and soil erosion from large factories and mining operations, which were built without consideration for ecology during the Communist era, threaten both Romania's cultural heritage and the health of its population. Earthquakes remain a constant threat, especially for buildings that are unsuited for seismic zones, as was evidenced in Bucharest in 1977.[10]

As in Bulgaria, the difficult transition from subsidized Soviet satellite to a free market economy leaves little funding available for the conservation of historic structures, though the preparations for joining the EU provided another base of technical and financial support from this multinational organization. The number of threatened sites is increasing, as impoverished rural sites are abandoned by families seeking urban jobs. A general lack of public education about the value of historic structures has had a broad impact: Some villagers, when faced with a deteriorating church, will simply construct another and abandon the original.[11] Industrial sites and former mansions with their gardens are two other types of Romanian heritage particularly at risk today.

Though the conclusions of a roundtable of concerned experts from local universities and ICOMOS Romania in 2002 argued that local disinterest was the single most important challenge for protecting the country's heritage—when that disinterest is combined

During the thirteenth century, Hungarian kings invited Germans from the Rhineland to settle in Transylvania, which they had recently acquired. These settlers, known as the Transylvania Saxons, introduced new building traditions to the region, including fortified churches and distinctive vernacular architecture. Over the centuries, they managed to retain their language and culture and remained staunchly resistant to Hungarian and Romanian influences. In 1993 the village of Biertan was inscribed on UNESCO's World Heritage List, because it had maintained its medieval layout, most of its sixteenth-century public buildings, and many of its historic dwellings. In 1999, six other well-preserved Saxon villages built between the thirteenth and sixteenth centuries were added to the nomination. That same year, the fortified medieval town of Sighişoara, with its City Hill and Lower Town, was added separately.[12]

The sites had been protected as a national monument by the Romanian government since the mid-twentieth century.[13] All were included on the first Romanian National List of Monuments, which was developed in 1959. In addition, they are all recognized at the highest level by the 2001 law. The fortified church in Biertan was restored in the 1930s and again in the 1980s; the Prejmer fortified church was repaired in the 1960s and Câlnic's castle in the 1970s, and the murals at Dârjiu were restored in the early 1980s. The fortified church at Saschiz had received the least attention and was in the worst condition, so the Ministry of Culture and National Heritage initiated its conservation and structural consolidation in 1999.

In the latter half of the twentieth century, political and social changes in Transylvania resulted in an exodus of its German-origin population to Germany. Now, few people of German extraction remain in this extremely impoverished area, leaving the region's fortified churches with reduced congregations, which threatens their futures. Squatters moved into abandoned eighteenth- and nineteenth-century Saxon dwellings, posing a difficult problem for those wishing to protect Romania's rural vernacular architecture. In January 2000, the Ministry of Culture and National Heritage passed a special decree to provide local and county administrations with funds needed to cover regular maintenance and training at these and other World Heritage Sites.

The plight of Romania's Saxon heritage has also been a catalyst for the receipt of significant help from abroad, including from the British-Romanian Mihai Eminescu Trust, whose "Whole Village Project" has revitalized communities with support from the World Bank. International support for this facet of Transylvania's heritage has especially come from Germany. Since 1979 the Siebenburgisch-Sachsische Stiftung (Transylvanian-Saxon Foundation), supported by the Habermann family, has restored fortified churches and other sites in Prejmer, Biertan, and other towns. Between 1991 and 1998, the Cultural Council of the Transylvanian Saxons in Germany completed a comprehensive survey of Saxon settlements in Transylvania, using current German conservation methodologies and with funding from the German government.[14] The Messerschmitt Foundation made a significant contribution in 1990 toward the restoration of Sighişoara citadel's thirteenth-century Stag House. In 1991 ICOMOS Germany and the Romanian Oficiul National al Monumentelor Istorice signed a partnership agreement covering the exchange of experience in all aspects of heritage protection and administration.[15] Many Romanian architectural conservationists have since been trained in German state conservation offices; however, their education has only slowly begun to influence Romania's heritage protection programs.

Despite these significant efforts, threats to Transylvania's Saxon heritage persist and conservationists remain vigilant. An exposé of the issue was published in 2010 in a booklet called *Silesia, The Land of Dying Country Houses* by the London-based SAVE Europe's Heritage, which dramatizes the race against time that is being faced in Transylvania by concerned conservationists.

with the government's lack of monitoring, planning, maintenance, and funding, indeed together they do pose the greatest threat to Romania's heritage today.[16] At the local government level, this has translated into a lack of political will to take protective initiatives, and at senior governmental levels it leaves heritage vulnerable to inappropriate decisions.

While such threats pose great risks to the innumerable historic sites found within Romania's borders, there have also been success stories. One high-profile project was the effort to preserve the famous Romanian sculptor Constantin Brancusi's monumental ensemble in his hometown Târgu Jiu. His famous sculpture *Endless Column* is almost 98 feet (30 meters) high, and it is composed of sixteen specially shaped cast iron mod-

Figure 27-2 Significant examples of Saxon heritage in Transylvania that have been conserved or restored as a result of the outpouring of international interest, especially from German organizations, include villages—such as Viscri—known for their fortified churches and well-preserved Saxon houses (a) and larger towns like Sibiu, with its network of interlocking public squares surrounded by medieval, Renaissance, and baroque architecture (b). Images courtesy and copyright Dennis Rodwell.

ules finished in bronze. Along with two accompanying works in travertine, the *Table of Silence* and the *Gate of the Kiss*, the *Endless Column* was built in 1938 to commemorate Romania's immense World War I casualties. Time and nature had taken their toll on the sculpture's bronzed modules, and the Romanian government, helped by a $2.6 million contribution from the World Bank and matching funds and technical assistance from the World Monuments Fund, restored the *Endless Column* ensemble within a new park setting as an open air national monument. Plans have been made for an interpretive center to be located not far from Brancusi's art works and to further improve the urban context of the ensemble.

Figure 27-3 The *Endless Column* ensemble created by master sculptor Constantin Brancusi in 1931 was restored in 2005 by the Romania's Ministry of Culture and National Heritage with financial and technical assistance provided by World Monuments Fund and significant funding from the World Bank. These images depict: the *Endless Column* restored (a), spine of the column and scaffolding during restoration (b), a cast iron module showing loss of its bronze finish (c), a restored module (d), and landscape design for the upper park (e) by the American landscape architecture firm OLIN.

Other successful major restoration projects include the fourteenth-century, Byzantine-style Monastery of Horezu, a World Heritage Site, that was intended to be the tomb of Prince Constantin Brâncoveanu, who reigned in Wallachia from 1688 to 1714. He not only presided over a period of prosperity and peace but also ushered in a renaissance of art and building that saw the unique Brâncovan style of architecture, in which the Horezu Monastery is designed. Today, a well-known school of mural and icon painting operates out of the complex.

"Beautiful Bucharest" is another interesting project that addresses the dual goals of employment for institutionalized young adults and historic preservation. In the same vein as in neighboring Bulgaria, which also participates in this UNDP sponsored program, teenagers emerging from state institutions are trained as construction and restoration workers, and they are given projects on which to practice their learned skills. By 2003 six historic buildings and three streets had been restored in Bucharest, and the program was expanded to include ten additional cities with the launch of the "Beautiful Romania" project.[17] For example, in Târgoviște and Sighișoara new employment opportunities have been generated, helping the local economy while simultaneously preserving the historic town center. In 2009 planning began for a "Beautiful Rural Romania," the third phase of this initiative, which seeks to expand urban successes to the whole of the country.

NGOs have also emerged in contemporary Romania to assist with the conservation of the country's architectural heritage. For example, the Mihai Eminescu Trust (MET), largely funded by the U.S.-based Packard Humanities Institute, has focused on rural and village conservation in Transylvania since 1989. In 2006 the MET was awarded the EU/Europa Nostra Prize for Dedicated Service for all its work, especially including its Village Project, which trained local craftsmen in traditional methods and preserved more than three hundred buildings in fifteen villages.[18]

Figure 27-4 Development pressures pose serious contemporary challenges for the protection of late nineteenth- and early twentieth-century architecture in Bucharest and in Romania's smaller cities and towns. The "Beautiful Bucharest" program, sponsored by the UNDP, restored six historic buildings and three streets in the capital by 2003. The program was designed to produce helpful "demonstration projects" that could be followed elsewhere, and was soon expanded to include other cities in Romania.

a

Figure 27-5 The ongoing, phased restoration of the sixteenth-century Bánffy Castle (a), which was significantly damaged in World War II, was begun by the Transylvania Trust in the late 1990s. The castle now serves as home to the Built Heritage Conservation Training Center, whose students (b and c) get hands-on experience in architectural conservation while working to restore its complex of buildings.

b

c

Based on the British Natural Trust model, the Pro Patrimonio Foundation was founded in 2001 by the eminent architectural conservation advocate Serban Cantacuzino to acquire, restore, and open both natural and built sites to the public in Romania.[19] Branch offices in London, Paris, and New York help raise funds to carry out the Foundation's mission of promoting diversity and multiculturalism and interesting new generations in Romania's heritage. Its "Route of Merchant Caravans" project linked a series of Pro Patrimonio properties to create a cultural itinerary from central Bucharest to Câmpulung Muscel, its home base.[20]

One of the most important NGOs concerned with heritage in Romania in recent years has been the Transylvania Trust, established in 1996, which like the MET, focuses on researching and restoring the built legacy of this single region of Romania. The Trust receives support from several governmental and private sources, and its work includes owning and managing properties, running training workshops and a post-graduate conservation program, and conducting surveys and research studies. One of the Transylvania Trust's highest profile projects has been the innovative conversion of the Bánffy Castle in Bonțida, which had been included on the World Monument Watch list of endangered sites in 1999, into the Built Heritage Conservation Training Center (BHTC). The Ministries of Culture of Romania and Hungary cooperated to complete the project, and since 2006 Princess Margarita of Romania became an official sponsor.

The phased restoration of Bánffy Castle has approached the complex's buildings one by one: In 2001, work began at the former kitchen block, which was converted into dormitories and a cafeteria for the students; the entrance gatehouse has become a visitor center as well as an Internet facility for the local community; and the Miklos building became the BHTC headquarters, including a library, lecture hall, offices, and workshops.[21] Craftspeople and university students from Romania as well as from other regional countries and Western Europe and the United States have studied at Bánffy Castle's BHTC, whose program focuses on minimal intervention, use of local resources, and practical experience with masonry consolidation, stonemasonry, and restoration carpentry.[22] In 2008 the BHTC won an EU/Europa Nostra Prize for Cultural Heritage in the category for Education, Training, and Awareness Raising.

Through this project, students at the BHTC have gained hands-on experience, and Bánffy Castle has been conserved and restored. Recent work, supported by the Headley Trust, has resulted in the conversion of the former stables into workshops for local craftspeople as well as a community hall, indicating a new phase at the BHTC that involves outreach to the local community through programs at local schools and sponsorship of annual cultural days for nearby Bonita.[23]

Architectural conservationists face an uphill battle providing care and restoration for Romania's wealth of historic buildings, as they do throughout southeastern Europe. During the Ceaușescu era, some put their lives on the line to protect historic sites when such action was expressly forbidden by the government. Today's challenges, while numerous, are less dire, and it is therefore unlikely that they are insurmountable for Romania's dedicated experts, especially as full EU membership has meant increased collaboration with Europe's cultural institutions and integration of Romania's policies with pan-European standards and norms.

ENDNOTES

1. Paul MacKendrick, *The Dacian Stones Speak* (Chapel Hill: University of North Carolina Press, 1975), 152.
2. Jokilehto, *A History of Architectural Conservation*. Oxford: Elsevier Butterworth-Heinemann, 2004, p. 260; first published in 1999.
3. Dinu C. Giurescu, *The Razing of Romania's Past* (New York: World Monuments Fund, 1989), 35.

4. Ibid., 39, 51–52.

5. Dorothy Bell, "Post-Ceauşescu Conservation in Romania," *Journal of Architectural Conservation* 7, no. 3 (November 2001): 55.

6. "Romania," *Heritage@Risk 2001–2002* (Paris: ICOMOS, 2001), www.international.icomos.org/risk/2001/roma2001.htm (accessed December 2, 2009).

7. ICOMOS, "Sighişoara (Romania), No. 902," in *Advisory Body Evaluation*, 156–169 (Paris: ICOMOS, June 28, 1998), http://whc.unesco.org/archive/advisory_body_evaluation/902.pdf (accessed July 3,2010).

8. "Scurt istoric," Institutul National al Patrimoniului, www.monumenteistorice.ro/index.php?option=com_content&task=view&id=2&Itemid=74&lang=RO (accessed January 4, 2011).

9. "Activities of the Institute for Cultural Memory," Institute for Cultural Memory, www.cimec.ro/DespreCIMEC/e_-Activitati.htm (accessed December 1, 2009).

10. Zsolt Visy, "Romania" *Heritage@Risk 2002–2003* (Paris: ICOMOS, 2002), www.international.icomos.org/risk/2002/romania2002.htm (accessed December 2, 2009).

11. Ibid.

12. ICOMOS, "Villages in Transylvania (Romania)," in *Advisory Body Evaluation*, 99–106 (Paris: ICOMOS, June 28, 1998), http://whc.unesco.org/archive/advisory_body_evaluation/596.pdf (accessed July 3, 2010).

13. During the 1950s, the Lutheran Superior Council recognized the importance of the many medieval churches it owned and established a Department for Architecture and Historic Monuments to coordinate their maintenance and repair. A Conservation Workshop was established in Brasov during the 1970s to restore altarpieces and other church furniture.

14. Christoph Machat, "Romania," *Heritage@Risk 2000* (Paris: ICOMOS, 2000), www.international.icomos.org/risk/world_report/2000/roman_2000.htm (accessed December 2, 2009).

15. Ibid.

16. Visy, "Romania."

17. United Nations Development Programme (UNDP) Romania, "UNDP Romania Launches 'Beautiful Romania' Project," *Newsletter* 9 (May 12, 2003), www.undp.ro/download/files/newsletters/2003/No09-Launch of Beautiful Romania.pdf.

18. "The Mihai Eminescu Trust (Romania-United Kingdom)," *European Union Prize for Cultural Heritage / Europa Nostra Awards 2006* (Paris: Europa Nostra, 2007), 36.

19. Maria Berza, "Heritage, Regeneration and Cultural Diversity: A Romanian Experience," in *Cultural Heritage in the 21st Century: Opportunities and Challenges*, eds. Monika A. Murzyn and Jacek Purchla (Kraków: International Cultural Center, 2007), 262–263.

20. Ibid., 264.

21. David Baxter, "Conservation Training at Bánffy Castle," *Context* 97 (November 2006): 37–8.

22. Ibid.

23. Ibid.

Conclusion to Part I

The collective experience of the European countries in conserving their architectural heritage in the post–World War II era is intrinsically a social phenomenon. With the architectural heritage of every country having been affected in one way or another by that catastrophic conflict, the continent's nearly uniform response to rebuilding, restoring, and accommodating heritage protection in building today's Europe represents a benchmark in the physical development of one of the world's most affluent continents. Despite the vast differences that occur across Europe in terms of approaches to heritage conservation, availability of resources, and culture in general, every country has taken remarkably similar steps in the interest of its historic sites. Though the relative strengths and exact parameters may vary, protective legislation, responsible administrative agencies, and international cooperation has been initiated in every European country.

Though it appeared that approaches and priorities fractured in Europe during the Cold War, concerted cultural heritage protection not only persisted in both East and West, but has evolved to become an important agenda item throughout Europe in the past two decades. For reasons ranging from natural interest and respect for the past, to defiance, to commercial interest and national pride, the motives for rebuilding, restoring, and conserving Europe's built patrimony are strongly present and will be for the foreseeable future. Because the commitment to the cause is now widely understood, today the principal challenges in architetural conservation's future in Europe has evolved to include more widely accommodating shared heritages, planning for sustainable development, and the conservation of resources.

Consensus and cooperation in architectural heritage protection in today's peaceful Europe is more sophisticated than ever via the many heritage protection and advocacy programs of the European Commission, the European Union, and other pan-European advocacy programs, especially NGOs. At the same time, each European country has its distinctive history, architectural patrimony, and experiences in architectural conservation that make examination of each country interesting and worthwhile. Nonetheless, it is Europe's cumulative experience in architectural heritage protection and conservation—whether viewed as a whole or in its particularities—that distinguishes it as both the originator and leader in the field today.

PART II

The Americas

North, Central, and South America

In the Americas today, the protection of cultural heritage, including architectural conservation, reflects the hemisphere's distinct history and social and economic development. Since discovery by European explorers in the late fifteenth century and gradual settlement thereafter, the regions broadly referred to today as North, Central, and South America have shared remarkably similar developments. European colonizers in search of riches, religious freedom, and space to expand arrived and imposed themselves on lands inhabited by indigenous peoples. In subsequent centuries this was followed by well-documented agricultural, urban, and industrial development, waves of immigration, including the non-voluntary arrival of slaves, and independence movements and nation-building throughout the Americas. The reconciliation of ideas and ways of life, as well as their accommodations in the New World within the milieu of resident cultures, shaped the modern countries of the Americas, creating extraordinary and valuable histories, physical artifacts, and legacies that merit careful documentation, understanding, and conservation.

Among the many European traditions shared in the Americas is the sense that this significant historic, artistic, and architectural heritage should be preserved, ideally by organized means. Models for such action were increasingly apparent in Western Europe from the mid-nineteenth century onward, at which time both ancient and more recent remains were being conserved and presented for a variety of reasons. Partly inspired by observing these examples and partly by desires to conserve their own legacy, interested individuals throughout the Americas addressed the tasks themselves, first as individual activists and later through institutions. Despite the similarities in their historical development, the United States and Canada have somewhat different experiences in architectural conservation practice than most of Mexico, the Caribbean Sea region, and Central and South America. These differences are mainly due to varied cultural ties to the Old World, development patterns, systems of governance, and economic strengths.[2]

Though the experiences and capacities of public and private interests in cultural heritage protection throughout the Americas vary from country to country, each has a government institution charged with protecting its architectural heritage; importantly, every country has counterpart nongovernmental entities that aid in the process as well. In most of the Americas, the model is the classic cultural ministry with its principal monuments and museums divisions, while the U.S. Department of the Interior or Parks Canada are concerned with built as well as natural heritage. Nevertheless, the conservation aims and strategies are strikingly similar throughout the Americas due to the common source of theoretical approaches and techniques: western Europe. The similarity of approach is also due to the internationality of the subject itself, because in a broad sense the protection of valuable historic resources—especially those which are publicly accessible—is a concern shared with the rest of the world. This is well illustrated by the actions of international organizations such as the United Nations Educational, Scientific, and Cultural Organization (UNESCO), the International Council on Monuments and Sites (ICOMOS), the International National Trust Organization (INTO; formerly the Association of National Trusts), the Organization of American States (OAS), and a plethora of smaller organizations working practically throughout every region with high degrees of fluidity.

In 1996 the presidents of the ICOMOS national committees from throughout the Americas met in San Antonio, Texas, primarily to discuss the issue of authenticity and cultural heritage management. Collectively, the participants agreed and stated that:

> The cultures and the heritage of the Americas are distinct from those of other continents because of their unique development and influences. Our languages, our societal structures, our economic means, and our spiritual beliefs vary within our continent, and yet, there are strong common threats that unify the Americas.... Within the cultural diversity of the Americas, groups with separate

identities co-exist in the same space and time and at times across space and time, sharing cultural manifestations, but often assigning different values to them. No nation in the Americas has a single national identity; our diversity makes up the totality of our national identities.[3]

Following the conference, its participants issued the Declaration of San Antonio, which included recommendations for a comprehensive and detailed document to guide conservation practice and to better define and protect authenticity and heritage in the western hemisphere. The declaration looked to Japan's Nara Document and Australia's Burra Charter as models of more inclusive policies that reflect a sophisticated understanding of the meaning of authenticity and identity as they relate to historic sites.[4]

In addition to UNESCO and ICOMOS, the OAS (which was originally established in the late nineteenth century but took on its modern form in 1948 and today has thirty-five member states) has been particularly active in supporting architectural conservation collaboration in the Americas. In 1976 OAS member countries drafted the Convention on the Protection of the Archaeological, Historic, and Artistic Heritage of the American Nations, known as the Convention of San Salvador.[5] Though signed subsequently by only thirteen Latin American countries, the Convention's principles set the stage early for the OAS's interest and involvement in architectural conservation issues. The OAS's Department of Education and Culture sees cultural heritage protection as one of its priority topics and promotes this agenda mostly through ministerial-level meetings, bilateral and multilateral workshops on specific issues, and direct funding of architectural conservation projects.

The Inter-American Development Bank (IDB) has been involved in cultural heritage conservation in the Americas to an even greater degree. Like the OAS, its active involvement began in the 1970s when it issued the first loans to member governments focused on conserving major historic sites as part of tourism development plans—such as a $26.5 million loan in 1974 to Peru for the conservation of Cuzco and a $13 million loan in 1977 to Panama to restore historic Panama City. Due to the growing interest of member states in the mid-1990s, the IDB began offering loans that emphasized the potential role of cultural heritage in socioeconomic development and has focused especially on urban heritage rehabilitation and conservation. As a means of better understanding cultural heritage conservation challenges in Latin America and the Caribbean region, the IDB, as well as other bilateral and governmental national institutions, facilitated the development of the UNDP/UNESCO Regional Project for Cultural, Urban, and Environmental Heritage, coordinated by the prominent architect and heritage conservation planner Sylvio Mutal.[6] In relation to this, a second generation of loans was geared more toward promoting public and private partnerships, such as the 1994 loan of $42 million to the municipality of Quito, Ecuador, for a joint venture that included private investors to preserve buildings in its historic center. The IDB has sought funding projects that are self-sustainable, locally supported, and that have additional funders and maximum potential impact. In 2000 the IDB demonstrated its commitment to this new area of lending and cooperation by devoting a seminar to the topic at the joint annual meeting of the IDB and the Inter-American Investment Corporation (IIC). It similarly sponsored a conference on conservation of World Heritage Cities in 2010. In addition, the IDB has a technical collaboration program to support institutional development and program design throughout the Americas.

As one of the wealthiest and most influential countries in the Americas, the United States has been supportive of cultural heritage protection efforts throughout the western hemisphere. For over three decades the United States has worked toward eliminating the illegal trafficking of archaeological materials, mostly through bilateral agreements with individual countries in Latin America. In addition, through the Ambassador's Fund for Cultural Preservation, the U.S. Department of State has funded over ninety restoration projects in the Americas since 2001.

To further promote the region's heritage, at the Second Ministerial Trade Meeting at the Summit of the Americas in Cartagena, Colombia, in March 1996, the United States suggested creating a List of the Americas to serve as a billboard to promote the hemisphere's cultural heritage at a level between the World Heritage List and the registers of individual countries.[7] The proposed List of the Americas would carry no obligations or restrictions on property owners, and include no management expectations or conservation commitments; rather, it would be a strictly honorary designation not unlike the United States' own National Register of Historic Places. The criteria for inclusion was to be worked out by ICOMOS, and nominations were to be open to the public, not solicited from the states' parties. This was meant to make the list more inclusive of the hemisphere's range of historic sites and to prevent it from duplicating the World Heritage List. Unfortunately, this uniquely designed opportunity for shared and expanded promotion of heritage throughout the Americas was not implemented as planned.

Through the Instituto de Cooperación para Iberoamérica (Institute for Latin American Cooperation) of the Agencia Española de Cooperación Internacional para el Desarrolla (AECID, Spanish Agency for International Cooperation for Development), the former seat of control of much of the Americas has contributed to promoting cultural heritage conservation in its former dependencies.[8] In 1984, the AECI (Agencia Española de Cooperación Internacional), as the AECID was formerly known, launched its Programa de Preservación del Patrimonio Cultural en Iberoamérica (Program for Conservation of Cultural Heritage of Latin America), which is focused on sites officially designated as national monuments, locally identified as priorities, and whose restoration would contribute to social and economic development. The AECID expects local institutions to match funding for most projects. AECID-sponsored projects have primarily sought to conserve the common history of Spain and the Americas, and therefore have focused on colonial heritage, typically religious or institutional buildings ranging from the Loreto Mission in Argentina to the ruins of La Isabela fortress in the Dominican Republic. However, a number of republican-era and pre-Hispanic sites, such as the ancient Mayan city of Tikal in Guatemala, have also been conserved and presented with funding from AECID.

A similar highly effective Spanish government initiative to assist with architectural conservation in Latin America since 1993 has been its *Escuelas Tallers* (training workshops). The program's success at training young people in architectural conservation trades in Spain, where it had begun a decade earlier, encouraged the extension of the program abroad. Today, twenty-seven workshop-schools have been founded in sixteen countries, and their programs have trained thousands of sixteen- to twenty-five-year-olds in restoration trades.

Despite the successes and collaboration in architectural conservation throughout the Americas, significant threats and difficulties persist in the western hemisphere, particularly in Latin America. In 2004, UNESCO published a report titled *The State of the World Heritage in Latin America and the Caribbean* that included the results of a poll taken among governmental heritage protection institutions and managers of World Heritage sites throughout the region. According to this report, 72 percent believed that policy and/or legal reform was necessary in their country, especially in Central America. In addition, UNESCO's report revealed that 52 percent of the recognized World Heritage sites in Latin America had no monitoring systems, 60 percent did not have emergency plans, 36 percent had no specific heritage protection plan at all, and less than half of the heritage site managers felt their properties were sufficiently protected from potential threats.[9] This report indicated that throughout Latin America and the Caribbean region significantly more could be done to further conservation efforts, and that the increasing attention the artistic and architectural heritage of the Americas have received in recent decades has not necessarily translated into a secure climate for most of the hemisphere's historic sites.

Practitioners and analysts of architectural conservation in the Americas have studied the issues facing the field in Latin America and have sought solutions to the most pressing problems. Norma Barbacci, who oversees field projects and initiatives in the Americas for the New York-based non-profit international organization the World Monuments Fund, suggests the greatest challenges facing architectural conservation professionals in the Americas today include the lack of available economic resources and political instability, which continue to interrupt preservation initiatives in the region.[10] However, for Venezuelan architectural conservationist Graziano Gasparini, improving the state of cultural heritage in the Americas is not just a question of additional financial resources; in general it is "facing a declining sense of cultural responsibility and a disturbing collective lack of interest."[11]

Eduardo Rojas, principal housing and urban development specialist in the IDB's Sustainable Development Department, argues that most Latin American countries have only partially developed their heritage-protection systems.[12] He suggests that they have moved from an initial phase of high concern focused on key, threatened sites into a period of proactive government involvement. Legislation has been passed and agencies have been created, but these are typically insufficient, especially as they are unable to fund their own programs and lack professionals with the technical expertise to carry them out. Rojas argues that Latin America needs to move into a period where architectural conservation becomes a wider concern, where a variety of social actors are involved, because today governments are "still shouldering most of the costs and are unable to make a noticeable dent in the large task of preserving the urban heritage."[13]

The cultural ministries and national heritage-protection agencies of the Americas might continue to provide the regulatory environment for architectural conservation, but they should do more to encourage private sector involvement and to realize the commercial potential of rehabilitation. In addition, the governments in the Americas must do more to work with local and regional governments and to facilitate the decentralization of heritage activities. Cultural tourism provides the best opportunity to bring both recognition and funding for the historic sites of the developing countries of the Americas, as it does throughout the world, but in the process more must be done to balance and meet the needs of local residents as well as those of visitors. In addition, international support and expertise will continue to play an important role in the promotion and conservation of architectural heritage in Latin America for the foreseeable future.

Endnotes

1. In contrast, many details of the histories of indigenous peoples ranging from the First Nations peoples of Canada to the Aztec, Maya, Inca, and others are less fully understood and have mainly been researched through modern archaeology and ethnoarchaeology.

2. For this reason the chapters of Part II of this book are divided into three sections, with Canada and the United States discussed together and Mexico discussed along with the Caribbean region and Central America, although geographically speaking North America is divided from South America at Panama.

3. Declaration of San Antonio (ICOMOS document, San Antonio, Texas, March 30, 1996), www. icomos.org/docs/san_antonio.html (accessed January 26, 2010).

4. Declaration of San Antonio. For information on two of the Declaration's inspirational sources see: "The Australia ICOMOS Charter for the Conservation of Places of Cultural Significance (the Burra Charter, 1999)," ICOMOS, www.icomos.org/burra_charter.html (accessed July 21, 2010); and "The Nara Document on Authenticity (1994)," ICOMOS, www.international.ico-mos.org/charters/nara_e.htm (accessed July 21, 2010).

5. Convention on the Protection of the Archaeological, Historical, and Artistic Heritage of the American Nations, Department of International Law, Organization of American States Treaty

C-16, Washington, DC, June 16, 1976, www.oas.org/juridico/English/treaties/c-16.html (accessed January 26, 2010).

6. One of the final activities of the long term UNDP/UNESCO regional project entailed a systematic project monitoring exercise that was conducted between 1991-1994. Developed by an interdisciplinary team experts and collaborators and implemented through a system of project-specific partnerships, the study involved methodical monitoring of the state of conservation of 39 World Heritage Sites in Latin America and the Caribbean, and one from Mozambique. Conclusions were formulated and recommendations were proposed.

7. "United States non-paper on OAS Heritage Sites List," www.oas.org/udse/cic/ingles/web_cic/USAnonpaperOASHeritageSites.doc (accessed January 26, 2010).

8. Maria Rosa Suárez-Inclán Ducassi, "Spain's Ongoing Foreign Technical Assistance for the Conservation of Hispanic Heritage Worldwide" (paper, US/ICOMOS 2nd Annual Symposium: Culture, Environment, and Heritage, Washington, DC, 1999).

9. World Heritage Center, *The State of the World Heritage in Latin America and the Caribbean: Periodic Report 2004* (Paris: UNESCO, 2006).

10. Norma Barbacci, "World Monuments Fund: Latin American Preservation: Overview and Case Studies" (presentation at course entitled International Architectural Preservation Practice, Columbia University, New York, April 24, 2007).

11. Graziano Gasparini, "Monument Heritage in South America: Treasures Beyond Measure," in *Heritage Conservation in South America: Challenges and Solutions* (New York: World Monuments Fund, 2002), 44.

12. Eduardo Rojas and Claudio de Moura Castro, *Lending for Urban Heritage Conservation: Issues and Opportunities*, no. SOC–105 (Washington, DC: Inter-American Development Bank, 1999), www.iadb.org/sds/SOC/publication/publication_78_1316_e.htm (accessed January 2010).

13. Rojas and de Moura Castro, "Lending for Urban Heritage Conservation."

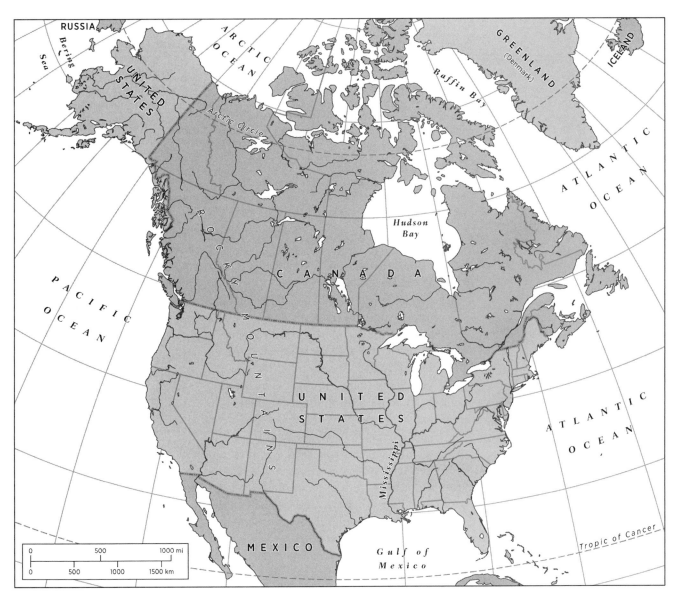

The United States and Canada.

The United States and Canada share many physical, historic, and cultural qualities: both vast countries nearly equal the size of the European continent; both were colonized by various European powers but ultimately controlled by the British; and both secured their independence and emerged as global financial and political leaders. However, at the same time, other elements in their past and present have differed significantly. Three-quarters of Canadians inhabit less than 10 percent of the country's land area, concentrated within one hundred miles of the United States border, because much of the land in the subarctic and arctic north is uninhabitable. This harsher climate and more difficult access meant that Canada was settled and developed more slowly than the United States. Both countries, however, were established by the union of numerous separate territories, and therefore regional differences and powers have remained important in both.

The similarities in American and Canadian histories in large part explain the shared attributes of their contemporary architectural conservation practices. Today both countries have decentralized heritage systems that delegate much authority and responsibility to the state or provincial or territorial level. The impressive and extensive natural landscapes attracted government attention and respect before the historic built environments of both of these young countries, and since the mid-twentieth century architectural conservation is carried out by specialists within the U.S. National Park Service and Parks Canada. These two federal agencies have a broad conservation mandate in their respective countries, covering both natural and cultural resources. Activists as well as the government in both the United States and Canada looked to European models, especially Great Britain, when designing protective mechanisms, legislation, and voluntary associations for their historic sites and cities.

At the same time, the nuanced differences between the United States and Canada also reveal the different character of their heritage and their systems for its protection. Canada's French tradition has remained an important aspect of its history, and though France lost its holdings in North America in the mid-eighteenth century, French cultural, linguistic, and architectural influences remain strong, especially in the province of Quebec.[1] While the United States fought a protracted war for its independence from Britain from 1776 to 1781, the Canadians negotiated self-rule peacefully in 1867, and their different attitudes toward their former colonizers have influenced their architectural conservation movements. The massive fortifications built by both the French and British were among the first historic sites to garner public interest and conservation attention in Canada, while it was sites associated with the founding fathers and the Revolutionary War that were first protected in the United States.

While in western Europe broad-reaching governments centrally decide on and fund architectural heritage conservation programs, in the United States the task of preserving historic architecture mainly rests with the people at large. Local, popular efforts are enhanced by a formalized and unified support network that has developed over the course of the twentieth century. Though it emerged later, Canada has similarly witnessed a popular architectural conservation movement driven primarily by local community networks rather than by professionally trained preservationists.[2] Voluntary membership organizations like the U.S. National Trust for Historic Preservation and Heritage Canada play crucial roles in conservation advocacy and practice in both countries today. However, the pragmatic, business-focused, and future-oriented citizenry of the United States, more so than in Canada and most other countries, requires that preservation efforts be economically justifiable and coexist with "progress."

a

b

c

Figure 28-1 North American building dating from approximately 1700 BCE through 1700 CE is represented in the Native American ceremonial mounds and trading center of Poverty Point in Northeast Louisiana (1650 BCE) that covers over two square kilometers (a), Taos Pueblo (c. 1200 CE) in northern New Mexico that is one of the oldest continuously inhabited communities in the United States (b), and the Adam Thoroughgood House in southeastern Virginia (c.1720)—seen here before it was restored—that reflects architecture of the English colonial era (c). All are listed as U.S. National Historic Landmarks. Taos Pueblo is a World Heritage Site and in 2010 Poverty Point was nominated to the World Heritage List.

Figure 28-II The first restoration of Independence Hall (a) in Philadelphia in 1828 and recent revitalization of whole urban areas, such as the Gooderham and Worts Distillery mixed residential and commercial district (b) in Toronto, represent the evolution of thinking about the values and physical scales of architectural conservation practice in North American over nearly two centuries.

a

b

Private voluntary organizations have also been instrumental to advances in the field in North America. For example, the Association for Preservation Technology (APT), now based in Springfield, Illinois, was founded in Canada in 1968 by Canadian and American architectural preservationist professionals to provide a cross-disciplinary platform for discussing the technical aspects of the field. Its many activities include offering specialized courses on the conservation of dozens of specific materials or historic building elements, ranging from stained glass to decorative hardware to terra-cotta facades. The APT also publishes a bulletin to "showcase cutting-edge architectural preservation techniques, as well as innovative applications of established restoration technologies."[3] In addition, thematic topics discussed at the annual APT conferences highlight key issues in contemporary preservation practice and bring professionals together to share experiences.

Though comprising only a few countries today, the North American continent was home to hundreds of indigenous cultures before settlement by Europeans. Though the built legacies of many Native American (in the United States) and First Nation (in Canada) cultures in North America were not always among the most appreciated heritage of the continent, today these sites and cultural landscapes are increasingly protected and conserved. Many active and organized Native American and First Nation communities have been involved in these efforts.

North America's contemporary architectural conservation practice is focused on the rich mix of heritage that resulted from its history of indigenous peoples, colonial settlements, rapid expansion, and more recent developments. In both the United States and Canada, the initially narrow focus on historically significant individual buildings from the colonial-era forward has increasingly broadened to encompass not only Native American sites but also those reflecting other minorities, as well as vernacular architecture, historic districts, and modern marvels. As American historian and preservationist David Lowenthal has noted, heritage has expanded "from the elite and grand to the vernacular and everyday; from the remote to the recent; and from the material to the intangible."[4] The growing multiculturalism in both the United States and Canada, and the need to keep heritage protection relevant to a diffuse mixed population, is clearly evident in contemporary North American architectural conservation practice.

ENDNOTES

1. To a lesser extent the same could be said of southwestern Louisiana for the past 250 years.
2. Frits Pannekoek, "The Rise of a Heritage Priesthood," in *Preservation of What, for Whom?* Michael A Tomlan, ed. Ithaca, NY: The National Council for Preservation Education, 1999, 35.
3. "APT Bulletin: The Journal of Preservation Technology," The Association for Preservation Technology, www.apti.org/publications/bulletin.cfm (accessed January 26, 2010).
4. David Lowenthal, "The Heritage Crusade and Its Contradictions," in *Giving Preservation a History: Histories of Historic Preservation in the United States.* Max Page and Randall Mason, eds. London: Taylor and Francis, 2004, 27.

a

b

CHAPTER 28

The United States

Public recognition of the importance of the historic built environment and the need to protect it has never been stronger in the United States than it is today. Yet, as historian Robin Winks notes, Americans are still obsessed with the future, not the past, suggesting that careful vigilance on the part of historic preservationists—the preferred term for architectural conservationists in the United States—is necessary to ensure that the past is not lost in moves toward the future. The pragmatic efforts of preservationists in the United States have enabled the successful meeting of important challenges faced thus far, and they are likely to continue doing so in the twenty-first century.

The concern for honoring and protecting historic sites in the United States has a long history, predating even the creation of the country in 1776. As early as 1749, the value of retaining sites as physical artifacts of memory was recognized, when in the country's earliest recorded instance of preservation for preservation's sake a lone-surviving log cabin in Philadelphia was saved because it was believed to be the last of its type.[1] Despite early instances such as this example, historic preservation did not become a popular movement in the United States until more recently. The country's youth contributed to the slow maturation of its heritage protection ethos. Before the twentieth century, relatively few historic buildings were viewed as valued historic resources, since most had been built only a few decades prior to that time. The United States' future-oriented attitude also encouraged what Wink calls a "bias of utility" in which historic resources have been valued less for their intrinsic qualities and primarily for their usefulness, including their economic value and their role in defining the "goals of the nation."[2]

Beginning in the sixteenth century, North America's European settlers exploited a seemingly boundless wilderness, putting it to practical use and creating an extensive built environment within just a few generations. But after nearly four centuries of ambitious building, the American "land of plenty" syndrome began to be questioned. Concern about the depletion of the country's natural resources grew in the late nineteenth century and gradually expanded to include historic sites as well. As the cause became more popular, dedicated volunteers and all levels of government began to act on behalf of important sites.

World War II and the postwar building boom interrupted the early progress the United States had made in the identification, documentation, and evaluation of its historic sites, and it was not until the 1960s and 1970s that more effective and broad-reaching mechanisms were established to protect significant historic American buildings and sites. Much has been accomplished since that time, and examples of good historic preservation practice abound—whole neighborhoods have been conserved and adaptive reuse projects have transformed derelict industrial warehouses into sought-after residences and shopping districts. Increasing attention has also been paid to the cultural heritage of various

◀**Figure 28-1** The restoration of Mount Vernon, home of the first U.S. president George Washington, began with its purchase and protection by the Mount Vernon Ladies' Association in 1854, which figures in the history of international architectural heritage protection as it is the first known nationwide citizens' effort to protect a heritage site by public subscription. After decades of effort, the association restored Mount Vernon's exterior (a), its interiors, and the grounds of the estate including several outbuildings. Over a century and a half later, this still–privately held initiative continues, a recent project being the installation of the new multimedia interpretive center named after its donors: the Gay Hart Gaines Legacy Theater and the Donald W. Reynolds Education Center (b). Photographer Robert Creamer. Courtesy of The Mount Vernon Ladies' Association.

minorities, especially Native Americans and African Americans, but also sites associated with the histories of Latinos, women, and gay rights. Contemporary architectural preservation practice in the United States is comprised primarily of issue-driven and innovative programs and firmly established policies and tools created by past generations.

PRIVATE INITIATIVES, ORGANIZATIONS, AND PHILANTHROPISTS

Though its various phases have been characterized by a different combination of participants, changing socioeconomic contexts, and an ever-broadening scope of sites considered, the historic preservation movement in the United States has continuously witnessed a remarkable amount of private initiative and effort. Individual pioneers started campaigning in defense of specific threatened historic properties in the early nineteenth century, beginning with concerned citizens who successfully lobbied the city of Philadelphia in 1813 to save Independence Hall, the building in which the United States' Declaration of Independence had been signed in 1776.[3] Activists, genealogists, and antiquarians saved many other major sites associated with the country's founding fathers and other Revolutionary-era heroes, often making them shrinelike tourist destinations. Following the 1876 Centennial Exhibition in Philadelphia, the community interested in historic preservation expanded as did the sites of interest. Individual buildings were preserved as were eventually entire battlefields, landscapes, villages, and urban centers. The private initiative that marked these earliest attempts to preserve sites in the late nineteenth and early twentieth centuries has remained central to the American heritage conservation ethos ever since. Indeed, unlike in other countries, historic preservation in the United States has always been considered the responsibility of the citizenry in general rather than a state-supported and state-controlled enterprise. Private individuals, including both property owners and philanthropists, were involved long before the government took a systematic interest in historic preservation, and they remain important components of the field today.

The populist approach of the American preservation scene is rooted in the many factors that have shaped the country's character from its very beginning: the take-charge attitude, cooperative spirit, and willingness to embrace causes and work for the public good exhibited by the first colonists remain defining American traits. These factors—combined with freedom to organize, an emphasis on private property, strong patriotic tendencies, and the accumulation of vast wealth—have engendered a tradition of generosity and philanthropic support for ventures such as historic preservation.

As one preservationist aptly put it, U.S. citizens are "joiners and organizers," who look to "the private sector rather than government for solutions to problems."[4] As a result, a wide range of special-purpose organizations have developed through most of the country's history to address a variety of local, regional, and national concerns. Nonprofit organizations have always been a significant force in American preservation, second only to private property owners, in the role they have played in protecting historic sites.[5]

The remarkable story behind the salvation of Washington's home and tomb at Mount Vernon, Virginia, by a dynamic and prescient individual vividly illustrates the importance of private initiatives and nonprofits in American historic preservation. Upon his retirement from the presidency in 1797, Washington had returned to his plantation on the Potomac River, where he died and was buried in 1799. For half a century afterward, riverboats passing the tomb tolled their bells as a sign of respect, but by the 1840s, the house was in disrepair because Washington's descendants could not afford its maintenance, and various proposals for selling the property to the federal government and the state of Virginia proved unsuccessful.

The future of Mount Vernon looked bleak until Ann Pamela Cunningham from South Carolina learned of its dilapidation and formed the Mount Vernon Ladies' Association (MVLA) to take up its cause. In doing so, Cunningham mobilized her private resources and social network via a patriotic appeal to the heretofore untapped administrative and financial potential of American gentlewomen. She invited them to join the first national women's organization and aid her innovative awareness and fundraising campaign. She was able to quickly raise enough money to purchase Mont Vernon, and since 1858, the nonprofit MVLA has been the site's proprietor, maintaining Mount Vernon without federal or state aid and making it available to visitors, which today average one million annually.[6]

Using the meticulous inventory lists and records Washington had kept, as well as drawings of the house and property from Washington's time, the MVLA restored Mount Vernon to its appearance in 1799, the year of his death.[7] The MVLA's efforts to preserve and present Washington's home have continued throughout their 150 years of stewardship, and it has faithfully adhered to Cunningham's retirement request that "no irreverent hand change it; no vandal hands desecrate it with the fingers of progress. Those who go to the home in which he [Washington] lived and died wish to see in what he lived and died."[8] Both the interpretation presented at Mount Vernon and the MVLA itself have mirrored America's evolving heritage conservation preferences and attitudes by broadening their focus from the house itself to its contextual setting in the past century and a half.[9] Most recently, a multimedia, interactive interpretive center and museum was built on Mount Vernon's grounds out of sight of the house itself, where interventions continue to respect Cunningham's request.

The Mount Vernon Ladies' Association's early success in saving a specific historic site became an inspiration and model for thousands of subsequent historic preservation campaigns in the United States. The country's other early-organized preservation efforts were also initiated by its financial and social elites, who had the time, money, and education needed for the task. Women played a predominant role in these activities throughout the nineteenth century. The Daughters of the American Revolution (DAR), the National Society of the Colonial Dames of America, and the Mayflower Society are but a few of the select groups that developed at that time to pursue preservation activities for its instructive value and as a means of distinguishing their lineage.

The effort that most closely followed the precedent of the MVLA was the campaign to save the Hermitage, the Nashville residence of Andrew Jackson, a War of 1812 hero and the seventh president of the United States. After consulting with the MVLA in the late 1880s, Jackson's descendents created the Ladies' Hermitage Association, which eventually took over stewardship of the historic home.[10] As at Mount Vernon, the Ladies' Hermitage Association's operations have evolved over the past century, along with the general preservation movement and its best practices. Today, in addition to the house itself and its outbuildings, the association also manages the site's original 1804 log cabin and the family tomb and church. An archaeological program begun in the 1970s excavated over a dozen other structures, including several relating to the lives of the Jackson family's slave community. In 2002 the Ladies' Heritage Association received one of the nation's highest preservation awards for its carefully researched restoration of the Hermitage's historic landscape following devastation from a tornado in 1998.[11]

Later in the nineteenth century, several new organizations emerged, and house museums were established to immortalize other aspects of American heritage than just its early political heroes.[12] One of the earliest of these organizations was the Association for the Preservation of Virginia Antiquities (APVA), which since 1889 has been "dedicated to preserving and promoting the state's irreplaceable historic structures, landscapes, collections, communities, and archaeological sites."[13] The APVA's branch structure allowed it to quickly broaden its base of support—as did MVLA's—but also to advocate for historic sites at the community level.

The first established regional preservation organization, and one of the most distinguished of the early private institutions active in the field, was the Society for the Preservation of New England Antiquities (SPNEA). SPNEA was founded in 1910 by Charles Sumner Appleton, a wealthy Bostonian and an avid disciple of the movement named for English critic and theorist John Ruskin, the Ruskinian movement, that argued for minimal intervention at historic sites.[14] Unlike most American preservationists of his time, Appleton was well informed about the range of restoration choices and theories, which he had observed in Europe. He created SPNEA in reaction to the destruction of the John Hancock House, one of Boston's most important colonial domestic buildings. For him this loss revealed that civil authorities were incapable of safeguarding heritage and that effective preservation must be spearheaded by citizen action. Appleton's focus on New England's domestic architecture helped shift the general focus of architectural preservation in the United States from exceptional historic sites to those that reflected the everyday life of early Americans.

SPNEA's activities, spread over five states, have been complemented by the Massachusetts Trustees of Reservations (MTR), another regional organization established in 1890 by Appleton's contemporary, landscape architect Charles Eliot. The MTR's regional landscape preservation work paralleled SPNEA's built heritage activities; together, these two organizations formally linked historic sites with their natural surroundings for the first time.[15] Over the course of the past century, SPNEA (renamed Historic New England in 2004) has preserved numerous heritage sites without using public funds or assistance, and it is therefore not compelled to open any of its thirty-five historic houses to the public. This has allowed it to better manage the wear inflicted on its properties than is possible at many federally or state-funded institutions. Historic New England's private consciousness, motivated by a respect for craftsmanship and the character of old structures, remains rare today, as education, recreation, patriotism, nostalgia, and financial viability have become the major concerns dominating the preservation field in the United States.

In the first few decades of the twentieth century, a number of America's first millionaires enthusiastically joined in the campaign to save the historic architecture of the United States, paying particular attention to the creation of open air architectural museums. The most widely known and influential example is John D. Rockefeller Jr.'s establishment of Colonial Williamsburg, a restoration project encompassing more than three hundred acres.[16] First settled in 1633, Williamsburg became the capital of Virginia, England's largest and richest colony, in 1699. After the Revolutionary War and the moving of Virginia's capital to Richmond in 1780, Williamsburg sank into an obscurity that proved fortunate for its built environment. Nearly 85 percent of its eighteenth-century buildings were intact, though neglected, upon Rockefeller's arrival in the early twentieth century.

The idea for Williamsburg's restoration originated with the Reverend Dr. W. A. R. Goodwin, an activist, antiquarian, and rector of the town's Bruton Parish Church. In 1906 Goodwin's appetite for restoration was whetted while overseeing a project on his own church, and in 1923 he presented his vision of a restored Williamsburg to Rockefeller. The millionaire was intrigued by the idea of creating a living historical landscape to teach the public about America's colonial and revolutionary past.

Over the next decade, Rockefeller invested approximately $40 million toward restoring the town to its appearance in the 1770s.[17] Interdisciplinary teams of historians, architects, archaeologists, landscape architects, and museum experts began researching, acquiring properties, and drafting planning and feasibility studies. Though historical accuracy was always their primary goal, informed conjectures were often required, and today only 88 of the nearly 500 structures in Williamsburg's historic area are original.[18] In keeping with "stylistic unity" restoration approaches still popular at the time, others were reconstructed and scores of post-1790 buildings and structures were removed from the area in the 1920s and 1930s. Many projects for which there was little surviving material or documentation, such as the restoration of historic landscapes, were approached more as sympathetic design processes than as preservation.

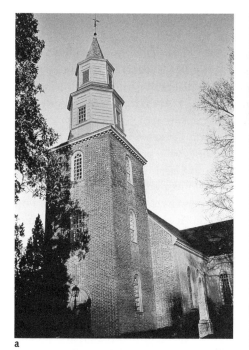

a

b

c

Figure 28-2 Restoration of Bruton Parish Church (a) in Colonial Williamsburg in 1906 helped inspire a vision of how the whole substantially intact colonial town might likewise be restored. The rector of the church, Reverend Dr. W. A. R. Goodwin, an activist and antiquarian, is credited with convincing philanthropist John D. Rockefeller Jr. to finance the restoration that began with payment for a plan only and ended with an expenditure of approximately $40 million by the time of Colonial Williamsburg's opening to the public in the late 1920s. At the head of Palace Street (b) is the reconstructed Governor's Palace (c).

While the restored town was designed to be as accurate a representation of colonial-era Williamsburg as possible, at times preservation purists have denigrated its authenticity. It has been described as too antiseptic and overly romanticized for avoiding many of the unpleasant realities of colonial life in its presentations, such as evidence of slavery or the squalor and odors of dusty and muddy streets where animals roamed freely. To the credit of the professional staff at Colonial Williamsburg, however, these and similar issues have been addressed in recent years, and today's visitors enjoy a more accurate interpretation of the town's realities than was originally presented.

Despite its critics, the methodologies of Colonial Williamsburg's restoration set certain precedents for American preservation, especially in the areas of historical and architectural research and conservation technology. The field of historical archaeology was born there, at the hands of Ivor Noel Hume, an English archaeologist.[19] In addition, Colonial Williamsburg stirred interest in preserving enclaves of buildings rather than just individual, isolated buildings and also encouraged other preservation projects that were similarly conceived of as places of learning.

Colonial Williamsburg is also a landmark in the development in the consciousness of American social history. Since it opened in the late 1920s, it has become a popular tourist site for American and foreign visitors alike, offering them the chance to visit more than two hundred period rooms. Rockefeller's project also inspired other philanthropists to embark on similar patriotic and educational ventures. Many of the architectural heritage sites in the United States today similarly evolved from an individual or family's private passion into fully staffed, nonprofit education organizations.

Some of these other outdoor architectural museums were conceived of in the same way as Colonial Williamsburg, where original buildings were preserved on their original sites, such as at Old Salem in Winston-Salem, North Carolina. However, many other projects involved the transport of historic structures to new sites, such as at Greenfield Village in Dearborn, Michigan. Greenfield Village was created in the 1930s almost contemporaneously with Colonial Williamsburg, but it was designed along the lines of Scandinavian open air museums like Skansen and the Norsk Folkemuseum, which brought together old buildings from disparate locations and organized them as if they were a historic village.

Ironically, Greenfield Village was the idea of automobile pioneer and industrialist Henry Ford, who reputedly declared: "History is more or less bunk" and "the only history worth a tinker's damn is the history we make today."[20] Ford's confident vision of a future country made widely accessible by his automobiles apparently also included a realization of the need to maintain some links with a rapidly receding past. The collection of over a hundred buildings at Ford's museum reflect his interests in innovation and enterprise: it includes the original laboratory of inventor Thomas Edison, the courthouse where Abraham Lincoln first practiced law, and the house where Noah Webster compiled his dictionary, as well as entire factories, mills, and brickworks tracing the course of American industrial development. Other parts of Greenfield Village were designed purely for entertainment and pleasure, anticipating Walt Disney's postwar re-creations of themed historic built environments and events.

Other early open air museums involved the complete reconstruction of no-longer extant structures from the past, such as at Plimoth Plantation, founded in 1947 by Boston stockbroker Henry Hornblower II to make the story of the Pilgrims' 1620 arrival in America publicly accessible. Plimoth Plantation is a compilation of imaginative and authentic reproductions set on a site miles away from the original landing place and settlement. Nearby, a seventeenth-century Wampanoag village has also been recreated, with exhibits focusing on the daily lives of the Native American people who first interacted with the Pilgrims. A full-size replica of one of the Pilgrim vessels, the Mayflower II, and exhibitions of crafts and animal husbandry round out Plimoth Plantation's offerings, which are explained by costumed staff who speak in period dialects.

The approach to preserving and presenting history at outdoor museums, such as Plimoth Plantation and Greenfield Village, raises serious questions of authenticity, especially with regard to the importance of the original physical contexts of the buildings and objects on display. Indeed, the idea of re-creating or collecting whole historic buildings or parts thereof in a seemingly idiosyncratic fashion and creating an unreal wonderland of history has been held by many experts as precisely what *not* to do. Nonetheless, in the case of Greenfield Village, many of the relocated buildings probably have more secure futures than had they been left in their original settings. In addition, the restorations at Greenfield Village and Colonial Williamsburg, as well as Old Sturbridge and Deerfield Villages in Massachusetts, encouraged popular interest in history and preserving enclaves of buildings.[21] For this, as well as for their interactive and engaging educational possibilities, these projects can be considered successful.

EARLY FEDERAL AND MUNICIPAL GOVERNMENT EFFORTS

Direct government participation in historic preservation has been relatively minimal in the United States when compared to other western countries and has only supplemented the overwhelming activities of private individuals, institutions, corporations, and nonprofit organizations. However, beginning in the late nineteenth century, the U.S. federal government began creating institutions and establishing policies for the protection of the country's resources—both natural and built. In the period between the two World Wars, American cities developed tools to restrict changes and therefore protect and preserve their historic sites and spaces. Thanks to these municipal and federal initiatives, by the 1930s organized efforts to identify, document, and restore historic buildings had become common and had replaced the sporadic and individual site-focused nature of nineteenth-century architectural heritage protection in the United States.

The federal government's involvement in historic preservation began shortly after the American Civil War of the 1860s, when in shock and sorrow it swiftly acquired Ford's Theatre in Washington, DC, where President Abraham Lincoln had been shot in 1864. The War Department maintained the building for nearly a century as a memorial, but today it is again a working theatre that calls itself "a living tribute of President Lincoln's love of the performing arts."[22] The nearby William Petersen house where Lincoln died has been preserved by the federal government as a museum since 1896.

Compared with the rapid decisions taken to protect sites sacred to President Lincoln's memory, government interest in other historically significant buildings came slowly, long after the first federal efforts to protect and conserve historic and natural landscapes and precolonial archaeological sites. As the country's territory expanded westward, its population became cognizant of the continent's natural beauty and wealth, and government attention turned to preserving its natural wonders.[23] This natural landscape preservation movement of the late nineteenth century preceded and paved the way for more comprehensive government participation in architectural preservation.

Figure 28-3 Interest from the 1860s in the conservation of America's natural heritage by prescient activists such as John Muir and Clifford Pinchot (founding director of the U.S. Forestry Service) worked in tandem with the country's nascent interest in protecting its architectural heritage. Designation of the geysers of Yellowstone National Park and its environs, which eventually included some 230 million acres of land, as a U.S. National Park in 1872 proved to be the world's first protected park of its kind. Image courtesy U.S. National Archives (photo no. 79-AAT-2).

One of the earliest and largest land conservation actions taken by the U.S. government was the establishment of the world's first national park at Yellowstone in 1872, an initiative fostered by naturalist John Muir, founder of the United States' oldest, largest, and most influential grassroots environmental organization, the Sierra Club.[24] During Theodore Roosevelt's tenure in the White House in the early 1900s, federal protection was extended to almost 230 million acres of land, an area greater than the thirteen original colonies.[25] No other president—before or since—has done so much for land conservation in the United States.

In 1889, following a decade of field research on Native American cultures carried out by the Smithsonian Institution's Bureau of Ethnology (now the Bureau of American Ethnology), the federal government extended funding for the first time to preserve a cultural landscape, when Congress appropriated $2,000 to protect the earthen archaeological remains of the ancient Sonoran Desert people's Casa Grande Ruins in Arizona. In 1906 the United States passed its first preservation legislation, the Antiquities Act, to allow for similar recognition and protection of historic sites on federally owned land and to establish penalties for their destruction. The creation of Mesa Verde National Park in Colorado, which encompasses the cliff dwellings built by the Ancestral Puebloans (formerly called Anasazi, a Navajo word, by archaeologists), was the Act's first success.

Civil War battlefields were the next historic landscapes to benefit from federal attention, but congressional approval for their preservation was slowed by conflicts with private landowners and other local groups. For example, despite the pivotal role of Gettysburg, Pennsylvania, in the American Civil War and the tragic loss there of more than 51,000 lives, efforts to ensure the preservation of that battlefield encountered massive local resistance. After a thirty-year stalemate, Gettysburg National Military Park was finally established in 1895, five years after the first and largest military park, Chickamauga and Chattanooga National Military Park, was created on thirteen square miles along the Georgia-Tennessee border.[26]

The U.S. government more formally accepted a role of overseeing historic preservation in 1916, when the National Park Service was established within the Department of the Interior. The National Park Service assumed caretaking responsibilities for the nine national monuments that had already been designated, as well as for the administration of national parks and historic sites. The National Park Service quickly became the United States' principal source of governmental preservation expertise, due in part to

Figure 28-4 The establishment of Gettysburg National Military Park in 1895 to commemorate the definitive turning point in the American Civil War and the loss of 51,000 lives exemplifies the U.S. government's early interest in protecting such cultural heritage sites. Illustrated here is a fence line marking the extent of Confederate Major General George Pickett's charge.

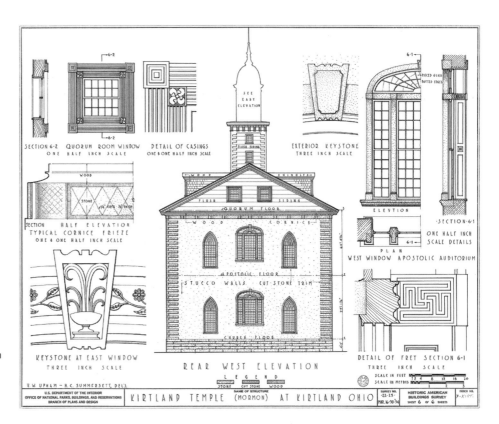

Figure 28-5 Photographic and written documentation of the Kirtland Temple in Kirtland, Ohio, in March 1934, from the Historic American Buildings Survey (HABS) project. The temple was one of hundreds of buildings documented as part of a program that was originally intended to provide work for unemployed architects and historians during the Great Depression. The idea proved to have a much greater effect, including establishment of the Historic Sites Act of 1935, which created a national inventory of historic architecture (later called the National Register of Historic Places) and a viable mechanism for broad legal and administrative protection involving federal and state governments.

the momentum and visibility gained by various Depression-era public works programs and through its close collaboration with private experts, especially those employed on the restoration of Colonial Williamsburg.[27]

In the 1930s, President Franklin D. Roosevelt attempted to alleviate some of the financial hardships of the Great Depression by creating federally sponsored work programs. One in particular, the Works Progress Administration (WPA), proved invaluable to the National Park Service's heritage protection efforts. Through the WPA, unemployed architects were mobilized to collect photographic and textual documentation regarding historic buildings as well as to create high-quality, professional, and measured drawings of these sites. This work, maintained in government archives, is still regularly consulted today.[28] This temporary emergency employment project became the core of an archival record called the Historic American Buildings Survey (HABS), and eventually evolved into a permanent national inventory. The program was temporarily halted during World War II, but it resumed in 1957. Since that time, the survey has been refined with the cooperative efforts of the American Institute of Architects (AIA), the Society of Architectural Historians (SAH), and the National Trust for Historic Preservation.

The HABS project underscored not only the wealth of America's built patrimony but also how quickly it was deteriorating. In 1933 all significant architectural and archaeological properties owned by the federal government were therefore turned over to the National Park Service, allowing for more consistent curatorial management. Shortly thereafter the National Park Service initiated a survey and status report of its holdings, which was funded by philanthropist John D. Rockefeller, Jr. The findings were largely embodied in the Historic Sites Act of 1935, which recognized the broad and complex interests of twentieth-century preservation by delineating a policy of protecting historic sites of national significance and making them publicly accessible. It also helped define guidelines for the federal acquisition of historic properties through the National Park Service and for the development of educational programs. The 1935 Historic Sites Act formalized the concept of the historic landmark in the United States by empowering the Secretary of the Interior to erect commemorative markers at significant historical and archaeological sites.[29]

Conserving Historic Engineering Structures: Bridges
Eric DeLony

Although the American Society of Civil Engineers (ASCE) was responsible for helping create the Historic American Engineering Record (HAER) in the late 1960s, few engineers at that time embraced or practiced the preservation of their own heritage. Historic preservation in the United States then was not a widespread concept, with only a few having knowledge that it was a new discipline that held significant ramifications for the future. In the United States today it generally is recognized that architectural preservation—which includes engineering monuments such as bridges—is a worthwhile endeavor.

Indeed, bridges not only illustrate economic development and engineering prowess, but they are sustainable components of the nation's transportation infrastructure that play a role in distinguishing the cultural landscape of the large country. Most people recognize engineering icons like the Brooklyn Bridge, the Golden Gate Bridge, or the steel-and-wrought iron arches of James Buchanan Eads's magnificent span across the Mississippi River at St. Louis. In thinking of bridges, those who may be nostalgic about such things may first think of the covered bridges of New England or bridges supported by graceful stone arches, while others marvel at the Erector-Set-like exactness of a metal truss bridge or one supported by soaring concrete arches. While the United States has more covered bridges than any other country—about 750—the types of bridge heritage that is most at risk are the iron-and-steel truss bridge and spans composed of concrete arches fabricated during the late nineteenth and early twentieth centuries by bridge companies and often sold through catalogs. Hundreds of patents were granted. No other country experimented with the truss type or concrete arch form so widely as did the United States. Americans depended on these structures to tie their growing communities together and link them to larger cities. Many of these bridges have survived, with some still carrying traffic. Many have passed the one-hundred-year age mark, and some are wearing out.

The U.S. Congress mandated a national historic bridge survey in 1987, when most states inventoried their bridges. Since the completion of the survey, attention has been given to identifying the most historically significant ones and their relative conditions. The question remains, in many instances, what to do with them? Some are not practical to repair and retain, while others could be bypassed by new structures and assigned to other purposes. It is encouraging that there are funding sources for preserving historic bridges and interest in the subject by most highway departments at local, state, and federal levels. It is encouraging as well that today there are engineering firms, builders, and craftsmen that have the knowledge to properly restore and rehabilitate these structures.

A sizable bridge disaster in August 2007 drew wide attention to the question of to America's highway bridges. This was collapse of the I-35W St. Anthony Falls Bridge spanning the Mississippi River in Minneapolis. The disaster occurred during an evening rush hour killing 13 people and injuring 145. Metal fatigue of an undersized gusset plate connecting beams compounded by several additional factors caused the span to fail and fall into the river.[30] Contributing to the problem was the fact that 2 inches (51 mm) of concrete had been added to the road surface over the years, increasing the constant dead load on the structure by 20 percent.

While there have been other bridge failures—such as the collapse of the Silver Bridge into the Ohio River at Point Pleasant, West Virginia in 1967, where 46 lives were lost—these incidents are rare. The American public may feel secure knowing that America's bridges are not dangerous, although many need rehabilitation and maintenance. One reason for the rare number of bridge collapses is due to the relatively high level of inspection and monitoring by the country's various departments of highways. This fact aside, according to the publication *Better Bridges,* out a total of approximately 560,000 interstate and state bridges surveyed by November 2009 some 62,504 (21.6 percent) were evaluated as being structurally deficient or functionally obsolete.[31] The safety of highway bridges is mainly a matter of proper upkeep that greatly depends on both funding and the training of maintenance personnel. Other considerations are the age of the structures in question, possibilities of controlling traffic flow, various corrosion factors, and even some environmental restrictions.

Though there has been some progress saving historic bridges, it is not enough. Over half the historic bridges of the United States were destroyed in the last three decades of the twentieth century and the first decade of the twenty-first century, during which awareness and capacity for preserving historic bridges and structures was at its highest level.[32] More work must be done to better protect historically significant American bridges. Until there is a national policy with specific legislative protection and funding incentives, bridges will remain an architectural and engineering heritage at risk.

A new challenge in this effort is the assessment and selective preservation of the thousands of "bridges of the recent past," built in the decades following World War II as part of the nation's interstate highway system.[33] It is the bridges built during the frenzy to complete the interstate highway system in the 1960s, the decade construction commenced on the I-35W, that are most at risk. Historians have only recently begun to document the steel beams and cantilevers, concrete slabs and girders, reinforced and prestressed concrete beams highway departments developed for overpasses, short and mid-length spans. The majority of bridges and other structures (including interchanges, tunnels, and rest areas) located within the 46,700 miles of interstate highway system have been exempted from eligibility for designation in the National Register of Historic Places. Certain examples of national or exceptional significance will become eligible for consideration as historic properties in the coming years.[34]

As greater numbers of engineers develop expertise in the rehabilitation of historic bridges as part of their everyday practice and more state departments of transportation recognize that the preservation of historic bridges is integral to highway planning, a rich potential exists for extending the lives of historic bridges in the United States and in other countries. There is also the rich potential for effectively and safely and aesthetically incorporating new bridge structures with the old.

Saving historic bridges of fine materials, humanly scaled proportions, notable craftsmanship, and varied textures not only preserves cherished historic structures and enhances the built environment but also makes economic sense. Bridges and the road systems they serve offer a cultural, educational, and recreational experience that is increasingly valued by Americans and foreign visitors alike who discover the fascinating matrix of scenic highways and byways that knit America together. Most well-maintained historic bridges can likely stay in service as vehicular roadways. For others, the solution may be relocation to lesser-used roads, trailways, or bikeways.

Rehabilitated bridges, especially the older ones, are among the best examples of "sustainability." There is ample evidence that archaic materials such as cast and wrought iron, wood, early steels, and concrete are durable for several generations—even centuries. Both engineering and conservation science literature attest to this. New materials, improvements in engineering and conservation science, and computer-assisted diagnostic and monitoring methods are also available. In addition, there is a corpus of experience in preserving engineering structures—the field is robust today and there are many examples that can be drawn from.

As a bridge engineer recently said, "I think it is inevitable that a 'green standard' (a sustainability project-rating system) will be applied to the bridge industry. In this scenario the rehabilitation of older historic bridges would be an important consideration. Such a green bridge standard, if developed properly, can be another tool to encourage the preservation of historic bridges. Such an approach will help save more of America's historic bridges and more of the world's historic bridges as well."[35]

FURTHER READING

DeLony, Eric. *Context for World Heritage Bridges,* Occasional Papers for the World Heritage Convention, International Council on Monuments and Sites, (A joint publication with TICCIH: The International Committee for the Conservation of Industrial Heritage), Paris, 1997. Published on-line 2008. www.icomos.org/studies/bridges.htm (accessed January 10, 2011).

DeLony, Eric, Terry H. Klein. *Historic Bridges: A Heritage at Risk, a Report on a Workshop on the Preservation and Management of Historic Bridges, Washington, DC, December 3–4, 2003,* SRI Foundation, Rio Rancho, NM. www.srifoundation.org/pdf/bridge_report.pdf, 2004 (accessed January 10, 2011).

Figure 28-6 Three types of historic bridges that have been conserved with the involvement of the Historic American Engineering Record (HAER) include the 2,184 feet (666 m) Lake Champlain Bridge (a), which connected New York with Vermont between 1929 and 2009 (when it was demolished for eventual replacement by a newer bridge); the bridge over Freeway 101 at 6th Street in Los Angeles, dating from 1932, a significant bridge in its genre, which has inherent problems with its original concrete mix—which poses the question: repair or replace? (b); and the 1861 Bridle Path Bridge designed by Calvert Vaux, one of fifty-one ornamental bridges in Central Park, New York City (c). Image (a) copyright 2009 Eric Bessette, photographer; image (b) HAER Collection (CA-1-176-1), U.S. Library of Congress. Taro Olmos, photographer, 1966; (c) is a vintage photo attributed to Calvin Vaux.

a

b

c

Advances made in historic preservation ground to a halt in 1941, when the United States' entry into World War II drained funds, personnel, and attention away from causes such as heritage conservation. It was not until the return of peace that the country was able to refocus on its historic sites. In 1949 the United States' historic preservation efforts were revitalized when Congress chartered the National Trust for Historic Preservation as a charitable, educational, and nonprofit corporation to facilitate and encourage public participation in the protection and conservation of historic buildings. The National Park Service had realized a need for such an organization and recommended its formation, as most of the historic buildings in America were privately owned and only a small fraction could be acquired and preserved by the government.[36]

Since its inception, the National Trust has performed essential work in raising awareness of the value of historic architecture. Through its regional office network, it educates the public about architectural preservation issues, especially the potential of adaptive use for saving historic buildings.[37] It owns and maintains twenty-nine historic sites, each of which is supported by a separate endowment. Though membership in this private organization seems slight compared with its British equivalent, through its affiliation with over five hundred other organizations and its privileged relationship with the government, the National Trust has been very influential.[38] In particular, it has played an important role in the passage of preservation legislation, especially since its profile and influence increased in the 1960s.

When the federal government first became interested in documenting and preserving the built environment in the early twentieth century, many U.S. cities also began to develop tools to protect their own architectural resources. At the municipal level, historic districts and zoning legislation were employed to restrict changes to historic buildings and streetscapes beginning in the 1920s and 1930s.

The first of these municipal level tools to emerge was the protected historic district, which has become one of the most important and effective preservation mechanisms in the United States. While the original idea for protecting enclaves of buildings within historic cities was related to the experiences of outdoor museums like Colonial Williamsburg, historic districts differed significantly because their enabling legislation did not call for cities to purchase buildings in a historic downtown but rather to restrict changes that could be made within a designated area by individual property owners. Government protection of enclaves of buildings and historic cities thus occurred decades before the listing of privately owned, individual landmark buildings in the United States.

The first official historic district in the United States was established in Charleston, South Carolina, largely due to the initiative of yet another dynamic individual preservation advocate, Susan Pringle Frost. After more than two decades of personal activism conserving individual buildings in Charleston, in 1931 she encouraged the revision of the town's ordinance to protect a twenty-three-block area known as the Old and Historic Charleston district. The ordinance also established the country's first Architectural Board of Review, which was staffed by five citizens to approve or reject proposals concerning changes to the exterior of the district's four hundred residences to ensure the preservation of the neighborhood's historic character.

The Vieux Carré, or Old Quarter, in New Orleans was the second designated historic district in the United States. After a decade of lobbying by the American Institute of Architects, the state and city council successfully created a historic preservation commission to safeguard the Vieux Carré, which is the site of an early eighteenth-century French colonial settlement and one of North America's first planned cities. While much of the original colonial fabric had not survived, the European baroque-period plan and over two-thousand architecturally significant buildings were still intact when the district was designated in 1936. The City of New Orleans received broad powers to protect and preserve this treasure, including the right to purchase or expropriate threatened buildings and to exempt others from taxation if owners complied with regulations of the Vieux Carré Historic District Commission. While most historic districts only regulate the publicly visible exteriors of buildings, in the Vieux Carré the appearance of sidewalls and back walls as well as of roofs are also protected.[39]

The prototype historic districts and commissions in Charleston and New Orleans—with their design-review processes, financial and technical assistance for property owners, and combination of incentives and deterrents—have inspired hundreds of other cities across the United States similarly searching for ways to retain their distinctive characters and histories. Numerous other cities also successfully established

Figure 28-7 Enhancements of an existing city ordinance in 1931 in Charleston, South Carolina, to protect a twenty-three block area known as the Old and Historic Charleston district, entailed the creation of America's first official historic district. Some of the city ordinance's provisions, such as the creation of an architectural board of review, likely represent "firsts" in architectural conservation practice in the world.

historic districts and rehabilitated their historic centers in the following decades, including Alexandria, Virginia (1946); Boston, Massachusetts (1955); Santa Fe, New Mexico (1957); Litchfield, Connecticut (1959); and Annapolis, Maryland (1965). By the time Santa Barbara, California, and San Antonio, Texas, officially established historic districts in the 1960s, both had already spent decades preserving their historic architecture. Santa Barbara had identified and conserved its local character, including defining features of its Spanish mission architecture, and promoted continued building in that idiom beginning in the 1920s and therefore had preserved a remarkably harmonious environment.[40] San Antonio's River Bend and La Villita areas had been rehabilitated with federal assistance in 1939, and the local Conservation Society had purchased and restored numerous historically significant structures throughout the city.

In a number of the earliest districts, regulations had to be strengthened as natural wear, repairs, alterations, and additions led to the loss of some of their historic character and fabric. Stricter guidelines have also been used when new districts have been designated to maintain greater control and retention of their appearances. Zoning regulations on use, massing, and other architectural aspects have also been frequently employed to add an extra layer of protection for historic districts to help control building heights, views, and scales.[41] The results of the restrictions required by both zoning and historic districts regulations have boosted property values, encouraged tourism, and enhanced local values, appearances, and economies in many cities. These positive benefits of urban conservation had to be learned though: the first American historic districts to be created were based on aesthetic and historic values, criteria that may be secondary considerations today. The designated historic district remains one of the most successful and prevalent architectural preservation tools in the United States for protecting enclaves of buildings, with nearly twelve thousand historic districts existing in American cities today.

EMERGENCE OF AN HISTORIC PRESERVATION SYSTEM IN THE 1960S

Following World War II, America was more preoccupied than ever with rapid progress. Encouraged by the triumph of war and the increased industrial production that had enabled that victory, returning soldiers and civilians were all eager to resume peacetime endeavors and build a new future. Postwar interests stressed modernization, and the building industry—including architects, planners, and educators—fully embraced and promoted new forward-looking trends. Architecture benefited from a great number of new building materials and manufacturing processes developed during and after the war. Planning witnessed the creation of new towns and an explosion of growth in suburban developments.

Despite the historic preservation movement's successes before World War II, this postwar building boom and focus on future-oriented progress, coupled with changing social trends and stylistic preferences, conspired against many American city centers and their historic buildings. Urban renewal projects posed a new threat, as they did in Europe, but also inspired the emergence of a modern field of historic preservation professionals in the United States and encouraged the updating and enhancement of protective legislation and government oversight agencies in the 1960s. By the 1970s, the basis of today's architectural preservation system in the United States had been firmly established: revised urban planning efforts had begun to reduce the disappearance of many historic cityscapes, the growing popular preservation movement and progressing methodologies had improved abilities to protect and restore historic sites, and new tools and economic incentives had been developed to engage even more participants in architectural heritage protection.

Throughout the 1950s and 1960s, most architects and planners held dim views of the possibilities for old buildings and neighborhoods. In the decades after World War II, afflu-

a

You're looking at
the most promising trend
in modern architecture.

This magnificent office building was once Boston's magnificent City Hall.
It came dangerously close to becoming magnificent rubble.
Who saved it? Some concerned ad hoc groups, a quickly-formed development

b

Figure 28-8 America's postwar enchantment with building a bright new world did not favor architectural heritage protection through the mid-1970s. Modern storefronts, if not whole new buildings, were in vogue as is humorously depicted in a Charles Addams cartoon "Last Brownstone" (a) in the *New Yorker* (5 September 1977). The trend led to losses and near-losses, such as the former Boston City Hall, which was saved and redeveloped as office space in the early 1970s (b) as well as the insensitive treatment of ornate historic buildings exteriors, such as this Washington, DC building that was covered with aluminum cladding (c). Image (a) copyright Charles Addams. With permission, Tee and Charles Addams Foundation.

c

ent urban dwellers fled inner cities to newly created suburbs, and businesses followed their customers to suburban malls. The proposed solution to address the desolated inner cities was termed "urban renewal," which often entailed radical interventions into depopulated urban areas to furnish them with updated housing projects or to drive interstate highways through them.[42] Though initially regarded as a sensible and socially responsible cause, by the 1960s the negative consequences of urban renewal were readily apparent. It did not take long for the inferior housing and industrial developments that replaced historic neighborhoods, the accompanying environmental pollution, and the loss of familiar urban places and identities to lead to public concern for the fate of American cities.

Among the first to recognize the waste and social problems of urban renewal were urbanists with long-range visions such as Jane Jacobs. In her seminal work, *The Death and Life of Great American Cities* (1961), Jacobs gave a loud, brave cry of opposition to the wholesale remaking of America's older cites and argued that the country's existing historical, physical, and social fabric provided valuable resources with which urban planners could work, rather than obstacles to be overcome or destroyed.[43] Jacobs was not alone in her concerns about wasteful change. At the same time she was educating Americans about urban issues, an early environmentalist, Rachel Carson, was writing her prescient book *Silent Spring*.[44] The early warnings of the hazards and limits of uncontrolled resource exploitation expounded in this book were echoed two decades later in James Marston Fitch's *Historic Preservation: Curatorial Management of the Built World*: Fitch is in many ways Carson's counterpart in the architectural preservation field.[45] As the ideas of Jacobs and others were disseminated in the 1960s, historic preservation became of interest to more and more city planners and citizens. The inadequacy and absence of existing protective mechanisms and frameworks inspired a new generation of concerned activists who reacted in effective and tangible ways.[46]

Important new tools for preserving historic areas within cities, which had developed in the decade since the war, were implemented on a greater scale, most notably the use of revolving funds. Like the historic district concept, the revolving fund was first tested in Charleston, and it also emerged out of the ideas of Susan Pringle Frost. Throughout the first half of the twentieth century, Frost had been privately rescuing derelict buildings in Charleston's oldest neighborhoods by buying structures, rehabilitating them, and selling the improved sites to generate capital for additional purchases in a continuous reinvestment cycle.[47] In 1947 the nonprofit Historic Charleston Foundation, which had been founded ten years earlier, established a fund based on Frost's model to purchase, restore, and resell buildings and reinvest the profits in additional preservation projects.[48] The fund is still active today. The resold buildings come with protective covenants to ensure that their new and future owners continue to maintain these historic sites. In the 1960s other city governments or private organizations established similar revolving funds focused on the heritage of particular cities, beginning with Savannah, Georgia, and Pittsburgh, Pennsylvania.

Municipalities within the United States also embraced the concept of protecting individual buildings by designating them as landmarks during the 1960s. While Europeans had been inventorying, listing, and restricting changes to individual historic structures since the nineteenth century, it was not until after a decade of general urban destruction in the mid-twentieth century that American cities began employing this important conservation tool. Individual buildings, especially house museums, had been preserved via ownership by trusts, organizations, individuals, and governments, but requiring owners to maintain and restore their privately held buildings located outside of historic districts was a new and daring approach in the United States. Cities in California, including Los Angeles in 1962, were among the first to establish Landmarks Commissions, followed quickly by New York City (1965), San Francisco (1967), Chicago (1968), Cleveland (1972), and Boston (1975).

The process of landmarking was first thoroughly worked out and tested through the New York City Landmarks Preservation Commission (LPC), whose authority to designate and protect historic districts and individual buildings was extended to historic interiors in 1973. The resolve with which the LPC has met and overcome the political and legal complexities it has faced have led to innovative policies that have influenced preservation theory and practice in other American cities.[49] At the time of the LPC's inception, the greatest threat facing New York City's historic architecture, and especially that of Manhattan Island, was the economic pressure to tear down lower-scaled, older buildings and replace them with vastly larger new structures. High real estate values and limited space rapidly led the LPC to the conclusion that the only way to save these

a

b

Figure 28-9 The sad and failed effort to protect New York City's Pennsylvania Station in 1963 had an unintended positive consequence—passage of the New York City Landmarks Law of 1964, which established the New York Landmarks Commission. Prominent preservation advocates Jane Jacobs and Philip Johnson (second from left and far right in image) are shown here on the picket line protesting Pennsylvania Station's destruction (a). Three decades later, the fully restored Grand Central Terminal (b), about which several important preservation battles were also fought, proved to have a more successful outcome. Figure 28-9a courtesy of Getty/Hulton Archives/Walter Daran, photographer.

endangered historic structures from demolition was to allow the transfer of development rights from designated landmarks to adjacent or nearby sites. Thus, a two-story landmark threatened with replacement by a taller building could permanently give up its right to expand upward, and a larger than usually permissible tower could be constructed next door. Though creating new problems of altered views and contexts, this eased the perceived tension between preservation and economic development in New York City.

The battle over the fate of one historic building in New York City, Grand Central Terminal, whose owners wanted to replace it with a taller structure, became one of the most well-known and influential legal decisions in the history of American historic preservation. In 1978, the U.S. Supreme Court ultimately ruled in favor of the city's right to designate the train station, or any site, as a landmark and to forbid its demolition or alteration.[50] Hailed as a major victory for preservationists, this case laid to rest the legality of landmarks designation, which had been challenged as uncompensated expropriation, violation of private property, and discriminatory "spot" zoning.[51] The overwhelming importance of individual rights, private property, and economic freedom in the United States had led to this late resolution and acceptance of landmarking compared to western Europe.

The rehabilitation of many inner cities was also aided in the 1970s by the return of affluent, young, and adventurous urban pioneers undeterred by the poor condition of many historic districts and attracted by the low real estate prices. Their purchases and rehabilitations of well-constructed but rundown older housing raised property values and reinvigorated neighborhoods. The restored "Creole cottages" in the newly fashionable Faubourg Treme district adjacent to New Orleans' Vieux Carré and the rehabilitated nineteenth-century brownstones in New York's Harlem and Brooklyn provide examples of how value has soared for properties in formerly blighted neighborhoods.

The arrival of these new owners to American city centers and their piecemeal rehabilitation of buildings and houses also had some unintended negative consequences in many places. The rising property values caused by their improvements displaced their economically disadvantaged neighbors, who were often longtime or characteristic residents of these districts. For example, in New York's SoHo neighborhood, a thriving community of artists attracted to the large open spaces of the area's nineteenth-century loft buildings in the 1960s and 1970s led to the proliferation of studios, galleries, and shops from that point forward. At the same time, the SoHo Cast Iron Historic District was designated in response to the outcry against threats to demolish parts of the neighborhood to make way for new developments. As buildings were restored and property values rose in the 1980s, the artists who had given SoHo its interesting character as well as the light manufacturing businesses that had continued to operate in the district were driven out and replaced by tourists, expensive chain stores, and trendy boutiques and restaurants. A new word was created to describe this phenomenon born out of the success of historic preservation in historic districts like SoHo across the United States: gentrification. The term is now widely understood to mean the displacement of lower-income inhabitants and small businesses by a more affluent population during the renewal of a neighborhood.

As a result of the same biting criticism of postwar urbanism that inspired new urban conservation efforts, President Lyndon Johnson established a Special Committee on Historic Preservation in 1965 to examine European modernization efforts and architectural conservation practices and to comprehensively analyze the problem. The Committee's recommendations for federal preservation leadership were outlined in the publication *With Heritage So Rich*, which suggested the government channel its efforts into four broad areas: (1) compilation of a comprehensive heritage inventory; (2) creation of a mechanism to protect historic properties from damage by federal actions; (3) development of a system of financial incentives to encourage preservation of privately owned sites; and (4) establishment of an independent advisory body to coordinate actions affecting historic preservation issues taken by any federal agency.[52]

The federal leadership role envisioned by the authors of *With Heritage So Rich* is embodied in the National Historic Preservation Act of 1966, which created a system whose strength lies in the symbiotic, layered partnership among many players. This legislation firmly placed historic preservation on national, state, and community agendas and instituted a comprehensive organizational framework for the first time. The 1966 act established State Historic Preservation Officers (SHPOs) charged with surveying all significant historic buildings and sites within each state, district, or territory; administering modest grants-in-aid; and providing technical assistance to historic property owners. Each individual state had to pass its own legislation to establish agencies to support their SHPOs, and most have typically chosen to do so through a parks department, often modeled on the National Park Service.[53] New York was the first state to create an historic preservation agency, the Office of Parks and Recreation, and today has an elaborate preservation program that protects and controls the appearance of sites of historic or aesthetic interest, qualifies rehabilitation work undertaken by citizens and businesses for federally sponsored tax incentives, and requires each town and village to have a historian.

Figure 28-10 The 1966 National Historic Preservation Act established the U.S. National Register of Historic Places, the President's Advisory Council on Historic Preservation, State Historic Preservation Officers, and expanded legal protection, including at archaeological sites affected by federally funded projects such as interstate highways. Illustrated here is archaeological salvage work along Historic Highway 91 in Corona, New Mexico, being conducted in compliance with the National Historic Preservation Act.

The 1966 Historic Preservation Act also authorized the formation of a National Register of Historic Places to coordinate and support public and private efforts to list cultural resources worthy of preservation. Unlike its many foreign counterparts, National Register listing in the United States does not automatically confer protection for sites, as it carries no restrictions or obligations for property owners. Rather, it is a sought-after honorary recognition that can add value and augment the reputation of a historic property.

Compiling the National Register for a country as large and diverse as the United States is a herculean task, and the expanding parameters of historic significance have ensured that it continues to evolve as America's preservation movement grows. The National Register's initial listings reflected earlier traditions, including mostly built sites of historic or architectural interest, especially those associated with prominent historic figures and events. Since its establishment, however, its scope has gradually broadened to include eighty thousand parks, districts, buildings, and objects reflecting all aspects of American history, architecture, archaeology, engineering, and culture. Today the National Register includes such varied resources as landscapes, lighthouses, and prototypical suburban strip malls.[54]

While generally a building or district must have been built or acquired significance more than fifty years ago to be included on the National Register of Historic Places, more recent sites have been added under exceptional circumstances. For example, in 1984 the mission control room and several launch pads at Cape Canaveral Air Force Station in Florida were listed just twenty-five years after witnessing the launching of the United States' first satellite in 1958 and first person into orbit four years later. In addition, the site of the former World Trade Center in New York was added to the National Register in 2004, only three years after the destruction of the two towers by a terrorist attack with particularly far-reaching historic, social, and political ramifications.

In addition to the SHPOs and the National Register, the 1966 act also created the Advisory Council on Historic Preservation, which has played a key role in government conservation efforts. This twenty-person independent federal agency helps coordinate preservation legislation and advises the President and Congress on national historic preservation policy. As part of its educational mandate, the Advisory Council also provides training for federal, tribal, state, and local officials regarding the inclusion of preservation values into their planning processes. It is the official point of contact between the United

a

Figure 28-11 The U.S. National Register of Historic Places, which lists over 85,000 individual historic sites and over 13,500 historic districts occasionally exercises flexibility in some of its listing criteria. Several rocket launch pads at Florida's Cape Canaveral Air Force Station (a) were exceptionally designated just twenty-five years after witnessing the U.S.'s first satellite launch and twenty-one years after the U.S.'s first manned space flight, as opposed to the normal minimum required age of fifty years. Since 1994 the history of the National Aeronautics and Space Administration (NASA) has been represented in the form of restored and replicated space vehicles (b) in an outdoor setting at Cape Canaveral.

b

States government and international organizations such as the International Centre for the Study of the Preservation and Restoration of Cultural Property (ICCROM) and the United Nations Educational, Scientific, and Cultural Organization (UNESCO).

One of the Advisory Council's most public responsibilities is to administer the Section 106 Review process, which is also outlined in the National Historic Preservation Act. This review ensures that all federal agencies fully evaluate the implications of any proposed actions on historically significant sites and the built environment in general. Since passage of the National Environmental Policy Act in 1969, environmental impact statements are also required for any federally funded project. The Federal Preservation Institute was established within the National Park Service to help federal agencies understand the requirements and processes of the Section 106 Review and to meet their technical requirements. In 1971, this review process was further strengthened when President Richard Nixon signed an executive order requiring all federal agencies to preserve, restore, and maintain cultural properties under their control.

The National Register of Historic Places of the United States
Carol D. Shull

The National Register of Historic Places of the United States is the official list of historic places worthy of preservation and the centerpiece of a national historic preservation program authorized by the National Historic Preservation Act of 1966. That law declared that for the United States "the spirit and direction of the Nation are founded upon and reflected in its historic heritage" and that "the historical and cultural foundations of the Nation should be preserved as a living part of our community life and development in order to give a sense of orientation to the American people."[55] To help meet this goal, the law authorizes expanding and maintaining a national register of buildings, sites, districts, structures, and objects significant in American history, architecture, archaeology, engineering, and culture. The National Register fosters a national preservation ethic, promotes a greater appreciation of heritage, and increases and broadens the public's understanding and appreciation of historic places.

Prior to 1966 the United States government recognized only places of national significance—historic units of the National Park System and National Historic Landmarks designated by the secretary of the interior. The National Historic Preservation Act allowed for a broadening of the National Register of Historic Places to include historic properties that are important to states and communities. The act lays out a role for each level of government and for individuals and community groups, creating a remarkably open system of public participation in the registration process. Federal grants from the Historic Preservation Fund provide modest financial support to states, local governments, and American Indian tribes to assist in the work of identifying and recognizing historic properties.

The law gives the secretary of interior the authority to expand and maintain the National Register. Within the Department of the Interior, the National Park Service has been delegated this responsibility. The keeper of the National Register and a staff of historians, architectural historians, archaeologists, and others list and determine the eligibility of properties and otherwise administer the National Register. The National Park Service has developed regulations, criteria for evaluation, and a wide range of published and audiovisual technical assistance materials, such as a series of National Register *Bulletins* that provide guidance on all aspects of the nomination process.

Today, the Internet is the primary means of making this information available.

Federal agencies are required to locate, inventory, and nominate properties under their ownership or control. National parks and wildlife refuges, military reservations, Federal buildings, and public domain land are examples of property by the government of the United States. The agency's federal preservation officer nominates its properties to the National Register.

The states nominate most historic properties to the National Register. The National Historic Preservation Act and its amendments charge states, territories, tribes and the District of Columbia to establish historic preservation programs, which the National Park Service approves. Each appoints a state (or tribal) historic preservation officer responsible for conducting a survey of historic properties and nominating properties to the National Register. Each also appoints a professionally qualified staff to administer its historic preservation program and a review board of experts in history, archaeology, architectural history, architecture, and related disciplines, who participate in the nomination process.

While National Register nominations are under consideration, property owners and local officials receive notice and have an opportunity to comment, and owners of private property have an opportunity to concur with or object to listing. The state, territorial or tribal review board reviews each nomination and considers public input. If the review board recommends the property, the state historic preservation officer generally signs the nomination and forwards it to the National Park Service. The Act also provides for the certification of local governments to participate in the nomination of properties in their communities. If the chief local elected official and the local preservation commission of the certified local government object to listing, the state cannot nominate the property to the National Register unless someone files an appeal. The law also allows individuals and local governments to nominate properties directly to the National Register if a state or territory does not have an approved program.

In fact, citizens everywhere in the United States participate in the National Register. Any person can propose or prepare a nomination and ask the nominating authority to process it, and anyone can comment. Many nomi-

(continued)

nations come from property owners and preservation advocates, although others are the result of government-sponsored surveys. Anyone can appeal nominations, removals, and designations or the failure or refusal of a nominating authority to nominate. The National Park Service also provides a comment period while considering nominations and notifies the public through the *Federal Register* and the National Register Web site of listings, determinations of eligibility, and removals from the National Register.

Because of the sanctity of private property rights in the United States, if the private property owner, or a majority of private owners for a property with multiple owners, objects to listing during the nomination process, the law does not allow the listing of the property. It can be determined eligible for listing, however. This assures that its historic values are recognized and considered in the planning of federal and federally assisted projects.

Most properties included in the National Register listings are in private ownership. Listing does not give the federal government control over private property nor are private property owners required to preserve or maintain their listed property or open it to public. They can do whatever they choose with it under federal law, although they may be subject to local land use controls for historic properties.

Federal agencies proposing projects that may affect a property listed in or eligible for the National Register must allow the Advisory Council on Historic Preservation established by the National Historic Preservation Act an opportunity to comment on the effects of the project. The law does not mandate preservation but ensures the consideration of historic properties in planning federal projects.

National Register listing recognizes and honors the value of historic properties and encourages communities and property owners to preserve these irreplaceable assets. Travel and tourism promotion, real estate advertisements, and other publications cite the listed status of properties to demonstrate their importance and desirability. The National Park Service educates people of all ages about National Register listings not only through the National Register Web site, but also through publications, other media, and the *Discover Our Shared Heritage* Travel Itinerary Series and Teaching with Historic Places lesson plans on the National Park Service Web site.

Owners can apply for federal investment tax credits for rehabilitating income-producing buildings listed in the National Register and may be eligible for federal income, estate, and gift tax deductions for making charitable contributions of partial interests in listed properties. Owners of registered historic places may be able to obtain federal historic preservation funding, when funds are available. Some states and local governments provide their own tax incentives and grants to assist in preserving and rehabilitating properties listed in the National Register.

The National Register criteria by which properties are evaluated are broadly stated and intended to qualify historic places that reflect the contributions of all people to the United States' history and heritage. Properties are evaluated using documentation that describes and explains their significance within specific contexts. The Criteria for Evaluation specifically state:

> The quality of significance in American history, architecture, archaeology, engineering, and culture is present in districts, sites, buildings, structures, and objects that possess integrity of location, design, setting, materials, workmanship, feeling, and association, and
>
> a. *that are associated with events* that have made a significant contribution to the broad patterns of our history; or
>
> b. *that are associated with the lives of persons* significant in our past; or
>
> c. *that embody the distinctive characteristics* of a type, period, or method of construction, or that represent the work of a master, or that possess high artistic values, or that represent a significant and distinguishable entity whose components may lack individual distinction; or
>
> d. *that have yielded, or may be likely to yield, information* about the nation's past.[56]

Special criteria considerations apply to religious properties, moved or reconstructed buildings or structures, birthplaces or graves, cemeteries, commemorative properties. In addition, in general a property must have achieved significance more than fifty years ago to qualify, but the criteria provide for the listing of exceptionally important properties from the past half century.

Nominations to the National Register use standard registration forms, available electronically, that include descriptions, statements of significance, a bibliography, and other data. Maps and photographs are also required. The

National Park Service digitizes registration documentation, which becomes part of a national database used for research, planning, management, education, and interpretation and which is available on the National Register Web site.

Most communities in the United States and its territories have properties included in the National Register. Listing of historic properties continues as the result of ongoing surveys, the passage of time, new scholarship, changing public perceptions about what is historic, and the commitment of property owners and others to recognize and preserve these irreplaceable American assets. Listings include ancient habitation sites; residential, commercial, and rural historic districts; designed and vernacular landscapes; traditional cultural properties; battlefields and forts; homes and work places of political figures, inventors, civil rights leaders, artists, and writers; industrial facilities; farms; canals; ships; airplanes; Cold War missile silos; and examples of many architectural styles and periods of construction. These and other listings demonstrate how the National Register of the United States recognizes the sweeping diversity of its heritage and the magnitude of the American experience.

FURTHER READING

"Discover Our Shared Heritage, Travel Itinerary Series," National Park Service, www.nps.gov/history/nr/travel/ (accessed July 21, 2010).

"Historic Preservation Grants," National Park Service, www.nps.gov/history/hps/hpg/ (accessed July 21, 2010).

"Historic Preservation Tax Incentives," National Park Service, www.nps.gov/hps/tps/tax/ (accessed July 21, 2010).

Federal Historic Preservation Laws (Washington, DC: U.S. Department of the Interior/National Park Service, 2006), www.nps.gov/history/history/hisnps/fhpl.htm (accessed July 21, 2010).

"National Register of Historic Places," National Park Service, www.nps.gov/nr/ (accessed July 21, 2010).

Shull, Carol D. "The National Register of Historic Places." *Cultural Resources Management (CRM)* 25, no. 1 (2002): 3–5; http://crm.cr.nps.gov/archive/25-01/25-01-1.pdf (accessed July 21, 2010).

"Teaching with Historic Places," National Park Service, www.nps.gov/history/nr/twhp.(accessed July 21, 2010).

THE ECONOMICS AND STANDARDS OF HISTORIC PRESERVATION

By establishing an inventory, creating an advisory body, and instituting a process for ensuring that federal projects did not unnecessarily damage historic sites, the National Historic Preservation Act of 1966 successfully addressed three of the four main recommendations of the 1965 report *With Heritage So Rich*. The question of providing financial incentives to encourage private sector participation in historic preservation was addressed a decade later by the Tax Reform Act of 1976. The passage of this act marked a new phase in American historic preservation history; federal tax incentives were made available to those who rehabilitated qualified, income-producing historic buildings, especially in underutilized inner-city areas, and preservation as business was born. The Tax Reform Act of 1976 initially offered a five-year amortization of rehabilitation costs, which attracted many owners and developers to the benefit of America's historic built environment. The U.S. government's tax incentive program is administered by each state's SHPO, who reviews and approves applications from property owners and developers for tax credits based on their rehabilitation efforts.

One of the most important aspects of the 1976 Tax Act was the institution of a system to ensure that the quality of the restoration projects seeking tax relief were of the highest caliber. Projects are only eligible if they meet the criteria outlined within *The Secretary of the Interior's Standards and Guidelines for Rehabilitation*, which was developed based on the tenets of earlier international charters and guidelines, including the Venice Charter. While the *Secretary of the Interior's Standards* were drafted in relatively general terms, a variety of publications and advisories about their implementation give a wealth of highly specific details about conservation—for example, information on the cleaning and repairing of masonry, on the repair (or the replacement "in kind") of historic wooden windows, and on new building systems that do not compromise architectural character.[57]

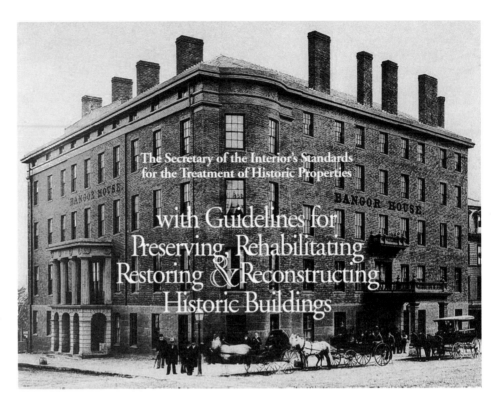

Historic preservation educator Michael A. Tomlan argues that, with the *Secretary of the Interior's Standards*, architectural preservation in the United States "really came of age."[58] Many architectural firms and builders distinguished themselves as specialized experts in restoration and rehabilitation. The response of the construction industry to these parameters was the advent of compatible new construction materials and increased training in restoration craft specialties. University graduate programs in historic preservation continued to expand, and new specialties in allied fields quickly emerged, including preservation engineering and historic landscape restoration. Architectural conservation theory and practice in the United States reached new levels of sophistication at that time, and the benefits of preservation were widely recognized and appreciated.

At first, however, much advocacy work was needed to convince a larger segment of the American population of the merits of historic preservation. Bitter struggles between preservationists, government officials, and developers resulted in the hard-won understanding that some of the best new housing and commercial redevelopment schemes in historic urban areas are those that successfully integrate new and old buildings. New perceptions of old buildings and their potential were demonstrated through the increasing number of creative adaptive-use schemes. Designers and government decision makers discovered that including sensitively rehabilitated old buildings into redevelopment schemes not only increased their options and appealed to the public, but also generated profits. Many city residents were especially enthusiastic about the increased commitments to urban preservation, because only shortly before their neighborhoods could have been targets of urban renewal.

One of the first large scale urban rehabilitation and reuse projects completed was also one of the most commercially successful in United States history: the preservation of the Quincy Market-Faneuil Hall Marketplace in Boston and its three-year conversion into a contemporary shopping center in 1976. Faneuil Hall, built in 1742, served originally as both a meeting space and market for colonial-era Bostonians until Quincy Market was built on the adjacent site in 1826. The complex continued as a bustling center until the 1950s, when it declined rapidly as its users moved from the inner city. In the

Figure 28-13 Restoration and adaptive use in 1976 of the dilapidated early nineteenth-century Quincy Market (a) and the mid-eighteenth-century Faneuil Hall (b) in downtown Boston by a partnership of developers, marketing experts and especially creative architects launched the revival of Boston's urban center in a method that was copied in several other cities in the United States. A carefully considered array of commercial spaces and amenities were provided in the large facility ranging from anchor stores, name restaurants, and other venues (c) to smaller stalls and push carts—even a full-service post office served local and out-of-town visitors in a "festival marketplace" atmosphere.

a

b

c

late 1960s, the Boston Redevelopment Authority acquired the structures and planned their demolition, but it was persuaded to consider redeveloping the site instead. Boston architect Ben Thompson and developer James Rouse suggested rehabilitating the buildings to create a new kind of "festival marketplace" that would revive the neighborhood and pay for itself through lease income. This pioneering initiative was undertaken even before the federal tax credits had been introduced. It has indeed been a popular and commercial success ever since it opened on August 26, 1976, 153 years to the day after Quincy Market's original dedication.

With the marketplace's reopening, Boston regained two important missing components of its downtown commercial area: its "livability" and appeal as a public amenity for longer hours, including weekends. Not only was downtown Boston's image revived but the historic marketplace was restored to its original character as a commercially viable enterprise. The project soon stimulated the renewal of neighboring areas. In addition, it also inspired many major urban rehabilitation projects in other cities, several of which were developed by the Rouse Company, including the South Street Seaport in New York and Harbor Place in Baltimore, Maryland.[59] Boston's success undoubtedly also influenced some well-known European urban marketplace conservation and adaptive use projects, such as Covent Garden in London.

As a result of the financial opportunities provided by tax incentives and the example of Rouse's success in Boston, several types of new players who had typically shied away from preservation entered the field, including more and more commercial property owners and real estate developers. The entrepreneurial opportunities contained in the 1976 Tax Reform Act and subsequent related legislation encouraged a new business-oriented approach to preservation. The economic benefits of historic preservation proved to be massive, with investors putting over $55.5 billion into over 36,400 rehabilitation projects through March 2010.[60]

Across the United States, thousands of architectural preservation projects benefited from the stimulus of the tax incentives, including Pioneer Square in Seattle, Larimer Square in Denver, and Ybor City in Tampa. In addition, the radically improved technical and administrative apparatus created to handle government-supported historic preservation at the local, state, and federal levels assisted many large-scale projects, including the restoration of Grand Central Terminal in New York City.

Although they were somewhat diluted in 1986 by the U.S. Treasury Department, tax credits for qualified rehabilitation are still considered to be one of the country's most effective preservation instruments. Another tax-based incentive scheme was launched in 1981, the Investment Tax Credit for Rehabilitation, whose mix of credits and favorable accounting treatment of expenses made historic rehabilitation projects even more economically competitive with new high-rise buildings with larger rentable spaces.[61] Unfortunately, despite much lobbying, privately owned historic properties remain ineligible for federal tax relief, although several states offer tax credit assistance for eligible commercial properties. Rehabilitation tax credits are also available under certain conditions to owners of properties that offer low-income rental housing.

IMPROVING AND ENHANCING THE SYSTEM

Contemporary historic preservation practice in the United States is still formed on the basis of the important tools and institutions established in the 1960s and 1970s, including municipal landmarks commissions, the SHPOs, the National Register, the Advisory Council and its Section 106 Review process, the *Secretary of the Interior's Standards*, and tax-based incentives. In addition, even earlier programs and policies such as state- and city-level historic districting, the National Park Service, the Historic American Buildings Survey (HABS), and the National Trust for Historic Preservation are all still active, though many have been updated and expanded. Thus in the final quarter of the twentieth century and the early twenty-first century, developments in historic preservation protection in the United States have served as enhancements to the existing, established system.

Since its inception, the National Park Service's agenda has included the sometimes antithetical goals of providing for public recreation and minimizing intrusions at the historic and natural sites it protects. At first, it also attempted rehabilitation and restoration, but in more recent decades activities have focused more on reconstruction for educational purposes. The National Park Service's HABS program was enhanced in

1969 with the addition of the Historic American Engineering Record (HAER) and in 2000 with the Historic American Landscape Survey (HALS), expanding the scope of the United States' heritage that is documented for posterity. For example, HAER has documented hundreds of historic bridges as well as maritime sites, highways, machinery, and industrial buildings. HALS has already made progress photographing, drawing, and writing up descriptions of the cemeteries, parks, gardens, and other human-shaped landscapes important to U.S. history.

Beginning in the 1970s, wholly new historic preservation schemes and regulations improved the climate of architectural conservation in the United States. Cultural resources were inventoried and addressed more thoroughly than ever before, and a myriad of new examples of good preservation practice emerged. The elaborate and extensive celebrations of the U.S. bicentennial in 1976 gave preservationists a perfect opportunity to highlight the significance of the country's cultural heritage and launch numerous new projects for the research, restoration, and presentation of all kinds of Americana.

Among the architectural conservation methods that became popular after passage of the 1976 Tax Reform Act were three pilot projects initiated in 1977, which encouraged the establishment of the National Trust's Main Street Center in 1980. The Main Street program helps communities across the country revitalize their downtown business districts while preserving historic buildings and regaining community spirit.[62] Since 1980 nearly 2,000 American communities have participated in the Main Street program. Investment in this effective public and private partnership program has reached $48.9 billion, restored over 214,000 individual buildings, and created over 94,000 new businesses and over 417,000 new jobs.[63]

The Main Street program's innovative approach continues to enhance historic preservation in the United States through its broad objectives: rehabilitate buildings, attract new businesses, create adequate parking, and make coming to the shopping district a pleasurable family activity. Efforts are channeled into four broadly defined areas: design (enhancement of the physical appearance of the commercial district), organization (creation of cooperative interaction between the various groups involved in a community's revitalization scheme), promotion (marketing and public relation issues), and economic restructuring (ways to strengthen the area's economy and more successfully meet outside challenges from traditional malls and other development schemes).

The success of the Main Street program during the 1980s emphasizes the country's shortfalls in rural preservation, which emerged as the new problem area to be addressed by conservationists interested in both cultural and natural heritage. The National Trust initiated three programs to help communities battle against the detrimental effects of urban and rural sprawl: demonstration projects for rural communities beginning in 1979, the Barn Again! program in 1987, and the Rural Heritage Program in the 1990s. The Barn Again! program, for example, combined publications, an awards program, and technical assistance to encourage the innovative transformation of seemingly obsolete barns to new farm uses. Numerous states, especially in the Midwest, were inspired to create their own organizations and trusts to focus on preserving barns and other components of rural heritage.

The National Center for Preservation Technology and Training was created in 1992 through amendments to the National Historic Preservation Act, which allowed the National Park Service to expand its mission from educating the public about American history through historic sites to also training architects, engineers, developers, and other interested parties in proper architectural conservation techniques via workshops and publications. In addition, the National Center for Preservation Technology and Training has become the materials and technologies research branch of the National Park Service, developing new methods of studying and monitoring threats and of materials conservation. Its focal areas reflect the National Park Service's broad responsibilities and include archaeology and museum collections, architecture and engineering, historic landscapes, materials, and heritage education.

The emergence and growth of historic preservation as a profession in the United States since the 1960s was due in large part to extensive developments in conservation science and technology. This technical side of the profession developed from the work of a few scientists, art restorers, and restoration architects to become the core of the field today. While scientific applications for architectural conservation have developed along similar lines in other parts of the world, especially in Europe, the explosion of scientific and technological developments in response to the burgeioning demands of the field is particularly impressive in the United States from the 1970s on.

Modern conservation science and its practical applications in the United States derives from four main sources: the conservation divisions of museums, the American building industry, observations and importations from abroad, and firsthand experiences in technical problem solving by restoration architects, chemists, engineers, archaeologists, and craftspeople. It was this latter group, in particular, whose job it was to preserve authentic historic materials (and historic building systems) at projects in which they were involved.

The earliest experts involved in the scientific aspects of architectural conservation were art restorers. Restoring and conserving works of art can be traced at least back to the Italian Renaissance, when artists themselves became experienced in the repair and rejuvenation of extant works of art. Along the way, the attendant issues of theory, technique, and their wider implications of both evolved. Concerns from the beginning have included the issue of preserving authenticity, dealing with lacunae (missing elements), and distinguishing old and new materials and elements in all interventions. In both art and architectural conservation these issues can be of enormous importance, and as a result expertise and specialization in restoration and conservation developed. Because it was in art collections where the need for conservation was greatest, the early leaders in the field of conservation science were usually restorers, scientists, and technicians at museums and occasionally at academic institutions who found themselves in increasing demand to address "immovable" as well as "movable" heritage. Some of these early experts in the United States

include Sheldon Keck at the Brooklyn Museum of Art and Craig Hugh Smyth, Seymour Lewin, and Lawrence Majewski at New York University's Institute of Fine Arts. They continued the work of their numerous counterparts in Europe, such as Paul Coremans at the Institute Royal Partrimoine in Paris and Harold Plenderleith at the British Museum and after 1959, first director of the International Centre for the Study of the Preservation and Restoration of Cultural Property (ICCROM).[64] These names in fact follow the groundbreaking work in restoration and conservation theory and practice of Alois Reigl (Austria), Roberto Longhi and Cesare Brandi (Italy), Paul Philippot (Belgium), Max Doerner (Germany), and George Stout and Rutherford Gettens at the Fogg Art Museum (Boston).[65]

The American building industry also played a key role in the development of conservation science through manufacturers' research and development branches of product manufacturers in response to market needs. Various independent chemists, scientists, and technicians became associated with the field via their interests in the building trades, and the building products industry made contributions in the areas of masonry, wood, glass, and paint conservation. The proliferation of the architectural restoration and preservation industry in North America can be easily traced by examining the increasing presence of references to preservation projects, products, and services within architectural trade magazines such as *Architecture, Architectural Record, Traditional Building,* and the *Old-House Journal.*

Importation of techniques from conservation professionals who had already faced similar problems, especially from Europe, led to the transmission of ideas and methods of architectural conservation.[66] Various American fact-finding missions went to Europe to observe architectural restoration practice and brought back news of established government commitment to the issue and of academic institutions that were teaching conservation. Such examples were noted and followed in several instances. A related form of transmission was the importation of scientists, restorers, and craftsmen themselves.

Practitioners involved in actual hands-on projects have also made significant contributions to architectural conservation science. These individuals may range from specialist architects, engineers, chemists, stone conservators, and other scientists to specialized craftspeople. Examples of high-profile restoration projects from the founding years of conservation science as a profession include Colonial Williamsburg in the early 1930s, restoration of Independence Hall in the 1960s, the experiences of restorers at the Society for the Preservation of New England Antiquities, and experiences of building technology experts within the National Park Service's Technical Preservation Services division.

The graduate-level training programs in historic preservation at Columbia University and the University of Pennsylvania have taught conservation sciences and technology almost from the years of their founding, 1964 and 1982 respectively. Distinguished professors of architectural conservation at both universities have included Norman Weiss, Frank G. Matero, Martin Weaver, and George Wheeler, and additional instructors have included Jeanne Marie Teutonico, Elena E. Charola, Fran Gale, Glenn Boornazian, and Mary Jablonski. At New York University's Institute of Fine Arts, which focuses on objects conservation as well as architectural conservation, scientists such as Norbert S. Baer and Margaret Ellis have carried on the traditions of Lewin and Majewski. In their influential positions, such professors have taught two generations of conservation scientists and technicians. The very nature of university research-based instruction led to the development of a variety of conservation materials and techniques that inspired enterprising graduates to enter the profession as specialty consultants to government agencies, specialists within cultural institutions and architectural firms, and as professional staff at the specific heritage sites.[67]

Even with these higher education programs, in the 1980s it became apparent that some of the technical skills essential for architectural conservation were no longer easily found. For example, the fabrication of stained glass windows had declined since the nineteenth century when countless ecclesiastical structures were built across the country. And even fewer were trained as stained glass conservators. This realization of the need for more trained materials conservation specialists led to the formation of a variety of ad hoc training programs, often around specific projects, such as at the Church of St. Ann and Holy Trinity in Brooklyn, St. Marks in the Bowery, and the Cathedral of St. John the Divine in Morningside Heights—all in New York City. By the 1990s the need for more systematic approaches was clear. Boston's North Bennet Street School, founded in the nineteenth century as an industrial training program, emerged as a beacon for teaching conservation skills. Over the last thirty years, other programs have formed the groups addressing the need for continuing expansion of hands-on experience, including the Preservation Trades Network and the American College of the Building Arts.[68]

Architectural conservation science in the United States today is served by several institutions and professional interest groups. The most prominent federally supported facilities are the National Center for Preservation Technology and Training (NCPTT) and the Museum Conservation Institute (MCI) of the Smithsonian Institution. Among the private not-for-profit institutions with in-house technical capacity, the leader in both American and international conservation practice is the Getty Conservation Institute (GCI) in Los Angeles, California, and its counterpart in Canada, the Canadian Conservation Institute (CCI) based in Ottawa, Ontario. North American professional conservation membership organizations include the Association for Preservation Technology (APT) and the American Institute for Conservation (AIC).

All of these individuals, institutions, and companies have participated in the sophisticated technical problem solving that is conservation science and which aims to meet architectural conservation practice's primary aim of slowing or arresting the decay process. Their focus has been on the great variety of building materials, each with its own physical characteristics, threats, and problems, as well as with their own solutions. The application of these developments in materials conservation as well as in documentation of as-found conditions, testing, and monitoring, have been perfected through experimentation.

Numerous sources have thoroughly documented the discoveries and solutions that conservation has found regarding the range of threats to building materials and built heritage. Examples include Bernard Fielden's *Architectural Conservation*, Martin Weaver's *Conserving Buildings*, Giorgio Croce's *The Conservation and Structural Restoration of Architectural Heritage*, Harold Plenderleith's *The Conservation of Antiquities*

(continued)

and *Works of Art,* and a plethora of journals and occasional publications such as the *APT Bulletin: Journal of Preservation Technology,* the *Journal of Architectural Conservation,* the *Journal of the American Institute of Conservation,* and the Technical Brief Series of the National Park Service's Technical Preservation Services division. It is among these sources and others, especially the well-indexed bibliographies on the World Wide Web, that the constantly evolving developments in architectural conservation science and methodology are best researched.

FURTHER READING

Getty Conservation Institute (GCI) Bulletin and *Conservation Perspectives: The GCI Newsletter,* www.getty.edu/conservation/publications/ (accessed July 22, 2010).

Matero, Frank G. "Loss, Compensation, Authenticity: The Contribution of Cesare Brandi to Architectural Conservation in America." *Future Anteriors: Journal of the Historic Preservation History, Theory, and Criticism* 4, no. 1 (Summer 2007): 45–63.

Weaver, Martin E. with F. G. Matero. *Conserving Buildings: A Guide to Techniques and Materials.* (New York: John Wiley & Sons, 1993).

Figure 28-14 Architectural conservator Morgan Phillips repairing an historic window sash in the laboratory of the Northeast Regional Office of the U.S. National Park Service (a). The chemical cleaning of the granite base of the Post Office Building, Washington, DC (b). Images courtesy U.S. National Park Service, Washington, DC.

There has been a slow but sure increase in advanced technical training for crafts-people in the United States in recent decades. Some of the most important examples include the National Center for Preservation Technology and Training, established within the National Park Service in 1992, and the preservation carpentry program at the North Bennet Street School in Boston. Though in the United States most training programs are more directly associated with the building industry, professional organizations, and the government than they are with academia, since the mid-twentieth century, professional graduate programs in historic preservation have augmented the field and replaced earlier traditions of training in Europe or self-study.

The first such program in the United States was created by architect and architectural historian James Marston Fitch in 1964 at Columbia University. Still a leader in the field, Columbia's program has served as a precedent for the more than fifty U.S. institutions that today offer undergraduate or graduate-level education in architectural preservation and allied disciplines. Subfields such as preservation planning, archaeological site management, and conservation technology have evolved as these programs have matured, and the increased number of professionals has allowed for specialization. The proliferation of opportunities in preservation education is evidence of the maturity of American architectural preservation practice by the turn of the twenty-first century.

To celebrate the Millennium, the National Trust joined with the National Park Service and the U.S. presidency to establish another important public and private partnership to preserve and celebrate some of the most important American cultural resources, including threatened historic structures, documents, objects, and collections. The program, called Save America's Treasures, was introduced by President William J. Clinton in 1998. One of the first grants awarded through this program helped further preserve the ancient cliff dwellings of Mesa Verde National Park, which a century earlier had provided inspiration for the landmark 1906 Antiquities Act. Today the Save America's Treasures program continues to identify and designate official projects and raise funds and advocate on their behalf. These projects address a wide range of American cultural heritage, including the Declaration of Independence, the specific American flag that inspired the American national anthem, the oldest standing African-American church in the country, and President Lincoln's summer cottage. In 2003 another federal initiative, Preserve America, was established by President George W. Bush to assist local communities foster an appreciation for the preservation of their sites of historic importance.

Nonprofit organizations have continued to play a vital role in historic preservation in the United States, and in fact in the late twentieth century, professional and non-professional groups have become more involved than ever. Though this involvement reflects the continued importance of an engaged public to the history of architectural conservation in the United States, though today these groups represent a broad base of support rather than just a few social and economic elites as at the movement's beginning in the nineteenth century. For example, the American Institute of Architects (AIA), encouraged by its early successes lobbying on behalf of New Orleans' Vieux Carré in the 1930s and New York's Grand Central Terminal in the 1970s, has begun addressing other preservation issues in recent years. Through its well-known and effective Committee on Historic Resources, the AIA publishes newsletters with updates on preservation activities and best practices as well as seeks to provide resources for preservation architects and share the expertise of its professionals with preservation organizations.

The Washington, D.C.–based advocacy group, Preservation Action, was established in 1974 to lobby the federal government on behalf of preservation causes and has been instrumental in facilitating the passage of various laws and amendments, including the seminal Tax Reform Act of 1976. More recently, Preservation Action has focused on helping local organizations advocate for preservation in their own communities and states as well as continuing to lobby Congress for increased funding for federal preservation projects and agencies.

a

Figure 28-15 The largest single architectural preservation project to date in the United States is restoration of the north half of the Ellis Island Immigration Station in New York Harbor (a, b, and c), costing approximately $275 million in the late 1980s. There are current plans to stabilize and restore the remainder of the structures on the island. Ellis Island is a cultural heritage site of world importance as the location where over 12 million immigrants arrived to begin a new life in the New World. A different type of heritage site where major historical events also happened is Pearl Harbor, Hawaii. The *USS Arizona* war memorial (d) in Pearl Harbor commemorates those who died in the attack of December 7, 1941, and the onset of the United States' entry into World War II. The viewing pavilion straddling the sunken warship (e) accommodates visitors who arrive by boat.

b

New challenges face contemporary architectural conservationists in the United States, but innovative new initiatives to raise interest and awareness of historic preservation have also been launched in the early twenty-first century. Historic house museums, the foundation on which the U.S. preservation movement began, have lost visitors and revenue in recent years, leading to the closure of some properties and their return to private ownership. Even Colonial Williamsburg sold in 2010 the 400-acre Carter's Grove Plantation with a preservation easement to ensure its continued protection by its future resident-owner. Some $20 million from the plantation's sale will be used to fund a new museum wing reflecting a shift in Colonial Williamsburg's priorities to more engaging and interactive educational experiences than can be offered by (some say) "boring" house museums.[69]

c

d

e

Other major sites, such as Mount Vernon, have combined continued stewardship of historic homes with the latest in multimedia didactic experiences. A major new orientation center and educational complex was opened in 2006 at Mount Vernon after the MVLA successfully raised over $110 million, including generous contributions from the Ford Motor Company and the Donald W. Reynolds Foundation. Over 65 percent of this 66,700-square-foot complex was built underground to mitigate its impact on Mount Vernon's historic setting.[70]

Rethinking the approach to house museums is not the only early twenty-first century innovation to further historic preservation efforts in the United States. Other new programs have helped raise funds and awareness of the needs of the country's architectural heritage. For example, many states have begun selling specialized license plates whose proceeds are used to support either a specific historic site or to fund matching grant programs for restoration projects at sites throughout their territory. In 2006 the National Trust for Historic Preservation and American Express launched an online competition in the city of San Francisco where Bay Area residents could vote on which of twelve local historic sites should be the beneficiary of part of a $1 million restoration grant. Due to the program's success and the level of public interest and participation, it will be continued in other U.S. cities in future years.

PRESERVING A MOSAIC OF HERITAGES IN THE UNITED STATES AND ITS TERRITORIES

Like many countries, the United States is a cultural mélange with diverse people forming its dynamic multicultural population, and its architecture also strongly reflects influences from various places and cultural backgrounds. Despite this diversity, America's colonial past and the heritage of its European immigrants and their descendants dominated historic preservation efforts for most of the nineteenth and twentieth centuries. It was not until the 1970s that other American heritages became increasingly valued and appreciated, and more and more sites associated with minorities and special interests groups were restored and protected. Changing views toward race, gender, and minorities have influenced all American social and political institutions, including those concerned with the preservation of cultural heritage.

Often overlooked in the history of the United States, and still little understood by outsiders, are the traditions of North America's original inhabitants. The relationship between the cultures of European settlers and Native Americans was for centuries characterized by appropriation and displacement by the newcomers, and these policies are still being uncomfortably reconciled and overcome today.

There is no lack of monumental and impressive remains of American civilizations that predate the European conquest of the western hemisphere. The extraordinary sites of Chaco Canyon, Mesa Verde, and others in the southwestern United States, as well as numerous impressive earthworks in the Mississippi River valley and eastward, attest to the cultural richness of various Native American communities. These settlements and earthworks were occasionally noted as curiosities by the earliest Europeans, and later some were protected among the federal government's earliest national park or land-conservation initiatives. For the most part; however, little attention has been paid to the considerable range of less dramatic, but no less important, Native American sites.

Though both professional and amateur archaeologists have documented the widespread presence of Native American heritage, public interest in these places and their interpretation remains limited. In the past two decades, several federal, state, and even local efforts to conserve Native American heritage have tried to focus attention and funding on these long overlooked sites and cultures. The National Park Service began administering grants directly to Native American communities to preserve historic sites in 1990, and more importantly a 1992 amendment to the National Historic Preservation Act authorized the establishment of Tribal Historic Preservation Officers (THPOs) for federally recognized Indian tribes. A Tribal Preservation Officer is nominated by the governing authority of a tribe and assumes the same responsibilities within a tribal land as a SHPO does within a state. By 2010, 102 Native American communities had THPOs responsible for surveying and inventorying historic sites and nominating properties to the National Register.[71] These organizations coordinate activities and share experiences through the National Association of Tribal Historic Preservation Officers.

In addition to providing a sovereign administrative framework through which Native Americans could preserve their heritage in the United States, the 1992 amendment to the Historic Preservation Act also expanded the types of sites eligible for National Register listing to embrace specific Native American concerns. A new "traditional places" category allows for the inclusion of religiously or culturally important sites that might not meet earlier, perhaps western-biased criteria.[72] Many sites already protected for their natural beauty are now also appreciated for their cultural and historic importance to Native Americans.

Beginning in 2003, the bicentennial celebrations of Meriwether Lewis and William Clark's expedition, which explored and documented a large portion of the North American continent in the early nineteenth century, provided an important opportunity for raising awareness of Native American heritage as well as for its protection.[73] Though many Native American communities have mixed feelings about the Lewis and Clark legacy, many have been eager to capitalize on the financial opportunity that tourism may bring as well as for the chance to tell their side of the historical story, complete with the indignities and their interpretation of their own cultures.[74] For example, a number of Native American reservations in North Dakota have trained tour guides and craft demonstrators, produced maps and audio tours of their regions, and re-created traditional buildings to help overcome stereotypes and present their own heritage. At Idaho's Lemhi Pass, Native American and non-Native American organizations and agencies partnered to preserve this culturally important natural landmark where Lewis and Clark, with the aid of Native American guides, became the first United States citizens to cross the Continental Divide two centuries ago.

The native populations of Hawaii and Alaska present another unique challenge to U.S. heritage conservation efforts. Under the National Park Service provisions for all Native Americans these communities are eligible for federal grants and can establish Tribal Historic Preservation Officers; however, they have more often tended to work for architectural preservation within the parameters of their state SHPOs. Despite this, Hawaii's SHPO has protected and carried out projects at natural and cultural sites that reflect traditional Hawaiian religious and political history, such as Keahualaka Halau Hula preserve, associated with the goddess of the hula dance, and Kaniakapupu, the ruins of the nineteenth-century summer home of the Hawaiian royal family. The nonprofit Historic Hawaii Foundation, established in 1974, is devoted to preserving native Hawaiian archaeological sites, objects, and buildings as well as popularizing and encouraging respect for this long-overlooked facet of American history. It also works as an advocacy group to lobby on behalf of threatened sites, such as the Keakealaniwahine archaeological complex, which include the foundations of sixteenth-century stone structures. Though donated to the state in 1998, this complex suffered for over a decade from a lack of maintenance, conservation, and interpretation.

Since the 1970s, prehistoric and historic native Alaskan sites have been added to the National Register, including the Sitka Camp, built in 1914 as a meeting hall for the founding chapter of the Alaska Native Brotherhood, the first organization promoting rights and recognition of Native Alaskans. The Alaska Native Brotherhood and Sisterhood is still active today and has worked diligently to promote historic preservation in their state, launching projects focused on community houses, totem poles, and other legacies of Aleutian and Tlingit heritage. In relation to this recent archaeological excavations at Castle Hill in Alaska have unearthed important evidence of the Sitka Tlingit Tribe as well as eighteenth- and early nineteenth-century Russian settlements and workshops.

While the late twentieth century has witnessed efforts to assert the rights and contributions of America's native peoples, years of neglect cannot be easily eradicated. Numerous sites have yet to be protected. Given their antiquity, or "age value" alone, each of these sites deserves careful consideration for their protection. The slow appreciation and interpretation of Native American sites is in part the result of the complicated issues they raise:

Figure 28-16 Since the 1960s the U.S. National Park Service has worked with local artisans to reconstruct and maintain the temple and burial site Hale o keawe heiau, in Puʻuhonua O Honaunau National Historical Park on the Big Island of Hawaii.

they require treatments reflective of native oral traditions and concepts of spirituality, land, and human relations, both at the time of their earliest encounters with European settlers and today. In these aspects, American cultural resource managers could learn from their Australian counterparts, who have wholly reassessed the significance of their aboriginal past and now handle it with greater sensitivity and innovation.

In recent decades increasing attention has also been paid to culturally important historic places associated with non-European immigrants in the United States, as well as with other minority communities. Certainly among the most important and pervasive of these groups of places have been those related to African American history, beginning with sites associated with slavery but also to important individuals, the civil rights movement, and black communities and institutions. Southern plantations and house museums, such as George Washington's Mount Vernon and Thomas Jefferson's Monticello, have begun to uncover and interpret their slave quarters and to present this aspect of their history alongside the long-appreciated history of their stately mansions. In New York City, a slave cemetery was discovered in Lower Manhattan during construction of a federal office building in 1991, and it has since been preserved as the African Burial Ground National Monument. After ten years of archaeological research, many of the unearthed artifacts were documented and reproduced before they (and the recovered human remains) were reinterred. Today the site features a visitor center and an outdoor memorial.

In 1990 the National Park Service began studying the Underground Railroad and sponsored a program to identify, protect, and present sites related to this important secret organization that enabled many slaves to find their way to freedom through a series of safe houses and passages. The initial National Park Service study found nearly four hundred sites in thirty-four states and two territories that were linked to the Underground Railroad and that should be recognized as important American historical sites.[75] In recent years, a number of states have sponsored their own initiatives to restore these sites. For example, Eleutherian College in Lancaster, Indiana, where fugitive slaves were hidden and educated on their way north, and Quaker Meeting Houses in Delaware, which were often the last stop before the final journey to freedom in the northern states, have been protected and opened to the public.

Sites associated with slavery and the quest for its abolition are not the only important components of African American history to have been preserved. Later developments have been remembered through the restoration of sites such as the Ferris District in Jackson, Mississippi, the oldest continuing black community in the United States. Preserved sites associated with the civil rights movement include a lunch counter in the F. W. Woolworth store in Greensboro, North Carolina, where black college students in 1960 staged a groundbreaking sit-in to demand equal service, an action that encouraged similar protests in numerous other states. An additional preserved portion of the historic lunch counter is also on display in the Smithsonian Institution Museum of American History in Washington, D.C. The entire Woolworth's building in Greensboro has been converted into an International Civil Rights Center and Museum. Similarly, the Lorraine Motel in Memphis, Tennessee, where the human rights advocate Dr. Martin Luther King Jr. was assassinated on April 4, 1968, was initially preserved as a shrine by its owner. It was later purchased by a locally established memorial foundation and transformed into the National Civil Rights Museum with support from the city, county, and state governments.

Figure 28-17 A binational effort to preserve the river towns of the Lower Rio Grande between Laredo and Brownsville, Texas, is an award-winning program of the Texas Historical Commission and the Mexican Secretariat of Tourism called Los Caminos del Rio/Roads of the River. Its approach has been to promote the protection and economic revitalization of an entire historic trade and transportation system in part via heritage tourism. In addition to its multicultural nature, the project has also been appealing because it promotes positive cooperation between United States and Mexican border and heritage protection agencies. Viewed here is the main street of Roma, Texas, before its restoration, one of several pairs of historic Rio Grande towns situated along the historic transportation route.

Figure 28-18 Some of America's historic highways are increasingly being viewed as heritage routes worth conserving. Route 66, that has connected Chicago to Los Angeles since 1927 and runs through some of the country's most picturesque landscapes, is an example of an iconic highway. The Route 66 Associations consist of preservation advocacy groups located in the eight states through which the "Mother Road," with its array of historic architecture and amenities, passes.

Other American minority and special interest groups have also gained greater appreciation of their own heritage as sites important to their histories became protected and valued by American society at large. Examples of recognized historic places today include Wesleyan Chapel in Seneca Falls, New York, where the women's suffrage movement began in 1848; the Stonewall Inn in Greenwich Village, New York, where a 1969 uprising launched the gay and lesbian rights movement; and César E. Chávez' home near Bakersfield, California, from which the legendary activist worked tirelessly for the rights of Hispanic migrant farm workers. In the 1990s, Spanish colonial and Hispanic heritage on both sides of the Rio Grande River was also preserved as part of a cooperative project between the Texas Historic Commission and the Mexican Secretariat of Tourism. Through this Los Caminos del Rio/Roads of the River project, the central plaza and rich collection of eighteenth-century buildings in Roma, the Our Lady of Refuge Catholic Church in San Ygnacio, and numerous other sites were restored on the U.S. side of the border, while Guerrero Vijeo and other towns on the Mexican side also received attention from local and state heritage conservationist organizations.

The panorama of cultures, peoples, histories, and sites in the territories of the United States, including American Samoa, Guam, the Northern Mariana Islands, Puerto Rico, and the U.S. Virgin Islands, constitutes another significant component of recognized American cultural heritage.[76] According to the 1966 National Historic Preservation Act, territories are equivalent to states with regard to preservation issues, and so Historic Preservation Offices have been established in each. As a result, hundreds of National Register sites and several National Historic Districts have been designated among these islands.

The tropical climates of these Caribbean and Pacific island countries pose special challenges for architectural conservationists in these regions as compared with elsewhere in the United States. Atypical historic building types and techniques for the United States also exist in these territories. For instance, the U.S. Virgin Islands are home to some eighteenth-century Danish colonial residential architecture and the remains of wind-driven sugar mills. In Puerto Rico's capital, the La Fortaleza and San Juan Historic Site is one of the best-preserved colonial landscapes in the Caribbean, and it is the only American territorial structure on UNESCO's World Heritage List. Puerto Rico is also home to a wealth of Spanish colonial residential architecture and historic agricultural and industrial structures.

In the Caribbean, the greatest threats to built heritage include hurricanes, suburban sprawl, unchecked urban development, and tourism.[77] In addition, many undocument-

Figure 28-19 In Charlotte Amalie on the island of St. Thomas in the U.S. Virgin Islands, the restoration of the 1830s Kathrineberg governor's house (illustrated) and the seventeenth-century Danish-built Fort Christian—the island's history museum—are among the several heritage sites being protected in the U.S. territories in the Caribbean.

ed archaeological sites associated with the indigenous people of the U.S. Virgin Islands are at risk from tourism-related commercial developments. Tourism in Puerto Rico employs about half of its population and is therefore the country's economic lifeline, but it has also led to the over-commercialization of some of its architectural heritage. This is especially the case in Old San Juan, where historic authenticity has been seriously compromised in places. This historic district's former sense of local life and variety is largely gone because its original inhabitants—a vital part of the living heritage of this site—were driven out by high property values and replaced by tourist boutiques and hotels.

Recent work on the Kathrineberg in St. Thomas, U.S. Virgin Islands, demonstrates conservation efforts to rehabilitate this 1830s plantation home's original cross-ventilation system, which was carefully designed to maintain cool temperatures.[78] This structure is one of the oldest private residences of the U.S. Virgin Islands, and today it serves as the governor's residence. The classically derived Danish colonial facade and interior decorations, while predominately a reflection of European designs and techniques, also incorporate elements that respond to the Caribbean climate, such as high ceilings, louvered shutters, and generously sized openings. In 2000 Kathrineberg underwent a major restoration that reversed many later additions and changes that had altered the buildings ventilation capacity and led to increased moisture and mold.[79]

The U.S. tax incentive programs of the mid-1970s and 1980s have helped to preserve sensitively the historic buildings and townscapes of the Caribbean islands that are U.S. territories. The U.S. Virgin Islands also have their share of especially successful at adaptive reuse schemes, including the transformation of the oldest surviving building in the territory, Fort Christian in the harbor area of Charlotte Amalie, that was built by the Danes in the seventeenth century, into the St. Thomas Museum.[80] Over the past half century, local political and grassroots actions, supported by several government and nongovernmental organizations, have also encouraged many preservation successes on these islands. The Institute of Puerto Rican Culture, the Puerto Rican Conservation Trust, the St. Croix Landmarks Society, and the St. Croix Foundation are among the most active and important of these organizations.[81]

Preservation challenges in United States' Pacific territories are similar to those found in the Caribbean, but they are compounded by the unusual cultural mix of their populations. While some islands were uninhabited until World War II, others were regularly used by a variety of nations and cultures as shipping way stations, military depots, and hunting grounds. Most of these bear the architectural imprints of indigenous people along with those of the Spanish, Japanese, Dutch, and American colonizers.

Conservation efforts in both Guam and the Northern Mariana Islands today are hampered by land competition, development pressures, and U.S. military activities. A growing tourism industry in both territories may aid but also may hinder preservation efforts. Most of the inhabited islands contain communities and advocates interested in preservation of both indigenous and colonial heritage. In American Samoa, several locally built stone quarries, villages, archaeological sites, and defensive structures are listed on the National Register, along with World War II era structures and early American naval administration buildings within the U.S. Naval Station Tutuila Historic District.[82] World War II military installations make up a significant component of the region's architectural heritage; however, this important architectural evidence of American and Pacific regional history was abandoned in the 1950s and has mostly fallen into disrepair.

Throughout the United States' overseas territories, the influx of mainland ideas, products, and practices threatens both their distinctive local cultures and their historic buildings and sites. In addition, local attempts at modernization, quests for short-term profits, and focus on commercial and tourist development also pose frequent threats. But these communities also seek to maintain their special cultural identities, and this is a natural ally of historic preservation. Through the joint efforts of both the resident SHPOs and the local cultural organizations, the key historic characteristics of these islands will likely be sustained.

Figure 28-20 Historic preservation in the U.S. territories in the Pacific Region usually entails accommodating cultural differences. Preserving former U.S. Navy administrative buildings in Guam (a) must be balanced with the concerns of the local community and their indigenous heritage. In Pago Pago, Samoa, traditional domestic architectural forms (b), which have mixed with early-twentieth-century mainland, American-style residential forms, have been preserved.

a

b

NEW CONCERNS IN THE TWENTY-FIRST CENTURY

In the early twenty-first century, historic preservation in the United States has continued many of the trends and continues to use many of the tools and policies developed by earlier generations, but it has also begun moving in new directions. In looking forward, there is still much more to do in the field.

While in the final decades of the twentieth century there were a few conservation projects focused on the architecture of the recent past, this kind of work is a burgeoning new specialty in the twenty-first century. Many of the designs and materials used in the creation of modernist architecture are quite different from the relatively simple palate of traditional construction materials that preceded it. Thus, conserving some of the more specialized building designs of the twentieth century poses new questions in both conservation theory and practices. Fortunately, today's architectural conservation practice is rising to the occasion, as several specialty architectural and engineering firms have developed expertise in this area. Further signs of the response to the need for architectural conservators can be seen in exhibitions, literature, and advocacy schemes devoted to preserving significant twentieth-century architecture and in the increasing number of training opportunities for both young and established professionals alike.

Figure 28-21 The restoration in 2005 of Frank Lloyd Wright's most famous residential design, Fallingwater (a) at Bear Run, Pennsylvania, well represents one of the most important recent trends in architectural conservation—restoration of modern architecture. For architects, engineers, and conservators, such work requires new understandings of the proliferation of new construction materials, systems, and methods developed during the interwar and immediate post-World War II era, and offers some of the most exciting research and problem-solving work in the field today. The team effort to conserve Fallingwater, led by Wank Adams Slavin, Architects, and engineers Robert Silman, Associates (New York), addressed several vexing problems, most notably the sagging of the cantilevered-beam systems that form two of the building's distinctive terraces. The solution involved the temporary shoring and protection of the lower southwest terrace (b), exposure of the original concrete floor and beam system on the main floor (c), and the posttensioning of principal slab beams (d) to prevent further movement. Images b, c, and d courtesy of the Western Pennsylvania Conservancy.

a

b

c

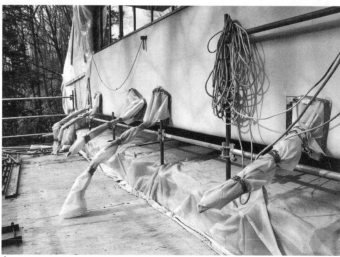

d

a

b

c

d

Figure 28-22 A special aspect of conserving modern buildings is the shear enormity of the problem in some circumstances, especially in relation to the height of some structures that periodically must be maintained and restored. The restoration of the Town Hall (1929-31) in Buffalo, New York (a), entailed the replacement of brick- and terra-cotta masonry units, after in situ testing using various nondestructive techniques (b). Daniel Burnham's 1894 Reliance Building (c) in Chicago was one of the world's first skyscrapers. The building's exterior, which was completely clad in terra-cotta (d), underwent a restoration similar to that of the Buffalo Town Hall. Images (a) and (b) courtesy of Jon Reis, Vertical Access.

Special interest groups and an appreciation for the heritage of minorities have fueled the expansion of new programs and the development of important new mechanisms and programs that have benefited preservation efforts throughout the country. The vulnerability of historic sites and cities to large-scale threats was revealed by the terrorist attacks of September 11, 2001, and by the hurricanes that battered the Gulf coast in 2005. In the years since, security and emergency preparedness have become special concerns in preservation planning and site management in the United States.

In those attacks of September 2001 two American cultural symbols and unofficial landmarks were targeted by foreign terrorist groups: the World Trade Center office complex in New York City was destroyed and the Pentagon, the headquarters of the U.S. Department of Defense near Washington, D.C., was damaged. Not only did the groundswell of patriotism following these attacks increase appreciation of the importance of historic sites across the country—as well as the numbers of persons visiting them—but there was an immediate increase in protection of the country's key buildings and spaces, many of which are historic. In response, the federal government has delegated billions of dollars to improve security at major infrastructure facilities, vulnerable public buildings and spaces, and national landmarks. Thus, in the United States, the first few years of the twenty-first century have been characterized by a heightened appreciation of the country's cultural heritage and increased funding for specific types of interventions at select historic sites.

In early 2002 the Federal Preservation Institute (FPI) organized two conferences on "balancing public safety and protection of historic places," at which the country's experts met to discuss how sites and their visitors could be protected from future attacks without compromising the integrity or aesthetics of these important places.[83] The conferences led to the development of a set of standards to be considered during security infrastructure upgrades, which were jointly drafted by the FPI, the National Park Service, the Advisory Council on Historic Preservation, and the National Center for Preservation Technology and Training.[84]

Historic sites across the country, and visitor experiences at them, have been altered by the changed security climate in the United States. The Statue of Liberty in New York harbor was closed to the public in 2001—after new screening and security checkpoints and new means of egress were constructed, tourists were allowed to reenter the statue's massive stone pedestal in August 2004; however, the observation platforms in the crown remained closed until July 2009. Even at less iconic sites, visitors are subjected to increased searches and screening processes that are often added as unsightly intrusions to existing reception areas, and more importantly, the reallocation of resources from maintenance and interpretation to security has posed a new threat to some sites.

The city most probably significantly affected by the new security measures is Washington, D.C., because of its concentration of politically, symbolically, historically, and architecturally significant sites such as the White House, the U.S. Capitol, and the numerous monuments commemorating the most important persons and events in U.S. history. The National Capital Planning Commission, the federal agency responsible for preserving and planning in the District of Columbia, prepared a report on the city's preparedness for future threats as early as October 2001.[85] The report assessed the city's security needs and proposed designs for added security at the urban scale, with a particular focus on the area around the White House, the residence and office of the U.S. president. Permanent security upgrades and barriers have been devised for other downtown Washington landmarks, including the Lincoln and Jefferson memorials. At the U.S. Capitol building, a new visitor's entrance with expanded screening facilities and enhanced monitoring was constructed beneath its east lawn. The Washington Monument was closed for a few months in 2001 and concrete barriers and unsightly fencing were immediately erected to protect it; however, a $15 million project in 2005 involving less obtrusive, aesthetically appropriate landscaping now deters vehicular traffic, potentially containing threats, from approaching the monument.[86]

Emergency preparedness planning at historic sites in the United States took yet another turn after a systemic weakness in disaster preparedness and response was revealed by the destruction of New Orleans, Louisiana; Biloxi, Mississippi; and other Gulf Coast cities and sites caused by Hurricanes Katrina and Rita in 2005. Planning for natural disasters has, therefore, also moved to the forefront of historic preservation discussions in the United States. After Hurricane Katrina, the city of New Orleans and the affected Mississippi Gulf Coast were placed on the 2006 World Monuments Watch List and demonstration restoration projects were conducted in both places. New Orleans' twenty historic districts, which are also on the National Register of Historic Places, were included on the National Trust's 2006 list of most endangered sites. Looking beyond the exceptional buildings of these districts, the National Trust also quickly published guides for homeowners to explain how to evaluate and to repair their historic homes. In partnership with other organizations and corporate donors, it also established a long-term Hurricane Recovery Fund to help them financially in the years of neighborhood-rebuilding ahead. In the spring of 2006 the National Trust and Tulane University in New Orleans organized a conference to discuss the role cultural heritage could play in the city's renewal.[87]

Though disaster planning and recovery have driven architectural preservation efforts in the United States in recent years, it remains to be seen what long-term influence these two especially costly disasters will have on American cultural heritage protection. The future will reveal whether this new focus is reflective of a short-term reaction or a greater paradigm shift; nonetheless, at present it is clear that architectural preservationists in the United States have both popular support and access to the resources necessary to respond effectively to threats against the country's considerable historic resources.

a

b

Figure 28-23 The problems of postdisaster response and recovery in New Orleans, Louisiana, after Hurricane Katrina on August 29, 2005, were witnessed in the media around the world. Typically, historic preservation organizations are among the first to move in and try to help, even if the task seems overwhelming. The Preservation Resource Center, the National Trust for Historic Preservation, and the World Monuments Fund launched representative heritage-property rescue and recovery efforts along the Gulf Coast. For example, WMF helped in Biloxi, Mississippi, by saving a badly damaged eighteenth-century home (a) and a relatively intact surviving nineteenth century home (b) from final demolition by recovery authorities (illustrated). This work was aided by volunteer craftspeople from the Preservation Trades Network.

Historic Preservation and Sustainable Development
Donovan Rypkema

Every fifth grader in the United States learns that to save the environment we need to reduce, reuse, and recycle. What does historic preservation do? Rehabilitation of historic buildings reduces the demand for land and new materials; reuses energy embodied in the existing materials; and recycles rather than produces waste because 40 percent of what goes into landfills is construction debris. That is, historic preservation reuses the labor and materials, as well as the skills and principles of past generations, while recycling entire buildings and reducing the need for constructing new ones. Internationally the concept of *sustainable development* is viewed much more broadly than in the United States. Most of the world concerned with this matter sees sustainable development as the combination of three responsibilities: environmental responsibility, economic responsibility, and social/cultural responsibility. In the United States the environmental third of the equation has largely co-opted the other two, with environmentalists using "green building" and "sustainable development" as synonyms. They are not. While going to the dentist is an important part of health care, it is far from the whole picture. While green buildings are an important part of sustainable development, they are far from the whole picture.[88]

This has adversely affected historic preservation on two levels. First, the significant contribution of preserved buildings to the economic and social/cultural responsibilities of sustainable development is often unrecognized. Second, even the "green building" attributes of existing historic buildings rate scant credit. In recent years, however, the preservation movement in America has begun to make its own sustainable development case.

According to many advocates of "green" building, energy efficiency is the key component of green building, or ought to be. On the environmental side, the green building approach focuses almost entirely on the annual energy use of a building. Preservation advocates point out, however, that the energy expended to build the structure is fifteen to thirty times the annual energy use. This is called *embodied energy* and is defined as the total expenditure of energy involved in the creation of the building and its constituent materials.[89] None of the measurements of annual operating costs account for this embodied energy.

Certainly there can be improvements in energy efficiency of some historic buildings—and preservation architects and conservationists are developing methods to make those improvements without sacrificing the character defining features of the building. But because of the embodied energy in a structure, a 100-year-old building could use 25 percent more energy each year and still have less lifetime energy consumption than a building that lasts only four or five decades, and there are plenty of buildings around built with that kind of life expectancy.

The environmental impact of demolition must also be considered. Landfill is increasingly expensive in the United States in both dollars and environmental quality, and over a third of everything dumped at landfills is construction debris, including the remnants of razed historic structures. Americans diligently recycle their soda cans. But demolishing one small masonry commercial structure—two stories, 25 feet wide, and 120 feet deep—wipes out the entire environmental benefit of the last 1,344,000 aluminum cans that were recycled.

The closest to a comprehensive sustainable development movement in the United States is known as Smart Growth. The Smart Growth movement has established an excellent set of principles:

- Create a range of housing opportunities and choices
- Create walkable neighborhoods
- Encourage community and stakeholder collaboration
- Foster distinctive, attractive places with a Sense of Place
- Make development decisions predictable, fair, and cost effective
- Mix land uses
- Preserve open space, farmland, natural beauty, and critical environmental areas
- Provide a variety of transportation choices
- Strengthen and direct development toward existing communities
- Preserve and plan for more densely built designs.[90]

Preservationists have been making the case that historic preservation is inherently Smart Growth. In fact, if a

(continued)

community did nothing but save its historic buildings and neighborhoods, nearly every Smart Growth principle would be advanced.

The standard international definition of *sustainable development* is: the ability to meet our own needs without prejudicing the ability of future generations to meet their own needs. The rehabilitation of historic buildings does just that. Demolition is the polar opposite of sustainable development; once buildings are razed they cannot possibly be available to meet the needs of future generations. Buying solar panels and waterless toilets are important contributions that allow Americans to feel they are doing something as individuals towards sustainable development, but getting involved in the historic preservation movement has allowed others to have a substantially more significant impact. So go and buy a solar panel and a waterless toilet if it makes you feel good. But if you really want to be part of sustainable development rehabilitate an historic home.

In past two decades, especially, a fundamental change has occurred in the way many Americans relate to their environment, and historic preservationists have played a key role in these developments. For the United States' first two hundred years, aggressive economic growth was fueled by the enthusiasm of its initial immigrants, coupled with a perception of infinite natural wealth. The concept of "limitless expansion" is today considered not only unsustainable but also irresponsible. Growing conservation-mindedness means more Americans are embracing more resourceful patterns of living. While still not as "green" as their counterparts in some European countries, the American population has continued to make strides in restraining the country's wasteful habits. If past experiences are an accurate indicator, as popular perceptions change, government policies will follow.

Today, a historic preservation ethic has been internalized by a broader base of the U.S. population than ever before, with people viewing it as a desirable element within their search for cleaner and more attractive environments. The public seems more prepared and willing than ever to profit from the educational and cultural benefits derived from visits to, or associations with, historic sites and protected areas. There are an unprecedented number of professionals, professional organizations, and knowledgeable lay people who can provide historic property owners with information and technical assistance.

As it matured and evolved, American preservation has contributed more and more to the international community. In addition to the more recent Department of State's Ambassador's Fund for Cultural Preservation initiative, professionals from the United States were a driving force in the drafting of UNESCO's World Heritage Convention over three decades ago.[91] Several American NGOs have made considerable contributions to international architectural conservation practice—the World Monuments Fund, the Getty Trust, and the Samuel H. Kress Foundation have all given generously to heritage preservation projects in other countries. American private and corporate contributions for international heritage protection have been considerable as well.

Cultural heritage conservationists in other parts of the world may be inspired today to broaden their definition of what is historically important based on U.S. practices: not only landscape vistas, historic districts, and innovative adaptive reuse but also postwar shopping malls, suburban housing developments, and landmarks to science and technology. Typical U.S. approaches to heritage protection issues have also been introduced throughout the world, especially including the potency of tax incentives and the efficacy of grassroots volunteerism and the related network of nonprofit organizations willing to fill the gap between governmental capacity and local needs.

a

b

Figure 28-24 New buildings of the same size could hardly be more space efficient than these open-plan commercial buildings in Louisville, Kentucky (a), which have been restored, are fully occupied, and add to the historic character and commercial viability of the city's historic center. Reuse value and replacement cost in terms of resources and energy consumption should be taken into account when such structures are considered for retention or replacement. Yet thousands of historic buildings with character and reuse potential are destroyed in the United States annually as was the case at this other Louisville site (b). Instead, every historic building being considered for demolition should be given its day in court, so to speak, when the pros and cons—including honest evaluations of the true cost of replacement—are taken into account. Key to figuring replacement cost of existing buildings is consideration of total energy and resources consumed. Images courtesy Donovan Rypkema.

a

▲▶▼▶ **Figure 28-25** The adaptive use of a half-mile stretch of derelict elevated railroad called the Highline on the Lower West Side in New York City as a smartly landscaped urban park (a, b, c) is a recent American preservation project that combines environmental and architectural conservation concerns and reflects the exciting new directions and broadening audience for preservation. The project was the idea of two local residents concerned about the Highline's demolition and the idea grew to include local property owners and the city of New York, especially its Parks Department, as well as some celebrities. The project, designed by landscape architects James Corner Field Operations and architects Diller Scofidio + Renfro, has revitalized an underused area of the city (d) and has provided an attractive new destination for New Yorkers and visitors alike.

b

The cultural heritage protection movement in the United States has come full circle. Many of the country's early preservationists who crusaded for protection of the country's architectural and historic resources were initially reviled as impeding progress and wasting financial resources. However, the importance of engaging the public in historic preservation has steadily increased in the past century and architectural conservation is now the norm. Being preservation minded in the United States today is synonymous with good citizenship, and the economic and developmental benefits of conserving existing buildings are widely accepted. Through decades of hard work, the

c

d

national and local level preservation advocates in the United States have raised the stakes for government decision makers and planners responsible for shaping the country's built environment in an irreversible trend. The traditional ingenuity and adaptability of American preservationists and the country's wealth and generosity has ensured that challenges such as these have been quickly addressed in the past, and therefore the future for many historic sites in the United States is secure. Organized and effective cultural heritage protection is a fact of life in the United States today, and the roles of historic preservationists in the future will only become more important.

ENDNOTES

1. In 1749 Peter Kalm, a Swedish explorer, noted the existence of a log cabin in Philadelphia, which was preserved to remind citizens of the privations and makeshift circumstances of colonial pioneer days half a century prior. Charles E. Peterson, "Historic Preservation USA: Some Significant Dates," *Antiques* vol. 89, no. 2 (February 1966), 229–232.

2. Robin Winks, "Conservation in America: National Character as Revealed by Preservation," in *The Future of the Past: Attitudes towards Conservation*, ed. Jane Fawcett (London: Thames and Hudson, 1976), 142.

3. Independence Hall, a National Register and UNESCO World Heritage List site, is one of the most frequently visited historic locations in the United States. In 1828 architect William Strickland rebuilt its steeple in the form that is seen today, a compromise for those who wanted an authentic restoration and those who wanted a town clock. This building has probably been restored more than any other building in the United States.

4. J. Myrick Howard, "Nonprofits in the American Preservation Movement," in *A Richer Heritage*, ed. Robert E. Stipe (Chapel Hill: University of North Carolina Press, 2003), 314.

5. Ibid.

6. The MVLA paid the $200,000 asking price for Mount Vernon, twice the amount the Washington family had originally quoted to the federal and state governments. The home today is a center for learning about George Washington but also colonial American life more generally. Visitors can see not only the main house but also the property's scrupulously restored outbuildings and grounds, including the blacksmith shop, kitchen gardens, and slave quarters. Even important trees, some of which were planted by Washington, are protected against lightning. The site's careful maintenance poses a problem for some purists, who argue its pristine condition inaccurately represents what existed in Washington's day.

7. Mount Vernon has been restored many times to the then-highest aesthetic, historical, and technical standards. Because the MVLA was a pioneer in its field, it had to develop its own pragmatic approach toward many preservation decisions that we now take for granted. For example, to retain all of the structure's visual appearance while strengthening it for the expected increase in tourism, an invisible steel support system for the stairways was installed. Fitch, *Historic Preservation: Curatorial Management of the Built World*, 90.

8. Fitch, *Historic Preservation*, 89–90.

9. In the 1940s, 750 acres of shoreline across the Potomac River were purchased to preserve the view that Washington would have had. Thirty years later, a proposed nearby industrial park further threatened Mount Vernon's historic setting, and preservationists rallied once again. Congress purchased the adjacent property and created the 4,000-acre Piscataway National Park to ensure Mount Vernon's vista for posterity.

10. Though the State of Tennessee had purchased the Hermitage from Jackson's descendants in 1856, the family continued to live in the house undisturbed until 1888, when the state legislature proposed turning it into a Confederate veterans' hospital. W. Brown Morton III, "What Do We Preserve and Why?" in Robert E. Stipe and Antoinette J. Lee, eds. *The American Mosaic: Preserving a Nation's Heritage* (Detroit: Wayne State University Press, 1997), 152.

11. The Ladies' Hermitage Association received the National Trust for Historic Preservation's Trustee Emeritus Award for Excellence in the Stewardship of Historic Sites.

12. Two notable examples include Sunnyside and Olana, the Hudson River estates of writer Washington Irving and artist Frederic Church. While these sites were initially preserved primarily because of the historic importance of their owners, each property also has its own aesthetic merits and various interpretive offerings for today's visitor.

13. "About Us: Mission Statement," Association for the Preservation of Virginia Antiquities, www.apva.org/aboutus/ (accessed January 26, 2010).

14. Brown Morton III, "What Do We Preserve and Why?," 152.

15. Diane Lea, "America's Preservation Ethos: A Tribute to Enduring Ideals," in Stipe, *A Richer Heritage*, 4.

16. The magnitude of the restoration project is suggested in the statistics: some 440 buildings of modern Williamsburg were torn down, a highway was rerouted, 18 buildings were moved, 66 buildings were restored, and 84 buildings were reproduced based on archaeological evidence. Today there are nearly 900 guides in period costume and some 350 professionals, including

archaeologists, historians, architects, curators, and costumiers who help to maintain historical authenticity. Some 400 carpenters, mechanics, painters, gardeners, and the like maintain the complex's physical structure. In addition, some 1,400 people are engaged in maintaining and interpreting the historic appearance, and another 1,800 are dedicated to feeding, transporting, and sheltering tourists and staffing sales operations.

17. Deciding to what period to restore the Governor's Palace posed a serious dilemma for the architects. Completed in 1722, the Governor's Palace burned in 1747 and was rebuilt in 1753 and finally destroyed in 1831. Architecturally, the first palace was more interesting, but it was in the second palace that history was made, because it spanned the historic events before, during, and immediately after the Revolution. Nonetheless, since more extensive documentation existed for the first building, it was ultimately selected to be reconstructed.

18 "88 Original Buildings in the Historic Area," Colonial Williamsburg, http://research.history. org/JDRLibrary/Public_Services/FAQ88original.cfm (accessed July 21, 2010).

19. Historical archaeology as a new discipline in the United States was largely developed at Williamsburg through the great attention Ivor Noel Hume and his staff gave to the site's early excavations. Of prime interest was evidence necessary for an accurate architectural restoration. In the process nail-dating, typological analyses of eighteenth-century brickwork, and paint archaeology were developed for the first time, in ways which may be considered early modern conservation science.

20. Henry Ford, "Interview in *Chicago Tribune*," May 25, 1916, as cited in Quotation #24950 in Classic Quotes, The Quotations Page, www.quotationspage.com/quote/24950.html (accessed January 26, 2010).

21. Old Sturbridge Village in Massachusetts, created through the accumulation of anonymous homes and buildings typical of New England vernacular architecture, even more closely followed the Skansen model. Three industrialist brothers purchased, transported, and reerected these buildings, and they used them to showcase their collections of historic American artifacts. Costumed docents and craftspeople were employed from the very beginning to teach visitors about everyday life in colonial America. At nearby Deerfield Village, Mr. and Mrs. Henry Flint preserved the eighteenth- and nineteenth-century houses and buildings of a typical New England town in situ, as had been done at Colonial Williamsburg. The fourteen historic buildings and a modern exposition center at today's Deerfield Village display more than 25,000 artifacts used or made in the United States between 1650 and 1850.

22. Following a 1931 renovation, an exhibition on Lincoln was installed and remained until the National Park Service restored Ford's Theatre to its 1865 appearance in the 1960s. "About Ford's," Ford's Theatre, www.fordstheatre.org/home/about-fords (accessed January 26, 2010).

23. Two men were largely responsible for this interest: President Theodore Roosevelt and landscape architect Frederick Law Olmsted. Olmsted designed New York City's Central Park and many other treasured landscapes, including the U. S. Capitol and White House grounds; and whole park systems in cities such as Seattle, Boston, and Louisville. He and his sons played an influential role in the creation of the National Park Service, and he created designs for the Great Smoky Mountains National Park and Acadia National Park as well as Yosemite Valley.

24. The Park's existence, massive size, and pristine natural landscape owe much to the naturalist John Muir, who vigorously advocated land conservation and successfully lobbied Congress in 1890 to create Yosemite National Park. Today, more than 3,000 square miles in Idaho, Montana, and Wyoming remain "dedicated and set apart as a public park or pleasure ground for the benefit and enjoyment of the people." Federal Interagency Committee on Recreation, *The Role of the Federal Government in the Field of Public Education*, No. 3 (Washington, DC: 1961), 5.

25. Theodore Roosevelt designated 150 new national forests, along with 5 more national parks and the first 51 federal bird reservations, the first 18 national monuments, the first 4 national game preserves, and the first 21 reclamation projects. "Conservationist," Theodore Roosevelt Association, www.theodoreroosevelt.org/life/conservation.htm (accessed January 26, 2010).

26. Creation of Gettysburg National Military Park began when local residents donated 600 acres of the original battlefield to the government in 1895. Expanding the park to 3,400 acres later became the task of the volunteer Gettysburg Battlefield Association, whose successful publicity campaign allowed it to forestall unsuitable commercial development on privately owned land within the projected park area.

27. Lea, "America's Preservation Ethos," 5.

28. Many of the documented sites were not federally owned but rather belonged to a wide variety of groups, including state, county, and city agencies, historical societies, preservation associations, churches, and business corporations.

29. Morton, "What Do We Preserve and Why?" 163.

30. The primary cause of collapse was an undersized gusset plate used to connect beams or truss members along the top chord to a load-bearing column of the structure's continuous arched deck trusses. Rather than the gusset plate being 1-inch (25 mm) thick, it was only 0.5 inches (13 mm). The weight of construction equipment resting on the bridge just above its weakest point also likely contributed to the collapse.

31. "Better Roads: Bridge Inventory," November 1, 2009. The Better Roads Bridge Inventory is an exclusive, award-winning annual survey that has been conducted since 1979 by Contech Construction Products, Inc.

32. Eric DeLony and Terry H. Klein, *Historic Bridges: A Heritage at Risk, A Report on a Workshop on the Preservation and Management of Historic Bridges, Washington, DC, December 3–4, 2003*, SRI Preservation Conference Series 1 (Rio Rancho, NM: SRI Foundation, 2004), 18; www. srifoundation.org/pdf/bridge_report.pdf (accessed July 21, 2010). Probably half the bridges illustrated in this book have been destroyed.

33. The Dwight D. Eisenhower National System of Interstate and Defense Highways celebrated its fiftieth anniversary in June 29, 2006.

34. Reinforced and prestressed concrete and steel slabs, beams, and girders have become the most common bridge types, numbering in the thousands, and superseding the once ubiquitous single-intersection Pratt and Warren through and pony trusses. Source: Parsons Brinkerhoff, Engineering & Industrial Heritage, PC, A *Context for Common Historic Bridge Types* (Washington, DC: National Cooperative Highway Research Program, Transportation Research Council, 2005).

35. Private conversation with Scott Snelling, PE, senior engineer with Hardesty & Hanover, LLP, New York City, and author of *Towards Green Bridges*, (Washington, DC: Transportation Research Board, 2010).

36. North American historic preservation's roots lie firmly in western Europe: The National Trust was formed after a group of U.S. congressmen completed a tour of Europe undertaken to help them better understand how built heritage preservation was handled in other countries.

37. It devotes considerable effort to informing city officials and businessmen's groups about local preservation issues and projects and to encouraging suitable preservation legislation. The Trust offers lectures, seminars, workshops, and short courses, including courses for historic property managers and administrators of historic preservation projects. Serving as a clearinghouse for individuals, groups, agencies, and institutions concerned with preservation, the National Trust publishes a monthly magazine, *Historic Preservation*, for its general membership and *Forum* for special subscribers and principal donors.

38. The NTHP has approximately 270,000 members, representing one one-thousandth of the American population, while the 3.6 million members of the National Trust in the United Kingdom equal over 6 percent of the population of England, Wales and Northern Ireland (Scotland has its own National Trust).

39. Legislation also details policies for balconies, including which ironwork should be preserved or restored, and rules for artificial lighting, paint colors, and sign placement. A 1958 amendment gives the Commission the authority to prevent demolition by neglect and to force owners to maintain or restore their properties. Louisiana Legislature, Acts 1936, no. 139, sect. 1 (adopted November 3, 1936).

40. Jacobs, *Death and Life of Great American Cities*, 216.

41. Many historic district ordinances are incorporated within local zoning regulations, but in other cities these are separate. Howard, "Where the Action Is: Preservation and Local Governments," in Stipe and Lee, *The American Mosaic*, 130-1; Linda Cofresi and Rosetta Radtke, "Local Government Programs," in Stipe, *A Richer Heritage*, 131; and Tersh Boasberg, "A New Paradigm for Preservation," in Lee, *Past Meets Future: Saving America's Historic Environments*, 146.

42. Based on new eminent domain laws that authorized public seizure of land with compensation, typical planning solutions included: street-widening projects, new roads, the razing of whole blocks of existing buildings for new high-rise residential or commercial structures, and the creation of extensive parking areas. Parks and plazas often of incongruous designs were seen as the most viable alternative to rehabilitating underused buildings.

43. The book's closing paragraph succinctly summarized her thesis: "Dull, inert cities, it is true, do contain the seeds of their own destruction and little else. But lively, diverse, intense cities contain the seeds of their own regeneration, with energy enough to carry over for problems and needs outside themselves." Jacobs, *Death and Life of Great American Cities*, 448.

44. Rachel Carsen, *Silent Spring* (Boston: Houghton Mifflin, 1962).

45. Fitch, *Historic Preservation: Curatorial Management of the Built World*. (Charlottesville: University Press of Virginia, 1990).

46. In 1959 one of the first proposals suggested that the federal government begin by examining the historic structures threatened by its own major building programs, such as the creation of an interstate highway system.

47. In 1920, when her own finances were not enough to save the early nineteenth-century Joseph Manigault House, Frost founded the Society for the Preservation of Old Dwellings (renamed the Preservation Society of Charleston in 1957) to help finance her work by sourcing external capital. Jacobs, *Death and Life of Great American Cities*, 384.

48. Jacobs, *Death and Life of Great American Cities*, 394.

49. Tung, *Preserving the World's Great Cities*, 348.

50. *Penn Central Transportation Co. v. New York City*, 438 U.S. 104 (1978).

51. Spot zoning occurs when a single building or small parcel of land are zoned differently than neighboring buildings and sites. The 1980 amendment to the Preservation Act of 1966, which requires owner consent for National Register listing, is directly related to this ruling. Howard, "Where the Action Is," 131, 136, and 137.

52. John M. Fowler, "The Federal Government as Standard Bearer," in Stipe and Lee, *The American Mosaic*, 35.

53. The SHPO is therefore in a politically sensitive position: Though administering federal regulations, the officer is appointed by the governor of a state and oversees a state-level agency whose practices can come into conflict with local interests.

54. "National Register of Historic Places Fundamentals," National Park Service, www.nps.gov/history/NR/national_register_fundamentals.htm (accessed January 26, 2010).

55. "National Historic Preservation Act of 1996, as Amended," Advisory Council on Historic Preservation, http://www.achp.gov/nhpa.html (accessed July 21, 2010).

56. "National Register Evaluation Criteria," Advisory Council on Historic Preservation, http://www.achp.gov/nrctriteria.html (accessed July 21, 2010).

57. On behalf of the Technical Preservation Services Division of the U.S. National Park Service, architectural historian W. Brown Morton III and architect Gary Hume produced the original, complete version of the *Secretary of the Interior's Standards and Guidelines* in 1976; the Guidelines have evolved considerably in later versions with detailed explanations of "recommended" and "not recommended" approaches to architectural preservation.

58. Michael A. Tomlin, "Preservation Practice Comes of Age," in Lee, *Past Meets Future*, 73.

59. These examples less directly inspired the initiation of a number of other large heritage conservation schemes involving the reestablishment of waterfront districts and towns to the waterways that enabled their existence. Notable among them are: the San Antonio, Texas riverfront cleanup and restoration scheme; the Los Caminos del Rio binational (United States and Mexico) river town conservation program, also in Texas; the renovation of the Louisville, Kentucky urban waterfront; and historic harbor place improvements in San Francisco, New York City, Baltimore, and New Orleans.

60. "Tax Incentives," National Park Service, www.nps.gov/history/tax.htm (accessed January 26, 2010) and updated by e-mail correspondence with Charles Fisher, Technical Preservation Services, National Park Service.

61. The ITC's generous financial incentives allow private investors to rehabilitate historic properties for modern usage on an after-tax basis that is competitive with new construction. A generous 25 percent tax credit (20 percent since 1986) is fully available when a project is put into use; accounting treatments qualify almost all costs as rehabilitation expenditures, which are tax deductible.

62. In Roslindale Village in Boston, a 1985 pilot Main Street project site, guidelines were developed to maintain the historic architecture, numerous facade, and signage improvements were completed, public and private partnerships were formed, new businesses were recruited while existing ones were retained, and the commercial vacancy rate dropped. Roslindale's successes inspired Boston's mayor to institute similar projects in more than twenty other neighborhoods. Tom Litke, correspondence with J. H. Stubbs, August 2002.

63. "Reinvestment Statistics: The Main Street Program's Economic Success," Main Street: National Trust for Historic Preservation, www.preservationnation.org/main-street/about-main-street/reinvestment-statistics.html (accessed July 22, 2010).

64. Based on lecture given by Dr. George Wheeler at J. H. Stubbs's Historic Preservation Theory and Practice course, Columbia Graduate School of Architecture, Planning, and Preservation, New York City, November 10, 2006.

65. Laurence Kantner, "The Reception and Non-Reception of Cesare Brandi in America," Future Anterior: Journal of the Historic Preservation; History, Theory and Criticism 4, no. 1 (Summer 2007): 31–43.

66. Earlier histories of architectural conservation especially in Italy, France, England and Germany are found in this book's preceding title: J. H. Stubbs, Time Honored; A Global View of Architectural Conservation (2009).

67. Among the earlier more generally oriented architectural conservation experts who played influential roles in advocating conservation science from their positions either in academia or government were Harley J. McKee, Lee H. Nelson, Hugh Miller and James Marston Fitch. Government-based conservation scientists include Penelope Bachelor and Morgan Phillips. The various architectural conservation experts operating in the private sector are too many to name here, although they are easily found through the professional conservation networks and bibliographies.

68. Lisa Ackerman contributed this paragraph on restoration education.

69. Tracie Rozhon, "Homes Sell, And History Goes Private," The New York Times, December 31, 2006, 1.

70. In addition, after nearly a decade of archaeological excavation and research, the reconstruction of George Washington's gristmill and distillery was completed in the fall of 2006. The operational mill was opened to the public at the same time as the new orientation center and museum, and the distillery opened a few months later in spring 2007.

71. Maps of Federally Recognized THPOs, National Association for Tribal Historic Preservation Officers, http://www.nathpo.org/map.html (accessed January 26, 2010).

72. Alan Downer, "Native Americans and Historic Preservation," in Stipe, A Richer Heritage, 417.

73. As planning and festivities began in 2002, the National Association of Tribal Historic Preservation Officers (NATHPO) published a Tribal Tourism Toolkit with advice for how Native American communities could plan and market their cultural assets for the many visitors who would follow the trail of Lewis and Clark and be interested in the many Midwestern tribes they encountered. NATHPO, Tribal Tourism Toolkit: For the Lewis and Clark Bicentennial and other Tribal Opportunities (Washington, DC: NATHPO, 2002).

74. Angie Wagener, "Tribes Eager to Capitalize on Lewis and Clark Tourists," (Associated Press, 2003), National Association of Tribal Historic Preservation Officers, www.nathpo.org/News/Lewis_Clark/News_Lewis26.htm (accessed January 26. 2010).

75. "Underground Railroad: Special Resources Study," National Park Service, www.nps.gov/undergroundrr/ugsum.htm (accessed January 26, 2010).

76. Special thanks to Rob Thompsan from whose unpublished paper "Islands in America: Historic Preservation Practice, Policy and Organization in the U.S. Territories" (2004) large portions of this text on preservation in overseas territories has been extracted with permission.

77. "Plan Profile: Puerto Rico," Historic Preservation Planning Program: National Park Service, www.nps.gov/history/hps/pad/stateplans/puerto.htm (accessed January 26, 2010).

78. Martin E. Weaver, "Conservation vs. Disasters: The Restoration of the Kathrineberg," *Cultural Resource Management* 23, no. 6 (2000): 26–29.

79. The project included the removal of its heating, ventilating, and air-conditioning system and restoration of interior painted-canvas wall finishes that allow moisture to move through them. Weaver, "Conservation vs. Disasters," 26–29.

80. "St. Thomas: Culture and History," United States Virgin Islands, www.usvitourism.vi/stthomas/culture_history (accessed January 26, 2010).

81. Conservation Trust of Puerto Rico, www.fideicomiso.org (accessed January 26, 2010); Saint Croix Foundation, www.stxfoundation.org (accessed January 26, 2010); St. Croix Landmarks Society, www.stcroixlandmarks.com (accessed January 26, 2010).

82. "Cultural History of American Samoa," American Samoa Historic Preservation Office, www.ashpo.org/history.htm (January 26, 2010).

83. Conference on Balancing Public Safety and Protection of Historic Places, organized by the Federal Preservation Institute, in Washington, DC, January 22, 2002, and San Francisco, CA, July 25, 2002.

84. "Principles for Development of Security Measures for Historic Places," Federal Preservation Institute, http://fpi.historicpreservation.gov/TechnicalInfo/Riskpreparedness/Principles.aspx (accessed January 26, 2010).

85. National Capital Planning Commission, *Designing for Security in the Nation's Capital* (Washington, DC: NCPC, 2001).

86. See Figure 17-94, in Stubbs, *Time Honored*, 347.

87. Mary Ann Travis, "Rebirth Conference Calls for One City, One Plan," June 2, 2006, www2.tulane.edu/article_news_details.cfm?ArticleID=6558 (accessed January 26, 2010).

88. "Green building" and "sustainable development" are broad terms that are often defined to the convenience of the one using them.

89. Current research seeks to quantify the energy embodied in historic structures; however, the process of attaining accuracy is a complex and challenging one. Further information on this and related topics is contained within: Jean Carroon, *Sustainable Preservation: Greening Historic Buildings*, Wiley, 2010.

90. "Smart Growth Principles," Smarth Growth Online, www.smartgrowth.org/about/principles/default.asp?res=1429 (accessed July 22, 2010).

91. The idea of a World Register of Heritage Places was born during the Nixon administration. Douglas Comer, presentation in the panel discussion, "Innovative Approaches to Policy and Management of Archaeological Sites" (Fifth World Archaeological Congress, Washington, DC, June 21–22, 2003).

Canada

Because it is such a large country, Canada's history has been dominated by the twin challenges of traversing its expanses and holding its regions together. Today, nearly two-thirds of the population resides in the central provinces of Ontario and Quebec, where European settlement began in the early seventeenth century. The remaining third is dispersed from the Pacific Coast to the Arctic Circle to the Atlantic Maritime region. The long-standing cultural influences from Great Britain and France continue to be strong; however, approximately 20 percent of Canadians now cite a language other than English or French as their mother tongue.[1] Heritage places are now being identified, throughout Canada's diverse types of terrain, to reflect all of the traditions in its cultural mosaic—from the traditions of First Nations peoples to twentieth- and twenty-first century entrepreneurs.

Canadian architectural heritage conservation professionals face a harsh climate, including extreme seasonal and daily temperature swings. Also, the mindset of resource extraction is well entrenched. Nine in ten Canadians say that heritage conservation is very important to maintaining a distinct cultural identity and that conserving heritage buildings is a way of increasing community pride.[2] However, the day-to-day pragmatism of a country that has an abundance of space often argues against the careful management of the built—or any—environment.

Legislative control of heritage properties in Canada is exerted mainly at the provincial and municipal level, not at the federal level. Nevertheless, the government of Canada has led the way by establishing guidelines that provinces may elect to follow and by helping to develop the "know-how" of conservation professionals.

EARLY CONSERVATION EFFORTS

Heritage conservation was closely tied to nation building when an act of the British parliament in 1867 declared the Dominion of Canada a confederated union.[3] The commemoration of significant sites and buildings began very shortly afterwards, in both the settlements of central and eastern Canada (which had been established nearly three centuries earlier) and in the westerly regions that were then inhabited mainly by indigenous peoples.

One of the ideas essential to Canada is its loyalty to the Crown of England, though recently the relevance of that Crown to today's society has been debated in some quarters. However, throughout the nineteenth and twentieth centuries, a strong sense of this allegiance—in contrast to the direction taken in the United States—has defined what it is to be a Canadian. Many of the early initiatives to conserve heritage buildings were taken by descendents of the United Empire Loyalists—colonists who supported the British cause in the American Revolution, and then fled from the United States after 1776.

With a determination to consolidate a pluralistic, nonrevolutionary society north of the border, the Loyalist perspective added extra emphasis to this defining concept.

As early as 1895, both government and the citizenry were recording the history of the European settlers in this new land. Along the Lake Ontario and St. Lawrence River waterways, the government erected stone monuments at the battlefields where Canadian militiamen had defended against American invasion during the War of 1812.[4] The local historical societies, and organizations such as the Imperial Order of Daughters of the Empire and the St. Jean Baptiste Society also were active in preserving and restoring buildings.[5] In addition, the churches sought to preserve the memory of earlier days by preserving the fabric of their buildings—a very early example being the 1910 restoration of late-eighteenth-century wooden church at Hay Bay, Ontario, by the Methodist Church.

When the British National Trust appealed to expatriates in Canada, some members of the Royal Society reacted by rededicating their energies closer to home, forming a Committee for the Preservation of Scenic and Historic Places in Canada in 1901 and the Historic Landmarks Association in 1907.[6] Members of the Royal Society of Canada observed the way the United States was preserving its significant buildings, and they argued that Canada ought to care for its own heritage to a similar degree.[7]

In 1911 the Canadian Parliament established the Dominion Parks Branch of the Department of the Interior, the first national parks agency in the world. The first national park in Canada had been established in 1885 at Banff, Alberta, to conserve the natural hot springs there. The Parks Branch's first leader, James B. Harkin, would play an important role in Canada's early efforts to conserve heritage buildings. Harkin is regarded as an enormously successful salesman of the national parks idea. When he was able to tie leisure and scenery to education and history, he felt Canadian identity would be promoted. Also, for Harkin, the unification of historic sites with parks was a way of extending the National Parks network eastward.[8]

Commissioner Harkin developed the branch to carry out the conservation work at government-controlled properties, and he established an internal advisory board to acknowledge the significance of heritage sites across Canada regardless of their ownership. The latter agency, the Historic Sites and Monuments Board, was established in 1919.[9] The Royal Society's Historic Landmarks Association shifted its purpose and renamed itself the Canadian Historical Society in 1922.

The Historic Sites and Monuments Board's first project was to compile a list of sites associated with Canada's history, especially those related to important persons and events. The places identified as National Historic Sites were marked with bronze plaques. The Board was comprised of members that reflect various perspectives on conservation issues, and it continues to operate today in much the same role as when it began. In the meantime, the Parks Branch began stabilization efforts at properties that were in particular need of attention, including the complex at Annapolis Royal in Nova Scotia, where Samuel de Champlain's original 1604 settlement is located.[10]

An active interest also was taken in the early twentieth century in the heritage of Canada's first peoples, arising from the urge to collect artifacts, as much as any other motive. Between 1897 and 1913, Charles Newcombe, a British botanist and ethnographer based in Victoria, British Columbia, took a photographic inventory of the Haida village of Ninstints (on SGang Gwaay, also known as Anthony Island). In 1947 Marius Barbeau's team of archaeologists from the National Museum of Man photographed the Haida villages and made the first plan to salvage the monuments themselves. During the 1950s, a more thorough mapping project, as well as the removal of some of the totem poles, would be undertaken by the Provincial Museum and the University of British Columbia.[11]

The fledgling architectural profession soon began to record Canada's built heritage as well. The School of Architecture at McGill University started to collect documentation related to historic structures in 1917. Together with the earlier measured drawings by Professor Ramsay Traquair, this became the Canadian Architectural Collection, which remains an important resource for architectural conservationists today.[12]

Figure 29-2 In 1910, when the Methodist Church restored the late-eighteenth-century Hay Bay Church, it acknowledged the importance of the United Empire Loyalist heritage and in so doing expressed Canada's continued allegiance to the Crown of England. The church had fallen into disuse after a century of service, instead serving as a farmer's storehouse; today it is used for regular worship, and it proudly flies the flag of Great Britain. Photo courtesy Barbara Ross.

Figure 29-3 The heritage of Canada's First Nations was an object of curiosity for European settlers "opening" the west. In the late nineteenth century, an effort was made to record the vanishing settlements of the Haida people, particularly at the nineteenth-century village of SGang Gwaay 'Ilnagaay (formerly Ninstints) on the Queen Charlotte Islands (Haida Gwaii). It is now a National Historic Site, within a national park, that is inscribed on the World Heritage List. Photo George Mercer Dawson, 1878, courtesy of the Canadian Museum of Civilization.

These activities show that Canadians have been mindful of their distinct heritage since very early on. Heritage legislation specialist Marc Denhez notes that Manitobans formed an historical society in 1870, only nine years after the province was formed.[13] However, the emphasis on taking inventory, before taking action, also shows the challenge that faces the federal government in a country as big and diverse as Canada.

Local agencies have been essential to the substantive work of conserving Canadian buildings. For instance, the Chateau de Ramezay, the home of Montreal's governor in 1705, became in 1895 the first building in Quebec to be proclaimed an historical monument and the first private history museum established in the province. In 1929 it was the first Montreal building to be classified under Quebec's new conservation act, which was the first of such statutes to be drawn up in Canada.[14] In the interwar period, provincial-level organizations also emerged, such as the Architectural Conservancy of Ontario, which was founded in 1933 by Eric Ross Arthur, who was born in New Zealand, trained in England as an architect, and became a tireless advocate for the preservation of historic buildings in Canada.

THE MASSEY COMMISSION AND THE HISTORIC SITES AND MONUMENTS ACT

In 1949 the Royal Commission on National Development in the Arts, Letters, and Sciences examined the general state of culture in post–World War II Canada. Under the leadership of the Canadian diplomat Vincent Massey, the Commission's 1951 report applauded the work done up until that time by the Historic Site and Monuments Board, but it noted that the stone cairns typically used to mark historic sites had "the melancholy of an old grave-yard without its charm.[15] Once again, the Commission declared it an urgent matter to restore historic sites and present them in such a way that Canadians might find greater appeal in the enjoyment of their own history.[16] The report called for legislation respecting the treatment of Canadian heritage sites, as well as a designation system modeled on that of Britain or France; it also called for an expanded list of protected sites, which would include buildings of purely architectural significance as well as those of historical importance.[17]

As a result of the Massey Commission, all federally owned buildings and sites, including the historic fortresses held by the Department of Defense, were transferred to the jurisdiction of the Dominion Parks Branch. Special attention was called to Halifax's Citadel Hill, a star-shaped fortress constructed in 1856 to defend against attacks from the United States. As soon as it was transferred to the Parks Branch in 1951, Citadel Hill was designated as a National Historic Site and a comprehensive restoration program began.

At Louisbourg in Nova Scotia, the Parks Branch undertook the largest reconstruction so-far contemplated in Canada, looking southward to the project at Williamsburg as an impetus. Through the late 1960s and early 1970s, the project at Louisbourg fueled an intense period in the development of restoration know-how among Canadian architects, engineers, and craftspeople. For nearly a decade, it enjoyed a substantial yearly investment of federal funds and raised many important issues with respect to the interplay between archival research and reconstruction in the field.[18]

Figure 29-4 Vincent Massey, champion of Canadian cultural identity, authored the 1951 Royal Commission report calling for the establishment of a full range of heritage conservation strategies. As the first Canadian-born Governor-General of Canada, Massey travelled widely—he is shown here, visiting with an Inuk in Iqaluit (formerly Frobisher Bay) in 1956. Image courtesy of Phototeque Library and Archives Canada/National Film Board of Canada. Gar Lunney photographer.

Figure 29-5 The fortress town of Louisbourg, in Nova Scotia, constructed circa 1730, was reconstructed by Parks Canada during the 1960s and 1970s. This project established a new standard for national historic parks for the second half of the twentieth century. Image courtesy and copyright Parks Canada/Fortress of Louisbourg.

The 1951 report of the Royal Commission was comprehensive in scope, and its spirit foreshadowed Massey's later tenure as the first Canadian-born governor-general. Massey had a keen interest in uniting Canada's diverse cultures, and in encouraging cooperation between national and provincial governments. While the 1951 report called for immediate action with respect to older sites, which are located mainly in central Canada and the east, it also invited all Canadians to think about preserving the evidence of their cultures. When it noted that "in the thinly settled regions of the country, certain places still have the history of the past written on the very surface of the land, but this history is threatened every day with obliteration," the Commission implied that there was important, urgent work to be done in a westward and northward direction.[19]

Many of the recommendations made by the Massey Commission were reflected in a new Historic Sites and Monuments Act, passed in 1953 and amended in 1955. Expanded authority and increased resources were committed, and architectural structures, as well as historic districts, gardens, and landscapes were placed officially in the purview of the Historic Sites and Monuments Board. However, to this day, sites are nominated for designation by ordinary citizens and, as in the United States, recognition as a National Historic Site is primarily honorary.[20] A bronze plaque may mark a location, but funding for conservation of many of these sites is scarce.[21]

The Massey Commission also reminded the federal government to suggest to the provincial governments that they take suitable legislative action to protect historic sites and buildings. In 1954, New Brunswick passed a Historic Sites Protection Act, which called for the designation and protection of sites of historical importance to the province and strengthened the oversight of federally recognized sites within its borders. In 1952 Quebec's 1922 heritage act was redrafted; the same year the Commission Viger was formed to study sites deemed worthy of conservation in Old Montreal, which was declared an historic district in 1964. It would take twenty years for similar legislation to be passed in Ontario and the other provinces.

INSTITUTION BUILDING IN THE SECOND HALF OF THE 20TH CENTURY

Beginning in the 1950s, rapidly expanding commercial enterprise brought with it a building boom in Canada. Cities across the country started to sprawl, and older structures in the urban cores were perceived as less valuable than the land they occupied. Widespread demolition was permitted in the name of urban renewal and no major Canadian city was left unscathed.

During the celebration of the Centennial of Confederation, in 1967, the general awareness of Canadian history seemed to have increased. Yet, in 1973, in Hamilton, Ontario, an observer predicted that all of the city's designated heritage buildings would be gone within fifteen years, if demolitions were to continue at the rate they were then occurring.[22] To try to stop the wrecker's ball, volunteer citizens' coalitions, such as Time and Place in Toronto and Save Montreal (later Heritage Montreal), were galvanized into action. There were many regrettable losses, such as the Van Horne Mansion in Montreal, which was bulldozed by a developer in the middle of the night, amid cries of protest. However, other important structures were conserved, often after a planning commission or a consultant's report had recommended its demolition, such as the St. Lawrence Market in Toronto. During this era, very few private investors had an interest in capitalizing on the growing niche market for reuse of heritage buildings.[23]

A popular means of preserving a building and using it for educational purposes was the "pioneer village." As in the United States and based on the European open air museum model, buildings that were representative of an historic type—such as a gristmill, a bakery, or a blacksmiths shop—were removed from the paths of encroaching development, taken to safer ground, and grouped with other buildings found in similar plights. For instance, when the construction of the St. Lawrence Seaway commenced, twenty-eight typical and everyday buildings of the eighteenth and nineteenth century were gathered from the townships in eastern Ontario that were to be flooded and taken to a position above the new water line. Together, the buildings were presented as Upper Canada Village, a tourist site that still operates today.

Also during this era, the practice of archaeology on Canadian soil increased markedly, in both scope and expertise. On the east coast, a Norwegian team discovered the eleventh-century Viking settlement at L'Anse aux Meadows, and archaeologists quickly came from Iceland, Sweden, Norway, and the United States to study its remains. Meanwhile, in Ontario, researchers from the University of Toronto examined the remains of the nineteenth-century Jesuit settlement at Sainte Marie among the Hurons and located several clusters of Iroquoian longhouses in the province. Within the federal Department of Indian and Northern Affairs, the Canadian Conservation Institute was formed—a scientific facility that is now recognized worldwide for its expertise in materials testing, analysis, and research.

◄◄**Figure 29-6** The St. Lawrence Market (a, b) in Toronto, saved in 1974 by citizen advocacy, is functioning fully today as an essential and vibrant focal point in the downtown core. Used with permission of the City of Toronto.

Internationally, Canadians played a leadership role in conservation organizations, and have been quick to implement international best practices at home.[24] ICOMOS Canada was founded in the late 1960s, and Canada participated in drafting and ratifying the World Heritage Convention in 1976. In 1982, ICOMOS Canada's French-speaking committee, in collaboration with the Conseil des monuments et des sites du Quebec (Council on the Monuments and Sites of Quebec), prepared the Declaration of Deschambault. Inspired by the Venice Charter, this document emphasizes the importance of community involvement and the need to show respect for the significant contributions of every period of history when doing conservation work. In 1983, the English-speaking committee drafted the Appleton Charter, which was heavily influenced by early versions of Australia's Burra Charter.[25] In 1986 a Code of Ethics for Canadian conservators was first published; it is now in its third edition.

▶**Figure 29-7** A period of intense industrial and economic growth threatened heritage structures in Canada during the 1950s. When the construction of the St. Lawrence Seaway flooded counties around Morrisburg, Ontario, a collection of ordinary eighteenth- and nineteenth-century buildings were moved to higher ground and presented to the public as an open air museum, called Upper Canada Village. Photo Fred Perry.

▼**Figure 29-8** An archaeological find at L'Anse aux Meadows, an eleventh-century Viking settlement on the Labrador coast, led to a project involving international experts during the 1970s. The site was inscribed on the World Heritage List in 1978, the year the list began. Photo Dylan Kereluk.

An ongoing interest in listing heritage buildings gained impetus during this time as well. In 1970, in response to a recommendation of the Historic Sites and Monuments Board, the Canadian Inventory of Historic Buildings was launched. This first computerized inventory of heritage architecture in the world was searchable using a variety of keywords. Because young recorders collected most of the data, the project also served as a teaching tool. In just six years, more than 160,000 buildings were photographed and described; the visual record alone will serve as an important resource for future generations of researchers.[26]

In 1973, as the Parks Branch (which was renamed Parks Canada by decade's end) and the Historic Sites and Monuments Board continued their work, the Government of Canada established an independent agency, that is now called the Heritage Canada Foundation. Modeled on the U.K. National Trust, this membership-based, not-for-profit, registered charity was given an initial endowment, and it operates today on a blend of interest from that endowment and project-specific private donations. Heritage Canada's mandate is to encourage the preservation of "significant historic, architectural, natural, and scenic heritage of Canada with a view to stimulating and promoting the interest of the people of Canada in that heritage."[27]

As an NGO, Heritage Canada has the flexibility to get involved in a wide variety of conservation projects at a level of its own choosing. It administers a prestigious award program and publishes guides and media reviews, and it advocates forcefully when historic structures are threatened. It publishes an annual list of what it considers Canada's Top Ten Endangered Places and Worst Losses and provides support for various organizations on an as-needed basis. Since the 1970s, it has been lobbying the federal government to create tax incentives for heritage conservation, and it continues to encourage provincial governments to strengthen their legislation.

Heritage Canada launched its Main Street program in 1978, using the four-point approach that is well known in Britain and the United States.[28] By 1988 Main Street Canada had achieved international recognition, and over seventy small towns had participated in the program. In 1990, when federal funding was terminated, the Quebec Ministry of Culture contributed funds to keep the program running nationally for another three years. Through the creation of an endowment fund, Quebec established La Fondation Rues Principales (Main Street Foundation), which is still in operation. The province of Alberta likewise established its own Main Street program, which continued to operate into the new millennium. In 2009 Heritage Canada undertook a study that reflected on the experience with Main Streets programs across the country and presented to the Province of Saskatchewan a strong argument in favor of the establishment of a new program there.

At the provincial and municipal levels, a bewildering array of heritage organizations came into being during the 1970s and 1980s—either by government decree or out of citizen concern. For instance, the Ontario Heritage Trust, established in 1967 as the Ontario Heritage Foundation, is an agency of the provincial government. Like the federal Historic Sites and Monuments Board, it places markers at sites of historic interest, be they for their natural, architectural, or sociocultural significance.[29] Like Heritage Canada, it also publishes a magazine, holds conferences and symposia, and helps to promotes events such as Doors Open, an annual weekend during which interesting buildings of all eras are open to the public for tours. Also, having helped channel funding to help restore particular properties, such as the Apothecary at Niagara on the Lake, the Ontario Heritage Trust owns and operates such sites as places of public interest.[30] Another agency, the Architectural Conservancy of Ontario, noted earlier, is a nonprofit organization with a network of branches in communities throughout the province; operating outside of government, it too can take a more adversarial approach.[31] Similar stories can be told across the country: the proliferation of these agencies attests to the ongoing efforts of many Canadians to find the most effective means to conserve heritage places.[32]

Heritage legislation had been enacted in some form in most provinces and territories in Canada by the mid-1970s; however, concerns about the degree of enforcement continued. The legal and financial aspects of Canada's efforts to save its architecture and historic sites is portrayed lucidly by noted Canadian architectural conservation educator, author and practitioner Marc Denhez, who points to a number of the issues.[33] For instance, with the notable exceptions of Nova Scotia and Ontario, definitive protection against demolition was a part of each statute, but the fines for an offense, at the outset, were miniscule. Further, in only a few provinces (Prince Edward Island, Quebec, and Alberta) did laws enable enforced maintenance of a heritage property.

The tendency of some of these statutes to provide little more than "a stay of execution" for a heritage structure facing demolition may be changing. In Ontario, conservation advocates now are hopeful that the 2005 revision of the 1974 Heritage Act will have a more lasting effect. In 2006, the provincial Ministry of Culture exercised its new powers to intervene in the affairs of a municipal council, when it directed the City of Hamilton to reverse an earlier decision and, in so doing, prevented the demolition of a nineteenth-century commercial building in the downtown core called the Lister Block.

▶**Figure 29-9** Famed French Canadian explorer Louis Jolliet used this house in Vieux Quebec as a base of operations for exploration of lands to the west. It now serves as the base of the funicular of old Quebec.

◀**Figure 29-10** The Apothecary at Niagara-on-the-Lake, circa 1820, was exactingly restored to its 1869 appearance, with advice from local architect P. J. Stokes and support from the Ontario Heritage Foundation. The restoration, begun as a Centennial Project in 1967, involved approaches that set a new model for conservation practitioners in Canada. Photo Barbara Ross.

Figure 29-11 Main Streets throughout Canada, like the one in Quebec City shown here, benefited from a program coordinated by Heritage Canada from 1978 to 1994, known as La Fondation Rue Principales. Successful similar programs are still running, under the aegis of provincial agencies in Alberta and Ontario, as well as in Quebec.

Figure 29-12 The largest underwater archaeological project ever undertaken in Canada ran from 1978 to 1985 at Red Bay, Labrador, the site of a mid-16th-century Basque whaling station. Among the many finds was an 8-meter-long craft, called a chalupa, which was excavated from beneath a galleon, disassembled underwater, meticulously documented, and then transported more than 1,500 kilometers to the conservators' laboratories in Ottawa, where it was stabilized and reassembled. In 1998, the chalupa was returned to Labrador where it is now on public display. Photograph courtesy and copyright Parks Canada/GMNP, P. Waddell photographer.

In 1983 the Federal Heritage Buildings Review Office (FHBRO) began to oversee the treatment of all federally owned historic properties, following an assessment of the historic, aesthetic, and environmental significance of over sixty thousand Crown-owned buildings.[34] In the graded system, each historic federal property is designated either as "classified," "recognized," or "not Federal Heritage." At the outset of each proposed intervention, the potential impact on "heritage character" is evaluated. The FHBRO Code of Practice was consolidated in 1993, after wide consultation with numerous government agencies, including project managers with field experience in conserving federal buildings. The FHBRO Code promotes a balance between international heritage conservation principles and the practical necessities of property and building management.[35]

TORONTO'S FIRST CHINATOWN
多倫多的首個唐人街

The first Chinese resident recorded in Toronto was Sam Ching, the owner of a hand laundry business on Adelaide Street in 1878. Though immigration to Canada directly from China was restricted after 1885, Ching was eventually joined by Chinese men who migrated from western Canada after helping to build the transcontinental Canadian Pacific Railway.

Between 1900 and 1925, Toronto's first Chinese community took shape here, around Elizabeth Street which once ran all the way south to Queen Street. 'Chinatown' was a bustling commercial and residential area that included restaurants, grocery stores, and traditional clan associations.

Detail of 1923 Goad's Fire Insurance Plan showing the streets of Toronto's first Chinatown. Chinatown's main street, Elizabeth Street, is coloured red. The area shaded in grey was demolished in the 1950s for Nathan Phillips Square and City Hall.
City of Toronto Archives; © CGI.

根據記載，多倫多的第一個華商居民是 "Sam Ching"。一八七八年，他在 Adelaide 街經營洗衣店。一八八五年後，雖然加拿大政府限制華人從中國直接移居加國，但參與興建橫跨加拿大太平洋鐵路的華人在鐵路完成後，從加拿大西部移居多倫多，最終與 "Sam Ching" 一同居於此地。

在一九零零年至一九二五年之間，多倫多的第一個華人社區在伊麗莎白街一帶建立起來。伊麗莎白街一度向南伸延至皇后街。當時的 "唐人街" 是一個熙來攘往的商業和住宅區，餐館、雜貨店和宗親會比比皆是。

Figure 29-13 In keeping with a popular interest in celebrating cultural diversity, the markers of historic places in the Province of Ontario appear in languages other than English or French, where meaningful. For example, located beside Toronto's New City Hall, this plaque speaks to the established Chinese community. Photo Barbara Ross.

Figure 29-14 Students in the Heritage Masonry Program at Algonquin College in Ottawa working with experienced masons at Fort Prince of Wales, Churchill, Manitoba, during the summer of 2009 faced a new problem in preservation technology arising from climate change—a freeze-thaw cycle that did not exist so extensively in the past. Photo courtesy of Algonquin College.

Looking back, some commentators observe that an interest in heritage seemed to be sweeping the nation in the last quarter of the twentieth century. In the midst of a building boom, citizens became active advocates for architectural conservation, a Canada-wide inventory made use of new computer technology, arm's-length advocacy groups gained in strength, archaeology increased in scope, commitment, and expertise, the Main Streets program was considered a success, and legislation to conserve privately owned historic structures was enacted at a level that the constitution of Canada allows. Some bemoan the lack of a strong legislative response at the federal level, pointing to the 1966 legislation in the United States as a better model. However, Denhez argues that legislation alone is not a solution to everything and that in Canada, as in other places, there is no such thing as an single, easy remedy to ensure that heritage is conserved.[36]

The Spirit of Place as Conceived by the First Nations
Barbara Ross

Topography and the harsh realities of the changing seasons have always occupied a prominent place in the Canadian psyche. For Canada's indigenous peoples, "the land is alive, a dynamic force to be embraced and transformed by the human imagination."[37] Whether one is a member of a First Nations band (a status Indian, as defined in the controversial Indian Act, from any one of hundreds of clans), a Métis (a person of mixed heritage, usually Indian and French), or an Inuk (one of the people of the north), one's cultural identity always has been defined, in very large measure, by a relationship with the land.

Whenever the connections between an aboriginal society and its territory were damaged or broken, the cultural heritage of that society was also severely damaged or broken. Yet the perception that the spirit of a culture remains alive in certain places is upheld—and it has become the reason why preserving these places is of such vital importance to the preservation of the cultures themselves. The idea that a place itself retains a spirit, or cultural memory, may not be appreciated fully by the general public today, yet it is evident whenever a place of significance to an aboriginal culture is conserved.

There is emerging evidence that the spirit of certain places in Canada will be respected by future generations. However, it remains important to avoid romanticizing the unique character of such places to a point that a Haida or a Blackfoot or an Iroquois would not recognize.

On the Pacific Coast islands formerly known as the Queen Charlotte Islands, there is an area recently dubbed the "Galapagos of the North." The aim there is to preserve an entire ecosystem, from the mountain ridge to the ocean floor. As a 1993 declaration, jointly made by the Council of the Haida Nation and the Government of Canada states, "the two parties strongly agree on the need to protect Gwaii Haanas, even though the question of ownership is unresolved."[38]

The nineteenth century village of SGang Gwaay 'Ilnagaay (formerly Ninstints) on the Queen Charlotte Islands (Haida Gwaii), British Columbia, which contains thirty-two totemic and mortuary columns and the remains of ten cedar longhouses, is a place with a unique spirit. Norman Tait, a Nisga'a carver says, "you treat a totem pole with respect, just like a person, because in our culture that's what it is. A pole is just another person that is born into the family, except he is the storyteller."[39] As a testament to the

Figure 29-15 The heritage landscape at Head-Smashed-In Buffalo Jump begins 9 kilometers (5.59 miles) behind this precipice and includes some eight-thousand lines of stone cairns, comprising guide barriers through which bison were channeled. The site is believed to be the oldest and largest of thousands of such sites on the central plains of North America; it was inscribed on the World Heritage List in 1981. Photo by and copyright 2006 Ken Thomas.

artistry of the Haida people, and the spirit that remains on the shores they call "place of wonder," SGang Gwaay 'Ilnagaay now is a National Historic Site, inside a National Park, and is inscribed on the World Heritage List.

Conservation of the spirit of a culture is immensely challenging when the physical remains of the culture are scant, and the "old ways," once transmitted by storytelling, have been largely forgotten. This is the unfortunate reality of the once great aboriginal civilizations of central Canada. In 1981, the Iroquoian Village at Crawford Lake Conservation Area in Halton, Ontario, was reconstructed through a combination of excavation, analysis of the written records of early settlers, and consultation with nearby First Nations communities. Like all parts of the Greater Toronto Area, Halton continues to experience intense development pressures. Yet, the blending of cultures that began with this restoration project continues—a visit to the longhouses of the Turtle and Wolf clans now is a mandatory part of the local elementary school curriculum.

The site called Head-Smashed-In Buffalo Jump, near Fort Macleod, Alberta, shows how the Blackfoot people used a natural landscape formation to assist with communal hunting. Prior to its inscription on the World Heritage List, it may have been hard to imagine that a lonely field in the Canadian prairies might share company with the great achievements of human civilization. Yet, as one of the oldest, largest, and best preserved such sites in North America, Head-Smashed-In sheds light on the cunning, courage, and organization of First Nations cultures.

FURTHER READING

Brink, Jack W. *Imagining Head-Smashed-In: Aboriginal Buffalo Hunting on the Northern Plains* (Edmonton: Athabaska University Press, 2008).

Cameron, Christina. "The Spirit of Place: The Physical Memory of Canada." In *Journal of Canadian Studies*, vol. 35, no. 1 (Spring) pp. 77–94, 2000.

Davis, Wade. *The Wayfinders: Why Ancient Wisdom Matters in the Modern World*, CBC Massey Lectures (Toronto: House of Anansi Press Inc., Toronto, 2009).

Denhez, Marc C. *The Heritage Strategy Planning Handbook: An International Primer.* (Toronto: Dundurn Press, 1997).

Government of Canada. *Report of the Royal Commission on Aboriginal Peoples,* 1996. http://www.ainc-inac.gc.ca/ap/rrc-eng.asp.

Grace, Sherrill 2001. *Canada and the Idea of North.* (Montreal/Kingston: McGill-Queen's University Press, 2002).

Kalman, Harold. *A History of Canadian Architecture.* (Don Mills, Ontario: Oxford University Press, 1994).

MacDonald, George F. *Ninstints Haida World Heritage Site.* (Vancouver: University of British Columbia Press/UBC Museum of Anthropology, ca. 1983).

Stewart, Hilary. *Looking at Totem Poles.* (Seattle: Douglas & McIntyre Vancouver/Toronto and University of Washington Press, 1993).

Figure 29-16 The longhouse at Crawford Lake in Halton, Ontario, presents an Iroquoian settlement of the eleventh century. During the 1980s, reconstructions at the site entailed the excavation of archaeological remains (which were scant), the study of written reports made by European settlers, as well as consultation with members of the nearby Six Nations community. Photo Barbara Ross.

LOOKING FORWARD IN CANADIAN HERITAGE CONSERVATION

The twenty-first century brings new challenges, yet many of the original issues remain. Canada encompasses a vast territory with diverse heritage and cultures, and conservation approaches that are successful in a community in one part of the country may not be applied easily in another. Also, working in a cold environment is becoming more complex, as the far north witnesses the effects of climate change. As the Canadian economy shifts from one with a robust manufacturing sector to one with a more dominant service sector, the existing building stock must respond.

The challenges of distance and diversity are being recognized in federal legislation that addresses specific types of historic buildings, in the priorities established by Parks Canada for its projects, and by advocacy groups interested in redefining Canadian heritage. For example, Canadian architectural conservationists began to focus on specific components of their heritage, notably with the federal government's passage of the Heritage Railway Stations Protection Act in 1985.[40] This act not only protected these important symbols of national unity, but was also a significant milestone in the development of Canadian architectural conservation practice because it has inspired protection for other buildings types as well, including lighthouses in the early 1990s. While such legislation provides welcome support for these two specific building types, many other important sites are left unprotected and there is a continuing need to develop a more coherent approach to protection at the federal level.

During the 1990s, aboriginal history, cultural communities, and women's history were identified as Parks Canada's main priorities. Cultural communities already recognized include Ukrainian and Mennonite settlements on the western prairies and a Chinese cemetery in British Columbia. Places associated with the Underground Railroad also have been recognized, including the Buxton Settlement in southwest Ontario, which provided refuge and opportunity for freed and fugitive slaves from the United States during the mid-nineteenth century.[41] Midcentury modern architecture has been the focus of a number of recent symposia and exhibitions.[42] In Ontario the informal assumption that a "heritage" building must be more than forty years old did not prevent many post-1960 structures from being designated under the Ontario Heritage Act in recent decades; however, the same cannot be said of all of the heritage lists. Redevelopment threatens modern buildings, just as it does older ones; the Bata building and Terminal One at Pearson Airport in Toronto are among the significant losses in recent years. Currently, the fate of the Winnipeg Airport hangs in the balance.

Climate change is also a factor, particularly in the far north, where some low-lying areas are threatened by sea level changes.[43] When the ground begins to thaw, buildings that were constructed on permafrost are severely distorted by settlement. Where freeze-thaw cycles that did not exist in the past become the new normal, accelerated deterioration is a challenge. For instance, at the Fort Prince of Wales in Churchill, Manitoba, some of the massive masonry walls, constructed during the eighteenth century, collapsed during the 1990s. Parks Canada now has an ongoing project that entails disassembling and reconstructing the inner rubble core of the fortress walls and installing a drainage system to try to minimize future water damage.[42] At this fort in Churchill, students from the traditional masonry program in the Heritage Institute at Algonquin College in Perth, Ontario, contributed labor and expertise to the Parks Canada project and had a learning experience that is wholly unique, even in the Canadian north.[45]

The changing economy suggests that Canada's industrial heritage should be recognized, preserved, and adapted to today's realities. For instance, many of yesterday's mills and garment factories stand ready for reuse; their large floor areas, high ceilings, and wood structures provide flexible, potentially interesting space for any number of future uses. Mere legislation does not seem to be enough to launch these buildings into the twenty-first

Figure 29-17 The Distillery District in Toronto, once the largest whiskey producing site in the British empire, is now the largest collection of preserved Victorian-era industrial buildings in North America, accommodating artists' studios, theatres, new housing, and public activities to suit tourists and local inhabitants alike.

century; imagination and a creative approach to development are required. For example, the Gooderham & Worts Distillery in Toronto, which closed operations in 1990, has been adapted through the efforts of a private developer in partnership with the city. Some have criticized the compromises to pure heritage conservation that were made at the Distillery District, while others celebrate the revitalization of an historic district into a twenty-first century neighborhood that accommodates a full range of urban experiences.

Within government, Parks Canada began a review of all of its policies in the early 1990s, and has upgraded its approaches in a number of important ways since then.[46] In 1993, the Cultural Resource Management Policy was adopted; that philosophy and the accompanying conservation principles and tools (including the use of Commemorative Integrity Statements as management tools) are used at national historic sites across the country. In 2001, after a decade of consultation with numerous agencies, Parks Canada launched its Historic Places Initiative. This sought to build a pan-Canadian approach to heritage management and conservation, by fostering "co-operative federalism" between the federal government, the provinces, and the territories.[47] The first phase of the Historic Places Initiative involved the creation of new Conservation Standards and Guidelines, based on the model of the United States' *Secretary of the Interior's Standards*. It also also aimed to institute improved financial assistance for conservation works. In addition, the Historic Places Initiative also produced more detailed criteria for a newly consolidated Canadian Register of Historic Places, which aims to consolidate existing lists held at municipal, provincial, and federal levels, and to "provide a single source of information for historic places formally recognized by all levels of government."[48]

New legislation was also drafted in the early twenty-first century: the Canada Historic Places Act proposed to provide legal protection for all historic properties and archaeological resources on federal lands or in federal waters and to demand that they comply with the new Conservation Standards and Guidelines. Under the proposed statute, demolition of any "classified," federally owned building would have required the consent of the Parliament of Canada.[49] However, all federal funding for the Historic Places Initiative and support for passage of the proposed act were terminated in 2007 and 2008.

a

b

c

Figure 29-18 In Canada a railway station is a symbol of the settlement and consolidation of the country. The architecture of the Ottawa Station (a, b, c) is representative of the late 1960s period of heroic modernism. Because it is a Designated Heritage Railway Station, any future alterations to this building are controlled under the Heritage Railway Stations Protection Act. Images Panda Photography; Hugh Robertson, photographer.

For some who have worked on behalf of architectural conservation in Canada, the future may now appear disheartening. Despite the gains that have been made throughout the twentieth century, experts estimate that 21 percent of Canada's built heritage has been lost in the past thirty years.[50] In comparison to the headier days of the 1970s, when government programs were expanding, new agencies were being formed, and many excellent projects were realized, some of today's heritage conservationists feel overburdened by the remaining challenges. As federal funding dwindles, sprawl seems to continue unabated while much of Canada's most interesting heritage buildings stand empty. Shoreline erosion threatens to erase important archaeological sites, appropriate new uses for abandoned churches and historic industrial buildings are elusive, and development pressures jeopardize many historic urban environments, even within the World Heritage Site of Quebec City. Current institutions and legislation meant to protect heritage structures are strong in Canada; however, architectural conservationists and others concerned with heritage protetion in Canada have to remain vigilant in the face of ever-present threats.[51]

On the other hand, architectural conservation in Canada has come a very long way in a relatively short period of time. The subject is no longer limited to the history of a small group of European colonists; it now includes a rich array of sites that are compelling to the imagination and unique in the world. Public appreciation for architecture in general, and the ingenuity of the commercial developer concerning the adaptive reuse potential of older buildings, seems to be at an all-time high. At two of Canada's universities, specialist degree courses in architectural heritage conservation are now offered. At other institutions, specialists in the conservation trades can receive expert training and are in high demand. The Canadian Association of Heritage Professionals has been active since 1987. Relevant legislation has been enacted at all levels—and, while it is imperfect in many respects, it will likely be improved in the future. Perhaps most importantly, Canada's traditional inclusiveness, and its tendency to blur the lines between built, natural, and intangible heritage allows concerns about protecting the built heritage to mingle naturally with concerns about preserving significant ecosystems. Important structures and sites still are threatened by multiple factors, but Canada's willingness to engage in continuous reevaluation of its conservation practices, the capabilities of its professions and trades, and a growing appreciation for heritage sites bodes very well for the future.

ENDNOTES

1. Since the mid-1980s, the demographic pattern has shifted dramatically; immigration from Asia and the Caribbean has risen sharply, while immigration from Europe has lessened. "Canada's Population Estimates," Statistics Canada, http://www.statcan.gc.ca/daily-quotidien/100628/dq100628a-eng.htm (accessed January 9, 2011).

2 Heritage Canada Foundation, *Canadians and their Attitudes on Heritage: Pollara Survey Results* (Ottawa: Heritage Canada Foundation, 2000).

3. The lands along the St. Lawrence River were first called "Canada" by the explorer Jacques Cartier in 1535. The first session of parliament was held in 1841, and a treaty with the United States in 1846 established the western boundary between the two countries along the 49th parallel.

4. These are at Châteauguay (near Montreal), Crysler's Farm (the later site of Upper Canada Village), Stoney Creek, and Lundy's Lane in Niagara.

5. For instance, the Niagara Historical Society was formed with the explicit purpose of "preserving Canadian historical records and relics, and the building of Canadian loyalty and patriotism." In 1907, it would open the first building in Ontario designed solely for use as a museum. "Society and Museum History," Niagara Historical Society & Museum, http://www.niagarahistorical.museum/about/history.html (accessed July 21, 2010).

6. This committee defined "landmark" as "a building or a ruin, or a site...or a poet's walk, any natural object...or even the mere local habitation of a legend or a man." Cited in C. J. Taylor, *Negotiating the Past: The Making of Canada's National Historic Parks and Sites* (Montreal, Quebec, and Buffalo, New York: McGill-Queen's University Press, 1990), 23.

7. The Royal Society of Canada was founded in 1882. Today, it continues to recognize excellence, advise governments and organizations, and promote Canadian culture; presently it consists of approximately two thousand fellows—men and women who are distinguished scholars, artists, and scientists.

8. For a thorough discussion of how the Canadian federal bureaucracy evolved, as well as numerous reflections on the political sentiments that drove heritage policy during the first half of the twentieth century, see Taylor, *Negotiating the Past*. Taylor also describes attitudes for and against the United Empire Loyalists.

9. M. H. Long, "The Historic Sites and Monuments Board of Canada," *Report of the Annual Meeting of the Canadian Historical Association* 33, no. 1 (1954):1–11; www.erudit.org/revue/ram/1954/v33/n1/300356ar.pdf (accessed July 8, 2010).

10. "History of the Board," Historic Sites and Monuments Board of Canada, www.pc.gc.ca/clmhc-hsmbc/clmhc-hsmbc/clmhc-hsmbc1_E.asp (accessed January 26, 2010).

11. Ninstints (from *Nan Sdins*) on Anthony Island (SGang Gwaay) in the Queen Charlotte Islands, British Columbia is now known by its Haida name, SGang Gwaay 'Ilnagaay. The Museum of Man has been renamed the Museum of Civilization.

12. The collection is still located at McGill, in Montreal.

13. Denhez, *Heritage Fights Back*, 16.

14. In 1922, Quebec established a Historic Monuments Commission, along with its first heritage act. Quebec's unique perspective is evident in its very title: "*Loi relative à la conservation des monuments et des objets d'art ayant un intérêt historique et artistique.*"

15. The Massey Commission, as it has become known, led to the establishment of several new cultural institutions, including the National Library of Canada and the Canada Council for the Arts.

16. *Report: Royal Commission on National Development in the Arts, Letters, and Sciences* (Ottawa: Edmond Cloutier, Printer to the King's Most Excellent Majesty, 1951), 347, www.collectionscanada.gc.ca/2/5/h5-400-e.html (accessed July 20, 2010).

17. Ibid., 350.

18. Covering nearly 60 acres, Louisbourg was France's last and largest economic and military foothold in North America, at one time housing four thousand civilians and four thousand soldiers. In 1902 the condition of the ruined French Fortress of Louisbourg was noted by the Royal Society, yet it would be nearly sixty years before any substantial reconstruction work would begin there. The reconstructed Fortress of Louisbourg on Cape Breton in Nova Scotia is the most elaborate example of a French colonial military structure in Canada today. Within its walls are found numerous houses built in a French vernacular style. See "Its Reconstruction," Parks Canada, www.pc.gc.ca/eng/lhn-nhs/ns/louisbourg/natcul/natcul3.aspx (accessed January 26, 2010). C. J. Taylor, *Negotiating the Past*, provides a summary of the challenges encountered at Louisbourg in establishing the scope of the area to be reconstructed and in scheduling; he also reflects on certain internal differences between the Historic Sites and Monuments Board and the Parks Branch.

19. *Report: Royal Commission*, 347.

20. "Designation Process" and "Implications of the Designation," Historic Sites and Monuments Board of Canada, www.pc.gc.ca/clmhc-hsmbc (accessed January 26, 2010).

21. Because private property regulations in Canada fall under the jurisdiction of provincial and territorial governments, the federal government cannot place restrictions on the treatment of designated sites, unless they are controlled by the Crown. See Denhez, *Heritage Fights Back*, 70.

22. Anne Faulkner, *Without Our Past? A Handbook for the Preservation of Canada's Architectural Heritage* (Toronto: University of Toronto Press, 1979), 6–7.

23. "Heritage Conservation," *The Canadian Encyclopedia*, www.thecanadianencyclopedia.com/index.cfm?PgNm=TCE&Params=A1ARTA0003726 (accessed January 26, 2010).

24. Herb Stovel, "ICOMOS Canada and International Outreach," *Momentum: ICOMOS Canada Bulletin* 10, no. 1 (2002): 17–8.

25. ICOMOS Canada, "The Appleton Charter for the Protection and Enhancement of the Built Environment" (Ottawa: ICOMOS Canada, 1983).

26. Denhez remarks wryly that the principal criterion used in the CIHB exercise—that the building to be recorded must be older that 1914—rarely fails to make conservationists from other countries smile. Denhez, *Heritage Fights Back*, 36.

27. "Who We Are," Heritage Canada, www.heritagecanada.org/eng/about/who.html (accessed January 26, 2010).

28. Deryck Holdsworth and Jacques Dalibard, eds. *Reviving Main Street* (Toronto: University of Toronto Press, 1985).

29. This program began in 1956 under the agency's progenitor, the Archaeological and Historical Sites Board of Ontario, and now has over two thousand markers in its roster. "Plaques & markers," Ontario Heritage Trust, www.heritagefdn.on.ca/userfiles/HTML/nts_1_2638_1.html (accessed July 20, 2010).

30. The Ontario Heritage Trust currently manages 140 natural heritage properties and owns and operates 24 built heritage sites, 11 of which are also designated as national Heritage Sites.

31. The Architectural Conservancy of Ontario is the continuing organization founded by Eric Arthur in 1933 "About," Architectural Conservancy of Ontario, www.arconserv.ca/about (accessed July 20, 2010).

32. For instance, the Heritage Trust of Nova Scotia was founded in 1959, modeled on the structure of the British National Trust, to purchase and restore historic sites and accept donated conservation easements from private property owners. The establishment of the Heritage Trust of Nova Scotia was a direct result of local community reaction to the demolition of the eighteenth-century Gorsebrook estate, the home of Enos Collins (one of Nova Scotia's most famous privateers and bankers) by St. Mary's University. "About the Trust," The Heritage Trust of Nova Scotia, www.lizmacdougall.netfirms.com/htns.ca/about.html (accessed January 26, 2010).

33. Denhez presents a thorough comparison of the efficacy of provincial and municipal statutes in Canada, as they existed in 1978, in *Heritage Fights Back*, 80 and 106.

34. "Federal Heritage Buildings Review Office," Parks Canada, www.pc.gc.ca/progs/beefp-fhbro/index_e.asp (accessed January 26, 2010).

35. Herb Stovel and Julian Smith, *Federal Heritage Buildings Review Office Code of Practice*, revised edition. Ed. Jean-Pierre W. Landry and Lyette A.M. Fortin (Ottawa: Parks Canada, 2004), 1.

36. Denhez concludes *The Heritage Strategy Planning Handbook an International Primer* (p. 63) with the suggestion that legislation ought take care of only the 10 percent of heritage conservation projects that are not enabled by more "natural" approaches.

37. Wade Davis, *The Wayfinders: Why Ancient Wisdom Matters in the Modern World* (Toronto: House of Anansi Press, 2009).

38. "Gwaii Haanas National Park Reserve and Haida Heritage Site," Parks Canada, http://www.pc.gc.ca/eng/pn-np/bc/gwaiihaanas/index.aspx (accessed January 10, 2011).

39. Stewart, *Looking at Totem Poles*, 9.

40. Federal legislation respecting train stations and lighthouses received royal assent in 1988 and 2008, respectively. The HRSPA offered the highest level of protection to historic railway stations throughout the country, thereby preventing their demolition and regulating the use and conservation of this specific building type.

41. Sharon A. Roger Hepburn, *Crossing the Border: A Free Black Community in Canada* (Chicago: University of Illinois Press, 2007); Nancy Pollock-Ellwand, "The Path to the Promised Land: A Terminus to the Underground Railroad" *Momentum: ICOMOS Canada Bulletin* 10, no. 1 (2002): 52.

42. See, for example, Susan Algie and James Ashby, eds., *Conserving the Modern in Canada—Buildings Ensembles and Sites 1945–2005*, conference proceedings May 6–8, 2005, Trent University, Peterborough, Ontario (Winnipeg, Manitoba: Winnipeg Architecture Foundation, 2007).

43. Stubbs, *Time Honored*, 360.

44. "Prince of Wales Fort Wall Stabilization Project," Parks Canada, www.pc.gc.ca/lhn-nhs/mb/prince/ne/ne2.aspx (accessed January 26, 2010).

45. "Masonry—Heritage and Traditional: Traditional," Algonquin College Heritage Institute, www.algonquincollege.com/Perth/programs/heritage_masonry/project.html (accessed July 20, 2010); and "Prince of Wales Fort National Historic Site of Canada," Parks Canada, www.pc.gc.ca/lhn-nhs/mb/prince/ne/ne3.aspx (accessed July 20, 2010).

46. Between 1994 and 2003, Parks Canada was part of the newly established ministry-level Department for Canadian Heritage, which also oversaw the Historic Sites and Monuments Board. However, during the most recent restructuring in 2003, Parks Canada became an independent agency within the Ministry of the Environment.

47. The Canadian Register of Historic Places is intended to encompass all scales and types of heritage, including "buildings, battlefields, shipwrecks, parks, archaeological sites and cultural landscapes, bridges, homes, grave sites, railway stations, historic districts, ruins, engineering wonders, schools, canals, courthouses, theatres or markets." See "Frequently Asked Questions," Canada's Historic Places, www.historicplaces.ca/en/pages/more-plus/faq.aspx (accessed January 26, 2010).

48. "About Us," Canada's Historic Places, www.historicplaces.ca/en/pages/about-apropos.aspx (accessed January 26, 2011).

49. Department of Canadian Heritage, Towards a New Act: Protecting Canada's Historic Places. (Ottowa: Minister of Public Works and Government Services Canada, 2002): 6.

50. ICOMOS Canada, "Canada," *Heritage@Risk 2001–2002* (Paris: ICOMOS, 2002), www.international.icomos.org/risk/2001/cana2001.htm (accessed January 26, 2010).

51. For example, in 1994, the early nineteenth-century St. George's Church in Halifax was severely damaged by arson, which also led to the near total destruction of St. John's Anglican Church in the World Heritage City of Lunenburg, Nova Scotia, in 2001. Both churches have since been reconstructed.

MEXICO, THE CARIBBEAN, AND CENTRAL AMERICA

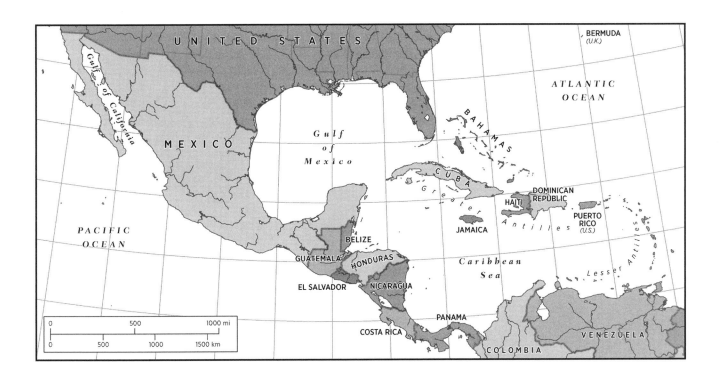

The countries of Central America and the Caribbean, as well as Mexico, share a rich continuity with the past in which both the preconquest and colonial periods are fused with the present. It is a region of cultural contrasts, where the traditional and contemporary coexist and where the layers of heritage include Mayan ruins, neoclassical and baroque facades and cities, and noteworthy modern architecture. History also lives on in the traditional practices of the indigenous people of the region. While some Central American and Caribbean countries have just begun to protect their cultural heritage resources in recent decades, others have long histories of architectural conservation. Today, the shared challenges facing the region's cultural heritage conservationists and a strong spirit of cooperation have led to important developments in the field.[1]

The most advanced ancient civilizations in the Americas were primarily centered in Mesoamerica, including the Zapotecs, Toltecs, Olmecs, Maya, and Aztecs.[2] These cultures built monumental temple complexes and extensive cities throughout the region. Though many had already declined by the fifteenth century, others were still strong and vibrant when Europeans first encountered this New World. On Christopher Columbus's first two voyages in the 1490s he explored the Caribbean islands, and in 1508 Vicente Yáñez Pinzón sailed the Caribbean sea looking for a pass to the Pacific

Figure 30-I An early-eighteenth-century engraving depicts the Temple of the Sun in Tenochtitlán, the grandest of several pre-Columbian cities in the Americas, which was comprised of numerous natural and human-made islands and canals in the middle of Lake of Texcoco. Spanish conquistador Hernán Cortés destroyed the Aztec city and built over it what soon became the most important European city in the New World. Today the ruins of Tenochtitlán's Temple of the Sun are buried beneath the center of modern Mexico City (see Figure 30-9). Source: Jan Karel Donatus van Beecq, *Illustrations de Histoire de la conquête du Mexique ou de la Nouvelle Espagne* (Gallica-BNF) c. 1705.

Ocean and explored Mexico's Yucatan Peninsula and Central America's eastern coast. The contact between Europe and the Americas that began with these early explorations had such a dramatic effect on the Americas, and changed its course so radically, that its history is typically divided into the pre- and post-Columbian eras.

By the mid-sixteenth century, Spain had conquered and claimed the region, establishing a viceroyalty of New Spain to administer it, and built an impressive new capital—Mexico City—on the foundations of the Aztec capital of Tenochtitlán. Hundreds of other new cities were founded throughout Central America; they were mostly laid out according to the sixteenth-century Leyes de Indias (Laws of the Indies), with grid patterns and central squares dominated by religious and civic structures. In the seventeenth and eighteenth century, elaborate and monumental baroque churches, convents, and monasteries were built throughout the region by the members of the Catholic clergy who quickly followed the conquistadors to the Americas. In the Caribbean region, it was not only the Spanish but also the Dutch, French, and British who established colonies, bringing very different styles of architecture and cultural influences along with them.

Independence was won by Mexico, the countries of Central America, and Haiti in the early nineteenth century and came to most of the rest of the Caribbean in the mid- to late-twentieth century. Several Caribbean islands, however, are still part of the United Kingdom, France, the Netherlands, or the United States. Today the population of Central America is a complex mixture. While some countries, such as Costa Rica, El Salvador, and nearly all in the Caribbean have very few indigenous persons left; in other countries, such as Guatemala, Belize, and especially Mexico, these groups form a large percentage of the contemporary population. In Mexico and Central America, people of mixed European and indigenous ancestry, called mestizos, comprise the majority of the population, but in the Caribbean, the overwhelming majority of people are of African descent, their ancestors having been brought to the region as slaves between the sixteenth and nineteenth centuries.

The isolation of the over seven thousand islands of the Caribbean, the deserts of northern Mexico, and the tropical rainforests of Central America have all influenced the fate of architectural heritage in the region. In addition, natural disasters have repeatedly destroyed sites and even cities throughout the region, most recently in Port-au-Prince, Haiti, in January 2010. Earthquakes are a reoccurring threat in Central America, and in the Caribbean Sea and along the Caribbean and Gulf coasts of Central America and Mexico hurricanes have battered the region's historic cities and sites with increasing intensity and frequency.

The lack of financial resources and formal training for professionals in the region also plagues historic sites throughout most of the Caribbean and Central America, as does the looting of archaeological sites. Migration to metropolitan centers has caused problems for historic sites in both the abandoned rural areas and the overwhelmed cities. Finally, as in many developing regions of the world, tourism has both solved and contributed to the problems of architectural conservationists, bringing funding and incentives, yet also new threats and complications.

Since the nineteenth century, Mexico has emerged as a world leader in archaeology, and its architectural conservation movement evolved out of this tradition. As a result of this expertise and because of strong nationalist and antiforeign biases, Mexican cultural heritage specialists have overwhelmingly focused on pre-Columbian sites and only relatively recently begun to appreciate the wealth of Spanish colonial cities, churches, and other building complexes throughout the country. Mexico's dedication to its historic resources, strong protective legislation, and experienced professionals have proven a successful model throughout the region.

The countries of the Caribbean have had the opposite experience: there are very few surviving pre-Columbian sites or communities, and with lingering relationships with former colonial powers in Europe and the United States, architectural conservationists have predominately focused on the islands' wealth of colonial cities, plantations, and fortresses. In recent decades, the vernacular heritage of the Caribbean's African descendants as well as sites documenting the history of slavery in the region have begun to attract attention both internationally and locally. Balancing the competing expectations and needs of local populations and tourists with the integrity of the historic sites themselves has been among the greatest challenges in the Caribbean.

Mexico and Central America have struck a balance in their conservation efforts, examining their pre-Columbian sites as well as their colonial heritage, appreciating contemporary indigenous cultures, and integrating natural and cultural heritage conservation successfully in innovative programs. Though most of the region's countries have only begun to address architectural conservation in a comprehensive and systematic way with the wave of new and radically strengthened legislation in the 1980s and 1990s, they are incorporating inventive policies and a cooperative spirit to quickly secure the future of the region's architectural heritage.

ENDNOTES

1. It is for this reason and the commonality of their histories in cultural heritage protection that Mexico's experiences in architectural conservation are being discussed together with those of Caribbean and Central American countries.

2. Mesoamerica, which refers to the lands of pre-Hispanic cultures in parts of today's Mexico, Nicaragua, and Costa Rica, will be referred to only in its historical geographical sense.

Figure 30-1 Early Spanish settlement of Mexico entailed the replacement of indigenous religious buildings with Christian churches and imposition of new administrative and residential districts on top of predecessor settlements. The erection of the Church of Our Lady of the Remedies atop the Tlachihualtepetl, or the Great Pyramid of Cholula in Puebla State is one such example. Excavations at different times in the twentieth century have vividly displayed this cultural palimpsest.

CHAPTER 30

Mexico

As one of the largest Latin American countries, Mexico is endowed with diverse geographical and cultural landscapes as well as extensive arrays of archaeological sites that rival any in the world. Mexico's territory witnessed the flourishing and fall of great indigenous civilizations, such as the Olmecs, Maya, and Aztecs. and grew into a regional power as one of the main seats of the Spanish colonial empire in the Americas. Since its independence in the early nineteenth century, Mexico has continued to develop as a cultural center of the Spanish-speaking world.

Today architectural conservationists in Mexico work diligently to protect the country's towering pyramids, adobe dwellings sheltered within cliff sides, open-air chapels erected over indigenous temples, gilded baroque churches, and more recent architectural heritage. The country's museums, galleries, public art, conserved historic town centers, and numerous accessible archaeological sites reveal that Mexico truly recognizes the value of its heritage and has taken significant steps to protect this legacy. Architectural conservation has a long history in Mexico, but the practice especially gathered strength in the nineteenth century due to the interrelated forces of a strong national movement and a quickly developing field of archaeology. Unlike most other countries, Mexico's contemporary architectural conservation practice emerged out of—and is still intimately linked to—archaeology.

A LEGACY OF GOVERNMENT LEGISLATION AND PROTECTION

Mexico's contemporary centralized archaeological and architectural conservation policies and practices are built on a long tradition of government ownership and legal protection for historic and archaeological sites. This state dominance has marked every period of Mexico's history and has always been highly politicized. The impetus to preserve the extensive archaeological remains of the lost and ancient civilizations of the region and to incorporate them into present state policies predated even the European conquest. After settling in Tenochtitlán, the Aztecs respected the nearby ruins of the cultures of Teotihuacán and Tula and believed the evidence of this illustrious past should be maintained, because it was the legacy on which their own authority and importance was based.[1]

For very different reasons, the Spanish colonial government also took an interest in the region's cultural heritage after conquering the territory of today's Mexico in the sixteenth century. The colonial government's interest was rarely, if ever, in the best interests of these sites and objects: cities were razed to the ground, found objects were destroyed as idolatrous icons, and others were melted down for their precious metals, but some objects were saved and taken back to Spain as representative treasures. Spanish practices were institutionalized in 1573, when a set of ordinances was passed by King Phillip II of Spain to govern the building and design of towns throughout the Americas, as these ordinances also claimed all indigenous heritage as property of the Spanish crown.[2]

Figure 30-2 Illustration of "Indigenas" (indigenous peoples) constructing a building for the Spanish from Francisco Xavier Clavijero's *Atraidos por la Nueva España* (Ancient History of Mexico) reflecting mid-eighteenth-century antiquarian interest in Mexico's pre-Columbian and colonial history. *The Atraidos por la Nueva España (Codice Florentino)*, Biblioteca Nacional de Anthropología e Historia, INAH-CNCA.

For a few missionaries there was a special interest in understanding and documenting the indigenous past. Among them was Bernardino de Sahagún, a Franciscan friar who organized and supervised his Aztec students in the mid-sixteenth century in the creation of the so-called Florentine Codex, a major source on Aztec life in the years before the Spanish conquest. By the mid-eighteenth century, many educated persons born in Mexico but of Spanish descent, known as criollos, were unsatisfied with Spanish policies. They began arguing on behalf of a Mexican national culture that celebrated the achievements of New Spain's pre-Colombian past. New histories were written, including Mexican Jesuit priest Francisco Xavier Clavijero's *Ancient History of Mexico*. His book, published in Italy in 1780-81, promoted a positive view of the American indigenous and argued for the importance of excavating and protecting ancient statues, structures, and mosaics as well as for the copying of historic manuscripts representative of both indigenous and early colonial missionary cultures.[3] Active planning for a museum and council focused on Mexico's antiquities began in 1790 after the discovery of some Aztec carved monolithic figures during a construction project in the Zócalo, the principal square of Mexico City. Information about these carvings and other archaeological sites encouraged more and more European and local visitors to come to examine and study them. However, without protective mechanisms, this attention led to the gradual disappearance of numerous pre-Columbian objects across Mexico.

After a long but successful War for Independence in the early nineteenth century, the newly established Mexican government assumed responsibility for protecting the republic's heritage. The exporting of antiquities was prohibited by a federal law in 1826 more broadly aimed at regulating the maritime and border customs of Mexico. A presidential decree calling for the formation of the Museo Nacional (National Museum) was issued about the same time. After the Mexican American War at mid-century, and the consequent loss of more than half of Mexico's territory, followed by a brief return of a European-controlled monarchy under the French in the 1860s, feelings of national pride and confidence increased. The Museo Nacional had been established in a hall of the university in 1831 during the first republic, and in 1865, during the brief monarchical period, Emperor Maximilian I ordered its move to the former Casa de Moneda, the eighteenth-century building that had housed the colonial-era mint.

The illicit antiquities trade remained an imperative concern as much for liberal as for conservative governments in the mid-nineteenth century: in 1864 Maximilian I ordered the prohibition of any excavation in the Yucatan peninsula and in 1868, after the restoration of the republic, Benito Juarez's legislation established that any antiquities found throughout the country belonged to the Mexican government. Like the Spanish decree of the previous century, the state thus claimed ownership of these sites and objects; however, this time the law also obligated the government to ensure their protection and conservation.[4]

In the late-nineteenth century, during the regime of Porfirio Díaz, Mexican heritage conservation practices further developed. Díaz was a mestizo—of mixed Spanish and indigenous descent—as well as a Mexican patriot and military hero, having opposed first the Antonio López de Santa Anna dictatorship and later serving as commander of the army in the war that repelled the French invasion and Emperor Maximilian I. His presidency lasted from 1876 to 1911, and it was increasingly viewed as a dictatorship in its later years.

The centennial anniversary of Mexican independence coincided with the anniversary of thirty years of Porfirio Díaz's presidency. Díaz conceived the centennial celebrations as the stage to display the industrialized and modern country he had helped develop. Events held in conjunction with the centennial included inaugurations of new and restored public buildings, gardens, streets and boulevards, as well as dedications of new commemorative monuments. The period also included a renewed embracing of ideas imported from Europe, including architectural styles, urban planning techniques, and philosophies, especially *positivism* that promoted education as a method of constructing national identity and cohesion.

At the same time, Díaz oversaw increased support for archaeology, the growing study of indigenous peoples, and even a neo-indigenous movement in professional art. Pre-Colombian antiquities were lent to foreign museums and international exhibitions to promote Mexico's history and culture abroad. The systematic documentation of significant sites began in 1885 with the establishment of the Inspección de Monumentos Arqueológicos (Archaeological Monument Inspection) that became Mexico's first formal government institution for archaeology. In 1897 additional legislation reinforced earlier policies and enhanced the government's control by criminalizing the destruction of

Figure 30-3 Late nineteenth-century archaeological and architectural restorations of Aztec remains at Teotihuacán and at the Zapotec site of Mitla in Oaxaca by Leopoldo Batres, chief archaeologist of the Inspección de Monumentos Arqueológicos, reflected Viollet-le-Duc's "unity of style" approach to monument conservation, which developed in France in the mid-nineteenth century.

archaeological sites, strengthening restrictions on the export of objects without a federal permit, and requiring the placement of all found objects in the Museo Nacional.[5]

Site conservation also increased at the turn of the twentieth century; however, in most cases, such as the Zapotec city of Mitla in Oaxaca, this meant they were wholly reconstructed. Most of these projects were supervised by the government's chief archaeologist, Leopoldo Batres, who had studied archaeology in Paris and was an adamant follower of Viollet-le-Duc's approach of extensive rebuilding and "unity of style" restoration. Batres's projects at Mitla, as well as at Monte Albán, Xochicalco, and Teotihuacán, introduced romanticized reconstruction to Mexico, and this practice lingered long into the twentieth century.[6] Noted as the most ambitious of early architectural reconstruction and conservation projects, Batres's work at Teotihuacán began in 1905 and lasted more than six years. The project was unique for its time in its goal of integrating the site into a useful public space for education and tourism.[7]

TWENTIETH-CENTURY INSTITUTIONS AND POLICIES

By the early twentieth century, the foundations had been firmly laid for the strong conservation ethic and practices that have continued to develop in modern Mexico through today. The first decade of the twentieth century, however, was a period of political turmoil as Díaz's modernization policies were increasingly pursued at the cost of social improvements. Discontent culminated in the Mexican Revolution, the 1910 through 1920 armed struggle that led to the 1917 constitution and resulted in the creation of the National Revolution Party in 1929 (in 1946 renamed the Institutional Revolutionary Party, the Partido Revolucionario Institucional, known commonly as the PRI) that would govern Mexico nearly unchallenged until the year 2000. The post-revolution change in regime was accompanied by a renewed focus on forging a Mexican national identity that concentrated on the country's indigenous heritage and the recognition of its colonial past. These ideals were clearly visible in the arts, which were encouraged and flourished throughout the twentieth century.

Thus even after the revolution, much of the archaeological and conservation work initiated under Díaz was continued by the new regime. Even during the period of conflict in the second decade of the twentieth century, legislation was passed in 1914 protecting colonial and natural heritage and two government agencies focused on these components of Mexican heritage were combined in 1916 into the Inspección General de Monumentos Artísticos e Históricos y Bellezas Naturales (General Inspection of Artistic and Historic Monuments and Natural Beauties). Both this new agency and the 1895 Inspección de Monumentos Arqueológicos were incorporated into the Museo Nacional, which had grown to become one of the most extensive and respected ethnographic and archaeological collections in the world.

Though political preoccupations and economic hardships in the early years of the Inspección de Monumentos Artísticos prevented much architectural conservation from actually being completed, another large project of excavation, study, and conservation was launched at Teotihuacán in the 1920s under Manuel Gamio. Gamio led the museum's Dirección de Antropología (department of anthropology, formed in 1917 as the archaeology an ethnography department) and was an avid promoter of national identity and one of the leading archaeologists and anthropologists of post revolutionary Mexico. He argued for anthropology as a science and introduced the stratigraphic method to Mexican archaeology, encouraging archaeologists to trace the historic and cultural sequences of civilizations at sites they studied. Between 1918 and 1920 Gamio explored Teotihuacán with a large team of workers and an interdisciplinary professionals group and in 1922 he published the results of his research under the title *La Población del Valle de Teotihuacán* (*The Population of the Valley of Teotihuacán*). This publication

a

b

Figure 30-4 Lawyer, anthropologist, and archaeologist Alfonso Caso, on behalf of the Instituto Nacional de Anthropologiá e Historia (INAH), conducted restorations at Monte Albán (a) in the 1930s and 1940s that refined earlier, more extensive restoration of Mexico's ancient monuments by purposefully distinguishing his interventions, including using lines of small stones pressed into mortar at new construction joints to differentiate original and later building fabric (b).

and other works promoted Gamio´s thesis about the importance of understanding the social impact in archaeological and anthropological research.

In 1934, in accordance with the international principles of the Athens Charter, Mexico passed the new federal Law for Protection and Conservation of Archaeological and Historical Monuments, Typical Towns and Natural Beauty Sites, combining architectural, archaeological and natural heritage under a single law. The cultural heritage protection system was overhauled further in 1939 with the creation of the Instituto Nacional de Antropología e Historia (INAH, National Institute of Anthropology and History). INAH was entrusted with Mexico's cultural heritage, and still today it remains the primary government agency concerned with "researching, preserving and diffusing the archaeological, anthropological, historic, and paleontological heritage of the nation for strengthening the identity and the memory of the society."[8] One of the most important early projects completed by INAH was the restoration of the palace complex tower at the Palenque Mayan site in Chiapas.

It was during the mid-twentieth century that Alfonso Caso ushered in Mexico's golden age of archaeology and site conservation, especially in projects such as the excavation and protection of Monte Albán, an extensive site near Oaxaca that was constructed over the course of two thousand years and shows evidence of the Olmec and Mixtec peoples, but most notably of its last occupant culture, the Zapotec. Caso continued earlier tendencies toward extensive reconstruction, but his archaeological work was more systematic and his interventions were more easily distinguishable from the original material than the work of previous Mexican archaeological site conservationists.[9]

In 1972, a new federal Law of Monuments, Archaeological, Artistic, and Historic Zones strengthened existing prohibitions on selling or trading movable objects and reinforced state ownership of archaeological sites while extending this status to additional buildings and monuments. The new law also introduced the concept of monument zones as areas in which several protected sites were located. In addition, the law clarified the distinctive roles of INAH and the Instituto Nacional de Bellas Artes y Literatura (INBA, National Institute of Fine Arts and Literature), which had been created soon after its counterpart.[10] INAH's jurisdiction was outlined as encompassing all archaeological and historical monuments. Archaeological monuments are defined by the same law as artifacts, buildings, sculptures, and any other remnants associated with the period prior to the establishment of Spanish culture. Historic monuments are the properties (and their contents) associated with the country's colonial and post-colonial history from sixteenth through the nineteenth centuries. This category also included all documents of local or federal offices and all books and other printed material in Mexico from the same period that are worthy of conservation due to their importance or rarity. INBA, on the other hand, was given authority over all artistic monuments recognized by the law as movable or immovable properties valued primarily for their aesthetic qualities. In cases of overlapping values, the law stated that archaeological value has precedence over historic value, which in turn has precedence over artistic value.

In 1989 the Consejo Nacional para la Cultura y las Artes (CONACULTA, National Council for Culture and Arts) was created to coordinate the multiple organisms and offices of cultural and artistic nature throughout Mexico, and it continues to serve as an umbrella organization in the country today. CONACULTA has multiple departments focused on various aspects of culture, a number of which are related to heritage, including one dedicated to cultural heritage tourism, one to historic railroads, and the Dirección General de Sitios y Monumentos del Patrimonio Cultural (General Department of Monuments and Sites of Cultural Heritage), which catalogs and carries out conservation projects at federally-owned sites. It maintains the Catalog and Inventory of Movable and Immovable Monuments of Federal Property in its charge, which includes 817 researched entries with detailed descriptions of the building and its restoration interventions.[11] In 2003, CONACULTA initiated the Fondo de Apoyo a Comunidades para la Restauración de Monumentos y Bienes Artísticos de Propiedad Federal (FOREMOBA, Fund for Supporting Communities for the Restoration of Monuments and Works of Art of Federal Properties) to provide matching funds for projects at federally owned properties that are also supported by municipal governments and local communities. In its first five years over US $3.5 million was spent for the preservation of liturgical objects, paintings, altarpieces, and sculptures as well as religious and other buildings.[12]

Today, INAH is responsible for the maintenance and conservation of over 110,000 historical monuments, 29,000 archaeological zones, and over 100 museums.[13] To address the diverse needs of these sites, INAH is organized into the central Technical Secretariat whose work is carried out through offices in each of Mexico's thirty-one states.

To improve its efficiency, INAH has spent decades compiling catalogs of information about all Mexico's archaeological and historic sites. The Public Register of Archaeological Sites and Monuments is the repository for information about particular collections, archaeological sites and museums while the National Historical Immovable Monuments Catalogue lists, to date, over 89,000 of the estimated 110,000 eligible properties and intends to catalog the additional buildings in the coming years.[14]

Other current projects of INAH include investigation into the development of numerous cultural routes, such as the Camino Real de Tierra Adentro (Royal Trail of the Interior Lands), which traces the colonial-era path from Mexico City to the former provincial capital or Santa Fe, now in New Mexico, in the United States: The trail includes numerous historic towns, estates, churches, and roads.[15] Another, the Liberation Trail, traces the route followed by the father of Mexican independence, Miguel Hidalgo y Costilla, and stretches from Dolores town in Guanajuato to Chihuahua city in northern Mexico. In addition, in 2006 Mexico's first regionally focused initiative successfully nominated the country's blue agave region around the city of Tequila to the World Heritage List as an important cultural landscape demonstrating the continuity in agricultural and beverage production techniques from the pre-Columbian period to the present.[16] The architectural heritage sites protected under this initiative include pre-Columbian wells, ovens and mills; late-seventeenth-century secret *tabernas* (taverns); and nineteenth-century estates and factories.

Ongoing archaeological work in Mexico also includes the monitoring and maintenance of sites such as Mexico City's Templo Mayor. In an episode reminiscent of the discovery of the carved monolith nearly two hundred years prior, a service professional accidentally uncovered an important Aztec stone carving in the center of Mexico City

a

b

Figure 30-5 Among the hundreds of impressive cultural heritage conservation projects in Mexico conducted under the aegis of INAH are cultural landscapes and heritage routes. An example of a conserved agricultural landscape, and Mexico's first regionally focused conservation initiative, is seen in the Cultural Landscape of the Agave and the Production of Tequila (a and b) in the blue agave region of western Mexico. This site demonstrates the continuity in agricultural and beverage production techniques from the pre-Columbian period to the present and was placed on the UNESCO World Heritage List in 2006. Image (a) UNESCO/Carlo Tomas, photographer.

in 1978. This discovery led to the excavation of extensive ruins adjacent to the northeast side of the Zócalo in the very center of Mexico City. The find included the Templo Mayor, a monumental complex dedicated to the Aztec god of war and decorated with hundreds of stone carvings of skulls. The precise location of this legendary temple had previously been unknown. After its rediscovery, the demolition of buildings deemed less historically significant was authorized to reveal the pre-Columbian structure, even though many of the destroyed buildings dated to the early colonial era and were themselves architecturally and historically significant.[17]

COLLABORATIVE PROJECTS

The clear policies, strong mandates, and consistent funding of the INAH and other government agencies in Mexico have enabled the protection and conservation of a significant amount of the country's historic and archaeological sites. But at the same time, strong centralized control and the volume of sites with which they are concerned have also presented challenges for contemporary archaeologists and architectural conservationists in Mexico. Most important among the challenges with which these state organizations continue to struggle is the need for local groups, indigenous peoples, and even state and municipal governments to play an increased role in prioritizing, selecting, and carrying out projects in their own communities.

The need for increased collaboration has arisen from conflicts surrounding conservation projects with multiple interested parties. For example, complications at the archaeological site of Mitla, noted for its stone mosaic decorations, began when conservation efforts were initiated in the early 1990s. Within five years, multiple distinct groups were disputing Mitla's fate. Some were concerned with the site's income-producing potential from tourism; others were concerned with its sacred character for indigenous peoples, and still others were advocates of property rights, concerned with the extension of the boundaries of the official archaeological zone. In addition, competing jurisdictions between the municipal government and the Catholic Church over responsibility for parts of the site have in the past led to slowdowns in conservation work planned for the area.[18] The challenge in this and other similar situations consists in developing strategies to promote the protection and preservation of heritage in general, as well as respect and mutual understanding among archaeologists, architectural conservationists, institutions, and communities.[19]

In many cases the protected zones or sites are still inhabited, and the communities themselves have played an increasingly important role in their protection as concern for their ancestors' heritage and feelings of belonging have proven valuable incentives for conservation. Good examples of collaborative projects involving enterprising local communities include the 2005 initiatives of the Mixtec populations in Tidaá and Tejupan in Oaxaca State for the restoration of their polychromatic, seventeenth-century baroque altarpieces. Funds for both projects came from CONACULTA's FOREMOBA program, subscriptions from the community, and INAH, whose experts were also responsible for the actual conservation work.[20] These projects were not only collaborations of multiple institutions with local communities, but both restorations were also interdisciplinary collaborations involving architects, anthropologists, and conservation specialists.

An increasing number of cooperative projects and initiatives have been undertaken in Mexico in recent years to supplement the efforts of the government with the involvement of private parties, international donors, nonprofit groups, and municipal governments. For example, a nonprofit agency called Fideicomiso del Centro Histórico (Historic Center Trust) was created in Mexico City in 1990 to serve as a link between the government, cultural groups, businesses, and the inhabitants of the city's Centro Histórico, or central historic district. The district encompasses 680 square blocks, and its architecture reflects the long span of Mexican history. Noted sites around its massive central square, the Zócalo, include not only the pre-Columbian Templo Mayor but also the Metropolitan Cathedral, built between 1573 and 1813 and still one of the largest churches in Latin America. In addition, the eastern side of the Zócalo is the site of the seventeenth-century Palacio Nacional, built over the ruins of Montezuma II's palace and later adorned with murals painted by Mexican painter Diego Rivera depicting important moments in Mexican history. Nearby in the Centro Histórico is the Palacio de Bellas Artes, a blend of neoclassical and art nouveau styles, built between 1904 and 1934.

Due to innovative and creative projects that have involved multiple constituencies, the Historic Center Trust, and especially its funding or sponsor division, Patronato del Centro Histórico, was able to involve different actors in the recovery programs for the historic center. The catchy slogan of the Trust's ¡Échame una Manita! (Lend Me a Hand!) program in 1991, for example, encouraged local residents to participate in conservation and promoted private support for projects at individual sites. The program also provided technical and administrative assistance as well as funding and financial incentives for conservation work on historic structures in the district.[21] After three years, the ¡Échame una Manita! program had led to the rehabilitation of over six hundred residential and commercial buildings, more than half of which were listed as historic or artistic monuments by INAH. Mexico City's municipal government contributed $50 million for infrastructural and conservation projects, but it was private investors who were essential in this process, supplying nearly $150 million. In 2002, the Trust became a public organization integrated into the government of Mexico City. At the same time, the nonprofit Fundación del Centro Histórico de la Ciudad de México (Mexico City Historic Center Foundation) was established to promote the revitalization and restoration of the historic center by facilitating collaborative projects with other private institutions and social organizations.

In the colonial city of Oaxaca, the Fundación del Patronato Prodefensa del Patrimonio Cultural y Natural del Estado de Oaxaca (PROAX, Council for the Defense and Conservation of the Cultural and Natural Patrimony of the State of Oaxaca), which is run by one of Mexico's most acclaimed contemporary painters, Francisco Toledo, has joined forces with the local office of the INAH to work for the conservation of this World Heritage city. In addition, it has spearheaded public protest campaigns against threats to the city's historic district and has participated in the restoration of historic sites, such as the colonial-era ex-Convent of Santo Domingo.

Adopte una Obra de Arte (Adopt a Work of Art) is another highly successful not-for-profit organization that has become an important participant in the field of architectural conservation in Mexico. This organization grew out of the Friends of the National Museum of the Viceroyalty of Tepotzlán, which had formed in 1988 to identify private citizens willing to provide financial support for the conservation of a series of paintings in that museum. By 1991 a total of fifty-six paintings had been conserved and the program continued to grow: it adopted its current name and established representative councils in other Mexican states and in the Federal District of Mexico City.[22] These branches review and accept project proposals from community groups and connect funders with a needy site or object. Selection criteria for preservation projects include the object or site's historical and cultural significance, level of deterioration, and potential to benefit the community.

To date, Adopte una Obra de Arte has facilitated the sponsorship of over seventy projects that reflect the diversity of Mexican heritage. The adoptive parents, or patrons of these projects, have come from the private sector in Mexico and abroad, as well as from the Mexican government. The conservation projects have included streetscapes, civil and religious buildings, cave paintings, museums and cultural centers among many other types of sites. Some of the most important sites in Mexico have been restored

a

b

c

Figure 30-6 An example of a collaborative project organized by Adopte una Obre de Arte (Adopt a Work of Art) involving the public and private sectors, which also included international funding, is the restoration of the Sanctuary Church of Jésus Nazareno in Atotonilco (a), near San Miguel Allende in the state of Guanajuato. Aided by placement of the site on the World Monuments Fund Watch list, attention and funding was mobilized and the seven year-restoration restoration was completed in 2005. The exterior of the church was addressed before the phased restoration of the church's highly ornate interiors (b and c).

through the efforts of this program, including important eighteenth-century altarpieces in the chapels of Huáncito, Zacán and Nurío, Michoacán and the unique, wooden *mudéjar*-style roofs Church of San Francisco in Tlaxcala city, Tlaxcala.

Collaboration with the state and federal governments in Mexico as well as with international organizations has been an essential component of the success of Adopte una Obra de Arte. For example, the organization has worked with various other entities in the restoration of the recently discovered mural paintings at the sixteenth-century ex-Convent of San Gabriel in Cholula Puebla. The conservation of the richly decorated interiors of the Jésus Nazareno Church in Atotonilco was accomplished in a tripartite funding arrangement involving the state and national government, Adopte una Obra de Arte, and the World Monuments Fund (WMF).[23] In addition, Adopte una Obra de Arte and the WMF have cooperated with the Mexican government and the State of Jalisco in the establishment of the Escuela de Conservación y Restauración de Occidente (ECRO, School of Conservation and Restoration of the West) in Guadalajara in 2000.[24] ECRO was established as a public agency of the Government of Jalisco state for technical training of conservation specialists for movable heritage objects.

Mexico has a long tradition of training and educating restoration specialists, including the first graduate program in conservation in Latin America in 1963, the Institute of Restoration in Guanajuato University. In 1966, the Mexican government and UNESCO joined forces to create the School of Restoration and Conservation of Artistic Heritage that in 1977 became the INAH National School of Conservation, Restoration, and Museography.[25] The school's five-year undergraduate program in building conservation was among the first of its kind in the world. A second program for the formation of professional postgraduates was inaugurated at the time, in 1967, at the Architecture Faculty of the National University of Mexico. Since then, several other postgraduate programs have merged nationwide, in public and private universities, supporting the necessity of regional formation of restoration professionals.

A key challenge for the architectural conservation establishment in Mexico is the task of looking after the country's extraordinary and extensive collection of historic churches and associated structures. Mexico's first *conventos,* or friaries, were erected by missionaries of the Spanish mendicant orders beginning in the 1530s in Puebla and Mexico City. Because of their symbolic and social role, it is in religious buildings, more consistently than any other building type, that one finds loving and frequently lavish attention to detail in artistic finishes. Today, as a result of their scale and grandeur, church buildings are still typically the character-defining feature of most of Mexico's cities and towns.

The success and popularity of the Christian faith in Mexico has resulted in many historic religious structures being replaced by newer, larger structures in recent centuries. In addition, many churches and associated structures have been neglected or have been lost to the hazards of time. Regardless of their condition, religious monuments are usually considered as having special historic and religious associations, especially for those who worship in these buildings, there is a sense of pride, respect, and strong personal associations.

Some of the most challenging sites for conservationists in Mexico today are the Christian churches that were superimposed on predecessor buildings of the pre-Columbian period, as frequently occurred in the early colonial period. The grandest example of this is the Cathedral of Mexico, which was erected above the partially leveled Temple Mayor of the Aztec capital of Tenochtitlán. The grandness of the Mexico City Metropolitan Cathedral and the history of the site as the spot where the Aztec empire was vanquished, all add to its extreme cultural significance, hence its status as both a national symbol and a UNESCO World Heritage Site. Addressing the layers of history found in the church, which was built from the sixteenth through the nineteenth centuries, as well as of history beneath and around the church has kept art and architectural conservationists and structural engineers busy for decades.

Churches almost always form the centerpieces of larger enclaves of historic religious buildings as found at the sixteenth-century churches of Tzintzuntzan and Metztitlán in the states of Michoacán and Hidalgo, respectively. There are smaller but equally distinguished individual constructions such as Santa Prisca and Templo del Apóstol Santiago that serve as the proud symbols of Taxco, Guerrero, and Nurio, Michoacán. From the onset of church buildings in Mexico, new forms of religious complexes evolved to facilitate special needs, such as *conventos* that consisted of chapels able to accommodate open air worship within large-walled enclosures and formulaic building programs that featured churches as centerpieces in frontier settlements.

Styles ranged from the earliest, relatively severe late–Spanish Renaissance styles in the manner of Juan de Herrera, architect of Philip II's El Escorial, to the grander baroque style that developed from the second half of the seventeenth century to the ultra-baroque that emerged at the turn of the eighteenth century in which no effort was spared in elaborate design and in the application of ornamentation in both exteriors and interiors. From the nineteenth century forward, as in Europe, the designs of most religious buildings were exercises in historicism. All, however, were informed and probably strictly guided by the authority behind their construction, either the set rules within the Laws of the Indies or the subtly different and somewhat competitive building programs of the Jesuit, Augustinian, or the Dominican orders.

Mexican church architecture that displays high degrees of vernacular style and decoration are commonplace (e.g., Sanctuary Church of Jésus Nazareno in Atotonilco, and Santa María Tonantzintla, Puebla). In contrast, elsewhere there are religious buildings that represent simple, unpretentious local building customs and life ways. There are other forms of religious architecture, including shrines, cemeteries, and heritage routes that have special religious associations. Among the numerous former religious sites abandoned, or damaged by earthquake or some other calamity, are the Pimería Alta missions in Sonora and the Santo Domingo de Guzmán church in Tecpatán, Chiapas.

Specific architectural conservation challenges facing religious buildings in Mexico, as elsewhere in the world, may range from a lack of local, trained personnel to maintain such structures, to problems that pose very complex technical challenges. An example of a church that was preserved by conversion into a museum is

(continued)

a

b

c

Figure 30-7 Templo del Apóstol Santiago in Nurío, Michoacán (a, b, and c), and the Santo Domingo de Guzmán Church (d) in Tecpatán, Chiapas.

Santa Ana de Chinarras, Chihuahua. An extreme conservation intervention was required in the case of the Cathedral of Mexico City, which suffered from settlement of its foundations.

Assets within Mexico that are brought to such projects include the long experience and capacity of the Instituto Nacional de Antropología e Historia (INAH), the present robust array of architectural and architectural conservation talent, and the country's artisanal restoration capacities. The persistent challenge, however, is that there is always so much to do. In any case, the most important element in the equation of conserving Mexico's religious architectural heritage is the role that supporting communities play. As with architectural heritage protection elsewhere, the stronger the interest and participation of local constituencies, the more promising the results. This is the main reason why Mexico's experience in conserving its religious buildings is on the whole successful.

Foreign governments have been involved in specific architectural conservation projects elsewhere in Mexico. For example, the La Agencia Española de Cooperación Internacional para el Desarrollo (AECID, Spanish Agency for International Cooperation for Development) has funded various projects, including the restoration of the market building in the World Heritage City of Tlacotalpan, Veracruz.[26] In addition, the United States National Park Service has worked with INAH since 1998, providing exchange opportunities, technical assistance, site-management training, and on the related topic of cooperation to halt illicit trafficking of cultural heritage.

d

CONTEMPORARY CONSERVATION ISSUES IN MEXICO

Despite the extensive government structure, comprehensive policies, numerous organizations, and long-standing commitment to cultural heritage protection, conservation professionals in Mexico continue to face challenging threats. Historical biases and differing government priorities as well as natural disasters, rural migration, and tourism all contribute to the need for continued vigilance over Mexican heritage today. INAH's task of managing thousands of architectural, archaeological, and historic sites and interpreting those that are open to the public exhausts the agency's resources, even though it is better funded than many other parallel institutions in Latin America. Since nearly 90 percent of INAH's budget is devoted to operational costs, little is left over for excavation, research, or conservation.[27] In addition, land ownership problems plague many of Mexico's extensive archaeological areas, since the government cannot afford to compensate private owners for properties of archaeological interest and value that are adjacent to or within protected zones, such as at Chichén Itzá in the state of Yucatán.

Also of concern in Mexico today is the loss of some indigenous traditions and cultural practices due to modernization efforts as well as due to neglect and disinterest in this intangible heritage by various government agencies. Mexican nationalism throughout the nineteenth and twentieth centuries, and the Museo Nacional in particular, may have celebrated and exalted pre-Colombian archaeological sites but simultaneously, largely ignored present-day indigenous communities and their living cultures for most of that time period. Today, ruins of the Aztec, Mayan, and Zapotec civilizations are integral to Mexico's heritage and identity, while Mayan communities in Chiapas and the Yucatán and those of other indigenous groups in the western and northern regions tend to be marginalized from the predominate population.

In 1971, the National Bank of Mexico (BANAMEX), established Fomento Cultural Banamex, a nonprofit agency to support the diffusion and development of Mexican culture. To achieve these goals, Fomento Cultural Banamex has directly funded architectural conservation projects such as at the Convent of San Miguel Arcángel in Mani, Yucatán, and the San Gabriel Convent in Cholula. In addition, Fomento Cultural Banamex created diverse programs, including Apoyo al Arte Popular (Support for Popular/Folk Arts) that has recognized the importance of maintaining not only the

Figure 30-8 Although certain iconic heritage sites such as the Mayan complex of Chichén Itzá, Yucatán, are well conserved and highly protected, such extensive archaeological zones often face development pressures and encroachment in their buffer zones.

a

b

Figure 30-9 Conservation and presentation of the Zócalo—the square which is at the heart of Mexico City and is built above the area of the Aztec palaces and temples—is compounded by extensive ground-settlement problems and damage from the disastrous September 1985 earthquake. Nonetheless, recent projects around the Zócalo have entailed the stabilization of the foundations of the Metropolitan Cathedral (a), requiring the installation of structural scaffolding in 1998 (b), as well as excavations and other work to improve presentation of the remains of the Aztec Templo Mayor. In addition, plans have been developed to convert the Rule Building, a ruined early-twentieth-century movie theatre, into a state-of-the-art visitor's center (c) featuring the complex history of the Zócalo area in interactive, interperative exhibits (d) which permit all manner of "virtual touring" and information downloads. Interpretive center model section image (c) and screen view (d) courtesy of Alfonso Govela Thomae.

c

d

tangible artifacts but also the techniques and processes of creating the arts that characterize Mexico's different regions through education programs, workshops, publications and exhibitions. However, even as attention has begun to turn to protecting traditional practices and recognizing the value of these indigenous communities and even though examples of community-based initiatives can be found, the centralized nature of the Mexican conservation system still offers little opportunity for these groups to get actively involved in the process of protecting their own heritage, whether intangible traditions or archaeological sites inhabited by their ancestors.

Hurricanes frequently batter Mexico's extensive coastline on both the Pacific and Atlantic sides, and volcanoes and destructive earthquakes are prevalent in the center and the south of Mexico as well as on the Baja California Peninsula. These natural disasters cause significant damage to the country's archaeological sites and historic cities, from which recovery is often slow. For example, damage caused by the earthquake of September 1985 is still apparent in Mexico City today. The World Heritage city of Puebla, on the other hand, recovered quickly from a 1999 earthquake; however, its position in the shadow of four active volcanoes keeps it under constant threat. In addition, the precariously located sixteenth-century monasteries and churches in the foothills of Popocatépetl volcano, which regularly spouts ash and water, are also at risk from seismic and volcanic activity.

Rural migrations in the second half of the twentieth century have resulted in the rapid growth of Mexican cities as economic needs and changing technologies have forced large numbers of people to move to them in search of employment. In addition, the rapid construction of roads, factories, and infrastructure that has supported and encouraged these rural to urban migrations has not only rapidly changed Mexico's landscapes but also inadequately provided for the documentation and examination of archaeological finds and historic sites in the path of these new developments. The high pollution rates caused by the increased traffic in Mexico's cities, especially its capital, are also a primary concern to those charged with conserving their historic buildings and sites.

The extensive growth of Mexico City in particular, with its metropolitan area exceeding twenty-one million people today, has also compounded existing threats to the city's central historic district. Even at the moment of its inclusion on the World Heritage List in 1986, ICOMOS noted that the Centro Histórico was a site "whose universal value is obvious but whose integrity is threatened."[28] Mexico City's increasing population has depleted underground water sources, causing the gradual sinking of the historic district, whose construction was originally begun in the late sixteenth century on the unstable ground of the drained Lake Texcoco. Over the course of the twentieth century, the Centro Histórico sank almost ten meters, and it continues to do so today, because the city's water-supply problem has not been solved. As a result of this alarming situation, which is not being mitigated, the World Monuments Fund added Mexico's historic center to its Watch List in 2006.[29]

While Mexico City and other major centers suffer from overcrowding, Mexico's villages and once-bustling nineteenth-century mining towns are losing their populations and their vernacular architecture. Many rural areas and smaller towns in Mexico have turned to tourism to stimulate their economies, which has introduced new threats and challenges. At Angahuan in Michoacán, wooden structures called *trojes* have been abandoned, and others have been renovated using insensitive modern materials such as cement blocks and asphalt cardboard. These unique buildings used simultaneously as family houses and granaries are constructed of untreated wood without nails and characterized by large porches and overhanging eaves—are also at risk due to redevelopment pressures to accommodate the increased number of visitors to the Angahuan's sixteenth-century temple. Thus tourism at one heritage site is contributing to the destruction of another less appreciated historic resource, leading ICOMOS to highlight this problem in their 2004–2005 report on heritage at risk.[30] Conservationists and archaeologists alike have lamented efforts to encourage mass tourism in many other environmentally and

Figure 30-10 Mexico is among the first countries in the Americas to begin conserving its most recent architectural heritage. Conservation of Mexican architectural modernism and other artistic works of the period have included research and stabilization of failing glass mosaics applied to the facade of Juan O'Gorman's Central Library (a) at Universidad Nacional Autónoma de México (UNAM) as well as the conservation of murals (b) by master artists of the Mexican Muralist Movement in the former Convent of Colegio Máximo de San Pedro y Pablo near the Zócalo. Both of these projects were carried out by local specialists, with financial assistance from the World Monuments Fund.

a

b

culturally important regions of Mexico, and some excessively visited sites have even been closed to the public to prevent further deterioration.[31]

Despite the challenges faced by today's architectural conservation professionals, Mexico remains a country whose dedicated commitment to its heritage protection ranks among the highest in the world. Archaeological sites, churches, historic centers, murals, and public art all express the country's past, present, and future. Architectural heritage conservation in Mexico is based on the country's long experience and reflects a multidimensional system that includes both public and private efforts to maintain the many strands of its cultural patrimony. As a pioneer in regional heritage conservation education and an active member of numerous international organizations such as ICOMOS, UNESCO, and the Organization of the Greater Caribbean on Monuments and Sites (CARIMOS), Mexico is one of Latin America's leaders in heritage protection and conservation.

Like many other aspects of Mexico's contemporary culture, its architectural conservation practices have already begun to expand to incorporate more constituencies and types of heritage sites. Combined with its popular appreciation of the value of cultural heritage and its long-standing government support for conservation, this broadened practice should keep Mexico at the forefront of cultural heritage management not only regionally but also globally.

ENDNOTES

1. James Early, *The Colonial Architecture of Mexico* (Dallas, TX: Southern Methodist University Press, 1994), 2.

2. Salvador Díaz-Berrio Fernández, *Conservación del Patrimonio Cultural en México* [Conservation of Cultural Heritage in Mexico] (México: Instituto Nacional de Antropología e Historia, 1990), 83.

3. Luis Gerardo Morales-Moreno, "History and Patriotism in the National Museum of Mexico," in *Museums and the Making of "Ourselves": The Role of Objects in National Identity*, ed. Flora E. S. Kaplan (London: Leicester University Press, 1994), 173.

4. Díaz-Berrio Fernández, *Conservación del Patrimonio Cultural*, 87.

5. Julio Cesar Olive Negrette and Augusto Urteaga Castro-Pozo, eds., *INAH: Una Historia* (México: Instituto Nacional de Antropología e Historia [INAH], 1988).

6. Nelly M. Robles Garcia, *The Management of Archaeological Resources in Mexico: Oaxaca as a Case Study*, trans. Jack Corbett (Washington, DC: Society for American Archaeology [SAA], 2004), www.saa.org/AbouttheSociety/Publications/TheManagementofArchaeological-ResourcesinMexi/MonteAlbanandMitlaasThemesintheFieldsofA/tabid/1106/Default.aspx (accessed March 21, 2010); and Jaime Litvak King, "Mexican Archaeology: Challenges at the End of the Century," *SAA Bulletin* 15, no. 4 (September 1997); www.saa.org/Portals/0/SAA/publications/SAAbulletin/15-4/SAA7.html (accessed July 10, 2010).

7. José Roberto Gallegos Tellez Rojo, "Teotihuacán: La Formación de la Primera Zona Arqueológica en México" [Teotihuacán: Formation of the First Archaeological Zone in Mexico], in *Patrimonio Histórico y Cultural de México: IV Semana Cultural de la Dirección de Etnología y Antropología Social* (Historical and Cultural Heritage of Mexico: IV Cultural Week of the Directorate of Ethnography and Social Anthropology), eds. María Elena Morales Anduaga and Francisco J. Zamora Quintana, 255–79 (México: Instituto Nacional de Antropología e Historia, 2001).

8. "Misión y Vision" [Mission and Vision], Instituto Nacional de Antropología e Historia, http://dti.inah.gob.mx/index.php?option=com_content&task=view&id=2843&Itemid=467 (accessed March 21, 2010).

9. King, "Mexican Archaeology."

10. The Instituto Nacional de Bellas Artes y Literatura (INBA) was established to encourage the development and study of the fine arts, including painting, sculpture, music, theater, dance, literature, and architecture. With the goals of educating and promoting research, as well as supporting new art and design, the INBA has also proven an essential supporting element in Mexican architectural conservation.

11. "Programa Nacional de Catálogo e Inventario de Monumentos muebles e inmuebles de Propiedad Federal," Dirección General de Sitios y Monumentos del Patrimonio Cultural, http://www.conaculta.gob.mx/monumentos/catalogo.htm (accessed July 24, 2010).

12. "FOREMOBA: Informes Anuales," Dirección General de Sitios y Monumentos del Patrimonio Nacional, www.conaculta.gob.mx/monumentos/foremoba/informes.html (accesed June 22 2010).

13. "Quiénes somos?" Instituto Nacional de Antropología e Historia, http://dti.inah.gob.mx/index.php?option=com_content&task=view&id=2842&Itemid=317 (accessed July 24, 2010).

14. "Catalogación de monumentos históricos," Instituto Nacional de Antropología e Historia, http://www.cnmh.inah.gob.mx/4001.html (accessed July 24, 2010).

15. The portion of the Camino Real in the United States is also recognized as a cultural route by the National Park Service. Carlos Flores Marini, *Seis Años en la Conservación del Patrimonio Monumental, ICOMOS Mexicano AC* [Six Years in the Conservation of Monumental Heritage, ICOMOS Mexico] (México: Arte e Imagen, 2000).

16. Ignacio Gomez Arriola and Francisco Javier Lopez Morales, "The Cultural Landscape of the Agave and the Production of Tequila," in *Art and Cultural Heritage: Law, Policy and Practice,* ed. Barbara T. Hoffman (Cambridge and New York: Cambridge University Press, 2004) , 214–219

17. Tung, *Preserving the World's Great Cities,* 410.

18. Jack Corbett and Nelly M. Robles Garcia, "Problematica Social del Manejo de Recursos Arqueólogicos" [Problems in the Social Management of Archaeological Resources], in Morales Anduaga and Zamora Quintana, *Patrimonio Histórico y Cultural de México,* 53–43.

19. Olivé Negrete y Cotton, *Leyes Estatales en Materia del Patrimonio Cultural* (Mexico City: INAH, 1997).

20. " Rescate de Retablos Mixtecas," Instituto Nacional de Antropología e Historia, http://dti.inah.gob.mx/index.php?option=com_content&task=view&id=909&Itemid=329 (accesed June 22 2010).

21. Extensive financial incentives included the ability to deduct 77 percent of the investment for conservation from annual federal taxes and to suspend various other taxes associated with the investment in real estate. Other incentives included the transfer of development rights from one structure to another due to the height limit on structures in the district. "El Programa 'Échame Una Manita,' 1991–1994" [The "Lend-a-Hand" Program], Ciudad y Patrimonio [City and Heritage], www.cyp.org.mx/chcm/echame.html (accessed July 10, 2010).

22. Efraín Castro Morales, *Adopte una Obra de Arte Patrimonio Recuperado* [Adopt a Work of Art: Heritage Recovered] (México: CONACULTA, 2000), 11.

23. See also Stubbs, *Time Honored,* 14, 15, and 355.

24. Morales, *Adopte una Obra de Arte,* 15.

25. Alfonso Govela, "Adaptive Reuse of Mexico's Historic Architecture: Tampico and Tlacotalpan," in Serageldin, Shluger, and Martin-Brown, *Historic Cities and Sacred Sites,* 121.

26. Anahi Rama, "Mexico Struggles to Preserve Ancient Ruins," *Reuters,* October 22, 2004, www.globalheritagefund.org/news/conservation_news/oct_22_mexico_struggles_2004.asp (accessed March 21, 2010).

27. ICOMOS, "The Historic Centre of Mexico City and Xochimilco," *Advisory Body Report* no. 412 (December 2, 1984); http://whc.unesco.org/archive/advisory_body_evaluation/ 412.pdf (accessed March 21, 2010).

28. "Mexico City Historic Center," *World Monuments Watch: 100 Endangered Sites 2004* (New York: World Monuments Fund, 2004); www.wmf.org/project/mexico-city-historic-center (accessed March 21, 2010).

29. Valeria Prieto, "Mexico: Vernacular Mexican Architecture in Danger," in *Heritage at Risk: ICOMOS World Report 2004/2005 on Monuments and Sites in Danger,* eds. Marilyn Truscott, Michael Petzet, and John Ziesemer (Munich: K. G. Saur, 2005), 172.

30. Jesus Antonio Machuca Ramirez, "El Proyecto Turistico *Mundo Maya:* Un Modelo Promisorio de Integracion Regional?" [The Mundo Maya Tourist Project: A Promising Model of Regional Integration?], in Morales Anduaga and Zamora Quintana, *Patrimonio Histórico y Cultural de México,* 255–79 and 101–12.

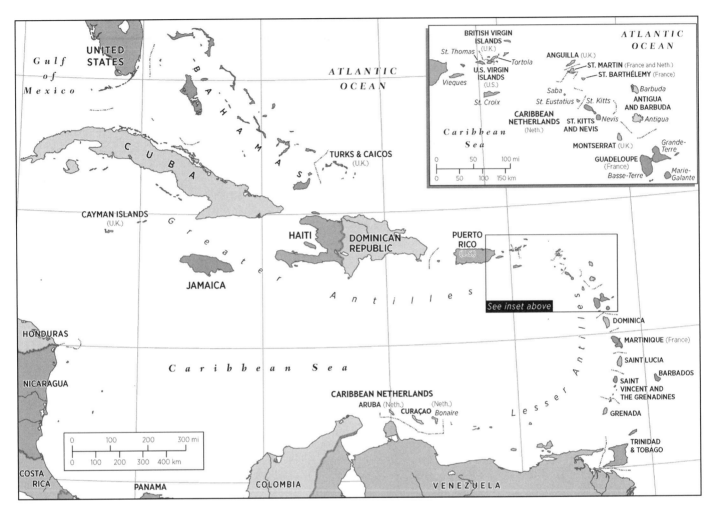

Figure 31-1 Greater Caribbean region.

CHAPTER 31

The Caribbean

Figure 31-2 One of numerous carved petroglyphs in Los Haitises, Dominican Republic, that exemplify the wide distribution of indigenous islanders in the Caribbean in pre-Hispanic times.

The Caribbean Sea is approximately 750,000 square miles and encompasses thirty larger islands and hundreds of smaller ones. The shared histories and building traditions of these islands make broad discussion of them possible; however, each island's specific individual characteristics also define its distinctive cultural policies and practices today. Current cultural heritage conservation efforts in the Caribbean reflect a balance between the isolation of each island and the shared challenges faced throughout the region.

The architectural heritage of the Caribbean is heavily influenced by Spanish, French, English, and Dutch traditions, as it was mostly these European powers that struggled for control of its islands. Spanish cities and forts were built in the sixteenth and seventeenth centuries, and as the balance of power shifted, the English and French dominated the region in the eighteenth and nineteenth centuries, building cities, agricultural plantations, and industrial structures. The imported elements of European architecture were progressively adapted to the local environment, influenced by the tropical climate and the vernacular traditions of local populations. Historic accounts document the presence of the indigenous people of the Caribbean, especially the Arawak, Carib, and the Taino, who were largely decimated by European diseases and attacks. Only a few pre-Columbian archaeological sites have survived in the Caribbean as the indigenous communities of the islands built primarily in wood.

In 1804, Haiti was the first country in the Caribbean region, and the second in all the Americas, to win its independence from colonial rule. In the early twentieth century, other islands and archipelagos in the region gained political and economic independence or autonomy from European and American domination, beginning with Cuba and the Dominican Republic. After World War II, Guadeloupe and Martinique were elevated to the status of official overseas departments of France and the Netherlands Antilles became an associated state of Holland. Some islands have since become independent Dutch countries, and the remaining were reorganized in 2010 into the Caribbean Netherlands.[1] Most other Caribbean islands continue to be British Overseas Territories, though they gained autonomous self-rule in the 1960s, and some have opted for full independence in the decades since.[2]

Many Caribbean islands have retained strong ties with their former European colonizers, whether through ongoing political relationships or continuing cultural connections. These ties are evident in their contemporary architectural conservation practices. Across the Caribbean, current preservation activities span a wide range of approaches and levels of political and economic commitment. Many islands have governments and nonprofit organizations working to catalog, document, and restore their historic sites. But others have had little resources or expertise to devote to preserving historic architecture and have only recently begun organized

Figure 31-3 An example of early architectural conservation of colonial heritage in Willemstad, Curaçao. The project derived from the country's long ties with the Netherlands, from which it obtained full independence in 2010, and conservation work was performed in accordance with Dutch conservation practice.

conservation activities. During the mid- and later part of the twentieth century, tourism began to dominate the economies of most Caribbean islands, and this has had a lasting influence on architectural conservation practices in the region.

The Caribbean islands are traditionally grouped into the Greater Antilles—including Cuba, the Cayman Islands, Jamaica, Hispaniola, and Puerto Rico—and the Lesser Antilles, which are divided into the Leeward and Westward islands. The Leeward Islands are located just east of Puerto Rico and include the Virgin Islands, Saint Martin, Saint Eustatius, Saba, St. Kitts and Nevis, Montserrat, Antigua and Barbuda, Guadeloupe, and Dominica. The Windward Islands are located further south, approaching South America, and include Martinique, St. Lucia, St. Vincent and the Grenadines, Grenada, Barbados, Trinidad and Tobago, Aruba, Curaçao, and Bonaire. Though Bermuda and the Bahamas are technically located in the Atlantic Ocean to the north of the Caribbean Sea, discussion of their contemporary architectural conservation practices has been included here, because they share the same history, architectural traditions, and current conservation challenges as the island countries of the Caribbean proper. Architectural conservation in Puerto Rico and the U.S. Virgin Islands is discussed along with the other overseas territories of the United States because of their related preservation histories.[3]

GOVERNMENT CONSERVATION EFFORTS AND NATIONAL TRUSTS

As in North America, the protection of natural heritage preceded that of historic architectural sites on many Caribbean islands. In fact, the first legislation designating a protected area anywhere in the Americas was passed in 1791 by the British governor general of the island of St. Vincent to set aside Kingshill Forest Reserve outside of Kingstown. In addition, the southern Caribbean island of Tobago is home to the western hemisphere's oldest protected rainforest.[4] The earliest recognition of the value of Caribbean historic sites and the first steps to ensure their protection came in the final years of colonial rule in the early and mid-twentieth century. The British began inventorying sites in Jamaica in 1909, Martinique and Guadeloupe fell under the jurisdiction of French heritage legislation in 1913, and the United States passed a law in 1927 nationalizing and protecting historic sites in Haiti, which it occupied between 1915 and 1934.

The Dominican Republic and Cuba were the first independent Caribbean countries to pass architectural conservation legislation in the 1960s, and these laws were strengthened and enhanced in 1994 and 2002, respectively. In Cuba, the Oficina del Historiador de la Ciudad de La Habana (Office of the Historian of the City of Havana) was authorized to carry out conservation efforts in innovative ways that balance the needs of the community, tourists, and historic sites.

The City Historian's Office and the Conservation of Old Havana

In the early 1990s, a building collapsed in Cuba's capital city of Havana every few days, or so the saying went. Though perhaps an exaggeration, this saying reflected the urgent need for architectural conservation efforts to protect the colonial and early-twentieth-century heritage of the city. Before the Cuban Revolution in 1959, Old Havana had been hailed as one of the Caribbean's most vibrant and beautiful urban centers, but afterward it was neglected while the new regime focused on rural improvements. Havana's buildings quickly deteriorated as many wealthy property owners fled Cuba and upkeep of their business and residential properties was neglected.

To inventory the richness of Old Havana and address its deteriorating conditions, the Oficina del Historiador de la Ciudad de La Habana (Office of the Historian of the City of Havana) was established in 1967 but was given little financial or political support and did not even produce a restoration plan for the city until 1979. When completed, this plan identified a historic core in which 90 percent of the buildings were considered architecturally valuable, and a successful nomination of Old Havana to the World Heritage List followed in 1982. In the early 1990s, the already underfunded Oficina del Historiador de la Ciudad witnessed a decline in its support from the Cuban government, which was hit hard by the loss of Cuba's Eastern European trading partners due to political transformations in that region.

In 1994, in response to the lack of financial resources and the precarious condition of Old Havana's architecture, in 1994 the Oficina del Historiador de la Ciudad was given permission to deal directly with foreign real estate investors and financiers to restore historic structures.[5] The Oficina del Historiador de la Ciudad devised a program that reaps full advantage of the funds generated by tourism in the form of a sophisticated revolving fund where profits are reinvested in new conservation projects. Additional funds have been solicited from major foreign investors, including the Spanish government. Recent projects include restoring fourteen blocks of the famous seawall, the Malecón, and the oldest neighborhood of Old Havana, San Isidro.

Though protecting and restoring one of the primary tourist attractions in Cuba, the Oficina del Historiador de la Ciudad has not allowed the Old Havana district to become a museum. Instead, in addition to funding conservation projects, it has financed social programs and ensured the maintenance and revival of the district's viability and local vibrancy, because Old Havana is one of the poorest and most densely populated parts of the city. Most projects have rehabilitated historic buildings and adapted them to provide quality housing for the poor and elderly and medical facilities for needy families. In addition, the Office of the Historian of the City publishes a magazine, produces a television program, and encourages students to visit museums. With support from the Spanish Agency for International Cooperation in 1992, the Oficina del Historiador de la Ciudad founded a workshop school to educate high school students about the importance and care of their cultural heritage. Many of the young people who are trained in restoration techniques through the workshop school's two-year program are later employed by the Oficina del Historiador de la Ciudad on conservation projects.

The success of restoration efforts in Old Havana are the result of the work and diligence of a number of architects, historians, planners, and conservation professionals. However, one man, who frequently walks the streets to check the work and note progress, has been the cornerstone of the district's revitalization. Eusebio Leal Spengler, the City Historian, has overseen all major restoration and conservation projects in Old Havana since 1967. Leal's membership in the Cuban Communist Party and participation in the country's government institutions enabled him to garner the autonomy necessary for his institution to effectively complete its remarkable rehabilitation work.

Despite all its efforts and innovative programs, the remaining poor conditions of Old Havana and funding shortfalls continue to challenge the Oficina del Historiador de la Ciudad. Over three-thousand projects have been completed, but 45 percent of Old Havana is still considered uninhabitable.[6] Nevertheless, the revitalization of Old Havana with such limited resources remains a remarkable achievement, and portions of the work of the Oficina del Historiador de la Ciudad could serve as a model to be adapted in the interests of restoring and renewing other deteriorated cities in the Caribbean and throughout the world. The success and commendability of the restoration of Old Havana was documented and celebrated in a UNESCO sponsored monograph in 2006: *A Singular Experience: Appraisal of the Integral Management Model of Old Havana, World Heritage Site.*[7] Architectural conservation success in Old Havana has resulted from the synergetic combination of circumstances—including Leal's innate leadership abilities, his determination and lust for hard work, and the rare authority vested in his office by the regime it has served.

a

b

c

Figure 31-4 In Cuba, the success of the Office of the Historian of the City in restoring and revitalizing Old Havana (a and b) through a resourcefully managed revolving fund is exemplified by the rehabilitation of eight blocks of buildings in the Malecón district along Havana's waterfront (c) beginning in 1998. The task in Old Havana has been one of rehabilitating the public and commercial buildings that comprise the historic center of the country's capital in ways which are sustainable. The restored Malecón district addresses less densely arranged residential and commercial buildings. The leadership exemplified by City Historian Eusebio Leal Spengler (d) in addressing the huge task of conserving hundreds of buildings within these districts from an extremely minimal original budget is extraordinary.

d

Although private efforts began in the Netherlands Antilles in the 1950s, preservation legislation was not enacted until 1971, when historic sites in these Caribbean territories were protected under a new Dutch law.[8] The Dutch government began extensive documentation efforts throughout the following decades; complete inventories were carried out in 1966 and 1976, resulting in numerous publications on the historic architecture of the Netherlands Antilles and inspiring further conservation efforts there.[9]

In the 1990s, Curaçao, while still part of the Netherlands Antilles, passed heritage legislation that established both a Monuments Council and a Monuments Bureau.[10] The former is a government-appointed professional advisory board and the later is a policy development and implementation agency within the Department of Urban and Regional Development Planning and Housing. A Register of Protected Monuments was inaugurated and a fund was established to administer loans to help owners of listed buildings with the costs of restoration and rehabilitation projects. Tax relief was enacted as a further incentive. Within a decade, nearly two hundred projects had been completed and more than half were financed in part by the Curaçao Monuments Fund. The success of the program led to an updated Monuments Plan in 2001, which broadened efforts to focus more on public awareness campaigns and advocated the establishment of a Monumentenwacht (Monuments Watch) program based on the long-standing Dutch model.[11]

Curaçao's comprehensive legislation and protective agencies encouraged other islands in the then Netherlands Antilles, such as St. Eustatius, to begin designing their own architectural conservation plans and drafting protective laws. However, though state-owned properties are now protected on the small island of St. Eustatius, an ordinance for designating privately owned properties as key historic sites and restricting changes to them is still pending approval at the executive level of the Monuments Council. Today, the St. Eustatius government is working to restore the colonial character of the cliff-top town of Oranjestad, while the nearby island of Saba has been recognized for its carefully managed development and tourism policies that have aided its conservation efforts.[12] In Bonaire, another island of the Caribbean Netherlands, conservation efforts have focused on the natural environment, but the park system created in the 1970s to protect large portions of its territory from development also extends to historic sites.

The British authorities began establishing National Trusts in Jamaica, the Bahamas, Barbados, and the Virgin Islands in the late 1950s and early 1960s. These trusts combined responsibilities for the protection and conservation of cultural and natural heritage sites within a single institution. All were set up by the legislatures of the United Kingdom or of the islands themselves, but they have mostly operated as independent membership organizations. These trusts, however, have been so thorough in their missions to inventory, acquire, restore, and protect historic sites that government oversight agencies were not separately established in most of these countries. The Barbados National Trust, for example, was established by the British Parliament in 1961, four years before Barbados's independence, and it has in the past half century purchased properties reflecting the island's—and the region's—wide-ranging heritage. These sites include wind-driven sugar mills, Georgian mansions, early-nineteenth-century signal stations, and the seventeenth-century Bridgetown Synagogue, one of the oldest in the western hemisphere.

In the 1970s and early 1980s, National Trusts with similar mandates, but varying strengths and foci, were established in the newly autonomous territories of Grenada, St. Vincent and the Grenadines, Montserrat, Bermuda, St. Lucia, St. Kitts and Nevis, and Dominica. The Bermuda National Trust, for example, was founded in 1970 with a mission to preserve natural, architectural, and historic treasures and to encourage public appreciation of them. Today, it manages seventy historic properties, including homes, an unfinished church, an old rectory, and a hotel that is one of Bermuda's first stone buildings. To generate awareness of the heritage of the islands, it has instituted several creative education programs that include summer camps that focus on history and archaeology.

Figure 31-5 The Bermuda National Trust is among the oldest organizations for heritage protection in the Greater Caribbean and has among its responsibilities the protection of the unfinished church located in the town of St. George's. Construction began on the church in the 1870s to replace St. Peter's Church, but it was abandoned before it was completed. The Bermuda National Trust has worked with the St. George's Foundation to ensure the unfished church's conservation. The establishment of numerous National Trusts for many island countries of the Caribbean has made a significant difference in enhancing heritage protection capacities in the region, especially in cases where these organizations collaborate with others, as occurred in St. George's.

Educational and promotional programs have been the primary focus of the National Trusts of many of the smaller island countries, such as in St. Lucia, where this institution not only manages parks and sites but also organizes guided tours and even "destination weddings" at historic sites. Education has also been a major component of the programs of the National Trust for the Cayman Islands, which has been involved in incorporating natural and cultural heritage into elementary school science and social studies curricula. Though it was the last British territory in the region to establish such an organization, since its founding in 1987, the Cayman National Trust has become one of the most vibrant. It quickly began documentation and inventory programs, the acquisition and management of endangered sites, and the placement plaques on sites of historic interest throughout the islands. The National Trust for the Cayman Islands also administers an awards program to recognize well-restored buildings and sensitive new designs for historic architecture.

By the 1980s, the documentation of architectural heritage was underway and national trusts or government oversight organizations had been established on most Caribbean islands, but essential protection and maintenance policies for all historic structures had only been enacted in a few Caribbean countries.[13] In the 1990s, however, more of the region's governments got involved and passed legislation. For example, in the Bahamas, the Antiquities, Monuments, and Museum Act of 1998 provided guidelines and incentives for the protection of cultural heritage. Previously, architectural conservation had fallen under the purview of the Department of Archives, which had successfully combined its many mandates by restoring buildings to serve as galleries and museums to house the objects found in the archaeological excavations it was also responsible for overseeing.[14] The 1998 Act established a National Museum and managing board, which has continued the process of identifying, acquiring, and ensuring the protection of historic sites and artifacts of the Bahamas. To date, a number of historic manor houses and smaller residential buildings, some in historic districts, on the island of Eleuthera have been restored with partial funding from the National Museum.

The government of the Cayman Islands also became actively involved in architectural conservation in the 1990s, beginning with the restoration and reconstruction of the Pedro St. James in Savannah, Grand Cayman. Billed as a "heritage attraction" and

Figure 31-6 The restoration of scores of residences in Harbour Island (a) at the north end of Eleuthera, Bahamas, serves a thriving high-end international tourist trade, while throughout most of the rest of the island—as at Tarpum Bay (b)—numerous eighteenth- and nineteenth-century colonial buildings remain unrestored. The island's uneven socioeconomic conditions partly explain the differing conditions, suggesting the need for more effective islandwide heritage conservation.

the Cayman's "first national landmark," this house, built between 1780 and the early nineteenth century, was the oldest surviving stone building in the Caymans until devastated by fire in 1989. The government purchased the ruined property and embarked on a multimillion dollar reconstruction that began with years of archaeological research and incorporated historic building techniques.[15]

Though it had taken an active interest in its natural heritage since its independence in the 1960s, Trinidad and Tobago's was the last Anglophone government in the Caribbean to begin conserving and protecting its architectural heritage. Discussion of creating a national trust began in earnest in the 1980s—but when little happened for years, frustrated preservationists on the island of Tobago formed their own trust in 1990, and a Historical Restoration Unit was established within the Ministry of Works and Transportation. Legislation establishing a National Trust of Trinidad and Tobago was finally enacted the following year; however, it was not implemented until the year 2000.[16] At the outset of the twenty-first century, architectural heritage protection became a clearer priority of Trinidad and Tobago's government. The country's National Heritage Parks began to prioritize valuable historic as well as natural sites, and in 2005 it ratified the World Heritage Convention. To demonstrate the serious spirit with which this convention was signed, on the island of Tobago, efforts to complete the decades-long restoration of the Fort King George were enhanced with increased funding and attention. Along with this eighteenth-century fortress, an eclectic group of late nineteenth-century residential and institutional buildings—known as the "Magnificent Seven"—in the capital city of Port of Spain, Trinidad, became the country's first protected historic sites.

NONGOVERNMENTAL ORGANIZATIONS

Nongovernmental organizations have played an especially important role in the protection of Caribbean architectural heritage, and they have also done much to increase international recognition of the region's important sites. Most Caribbean islands are active members of the Organización del Gran Caribe para los Monumentos y Sitios (CARIMOS, Organization of the Wider Caribbean Monuments and Sites), which was founded in 1982 as a ten-year project to encourage conservation awareness and the documentation of cultural heritage. CARIMOS also carried out individual restoration projects, promoted educational exchanges and training programs, and completed a regional survey.

Due to its success and the growing consciousness of the benefits of regional cooperation, CARIMOS' mandate was extended and it was more firmly established as a non-profit organization in 1994 with its headquarters in the Dominican capital of Santo Domingo. Today the organization works with over forty countries and territories to promote conservation projects as an integral part of cultural heritage management and tourism in the region. Its multilingual publications allow for wide dissemination of information, and its broad influence and network has proven especially important for the smaller and less developed countries of the Lesser Antilles, where architectural conservation resources are not as available as in the larger and more prosperous islands.

The work of CARIMOS represents the broadest-based efforts to recognize the architectural heritage of the Caribbean; however, other NGOs dedicated to a single island, city, or site have also become increasingly popular in the Caribbean. Their perseverance and the quality of their work have often attracted international attention and support. The St. Eustatius Historical Foundation, for example, has advocated restoration and protection of the small wooden houses in the historic core of Oranjestad. The Foundation also established a historical museum in one of the district's oldest and most prominent buildings with assistance from the College of William and Mary in the United States and Leiden University in the Netherlands.

In Bermuda the St. George's Foundation was established in 1997 to promote and protect the town of St. George's, which was founded as a British settlement in 1612 and is the oldest continuously populated English town in the Americas. By 2000 the Foundation had successfully campaigned to have the historic town and its surrounding fortifications added to the World Heritage List as important examples of the development of English planning and military engineering from the seventeenth through the twentieth century. Efforts have been made by the Bermudan government to restrict new development in St. George's and to sensitively integrate new additions and modernizations in this historic city. Today, the St. George's Foundation works on capital improvement projects identified in the Town Heritage Plan, maintains a revolving fund to help owners rehabilitate deteriorated properties, and promotes awareness of the city's architectural heritage through educational opportunities and a series of short radio features called "Historic Monuments."

Figure 31-7 Since the 1960s, Falmouth, Jamaica's eighteenth- and nineteenth-century British colonial buildings—including houses and port facilities—have been restored to very high standards with the aid of various affiliated international organizations, including the U.S.-based Falmouth Heritage Renewal. The Falmouth Government House (a) is the port's most prominent structure in the Jamaican Georgian style and is considered one of the finest English neoclassical buildings in the Caribbean. Preservation efforts over the past decades have also saved scores of distinctive residential buildings. The effects of recent restoration efforts are seen here in these pair of "before" and "after" images (b, c, d, and e). Images courtesy and copyright 1999 Nigel D. Lord.

a

b

c

d

e

Jamaica is also home to numerous NGOs concerned with architectural conservation that have worked with the Jamaican National Trust in its efforts to preserve two important eighteenth-century cities: Spanish Town and Falmouth. Both contain outstanding examples of the Georgian architecture and planning that characterized Jamaica during the period in which it was the most prosperous British Caribbean colony. Much of the restoration work, particularly at Falmouth, was sponsored by the Friends of Georgian Society of Jamaica, which was founded in 1967. In addition, the University of Virginia and the Colonial Williamsburg Foundation have worked for a number of years with the American charity Falmouth Heritage Renewal to support its efforts to restore and protect the architecture of the historic district of Falmouth, Jamaica.

In 1994 the Jamaica Heritage Trail Limited received a Caribbean Preservation Award from the American Express Foundation in New York to fund the rehabilitation of small privately owned vernacular buildings in the Falmouth Historic District. American Express had begun sponsoring these annual Caribbean Preservation Awards in conjunction with the Caribbean Tourism Organization in 1990 to encourage the protection of the region's architectural and cultural heritage. US/ICOMOS administers the program with a professional jury of experts that selects the recipients and awards grants to finance restoration projects. The project in Falmouth, Jamaica, involved local conservation advocates and community members, served as a training ground for introduction of additional conservation techniques, and encouraged responsible heritage tourism.

Curaçao boasts numerous NGOs dedicated to the island's historic cities and architecture. The first, Action Willemstad, was established in 1988 to lobby on behalf of that city's Dutch colonial center. Within a decade, a historic district had been established with special protective legislation, and numerous community groups had emerged to

Figure 31-8 The Old Iron Bridge over the Rio Cobre in St. Catherine, Jamaica, is believed to be the oldest industrially fabricated bridge in the Americas. It was designed by Thomas Wilson, manufactured by the Walker Ironworks in Rotherham, England, shipped to the island, and erected in 1803. The structure remains sound today, although serious damage to the roadway and other components have placed it in danger of increased deterioration. However, adjacent neighborhoods have been unwilling to permit the proper restoration of this important industrial heritage site.

assist with the conservation of Willemstad's colonial buildings.[17] Located on the largest harbor in the Caribbean, Willemstad thrived as a central port for the slave trade and for general commerce between South America and Europe during the eighteenth and most of the nineteenth century. The discovery of oil on Curaçao and its refinement by Royal Dutch Shell since 1914 has fostered a robust economy and allowed Willemstad to become the principal city in the former Netherlands Antilles. The architecture of Willemstad reflects the fusion of Dutch traditions with the local climate, with older merchant houses emulating the high structures popular in Holland in the seventeenth and eighteenth century and more recent buildings with lower scales and sweeping roofs.[18]

In 1993, another NGO, the Fundashon Pro Monumento, known as ProMo, was established to raise awareness of destruction and fundamental changes in the historic district of Willemstad.[19] ProMo has sponsored educational campaigns, tours, and "open monument days," as well as staged rallies and initiated legal action in response to specific threats. In recent years the scope of its activities has been extended to other cities, including Scharloo. Another nongovernmental organization, the Stichting Monumentenzorg (Monument Care Foundation), played an important role in the successful nomination of Willemstad to the World Heritage List in 1997. Particularly focused on Curaçao's colonial domestic architecture, including country estates and townhouses, this private organization has been active in acquiring and restoring historic architecture since the 1950s.

CONSERVING COLONIAL CITIES, PLANTATIONS, AND FORTRESSES

Unlike in Mexico, where the architectural value of the built legacy of colonialism was appreciated relatively late, in the Caribbean, it is precisely this component of heritage that has received the most attention from conservationists. The predominant interest in colonial heritage has in part resulted from the continued relationships between most islands and their former colonizers, as well as from the relative obscurity of pre-Columbian sites in the Caribbean. In addition, several recent studies have concluded that colonial-era sites represent the region's greatest potential cultural tourist attractions. These structures, built from the mid-sixteenth century to the end of the nineteenth century, are typically found in the coastal cities frequented today by cruise ships and other travelers and include fortifications, monasteries, churches, civic buildings, and plantation houses. The previously mentioned historic districts that have been the focus of the region's government and nonprofit efforts, such as Havana, Willemstad, and Falmouth, are Spanish, Dutch, and British colonial settlements, respectively.

In the Dominican capital of Santo Domingo, the Alcázar de Colón, the residence of Christopher Columbus's son, was restored in the 1950s and inspired efforts to protect and rehabilitate more of the city and to designate its historic center as a World Heritage Site. Santo Domingo is not only the oldest colonial city in the Americas, but it is also home to the Americas' first cathedral, hospital, monastery, and university. Today, many of these sixteenth-century buildings have been restored and are open to the public. Work in Santo Domingo created a foundation upon which the conservation efforts in the Dominican Republic have continued to build; the government later turned its attention to the historic centers of outlying cities, including Santiago and Puerto Plata.

Much of the architecture of the French colonial city of St. Pierre, Martinique, has been preserved, though uninhabited since a disastrous volcanic eruption in the early twentieth century. The city was founded in 1635 and served as a base for further French colonization and exploration of the Caribbean. After centuries of development as a prosperous port city, it was destroyed by the eruption of nearby Mount Pelée in 1902. The ruins of St. Pierre's houses, churches, warehouses, and other buildings reveal much

Figure 31-9 The the Morgan Lewis Sugar Mill (a) in Barbados, dating from 1827, is the oldest suriving wind-driven sugar mill in the Caribbean. The effort to conserve it was organized by the Barbados National Trust in 1997 and was aided by funding from the American Express Corporation and the World Monuments Fund. Only the masonry base remained in 1995. The restoration entailed repairing the machinery and reproducing the cap and wooden enframement (b) of the windmill's sails.

about nineteenth-century life in the Caribbean as well as about the French colonial architecture of the region.

Eighteenth- and early nineteenth-century plantation sites have been the focus of conservation efforts in several of the Anglophone and Francophone islands. One of the region's largest, oldest, and most intact sugar mills was acquired by the Barbados National Trust in 1962. Constructed in 1727, the Morgan Lewis Mill remained in a nonfunctional, dilapidated state until 1996, when recognition by the World Monument Fund's Watch as an endangered site led to its complete restoration. The project was funded by multiple donors, including a British firm that had manufactured machinery for the mill in the 1850s.[20] In Martinique, numerous centuries-old rum plantations and distilleries—such as Habitation Clement in La Trinité—as well as sugar mills and plantations—including Josephine Bonaparte's birthplace at La Pagerie—have been restored and are today operated as museums.

The many impressive fortresses of the Caribbean stand both individually and collectively as monuments of importance to the colonial as well as postcolonial periods and today serve as valuable tourism destinations and a reminder of the region's maritime history. As a result of their significance and often imposing physical presence, many fortresses have been conserved and protected by the various Caribbean governments. For example, Pigeon Island in St. Lucia, which encompasses the ruins of the military buildings used by both the French and the British during their battles for naval superiority in the Caribbean in the 1790s, was recognized as a national park in 1979 and a national landmark in 1992.

Haiti is home to impressive fortresses built by the Spanish, French, and English in addition to twenty others built after the Haitian revolution, including the early-nineteenth-century Citadelle Henri Christophe, located on the peak of a 900-meter-high mountain.[21] The Citadel and the Sans Souci Palace at the mountain's base were built as strongholds and symbols soon after Haitian independence. The sites were designated as a national history park in 1978 and added to the World Heritage List in 1982. Conservation work began at this fortress and palace in the 1930s during the American occupation, and the work began anew in the 1950s by the Haitian Ministry of Public Works and again through a World Monuments Fund project in the 1980s. Improved interpretative signage and other visitor enhancements were recently financed by the U.S. Ambassador's Fund for Cultural Preservation, which has also supporting projects at other fortresses throughout Haiti.

Other Caribbean fortresses have also received international attention. The impressive stone fortifications of Havana, Cuba, and San Juan, Puerto Rico, built by the Spanish between the fifteenth and nineteenth centuries, were both integral components of the World Heritage List nominations of these historic cities in the early 1980s.[22] In the late 1990s, efforts to collectively nominate Caribbean Fortifications to the World Heritage List were initiated by the Ministers of Cultural Heritage of Latin America and the Caribbean, CARIMOS, and the ICOMOS International Committee on Cultural Routes.

a

Figure 31-10 The Citadelle Henri Christophe in Haiti (a) is emblematic of a series of numerous historic fortifications in the Caribbean. It was restored in the early 1980s (b) with financial assistance from the International Fund for Monuments (later renamed the World Monuments Fund). Its example was followed by the restoration of several other Caribbean fortifications in recent years.

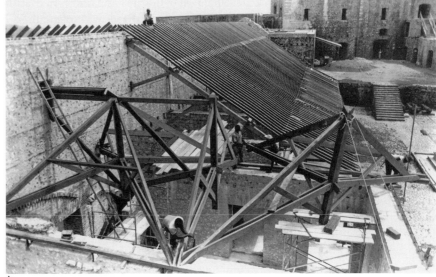

b

CONSERVING OTHER CARIBBEAN HERITAGE

Architectural conservation interests in the Caribbean have begun to move away from addressing only the most imposing and famous structures and cities built by the European colonists to recognizing a broader panorama of the region's heritage. Many Caribbean citizens have been frustrated by the focus only on sites that will attract foreign visitors as well as on sites from the colonial era, which they often associate with exploitation and oppression. As a result, sites of local significance and that emphasize the hard-won independence of many islands have become of increasing importance to Caribbean architectural conservationists. In recent decades, for example, organizations such as CARIMOS have turned their attention and conservation efforts to vernacular architecture and sites reflecting the history of slavery, which dominated the region between the sixteenth and mid-nineteenth centuries. In addition, some of the Caribbean's twentieth-century built heritage has begun to attract regional and international interest.

Jamaica's current heritage protection efforts well illustrate broader views of architectural heritage protection. As part of the ten-year tourism development plan adopted by the Jamaican government in 2001, the promotion of ten thematic heritage trails became a priority. While some trails focused on famed plantation houses and fortifications, others focused on pre-Columbian sites, industrial heritage, sites associated with slavery and the quest for emancipation, and the maroons, the free blacks who have lived independently in the country's inland mountains for centuries.

In Nassau, the Bahamas, and Roseau, Dominica, eighteenth-century slave markets were recently restored and converted into museums dedicated to slavery, emancipation, and local history. Since the early 1990s, academic studies and archaeological excavations at Caribbean plantations have begun to analyze and explore the life and accomplishments of the region's enslaved people and their descendants. At the Seville Great House and Heritage Park at St. Ann's Bay in Jamaica, the island's entire history is presented, including not only the plantation house but also the village where slaves lived.[23] The nearby town of St. Ann's is also the site of the shipwreck of Christopher Columbus, the brief Spanish capital of the island, and the birthplace of Jamaican civil rights leader Marcus Garvey. In 1994 the Seville Park was restored and opened to the public by the Jamaican National Heritage Trust, providing architectural evidence of this multifaceted history of the island.

Conservation of historic architecture and sites reflecting the African heritage of the Caribbean has not been immune from the tourist and development pressures that influence all projects in the region. In Haiti, for example, community efforts to conserve the pier where ships from Africa docked and unloaded slaves are set against interest in development of the area as a resort. In Martinique, slave heritage has occasionally been curiously commercialized, with plantations like Lyritz in Basse-Pointe converted into a bed-and-breakfast where visitors can sleep in former slave huts.[24] Martinique is also home to an open air museum near Les Trois-Ilets, where a group of wattle-and-mud houses was built to represent and educate about life in a typical slave village.

Development of a cultural route through the Caribbean as an extension of the Slave Route previously established on the west coast of Africa was launched by UNESCO and the World Tourism Organization (WTO) in 1994 and expanded in 2000.[25] Today the Slave Route connects the islands and their waterways and recognizes the important role that the region's colonization and slaves played in world history. This route encourages cultural heritage conservation throughout the Caribbean and provides an unparalleled opportunity for the smaller islands of the Lesser Antilles, which are home to fewer major historic buildings but do possess numerous vernacular sites related to the history of slavery that deserve protection and recognition.

Many of the surviving pre-Columbian sites in the region have not fared as well as those associated with slavery and Afro-Caribbean history. For example, during the recent construction of a hotel in Saint Martin in the Carribean Netherlands, workers discovered caves that were probably places of worship for the indigenous Taino peoples and that were decorated with petroglyphs and stone sculptures dating from the early fourteenth century.[26] The local government expressed no interest in the site, and so construction continued, leading to the destruction of some caves and their artifacts.

Indigenous architectural traditions have been better respected in the small island country of Dominica. Though visited and claimed by the Spanish, French, and British, Dominica's mountainous terrain and small size made it one of the last Caribbean islands to be formally colonized. It therefore became a refuge for indigenous peoples and runaway slaves from throughout the region. Because the Carib and Kalingo population of the island had become so significant by the early twentieth century, a reservation comprised of multiple villages was set aside for them by the British governor in 1903.

As the only organized community of native islanders in the Caribbean today, this reservation has felt a responsibility to share its traditional culture. Though their indigenous pre-Columbian architecture has not survived and the more recent buildings of these communities reflect the general vernacular of the region, visitors can now view reconstructions of traditional oval *karbay* communal longhouses. Plans have been underway for decades to build an entire Carib Cultural Village, with multiple thatched karbays as well as craft workshops.[27] Though the village is being built by the government of Dominica, the indigenous community has been involved in this project since the outset and made the original proposal for the village in 1976. Today, the community has accepted the cultural changes that will accompany the increased visitors in exchange for the income the project is expected to generate for their reservation.

In addition to slave and pre-Columbian heritage becoming increasingly recognized in the Caribbean, postcolonial architecture has also recently become the focus of heritage protection efforts in the region. Community rallies for the protection of the modern neighborhood of Gacuze, in the suburbs of the capital of Santo Domingo, began in the early 1980s and grew into a full-scale effort ten years later. This affluent neighborhood embodies the suburbanization that took place in Santo Domingo from the 1930s to 1960s, and works of several leading Dominican architects from this period can be found there. The community activism that saved Gacuze encouraged dialogue within the Dominican national chapters of DOCOMOMO and ICOMOS about the conservation of other examples of modern architecture.

Figure 31-11 Architecture dating from the 1930s to the 1960s in Santo Domingo, capital of the Dominican Republic, is the focus of architectural conservationists there with the aid of DOCOMOMO and ICOMOS. The Banco de Reservas de la Isabel La Católica building is a leading example of modern commercial architecture that has recently been restored. Courtesy and copyright Ricardo Briones/ DOCOMOMO Dominicano.

Figure 31-12 One of the most notable efforts to save exemplary modern architecture in the Americas is the case of Cuba's National Schools of Art in Havana. Built between 1964 and 1966 as the utopian visions of Ricardo Porro, Roberto Gottardi, and Vittorio Garatti, the partially completed complex, consisting of schools for dance, the plastic arts, music, and drama (a, b, c) fell into serious disrepair through the 1990s due to neglect and harsh environmental conditions, and the complex has only recently begun to witness proper architectural restoration interventions. The mobilization of the restoration work at the Art Schools has benefited from the participation of the project's original three architects.

a

b

c

Following the Dominican Republic's example, other Caribbean countries are beginning to address the conservation of their twentieth-century heritage. In Cuba the never-completed National Art Schools in Havana recently gained international recognition as one of the most important landmarks of modernism in the region. The construction of three of five planned buildings began in 1961 in the heroic early years of the Cuban revolution but stopped after only four years due to a lack of funding and different government priorities. The architectural designs for each of the National Art Schools were always intended to connect with the landscape (the grounds of the former Havana Country Club), but this relationship took on new meaning when parts of the complex became overgrown and were subjected to the regular flooding of the adjacent Quibu River.

Interest in the site was renewed after American architectural historian John Loomis wrote a book about the forgotten schools in 1998 and the World Monuments Fund placed the complex on their Watch list of most endangered buildings the following year.[28] Initial planning for the completion and restoration of the schools began in dialogue with the three original architects, Ricardo Porro, Roberto Gottardi, and Vittorio Garatti. The Cuban government reportedly contributed $20 million, and the Ministry of Culture assumed responsibility for the project. Rubble and vegetation clearance began and scaffolds were erected, but again, funding reassignment and other priorities have evidently thwarted progress in restoring and preserving the Arts Schools.[29]

CURRENT CHALLENGES AND PROSPECTS

Although protective legal mechanisms and dedicated organizations have been established in many of the Caribbean islands, issues such as a lack of economic resources and climatic factors continue to limit many conservation efforts. The region's tropical climate and geography includes humid jungles, coastal plains, and arid deserts on the southernmost islands. Most of the Caribbean's architectural heritage is constantly exposed to intense sun and high precipitation levels. The cyclical wet and dry seasons, coupled with the fact that much of the Caribbean is a seismic zone, create continuous pressure on the region's architectural heritage. For example, an earthquake in the Guadeloupe channel in 2004 destroyed two nineteenth-century churches built of rough volcanic stone in Dominica.

More recently, on January 12, 2010, an earthquake devastated Port-au-Prince, Haiti, and killed over 230,000 people. There was also serious damage in nearby Jacmel and Léogâne. Initial responses, of course, addressed relief for the earthquake's survivors, although not long afterward teams of conservation specialists under the aegis of ICOMOS arrived to assess structural damage. Their timing proved good since several restorable buildings that were marked for demolition were reclassified as restorable after all, and an action plan for creating a custom-made repair-and-conservation manual for earthquake-damaged buildings in the area was formulated.

Hurricanes also pose a major threat to Caribbean architectural heritage, and some of the most severe on record have occurred in the past few decades. The Lesser Antilles were battered by both Hurricane Hugo in 1989 and Hurricane Mitch in 1998. The high winds and flooding associated with Hurricane Fabian caused widespread damage in St. George's, Bermuda, in 2003. The Bermuda Historic Museum lost part of its roof, and one-quarter of the historic properties owned by Bermuda National Trust were flooded, including the Verdmont Historic House Museum. In 2004 Hurricane Ivan damaged 90 percent of all buildings in Grenada and 70 percent of those in the Cayman Islands. A late-nineteenth-century wattle-and-daub schoolhouse owned by the Cayman National Trust and recognized as a national landmark was nearly destroyed. It has still not been restored and reopened to the public.

Although Cuba is the country in the region with the most World Heritage Sites and a well-established cultural heritage conservation tradition, its economic stagnation due to a U.S.-imposed trade embargo, in place since 1962, has meant the country can turn to neither investment from the nearby United States nor major tourism as potential financial resources for architectural conservation beyond the special case of Old Havana. Even projects for which there is significant political will, such as the National Schools of Arts, languish due to a lack of available funds.

Cuba is not the only island in the region with financial problems: in the early decades of the twenty-first century, many Caribbean countries find themselves in an economic downturn. Even the traditionally wealthy islands that have benefited financially from tourism since the 1960s have experienced funding shortfalls in recent years. Carib-

a

b

c

Figure 31-13 Earthquakes pose a threat to most islands in the Caribbean, as was tragically displayed on January 12, 2010, when an earthquake measuring 7.0 on the Richter scale struck near the Haitian capital of Port-au-Prince, killing an estimated 230,000 people and leaving over 1 million people homeless. Practically every building in the city was damaged. In Port-au-Prince, the National Palace partially collapsed (a and b). The entirety of the roof and upper stories of the Cathedral of Our Lady of the Assumption also collapsed (c). It is worth noting that several lessons from other earthquake-affected historic cities were not heeded here. For example, there had been a determination by the first technical teams on-site to demolish and clear a number of damaged historic structures that could be feasibly restored. A subsequent team of experts on post-earthquake rebuilding determined that fewer damaged historic structures required demolition. Images (a) and (c) courtesy UN Photo/Logan Abass

bean exports and tourist destinations have been marginalized by larger competitors like Mexico. In addition, national debts are high in the region, and destructive hurricanes have caused extensive damage and deterred visitors in some areas. In some cases, such as in the Caribbean Netherlands, the global economic crisis has led to a near halt in conservation work.[30]

In many Caribbean countries, however, the lack of available funding for architectural conservation has meant rethinking the identity of the islands and their historic sites and districts in order to attract more visitors and generate revenue. CARIMOS, UNESCO, and many Caribbean governments have argued that conservation efforts could be more explicitly linked with regional and touristic development. Numerous sites have received attention—but as William Chapman, an expert on Caribbean architecture and conservation practices, argues, sometimes interventions "follow a somewhat romantic approach to architectural conservation that is usually only loosely grounded in recognized preservation and conservation techniques."[31] This has meant that elements not necessarily local to a specific island but associated with a generalized "Caribbean style"—such as bright colors, sawn-wood "gingerbread" decorations, and shutters—are added to buildings and towns where they may have never existed. The region's architectural conservationists, however, are doing an increasingly better job of using the local heritage to promote tourism and to meet the interests and expectations of visitors, while at the same time preventing historic sites from being overvisited and losing their authenticity or local particularities.[32]

In addition to financial challenges, in some Anglophone island countries of the Caribbean region, such as the Bahamas, conservation efforts have been hampered by the cumbersome requirements of inheritance laws, which in cases without clear wills require property be shared among all heirs. Though legal changes made in 2002 were an important step in women's and human rights since they allowed women and children born out of wedlock to inherit property, they have complicated the situation further by increasing the number of joint owners for each property. Within just a few generations this could mean a historic home is shared between dozens of owners, who must all be in agreement before sales or restoration decisions can be made. Valuable properties are therefore at risk of falling into disrepair as consensus is difficult to reach. Neglect of privately owned historic sites has also been a problem in the Bahamas, because local owners are not required to pay taxes on derelict or abandoned properties and there is no system for imposing penalties for violations.[33]

Increasing interest in the architectural heritage of the Caribbean by international organizations and donors has proven invaluable for offsetting the financial difficulties of the islands themselves. CARIMOS recently proposed nineteen possible restoration projects to be financed by the European Union through the Regional Tourism Program of the Caribbean Forum (CARIFORUM), a political organization. The proposal aims to restore key historic sites to encourage cultural tourism in individual cities and countries throughout the region. UNESCO's support for policy development has also continuously helped shape regional efforts in the field of architectural conservation. During the mid-1990s, the lack of broad Caribbean representation on the World Heritage List motivated UNESCO to sponsor a series of conferences focused on broadening regional recognition.[34] Extensive discussion was given to developing further conservation efforts not only at Caribbean fortifications but also expressions of living cultures. There is also interest in examining more recent aspects of the built environment, such as industrial heritage, nineteenth- and twentieth-century architecture, and cultural landscapes.[35]

Current efforts to conserve the rich architectural heritage of the Caribbean represent a number of innovative policies, well-established legal mechanisms, and recognition of a variety of components of heritage worthy of attention. But while important work has been accomplished and community support is growing, financial realities and the continued belief that the colonial period is the primary tourist attraction still hamper preservation efforts. As more and more Caribbean countries supplement their active nonprofit sectors by legally establishing registers of historic sites and oversight organizations to ensure their protection, many of today's challenges will be overcome. Cause for optimism also results from the pooling of resources and experiences among the Caribbean's small countries based on an awareness of the shared elements of their history and heritage. A most notable example of this cooperation has been the creation of cultural roots linking historic sites throughout the Caribbean, especially as these efforts have included vernacular structures as well as monuments. In addition, regional collaboration through organizations such as CARIMOS have already begun to enhance the work of the region's professionals and offer models of cooperation from which other global regions could learn.

ENDNOTES

1. Bonaire, Saint Eustatius, and Saba remain part of the Caribbean Netherlands. The former Dutch colonies that opted for independence include Aruba (1986), Curaçao (2010) and Saint Marten (2010).

2. The Cayman Islands, Montserrat, Anguilla, the British Virgin Islands, and Bermuda remain British Overseas Territories. The former British colonies that opted for independence include Jamaica (1942), Barbados (1944), the Bahamas (1973), Grenada (1974), Dominica (1978), St. Vincent and the Grenadines (1979), St. Lucia (1979), and St. Kitts and Nevis (1983).

3. See Chapter 28, "The United States," 460–466.

4. Chris Leadbeater, "Tempted by Tobago," Daily Mail Online, December 2008, http://www.dailymail.co.uk/travel/article-617537/Tempted-tranquil-Tobago.html (accessed July 24, 2010).

5. "As Havana Crumbles, Castro's Agencies Struggle to Preserve a Rich Legacy while Controlling New Development," *Architectural Record* 187, no. 3 (1999): 43. Also, see: Stubbs, *Time Honored*, 344.

6. Dalia Acosta, "Restoring Old Havana: With a Social Twist," *Arts Weekly*, December 2005, http://ipsnews.net/news.asp?idnews=31254 (accessed July 12, 2010).

7. Sylvio Mutal and Fernando Carrión, A *Singular Experience: Appraisal of the Integral Management Model of Old Havana, World Heritage Site* (Paris: UNESCO, 2006).

8. Jashina Alexandra Tarr, A *Collaborative Caribbean Preservation Strategy* (Washington, DC: Partners for Livable Spaces, 1982), 42.

9. Ibid., 42.

10. "Monuments Policy and Strategies," Curaçao Monuments, n.d., www.curacaomonuments.org/monuments-policy.shtml (accessed March 21, 2010).

11. See Chapter 6, "Belgium, Luxembourg, and Netherlands."

12. Frans H. Brugman, *The Monuments of Saba: The Island of Saba, a Caribbean Example* (Zutphen, Netherlands: Uitgeversmaatschappij Walburg Pers, 1995).

13. Tarr, A *Collaborative Caribbean Preservation Strategy*, 39.

14. Gail Saunders, "Preserving Bahamian Heritage," in *Safeguarding Traditional Cultures: A Global Assessment*, ed. Peter Seitel, 190–3 (Washington, DC: Center for Folklife and Cultural Heritage, Smithsonian Institution, 2001); http://unesdoc.unesco.org/images/0013/001323/132327m.pdf (accessed July 12, 2010).

15. "Pedro St. James Historic Site," Cayman Islands, www.caymanislands.ky/to_do/activities_pedro.aspx (accessed July 12, 2010).

16. Vel A. Lewis, "Protecting the Wooden Urban Heritage in Trinidad and Tobago," *Caribbean Wooden Treasures, Proceedings of the Thematic Expert Meeting on Wooden Heritage in the Caribbean Region, 4–7 February 2003, Georgetown, Guyana.* World Heritage Papers 15 (Paris: UNESCO World Heritage Center, 2005), 77.

17. "More about 'Action Willemstad,'" Old Willemstad, www.oldwillemstad.info/action.htm (accessed March 21, 2010).

18. Tarr, A *Collaborative Caribbean Preservation Strategy*, 42.

19. "About ProMo," Fundashon Pro Monumento, www.monumento.com (accessed March 21, 2010).

20. "Morgan Lewis Mill Re-Opens," The Barbados National Trust, http://trust.funbarbados.com/conservation.html (accessed March 21, 2010).

21. Jean Julien Olsen, "Preservation Practice in Haiti" (paper, International Preservation Practice Course, Graduate School of Architecture, Planning and Preservation, Columbia University, May 2003).

22. Herman Van Hooff, "The State of the Implementation of the World Heritage Convention in the Caribbean," in *Le Patrimoine Culturel des Caraïbes et la Convention du Patrimoine Mondial* [The Cultural Heritage of the Caribbean and the World Heritage Convention], ed. Herman Van Hooff, 187–196 (Paris: Comité des travaux historiques et scientifiques [CTHS] and UNESCO, 2000), 191–4.

23. Polly Pattullo, *Last Resorts: The Cost of Tourism in the Caribbean* (New York: Monthly Review Press, 2005), 189.

24. Renée K. Gosson, "What Lies Beneath: Cultural Excavation in Neocolonial Martinique," n.d., www.facstaff.bucknell.edu/rgosson/beneath/ (accessed March 21, 2010).

25. Patricia Green, "Caribbean Monuments and Sites Inventory: On the Trans-Atlantic Slave Trade" (The UNESCO Slave Route Project, UNESCO-WTO Joint Caribbean Programme of Cultural Tourism, ICOMOS-CIIC, 1994), www.icomos-ciic.org/CIIC/pamplona/PROYECTOS_Patricia_Green.htm (accessed March 21, 2010).

26. Pattullo, *Last Resorts*, 193.

27. Lennox Honychurch, "A Carib Opportunity: A Cultural Village," The Caribs of Dominica, n.d., www.da-academy.org/kalinago_village.html (accessed March 21, 2010).

28. John A. Loomis, *Revolution of Forms: Cuba's Forgotten Art Schools* (New York: Princeton Architectural Press, 1998), and "Castro's Dream: The Rediscovery of Cuba's National Art Schools," *ICON World Monuments* (Winter 2002/2003): 26–33.

29. Gary Marx, "Academic Ruins: Cuba's National Art Schools," *Havana Journal*, January 4, 2004, http://havanajournal.com/culture/entry/academic_ruins_cuba_national_art_schools (accessed March 21, 2010).

30. "Netherlands," *ICOMOS World Report on Monuments and Sites in Danger 2001* (Paris: ICOMOS, 2001), www.international.icomos.org/risk/2001/neth2001.htm (accessed March 21, 2010).

31. William R. Chapman, "A Little More Gingerbread: Tourism, Design and Preservation in the Caribbean," *Places* 8, no. 1 (1992): 63.

32. Leon Pressouyre, "The World Heritage Convention and Cultural Property: Potential Value of an Open-Ended Concept for the Caribbean Region," in *Le Patrimoine Culturel des Caraïbes*, 211.

33. Another problem is the lack of wood for restoration in Haiti, Cuba, and other islands.

34. Cuba is home to half of the Caribbean's twelve cultural properties on the World Heritage List. The non-Cuban World Heritage sites in the Caribbean include: the city and fortifications of Santo Domingo in the Dominican Republic, La Fortaleza and San Juan National Historic Site in Puerto Rico, Historic Town of St. George's (and related fortifications) in Bermuda, and the Historic Area of Willemstad, Inner City, and Harbour in the Curaçao Antilles, the Brimstone Hill Fortress in St. Kitts and Nevis, and the National History Park (Citadel, Sans Souci, Ramiers) in Haiti.

35. Van Hooff, "State of the Implementation," 194.

CHAPTER 32

Central America

The isthmus of Central America connects the continents of North and South America and is marked by a central mountainous spine that unfolds into tropical rain forests, mangrove swamps, and white sand beaches on the eastern Caribbean Sea side and rock cliffs over the Pacific Ocean in the west. This land bridge is defined by its strikingly beautiful geography and ecological diversity. The region's indigenous people and heritage included the Mesoamerican cultures of the Maya and Aztec in the north as well as the Cueva and other peoples in the area known as Panama today.

Foreigners first arrived in Central America in 1502, when Christopher Columbus claimed the Gulf of Honduras and surrounding territories as property of the Spanish crown. During the ensuing colonial period, the Captaincy General of Guatemala was established to administer most of Central America as well as Chiapas, in today's southern Mexico. Panama, however, was part of the Viceroyalty of New Grenada centered in Bogotá. In 1821 the region gained its independence from Spain, and after a brief period as the United Provinces of Central America, a federal republic modeled on the organization of the United States, the region separated into independent countries in 1838. Guatemala, El Salvador, Honduras, Nicaragua, and Costa Rica emerged as separate entities, yet they continued to share aspects of their cultural history in the later nineteenth and twentieth centuries. Panama and Belize gained their independence later than their neighbors in Central America: Panama remained part of Colombia until 1903, and Belize did not separate from Britain until 1981.

In the 1960s guerilla movements opposed to the autocratic governments in Guatemala and Nicaragua became increasingly active, and conflict spread to El Salvador. The ensuing decades brought numerous challenges, as most of the region struggled with civil unrest. The Guatemalan civil war of the early 1980s was the most violent and destructive, resulting in the killing of some 75,000 Maya and the systematic destruction of their material culture, including 440 villages.[1] Peace and relative stability returned to most of the region by the mid-1990s, and afterward many Central American countries experienced a rebirth of cultural expression and traditions. The protection of cultural diversity and heritage in each of the countries of the region has also become increasingly important since that time. Attacks on indigenous communities raised awareness of their threatened culture both within the region and internationally.

Exemplary restoration projects and isolated heritage projection laws have had positive effects in Central America over the past century and a half, but it was primarily in the 1970s that the governments of the region became actively involved in architectural conservation. Through the Organization of American States (OAS) in 1976, they participated in drafting the "Convention on the Protection of Archaeological, Historical and

◄ **Figure 32–1** The historic town of Antigua, situated in the highlands of Guatemala, represents a special blend of both indigenous Mayan and Spanish colonial culture that is well reflected in the town's architecture and modern ways of life. Antigua was placed on the UNESCO World Heritage List in 1979.

Artistic Heritage of the American Nations."[2] Known as the Convention of San Salvador, this agreement was primarily concerned with reducing the illegal export and trafficking of antiquities, but it also reinvigorated the regional commitment to conserving cultural heritage in general by requiring that each country ensure excavation and conservation projects follow recognized best practices, maintain inventories of cultural property, and pass legislation safeguarding sites from destruction or inappropriate alterations. Though open to all members of the OAS, it has primarily been the countries of Central America that have ratified this treaty and that were inspired by it to update or pass relevant legislation.

Civil conflicts no longer threaten historic sites in Central America, but the region's heritage is continually at risk from other factors: the pillaging of archaeological sites is not uncommon, economic circumstances limit funding for conservation efforts, and uncontrolled development encroaches on both natural and cultural resources. The natural environment of Central America also poses one of the greatest threats to the region's cultural heritage. The isthmus' mountainous spine includes more than forty volcanoes, along the Pacific coast, whose eruptions have been known to destroy entire cities. The increasing intensity and frequency of hurricanes are also of concern for Central American communities. But earthquakes—even more than volcanic activity or hurricanes—have caused the most harm to the built environment in Central America, both historically and today. Though natural disasters have been a constant threat in the region, they have also repeatedly proven to encourage and trigger architectural conservation movements and public interest in historic sites.

In the northern part of the Central America, which is richly endowed with pre-Columbian archaeological remains, these sites provided the impetus for early conservation efforts, as they did in Mexico. Alternatively, in the southern part of the region, it has been the remarkable colonial centers of ever-growing cities that have been the primary focus of conservation efforts. Central America has made increasing progress since the mid-twentieth century, placing ever greater significance on the protection of its architectural heritage. In addition, visitors to the region have begun to discover and appreciate its natural and cultural wonders. By the 1990s, cultural heritage conservation in Central America had become an active field with policies demonstrating a sophisticated integration of environmental and cultural heritage protection.

BELIZE

Belize shares many characteristics with other countries of Central America, in particular its large number of pre-Columbian archaeological sites and its spectacular natural landscapes, yet it is also culturally and politically distinct from its neighbors because of the extensive influence of Great Britain. The Spanish ceded this small territory to the British after a fierce battle in 1798; therefore, Belizean cities developed alongside the other Caribbean countries that were also under British control. The youngest country in Central America, Belize was known as British Honduras until 1973. It only gained independence from the United Kingdom in 1981, though it had practiced self-rule since the 1960s, as did most former British colonies in the Caribbean region.

Belize's first organized architectural conservation efforts took place following Hurricane Hattie, which devastated the capital of Belize City in 1961. One-third of the city's buildings were completely destroyed, one-third seriously damaged, and the other third partially damaged.[3] Because of its precarious location at the delta of the Belize River on the Caribbean coast, surrounded on three sides by water and nowhere more than a few feet above sea level, Belize City had often been inundated. But after the particularly devastating storm of 1961, it lost its status as capital to Belmopan, which was newly founded on an inland site.

Figure 32–2 The extensive damage (a) in Belize City caused by Hurricane Hattie in 1961 led not only to the gradual rebuilding and restoration of the city (b) but also marked the beginning of architectural conservation policy and practice in the country of Belize as a whole.

Because timber is one of the country's most important resources, Belize City's architecture was—and is still—mostly wooden. In fact, the city was founded in the late seventeenth century as a trading post for logwood merchants, and most of its history has been dominated by its role as an export center for logwood and later mahogany. However, some of Belize City's most significant buildings, including St. John's Cathedral, were built in the early nineteenth century of brick, which had been brought over as ballast on ships from Europe. In addition, a number of the wealthier merchants in the city had built their homes using these same European bricks. Nearly all buildings of Belize City are built either on infill sites or wooden stilts that raise them above sea level.

These structures were not, however, protected from the tidal waves and high winds that accompanied Hurricane Hattie. With funds diverted to the construction of the new capital, Belize City's reconstruction was less organized and slower than it had been after a 1931 hurricane, when its rebuilding work was generously supported by the British government. The city's slow recovery from the 1961 disaster meant that by the mid 1980s it was still dilapidated and had become a drain on the country's financial resources. Though much of Belize City still shows evidence of damage and neglect today, some sections have been restored, including the City Market and the wealthy Fort George neighborhood. In addition, new concrete structures have replaced the traditional wooden homes in the commercial center.

The period after Hurricane Hattie witnessed increasing interest in Belizean heritage, especially of Belize City and its numerous Mayan ruins. After gaining self-rule, Belize passed the Ancient Monuments and Antiquities Act in 1972, protecting ancient monuments (defined as any "structure or building erected by man and any natural feature transformed or worked by man" that is more than one hundred years old) as well as antiquities (defined as any "article manufactured or worked by man" that is over 150 years old).[4] This legislation, which was revised in 2000, requires all such buildings and objects in private possession be registered and licensed, and it gives the government the right to acquire those it wants. The act also instituted fines for the willful damage, disturbance, or destruction of these historic sites and objects, forbade transfer of ownership without government permission, and forbade the export of such objects.

Though Belize's architectural conservation legislation provides strict mechanisms for preventing changes or demolitions, the law neither required the restoration or maintenance of these cultural resources by either the government or licensed private owners, nor did it establish a system by which their conservation would be ensured. However, within Belize's Ministry of National Development, Investment, and Culture, there are a number of departments and agencies that participate in the management and conservation of the country's historic sites. In 2003 the National Institute of Culture and History (NICH) was established to bring these agencies together and coordinate their efforts.[5] Today, the NICH's four branches focus on contemporary creative arts, museums and cultural centers, social and cultural research, and archaeology. The Institute of Archaeology, for example, issues permits for excavation at ancient sites and manages the country's numerous publicly accessible archaeological parks.

The Getty Conservation Institute (GCI) helped conserve Xunantunich, a Mayan complex, that dates from the eighth through eleventh centuries and is dominated by the Castillo, a 130-foot-high pyramid that is still the tallest building in Belize. Beginning in 1992, the GCI worked with the University of California, Los Angeles and the Belizean government on a long-term archaeological research project that incorporated conservation into the excavation process and especially focused on the deterioration problems caused by the humid Central American climate. The GCI also used the project as an opportunity to train authorities from the Belizean Department of Archaeology in site management and conservation techniques. The GCI helped develop a laboratory- and field-testing program to research chemical consolidants (to strengthen limestone) and biocides (to control microfloral growth). Short courses and workshops held at the site spread this expertise to the region's professionals and benefited other Mayan sites suffering from similar problems related to the region's humid climate.

The U.S. Ambassador's Fund for Cultural Preservation has also offered assistance for a range of sites in Belize through grants that have been among the largest offered by the fund anywhere in the world (up to $54,000). In 2003 a grant aided a public education campaign to discourage looting and increase respect for Mayan heritage and helped establish a citizens group to encourage architectural conservation in the El Pilar region. In 2005 another grant supported a number of projects at the Cerro Maya Temple, including a tourism-management plan, limestone-consolidation efforts, increased site protection, and the manufacture of fiberglass replicas as substitutes for stucco masks on the temple. In 2006 two Spanish colonial churches and a sugar mill in Lamanai were also restored by the Ambassador's Fund.

Figure 32–3 The Mayan complex of Xunantunich dating from the eighth through eleventh centuries is dominated by its distinctive Castillo (a) and was the subject of an archaeological research project that incorporated conservation (b) and (c) under the direction of the Belizean government as assisted by the Getty Conservation Institute in association with the University of California, Los Angeles. Images b and c copyright the J.P. Getty Trust 2010. Guillermo Aldana, photographer.

b

c

Today nineteen pre-Columbian archaeological sites and numerous caves used for ceremonial purposes have been documented in Belize; however, excavation and conservation is only beginning at most of these sites. Due to its own limited resources for research, the Belizean government has used archaeological sites in the country—including the Lamanai Maya ceremonial center, whose extensive ruins include more than one hundred buildings—to encourage exploration and excavation by archaeological field schools from foreign academic institutions, mostly from North America. Most of Belize's archaeological wonders are not open to the public due to the lack of facilities and management resources.

Though there is still much to be done to conserve the wealth of archaeological sites and historic buildings in Belize, through its legislation and agencies and by soliciting international investment and participation, the government has begun to create protective areas and to ensure the future of its built heritage.

GUATEMALA

Architectural conservation in Guatemala has traditionally been a state-centered and state-controlled enterprise with a long history, as in Mexico, its large, northeastern neighbor. The first efforts in Guatemala were made soon after independence from Spain in the 1820s, and in 1898 a Museo Nacional de Arqueología y Etnología (MUNAE, National Museum of Archaeology and Ethnography) was established. It moved to its present location in the 1940s. At that time numerous laws and statutes related to archaeological and other heritage were enacted, and in 1946 the Instituto de Antropología e Historia (IDAEH, Institute of Anthropology and History) was founded to take responsibility for Guatemala's architectural, archaeological, and other heritage.

In the mid-1950s, Guatemala passed its first legislation establishing state ownership of "archaeological, historic, and artistic riches" as well as government responsibility for their protection and conservation. This legislation also forbade the export of these items without permission.[6] The inadequacies of this legislation and the lack of consistency in architectural conservation projects was criticized in Guatemala in the 1960s and early 1970s, leading to the establishment of a Registro de la Propiedad Arqueológica, Histórica y Artística (Register of Archaeological, Historic, and Artistic Property) in 1976. Today this register is divided into three categories: pre-Hispanic heritage, Spanish colonial and republican-era heritage, and folklore. As of 2004, the Guatemalan register totaled over 114,000 sites, buildings, and objects, including 2,400 archaeological sites.

Guatemala's capital, Guatemala City, was devastated by an earthquake in 1976, after which strict regulations for new designs in the city were required based on building regulations in San Francisco, California. The earthquake's damage also resulted in increased interest in the city's historic structures. Numerous Guatemalan architects dedicated themselves to the completion of detailed surveys, documentation, and restoration projects in their capital, which in turn encouraged local communities to organize and effectively promote conservation efforts elsewhere in the country.

In direct response to the 1976 earthquake, the Cultural Property Conservation Center—later renamed the Centro de Conservación y Restauración de Bienes Muebles (Center for the Conservation and Restoration of Movable Cultural Property)—was founded with support from the OAS. In 1978 a parallel Programa de Conservación y Restauración de Bienes Culturales Inmuebles (Program for the Conservation and Restoration of Immovable Cultural Property) was established to restore and promote appreciation of Guatemala's archaeological and architectural sites. Both the movable and immovable heritage programs were absorbed into Guatemala's IDAEH in 1979 but made independent centers within the Dirección General del Patrimonio Cultural y Natural (General Directorate of Cultural and Natural Heritage) in 1984. The following year the Dirección became a department of the newly created Ministry of Culture and Sport. The work of both the ministry and the Dirección has been slowed by their excessive bureaucracies, inadequate training for professionals, and frequent management turnovers, which have led to abandoned projects and internal confusion.[7]

In 1997 a new Law for the Protection of the Cultural Heritage of the Nation was enacted in Guatemala and it significantly raised public awareness of the issue. It was drafted by a consensus of interested parties in the country under the direction of the Ministry of Culture and Sport. This law was more detailed in its provisions, broader in its scope, and established a more active regulatory system than had previous laws. One of its most important provisions was the creation

Figure 32–4 As a conservation measure meant to prevent looting, original stone stelae at the Mayan site of Ceibal in eastern Guatemala were removed and placed in a museum setting, and replicas of the stelae were installed in their place.

of a department within the State Prosecutor's Office specifically concerned with crimes against cultural property.

Because of increased looting of archaeological sites during the 1990s, the Ministry of Culture and Sport began taking preventative measures by replacing objects, such as carved relief stelae at the ruins of Ceibal, with replicas and placing the originals in museums. Decisions to move cultural property to museums have been debated by heritage conservationists and archaeologists alike in Guatemala, because valuable contextual information is lost whether objects are removed for safekeeping or by looters. Experts cannot agree whether it would be better to house objects in a museum or simply allocate funds for better management and security at the sites.[8]

Through the efforts of archaeologists at the University of California, Santa Barbara, progress was made in the conservation of the ancient Mayan city of El Pilar on the border between Belize and Guatemala. A binational conservation plan, called the BRASS/El

a

Figure 32–5 The magnificent ruins at the National Park of Tikal (a) in central Guatemala are emblematic of the country's rich archaeological heritage. Tikal's pristinely maintained park setting allows ample site visitation and includes overnight guest facilities. Other important Mayan sites, such as Naranjo (b) in western Guatemala, are purposefully kept less accessible and left in their more natural jungle context to provide visitors experiences of a different kind. The combination of both types of offerings adds to the appeal of Guatemala's Mayan heritage and helps divert attention from just a few of the country's most famous sites.

b

Pilar project (Belize River Archaeological Settlement Survey and El Pilar Archaeological Reserve for Maya Flora and Fauna), was developed in 1999 to protect the rainforest and the historic site and to curtail looting. In addition, the plan for El Pilar promoted the development of traditional Mayan forest gardens as more sustainable agricultural practices. The plan also incorporated the local community and government agencies and included a development agenda that provides for the construction of sensitive new housing. The BRASS/El Pilar program also called for using the site to introduce tourists to more of Mayan cultural heritage than just pre-Columbian archaeological sites. Through explanations of the forest gardens and participation in annual festivals, visitors are now afforded new experiences that deal with the contemporary and its continuity with the past.

Guatemala's most iconic architectural heritage is located in Tikal National Park, which covers 222 square miles in the country's north-central region and is a popular visitor destination today. The preservation and display of this Mayan site, whose peak was between the third and tenth centuries, is emblematic of other evocative presentations of Mayan heritage in the country, such as at Ceibal, Piedras Negras, and Naranjo.

The Guatemalan city of Antigua, which was known as Santiago de Guatemala when it was the capital of the Spanish Central America colonies, was at one time an important agricultural export center and one of the largest cities in Latin America. After being damaged repeatedly by earthquakes and after an especially destructive one in the 1770s, Antigua lost its status as capital to Guatemala City, but it is still known today as the country's colonial architectural jewel. After that earthquake, much of the damaged ornamentation on the city's baroque churches was never replaced, but most of the buildings themselves have survived as impressive structures or romantic ruins. Antigua was one of the first Latin American cities to be recognized as a national historic site in 1944 and to receive World Heritage designation in 1979. Ten years later, the Consejo Nacional para la Protección de Antigua Guatemala (National Council for the Protection of Antigua Guatemala) was formed, which still monitors changes and sets guidelines for new construction in the historic city today.[9]

In 2003 Antigua was embroiled in controversy as developers planned a multiblock shopping complex, causing concern among local conservationists and UNESCO. The mayor and the Consejo Nacional for Antigua had approved the project, because the complex would be located outside of the protected area and would house numerous businesses, such

Figure 32–6 The partially ruined Capuchin Convent (a) in the historic district of Antigua, Guatemala, was adaptively used as offices for the National Council for the Protection of Antigua Guatemala. Other similarly earthquake-damaged buildings—such as the Palacio de los Capitanes Generales (b), which faces the main town square—have yet to be fully restored.

a

b

a

b

c

Figure 32–7 Architectural conservation in Guatemala City, Guatemala, entails projects ranging from facade restorations of the National Palace (a) to the preservation and presentation of a fraction of the remains of the extensive ancient earthen Mayan city of Kaminaljuyu (b and c) in what is now the principal city park.

as movie theatres and sports facilities, that were desirable, but not appropriate the historic center itself.[10] However, critics argued that the plan would nonetheless exacerbate the city's traffic problems and alter the historic cityscape. The controversy led to the development of a new master plan for Antigua Guatemala, which had not been updated since 1972.

During the presidency of Álvaro Arzú in the late 1990s, tourism was increasingly promoted in Guatemala in the hope of reaping some of the economic benefits Mexico was enjoying. Cultural and ecological tourism became Guatemala's focus, and within a few years the country had already increased its revenues from foreign visitors. As elsewhere in the world, tourism has raised new concerns in the country's historic cities and at its archaeological sites, even as the presence of visitors has reduced looting and their funds improved security measures and supported conservation projects.

A task force was established in the year 2000 to study possible revisions to existing architectural conservation legislation and to reevaluate Guatemala's complicated heritage-management system. The Guatemalan government has recognized that monopolizing conservation efforts without adequate financial resources is not the best long-term solution for its heritage, and it has begun to seek partnerships with private institutions and foundations. This new strategy indicates a positive future for Guatemala's architectural and archaeological sites, even though most partnerships so far have been within the country and more could be done to promote international support and involvement in the conservation of Guatemala's heritage.

EL SALVADOR

As in many other Central American countries, concern for architectural heritage in El Salvador began with its archaeological sites and interest has grown steadily over the course of the twentieth century. In the 1920s Salvadoran archaeologist Antonio Sol began excavations at seventh- or eighth-century Cihuatán, one of the most impressive late Mayan cities in the region. El Salvador has also continuously passed legislation to protect and provide for the conservation of its architectural and archaeological heritage. It was the first country in the region to legally prevent the exportation of antiquities and other archaeological objects in 1903. In 1935 a law protecting historic sites was enacted, and three years later its coverage was extended to movable objects as well.

Beginning in the 1940s, Stanley Boggs, a then-recent graduate of Harvard University, introduced more scientific archaeological methods to El Salvador as well as guided and encouraged the protection of those sites until his death in 1991.[11] In the 1940s and 1950s, Boggs excavated and founded a museum at Tazumal, another late Mayan site, and he led the Ministry of Culture's Department of Archaeological Excavations. In the 1960s he served as head of the national museum as well as head of the Archaeology Department of the University of El Salvador. In the 1970s El Salvador ratified the UNESCO World Heritage convention, and Boggs encouraged the country to update and expand the provisions of its architectural conservation legislation and to create a register of protected sites.

Civil war in the 1980s and early 1990s interrupted architectural conservation efforts in El Salvador, but peace brought new legislation and organizations and renewed vigor to the task of protecting Salvadoran sites. In 1993 the Special Cultural Heritage Act was passed, which augmented earlier laws by establishing a registry of significant sites as well as a process for state acquisition of privately owned objects and buildings of cultural importance. In 1996 this law was refined and a process was outlined by which municipal governments would safeguard sites of national significance within their jurisdictions. The 1996 Special Cultural Heritage Act also provided an explicit and all-encompassing definition of cultural property that included objects and sites of "anthropological, paleontological, archaeological, prehistorical, historical, ethnographic, religious, artistic, technical, scientific, philosophical, bibliographical, or documentary nature."[12]

Figure 32–8 As with most other Central American countries, laws and efforts to protect cultural heritage in El Salvador initially focused on archaeological sites that had been discovered in modern times. Excavation work beginning in the 1920s at the seventh- or eighth-century Mayan site of Cihuatán and in the 1940s and 1950s at the late Mayan site of Tazumal (illustrated) helped provide the impetus for establishing the country's Department of Archaeological Excavation within its Ministry of Culture and the Archaeology Department at the University of El Salvador, as well as the passage of relevant cultural heritage protection laws.

Figure 32–9 At the small, pre-Columbian Mayan farming village of Joya de Cerén, which was very well preserved after inundation by ash from a volcanic eruption around 600 CE, much has been learned about everyday life at the time through advanced archaeological investigation techniques. International organizations have assisted in planning for the protection and presentation of this site in El Salvador.

The primary governmental organization responsible for cultural heritage conservation in El Salvador today is the Consejo Nacional para el Arte y la Cultura (CONCULTURA, National Council for Culture and Arts). CONCULTURA was founded in 1991 within the Salvadorian Ministry of Culture and Communications as an agency to study, preserve, and promote culture and the fine arts throughout the country. Its objectives are twofold: On the one hand, it is engaged in encouraging and disseminating contemporary art and culture, and on the other with the protection of the heritage of the past.

In 1995 CONCULTURA began a program of partnership with private organizations in which it transferred funds to them and entrusted them with the implementation of projects. Within a decade, CONCULTURA had granted funds to thirty-eight different NGOs for a range of projects. The results of this partnership and grant program have been to increase popular participation in cultural production and protection in general, as well as to broaden the geographic range of sites and the types of people and organizations interested and involved in Salvadoran culture.[13]

One of the most successful of these partnerships has been between CONCULTURA and the Fundación Nacional de Arqueología (FUNDAR, National Foundation for Archaeology), an NGO established in 1996. FUNDAR's first major project was at Cihuatán, where movable metal stairs were installed to protect the steps of the Temple of the Idols, which were constructed of volcanic material before the tenth century and had been worn down by fifty years of visitor use. Due to their successful conservation efforts at Cihuatán, in 2005 CONCULTURA granted FUNDAR supervisory control over two additional Mayan sites: San Andrés and Joya de Cerén. At San Andrés, FUNDAR increased the lighting, controlled access, and simultaneously improved the visitor experience and better protected the ruins by requiring tours to take place only in organized groups.

Unlike Cihuatán and San Andrés, Joya de Cerén is a smaller, pre-Columbian farming village rather than a large-scale town. Nevertheless, it is one of Central America's most important Mayan archaeological sites, because it is one of the best-preserved examples of the remains of the everyday lives of the people of pre-Columbian Mesoamerica. The site, which was discovered in 1979, was first inhabited in 900 BCE and has sometimes been called the "Pompeii of the Americas," as archaeologists believe an abrupt volcanic eruption buried its houses, community structures, artifacts, gardens, and cultivated fields around the year 600 CE. More than eighteen buildings have been discovered at Joya de Cerén thus far, and ten of these have been fully excavated.

Figure 32–10 The remarkably intact colonial town of Suchitoto, El Salvador, lacked a conservation management plan until after 1998 when listing on the World Monument Fund's Watch List stimulated action and funding to produce a comprehensive plan and phased conservation work in the town.

CONCULTURA began drafting a comprehensive management and conservation plan for Joya de Cerén in 1997, and UNESCO supported an international conference to discuss guidelines for the site. Since 1999, the Getty Conservation Institute has participated in this planning process, offering a model that encompasses conservation, presentation, publicity, and administration and can be adapted for other archaeological sites in El Salvador. An unsightly temporary shelter had been erected over the archaeological site at Joya de Cerén to help protect it from the elements during excavation. After assuming management responsibility in 2005, FUNDAR replaced its sheathing with more permanent panels that filter the sunlight and protect the site's remains without obstructing views.[14]

In recent decades, El Salvador has paid increasing attention to its colonial heritage, and Suchitoto—one of the county's most intact Spanish-era towns—has also been of growing concern for international heritage protection organizations. Suchitoto was designated as a national historic site in 1997, but the lack of a master plan for its conservation and the municipal government's lack of financial resources led to Suchitoto's inclusion on the World Monument Fund's Watch List in 1998 and 2000. Suchitoto is also home to a teaching workshop established by CONCULTURA and partially funded by the Spanish Agency for International Cooperation for Development (AECID). At this workshop, students can learn traditional bricklaying, ironworking, and carpentry skills and be trained to work on architectural conservation projects.[15] However, plans for the conservation and sustainable growth of the city are still lacking, infill buildings continue to alter its character, and there are little funds to initiate restoration projects at priority buildings.

CONCULTURA has been generously supported by numerous foreign governments and agencies, including the AECID, which has funded not only the workshop schools but also the publication of reports and archaeological findings and individual projects, such as the restoration of the endangered Church of Santa Lucia, Cathedral of Suchitoto. In 2001 the U.S. Ambassador's Fund for Cultural Preservation funded the restoration of the Manuel Gallardo Library in San Salvador, as well as the development of an online catalog of its historic collections. In 2004 this same fund supported the restoration of the early twentieth-century cathedral in Santa Ana. In addition, after a January 2001 earthquake, UNESCO began working in cooperation with CONCULTURA to repair its offices, which were damaged. After that same earthquake, emergency repairs were also undertaken at two of the few remaining colonial churches in El Salvador, San Miguel Arcángel Church in Huizucar and Santa Cruz de Roma Church in Panchimalco. But financing was lacking for more comprehensive conservation measures at these Salvadorian national heritage sites, and the plight of both was highlighted by the World Monuments Fund in 2004, which raised concern about the deteriorated state of their wooden altarpieces and coffered ceilings.

The lack of human resources ranks among CONCULTURA's greatest challenges today, because there are only a handful of trained archaeologists in a country with over 750 archaeological sites to care for. Though many historic buildings are protected or state owned and have comprehensive management plans, the continuing deterioration of the county's significant historic earthen structures is a primary concerns in El Salvador. On the other hand, CONCULTURA's innovative partnership program with private Salvadorian organizations, as well as its successful solicitation of international assistance, indicate positive trends for the country's architectural heritage.

HONDURAS

Architectural conservation efforts in Honduras also began more than a century ago as a result of interest in archaeological sites. The first modern excavation and conservation project in the country took place between 1891 and 1900 at the Mayan ruins of Copán under the direction of Harvard University's Peabody Museum of Archaeology and Ethnography. In the 1930s the Norwegian archaeologist Gustav Stromsvik, working for the Carnegie Institute of Washington, continued the work at Copán, which is known for its main acropolis, five major plazas, imposing hieroglyph staircase, and numerous well-preserved stelae.

Figure 32–11 Documentation of the discoveries of the ancient Mayan remains at Copán, Honduras, in 1839 by architect and explorer Frederick Catherwood helped define and popularize study of the Maya for decades to follow. Frederick Catherwood. *Incidents of Travel in Central America,* Virtue & Co. London, 1854, plate IX.

The first law protecting historic sites in Honduras was enacted in 1935, partly in response to a particularly destructive earthquake in 1934. By 1940 this legislation was extended to also protect movable objects of historic value. A new Law for the Protection of the Nation's Cultural Heritage was passed in 1984 and revised in 1997. This law identified five categories of heritage that encompass the tangible and intangible as well as the movable and immovable. These categories include objects, manuscripts, folklore, colonial and nineteenth-century buildings, and groups of buildings (including archaeological sites).

The 1984 law vested exclusive authority over excavations, alterations, and demolition of designated heritage in the Instituto Hondureño de Antropología e Historia (IHAH, Honduran Institute of Anthropology and History), which had been established in 1952 and in the 1980s was a division of the Secretariat of State for Culture and Tourism. Today the IHAH maintains central offices in the capital of Tegucigalpa as well as regional and subregional centers throughout the country. Its central offices include five departments focused on anthropological research, historical research, museums, restoration, and protection. The IHAH's restoration department is responsible for the actual rehabilitation and conservation work done in Honduras, as well as for technical consulting, training local personnel, conditions inventories, studies of conservation practices, and implementing master

Figure 32–12 Development of a new conservation plan in 2001 for the conservation and presentation of Copán, Honduras, was a process that involved national and foreign experts and local stakeholders and resulted in the present effective program to preserve and display the Copán historic site in a sustainable way.

plans for recognized historic city centers. The protection department of the IHAH is responsible for creating and maintaining the national inventory of cultural heritage, dealing with regulation of designated buildings and objects that are privately owned, and implementing programs to raise awareness of cultural heritage in Honduras.

As in the early years of Honduran archaeology, Copán has dominated cultural heritage conservation efforts in recent decades, following its inscription on UNESCO'S World Heritage List in 1980. In 1985 the IHAH initiated the Copán Mosaic Project to catalog fragments of sculptures found at the site, to analyze and conserve these fragments, and to reconstruct sculptures when possible. This project was followed by the restoration of the site's hieroglyph staircase—the longest surviving pre-Columbian hieroglyphic inscription in the Americas. The Getty Conservation Institute funded a study of the stairway to investigate its conditions and plan for its preservation. The U.S. Agency for International Development (USAID) also funded work at Copán between 1988 and 1995.

In 1993 the IHAH joined forces with the Copán Acropolis Archaeological Project and the local nonprofit, Copán Association, to construct the Museum of Maya Sculpture, adjacent to the site. The climate-controlled museum opened three years later to display the original sculptures, stelae, and facades from Copán, while replicas of the artifacts have been placed at the actual site. A program to digitally record Copán's hieroglyphics using photogrammetric techniques, combined with glass plate negatives used in nineteenth-century photography of the site, was initiated to document the inscription. In 2001 a new management plan for Copán replaced the one created in 1984. Development of the new plan involved the IHAH and foreign experts as well as regional authorities, representatives from related tourist businesses, and members of indigenous communities.[16]

In the early twenty-first century, the Copán archaeological complex was the center of a controversy between UNESCO and the Honduran government, whose Ministry of Tourism planned to construct an international airport in Rio Amarillo, twenty kilometers from the World Heritage Site. The airport aimed to ease and increase tourist access to the country's best-known site, as well as to link it to other Mayan sites in Central America. However, environmental impact studies and the ICOMOS evaluation missions argued that the airport would be detrimental to the valley's social networks, landscapes, and cultural heritage. UNESCO's World Heritage Committee repeatedly urged the Honduran government to reconsider its plans and to locate the airport significantly further from the protected zone so as not to preclude its future extension to include other parts of the Rio Amarillo valley. In early 2007, at the Honduran President's request, the Ministry of Tourism decided to build the airport forty kilometers from the ruins in the town of La Concepción and to construct a new highway between the airport and Copán Park.

The cultural heritage of Honduras also encompasses non-Mayan archaeological sites as well as colonial cities. Among the former is the Los Naranjos Archaeological Park on Lake Yojoa, which includes multiple settlements inhabited by a pre-Columbian people about which little is known other than that they were a fairly isolated society that occupied the area between 800 BCE and 1200 CE. The IHAH is currently excavating and preparing the Los Naranjos area to be publicly accessible. In addition, prehistoric pictographic rock art can be found throughout Honduras, and initial efforts have been made to protect some of these sites.

a

b

c

Figure 32–13 The installation of modern urban infrastructure and the rehabilitation of historic streets and buildings in the town of Trujillo on the north coast of Honduras was financed by the World Bank in 2001. The Casa Melhado (a) has been restored (b) and transformed (c) for use as a hospitality industry training center.

The coastal city of Trujillo, near where Christopher Columbus arrived on his fourth voyage to the Americas in 1502, as well as Tegucigalpa, rank among Honduras' best-preserved colonial cities. Through the World Bank's North Coast Sustainable Tourism Project, Trujillo's cobblestone streets have been repaved and its Casa Melhado has been restored and transformed into a hospitality industry training center. In addition, since 2002, the IHAH has rehabilitated the Santa Barbara Fort, Commandante's House, and Courthouse.

The late seventeenth- and eighteenth-century architecture of the Honduran capital of Tegucigalpa has also received recent conservation attention: the San Pedro Nolasco Convent was restored in 1984 and reopened as the National Art Gallery in 1994, the former gold-and-silver processing building (and later National Mint) was rehabilitated and transformed into the National Library, and the Church of San Francisco

a

b

c

Figure 32–14 The adaptive reuse of the San Pedro Nolasco Convent (a and b) in Tegucigalpa as the Honduran National Gallery of Art and the rehabilitation of the National Mint building and its conversion into the National Library (c) are considered to be two of the country's most successful restoration projects.

has been returned to its former splendor. On the other hand, an impressive colonial-era building, which served as the American Embassy in the early twentieth century, began to deteriorate due to neglect in the late 1990s. As a result of safety concerns, the Honduran government granted permission for the owners to demolish the deteriorated adobe structure even though it was located within the protected Tegucigalpa Historic District.

As the poorest country in Central America, Honduras has struggled even more than its neighbors to finance its architectural conservation institutions and projects. In addition, in 1998 Hurricane Mitch damaged several cities and historic sites and further set back the country's economy. As a result, the IHAH's mission of investigating and conserving sites has been superseded by urgent, short-term rescue projects.[17] Yet Honduras has been particularly active in discussions concerning the intellectual property rights of collective indigenous communities, and has engaged these groups—as well as local governments—in the architectural conservation process to a greater extent than most of its neighbors.

COSTA RICA

Interest in cultural heritage conservation in Costa Rica began in 1887 with the founding of the Museo Nacional (National Museum) in San José, which initiated the documentation, protection, and display of the country's cultural and natural patrimony. Since its creation, the museum has maintained a department for the defense and conservation of heritage that supports the preservation legislation and the dedicated government agencies that Costa Rica has created over the course of the twentieth century.

Costa Rica passed its first law related to the protection of its cultural heritage in 1938, and like many of its neighbors, this legislation was concerned with regulating the excavation of archaeological sites and restricting the export of objects from those sites. The country's 1949 constitution reinforced this law by stating that it was the government's responsibility to protect, conserve, and develop the country's natural, artistic, and historic heritage. Additional laws in 1982 and 1995 established a modern system to ensure conservation of the country's cultural patrimony. The 1982 law for the Defense and Conservation of the National Archaeological Heritage created a Comisión Arqueológica Nacional (National Archaeological Commission), which was entrusted with creating an inventory of archaeological sites in Costa Rica. The Commission's five members include representatives of the Museo Nacional, the University of Costa Rica, the National Committee of Indigenous Matters, the Ministry of Education, and the Ministry of Cultural, Youth, and Sport.

The 1995 law for the Historic and Architectural Heritage of Costa Rica created a parallel Comisión Nacional de Patrimonio Histórico-Arquitectónico (National Historic-Architectural Commission) that was mandated to designate protected buildings, monuments, sites, groups, and historic centers and to impose fines for altering or damaging them. The law also created the Centro de Investigación y Conservación del Patrimonio Cultural (Center for Investigation and Conservation of Cultural Heritage) to carry out research and restoration projects, provide technical advice to property owners, and inspect and authenticate work on protected sites. The Center is divided into five sections focused on technical studies, historical and anthropological investigations, training, cul-

Figure 32–15 Costa Rica's efforts to protect the environment are in balance with those focused on culture and the arts in such a way that attracts numerous foreign visitors. Presentation of historic architectural sites, such as the ruins of church of Ujarrás, Cartago, within lightly managed natural settings symbolizes this balance and shared valuation.

tural inventories, and promotion. It is also the Center's responsibility to prepare reports on the value and state of conservation of sites deserving protection and submit them to the Comisión Histórico-Arquitectónico for approval. The 1995 law, and its 2005 amendments, define fourteen different criteria for which historic buildings, sites, or cities can be designated. These criteria range from historic, cultural, and artistic values to representative example, symbolic value, documentary evidence, and age.

Beginning with the 1995 law, Costa Rica no longer encouraged state purchase of sites it sought to preserve but rather introduced a series of incentives to encourage property owners and private organizations and companies to get involved in architectural conservation.[18] These incentives included income tax deductions, property tax exemptions, and favorable loan terms for investments in historic properties. In addition, money collected from fines for violations of this legislation as well as from the sale of a special issue of stamps depicting important Costa Rican heritage sites was earmarked for use only for architectural conservation projects.

An indicator of the growing public commitment to architectural conservation in Costa Rica was the establishment of an active national chapter of ICOMOS in the 1980s. Since 1988, ICOMOS Costa Rica, in conjunction with the Ministry of Culture, Youth and Sport, has celebrated April 18 as the National Day of Monuments and Historic Sites and has given awards to recognize exemplary conservation practices within the country. In the 1990s, ICOMOS Costa Rica organized a series of conferences to promote awareness of architectural heritage and conservation, some of which were focused on specific themes such as traditional building types and materials, natural disasters, and tourism.

Though Costa Rica has recognized the importance of its historic archaeological sites and architecture, it has been better known in the twentieth century for its remarkable work toward the conservation of its rich and largely unspoiled biological and geographical diversity and for the encouragement of a thriving ecotourism industry around its nature and wildlife reserves. In recent decades, however, interest in the country's built heritage has steadily increased, and its plans for sustainable development have broadened to also include the country's cultural tourism potential.

Figure 32–16 Resourceful land use and maintenance of the natural ecology include the preservation of traditional land settlement patterns and farmsteads in Costa Rica so much so that it is an international "brand" of the country. A roadside sign advertising an eco-friendly coffee plantation near Monteverde in the central highlands of Costa Rica exemplifies this. The ecocultural assets in a country so well endowed with natural wonders is an aspect of Costa Rica that ensures both economic stability and the sustainability of both its cultural and natural heritage resources.

NICARAGUA

The first government interest in historic sites in Nicaragua came during the early 1940s, during a period when the dictatorship of the Somoza family was nationalizing and confiscating much of the country's resources. When the eighteen-year civil war between the Somocistas and the leftist Sandinistas ended in 1979, the victorious new Sandinista government also took an immediate interest in the country's natural heritage, which had been damaged during the conflict. Five years later, they broadened state protection to also include the country's architectural and archaeological heritage by enacting Nicaragua's first legislation specifically aimed at safeguarding these sites—the Law on the Protection of the Cultural Heritage of the Nation.

The 1990s brought political stability, more democratic institutions, increased tourism, and a generally growing economy to Nicaragua, and these developments enabled increased attention and funding to be focused on architectural conservation. Within the Ministry of Education, Culture, and Sport, the Instituto Nicaragüense de Cultura (INC, Nicaraguan Institute of Culture) was established, complete with a Dirección de Patrimonio Cultural (Directorate of Cultural Patrimony). This new agency was in part created in response to the deterioration of numerous historic sites during the decades of unrest. In addition, a National Plan for the Arts and Culture that integrates the protection of historic sites with the National Plan for the Protection of the Environment was called for at that time.

Nicaragua is home to fewer monumental pre-Columbian archaeological sites than other countries of Latin America, though it has paid special attention to the rock art sites it has discovered. As a result, Nicaragua has focused its conservation efforts on its remarkable Spanish colonial cities, including León and Granada, as well as the nineteenth- and twentieth-century city of Managua. The extensive ruins of León Viejo (Old León), which the Spanish deserted in 1609 after a severe earthquake, were left buried beneath the jungle and untouched for centuries until accidentally discovered in 1968. Excavations by the Universidad Nacional Autonóma (National Autonomous University) in León began immediately, and the government assumed responsibility for the site in 1979. The OAS funded a conservation master plan for León Viejo in 1987 and an on-site directorate was established ten years later.

To date, the ruins of a cathedral, several churches, a convent, a foundry, and numerous private homes have been excavated at León Viejo. As these ruins have been uncovered, consolidation and waterproofing treatments have reflected the changing technologies and philosophies of archaeological site conservation from the late 1960s to the present. The walls were first capped with bricks and hard cement mortar, which were removed and replaced with ceramic tiles in the 1980s, which in turn were removed and replaced with a lime, earth, and cement mixture in the 1990s.[19] In recent decades, numerous sites in "New" León, whose oldest structures date from the early seventeenth century, have also been restored, including the elaborate baroque Cathedral of the Annunciation, the largest in Central America, and the turn-of-the-eighteenth century Church of John the Baptist of Sutiava, the oldest church in "New" León with its simple façade and carved wooden interior.

Granada, one of the oldest mainland cities in the Americas and a recognized national cultural heritage site in Nicaragua, is one of the best preserved colonial cities in the country. Located on the shores of Lake Nicaragua, Granada's picturesque streets are lined with brightly colored buildings and ornate metal balconies. Despite their Spanish colonial appearance, most of these buildings actually date from the late nineteenth century, when they were rebuilt after a devastating fire in 1857. Sites like the Fuerte la Pólvora, the central plaza, the neoclassical cathedral, and the Guadeloupe Church have all been restored in recent decades. Beginning in 1990, the Swedish International Development Cooperation Agency promoted and funded restoration of the

Figure 32–17 In Nicaragua, the accidental discovery in 1968 of León Viejo (Old León), which the Spanish deserted in 1609 after a severe earthquake, posed challenges for the stabilization of the ruins and presentation of the site that have been addressed in three separate conservation campaigns. The present system of wall capping using a softer more organic mix of lime, mud, and cement is based on successful experiences with this approach elsewhere.

Church and Convent of San Francisco, which is operated as a museum today by the Nicaraguan Institute of Culture.

In 2000, an earthquake caused extensive damage to Granada and other Nicaraguan colonial cities, and immediately afterward homeowners began ad hoc repairs or demolitions of their properties, many of which were of historic value. The Instituto Nicaragüense de Cultura was concerned that proper procedures and materials were not being used and that many of the designs leading to structural failures at the time were being repeated in repair work. However, without funding to assist homeowners or to enforce regulations, and with the more pressing needs for sheltering victims at the time, Nicaraguan conservationists found they could do little to prevent such interventions.[20] Despite these developments, in 2003, Nicaragua nominated Granada for inclusion on the World Heritage List and its application is still pending.

In the capital city of Managua, inspiration for architectural conservation grew following President Violeta Barrios de Chamorro's initiatives in 1994 to restore the neoclassical Palacio Nacional (National Palace), which housed Nicaragua's legislature for half a century. Managua was founded in 1819 as a fishing village, and became Nicaragua's capital in 1857 to balance a long-standing dispute between León and Granada. Managua grew substantially during the Somoza regime, which built numerous government structures there after a devastating earthquake in 1931, including the Palacio Nacional, which was completed in 1935.

Many of the nineteenth- and early twentieth-century buildings of Managua were damaged by another earthquake in 1972, but little interest was expressed in repairing these sites until after the successful restoration of the Palacio Nacional and its adaptation into spaces for the National Library, Archives, and Museum in 1994. This project was intended as a first step in a larger plan to invest in the protection of the city's historic core and to reinforce its position as a cultural center.[21] Once the palace project was complete, plans were made to rehabilitate the Old Cathedral, Nicaragua's first steel-framed building, which was designed and constructed by Belgian engineers in the 1920s—but little restoration work was actually completed at the cathedral. Legislation for the designation and protection of Managua's center

Figure 32–18 Urban conservation in Granada (a) and in Managua, including at the Palacio Nacional (b), has faced persistent difficulties from the need to make appropriate and effective repairs to historic buildings damaged in earthquake-prone Nicaragua. Since the 2000 earthquake, continuing challenges range from finding the proper repair techniques in both cities to forming a critical mass of effort and financing to restore the character of whole neighborhoods.

a

b

was enacted in 1996 and revised in 2000. This law also includes provisions for the promotion of the intangible cultural heritage that is part of this zone of the city, such as its annual festivals.

Nicaragua's commitment to architectural conservation since its first laws on the matter were drafted in the 1940s is a good example of how despite periods of social turmoil, a country can rise to the challenges posed within a few decades and include cultural heritage protection as national agenda item.

PANAMA

Government interest in architectural conservation occurred later in Panama than in most other Central American countries, but in 1972 a new constitution raised awareness of Panama's architectural heritage and a new master plan initiated the renewal of the historic core of Panama City. The new constitution obliged the government to promote, develop, and safeguard the country's national culture, which it defined as all human artistic and scientific demonstrations, including archaeological and historic sites. A series of constitutional amendments and new legislation concerning cultural heritage protection in Panama were passed on five occasions between 1976 and 2002.

Today, a number of state agencies carry out the mission outlined in the constitution, including the Instituto Nacional de Cultura (INAC, National Institute of Culture), its Dirección del Patrimonio Histórico (Directorate of Historic Patrimony), and the Comisión Nacional de Arqueología y Monumentos Históricos (National Commission for Archaeology and Historic Monuments). The Dirección is charged with classifying, preserving, and promoting Panamanian heritage, while the Comisión serves as an advisory body that also oversees and approves rehabilitation projects at listed historic sites. By the early twenty-first century, the Dirección had extended state protection to about forty key historic buildings, four historic districts, and numerous archaeological sites in the country. Since the passage of a tourism promotion law in 1994, private owners and developers can have their property and income taxes reduced as an incentive to properly restore and maintain designated sites.

Due to the combined interests of the Dirección del Patrimonio Histórico, private investors, and the city's mayor, Panama City's Casa Góngora was one of the first major restoration projects in the country.[22] This eighteenth-century house was converted into an arts center, and its renewal inspired planning for an historic district that encompassed the surrounding colonial Old Town, or Casco Antiguo. The Inter-American Development Bank sponsored this master plan in 1972, which in turn led to the restoration of the National Theater, the Cathedral, and the Town Hall in the late 1970s. In addition, the Old Town was officially designated for protection at the national level in 1976 and placed on the World Heritage List in 1997.

Figure 32–19 In the late 1970s, a master plan funded by the Inter-American Development Bank led to the restoration of three key buildings in Panama City, Panama: the National Theater, the Cathedral, and the Town Hall. The ensuing protection of the area (illustrated) by additional heritage legislation and eventual placement of historic Panama City on the UNESCO World Heritage List in 1997 is a clear demonstration of the positive progress that urban conservation can take when both government and citizens commit to cultural heritage protection of this kind.

a

Figure 32–20 In Panama, the seventeenth- and eighteenth-century fortresses of San Lorenzo (a) on the Pacific Coast and San Jerónimo of Portobelo (b) on the Caribbean coast are joined by a stone highway across the isthmus of Panama and are included together on the World Heritage List as Portobelo-San Lorenzo. Due to their ruinous conditions, they have both required extensive conservation interventions, including roof repairs and improvements to water drainage systems (c) at the San Jerónimo fortress.

b

c

The historic district in Panama City preserves traces of the country's numerous foreign influences, including the monastic complexes, houses, and tenements built during the Spanish colonial era as well as buildings reflecting the brief French and long United States involvement in the country in relation to their interests in the Panama Canal. In the early 1990s, the 1972 Master Plan for Panama City was revised, with attention to issues that had developed in recent decades, including parking, housing shortages, and the declining socioeconomic status of most of the district's residents.[23] In 2002 the Japanese Center for International Cooperation in Conservation supported work on a new master plan for conserving Panama City's Old Town historic district as well as conditions surveys and training workshops. Today Panama City's center is the most intact and best managed historic district in the country, with significant private participation thanks to tax incentives as well as an established Oficina del Casco Antiguo (Office of the Old Town) that actively guides all proposed interventions.[24]

In 2003 the boundaries of the Panama City World Heritage List site were extended to also include the ruins of Panamá Viejo (Old Panama), founded in the early sixteenth century but abandoned after a fire in 1672 when Panama City was moved to its present location. Panamá Viejo includes the well-preserved ruins of the main plaza, its cathedral, and several other churches, as well as the Town Hall and numerous residential buildings.[25] Abandoned for centuries, the ruins are now a park maintained by a public-private entity established in 1995 called the Patronato Panamá Viejo (Trust for Old Panama).

Panama's other World Heritage Site is a pair of important fortifications; the seventeenth- and eighteenth-century fortresses of San Lorenzo on the Pacific Coast and San Jerónimo of Portobelo on the Caribbean coast. By the time of their inscription in 1980, both fortifications had fallen into disrepair. After placement on their Watch list of endangered sites in 1998, the World Monuments Fund supported a study on integrating natural and cultural conservation at these fortifications and offered technical assistance toward securing their futures.[26]

Panama is best known not for its seventeenth- and eighteenth-century fortifications but for its modern military and engineering marvel connecting the Atlantic and Pacific oceans—the Panama Canal. Due to the important global economic influence of the canal since its completion in 1914, its lock systems and massive support complex have attracted the interest of conservationists and historians. The architectural, urban, and landscape design of the ten-mile wide Canal Zone are also of interest. The canal was constructed by the United States, which managed it and the surrounding zone until December 31, 1999, when complete control was handed over to the Panamanian government (the Canal Zone itself had ceased to exist as of 1979).[27]

While still owned and administered by the United States, a few isolated conservation projects were initiated on the Canal Zone's numerous structures. These included the 1993 restoration of the four massive murals depicting scenes from the canal's construction, which adorned the impressive Canal Administration Building that was built to resemble an Italian Renaissance palazzo. By the time of the handover of the canal at the end of 1999, most of the buildings were in need of repair, and the lack of restrictions on their care worried the international conservation community as well as locals involved with ICOMOS Panama.

The property acquired by Panama included the two towns founded by the United States to house its support personnel: Balboa, a suburb of Panama City on the Pacific entrance to the canal, and Gamboa on Gatun Lake in the middle of the Canal Zone. The buildings in these modernist planned communities were all designed in a homogeneous and coherent style—mostly of concrete with red tile roofs.[28] After acquiring the houses, civic, and entertainment buildings, the Panamanian government began privatizing them on a piecemeal basis. Many were concerned that the integrity of these largely unaltered communities would be lost. For this reason, the Panama Canal Zone was included on the World Monuments Fund's Watch list in 2004.[29] To ensure its pro-

a

b

c

Figure 32–21 The enormity of the engineering feat that was the building of the Panama Canal (a) is reflected in the conservation challenges that this world-renowned and important site faces today. Recent conservation issues have included threats to the canal's older structures (b) from modern efforts to widen the canal, insensitive plans for privatizing some of its historic structures and views (c), and ambiguity over responsibilities for maintaining the districts historic cemeteries. The Panama Canal is an emblem of early-twentieth-century American (and earlier French) engineering, a theme in heritage protection that has particular resonance throughout the Americas where numerous other extraordinary engineering marvels were accomplished.

tection, there have been calls for designation of the Panama Canal Zone as a historic district or a cultural landscape, on either the national or international level.

In Panama, the acquisition of the canal and its supportive structures has been viewed as an opportunity for development. The new Master Plan for the Panama Canal approved in 2005 reflects local priorities: while it details extensive strategies for adding a new container terminal and building a third set of locks to increase the canal's capacity and revenue-producing potential, it does not mention the historic resources of the Canal Zone.[30] While important for the architectural, urban, and economic history of the United States, for many Panamanians the canal evokes images of foreign dominance and exploitation, which they would prefer to appropriate rather than preserve. In fact, the Autoridad del Canal de Panamá (ACP, Panama Canal Authority), the autonomous entity that manages the canal's operations today, has on several occasions banned the designation of historic sites within the former Canal Zone to maintain control over the area, and its current expansion plans to accommodate larger ships threaten some adjacent sites. At the same time, Panama has recognized the importance of the canal, having opened an Interoceanic Canal Museum in 1997, before even acquiring control of the canal itself. Located in the restored Casco Viejo building in Panama City, the museum has attempted to generate scholarly and tourist interest in the canal and to acquire and display objects and documents associated with its history.[31]

Like Nicaragua, Panama is home to fewer large-scale archaeological sites than more northern countries in Central America, so conservation efforts have focused more on Spanish colonial heritage. However, numerous examples of pre-Columbian rock art have also been found in Panama, and important measures have been taken to safeguard these sites. In 2002, a law was passed making their destruction illegal and calling for their protection, which led to the designation of many prehistoric rock art sites as national monuments. Unfortunately, widespread appreciation of the value and importance of protecting these sites has not yet permeated the Panamanian public, and in some cases, such as at El Nancito, community residents allegedly destroyed recently discovered rock paintings because of fears that the government would confiscate their land and create an archaeological park.

The lack of public awareness and community participation in cultural heritage is not the only challenge facing architectural conservationists in contemporary Panama. The state conservation institutions in Panama have also been criticized for their lack of inter-cooperation, inadequate monitoring and control of protected sites, and the absence of qualified or experienced staff. In part, these shortcomings result from the failure of the government to provide these institutions with sufficient financial resources to carry out their missions. But critics argue that the INAC, Dirección, and Comisión have done little more than identify and designate historic sites and districts and could be developing effective management policies and completing conservation projects at these sites.[32]

Nonetheless, the legislation and administrative structures for architectural conservation in Panama are thorough and, if implemented through increased will and funding, could certainly ensure the protection of the country's cultural heritage. Because its amazing architectural and engineering heritage testifies to the important place Panama holds in world history, the country will hopefully soon recognize how its canal, if preserved and exploited more wisely, could act as an important economic force in the country's future—not only from the shipping that passes through its locks but also from the visitors who would come to appreciate its design and historical significance.

CONTEMPORARY CHALLENGES AND OPPORTUNITIES IN CENTRAL AMERICA

Architectural conservation activities and legislation experiences vary from country to country in Central America, yet these countries also share many aspects of their histories and face many of the same challenges today. Though many Central American governments have made serious commitments to protecting their built heritage in recent years, conservation efforts have been slowed due to a lack of financial resources. In many cases, this has meant facades are restored, but there is no funding for interiors or long-term planning and maintenance. Most Central American countries have some distance to go in having full capacities for adequately conserving their extensive architectural heritage, and training opportunities in the region are limited even with the programs of the GCI and the AECID. Another concern experienced by architectural conservationists throughout Central America today is the low level of public interest and participation in heritage protection. In addition, the illicit trade of historic objects has been an important legal issue with which all Central American countries have struggled throughout the twentieth century, and looting of archaeological sites continues to be a serious problem throughout the region.[33]

The extraordinary built heritage of Central America has prompted international organizations and foreign governments to get involved in an effort to make up for the lack

Figure 32–22 New directions in cultural heritage conservation in Central America include protection of some of the region's intangible heritage, including music such as that performed by Guatemalan street musicians. As a result of various national legislation and further bolstered by the passage of the UNESCO Convention on Intangible Heritage in 2002, there will be heritage protection work of this kind in Central America and other Latin American countries for decades to come. Where built cultural patrimony is involved, there is an opportunity for these two kinds of heritage protection to be mutually reinforing.

of financial resources of the Central American countries. Foreign universities, especially from the United States, have actively participated in the excavation and conservation of archaeological sites in the region throughout the twentieth century. Interest in Central American heritage now extends far beyond the region's North American neighbors, though. Because of its cultural and historic connections with the region, Spain, through the AECID, has also been active in promoting and conserving Central American cultural heritage. In 1999 representatives of the European Union met with leaders from throughout Latin America and committed to help with the conservation of cultural heritage among other improvements in relations between the two regions. Soon thereafter, the German Agency for Technical Cooperation initiated a project called FODESTUR (Fomento al Desarrollo Sostenible mediante el Turismo en Centroamérica) to promote the use of natural and cultural heritage in sustainable development and tourism in various Central American countries. The successful program was renewed in 2003 with an additional investment of $3 million.[34] In addition, in its first ever bilateral cultural project, Taiwan offered to restore a museum and monastery complex in Antigua, Guatemala, in 2005.

There have been other regional cooperative initiatives that addressed the broader scope of conserving both natural and cultural heritage. One is the Corredor Biológico Mesoamericano (Mesoamerican Biological Corridor), which was established in 2000 as a six-year trial conservation accord uniting the Central American governments with those of five states in southern Mexico to promote sustainable development. Though the proposed corridor's primary emphasis is on environmental protection, cultural heritage conservation has clearly been an important component of its planning as well. Within the Corridor, the Sierra del Lacandón National Park in Guatemala, including the ruins of the Mayan city of Piedras Negras, is managed by the private organization Defensores de la Naturaleza (Defenders of Wildlife). This organization has developed an initiative called the Binational Cooperation for the Development of Community Ecotourism on the Usumacinta River in conjunction with Conservation International in Chiapas and the support of USAID-México. This project seeks to build cooperative regional efforts for increasing responsible tourism through the participation of local communities and stimulation of greater investments in local populations.

Throughout Central America, the protection of intangible cultural heritage, including traditional knowledge, practices, languages, and festivals, has been at the forefront of conservation movements since the 1990s.[35] The loss of indigenous peoples reached unprecedented numbers in the twentieth century with the extinction of more native groups than in any other period of history.[36] These Central American populations were targets of civil wars and have had to struggle to maintain their land and identities. Increased awareness and discussion of these issues has led to a broader definition of cultural property within the region, and much of the legislation passed in the 1990s reflects these concerns. In addition, the region's indigenous communities themselves have increased efforts to protect their own cultural heritage.

The countries of Central America are the caretakers of a complex combination of culture, history, and biodiversity. The ways in which protecting environmental and cultural sites have been intertwined in Central America represent a unified effort to safeguard its heritage and could provide models for other regions. As the region's heritage conservation movement has matured, the importance of its historic sites has been integrated into government policies and numerous organizations have established international conservation partnerships. The innovative policies and projects that have emerged from recent regional cooperation have improved the conditions of Central American heritage sites as well as their prospects for the future. Clearly, the multilateral approaches to the various complicated issues in the region reveal that despite limited resources, Central America will soon match global conservation standards and practices.

Endnotes

1. Edelberto Rivas Torres, "Crisis and Conflict, 1930 to the Present," in *Central America since Independence*, ed. Leslie Bethell (Cambridge: Cambridge University Press, 1991), 49–118.

2. "Convention on the Protection of the Archaeological, Historical, and Artistic Heritage of the American Nations," Organization of American States, Office of International Law, www.oas.org/juridico/English/treaties/c-14.html (accessed March 22, 2010).

3. John C. Everitt, "The Growth and Development of Belize City," *Journal of Latin American Studies* 18, no. 1 (May 1984): 107.

4. "The Ancient Monuments and Antiquities Act," 1972, Substantive Laws of Belize, www.belizelaw.org/lawadmin/index2.html (accessed March 22, 2010).

5. "Welcome to the NICH," National Institute of Culture and History, http://www.nichbelize.org (accessed March 22, 2010).

6. "Tráfico Ilícito de Patrimonio Cultural de Guatemala: Base Legal," Comercialización de Objetos del Patrimonio Cultural, www.minex.gob.gt/index.php?option=com_content&task=view&id=82&Itemid=68 (accessed March 22, 2010).

7. Juan Antonio Valdes, "Management and Conservation of Guatemala's Cultural Heritage: A Challenge to Keep History Alive," in *Art and Cultural Heritage: Law, Policy, and Practice*, ed. Barbara T. Hoffman (Cambridge and New York: Cambridge University Press, 2004), 99.

8. Judith Dobrzynski, "To Save Mayan Artifacts from Looters, a Form of Protective Custody," *New York Times*, March 31, 1998, E1.

9. Elizabeth Bell, *Antigua Guatemala: The City and Its Heritage* (Antigua: Antigua Tours, 1999), 189–92.

10. Edin Hernández, "Guatemala: Retail Project Spells Dispute in Antigua," *Tierramerica*, February 17, 2003; www.tierramerica.info/nota.php?lang=eng&idnews=1840&olt=252 (accessed March 22, 2010).

11. E. Wyllys Andrews V, "Obituary: Stanley Harding Boggs, 1914–1991," *American Antiquity* 61 no. 1 (January 1996): 57–61.

12. Government of El Salvador, "El Salvador," *Implementation of the International Covenant on Economic, Social and Cultural Rights*, Addendum to the UN Committee on Economic, Social, and Cultural Rights Regular Session of 2005, December 4, 2004 (Geneva: Office of the UN High Commissioner for Human Rights, 2005), 133.

13. Ibid.

14. ICOMOS, "Joya de Cerén Archaeological Site," Advisory Body Evaluation, no. 675, October 12, 1992, http://whc.unesco.org/archive/advisory_body_evaluation/675.pdf (accessed July 15, 2010).

15. The traditional building schools, known as workshop schools, or *Escuela Talleres*, are part of Spain's effort to conserve Iberian heritage in the Americas. Located in numerous cities of Latin

America, the schools train students of high school age to become architectural conservators. There are six of these workshop schools in Central America: in León and Granada (Nicaragua), Antigua and Quetzaltenango (Guatemala), Comayagua (Honduras), and Suchitoto (El Salvador).

16. Gloria Lara-Pinto, "Honduras: Cultural Heritage at the Crossroads of Modernity," ICOMOS World Report on Monuments and Sites in Danger 2002, www.international.icomos.org/risk/2002/honduras2002.htm (accessed March 22, 2010).

17. Carmen Julia Fajardo Cardona, "Archaeological Investigation and Conservation in Honduras," *SAA Bulletin* 15 no. 1 (January 1997), www.saa.org/Portals/0/SAA/publications/SAAbulletin/15-1/SAA14.html (accessed July 13, 2010).

18. Sara Castillo Vagas, "Costa Rica's Legal Framework for the Sponsorship and Protection of its Cultural Heritage," in Hoffman, *Art and Cultural Heritage*, 452.

19. ICOMOS, "León Viejo (Nicaragua)," Advisory Body Report, no. 613 rev., October 7, 1994, http://whc.unesco.org/archive/advisory_body_evaluation/613rev.pdf (accessed March 22, 2010).

20. ICOMOS Nicaragua, "Nicaragua," *Heritage@Risk 2000* (Paris: ICOMOS, 2000), www.international.icomos.org/risk/world_report/2000/nicar_2000.htm (accessed March 22, 2010).

21. Government of Nicaragua, *Palacio Nacional de la Cultura Reconstrucción e Historia* (Managua: Gobierno de Nicaragua. 1996).

22. Shoshanna Levy, ed., *Panamá, el Casco Antiguo* [Panama, the Old Quarter] (Panama: Editart, 1999), 71.

23. Oficina del Casco Antiguo Ciudad de Panama, http://www.cascoantiguo.gob.pa/ (accessed July 24, 2010).

24. ICOMOS, "The Historic District of Panamá City, with the Salon Bolivar," Advisory Body Report, no. 790, September 29, 1995, http://whc.unesco.org/archive/advisory_body evaluation/790bis.pdf (accessed March 22, 2010).

25. ICOMOS, "Panama Viejo (Panama)," Advisory Body Report, no. 790 bis., February 1, 2002, http://whc.unesco.org/archive/advisory_body_evaluation/790bis.pdf (accessed March 22, 2010).

26. The San Lorenzo Fortress was neglected during the decades it was incorporated within the U.S. Army base of Fort Sherman. Once returned to Panama in 1979, it was immediately recognized at the national and international level, but no management plans or institutions were established, no tourist facilities were built, and no conservation activities were carried out. In July 2001, USAID and the U.S. National Forest Service sponsored a report that proposed ideas for the fortress' interpretation and long-term care. Today a comprehensive San Lorenzo Project is working to protect the fortress in association with the surrounding wetlands, forests, and the Chagres River. ICOMOS, "Panama," *Heritage@Risk 2000* (Paris: ICOMOS, 2000), www.international.icomos.org/risk/world_report/2000/panama_2000.htm (accessed July 13, 2010); Daniel Mattson and Ramiro Villalvazo, *Castillo San Lorenzo Panama Concepts for Interpretation and Site Planning: A Prelude to Master Planning*, July 2001 (report, USAID/Panama by the USDA Forest Service International Institute of Tropical Forestry, July 2001), www.sanlorenzo.org.pa/docs/Concepts for Interpretation and the Site Planning.pdf (accessed March 22, 2010).

27. The phased turnover of the Canal Zone's support structures actually began in 1977.

28. Samuel A. Gutiérrez, *Arquitectura de la época del Canal 1880–1914* (Panama: EUPAN, 1984), 124.

29. James Conaway, "Zoning Out," *Historic Preservation* 50, no. 4 (1998): 38–47.

30. "Master Plan 2005–2025," Panama Canal Authority, www.pancanal.com/eng/plan/temas/plan-maestro/ (accessed July 13, 2010). The Master Plan expresses concern for protecting the surrounding natural environment, which makes the lack of provision for the built heritage of the zone all the more obvious.

31. Though not housed in any of the Canal Zone properties, this building is important to the canal's history. It was built in the 1870s as a hotel, but it served as the headquarters for the French company that started the canal in the 1880s as well as that of the Americans, until their Canal Administration Building was completed in 1910.

32. ICOMOS, "Panama."

33. For example, more than 90 percent of Guatemalan archaeological sites and 75 percent of the sites in neighboring Belize have been looted. This issue is exacerbated by deforestation, resulting in increased visibility and access to sites that were once protected by the dense forest canopy. Due to the lucrative trade in antiquities, generating $4.5 billion worldwide annually, even protected sites and archaeological museums are at risk. Manus Brinkman, "The Causes of Illicit Traffic in Cultural Property," *Legal and Other Issues in Protecting Cultural Heritage: The Latin American and Caribbean Experience in Context*, ed. Barbara T. Hoffman (London: International Bar Association, 2003).

34. Yashpal Rao, "Development: German Aid for Promoting Tourism in Central America," *Global Information Network*, March 21, 2002, 1.

35. Lynn V. Foster, *A Brief History of Central America* (New York: Facts on File, 2000), 25.

36. IUCN (International Union for Conservation of Nature) Inter-Commission Task Force on Indigenous Peoples, *Indigenous Peoples and Sustainability: Cases and Actions* (Utrecht: IUCN and International Books, 1997), 57.

Caribbean Sea

ATLANTIC
OCEAN

VENEZUELA

GUYANA

SURINAME

FRENCH
GUIANA

COLOMBIA

Equator

ECUADOR

Amazon

P
E
R
U

A
N
D
E
S

B R A Z I L

BOLIVIA

PARAGUAY

Tropic of Capricorn

PACIFIC
OCEAN

C
H
I
L
E

A
N
D
E
S

A
R
G
E
N
T
I
N
A

URUGUAY

ATLANTIC
OCEAN

Falkland Islands
(Islas Malvinas)

0   500   1000 mi

0   500   1000   1500 km

South America's cultural heritage is a kaleidoscope of traditions, historic architecture, artifacts, and legacies that have marked the continent's dramatic landscapes and that stretch from the Caribbean Sea to the Antarctic Ocean. The cultural and geographic regions of the continent—the non-Iberian coast, the Andes, Brazil, and the Southern Cone—all have distinctive aspects but also overlapping characteristics based on their shared histories and the common influences of pre-Colombian societies and colonial regimes as well as cycles of economic and political growth and instability since independence in the early nineteenth century. The architectural heritage of South America includes complex stone and earthen architecture built by indigenous peoples; fortresses, churches, elaborate altar pieces, and ambitious city planning that reflect the arrival of the Spanish and other European powers; eclectic and neoclassical structures, wide tree-lined boulevards, and railroads that remain as evidence of the early independence period; and numerous examples of exemplary modern architecture and industrial engineering from the past century.

Although isolated instances of cultural heritage protection occurred in South America during the late colonial period, and early legislation on the subject was passed in the nineteenth century by countries such as Colombia, in general, architectural conservation on the continent has been an endeavor that has gained recognition and become a priority only since the mid-twentieth century. It was then that most major South American cities experienced a rapid expansion and intense development that threatened, destroyed, or abandoned the continent's historic architecture. This resulted in concern for architectural conservation as expressed in the Norms of Quito in 1967, the First Brazilian Seminar about the Preservation and Revitalization of Historic Centers in 1987, and the Declaration of San Antonio in 1996. As elsewhere in the Americas and throughout the world, the development of these charters reflects the growth of cultural heritage protection from a focus on monuments and districts to a broader definition for protection of cultural diversity and intangible expressions of culture.

The principal architectural conservation issue in South America today is the continued migration of the population from rural communities to urban centers, leading to unplanned development and loss of cultural identity. Capital cities such as Caracas, Venezuela, demonstrate this rapid unplanned development that has left sections of historic urban fabric in pockets surrounded by twentieth-century construction. The continued arrival of migrants from the rural areas of Venezuela has resulted in the construction of informal settlements on Caracas's hillsides and the transformation of many of the historic buildings of its center into overcrowded tenements. These results, which are common to all of South America's capital cities and other large metropolitan areas, have increasingly challenged conventional planning techniques. Furthermore, rapid changes in the urban environment exacerbated by migration have caused a loss of identity in these cities, as well as in the abandoned and neglected rural and traditional landscapes and in the smaller towns migrants leave behind.

Other issues facing architectural conservation professionals and government agencies in South America concerned with heritage protection in recent decades have included the pressing need to replace confusing and inefficient legislation, to create a public conservation consciousness, to increase funding for heritage conservation activities, and to develop additional training opportunities for heritage conservation professionals. Efforts to combat this trying situation developed increasingly through the 1990s and early twenty-first century with legislative reforms in many countries and the adoption of new master plans by numerous municipalities. Reforms in the management of historic resources also occurred at archaeological sites such as Machu Picchu in Peru. Work to raise public awareness and appreciation of cultural heritage are apparent in the recent formation of local and NGOs such as the Volunteers for Patrimony in Chile and the Jodensavanne Foundation in Suriname.

Increased funding for architectural conservation in South America has come from the involvement of an increasing number of international organizations and private sponsors. For example, Esso Chile (the Exxon Company's Chilean subsidiary) has provided funding and encouraged other donors to support the conservation of the wooden churches of the archipelago of Chiloé. Additionally, American Express has funded projects through the World Monuments Fund, which has in the past fifteen years especially increased its identification and support of conservation projects throughout South America. Since the 1970s, growing partnerships with the Organization of American States (OAS), UNESCO, ICOMOS, and the United Nations Development Program (UNDP) as well as with foreign governments—especially Spain and the United States—have provided funding, training, and models upon which the field has grown significantly in South America.

The wide range of cultural and natural assets of South America create an excellent opportunity for a burgeoning tourism industry that, as of yet, remains largely unrealized. With the United States and Canadian markets to the north and the official languages of Spanish and Portuguese making it accessible to Europeans and Central Americans, South America could easily compete with other tourist destinations. With the political stability that has returned to most South American countries in recent decades, such cultural tourism is beginning to develop alongside ecotourism as beneficial not only to the economy as a whole but also to those seeking to keep the continent's architectural heritage intact. Urban districts, civil and religious monuments, museums, archaeological sites, folklore, and arts and crafts have all figured prominently into this new form of tourism.

Yet, despite the increasing commitment to architectural conservation in South America in the past few decades, cultural heritage protection is still not a strong priority in this region. Much of what could be developed to attract tourist revenue is at risk, mostly due to the continuing lack of awareness of the value of preserving and presenting cultural heritage. Indeed, though much effort has been exerted to protect South America's historic sites, there are many historic towns and districts and works of architecture still in need of conservation attention or improved management. This leads many heritage protection professionals to argue that the future of South America's cultural heritage hinges on stronger legislation, increased government commitments, further regional accords, and improved public education—elements essential to protect the richness and diversity of the historic architecture of any region.

Figure 33-1 As a result of subordinization by European colonizers, only petroglyphs and scant archaeological evidence remain of the indigenous Arawak and Carib people who populated what is now Guyana and the surrounding Caribbean region. A petroglyph at the Arawak site of Mdoruka Waini is illustrated here.

C H A P T E R *33*

The Non-Iberian Coast
Guyana, Suriname, and French Guiana

The northeastern part of the South American continent was known as the "wild coast" by its earliest Spanish explorers because of its seemingly impenetrable jungles as well as its abundance of indigenous communities. As a result, it was largely passed over by the Spanish only to be subsequently colonized by the Dutch, English, and French, who quickly supplanted and enslaved the original inhabitants of the region. In 1615 the Dutch West India Company established the first settlement on this coast, while the English moved further into the interior, and the French focused on the east. Though their territories overlapped and individual settlements frequently changed hands, by the early nineteenth century, each of these European countries had established a firm colony in a portion of this area: the British controlled today's Guyana, the Dutch Suriname, and the French what is today's Guiana. As a result, these three countries are sometimes referred to as the non-Iberian coast, and they are historically, linguistically, and culturally aligned more with the Caribbean region than their mainland South American neighbors.

Due to the unique histories of Guyana, Suriname, and French Guiana, the region is also distinguished by the influence of the cultures of the subordinated indigenous people, enslaved Africans, and indentured laborers from China, India, and Indonesia, who were brought in to provide labor or immigrated there during the colonial era. In Guyana, where the British primarily brought laborers from India, more than half of the population today is of Indian descent. In contrast, French Guiana received a large number of African laborers from the French colonies, and more than 70 percent of the current population is of Creole African descent.[1] In Suriname no cultural group constitutes a majority today, and it remains a mosaic of indigenous, Creole, Indian, Javanese, and European traditions with highly diverse heritage, cuisine, language, and arts.

Actions to preserve this diverse heritage and the historic sites in these three countries began in the mid-twentieth century. Though the countries of the non-Iberian coast share similar histories, their architectural conservation policies and practices have been shaped by their different colonizers and the contemporary relationship of each with these former European powers. French Guiana remains part of France today, and its cultural heritage is thus protected by the strong French legislation and policies. Suriname is independent, but it continues to receive technical and financial support for heritage from the Netherlands. Alternatively, Guyana has forged a truly independent path since its separation from Great Britain, and it is now tackling national architectural conservation matters

585

on its own and in conjunction with international organizations. While Suriname has focused on its colonial sites, Guyana and French Guiana have struck a better balance between colonial heritage and that of its indigenous and non-European communities. But in all three countries, the past two decades have witnessed growing interest in and the development of increasingly sophisticated cultural heritage protection.

GUYANA

The Italian Amerigo Vespucci was among the first Europeans to see Guyana's coast in 1499, and its interior was explored a century later by Englishman Sir Walter Raleigh, who searched its rainforests in vain for the legendary city of El Dorado. Both the Dutch and British established settlements in the area in the early seventeenth century, enslaving and decimating most of the indigenous population. Control passed back and forth between the two European powers until 1803, after which Guyana remained consistently British.

After gaining self-rule in 1961, the government of Guyana began systematically conserving its cultural heritage. Within two years, a National History and Arts Council and a Standing Committee for the Preservation and Protection of Architectural Monuments and Historic Sites were established. After securing complete independence in 1966, further measures were taken, including the founding of museums dedicated to anthropology, African art, and the fine arts. In 1972 legislation was passed establishing the National Trust of Guyana, an institution similar to its counterparts elsewhere in the Anglophone Caribbean. Though experts and laymen alike argue Guyana's cultural heritage legislation and protective institutions could be more effective, the efforts marked an important step forward.

The 1990s witnessed renewed interest in cultural heritage in Guyana, beginning with the Department of Architecture of the University of Guyana receiving a grant from UNESCO in 1995 to record historic buildings and establish a Center for Architectural Heritage, Research, and Documentation (CAHRD).[2] An inventory of eighty important wooden structures in Guyana was compiled in 2003, and by 2007 nine official national monuments had been designated, including seventeenth- and eighteenth-century forts, nineteenth-century churches and public buildings, and twentieth-century commemorative monuments.

Responsibility for maintaining these sites today is vested in the National Trust, which has successfully protected them, yet has also been criticized for not acting proactively or vigorously on behalf of Guyana's cultural heritage in general. In large part, due to a lack of adequate funding to extend its activities, the Trust has forgone advocacy for many threatened sites (and similar duties) taken on by other Caribbean National Trusts.

Beginning in 2003, community activism fueled the recognition and consolidation of the historic fabric of Guyana's capital city of Georgetown. Its site on the mouth of the Demerara River was selected by the British in 1781, but it was quickly taken over by the French, who established building guidelines and paved its first roads with brick. Soon thereafter it fell under the control of the Dutch, who planned its gridiron layout and built drainage canals before the settlement was returned to the British, who renamed it Georgetown in 1812. The town grew significantly in the late nineteenth century, and most of its surviving historic structures are examples of the eclectic architecture of that period, including the neoclassical Parliament, the Tudor-revival Stabroek Market, and the neo-Gothic St. George's Cathedral—one of the world's tallest wooden structures at 143 feet high (43.6 meters). It was also during the late nineteenth century that the stilt architecture characteristic of the indigenous Arawak communities on the coast re-emerged as part of the Creole style in Georgetown. The designs of these wooden structures incorporated decorative balconies and louvered windows called jalousies.

Figure 33-2 The nineteenth-century Cara Lodge, with the region's characteristic jalousied windows, is representative of Georgetown, Guyana's wooden urban architectural heritage. Conserving the architecture of Guyana has mostly been the responsibility of the country's National Trust.

Since 2003 the Guyanese government has invested $6 million for the rehabilitation and reconstruction of ten government buildings in Georgetown's designated preservation zone.[4] Initiatives have also included establishing guidelines and limits for conservation intervention, supporting training programs in traditional timberworking skills, and educating the public about the economic benefits of architectural conservation. In an effort to promote the city on an international scale, in February of 2003 Georgetown hosted a "Thematic Expert Meeting on Wooden Urban Heritage in the Caribbean Region," which was organized by the Organization of the Wider Caribbean on Monuments and Sites (CARIMOS) and UNESCO's World Heritage Center. In addition, preliminary actions were taken to promote Georgetown's nomination to the World Heritage List, although the application is still pending today. A 2005 study carried out by the University of Guyana, with the assistance of international experts, argued that $20 million was needed to rehabilitate the city's historic buildings, implement the management plan drafted that same year, and to prepare the city for World Heritage status.

Fire has always been a major threat to the impressive wooden heritage of Guyana, with the most serious recent loss being the neo-Renaissance Church of the Sacred Heart, which was a noted landmark on Georgetown's Main Street for more than 140 years. It was devastated in half an hour by a fire on Christmas morning in 2004. The rapid loss of the church and three adjacent buildings raised concerns about the fire-preparedness of historic structures in the predominately wooden city. The disaster was followed by calls for improvements at key sites—especially others constructed of the same combustible pitch pine as the church—as well as for an assessment of the capabilities of the Guyana Fire Service, which had been unable to respond effectively and save the church.

Architectural conservation interest and activity in Guyana has focused on Georgetown, while many important structures elsewhere in the country have yet to be appreciated. Other concerns have not been addressed by Guyana's emerging architectural conservation community, such as the loss of the country's industrial heritage. The destruction of the Georgetown-Rosignol railway line—said to be the first railway in South

Figure 33-3 Urban conservation in Georgetown, Guyana, has entailed the full range of interventions from rehabilitations and adaptive use—such as a former residence restored and transformed into an office for an international NGO (a)—to complete restoration and reconstruction of key structures, such as the completely rebuilt neo-Renaissance Church of the Sacred Heart (b), which had been destroyed by a fire in 2004.

America—caused community alarm, but desires for a progressive new highway system sealed the fate of the historic railroad.[5]

While the Guyanese government has not protected all the assets of its built environment, it has made an effort to recognize the diversity of the population through heritage celebrations such as the "East Indian Arrival Day" in May, the dedication of the month of September to the recognition of its indigenous heritage, and of the month of August to African emancipation.[6] Guyana has also been actively involved in regional initiatives focused on cultural heritage. For example, the National Trust of Guyana has participated actively in the OAS and the heritage database project of CARIMOS.

SURINAME

Located between Guyana and French Guiana, Suriname was a Dutch colony until gaining self-rule in 1954 and independence in 1975. Originally settled by the British in the early seventeenth century, in 1667 Suriname was traded to the Netherlands in exchange for their North American colony of New Amsterdam (today's New York City). Like its neighbors, Suriname's history was dominated by prosperous sugar plantations, and its contemporary population reflects the same mixture of indigenous peoples, descendants of enslaved Africans, and Chinese, Indian, and Javanese laborers, and creoles of mixed European and other ancestry. However, unlike Guyana, which has sought to distance itself from Great Britain since independence, Suriname has continued to maintain close cultural and financial ties with the Netherlands.

The Dutch oversaw the founding of Suriname's first museums, which began collecting the colony's movable heritage in the late nineteenth century. In 1952, the Dutch administration also passed the first legislation for the protection of Suriname's historic sites and prohibiting the export of objects dating to before 1900. This legislation was updated in the early 1960s during the period of self-rule, and at that time the first heritage inventories were carried out, the Commissie tot behoud van voorwerpen welke historische, culturele dan wel wetenschappelijke waarde hebben voor Suriname (Commission to Preserve Objects of Historical, Cultural and Scientific Value of Suriname) was established, and the first examples of art, architecture, and archaeological sites were designated as protected.[7] Architectural conservation efforts in Suriname were furthered in 1967 with the creation of the nonprofit Foundation for Care and Maintenance of Monuments, whose working list of historic buildings was adopted by the government in 1987 as Suriname's official list of protected sites.[8] Since 1980 the Directoraat Cultuur (Cultural Directorate) of the Surinamese Ministry of Education and Community Development has assisted the Commissie in efforts to conserve the country's cultural heritage.

The twenty-first century began with a vigorous campaign to improve the condition and recognition of cultural heritage in Suriname. In 2001 a new countrywide cultural policy was drafted that included heritage conservation as one of its central pillars, and a new Monuments Bill was passed allowing for the protection of entire historic districts with design guidelines for interventions. This most recent legislation also provided for low-interest loans for property owners carrying out restoration projects on recognized historic sites. In addition, in 2001, Suriname signed a treaty with the Netherlands in which the former colonial power agreed to finance restoration projects at sites that reflected the two countries' shared heritage, beginning with the late-seventeenth-century Zeelandia Fortress.

In 2001 the Surinamese government also established the Surinaamse Monumenten Beheer Maatschappij NV(Suriname Heritage Management Corporation Limited) as an independent organization specifically focused on the sensitive development of the capital city of Paramaribo.[9] Paramaribo was originally an Arawak village on the Suriname River but was subsequently appropriated by the French who began construction of a fort in 1650 that became the cornerstone of the settlement. Unlike Georgetown in Guyana, Paramaribo's plan was more determined by topographical features, including the location of existing creeks, and as a result was less orthogonal and rigid.[10] Paramaribo was eventually inhabited by the English and then reclaimed by the Dutch, who rebuilt the predominantly wooden city after fires in 1821 and 1832 in a style typical of other Dutch Caribbean colonies.

Today, Independence Square, located behind Fort Zeelandia and surrounded by major public buildings, is the town's central civic amenity. Most of the architecture of the city is uniform in design: wooden houses above brick basements, with high-pitched roofs, green shutters, and white painted facades. However, the multicultural and multi-

a

b

Figure 33-4 The close ties between Suriname and the Netherlands since the South American country gained self-rule in 1954 and independence in 1975 has ensured continuity in the country's heritage protection and museum institutions. Restoration of the late-seventeenth-century Zeelandia Fortress situated on the Suriname River (a) and several of its key buildings (b) beginning in 2001 was celebrated as an example of conservation of the two countries' "shared heritage." The project was accomplished through an accord between the governments of Suriname and the Netherlands.

religious background of Suriname's population is revealed by Paramaribo's historic sites, which include two synagogues built by Brazilian Jewish settlers, a mosque built by Javanese immigrants, and numerous churches, including a late-nineteenth-century Roman Catholic cathedral.

In 1997 a temporary Stichting Gebouwd Erfgoed Suriname (Suriname Urban Heritage Foundation) began developing a master plan for the growth and conservation of Paramaribo. In 2001 this foundation's work was taken over by the government-mandated Surinaamse Monumenten Beheer Maatschappij, which today acquires, restores, and maintains sites in the city as well as completes conservation projects at privately owned sites on a contractual basis. In addition, a trust fund was established by the Dutch government, the Getty Conservation Institute, and the European Union to offer low-interest

Figure 33-5 The Surinaamse Monumentenbeheer Maatschappij (Suriname Heritage Management Corporation) has since 2001 acquired, restored, and maintained historic buildings in the capital city of Paramaribo. Planning for the growth and conservation of the mostly wooden Dutch and British colonial buildings in this now World Heritage city on a contractual basis has been a collaborative project based on urban civic trusts and revolving fund schemes developed in Amsterdam. A house and small church on Malebatrum Srtaat are representative of the capital's preserved urban architecture.

loans for restoration projects in the city.[11] Paramaribo was added to the World Heritage List in 2002 as a result of its strong new management plan and the clear commitment toward preserving architectural integrity, which had resulted from the continued maintenance of its building's throughout their history and the fact that most additions and repairs had been made using traditional materials and techniques.

Another of the most interesting and important historic sites in Suriname—and one that has also begun to attract international attention—is the settlement of Jodensavanne, founded in the seventeenth century by Sephardic Jews from Europe as well as fleeing persecution at that time in Brazil. Its Beracha Ve Shalom (Blessings and Peace) synagogue was built in 1685 of brick used as ballast in British ships, and it is among the earliest synagogues in the western hemisphere. After a devastating fire in 1832, the community was abandoned until 1971 when the Stichting Jodensavanne (Foundation for Jodensavanne) was founded with support from the Dutch government. The Stichting Jodensavanne began conserving what remained of the synagogue's foundations, clearing the overgrowth from the site's two cemeteries, and establishing a small visitor center and museum to display archaeological finds revealed during these processes.

Political instability in Suriname in the 1980s prevented the ongoing maintenance of Jodensavanne, which was quickly reclaimed by the jungle. The importance and precarious state of the site led to its placement on the World Monuments Fund's Watch list of endangered sites in 1996. Following this listing, the WMF Jewish Heritage Program assisted North American researchers who led renewed efforts to clear and document the synagogue's foundations and cemeteries. Since 2008 the ruins of the Jodensavanne settlement the site have been effectively preserved and presented.

In part due to the interests of the international parties that have primarily funded architectural conservation efforts in Suriname, the focus has been on Dutch colonial architecture as well as on exceptional sites like Jodensavanne. But as interest in architectural conservation broadens in Suriname and activities continue to expand, the Surinamese government has looked to the private and community sectors for help. These locally initiated and funded projects will certainly begin to address the heritage of the country's indigenous and non-European immigrant populations in a more systematic and thorough fashion and thus indicate a bright future for a movement that already has significant momentum.

a

Figure 33-6 Conservation of the seventeenth-century brick remains of the Beracha Ve Shalom synagogue in Jodensavanne (a), Suriname, founded by Sephardic Jews, has garnered interest and support from international organizations including the World Monuments Fund. Since 2008 the Jodensavanne synagogue remains and landscape features of the site have been maintained (b) and aided by an interpretive program (c). Images courtesy WMF and Rachel Frankel, Architect, on behalf of Jodensavanne Foundation.

b

c

FRENCH GUIANA

The easternmost country of the non-Iberian coast, French Guiana, was also settled by Europeans who established profitable sugar plantations, but it was not the Dutch and British who dominated its history, rather the French. The plantation economy declined significantly following the abolition of slavery in 1848, but the discovery of gold six years later encouraged new development in French Guiana. The cities of Régina and Saül, two of the primary gold-rush settlements, retain much of their original architectural fabric, including recently restored historic structures such as the cathedral of Saül. Evidence of the penal colony that France established in Guiana during the second half of the nineteenth century is even more prevalent than reminders of the gold rush. The prison of Devil's Island and the town of Saint-Laurent du Maroni are two of the best preserved and most-visited examples. Founded in 1858, Saint-Laurent du Maroni reportedly received 80,000 petty criminals from France, sent to populate the colony, and the town has since undergone a number of renovations and restorations.

In 1946 French Guiana was elevated to the status of an overseas department of France, and its cultural heritage came under the protection of existing French policies and legislation. The French heritage law of 1913 had established procedures for documenting and examining historic sites and objects, and authorized state funding for up to 40 percent of restoration projects.[12] In addition, the permission of the French government is required to excavate any archaeological site or to destroy, move, or modify designated historic sites.

The French government continues to provide financial support for architectural conservation activities in French Guiana today; however, in 1992, in a decentralizing effort to shift more responsibility to the overseas territories, the Direction Régionale des Affaires Culturelles (DRAC, Regional Directorate of Cultural Affairs) was established in Guiana as a division of the French Ministry of Culture. Like the Ministry itself, DRAC's mandate covers three broad areas: cultural production, education, and heritage. DRAC has four divisions dedicated to ensuring the protection of French Guiana's cultural heritage, which focus on inventorying, historic sites, archaeology, and ethnography.

Of these divisions, the Regional Service for the Conservation of Historic Monuments is responsible for the protection, restoration, and monitoring of the movable and immovable heritage of French Guiana. France's two-tiered system of *monument classés* (classified monuments) and *monuments inscrits* (registered monuments) also applies in its overseas departments. While classified monuments are those recognized at the national level by the French Ministry of Culture, registered monuments are recognized regionally by the Guianese government. Today there are more than 160 classified and registered buildings in Guiana, 60 percent of which are located in the capital city of Cayenne, 20 percent in the town of Remire-Montjoly, and 20 percent elsewhere in the department. These sites include pre-Columbian rock art, such as in Maripasoula; colonial fortresses, such as Fort Diamant in Remire-Montjoly; early industrial heritage, such as the ruined mills and sugar cane boilers of the Mount Favard Estate; and examples of Creole architecture, such as the Franconie Museum in Cayenne. In Guiana there is also a third category of recognized but not protected heritage, *patrimonie non protégé* (PRNP), which mostly includes indigenous and Creole vernacular architecture.

The Regional Service of the General Inventory, which was established in 1999 to extend the provisions of France's 1964 Malraux Act to French Guiana, is responsible for systematically studying and recording historic buildings and objects in the department. At present, its two main focal areas for research include documenting Creole houses and the diverse heritage of the Maroni River area along the Suriname border. The multicultural communities that have lived along this river include not only the distinctive

Figure 33-7 The diverse architectural heritage of French Guiana includes a range of forms, from planter's mansions to Creole vernacular architecture, from colonial-period fortresses to prehistoric rock art, and from industrial engineering heritage to penal institutions. The remains of a sugar mill and cane boiler on the nineteenth-century Mount Favard estate are illustrated here.

Figure 33-8 Rock art created by Carib, Arawak, and other indigenous peoples as found at coastal locations between the cities of Kourou and Carapa (illustrated) constitutes a significant component of the archaeological heritage of French Guiana.

Carib, Arawak, and other indigenous peoples but also the Bushinenge—descendants of runaway slaves who had formed their own communities—and the descendants of laborers brought from India in the nineteenth century.

In addition to studying Guiana's heritage, the General Inventory Service is also responsible for publicizing information about these sites and objects, and it fulfills this by maintaining a publicly accessible library and archives, known as the Centre d'Information et Documentation (CID, Information and Documentation Center). The Regional Service of the General Inventory also publishes pocket guides to popular sites, such as the 2004 guide to the elaborately painted St. Joseph Church in Iracoubo, as well as well-illustrated monographs on other key sites and towns, such as the 2005 book on the historic structures of the penal colony town of Saint Laurent du Maroni.

The Regional Services for Archaeology and Ethnography are primarily focused on protecting and studying French Guiana's indigenous heritage. Numerous archaeological sites reflecting the first inhabitants of Guiana are dotted along the coast and throughout the forests. Typically found near waterways, these sites reveal aspects of the indigenous people's daily lives, such as characteristic pottery and jewelry. Rock carvings, however, constitute the majority of French Guiana's archaeological heritage: 232 carvings have been found along the coast between the cities of Kourou and Carapa.[13]

French Guiana is one of the poorest French overseas departments and the poorest country in South America.[14] While its physical and cultural distance from Paris has often meant it has not received the same level of financing or attention for endeavors such as architectural conservation as have other departments of France, Guiana's distance—especially since the partial decentralization of cultural affairs in the early 1990s—has also allowed it to privilege its vernacular architecture reflective of the heritage of its indigenous, Creole, and non-European immigrant populations.

With its limited resources, DRAC has been able to take important steps for the conservation of the department's historic sites, but it could benefit from the experiences of its neighbors and promote its heritage on the international scale and seek funding for projects from international organizations, foreign governments, and institutions.

ENDNOTES

1. Jerry Egger, "The Non-Iberian Coast," *Trails to Treasures: A Tour of South America's Cultural Heritage* (Washington, DC: US/ICOMOS and the World Monuments Fund, 2001), 61.

2. In 1975 the Department of Architecture, University of Guyana, became the first institution to offer a degree in architecture in the Caribbean region.

3. Dennis Williams, "Guyana," *Trails to Treasures*, 65.

4. Miranda La Rose, "Create a Culture of Conservation: Workshop on Wooden Urban Heritage Hears Detailed Inventory Proposal," *Stabroek News*, February 7, 2003.

5. "Cost Constraints?" *Stabroek News*, September 22, 2002.

6. "Honoring Our Collective Heritage," *Guyana Chronicle*, September 2, 2002.

7. Benjamin Mitrasingh, "Suriname," *Trails to Treasures*, 67.

8. Ibid., 67.

9. ICOMOS, "Paramaribo (Suriname)," Advisory Body Evaluation, no. 940, July 1998, http://whc.unesco.org/archive/advisory_body_evaluation/940rev.pdf (accessed February 27, 2010).

10. Ron van Oers, "Wooden Caribbean Cities as World Heritage: Outline for a Comparative Analysis between Paramaribo (Suriname) and Georgetown (Guyana)," in *Caribbean Wooden Treasures: Proceedings of the Thematic Expert Meeting on Wooden Urban Heritage in the Caribbean Region, 4–7 February 2003, Georgetown, Guyana*, World Heritage Papers No. 15, eds. R. van Oers and S. Haraguchi, 33–39 (Paris: UNESCO, 2005), 37.

11. ICOMOS, "Paramaribo (Suriname)," 2.

12. Sylvie Reol, "French Guiana," *Trails to Treasures*, 63.

13. Ibid., 63.

14. Since 1965 French Guiana has benefited economically from hosting a French and later European satellite launch center; however, this has not yet meant increased funding for architectural conservation. The center's construction in the town of Kourou in the 1960s led to French financing of major infrastructural improvements in Guiana, including enlarging and modernizing its sea and airports, as well as French construction of support facilities such as housing and hospitals, which have benefited all Guyanese. Today, the Guiana Space Center (Centre Spatial Guyanais) accounts for more than a quarter of French Guiana's gross domestic product (GDP) and continues to benefit the country through a multiplier effect.

Figure 34-1 The small church of Igreja do Sangrado Coracas de Jesus in Igarassu (in the right portion of illustration) dates from 1535. During the inventory of historic buildings conducted by the Institute for National Artistic and Historical Heritage (IPHAN) in 1955, it was realized that this site was the oldest surviving church in Brazil.

CHAPTER 34

Brazil

The richness of Brazil's cultural and natural heritage results from its diverse geographies, cultures, and art forms, which have combined to create an array of extraordinary historic buildings and sites. Occupying over half of South America, Brazil is also the continent's most populous country and largest economy. Uniquely in the Americas, it was the Portuguese who dominated Brazil in the colonial period and whose language and culture still prevail today. Yet, like the neighboring non-Iberian coast, Brazil's population and culture is a mixture of indigenous, African, Asian, as well as European elements. In much the same spirit as in the United States, these waves of immigrants have left indelible marks on Brazilian society, adding to the culture and the architecture of the country.

Portuguese explorers first visited the coasts of today's Brazil in 1500 and settlers began to develop towns along the east and southeast coasts of South America, beginning with São Vicente in 1532. During that early colonial period, Brazil's towns were planned according to European baroque styles and architectural design principles. By 1700 Brazil boasted fifty-eight towns, almost all of which were near the coast and were supported by a network of sugar plantations. To work these immense plantations, enslaved people from the African coast were shipped to Brazil in large numbers, supplementing the labors of the enslaved indigenous people and further diversifying the territory's growing population.[1]

In 1808 the Portuguese royal family fled Napoleon and after arriving in Brazil quickly initiated building programs in many major cities. After the king's return to Portugal, his son orchestrated Brazilian independence and formed the Empire of Brazil as a separate constitutional monarchy in 1822. During the early imperial period, King Pedro brought in a group of artists known as the "French Mission" who supplanted the baroque aesthetic with the neoclassic style—especially in Rio de Janeiro, which was transformed into a grand capital city.[2] Since the monarch was ousted in 1889, Brazil has oscillated between democratic republics and military-style dictatorships, but both types of government have sponsored new building programs and consistently prioritized architectural conservation.

Brazil's climate, with its mostly high humidity and lush vegetation, has long threatened its historic buildings, and throughout history there has been a need to address their deterioration. Concern for protecting cultural heritage occurred early in Brazil and developed at an accelerated pace, leading to the well-developed architectural conservation practices of today. Brazil's long-standing respect for the historic built environment differentiates it from many of its South American neighbors. Today, the protection of Brazil's built heritage has taken center stage in an age of pressing change and urbanization.

FEDERAL EFFORTS AND ARCHITECTURAL CONSERVATION PARTNERS

One of the first deliberate acts of architectural heritage protection in the New World occurred in 1742, when Count Andre de Melo e Castro, the colonial viceroy of Brazil, ordered the preservation of the Palacio das duas Torres in Pernambuco (now Recife).[3] In the mid-nineteenth century, the imperial government gave further orders for the repair of key buildings and sites and the preservation of historic inscriptions in Brazil.

In the 1920s, a number of separate Brazilian states established commissions and inspectorates to oversee and restore historic sites within their territories. The first large scale modern architectural conservation projects were initiated at this time. For example, the foundations and other remains of the homes, schools, sacristy, and church of the village of São Miguel das Missões, which was founded in 1687 but abandoned in 1768, were consolidated in the 1920s. Toward the end of that decade, the president of the Sociedade Brasileira de Bellas Artes (Brazilian Society of Fine Arts) and the director of the recently founded National Museum began drafting federal protective legislation for built heritage. Despite a military coup in 1930, efforts to pass the law continued, and concern for natural and built heritage was expressed in the 1934 constitution.

In 1937 a constitutional decree on the Protection of Cultural Heritage was finally passed, and the Instituto do Patrimônio Histórico e Artístico Nacional (IPHAN, Institute for National Artistic and Historical Heritage) was established within a newly created Ministry of Education and Health. This law called for the registration of heritage sites at three levels—federal, state, and municipal—and obliged property owners to preserve any listed buildings and request permission to alter them. The 1937 law established the four categories of sites, called *Livros do Tombo*, still used for classifying heritage in Brazil today. These categories include the fine arts, applied arts, historical sites and objects, and sites of archaeological, ethnographic, or landscape value. The categories of fine art and historic interest have dominated Brazil's registry, and although the law covers everything from objects to landscapes, Brazil's protected heritage is overwhelmingly drawn from the built environment.[4] Within its first two years, IPHAN designated 261 monuments, six zones, and nine urban centers and initiated restoration projects at thirty-eight of these sites.[5] By 1940 IPHAN was also authorized to acquire properties for the purpose of their restoration and protection.

Brazil's president at the time of the 1937 law, Getulio Vargas, was an ardent nationalist whose regime focused on the country's Portuguese Catholic roots, and his policies also influenced the heritage sites of interest to IPHAN in its early years. Thus Brazil's historic churches and missions dominated early conservation efforts. In the 1940s, French art historian and Louvre curator Germain Bazin conducted a survey of Brazil's colonial religious architecture, which was supplemented by British scholar John B. Bury and became the basis for IPHAN's inventory of historic buildings in 1955.[6] The churches included in the initial survey and protected by IPHAN range from the extremely grand—such as the elaborate, mid-seventeenth-century Franciscan Convent of Santo Antônio in Igarassu—to the simple and humble—such as the Church of Igreja do Sangrado Coracas de Jesus in Igarassu, which was built in 1535 and is today the oldest standing church in Brazil.[7]

Since its creation, IPHAN has made impressive strides to secure Brazil's cultural patrimony by heightening public awareness of the importance of conserving the country's heritage before it disappears. Its activities focus on researching cultural heritage needs, improving its inventory database, making its database more accessible, and carrying out regularly planned conservation projects and emergency stabilization efforts at historic sites. Today IPHAN protects 960 buildings, twenty-nine historic centers, sixty-five architectural and landscape areas, and sixty-five art collections.[8] However, for this wide range of protected sites, there are no set regulations or norms, and IPHAN's decisions have

Figure 34-2 Since the mid-1990s the Monumenta program of Brazil's Ministry of Culture has been supported by the Inter-American Development Bank. In 2006 the program came under the purview of the country's Institute for National Artistic and Historical Heritage (IPHAN). Several buildings, including this streetscape in the historic town of Olinda, were restored via Monumenta's conservation program.

been seen by some as arbitrary. In addition, Brazil's vast size has often meant the process of designation and acquiring permission for alterations is slow, and distant property owners have often ignored IPHAN. Another major challenge faced by IPHAN today is the limitations of its resources, which are stretched thin by the number of sites in need of conservation.

To assist IPHAN in its concern for Brazil's heritage, several other agencies and institutions have stepped forward. UNESCO's World Heritage Center has helped by recognizing numerous historic cities and sites in Brazil.[9] One of the most important private initiatives for heritage protection in Brazil is that of the Roberto Marinho Foundation, which—since its creation in 1977—has addressed conservation projects that further its mission of promoting education and culture in Brazil. The Roberto Marinho Foundation has helped in the conservation of the Nossa Senhora do Rosario Church in Ouro Preto, the Matriz de São Antonio Church in Tiradentes, and the Portuguese Language Station in São Paulo.[10] More recently, the Foundation has worked with IPHAN on the restoration and interpretation of Rio de Janeiro's Church of the Madonna of the Merchants.

In the mid-1990s the Brazilian Ministry of Culture partnered with the Inter-American Development Bank (IDB) and UNESCO and began planning the Monumenta (Monuments) Program. In the year 2000, with a generous loan from IDB, Monumenta began projects in twenty priority cities and identified eighty additional cities for potential expansion of the program. Within five years, seventy-seven conservation projects were underway in forty-six cities. In 2006, the Monumenta program became part of IPHAN, and today it is funded 60 percent by Brazilian resources and 40 percent by the IDB.[11] This program has included a massive public education and awareness media campaign, including the production of six television documentaries focused on architectural heritage.

Moumenta's goals include improving awareness, management, and use of historic urban areas by combining heritage conservation with social and economic development. The program focuses on cities protected by IPHAN and works with local governments to establish municipal funds for conserving historic buildings, developing museums, and preserving and improving streets and public spaces.[12] Profits and rents generated from completed projects are returned to the revolving fund with the aim of making architectural conservation in each city self-sufficient. The focus of the municipal funds has been on federally listed, publicly owned buildings; however, the program has also successfully stimulated private sector involvement in conservation by offering loans to property owners and developers.

In addition to promoting local economies, the Monumenta program has also relieved the financial pressure on IPHAN by securing sustainable funding for sites that would have ordinarily fallen solely under its responsibilities. In addition, since 2001, the involved municipalities, local universities, and UNESCO have also assisted IPHAN with inventories of historic sites for potential designation as national monuments.

An example of Monumenta's success is clearly visible in the recent restoration and rehabilitation of the World Heritage city of Olinda, which in the twentieth century became part of the Recife metropolitan area. As the colonial-era capital of Brazil, Olinda (Portuguese for "how beautiful") is one of the finest surviving examples of architecture from that period in Brazil. Although the Dutch invasion of 1630 destroyed much of the town, the rebuilding resulted in a unique blend of baroque and African styles. Through the Monumenta program, numerous sixteenth- and seventeenth-century churches and houses have been restored, the latter accomplished by means of low-interest loans to private owners.[13] The Convent of São Francisco, which is located within the boundaries of the World Heritage site of Olinda, was added to the World Monuments Fund's Watch list in 2004 and 2006 because of weathering and biological growth as well as a lack of funds to stabilize the site. This international recognition proved helpful as preservation efforts followed immediately, including a conservation master plan and two campaigns of conservation work.

The Banco Nacional de Desenvolvimento Econômico e Social (BNDES, Brazilian Development Bank), a government agency associated with the Ministry of Development, Industry, and Foreign Trade, initiated a partnership with IPHAN in 1997 to preserve the country's heritage. In 2005 it began a program through which three cities would be selected as foci of BNDES architectural conservation projects for two-year periods. The first three cities selected included Olinda, Rio de Janeiro, and Ouro Preto.

Ouro Preto (Portuguese for "black gold") was one of the first towns founded after gold was discovered in Brazil in 1693 — it was named for the dark palladium surrounding the precious gold ore. Here Aleijadinho, considered the greatest Brazilian artist of the colonial era, labored to produce a rich corpus of art and architecture that has become known throughout the region. His Church of São Francisco de Assis, (built between 1765 and 1810), with interior paintings by Manoel da Costa Athayde, illustrates his mastery of the baroque style, which he adapted to specific local needs and building materials. In 2006 BDNES gave $287,000 for the restoration of the Ordem Terceira do Carmo Church and the Noviciado do Carmo house in Ouro Preto.[14] The roof and exterior masonry of the early eighteenth-century baroque church were restored, its interior paintings cleaned, and its electric systems upgraded. The facade and collections of the Noviciado, which houses a local museum, were similarly restored.

URBAN CONSERVATION AND REVITALIZATION IN BRAZIL

Brazil's protected architectural heritage is overwhelmingly urban, and historic cities have been a focus by more than the BDNES and Monumenta programs. By the mid-1980s, when IPHAN was absorbed into the newly established Ministry of Culture, it had designated more than fifty *conjuntos*, historic towns or historic districts within urban centers.[15] These include early coastal settlements and eighteenth-century gold rush towns in the north as well as twentieth-century wonders such as Brasília.

Overcrowding in urban areas has been an especially pressing urban planning and conservation issue in Brazil since the mid-twentieth century. During this period, Brazil experienced a mass migration of people from the countryside to its major coastal cities, which added to expansion and redevelopment pressures. By the early 1990s, more than 75 percent of Brazil's population lived in urban areas, and today the country has fifteen cities with a population exceeding one million people. In megacites, such as Rio de Janeiro and São Paulo, these metropolitan areas have populations in excess of ten- and twenty-million people, respectively. As the older areas of many of these cities have deteriorated developers have replaced historic areas with larger-scale buildings that accommodate greater numbers of inhabitants. In addition, the smaller inland towns that served as centers of no longer viable industries have been neglected as populations have shifted to the major coastal centers.

a

b

Figure 34-3 Some of the first large-scale urban conservation in Brazil occurred in the Bom Jesus area of Barreiro de Recife (a and b) in the 1970s, which served as an example to be followed elsewhere in Brazil. One of the more imaginative and successful schemes was instituted by the Roberto Marinho Foundation in a partnership with the city to sponsor the City Colors Projects to encourage façade restoration by painting buildings for free if owners repaired them.

Effective urban conservation therefore has presented the biggest challenge to architectural conservationists in Brazil as well as in many other countries of South America in recent decades. In 1973 IPHAN launched the Historic Cities Reconstruction Program of the Northeast, its first major, urban-focused initiative. Through this program, state funding helped spark local municipal and private interest in architectural conservation.

For example, in Recife, this program encouraged the development of the Historic Sites Preservation Plan, the passage of municipal heritage protection legislation, and the launch of a downtown revitalization program. An office to coordinate municipal investments was established in 1987, and in 1993 actual projects were first undertaken in the Bom Jesus area of Barreiro de Recife, a barrier island that forms part of the original seventeenth-century core of the city. These projects included improved urban infrastructure and public spaces as well as a handful of demonstration building restorations. The Roberto Marinho Foundation partnered with the city to sponsor the City Colors Projects to encourage facade restoration by painting buildings for free if owners repaired them. Soon thereafter other private sector investment followed.[16]

As there was only one national monument and a few state recognized historic sites in Recife, which were the focus of this conservation effort in Born Jesus, the restoration process was not subjected to strict regulations or scientific conservation principals. Though efforts were made to preserve rooflines and facades, many details were changed or removed, and most interiors were dramatically altered.[17] However, because the primary goals of preserving Barreiro de Recife included neighborhood revitalization and stimulating economic development, the initiative can be considered successful. Within three years, private investment in the Bom Jesus area exceeded public expenditures for architectural conservation, and the pattern was repeated in other neighborhoods in Barreiro de Recife.[18]

In response to more recent development pressures, IPHAN initiated the Programa de Reabilitação Urbana de Sítios Históricos (URBIS, Urban Rehabilitation Program for Historic Sites) in 2000 in an attempt to conserve historic centers of the country's ever-growing cities and simultaneously improve conditions for their current residents. Like the earlier Historic Cities Reconstruction Program, this initiative similarly combines the conservation of historic towns and cities with economic revitalization. In addition to stimulating renewal and improving residents' quality of life, the program's objectives include identifying and inventorying built cultural heritage and providing resources for its sustainable development. The rehabilitation and restoration of these historic centers assumes that tourism will play a significant part in the upkeep of these sites.

NEW DIRECTIONS IN ARCHITECTURAL CONSERVATION

Recent decades have also witnessed increasing attention in Brazil to sites that reflect cultural and architectural legacies other than the country's Portuguese and Catholic traditions. Despite years of expanding scope, Brazil's heritage conservationists are still struggling to overcome these early biases. Though two-thirds of the sites and objects protected by IPHAN date from the colonial era—and half of these are religious in nature—pre-Columbian and twentieth-century heritage sites, as well as those important to different components of the country's diverse population have finally begun to be recognized.

The impact of colonization on Brazil's indigenous people has become of increasing interest in recent decades. Most of the Guaraní peoples were converted to Catholicism by Jesuit and Franciscan missionaries, who established São Miguel das Missões and other large plantations and churches in the inland jungles of Brazil. Many of the remains of these developments still exist today. In the 1980s, São Miguel and other Jesuit missions along the Brazilian, Argentine, and Paraguayan border were added to the World Heritage List.

a

b

c

Figure 34-4 The prospects for preserving the the monumental core and numerous other structures comprising the new capital of Brasília, designed by urban planner Lúcio Costa and architect Oscar Niemeyer in the 1960s, have drawn attention from the architectural profession in general as well as from conservationists such as the international membership of DOCOMOMO. The iconic National Congress of Brazil (a), the Memorial of Indigenous Peoples (b), numerous other major buildings, and the site designs of landscape architects Roberto Burle Marx and Lina Bo Bardi (c) are all overseen by a special conservation group that ensures protection of this World Heritage site. Images (a) and (c) courtesy Theodore H. M. Prudon.

Conserving Modern Architecture in Latin America
Theodore H. M. Prudon

Architectural conservation is tied as much to the past as to the present in its perceptions. Never is this more apparent than in dealing with architecture of the recent past or, more specifically, with examples of modernism. Attitudes and approaches to modern heritage have varied between North and Latin America as well as within the various countries on the South American continent.

While much of the early scholarly discourse about Latin America followed West European historiography, this began to change in the early 1980s with the emergence of a greater recognition and appreciation of the unique regional accomplishments of the nineteenth and twentieth centuries.[19] Not surprisingly, at the time of this recognition, discussions about preserving modern architecture also became more common. In this context it is important to understand how and why modern architecture arrives in South America. In Canada and the United States, architectural modernism was initially more connected to corporate and institutional effectiveness. In many of the Latin American countries, the connections were more related to social and political issues from the outset and represented an assertion of independence, identity, and global modernity. Modern architecture symbolized a conscious break with the colonial past and suggested progress and advancement and a greater sense of self.

While in many ways the Latin American countries shared similar paths, the story about the emergence of modern architecture in Brazil is the best known case. Although Le Corbusier had visited the country earlier, it is his 1936 visit to work with a group of architects under the leadership of Lúcio Costa on the design of the Ministry of Health and Education in Rio de Janeiro that is often interpreted as a turning point. It is the particular brand of Brazilian modernism that evolved in the pre–World War II years that received so much attention in the United States and elsewhere, such as the exhibit Brazil Builds in January and February of 1943 at New York's Museum of Modern Art.[20]

Now Brazil is in the forefront in preserving this very architecture, including the work of Lúcio Costa and Oscar Niemeyer as well as the landscape architects Roberto Burle Marx and Lina Bo Bardi.[21] Brazil's capital city of Brasília, Costa and Niemeyer's masterpiece, exemplifies both the country's modernism and its recognition and protection, as it was one of the first examples of modernism to be placed on the World Heritage List in 1987, even before the listing of the Bauhaus in Dessau, Germany, which did not take place until 1996. The level of interest in preserving modern architecture in Brazil can also be gauged from its citizens' active participation in such international organizations as DOCOMOMO.[22]

While the initial trajectory for modern architecture in Argentina may be somewhat different and lesser known, it is certainly not less significant. Le Corbusier visited Argentina as early as 1929, but it was not so much his influence as the work of local architects and other émigrés that introduced modern architecture. Toward the end of the 1930s, design took a more classical turn until well after World War II when Brutalism exerted its influence.[23] Argentina was the first South American country to join DOCOMOMO, even before the orgnization's first international conference in Eindhoven, the Netherlands, in 1990.[24] Architectural preservation efforts, as in many other countries, have focused mostly on individual buildings with varying degrees of success. For instance, while the Casa Curutchet in La Plata—designed by Le Corbusier in 1954—became the headquarters of the local architectural association, the fate of the Casa del Puente—designed by the important Argentinean architect Amancio Williams in 1942—remains uncertain.

While both Brazil and Argentina were in the forefront of preserving modern architecture in the early 1990s, similar development in other Latin American countries did not begin until the turn of the twenty-first century. However today efforts in Venezuela, Colombia, Chile, and Mexico are gaining momentum and additional preservation projects are anticpated.[25] Like Brazil and Argentina, Venezuela had an early modernist tradition, as reflected in the work of Carlos Raúl Villanueva and his Ciudad Universitaria de Caracas, designed between 1940 and 1960 and placed on the World Heritage List in 2000. As in other South American countries, the design and construction of a university was one place this modern architecture could express the passage to a new future still connecting to the past. The Universidad Nacional Autónoma de México (UNAM) is another example where pre-Hispanic traditions are connected to modern architecture.[26] This site was placed on the World Heritage List in 2007.

Whereas South America shows the development of modern architecture after almost a century of independence, the picture in the Caribbean is quite different. Though it varies from country to country or island to island, in most instances, the European influence is more direct. Two exceptions are Puerto Rico and Cuba where more distinct modernist presences developed.[27] The results are remarkable and have become the subject of important preservation efforts. The National Schools of Arts in Havana have been a key site of interest in Cuba, while in Puerto Rico the work of Henri Klumb is receiving considerable attention.[28] On other Caribbean islands, government building and resort development were important stimuli for the introduction of modern architecture that still survives today.

The contrast in efforts to preserve modern architecture in Latin America, the Caribbean, and North America is interesting and striking. Whereas in many countries modern architecture is identified and accepted as progressive, and as a symbol of visual and physical acceptance of new cultural and social ideals, the attitude in North America initially lacked these annotations. Whereas in Latin America and the Caribbean it represented a break or separation from a more immediate colonial past and a search for an identity in a society with a great deal of immigration, in North America a similar process had occurred earlier and by the mid-twentieth century was seen as an often undesirable break with a more distant and idealized early history. Those very misconceptions about identity and history still play through the preservation dialogue when discussing what can and should be done with modern architecture. The intertwining of postcolonial and social and political ideals in Latin American and Caribbean countries as well as North America have led to different degrees of acceptance of cultural significance that allows for the preservation of modern architecture. For Latin America, the link between modern architecture, independence, and autonomous development has in many countries meant this heritage is privileged and appreciated by the government and population.

Brazilian Amerindian heritage is still dramatically underrepresented within the country's conservation efforts. Before the 1980s, the Ministry of Culture had not designated a single archaeological or architectural site associated with Brazil's pre-Columbian population—other than the missions and plantations where they were converted and labored. However, in 1979, the Instituto Brasileiro do Meio Ambiente e dos Recursos Naturais Renováeis (IBAMA, Brazilian Institute for the Environment and Renewable Natural Resources) established the Serra da Capivara National Park to protect the rock-hewn shelters decorated with paintings that had been discovered in the 1960s. These 300 plus sites date from 26,000 to 4,000 BCE and include the oldest traces of rock art in South America. Because of its uniqueness and importance, the park was added the World Heritage List in 1991.

Before Serra da Capivara could be added to UNESCO's list, however, measures had to be taken to ensure it was adequately protected. Therefore, in 1989, IBAMA asked the Brazilian nonprofit Fundação Museu do Homem Americano (FUNDHAM, Museum Foundation of the American Man) to oversee the park and create a management plan. With aid from the French Ministry of Culture, FUNDHAM is still responsible today for conservation within the park and has begun to address the main threats to the rock shelters and paintings, which include ceaseless biological growth and sunlight exposure. The difficulty of accessing the park has prevented it from being visited by many tourists, and that lack has also meant the absence of this potential source of funding for maintenance and conservation.

In 1988 the Brazilian government established the Fundação Cultural Palmares (Palmares Cultural Foundation) within the Ministry of Culture to focus specifically on promoting the contemporary culture and heritage of Afro-Brazilians.[29] At that time only a handful of sites related to the history of slavery in Brazil—such as the São Luis slave market and a *candomblé* religious center in Salvador de Bahia—had been recognized and protected as part of the country's heritage. Today, the Fundação Palmares's activities include promoting research on the history of Brazil's black population and disseminating this information through publications, at international forums, and in Brazilian schools. In addition, the Fundação Palmares protects and conserves the tangible and intangible heritage of Afro-Brazilians, including many of the over seven hundred documented archaeological remains of hiding places and communities established by runaway slaves during the colonial era.[30]

Only around forty sites from the past century have been protected by IPHAN thus far, and more than half of these are the major early twentieth-century public and commercial buildings built in Rio de Janeiro.[31] However, one Brazilian example of internationally important modern architecture—the city of Brasília—was quickly recognized as worthy of protection. Planning for Brasília began in 1956, and the design competition winner, urban planner Lúcio Costa, teamed with architect Oscar Niemeyer, director of the Brazilian Department of Architectural and Urban Affairs, to create the new capital city for Brazil.[32] Brasília is composed of self-contained superblock neighborhoods, each with their own commercial centers, schools, and churches. The city's monumental core is formed by the Plaza of Three Powers, which is surrounded by the Presidential Palace, Congress, Supreme Court. Nearby are located a cathedral, a national theater, and other institutions. As there was no master plan to dictate further growth or design guidelines to regulate changes within the city, concern for the urban and architectural integrity of Brasília was raised within twenty years of its becoming the official seat of government in 1960. A working group for the Preservation of the Historical and Cultural Heritage of Brasília formed in 1981, and the part of the city included in Costa's original plan—along with a green space buffer zone—was soon thereafter added to the World Heritage List.

Further evidence of the growing scope of heritage conservation efforts in Brazil in the 1990s and early twenty-first century is found in the expanded activities of local archaeologists, who have begun to investigate early industrial heritage such as sugar mills and mines as well as public places, harbors, and old roads in urban areas.[33] These and many other efforts in architectural conservation have stemmed the loss of hundreds of sites that represent the history and ingenuity of Brazilian culture.

The increase in private participation and the broadening of interests to encompass non-Portuguese immigrant communities has also led to important efforts at other historic sites in Brazil. For example, local heritage conservationists have begun championing Vila de Paranapiacaba (meaning "a place to view the sea"), a small town on a plateau overlooking São Paulo built between 1860 and 1890 by British settlers investing in the development of the regional railway. The town is characterized by wooden Victorian houses and brick industrial buildings and includes a clock tower that is a scaled-down version of London's Big Ben. Local activists in the mid-1990s encouraged the Brazilian Federal Railroad Network, which owns most of the site, to create a heritage park, and they involved the regional government in creating a development plan that will rehabilitate the town and promote cultural tourism.[34] Notable progress toward this goal has been made since 2002, when the municipality of Santo Andre acquired the Vila of Paranapiacaba and began implementing a comprehensive conservation and tourism development plan, with great visible results. International support for conserving the Vila de Paranapiacaba in the form of WMF Watch listing in 1996 and seed funding via the American Express Corporation were instrumental in launching this large industrial heritage conservation project.

Today architectural conservation is an important component of the work of the Brazilian Ministry of Culture, encompassing more than a quarter of its annual budget. Tax incentives since the 1980s have encouraged private sector participation and international organizations have also begun investing in Brazil's architectural heritage. This means IPHAN is no longer faced with safeguarding the country's vast cultural patrimony on its own. The past few decades have also witnessed increasing international

a

b

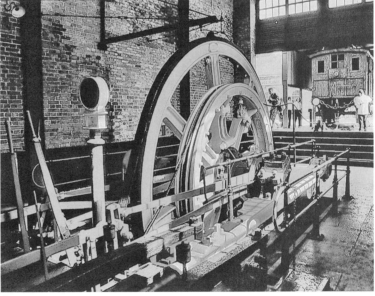

c

Figure 34-5 The mid-nineteenth century town of Vila de Paranapiacaba, located just north of São Paulo, is a planned industrial town (a) built in association with the installation of a British-designed rail transport system (b) that operated by pulling rail cars up and down a steep three-kilometer slope on a cable system in the manner of a funicular. The steam engine machinery (c) in the head house that pulled the cable, along with most all of the remainder of the industrial town, is remarkably well preserved.

recognition of Brazil's historic architecture and especially its historic cities, with ten cultural sites added to the World Heritage List since 1980. In addition, the movement toward decentralization of culture in Brazil has meant that architectural conservation responsibilities are increasingly being assumed by individual states and cities. These factors combine to suggest an optimistic future for the surviving architectural legacies of Brazil's past.

ENDNOTES

1. Boris Fausto, *A Concise History of Brazil* (Cambridge: Cambridge University Press, 1999), 11.

2. Buildings such as the Old Custom House (designed by French architect Auguste Henri Victor Grandjean de Montigny) and the Dom Pedro II Hospital and the Santa Casa de Misericórdia (designed by followers of Grandjean de Montigny) created a splendid urban ensemble in Rio de Janeiro. In addition, historicist architecture dominated the buildings of the king's summer residence in the newly founded town of Petropolis north of Rio de Janeiro.

3. Rodrigo Melo Franco de Andrade. Brazil, *Monumentos Archaeologicos Mexico City, Instituto Panamericana de Geographica e Historia*, 1952, 149. and Stephen W. Jacobs, "Architectural Preservation: American Developments and Antecedents Abroad," (doctoral dissertation), Princeton University, 1966), 338.

4. John Dickenson, "The Future of the Past in the Latin American City: The Case of Brazil," *Bulletin of Latin American Research* 13, no. 1 (1994): 17.

5. Rodrigo Melo Franco de Andrade, "Historical and Artistic Patrimony" (lecture, National School of Engineering, September 27, 1939).

6. William C. Brooks, "The Politics of Historic Preservation: João Pessoa: A Case Study" (master's thesis, Central Connecticut State University, May 2003), 54.

7. Lúcio Gomes Machado, "Brazil," in *Trails to Treasures: A Tour of South America's Cultural Heritage*, eds. US/ICOMOS and the World Monuments Fund (WMF) (Washington, DC: US/ICOMOS and the WMF, 2001), 13.

8. Jorge Werthein, Maria Dulce Almeida Borges, and Célio da Cunha, eds., *UNESCO Brazil: Framework for Action* (Brasília: UNESCO, 2001), 64.

9. Brazilian World Heritage cities include Brasília (Federal District), Salvador (Bahia), São Luís (Maranhão), Diamantina (Minas Gerais), Goiás (Goiás), Olinda (Pernambuco), and Ouro Preto (Minas Gerais).

10. Brazilian Development Bank, "Architectural Heritage: Projects," www.bndes.gov.br/English/projects6.asp (accessed February 27, 2010).

11. *UNESCO Brazil: Framework for Action*, 66.

12. Inter-American Development Bank, "Urban Heritage Preservation: Brazil," *IDB America Magazine*, November/December 1999, www.iadb.org/idbamerica/Archive/stories/1999/eng/e1299j3.htm (accessed February 27, 2010).

13. Kristina Shevory, "Restoring an Old Sugar Town…and Trying to Stymie Art Thieves," *Business Week*, May 21, 2001, www.businessweek.com/magazine/content/01_21/b3733149.htm (accessed February 27, 2010).

14. Brazilian Development Bank, "BNDES supports cultural restoration project with R\$ 591.5 thousand in Ouro Preto," May 22, 2006, www.bndes.gov.br/english/news/not070_06.asp (accessed February 27, 2010).

15. Dickenson, "The Future of the Past in the Latin American City," 17.

16. Eduardo Rojas, *Old Cities, New Assets: Preserving Latin America's Urban Heritage* (Washington, DC: Inter-American Development Bank, 1999), 71. Among the other organizations that have been active in heritage conservation in Brazil is the Vitae Foundation.

17. Ibid., 76.

18. Ibid., 63–64.

19. Fabio Grementieri, "The Preservation of Nineteenth- and Twentieth-century Heritage," in *Identification and Documentation of Modern Heritage*, eds. R. van Oers and S. Haraguchi, 82–90 (Paris: UNESCO, 2003); http://whc.unesco.org/documents/publi_wh_papers_05_en.pdf.

20. In addition to the MOMA Brazil Builds Exhibition No. 213, the media were in general very important in building the reputation of modern architecture in Brazil. Beatriz Santos de Oliveira, "1945–1970: How the Media Built Brazilian Architecture," in *Proceedings VIII International DOCOMOMO Conference*, eds. Theodore H. M. Prudon and Hélène Lipstadt, 121–128 (New York: DOCOMOMO US, 2008).

21. The work of Lina Bo Bardi has been the subject of a number of presentations at DOCOMOMO International conferences. See, for instance, Zeuler R. Lima, "Preservation as Confrontation in the Work of Lina Bo Bardi," or Marcos José, "Carrillo, The Saõ Paulo Museum of Art," in *Proceedings of the VIII International DOCOMOMO Conference*, 305–314 and 315–320.

22. Brazil, like Argentina, has been active in DOCOMOMO International for many years. In 2000 DOCOMOMO Brazil hosted the Sixth International DOCOMOMO Conference—"The Modern City Facing the Future"—in Brasília. This conference, because of its location, contained a number of papers and presentations dealing with preservation of modern architecture and planning in Latin America.

23. Examples of the pre-1940 architecture as well as that of the postwar period may be found in Dennis Sharp and Catherine Cooke, eds., *The Modern Movement in Architecture: Selection from the DOCOMOMO Registers* (Rotterdam: 010 Publishers, 2000), 18–24. Aside from Argentina and Brazil, no other Latin American country is included. For examples from Brazil, see *The Modern Movement in Architecture*, 41–48.

24. "DOCOMOMO Argentina: Twelve Years of Research and Education," *DOCOMOMO Journal* 27 (June 2002): 26–27. For a summary of Brazil's efforts, "DOCOMOMO Brazil: Ten Years After," *DOCOMOMO Journal* 27 (June 2002): 34–36.

25. One of the ways to measure interest is to be aware of the dialogue taking place in universities; for instance, conferences were held at Columbia University in 2008 on the topic and, more recently, in March of 2010 that addressed not only preservation, selection, and advocacy but also how they all relate to different cultural and ethnic groups. In most of the Latin American countries, DOCOMOMO chapters have been formed in recent years.

26. For a discussion of the preservation of the pre-Hispanic inspired murals by Juan O'Gorman on the facade of the main library, see Louise Noelle Gras, "The Restoration of Juan O'Gorman's Central Library of University City, National Autonomous University of Mexico," in *Restoring Postwar Heritage*, DOCOMOMO Preservation Technology Dossier No. 8, eds. Theodore H. M. Prudon and Kyle Normandin, 121–124 (New York: DOCOMOMO US, 2008).

27. A good summary of preservation of modern architecture in the Caribbean may be found in: *The Modern Movement in the Caribbean*, DOCOMOMO Journal 33 (September 2005). This issue, guest edited by Eduardo Luis Rodriguez and Gustavo Luis Moré, contains contributions from Cuba, Puerto Rico, Dominican Republic, Jamaica, Trinidad and Tobago, and the French West Indies. While Curaçao has since formed a DOCOMOMO chapter, there are no contributions from the Netherlands Antilles.

28. For a detailed history of the National Arts School in Havana, see John A. Loomis, *Revolution of Forms: Cuba's Forgotten Art Schools* (New York: Princeton Architectural Press, 1999). For the work of Henri Klumb in Puerto Rico, see Enrique Vivoni Farange, ed., *Klumb: Una Arquitectura de Impronta Social* [Klumb: Architecture of Social Concern] (San Juan, PR: La Editorial, Universidad de Puerto Rico, 2006).

29. Palmares Cultural Foundation, "Apresentação FCP—Ingles," www.palmares.gov.br/005/00502001.jsp?ttCD_CHAVE=67 (accessed February 27, 2010).

30. *UNESCO Brazil: Framework for Action*, 65.

31. Dickenson, "The Future of the Past in the Latin American City," 18.

32. Oscar Niemayer belonged to the "Rio Group," a society of architects who, along with Lúcio Costa, designed the Ministry of Education and Health building in 1938. While championing the modernist movement in the country, Niemayer and a number of his colleagues actively supported the preservation of Brazil's key historic buildings. Machado, "Brazil," in *Trails to Treasures*, 15.

33. Tania Andrade Lima, "Historical Archaeology in Brazil," *SAA Bulletin* 17, no. 2 (March 1999), www.saa.org/Portals/0/SAA/publications/SAAbulletin/17-2/SAA14.html (accessed February 27, 2010).

34. Colin Amery with Brian Curran, "Vila de Paranapiacaba," *Vanishing Histories: 100 Endangered Sites from the World Monuments Watch* (New York: World Monuments Fund, 2001), 152.

Figure 35-1 The historic town of Coro, Venezuela, is a UNESCO World Heritage Site that has been subject to uneven levels of upkeep and protection. Efforts have been made in recent years to improve the situation, but achieving a balance of viable socioeconomic activities and sustainability remains elusive. The restoration of this streetscape is one of the more successful.

CHAPTER 35

The Andean Countries

The South American continent is dominated by the presence of the Andes, the world's largest mountain range. Historically, the Andes have acted both as a barrier and as an agent of protection, stretching from the Caribbean Sea—4,300 miles southward—separating the interior jungles of the Amazon River basin from the tropical coastlines along the Pacific Ocean. The diversity of these climate zones within the Andean region resulted in some differing building traditions as well as some differing architectural conservation problems from the rest of the South American continent.

The Andean countries of Venezuela, Colombia, Ecuador, Peru, and Bolivia share not only geography and climate but also their historical and cultural development. Human settlements have created agricultural terraces and excavated mines of gold and silver in the mountains for millennia. The region's natural resources allowed for the accumulation of wealth and the development of city-states and large empires, which built monumental architecture. Numerous local cultures, including the renowned Inca, left testaments to their heritage in the arid coastal regions to the west of the Andes, in the mountains themselves, and in the Amazon basin that spreads to the east.

The Spanish arrived in the early sixteenth century under the leadership of one of the most ruthless conquistadors, Francisco Pizarro, who became the first governor of the Viceroyalty of Peru in 1542. The viceroyalty encompassed the five present-day Andean countries and was centered in the city of Lima, which had been founded in 1535. In 1717 this territory was divided, and its northern parts became a new viceroyalty centered in Bogotá. In 1776 Bolivia became part of the new viceroyalty in the southern part of the continent, centered in Buenos Aires.[1]

During the three hundred years of Spanish rule, indigenous and European cultures fused throughout the Andean region. As elsewhere in Latin America, the Spanish constructed new cities to serve as administrative centers, new missions to teach their religious beliefs, and new industrial and agricultural works to establish a culture of indentured land servants. In the typical practice of the Spanish empire, many of the towns it founded in South America were established on top of or in close proximity to the remnants of existing Amerindian settlements. Elaborate baroque churches and whitewashed adobe structures with interior courtyards dominated the construction in the Spanish period, and they are still found in the region's historic cities.

After Napoleon's defeat and occupation of Spain in 1808, the wealthy and educated *criollo* population of the region (persons of Spanish descent born in the Americas) initiated a series of revolts against the new French authorities. The rebellions continued even after the restoration of the Spanish king a few years later, as the Andean population sought political independence. In 1812 Simón Bolívar led a revolt to liberate his native Venezuela, and over the course of the next five years he led additional campaigns in Colombia and Ecuador. In 1821 he united all these territories into Gran Colombia, of which he was the president; however, within ten years this state separated into the individual republics of Colombia, Ecuador, and Venezuela. After decades of struggle, Peru and Bolivia were also finally independent in 1824 and 1825, respectively, with the latter naming itself after the revolutionary leader who had aided both countries in their struggles. Political instability and periodic civil wars have troubled the Andean region throughout the nineteenth and twentieth centuries, but they have been interspersed with periods of peace and development.

The heritage of the Andes region is rich, and the number of cultural assets that require protection has grown as the fields of archaeology and anthropology have expanded during the twentieth century. Modernity and development have had varying effects on the region. For example, while cities such as Lima and Bogotá have expanded to unrecognizable proportions, other colonial cities remain largely as they were a century ago. Nevertheless, similar problems are experienced by the region's architectural conservation professionals today. The lack of coherent legislation that addresses all of today's issues, training opportunities, and funds has hampered architectural conservation efforts in the Andean region of South America. In addition, there is a pressing need to raise public awareness concerning the value of cultural heritage. Initiatives to overcome these obstacles continue to develop, international collaboration has been forthcoming, and efforts to protect and promote the region's heritage have grown since the mid-twentieth century.

VENEZUELA

Architectural conservation in contemporary Venezuela is administered by numerous ministries and agencies with overlapping jurisdictions and without clear mandates for protecting historic sites. Numerous laws, and even the Venezuelan constitution, note the importance of cultural heritage, but the implementation of these ideas has often fallen short of expectations. The country's disjointed administrative context coupled with its weak legislation has left the fate of the country's cultural heritage in a suspended state. Increasing pressure and interest from private organizations and the Venezuelan public will hopefully encourage the government to organize the country's heritage system more effectively.

The indigenous groups that inhabited Venezuela at the time of the Spanish arrival belonged predominately to the Carib, Arawak, and Chibcha linguistic groups. The territory was never an important center of the Spanish empire, and its colonial cities are less impressive than in many neighboring countries. Instead, Venezuela remained a provincial agricultural region of small towns, which allowed for the relative isolation of the indigenous groups and the continuity of their cultures until the present. Today thirty-eight distinct indigenous communities live in Venezuela, and testaments to their pre-Colombian ancestors have also survived.

Even the country's name reflects the *palafitos* (or stilt architecture) used by the area's coastal communities, because these structures reminded late-fifteenth-century Spanish explorers of Venice when they arrived and claimed the territory as Spain's "Little Venice" ("Venezuela"). The palafitos and waddle-and-daub building techniques represent Venezuela's traditional building styles and can still be found in costal and rural regions of the country. In addition, contemporary interpretations of the palafitos are also common in the country's cities. The well-maintained palafito villages built over Maracaibo Lake and Sinamaica Lagoon near the city of Maracaibo have become popular tourist sites yet are also active communities of Añu peoples.

The Spanish established a number of towns in Venezuela, such as La Guaira, as well as the Fortress of Santiago de Arroyo in the eastern region; it is one of the few remaining

Spanish fortifications that once lined most of the Venezuelan coast. The town of Coro, added to the World Heritage List in 1993, prospered as an important trade center with the Caribbean islands in the eighteenth century, and the distinctive decorative styles of its architecture reflect the influence of its multicultural trading partners. Founded in 1527, Coro is located on the arid coast surrounded by large sand dunes, and uniquely for this northern region, most of its major historic buildings are built of adobe. The first conservation efforts in Coro occurred in the eighteenth century, but it was after the town was declared a national monument in the 1950s that extensive restoration work was completed. Among the projects completed at that time was the consolidation of the city's cathedral, including the reversal of alterations made to that structure in 1927 and 1928.[2]

In the late 1980s, the Ministry for Urban Development prepared a study on historic Coro and partnered with the Fundación para el Rescate y Conservación de Inmuebles, Localidades y Bienes de Valor Histórico, Religioso y Cultural (FUNRECO, Foundation for the Rescue and Conservation of Objects, Towns, and Sites of Historic, Religious, and Cultural Value) to prepare a plan for conserving Coro and other historic centers and to design relevant regulations and laws to protect these districts. Despite these implements, only sporadic actual conservation and restoration work has taken place in the city in recent decades.

In the early twenty-first century, UNESCO's World Heritage Committee issued a series of warnings to Venezuela because of its inadequate management and lack of conservation activities in Coro. In 2004 the Presidential Commission for the Protection of Coro, the Port of La Vela, and their Areas of Influence was established to focus on improving the mechanisms for protecting the city and other nearby sites of cultural and natural importance. However, the commission's slow progress, combined with heavy rains in the winter of 2004–2005, which caused considerable damage to the city, led UNESCO to place Coro on the List of World Heritage in Danger in 2005.[3] In 2006, the Plan Integral para la Conservación y Desarrollo de Coro, La Vela y sus áreas de influencia (PLINCODE, Integrated Conservation and Development plan for Coro, La Vega and Areas of Influence) was developed and an Oficina de Atención a la Emergencia (OTAE, Office of Emergency Attention) was created to temporarily oversee work at the Coro World Heritage Site. However, though a joint UNESCO and ICOMOS monitoring team in 2008 acknowledged the completion of key emergency projects and the continued prioritization of the site by Venuzela, that same team recommended the site remain on the List of World Heritage in Danger because the PLINCODE had still not been approved by the Venezuelan government, a permanent oversight body had not been created, and the necessary budget to ensure the site's maintenance and protection had not been allocated.[4]

Focused attention in the 1990s on supporting heritage conservation in the State of Vargas, in which Coro is located, did lead to one positive development: foundation of an important nonprofit organization, the Brigadas de Emergencia para el Patrimonio Cultural (Emergency Brigades for Cultural Heritage). The Brigadas de Emergencia came into existence in 2001 to help with postdisaster recovery work after heavy rains and resultant mudslides in the area two years prior caused a particularly significant amount of damage. The organization partially filled the gap left by the Venezuelan government's slow disaster relief work. Established by the Venezuelan Committee of International Council of Museums (ICOM), the project's initial focus was on movable heritage and on training people to carry out salvage missions following sudden disasters.[5] But the Brigadas de Emergencia also worked to protect public sculpture and historic sites, such as 1920s El Castillete, the home of famed modernist painter Armando Reverón, in La Guaira. Today the Brigadas de Emergencia project has crossed borders, involving professionals in Bolivia, Colombia, Ecuador, and Peru and promoting exchange and expertise sharing regarding this particular aspect of cultural heritage conservation.

In Venezuela's capital city of Caracas, the twentieth century was a period of hurried and drastic modernization that altered the cityscape, beginning with the oil boom of the 1920s, which helped launch a series of extensive building programs that eventually created today's metropolis. In the 1940s, President Marcos Peréz Jiménez embraced the rationalism of modern architecture as a symbol of his administration and initiated the construction of social housing, schools, hospitals, and other civic structures. The largest housing program in Latin America, the 23 January Project, was realized between 1954 and 1957 on the hills of the western section of the city to house sixty thousand residents in a self-contained city. Like numerous others at the time, this project aimed to solve housing deficiencies by eradicating the informal settlements that had multiplied with the rapid population increases.

Among the architects of the mid-twentieth-century public works programs in Venezuela was Carlos Raul Villanueva, whose most celebrated project was the City University of Caracas. Villanueva's design for the university recreated traditional architectural themes such as covered galleries and plazas with modern forms and materials, such as reinforced folded concrete roofs. He also adapted modern standards to the local climate through the profuse use of louvered windows to diffuse the tropical sun and create intense patterns of light. His original campus plan has been added to and changed slightly, but the ensemble retained enough of its original integrity to come under state protection in 1994, when a study of the campus' conditions was carried out and an ongoing monitoring process was implemented. The university campus was added to the World Heritage List in 2000, and due to recent long-term conservation concerns it was placed on the World Monuments Fund's Watch list in 2009.

The building programs of the Jiménez regime were not focused on the architectural heritage of Caracas, and in fact they often resulted in its destruction for redevelopment. Therefore, Caracas' skyline today is a testament to the goals of modernism and the prosperity that oil brought to the country in the early twentieth century. Much of the original colonial building fabric became fragmented due to intense construction and the introduction of high-rise modern buildings. Today Caracas retains a few isolated legacies of its colonial beginnings—such as the seventeenth-century cathedral on Plaza Bolívar—nestled in among its skyscrapers and highways.

Despite being an era in which much historic architecture was lost, it was Jiménez's regime that passed Venezuela's first legislation to safeguard the country's cultural heritage; the Protection and Conservation of Antiquities and Artistic Works Act of 1945 initiated the process of designating national monuments.[6] This legislation was not revised until 1993, when a new Law for Protection and Defense of the Cultural Heritage was finally passed in Venezuela. Critics have argued that certain provisions of the new law made it even less effective than the earlier one, but despite public discussion, little legislative debate on reforming the law has occurred in the past decade. Venezuela's ICOMOS chapter has continued to express concern regarding the legislation, especially for the loss of the Local Government Councils of Protection, the municipal agencies that previously aided with architectural conservation on the local level. Despite the increase in community awareness and participation that arose to fill this gap, ICOMOS Venezuela has argued the law represents a regression.[7]

The new law of 1993 did establish the Instituto del Patrimonio Cultural (Institute for Cultural Heritage) within the Ministry of Culture, Education, and Sport. The Instituto has worked to educate communities concerning the value of their heritage with pilot projects such as the Education of Cultural Heritage and Environmental Values program in the State of Vargas. In addition, the Instituto has devoted its energies to increasing the number of sites on the inventory of the country's heritage—for example, by compiling a list of 319 urban centers throughout the country of historic value in 2001.[8] However, with few trained professionals and few implemented restoration projects, the built heritage of Venezuela has not benefited as much as it could potentially from the Instituto's activities.[9] Continued demolition of structures for future redevelopment and neglect of others has led to the continued deterioration of Venezuela's heritage.

While the political turmoil of the past decade has captured much of the Venezuelan government's attention, the country continues to takes small steps toward recognizing the value and diversity of its cultural heritage. ICOMOS Venezuela reported a sizable increase in petitions concerning the built heritage of the country both from community and local government agencies, while the number of museums and their participation in conservation efforts is also growing. From its traditional architecture to its colonial towns to its modern university campus, the panorama of Venezuela's cultural history is diverse, and if the existing conservation institutions were made more effective and efficient and pressure for legislative reform more successful, the forecast for the country's historic sites would surely improve.

COLOMBIA

Despite Colombia's struggles to establish social, political, and economic stability throughout the twentieth century, it has managed to consistently focus attention on architectural conservation. In fact, interest in the cultural heritage of Colombia was established even prior to independence from Spain and grew steadily during the nineteenth and twentieth centuries. The first noted heritage protection event occurred in 1761 when a government accountant forbade the construction of a church over an existing precolonial structure.[10] Shortly after independence in 1823 the government established its first museum and the Comisión Cartográfica (Commission of Cartography) followed in 1850. The Comisión mapped the geography of the country, recorded aspects of the country's natural and cultural resources, and documented its archaeological sites, encouraging further investigations.[11]

Legal protection of cultural heritage in Colombia began in 1920, when destruction and theft from archaeological sites and export of documents or objects of artistic importance were forbidden. Museums and libraries were required to inventory their collections and a Academia Nacional de Historia (National Academy of History) was established to advise and oversee these public repositories. Colombia enacted more comprehensive cultural heritage policies in 1936 when the Roerich Pact was adopted as part of the country's new Constitution. The Roerich Pact was an international agreement stressing the importance of protecting the world's artistic and scientific institutions and historic sites and emphasizing their neutrality during times of conflict.[12] Though the pact was inspired by Europe's devastation during World War I and drafted by a Russian archaeologist, it was first signed by twenty-one countries of the Pan-American Union in 1935.

In Colombia, the provisions of the Roerich Pact substituted for a heritage law, outlining more clearly the different categories of objects and sites deserving protection than the 1920 law had done. In 1959 a new law expanded the protection of heritage even further to more explicitly include archaeological sites and immovable property and also allowed for government expropriation of sites when necessary for their protection. In addition, it established the Consejo Nacional de Monumentos (National Council of Monuments) to register private property of national importance and to impose penalties for illegal export of cultural goods.[13] In the following decade, numerous additional government institutions dedicated to culture, education, and the protection of indigenous heritage were founded as were private organizations interested in the promotion and conservation of the country's historic sites.

The Consejo Nacional de Monumentos has continuously advised the government on architectural and archaeological heritage conservation up until the present, but between the years of 1968 and 1997, the Instituto Colombiana de Cultura (Colombian Institute of Culture), known as Colcultura, was the agency responsible for overseeing the actual protection and restoration of the country's recognized historic sites. The 1980s were one of the darkest decades for Colombia politically, and although it was a period of intense urbanization, important architectural heritage conservation developments were realized at that time. Through collaboration with the Central Bank's Foundation for the Conservation and Restoration of Colombian Cultural Heritage, Colcultura was able to restore important individual structures throughout the country, including the Convento de San Agustín in Boyacá.

These initiatives took center stage in the 1990s as Colombia enacted constitutional reforms that directly improved efforts for cultural heritage protection. The new Colombian constitution of 1991 focused on the importance of the country's physical cultural heritage and identified one of the government's roles as safeguarding this legacy for the Colombian people. In 1997 a new General Law on Culture disbanded Colcultura and replaced it with a Dirección de Patrimonio (Heritage Directorate) within a new Ministry of Culture. Today, this Dirección is responsible for dozens of historic districts and more than four hundred protected properties.[14] The Dirección is organized into six departments, which focus on research and documentation, diffusion and promotion, movable heritage, intangible heritage, protection, and conservation interventions at historic sites.

The projects department, which is partly funded by a tax on cellular telephones, recently launched the National Plan for the Recovery of Historic Centers to promote state and municipal government cooperation in the conservation of Colombia's historic cities. In 2005 projects began in the plan's first three cities of Barranquilla, Santa Marta, and Manizales, and agreements in forty-two other historic centers recognized at the national level began planning their own projects. Most of these historic cities reflect the country's centuries of Spanish colonial rule, as this was the period during which 80 percent of Colombia's towns and cities were founded.[15] As elsewhere in Latin America, most have centrally organized grids, with major church and administrative structures located around a plaza.

a

Figure 35-3 Before its replacement in 1997 by the Dirección de Patrimonio (Heritage Directorate) within a new Ministry of Culture, Colcultura played a key role in architectural heritage protection in Columbia for over two decades. The restoration of the Convento de San Agustín in Boyacá (a) was organized by Colcultura in collaboration with the Central Bank's Foundation for the Conservation and Restoration of Colombian Cultural Heritage. The restoration of the convent's courtyard facades includes abstract representations of missing masonry arches in new painted steel (b). Images courtesy Rodolfo Vallin and Jairo H. Mora

b

Many of Colombia's colonial cities were significantly developed during the twentieth century; however, historic structures are found throughout their cityscapes and are protected by both federal and municipal legislation. For example, Cartagena de Indias, founded in 1533 on the Caribbean coast, still boasts the largest system of fortifications in South America. Within the city's fortified walls, the strict organization of the city involved a system of zones that divided it into distinct neighborhoods, each with a distinctive housing type. Cartagena was added to the World Heritage List in 1984, as a significant portion of the city's sixteenth- and seventeenth-century houses had survived, though many in severely deteriorated states.

Figure 35-4 As director of Colcultura's cultural heritage section for over a decade, Colombian architect Álvaro Barrera began restoring Cartagena's historic buildings in 1982, converting many of them to viable new uses. A hallmark of his work was the preservation of the patina and careful incorporation of surviving fragments of historic buildings into new structures, such as at the Hotel Santa Teresa, which he created by combining the remains a radically altered old convent (illustrated) with a church and adjacent houses. Image courtesy Alvaro Barrera

Beginning in 1982, Colombian architect Álvaro Barrera began restoring Cartagena's structures one by one, converting many of them to viable new uses. Barrera studied in Colombia and Spain, and he served as the director of Colcultura's cultural heritage section between 1974 and 1982. Barrera is also individually responsible for the restoration of much of the country's cultural heritage. His first project in Cartagena—in which he left signs of patina and damage in a house destroyed by fire while simultaneously converting it into four modern apartments and meticulously restoring the original plaster colors and decorative finishes—bore the signature of his restoration style that would be repeated until more than half of the city's historic structures had been restored.[16] His work has also carefully preserved important fragments and incorporated them into new structures, such as at the Hotel Santa Teresa, which he created from combining the remains of an old convent, church, and adjacent houses. Barrera's work has respected and preserved these Spanish colonial structures, and at the same time he has created useful public buildings and contemporary homes, significantly improving the fate of Cartagena's cultural heritage.

Though indigenous people in Colombia constitute less than 2 percent of the overall population today, they include eighty-seven distinct peoples speaking sixty-four different languages.[17] The cultures of ancient inhabitants of the country are recorded in pottery, metalwork, and archaeological sites. Between 500 BCE and 500 CE various cultures flourished in the territory of present-day Colombia. Artifacts such as the network of canals and ditches that extends across approximately 1,250 acres in the highlands were left by the Sinú culture; while evidence of their contemporaries, the Taironas, is found in the remnants of terraced agriculture in the Sierra Nevada. Intricate reliefs are found in the subterranean tombs and on the statues of the Tierradentro archaeological site. The World Heritage Committee describes the carvings as important examples of the social complexity and cultural wealth of the precolonial societies in the northern Andes. Designated in 1995, the park reflects the period from the sixth to the tenth century. The slightly older religious structures and megalithic carvings of human figures of the San Agustín Park were recognized the same year.

Locally based architectural conservation efforts have formed in Colombia, such as in the city of Cali. In response to increased development and the demolition of significant buildings in neighborhoods such as Centenario and Granada, many conservation professionals pushed for the Plan for the Protection of the Patrimony as part of the proposed Special Plan for Environmental and Landscape Protection. They noted the lack of a public consciousness concerning the value of heritage as a primary problem in the city; in their view, this has been exacerbated by a lack of incentives for preserving historic buildings and the absence of coherent regulations for designation.[18] Although many structures, such as the Church of San José, were already recognized national monuments, under the new Plan of Territorial Organization in 2000, the city of Cali additionally designated 120 private residences, forty other structures, and eight historic districts.

The tradition of heritage protection established in Colombia continues to develop as debates about reforming the new national cultural heritage polices of the early 1990s have encouraged municipal governments to take action and have slowly begun to increase efforts to improve public awareness concerning the riches of the country's heritage. For example, during the 1980s and 1990s, many important urban preservation interventions in Bogotá were spearheaded by administration leaders such as Enrique Peñaloza, whose efforts were key to the protection of the city's historic core, La Candelaria. In addition, in response to decades of civil strife, the new Colombian government in 2002 launched plans for using the country's culture, including its heritage, as an expression of and an opportunity for national unity.[19] These new initiatives are building on a solid foundation and a long tradition of architectural conservation and demonstrate that as long as the Colombian government has the resources it will continue to prioritize the country's cultural heritage.

a

b

Figure 35-5 The rehabilitation of emblematic buildings becomes sustainable when they are used more actively by the local population. The rehabilitated Old University Building (a) in García Moreno Street in Quito, Ecuador houses a museum supported by the national government and the municipal library which is heavily used by local students. The Quito Development Corporation partnered with the owners of a representative building to test the viability of bringing commerce back to the historic center. The rehabilitated Pasaje Baca building (b) has retail on the first floor, art galleries on the second floor, and an eatery on the third floor. Images: the photo library of the Inter American Development Bank courtesy Eduardo Royas

ECUADOR

Ecuador's central position on trade routes led to its flourishing both before and after the arrival of the Spanish. Following independence in the 1820s and the subsequent secession from Gran Colombia in 1830, Ecuador developed as a republic and emerged as a cultural center. Cultural resource policy and its enforcement in Ecuador has been strongly dependent on the personal interests of its leaders and therefore somewhat erratic during the past century, as different governments prioritized historic sites or focused efforts elsewhere. In the last quarter century, Ecuador has enjoyed increasingly consistent political support for architectural conservation. Especially in the capital city of Quito, heritage protection has become a priority and important public and private partnerships have been established to ensure a secure future for the country's architectural and urban legacies.

The first legislation related to cultural heritage was passed in 1945, but it was not until 1978 that a government agency was created to take responsibility for regulating protected historic sites. At that time, the Instituto Nacional de Patrimonio Cultural (INPC, National Institute for Cultural Heritage) was established within the Ministry of Education, Culture, Sports and Recreation and given a mandate to preserve, present, and promote Ecuador's cultural heritage. Its initial tasks included preparing an inventory of historic sites and urban centers. In its thirty years of existence, the INPC has often been handicapped by a shortage of professionally trained personnel as well as by insufficient funds.[20]

In 1984 new legislation established two important institutions to assist the INPC in safeguarding Ecuador's heritage: the Consejo Nacional de Cultura (National Council of Culture) and the Fondo Nacional de Cultura (FONCULTURA, National Fund for Culture). The Consejo's members are drawn from the leadership of the country's cultural institutions, including the secretary of education and culture and the director of INPC, as well as include representatives of other federal agencies, local universities, and private cultural heritage organizations. The Consejo establishes priorities for conservation, ensures the equitable regional distribution of public funds, advises the Ministry of Foreign Affairs on international agreements related to culture, suggests legislative reforms, approves annual plans, and oversees the FONCULTURA, which is used to directly finance conservation projects of national or regional interest, grant loans for similar private endeavors, and to coordinate all cultural heritage investment in Ecuador. With the creation of FONCULTURA, the first organized structure for government funding of architectural conservation projects was established in Ecuador.

As in many places in South America, architectural conservation efforts in Ecuador have focused primarily on the country's rich legacy of Spanish colonial architecture and cities. One of the most picturesque of these is the city of Cuenca, which was founded in 1577, and which still retains its original street pattern. The city's architecture is a combination of baroque, eclectic, and neoclassical styles and also includes numerous important structures from the republican period. In 1982 Cuenca was designated a national historic district and an urban development plan was created for the city. In the next decade a series of planning regulations followed, encompassing everything from setting up an administrative body for the district to regulating signage to declaring tax-exempt status for historic properties.[21] When declared a World Heritage Site in 1999, Cuenca's historic center had twenty-six buildings classified as national monuments, 602 buildings of architectural significance, and 830 that contributed to the cityscape.[22] Cuenca's central Plaza Calderón was painstakingly restored in 2002, and many of its fragile mud-brick residential structures were transformed into new boutique hotels and cafes catering to the increasing

Figure 35-6 Founded in 1577, the Spanish colonial town of Cuenca, located in the highlands of Ecuador, has survived remarkably intact with over fifteen hundred historic buildings categorized as either national monuments or contributing to the character of the town that was declared a World Heritage Site in 1999.

number of tourists. At the same time, a conservation project was undertaken at the sixteenth-century Iglesia del Sagario (Old Cathedral of Cuenca), that transformed it into a museum for religious art.

Ecuador's capital city of Quito is one of the oldest in South America. Founded in 1534 on the ruins of an Inca city, Quito immediately became an important regional center for missionary activity and for culture when a Franciscan art school was established the following year. The school attracted artists to the region and established a painting style known today as the School of Quito. The architecture of the colonial period developed along with the arts and adopted Moorish, Renaissance, and baroque elements imported from Spain. Significant eighteenth-century structures in Quito include the Hospital San Juan de Dios, one of the earliest hospitals of the Spanish colonies, and the Palacio de Gobierno (Governor's Palace), which was augmented in the mid-twentieth century with an abstract mural by Ecuadoran artist Oswaldo Guayasamín.

In the early 1940s, a master plan for Quito was established to regulate growth, and an Artistic Heritage Act was enacted to preserve individual buildings of historic importance. Though in the early twentieth century Quito had the same boundaries it had had for centuries, by the 1970s the historic core of the city was surrounded by development and had been abandoned by the city's wealthier citizens and businesses. Its stately mansions were subdivided into multifamily housing units and had begun to deteriorate. In addition, because of the city's location in a narrow valley, the city center has experienced traffic congestion and pollution problems that have also negatively impacted its historic sites.

In 1967 and 1971, the historic center was identified and protected as an entity, but important parts of the cityscape had already been lost to urban development schemes before the municipality began sponsoring the conservation of prominent sites in the 1970s. At that time the city also tried to restrict how historic properties were used and altered through a series of hastily drafted regulations that only encouraged property owners to neglect sites so they could later demolish them.[23] Yet today Quito's basic colonial plan remains intact and fifteen monasteries, thirty-eight churches, and numerous significant residential and administrative buildings have survived. In 1978 the seventy-two-block historic center of Quito as well as the Galapagos Islands off Ecuador's coast were inscribed on UNESCO's World Heritage List.

Quito has frequently been damaged by earthquake, with the most devastating effects seen at the Iglesia de la Compañía de Jesús (Church of the Company of Jesus [the Jesuits]).

a

b

Figure 35-7 Due to plunder, fire, and earthquakes, the Iglesia de la Compañía de Jesús (a) in Quito, Ecuador, has undergone more necessary restorations over its four-hundred year history than most buildings in South America. The latest entails recovery from a fire in 1997 and restoration of the church's interior in 2008 (b).

The church, whose design was based on the churches of the Gesù and St. Ignatius in Rome, was constructed by the Jesuits between 1605 and 1690, and its facade was finished in the 1720s. In the 1760s the Jesuits were expelled from Quito and the church was seized by the local government and most of its interior fittings and riches were sent to Spain. In 1850 the church was returned to the Jesuits who begun repairs on the long-neglected building until they were expelled again two years later. In 1859 an earthquake damaged the church's tower so severely that, when the Jesuits finally regained control of their church in 1862, they had to tear down the tower and completely rebuild it as well as restart their general restoration projects of the previous decade. In 1868 another earthquake destroyed the tower, and it was again rebuilt.

The Iglesia de la Compañía de Jesús was damaged by yet another earthquake in 1987. This time numerous state institutions aided the Jesuits in restoring the church, and the order established a foundation to maintain and conserve the church building as well as the adjacent school and residence. In addition to earthquake damage, the entire complex suffered from general deterioration and ineffective past interventions. A fire in 1996 caused significant additional damage to the church, but funds from international and local organizations helped with emergency repairs. After a slow start, in 1997 the foundation assembled a conservation team, prepared a comprehensive restoration plan, and solicited additional support. The restoration of the building began in 2008.

In response to the March 1987 earthquake, the Municipality of Quito took a more proactive approach to architectural conservation by establishing the Fund for the Preservation of the Historic City Center (FONSAL) to restore damaged structures throughout the city. The following year FONSAL was supplemented by the Empresa de Desarrollo del Centro Histórico (ECH, Corporation for the Development of the Historic Center), which produced a management plan to restore the city's historic residential architecture. The master plan was completed in 1989 and implementation began with improvements to the appearance, amenities, and infrastructure of the historic district's Plaza Grande. The ECH was initially financed through a $42 million loan from the IDB and functions as a semipublic corporation that facilitates partnerships between the city and private investors for the rehabilitation of Quito.[24] Its projects typically involve purchasing larger buildings, restoring their facades, and upgrading their interiors with modern amenities to serve as shops, theaters, restaurants, and hotels. However, the ECH has also restored the historic buildings inhabited by the city's lower-income population to ensure that they are not forced out of the revitalized district.

After the emergency earthquake-response period concluded, FONSAL continued on as the city agency responsible for overseeing the World Heritage Site and conserving the city's heritage. In addition to revitalizing and preserving the city's historic district, since the early 1990s, the objectives of the city government have also included educating citizens and tourists about the value and history of Quito's heritage.[25] Currently, FONSAL is busy with more than a dozen restoration projects throughout the city, ranging from hospitals to convents to bridges. In addition, in 1989, a local nonprofit organization called the Fundación Caspicara was established to focus on soliciting international contributions for conservation projects in Quito. A few years later another nonprofit, the Corporación del Centro Histórico (Historic Center Corporation) was established to encourage heritage education among schoolchildren and visitors to Quito by organizing volunteer opportunities, theater programs, and tours of the historic district

Figure 35-8 The organization FONSAL, in collaboration with the Corporation for the Development of the Historic Center, has conserved scores of damaged buildings in Quito's historic center since the late 1980s. Projects have included façade restorations around the Plaza Grande (illustrated), adaptive use of redundant religious buildings as commercial facilities, and other assistance to historic property owners. Image courtesy A. Ortiz.

that combine information about the heritage sites themselves with the living culture of the city's residents.

The Getty Conservation Institute (GCI) cosponsored a conference on historic cities held in Quito in 1990 and has worked with the municipality on specific conservation projects ever since. Initially the GCI focused its efforts on the Calle García Moreno, the main urban axis of the historic city, which is lined with many interesting colonial- and republican-era structures. Pollution from leaded gasoline, uncontrolled street vendor management, and overcrowding led to severe conservation problems along this central thoroughfare and adjacent areas in the early 1990s. In 1994 the GCI presented the city with a comprehensive survey of the street including a detailed conservation plan for each individual structure. The Banco Central del Ecuador began offering loans to individual property owners who wished to restore their buildings according to GCI's plans.

Despite the numerous local and international partners dedicated to the conservation and protection of Quito, the city continues to struggle with ongoing threats. Deterioration of the historic center as a result of overcrowding and limited-income residents who cannot afford regular maintenance have contributed to the ongoing need for proactive solutions to safeguard the architectural heritage that define the city's historic character. In addition, after three centuries of dormancy, the nearby La Pichincha volcano became active again in 1998, posing concerns among Quito's residents as well as for its historic architecture. Subsequent disaster response preparations were made for the World Heritage Site by the city and approved by UNESCO.

Though Ecuador's architectural conservation efforts have focused on colonial- and republican-era sites, especially in Quito, the country's more remote archaeological sites have in general received less attention from conservation institutions. Though archaeological investigations and conservation activities in Ecuador have privileged sites in the coastal region rather than the highlands or the Amazon interior, the most prominent archaeological site in Ecuador today is the ruins of the Inca town of Ingapirca, meaning "wall of the Incas," which is located in the mountains. At Ingapirca, the Inca's adaptation of the Cañari culture's semicircular architecture is clearly visible, as are the roadways, aqueducts, baths, and staircases they constructed after conquering the region in the 1470s.[26] Until the early twentieth century, the site long served as a quarry for building materials for the Spanish and, later, local generations. In 2004 the Instituto Nacional de Patrimonio Cultural signed an agreement with the Instituto Ingapirca del Pueblo Cañari (Ingapirca Institute of the Cañari Town) for the conservation of the walls of the elliptical temple of the sun, the site's most impressive surviving structure.

Though pre-Columbian archaeology has been carried out in Ecuador for more than a century, historical archaeology is a relatively new field. Archaeological excavations were mandated by the INPC in the early 1990s as part of all restoration projects at protected sites. Additionally, all new development projects must incorporate an archaeological impact survey. Excavations in both restoration and new development projects are overseen by professionals of INPC's Dirección de Arqueología (Archaeology Directorate); however, the large number of projects and limited staff has reduced the quality and thoroughness of some of this research.[27]

Communities have had a significant impact on archaeology as well, including in 1990 when several local archaeologists and others successfully protested construction of a dam at the Culebrillas Lagoon by the Ecuadorian government. The dam would have dramatically altered the appearance of the lagoon, which is a cultural landscape of great significance to the Cañari people, and it would also have inundated numerous pre-Columbian structures as well as part of the Inca Trail.

a

b

Figure 35-9 A notable, ongoing private-public architectural conservation initiative in Guayaquil, Ecuador, is the restoration of the historic Las Peñas neighborhood; the project is jointly sponsored by the Banco de Guayaquil and the local municipality. Restoration of two different street fronts in the district of Las Peñas in their pre- (a) and post-restoration (b) states are illustrated here. Image b. courtesy of Antonio Moncayo

In Ecuador today the legacy of decades of architectural conservation has shown positive results. ICOMOS Ecuador has emerged as active advocate of the country's heritage and has been involved in international discussions and professional exchange programs that have brought new ideas to the country. The government's cooperation with and encouragement of private sector involvement in cultural heritage through FONCULTURA has significantly aided architectural conservation efforts in Ecuador since the 1980s. The product of this conservation attention is especially visible in Quito, where private investment is similarly facilitated and where state and municipal agencies and international and local nonprofits are cooperating.

As in other countries of the region, Ecuador's architectural conservationists face important challenges—including mainly the still-nascent public consciousness of the full value of their cultural heritage and the lack of investors and government funds for architectural conservation due to various financial crises that have troubled South America since the 1990s. Nevertheless, the multiple strong institutions—both public and private—established in Ecuador in the past few decades indicate that the interest in architectural conservation is an established practice today.

Public-Private Partnerships and Urban Rehabilitation in Latin America
Eduardo Rojas

The deterioration of urban heritage areas is the result of complex social and economic trends whose reversal requires innovative and sustained interventions. Over time the abandonment of historic centers by the economic and cultural elite, following their preferences for suburban life, has been followed by the flight of the services and commerce and the middle classes. Urban sprawl has both fueled and facilitated this process. Unfortunately, no single actor working independently can prompt significant change in these trends. The government alone cannot rehabilitate all the private buildings in deteriorated urban heritage areas, while private investors shy away from taking on rehabilitation projects in these areas due to the high commercial risk involved. Furthermore, individual investors have incentives to wait for the rehabilitation process to gain traction before investing and reaping the benefits from the positive externalities generated by the pioneers. Without sufficient funding and coordinated efforts, it is difficult to initiate the rehabilitation process. Moreover, even if the process is launched, it often cannot gain sufficient scale to make a difference in the deteriorated areas.

Stakeholders need to coordinate their foci and actions to stop the deterioration process and achieve change. They must design and finance innovative interventions in urban development over extended periods of time to attract consumers and residents back to the historic centers. The implementation of these innovations, which take time to mature and show benefits, involves taking risks and securing long-term financing. To take on these challenges, well-structured partnerships between the private and public sectors are often necessary.

A good example is Quito, Ecuador's Empresa del Centro Histórico (ECH, Corporation for the Development of the Historic Center), established in the early 1990s by the Municipality of Quito and Fundación Caspicara. This partnership allowed the local government, which owned the majority of the shares, to contract directly with the corporation, while at the same time the ECH could also operate as a private real estate developer. This operational flexibility allowed the ECH to intervene in the conservation efforts of the historic center on a variety of fronts, including the improvement of the infrastructure and public spaces under contract with the municipality, the rehabilitation of public buildings, and the restoration of residential, commercial, and services buildings in partnership with land owners and private investors.

The ECH took risks in the rehabilitation of the historic center by pioneering the reintroduction of diversified commercial activities, and it shared the risks and returns on the investments with private partners by making the center once again appealing to middle- and upper-income households. When identifying the investments, the ECH saw the historic center as an area that should be able to compete commercially with the shopping malls of the periphery. To this end, the ECH promoted the diversification of the retail and service activities offered in the historic center and worked with the municipality to improve accessibility via public transportation and private vehicles. Also, the ECH, in conjunction with the municipal administration, was able to control the use of the rehabilitated public spaces, which led to a decrease in informal activities. These improvements contributed significantly to transform the historic center into an attractive place to visit, live, and conduct business. In just over fifteen years, the historic center of Quito has changed dramatically. Today it is a well-preserved functional area of the city that provides the population with ample services and a good living environment while still retaining its historic and cultural values.

The success of public private partnerships for the restoration and revitalization of Latin America's historic cities has been demonstrated in numerous other projects, each as diverse as the contexts in which they were conceived. For example, in Brazil, the municipal government of Recife has set up an office to promote conservation in the Bairrio do Recife neighborhood, oversee implementation of a rehabilitation plan, and restore sample properties to inspire homeowners and demonstrate the public commitment to rejuvenating the area. The Bairro do Recife Office also seeks out private investors and connects them with properties in need of conservation attention and helps them program those sites once restored.

FURTHER READING

Rojas, Eduardo (ed.). *Building Cities, Neighbourhood Upgrading and Urban Quality of Life*. (Washington, DC: Inter-American Development Bank, 2010).

PERU

Peru's name has its origin in the Quechua word *pirú*, which appropriately implies land of abundance—the country's wealth through the course of history is evident in the quantity and diversity of its cultural resources. As the center of the Inca empire in the fifteenth and sixteenth centuries and of a Spanish viceroyalty from the mid-sixteenth through the early nineteenth centuries, Peru flourished—and a rich legacy of important cities and sites from the pre-Columbian and colonial periods have survived to the present. Unlike in most neighboring countries, the first component of Peruvian heritage to be protected were some of the country's over five thousand recorded archaeological sites, and this heritage has continued to be the focus of conservation efforts up until the present. In the twentieth century, a body of protective legislation was passed and numerous government agencies established, though funding and enforcement challenges meant that Peru's heritage was continually at risk.

Heritage protection interests within the Peruvian government spent the early twentieth century trying to overcome the precedent set by its 1852 Civil Code, which stated that archaeological finds belonged to their discoverers and to private property owners. This led to damage and destruction of numerous sites as well as the exportation of valuable cultural property from Peru. State ownership of antiquities and the ability to expropriate sites from which these objects had been excavated was not established until 1929; however, the legislation was not retroactive for previously discovered finds. But after passage of the Law for the Protection of Archaeological Monuments in 1929, numerous recently discovered sites, such as Machu Picchu and Caral, were acquired by the government to ensure their protection.[28] In addition, this law initiated a registry of historical sites and objects of value within the country in either public or private hands.

In 1939 Peru's heritage legislation was expanded to include buildings from the colonial and republic periods in addition to the already protected archaeological sites. A 1958 law updated the register of historic sites and objects, which had never been completed because of the difficulty of recording private property. That list remains incomplete today due to a lack of financial resources and the fact that participation for private property owners was made voluntary in the mid-1980s. Indeed, a concern for private property rights and a lack of resources to enforce policies has led to the continual revisiting of Peru's heritage protection legislation.[29]

Today, protecting Peru's cultural heritage is the responsibility of the Instituto Nacional de Cultura (INC, National Institute of Culture), which was created in 1971 to replace agencies established in the early 1960s. Like similar state institutions around the world, the INC's mission includes encouraging Peruvian identity by protecting, conserving, and promoting the country's heritage. In addition, the INC aims explicitly to involve the private sector and other public institutions in this process.

In 2001 a Comisión Nacional de Cultura (National Commission of Culture) was established as a division of Peru's presidency, with a mandate to develop a reasoned state cultural policy that consolidates the country's efforts for heritage protection. In cooperation with the INC, the following year a new cultural plan for the period from 2003 to 2006 was developed. Among its broad goals were to incorporate more on cultural heritage protection in the country's education system; improve access to historic sites for children, seniors, and disabled people; improve the quality of regional museums; increase partnerships with private institutions, organizations, universities, and municipalities for the promotion and restoration of heritage; and produce new, high-quality interpretative materials and guidebooks for major sites.[30]

New cultural legislation was also passed in 2004 in an attempt to rectify the inconsistencies and deficiencies of earlier laws. The 2004 law clearly stated that all sites and objects from the pre-Hispanic, colonial, and pre-1850 republican periods were automatically presumed part of Peru's cultural heritage unless a specific written statement from the INC acknowledged its lack of value. This most recent law established state ownership over new discoveries and again made registration of sites and objects with the INC mandatory.

The categories under which cultural heritage in Peru can be classified include movable, intangible, underwater, industrial, documentary, and immovable, with this final category including archaeological sites as well as colonial and republican buildings and historic cities. The INC has numerous directorates focused on these different types of heritage or specific aspects of the field.[31] The Archaeology Directorate, for example, authorizes and supervises any excavations within Peru as well as coordinates the conservation and management of the country's pre-Columbian heritage. The Colonial and Republican Heritage Directorate similarly oversees and manages historic sites, including authorizing all alterations or restoration projects at privately owned properties. It includes subdirectories responsible for registration, research, conservation projects, and historic centers. A special World Heritage Directorate of the INC is responsible for Peru's eight cultural sites recognized by UNESCO, which include the cities of Lima, Cuzco, and Arequipa and the archaeological sites of Machu Picchu, Río Abiseo, Chavín, Nasca, and Chan Chan.

Cuzco, the Inca capital at the time of the Spanish invasion, was an old city that had been significantly redeveloped as an idealized capital in the fifteenth century by Pachacútec, a great Inca leader and patron of architecture. When they arrived in the city in 1534, the Spanish retained Cuzco's orthogonal plan, with its hierarchical organization and clearly delimited agricultural, artisan, and industrial areas. However, many of the monumental and ceremonial buildings were destroyed and replaced with new structures, such as the Convent of Santo Domingo, which was built on top of the Inca Temple of the Sun, and the Plaza de Armas, which sits atop the former Huaccapayta, the administrative center of the Inca empire. Similar examples of Spanish construction set on the foundation of the large stone masonry of Inca structures are found in churches and public buildings throughout the Andean region.

After Peru's independence in the nineteenth century, Cuzco declined as it no longer served as an important administrative center. As a result of its lack of development

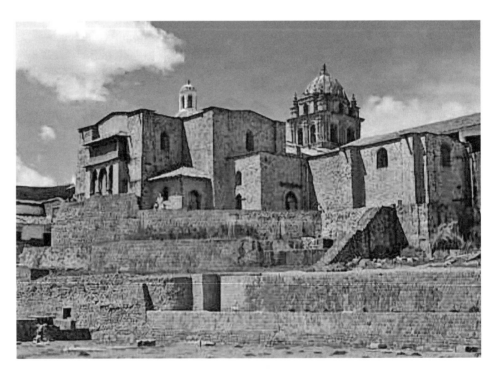

Figure 35-10 Cuzco, Peru, was already an historic town before it was enhanced with even grander fitted-stone construction during the Inca empire. After the Spanish arrival in 1533, temples were razed and replaced with churches, and administrative buildings were similarly destroyed and replaced with newer buildings in Spanish Renaissance and baroque styles. Examples include the Convent of Santo Domingo (illustrated), which was built atop Korikancha, the Incan Temple of the Sun.

and modernization, it survived nearly intact into the mid-twentieth century, when continued natural causes and unsympathetic alterations and additions began to erode its historic integrity. By the 1970s, the rise of tourism and the interest of international organizations, such as UNESCO and the OAS, began to reverse this trend. These efforts led to Cuzco's World Heritage designation in 1983, but the city still has not been prioritized by the INC, which has yet to develop a master plan for its conservation and development, and local authorities continue to be more reactive than proactive on conservation matters.

Along the coast of Peru, the Spanish established their principal new towns, such as Trujillo, Arequipa, and their capital of Lima, which were all planned on the typical grid and central plaza system found throughout the Spanish Americas. In most of these cities, the Andean or mestizo-baroque dominated the architectural language: Spanish-era buildings relied heavily on traditional construction techniques, and the era's masterpieces reflect a combination of Spanish and indigenous materials and methods as well as styles. The *quincha* tradition of wattle-and-daub adobe construction is common in historic parts of many cities, including Lima. This technique is readily visible in important buildings in the city, such as the complex of buildings that comprises the Convent of San Francisco, and it has proved resistant to the numerous earthquakes that have plagued the area.[32]

By the 1980s, Lima had grown to a population in the millions and had become known as one of Latin America's most challenged cities, with population pressures and uncontrolled development encroaching on its historic resources. After the addition of the Convent of San Francisco to the World Heritage List in 1987, a push for the inclusion of Lima's entire historic center was made by Patronato de Lima, a nonprofit coalition of local architects and other professionals founded in 1989. This organization drafted a regulation plan, which the municipal government and INC adopted in 1991 after the city's recognition by UNESCO. Many of the regulation plan's provisions—such as the use of zoning to link usage and permitted interventions, efficient integration of Peru's overlapping heritage policies and programs, and focus on management—have been successful and have made it a model for other historic cities. Some have argued that the conservation plan for Lima's historic center has been carried too far. The plan has been criticized for making the district more of a museum by restricting usage, focusing on tourism at the expense of local inhabitants, and removing later significant buildings and alterations to restore the area's eighteenth- and nineteenth-century appearance.

Today, a subsequent master plan developed by the INC in 1999 is being implemented by ProLima, a quasi-public organization affiliated with the municipality. The city's traffic and public transportation systems were altered and this has abated, though not completely eliminated, pollution in the historic core. Public spaces such as the Plaza de Armas have been restored, and new uses have been found to revitalize rehabilitated historic buildings. An "Adopt a Balcony" program encouraged investment from private sources, including Coca-Cola and the Backus Cultural Heritage Foundation, a division of Peru's Backus and Johnston Brewery. The adoption program has facilitated the restoration of many of Lima's three hundred colonial-era carved wood balconies, which reflect the influence of Arabic architecture on Spanish traditions. In recent years, efforts to encourage people to move back to the historic district through the conversion of unused historic structures has spelled a return of urban life to area.

Like Lima, the Spanish colonial city of Arequipa also suffered from pollution and neglect in the twentieth century, but due to its location near a boundary between tectonic plates, earthquakes have been the greatest threat to its architectural heritage. Known as the White City of the Andes, the seventeenth- and eighteenth-century structures of Arequipa are famous for their numerous arches and vaults, and they are mostly built from a light-colored stone made of consolidated volcanic ash, known locally as *sillar*.

a

b

Figure 35-11 The historic center of Lima, Peru, was restored in the 1990s primarily to appeal to tourists; ultimately, this created a relatively sterile environment. More recent efforts have encouraged the return of round-the-clock life to the historic center. All of these initiatives have meant attention has been paid in recent decades to Lima's stock of distinctive historic buildings, such as the Casa de las Columnas, illustrated before (a) and during restoration (b). Images courtesy Escuela Taller de Lima.

Though construction with this white stone has contributed to Arequipa's beauty, it has proven less resistant to seismic activity than the mud-brick architecture found elsewhere in Peru.

An intense earthquake in 1958 sparked the architectural conservation movement in Arequipa, leading to the establishment of a Committee for the Rehabilitation and Development of Arequipa, one of the first such agencies in Peru.[33] Restoration of key structures in the city followed. For example, the sixteenth-century Convent of Santa Catalina, whose interior is reminiscent of contemporaneous architecture of Spanish Andalusia, was skillfully restored, furnished with period pieces, and fitted with an important collection of religious art. The Peruvian government named the colonial center of Arequipa as a protected historic district in 1972, but a municipal agency to manage the district was not established until 1999 when a successful petition for World Heritage status was submitted to UNESCO. The Municipal Council and the INC began development of a master plan at that time.

An earthquake in June 2001 again caused significant damaged to the historic center of Arequipa and destroyed over 25,000 buildings in southwest Peru.[34] In Arequipa, it was the historic stone buildings that suffered the most significant damage, with 80 percent of its buildings damaged.[35] One of the towers of the Cathedral of Arequipa collapsed, falling into the church itself. Though the cathedral was originally built in the early seventeenth century, it had been rebuilt extensively in the nineteenth century and in the 1940s, following previous earthquakes. The walls of the library of the Franciscan Recoleta Convent-Museum also collapsed, burying historic manuscripts and books in the rubble. The vaults and domes of thousands of centuries-old houses in Arequipa also suffered damage and were weakened structurally by the earthquake.

The first on the scene to aid in Arequipa's recovery was the Peruvian Army, which cleared the rubble from the streets but was careful to classify and save carved stone fragments from the facades of important buildings.[36] Within days, ICCROM coordinated

Figure 35-12 Post-disaster restoration and reconstruction in historic Arequipa, Peru, after an earthquake in June 2001 destroyed or seriously damaged over 25,000 buildings in the area, was handled particularly well in a coordinated effort of the Peruvian Army and volunteer conservators working under the aegis of the Rome-based ICCROM. Illustrated here is earthquake-damaged building fabric before restoration (a) and a formerly damaged adjacent building after restoration (b).

a

b

Conserving Ancient Earthen Architecture: The Chan Chan Example

New master plans for conserving and presenting two of Peru's most famous historic sites, Chan Chan and Machu Picchu, were created by the National Institute of Culture (Instituto Nacional de Cultura, INC) in 2002, and these plans have broadly sought to integrate the local community with the world-famous sites. Chan Chan, the cultural and political center of the Chimú peoples, is comprised of nine citadels, or ceremonial centers with pyramids and temples, as well as extensive dwelling areas. The archaeological site represents the largest complex of earthen architecture in the Americas, spanning more than 20 square kilometers (7.7 square miles). The height of the Chimú culture occurred between 1250 and 1450, before they were overtaken by the Incas. After the Spanish conquest, the site was plundered by treasure hunters and also by early travelers and archaeologists. Chan Chan was first surveyed between 1755 and 1785 by Baltazar Martínez de Compa on and then again in the 1960s by a team from Harvard University. Because of the site's fragile adobe construction, which requires constant maintenance, centuries of abandonment, high winds, and heavy rainfall have led to the gradual disappearance of excavated features. Due to this ongoing natural threat, Chan Chan was placed on the list of World Heritage in Danger in 1986—the same year it was recognized by UNESCO.

The Project Terra initiative of the Getty Conservation Institute, ICCROM, and the International Center for Earth Construction—School of Architecture Grenoble (CRATerre-EAG) focused on Chan Chan as a site where it could develop and encourage the latest technologies and methodologies for the conservation of earthen architecture. Project Terra coordinated efforts with the INC to develop a master plan for the site's management and used this as a model for other earthen sites around the world.[37] The Chan Chan master plan was completed in 1999, identifying over 150 separate conservation projects required at the site, thirty-seven of which had been completed by 2007.

The international collaborative effort to investigate conservation issues and solutions and carry out a series of representative projects at Chan Chan over a period of years served as a demonstration project that informed conservation at several other sites in Peru and its neighboring countries. In the mid-1990s, Chan Chan hosted a series of international conferences and short courses on earthen architecture sponsored by the same international bodies responsible for the site's conservation as well as by UNESCO, the European Union, and Peru's INC. For example, in November 1996, the site hosted the one-month training course entitled PAT 96, the Pan-American course on Conservation and Management of Earthen Archaeological Heritage at Chan Chan.

and funded inventorying and packing supplies to be used to protect the interior fittings, paintings, and collections of the damaged buildings—it also sent a team of volunteer conservators to begin work in the city. Within a year, most of the city's historic structures were stabilized or restored with financial assistance coordinated through UNESCO. At the Cathedral of Arequipa, the structurally weakened but surviving tower was stabilized using a carbon-fiber laminate, and the collapsed tower was rebuilt.

In addition to the conservation of colonial cities, the twentieth century has witnessed the discovery of numerous archaeological sites and further understanding of the cultures that inhabited ancient Peru. The Caral site in the Supe Valley was discovered in 1905, but it was only recently dated to 2600 BCE and thus determined to be the oldest city in the Americas, debunking the long-held theory that the pre-Inca cultures only inhabited the coast region.[38] The presence of the Nasca Lines was realized in the 1930s when aviators spotted a thousand-mile long stretch of enormous depictions on ground surfaces of animals, birds, spirals, zigzags, triangles, and other motifs. Scholars have since dated these geoglyphs to the period between 1 CE and 750 CE and argue that they are actually pathways, as remnants of structures believed to be temporary dwellings and guideposts have been documented along them.[39] Even today, the number of known archaeological sites in Peru continues to grow. Therefore, the responsibilities of the INC and local agencies charged with protecting this pre-Columbian architectural heritage also continues to increase.

Figure 35–13 Due to the size and conditions of the pre-Columbian Chimú site of Chan Chan (a), located near Trujillo, Peru, its conservation has been ongoing since its placement on the World Heritage List in 1986. Considerable expertise was applied at Chan Chan during the Project Terra initiative of the Getty Conservation Institute, ICCROM, and the International Center for Earth Construction-School of Architecture Grenoble. This resulted in conservation plans, scores of successful conservation interventions, and conferences that helped to disseminate successful earthen architecture conservation technologies and methodologies used there to other parts of the world. Illustrated here are surface stabilization measures being conducted at an exterior wall fragment at Tschudi Palace (b), ICCROM expert Giacomo Chiari and training-course participants carrying out surface treatments (c), and a shelter system erected to protect adobe friezes (d). Images copyright ICCROM/Alejandro Balderamma

Since its rediscovery in 1911 and excavation in the 1920s by the National Geographic Society, Machu Picchu has been one of the most famous archaeological sites in the world and a testament to the legacy of the Inca. This planned mountain top city was constructed in the fifteenth century about 100 kilometers (approximately 62 miles) from the Inca capital of Cuzco, and it is attributed to Pachacútec, the same leader who redeveloped the city of Cuzco during the same time period. Little is known about why the city was built or the functions of many of the buildings whose ruins have survived. Environmental degradation in the surrounding valley has led to an increasing number of mudslides that have proven disastrous for other historic sites and modern dwellings in the Machu Picchu area.

But the lack of adequate policies to manage tourism at Machu Picchu and to protect it against overuse has proven to be the biggest challenge at this site. Machu Picchu is Peru's main tourist attraction, visited by 70 percent of all foreign visitors to the country. The number of tourists has increased annually since the end of political instability in the 1990s: In 2008 over 800,000 people visited Machu Picchu, twice as many as in 1998 and more than ten times as many as in 1991.[40] The presence of so many visitors to the site pushes the limits of its carrying capacity as a historic cultural resource. Concerned heritage conservationists have reported problems ranging from soil compaction from wear by tourists that may alter drainage patterns and soil-bearing capacities to the accidental damage to the Intihuatana, the ancient sun dial, following a mishap with a crane during filming for a beer commercial.[41]

Figure 35-14 Machu Picchu is Peru's most popular tourist attraction, receiving over 800,000 visitors per year today, up from around 70,000 in 1991. Overuse at times has threatened the stability of the archaeological remains and their mountainous landscape, while pressures to provide improved access—ranging from new bridges and helicopter access areas in the Vilcanota Valley to a cable car system—have threatened the integrity of this site.

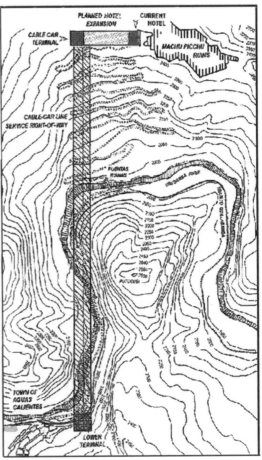

Figure 35-15 Concept renderings of a proposed new cable car system along the west side of the Machu Picchu site which would bring a greatly increased number of visitors to the mountaintop citadel from the Vilcanota Valley, some 450 meters (1,500 feet) below. Plans for this were vehemently opposed by concerned heritage conservationists from near and far. ICOMOS led the campaign internationally, and protests arose from different quarters in Peru. One of the more remarkable actions of protest was a heritage protection march on foot from Lima to Machu Picchu, a distance of over 425 kilometers (265 miles).

The INC's 1999 master plan for Machu Picchu, funded through the efforts of UNESCO and the Finnish government, sought to manage the site more effectively, but implementation initially met with limited success due to a lack of funding and preparedness for the complicated context. In 2004 the World Bank began a program for the rehabilitation of the entire Vilcanota Valley, above which Machu Picchu is sited, to comprehensively tackle the area's socioeconomic problems, environmental issues, and the conservation of Machu Picchu itself. Interventions at the archaeological site have included the installation of state-of-the-art equipment to monitor ground conditions and the application of a sealant to the stone to alleviate water damage.[42] In addition, the broad World Bank project includes improvements in waste management, transportation, and telecommunications; resettlement of households threatened by mudslides or that encroach on the protected site; enhancement of visitor services and increased capacity-building for tourists; and stimulation of the local economy. The National Geographic Society has partnered with the World Bank to create map guides to the area to promote a variety of destinations within the valley and alleviate the pressure on the main citadel.

The possibility of constructing a cable car to carry tourists from the valley town up to Machu Picchu and replace the current shuttle bus system was debated internationally in recent years. Many feared the construction of such a system would encourage additional landslides on the mountain, in addition to radically increasing the number of visitors to the site per day. UNESCO argued the cable car would ruin views of the site, which is recognized as both a natural and cultural site on the World Heritage List. Plans were tabled in 2001, but discussion has not completely disappeared. In addition, a Conservation Management Plan for Machu Picchu was developed in 2005 by the INC that was not fully implemented.

The legacy of the Moche culture that flourished on the northern coast of Peru before the eighth century was also revealed during the last century with the discovery of the Tombs of Sipán and the conservation work that began at the Huaca de la Luna in 1991. The Huaca de la Luna is an adobe brick complex of plazas and platforms built successively over six hundred years and decorated with a polychrome frieze. Portions of each of the six identified phases of its development have been excavated by a team from the National University of Trujillo, with evidence of each layer carefully conserved. The initial funder of this project, the Ford Foundation, was joined by the World Monuments Fund in 2001 although the work at the Huaca de la Luna has primarily been supported by the Backus Cultural Heritage Foundation.

In 1994 a ten-year plan for research and conservation at Huaca de la Luna was developed with a focus on involving the local private sector. After opening to the public that same year, the site has been successfully promoted so as to increase its number of visitors annually, but it has been carefully managed to mitigate the potentially harmful effects of this tourism. Today, Huaca de la Luna has almost become financially self-sufficient and has stimulated the economy and significantly alleviated the poverty of the surrounding valley, which is inhabited by the descendants of the ancient Moche who built the complex. The project provides an important model for the region as it successfully utilized funds from international and local organizations until it became sustainable on its own, thereby avoiding dependence on the underfunded, overworked government for support. The Peruvian government has not been significantly involved in protection or conservation at Huaca de la Luna, although it did fund the construction of a protective shelter system over part of the ruins. As part of the project, a large site museum was completed and opened in 2010.

The Backus Cultural Heritage Foundation is not the only NGO active in Peru today. Other private institutions have also contributed to improving the conditions of the country's cultural heritage. For example, the Fundación Telefónica, created in 1999 by a new Peruvian telecommunications company, has focused on using technology to promote culture and education in Peru to improve equality within the country. One of its primary support areas has been cultural heritage, and its projects have included funding a tourism study on rural sites, the digital recording of the collections of the Larco Herrera Archaeological Museum, and the restoration of the three churches of the Cuzco cathedral complex between 1997 and 2001.[43]

The Yachay Wasi Conservation and Restoration Institute, a division of the Círculo Amigos de la Cultura (CAC, Circle of Friends of Culture), is a private institution that combines education, research, and conservation projects. Its laboratories complete chemical analysis on materials and treatments for projects throughout the region, and its magazine *ICONOS* (icons) publishes the results of its scientific advances in conservation. Yachay Wasi also runs short workshops on pre-Hispanic building technologies for craftsmen and students, and since 1993 it has offered a three-year degree in conservation, with concentrations on specific materials, such as metals, painted wood, or murals.

Yachay Wasi has been particularly active in developing plans for the Cajamarquilla archaeological site outside of Lima. A settlement inhabited from the fifth century until the Spanish conquest by the Huari, Ychma, and Inca peoples, Cajamarquilla's extensive remains include mud-brick houses and pyramids. Though a protected site in Peru, in recent decades the site has been used as a dumping ground and residence for squatters and is threatened by urban development from Lima. Yachay Wasi's plans have not yet been implemented, and the dire conditions at Cajamarquilla led to its inclusion on the World Monuments Watch list of endangered sites in 2006.

Despite the intensive international interest in Peru's cultural heritage and the rise of local NGO and private initiatives, inconsistent legislation, funding needs, and challenged administrative agencies have created difficulties for architectural conservationists working in the country. Damage to a number of Peru's heritage sites by humans

a

b

Figure 35–16 Careful planning and integrated conservation practice at Huaca de la Luna, seat of the Moche culture on the north coast of Peru, has resulted in exemplary work on an ancient earthen site (a). Work at the large complex is notable for its incorporation of the local community (b) in the heritage protection process as well as for the effectiveness of the shelter for the site's fragile earthen remains, which also enhances the visitor's experience.

and through natural causes continues, and illegal trade of antiquities remains a serious problem. In the mid-1990s, ICOMOS warned that Peru's "policy to drastically increase tourism at archaeological sites and historic cities, precisely at a time when the protective mechanisms of these resources [were] at an all-time low" added significantly to their potential threats.[44] Critics argue the newest 2004 law is still deficient, because the criteria for removing sites and objects from protected status is unclear, and the registration system is complicated and inadequately enforced.[45] Peru's heritage policies are yet to be fully implemented, despite a dedicated Defense Directorate within the INC, which is charged with enforcing compliance with legislation, recovering and repatriating illicitly traded antiquities, and representing the state in legal matters concerning municipal or regional governments or private parties.

Indeed, protecting and conserving Peru's rich legacy of important historic architectural sites is a duty the country has both embraced and struggled to accomplish. Today Peru has a significant number of trained professionals who are highly active in international discussions concerning cultural heritage protection, and it sponsors international conferences and workshops to promote international dialogue on best practices in the field. Clearly, as long as international support and legislative and policy reform continues, the monumental task of protecting Peru's cultural heritage is within the reach of these dedicated professionals.

BOLIVIA

Bolivia's relatively small population of eight million and its slow pace of development in comparison to other South American countries has allowed for the survival of a significant portion of its architectural heritage, ranging from its pre-Columbian rock art to its colonial cities. Bolivia was the last country in South America to gain independence from Spain in 1825, and the government has created institutions concerned with protecting the country's heritage ever since. A Supreme Decree issued within the first year of the Bolivian republic's creation argued for the preservation and reuse of historic buildings for educational purposes.[46] However, the built heritage of this small, landlocked Andean country is continually at risk due to a lack of financial commitment and prioritization by the government as well as underappreciation by most of Bolivia's population of the importance of heritage protection.

Measures to protect Bolivia's architectural and archaeological heritage began in the early twentieth century and have grown considerably with the political stabilization of recent decades. In 1906 numerous archaeological sites were designated as property of the government, and funds were made available for their maintenance. New excavations followed soon thereafter. More formal cultural heritage policies were implemented through the National Monuments Act of 1927, which initiated the process of classifying and designating historic sites throughout the country. In 1961 a series of Supreme Decrees and Ministerial Resolutions further clarified this earlier legislation by establishing a comprehensive list of types of objects and sites that could be protected and establishing the legal norms that continue to provide for the protection of Bolivia's heritage today.[47]

The establishment of heritage protection entities in the 1970s laid the foundation for Bolivia's contemporary architectural conservation practice. ICOMOS Bolivia was established in 1973. The Instituto Boliviano de Cultura (Institute for Bolivian Culture) was created in 1975 and began documenting the country's art and architectural heritage and leading conservation projects at selected sites.[48] That same year also saw the founding of the Centro Nacional de Conservación y Restauración de Bienes Inmuebles (CENACORE-BI, National Conservation and Restoration Center for Immovable Heritage).[49] A number of major conservation projects were completed in Bolivia in the 1970s, such as the restoration of the Jesuit mission churches of Chiquitos and accompanying report on the site published by UNESCO. This exemplary project employed local craftspeople trained in traditional building techniques.

The Institute for Bolivian Culture was replaced with a new Secretaría Nacional de Cultura (National Secretary of Culture) in 1993, which four years later evolved to become the Viceministerio de Desarrollo de las Culturas (VDC, Vice Ministry of Cultural Development). The VDC was first a department of the Ministry of Education, Culture, and Sport, but since 2003 it has been one of three sections of the new Ministry of Education and Culture. The VDC's broad responsibilities include cultural policy development, compliance and coordination with international agreements and organizations, oversight of regional and municipal activities, supervision and direction of technical projects, and regulation of illicit trade in cultural goods.

Figure 35–17 Restoration of the Jesuit mission churches of Chiquitos in the state of Santa Cruz in eastern Bolivia, whose architecture fuses European and indigenous traditions, was carried out with the support of UNESCO in the 1970s. It is an early example of organized, internationally supported architectural conservation in Bolivia and its neighboring countries.

Within the VDC, the Dirección General de Patrimonio Cultural (Department of Cultural Patrimony) is directly responsible for managing Bolivia's tangible and intangible cultural heritage, including the country's five cultural World Heritage Sites and its over four hundred designated national architectural heritage sites.[50] The Dirección's four agencies focus on museums, archaeology, libraries, and historic sites. Bolivian legislation allows for strict penalties—including up to six years imprisonment—for the destruction of protected sites or the theft of protected objects.

Though the ministries and departments of the Bolivian government were repeatedly reorganized in the 1990s and early 2000s, CENACORE-BI continued to play a key role in the Bolivian government's efforts to study, inventory, and regulate interventions at its protected historic sites. Today a division of the VDC, CENACORE-BI also sponsors a few conservation projects around the country each year. In addition, throughout Bolivia, numerous municipalities, such as Potosí, Oruro, and La Paz, also have their own specialized agencies focused on architectural conservation and maintain local catalogues of their significant built heritage.[51]

Despite the Bolivian government's initial interest in researching and protecting its diverse wealth of archaeological sites, and the fact that its contemporary population is 60 percent indigenous, the country's colonial heritage has typically been the primary focus of its architectural conservation efforts and represents the majority of its recognized national monuments. Under the Spanish, the area of today's Bolivia quickly developed to be one of the wealthiest in the Americas with the discovery of silver in 1545 near Potosí. Mining provided the economic resources for Bolivia's prosperity for the next two centuries, and Potosí quickly became an institutional, governmental, and educational center. It was the largest city in the Americas in the seventeenth century—but as silver became more difficult to extract from the mines in the nineteenth century, the city began to decline.

The Potosí mines were finally closed in the 1980s, at the same time that the city was recognized as a World Heritage Site. With the assistance of the Agencia Española de Cooperación Internacional para el Desarrollo (AECID, Spanish Agency for International Cooperation for Development), the Potosí Historical Sites Rehabilitation Plan was drafted with regulations for intervention, development, and tourism as well as calls for inventories of the city's movable cultural heritage and further definition of its intangible heritage. Despite this comprehensive plan and the involvement of UNESCO and the AECID, few actual restoration projects have been carried out and Potosí remains a poverty-stricken city of unemployed miners with a derelict collection of public buildings, churches, and houses.

Nevertheless, the Potosí Plan quickly became a model for the conservation of other important urban centers in Bolivia. For example, in 1995, the Sucre Historical Sites Rehabilitation Plan was initiated based on the Potosí Plan and was similarly drafted through a partnership of the AECID, the municipality of Sucre, and the state of Chuquisaca. Nearly 60 percent of Bolivia's designated national monuments are located in Chuquisaca, and most of these are in Sucre. The numerous white-washed churches, important educational buildings, and patio houses of this early-sixteenth-century settlement and colonial capital, originally known as La Plata, demonstrate the architectural trends of the Spanish period. In the city's republican period it was renamed for the country's first president, Antonio José de Sucre, and its colonial center was supplemented with new architectural marvels, such as the circular church known as the Capilla de la Rotonda, which was built in 1852.

The Spanish government's interest in preserving the Iberian legacy in the Americas is also evident in the workshop schools—known as Escuelas Taller—it has sponsored in Bolivia's historic cities. Workshop schools established in the 1990s first in Potosí, then Sucre and Chiquitanía, and most recently in La Paz, have contributed significantly to restoration work in these cities. In Potosí, for example, the extensive restoration of the Church of San Francisco was completed through the Escuelas Taller. In Sucre, since its opening in 1998 fifteen rehabilitation projects have been completed and over three hundred students have graduated from the Escuelas Taller with specializations in various trades, and many of these students will use their new skills to work on other architectural conservation projects in the city.[52]

In Bolivia's smaller colonial cities, there is also architectural heritage in need of conservation that has received less planning attention than in Potosí and Sucre. For example, the central Church of Santiago in Callapa is noted as the one of the most intact sixteenth-century adobe religious complexes in the country and an important example of the mestizo baroque. However, due to the deterioration process of its earthen architecture, it and numerous churches in the region are in need of attention. Natural threats and the lack of maintenance resulted in the inclusion of both the Santiago de Callapa as well as the late baroque adobe Church of San Bartolomé in Arani on the World Monuments Watch list in 1998.

Although Bolivia's architectural conservation movement began with a focus on archaeological remains, for most of the twentieth century these sites suffered from a lack of maintenance and inadequate management. Their protection finally became a recognized issue in the past two decades, largely due to the interest of the international community. Since the mid-1990s, the Bolivian government and various foreign organizations have increasingly paid attention to the country's heritage reflective of its pre-Columbian and indigenous histories. Bolivia's new constitution of 1994 affirmed the responsibility of the state and its citizens to respect and protect the country's "artistic, colonial, archaeological, historical and documentary wealth" but also formally recognized and celebrated the country's multiethnicity for the first time.[53]

Two pre-Columbian sites in Bolivia were added to the World Heritage List in the late 1990s, Tiawanaku and Fuerte de Samaipata. The Tiawanaku people were one of the numerous cultures that have inhabited the Lake Titicaca region of Bolivia over the past 10,000 years. They settled the area beginning in 800 BCE and flourished for more than a millennium, evolving from small villages to an imperial society that peaked in the seventh century. Testaments to the history and development of the Tiawanaku are found in the architectural ruins of their spiritual center, such as the Gate of the Sun—with its well-preserved carvings of winged figures with the heads of condors, tigers, and serpents—as well as the Akapana, a pyramidal temple with seven platforms.

Figure 35–18 The prosperity of the nineteenth-century silver-mining town of Potosí is reflected in its elaborate architecture, though its inhabitants have faced difficult times since its mines were closed in the 1980s. AECID supported workshop schools, known as Escuelas Taller, for training in conservation trades, and it has conducted high-quality restoration work at the Church of San Francisco in Potosí that has elevated the deteriorating appearance and fortunes of the town. Young trainees learned on the job techniques, including reroofing in traditional materials (a), facade restoration (b), and stucco reproduction work (c). The Potosí Escuelas Taller's completed project at the Church of San Francisco (d) is one of scores of architectural conservation projects conducted throughout Latin America since 1984, and the AECID initiative is one of the most generous foreign-government-funded programs in architectural conservation in the world. Images courtesy La Agencia Española de Cooperación para el Desarollo (AECID)

Because of its archaeological importance, the Tiawanaku spiritual center was acquired by the Bolivian state in 1906, and the protected zone was extended in 1933 and 1945. Systematic archaeological exploration of the area did not begin until the 1950s though, and some areas of the site, such as the small subterranean temple and the open Kalasasaya temple were restored at that time. Later the Centro de Investigaciones Antropológicas y Arqueológicas (Center of Anthropological and Archaeological Research) was established to manage the site, and in 1997, a phased master plan for Tiawanaku was developed with financing from the IDB.

Known as "El Fuerte," the Samaipata archaeological site includes a sandstone ridge covered in carvings on both sides and surrounded by the archaeological remains of numerous buildings. As at Tiawanaku, in 1974 the Bolivian government established a Centro de Investigaciones Antropológicas y Arqueológicas de Samaipata (CIAAS, Center of Archaeological and Anthropological Investigations) to maintain and administer Samaipata; however, it has lacked the financial resources to properly protect the site from tourists and vandals or to combat the natural deterioration of the sandstone structures.[54] Even after the inclusion of this important example of pre-Columbian rock-art on the World Heritage List and the drafting of numerous studies of its conditions, the Samaipata complex has continued to deteriorate in the twenty-first century.[55] IDB funded a tourism development plan that included viewing platforms to prevent people from walking over the carvings.

Fortunately for Bolivia's heritage, private organizations have contributed to conservation efforts where government funding has fallen short. For example, the Sociedad de Investigación del Arte Rupestre de Bolivia (SIARB, Bolivian Rock Art Society) has emphasized educational campaigns, site preservation, and management in the Torotoro and Calacala national parks. This organization works to establish site management through the construction of circulation systems such as walkways, paths, and viewing platforms that intervene minimally within these parks. In addition, the World Monuments Fund has sought to draw attention to the threatened status of additional rock art

Figure 35-19 Rock art sites found throughout the world pose special conservation problems. Although some rock art sites in Bolivia are well protected and conserved, others, such as Saipina and Vallegrande (illustrated) are currently threatened. The Ministry of Culture of Bolivia, working in concert with the Bolivian Rock Art Society (known as SIARB) and the World Monuments Fund, are trying to address the problem by raising local awareness and ensuring that proper conservation techniques are used.

sites in Bolivia by including the complexes of Saipina and Vallegrande on its Watch list of endangered sites in 2004.

The Vice-Ministry of Culture of Bolivia unveiled a new Cultural Plan in 2005 that appears to take an important step toward improving the architectural conservation climate in the country. Through financing from the governments of numerous foreign countries, especially the Netherlands and Germany, the 2005 plan provides for restoration projects at ten recognized national monuments, the excavation and conservation of six archaeological sites, and the cataloging and documentation of additional sites throughout the country.[56] Though only focused on a few key locations, once completed these interventions at select historic and archaeological sites will hopefully provide an important catalyst for continued efforts in Bolivia.

Despite its long-standing policies and institutions, inadequate funding for the implementation of conservation projects has meant that Bolivia's built heritage continues to be challenged. Although planning controls and master plans have been developed for Bolivia's key historic and archaeological sites, few such tools have been enforced or carried out—as is true elsewhere in the region. As in neighboring countries, the local chapter of ICOMOS has recognized that cultural heritage conservation is a priority within the Bolivian government, and it has urged in recent decades the updating of legislation and the strengthening of heritage management policies.[57] Awareness of Bolivia's deficiencies has been raised and discussion on improvements continues while pressure is being applied to the government to ensure the country's built legacy is adequately preserved for future generations. Most importantly, measures have begun to be taken in Bolivia and throughout the Andes to encourage the general population to recognize the importance of architectural conservation. As this public interest grows and is combined with increasing attention and funding from international organizations and local governments, the fate of the architectural heritage of the Andes seems more promising today than ever before.

ENDNOTES

1. The Viceroyalty of New Granada, based in Bogotá, included today's Colombia, Venezuela, Ecuador, and Panama. The Viceroyalty of the Río de la Plata, based in Buenos Aires, included today's Argentina, Bolivia, Paraguay, and Uruguay.

2. Graziano Gasparini, *Coro: Patrimonio Mundial* [Coro: World Heritage] (Caracas: Armitano Editores, 1994), 61.

3. World Heritage Committee, "Decision 29COM 7B.92 - Coro and its Port (Venezuela)," World Heritage Center, http://whc.unesco.org/en/decisions/449 (accessed July 25, 2010).

4. "Mission Report: Coro and its Port (Bolivarian Republic of Venezuela) (658), May 9-13, 2008," World Heritage Committee, 32nd Session, Quebec, Canada, July 2-10, 2008 (Paris: UNESCO, 2008).

5. Maria Ismenia Toledo, "Management and Prevention of Risks to the Cultural Heritage: Case of Venezuela," *Cultural Heritage Disaster Preparedness and Response*, ed. Cristina Menegazzi (Paris: International Council of Museums [ICOM], 2004), 260; http://icom.museum/disaster_preparedness_book/country/ismenia_toledo.pdf (accessed July 17, 2010).

6. María Carlota Ibáñez and Ramon Paolini, "Venezuela," in *Trails to Treasures: A Tour of South America's Cultural Heritage*, eds. US/ICOMOS and the World Monuments Fund (WMF) (Washington, DC: US/ICOMOS and the WMF, 2001), 57–59.

7. ICOMOS, "Venezuela," *Heritage@Risk 2000* (Paris: ICOMOS, 2000), www.international.icomos.org/risk/world_report/2000/venez1_2000.htm (accessed February 27, 2010).

8. ICOMOS, "Venezuela," *Heritage@Risk 2002* (Paris: ICOMOS, 2002), www.international.icomos.org/risk/2002/venezuela2002_eng.htm (accessed February 27, 2010).

9. ICOMOS, "Venezuela," *Heritage@Risk 2000*.

10. Luis Dunque Goméz, "Defensa del Patrimonio Histórico y Artistico de Colombia Legislación," www.colciencias.gov.co/seiaal/congreso/Foro/DUQUE.htm (accessed February 27, 2010).

11. "Periodos históricos," Informe del Sistema Nacional de Cultura-Colombia, www.campus-oei.org/cultura/colombia/01.htm (accessed February 27, 2010).

12. The Roerich Pact, www.roerich.org/nr_RPact.html (accessed February 27, 2010).

13. Juan Carlos Uribe, "The Protection of Cultural Heritage in Colombia," in Hoffman, *Art and Cultural Heritage*, 119.

14. Rodolfo Ulloa, "Colombia," in *Trails to Treasures*, 46.

15. Ibid., 45.

16. Alberto Saldarriaga, *Restoring Architecture: The Work of Alvaro Barrera*, ed. Benjamin Villegas (Bogotá: Villegas Editores, 2003), 65.

17. "Perfil Actual," Informe del Sistema Nacional de Cultura-Colombia, www.sinic.gov.co/OEI/paginas/informe/informe_24.asp (accessed February 27, 2010).

18. Ricardo Moncada Esquivel, "El Patrimonio Indefenso," *Gaceta Dominical*, October 5, 2003.

19. "Periodos Históricos," Informe del Sistema Nacional de Cultura-Colombia, www.campus-oei.org/cultura/colombia/01.htm (accessed February 27, 2010).

20. Ernesto Salazar, "Between Crisis and Hope: Archaeology in Ecuador," *SAA Bulletin* 13, no. 4 (September/October 1995): www.saa.org/Portals/0/SAA/publications/SAAbulletin/14-3/SAA6.html (accessed February 27, 2010).

21. ICOMOS, "Cuenca (Ecuador)," Advisory Body Evaluation, no. 863, June 30, 1988, http://whc.unesco.org/archive/advisory_body_evaluation/863.pdf (accessed February 27, 2010).

22. Kintto Lucas,"Cuenca es Patrimonio Cultural de la Humanidad," *Nuevo Servicio Informativo Iberoamericano*, June 2000, www.oei.org.co/nuevo sii/nentrega5/art07.htm (accessed February 27, 2010).

23. David Mangurian. "All Dressed Up and Looking for Investors: Ecuadorian Capital Shows How Public Private Partnership Can Preserve Urban Heritage," *IDB América* (January 1, 2001), http://www.iadb.org/features-and-web-stories/2001-01/english/all-dressed-up-and-looking-for-investors-6107.html (accessed February 27, 2010).

24. Sylvio Mutal, "From Ideas to Action: the Challenge of Management and Economics," in *Trails to Treasures*, 75; and Mahasti Afshar, "Quito: Preserving a Historic City," *GCI Newsletter* 8, no. 3 (Fall 1993): www.getty.edu/conservation/publications/newsletters/8_3/quito.html (accessed February 27, 2010).

25. "A conversation with Jamil Mahuad Witt," *GCI Newsletter* 8, no. 3 (Fall 1993): www.getty.edu/conservation/publications/newsletters/8_3/witt.html (accessed February 27, 2010).

26. Wilson Herdoíza, "Ecuador," in *Trails to Treasures*, 49.

27. Salazar, "Between Crisis and Hope."

28. José Correa, "Peru," in *Trails to Treasures*, 55.

29. Jack Batievsky and Jorge Velarde, "The Protection of Cultural Patrimony in Peru," in Hoffman, *Art and Cultural Heritage*, 101.

30. "Qué es el INC?" Instituto Nacional de Cultura, http://inc.perucultural.org.pe/inst1.shtml (accessed February 27, 2010).

31. The complete list of directorates (*direcciones*) includes: historic colonial and republic heritage, museums, arts promotion, archaeology, defense, promotion and diffusion of culture, research, cultural landscapes, and world heritage sites, as well as the national directorate, which coordinates and oversees the others. "Áreas Técnicas," *Instituto Nacional de Cultura*, http://inc.perucultural.org.pe/areas_tecnicas.shtml?x=7 (accessed July 21, 2010).

32. Correa, "Peru," 53.

33. ICOMOS, "Arequipa (Peru)," Advisory Body Report, no. 1016, July 20, 1999, http://whc.unesco.org/archive/advisory_body_evaluation/1016.pdf (accessed February 27, 2010).

34. Eduardo Fierro, "Initial Report on 23 June 2001 Arequipa, Peru Earthquake," *Earthquake Engineering Research Center* (2002), www.eeri.org/lfe/pdf/peru_arequipa_initial_reconnaissance_part1.pdf (accessed February 27, 2010).

35. Franz Grupp, "The 2001 Earthquake in Arequipa: Lessons Learned and International Rescue Network for Endangered Cultural Heritage," in Menegazzi, *Cultural Heritage Disaster Preparedness and Response*, 213.

36. Grupp, "2001 Earthquake in Arequipa," 213.

37. Erica Avrami, "Project Terra," *GCI Newsletter* 16, no. 1 (Spring 2001): www.getty.edu/conservation/publications/newsletters/16_1/news_in_cons1.html (accessed February 27 2010).

38. Henry Fountain. "Archaeological Site in Peru is Called the Oldest City in the Americas," *New York Times*, April 27, 2001, A.6.

39. Anthony F. Aveni, "Solving the Mystery of the Nasca Lines," *Archaeology* (May/June 2000): 26–35.

40. "Experts Say Tourists Harm Machu Picchu: UNESCO May Add Ruins to List of Endangered World Heritage Sites," Associated Press, *MSNBC.com*, July 1, 2008, www.msnbc.msn.com/id/25481449/ (accessed February 28, 2010).

41. José Gabriel Chueca, "Can Peru Manage Machu Picchu?," *The Art Newspaper* no. 122 (February 2002): 12.

42. Patrick J. McDonnell, "Machu Picchu Shows Wear of Being on the Must-See List," *Los Angeles Times*, May 3, 2006, reprinted by the *Global Heritage Fund News*, www.globalheritagefund.org/news/conservation_news/la_times_machu_picchu_may3_06.asp (accessed February 27, 2010).

43. "Rescate del Patrimonio Histórico," Fundación Telefónica, www.fundaciontelefonica.org.pe/resca.htm (accessed February 27, 2010). An additional initiative has been conducted by the Fundación Wiese at Huaca Cao on the north coast of Peru, where a long-term commitment to conservation is underway involving a site museum and protective shelters.

44. US/ICOMOS, "Peru's Heritage Under Siege," *Newsletter* no. 3 (1996), www.icomos.org/usi-comos/news/usicomos396.html (accessed July 26, 2010). Due to the continuing threat of illicit trade of antiquities, ICOMOS began a ten-year program to combat the pillage of archaeological sites in Peru in 1992. The projects included many interventions and resulted in the recovery of more than three-thousand objects listed as for sale on the international market in just the first six months. In addition, ICOMOS has worked to educate local communities of the valleys of Lambayeque concerning the value of these artifacts. ICOMOS, "Peru," *Heritage@Risk*, 2002–2003 (Paris: ICOMOS, 2003), www.international.icomos.org/risk/2002/peru2002.htm (accessed February 27, 2010).

45. Alberto Martorell-Carreño, "Cultural Patrimony and Property Rights in Peru," in Hoffman, *Art and Cultural Heritage*, 106.

46. Elizabeth Torres, "Chronological Overview of Developments in Bolivian and Latin American Cultural Heritage Legislation with a Special Emphasis on the Protection of Indigenous Culture," in Hoffman, *Art and Cultural Heritage*, 124.

47. Ibid., 124–25.

48. "Breve Historia," Viceministerio de Desarrollo de las Culturas, www.bolivia.com/empresas/cultura/Breve_historia/index.asp (accessed February 27, 2010).

49. The National Conservation and Restoration Center for Movable a Heritage (Centro Nacional de Conservación y Restauración de Bienes Culturales Muebles, CENACORE-BM) and a National Cataloging Center (Centro Nacional de Catalogación, CENDCA) were also created at that time.

50. "Dirección General de Patrimonio Cultural," Viceministerio de Desarrollo de las Culturas, www.bolivia.com/empresas/cultura/Direccion_Patrimonio/index.asp (accessed February 27, 2010).

51. Mireya Muñoz, "Bolivia," in *Trails to Treasures*, 42.

52. "Escuela Taller de Sucre (Bolivia) Celebra su Décimo Aniversario, " AECID, http://www.aecid.es/web/es/cooperacion/prog_cooperacion/Patrimonio/noticias/noticia51.html (accessed July 26, 2010).

53. "Normas para la Protección Del Patrimonio Cultural Boliviano," Viceministerio de Desarrollo de las Cultura, www.bolivia.com/empresas/cultura/Patrimonio_Cultural/normas_proteccion.asp (accessed February 27, 2010).

54. A German architectural conservation company, Ars Restaurato, has begun assisting with the conservation of the sandstone. ICOMOS, "Bolivia," *Heritage@Risk 2000*, www.international.icomos.org/risk/world_report/2000/boliv_2000.htm (accessed February 27, 2010).

55. ICOMOS, "Bolivia."

56. "Viceministerio de Cultura Plan 2005," Viceministerio de Desarrollo de las Culturas, www.bolivia.com/Empresas/Cultura/Documentos/PLAN_2005_2.doc (accessed February 27 2010).

57. ICOMOS, "Bolivia."

CHAPTER 36

The Southern Cone

The Southern Cone of South America includes the countries of Uruguay, Paraguay, Argentina, and Chile. As elsewhere in Latin America, these countries share common histories—including pre-Columbian, Spanish colonial, and independent republican periods. In the twentieth century, the region witnessed cycles of instability, with dominating military dictatorships alternating with periods of democratic openness, and successive financial crises alternating with periods of economic prosperity. Until the 1990s, organized cultural heritage protection made little headway in South America's Southern Cone, but with the passage of protective legislation and founding of cultural heritage conservation agencies and organizations, it has gained momentum in recent decades. This region is richly endowed with architectural heritage, including sites revealing the region's diverse history. Evidence of Polynesian contacts can be found in Chile on Easter Island—while in Argentina's Patagonia, numerous traditional Welsh teahouses still exist, and in its capital of Buenos Aires, the large Italian population has influenced everything from the city's tango tradition to its architecture. The ruins of the Jesuit missions in Argentina, Chile, and Paraguay are among the strongest reflections of the region's colonial experience.

Despite the stability of the past two decades, South America's Southern Cone has had a history of massive foreign debt that has often led to periods of great fiscal restraint in which funding for architectural conservation programs and projects has been limited. However, as these countries move forward on their positive economic and political paths, the climate for cultural heritage protection in the region has never been stronger than it is today. With the increasing involvement of the private sector as well as international organizations, the conservation professionals and governments of these countries have begun initiating the multilateral programs necessary to ensure the future of the architectural heritage of the continent's southern half.

URUGUAY

The Spanish explored and claimed the area of today's Uruguay in 1525; however, this region, known as the Banda Oriental (Eastern Shore) until 1830, had few mineral resources and few inhabitants and was of little interest to the Spanish. As a result, Uruguay was settled and developed primarily in the past two centuries. One of the most European countries of South America, with few indigenous people and few mestizos, the population today is almost completely comprised of descendents of the Spanish and other immigrants who came in the eighteenth and nineteenth centuries. In the 1820s, Uruguay separated from Spain, first becoming part of Brazil then part

◀Figure 36-1 In a program conceived in 1968, the Uruguayan government established the Consejo Ejecutivo Honorario de las Obras de Preservación y Reconstrucción, which examined the architectural conservation potential of one of Uruguay's oldest cities, Colonia del Sacramento (founded in 1680). By 1970 the city's defensive walls were restored and advocacy actions such as the opening of an interpretative center were underway. Illustrated here are the restored lighthouse and the stabilized ruins of the 17th-century Convent of San Francisco. Such projects launched the conservation of even more of the town's architecture, especially historic residential buildings, and inspired conservation work elsewhere in Uruguay.

of Argentina, and finally an independent country in 1828. Throughout the nineteenth century, Uruguay witnessed further interventions from these two significantly larger and more powerful neighbors, as well as repeated civil wars. The first half of the twentieth century was relatively peaceful and development of the country began, but economic problems in the 1950s led to unrest and a military dictatorship from 1973 until 1984.

Despite the political and economic difficulties in Uruguay during the second half of the twentieth century, architectural conservation received increasing government and public attention, beginning with the establishment of a Commission on Historic Sites in 1950. Countrywide heritage-protection legislation was passed in the early 1970s that reorganized the Comisión del Patrimonio Histórico, Artístico y Cultural de la Nación (Commission on the Historical, Artistic, and Cultural Heritage of the Nation) within the Ministry of Education and Culture. A graduated system of national monuments was established and exemption from real estate taxes for designated sites through the Ministry of Industry soon followed. In 1987 an inventory of state-owned buildings was conducted to identify those of special cultural value.

This complicated system of overlapping jurisdictions of multiple ministries led to a reorganization of responsibilities in 1997, and today the Comisión del Patrimonio Cultural has the authority to declare national monuments, approve rehabilitation projects, supervise archaeological excavations, inspect sites, monitor exports, and keep an inventory of sites and objects. The Comisión is organized into three main departments: one focused on archaeology; another focused on architectural, urban, and landscape sites; and a restoration workshop primarily focused on movable heritage.

Uruguay's capital city Montevideo was not established until 1726 and only then in response to concern about the expanding Portuguese claim to the territory demonstrated by their founding of the settlement of Colonia del Sacramento on the northern bank of the Río de la Plata in 1680. These fortified cities are among the most important aspects of Uruguay's colonial heritage. Colonia has an organic form that follows the topography of the banks of the Río de la Plata and reveals the incremental growth and repeated destruction of this Portuguese outpost. Its whitewashed structures and narrow, cobblestone streets are now surrounded with eclectic combinations of nineteenth- and twentieth-century architecture, such as the neoclassical residences around the Plaza Mayor.

In 1968 the Uruguayan government established the Consejo Ejecutivo Honorario de las Obras de Preservación y Reconstrucción de la Antigua Ciudad de la Colonia del Sacramento (Honorary Executive Board for the Preservation and Reconstruction of Old Colonia del Sacramento). The Consejo immediately launched a survey of the city, staged an exhibition on its architectural history, and began planning for its rehabilitation. By 1970 it had restored the city's defensive walls and its Franciscan convent, opened an interpretative center, installed new street signage, and begun purchasing historic houses. More buildings were donated to the Consejo in the following years, and major restoration projects were undertaken at the Church of the Most Holy Sacrament, the Plaza Mayor, and the Casa de Palacios. The Consejo was reorganized in the 1980s but continued its active work in the city by documenting every structure in the historic district, repaving streets using traditional materials and techniques, and persuading utility companies to bury power and communication cables.

Colonia del Sacramento's designation as a World Heritage Site in 1995 launched a new wave of government interest in conserving and repairing structures in the historic heart of the city and in improving conditions and promoting tourism in this economically depressed district. Financial support for projects in Colonia has come from the governments of Portugal and Spain, the IDB, the United Nations Development Program (UNDP), and from a Lisbon-based nongovernment organization, the Calouste Gulbenkian Foundation.[1]

a

b

Figure 36-2 Restoration in the area of the Plaza de Independencia in Montevideo, Uruguay, included a six-year project to restore the grand Teatro Solís (a), built in 1856, and other structures on the square, such as the twenty-six-story Palacio Salvo (b), designed by Mario Palanti, which was the tallest building in South America after its completion in 1927.

Uruguay's Spanish colonial city of Montevideo was situated further west than Colonia along the Río de la Plata. Due to its natural harbor, it quickly became a bustling port and a buffer zone between Portuguese Brazil and Spanish Argentina. In an effort to keep these neighbors at bay, Uruguay sought British support in the nineteenth century, and evidence of this political relationship can be found in the city's architecture of the period. Though still little more than a village in 1860, within twenty-five years the city had tripled in size, and today it is home to 1.33 million inhabitants—nearly 40 percent of Uruguay's population.

Montevideo has an eclectic skyline of colonial, Italianate, neo-classical and art deco structures. The original city was built in haste with temporary structures between 1724 and 1795 and did not follow the traditional grid structure of most Spanish cities. However, beginning at the end of the eighteenth century, original buildings were replaced with more permanent structures of distinct styles, with the neoclassical dominating until 1860. The Plaza de Independencia reflects the juxtaposition and fusion of the city's distinct architectural periods. A black marble mausoleum and statue of the national hero of independence—José Gervasio Artigas, takes center stage in the plaza—while a colonial arched doorway is found on one side of the plaza, early twentieth-century buildings on another, and a taller, Corbusian curtain wall structures on *pilotis* from the mid-twentieth century on yet another side. The twenty-six-storey Palacio Salvo, designed by Mario Palanti, was the tallest building in South America for decades after its completion in 1927. In recent years the municipality has begun restoring these historic buildings—such as the 1856 Teatro Solis, one of South America's finest theaters, which was painstakingly restored between 1998 and 2004 for $14 million.

A major recent redevelopment project in Montevideo that aimed to rehabilitate the entire La Aguada neighborhood ended up as a preservation battle that activated the local community. The controversy focused on the fate of the city's central railway station (built in 1897). In 1998 the IDB extended a $28 million loan to improve the infrastructure of the neighborhood and to restore the facade and roof of the historic station. The building's owners, the Sociedad Fénix, a real estate corporation of the Banco Hipotecario of Uruguay, hoped to lease the building to developers who would sensitively create a residential, retail and entertainment complex in the station and the former rail yards. However, many citizens' organizations, especially the El Grupo de Pasajeros en Defensa de la Estación Central (Passengers' Group in Defense of the Central Station), opposed the redevelopment plan and moving the train service from its central city location. Though they agreed the railway station should be restored, they hoped also to retain its historic function. In May 2005, after years of public protest and lost revenue from the inconvenient new railway station on the outskirts of the city, the municipality abandoned the plan for the mixed-use complex and reopened the historic central station as a passenger and freight rail terminus. The remaining funds were redirected to provide low- and medium-income housing through the restoration of Montevideo's Goas neighborhood.

Some of Uruguay's heritage professionals have begun to explore the potential of agrotourism and the gaucho traditions associated with the large cattle ranches established by the Spanish in the eighteenth century as frontier posts in the northern part of the country. In addition, in recent years, new emphasis has been placed on the importance of archaeological research as understanding of Uruguay's indigenous heritage grows. As a member of ICOMOS, Uruguay has been involved in the growing discussion of the protection of underwater heritage, and it is primarily concerned with the protection of artifacts in the Bahía de Montevideo (Bay of Montevideo).

The banking crisis in Uruguay in 2002 lessened what little financial resources had begun to be dedicated to architectural conservation in the country, but there is growing evidence of a renewed commitment. In 2006 the Comisión del Patrimonio Cultural launched a Heritage Days program where historic sites are highlighted for a weekend in September or October and public participation and awareness of cultural heritage are promoted throughout Uruguay. In addition to many historic sites and museums being open free of charge, the Heritage Days also include dance performances, art exhibitions, and concerts. Through initiatives like this, the government can continue to involve the public in architectural conservation activities and help secure the future for the country's historic sites.

PARAGUAY

Paraguay is divided by its namesake river into the Chaco Plain in the west and the Paraná River plateau in the east. The still sparsely populated, harsh Chaco landscape was historically inhabited by nomadic cultures whose ancestors retain their independent identity. Settlement and colonization concentrated in the fertile plains of the Paraná River and centered on the Spanish town of Asunción. The war of the Triple Alliance between Argentina, Brazil, and Paraguay in the mid-nineteenth century was the bloodiest war in Latin American history, and it left Paraguay devastated with one-third of its population killed and much of its built fabric destroyed. Reconstruction and industrialization followed, but the twentieth century brought additional wars and new dictators. During the final quarter of the twentieth century, Paraguay finally achieved a stable government and began active participation in regional cultural heritage protection efforts.

Organized heritage conservation in Paraguay therefore began significantly later than in most of its neighboring countries. Rather than initial efforts occurring in the 1930s and 1940s, the Paraguayan government officially recognized the value of its natural landscapes by protecting designated areas and establishing several national parks first in 1973 and turned to archaeological and architectural sites only in the 1980s.[2] A 1982 law created the Dirección General de Patrimonio Histórico Cultural (General Directorate for Cultural Heritage) within the Ministry of Education and Culture. Today the Dirección General includes separate divisions focused on museums, archives, the national library, and cultural goods. The first government sponsored inventories, surveys, and restoration projects in Paraguay also were undertaken in the 1980s.

With the return to civilian rule in 1992, after nearly six decades of military dictatorships, a new constitution was drafted. Article 81 of that constitution identifies the government's role in the conservation and protection of the country's heritage as defining and registering objects and working for the reappropriation of objects found outside of the country.[3] To further these ends, in 1998 the Paraguayan government established the Fondo Nacional para la Cultura y las Artes (FONDEC, National Fund for Culture and the Arts) with an initial contribution of $500,000 and annual support from the state budget. FONDEC's mission is to support artistic production and heritage conservation in Paraguay as well as to encourage private sector involvement in these activities through tax incentives and loans.

Cultural heritage conservation efforts in Paraguay have concentrated on the colonial architecture and more recently on the tangible and intangible elements of the Guaraní culture, the indigenous peoples who inhabited the area before the arrival of the Spanish and remain an important element of the population today. Within the region, Paraguay retains the strongest ties to its pre-Hispanic culture, with more than seventeen distinctive indigenous communities, and Guaraní continuing as one of the country's two official languages. Modern Paraguayan society has in fact been formed over the past few centuries as a fusion of local Guaraní and imported Spanish traditions, most notably visible in its Jesuit missions that are among the most important historical and architectural sites in the country.

Although the Jesuit Guaraní missions constitute the most well known colonial architecture of Paraguay, the wooden churches built by the Franciscans are also significant. These churches were built in the sixteenth century as the initiating structures of small settlements, and they were uniquely placed in the middle of the main squares rather than along one of the sides.[4] The wooden churches were generally rebuilt during the eighteenth century using original construction techniques, and some house exceptional *retablos* (altars) and baroque polychrome religious images. Surrounding the churches were indigenous dwellings referred to as *tiras*, which are characterized by continuous porches on their front facades. During the nineteenth century this vernacular style evolved into the continuous porches typical of the neoclassical streets seen in San Lorenzo.[5]

Paraguay's capital of Asunción is one of the oldest cities in the Americas. Founded in 1537, it served as the starting point for expeditions to explore the Southern Cone of the continent and to establish other cities, such as Buenos Aires. Because its origins predate the Laws of the Indies, its original layout is more organic and fitted to the landscape than the typical Spanish colonial cities of Latin America. Paraguay was a peripheral region for much of the colonial era, not tightly controlled and known for its rebelliousness, and as a result, the city of Asunción remained quite undeveloped even in the early nineteenth century. In the 1820s, after Paraguayan independence, Asunción's streets were paved and a massive construction campaign eradicated much of the historic city, replacing it with an imposed geometric grid and new buildings. This urban redevelopment was organized by independent Paraguay's first leader, the dictator José Gaspar Rodríguez de

Figure 36-3 One of the few buildings from the colonial period to have survived the almost complete rebuilding of Paraguay's capital city of Asunción is the home of Juana Maria de Lara, who led the country's revolution in 1811. In the 1960s it opened as the Casa de la Independencia museum, and it was restored in 2003 thanks to local philanthropist Nicolás Darío Latourrete Bo.

Francia, who presided over a period of political and cultural isolation in the first half of the nineteenth century during which foreign trade and travel were forbidden and arts and architecture stagnated.[6] Economic reforms in the mid-nineteenth century led to Asunción's rapid growth, but even today the city's population is only around 550,000, unlike the mega-cities many other South American capitals have become since the mid-twentieth century.

Few colonial-era buildings have survived in Asunción, but one important colonial structure that has been conserved because of the important historic role it played during the revolution in 1811 is the home of Juana Maria de Lara, now known as the Casa de la Independencia. In addition, Spain's AECID has provided funding to preserve Spanish colonial heritage as well as for the restoration of the 1860s Carlos A. López Train Station in Asunción, the terminus of one of the first rail systems in South America, which now serves as a rail museum. In addition, the AECID established a workshop-school, Escuela Taller, to train high school students in conservation crafts similar to those established in other South American countries.

One of the first areas of the city to receive attention from the public and the municipal government, as soon as the transition to democracy began in the late 1980s, was the area known as the Manzan de la Riviera. This complex of historic houses, built from the mid-eighteenth to the early-twentieth century, is directly across the street from the Palacio de López, the presidential palace constructed in 1857, which was itself restored and fitted with sensitively installed, modern air-conditioning systems in the 1990s. The idea to restore and reuse the houses of Manzan de la Riviera originated with architectural students and local architectural organizations in 1989, and the city soon began acquiring the buildings and took the idea to the AECID, which contributed to their restoration beginning in 1991. The Casa Viola was one of the oldest structures and the first to be rehabilitated and transformed into a historical museum for the city. Other projects soon followed: For example, the early twentieth-century art nouveau Casa Clari became a coffee shop, the drastically altered 1912 neoclassical Casa Clari-Mestre became an auditorium, and the well-preserved 1804 Casa Castelví became an exhibition space and children's recreation center.

Figure 36-4 Restoration of houses in the late 1980s in the area known as the Manzan de la Riviera in Asunción, Paraguay, originated as a project of architecture students and local heritage conservationists. The eventual restoration of the entire district was launched with funding and technical support from the AECID.

In 1991 the municipality of Asunción participated in the chartering of an independent organization, the Centro de Conservación del Patrimonio Cultural (CCPC, Center for the Conservation of Cultural Heritage). Today the CCPC is active in strengthening government capacities and promoting public participation in preservation activities as well as in organizing conferences and completing actual restoration projects at key sites. Through a grant from the U.S. Ambassador's Fund for Cultural Preservation, it began the compilation of a digital database of all historic buildings along Asunción's waterfront in 2001. The project has since been expanded to encompass other sites within the country. More recently, CCPC has entered into a partnership with the National University of Mar del Plata in Argentina to offer a master's degree in architectural and urban conservation.

Though the Paraguayan Ministry of Education and Culture identifies the three primary elements of its heritage as its natural parks, sites related to the Guaraní and other indigenous communities, and the Jesuit missions, conservation work in the country has not been limited to these categories. Paraguay has established a cultural heritage conservation agenda that also embraces nineteenth- and twentieth-century sites. Since the early 1990s, several new private organizations have also joined in architectural conservation activities, such as the Cabildo Fundación, established in 1991, which primarily focuses on education and founding of libraries in rural areas, but it has also notably promoted cultural heritage protection. In addition, in 2008 the Foundation Nicolás Darío Latourrete Bo was established to promote Paraguayan art, culture, and heritage at home and abroad, and it has been working on numerous projects, including the creation of a Sacred Art Museum in the restored, Italianate turn-of-the-twentieth-century Villa Lina in Asunción. In addition, municipal governments and international organizations have also participated in the protection and promotion of Paraguay's architectural heritage in recent decades, indicating an increasingly positive future for the country's historic sites.

Figure 36–5 Map of the Guaraní missions of Paraguay. Image source *The Missions Guaraní Universe*, Esteban Angel Snihur, Golden Company SRL, Misiones Province Government, 2007.

Conserving South America's Guaraní Missions
Norma Barbacci

A unique collection of architectural assets with similar conservation challenges shared by a number of South American countries are the Jesuit Guaraní missions, or *reducciónes,* built in the seventeenth and eighteenth centuries near the Paraná and Uruguay rivers. Catholic missions are found throughout Latin America, but the Jesuit missions of the Guaraní peoples were special because of their independence and economic strength, which lasted until the order was expelled from Spanish territories in 1767.

The Society of Jesus, better known as the Jesuits, was founded in 1540 by Ignatius of Loyola as a new missionary order within the Catholic Church. In 1607 the Spanish monk Diego de Torres was granted permission from the Spanish crown to establish missions to the Guaraní in a frontier zone devoid of the mineral resources the Spanish exploited elsewhere in South America. The mission system they established involved communal property and land planning for residential, commercial, and agricultural purposes.

During its height, the entire Jesuit system in the region was based in the city of Córdoba in today's Argentina. When the city was originally laid out in 1573, the Jesuits were given one of the city's seventy blocks, as were the other religious orders. Construction in the Jesuit block did not begin until the early seventeenth century, but at that time a number of major institutional buildings were built in quick succession. The first completed was the stone and brick Colegio Máximo, organized around a colonnaded central courtyard. This later became the Royal and Pontifical University and is today part of the National University of Córdoba. The second building constructed was the church, with a massive dome, two towers, elaborate baroque *retablo,* and a wooden roof reminiscent of a ship's hull. The richly decorated facades of the college completed the Jesuit complex of Córdoba.

The Jesuit block in Córdoba was recognized as a national monument of Argentina in the 1930s, and overly interventionist restoration projects were carried out at that time. The block, as well as five of the *estancias* (rural settlements) that supported it, were added to the World Heritage List in 2000. The estancias, which focused on specific activities such as textile production, agriculture, or cattle breeding, were privatized after the Jesuit's expulsion in the late eighteenth century, but they have all been protected by local and national preservation ordinances in the twentieth century. Many have been recently restored and opened as museums.

Though the central Jesuit block in Córdoba is of great importance to the historical and architectural history of South America, the even greater Jesuit contribution to the region were thirty Jesuit Guaraní missions. The missions were established during the seventeenth and eighteenth centuries throughout the independent province of Paraguay, which encompassed parts of present-day Argentina, Brazil, and Paraguay (eight in Paraguay, seven in Brazil, and fifteen in Argentina). Other Catholic orders had been ministering in South America for more than a century, but the Southern Cone of the continent was only just being explored, and the Jesuits were among the first to interact with the peoples of this region and to develop its potential. Though the Jesuits converted the Guaraní to Christianity and encouraged these formerly nomadic hunters to live in organized settlements and focus their efforts on animal husbandry and agriculture, much of their culture, including their language and social structure, were respected and preserved by the Jesuits. The prosperity of the reducciónes allowed for increased specialization, including training in the arts and in the woodcarvings that decorate the mission churches. The carvings that have survived demonstrate the high level of artistic skill the Guaraní achieved.

The architecture of each of the reducciónes in the region presents perhaps the richest examples of the fusing of cultures found anywhere in South America. The baroque architecture patronized by the Jesuits around the world combined with the techniques, traditions, and motifs of the Guaraní to create interesting, unique, and beautiful architecture. For example, the elaborate carved stone figures on the church facades included the physical features of the indigenous people, including long hair and large foreheads, as well as combined elements of their traditional culture with new, imported ideas—such as angels holding maracas. Each reducción was organized around a large central plaza dominated by a church flanked by a cloister, school, and a house for the two priests on one of its sides and a cemetery, hospital, and orphanage on its other. The other sides of the square were lined with parallel rows of *casas de indios,* or residential structures, housing the four to six thousand Guaraní who lived and worked in each reducción. These large stone buildings had tiled roofs and covered verandas and included rooms for eight to ten families.

(continued)

The economic success of the Jesuit mission system led to direct competition with the landowners of the Spanish colonies in the region, especially because the Jesuits protected the Guaraní from those who sold them to the landowners as slaves, or *bandeirantes*. In Europe, the political and economic power of the Jesuits also led to envy and distrust, and they were expelled from various countries, including from all Spanish territories by King Carlos III in 1767. Their missions in South America were taken over by other congregations who did not understand the complex management system of the mission network and tried to operate them as self-sufficient units, which quickly led to the economic ruin and abandonment of these once prosperous settlements. During the independence and civil wars of the early nineteenth century, many of the reducciónes were completely destroyed.

In 1983 the São Miguel das Missões site in Brazil was added to the World Heritage List. The mission was moved twice before construction began at its present site in 1687, and its church was completed in 1750 according to the designs of a Jesuit architect from Milan, Giovanni Battista Primoli, who worked in Buenos Aires, Córdoba, and Concepción. The church burned shortly after its construction and was rebuilt quickly before the Jesuit expulsion, and its ruins were restored by the Brazilian government in the 1920s as well as with UNESCO's assistance in the 1980s.

In 1983 the São Miguel World Heritage List site was expanded to include four other similar Jesuit missions in Argentina, and the importance of protecting the surviving Jesuit Guaraní missions was recognized by local and international architectural conservationists. One of the most complete of these complexes was the San Ignacio Miní mission in Argentina, built in 1666, rediscovered in the jungle in 1944, and immediately protected and restored by the Argentine government. Visitation to the site was not controlled and looting, graffiti, and other damage were problems for decades. In 1996 the site was added to the World Monuments Fund Watch list. The American Express Corporation and the Inter-American Development Bank (IDB) helped fund interventions at the San Ignacio Miní mission. However, in the early twenty-first century, some of its walls were still so near collapse they had to be buttressed with extensive wooden scaffolding, and the expansion of the town of San Ignacio Miní was beginning to encroach on the protected area.

Numerous other organizations got involved at other mission sites in the region. In the late 1990s, a new visitor's center, entrance, and protective shelter for the ruins were built for the Nuestra Señora de Loreto Mission and Santa Ana Mission in Argentina. With financial assistance from Germany, the nonprofit Paracuaria Foundation in Asunción stabilized the ruins, restored the wall carvings, and used fragments to rebuild the pulpit of the Santísima Trinidad de Paraná mission. This early eighteenth-century mission is the best preserved example in Paraguay, retaining much of its urban structure and its buildings. A museum and interpretive center as well as conservation workshop are planned for the site. The Spanish government funded the cleaning of the Jesús de Tavarangüe mission, which was still incomplete when the Jesuits left it in 1767 and had been previously restored in the 1960s. In 1993 these two missions together became Paraguay's first and only recognized World Heritage Site. Due to its additions and reconstructions, a third Jesuit Guaraní mission in Paraguay was considered lacking in authenticity, and therefore it was not included in the World Heritage designation. This site, the Mission San Cosme y Damián, was recently restored with the assistance of the German Catholic Church. In addition, in 2004, the U.S. Ambassador's Fund for Cultural Preservation extended a $27,000 grant for conservation, community outreach, and traditional craft training at three other Jesuit missions in Paraguay.

In Bolivia in the first half of the eighteenth century the Jesuits built the churches of six additional reducciónes as similar missionary settlements for the Chiquito peoples, and these missions were also added to the World Heritage List. Like the Guaraní missions in the province of Paraguay, the Chiquito missions were similar agricultural-based communities that converted the local population to Christianity but retained much of their traditional cultural and language. The Bolivian missions survived the Jesuit expulsion, however, and continue as villages even today. The World Heritage nomination noted their continuation as living heritage, still inhabited and used by local communities, rather than as archaeological sites like those in Paraguay, Argentina, and Brazil. In the 1970s, a UNESCO-led project involved the restoration of the central churches of these six Bolivian missions.

In 2002 the World Monuments Fund organized an international workshop to discuss the fate of all of the surviving Jesuit Guaraní missions in Brazil, Argentina, and Paraguay, which—despite all the attention and recognition—were still in a poor state of conservation. The workshop ended with a set of recommendations, which were accepted by the regional governments and were quickly followed by a number of pilot projects. The workshop also led to a number of training seminars in which local site managers and international experts discussed archaeology, conservation, management, and public use of the sites. The joint nomination to the World Heritage List was encouraged in order to include representative missions from all three countries and thus develop a shared vision. In 2005 the IDB offered a $33 million loan to Argentina for conservation and development of the Jesuit missions as well Iguazú Falls and the lakes of Patagonia to promote foreign tourism.[7] The loan details stipulated that the Argentine government provide an additional $25 million. This important development demonstrates that this recently appreciated heritage shared by numerous Southern Cone countries is entering a new phase where it may more reliably receive adequate funding to ensure it will survive for future generations to cherish.

a

b

c

d

Figure 36–6 The 1996 conservation work that entailed project identification, planning, and structural stabilization of the surviving Jesuit Guaraní missions found in contiguous regions of present-day Argentina, Brazil, and Paraguay has proven to be a model of international cooperation in cultural heritage conservation practice. The signature project of San Ignacio Miní (a, b, and d) benefited from some re-restoration, using physically and visually compatible repair mortars and pinning with nonferrous dowels. Parts of the ruins of the Nuestra Señora de Loreto Mission have been temporarily shored with timber (c), and the sandstone masonry (d) of the main portal of San Ignacio Miní church was fully conserved using the highest standards in stone conservation as a demonstration project.

ARGENTINA

Before the Spanish conquest, today's Argentina was sparsely populated, as it only slightly overlapped with the edges of the Inca empire in the northern highlands and parts of the Guaraní territory in the northeast. Though the city of Buenos Aires was established by the Spanish in 1580, its development, and that of the surrounding region, was stifled as all trade went through Lima until the new Viceroyalty of Río de la Plata was established in 1776. After becoming the seat of this new Spanish administrative district, Argentina grew and prospered rapidly in the late eighteenth and early nineteenth century and continued to develop after independence from Spain in 1816. Waves of immigration from Europe in the late nineteenth and early twentieth century gave Argentina the multicultural character for which it is celebrated today.

Because of its relatively late development, the richest components of Argentina's architectural heritage are the structures and cities of the past two centuries, but the country does also boast important precolonial cave paintings and colonial-era missions and towns. Efforts to protect Argentina's built heritage have developed quickly since the country's return to democracy in the late 1980s but originated in the early twentieth century. In 1913 archaeological sites in Argentina were legally protected in one of the first such acts in the region. The appreciation and protection of Argentina's cultural heritage gained momentum beginning in the 1930s and an informal monuments commission was established in Buenos Aires in 1938.

With Law No. 12.665 in 1940, this agency was formalized into the Comisión Nacional de Museos y Monumentos y Lugares Históricos (National Commission of Museums, Monuments, and Historic Sites). Originally a department within the Ministry of Justice and Public Education, the Comisión Nacional became part of the Ministry of Culture in 1981. From the outset, the Comisión Nacional was charged with designating historic sites and objects as national monuments and was responsible for overseeing any alterations, changes in ownership, or export plans involving this heritage. The Comisión Nacional also assumed financial responsibility for the maintenance of state-owned historic sites.

The Comisión Nacional began compiling a List of Monuments and Sites that in the year 2000 only included four hundred entries, but has more than doubled since then as efforts to document and research Argentina's heritage have increased in recent years. In addition, the list has slowly begun to move away from its initial focus on the country's few colonial and pre-Columbian archaeological sites that dominated interests for most of the twentieth century. The Comisión Nacional has recently expanded its range to recognize Argentina's more recent heritage, including its cultural landscapes, vernacular architecture, industrial sites, and the influence of its non-Hispanic immigrant communities. Unfortunately, the Comisión Nacional has faced significant challenges in fulfilling its mandate, and its control over historic sites in the country is weak because its role has always been more oversight than direct management. In addition, the institution has always been poorly funded.

Although the influence of pre-Columbian cultures is not as prevalent in Argentina as elsewhere in South America, tangible remnants of the communities of Patagonia, the territory embracing parts of southern Argentina and Chile, can be found in numerous caves decorated with wall paintings. The most imprssive of these is the Cueva de las Manos (Cave of Hands), whose walls are decorated with more than eight hundred red-hand impressions coupled with simple geometric figures. Evidence of the country's earliest inhabitants is predominately concentrated in the northern, more arid regions where nomadic hunting and fishing communities emerged and where connections were made with the Inca Empire in the highlands. The colonial population of Argentina also remained concentrated in the northern region until the eighteenth century, and it is here that the fusion of indigenous cultures and the Spanish colonists is most evident. For

Figure 36–7 While prehistoric rock art is a component of the heritage of all countries in the Americas, one of the most amazing examples is seen in the Cueva de las Manos in southern Argentina where over eight hundred images of human hands outlined in paint applied with a spray pipe decorate the cave walls. The idea of actual human handprints dating from about 2,500 years ago and their pristine condition makes deep human history in the Patagonia region palpable to modern viewers.

example, the *pirca* architectural tradition of rough stones set in mud was commonly employed in Spanish-era buildings. The Quebrada de Humahuaca Inca Trade Route—a cultural pathway some 10,000 years old in which evidence of hunter-gatherer communities, the Inca empire, and the Argentine struggle for independence can all be found—is located in the northern region of the country. It was recognized as a World Heritage Site in 2003.

A group of Argentine towns on the World Heritage List that grew from the sixteenth- and seventeenth-century *encomienda* estates granted by the king of Spain are found between La Quebrada and Puna Jujeña. Each village features a church as a focal point and demonstrates similar architectural styles and construction techniques. Many of these buildings, including the seventeenth-century churches of San Francisco de Yavi and Purmamarca, were restored during the 1990s.[8]

The town of La Plata, located thirty-five miles southeast of Buenos Aires, was founded in 1882 as a model administrative center with wide thoroughfares, diagonal avenues, and abundant public spaces and parks. La Plata influenced urban planning elsewhere in South America, and international competitions were held for the design of its major buildings, which included a municipal palace, museum, parliament, cathedral, railway station, and numerous other institutions. In the second half of the twentieth century, the integrity and authenticity of the city has been gradually eroded, as demolitions and insensitive restoration projects have been carried out at many of these structures. La Plata was nominated to the World Heritage List in 1998, but it has not yet been approved. Local architectural conservationists argue it is because not enough has been done to preserve this undoubtedly important city.

Argentina's architectural conservation challenges are nowhere more apparent than in its capital city of Buenos Aires. The understaffed office of the City Planning Secretary is responsible for the protection of the architectural heritage in Buenos Aires, which has no preservation legislation and only two historic districts designated through its Urban Planning Code.[9] Many of the city's most architecturally interesting and historically

a

b

Figure 36–8 An impressive conservation project began in 2000 in the industrial neighborhood of La Boca in Buenos Aires. La Boca's Caminito Street (a and b), famous as the birthplace of tango, is a symbol of the capital city and of the Italian immigrants community in Argentina.

significant buildings are not included on Argentina's list of protected sites. In the late 1990s, numerous losses of early-twentieth-century buildings, such as of the Beaux-Art Spanish Bank Central Headquarters and the Bunge y Born Grain Elevator, were approved by the City Planning Secretary. In addition, numerous unsympathetic adaptive reuse projects have been carried out, such as the renovation of the subway system (built between 1908 and 1938 as the first in Latin America), which was decorated with extensive ceramic murals.[10]

Buenos Aires flourished throughout the nineteenth century as its development policies favored European immigration and foreign investment. Between 1856 and 1930, more than ten million immigrants arrived in Argentina. Of those, one-half were Italian, one-third were Spanish, and other major groups included the English and Welsh. The influence of these numerous communities is readily apparent throughout Argentina, but especially in Buenos Aires, through whose port most of these immigrants arrived. These first-generation immigrant communities encouraged historicist architectural styles reminiscent of the traditions of their homelands and reflecting their fusion with local cultures. For example, after the construction of the railroad in the late nineteenth century, Welsh immigrants helped populate and develop the newly accessible frontier, founding numerous towns between 1865 and 1914 that have characteristic Welsh-style churches, tea houses, and mills.[11]

In Buenos Aires' industrial neighborhood of La Boca, which served as a primary destination for Italian immigrants, brightly colored corrugated iron facades were built using leftover materials found on boats in the city's port. In 2000 the Instituto Italo-Latino Americano (Italian Latin American Institute) launched a project to conserve La Boca neighborhood, and today its picturesque Caminito Street—known as the birthplace of the tango—is one of the prime tourist destinations in Buenos Aires. The first stage of the neighborhood's renovation was completed in December 2003, with the establishment of a conservation training course for professionals and artisans. Actual work began with the restoration of the Giuseppe Verdi Theater and fifteen nearby facades. This was followed by a second phase that dealt with interiors and involved the collaboration of Argentine and Italian materials conservationists.

The twentieth-century first brought prosperity, then repression under military rule with the election of Juan Perón first in 1946, then a return to a democracy plagued with economic strife. Throughout these changes, though, Argentina continued to embrace international architectural trends, and wide avenues replaced colonial streets in the 1930s and 1940s while art deco became the architectural language of movie houses and theaters. Two of the most noted international style modernist structures in Buenos Aires province include the Curutchet House in La Plata, designed in the mid-1950s by Le Corbusier, and the Kavanagh Building in the Retiro neighborhood, the first skyscraper in South America and the world's tallest concrete structure when it was completed 1936. Since 1990, advocacy for the conservation of Buenos Aires' modern architecture is provided by the Argentine chapter of DOCOMOMO.[12]

Numerous other public and private organizations are currently working to promote cultural heritage conservation and protection in Buenos Aires and throughout Argentina. The Program for the Revitalization of the Avenida de

Figure 36-9 Dating from the mid-1950s, the Curutchet House in La Plata, Buenos Aires, was designed by Le Corbusier and is a protected national landmark. It now serves as the headquarters of the Colegio de Arquitectos de la Provincia de Buenos Aires (Architects Association of Buenos Aires Province).

Figure 36-10 More orthodox architectural conservation has occurred in Buenos Aires through the Program for the Revitalization of the Avenida de Mayo that has addressed the city's most prominent nineteenth-century boulevard, which is lined with elaborate Beaux-Arts structures, such as the Teatro Colón, the National Congress (illustrated), and the Anchorena and Paz palaces.

Mayo has concentrated its efforts on one nineteenth-century boulevard in the capital, which is lined with elaborate Beaux-Arts structures, including the Teatro Colón, the National Congress, and the Anchorena and Paz Palaces. This program also identifies and works to conserve the city's defining elements, including art that is integral to the city's architecture, sites related to the railroad, immigrant neighborhoods, archaeological sites, and cultural landscapes.[13] Other conservation activities in Buenos Aires have been funded by the Spanish government, and specialized training for the construction and rehabilitation of wood architecture has been provided by the National Construction Department.[14]

Provincial and municipal level governments have established secretariats and committees to assume some of the burden for local architectural conservation efforts, and in the 1970s the revitalization of historic centers such as Córdoba began. However, these regional and local organizations led to inconsistent policies and encouraged the centralization of information on Argentina's historic sites in 1999 through a new National Record of Cultural Heritage. In addition, NGOs such as El Centro Internacional para la Conservación del Patrimonio Argentina (CICOP, International Center for the Preservation of the Architectural Heritage of Argentina), have worked to coordinate local, national, and international conservation efforts in the country. CICOP has also sponsored extensive research on Argentina's architectural history from an interdisciplinary perspective and is broadly interested in all aspects of the country's culture.

In 2002 ICOMOS Argentina noted that architectural heritage protection and conservation remains inadequate in most places in the country and cited a number of issues in urgent need of attention. These included the need for greater involvement of NGOs in heritage protection, for legal reform, for significantly increased budget allocations for architectural conservation, for the creation of standardized principles and procedures for cultural heritage protection, and for improved training opportunities for conservation professionals.[15] Despite these shortcomings, which Argentina is still working to overcome, the past two decades have witnessed the progressive development of cultural heritage protection in Argentina. The types and styles of sites valued in Argentina are broad, regional-level standards have been drafted, and conservation courses are offered at various universities. Argentina's cultural heritage professionals have accomplished much and seem well aware of the challenges that lie ahead.

CHILE

The geography of Chile has strongly influenced its culture and has encouraged a feeling of isolation among the country's distinct regions as well as from the rest of the continent and world. Situated in a long, narrow strip between the Andes and the Pacific Ocean, Chile is dominated in the north by the driest desert in the world, while its fertile central zone has attracted settlement, and its south is a lush, ecological paradise that is now largely protected natural preserves. The fusion of pre-Columbian cultures and Spanish traditions is demonstrated in the homogeneity of the Chilean population, 90 percent of which is mestizo. However, indigenous communities such as the Mapuche in the south and the Aymara in the north have also maintained strong, independent cultural identities.

Though measures to protect Chile's built heritage have been undertaken for nearly a century, architectural and urban conservation have only recently matured in the country, and the rapid developments of recent decades have included increasing recognition of the value of Chilean cultural heritage and of actions to protect it. The twentieth century has witnessed unregulated development as foreign investment has dominated the economy, and policies have promoted urban development and the depletion of natural resources. The Consejo de Monumentos Nacionales (Council of National Monuments) was established in 1925 but was provided no funding. During its first half century, the Consejo oscillated between periods characterized by high amounts of concern and conservation and those with little or no activity due to the country's political, social, and economic difficulties.[16]

In 1970, a new Law 17.288 of National Monuments expanded the early twentieth-century legislation by defining five categories of protected sites: historic, public, and archaeological monuments, typical zones, and natural sanctuaries or reserves. In the late 1970s and early 1980s, the Consejo de Monumentos Nacionales was consolidated and designated numerous additional sites as protected national heritage. In 1977 the Consejo established financial incentives to exempt these sites from real estate taxes.

The social and political stability in Chile that has lasted since General Augusto Pinochet lost power in 1989 has encouraged efforts to better understand and interpret the country's cultural heritage. The Consejo de Monumentos Nacionales and Chilean heritage policies in general were reformed in 1994 to create a more effective system that relied on multiple actors. Four regional councils were organized and work was delegated to entities such as universities, the Ministry of Housing and Urbanism, and the Department of Architecture in the Ministry of Public Works. Growing interest in architectural conservation in Chile has led to the declaration of record numbers of national monuments since 1997. In addition, during the 1990s, Environmental Impact Reviews began to be required before construction or development projects in areas sur-

Figure 36–11 Preserving remains of Neolithic earthen buildings as found at the ruins of Tulor in the northern Atacama Desert of Chile is difficult under any conditions. The extreme remoteness of the Tulor ruins makes constant site monitoring a challenge, an issue of special concern to Chile's Council of National Monuments.

rounding national monuments. This quickly led to a renewed interest in archaeological sites and their excavation and conservation, as is demonstrated in the careful exploration of the area designated for the expansion of the subway in Santiago. The recovered objects ranged from Inca ceramics to remnants of a colonial aqueduct and an eighteenth-century market.

Today the Consejo de Monumentos Nacionales—now a division of the Ministry of Education—encourages community involvement in architectural conservation by hosting a Día Nacional del Patrimonio Cultural (National Cultural Heritage Day) in May as well as through programs such as Volunteers for Patrimony, which organize lectures and tours in individual communities. In 2001 the Council also initiated a Cultural Patrimony of the Indigenous Communities program based on the recent legal recognition of these groups as descendants of the original inhabitants of Chile and as key components of the country's foundation and current culture. The Consejo has worked to protect both the tangible and intangible element of the cultures of groups such as the Mapuche in the Bío-Bío district. Testaments to the long inhabitation of Chile are found in archaeological sites such as Monte Verde and Fell's Cave, which flourished more than ten millennia ago. In the northern Atacama Desert, the ruins of Tulor, one of South America's best preserved Neolithic villages, are threatened by wind erosion and a lack of funding for conservation. The Consejo de Monumentos Nacionales increasingly works to protect this and other archaeological sites and objects from poor excavation and from looting.

The Rapa Nui National Park that occupies over half of Easter Island represents one of Chile's most-renowned and studied archaeological sites. Between the fifth and ninth centuries, it was settled by Polynesian communities who carved petroglyphs and erected hundreds of large *moai* statues, the megalithic figural sculptures carved out of volcanic tuff. The island was discovered by a Dutch explorer in 1722, and it became a colony of Chile in 1888, only becoming a full part of the country in 1960. Over one-thousand examples of rock art have been found on Easter Island, with the largest concentration in Orongo. The island was declared a national monument in 1935, and systematic research followed, but the first management plan for the island was not drafted by Chile's Corporación Nacional Forestal (CONAF, National Forest Corporation) until the 1970s. By the 1990s, insufficient resources and overlapping government agencies complicated the completion of necessary conservation and management activities at the site. Concerns for this site led to the involvement of international conservation organizations whose interest and financial support encouraged the Chilean government to form the Rapa Nui Monuments Board to decentralize decision making to the site. In 1995 Rapa Nui was added to the World Heritage List. Several international scholars and foreign missions have researched and helped to conserve the stone remains and the cultures of Rapa Nui since the island became accessible by airplane in the 1960s, most notably the World Monuments Fund (WMF) that began its work in 1968 and continues today.

The cities of modern Chile were predominately established during the Spanish colonial period, which began in the 1530s and lasted more than three hundred years. The adobe buildings were organized in a grid structure around a central plaza as established by the Laws of the Indies. Conservation efforts throughout most of the twentieth century focused on the colonial heritage in cities such as La Serena and Old Chillán in the north, Santiago and Valparaíso in the central zone, and Concepción in the south, which was badly damaged on February 27, 2010, by a powerful earthquake.

An outstanding example of Chilean architectural heritage established during the colonial period is the group of wooden churches on the archipelago of Chiloé. Noted by WMF as the "most important assemblage of wooden sanctuaries in Latin America," the churches of this small Pacific island are architecturally and culturally unique and serve as the centers of small villages that developed around them. Constructed between 1608 and 1767 by Jesuit missionaries and taken over by Franciscans once the Jesuits were expelled, most were rebuilt in the eighteenth and nineteenth centuries. At the beginning of the twentieth century there were 150 churches, but today sixty remain. In 1993, the nonprofit Friends of the Churches of Chiloé Foundation was established to work with local communities to promote awareness of the value of the churches and carry out emergency repairs—especially after a damaging storm in 2002. The Foundation, in concert with WMF, has also sponsored a carpentry training program and actively promoted a tourism management plan for the island with funding from the IDB. The WMF has also been involved in the restoration of a few churches, and sixteen of them were added to the World Heritage List in 2000.

a

Figure 36–12 Although located some 3,500 miles west of mainland Chile, the protection of the entire island of Rapa Nui (Easter Island), its built heritage, and its native population has been one of main projects of Chile's Consejo de Monumentos Nacionales and its related agencies, particularly its National Forest Corporation. After many years of work in documenting the over one-thousand stone *moai* (a and b) and other built features of Rapa Nui, such as its remarkable main quarry area at Ranoraraku (b) that reveals moai in the process of being cut (c), and recent efforts to effectively engage the local population in the conservation and interpretation process (d), positive achievements in protecting the islands famous cultural heritage is currently underway. Conservation issues being faced range from monitoring deterioration rates of the volcanic tuff moai in their windy and salt-laden environment to guarding against the "tourist wear" that threatened petroglyphs on the site of Orongo (e).

b

Though Chile was largely undeveloped prior to its independence from Spain in 1817, the subsequent rapid construction of the railroad connected the existing cities and pushed development into the frontiers. As a port city, Valparaíso flourished as the interior's agricultural products and the north's mining industries fed it exports. The city's significance in the development of trade, in addition to unique elements such as the funicular elevators built between 1883 and 1915 to connect the port with neighborhoods on top of the city's steep hillsides, contributed to the recognition of Valparaíso on the World Heritage List in 2003. In February 2007 a gas explosion caused by inadequate maintenance led to a fire that destroyed dozens of buildings in Valparaíso's historic city center, encouraging calls for better protection and proactive conservation both there and throughout the country.

c

d

e

Initiatives have been launched to promote the other aspects of Chile's nineteenth- and twentieth-century heritage, such as the efforts of the local chapter of DOCOMO-MO to increase the recognition and state of conservation of the country's modern architecture. In addition, the School of Architecture of the University of Chile in Santiago organized an international seminar in 2004 dedicated to the Industrial Architecture and Patrimony of Chile. The significance of numerous industrial sites in the country and their increasing state of abandonment and demolition served as inspiration for holding the seminar. A number of Chilean industrial sites have since been successfully nominated to the World Heritage List—the Humberstone and Santa Laura Saltpeter Works were added in 2005 and the mining town of Sewell was added in 2006.

a

b

Figure 36–13 The sixty surviving wooden churches on the archipelago of Chiloé represent a cultural landscape that reflects the influence of the Christian faith and international maritime trade in this remote region of southern Chile. No two churches were built alike, and many contain construction detailing, even recycled wooden ship parts, that were likely built by ship carpenters. In 1993 the nonprofit Friends of the Churches of Chiloé Foundation was established to work with local communities. Shown here are the churches of Conchi (a, b, and c) and Ichuac (d and e), during and after conservation measures were taken.

c

As in Argentina, the greatest challenges facing Chilean architectural conservationists include the lack of funds and trained professionals and a need for more specific regulations regarding archaeological excavations and best conservation practices. An important positive development in Chile is a financial incentive called the Ley Valdés (Valdés Law), which is a tax-incentive law designed to encourage private participation in the conservation of sites. It is a program that is being emulated by other countries. In addition, community participation in cultural heritage in Chile is growing and nonprofit organizations have become involved. International appreciation of Chilean heritage has also emerged—though the country's first World Heritage List site—Rapa Nui National Park—was recognized only in 1995, four others have been designated since the year 2000. This growth of concern, advocacy, and participation by multiple institutional and private participants in the conservation of the cultural heritage of Chile is an important characteristic this country shares with most other countries in Latin America and Caribbean.

d

e

ENDNOTES

1. Antonio Cravotto, "Uruguay," in *Trails to Treasures: A Tour of South America's Cultural Heritage*, eds. World Monuments Fund (WMF) and US/ICOMOS (Washington, DC, and New York: US/ICOMOS and WMF, 2001), 33.

2. Elizabeth Prats Gil, "Paraguay," in *Trails to Treasures*, 29.

3. Republic of Paraguay, "Constitución Política de 1992," Political Database of the Americas, Georgetown University, http://pdba.georgetown.edu/Constitutions/Paraguay/para1992.html (accessed February 27, 2010).

4. Ramón Gutiérrez, "Paraguay: The Jesuit Missions," *The Urban Architectural Heritage of Latin America* (Paris: International Council on Monuments and Sites [ICOMOS], 1998; www.icomos.org/studies/latin-towns.htm (accessed July 21, 2010).

5. Gil, "Paraguay," in *Trails to Treasures*, 29.

6. Ibid., 31.

7. "IDB Approves $33 million to Argentina to Promote Competitiveness in the Tourism Sector," *Inter-American Development Bank*, July 26, 2005, www.iadb.org/news/articledetail.cfm?artid=542&language=english (accessed February 27, 2010).

8. Gutiérrez, "Argentina: The Towns of La Quebrada de Humahuaca and Puna Jujena (Province of Jujuy)," *Urban Architectural Heritage of Latin America*, www.icomos.org/studies/latin-towns.htm#5 (accessed July 21, 2010).

9. Fabio Grementieri, "Argentina," *Heritage@Risk 2000* (Paris: ICOMOS, 2000), www.international.icomos.org/risk/world_report/2000/argen_2000.htm (accessed February 27, 2010).

10. Another example of insensitive treatment of Buenos Aires's architectural heritage is seen at the Casa Rosada (Pink House), the Italianate palace that houses Argentina's office of the president and serves as an important anchor on the city's main urban axis. It was repainted by the National Commission in colors that are not historically accurate to reinforce its "pinkness."

11. María de las Nieves Arias Incollá, "Argentina," in *Trails to Treasures*, 21.

12. DOCOMOMO Argentina, www.fadu.uba.ar/sitios/docomomo/paginas/textoscompletos.htm (accessed February 27, 2010).

13. "Buenos Aires Ciudad de Identidades: Reflexiones sobre el Patrimonio Para el Plan Urbano Ambiental," a conference organized by ICOMOS Argentina and El Centro Internacional para la Conservación del Patrimonio (CICOP) Argentina, Buenos Aires, August 22, 2000, http://webs.sinectis.com.ar/cicop/conclu.html#perfec (accessed February 27, 2010).

14. "Buenos Aires Ciudad de Identidades."

15. ICOMOS Argentina, "Argentina," *Heritage@Risk 2001–2002* (Paris: ICOMOS, 2002), www.international.icomos.org/risk/2001/arge2001.htm (accessed February 27, 2010).

16. "Historia del CMN," Consejo de Monumentos Nacionales (CMN), www.monumentos.cl/OpenDocs/asp/pagDefault.asp?boton=Doc54&argInstanciaId=54&argCarpetaId=7&argTreeNodosAbiertos=(0)(7)&argTreeNodoSel=7&argTreeNodoActual=7&argRegistroId=3044 (accessed February 27, 2010).

Conclusion to Part II

Architectural conservation in South America and the Caribbean has made great progress in recent years from being a topic that was generally under-appreciated and practiced only a few decades ago. The history of organized cultural heritage protection in Latin America is notably complex due in large part to the numbers of countries involved, varied social context, economic instability, and legacies of political differences among many of the region's nations. At the sociocultural level there have been miscellaneous appreciations for both indigenous and colonial heritage for most of the past four centuries that only recently have come to be valued widely as rich cultural assets that characterize Latin America's modern ways of life.

Architectural conservation in the Americas has progressed significantly in recent years. In North America, including Mexico, key national anniversaries and other historic commemorations inspired early interest, and losses resulting from mid-twentieth-century urban renewal spurred development and institutionalization of the field. In the Caribbean and Central and South America, organized and sustained efforts for cultural heritage protection and architectural conservation are even more recent developments.

Throughout the Americas, the procedures and mechanisms for architectural conservation that are in operation today, in both the public and private sectors, are mostly informed by principles and practices developed in Europe. However, over the past half century the field of cultural heritage protection has reached a maturity that has included the questioning of philosophies and systems imported from abroad and the assertion of ideas and practices tailored to local and regional needs, especially in Latin America. As a result, well-tempered basic systems of heritage protection have been adapted, expanded upon, and enriched with locally derived solutions.

Various experts on Latin American cultural heritage have observed how, despite the region's rich history and heritage, ambivalence about cultural heritage continues and in many countries participation and appreciation are not pervasive.[1]

At a conference in 2002 on Latin American comparative methods and the further engaging the private sector, several conclusions of both a general and a practical nature were drawn, and specific goals for the coming decades were proposed: raising the profile of cultural heritage protection; embracing allied disciplines, especially the social sciences; promoting wider diversity of heritage; engaging the public more effectively; and improving the training of future professionals. The means to these ends were presented by then-U.S./ICOMOS executive director (and presently director general of ICOMOS International) Gustavo Araoz, who offered concluding remarks at the conference, where he stressed--among other things--the need for new and more realistic roles for governments, the importance of public participation, the need for new strategies for paying for heritage conservation, and a general need for a reappraisal of the social role of the built cultural heritage.[2]

These are sizable challenges for the dedicated though typically underfunded activists, professionals, and state institutions of Latin America. But stability has returned to the region and prospects looking forward are positive. Regional cooperation through the Organization of American States and the Interamerican Development Bank continues to significantly strengthen the architectural conservation field in Central and South America and the Caribbean. As many Latin American countries look toward marking the bicentennial of their independence, discussion has already begun to focus on how cultural heritage can be incorporated into the celebrations. The programs developed in this context should increase awareness of the value of cultural heritage in general and encourage new research and architectural restoration and conservation projects in much the same way that similar celebrations did in North America.

ENDNOTES

1. For example, regarding his own continent, the eminent Venezuelan architectural historian Graziano Gasparini has pointedly described the state of heritage conservation practice: "South America has suffered through a century of confusing and mostly mediocre efforts to rescue and safeguard its monumental heritage." Gasparini also laments the inexactness of efforts to respect and conserve authenticity in modern conservation practice, and additionally he worries about an apparent lack of awareness of the talent and sensitivity needed to effectively conserve monumental heritage. Graziano Gasparini, "Monumental Heritage in South America: Treasures Beyond Measure," in *Conference Abstracts of Heritage Conservation in South America Challenges and Solutions*, organized by the World Monuments Fund, São Paolo, Brazil, April 11–14, 2002 (New York: World Monument Fund, 2002), 44.

2. Araoz, Gustavo. "Concluding Remarks," in *Conference Abstracts of Heritage Conservation in South America Challenges and Solutions*, 52.

Looking Ahead

The shared histories, linguistic and cultural ties, and modern fates of Europe and the Americas have led the over ninety countries of these three vast continents to develop and institutionalize heritage management systems with much in common in the past century. Though no countries address architectural conservation exactly the same way, and some of the challenges they face vary widely, remarkably similar architectural conservation threats, objectives, and practices are shared worldwide. Respecting, understanding, documenting, and learning from the simultaneously unique and collective architectural heritage conservation experiences of the countries of Europe and the Americas has been the principal aim of this book.

The list of shared, active challenges to architectural heritage in Europe and the Americas is ever-expanding. Four categories of threats are gaining new prominence as special issues to address, including the effects of global warming on cultural heritage; the targeting of the past though vandalism, iconoclasm, and terrorism; the commodification and marketing the past in insensitive ways; and the dilution of history through inaccurate treatment and interventions. In addition, all countries — including even the wealthiest — continuously require additional resources, including both funding and dedicated individuals and organizations, and this is likely to continue as costs rise and the range of sites conserved expands.

In today's globalizing era, individuals, institutions, organizations, and governments from Europe and the Americas are in constant cultural and informational exchange with one another and the rest of the world, and traditional boundaries in architectural conservation and many other fields have melted away. Recent telling trends include increased demand for the conservation of structures of all types and ages, including indigenous, industrial, and vernacular architectural heritage; increased sophistication of historic urban conservation schemes to address larger areas and their sense of place; and increased participation in architectural conservation by the allied technical fields of engineering, landscape architecture, and planning as well as the allied socio-humanistic disciplines of archaeology, anthropology, museology, and sociology.

Today's conservation ethos in Europe and Americas includes a clear understanding of the links between architectural conservation and natural resources protection as well as between built and intangible heritage. One concrete result has been the increased recognition of cultural landscapes in recent years. In addition, cultural heritage education today operates at all levels, from young school children to curious senior citizens, and site interpretation is ever-improving as a result. Heritage-related programming of events in historic places is also more robust than ever. And professionals in architectural conservation have more educational and training opportunities than ever previously, including craft workshops, thorough graduate programs, and specialized short courses offered by organizations such as ICCROM.

Recognizing and stressing the importance and interconnection of social issues and architectural conservation will continue to be a priority in Europe and the Americas in the future. Awareness of the limits of growth and the relationship between cultural diversity and sustainable development, as well as new demands for sustainable urban conservation and environmental protection, will continue to change architectural conservation practice. New cultural policies will be formed that reflect social change and the expanding definitions of culture. Efforts to address cultures in transition, threats to traditional rights and usage, and pursuit of equal opportunity will be enhanced, and addressing social fracturing, and marginalization, especially in areas of conflict, will continue to grow.

Since their founding until the past one or two decades, the international practice of architectural conservation was led by the supra-national organizations of UNESCO and ICOMOS, created in the wake of World War II to facilitate cooperation and improve international relations via exemplary projects and the advocacy of sound conservation principles and best practices. The accomplishments in the field of these organizations and allied others such as ICOM have been instrumental. Across Europe and the Americas, the successes and unifying influences of regional intergovernmental organizations have also advanced heritage protection for decades. Gradually, the global architectural conservation scene has shifted such that these top-down, governmental and intergovernmental programs have nearly been overtaken by the proliferation of countless nongovernmental organizations and less formal grassroots initiatives, large and small, devoted to niches of need and interest that form a network of participation and concern throughout Europe and the Americas and beyond. These bottom-up architectural conservation efforts are more widespread and effective today than ever, and they continue to grow. Most governments in Europe and the Americas have willingly and increasingly sought to share architectural conservation responsibilities with this burgeoning private sector, especially as political change and economic crisis cause cuts to government-supported cultural programs.

Decentralization of architectural conservation from the federal to the regional and municipal levels, in combination with the growth of nongovernmental organizations, has meant that the trajectory of local awareness, commitment, and capacities is ever-strengthening. In the future, larger-scale international organizations will likely continue the adaptation process already underway to support these new local institutions and organizations, as well as the new structures of heritage management and conservation they reflect. Thus architectural conservation today truly epitomizes twenty-first-century globalization; in its purpose and its practice it is simultaneously local and global. Not only do the conserved sites range from community landmarks to World Heritage Sites, but its participants range from the concerned local citizen to intergovernmental organizations. More important, it is the constant interaction between these values and participants that have enriched the field.

Heritage conservation is a broad ethos, not limited to a specific discipline or profession, which involves being resourceful, respectful, appreciative, and otherwise engaged in preserving and effectively utilizing the human built environment. This inclusive definition has emerged from the millions of people who enjoy the benefits of architectural heritage protection and who can be counted among its constituents and supporters. Naturally, among the most committed are the members of the multidisciplinary teams involved in every conservation project, including owners, patrons, officials, advocates, architects, engineers, scientists, contractors, craftsmen, the supportive public, and others. Each of these participants in architectural conservation has a specific contribution and a particular perspective, and has played a pivotal role in shaping the field in every corner of Europe and the Americas.

Examining representative experiences and accomplishments of these participants in each country of Europe and the Americas alongside one another, as has been done in *Architectural Conservation in Europe and the Americas*, allows for this general understanding of architectural conservation's local and global aspects as well as its position in world culture today. Throughout Europe and the Americas, and the world at large, the bar has been raised by the field's achievements to date; new and high standards are set. Many possibilities have yet to be realized and there is an unending list of sites in need, but the field's best practices, doctrine, and growing supply of participants and expertise are all harbingers of a positive future for the built heritage of Europe and the Americas.

Further Reading on Architectural Conservation by Region

The following list of titles on architectural heritage conservation follows the order of the contents of *Architectural Conservation in Europe and the Americas* and is meant to serve as a supplement to the books cited in Further Reading lists and the endnotes. Most of the following titles are in book form, as it is assumed that information contained within journals, conference proceedings, news outlets, and solely electronically published material are better searched via Internet databases.

Key Web-based sources for architectural conservation bibliographies include:

- Art and Archaeology Technical Abstracts (AATA), an on-line service of the Getty Conservation Institute in association with the International Institute for Conservation of Historic and Artistic Works, http://aata.getty.edu.

- The Bibliographic Database of the Conservation Information Network (BCIN), www.bcin.ca.

- International Council on Monuments and Sites (ICOMOS) Documentation Centre Catalogue, http://databases.unesco.org/icomos

SECTION 1 (WESTERN EUROPE)

Aebischer, P. *L'Ottocento. Gli stati tedeschi e la Svizzera.* In *Il restauro dei monumenti nei paesi europei.* Edited by Mariani G. Miarelli. Rome: Dipartimento de Storia dell'Architettura, Conservazione e Restauro, 2003.

Agnew, Neville, and Janet Bridgland, eds. *Of the Past, for the Future: Integrating Archaeology and Conservation, Proceedings of the Conservation Theme at the 5th World Archaeological Congress, Washington DC, 22–26 June 2003.* Los Angeles, CA: Getty Conservation Institute, 2006.

Ago, Fabrizio (ed.). *Culture in Sustainable Development: An Italian Strategy.* Vol. 1, Development Cooperation Programmes; vol. 2, Policy Objectives and Major Results; vol. 3, Research and Pilot Projects on Archaeology and Anthropology. Translated by Christopher McDowell. Rome: Chrisengraf 1999.

Alfrey, Judith, and Tim Putnam. *The Industrial Heritage: Managing Resources and Uses.* London: Routledge, 1992.

Alpin, Graeme. *Heritage: Identification, Conservation and Management.* Oxford and New York: Oxford University Press, 2002.

Andrieux, Jean-Yves (ed.). *Patrimoine and Société. Actes du cycle de conférences prononcées à l'université de Haute-Bretagne en 1996–1997.* Lyon, France: Presses Universitaires de Rennes, 1998.

Appleyard, Donald, (ed.). *The Conservation of European Cities.* Cambridge, MA: MIT Press, 1979.

Architectural Association of Ireland. *Architectural Conservation: An Irish Viewpoint: A Series of Papers Read to the Architectural Association of Ireland by Irish Authorities between October and December 1974.* Dublin: Architectural Association of Ireland, 1975.

Ashurst, John. *Conservation of Ruins.* Amsterdam and London: Elsevier/Butterworth-Heinemann, 2007.

Ashurst, John, and Francis G. Dimes. *Conservation of Building and Decorative Stone.* Oxford: Butterworth-Heinemann, 1990.

Ashurst, John, and Nicola Ashurst. *Practical Building Conservation: English Heritage Technical Handbook.* Volumes 1–5. London: Gower Technical Press, 1988.

Ashworth, G. J., and J. E. Turnbridge (eds.). *Building a New Heritage: Tourism, Culture and Identity in the New Europe.* London: Routledge, 1994.

Baer, N. S., and F. Snickars (eds.). *Rational Decision-Making in the Preservation of Cultural Property.* Berlin: Dahlem University Press, 2001.

Baker, David. *Living with the Past: The Historic Environment.* Bletsoe, Bedford, UK: David Baker, 1983.

Ballardini, Romeo, and Pasquale Ventrice, eds. *Restauro Tecnologia e Architectura: Epistemologia Storica delle Tecniche tra Tecnologia e Progetto di Architettura-Restauro.* Venice: Il Cardo Editore., 1995.

Bandinelli, R. Bianchi. "Come Non Ricostruire Firenze." *Il Ponte* 1, no. 2 (1945): 114–118.

Barbacci, Alfredo. *Il Restauro dei Monumenti in Italia.* Roma: Instituto Poligrafico dello Stato, Liberería dello Stato, 1956.

Bardeschi, Marco (ed.). *Ex Fabrica: Storia e Tecniche della Conservazione.* Vol. 1, "Restauro Architettonico: Padri, Teorie, Immagini," and Vol. 2, "Sur Restauro dei Monumenti." Milano: Franco Angeli Libre.

Bell, D. *The Historic Scotland Guide to International Conservation Charters*. Edinburgh: Historic Scotland, 1997.

Bercé, Françoise. *Les premiers travaux de la commission des monuments historiques 1837–1848*. Paris: Picard, 1979.

Berenson, Bernard. "Come Ricostruire la Firenzie Demolita." *Il Ponte* 1, no. 2 (1945): 33–38.

Bergeon, S., G. Brunel, and E. Mognetti. *La conservation restauration en France/Conservation restoration in France*. Rome: ICOM, 1999.

Biasini, Emile, Jean Lebrat, Dominique Bezombes, and Jean-Michel Vincent. *Le Grand Louvre*. Paris: Electa Moniteur, 1989.

Binney, Marcus. *Our Vanishing Heritage*. London: Arlington Books, 1984.

Binney, Marcus, Francis Macin, and Ken Powell. *Bright Future: The Re-use of Industrial Buildings*. London: SAVE Britain's Heritage, 1990.

Binney, Marcus and Marianne Watson-Smyth. *The SAVE Britan's Heritage Action Guide*. London: Collins and Brown, 1991.

Binney, Marcus, and Peter Burman. *Change and Decay: The Future of Churches*. London: Studio Vista, 1977.

Bitelli, Luisa Masetti, and Marta Cuoghi Constantinin. *Ripristino Architettonico: Restauro o Restaurazione? Ferrara 4–5 April 1997. Convegno Organizzato in Occasione de: Restauro 97 Salon dell'Arte, del Restauro e della Conservazione*. Fiesole: Nardini Editore 1997.

Blanco, Javier Rivera. *De Varia Restauratione: Teoria e Historia de la Restauración Arquitectónica*. Madrid: Valladolid, 2001.

Boito, Camillo. *I Restauratori*. Florence: G. Barbèra, 1884.

———. *Questioni Pratiche di Belle Arti: Restauri, Concorsi, Legislazione, Professione, Insegnamento*. Milano: Ulrico Hoepli, 1893.

Bonelli, Renato. *Scritti sul Restauro e sulla Critica Architettonica*. Introduction by Giovanni Carbonara. Series no. 14, produced by the Studio for the Restoration of Monuments, University of Rome "La Sapienza. Rome: Bonsignori Editore, 1995.

Bonsanti, Giorgio. *The Basilica of St. Francis of Assisi: Glory and Destruction*. New York: Harry N. Abrams, Inc., 1997. Originally published in Italy by Franco Cosimo Panini Editore.

Brandi, Cesare. *Il Restauro: Theorie Practica*. Preface by Michele Cordano, Rome: Editori Riuniti, 1995.

———. *Theory of Restoration*. Translated by Cynthia Rockwell. Florence: Nardini Editore, 2005.

Brandon, Peter, and Patrizia Lombardi. *Evaluating Sustainable Development in the Built Environment*. Oxford: Blackwell Publishing, 2005

Brereton, Christopher. *The Repair of Historic Buildings—Advice, Principles, and Methods* (2nd ed.). London: English Heritage, 1995.

British Standards Institute. *Guide to the Principles of Conservation of Historic Buildings*. BS 7913:1998. London: British Standards Institute, 1998.

Bruno, Andrea, Ida Gianelli, and Claudio Bertolotto. *Il Castello di Rivoli: Le Grandi Residenze Sabaude*. Torino: Umberto Allemandi & C. Spa, 2007.

Buchanan, Colin and Partners. *Bath: A Study in Conservation. Report to the Minister of Housing and Local Government and Bath City Council*. London: Her Majesty's Stationery Office, 1968.

Buls, Charles. *I Principi dell'arte Urbana*. Rome: Officina Edizioni, 1999. Originally published as *Les principes de l'art urbain* (1893). Translated by Barbara Barbini. Edited by Marcel Smets. Liège: Mardaga, 1995.

Buls, Charles "La Restauration des Monuments Anciens." *Revue de l'Art Chrétien* 44 (1901): 498–503 and 45 (1902).

Burman, Peter, Rob Pickard, and Sue Taylor (eds.). *The Economics of Architectural Conservation*. York, England: The University of York Institute of Advanced Architectural Studies, 1995.

Butcher-Younghans, Sherry. *Historic House Museums: A Practical Handbook for their Care, Preservation, and Management*. Oxford: Oxford University Press, 1993.

Butt, John, and Ian Donnachie. *Industrial Archaeology in the British Isles*. London: Paul Elek, Ltd, 1979.

Cantacuzino, Sherban (ed.). *Architectural Conservation in Europe*. London: Architectural Press, 1975.

———. *Re-Architecture: Old Buildings/New Uses*. London: Thames and Hudson, 1989.

Cantacuzino, Sherban, and Susan Brandt. *Saving Old Buildings*. London: The Architectural Press, 1980.

Carbonara, Giovanni. *Avvicinamento al Restauro: Teoria, Storia, Monumenti*. Naples: Liguori Editore, 1997.

———. *Il Pensiero di Paul Philippot e Altri Contribute Europei*. In *Avvicinamento al Restauro:Teoria, Storia, Monumenti*. Naples: Liguori Editore, 1997.

———. (ed.) *Teoria e Metodi del Restauro*. In *Trattato di Restauro Architettonico*. Vol. 1, 1–107. Torino: UTET, 1996.

———. (ed.). *Trattato di Restauro Architettonico, Primo Aggiornamento. Grandi Termi di Restauro*. Vols. 1–10; Vol. 8, International Practice, 1–208. Milan: UTET Giuridica, 2007.

Celada, M., and A. Faria da Costa. *Filosofia di Intervento in Portogallo*. In *Progettare I Restauri: Orientamenti e Metodi Indagini e Materiali, Atti del Convegno (Bressanone, 30 June–3 July 1998)*. Marghera (Venezia): Arcadia Richerche, 1998.

Cervellati, P., and R. Scannarini. *Bologna: Politica e Metodologia del Restaurone I Centro Storica*. Bologna, 1973.

Ceschi, Carlo. *Teoria e Storia del Restauro*. Rome: M. Bulzoni, Editore, 1970.

Chamberlin, E. R. *Preserving the Past*. London: J. M. Dent & Sons, 1979.

Chitty, Gill, and David Baker, (eds.). *Managing Historic Sites and Buildings: Reconciling Presentation and Preservation*. London: Routledge, 1999.

Choay, Françoise. *The Invention of the Historic Monument*. Translated by Lauren M. O'Connell. Cambridge: Cambridge University Press, 2001; orig., Paris: Éditions du Seuil, 1992.

Christie, Trevor L. *Antiquities in Peril*. Philadelphia: Lippincott, 1967.

Cleere, Henry (ed.). *Archaeological Heritage Management in the Modern World*. London: Unwin Hyman, 1989.

Cnattingius, L. D. "Problemi di Restauro dei Monumenti in Svezia." in *La Tutela del Partimonio Architettonico in Svezia*, in *Restauro*, Vol. 24, 1976.

Cody, Jeff, and Kecia Fong (eds.). "Built Heritage Conservation Education." *Built Environment* 33, no. 3 (2004).

Colenbrander, B. W. *Chiado Lisbon: Alvaro Siza and the Strategy of Memory*. Rotterdam: Dutch Architectural Institute, 1991.

Comune di Firenze. *Ufficio Belle Arti, Centro Anni di Restauro a Firenze*. Florence: Edizioni Polistampa, 2007.

Conti, Alessandro. *History of the Restoration and Conservation of Works of Art*. Translated by Helen Glanville. Oxford: Elsevier, 2007. First edition published in 1988.

Contorni, Gabriella. *Erre Come Restaruro*; degli Interventi sul Patrimonio Architettonico. Florence: Alinea Editrice, 1993.

Council of Europe. *Compendium of Basic Texts of the Council of Europe in the Field of Cultural Heritage (provisional version September 1998)*. Strasbourg: Council of Europe, 1998.

———. *Heritage and Successful Regeneration*. Strasbourg: Council of Europe, 1998.

———. *Monument Protection in Europe*.; Boston and Deventer: Kluwer, 1979.

Council of Europe, and Pierre-Yves Ligen. *Dangers and Perils: Analysis of Factors which Constitute a Danger to Groups and Areas of Buildings of Historical or Artistic Interest*. Strasbourg: Council of Europe, 1968.

Crosby, Theo. *The Necessary Monument: Its Future in a Civilized City*. New York Graphics Society, Greenwich, CT, 1970.

Cubero, María Luisa de Vega et al, *Junta de Castilla y León*, Castilla: Consejería de Cultura y Turiamo, 2004.

Cunningham, Allen (ed.). *Modern Movement Heritage*. (DOCOMOMO). E & FN Spon, Routledge, London, 1998.

Dale, Antony. "France, Great Britain, Ireland, the Netherlands,. in vol. 1, *Historic Preservation in Other Countries*, Robert E. Stipe (ed.). Washington, DC: US/ICOMOS, 1982.

D'Ayala, Dina, and Enrico Fodde, (eds.). *Structural Analysis of Historic Construction: Preseving Safety and Significance. Proceedings of the Sixth International Conference on Structural Analysis of Historic Construction, 2–4 July, Bath, United Kingdom*. Vol 1. London: CRC Press/Balkema, 2008.

De Angelis d'Ossat, Guglielmo. *Sul Restauro dei Monumenti Architettonici: Concetti, Operatività, Didattica*. Series no. 13, School for the Restoration of Monuments, University of Rome "La Sapienza." Rome: Bonsignori Editore, 1995.

D'Angelo, Donatello, and Silvia Moretti, (eds.). *Storia del Restauro Archeologico Appunti*. Firenze: Alinea Editrice, 2004.

Delafons, John. *Politics and Preservation: A Policy History of the Built Heritage, 1882–1996*. London: E. and F. N. Spon, 1997.

De la Torre, Marta, (ed.). *Assessing the Values of Cultural Heritage*. Los Angeles: Getty Conservation Institute, 2002.

———. *The Conservation of Archaeological Sites in the Mediterranean Region, Proceedings of an International Conference Organized by the Getty Conservation Institute and the J. Paul Getty Museum, 6–12 May 1995*. Los Angeles: Getty Conservation Institute, 1997.

———. *Heritage Values in Site Management: Four Case Studies*, Los Angeles: Getty Conservation Institute, 2005.

de Jong, E. *Restoration of Baroque Gardens: the UNESCO Conference on Neercanne*. Dutch Yearbook of the History of Garden and Landscape Architecture 2. Amsterdam: Architectura & Natura, 1996.

De Naeyer, André, (ed.). *Restoration Principles for a New Europe. International Symposium Ghent 2–3 February 2001*. Ghent: Ghent University, 2001.

Denhez, Marc, and Stephen Neal Dennis (eds.). *Legal and Financial Aspects of Architectural Conservation, The Smolenice Castle Conference Central Europe*. Toronto and Oxford: Dundurn Press, 1997.

Denslagen, Wim. *Architectural Restoration in Western Europe: Controversy and Continuity*. Amsterdam: Architectura and Natura, 1994.

———. "Restoration Theories, East and West." *Transactions/ Association for Studies in the Conservation of Historic Buildings* 18 (1993): 3–7.

———. *Romantic Modernism: Nostalgia in the World of Conservation*. Amsterdam: Amsterdam University Press, 2009.

Denslagen, Wim, and Niels Gutschow, (eds.). *Architectural Imitations: Reproductions and Pastiches in East and West*. Maastricht, Netherlands: Shaker Publishing, 2005.

Díez, Isalbel Ordieres. *Historia del la Restauración Monumental en España (1835–1936)*. Instituo de Conservación y Restauración de Bienes Culturales. Madrid: Ministerio de Cultura, 1995.

Drdácký, Miloš, and Michel Chapuis, (eds.). *Safeguarded Cultural Heritage: Understanding and Viability for the Enlarged Europe. Proceedings of the 7th European Conference "SAUVEUR," 31st May–3rd June 2006, Prague*. Vols. 1 and 2. Prague: ITAM, 2007.

Ducassi, Maria Rosa Suárez-Inclán. "Spain's Ongoing Foreign Technical Assistance for the Conservation of Historic Heritage Worldwide," www.icomos.org/usicomos/symp99/ suarez-inclan.htm.

Dunn, Nigel. "Maintaining Europe's Built Cultural Heritage." In From Cataloguing to Planned Preservation (Conference, November 23–25, 2000, Milan, Italy). www.medicif.org/ Events/MEDICI_ events/Milan_nov00/Proposals/Nigel_ Dunn.htm (accessed October 14, 2005.)

Earl, John. *Building Conservation Philosophy*. 3rd ed. Preface by Bernard Feilden. Shaftesbury, UK: Donhead and College of Estate Management, 2003.

English Heritage. *Conservation-led Regeneration*. London: English Heritage, 1998.

English Heritage. *Monuments of War: The Evaluation, Recording and of Twentieth-Century Military Sites*. Edited by John Schofield. London: English Heritage, 1998.

Erder, Cevat. *Our Architectural Heritage: From Consciousness to Conservation*. Paris: UNESCO, 1986.

European Commision. *Preserving Our Heritage, Improving Our Environment—20 Years of EU Research into Cultural Heritage*. Edited by Michel Chapuis. Luxembourg and Brussels: Council of Europe, 2009.

Evans, David. M., Peter Salway, and David Thakeray. *"The Remains of Distant Times" Archaeology and the National Trust*. Suffolk, UK: The Society of Antiquaries of London and the National Trust, The Boydell Press, 1996.

Fairclough, Graham, Rodney Harrison, John H. Jameson Jr., and John Schoenfield (eds.). *The Heritage Reader*. London and New York: Routledge, 2008.

Fawcett, Jane (ed.). *The Future of the Past: Attitudes to Conservation 1174–1974*. London: Thames and Hudson, 1976.

Feilden, Bernard. *Between Two Earthquakes: Cultural Property in Seismic Zones*. Rome and Marina del Rey: ICCROM and Getty Conservation Institute, 1987.

———. *Conservation of Historic Buildings*. 3rd ed. Oxford: Architectural Press, 3rd ed., 2003. First published in 1982 by Butterworth Scientific.

Feilden, Bernard M., and Jukka Jokilehto. *Management Guidelines for World Cultural Heritage Sites*. Rome: ICCROM, 1993.

Feliú, Carmen Añón, (ed.). *Culture and Nature: International Legislative Texts referring to the Safeguard of Natural and Cultural Heritage*. Madrid: Leo. S. Olshki, 2003.

Findlay, Donald. *The Protection of our English Churches: The History of the Council for the Care of Churches 1921–1996*. Bristol: The Longdunn Press, 1996.

Fishlock, Michael. *The Great Fire at Hampton Court*. London: The Herbert Press, 1992.

Fitch, James Marston. *Historic Preservation: Curatorial Management of the Built World*. 5th ed. Charlottesville, VA: University of Virginia Press, 2001. First published in 1982 by McGraw-Hill.

Fladmark, J. M. (ed.). *Cultural Tourism*. Papers presented at the Robert Gordon University Heritage Convention 1994. Oxford: Donhead Publishing, 1994.

———. (ed.) *Heritage: Conservation: Interpretation and Enterprise: Papers presented at the Robert Gordon Heritage Convention, 1993*. London: Donhead, 1993.

Fletcher, Caroline, and Jane Da Mosto. *The Science of Saving Venice*. Turin: Umberto Allemandi e C., 2004.

Forsyth, Michael (ed.). *Materials and Skills for Historic Building Conservation*. Oxford: Blackwell Publishing 2008.

———. (ed.) *Structures & Construction in Historic Building Conservation*. OxfordUK, and Malden, MA: Blackwell, 2007.

———. (ed.) *Understanding Historic Building Conservation*. Oxford, UK, and Malden, MA: Blackwell Publishing Ltd. 2007.

Fowler, Peter J. *The Past in Contemporary Society: Then, Now*. London: Routledge, 1992.

Galan, Emilio, and Fulvio Zezza (eds.). *Protection and Conservation of the Cultural Heritage of the Mediterranean Cities, Proceedings of the 5th International Symposium on the Conservation of Monuments in the Mediterranean Basin, Sevilla, Spain, 5–8 April, 2000*. Lisse, Netherlands: Swets & Zeitlinger B.V., 2002.

Galeazzi, Andrea (ed.).*Ripristino Architettonico: Restauro o Restaurazione?* Fiesole: Nardini Editore, 1999.

Gamboni, Dario. *The Destruction of Art: Iconoclasm and Vandalism since the French Revolution*. London: Reaktion Books, 1997

Gaze, John. *Figures in a Landscape; A History of the National Trust*. London: Barrie & Jenkins in Association with the National Trust, 1988.

Gerstenblith, Patty. *Art, Cultural Heritage, and the Law: Cases and Materials*, 2nd ed. Durham, NC: Carolina Academic Press, 2008. First edition published in 2004.

Gli Anni del Governatorato (1926–1944) Interventi Urbanistici Scoperte Archaeologiche Arredo Urbano Restauri. Roma: Quaderni dei Monumenti, Edizioni Kappa, 1995.

Global Heritage Fund. *Saving our Global Heritage*. Palo Alto, CA: GHF Press, 2004.

Giannattasio, C. *Il Restauro Urbanistico in Francia: 1962–2002. Piani e Interventi nei Secteurs Sauvegardés*. Naples: Graffiti, 2003.

Giordano, E. *Luxembourg*. In *Les Monuments et Leurs Abords, entre Conservation et Développement: L'Exemple des Villes de Bordeaux, Luxembourg, Mons et Valladolid*. Brussels: Société d'Architecture, de Rénovation et d'Urbanisme, 2000.

Giovannoni, Gustavo. *Dal Capitello alla Città*. Milano: Jaca Book SpA, 1997.

Godefroid, J. "Creation and Restoration in Classical Paris." In *Paris: La Ville et Ses Projets*. Edited by J. L. Cohen and B. Fortier. Paris: Babylone, 1988.

Goulty, Sheena Mackellar. *Heritage Gardens: Care, Conservation, and Management*. London: Routledge, 1993.

Greffe, Xavier. *La Valorisation Économique du Patrimoine*. Paris: Ministère de la Culture et de la Communication, DAG, Département des etudes et de la perspective, 2003.

Grenville, J. ed. *Managing the Historic Rural Landscape*. London: Routledge, 1999.

Guidi, E. "Conservazione e Restauro in Francia: L'Organizzazione del Sistema della Tutela e del Restauro." *Kermes: Arte, Conservazione, Restauro* 12 no. 35 (1999): 59–65.

Gulber, Jacques, et al. *Viollet-le-Duc: Centenaire de la Mort à Lausanne*. Lausanne: Musèe historique de l'Ancien-Evêché, 1979.

Hardy, Matthew (ed.). *The Venice Charter Revisited: Modernism, Conservation and Tradition in the 21st Century*. Newcastle upon Tyne: Cambridge Scholars Publishing, 2008.

Harrison, Richard (ed.). *Manual of Heritage Management*. Oxford: Butterworth-Heinemann, 1994.

Harrison, Richard, ed. *Manual of Heritage Management (Conservation and Museology)*. Oxford: Elsevier Architectural Press, 1995.

Harvey, John. "The Origin of Listed Buildings." *Transactions of the Ancient Monuments Society* 37 (1993): 1–20.

Haskell, Tony (ed.). *Caring for Our Built Heritage: Conservation in Practice*. London: E. and F. N. Spon, 1993.

Henket, Hubert-Jan, and Wessel de Jonge. *First International DOCOMOMO Conference Proceedings*, September 12–15 1990. Eindhoven University of Technology, Netherlands, 1991.

Herbert, David T. (ed.). *Heritage, Tourism and Society*. London: Mansell, 1995.

Heritage Policy Group. *The Conservation of Architectural Ancient Monuments in Scotland (Heritage Policy Papers)* Edinburgh: Historic Scotland (December 31, 2001).

Hernández, Josep Ballart, Jordi Juan I Tresserras, *Gestión del Patrimonio cultural*, Barcelona: Ed.Ariel S.A., 2001

Hewison, Robert. *The Heritage Industry: Britain in a Climate of Decline*. London: Methuen, 1987.

Horta, V. *L'Entourage des Monuments: Principes Genereaux*. Paris, 1933.

Hunter, Michael (ed.). *Preserving the Past: The Rise of Heritage in Modern Britain*. Stroud, Gloucestershire, UK: Alan Sutton, 1996.

Hutter, Michael and Ilde Rizzo (eds.). *Economic Perspectives on Cultural Heritage*. Hampshire and London: Macmillan Press, 1997.

ICOMOS. *First Conference on The Conservation, Restoration and Revival of Areas and Groups of Buildings of Historic Interest*. Caceres, Spain, 15–19, 1967. n.p., 1968.

———. *Guidelines on Education and Training in the Conservation of Monuments, Ensembles and Sites* (Paris: ICOMOS, 1993). www.icomos.org/docs/guidelines_for_education.html

———. *Monuments for People: Records of the II International Congress of Restoration*. Venice, 25–31 May, 1964. Marsilio Editori, Padua, 1971.

———. *Proceedings of the First International Symposium on Protection and Restoration of Historical Gardens*. Fontainebleu, France, 13–18 September 1971. ICOMOS Paris, 1973.

Insall, Donald. *The Care of Old Buildings Today: A Practical Guide*. London: Architectural Press, 1972.

———. *Living Buildings*. London: Images Publishing Group Pty Ltd., 2008.

International Fund for Monuments. (former World Monuments Fund) *Venice in Peril*. Translated by Diana Sears. Florence: Sansone Editore, 1970.

Irish Architecture....A Future for Our Heritage. Published by the National Committee for European Architectural Heritage Year, 1975. George Sheppard, Ltd.1975.

Istituto Veneto de Scienze, Lettere ed Arti. *A Future for Venice? Considerations 40 years after the 1966 flood*. Venice: Umberto Allemandi & C. 2006.

Jenkins, J. and James, P. *From Acorns to Oak Trees: the Growth of the National Trust 1895–1994*. London: Macmillan, 1994.

Jokilehto, Jukka. *A History of Architectural Conservation*. Oxford: Butterworth-Heinemann, 1999.

———. *A History of Architectural Conservation: The Contribution of English, French, German,and Italian Thought Towards an International Approach to the Conservation of Cultural Property*. D.Phil Thesis, The Institute for Advanced Studies, University of York, 3 Vol., 1986.

Journal of Architectural Conservation. Since 1995.

Junta de Andalucia, *Programa de Cooperacion Internacional, Consejeria de Obras Publicas y Transportes*, Sevilla: Consejeria de Obras Publicas y Transportes, 2000.

Kain, R.J.P. "Conservation and Planning in France: Policy and Practice in the Marais, Paris," in R.J.P. Kain (ed.), *Planning for Conservation: An International Perspective*. London: Mansell, 1981.

Knight, John (ed.). *The Repair of Historic Buildings in Scotland: advice on principles and methods*. Edinburgh: Historic Scotland 1995. First published as *The Repair of Historic Buildings: Advice on Principles and Methods*. Christopher Brereton. London: English Heritage 1991.

The Knight of Glin, Desmond Fitzgerald and David J. Griffin, Nicholas K. Robinson. *Vanishing Country Houses of Ireland* (2nd ed.). Dublin: The Irish Architectural Archive and The Irish Georgian Society, 1989.

Kuipers, M. "The Long Path to Preservation in the Netherlands." *Transactions of the Ancient Monuments Society*, vol 42,13–34.

de Lagarde, Pierre. *La Mémoire des Pierres*. Editions Albin Michel, Paris, 1979.

La Regina, Francesco. *Come Un Ferro Rovente: Cultura e Prassi del Restauro Archittonico*. Clean Edizione. Naples, 1992.

Larkham, Peter. *Conservation and the City*. London: Routledge, 1996.

Larsen, K. (ed). *Nara Conference on Authenticity*, UNESCO World Heritage Centre, Agency for Cultural Affairs, ICCROM and ICOMOS, 1995.

Latham, Derek. *Creative Re-use of Buildings*. 2 vols. Shaftesbury, UK: Donhead Publishing, 2000.

Layton, Robert, Peter G. Stone and Julian Thomas (eds.). *Destruction and Conservation of Cultural Property*. London: Routledge, 2001.

Lemaire, Chan R. *La Restauration des Monuments Anciens*. Anvers: Steenlandt 1938.

Leniaud, Jean-Michel. *L'Utopie Française: Essai sur le Patrimoine*. Paris: Editions Mengès, 1992.

Lichfield, Nathaniel. *Economics in Urban Conservation*. Cambridge: Cambridge University Press, 1988.

Ligen, Pierre-Yves. *Dangers and Perils: Analysis of Factors which Constitute a Danger to Groups and Areas of Buildings of Historical or Artistic Interest*. Strasbourg: Council for Cultural Co-operation, 1968.

Linstrum, Derek. "Conservation and the British". The Commonwealth Foundation Occasional Paper XXXVIII, pp. 26–36, London, 1976.

Littlejohn, David. *The Fate of the English Country House*. Oxford University Press, London, 1997.

Loew, S., *Modern Architecture in Historic Cities: Policy, Planning and Building in Contemporary France*. London: Routledge, 1998.

Lowenthal, David. *The Past is a Foreign Country*. Cambridge: Cambridge University Press, 1985.

———. *The Heritage Crusade and the Spoils of History*. Cambridge: Cambridge University Press, 1998.

———. *Possessed by the Past: The Heritage Crusade and the Spoils of Modern History*. Viking, London, 1996.

Lutz, Thomas and Gerhard Wesselkamp. *Dächer der Stadt Basel*. Basel: Basler Dachlandschaft 2005.

MacDonald, S (ed.).*Preserving Post-War Heritage: The Care and Conservation of Modern Architecture*, Shaftsbury: Donhead, in association with English Heritage, 2001.

Macdonald, Susan, Kyle Normandin, Bob Kindred (eds.). *Conservation of Modern Architecture*. Shaftesbury: Donhead, 2007.

Macdonald, Susan. (ed.). *Modern Matters, Principles and Practice in Conserving Recent Architecture*. Donhead with English Heritage, Shaftesbury, 1994.

Machatschek, Alois. *Denkmalpflege in Europa, Der Europa-Preis fur Denkmalpflege der Alfred Toepfer Stiftung F.V.S*, Hamburg: Christians verlag, 2001.

Maderna, Marco. *Camillo Boito: Pensiero sull-architettura e dibattito coevo*. Milano: Edizione Angelo Guerini, 1995.

Malraux, Andre. *La Grande Pitie des Monuments de France: Andre Malreaux: Debats Parlementaires (1960/1968)*. Reunis et commentes par Michel Lanteleme. Perspectives series, Septentrion Universitaires Presses, Paris, 1998.

Marasovič, Duško. *Povijesna Jezgra Splita Studije-Programi-Realizacije* [Historic Core of Split, Studie-Programmes-Realized Projects.] Split: City of Split, Department for the Old City Core, 2009.

Marconi, Paolo. *Arte e Cultura della Manutenzione dei Monumenti* (2nd ed.). Rome: Editori Laterza, 1990.

———. *Il Restauro e L'Architetto: Teoria e Practica in Due Secoli di Dibattito*. Saggi Marsilio Editore, Venice, 1993.

———. *Materia e Significato: La Questione del Restauro Architettonico*. Rome: Editori Laterza, 1999.

Marsillo, Saggi. *La Cultura del Restauro*; Teorie e Fondatori a cura di Stella Casiello. Marsilio Editori, Venezia. 1996.

Marino, Bianca Gioia. *Victor Horta: Conservazione e Restauro in Belgio*. Napoli: Edizioni Scientifiche Italiane, 2000.

Marks, Stephen (ed.). *Concerning Buildings: Studies in Honor of Sir Bernard Feilden*, Oxford: Butterworth-Heinemann, 1996.

Martin-Brown, Joan (ed.). *Culture Counts, Financing, Resources, and the Economics of Culture in Sustainable Development*, Proceedings of the Conference held in Florence, Italy October 4–7, 1999, Washington DC: IBRD, 2000.

McGee, Mark. *Berlin: A Visual and Historical Documentation form 1925 to the Present*. New York: The Overlook Press, 2002.

McManamon, Francis P. and Alf Hatton (eds.). *Cultural Resource Management in Contemporary Society, Perspectives on Managing and Presenting the Past*. London: Routledge, 2000.

Melucco Vaccaro, Alessandra. *Archeologia e Restauro: Tradizione e Attualitá*. Il Saggiatore, 1989.

Mills, Edward. *Building Maintenance & Preservation: A Guide to Design and Management* (2nd ed.). Oxford: Butterworth Architecture, 1994. First published 1980.

Ministerio de Cultura. *Intervenciones en el Patrimonio Arquitectonico (1980–1985)*. Madrid: Ministerio de Cultura, 1986.

Ministero della Pubblica Istruzione. *La Ricostruzione del Patrimonio Artistico Italiano*. Rome: La Libreria dello Stato, 1950.

Moneo, Rafael. *La solitude e degli edifici e altri scritti. Questioni intorno all' architettura*. Torino-London: Umberto Allemandi & C., 1999.

Monuments Historiques. "Les Restaurations Françaises et la Charte de Venise." *Les Monuments Historiques*, special issue covering a conference held in Paris on 13–16 October, 1977.

Munoz, Angel Luis (ed.). "Restauracion Arquitectonica" in *Serie Arquitectura y Urbanismo*, no. 19. Univesidad de Valladolid, Liberia General, Zaragosa, 1992.

Muñoz Cosme, Alfonzo. *La Conservacion del Patrimonio Arquitectonico Español*. Madrid: Ministerio de Cultura, 1989.

Muñoz Viñas, S. *Contemporary Theory of Conservation*. Oxford: Elsevier, 2005.

Murphy, Richard. *Carlo Scarpa & Castelvecchio, testi di Alba Di Lieto e Arrigo Rudi*. Venezia: Arsenale Editrice, 1991.

———. *Carlo Scarpa and the Castelvecchio*. Butterworth, Oxford, 1990.

N.A. *Le Portail de Saint-Trophime d'Arles, Naissance et Renaissance d'Un Chef d'Oeuvre Roman*. Arles: Actes Sud. 1999.

The National Trust. *Manual of Housekeeping: The Care of Collections in Historic Houses Open to the Public*. Oxford: Butterworth-Heinemann, 2006.

Nationale Informationsstelle fur Kulturguter-Erhaltung (eds.). *Schweizerische Verband fur Konservierung und Restaurierung, Vereinigung der Kunsthistoriker in der Schweiz, Geschichte der Restaurierung in Europa/Histoire de la Restauration en Europe*, Vol. 1–2. Worms: Wernersche Verlgesellaschaft, 1991.

Navrud, Stale and Richard C. Ready (eds.). *Valuing Cultural Heritage: Applying Environmental Valuation Techniques to Historic Buildings, Monuments and Artifacts*. Cheltenham UK/Northampton, MA: Edward Elgar Publishing Ltd., 2002.

Nicholas, Lynn H. *The Rape of Europa: The Fate of Europe's Treasures in the Third Reich and the Second World War*. New York: Vintage Books, 1995.

Nicolson, A. *Restoration: The Rebuilding of Windsor Castle*. London: Michael Joseph, 1997.

O'Byrne, Robert. *The Irish Georgian Society: A Celebration*. Dublin: The Irish Georgian Society, 2008.

Ogrin, Dušan. *The World Heritage of Gardens*. London: Thames and Hudson 1993. Translated by Margaret Davies, Maja Bilbija and Milan Mlačnik.

Orbaşli, Aylin. *Architectural Conservation*. Oxford: Blackwell Science Ltd., 2008.

———. *Tourists in Historic Towns: Urban Conservation and Heritage Management*. London: E & FN Spon, 2000.

Ost, Chr. *Les dimensions économiques du patrimoine, Entretiens du Patrimoine, Collection des Actes de Colloques de la Direction du Patrimoine*. Paris: La Documentation Française, 1992.

Otero, Carlos and T. Bailey. Europe's Natural and Cultural Heritage: The European Estate. Brussels: Friends of the Countryside, 2003.

Pane, Roberto. *Il Canto dei Tamburi de Pietra: Restauro dei Monumenti e Urbanistica de Centri Antichi*. Napoli: Guida Editori, 1980.

Peacock, Alan and Ilde Rizzo. *The Heritage Game: Economics, Policy, and Practice.* New York: Oxford University Press, 2008.

Pearson, Michael, and Sharon Sullivan. *Looking after Heritage Places: The Basics of Heritage Planning for Managers, Landowners and Administrators.* Carlton, Victoria, Australia: Melbourne University Press, 1995.

Pérez Arroyo, S. "10 anni dopo: il restauro in Spagna," in *Dossier restauro in Spagna,* in "TeMa. Tempo Materia Architettura," 1. 1997.

Périer-D'ieteren, Cathline. *Pénétrer l'Art Restaurer l'Oeuvre: Une Vision Humaniste.* Homage en Forme de Florilège, Belgium: Groeninghe Eds, 1990.

Périer-D'Ieteren, Cathline (ed.). *Restoration in Belgium from 1830 to the Present: Painting, Sculpture, Architecture.* Liege: Mardaga, 1991.

Perschler, Martin."John D. Rockefeller Jr.'s 'Gift to France' and the Restoration of Monuments, 1924–36," Research Reports from the Rockefeller Archive Center (Spring 1977).

Pesaresi, Paola and Gionata Rizzi. "New and Existing Forms of Protective Shelter at Herculaneum: Towards Improving the Continuous Care of the Site," *Conservation and Management of Archaeological Sites,* vol. 8, no. 4 (2006), p. 237–252.

Pickard, R.D. *Conservation in the Built Environment,* Essex: Addison Wesley Longman Limited, 1996.

Pickard, Robert (ed.). *Management of Historic Centres* (Conservation of the European Built Heritage Series). Rome: Taylor & Francis; 2001.

———. (ed.). *Policy and Law in Heritage Conservation.* London: Spon, 2001.

Pierattini, Alessandro. *Manuale del Restauro Archeologico di Ercolano: tipi, techniche costruttive e schede progettuali di indrizzo al restauro.* Roma: Editrice Dedalo Roma, 2009.

Piqué, Francesca and Dusan C. Stulik (eds.). *Conservation of the Last Judgment Mosaic, St. Vitus Cathedral, Prague* Los Angeles: Getty Publications, 2005.

Pour Notre Patrimoine. Alliance Culturelle Romande, No. 21, Octobre 1975. Genève.

Poulot, Dominique (ed.). *Patrimoine et Modernité.* Conference proceedings. Paris: L'Harmattan, 1998.

Prentice, R.J. *Conserve and Provide: a Brief History of the National Trust of Scotland and its Properites.* National Trust of Scotland, c. 1971.

HRH The Prince of Wales. A *Vision of Britain: A Personal View of Architecture.* London: Doubleday, 1989.

Prudon, Theodore H.M. "Architectural Preservation in the Netherlands," in *Curator,* A Quarterly Publication of the Museum of Natural History), vol. XVI, no. 2 (June 1973).

———. *Preservation of Modern Architecture.* Hoboken, NJ: John Wiley & Sons, 2008.

Quaedvlieg-Mihailovic, Sneška and Rupert Graf Strachwitz (eds.). *Heritage and the Building of Europe,* Europa Nostra/Kulturstiftung Haus Europa, The Hague/Berlin: Maecenata Verlag, 2004.

Rab, Samia. 'The "Monument" in 'Architecture and Conservation: Theories of architectural significance and their influence on restoration, preservation and conservation.' A Thesis presented to The Academic Faculty in partial fulfillment of the requirements for the Degree Doctor of Philosophy in Architecture, Georgia Institute of Technology, Spring 1997.

Ranellucci, Sandro. *Restauro e Museografia: Centralità della Storia.* Rome: Multigrafica Editrice, 1990.

Recco, Javier Ruiz et al. (ed.). *Conservación y Restauración de Biens Culturales en Andalucía, Primeras Experiencias,* Sevilla: Estudio ADD, 2000.

Reynolds, Donald M. (ed.). "*Remove not the Ancient Landmark,*" *Public Monuments and Moral Values,* volume 3. Amsterdam: Gordon and Breach Publishers, 1996.

Richmond, Alison, Alison Bracker (eds.). *Conservation: Principles, Dilemmas and Uncomfortable Truths.* Oxford: Butterworth Heinemann, 2009.

Riegl, Alois. "The Modern Cult of Monuments: Its Character and Its Origin." Translated by Kurt W. Forster and Diane Ghirardo. *Oppositions* 25 (Fall 1982): 21–51.

———. *Il Culto Moderno dei Monumenti: Il suo carattere e I suoi inizi* (3rd ed.). Translated by Renate Trost and Sandro Scarrocchia. Bologna: Nuova Alfa Editorale, 1990. Originally published in 1903 as *Der modern Denkmalkultus. Sein Wesen und seine Entstehung* in Verlage von W. Braumüller, Wein und Leipzig, 1903.

Rodríguez, Jose María Calama and Amparo Graciani García. *La Restauración Decimonónica en España.* Sevilla:Universidad de Sevilla, Insituto Universitario de Ciencias de la Construcción, 1998.

———. *La Restauracion Monumental en Espana, de 1900 a 1936,* Sevilla: Universidad de Sevilla, 2000.

Rodwell, Dennis. *Conservation and Sustainability in Historic Cities.* Oxford: Blackwell Publishing, 2007.

———. "Conservation in a Changing Climate." *Context,* Institute of Historic Building Conservation (May 2009).

———. "From globalisation to localisation," *Context,* Institute of Historic Building Conservation (March 2008).

———. "Industrial World Heritage Sites in the United Kingdom." *World Heritage Review,* UNESCO, Paris, December 2002.

———. "Urban Regeneration and the Management of Change: Liverpool and the Historic Urban Landscape." *Journal of Architectural Conservation,* July 2008.

———. "The World Heritage Convention and the Exemplary Management of Complex Heritage Sites," *Journal of Architectural Conservation,* November 2002.

Ronchi, Alfredo M. (ed.). *European Legislation and Cultural Heritage: A Growing Challenge for Sustainable Cultural Heritage Management and Use.* Brussels: European Working Group on EU Directives and Cultural Heritage, 2006.

Rowan, Yorke and Uzi Baram. *Marketing Heritage: Archaeology and the Consumption of the Past.* Walnut Creek, CA: AltaMira Press, 2004.

Rowell, C. and J. M. Robinson. *Uppark Restored.* London: National Trust, 1996.

Ruiz, Dimas Fernandez-Galiano. *Restaurar Hispana*. Madrid: Ministerio de Fomento con la colaboracion de Patronato del Real Alcazar, 2002.

Sasone, Vito. *Pietre da Salvare*. Societa Editrice Internazionale, Torino, 1978.

Sawin, Martica (ed.). *James Marston Fitch, Selected Writings on Architecture, Preservation and the Built Environment*. New York/London: W.W. Norton & Co., 2008.

Semes, Steven W. *The Future of the Past: A Conservation Ethic for Architecture*. New York / London: W.W. Norton, 2009.

Urbanism, and Historic Preservation. New York/London: W.W. Norton in association with the Institute of Classical Architecture and Classical America. 2009.

Shacklock, Vincent, *Architectural Conservation: Issues and Developments*. Donhead St. Marh: Donhead Publishing, 2006.

Sire, Marie-Anne. *La France du Patrimoine: Les choix de la mémoire*. Paris: Gallimard, 2005.

———. *La France du Patrimoine, Les Choix de la Mémoire*. Caisse Nationale des Monuments Historiques et des Sites. Decouvertes Gallimard/CNMHS, Memoire des Lieux series, no. 291, Paris 2000.

Society for the Protection of Ancient Buildings (SPAB). *Repair Not Restoration*. Printed for the centenary of SPAB. London: SPAB, 1977.

Stanley-Price, Nicholas (ed.). *Conservation on Archaeological Excavations with Particular Reference to the Mediterranean Area*. Rome: ICCROM, 1995. First published in 1984.

———. "Special Issue on Protective Shelters," *Conservation and Management of Archaeological Sites* 5:1–2 (2001).

Stanley-Price, Nicholas and Joseph King (eds.). *Conserving the Authentic: Essays in Honour of Jukka Jokilehto*, ICCROM Conservation Studies 10. Rome: ICCROM, 2009.

Stanley-Price, Nicholas, M. Kirby Talley, Jr., and Allesandra Melucco Vaccaro (eds.). *Historical and Philosophical Issues in the Conservation of Cultural Heritage. Readings in Conservation*. Los Angeles: Getty Conservation Institute, 1996.

Stipe, Robert (ed.). *Historic Preservation in Other Countries. Vol. I: France, Great Britain, Ireland, the Netherlands and Denmark*, Anthony Dale, 1982.; Vol. II: *Federal Republic of Germany, Switzerland, and Austria* by Margaret Thomas, 1984.;. III: *Poland* by Paul H. Gleye and Waldemar Szczerba.; Vol. IV: *Turkey* by Jo Ramsey Leimenstoll, 1989. Washington, DC: US/ICOMOS, 1982–.

Strike, James. *Architecture in Conservation: Managing Development at Historic Sites*. London: Routledge, 1994.

Stovel, Herb. *Risk Preparedness: A Management Manual for World Cultural Heritage*. Rome: ICCROM, 1998.

Strong, Peter G. and Philippe G Planel. *The Constructed Past: Experimental Archaeology, Education, and the Public*. London: Routledge, 1999.

Stubbs, John H. *Time Honored: A Global View of Architectural Conservation*. Hoboken, NJ: John Wiley and Sons, 2009.

Stubbs, Michael. "Heritage-sustainability: Developing a Methodology for the Sustainable Appraisal of the Historic Environment," in *Planning Practice and Research*, vol. 19 no.3, 285–305.

Stungo, A. "The Malraux Act 1962–72." *Journal of the Royal Town Planning Institute* vol. 59, 357–362 1972.

Stratton, Michael. (ed.). *Structure and Style: Conserving 20th Century Buildings*. London: Spon, 1997.

Strike, James. *Architecture in Conservation: Managing Development at Historic Sites*. London: Routledge, 1994.

Suarez, Florencio Friera, *Patrimonio Historico y Cutural del concejo de Sariego (Asturias)*, Oviedo: Real Instituto de Estudios Asturianos, 2001.

Suddards, Roger W. *Listed Buildings, The Law and Practice*. London: Sweet & Maxwell, 1982.

Teutonico, Jeanne Marie (ed.). *A Future for the Past: A Joint Conference of English Heritage and the Cathedral Architects Association*. London: English Heritage, James & James, Ltd., 1996.

Teutonico, Jeanne Marie, and Frank Matero (eds.). *Managing Change: Sustainable Approaches to the Conservation of the Built Environment*. Los Angeles: Getty Conservation Institute, 2003.

Teutonico, Jeanne-Marie and John Fidler (eds.). *Monuments and the Millennium*, Proceedings of a joint conference organized by English Heritage and the United Kingdom Institute for Conservation. Slough: English Heritage, 2001.

Teutonico, Jeanne Marie and Gaetano Palumbo (eds.). *Management Planning for Archaeological Sites*, An International Workshop Organized by the Getty Conservation Institute and Loyola Marymount University, 19–22 May 2000 Corinth, Greece. Los Angeles: The Getty Conservation Institute, 2000.

Thorne, Robert. *Covent Garden and Market, its History and Restoration*. London: Architectural Press, 1980.

Tillema, J. A. C. *Schetsen uit de Geshiedenis van de Monumentenzorg in Nederland*. Staatsuitgeverij, Gravenhage, 1975.

Toscano, Gennaro with Fabien Jamois. *Victor Hugo et le débat patrimonial*. Acts du colloque organize par l'Institut national du patrimoine sous la direction de Roland Recht, Paris, Maison de l'UNESCO, 5–6 décembre 2002. Paris: Somogy editions d'Art, 2003.

Tomlan, Michael A. (ed.). *Preservation of What, for Whom?: A Critical Look at Historical Significance*. Ithaca, NY: National Council for Preservation Education, 1998.

Tschudi-Madsen, Stephan. *Restoration and Anti-Restoration: A Study in English Restoration Philosophy*. Oslo: Universitetsforlaget, 1976.

Tung, Anthony M. *Preserving the World's Great Cities: The Destruction and Renewal of the Historic Metropolis*. New York: Clarkson Potter, 2001.

UNESCO. *Operation for the Implementation of the World Cultural and Natural Heritage Convention*. Intergovernmental Committee for the Protection of the World Cultural and Natural Heritage, Paris, 1988.

———. *UNESCO for Venice. International Campaign for the Safeguarding of Venice, 1966–1992*. By Rolande Cuvillier and Edward Thompson. Department of Information and

Publications, President's Council of the Ministries, Roma, 1993.

———. *Venice Restored 1966–1986.* Milan: Electa, Elemond Editori Associati, 1991.

———. *World Heritage 2002 Shared Legacy, Common Responsibility.* Proceedings of An International Congress organized by UNESCO's World Heritage Centre and Regional Bureau for Science in Europe (ROSTE), UNESCO: Paris, 2003.

Van der Wee B. *L'Hôtel Van Eetvelde di Victor Horta a Bruxelles. Il restauro del pozzo di luce,* in "TeMa Tempo Materia Architettura," 1. 1999.

Van Jole, Marcel (ed.). *The Power of Example, 40 Years of Europa Nostra.* Den Haag: Europa Nostra, 2002.

Van Riel, Silvio. *Monumenti e Centri Storici: Note Bibliografiche sul Restauro e La Tutela dei Monumenti e dei Centri Storici.* UNIEDIT S.p.A., Firenze, 1996.

Van Santvoort, L. *Gestion, conservation et Restauration du Patrimoine de la Region Bruxelloise,* in De Naeyer A. (directed by) *Restoration Principles for a new Europe: International Symposium* (Ghent, 3 February 2001). Ghent: University Faculty of Engineering, Department Architecure and Urban Planning. 2001.

Viollet-le-Duc "On Restoration," from *Dictionnaire Raisonné,* vol.8., as cited in M.F. Hearn (ed.), *The Architectural Theory of Viollet-le-Duc: Readings and Commentary* Cambridge, MA: MIT Press, 1992.

Vitale, M.R. *Restauri in Francia, 1970–2000: storia, politiche, interventi.* Palermo: Medina, 2001.

Von Droste, Bernd, Harald Plachter and Mechtild Rössler (eds.). *Cultural Landscapes of Universal Value: Components of a Global Strategy.* Jena, Germany: Fischer Verlag in cooperation with UNESCO, 1995.

Von Droste, Bernd, Mechtild Rössler and Sarah Titchen (eds.). *Linking Nature and Culture: Report of the Global Strategy, Natural and Cultural Heritage,* Expert Meeting. Held in Amsterdam, March 25–29, 1998.

Von Tr tzschler, Werner and Florian Fiedler. *Legal Structures of Private Sponsorship.* ICOMOS International Seminar on Legal Structures of Private Sponsorship and Participation in the Protection and Maintenance of Monuments, Weimar, April 17–19, 1997. Munich: Karl M. Lipp Verlag, 1997.

Warren, John, John Worthington and Sue Taylor (eds.). *Context: New Buildings in Historic Settings,* Oxford. London: Architectural Press, 1998.

Waterson, Merlin and Wyndham, Samantha. *The National Trust: the First Hundred Years.* London: The National Trust/BBC Books, 1994.

Watt, John, Johan Tidblad, Vladimir Kucera, Ron Hamilton (eds.). *The Effects of Air Pollution on Cultural Heritage.* New York: Springer Science and Business Media LLC, 2009.

Weideger, Paula, *Gilding the Acorn, Behind the Façade of the National Trust.* London: Simon & Schuster Ltd., 1994.

Weyer, Angela (ed.). *Rettung des Kulturerbes, Projekte rund ums Mittelmeer/Saving Cultural Heritage, Projects around the Mediterranean/Sauvetage du Patrimoine Culturel, Projets autour de la Mediterranee,* Series of the Hornemann Institute, volume 3, Hamburg: Gloss Verlag, 2000.

Whitehand, J.W.R. and P.J. Larkham (eds.). *Urban Landscapes: International Perspectives.* London: Routledge, 1992.

Whittle, E. *The Conservation of Historic Gardens in Europe.* London: The Garden History Society, 1995.

Williams, Kenneth. *Development and Design of Heritage Sensitive Sites: Strategies for Listed Buildings and Conservation Areas.* London: Routledge, 2010.

Wines, James, *Green Architecture.* Köln: Taschen, 2000.

World Monuments Fund. (by Colin Amery and Brian Curran). *Vanishing Histories* New York; Abrams, 2002.

World Monuments Fund. (formerly International Fund for Monuments). *Venice in Peril.* Sasoni, Florence, 1970.

Zaki Aslan. "Protective Structures for the Conservation and Presentation of Archeological Sites," *Journal of Conservation and Museum Studies* 3 (November 1997).

Zander, G. *Scritti sul restauro dei monumenti architettonici,* Scuola de specializzazione per lo studio ed il restauro dei monumenti, Università degli studi di Roma "La Sapienza" (Strumenti 10). Rome: Bonsignori, 1993.

Zilhão, João. Arte Rupestre e Pré-História do Vale de Côa: Trabalhos de 1995–1996. Lisboa: Ministerio de Cultura, 1997.

SECTION 2 (NORTHERN EUROPE)

Adlercreutz, Eric, Leif Englund, Maija Kairamo, Tapani Mustonen and Vezio Nava/The Finnish Committee for the Restoration of Viipuri Library. *Alvar Aalto Library in Vyborg: Saving a Modern Masterpiece.* Helskinki: Pakennustieto Publishing, 2009.

Aluve, K. *Restoration of the Kuressaare castle and its adaptation for new functions,* in *Problems of the Protection and Present-Day Usage of Architectural Monuments.* Colloquio internazionale ICOMOS (Tallinn, June 4–7 1985). Tallinn: Gosstroj, 1987.

Anker, Leif and Jiri Havran. *The Norwegian Stave Churches,* Translated by Tim Challman. Oslo: Arfo, 2005.

Anker, Leif. *Our Nordic Heritage: World Heritage Sites in the Nordic Countries.* Translated by V.F. Stokke and Melody Favish. Vågeveìen: KOM Forlag as, 1997.

Appleyard, Donald (ed.). *The Conservation of European Cities.* Cambridge, MA: MIT Press, 1979.

Ashworth, G.J. and J.E. Turnbridge (eds.). *Building a New Heritage: Tourism, Culture and Identity in the New Europe.* London: Routledge, 1994.

Brock-Nannestad, G. *The rationale behind operational conservation theory,* in *Conservation without Limits*; IIC Nordic Group XV Congress, Helsinki, 23–26 August 2000. Helsinki: IIC Nordic Group, 2000.

By & Bolig Ministeriet. *Urban Renewal in Denmark.* Copenhagen: Ministry of Housing and Urban Affairs, 2001.

Cantacuzino, Sherban (ed.). *Architectural Conservation in Europe.* London: Architectural Press, 1975.

Carbonara, Giovanni (ed.). *Trattato di Restauro Architettonico,* Primo Aggornamento. Grandi termi di restauro, Vols. 1–10 (esp. vol. 8 on *International Practice,* pp 1–208). Milan: UTET Scienze Techniche, 2007.

De la Torre, Marta (ed.). *Assessing the Values of Cultural Heritage*, Los Angeles: the Getty Conservation Institute, 2002.

Denslagen, Wim. *Romantic Modernism: Nostalgia in the World of Conservation*. Amsterdam: Amsterdam University Press, 2009.

Denslagen, Wim. *Architectural Restoration in Western Europe: Controversy and Continuity*. Amsterdam: Architectura and Natura, 1994.

Denslagen, Wim and Neils Gutschow (eds). *Architectural Imitations: Reproductions and Pastiches in East and West*. Maastricht, Neth.: Shaker Publishing, 2005.

Drdácký, Miloš, Michel Chapuis et al. (eds). *Safeguarded Cultural Heritage, Understanding and Viability for the Enlarged Europe*. Proceedings of the 7th European Conference "SAUVEUR," May 31–June 3, 2006.

Dromgoole, Sarah. *Legal Protection of the Underwater Cultural Heritage: National and International Perspectives*. London: Kluwer Law International Ltd., 1999.

Fladmark, J.M. (ed.). *Heritage and Identity: Shaping the Nations of the North*. Papers presented at the 2001 Heritage Convention, Shaftesbury: Donhead, 2002.

Hinsch, Luce and Hans-Emil Lidén, Dag Myklebust, Stephan Tschudi-Madsen. *Norway: A Cultural Heritage/Norvège: Un Patrimoine Culturel*. Oslo: Univversitetsforlanget A/S, 1987.

Jokilehto, Jukka. *A History of Architectural Conservation*. Oxford: Butterworth-Heinemann, 1999.

Kairamo, Maija and Hanni Sippo. "Repairing Alvar Aalto's Buildings". Arkkitehti. 2001, n.5, 24–25.

Kairamo, M. *Developments in Restoration and Building Conservation in Finland since the Second World War*, in *Monuments and Sites. Finland*, ICOMOS 12th General Assembly (Mexico 1999). Helsinki: ICOMOS, 1999.

Krastins, J. *Conservation and architectural restoration in Latvia*, in Ahoniemi A (directed by) *Conservation Training—Needs and Ethics*, Atti del seminario (Suomenlinna, Helsinki, Finland, 12–17 June 1995). Helsinki: ICOMOS, 1995.

Larrson, Henrik. "Conservation of Wooden Architecture in Sweden" in *Living Wooden Culture Throughout Europe*. Nuria Sanz (ed.). Strasbourg: Council of Europe Publishing, 2002.

Larsen, Knut Einar and Nils Marstein (eds). *Conference on Authenticity in Relation to the World Heritage Convention*. Prepatory Workshop Bergen, Norway, 31 January–2 February 1994. Directorate for Cultural Heritage, Tapir Forlag, Trondheim, 1994.

Lass, Anne and Juhan Maiste. *Architectural Monuments in Estonia and Scandinavia: Restoration in Theory and Practice*. Architectural Conservation Methodology Conference, Tallinn 9–10 October 1989. Tallinn: Tallinna Raamatutrükikoda, 1993.

Lehtimäki, Marianne (ed.). *Urban Heritage—Collective Privilege*. Helsinki: National Board of Antiquities of Finland, 2005.

Lejnieks, J. *Threats of Development of Urban and Rural Landscaper in Latvia, Conservation Training—Needs and Ethics*, Atti del seminario (Suomenlinna, Helsinki, Finland, June 12–17, 1995). Rome: ICOMOS, 1995.

Lemaire, C. R. *La Restauration des Monuments Anciens*. Antwerp: De Sikkel, 1938.

Macdonald, Susan (ed.). *Preserving Post-War Heritage: The Care and Conservation of Mid-Twentieth Century Architecture*. Shaftesbury: Donhead, in association with English Heritage, 2001.

Magnusson, T. "Conservation of Industrial Monuments on Iceland," in *The Industrial Heritage in Scandinavia*, the Third International Conference on the Conservation of Iindustrial Monuments (Sweden, May 30–June 5, 1978). Stockholm: Nordiska museet, 1978.

Maiste, Juhan. *Eestimaa Mõisad, Manorial Architecture in Estonia*. Tallin: Trűkitud Tallinna Ramatutrűkikojas 1996.

———. *Estonian Manorial Architecture, A Look at the History, Research, Problems of Use and Restoration*, in Ivars M. (ed.), *Building Conservation*, Atti dell'88e Simposio (Helsinki, August 22–26, 1988). Helsinki: Finnish National Commission for UNESCO, 1989.

———. *Retracing Steps/Tuldud Teed Tagasi*. A publication of the Estonian Academy of Arts Restoration School No.1, Proceedings of the Estonian Academy of Arts, vol 12. Tallinn: Tallinna Raamàtutrükikoja OÜ, 1995.

Martin-Brown, Joan (ed.). *Culture Counts, Financing, Resources, and the Economics of Culture in Sustainable Development*, Proceedings of the Conference held in Florence, Italy October 4–7, 1999, Washington DC: IBRD, 2000.

Nielsen, Jens V. *Urban Renewal in Denmark*. Copenhagen: Danish Ministry in Housing and Urban Affairs, 2001.

1960 Års Kommitté för Gamla Stan: *Saneringen Inom Staden Mellan Broarna*. Stockholm: Bröderna Siösteens Boktryckeri AB 1965.

Öiger, K. *Building Conservation, Restoration and Renovation in Estonia*, in A. Ahoniemi (ed.), *Conservation Training—Needs and Ethics*, Atti del seminario (Suomenlinna, Helsinki, June 12–17, 1995) Helsinki: ICOMOS, 1995.

Prudon, Theodore H. M. *Preservation of Modern Architecture*. Hoboken, NJ: John Wiley & Sons, 2008.

Quaedvlieg-Mihailovic, Sneška and Rupert Graf Strachwitz (eds.). *Heritage and the Building of Europe*, Europa Nostra/Kulturstiftung Haus Europa, The Hague/Berlin: Maecenata Verlag, 2004.

Slava, Laima (ed.). *The Wooden Heritage of Riga*, Riga: Neptuns, 2001.

Stanley-Price, Nicholas, M. Kirby Talley, Jr., and Allesandra Melucco Vaccaro (eds.). *Historical and Philosophical Issues in the Conservation of Cultural Heritage. Readings in Conservation*. Los Angeles: Getty Conservation Institute, 1996.

Swensen, G. *A Sustainable City: the Example of Talinn*, in R. Kozlowski (ed.), *Cultural Heritage research: a Pan-European challenge*, Atti della V Conferenza (Cracow, May 16–18 2002). Cracow: European Communities ICSC, 2003.

Tung, Anthony M. *Preserving the World's Great Cities: The Destruction and Renewal of the Historic Metropolis*. New York: Clarkson Potter, 2001.

UNESCO: Ryszkiewicz, Andrezej (Directeur de la publication). *Bois dans l'architecture et la sculpture slaves*. Lausanne: Imprimeries Populaires, 1981.

UNESCO, *World Heritage 2002: Shared Legacy, Common Responsibility*. An International Congress, 14–16 November 2002, Venice, Italy. Paris: UNESCO 2003.

Warren, J., J. Worthington and S. Taylor (eds.). *Context: New Buildings in Historic Settings*. London: Architectural Press, 1998.

Whittle, E. *The Conservation of Historic Gardens in Europe*. London: The Garden History Society, 1995.

World Commission on Environment and Development. *Our Common Future* (known as *The Bruntland Report*). Oxford: Oxford University Press, 1987.

Zobel, R. "On the Study and Restoration of Tallinn's Ancient Fortification," in *Problems of the Protection and Present-Day Usage of Architectural Monuments*, Colloquio internazionale ICOMOS (Tallinn, June 4–7 1985), Tallinn: Gostroj, 1987.

SECTION 3 (CENTRAL EUROPE)

Aebischer, P. *L'Ottocento. Il regno di Prussia*, in Miarelli Mariani G. (a cura di) *Il restauro dei monumenti nei paesi europei*, Dipartimento do Storia dell'Architettura, Conservazione e Restauro. Rome, 2001.

Ashworth, G.J. and J.E.Turnbridge (eds.). *Building a New Heritage: Tourism, Culture and Identity in the New Europe*. London: Routledge, 1994.

Bakoš, Ján. "Monuments and Ideologies." *Centropia: A Journal of Central European Architecture and Related Arts* 1, no. 2 (May 2001): 101–7. Previously published by the Slovak Academy of Sciences in its journal Human Affairs 1, no. 2 (December 1991).

Baranski, Marek. "The Monuments of Warsaw 50 Years After." *Transactions: Association for Studies in the Conservation of Historic Buildings* 19 (1994): 39–49.

———. "Foreign Views on the Reconstruction," in M. Konopka (ed.), *Destroyed but Not Lost*, 129–135. Warsaw: 2006.

Bieganski, Piotr et al. *Zabytki Urbanistykii Achitektury w Polsce: Odbudowa I Konserwacja. Miasta Historyczne*. Warsawa: Arkady, 1986.

Binney, Marcus, Kit Martin and Wojciech Wagner. *Silesia The Land of Dying Country Houses: A SAVE Europe's Heritage Report*, London 2009

Borowiec, Andrew. *Destroy Warsaw! Hitler's Punishment, Stalin's Revenge*. Westport, CT/London: Praeger, 2001.

Burian, Miroslav. *La Protection des Monuments Historiques en Tshécoslavaquie. L'Administration Nationale des Monuments Historiques*. Prague, 1957.

Burman, Peter. "Conservation in Poland," *Transactions*, vol. 10 (1985).

Cantacuzino, Sherban (ed.). *Architectural Conservation in Europe*. London: Architectural Press, 1975.

Carbonara, Giovanni (ed.). *Trattato di Restauro Architettonico, Primo Aggornamento. Grandi termi di restauro*, Vols. 1–10 (Vol. 8 on International Practice, pp 1–208). Milan: UTET Scienze Techniche, 2007.

Clayton, A. and A. Russell (eds.). *Dresden: A City Reborn*. Oxford: Berg, 1999.

The Conservation of Historical Monuments in the Federal Republic of Germany: History, Organization, Tasks, Case Histories. 'A Contribution to European Architectural Heritage Year 1975'. Inter Nationes Bonn-Bad Godesberg, Munich, 1974.

De la Torre, Marta (ed.). *Assessing the Values of Cultural Heritage*, Los Angeles: the Getty Conservation Institute, 2002.

Denhez, Marc and Stephen Neal Dennis (eds.). *Legal and Financial Aspects of Architectural Conservation*, The Smolenice Castle Conference Central Europe. Toronto/Oxford: Dundurn Press, 1997.

Denslagen, Wim. *Architectural Restoration in Western Europe: Controversy and Continuity*. Amsterdam: Architectura and Natura, 1994.

———. *Romantic Modernism: Nostalgia in the World of Conservation*. Amsterdam: Amsterdam University Press, 2009.

Denslagen, Wim and Neils Gutschow (eds.). *Architectural Imitations: Reproductions and Pastiches in East and West*. Maastricht, Neth.: Shaker Publishing, 2005.

Dercsényi, Dezso. *Historical Monuments and Their Protection in Hungary*. Egyetemi Nyomda, Budapest, 1984

Dölling, R. (ed.). *The Conservation of Historical Monuments in the Federal Republic of Germany*. Munich: 1974.

Drdácký, Miloš and Michel Chapuis and others (eds.). *Safeguarded Cultural Heritage, Understanding & Viability for the Enlarged Europe*. Proceedings of the 7th European Conference "SAUVEUR," 31st May–3rd June 2006, Prague. Volume and volume 2, Prague: ITAM, 2007.

The Dresden Frauenkirche Foundation (ed.). *The Frauenkirche in Dresden*, Dresden: Michel Sandstein Verlag, 2005.

Federal German Ministry for Regional Planning, Building and Urban Development. *Renewal of Historic Town Centres in Nine European Countries*. Bonn, 1975.

Fitch, James Marston. *Historic Preservation: Curatorial Management of the Built World*. Charlottesville, VA: University of Virginia Press, 5th Edition, 2001.

Frycz, Jerzy. *Restauracja I Konserwacja Zabytków Architektury w Polsce w Latach 1795–1918*. Warszawa: PW Naukowe, 1975.

"The Future of Jewish Heritage in Europe: An International Conference," Prague, April, 24–27, 2004 (www.jewish-heritage-europe.eu/confer/prague04/papers.htm).

Geschichte der Denkmalpflege. VEB, Verlag für Bauwesen, Berlin, 1989.

Glemža, J. and R. Jaloveckas. *The Renewal and Restoration of Part of the Old Town of Vilnius*, in "Monumentum" 1984:1, 27.

Gleye, P. and W. Szczerba. *Poland*, vol. 3 of R. Stipe (ed.), *Historic Preservation in Other Countries*. Washington DC: ICOMOS, 1989.

Gruber, Ruth Ellen. *Jewish Heritage Travel: A Guide to Eastern Europe*. Washington, DC: National Geographic, 2007.

Grüne Gewölbe im Schloss zu Dresden, Rückkehr eines barocken Gestamtkunstwerkes. Dresden: Seemann, 2006.

Hernández, Josep Ballart, Jordi Juan I Tresserras, *Gestión del Patrimonio cultural*, Barcelona: Ed.Ariel S.A., 2001

Hruška, E. "The Architectural Heritage of the Czechoslovak Socialist Republic and Its Preservation," in *Proceedings of the Seminar on Architecture and Historic Preservation in Central and Eastern Europe* (New York, 28–30 November 1979), published in *Journal of the Society of the Architectural Historians*," 38, 2.

Jacques and Jacqueline Levy-Willard Foundation. *The Cultural Guide to Jewish Europe*. Paris: Editions du Seuil, 2004.

Jäger, W. and C.B. Brebbia (eds.). *The Revival of Dresden*. Advances in Architecture Series. Southampton: WIT Press, 2000.

Jankowski, Stanislaw. "Warsaw: Destruction, Secret Town Planning 1939–44, and Postwar Reconstruction." in J.M. Diefendorf (ed.), *Rebuilding Europe's Bombed Cities*. New York: St. Martin's Press, 1990.

Jirì, J. *The Development of the Czechoslovak Restoration School in the Years 1945–65*, in ICOM Committee for Conservation 4th Technical Meeting (Venice, 13–18 October). Preprints Paris: ICOM, 1975.

Jokilehto, Jukka. *A History of Architectural Conservation*. Oxford: Butterworth-Heinemann, 1999.

Kiadó, Corvina. *Historical Monuments and their Protection in Hungary*. Translated by Zsuzsa Béres. Budapest: Egyetemi Nyomda, 1984.

Knoepfli, Albert, *Schweizerische Denkmalpflege: Geschichte und Doktrinen*. Jahrbuch 1970/71. Zurich: Schweizerisches Institut für Kunstwissenschaft 1972.

Konopka, M. (ed.). *Destroyed but Not Lost*, Warsaw: 2006.

Koshar, Rudy J. *From Monuments to Traces: Artifacts of German Memory, 1870–1990*. Berkeley: University of California Press, 2000.

_____. *Germany's Transient Past: Preservation and National Memory in Twentieth Century Germany*. Chapel Hill: University of North Carolina Press, 1998.

Kowalski, Wojciech. *Liquidation of the Effects of World War II in the Area of Culture*, Warsaw: Institute of Culture, 1994.

Krestev, T. *Le Rôle de la Charte de Venise dans le contexte est-europeen: le cas bulgare*, in "Restauro," 133–134, in *Attualità della conservazione dei monumenti*, Atti dell'incontro internazionale de Studio su La Carta de Venezia trenta anni dopo (Naples, 6–7 November 1995).

Krestev, T. *Protection et developpement des villes historiques en Bulgarie*, in "Restauro," 144.

Krzyżanowski, Lech (ed.). *Polish Conservators of Monuments in Asia*. Warsaw: DTP Studio BIGRAF, 1994.

Ledanff, S. "The Palace of the Republic versus the Stadtschloss," in *German Politics and Society*, vol.21 no.4, p.30–73.

Libál, D. *Le centre historique de Prague. Cinq décennies pour sa régénération*, in " Monuments Historiques," 1993, 188.

Lottman, H.R. *How Cities are Saved*. New York: Universe, 1976.

MacDonald, S. (ed.). *Preserving Post-War Heritage: The Care and Conservation of Modern Architecture*, Shaftsbury: Donhead, 2001.

Machat, Christoph. *Denkmaltopographie Siebenbürgen Kreis Kronstadt 3.3*. Sibiu: Wort und Welt Verlag, 1995.

Machatschek, Alois. *Denkmalpflege in Europa, Der Europa-Preis fur Denkmalpflege der Alfred Toepfer Stiftung F.V.S*, Hamburg: Christians verlag, 2001.

Mohr de Perez, Rita. *Die Anfange der Staatlichen Denkmalpflege in Preussen, Emittlung und Erhaltung alterhumlicher Merkwurdigkeiten*, Worms: Wernesche Verlagsgellschaft, 2001.

Monument Preservation in the German Democratic Republic. Verlag Zeit Im Bild Dresden, Dresden, 1982.

Nicholas, Lynn H. *The Rape of Europa, The Fate of Europe's Treasures in the Third Reich and the Second World War*. New York: Vintage Books, 1995.

Ostrowski, Waclaw. *Historic Areas in City Planning: Present Trends*. Centre de Recherche d'Urbanisme. Warsaw: Warsaw Technical University, 1994.

Parzinger, Hermann, Michael Eissenhauer, Florian Mausbach, Jörg Haspel. *Das Neue Museum Berlin: Konservieren, Restaurieren, Weiterbauen im Welterbe*. Leipzig: E.A.Seeman Verlag, 2009.

Penkova, I. *Les monuments historiques, mémoire de Sofia: le rôle de l'architecte lors de leur rehabilitation*, in De l'utilité du patrimoine, Actes des Colloques de la Direction du Patrimoine (Fontevraud, novembre 1991). Paris: Picard, 1992.

Podraza, A. *How Should We Understand the Term "Central Europe" at the Turn of the 21st Century?* In S. Quaedvlieg-Mihailović (a cura di) *Heritage and the Building of Europe*, Europa Nostra/Kulturstiftung Haus Europa, The Hague/Berlin: Maecenata Verlag 2004.

Price, Talley and Melucco (eds.). *Historical and Philosophical Issues in the Conservation of Cultural Heritage*. Los Angeles: Getty Trust, 1997.

Puc, Krystyna. *Poland's Commitment to Its Past. A Report of Two Study Tours*. Partners for Livable Places. Washington, DC. 1985.

Purchla, J. *Heritage and Transformation: the Experience of Poland*, in Quaedvlieg-Mihailović S. (a cura di) *Heritage and the Building of Europe*, Europa Nostra/Kulturstiftung Haus Europa. The Hague/Berlin: Maecenata Verlag 2004.

_____. (ed.). *The Historical Metropolis: A Hidden Potential*. International Conference Proceedings, 26–29 May 1996. Cracow: International Cultural Centre, 1996.

Quaedvlieg-Mihailović, Sneška, and Rupert Graf Strachwitz (eds.). *Heritage and the Building of Europe*. Europa Nostra/Kulturstiftung Haus Europa, The Hague/Berlin: Maecenata Verlag, 2004.

Riegl, Alois. *Der moderne Denkmallkultus, sein Weisen, seine Enstehung (Einleitung zum Denkmalschutz)*. Wien: Braumuller, 1903.

_____. "The Modern Cult of Monuments: Its Character and Its Origin." Translated by Kurt W. Forster and Diane Ghirardo. *Oppositions* 25 (Fall 1982): 21–51.

Rodwell, Dennis. *Conservation and Sustainability in Historic Cities*. Oxford: Blackwell Publishing, 2007.

Román, Andras. *Changement de régime dans les anciens pays socialistes d'Europe centrale st orientale et protection des monuments historiques*, in "Restauro," 133–134, in *Attualità della Conservazione die Monumenti*, Atti dell'incontro internazionale de Studio su La Carta de Venezia trenta anni dopo (Naples, 6–7 November 1995).

Scarrocchia, Sandro. *Alois Riegel: Teoria e Prassi della Conservazione de Monumenti: Antologia de Scritti, Discorsi, Rapporti 1898–1905, con una Scelta di Saggi Critici*. Accademia Clementina di Bologna. Clueb, Bologna, 1995.

Schmidt, Hartwig. *Wiederaufbau: Denkmalpflege an Archäologischen Stätten Band 2*. Stuttgart, Germany: Konrad Theiss, 1993.

Stanley-Price, Nicholas, M. Kirby Talley, Jr., and Allesandra Melucco Vaccaro (eds.). *Historical and Philosophical Issues in the Conservation of Cultural Heritage. Readings in Conservation*. Los Angeles: Getty Conservation Institute, 1996.

Stipe, Robert (ed.). *Historic Preservation in Other Countries* series. US/ICOMOS, Washington, DC. Vol. II: *Federal Republic of Germany, Switzerland, and Austria* by Margaret Thomas, 1984; III: *Poland* by Paul H. Gleye and Waldermar Szczerba.

Stubbs, John H. and Stefan Yarabek. "Lednice-Valtice: A Monumental Liechtenstein Landscape within the Prague-Vienna Greenway," in *SiteLines, a Journal of Place*, vol. VI, number 1 (Fall 2010). A publication of the Foundation for Landscape Studies, New York.

Syndram, Dirk and Joachim Hübner. *Das Grüne Gewölbe im Schloss zu Dresden, Rückkehr eines barocken gesamtkunstwerkes*. Dresden: E.A. Seeman in der Seeman Henschel GmbH & Co KG, 2006.

Teutonico, Jeanne Marie and Gaetano Palumbo (eds.). *Management Planning for Archaeological Sites*, An International Workshop Organized by the Getty Conservation Institute and Loyola Marymount University, 19–22 May 2000 Corinth, Greece. Los Angeles: The Getty Conservation Institute, 2000.

Tung, Anthony M. *Preserving the World's Great Cities: The Destruction and Renewal of the Historic Metropolis*. New York: Clarkson Potter, 2001.

UNESCO, *World Heritage 2002: Shared Legacy, Common Responsibility*. Proceedings of an International Congress organized by UNESCO's World Heritage Centre and Regional Bureau for Science in Europe, 14–16 November 2002. Paris: UNESCO, 2003.

Urbanová, Norma and Margita Šukajlová, *Slovakia's Cultural Heritage: Architectural Monuments/Kulturerbe der Slowakei Architektonische Denkmäler*. Bratislava: ARS Monument 1996.

Von Droste, Bernd, Harald Plachter, and Mechtild Rössler (eds.). *Cultural Landscapes of Universal Value: Components of a Global Strategy*. Jena, Germany: Fischer Verlag in cooperation with UNESCO, 1995.

Von Droste, Bernd, Mechtild Rössler, and Sarah Titchen (eds.). *Linking Nature and Culture: Report of the Global Strategy*, Natural and Cultural Heritage, Expert Meeting, Amsterdam, March 25–29, 1998.

Von Trützschler, Werner and Florian Fiedler. *Legal Structures of Private Sponsorship*. ICOMOS International Seminar on Legal Structures of Private Sponsorship and Participation in the Protection and Maintenance of Monuments, Weimar, April 17–19, 1997. Munich: Karl M. Lipp Verlag, 1997.

Will, Margaret T., "Federal Republic of Germany, Switzerland, Austria," vol. 2 of Stipe, R. (ed.). *Historic Preservation in Other Countries*. Washington DC: ICOMOS, 1984.

Wines, James. *Green Architecture*. Köln: Taschen, 2000.

Wohlleben, Marion. *Konservieren Oder Restaurieren?* Zur Diskussion über Aufgaben, Ziele und Probleme der Denkmalpflege um die Jahrhundertwende. Verlag der Fachvereine, Zurich, 1989.

World Monuments Fund. (J. H. Stubbs, rapporteur) *Architectural Conservation in the Czech and Slovak Republics*. Proceedings of a Symposium held at Prague, Olomouc, Banská Štiavnica and Bratislava, May 24–30, 1992. New York: World Monuments Fund, 1993.

World Monuments Fund. (J. H. Stubbs, rapporteur) *Preservation of Art and Architecture*. Proceedings of Salzburg Seminar No. 285. June 26–July 4, 1990. Schoss Leopoldskron, Salzburg, Austria.

Weyer, Angela (ed.). *Rettung des Kulturerbes, Projekte rund ums Mittelmeer/Saving Cultural Heritage, Projects around the Mediterranean/Sauvetage du Patrimoine Culturel, Projets autour de la Mediterranee*, Series of the Hornemann Institute, volume 3, Hamburg: Gloss Verlag, 2000.

Zieliński, Jarosław, *Warsaw: Ruined and Rebuild*. Warszawa: Wydawnictwo FESTINA, 1997.

Zuziak, Zbigniew (ed.). *Managing Historic Cities*. Cracow: International Centre, 1993.

SECTION 4 (EASTERN EUROPE AND THE CAUCASUS)

Ahunbay, Zeynep. *Tarihi Çevre Koruma ve Restorasyon* Istanbul: YEM Yayen, 1996.

Amery, Colin and Brian Curran. *St. Petersburg*. London: Frances Lincoln Ltd., 2006.

Ballester, José-Maria. *Urban Rehabilitation Policy in Tbilisi (Georgia)/Etat de la politique de rehabilitation urbaine de Tbilissi (Géorgie)*. Strasbourg: Council of Europe Publishing, 2002.

Barakat, Sultan and Jon Calame, and Esther Charlesworth. "Urban Triumph or Urban Disaster?" In *Dilemmas of Contemporary Post-War Reconstruction*. Report of the Symposium hosted by the Aga Khan Program at MIT, Cambridge, MA, 27–29 September 1996. York, UK: The University of York, 1997.

Brumfield, William Craft. *Lost Russia, Photographing the Ruins of Russian Architecture*, Durham, NC: Duke University Press, 1995.

Bulia, Marina and Mzia Janjalia, *Mtskheta*. Tbilisi: Medicopy Ltd, 2000

Carbonara, Giovanni (ed.). *Trattato di Restauro Architettonico, Primo Aggiornamento. Grandi termi di restauro*, Vols. 1–10 (Vol. 8 on International Practice, pp 1–208). Milan: UTET Scienze Techniche, 2007.

De la Torre, Marta (ed.). *Assessing the Values of Cultural Heritage*, Los Angeles: The Getty Conservation Institute, 2002.

Denslagen, Wim, and Neils Gutchow (eds.). *Architectural Imitations: Reproductions and Reproductions in East and West*. 2005.

Dushkina, Natalia (ed.). Collection of papers for 2006 conference "Twentieth Century: Preservation of Cultural Heritage." ICOMOS, Moscow 2006.

Erder, Cevat. *Our Architectural Heritage: From Consciousness to Conservation*. Museums and Monuments series. Paris: UNESCO, 1986.

Feilden, Bernard. *Between Two Earthquakes, Cultural Property in Seismic Zones.* Rome/Marina del Rey: ICCROM/Getty Conservation Institute, 1987.

Fiorani, D. *Transiti in Russia: restauro e architettura storico in un paese di frontiera,* in "Palladio," 1999:12, 24.

Galan, Emilio and Fulvio Zezza (eds.). *Protection and Conservation of the Cultural Heritage of the Mediterranean Cities,* Proceedings of the 5th International Symposium on the Conservation of Monuments in the Mediterranean Basin, Sevilla, Spain, 5–8 April, 2000. Lisse, The Netherlands: Swets & Zeitlinger B.V., 2002.

Giyasi, Jaffar. *Azerbaijan Fortresses—Castles.* Baku: Interturan Inc, 1994.

Gyrov, M.K. *The Development Strategy and 2002 Report on the Operations of the Perm—36 Memorial Center of the History of Political Repression.* Moscow: Izdatelstvo Referendym, 2003.

Harris, Edmund, Clementine Cecil and Mariana Khrustaleva (eds.). *MAPS and Save Europe's Heritage,* "Moscow Heritage at Crisis Point, updated expanded edition" (Moscow, 2009). NFP, Moscow. [www.maps-moscow. com/ index.php? chapter _ id=173&data_id=237&do=view_single].

Haspel, Jörg, Michael Petzet, Anke Zalivako and John Ziesemer (eds.), "Heritage at Risk Special Edition: The Soviet Heritage and European Modernism" (ICOMOS, 2006) [www.international.icomos.org/risk/2007/pdf/Soviet_Heritage _FULL_100dpi.pdf].

Hernández, Josep Ballart, Jordi Juan I Tresserras, *Gestión del Patrimonio cultural.* Barcelona: Ed.Ariel S.A., 2001

Hewryk, Titus D. *Masterpieces in Wood: Houses of Worship in Ukraine.* New York: The Ukrainian Museum, 1989.

ICOMOS. *Colloque de Leningrad.* 2–8 September 1969, Vol. III, International Council on Monuments and Sites, 1971.

————. *Heritage at Risk ICOMOS World Report 2004/2005 on Monuments and Sites in Danger.* Munich: K.G. Saur, 2005.

Jokilehto, Jukka. *A History of Architectural Conservation.* Oxford: Butterworth-Heinemann, 1999.

Macdonald, Susan (ed.). *Preserving Post-War Heritage, The Care and Conservation of Mid-Twentieth Century Architecture,* Shaftesbury: Donhead, in association with English Heritage, 2001.

Mainstone, Rowland J. *Hagia Sophia: Architecture, Structure and Liturgy of Justinian's Great Church.* London: Thames and Hudson, 1988.

Martin-Brown, Joan (ed.). *Culture Counts, Financing, Resources, and the Economics of Culture in Sustainable Development,* Proceedings of the Conference held in Florence, Italy, October 4–7, 1999. Washington DC: IBRD, 2000.

Massie, Suzanne. *Pavlovsk: The Life of a Russian Palace.* Boston: Little, Brown and Company, 1990.

Mihailovic, Sneška Quaedvlieg-Mihailovic and Rupert Graf Strachwitz (eds.). *Heritage and the Building of Europe,* Europa Nostra/Kulturstiftung Haus Europa, The Hague/Berlin: Maecenata Verlag 2004.

Morgan, Christopher and Irina Orlova. *Saving the Tsar's Palaces.* Clifton-upon-Teme, Polperro Heritage Press, 2005.

Museum of Modern Art, "Lost Vanguard: Soviet Modernist Architecture, 1922–1932, Photographs by Richard Pare, July 18 – October 29, 2007" [www.moma.org /visit/calendar/ exhibitions/47].

Narkomfin Foundation, "Narkomfin," and "Monuments of Constructivism Today," [http://narkomfin.ru/Eng.aspx].

Petzet, Michael and John Ziesemer (eds.). *Heritage at Risk: ICOMOS World Report 2006/2007 on Monuments and Sites in Danger.* Paris: ICOMOS/E. Reinhold Verlag, 2008.

Shvidkovsky, O.A. "The Historical Characteristics of the Russian Architectural Heritage and the Problems of Its Relation to Modern City Planning Practice," in *Proceedings of the Seminar on Architectural and Historic Preservation in Central and Eastern Europe* (New York, 28–30 November 1979). Published in the *Journal of the Society of the Architectural Historians* 38, 2.

Stanley-Price, Nicholas (ed.). *Conservation on Archaeological Excavations with Particular Reference to the Mediterranean Area.* Rome: ICCROM, 1995. First published in 1984.

Stanley Price, Nicholas, "The Reconstruction of Ruins: Principles and Practice," in *Conservation Principles, Dilemmas and Uncomfortable Truths,* Alison Richmond and Alison Bracker (eds.). Oxford: Butterworth-Heinemann, 2009.

Teutonico, Jeanne Marie and Gaetano Palumbo (eds.). *Management Planning for Archaeological Sites,* An International Workshop Organized by the Getty Conservation Institute and Loyola Marymount University, 19–22 May 2000 Corinth, Greece. Los Angeles: The Getty Conservation Institute, 2000.

Tung, Anthony M. *Preserving the World's Great Cities: The Destruction and Renewal of the Historic Metropolis.* New York: Clarkson Potter, 2001.

UNESCO. *World Heritage 2002: Shared Legacy, Common Responsibility.* An International Congress, 14–16 November 2002, Venice, Italy. Paris: UNESCO,2003.

U.S. Department of the Interior. *A Report by the U.S. Historic Preservation Team of the US-USSR Joint Working Group on Enhancement of the Urban Environment.* May 25–June 14, 1974, Washington, DC, 1975.

Wines, James. *Green Architecture.* Köln: Taschen, 2000.

SECTION 5 (SOUTHEASTERN EUROPE)

Agnew, Neville and Janet Bridgland (eds.). *Of the Past, for the Future: Integrating Archaeology and Conservation,* Proceedings of the Conservation Theme at the 5th World Archaeological Congress, Washington DC, 22–26 June 2003. Los Angeles, CA: The Getty Conservation Institute, 2006.

Ashurst, John. *Conservation of Ruins.* Oxford: Butterworth-Heinemann/Elsevier: 2007.

Astrinidou, P. (ed.). *Restoration of Byzantine and Post-Byzantine Monuments.* Proceedings of the International Symposium of Thessaloniki 11–13 December 1985. Thessaloniki: ΤΥΠΟ-ΜΟΥΓΚΟΣ, 1986.

Bakoš, Ján. "Monuments and Ideologies." *Centropia: A Journal of Central European Architecture and Related Arts* 1, no. 2 (May 2001): 101–7. Previously published by the Slovak Academy of Sciences in its journal Human Affairs 1, no. 2 (December 1991).

Banca Intesa (with UNESCO and Skira Editore Spa). *Treasury of World Culture, Monumental Sites, UNESCO World Heritage.* Milan: UNESCO and Skira Editore Spa, 2003.

Barakat S., C. Wilson. *The revitalization of Pocitelj, a war damaged historic settlement in Bosnia-Herzegovina.* York: PRDU, 1997.

Bogosavljevic-Petrovic V., T. Mihailovic, *Archaeology and Preservation of Monuments in Serbia in 1994,* in "Monument and Environment," 1996, 3.

Bold, John. "The Built Heritage of the Balkans: A Rehabilitation Project." *Transactions,* vol. 52 (2008), 49–64.

Bouras, Ch. and K. Zambas. *The Works of the Committee for the Preservation of the Acropolis Monuments on the Acropolis of Athens.* Athens: Epikoinonia, 2002.

Calame, Jon and Esther Charlesworth. *Divided Cities Belfast, Beirut, Jerusalem, Mostar, and Nicosia.* A volume in the City in the Twenty-First Century series. Philadelphia: University of Pennsylvania Press, 2009.

Carbonara, Giovanni (ed.). *Trattato di Restauro Architettonico, Primo Aggiornamento. Grandi Termi di Restauro,* Vols. 1–10 (Vol. 8 on International Practice, pp 1–208). Milan: UTET Scienze Techniche, 2007.

Čausidis, Nikos, *Macedonia Cultural Heritage.* Translated by Zoran Ančevski. Skopje: MISLA, 1995.

Chamberlain, Kevin, *War and Cultural Heritage: An Analysis of the 1954 Convention for the Protection of Cultural Property in the Event of Armed Conflict and its Two Protocols.* Leicester: The Institute of Art and Law, 2004.

Cleere, Henry (ed.). *Archaeological Heritage Management in the Modern World.* London: Unwin Hyman, 1989.

Curuni, Spiridione Alessandro and Lucilla Donati. *Creta Bizantina.* Rome: University of Rome "La Sapienza," 1987.

Cvjeticanin, Tatjana and Mila Popovic-Zivancevic (eds.). *Condition of the Cultural and Natural Heritage in the Balkan Region: Proceedings of the Regional Conference Held in Kladovo, Serbia, from 23th to 27th October 2006.* vol. 1 (ICOM. Paris, France/UNESCO Venice. Venice, Italy, Belgrade: National Museum Belgrade, 2007.

De la Torre, Maria (ed.). *The Conservation of Archaeological Sites in the Mediterranean Region,* An International Conference Organized by the Getty Conservation Institute and the J. Paul Getty Museum, May 1995. Los Angeles: The Getty Conservation Institute, 1997.

Erder, Cevat. *Our Architectural Heritage: From Consciousness to Conservation.* Museums and Monuments series. Paris: UNESCO, 1986.

Filetici, M.G., F. Giovanetti, F. Mallouchou-Tufano, and E. Pallottino (directed by). *I restauri dell-Acropoli d'Atene—Restoration of the Athenian Acropolis (1975-2003).* Rome: Quaderni ARCo, Gangemi, 2003.

Gavrilovíc, Predrag and William S. Ginell, Veronika Sendova, Lazar Šumanov. *Conservation and Seismic Strengthening of Byzantine Churches in Macedonia.* GCI Scientific Reports series. Los Angeles: The Getty Conservation Institute, 2004.

Gerstenblith, Patty. *Art, Cultural Heritage and the Law: Cases and Materials* (2nd ed.). Durham, NC: Carolina Academic Press, 2008. First published in 2004.

Giurescu, D.C. *The Razing of Romania's Past.* London: Architecture, Design & Technology Press, 1989.

Haas, Hans. *Preservation and Rehabilitation of Historic Quarters in Bulgaria.* German Commission for UNESCO and the Academy of the Chamber of Architects, North-Rhine/Westphalia, Vol. 22, 1983.

International Bank for Reconstruction and Development. *Culture Counts: Financing, Resources, and the Economics of Culture in Sustainable Development,* Proceedings of the Conference held in Florence, Italy, October 4–7, 1999. Washington, DC: IBRD, 2000.

Jokilehto, Jukka. *A History of Architectural Conservation.* Oxford: Butterworth-Heinemann, 1999.

Lagrange, C. "Patrimoine sans frontières and Reconstruction of Heritage in War: Experiences in Lebanon, Croatia & Bosnia-Herzegovina," in S. Barakat, J. Calame, E. Charlesworth (eds.), *Urban Triumph or Urban Disaster? Dilemmas of Contemporary Post-war Reconstruction.* Report of the symposium (Cambridge, Massachusetts, September 27–29, 1996). York: University of York, 1998.

Lalošević, Ilija. *Kotor Fortress: Studies, Conservation and Revitalization.* Podgorica: YURAGRAFIC, 2000.

Letunić, Božo. *The Restoration of Dubrovnik 1979–1989.* Dubrovnik: Zavod za obnovu Dubrovnika, 1990.

Machat, Christoph. *Monuments en Roumanie: Propositions du Comité National Roumain de l'ICOMOS pour la Liste du Patrimoine Mondial.* ICOMOS with Editions FF Press, Bucarest 1995.

Marasović, Duško. *Rehabilitation of the Historic Core of Split-1.* Split, Croatia: City of Split—Agency for the Historic Core, 1996.

———. *Rehabilitation of the Historic Core of Split-2.* Split, Croatia: City of Split—Agency for the Historic Core, 1998.

Marosovic, Tomaslav. *An Active Approach to Architectural Heritage,* Split, 1984.

———. *The Preservation of Urban and Architectural Heritage,* Split, 1983.

———. *Diocletian's Palace The World Cultural Heritage Split-Croatia.* Zagreb: Edition Nedljiko Dominović, 1994.

Martin, Sally. *Butrint Management Plan 2000–2005.* Norwich: Morris Printing Co. Ltd, 2001.

Menegazzi, Cristina (ed.). *Disaster preparedness and Response/Patrimonio Cultural: Preparación y Reacción ante los Desastres/Patrimoine Culturel: prevention et gestion des risques.* Proceedings of an International Symposium held in Hyderabad 23–27 November 2003. Paris: ICOM, 2004.

Merryman, John Henry. *Thinking about the Elgin Marbles: Critical Essays on Cultural Property, Art and Law.* London: Kluwer Law International, 2000.

Mihailovic, Sneška Quaedvlieg-Mihailovic and Rupert Graf Strachwitz (eds.). *Heritage and the Building of Europe,* Europa Nostra/Kulturstiftung Haus Europa, The Hague/Berlin: Maecenata Verlag 2004.

Miltchik, Mikhail (ed.). *The Actual Problems of the Unique Russian Wooden Architecture Monuments' Researching and Saving.* St. Petersburg: Spetzproyectrestavratsia, 1999.

Ministry of Culture of Greece. *The New Acropolis Museum.* Athens: Ministry of Culture, 1991.

Nomikos M.E. (ed.). Apokatástasi epanákhrisii mnimeíon kai istorikón ktiríon sti Bóreia Elláda. *Restoration-Rehabilitation of Monuments and Historical Buildings in Northern Greece.* Athens: Ergon IV, 2001.

Ogrin, Dušan. *The World Heritage of Gardens.* London: Thames and Hudson 1993. Translated by Margaret Davies, Maja Bilbija and Milan Mlačnik.

Oliver, Paul. *Built to Meet Needs: Cultural Issues in Vernacular Architecture.* Oxford: Architectural Press, 2006.

Omčikus, Marko (ed.). *Cultural Heritage of Kosovo and Metohija* (2nd ed.). Belgrade: Institute for the Protection of Cultural Monuments of the Republic of Serbia, 2002.

Opris, I. *Protecting Romania's cultural heritage in a contemporary and changing context,* in *Kulturgüterschutz betriffft uns alle,* Bundesamt für Bevölkerungsschutz. Bern: Kulturgüterschutz, 2003.

Orbaşli, Aylin. *Architectural Conservation.* Oxford: Blackwell Science Ltd., 2008.

———. *Tourists in Historic Towns: Urban Conservation and Heritage Management.* London: Spon, 2000.

Pace, V. *Kosovo: Passato, presente e futuro dei suoi monumeni cristiani in pericolo,* in "Kunstchronick" (2004) 57, 12.

Petkova, Svetozara. "Cultural Heritage Legislation in the Transition Countries of Southeastern Europe," International Policy Fellowship Research Paper, Open Society Institute – Budapest (July 2005), www.policy.hu/petkova/Research%20Paper.htm.

Pickard, Robert (ed.). *Analysis and Reform of Cultural Heritage Policies in South East Europe.* Strasbourg: Council of Europe Publishing, 2008.

———. *Integrated Management Tools in the Heritage of South East Europe.* Strasbourg: Council of Europe Publishing, 2008.

———. *Sustainable Development Strategies in South East Europe.* Strasbourg: Council of Europe Publishing, 2008.

Quaedvlieg-Mihailovic, Sneška and Rupert Graf Strachwitz (eds.). *Heritage and the Building of Europe,* Europa Nostra/ Kulturstiftung Haus Europa. The Hague/Berlin: Maecenata Verlag, 2004.

Rayas, Georges (ed.). *Architecture Traditionelle des Pays Balkaniques.* Athènes: Éditions Melissa Aussi publié en grec.

Reclaiming Historic Mostar: Opportunities for Revitalization, 15 Donor Dossiers for Conservation of High Priority Sites in the Historic Core. A Joint Conservation Project of the Aga Khan Trust for Culture's Historic Cities Support Programme & The World Monument Fund, August 1999.

Serageldin, Ismail, Ephim Shluger, and Joan Martin-Brown (eds.). *Historic Cities and Sacred Sites: Cultural Roots for Urban Futures.* Washington, DC: World Bank, 2001.

Smithsonian Institute/Institute of Earthquake Engineering and Engineering Seismology, University "St. Cyril and Methodius," Skopje, Project Number 124/SI *Protection of Byzantine Churches against Earthquakes using Seismic Isolation.* Skopje: Macedonian-US Joint Board on Scientific and Technological Cooperation 2001.

Stanley-Price, Nicholas (ed.). *Conservation on Archaeological Excavations with Particular Reference to the Mediterranean Area.* Rome: ICCROM, 1995. First published in 1984.

Stovel, Herb. *Risk Preparedness: A Management Manual for World Cultural Heritage.* Rome: ICCROM, 1998.

Toman, Jiří. *The Protection of Cultural Property in The Event of Armed Conflict.* UNESCO and Dartmouth Publishing Company Ltd., 1996.

Tournikiotis, Panayostis (ed.). *The Parthenon and Its Impact in Modern Times.* Athens: Melissa Publishing House, 1994.

UNESCO. *World Heritage 2002: Shared Legacy, Common Responsibility.* Proceedings of an International Congress organized by UNESCO's World Heritage Centre and Regional Bureau for Science in Europe, 14–16 November 2002. Paris: UNESCO, 2003.

The World Bank. *Post-Conflict Reconstruction, The Role of the World Bank.* Washington DC, The World Bank, 1998

World Monument Fund, *Financing Cultural/Natural Heritage and Sustainable Development,* International Conference May 28–31, 1996. New York: World Monuments Fund, 1996.

———. *Reclaiming Historic Mostar: Opportunities for Revitalization.* A Joint Conservation Project of the Aga Khan Trust for Culture's Historic Cities Support Programme & the World Monuments Fund. New York: WMF, 1999.

SECTION 6 (THE UNITED STATES AND CANADA)

Adams, Annemarie, and Martin Bressani. "Canada: The Edge Condition." *Journal of the Society of Architectural Historians* 62, no. 1 (March 2003): 75–83.

Advisory Council on Historic Preservation. *National Historic Preservation Act of 1966, as Amended.* Washington, DC: Advisory Council on Historic Preservation, 1993.

Algie, Susan, Winnipeg Architecture Foundation, James Ashby, Docomomo Canada-Ontario (eds.). *Conserving the Modern in Canada: Buildings, ensembles, and sites: 1945–2005.* Conference proceedings, Trent University, Peterborough, May 6–8, 2005. Peterborough: Trent University, 2005. Aussi disponible en français.

Alpin, Graeme. *Heritage: Identification, Conservation and Management.* Oxford and New York: Oxford University Press, 2002.

Ames, David and Richard Wagner (eds.). *Design & Historic Preservation: The Challenge of Compatibility.* Newark: University of Delaware Press, 2009.

Ashurst, John and Francis G. Dimes. *Conservation of Building and Decorative Stone.* Oxford: Butterworth-Heinemann, 1990.

Ashurst, John and Nicola Ashurst. *Practical Building Conservation: English Heritage Technical Handbook,* volumes 1–5. London: Gower Technical Press, 1988.

Avrami, Erica, Randall Mason and Marta de la Torre. *Values and Heritage Conservation: Research Report.* Los Angeles: Getty Conservation Institute, 2000.

Baer, N.S. and R. Snethlage (eds.). *Saving Our Architectural Heritage: The Conservation of Historic Stone Structures.* New York: John Wiley & Sons, 1997.

Baker, David. *Living With the Past: The Historic Environment.* Bedford: Bledsoe, D. Baker, 1983.

Barnett, Jonathan (ed.). *Smart Growth in a Changing World.* Washington, DC: APA Planners Press, 2007.

Barthel, Diane. *Historic Preservation: Collective Memory and Historic Identity,* New Brunswick, NJ: Rutgers University Press, 1996.

Benson, Virginia O. and Richard Klein (eds.). *Historic Preservation for Professionals,* Kent, Ohio: Kent State University, 2004.

Bird, Jon, Barry Curtis, Tim Putnam, George Robertson and Lisa Tickner. *Mapping the Futures: Local Cultures, Global Change.* London: Routledge, 1993.

Bluestone, Daniel. *Buildings, Landscapes and Memory: Case Studies in Historic Preservation.* New York: W. W. Norton & Company, 2011.

Brolin, Brent C. *Architecture in Context: Fitting New Buildings with Old.* New York: Van Nostrand Reinhold, 1980.

Burns, John A. (ed.). *Recording Historic Structures (2nd ed.).* Hoboken, NJ: John Wiley & Sons, 2003.

Cameron, Christina. "The Spirit of Place: The Physical Memory of Canada." *Journal of Canadian Studies* 35, no. 1 (Spring 2000): 77–94.

Canadian Association for Conservation of Cultural Property and The Canadian Association of Professional Conservators (CAPC). *Code of Ethics and Guidance for Practice.* 3rd ed. Ottawa: CAC and CAPC, 2000; orig. 1986. www.cac-accr.ca/pdf/ecode.pdf (accessed July 27, 2010).

Canadian Conservation Institute/Institut canadien de conservation, *The Conservation of Heritage Interiors,* Preprints of a Conference Symposium 2000, The Conservation of Heritage Interiors, Ottawa, Canada, May 17–20 2000.

Chitty, Gill and David Baker (eds.). *Managing Historic Sites and Buildings: Reconciling Presentation and Preservation.* Issues in Heritage Management Series published by Routledge in association with English Heritage. London: Routledge, 1999.

Cleere, Henry (ed.). *Archaeological Heritage Management in the Modern World.* London: Unwin Hyman, 1989.

Coloquhoun, Ian. *Urban Regeration: An International Perspective.* London: B.T. Batsford

Crawford, Patricia, et al. *Architecture in Ontario: A Select Bibliography on Architectural Conservation and the History of Architecture With Special Relevance to the Province of Ontario.* Ontario Heritage Foundation, 1976.

Crosby, Theo. *The Necessary Monument: Its Future in a Civilized City.* Greenwich, CT: New York Graphics Society, 1970.

Cultural and Human Resources Council (CHRC). *Human Resources in Canada's Built Heritage Sector: Mapping the Work Force and Setting Strategic Priorities.* Ottawa: Cultural and Human Resources Council, 2004.

Davis, Wade. *The Wayfinders: Why Ancient Wisdom Matters in the Modern World: CBC Massey Lectures.* Toronto: House of Anansi Press Inc., 2009. www.cbc.ca/ideas/massey.html.

Delafons, John. *Politics and Preservation: A Policy History of the Built Heritage, 1882–1996.* London: E. and F. N. Spon, 1997.

De la Torre, Marta (ed.). *Assessing the Values of Cultural Heritage,* Los Angeles: the Getty Conservation Institute, 2002.

———. (ed.). *Heritage Values in Site Management: Four Case Studies.* Los Angeles: The Getty Conservation Institute, 2005.

DeLony, Eric. "A Call for Preservation," in Richard L. Cleary, *Bridges* (a volume in the Norton/Library of Congress Visual Sourcebook series). New York: W.W. Norton, 2007.

———. *Landmark American Bridges.* Boston: Bulfinche Press, 1993 (a copublication with American Society of Civil Engineers).

Denhez, Marc C. *Heritage Fights Back: Legal, Financial, and Promotional Aspects of Canada's Efforts to Save Its Architecture and Historic Sites.* Ottawa: Heritage Canada, 1978.

———. *The Heritage Strategy Planning Handbook an International Primer.* Toronto: Dundurn Press, 1997.

Denslagen, Wim. *Romantic Modernism: Nostalgia in the World of Conservation.* Amsterdam: Amsterdam University Press, 2011.

Denslagen, Wim, and Niels Gutschow (eds.) *Architectural Imitations: Reproductions and Pastiches in East and West.* Maastricht, Neth.: Shaker Publishing, 2005.

Dono, Andrea L. *Revitalizing Main Street: A Practitioner's Guide to Comprehensive Commercial District Revitalization.* Washington DC: National Trust Main Street Center, 2009.

Faulkner, Anne. *Without Our Past? A Handbook for the Preservation of Canada's Architectural Heritage.* Toronto: University of Toronto Press, 1979.

Fawcett, Jane (ed.). *The Future of the Past: Attitudes to Conservation 1174–1974.* London: Thames and Hudson, 1976.

Feilden, Bernard. *Between Two Earthquakes, Cultural Property in Seismic Zones,* Rome/Marina del Rey: ICCROM/Getty Conservation Institute, 1987.

Feilden, Bernard M. *Conservation of Historic Buildings.* Oxford: Architectural Press, 3rd ed., 2003. First published in 1982 by Butterworth Scientific.

Feilden, Bernard M. and Jukka Jokiletho. *Management Guidelines for World Cultural Heritage Sites.* Rome: ICCROM, 1993.

Fitch, James Marston with William Bobenhausen. *American Building, The Environmental Forces that Shape It.* New York/Oxford: Oxford University Press, 1999.

———. *Historic Preservation: Curatorial Management of the Built World.* Charlottesville: University of Virginia Press (5th ed.), 2001. First published in 1982 by McGraw-Hill.

———. "On Formulating New Parameters for Preservation Policy,". *Preservation and Conservation: Principles and Practices.* Proceedings of the North American International Regional Conference, Williamsburg, Virginia, September 10–16, 1972, National Trust for Historic Preservation, The Preservation Press, Washington, DC, 1976.

———. "The Philosophy of Restoration: Williamsburg to the Present." In Evolution of the Restoration Process: New Directions Symposium. Washington, DC: The American Architectural Foundation at the Octagon, 1992.

Fram, Mark. *Well-Preserved: The Ontario Heritage Foundation's Manual of Principles and Practice For Architectural Conservation* (3rd ed.). Boston: Mills Press, 2003.

Frank, Karolin, Patricia Petersen. *Historic Preservation in the USA*. Berlin Heidelberg: Springer-Verlag, 2002.

GCI Newsletter. Los Angeles: Getty Conservation Institute, thrice-yearly since 1985 (www.getty.edu/conservation/publications/newsletters/index.html).

Gerstenblith, Patty. *Art, Cultural Heritage, and the Law: Cases and Materials* (2nd ed.). Durham, NC: Carolina Academic Press, 2008. First edition published in 2004.

Getty Conservation Institute and US/ICOMOS. *Authenticity in the Conservation and Management of the Cultural Heritage of the Americas*. Proceedings of the Interamerican Symposium. San Antonio, Texas, March 1996. Los Angeles: GCI, 1999.

Government of Canada. *Report of the Royal Commission on Aboriginal Peoples*. Ottawa, Ontario: Government of Canada, 1996. www.ainc-inac.gc.ca/ap/rrc-eng.asp.

Grace, Sherrill E. *Canada and the Idea of North*. Montreal, Quebec, and Kingston, Ontario: McGill-Queen's University Press, 2001.

Gratz, Roberta Brandes. *The Battle for Gotham: New York in the Shadow of Robert Moses and Jane Jacobs*. New York: Nation Books, 2010.

———. *The Living City*. New York: Simon and Schuster, 1989.

Gratz, Roberta Brandes and Norman Mintz. *Cities Back From the Edge: New Life for Downtown*. Hoboken, NJ: John Wiley & Sons, 2000.

Greer, Nora Richter. *Architecture Transformed: New Life for Old Buildings*. Gloucester, MA: Rockport Publishers, 1998.

Gunn, Cynthia. *Built Heritage: Assessing a Tourism Resource*. Ottawa: Heritage Canada Foundation, 2002.

Harmon, David, Francis P. McManamon, and Dwight T. Pitcaithley (eds.). *The Antiquities Act: A Century of American Archaeology, Historic preservation and Nature Conservation*, Tucson: The University of Arizona, 2003.

Harris, Donna Ann. *New Solutions for House Museums, Ensuring the Long-term Preservation of America's Historic House*, American Association for State and Local History Book Series. Latham, MD: Alta Mira Press, 2007.

Hayden, Dolores. *The Power of Place: Urban Landscapes as Public History*, Cambridge: The MIT Press , 1997.

Heritage Canada Foundation. *Preservation Pays: The Economics of Heritage Conservation*. Ottawa: Heritage Canada Foundation, 2002.

Hoffman, Barbara. *Art and Cultural Heritage: Law, Policy, and Practice*. Cambridge: Cambridge University Press, 2005.

Holdsworth, Deryck, Jacques Dalibard, and Heritage Canada (eds.). *Reviving Main Street*. Toronto: Heritage Canada Foundation by University of Toronto Press, 1985.

Hosmer Jr., C.B. *Presence of the Past: A History of the Preservation Movement in the United States before Williamsburg*. New York: Putnam, 1965.

———. *Preservation Comes of Age: From Williamsburg to the National Trust, 1926–1949*. Charlottesville: University of Virginia Press, 1981.

Hudnut II, William H. *Cities on the Rebound: A Vision for Urban America*. Washington DC: Urban Land Institute, 1998.

Huth, Hans. *Observations Concerning the Conservation of Monumnents in Europe and America*. Washington: National Park Service, 1940.

ICOMOS. *Guidelines on Education and Training in the Conservation of Monuments, Ensembles and Sites*. Paris: ICOMOS, 1993. www.icomos.org/docs/guidelines_for_education.html.

———. *Monuments for People: Records of the II International Congress of Restoration*. Venice, 25–31 May, 1964. Padua: Marsilio Editori, 1971.

ICOMOS Canada. "My City, My Heritage, My Future: Conserving the Heritage of Canadian Cities in the 21st Century." *Momentum* 11, no.1 (2004–05).

J. Paul Getty Museum. *Managing Change: Sustainable Approaches to the Conservation of the Built Environment*. Los Angeles: Getty Trust Publications.

Jacobs, Jane. *The Death and Life of Great American Cities*. New York: Random House, 1961.

Jacobs, Stephen W. *Architectural Preservation: American Development and Antecedents Abroad*, vol. 1 and 2. Princeton University PhD thesis, 1974. Ann Arbor: University Microfilms Inc.

Jameson, Jr., John H. (ed.). *The Reconstructed Past: Reconstructions in the Public Interpretation of Archaeology and History*. Walnut Creek, CA: Alta Mira Press, 2004.

Jokilehto, Jukka. *A History of Architectural Conservation*. Oxford: Butterworth-Heinemann, 1999.

Journal of Architectural Conservation. Quarterly publication since 1995

Katz, Ron. *French America*. Singapore: Editions Didier Millet, 2004.

Kaufman, Ned, *Place, Race and Story, Essays on the Past and Future of Historic Preservation*. New York: Routledge, 2009.

Kelley, Stephen J. (ed.). *Preservation and Rehabilitation*. Papers originally presented at the International Symposium on Standards for Preservation and Rehabilitation, October 1993 in Dallas/Ft. Worth, Texas. Ann Arbor, MI: ASTM (American Society for Testing and Materials) Special technical publication 1996.

King, Thomas F. *Cultural Resource Laws and Practice* (3rd ed.). Heritage Resource Management Series. Lanham, MD: Alta Mira Press, 2008.

Leask, Anna and Alan Fyall (eds.). *Managing World Heritage Sites*. Burlington: Butterworth-Heinemnn, 2006.

Lee, Antoinette J. (ed.).*Past Meets Future: Saving America's Historic Environments*. Washington, DC: The Preservation Press, 1992.

Lindgren, James M. *Preserving the Old Dominion: Historic Preservation and Virginia Traditionalism*. Charlottesville: University Press of Virginia, 1993.

Longstreth, Richard (ed.). *Cultural Landscapes: Balancing Nature and Heritage in Preservation Practice*. Minneapolis: Univ Of Minnesota Press, 2008.

Lowenthal, David. *The Past is a Foreign Country*. Cambridge: Cambridge University Press, 1985.

_____. *The Heritage Crusade and the Spoils of History.* Cambridge: Cambridge University Press, 1998.

_____. *Possessed by the Past: The Heritage Crusade and the Spoils of Modern History.* Viking, London, 1996.

Lozny, Ludomir R. (ed.). *Landscapes under Pressure: Theory and Practice of Cultural Heritage Research and Preservation.* New York: Springer Science+Business Media, Inc. LLC, 2006.

Macdonald, Susan, Kyle Normandin, Bob Kindred (eds.). *Conservation of Modern Architecture.* Shaftesbury: Donhead, 2007.

Marks, Stephen (ed.). *Concerning Buildings: Studies in Honor of Sir Bernard Feilden,* Oxford: Butterworth-Heinemann, 1996.

Martin-Brown, Joan (ed.). *Culture Counts, Financing, Resources, and the Economics of Culture in Sustainable Development,* Proceedings of the Conference held in Florence, Italy October 4–7, 1999, Washington DC: IBRD, 2000.

Mason, Randall. *The Once and Future New York: Historic Preservation and the Modern City.* Minneapolis: University of Minnesota, 2009.

Matero, Frank. "Loss, Compensation, Authenticity: The Contribution of Cesare Brandi to Architectural Conservation in America," *Future Anterior: Journal of the Historic Preservation History, Theory and Criticism.* Vol 4, no. 1 (Summer 2007): 45–63.

de Monchaux, John and Charles A. Riley III (eds.). Preserving the Built Heritage: Tools for Implementation. Salzburg, 1997.

Murtagh, William J. *Keeping Time: The History and Theory of Preservation in America* (3rd ed.). New York: Sterling Publishing, 2005.

National Parks Service. Secretary of the Interior's Standards for the Treatment of Historic Properties. 36 CFR Part 68, July 12, 1995.

Nixon, Richard M. *World Heritage Convention, The President's Message to the Senate Transmitting the Convention Concerning the Protection of the World Cultural and Natural Heritage for Advice and Consent to Ratification* (March 28, 1973). Washington, DC: Washington, DC, The White House, 1973.

Oliver, Paul. "Re-Presenting the Vernacular: The Open-Air Museum," in Nezar Alsayyad (ed.), *Consuming Tradition, Manufacturing Heritage.* London: Routledge, 2001.

Page, Max and Randall Mason (eds.). *Giving Preservation a History: Histories of Historic Preservation in the United States.* London: Routledge, 2003.

Parks Canada. *Standards and Guidelines for the conservation of Historic Places in Canada/Normes et lignes directrices pour la conservation des lieux patrimoniaux du Canada.* Gatnieau: Parks Canada, 2003.

Peacock, Alan and Ilde Rizzo (eds.). *Cultural Economics and Cultural Politics.* Boston: Kluwer Academic Publishers, 1994.

_____. *The Heritage Game: Economics, Policy, and Practice.* New York: Oxford University Press, 2008.

Pearson, Michael, and Sharon Sullivan. *Looking after Heritage Places: The Basics of Heritage Planning for Managers, Landowners and Administrators.* Carlton, Victoria, Australia: Melbourne University Press, 1995.

The Preservation of Historic Architecture. The U.S. Government's Official Guidelines for Preserving Historic Homes. Guilford, CT: The Lyons Press, 2004.

Price, Talley and Melucco (eds.). *Historical and Philosophical Issues in the Conservation of Cultural Heritage.* Los Angeles: Getty Trust, 1997.

Proshansky, Harold M., William H. Ittelson, and Leanne G. Rivlin (eds.). *Environmental Psychology: People and their Physical Settings,* 2d edition. New York: Holt, Reinhart and Winston, 1976.

Prudon, Theodore H.M. *Preservation of Modern Architecture.* Hoboken, NJ: John Wiley & Sons, 2008.

Rapoport, Amos. *The Meaning of the Built Environment: A Nonverbal Communication Approach.* Tucson: University of Arizona Press, 1990.

Reny, Claude. *Principes et Critères de restauration et d'insertion.* Québec: Les Publications du Quebec, 1991.

Richmond, Alison, Alison Bracker (eds.). *Conservation: Principles, dilemmas and uncomfortable truths.* Oxford: Butterworth Heinemann, 2009.

Riegl, Alois. "The Modern Cult of Monuments: Its Character and Its Origin." Translated by Kurt W. Forster and Diane Ghirardo. *Oppositions* 25 (Fall 1982): 21–51.

Rifkind, Carole. *Main Street: The Face of Urban America.* New York: Harper and Row, 1977.

Rodwell, Dennis. *Conservation and Sustainability in Historic Cities.* Oxford: Blackwell Publishing, 2007.

Rowan, Yorke and Uzi Baram. *Marketing Heritage: Archaeology and the Consumption of the Past.* Walnut Creek, CA: Alta Mira Press, 2004.

The Royal Society of Canada/La Société Royale du Canada, Fourteenth Symposium: *Preserving the Canadian Heritage,* October 7–8, 1975. Ottawa: The Royal Society of Canada, 1975.

Rypkema, Donovan D. *The Economics of Historic Preservation: A Community Leader's Guide* (2nd ed.). Washington DC: National Trust for Historic Preservation, 2005.

Sánchez, Mario L. (ed.). *A Shared Experience: The History, Architecture and Historic Designations of the Lower Rio Grande Heritage Corridor.* Austin: Texas Historical Commission, 1991.

Sawin, Martika (ed.). *James Marston Fitch, Selected Writings on Architecture, Preservation and the Built Environment.* New York/London: W.W. Norton & Co., 2008.

Semes, Steven W. *The Future of the Past: A Conservation Ethic for Architecture, Urbanism, and Historic Preservation.* New York/London: W.W. Norton in association with the Institute of Classical Architecture and Classical America, 2009.

Shacklock, Vincent. *Architectural Conservation: Issues and Developments.* Shaftsbury, UK: Donhead, 2006.

Sherrill, Grace. *Canada and the Idea of North.* Montreal/Kingston: McGill-Queen's University Press, 2001.

Silverman, Helaine and D. Fairchild Ruggles (eds.). *Cultural Heritage and Human Rights,* Urbana Illinois: Springer Science + Business Media LLC, 2007.

Slayter, R.O. "The Origin and Evolution of the World Heritage Convention." *Ambio* vol.12 (1983).

Stanley-Price, Nicholas and Joseph King (eds.). *Conserving the Authentic: Essays in Honour of Jukka Jokilehto*, ICCROM Conservation Studies 10. Rome: ICCROM, 2009.

Stanley-Price, Nicholas, M. Kirby Talley, Jr., and Allesandra Melucco Vaccaro (eds.). *Historical and Philosophical Issues in the Conservation of Cultural Heritage. Readings in Conservation.* Los Angeles: Getty Conservation Institute, 1996.

Stipe, Robert E. *A Richer Heritage: Historic Preservation in the Twenty-First Century.* Chapel Hill: University of North Carolina Press, 2003.

Stipe, Robert E. and Antoinette J. Lee (eds.). *The American Mosaic: Preserving a Nation's Heritage.* Detroit, MI: Wayne State University Press, 1997.

Strike, James. *Architecture in Conservation: Managing Development at Historic Sites.* Routledge, London, 1994.

Stovel, Herb, *Risk Preparedness: A Management Manual for World Cultural Heritage.* Rome: ICCROM, 1998.

Strong, Peter G. and Philippe G Planel. *The Constructed Past: Experimental Archaeology, Education, and the Public.* London: Routledge, 1999.

Stratton, M. (ed.). *Structure and Style: Conserving 20th Century Buildings.* London: Spon, 1997.

Strike, James. *Architecture in Conservation: Managing Development at Historic Sites.* London: Routledge, 1994.

Teutonico, Jeanne Marie and Frank Matero (eds.). *Architectural Conservation: An Introduction.* Los Angeles: Getty Publications, 2003.

Teutonico, Jeanne Marie, and Frank Matero (eds.). *Managing Change: Sustainable Approaches to the Conservation of the Built Environment.* Los Angeles: Getty Conservation Institute, 2003.

Timmons, Sharon (ed.). *Preservation and Conservation: Principles and Practices*, Proceedings of the North American International Regional Conference, Williamsburg, Virginia, and Philadelphia, Pennsylvania, September 10–16, 1972. Washington, DC: The Smithsonian Institution Press, 1976.

Tomlan, Michael A. (ed.). *Preservation of What, for Whom? A Critical Look at Historical Significance.* Conference proceedings, Goucher College, Baltimore, Maryland, March 20–22, 1997. Ithaca, NY: National Council for Preservation Education, 1998.

Tomlan, Michael A. and David Listokin. *Historic Preservation: Caring For Our Expanding Legacy.* Hoboken: John Wiley & Sons, 2009.

Towse, Ruth (ed.). *A Handbook on Cultural Economics*, Northampton, MA: Edward Elgar, 2003.

Tung, Anthony M. *Preserving the World's Great Cities: The Destruction and Renewal of the Historic Metropolis.* New York: Clarkson Potter, 2001.

Tyler, Norman. *Historic Preservation.* New York: W.W. Norton & Co, 2000.

Tyler, Norman, Ted J. Ligibel, Ilene R. Tyler. *Historic Preservation: An Introduction to its History, Principles and Practice.* New York: Norton, 2009.

Urban Conservation in Europe and America: Planning, Conflict and Participation in the Inner City. Proceedings of a conference held in Rome, 1975. Rome: European Regional Conference of Fulbright Commissions, 1975.

UNESCO. *World Heritage Papers 19, American Fortifications and the World Heritage Convention.* International meeting Campeche (Mexico) 12–15 March 2004. Paris: UNESCO, 2004.

———. *World Heritage 2002, Shared Legacy, Common Responsibility.* An International Congress 14–16 November 2002, Venice, Italy. Paris: UNESCO, 2003.

———. *Operation for the Implementation of the World Cultural and Natural Heritage Convention.* Intergovernmental Committee for the Protection of the World Cultural and Natural Heritage, Paris, 1988.

U.S. Department of the Interior. *The Preservation of Historic Architecture: The U.S. Government's Official Guidelines for Preserving Historic Homes.* Guilford, CT: The Lyons Press, 2004.

Von Droste, B., Plachter, H., Rossler, M. (eds.). Cultural landscapes of Universal Value, Components of a Global Strategy. New York: Jena, 1995.

Wachs, Mary. *Recording a Vanishing Legacy, The Historic American Buildings Survey in New Mexico 1933 – Today.* Santa Fe: University of New Mexico Press, 2001.

Warren, John, John Worthington and Sue Taylor (eds.). *Context: New Buildings in Historic Settings*, Oxford. London: Architectural Press, 1998.

Weaver, Martin E. with F.G. Matero. *Conserving Buildings: A Guide to Techniques and Materials.* New York: John Wiley & Sons, 1993.

Whitehand, J.W.R. and P.J. Larkham (eds.). *Urban Landscapes: International Perspectives.* London: Routledge, 1992.

Wines, James. *Green Architecture.* New York: Taschen, 2000.

Wood, Anthony C. *Preserving New York, Winning the Right to Protect a City's Landmarks.* New York: Routledge, 2008.

World Monuments Fund. *5 Case Studies, Modernism at Risk.* New York: World Monuments Fund, 2010.

SECTION 7 (MEXICO, THE CARIBBEAN AND CENTRAL AMERICA)

Agencia Española de Cooperación Internacional, *Programa de Preservación del Patrimonio Cultural de Iberoamérica.* Madrid: AECI, 1999.

Amodio, Emanuele, R. N. Sanchez and C.R. Rodriguez Yilo. *El Camino de los Españoles: Approximaciones históricas y Arquelógicas al Camino Real Caracas—El Guarira en la Epoca Colonial.* Caracas: Instituto del Partimonio Cultural, 1997.

Arjona, Marta. *Patrimonio Cultural e Identidad.* Havana: Editorial Lettras Cubanas, 1986.

Araoz, Gustavo, Margaret MacLean and Lara Day Kozak (eds.). *Proceedings of the Interamerican Symposium on Authenticity in the Conservation and Management of the Cultural Heritage of the Americas*, San Antonio, Texas, March 1996. Washington DC/Los Angeles, CA: US/ICOMOS and the Getty Conservation Institute, 1999.

Becerril, Moro J.E. *El derecho del patrimonio histórico-artístico en México.* Mexico: Ed. Porrúa, 2003.

Bernali, I. *História de la arquelogía en México*, Mexico: Ed. Porrúa, 1979.

Brown, Susan Francis and Peter Francis. *The Old Iron Bridge: Spanish Town, Jamaica.* Caribbean Architectural Monograph Series No. 2, Faculty of the Built Environment, Caribbean School of Architecture, University of Technology, Jamaica, 2005.

Castellanos, Carolina and Françoise Descamps. *Joya de Cerén, Conservation Management Planning, Putting Theory into Practice*, Los Angeles: Getty Conservation Institute, 2008.

Chanfon Olmos, Carlos. *Fundamentos Teoricos de la Restauracion.* Vol 10, Facultad de Arquitectura, Universidad Nacional Autonoma de Mexico, 1996.

The Cultural Heritage of the Caribbean and the World Heritage Convention, Paris: UNESCO, 2000.

Coates, Anthony G. (ed.). *Central America, A Natural and Cultural History*, New Haven and London: Yale University Press, 1997.

Del Cid, Donald. "Conservation and Architecture in Guatemala: A Study of the History of Architecture and the Need for Conservation of Monuments in Guatemala." Thesis for the Diploma Course in Consevation Studies, University of York Intitute for Advanced Studies, York, 1974.

Días-Berrio Fernández Salvador with Olga Oetemirive and Francisco Zamora. *Conservación de Monumentos y Zonas Monumentales.* Mexico City: Secretary of Public Education, City, 1976.

Díaz-Berrio, Fernandez S. *Protección del Patrimonio cultural urbano.* México: INAH, 1986.

———. *Conservación y rehabilitación en zonas de monumentos,* in « Metodológia del trabajo de conservación de conjuntos históricos, Escuela Nacional de Conservación, Restauración y Museografia, Cuaderno de Trabajo, n. 2 ». México: INAH, 1989.

Díaz-Berrio, Salvador. *Conservacion del Patrimonio Cultural en Mexico.* Mexico: Instituto Nacional de Antropologia e Historia, 1990.

———. *El Patrimonio Mundial, Cultural y Natural, 25 anos de la Convencion de la UNESCO,* Mexico City: Universidad Autonomia Metropolitana-Xochimil co, 2001.

Díez, Isalbel Ordieres. *Historia del la Restauración Monumental en España (1835–1936).* Instituo de Conservación y Restauración de Bienes Culturales. Madrid: Ministerio de Cultura, 1995.

Early, James. *The Colonial Architecture of Mexico.* Dallas, TX: Southern Methodist University Press, 1994.

Espíndola Victor Manuel (ed.). *Património de la Humanidad, Ciudades Mexicanas*, México, D.F.: Fondo Editorial de la Plástica Mexicana, 1998.

Feilden, Bernard. *Between Two Earthquakes, Cultural Property in Seismic Zones*, Rome/Marina del Rey: ICCROM/Getty Conservation Institute, 1987.

First Latin America-Europe Heritage Encounters: Monuments, Sites and Historical Documents. Patrimoine du Ministère de la Région Wallone. Etudes et Documents, série Monuments et Sites, 3. Presses Universitaires de Namur, Belgium, 1996.

FONSAL. *El Fondo de Salvamento del Partimonio.1992–1996.* Distrito Metropolitano de Quito, Quito, 1996.

Gasparini, Gaspar. *Echuchar al Monumento.* Caracas: Editorial Arte, 2009.

Gendrop, Paul. *A Guide to Architecture in ancient Mexico* (3rd ed.), México, D.F.: Ed. Minutiae Mexicana, 1991.

González de Valcárcel, J.M. *Restauración monumental y 'puesta en valor' de la ciudades americanas/Architectural conservation and enhancement of historic towns in America*, Barcelona: Editorial Blume, 1977.

Gravette, Andrew Gerald. *Architectural Heritage of the Caribbean: An A–Z of Historic Buildings.* Princeton, NJ: Markus Wiener Publishers, 2000.

Hardoy, Jorge E. and Mario R. dos Santos. *Impacto de la urbanizacion en los contros historicos latinoamericanos*, Santo Domingo:, Proyecto Regional de Patrimonio Cultural y Desarrollo PNUD/UNESCO, 1983.

Heritage Conservation in South America: Challenges and Solutions, conference abstracts, Sao Paulo, Brazil, April 11–14, 2002. New York: World Monuments Fund, 2002.

Hernández, Josep Ballart, Jordi Juan I Tresserras. *Gestión del Patrimonio cultural*, Barcelona: Ed.Ariel S.A., 2001

Hoffman, Barbara T. (ed.). *Art and Cultural Heritage: Law, Policy and Practice* Cambridge: Cambridge University Press, 2006.

van Hoof, Herman (ed.). *Le Patrimoine Culturel des Caraibes et la Convention du Patrimoine mondial/The Cultural Heritage of the Caribbean and the World Heritage Convention.* Fort de France: Editions CTHS, 2000.

Hume, Enrique Elguero. *Restauracion y Remodelacion en al Arquitectura Mexicana.* Mexico City: Litoprocess S.A. de C.V., 1994.

ICOMOS, *Primer Congreso Internacional de Conservacaion del Patrimonio Cultural-Ponecias.* Riombamba 9–12 Nov. 94. Quito, Ecuador.

Instituto Colombiano de Cultura. *Normas Minimas Para La Conservacion de Los Bienes Culturales.* Bogota: Instituto Colombiano de Cultura, 1978.

Loomis, John A. *Revolution in Forms: Cuba's Forgotten Art Schools.* Princeton: Princeton Architectural Press, 1998.

López Morales, Francisco Javier, *Nuevas Miradas Sobre la Autenticidad e Integridad en el Patrimonio Mundial de la Américas/New Views on Authenticity and Integrity in the World Heritage of the Americas*, San Miguel de Allende, Guanajuato, Agosto 24–26, 2005. México: ICOMOS, 2005.

Marini, Carlos Flores. *Apuntes sobre Arquitectura*, numero ocho, serie ensayos, México: Secretaría de Educación Pública, Instituto Nacional de Bellas Artes, 1980.

Matos, Eduardo, Felipe Solis et al. *Cholula: The Great Pyramid*, México D.F.: Grupo Azabache S.A de C.V., 2009.

Martin-Brown, Joan (ed.). *Culture Counts, Financing, Resources, and the Economics of Culture in Sustainable Development*, Proceedings of the Conference held in Florence, Italy October 4–7, 1999, Washington DC: IBRD, 2000.

Molina Montes, A. *La restauración arquitectónica de edificiós arquelógicos*, « Colección Cientifica n. 21 », México: INAH Departamento de Restauración el Patrimonio Cultural, 1975.

Montás, Eugenio Pérez, Esteban Prieto Vicioso, José Chex Checo (eds.). *Monumentos y Sitios del Gran Caribe/ Greater Caribbean Monuments and Sites/ Monuments et Sites de la Grande Caraïbe.* Santo Domingo: MOGRAF, S.A., 2000.

Negrete, Julio Cesar Olive and Bolfy Cottom. *Leyes estatales en material del patrimonio cultural.* Mexico: Instituto Nacional de Antropologia e Historia, 1997.

Olmos, Carlos Chanfón. *Fundamentos Teoreticos de la Restauracion.* Universidad Nacional Autonoma de Mexico. Mexico: Edificios Unidad de Posgrado, 1988.

Pugh, Jonathan and Janet Henshall Momsen (eds.). *Environmental Planning in the Caribbean.* Surrey, UK: Ashgate Publishing, 2006.

Quintana, Leonardo Meraz. *Conservacion aquitectonica y arqueologia urbana.* Mexico: Universidad Autonoma Metropolitana-Xochimilco,1993.

Rettig, Jaime Migone and Antonino Pirozzi Villanueva. *Tercer Coloquio Latinoamericano sobre Rescate y Preservación del Patrimonio Industrial,* Santiago, Chile, 13–16 septiembre 2001. Santiago: CONPAL-Chile, 2001.

Rojas, Eduardo. *Old Cities, New Asset:, Preserving Latin America's Urban Heritage.* Washington, DC: IADB/The Johns Hopkins University Press.1999.

Sánchez, Mario L. (ed.). *A Shared Experience: The History, Architecture and Historic Designations of the Lower Rio Grande Heritage Corridor.* Austin, TX: Texas Historical Commission, 1991.

Sanoja. M. "Cultural Policy and the Preservation of Latin America's National Heritage," in *Rescue Archaeology: Papers from the First New World Conference on Rescue Archaeology.* R.L. Wilson & G. Loyola (eds.), 21–28. Washington, DC: Preservation Press, 1982.

La Sociedad Civil Frente al Patrimonio Cultural. Third Coloquio del Seminario de Estudio del Patrimonio Artístico. Conservación, Restauración y Defensa., Mexico: UNAM, 1997.

Tarr, Jashina Alexandra. *A Collaborative Caribbean Preservation Strategy.* Washington, DC: Partners for Livable Spaces, 1982.

Tazzer, Alejandro Mangino. *La Restauración Arquitectónica: Retrospectiva Historica en Mexico.* México: Editorial Trillas, 1991.

Tazzer, Alejandro Mangino. *Restrospectiva histórica de la arquitectura mexicana, su restauración.* México: UNAM, Facultad de Arquitectura, 1983.

Teutonico, Jeanne Marie and Gaetano Palumbo (eds.). *Management Planning for Archaeological Sites,* An International Workshop Organized by the Getty Conservation Institute and Loyola Marymount University, 19–22 May 2000 Corinth, Greece. Los Angeles: The Getty Conservation Institute, 2000.

Tomlan, Michael A. (ed.). *Preservation: Of What, For Whom?* The National Council for Preservation Education, 1997.

Tomlan, Michael A. and David Listokin. *Historic Preservation: Caring For Our Expanding Legacy.* Hoboken, NJ: John Wiley & Sons, 2009.

UNESCO. *World Heritage Papers 19, American Fortifications and the World Heritage Convention.* International meeting Campeche (Mexico) 12–15 March 2004. Paris: UNESCO, 2004.

_____. *World Heritage Papers 24, Rock Art in the Caribbean, Toward a Serial Transnational Nomination to the UNESCO World Heritage List.* Paris: UNESCO, 2008.

_____. *World Heritage 2002, Shared Legacy, Common Responsibility.* An international Congress 14–16 November 2002, Venice, Italy. Paris: UNESCO,2003.

UNESCO LA HABANA. *Una Experiencia Singular: Valoraciones Sobre El Modelo De Gestion Integral de La Habana Vieja,* Patrimonio De La Humanidad (A Singular Experience — Appraisals of the Integral Management Model of Old Havana, World Heritage Site). Havana: Officina del Historiador de la Ciudad de La Habana, 2006.

US/ICOMOS and the Getty Conservation Institute. MacLean, M. et al. *Proceedings of the Interamerican Symposium on Authenticity in the Conservation and Management of the Cultural Heritage of the Americas,* San Antonio, Texas, March 1996.

U.S. Department of the Interior. *The Preservation of Historic Architecture: The U.S. Government's Official Guidelines for Preserving Historic Homes.* Guilford, CT: The Lyons Press, 2004.

Wines, James. *Green Architecture.* Köln: Taschen, 2000.

World Heritage Center. *Caribbean Wooden Treasures,* World Heritage Series no. 15 Paris: UNESCO, 2005.

_____. *The State of the World Heritage in Latin America and the Caribbean,* World Heritage Papers No. 18 Paris: UNESCO, 2004.

World Monuments Fund (WMF) and US/ICOMOS. *Trails to Treasures: A Tour of South America's Cultural Heritage,* Washington, DC, and New York: US/ICOMOS and World Monuments Fund, 2001.

SECTION 8 (SOUTH AMERICA)

Agencia Española de Cooperación Internacional. *Programa de Preservación del Patrimonio Cultural de Iberoamérica.* Madrid: AECI, 1999.

Amodio, Emanuele, R. N. Sanchez and C.R. Rodriguez Yilo. *El Camino de los Españoles: Approximaciones históricas y Arquelógicas al Camino Real Caracas—El Guarira en la Epoca Colonial.* Caracas: Instituto del Patrimonio Cultural, 1997.

Araoz, Gustavo, Margaret MacLean and Lara Day Kozak (eds.). *Proceedings of the Interamerican Symposium on Authenticity in the Conservation and Management of the Cultural Heritage of the Americas,* San Antonio, Texas, March 27–30, 1996. Washington D.C./Los Angeles CA: US/ICOMOS and the Getty Conservation Institute, 1999.

Barreda, Elías Mujica. *Paisajes Culturales en Los Andes.* San Borja, Peru: UNESCO, 2002.

Buarque de Hollanda, Heloisa, Italo Campofiorito and others (eds.). *Revista do Patrimônio, Histórico e Artistico Nacional,* No. 26 1997. Brazil: Instituto do Patrimônio Histórico e Artistico Nacional do Ministério da Cultura, 1997.

Campos, Magdalena Pereira and Cristián Herinsern Planella. *Iglesias del fin del Mundo.* Santiago: Max Donoso, 2006.

Charola, A. Elena. *Easter Island, The Heritage and its Conservation.* New York: World Monuments Fund, 1994.

Compton, Edwin Binda and ICOMOS-Chile. *Monumentos y Sitios de Chile*. Santiago: Ediciones Altazor, 2000.

Crementieri, Fabio, Jorge Francisco Liernur, and Claudia Shmidt (eds.). *Architectural Culture Around 1900: Critical Reappraisal and Heritage Preservation*. Buenos Aires: Universidad Torcuato di Tella, 1999.

Dalto, Renato. *Missões, Jesuítico — Guaranis*. San Leopoldo: UNISINOS, 2002.

De la Torre, Marta (ed.). *Assessing the Values of Cultural Heritage*. Los Angeles: the Getty Conservation Institute, 2002.

Díez, Isalbel Ordieres. *Historia del la Restauración Monumental en España (1835–1936)*. Instituo de Conservación y Restauración de Bienes Culturales. Madrid: Ministerio de Cultura, 1995.

Distrito Metropolitano de Quito. Quito: El Fondo el Salvamento del Património Cultural, 1996–2000.

Ducassi, Maria Rosa Suárez-Inclán. "Spain's Ongoing Foreign Technical Assistance for the Conservation of Historic Heritage Worldwide." www.icomos.org/usicomos/sym99/suarez-inclan.htm.

Feilden, Bernard. *Between Two Earthquakes: Cultural Property in Seismic Zones*. Rome/Marina del Rey: ICCROM/Getty Conservation Institute, 1987.

FONSAL. *El Fondo de Salvamento del Partimonio.1992–1996*. Quito: Distrito Metropolitano de Quito,1996.

Gazaneo, Jorge Osvaldo. *Las Misiones Jesuíticas del Guayrá*. Buenos Aires: Manrique Zago, 1995.

Getty Conservation Institute and US/ICOMOS. *Authenticity in the Conservation and Management of the Cultural Heritage of the Americas*. Proceedings of the Interamerican Symposium. San Antonio, Texas, March 1996. Los Angeles: Getty Conservation Institute, 1999.

González de Valcárcel, J.M. *Restauración monumental y 'puesta en valor' de la ciudades americanas* (Architectural Conservation and Enhancement of Historic Towns in America). Barcelona: Editorial Blume, 1977.

Grementieri, Fabio, Jorge Francisco Liernur and Claudia Shmidt. *Architectural Culture Around 1900: Critical Reappraisal and Heritage Preservation*. Buenos Aires: Universidad Torguato Di Tella, 2000.

Gutiérrez, Ramón. "The Urban Architectural Heritage of Latin America," ICOMOS Regional Studies 1997–1998, www.icomos.org/studies/latin-towns.htm#5.

Hardoy, Jorge E., Diana Mitlin and David Satterthwaite. *Environmental Problems in an Urbanizing World: Finding Solutions in Africa, Asia, and Latin America* (2nd ed.). London: Earthscan Publications Ltd., 2001.

Hardoy, Jorge E. and Mario R. dos Santos. *Impacto de la urbanizacion en los contros historicos latinoamericanos*. Santo Domingo: Proyecto Regional de Patrimonio Cultural y Desarrollo PNUD/UNESCO, 1983.

Hernández, Josep Ballart, Jordi Juan I Tresserras, *Gestión del Patrimonio cultural*, Barcelona: Ed.Ariel S.A., 2001.

Hoffman, Barbara T. (ed.). *Art and Cultural Heritage: Law, Policy and Practice*. Cambridge, MA: Cambridge University Press, 2006.

ICOMOS. *Primer Congreso Internacional de Conservacaion del Patrimonio Cultural-Ponecias*. Riombamba 9–12 Nov. 1994. Quito, Ecuador.

Instituto Colombiano de Cultura. *Normas Minimas Para La Conservacion de Los Bienes Culturales*. Bogota: Instituto Colombiano de Cultura, 1978.

Legal and Other Issues in Protecting Cultural Heritage: The Latin American and Caribbean Experience in Context, www.ibaculturalheritage.com.

Londoño, Juan Luis Isaza, *Patrimonio Brasileño*, Publicación semestral de la Facultad de Arquitectura y Diseño, vol 19, no. 1. Enero-junio 2006. Bogotá.

López Morales, Francisco Javier. *Nuevas Miradas Sobre la Autenticidad e Integridad en el Patrimonio Mundial de la Américas/New Views on Authenticity and Integrity in the World Heritage of the Americas*, San Miguel de Allende, Guanajuato, Agosto 24–26, 2005. México: ICOMOS, 2005.

Martin-Brown, Joan (ed.). *Culture Counts, Financing, Resources, and the Economics of Culture in Sustainable Development*. Proceedings of the Conference held in Florence, Italy October 4–7, 1999. Washington DC: IBRD, 2000.

Meza, Manuel (ed.). *El Fondo de Savamento del Patrimonio Cultural 1992–1996*, Quito: Distrito Metropolitano de Quito-Fonsal, 1996.

Muñoz Viñas, Salvador. *Contemporary Theory of Conservation*. Elsevier Butterworth Heinemann, Oxford, 2005.

Organization of American States, Office of International Law. *Convention on the Protection of the Archeological, Historical, and Artistic Heritage of the American Nations*, www.oas.org/juridico/English/treaties/c-16.html.

La Preservación y Promoción del Patrimonio Cultural del Ecuador, s.d., Cooperación Técnica Ecuatoriana — Bélgica Proyecto Ecua-Bel, Convento de Santo Domingo de Quito.

Rettig, Jaime Migone and Antonino Pirozzi Villanueva. *Tercer Coloquio Latinoamericano sobre Rescate y Preservación del Patrimonio Industrial*, Santiago, Chile, 13–16 septiembre 2001, Santiago: CONPAL-Chile, 2001.

Rojas, Eduardo. *Old Cities, New Assets: Preserving Latin America's Urban Heritage*. Washington, DC: Inter-American Development Bank, 1999.

———. *"Urban Heritage Conservation in Latin America and the Caribbean: A Task for all Social Sectors."* IADB Sustainable Development Department Technical Studies Series, SOC-125, February 2002, www.iadb.org/sds/publication/publication_4561_e.htm.

Sanoja. M. "Cultural Policy and the Preservation of Latin America's National Heritage," in *Rescue Archaeology: Papers from the First New World Conference on Rescue Archaeology*. R.L. Wilson & G. Loyola (eds.), 21–28. Washington, DC: Preservation Press, 1982.

Silverman, Helaine. *Archaeological Site Museums in Latin America*. Gainesville FL USA: University Press of Florida 2006.

Snihur, Esteban Angel. *The Missions Guarini Universe, A Territory and a Heritage*. Buenos Aires: Golden Company, 2007.

La Sociedad Civil Frente al Patrimonio Cultural. 3rd Coloquio del Seminario de Estudio del Patrimonio Artístico. Conservación, Restauración y Defensa., UNAM, Mexico, 1997.

Teutonico, Jeanne Marie and Gaetano Palumbo (eds.). *Management Planning for Archaeological Sites*, An International Workshop Organized by the Getty Conservation Institute and Loyola Marymount University, 19–22 May 2000 Corinth, Greece. Los Angeles: The Getty Conservation Institute, 2000.

Toral, Hernán Crespo and María Alexandra Silva (eds.). *Seminario Taller: Rehabilitacion Integral en Areas o Sitios Historicos Latinoamericanos, Memorias del Seminario-Taller 10–14 de enero de 1994.* Quito: Ed. Abya-Yala, 1994.

UNESCO. *Brazil: Framework for Action.* Brasilia: UNESCO, 2001.

———. *World Heritage Papers 19, American Fortifications and the World Heritage Convention.* International meeting Campeche (Mexico) 12–15 March 2004. Paris: UNESCO, 2004.

———. *World Heritage 2002, Shared Legacy, Common Responsibility.* An International Congress, 14–16 November 2002, Venice, Italy. Paris: UNESCO, 2003.

US/ICOMOS and the Getty Conservation Institute. MacLean, M. et al. *Proceedings of the Interamerican Symposium on Authenticity in the Conservation and Management of the Cultural Heritage of the Americas*, San Antonio, TX, March 1996.

Van Tilburg, Jo Anne. *Easter Island, Archaeology, Ecology, and Culture.* Washington, DC: Smithsonian Institution Press, 1995.

Viñuales, Graciela Maria. *Bibliographia sobre Conservacion Arquitectonica en America Latina.* Instituto Argentino de Investigaciones de Historia de la Arquitectura y del Urbanismo, La Nueva Provincia, Bahia Blanca, 1981.

Warren, John. *Conservation of Earthen Structures.* Oxford: Butterworth-Heinemann, 1999.

———. "Introduction," in *Earthen Architecture: The Conservation of Brick and Earth Structures, A Handbook.* Sri Lanka: International Council on Monuments and Sites, 1993.

World Heritage Center. *The State of the World Heritage in Latin America and the Caribbean*, World Heritage Papers No. 18. Paris: UNESCO, 2004.

World Monuments Fund. *Heritage Conservation in South America: Challenges and Solutions*, conference abstracts, Sao Paulo, Brazil, April 11–14, 2002. New York: World Monuments Fund, 2002.

World Monuments Fund and UNESCO. *Manual Basilico de Conservacion para las Misiones Jesuiticas Guaranies.* New York: World Monuments Fund, 2009.

World Monuments Fund and US/ICOMOS. *Trails to Treasures: A Tour of South America's Cultural Heritage.* Washington, DC, and New York: US/ICOMOS and WMF, 2001.

Photo Credits

The authors wish to thank the institutions and individuals who have kindly provided photographic material for use in *Architectural Conservation in Europe and the Americas:* In all cases, every effort has been made to contact copyright holders but should there be any errors or omissions, the publisher would be pleased to insert the appropriate acknowledgements in reprints of this book.

Particular appreciation is given to the trustees and staff of the World Monuments Fund, which has generously allowed access to its image library. Gratitude is also expressed to ICCROM's Director General for allowing access to its image archives and the kind assistance its staff provided to the authors.

PART I: EUROPE

Divider, Section 1: John H. Stubbs

Chapter 1

1-1, 1-2a: John H. Stubbs

1-2b, c: Courtesy World Monuments Fund

1-3a: John H. Stubbs

1-3b, c: Courtesy World Monuments Fund

1-4a, b, c: Courtesy Lisa Ackerman

1-5a: Vintage image

1-5b: Courtesy World Monuments Fund

1-6: John H. Stubbs

1-7a: Source: *Carlo Scarpa and Castelvecchio*, Richard Murphy (London and Boston: Butterworth Architecture, 1990)

1-7b: Courtesy Castelvecchio City Museum of Verona, Italy

1-8, 1-9 a, b: John H. Stubbs

1-10a, c, d: Courtesy and copyright of Gionata Rizzi, architect.

1-10b: Vintage image, collection of James Marston Fitch

1-11a: Courtesy World Monuments Fund

1-11b: copyright ICCROM/Alejandro Alva Balderamma, 1990

1-11c: Virginia W. Mason/National Geographic stock

1-11d: Courtesy Enginería and Thetis

1-12: Courtesy Giovanni Carbonara and World Monuments Fund

1-13a, c: Courtesy Werner Schmid

1-13b: Courtesy Werner Schmid. Stencil study image by Valeria Valentini

1-14a, b, c, d and 1-15a, b, c, d: Courtesy Alessandro Re, SITI, Torino

1-16: Courtesy, Norma Barbacci

1-17: Courtesy World Monuments Fund by Thomas Litke

Chapter 2

2-1: Copyright Réunion des Musées Nationaux France/Art Resource NY

2-2: Courtesy and copyright Europa Nostra

2-3a, b, c: Courtesy and copyright Dennis Rodwell

2-4a, b: Sourced by Ken Feisel

2-5a: Courtesy World Monuments Fund

2-5b: Creative Commons Attribution share-alike license v.2.5.

2-5c: flickr applied GNU Free Documentation License, v1.2

2-5d: Courtesy World Monuments Fund

2-6: Delor de Masbou, 1845

2-7a, b: Copyright 2010 Artists' Rights Society (ARS) New York/ADAGP Paris/F.L.C.

2-7c: Courtesy Takashi Hirato

2-8a: Courtesy World Monuments Fund by A. Rheinberg

2-8b, c: Courtesy World Monuments Fund

2-9a, b: Courtesy World Monuments Fund and CyArk

2-10a, b: Courtesy World Monuments Fund

Chapter 3

3-1a: John Wiley & Sons

3-1b: Courtesy Ethan Prater

3-2: Courtesy and copyright Dennis Rodwell

3-3a: John H. Stubbs

3-3b: Courtesy World Monuments Fund

3-4: By permission of People's History Museum, Manchester, England

3-5:Courtesy Angus Bremner photographer/The Landmark Trust, United Kingdom

3-6: Creative Commons Attribution share-alike license v.2.5.

3-7: Jacket cover from A Vision of Britain (1989) by HRH The Prince of Wales. Used

by permission of Doubleday, a division of Random House

3-8, 3-9a, b: Creative Commons Attribution share-alike license v.2.5.

3-10a, b, c, d: Courtesy and copyright Dennis Rodwell

3-11a, b, c, d; 3-12a, b: Courtesy World Monuments Fund; Richard Houlttom, photographer

3-13a, b, c: Courtesy James D. Seger and Joanne O'Sullivan

3-14: Creative Commons Attribution share-alike license v.2.5.

3-15: John H. Stubbs

3-16a: Historic Buildings and Monuments Commission for England (English Heritage)/National Monuments Record

3-16b, c: Source: Living Buildings, Images Publishing, courtesy and copyright Donald Insall Associates Ltd.

Chapter 4

4-1: Creative Commons Attribution share-alike license v.2.5.

4-2: John H. Stubbs

4-3, 4-4: Creative Commons Attribution share-alike license v.2.5.

4-5: John H. Stubbs

Chapter 5

5-1: Courtesy Nigel Goodman

5-2: Courtesy Rui Ornelas

5-3: flickr applied GNU Free Documentation License, v1.2

5-4: Courtesy World Monuments Fund by Elena Charola

5-5: Courtesy World Monuments Fund

5-6: Getty Images, by Luis Davila 26.4.06

5-7a: John H. Stubbs

5-7b: Courtesy Pablo Longoria

5-8: Courtesy Mario Fernandes

5-9: Courtesy World Monuments Fund

5-10a, b: Courtesy Rosa Ruiz, Patrimonitos en Ávila.

5-11: John Wiley & Sons

Chapter 6

6-1a: Copyright, Musée de la Ville de Bruxelles-Hotel de Ville

6-1b: Copyright, Musée de la Ville de Bruxelles-Hotel de Ville/Mirjam Devriendt, photographer

6-2a: Copyright, Musée de la Ville de Bruxelles-Maison du Roi

6-2b: Creative Commons Attribution share-alike license v.2.5

6-3a, b: Vintage image; source: Belgium: Hero and Martyr (Paris, 1915), E. Van Hammée, photographer

6-4a, b, c: Courtesy and copyright T. K. McClintock

6-4d: Courtesy Van Nelle factory, Rotterdam, The Netherlands

6-5a: Copyright photo collection Bastin & Evrard/SOFAM

6-5b: Source: Victor Horta: Conservazione e Restauro in Belgio, by Bianca Gioia Marino. T. Demey/ Edizioni Scientifiche Italiane, 2000.

6-6: flickr applied GNU Free Documentation License, v1.2

6-7a, b, c: Courtesy World Monuments Fund

6-8: Courtesy Monumentenwacht

6-9: Courtesy World Monuments Fund by Guido Vanderhulst. Image: AIRPRINT

6-10a, b: Courtesy and copyright, Roos Aldershoff, photographer

Chapter 7

7-1a: Courtesy, Basler Denkmalpflege. copyright, Erik Schmidt, photographer, 2006

7-1b, c: Courtesy and copyright, Basle cathedral Construction Hut 2009

7-2a, b: Courtesy Kantonale Denkmalpflege St. Gallen/ Walter Fietz, photographer

7-3a, b: Courtesy Patrik Birrer, lic. phil. Art Historian and Curator of Monuments, Historical Preservation of the Principality of Liechtenstein, Building and Fire Authority of the Principality of Liechtenstein, Cultural Heritage Division

Chapter 8

8-1: Courtesy Antikvarisk-topografiska arkivet, Swedish National Heritage Board/photograph by Iwar Anderson

8-2a: Creative Commons Attribution share-alike license v.2.5

8-2b: Courtesy and copyright B. Kim Barnes

8-3: Courtesy John Hackston

8-4: Creative Commons Attribution share-alike license v.2.5

8-5a: Courtesy Jens Auer/Maritime Archaeology Programme at the University of Southern Denmark 2008

8-5b: Vintage photo, collection of James Marston Fitch

Chapter 17

17-1:   Courtesy World Monuments Fund

17-2a, b, c: Source *Varsovie Reconstruite*, Ciborowski, Ed. Polonia, Warsaw 1962.

17-3a, b, c, d: Courtesy Archive ppPKZ (Marek Barański)

17-4a, b, d: Courtesy World Monuments Fund; Pawel Gasior, photographer

17-4c: Courtesy World Monuments Fund; Jaroslaw Adamowicz, photographer

Chapter 18

18-1a: Courtesy Simon Summers

18-1b: flikr applied GNU Free Documentation License, v1.2

18-2; 18-3a, b: Courtesy World Monuments Fund

18-4: flickr applied GNU Free Documentation License, v1.2

18-5a: RIA Novosti-92198

18-5b: Courtesy, Polperro Press (2005). Source: *Saving the Tsar's Palaces*, Christopher Morgan and Irina Orlova (Clifton-upon-Teme, UK: Polperro Press, 2005).

18-5c: Courtesy World Monuments Fund by Tuck & Larvey

18-5d: RIA Novosti-75874

18-6: Courtesy World Monuments Fund

18-7a: Courtesy World Monuments Fund by Pokchalov

18-7b, 18-8a,b: Courtesy and copyright Richard Pare

18-9: Courtesy Jeri L. Taylor

18-10: Courtesy Igor Palmin, photographer

18-11a, b, c, d: Courtesy World Monuments Fund

18-12: 2008 DMJM Architects, London

18-13a, b, c: Courtesy World Monuments Fund

18-14: flickr applied GNU Free Documentation License, v1.2

18-15a, b: Courtesy World Monuments Fund and Gulag Museum (image 18-15a: Yuri Resmetnikov, photographer)

Chapter 19

19-1a: Courtesy Tatyana Kowal

19-1b: Creative Commons Attribution share-alike license v.2.5

19-2: Courtesy Ewelina Włostowska

19-3a, b, c: copyright ICCROM 1971

19-4: Creative Commons Attribution share-alike license v.2.5

19-5: Courtesy Alexander Smerdov 2008

Chapter 20

20-1: John Wiley & Sons

20-2: Creative Commons Attribution share-alike license v.2.5

20-3, 20-4: Courtesy World Monuments Fund

20-5: Creative Commons Attribution share-alike license v.2.5

20-6a, b: Courtesy World Monuments Fund by Merade Bochardze

20-7a, b: Courtesy World Monuments Fund

Chapter 21

21-1: Vintage image, John H. Stubbs's personal collection

21-2a, b, c, d, e: John H. Stubbs

21-3a: Courtesy Benbulbin Photography/Liam Benbulbin

21-3b: Courtesy Andrea Castello

21-4a, b, c: John H. Stubbs

21-5: Courtesy Pamela Jerome

21-6: Courtesy Alice Chang

Chapter 22

22-1, 22-2a: Courtesy World Monuments Fund by Cemal Hoyuk

22-2b, c: Courtesy World Monuments Fund

22-3a: Courtesy World Monuments Fund

22-3b, c: John H. Stubbs

22-4: Courtesy Richard Beck-www.flickr.com/photos/becklectic

22-5a, b: John H. Stubbs

22-6: Courtesy World Monuments Fund

Chapter 23

23-1: Courtesy Hadrian Darmajuwana Liem

23-2a: Courtesy Michael J. Walsh/Allan Langdale, photographer

23-2b, 23-3: Courtesy World Monuments Fund by Michael J. Walsh

23-4a, b: Courtesy World Monuments Fund

Chapter 24

24-1: Courtesy Sarajeva Tourist Board

24-2: Courtesy World Monuments Fund

24-3: Courtesy Roy E. Graham

24-4: Courtesy World Monuments Fund by Ph. Kiesmer Lednic

24-5: John H. Stubbs

28-18: Courtesy Paul Cloutier

28-19: Courtesy Robert English

28-20a: Vintage image, flickr applied GNU Free Documentation License, v1.2

28-20b: Courtesy Charles A. Bello, Historic Preservation Specialist – Archaeologist, U.S. Department of Homeland Security

28-21a: John H. Stubbs

28-21b, c, d: Courtesy the Western Pennsylvania Conservancy

28-22a, b: Courtesy Jon Reis, www.jonreis.com

28-22c: flickr applied GNU Free Documentation License, v1.2

28-22d: Courtesy Dani Noguera Berdran

28-23a, b: Courtesy World Monuments Fund

28-24a, b: Courtesy Donovan Rypkema

28-25a, b, c, d: John H. Stubbs

Chapter 29

29-1: Courtesy Simon Lunn, Parks Canada

29-2: Courtesy Barbara M. Ross

29-3: Permission of the Canadian Museum of Civilization/ George Dawson, photographer 1878

29-4: Courtesy Phototeque Library and Archives Canada/ National Film Board. Gary Lunney, photographer

29-5: Parks Canada/Fortress of Louisbourg

29-6a, b: With permission, City of Toronto

29-7: Fred Perry photographer

29-8: Dylan Kereluk, photographer

29-9: Courtesy Peter Radunzel

29-10: Courtesy Barbara M. Ross

29-11: Courtesy Martha Wilkie

29-12: Courtesy and copyright, Parks Canada GMNP. P. Waddell, photographer

29-13: Courtesy Barbara M. Ross

29-14: With permission, Algonquin College

29-15: Courtesy and copyright 2006 Ken Thomas at www. KenThomas.us

29-16, 29-17: Courtesy Barbara M. Ross

29-18a,b,c: Panda Photography/Hugh Robertson, photographer.

Chapter 30

30-I: Vintage image, Jan Karel Donatus van Beecq

30-1: Courtesy World Monuments Fund

30-2: Source: Xavier Calvijero's *Atraidos por le Nueva Espana Asedio e Tenochtitlan Codice Florentino* Biblioteca Nacional de Antropologia e Historia INAH-CNCA

30-3: Creative Commons Attribution share-alike license v.2.5

30-4a: flickr applied GNU Free Documentation License, v1.2

30-4b: Courtesy Kim Fleming/seabird

30-5a: Courtesy UNESCO/Carlo Tomas, photographer

30-5b: flickr applied GNU Free Documentation License, v1.2

30-6a, b, c, 30-7a,b, c, d, 30-8, 30-9a, b: Courtesy World Monuments Fund

30-9c,d: Courtesy Alfonso Govela Thomae

30-10a, b: Courtesy World Monuments Fund

Chapter 31

31-1: John Wiley & Sons

31-2: flickr applied GNU Free Documentation License, v1.2

31-3: Courtesy Mari Ward-Foster

31-4c: Creative Commons Attribution share-alike license v.2.5

31-5: flickr applied GNU Free Documentation License, v1.2

31-6a, b: John H. Stubbs

31-7a, b, c, d, e: Courtesy World Monuments Fund/ copyright 1999 Nigel D. Lord

31-7c, d, e: Courtesy World Monuments Fund

31-8: Courtesy World Monuments Fund by C. McGeachy

31-9a, b, 31-10a, b: Courtesy World Monuments Fund

31-11: Courtesy and copyright Ricardo Briones/ DOCOMOMO Dominicano

31-12a, b, c: Courtesy World Monuments Fund, copyright John A. Loomis

31-13a, c: Courtesy Milner Associates/Alfonso Narvaez: UN Photo/Logan Abass, the United Nations

31-13b: Courtesy Cat Lainé, AIDG

Chapter 32

32-1a: Courtesy Pedro Aycinena

32-1b: Courtesy, Pedro Szekely

32-2a: Creative Commons Attribution share-alike license v.2.5

32-2b, 32-3a: flickr applied GNU Free Documentation License, v1.2

35-14: Creative Commons Attribution share-alike license v.2.5

35-15a, b: Courtesy World Monuments Fund

35-16a, b: Courtesy World Monuments Fund

35-17: flickr applied GNU Free Documentation License, v1.2

35-18a, b, c, d: Courtesy Agencia Española de Cooperación para el Desarollo (AECID)

35-19: Courtesy Norma Barbacci

Chapter 36

36-1: Creative Commons Attribution share-alike license v.2.5

36-2a: Courtesy Raphael Alvez

36-2b: Courtesy Ivan Utz

36-3: Courtesy World Monuments Fund

36-4: Courtesy Marlene Rocio Zárate Betzel

36-5: Source: Esteban Ángel Snihur, *The Missions Guaraní Territory and a Heritage* (Golden Company, 2007).

36-6a: Courtesy World Monuments Fund; Carlos Pernaut, photographer

36-6b, c, d: Courtesy World Monuments Fund

36-7, 36-8a: Creative Commons Attribution share-alike license v.2.5

36-8b: Courtesy World Monuments Fund

36-9, 36-10: Creative Commons Attribution share-alike license v.2.5

36-11a, b, 36-12a, c, d, e: Courtesy World Monuments Fund

36-13a, c, d, e: Courtesy World Monuments Fund

36-13b: Courtesy World Monuments Fund/Amigos de las Iglesias de Chiloe

Index